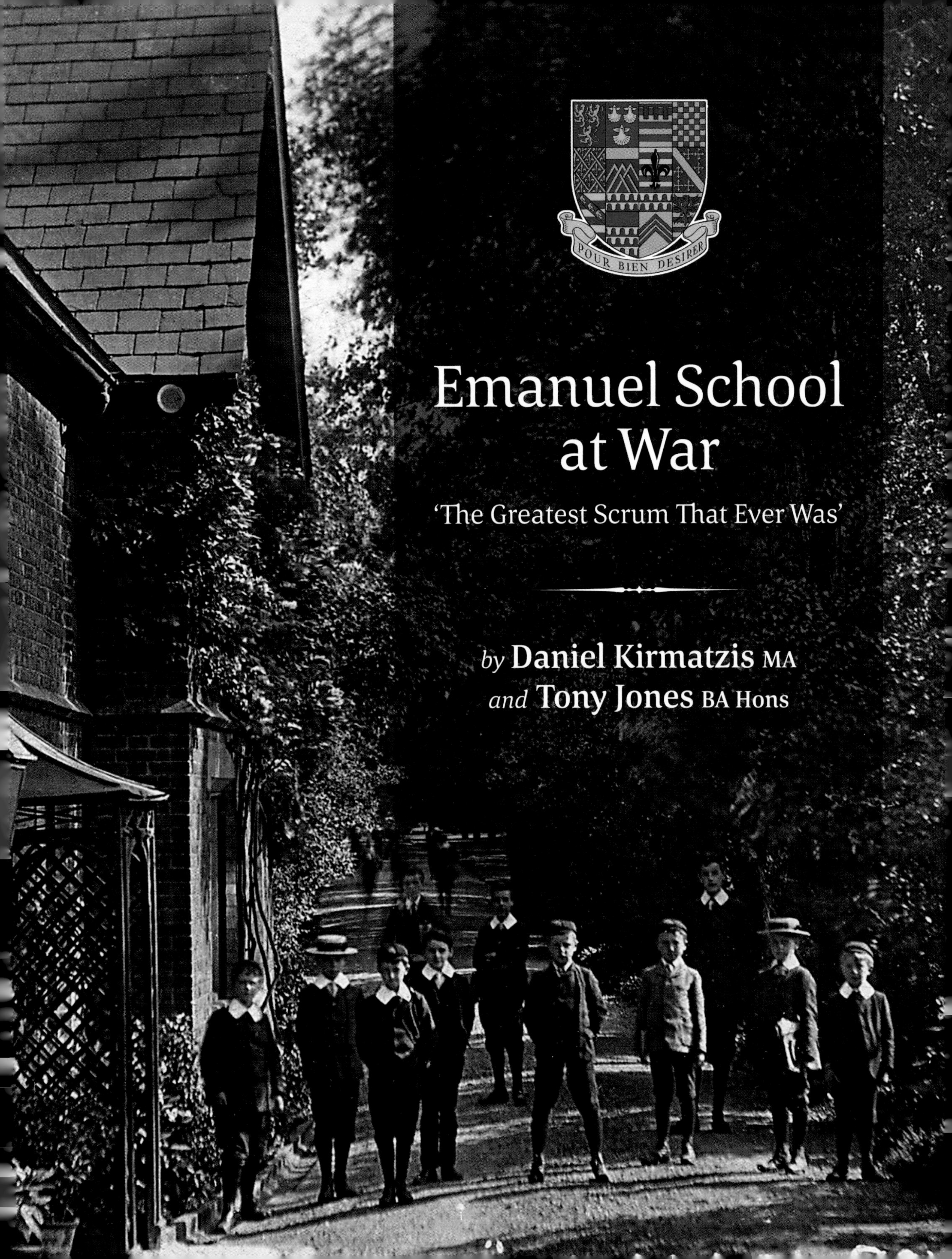
POUR BIEN DESIRER
Emanuel School at War
'The Greatest Scrum That Ever Was'
by Daniel Kirmatzis MA
and Tony Jones BA Hons

We would like to thank the following subscribers for their support in the publication of this book.

Edward Album, Jeremy Archer, William Arnold, William Attfield, Arthur Bailes, John Banbery, Stuart Barnett, Sharon Bierer, Kenneth Bouch, Andrew Boyle, Andrew Buchanan, Jon Butcher, Susan Chambers, Douglas Champ, Michael Christmas, Andrew Cobb, John Conway, Roy Crabtree, Colin Cracknell, Mary Davies, Peter Dudley, Ramon Edwards, Stafford Ellerman, Roger Ellis, William Farmer, Nicholas Fieller, Martin Flower, David Gallagher, Martin Graham, Raymond Grainger, Peter Harrington, John Harwood, Ronald Hayward, Andrew Hayward, Kenneth Headford, James Headford, Roger Hinxman, Edward Holland, Ronald Horlock, Peter Jacobsen, Nigel Johnson, Ronald Jordan, Mark Joyner, Polly Kemp, George Kingston, Nigel Kitchen, Vernon Leader, John Lee, George Locke, Jim Maile, Michael Markland, Paul Martin, Joanne Matthews, John Miell, Jonathan Mills, John Monkhouse, Paul Moore, Geoffrey Morris, Kenneth Moss, Richard Oakley, Frank Orford, Peter Osborne, John Parker, David Parton, Christopher Payne, Dennis Peck, Brian Prior, Stuart Raeburn, Richard Raine, Iain Reid, Rosemany Rowland, Megan Rowley, John Sales, Keith Sansom, Derek Saunders, Claude Scott, Brinsley Sheridan, John Somerville, Arshia Steele, Brian Stickland, Peter Sweetman, Anthony Sweetsur, Richard Tarling, Geoffrey Thorne, David Troup, Roy Veal, Harry Waddingham, John Walker, Robert Wardley, Loraine Watson, Peter Whiting, Nikolas Wilkinson, Ronald Williamson, John Windus, Graham Wood, Ronald Young and The Old Emanuel Association.

A further eleven subscribers have remained anonymous.

And to the memory of the following:

Allan Barnes (OE), Brian Cocks (Nephew of Horace Cocks OE), William Deeks (OE), Michael Fowle (Son of Colin Fowle OE), Roger Goodman (OE), William Michael Squire Jeffery (OE), Patrick Needham (OE)

And to all those Old Emanuels who served in the First and Second World Wars

General Sir Peter Wall GCB, CBE, ADC Gen

Foreword

This book is the remarkable record of the contribution of the masters and pupils of one intensely proud London school in the two wars that threatened Britain's survival during the first half of the twentieth century. Emanuel School in south London was not alone: any number of schools from middle England could file a similar record. But the scale and variety of Emanuel's vivid contribution is extraordinary and this book captures it wonderfully well. It covers a highly demanding and tragic era in the School's existence: ranging over three critical decades in over four hundred years of Emanuel's long history.

This mosaic of personal stories works at three distinct levels. The first level is a highly informative survey, of the range of campaigns, battles, actions and debacles that were spawned by the ebb and flow of these two protracted global conflicts: from Flanders to Gallipoli; from the Western Desert to Normandy; from the Home Front to Berlin; on land, at sea, and in the air.

The second level is the profound impact on particular generations of Old Emanuels: the cruel toll taken of entire year groups, rugby teams, rowing crews, groups of friends and of some of the more iconic individuals from the School. These collective tragedies are extremely poignant, reminding us how, in the Great War in particular, the country lost a generation of its talented youth.

The third level is the personal one, with the accounts of the commitment, courage, gallantry and honour of so many Old Emanuels in action in the heat of battle. Their conduct and ingenuity was so much a product of Emanuel Schools's culture of endeavour: its scholarship, its sporting prowess; its officer training corps, and ultimately its ethos and humility.

These proud former pupils were at the whim of events far beyond their personal control. They faced acute and unreasonable demands in the cause of the nation's freedom. Many did not return; many of those who did were changed and troubled people; either way these Old Emanuels were not found wanting.

A key part of the legacy of these Emanuels in wartime is the example they set to today's pupils. This immaculately researched book conveys that sense very strongly. Despite the inherent tragedy of war, the record of those who endured and fought to defend our values is one of which Emanuel School can be immensely proud.

General Sir Peter Wall GCB, CBE, ADC Gen
(Chief of the General Staff 2010–2014)

Matador
9 Priory Business Park
Kibworth Beauchamp
Leicestershire LE8 0RX, UK
Tel: (+44) 116 279 2299
Fax: (+44) 116 279 2277
Email: books@troubador.co.uk
Web: www.troubador.co.uk/matador

ISBN 978 1784621 568

British Library Cataloguing in Publication Data.
A catalogue record for this book is available from the British Library.

Book Design by Paul Hewitt and Mary Woolley, Battlefield Design
www.battlefield-design.co.uk

Printed and bound by Gutenberg Press Ltd

Matador is an imprint of Troubador Publishing Ltd

For Maxine Loader

‘Certainly no boy ever loved the School more’

Lt. Peter Harold Jackson MC
(Emanuel 1932–1938)

Full story on page 392

Contents

Features

Appendices 572

Emanuel! For the Noble Aim

On a December's evening in 1993 my mother and I walked down the Emanuel School drive for the first time. Prospective parents and pupils had been invited to attend the Emanuel Carol Concert. I turned to my mother and said that the School felt homely and that I would be very happy to attend. Fortunately fate was kind and I started my schooling at Emanuel the following year. Each Christmas, of the seven years I was in attendance, I read at the School Carol Concert. Readers would sit in the corner of the chapel, which in those days was adorned with a number of memorial plaques bearing the names of former pupils who fought for their country in the Great War. In addition to the plaques were two memorials, in the centre of the chapel, bearing the names of those who lost their lives in both world wars. During chapel assemblies I sat and read the long list of names, and I often wondered who the individuals were behind these names?

In his authoritative *History of Emanuel School* Wilfrid Scott-Giles wrote, 'In a few years the War will recede into the background of history and those who fell will be remembered only by their names on the memorial in the chapel, but the fact that the School as a whole and not merely individual members thereof, devoted all its resources and energies to a national purpose, should be a matter for lasting pride and inspiration.' Scott-Giles wrote this in the context of the First World War. Within a few years of penning these lines the Second World War broke out and once again Emanuel boys were called upon to defend their country. Another list of names of boys who apart from an occasional mention in the School magazine *The Portcullis*, remained largely anonymous for more than three-quarters of a century.

In 2009 I published the *History of Emanuel School Boat Club*. Whilst researching the Boat Club's history I spent hours perusing the School archive, so carefully assembled by the School Archivist, Tony Jones. I touched upon several stories of boys who rowed and subsequently fought in the wars and after the book was published I returned to look into Emanuel's contribution in these conflicts. I examined the School's 'Pro Patria' lists which have over 1700 names of OEs who fought in both world wars, and felt compelled to try and understand who these young men were and so Tony Jones and I sat down to discuss my initial idea of writing the School's war history.

In 2012 Tony began to assist me on the Emanuel School at War Project. Whilst I spent my time in external archives Tony searched the School archives in order to build a picture of OEs during their time at Emanuel. Tony pulled together vast resources and at the same time wrote articles on Vernon Richards, friend of George Orwell, and the Emanuel OTC, which appear here. He also began work on the School's 'Pro Patria' lists, ably assisted by Shan Johannson, whilst I researched new names and amended mistakes in the originals.

Perhaps the most rewarding aspect of this project is that I have been able to find the names of 24 OEs who were not included on the original chapel memorials, and with the assistance of the School Chaplain, the Reverend Paul Hunt, we have added five new memorial boards with these new names to be unveiled in the School chapel on a special Evensong on 9 November 2014 during the course of the 'Emanuel School at War' Exhibition.

Writing and editing this book has taken me on an incredible journey. Setting out to trace the lives of hundreds of young men, from Emanuel to the trenches of the First World War and the battlefields of the Second has on occasion been overwhelming and emotional. With my own Emanuel School friends, in particular Kwok Ho-Ip, who drove me across France and Belgium, I made four visits to the last resting places of Emanuel boys who fell in both world wars, visiting the Thiepval Memorial to the Missing on the Somme, the Menin Gate Memorial in Ypres and a significant number of Commonwealth War Graves Commission cemeteries, so beautifully tended. These were moving visits, not least when I saw the grave of Roland Walter Bullivant who died of his wounds on 1 May 1917, aged 21. The inscription at the bottom of his Commonwealth War Grave simply, but poignantly reads, 'Scholar Emanuel School Wandsworth.'

Many hours were spent in the reading rooms of the Imperial War Museum, the National Army Museum in Chelsea, the British Library and the Battersea Reference Library. But also in second-hand bookshops, where serendipitously, particular books would present themselves only for me to find that they contained a reference to an Old Emanuel who fought in the wars!

During my research I interviewed eight OEs who had served in the Second World War, striking up friendships across the generations. My admiration for these men has grown with every encounter and with each letter, memoir, postcard or account I have read. I have been in contact with hundreds of relatives of OEs, through the expert support of OE Stuart Cameron-Waller who helped Tony and I trace families across the globe. All relatives were so generous in giving of their time and gracious hospitality and Tony's and my appreciation goes to all of them; for searching their attics, cupboards and sheds for a wealth of documents that they allowed us to digitally preserve with many also donating objects to the School archive which not only richly add to this account but also provide a lasting legacy for future generations of Emanuel pupils, researchers and the wider community studying these periods.

Through this book and the 'Emanuel School at War' Exhibition, families have made their own emotional voyages of discovery, opening doors onto a past that their relatives, more often than not, had closed when they returned from the various fronts on which they fought. I have had the privilege of sharing these experiences, which were often extremely moving, especially those of the OE veterans I interviewed, walking through the corridors of their minds, out onto particular battlefields, or recalling lost friends; or as OEs' children, grandchildren, nieces and nephews read letters and memoirs, some for the first time, and others seeing with fresh eyes information Tony and I had been able to provide. More than a few tears have been shed as they read letters explaining the last moments of loved ones, many of whom sacrificed their lives for those of others, protecting their men on a battlefield or piloting an aircraft just long enough for their crew to jump to safety. Sons and daughters have also sought to understand how their fathers' wartime experiences affected the men that returned, especially when, as children, they had experienced moments when their fathers sat in silent contemplation, not fully appreciating why until they were much older.

But who were these individuals? They were like you and me. Ordinary people, who walked down the School drive, studied, played sports, laughed with friends and performed on stage. They learnt how to play musical instruments and memorised their Latin vocabulary for the weekly tests. But unlike the majority of the post-war generation they were called upon at a time of national and international crisis. They were thrown into a centrifuge that was 'Total War', experiencing untold hardships – sloshing through muddy fields, wading across fast flowing rivers and navigating through stormy skies, under heavy fire. Twice in the early twentieth century highly industrialised nations exhausted diplomacy and set upon each other utilising their technological advances to illogical and catastrophic ends. These young men became both the deliverers and the receivers of hellish judgement passed down upon the bodies of individuals that neither they nor their opponents knew personally but whom were constructed into abstractions such as 'Fritz' and 'Tommy' and who through propaganda, were classified as 'the enemy.'

In a letter to OE Lawrence Inkster, who was mistakenly reported as having died in the First World War, OE Wilfrid Scott-Giles wrote of Emanuel's role in that war, 'Emanuel has a right to be proud of its part in the war. We haven't done much that is "showy", but by jove! We've been sound to a man.' It may seem strange to associate individuals with the greater collective term of the School but this is essential to Emanuel's ethos. Its pupils represent the School both during their education and afterwards when they become OEs, and therefore the service and sacrifice of these individuals is also the School's. This was true of OEs in both wars.

To illustrate the impact the First World War had upon the School one need only to read the list of names in the School's prayer which gives thanks to the generosity of its benefactors for allowing it to continue to provide its pupils with 'the study of virtue and good learning.' Listed beside the names of the School's founders and those associated with its Charter, including Queen Elizabeth I, is that of OE Ronald Edwin Grundy, who eight months after his OE brother Cecil died of wounds at Bethune, was killed when a bullet hit him as he led a platoon of the Middlesex Regiment across no-man's land on the first day of the Battle of the Somme.

The School community as a whole was deeply affected by the loss of so many young men in the First World War. In the case of both wars masters wrote poems to fallen pupils and parents provided trophies to foster inter-house competitions in perpetual memory of lost loved ones.

One overriding theme throughout the stories in this book is the sense of how important Emanuel became in the lives of these young men who found themselves hundreds of miles away in wars they little understood but in which they did their duty. Even across vast distances the School remained close to their hearts. Many took *The Portcullis* with them into the trenches of the Western Front or to their barracks at various locations across the world. Two OEs illustrate this emotional connection to Emanuel – that the School was something much more than an educational establishment; for many it was an extension of their family. In the First World War Stanley Harvey wrote to the School whilst serving out in France, 'Dear Old Emanuel, what a treasure house of happy memories!' In a similar tone Walter Ward wrote a card to the School in the Second World War, 'Always with happy memories of the School.' Both young men lost their lives, Stanley during the German Spring Offensive of 1918 and Walter in a tragic incident when two anti-aircraft shells were accidentally fired from an adjacent troopship at Liverpool on 7 November 1944.

I too have always felt that the School is like an extended family and through Emanuel I have made many life-long friends and perhaps above all it was this that compelled me to find out what happened to those young men listed in the chapel so that future Emanuel pupils, whether this year or in a hundred years' time, will remember these OEs who fought in the world wars through their deeds, and as individuals with a zest for life, and not by their names alone. I think we owe these brave young men the dignity of being recognised appropriately.

Principally, this book was written for all those OEs who served, and especially those who never came home. I hope that this book will act as a fitting and lasting memorial to them and their families as well as both past and future generations of the School. We must never forget the sacrifices OEs made and it is right to honour their memory.

Those who have contributed towards this book and the many individuals who have made it possible receive their rightful thanks in the acknowledgements but here I would like to thank in particular, General Sir Peter Wall, for taking the time to compose a considered and fitting Foreword which stands as a testament to the service and sacrifice of so many OEs in the First and Second World Wars.

Daniel Kirmatzis *(Emanuel 1994–2001)* Battersea, August 2014

The Emanuel Boys

On a muddy field in Wandsworth
A whistle starts to blow
And the Emanuel boys play rugger
With courage much on show
Absorbing an ethos
That they would only recognise
After they had left the school
Of service and self sacrifice
On this muddy field in Wandsworth
They chase that leather ball
Egging their house mates on
As the young men give their all

Loyalty, teamwork, discipline
So much they'd learn from school
Humility, humanity
So much owed to Emanuel
Whilst on the river by Barnes Bridge
The Emanuel boys are afloat
Pulling all together
As one in the boat
And as they glide along
With the river shining blue
Relying on each other
Much more than just a crew

So when called upon in time of war
Or more likely volunteer
With thoughts of country uppermost
And all that they hold dear
Emanuel boys would take the field
Putting aside the fear
But taking Wandsworth in their hearts
Their rightful path so clear

Navy, Army, Air Force, Emanuel boys
were there
Never ones to shirk their task
Always ones to dare
To face any danger
On land, at sea or in the air
Emanuel boys gave their all
And some would reach the highest ranks
Whilst some, duty done, would fall

Paul Tofi, Sqn Ldr RAF (Ret'd)
(Emanuel 1969–1976)

CHAPTER 1

WAR CLOUDS

Letters from the Second Boer War 1899–1902

The Dutch East India Company founded a shipping station in the Cape of Good Hope in 1652 and their settlements were long established. The Boers (Boer meaning farmer) had descended from these original Dutch settlers, known as 'Afrikaners', and were defined by being from the poorest section of that community.

They established their own territory beyond the control of British interests in the Cape but throughout the late nineteenth century new discoveries including diamonds and gold started to attract British interest and it was this that led to increasing confrontation with the Boers who had settled in the resource-rich areas which the British coveted for themselves. The war itself had multiple causes but essentially it was a contest for a significant land mass, which held the key to vast riches. Over the course of two and three quarter years the British fought the Boers across the area of South Africa in a number of key battles. Around 400,000 British fought in the campaign between 1899 and 1902.

Emanuel Boys in the Second Boer War

Emanuel boys' experiences were reported in the *Emanuel School Magazine* in sections titled 'Letters from the Front.' These sections appeared again in the magazine some twelve years after the conflict ended and became the standard title for news about Old Emanuels (OEs) in the Great War of 1914–18.

During the Boer conflict the British garrison of Mafeking became a central battleground. Psychologically important to both sides in the conflict it was under siege by the Boers from 1899 but in May 1900 it was relieved by Imperial forces and made Robert Baden-Powell (founder of the Scout movement) a household name. Nevil Bursey Hodgson who attended Emanuel between 1887 and 1891 was at Mafeking and for his actions was Mentioned in Despatches. A mention occurred when a company commander would record notable acts during a campaign in the company's war diary or advertise them in the *London Gazette*. None other than Baden-Powell wrote Hodgson's mention, which follows:

EMANUEL . .
SCHOOL . . . .
MAGAZINE. .

EASTER, 1902.

Emanuel School Magazine, Easter 1902

MAFEKING, 13 October 1899 to 17 May 1900

From Major General Baden-Powell's despatch, 18 May 1900: 'Cape Police-Inspector Brown commanded detachment of Division 2; he and the splendid lot of men under his command did excellent work throughout, especially in occupation of trenches in brickfields, where for over a month they were within close range of enemy's works, and constantly on the alert and under fire. Inspector March commanded detachment of Division 1 throughout, and carried out his duties most efficiently and zealously. Trooper (local Sergeant Major) Hodgson acted as Sergeant Major to ASC, and was of the greatest help to Captain Ryan.'

Hodgson's brother, Conti, also an OE and in the Imperial Yeomanry, served under Lieutenant Colonel (later Field Marshal Lord) Herbert Plumer. Nevil died of typhoid in 1902 and is remembered on a plaque in the Emanuel School chapel. What follows is the announcement of his death in *The Sphere* newspaper of 14 June 1902: 'Lieutenant Nevil Bursey Hodgson of the Army Service Corps, who died at Pretoria on May 27 from en'eric [sic] fever, was formerly in the Cape Mounted Police and obtained his commission, but was gazetted to a commission in the Army Service Corps two days later, September 15, 1900, on recommendation of the Commander-in-Chief; he received his step in December, 1901. He served during the whole of the war, was in the siege of Mafeking, and for his services there he was Mentioned in Despatches. He was the eldest son of Mr. Nevil L. Hodgson of Woolwich and Blackheath.'[1]

The relief of Mafeking was celebrated across England and Emanuel had a thanksgiving service in the chapel. It was reported in the *School Magazine*, as was the donation of a new flag by a parent who attended the service. He wrote the Headmaster a letter, 'After attending your enjoyable and most patriotic service yesterday, I should like to do something for Emanuel boys, in honour of the relief of Mafeking. If your committee will allow me, I shall feel it a great pleasure to present the School with a new flag, of whatever kind most suitable'.[2] A new Union flag was bought by the School to replace its old one.

The Hodgsons were not the only Emanuel boys to have fought in the war. The School was left a diary, which unfortunately has long since been lost, given by Sergeant A. C. Hayton. Hayton received both the King and Queen's South Africa medals and bars for Diamond Hill, Belmont, Cape Colony, and Orange Free State. This meant he had either served or seen action in these areas during the course of the War. According to the *School Magazine*, 'he joined the Rough Riders, 79th Imperial Yeomanry, in March, 1900'.[3]

An interesting note was that a former nurse at the School, a Ms Marlow, who had left England for South Africa in 1898 to restore her health, then returned to England where she nursed troops who had been invalided out from the war. After staying a short while she returned to South Africa on a troopship.[4]

Other OEs wrote to the Headmaster detailing their experiences. H. J. Vincent who left Emanuel in 1898 wrote in one letter about one stormy night, which wreaked havoc in their camp, 'The town itself was a total wreck, roofs of houses blown off, and small shanties completely demolished. Fortunately, no one was killed'.[5] In another letter Vincent describes among other things the taking of guns and prisoners, 'The next day started the great drive – one of the worst marches I have ever had. It lasted three weeks; we generally started about 2am, halting at 12 noon for two hours, and halting at dusk, when everybody on the column was on outpost.' As many OEs would do later in the Great War, Vincent wrote about his thanks for receiving a copy of *The Portcullis*, 'I received the School Magazine yesterday, for which I hardly know how to express my thanks, as it is very interesting, indeed, to read of old friends.'

Nevil Bursey Hodgson

Memorial plaque in the Emanuel School Chapel

In a letter from A. S. Clare (who was at Emanuel for six years, and had three brothers and two nephews who also attended the School) we read of the raw realities of war.

Emanuel School Magazine.

"Let knowledge grow from more to more,
But more of reverence in us dwell."

No. 28. EASTER, 1902. [PER ANNUM, BY POST 10½d.

Emanuel School Magazine, Easter 1902

Clare was serving with the City Imperial Volunteers (CIV) and was a private in Number 1 Section. In an engagement near Brandfort he describes what happened when they were fired upon:

> Our horses were now brought up to us, and we advanced again in a quiet way, suddenly, without the slightest warning, a tremendous boom rang out, and in less than it takes to relate, two of our men on the left fell – struck dead by the fragments of the first bursting shell from the enemy. One poor fellow's head was completely shattered, and the other one, a sergeant was struck on the buckle of his belt, the shock killing him. After leaving these poor fellows safe in the hands of the stretcher-bearers, we proceeded with our duties.[6]

In a similar tone to Clare, Percy Wiseman wrote to the Headmaster in December 1901. The notes section of the *School Magazine* mentions the letter being reprinted later in the issue and the pride the School felt at seeing its former pupils in the service of the country can be found in the following lines, 'We have certainly done our share, with other Schools, in sending men to the front.'[7] Percy had been involved in actions five times and in the following letter describes his proximity to death:

> I have been in the country now since March, and feel like any old experienced soldier. I have only been in action five times, but the last time I was in a very tight corner. We are camping on the banks of the River Caledon, guarding the bridge which the Boers, sooner or later will try to cross. I think they will have a very hot time if they do try, as we are very strongly fortified, and have three 15-pounders, one of which we recaptured from the Boers some little time back. It was captured by them at the Vlakfontein fight, the gun belonging to 'V' Battery, RA. Every day four men and a corporal have to go off about five miles to keep a look-out for the safety of the camp. On November 26th, four other fellows and myself were told off for this work. We had been about half-an-hour out, and were approaching a farm, when we saw about ten of our black scouts galloping like mad over a ridge at the back of the farm. Then we heard heavy firing, and saw one of the scouts drop dead. We then knew that the Boers were firing at us, and immediately began to retire. The Boers then rose in a cluster and fired a volley at us, but it went harmlessly over our heads, and as we got farther away from them their firing became more accurate, and it seems a miracle to me that we were not all hit, as the bullets came all round us. I was shot right through the crown of the hat, and a fellow, named Winpenny, was shot through the water-bottle, the bullet grazing his side. The fellows seemed to think I had a very lucky escape, but I knew nothing about the bullet passing through my hat till afterwards. I am bringing the hat home, if I don't lose it, and will bring it to show you. I have no doubt that you have heard of Kritzinger's capture, which brings the war nearer the end. We are now in the midst of an African summer, and the weather is unbearably hot. The night before last I was on picket duty, and it rained an African rain; needless to say I was soaked to the skin, and had to stay in bed all the next day, while my clothes dried. It will be funny to me next Christmas, as it will be the first Christmas I have spent away from home.[8]

The *School Magazine* also mentions the death of the brother of two Emanuel boys. It is of interest because it shows the fascination this generation had in the lives of Emanuel boys outside of academia:

> All will be sorry to hear of the death of Staff-Sergt. John Carlyn Hill, of Thorneycroft's M.I., brother of Samson Hill and Rowland Hill, in South Africa. He had just recovered from fever, and on 12 January wrote home, "I am quite well, and returning to duty today." On the 20th January, at Konstanti, near Pietersdal, he received the wound, from which he died next day. He was not an Old Emanuel, but we are proud to have had the brothers of a hero with us. Rowland Hill, who is working in the General Post Office at Falmouth, writes, "There is one consolation, and that is that he died for his country, and that is a great honour." So it is.[9]

References

1 *The Sphere*, 14 June 1902, p. 254.
2 *Emanuel School Magazine*, Midsummer 1900, No. 23, p. 192.
3 For a general account of the Boer War see Thomas Pakenham, *The Boer War*, (1979)
4 *Emanuel School Magazine*, Midsummer 1900, No. 23, p. 192.
5 *Emanuel School Magazine*, Christmas 1901, No. 27, p. 244.
6 *Emanuel School Magazine*, Easter 1901, No. 25, p. 220.
7 *Emanuel School Magazine*, Easter 1902, No. 28, p. 252.
8 Ibid. p. 254.
9 Ibid. p. 253.

Emanuel School OTC Pre First World War with the Rev. H. B. Ryley

The Cadet Force and the OTC

'And the day has dawned of England's fate'

The pre-1914 generation lived under war clouds for a number of years. The rivalry between the European powers and the Boer War necessitated the training of officers for what some saw as an inevitable conflict between the major powers.

One such individual was the pre-war Headmaster Harold Buchanan Ryley, described in the *History of Emanuel School* by Charles 'Wilfrid' Scott-Giles as, 'a patriot who foresaw the war.'[1] In tones befitting a man steeped in Victorian notions of duty, Harold Buchanan Ryley wrote a number of poems in the School magazine. In 1911 the magazine reprinted a poem titled *Adsum*, Latin for 'I am present' which, whilst reflective of the Boer War, the last major conflict Britain had been embroiled in before 1914, suggests war clouds on the horizon and as Ryley held the position of commander of the Emanuel Officers' Training Corps (OTC) it can be seen as a recruiting call to Emanuel boys.

Emanuel OTC Camp Staffordshire 1913

Adsum

Charterhouse, Mafeking, Boy Scouts

The books are shut, and the game is done:
In the darkening cloistered walls of gray
A clear bell rings to the setting sun,
At the lingering close of a summer day.
For the high tradition, the peaceful rule,
The honoured name of the ancient School,
Who shall make answer? – say:
Out of the hundreds a voice rings clear:
Adsum! – I'm here!

A leaguered town of the Afric plain,
And war is red in the lowering sky.
There's the Queen's own flag to keep from stain,
And friends are far and the foe is nigh, –
An ancient banner to guard from shame,
The honour to keep of the ancient name:
Who is it makes reply? –
Out of the hundreds a voice rings clear:
Adsum! – I'm here!

The leaden days have trodden us down;
Our dead lie thick in their lowly graves;
Hand in hand through the little town
Gaunt famine stalks, fierce fever raves;
And the eyes of Europe strain afar
To see us sink in the tide of war: –
Where is the hand that saves?
One against thousands a voice rings clear:
Adsum! – I'm here!

So, when the banded nations stand,
And the day has dawned of England's fate;
When the war-clouds gather o'er sea and land,
And the foot of the foe is at our gate: –
Oh then, in the time of our Mother's need,
Be ours the will, be ours the deed,
Ours be the strength elate,
Ours be one voice outringing clear:
"England! – I'm here!"[2]

by Harold Buchanan Ryley,

The Portcullis, Easter Term 1911, p.401–402

The instruction of Emanuel boys in military systems can be traced to the late nineteenth century when, in addition to learning company drill, 'something more ambitious' was introduced. Under the instruction of Sergeant Evans a battalion drill was introduced in the summer of 1897 and henceforth was annually inspected by an official, in 1897 this being Colonel Hay, Warden of Christ's Hospital. On Thursday 22 July 1897 Colonel Hay witnessed a display by three companies of Emanuel boys consisting of, 'forming into line, forming quarter-column, deploying, retiring and advancing in line, in echelon, and in review order.'[3]

Bell tents at an OTC Camp, pre-1914

The drill was seen as an essential prerequisite for those seeking a military career and on Thursday 26 July 1900 the Emanuel Headmaster The Rev. Chilton 'addressed the boys on the advantages of battalion drill.' The *School Magazine* reported, 'In the present state of national feeling there would doubtless be many boys who, on leaving, might join some volunteer regiment, and the training received in their School drill would be of great assistance in their future duties as volunteers.'[4] The article continues with recognition of an esprit de corps being formed from the boys who partake in the battalion drill, 'Another great advantage was the knowledge that each boy's performance had something to do with the standard of excellence of the whole battalion – each boy would feel that he was "one of the line.'[5]

In 1906 a Cadet Corps was founded. It was constituted as Z Company of the Queen's Westminster Volunteers and was commanded by the Headmaster H. B. Ryley. The uniform worn by cadets, grey with red facings, was of particular pride as it was unique among other schools' cadet formations.[6] Prior to the Cadet formation was the institution of a Rifle Club in 1905, affiliated to the National Rifle Association.

Emanuel Cadet Corps c.1907

On a national level the army was being reformed under the direction of the Secretary of State for War, Richard Burdon Haldane. The Haldane Reforms, as they are more commonly known, made provisions for training officers for the army in time of war and more generally for the Auxiliary Forces.[7] It centralised the activities of the Cadet Corps and introduced regulations and official examinations. Emanuel's Cadet Corps was recognised as a contingent of the Officers' Training Corps in 1909.[8]

Life in the OTC up to and during the First World War consisted of route marches, lectures on military tactics, summer camps and drills of various kinds.[9] There was also the chance of gaining Certificate A, an award based upon military knowledge and its application. There can be little doubt that many boys who served in the Emanuel OTC were more than prepared to take commissions in the Regular Army when war broke out in the summer of 1914 and indeed when one looks at the names written on the mount of the photo of Emanuel's OTC in 1912 familiar faces stand out such as Ronald Grundy who became a Second Lieutenant in The Middlesex Regiment.

In the Summer Term *Portcullis* the headline for the OTC section read, 'The Corps is the back-bone of the School', [10] but even up to the First World War it appeared to lack sufficient numbers, as desired by senior members of the Corps and as expressed in the notes of the Christmas Term *Portcullis*, 'In a School of 600 boys it is somewhat disappointing, however, to find that only one-seventh or one-sixth join the Corps. Surely it is not too much to ask that at least one—third should join the contingent, and thereby keep up with other schools in maintaining a strong and efficient Corps.' [11]

The Cadet Corps and OTC can be seen to have been essential in training future officers for the Regular Army in the First World War but it becomes obvious reading the OTC notes that resentment towards their activities came from certain quarters. This last point is borne out in the Camp Notes in the Winter Term 1914 *Portcullis*, which illustrates the strongly held convictions that Corps members felt about the purpose of their training viz. that it had a greater purpose:

> We had, at any rate, stood on the fringe of the greatest event of all history, and all of us, it is to be hoped, resolved that, come what might, we should not stick to the Corps ourselves, and become efficient soldiers, but gather in as many of our comrades as possible.
>
> There is, at any rate, one good thing to be got out of it – we who are in the Corps have often been sneered at as toy soldiers, pretending to train for an event that would never come about, and we have been told by all sorts of wiseacres that war was impossible because it was inelegant and unbecoming, because it taught us to be brutal and coarse. We had lessons in Camp to prove that the latter statement was untrue, because no one could wish for a finer man than Major Stucley; and with regard to the first statement, we, who are now serving, have at any rate the satisfaction of being able to say to those who sneered at us, "I told you so, and I was right." [12]

References

1 C. Wilfrid Scott-Giles, *The History of Emanuel School,* (1948), p. 194.
2 *Adsum*, H. B. Ryley, *The Portcullis*, No. 52, Easter Term, 1911, pp. 401–402.
3 *Emanuel School Magazine*, No. 14, Midsummer 1897, p. 106.
4 *Emanuel School Magazine*, No. 23, Midsummer 1900, p. 193.
5 Ibid.
6 *History of Emanuel*, p. 172.
7 Col. J. K. Dunlop O.B.E., M.C., T.D., Ph.D., *The Development of the British Army 1899–1914*, (1938), pp. 294–295.
8 *The Portcullis*, No. 48, Easter Term 1909, p. 251.
9 Ibid. See the list of activities set out for OTC members.
10 *The Portcullis*, No. 62, Summer Term 1914, p. 59.
11 *The Portcullis*, No. 60, Christmas Term 1913, p. 32.
12 *The Portcullis*, No. 63, Winter Term 1914, p. 33.

CHAPTER 2

ADSUM! – I'M HERE

The Gallant Headmaster

Former Emanuel parent, Jeremy Archer writes about Emanuel's pre-war Headmaster.

Harold Buchanan Ryley senior, the eldest son of the Reverend George Buchanan Ryley, was born on 18 July 1868, educated at St Olave's Grammar School, Tooley Street, Southwark and awarded a scholarship to study at Exeter College, Oxford. On 14 March 1892 at the Congregational Church, Lewisham High Road, he was married by his father to Hughiena Lenny Florence, daughter of the late Donald Fraser.

Harold and Hughiena had two children: Donald Arthur George Buchanan, born on 5 July 1893 and Harold Buchanan junior, born on 6 June 1896. H. B. Ryley senior was ordained in 1893 and accepted a curacy at Grace Church, Colorado Springs. After a brief American interlude, he returned to his old school as an Assistant Master. His musical abilities soon shone through and he wrote the settings to a number of hymns in the *St Olave's Hymnal*.

In 1901 H. B. Ryley senior accepted a challenging new role as Headmaster of Sir Roger Manwood's Grammar School, Sandwich. A decade earlier, the Charity Commissioners had issued an ultimatum to the Trustees of the Sir Roger Manwood Charity: either the school – which had fallen into abeyance in the middle of the century – was successfully revived, or the charitable funds should be used for more general educational purposes. Six years after Sir Roger Manwood's Grammar School had reopened on a new site and the hundredth pupil had been admitted, Ryley's predecessor suddenly resigned, taking his two senior teaching assistants with him together with almost a quarter of the pupils.

The new Headmaster rose to the challenge, leaving the fine 'Big Hall' for his successor, restructuring the classes, changing the examination system, starting a school museum and establishing a preparatory school. The school's history records that 'perhaps the most significant event of Mr Ryley's régime was the founding of a Cadet Corps', commanded by the Headmaster. The entry in the Corps records book reads: 'The Cadet Corps was formed and put into working order some time before 27 July 1902, and was sanctioned as a Half-Company attached to the East Kent Volunteer Regiment, by the War Office, on 28 April 1903.'

Harold Buchanan Ryley

After four years of notable achievement, the Reverend H. B. Ryley returned to London in order to take up his new appointment as Headmaster of Emanuel School. During Ryley's tenure, there were enhancements and innovations in all aspects of Emanuel School life: pupil numbers increased from 359 in 1906 to a pre-war peak of 562 in 1912; examination results steadily improved; the school

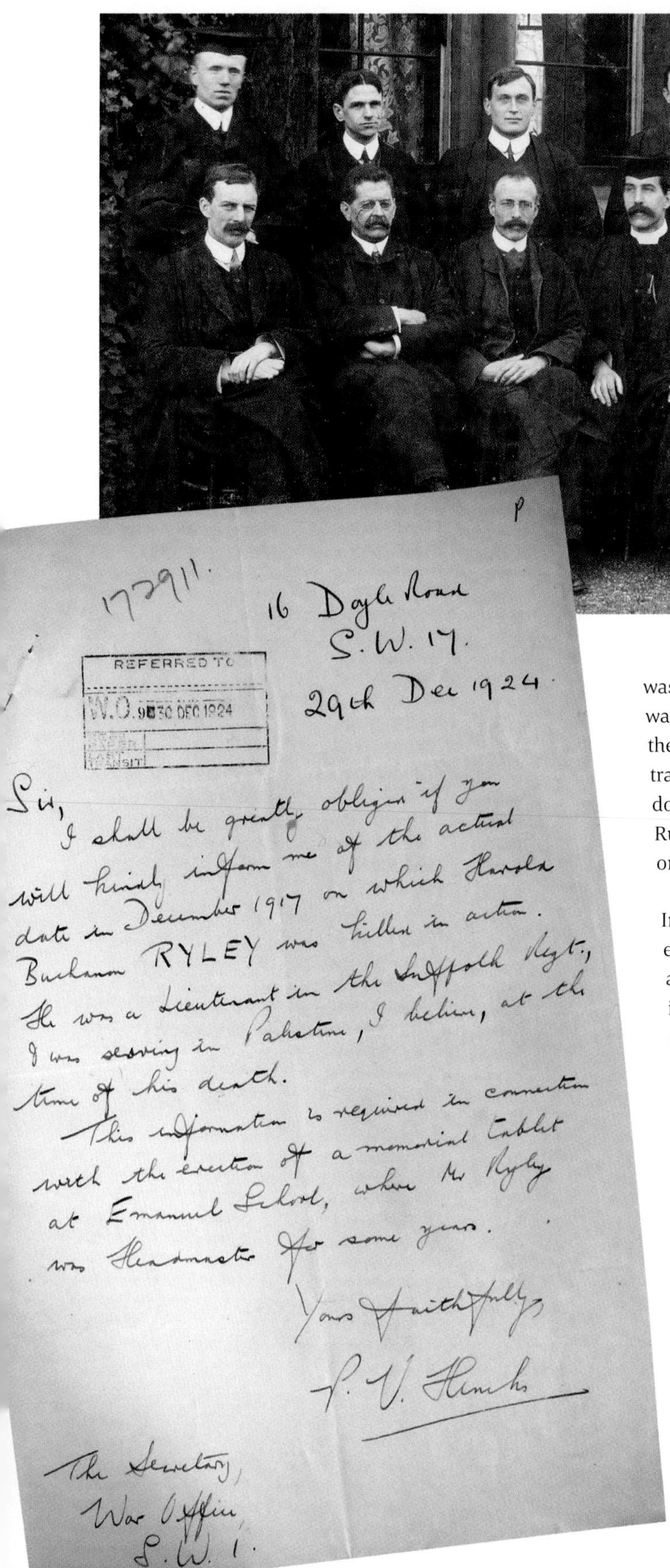

p

177911.

16 Doyle Road
S.W. 17.
29th Dec 1924.

REFERRED TO
W.O. 9 30 DEC 1924

Sir,
I shall be greatly obliged if you will kindly inform me of the actual date in December 1917 on which Harold Buchanan RYLEY was killed in action. He was a Lieutenant in the Suffolk Regt., & was serving in Palestine, I believe, at the time of his death.
This information is required in connection with the erection of a memorial tablet at Emanuel School, where Mr Ryley was Headmaster for some years.

Yours faithfully
P. V. Hincks

The Secretary,
War Office,
S.W. 1.

Harold Buchanan Ryley and Emanuel Masters 1906

was divided into 'classical' and 'modern' sides; the house system was adopted in 1906; a new school library was built in 1907; the Debating Society was founded in 1910, the same year that transition to a day school was completed with the boarding dormitories converted into classrooms; on the sporting front, Rugby Football was adopted as the school game, while the origins of Emanuel as a rowing school can be dated to 1913.

In the meantime, the Headmaster had lost none of his enthusiasm for military matters. In May 1906 he was appointed to command the Cadet Company at Emanuel School, initially with 82 members. On 11 February 1909 Ryley took command of Emanuel School OTC, when it 'emerged' from the Cadet Corps. It is noted in his Army records that 'Inspection Reports of Emanuel School OTC, which he commanded, were uniformly good for the years he was in command, viz: 1909, 1910, 1911 , 1912 & 1913.'

In the *History of Emanuel School*, Wilfrid Scott-Giles was naturally reticent, writing that 'private troubles and ill-health led Mr. Ryley to relinquish his headship in 1913'. The truth was slightly more complicated. On 17 March 1913 the minutes of the Governing Body reveal that his behaviour led to the resignations of two preparatory school mistresses. Meanwhile he readmitted as Scholars, on his own initiative, boys whose scholarships had already

Letter from Old Emanuel Percy Hincks to the War Office requesting the exact date on which Harold Buchanan Ryley was killed, for the purpose of erecting a memorial in the School chapel

been formally terminated. The Governing Body demanded Ryley's resignation, which was accepted on 28 July 1913. On 9 February 1914, by which time he had already sailed for the United States, the minutes reveal that the Headmaster's personal finances had become thoroughly intertwined with those of the School and that the School's financial situation was chaotic. In his new history, Nigel Watson summarised Ryley's period of office: 'A man of immense energy, he set

Harold Buchanan Ryley with Emanuel Masters and OTC Officers Gilbert Burnett (left) and J. Daniel (right)

himself such ambitious aims that, without any secretarial support, he often suffered from nervous exhaustion brought on by overwork.'

Ryley's two sons remained in England to complete their education. Donald Ryley was educated at Sir Roger Manwood's Grammar School and later at St Olave's, Southwark. In May 1912 he was awarded an Exhibition to read Classics at St John's College, Cambridge, joining the Cambridge University OTC as a private soldier in October 1912. However, he was never awarded his degree, applying instead for a special reserve commission in the Army on 26 August 1914. Posted initially to 1st/8th Manchester Regiment (Territorial Forces), he saw service in Gallipoli from 20 October 1915, it being noted that he did 'good reconnaissance work in Turkish trenches'. On 29 August 1916 he was 'order[ed] home from Egypt by first public opportunity', joining 3rd (Reserve) Battalion, The North Staffordshire Regiment, with a permanent commission, on 12 October 1916.

Harold Buchanan Ryley junior, Captain of Emanuel – popularly known as 'Bay' – spent three years in the OTC, achieving the rank of sergeant, before being commissioned into The North Staffordshire Regiment. On 16 September 1916 the War Office sent a telegram that was to set off a tragic sequence of events: 'Deeply regret to inform you that 2nd Lt. H. B. Ryley North Staffordshire Regiment was killed in action September 5. The Army Council express their sympathy.' 'Bay' Ryley was killed at Delville Wood on the Somme and, having no known grave, is commemorated on the Thiépval Memorial. Of the Emanuel School First Fifteen 1912–1913, eight were killed (including 'Bay' Ryley), three were wounded and one was missing in action, presumed dead.

When news of his younger son's death reached H. B. Ryley senior in Florida, his immediate reaction was to return to England and volunteer for active service. No-one should have been surprised. Many years earlier, Harold Buchanan Ryley had written a poem, *Adsum*, published in *The Portcullis*, the Emanuel School magazine, in 1911, a verse from which reads:

So when the banded nations stand,
And the day has dawned of England's fate;
When the war-clouds gather o'er sea and land,
And the foot of the foe is at our gate –
Oh then, in the time of our Mother's need,
Be ours the will, be ours the deed,
Ours be the strength elate,
Ours be one voice outringing clear:
'England! I'm here!'

On 16 November 1916, Ryley senior completed and signed his application for a commission and, shortly afterwards, was posted to 2nd Garrison Battalion, The Suffolk Regiment. The battalion's role was to defend the exposed coastline and vital installations and he formed part of the Shotley Barrier Guard.

Around that time, he wrote to the School: 'Perhaps you would like to add my name to *The Portcullis Pro Patria List*. If so, I am now Lieutenant of the above regiment.' Somewhat fatalistically, he added, 'I wish my name could go next to dear old Bay's, but ...' Of the over 800 Emanuel alumni listed on the *Pro Patria List*, 142 lost their lives, together with three of their teachers. With their natural dash, enthusiasm and flair for leadership, the School's most talented sportsmen were in the vanguard.

On 15 February 1917, Donald Ryley's paternal grandfather was sent a telegram by the War Office informing him that his grandson was 'missing'. On 21 August 1917 the Reverend G. B. Ryley wrote to the War Office, noting that 'since then

Harold Buchanan Ryley with Emanuel prefects

we have heard nothing, save that by private enquiry we find his brother Officers & others believe him to be killed.' On 13 September 1917, C. F. Watherston of C.2 Casualties Department at the War Office wrote to G. B. Ryley: 'I am directed to inform you that it is regretted that no further report has been received concerning Lieutenant D. A. G. B. Ryley, The North Staffordshire Regiment, reported Missing 11th February, 1917.' Lieutenant Donald Ryley is now officially recorded as having been killed in action near Hulluch in France and is commemorated on the Loos Memorial, since he also has no known grave.

Wilfrid Scott-Giles co-edited Harold Buchanan Ryley senior's obituary in *The Portcullis*, taking care to include extracts from one of his subject's last letters:

> I was over at Emanuel yesterday to see old Appleyard and look at the place for what, I doubt not, will be the last time ... I have been ordered to hold myself in readiness to go to the Front at short notice. There I shall be at first on 'lines of communication,' but I mean to wriggle up into the trenches somehow, somewhere. I said goodbye to my old mother and father on Sunday – a good day and a good place to say goodbye. You who know me can guess how eager I am for the Front, and how glad to have the chance. To all old boys of Emanuel and 'Stogs' give my 'Salvete, amici'.

Scott-Giles noted that 'perhaps the pith was in the postscript': 'Bay's sword was recovered and my mother has it now, thank goodness.'

On 18 October 1917, Lieutenant H. B. Ryley senior embarked on S.S. *Huntspill* to join the Egyptian Expeditionary Force. He reported to the 1st/5th Battalion, The Suffolk Regiment on 6 November 1917. During the next three weeks, the Suffolks made a series of long route marches until, by 1 December, they were established in trenches at Yehudiyah, opposite the final Turkish defence line in front of Jerusalem. On 13 December, the Battalion War Diary recorded 'warning received of intended attack on Kh Bornat W. 13 D. on the 15th.' It was to be a two-phase assault, with 1/5th Suffolks forming the left assault battalion during the second phase.

On 15 December 1917, 'at 0800 the Battalion debouches from the trees for attack – after a preliminary bombardment of 1st Objective – Sangar Hill – for 10 minutes. Met with heavy fire from 4 M.G.s causing about 30 casualties but they quickly get into dead ground and good cover among the rocks. The enemy is observed dismounting his gun and getting behind hill. Hill gained at 0820 – one prisoner – four dead observed – Total casualties during advance and after found to be one Officer & seven O.R. killed – two Officers 62 O.R. wounded. Positions improved at night by digging in, building up sangars etc. Night bitterly cold and the arrival of the blankets and greatcoats at 2300 gives the men a chance to rest.'

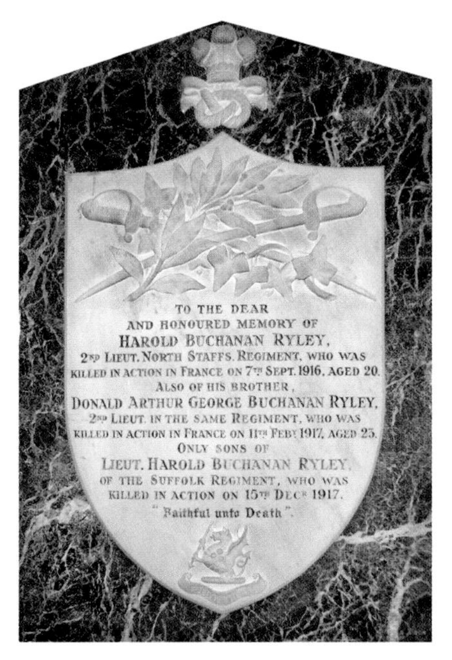

The Ryley Family Memorial, St Luke's, Whyteleafe

That rest was eternal for Lieutenant Harold Buchanan Ryley, who had managed to 'wriggle' his way forward, just as he had promised, and who was the only officer from 1/5th Suffolks to be killed that day. In 1929 Hedley J. Evans, Music Master at Emanuel School, wrote in *The Kipling Journal* that 'We were able to glean few details of his death beyond that he received a bullet through the head while gallantly leading his men.' His body now lies in Ramleh War Cemetery, some twenty miles south-east of Tel Aviv in Israel.

There was *An Appreciation* by the VI Form of Emanuel School in *The Portcullis*: 'One by one, with heavy hearts and loving memory, we have recorded the passing of many dear friends we have known and respected. And now the sad news has reached us that the Rev. H. Buchanan Ryley has laid down his life for King and Country, treading the path of honour and glory over which, only a few months previously, his two sons had walked and given their all for England ... We can almost imagine his tall, imposing figure, with his genial smile, coming across the playing fields to watch a match. Perhaps the most familiar sight of all when he was with us and one that showed a most human and gentle side of his character, was to see him walking along the corridors with his favourite collie.'

Harold Buchanan Ryley's application for a commission reveals an added dimension of sadness; he wrote, tersely: 'I lost my wife 11 years ago.' However, his Letters of Administration confirm that he died 'intestate without child leaving Hughiena Florence Ryley his lawful widow and relict who is now a person of unsound mind.' On 7 September 1918 the Reverend George Buchanan Ryley summarised the tragic situation in a letter to the War Office: 'My daughter-in-law, mother of these officers, has been many years in a lunatic asylum; and their father and after him, they, were her natural support.' Throughout his challenging time at Emanuel, Ryley therefore had no-one with whom to share the burden of his onerous responsibilities. On 29 July 1919 Hughiena Ryley died at the City of London Mental Hospital at Stone, near Dartford, Kent from 'septic inflammation of the liver and perforation of the stomach and gall bladder due to swallowing a bristle from a bass broom.'

One of the poems that H. B. Ryley set to music was *The Children's Song* from Rudyard Kipling's *Puck of Pook's Hill*:

Land of our Birth, we pledge to thee
Our love and toil in the years to be;
When we are grown and take our place
As men and women with our race.

In a fine epitaph in *The Kipling Journal*, Hedley J. Evans wrote: 'It is singularly fitting that the name of a brave man, who, after years devoted to the education of children, and giving himself and his sons to the land of their birth, should be associated with a song beloved by every child that has learnt it.'

Under the rules of the Commonwealth War Graves Commission, the family of the deceased may choose a modest inscription to appear at the foot of the Portland stone grave marker. The words engraved on Harold Buchanan Ryley senior's gravestone reflect the sentiments of his poem, *Adsum*:

For the Motherland

Sources

The History of Emanuel School by Charles Wilfrid Scott-Giles, published by *The Portcullis*, Redhill in 1935; revised editions published in 1948 and 1966.
Nigel Watson, *Emanuel School: An Illustrated History* (2008).
John Cavell and Brian Kennett, *A History of Sir Roger Manwood's School, Sandwich 1563–1963*.
The Kipling Journal, No. 8, January 1929.
The Times Digital Archive.
National Archives: WO95/4658 – War Diary of 1st/5th Battalion, The Suffolk Regiment, 163rd Infantry Brigade, January 1916 – October 1919.
National Archives: WO339/88635 – Papers of 172911 Second-Lieutenant Harold Buchanan Ryley, North Staffordshire Regiment.
National Archives: WO339/65416 – Papers of 140489 Lieutenant Donald Arthur George Buchanan Ryley, North Staffordshire Regiment.
National Archives: WO339/27426 – Papers of 49049 Lieutenant Harold Buchanan Ryley, Suffolk Regiment.
The Commonwealth War Graves Commission: www.cwgc.org.

Emanuel Masters in the First World War

Captain (acting) Grantley Adolphe Le Chavetois MC *(Staff 1909–1912)*

Grantley Adolphe Le Chavetois, 'Chavvy' as he was affectionately known, was Assistant Master at Emanuel 1909–1912. He was Head of Howe House and was an influential leader and popular teacher. Whilst he worked at Emanuel he was also studying for an MA, submitting a thesis on *The Legislation of Caius Gracchus*. When he left Emanuel he rejoined St Olave's Grammar School of which he was an Old Boy, as was the Headmaster he served under, Harold Buchanan Ryley.

Grantley Adolphe Le Chavetois

When war broke out Grantley took a commission in the London Regiment, eventually joining the 22nd Battalion. Whilst in France he went through an anti-gas course under the tutelage of Emanuel Master William Elder.

He served in both Salonika and Palestine winning the MC. He wrote to the School on more than one occasion. In one letter he wrote from the front line:

> You would be amused to see me now...It is 11pm and I am sitting shivering in a dug-out. I am on duty in a short time and it's not worth turning in. Every now and then I break away to give a vicious kick in the hope of disconcerting various rats that are making love somewhere at the back of my bed, which is behind me. On the dug-out table are mugs, whisky bottles and various tins. As I write, I, a peace time teetotaller, am sipping a liqueur. Fancy liqueur in the firing line! Last

time we were up we managed to get a bottle. We buried it while we were away and unearthed it on our return. Round the dug-out walls hang Very pistols, waders, bags of rockets etc. On a shelf in front are various souvenirs in the shape of bits of bombs and shells and a stock of bombs and Very lights. High up above is the sharp rattle of machine guns and the low rumble of the heavy guns in the south. The nights are very bad here and unfortunately they grow longer. I often think of Newbolt's line: "I love the daylight as dearly as any alive. You want a night in the trenches to appreciate the beauty of the day, any day, whether wet or fine..." Love to all friends at Emanuel.[1]

On 6 November 1917 he received a shrapnel wound to the head — a bullet entered in through his forehead and lodged into the back of his skull. After the extraction of the bullet he seemed to be recovering and he returned to England.

In one of his final letters to the OEA he wrote on 4 January 1918: 'I am very fit, except that one of the head wounds wants another operation.' He died eighteen days after writing this letter.

William Gardner Elder

Lieutenant William Gardner Elder

(Staff 1911–1915)

William was an Old Boy of Christ's Hospital in Horsham, attending 1902–1906. He joined Emanuel as a mathematics and geography master with a passion for games. William was House Master of Drake and President and Coach of the Rugby Fifteen.

Having served in the OTC he was commissioned a 2nd Lt. in the 2nd/20th Battalion London Regiment, advancing to Temporary Lieutenant in July 1916. The Board of Education had requested him to remain at his post but as *The Portcullis* noted, 'Mr. Elder's conscience would not allow him to do so.'[2] He served widely, including in France, Salonika and Palestine. He was Gas Officer to the 60th Division in France during the latter part of 1916. Having contracted consumption caused by getting sand into his lungs in Egypt, he returned to England in October 1917. He was originally taken ill whilst preparing for an attack on Beersheba. He died at the 3rd London General Hospital (adjacent to Emanuel in the Royal Victoria Patriotic building) on 10 February 1918, aged 28 years. He was buried in Eltham Churchyard. In a tribute the Drake House notes praised William's time as a master, 'While at Emanuel his unflagging enthusiasm did much to improve both School and House football. Nor were his energies only directed towards football. In every branch of School life he left a mark which cannot be erased. In fact, it may well be said...that in all that he did he gave of his best.' *The Portcullis* also commented, 'Mr. Elder was in all things an optimist. Throughout his long illness he never seemed to lose heart and was always ready to enter into discussions so far as his strength would permit. The prospects of Emanuel always interested him...'

James Edward Whitehead *(Staff 1909–1916)*

In his day 'Joey' was a much beloved history teacher who took a full part in the life of the school. He left to serve in the First World War and served in Palestine with William Elder. Although he never returned to employment at Emanuel, he was known to visit for Speech Days and Old Boy Dinners. When he died in 1977 he was one of the last surviving teachers to have taught during the headship of Harold Buchanan Ryley.

Lt-Colonel Stewart Montagu Cleeve

Viola Teacher and Commander of the 'Boche Buster'

Stewart Montagu Cleeve was a visiting music teacher at Emanuel for 25 years after the Second World War. He died in 1993, at the age of 98. He attended Dean Close School, a Public School in Cheltenham after growing up in Wimbledon. He later remembered that almost all the friends he had made at Dean Close were killed in the First World War.

In the First World War Montagu served with the Royal Garrison Artillery and in 1916 saw action on the Somme as he remembered:

> One thing I shall never forget was my first experience of dead bodies. On the first day at Albert, the weather was very hot and I was sent up to an observation post and literally couldn't walk along the trenches without treading on dead bodies, German. The stench and the flies were simply appalling. That was one of the most miserable memories I have of the Somme. It was pathetic really. Eventually one just got over it and thought nothing of it. We couldn't help it, we were alive and that's what mattered. And being alive, we jolly well had to get on with it.
>
> It was a complete and utter surprise to the Germans that we had ever devised such a thing as a tank. They were so shattered when they first appeared on the Somme that all resistance in the German section where they were used collapsed. The mistake we made then was not to have prepared for this lack of opposition. We should have had our cavalry all ready to take over from the tanks and wipe the whole thing out. We could have turned the flank of the Germans in no time. But the success of the tank took us by surprise and we were so ill-prepared that nobody followed.

Montagu recalled moments from his service experiences:

> **Dinner with the Brigadier** – I was asked to dinner at the Brigade Headquarters of the Infantry Brigadier. There was a terrible din from the machine-guns and shells bursting all around us, but he insisted on having an old-fashioned mess dinner. And we sat at a large table in this dugout and the wine was brought around in decanters. This was a contrast to trench life, where we often had to cook our own meals and I used a little bivvy tin that I had. It was a tiny wee saucepan with a lid, and inside the saucepan was a methylated spirits lamp.
>
> **Communication on the front line** – Before the wireless was invented we had to do the whole thing by telephone lines. We put them in the trenches for protection, but you can just imagine the confusion. In some trenches there may have been up to twenty lines all mixed up. Occasionally I think they may have been coloured red, blue and yellow, or something like that, but not always. And whenever a shell burst in a trench, as thousands did, they bust all the lines and there'd be complete confusion, with mud and lines and debris everywhere.
>
> The signallers, who were marvellous in our battery had a terrible job to find all the bits and pieces and to join them together again. It was absolutely hopeless in those seven days before the bombardment of the Somme, because the Germans knew exactly what was going to happen and shelled the place to blazes, so nobody had any communications after that. So the telephone system was a complete failure.[3]

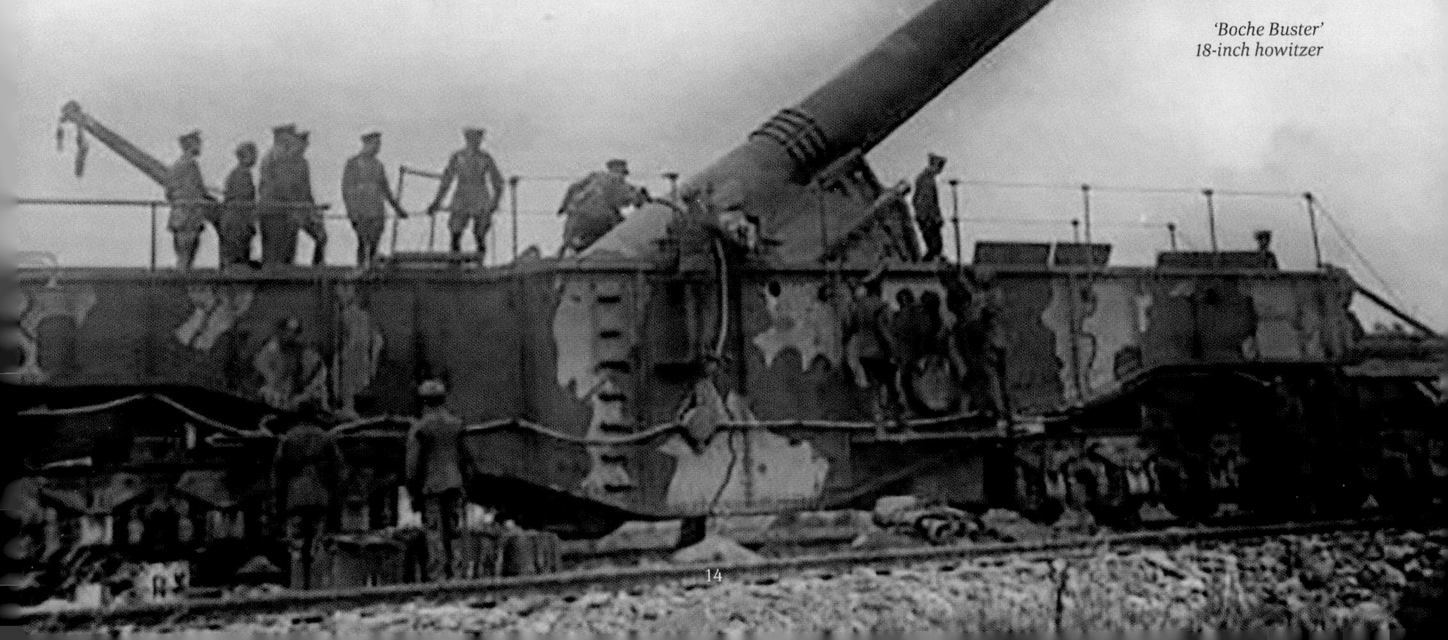

'Boche Buster' 18-inch howitzer

It was during the Somme Offensive that Montagu was injured when a German shell landed near a convoy of lorries filled with ammunition and the whole place became ablaze. He decided the shelter he had chosen to gain cover wasn't offering adequate protection and shortly after leaving it he was hit. He was sent to England to recuperate and when he got better he was sent on a battery commanders course at Larkhill. His success at the course led to the War Office offering him a special assignment. In 1917 GHQ France was concerned about the strength of the Hindenburg Line and they were looking for heavier guns to penetrate it. It was at this time that the Admiralty offered the War Office sixteen 14-inch Mark Three barrel guns which had come out of the turrets of the Chilean Battleship *Almirante Cochrane* which at that time was being converted into the first aircraft carrier HMS *Eagle*. The guns were not needed for the aircraft carrier and so the Admiralty offered them to the War Office. The War Office ordered twelve railway mountings to be built which would take these 14-inch guns. The problem they had was what to do with the recoil of the gun when fired. They got over the problem by making a balancing system, which consisted of two large hydro pneumatic cylinders, which helped elevate the gun.

There was a competition to name two of the guns which subsequently travelled to France. Montagu chose the names 'Boche Buster' and 'Scene Shifter'. He commanded His Majesty's Gun 'Boche Buster' in the neighbourhood of Arras. At this time he was a Major in the 471st Siege Battery Royal Garrison Artillery, under which the gun operated. After some initial technical difficulties, 'Boche Buster' saw action in June 1918 against the German railway system and then saw more serious action by the end of July. The maximum range of the gun was 34,000 yards and it was operated along a railway line. The 'Boche Buster' with the 'Scene Shifter' were the largest guns of any the army possessed. Montagu remembered what he did when called into action, 'I used to blow a whistle and that was the go into action signal and all the men jumped to their positions on the gun ...'

At Maroeuil on 8 August 1918 Montagu received a phone call saying that he was to receive a VIP and was told to get the gun ready to fire. Later that day he saw King George V step out from the first car of a motorcade. The King walked all over the gun with Montagu in a visit that was filmed and asked him about the life of the gun and Montagu informed the King that it would take 250 rounds before it needed retuning. To his astonishment the King possessed a wealth of knowledge about guns and told Montagu that the life of the guns was always underestimated saying that the gun would fire 350 rounds before she had to be retuned and at the 300th round she would still be firing just as accurately as she was firing that day. King George asked Montagu to fire the gun, a moment known as the 'King's shot.' The King then proceeded to look over the railway map and engaged Stewart in conversation about German movements and how Douai Station should be attacked at night, which Montagu thought insurmountable as the flash would be too large and draw German shelling, but orders were orders and they had to fire at Douai Station, night after night. It wasn't until after the War that he visited Douai and was informed that the 'King's shot' had damaged a German troop train but the King never knew, although later Montagu did inform his son, King George VI.

During the Second World War, Montagu was stationed in Hong Kong. He wrote a letter to the War Office and offered his services as the only serving officer left who had knowledge of mobile heavy artillery but a letter came back and he was notified that his services were no longer required. Soon war was declared, however, and he was personally recalled by Winston Churchill to reorganise Britain's heavy artillery guns which had been hidden away since the end of the First World War. Montagu found both 'Boche Buster' and 'Scene Shifter' in a transport shed where they had rested since the end of the First World War. They were requisitioned and used in the defence of the Kent coast. He described finding 'Boche Buster' again thus, 'Most excited, I couldn't contain myself with excitement, having found it I was thrilled, I went back and reported my discovery to the War Office and they were equally thrilled.'

Montagu moved to Catterick and helped set up the School of Super Heavy Artillery Railway. He chose his own personnel as instructors in gunnery and with lots of help from the War Office he established trains for training and living quarters. On Winston Churchill's direct orders the guns were sent to Dover in case of invasion.

After the Second World War Montagu continued to teach privately until the age of 90 and worked in local schools including Battersea Grammar School. In addition to teaching violin and piano Montagu promoted the *viola d'amore*, an old form of viola with six strings, later forming the Viola d'Amore Society in 1964. When he was 90 he said 'I don't believe in old age, only in being fit and doing what I love best – and in my case it's music.'

Alfred Mason Eade

Regimental Sergeant-Major Alfred Mason Eade

Alfred Eade had a colourful service career. For eighteen years he was caretaker of Emanuel School and was also the Small Arms Instructor of the School's OTC and was popularly known to Emanuel boys as 'the Sergeant-Major.'

In 1941 he collapsed while working in his garden and died before he reached the hospital.

His service career began when he gave a false age to join the Army Medical Corps and during his 25 years' service he served both in the South African War and the First World War in the Royal Marines Light Infantry attached to the Royal Marine Labour Company, obtaining the rank of Regimental Sergeant-Major.

In the First World War he fought alongside Indian troops for whom he always expressed his greatest admiration. He saw action at Mons, the Somme, Ypres, and also served with the Mediterranean Expeditionary Force in the Dardanelles.

His medals included the South African Medal, the Long Service and Good Conduct Medals, the 1914–15 Star and the Victory Medal.

Alfred was also a Freemason, a warden and an instructor in the local Home Guard. One of his sons-in-law, Mr S. W. Burton, was a private in the Royal Army Service Corps and was at the evacuation of Dunkirk, being on the beaches for two days before being rescued by a destroyer.

After Alfred's death Cyril Broom paid tribute to him writing in *The Portcullis*:

> Emanuel has suffered a great loss by the tragically sudden death of Sergeant-Major Eade, who for some twenty years served the School with characteristic loyalty, and enjoyed the full confidence of the Governors and Headmaster, and the respect and esteem of parents and boys. Officially the resident curator of the School buildings he performed a variety of other duties, supervising the domestic staff, organising for many years the provision of lunches, helping the OTC contingent, and controlling the issue of stationery. When evacuation transferred the School's work to Petersfield, he remained behind and bore the main responsibility for initiating protective measures when the premises were threatened by air raids. His prompt action on several occasions doubtless prevented serious fires, and once when the tower was directly hit he had a narrow escape from falling debris. As was to be expected from his service record, he had an invariable courtesy and an unshakable devotion to duty, and was closely identified with the life of the School. He took the keenest interest in the successes of boys past and present, and Old Boys visiting the place naturally gravitated to his office to talk of School affairs. Everyone associated with Emanuel will mourn the passing of a staunch friend who had become an intimate part of the tradition of the School, and will feel the sincerest sympathy with his widow and family.

References

1. *The Portcullis*, Christmas Term, 1916, p. 47.
2. *The Portcullis*, Lent Term, 1918, p. 62.
3. These extracts are part of the Montagu Cleeve papers and sound recording Catalogue number 7310 held by the Imperial War Museum. They were also published in *Forgotten Voices of the Great War* by Max Arthur. Published by Ebury Press in 2002 an imprint of Penguin Random House.

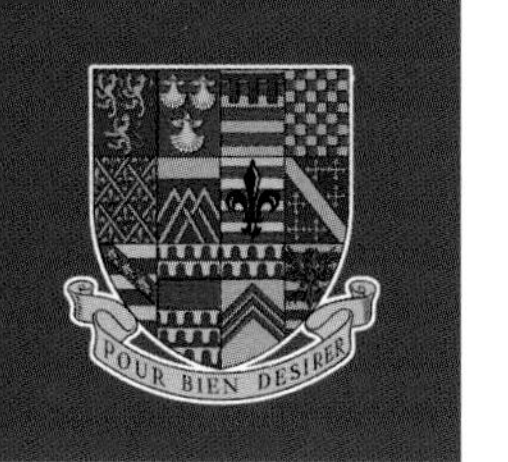

CHAPTER 3

FATEFUL 14 *'This will always be looked back upon as the most memorable term in the history of Emanuel. We broke up in July under the shadow of Armageddon and re-assembled to find it a reality.'*

Two Sides of a Postcard

The Emanuel Master Mr. Parkinson held back no punches in his criticism of his Emanuel First Fifteen side of the 1912–1913 season commenting in *The Portcullis*, 'The chief causes of weakness in the First Fifteen have been a deplorable lack of 'three-quarters' of any size or weight and a want of 'grit' and 'backbone' in the team generally; it was at its worst in an uphill fight and should have done much better.'[1]

The team was photographed outside the main School entrance and the image was subsequently turned into a postcard. There are always two sides to every postcard and similarly there are two sides to the story of these boys whom Parkinson thought lacked a certain something on the rugby pitch. Within a couple of years of the photo being taken the majority of these boys were in a far greater conflict in which they displayed all the 'grit' and 'backbone' any human could face with the trials of combat in the First World War.

The other side of the postcard shows the fate of this Fifteen. It is now known that eight of these young men were killed in the war. The captain of the side Eric William Dilnutt played forward in the team and was captain of it up to Christmas 1913. Parkinson described him thus, 'Did excellent work in the 'Scrum', a trifle wild in open play.'

The University of London Officers' Training Corps Roll of War Service records Eric's fate:

> Captain Royal Fusiliers son of Mr. and Mrs. C. J. Dilnutt of Balham killed instantly by a bullet in the head while attempting to occupy craters formed by the explosion of mines under the enemy's lines in France on 2 March 1916. Buried at the bottom of the crater No, 4 gained by his men near Hohenzollern Redoubt.[2]

The 8th and 9th Battalions' objective was *The Chord* which connected two German trenches, *Little Willie* and *Big Willie*.[3] Eric, who was aged only 19, is remembered on the Loos Memorial.

Basil Horswell was described in the rugby notes as, 'Flying Half. An excellent player; rather apt at holding onto the ball too long. Defence good.' In the Christmas Term *Portcullis* we learn that Basil was killed on 11 October 1917, 'while flying a new and difficult type of machine.'[4] That machine was an F.B.A. 'B' Pusher Biplane Flying Boat. From the Admiralty Basil entered the Royal Naval Air Service as a Probationary Flight Officer in March 1917. He returned from a post at Vendôme to an appointment at Cranwell in the summer of 1917 being described as, 'a very good pilot recommended for seaplanes.' His rank at the time of death was Flight Sub-Lt. *The Portcullis* recorded his last flight which occurred just off Calshot, 'He had made a successful flight of ten minutes duration, at a height of 600 feet and was on the point of descending, when the machine 'nose dived' and Horswell was thrown 300 feet into the sea.

B. Horswell's British War Medal

Emanuel First XV 1912–1913

Although speedily rescued from the water, he succumbed to his injuries.'[5] He is buried in Paddington.

Little is known about Frederick Kimber and John Roberts. In the Fifteen critiques Frederick was noted as 'Three Quarter. Has also filled the position of back; was improving every match, but unfortunately left us.' And John's critique noted, 'Three Quarter. Has played consistently well through the season, but has had very little support. Takes a pass wonderfully well.'[6] These two young men died just two days apart in the Battle of the Ancre, 13–18 November, 1916. It was the last major British offensive in the Battle of the Somme and the last of 1916 before winter set in. Both served in the Honourable Artillery Company, Frederick as a Private and John as a Lance Corporal.

Kenneth Newton, 'Forward. A good and keen forward who should do well when he has more weight.' On leaving School Kenneth joined the 1/4th Seaforths "B" Company and made his journey to the Front on 5 November 1914. Kenneth saw action at Neuve Chapelle and Aubers Ridge in 1915 and experienced three winters on the Western Front. He rose to the rank of Corporal and was attached to a Trench Mortar Battery when on 24 April 1917 at the age of 20 he was killed. The Captain of the Trench Mortar Battery wrote to Kenneth's parents:

John Roberts, Captain of Emanuel School 1914

> I deeply regret to inform you that your son, Corporal K. F. C. Newton, of this Battery, was killed in the heavy fighting on the afternoon of the 24th. He accompanied the officer in charge of his detachment on a reconnaissance of a very difficult and dangerous enemy position from which our troops were being held up by a party of snipers; and, while crossing the open, Kenneth was shot through the head and killed instantaneously. His death was a tremendous blow to the Battery, and from our own grief we can form some idea of what his loss will be to you. Please accept for yourself and for the other members of the family our very deepest sympathy.

did not come through. And if he had survived he would certainly have been recommended for the day's work in which he met his death. I had also written to his battalion asking them to put him forward for nomination to an Officer's Cadet School with a view to promotion to a commission. If he had only lived the splendid work of the last two years might have been more adequately rewarded. But, after all, the truest reward lies in the knowledge that the work was done, and that your son's life was continually devoted to the highest ends. He lived and died a brave soldier and a good man.

Owing to the peculiar difficulties of the situation, the officer who was with him was unable to recover any of his personal belongings that afternoon, and as our place was taken a few hours later by another division, we were withdrawn before any opportunity arose. The Commanding Officer of the relieving unit, however, promised faithfully to have his body taken in and his belongings forwarded to us as soon as the exigencies of the situation would permit. We shall write [to] you again, therefore, in a few days, and by then we hope to be able to send any little things of value that he carried with him.

Kenneth had not been home on leave for sixteen months. He was his parents' only son and fittingly a newspaper article described him as, 'A brave and intrepid, although youthful soldier, loving and beloved, with strong home instincts, and the soul of honour.'

The other side of the postcard detailing the fates of the 1912–1913 First XV

As an NCO your son was in a class by himself. All his work was done with exceptional thoroughness and care; and no one could help being struck by his constant and ungrudging efforts in the service of the battery and by his steadfast devotion to duty. He gave himself at all times without hesitation and without reserve to the work that came to his hands. His place will be hard indeed to fill; for we had come to rely upon him in every emergency, and he never failed to rise to any task. It may be of some help to you in your sorrow to know that he was recommended for recognition in the New Year Honours, but for some reason or other his award

Harold Buchanan 'Bay' Ryley, Captain of Emanuel, was the son of the pre-war Headmaster H. B. Ryley and was killed at Delville Wood on 5 September 1916. Bay served in the North Staffordshire Regiment, as did another boy in the 1912–13 Fifteen, Ivor Austin While, whose brother Eric is also pictured in the postcard. Ivor played a full part in Emanuel life being a Prefect, Captain of Lyons House, a Senior-Cadet Officer and was elected Captain of the First Fifteen in 1913 but left School to take a Commission in the North Staffs. Ivor wrote to the School in 1915:

Things at School are as per usual my brother gives me to understand, though I am rather disappointed that the

Eric William Dilnutt in 1912

Daniel Kirmatzis searching for Eric on the Loos Memorial

> whole School has not joined the OTC. Surely the Senior boys can see that the war will last years and that they will all be wanted badly in a few years.
>
> The great thing that strikes me here is the cheerfulness of the Tommies. They march all day, are on fatigue and in the night go as working parties to dig trenches and yet they are cheerful. None like the war, but we have never had a single case of discontent.
>
> I am engaged in tabulating the different sounds, but my list is not complete as I pen different ones practically every day.[7]

Ivor would have been able to compile quite a list of sounds from the Front from the noises made by guns, whistles, orders and tunes hummed by soldiers, but within a year there would only be the sound of silence. Ivor was killed on 31 August 1916 whilst meeting an enemy advance in his trench. Bay Ryley and Ivor's names appear on the same panel on the Thiepval Memorial to the Missing. Sadly neither has a known grave.

Harold Norton White was another whose rugby critique was far from glorious but who returned to France three times to serve in the War. The critique noted, 'Scrum Half. A player with more pluck than science; very prone to get off-side, passing with faulty lines at times.' In the Summer Term *Portcullis* we learn that Harold 'is suffering from trench feet, having been out through a period of very bad weather.'[8] Harold had three brothers and was distinguished from them by being known as 'dark-haired White'. He served in the Machine Gun Corps and had returned for his third duty in France in early September 1918 when on 6 September he was killed, 'by the bursting of a shell in the room which he, with six other officers, used as a mess.'[9]

The story does not end with those who lost their lives for seven others also served in the war and survived. There is minimal information on Cuthbert Harvey who is seen as the touch judge in the photo and Serge Trechatney, founder of Emanuel School rowing, is believed to have emigrated to the USA, marrying the actress Mae West's sister Beverly in 1917 and divorcing in 1927.[10] More information is available for Leslie Clinton who was Emanuel's first recipient of the MC and whose story can be read elsewhere. Percy Knight gained the rank of Captain in the Loyal North Lancashire Regiment and fought in the Battle of the Somme. He was injured during the war but he survived and moved to Dorset working for the auctioneer Rumsey and Rumsey in Bournemouth between 1923 and 1976. He became a Freemason being initiated into St Aldhelm's Lodge and was Director of Ceremonies for fourteen years. Percy was also curator of the Masonic Museum.

As a rugby team they may have lacked 'grit' and 'backbone' but as individuals in a far greater test of endurance they proved to have real guts and determination, giving themselves fully to their teammates on the front lines.

References

1 *The Portcullis*, Spring Term, 1913, p. 21.
2 University of London, Officers' Training Corps, Roll of War Service 1914–1919, 1921, p.17.
3 For a description of the action see H. C. O'Neill, *The Royal Fusiliers in the Great War*, pp. 82–83.
4 *The Portcullis*, Christmas Term, 1917, p. 51.
5 Ibid.
6 *The Portcullis*, Spring Term, 1913, p. 22.
7 *The Portcullis*, Summer Term, 1915, pp. 51–52.
8 *The Portcullis*, Summer Term, 1917, p. 55.
9 *The Portcullis*, Trinity Term, 1920, p. 46.
10 There are various spellings of Trechatney's surname.

Letters from the Front

In the late spring of 1914 Emanuel, its students and staff and their families and alumni went about their ordinary business. In the spring the School Boat Club had been founded and before the summer recess the School Music Society gave a concert on 17 June in the Battersea Town Hall. Just eleven days later Gavrilo Princip, a young Serbian nationalist, would set off a chain of events that turned the world upside down. On 4 August 1914 England went to war.

The experiences of the Emanuel School community in the First World War were not unique, for every school, town, village and community felt the War's impact. The surviving evidence from letters, photos, memorials, interviews and more allows us to form a picture of the way in which the war shaped the School community from the thoughts and feelings of Emanuel boys writing from the trenches to the ubiquitous obituary notices reprinted in both local and national newspapers throughout the war years.

To understand these boys' experiences you must understand something about the School which formed such an important part of their lives. Emanuel was based on the Victorian public school system, although technically it was never a public school in the league of Eton and Harrow. Its pupils came from a variety of economic backgrounds. Boys from all walks of society were educated within the familiar bounds of the two railway lines bordering the School's grounds.

Emanuel had a House system; each pupil was placed into one of eight houses named after English military figures: Clyde, Drake, Howe, Lyons, Marlborough, Nelson, Rodney and Wellington. The Houses would compete against each other each academic year in a number of events, largely sporting in nature. Each boy was also expected to participate in one of the School sports, which from 1914 were mainly cricket, rowing and rugby.

Emanuel School Sports Day c.1910

From 1906 to the late 1990s the School had a Cadet Force, originally known as the Officers' Training Corps. Many of the boys of the pre-1914 generation who went on to serve in the war had already spent many hours on shooting practice, undertaking route marches and kit inspections. The School also had societies such as Debating and Engineering. For alumni there was an Old Emanuel Association (OEA), which kept former pupils in contact with each other and provided a way for them to continue playing Rugby and Cricket with their friends at a specially designated ground called Blagdons. All of these elements of the School's life were reported at the end of each term in the School magazine *The Portcullis*.

Between winter 1914 and summer 1920 *The Portcullis* became a repository for news about Old Emanuels and their war service including reflections on operations and battles, news on awards and promotions, injuries, comedic escapades, requests for news on others and notices of deaths in action. The majority of news was reported in the Old Emanuel Notes. In 1915 a section titled, 'Letters From The Front' appeared, which would have been familiar to those OEs who remembered *The Portcullis* of the Second Boer War era.

The letters paraphrased in *The Portcullis* from OEs on active service were either written to the Headmaster or the editors of the Old Emanuel Association. They would have numbered in the hundreds. Sadly, the only evidence we have of these letters are the parts quoted in *The Portcullis*. It is firmly believed that the originals have been lost, most likely when the School was evacuated in the Second World War or in one of the refurbishment programmes in the past century.

The letters express the personal thoughts of Emanuel boys and many are furnished with news of chance encounters between friends, life in the trenches and thoughts on the War's progress. The reader must be made aware that they have gone through several layers of editing, not only the censor's, but also the editor of the OE notes and finally the current author. The selections chosen offer a timeline of the experiences of Emanuel boys through the course of the war and are themselves accompanied with other news from *The Portcullis* on awards, movements, injuries and obituaries as the War proceeded.

The winter term *Portcullis* of 1914 opened with the following:

> This will always be looked back upon as the most memorable term in the history of Emanuel. We broke up in July under the shadow of Armageddon and re-assembled to find it a reality.

The Portcullis No. 65 Summer 1915

Lt. Alfred Martin Smith: We've moved again, North. i.e. our Brigade. We left billets.... Marched about ten miles in rain and mud getting quite wet and then went in the trenches. We had four days in, very quiet in our trench, only one shell fell, burying my Sergeant, but we got him out in time, second time he had been buried.

My first day out I was in a shelled out farm in reserve – I then (after midnight) fell into my first Jack Johnson hole – you can't see the beastly things in the dark and you emerge soaking wet and slimy with mud.

The next night and day my platoon was in the fire-trench; I went out at night with my Sergeant to see that the Germans were up to no dirty tricks – we went about eighty yards – their trench is 120 yards from ours. They sent up a few fire balloons and their snipers were firing a little so we had to lie down in the mud and wet for a time.

In the day we sat quiet all the time – to put your head up for [more] than a few seconds is certain death. The men are very careless and that's how we lose them.

Since the 12th we've been in the trenches again. The latest arrangement is our Brigade is four days in trench and four days out, back in billets for rest which consists of fatigues and cleaning up etc. So after resting we are quite tired, but clean which is luxury.

You will be surprised to know that we've had several concerts here in the Concert Hall, tho' only three miles from the firing line. There's a platform, scenery, piano just like in the Hall at School. It made me think I was back there once more. Holy Communion was celebrated yesterday, it was a great pleasure, the one real link with home.

Memorial plaque to Leslie W. T. Pine in the Emanuel School chapel

Emanuel First XV 1913–1914

Back Row (left to right) K.F.C. Newton, W.G. Elder (Vice-Pres.), H.W. Vaughan, W.T. Vaughan, C.G. Bartram, J. Gibson, C.L. Croft, R. Urquhart, W.W. Parkinson (Vice-Pres.), E.B. Wrench

Middle Row - C. Harvey (Hon. Sec.), H.B. Ryley (Vice-Captain), P.J. Knight (Captain), J.H. Roberts, I.A. While

Front Row - W.T. Williams, R.R. Turner, W.H. Morgan

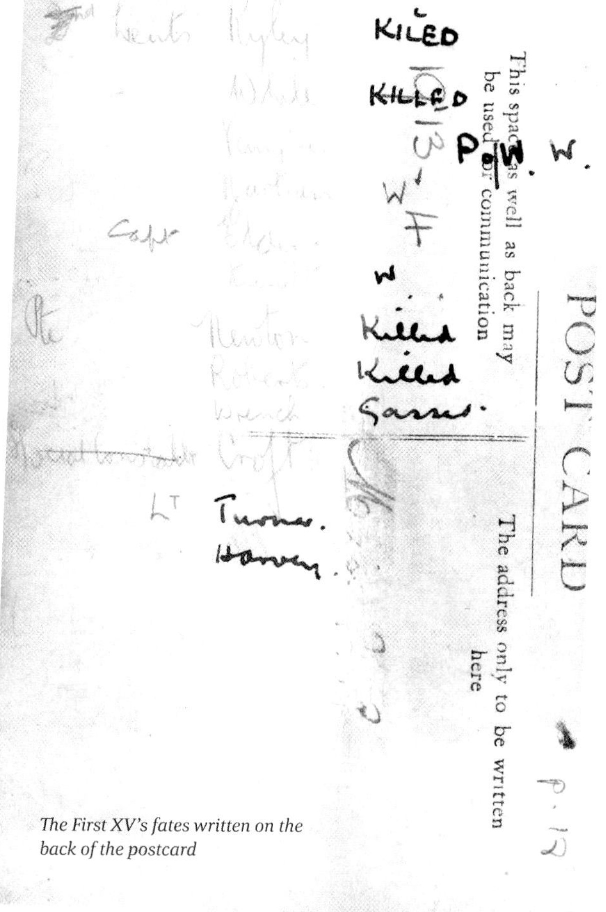

The First XV's fates written on the back of the postcard

Alfred Smith was Captain of Howe at Emanuel and a Senior Prefect. He was the younger brother of Geoffrey Cholerton Smith. Alfred served with the Manchester Regiment and whilst in action in the Dardanelles he was wounded. He was later promoted to the rank of Captain in the Worcester Regiment and in November 1918 was gazetted for 'The Order of the Redeemer, 5th Class, Chevalier'. The award is the highest decoration awarded by the Greek government and was bestowed upon Alfred by the King of Greece in 1918. Alfred Smith died in 1930 during an operation for appendicitis.

2nd Lt. L. W. T. Pine: I am now in the thickest of the fight. The others, meaning the Germans sent over clouds of gas which forced us to retire and men were lying on the ground gasping for breath, while the Germans stood on the parapets and shot them – under murderous shell and machine gun fire our men fell like flies. Between 3am and 5am the Germans sent 2000 shells at us. Twelve men of the Dublin Fusiliers were forced to surrender, but the Germans killed them on the spot.

I saw one man milking a cow while shrapnel was bursting all round him.

Lt. Harold Allen: We were under canvas for one night at our landing place and then we moved on to our station in cattle trucks. After being in these for nearly seven hours (45 men with full equipment, per trench) we were rather cramped, I can tell you. Since then we have been billeted in barns, but we are very comfortable indeed, and anyone who says you are badly fed at the front is a l—r.

Roland G. Harris: We were heavily shelled yesterday by some large shells and the Huns destroyed the church and killed the curé who was going to rescue the consecrated vessels. He had nobly stayed in the place and ministered to the peasants and the firing line.

The Portcullis No. 66 Christmas 1915

Gerald William West

In Memoriam:

News was received that Lt. Gerald William West was killed – Gerry, as he was more commonly known was a School Prefect, Captain of Howe, Colour-Sergeant in the OTC and Captain of the Old Emanuel Rugger Team.

'Charlie' Chewter wrote: On October 12th we came back into action, somewhat to our surprise as we had anticipated a rest after our long spell and here we are still. That was twenty days ago and as in this time I haven't washed or shaved I leave you to guess at my present state of trampy disreputableness. My beard is almost patriarchal, my hair is quite marked as Twain's (pardon!) and as it has rained almost incessantly, I can give you a most glorious selection of French mud from any portion of my clothing, hands or face. My moustache has grown from the most approved tooth brush order to a diabolical Chinaman's monstrosity, running round my mouth after the style of the immortal serpent that commenced eating itself. I'm not a bit like Regent Street or Piccadilly and I feel confident that you wouldn't recognise the Old Marlborough skipper anywhere, or anyhow.

This is doing one's bit, but sometimes I begin to find myself hankering after the fleshpots of Egypt – the unspeakable luxuries of a bath, a decent meal, daintily served and a good sleep. You see, I've had eight months of this, in which time I have been once wounded, had many narrow squeaks, lost some of the best around me and seen some rotten sights and now I'm beginning to thank God for preserved reason. However, I am fit and well and, somehow, no time has been so bad that we could not joke and sing our way through it.

Billy Poundall gives the following description of a night attack: We started at 6.30 for the trenches (assembly). Arrived about 11pm and had a look at the position as well as the light would permit. A Scotch regiment was on our right and an Irish one on our left and we all were to attack at 4.20am. At 3.50am our Artillery let fly and it was just as if Hell had been let loose all at once. At 4.19 four mines were exploded and 4.20 we all went over as silent as mice.

The Hun spotted us and opened fire with machine gun and rifle fire, not to mention bombs etc. We rushed on until we got to the German wire and there found a lot of Jocks hanging onto it. I immediately realised what had happened. The bombardment had been a complete failure and the enemy were holding the trenches in great force and their barbed wire, which was in a wide trench, was intact. I had a look to see how my men were going on and found them all knocked out or retiring, so back I started.

It was while turning to go back that I had a very funny experience. As I turned I bust my brace button and it made me swear in an awful manner and worried me all the way back. I just tell you this little bit to show you in what kind of a state I was in. I must have gone mad for a bit to worry over a trifle like that when I was as near death as I am ever likely to be without actually being killed. When I got back the Jocks were calling for assistance, so I took about twenty men and joined them. Then came the ordeal of holding on while the Germans gave us hell all day, till we were relieved at night.

Before we made the charge the place was absolutely covered with smoke and one could not see a couple of feet in front of one's face. And then the return. The shells were bursting like blazes and had ploughed the place up like nothing on earth. Here and there, in the holes made by shells, were little groups of men, mostly wounded.

Lt. E. Jerwood (1st Royal Berkshire Regt.) explains how Ranulph Summers (Old Emanuel) died in the Battle of Loos: Hurriedly in the morning of September 28th we were ordered to attack a strong German position which held up the whole British line. "A" Company led the attack. When Mr. Eager was wounded, Summers took over the command and led the attack. On reaching the Fosse, they were forced to retire, with fourteen officer casualties, among whom was Lt Summers. He died a very gallant soldier's death. We of the Berkshires are very proud of him and feel his loss very keenly. His general experience before the war made him very cool and quick to act. At Cuinchy he frequently showed great courage and coolness when mines were exploded. Our CO was very pleased with the way he carried on the company when poor Weston was killed and with his work in reconnoitring the mine craters in front of our line, a very nervous and hazardous undertaking. He is a great and real loss. All the Officers send their sincere sympathy. He died indeed a soldier's death.

Ranulph Summers was one of the 'missing' and as such has no known grave. He is remembered on the Loos Memorial.

2nd Lt. William Morgan writes about his experiences:

William Morgan

I was in the show at Hooge on September 25th with my trench mortars. We had another scrap on the 29th, when the Hun blew up a mine and took our trenches (front line only for about 200 yards frontage). On the 30th we tried to get him out and that night about 8pm I got a slight cut on the head by a piece of shell. The cut was described as a 'GS wound, shrapnel slight'. It was not a piece of shrapnel that hit me, but a piece of shell. If it had been shrapnel, it would have been 'bye bye'. However, I went to hospital and enjoyed myself fine.

Am very pleased to hear of the School's achievements in sports. Hope you are as successful in rugger as in cricket. The School is certainly doing well in this war. Was very pleased to hear they did so well at Tadworth. Best of luck to the OTC.

The Editor added, 'Jimmy also tells of meeting Moseley (who came to Emanuel from The Merchant Taylors...) in the trenches with the HAC (Machine Gun Section).'

Pte. Harold Allen: I never want to lose touch with the old School that has been the making of me...The idea for the improvement of the Old Boys' Club is jolly and I think it was needed. All being well, when the War is over, if I come back safe and sound, as sincerely hope I shall, I shall become a member of it.

In another letter Harold writes:

The last time we were in the trenches, the enemy's artillery gave us a hot time. They usually send us over a nice little variety. The 'coal boxes' or high explosives get the preference some days, but the 'cheeky Charlies', a smaller variety, usually come over in largest numbers. Of all shells, though, I think shrapnel is the worst, especially if you are in the open or in a half-built trench... Altogether we are very happy indeed and have quite a jolly time. A cheap accordion and odd mouth-organs often help to liven up proceedings. The food is quite good and there is usually tons of it.

The Portcullis No. 67 Spring 1916

Pte. Harold Allen: We had a long route march the other day, and in a passing car I noticed Jimmy Morgan. Of course we didn't get time to speak as we were on the march. It is a curious thing, but he is the first OE that I have seen out here.

The Portcullis No. 68 Summer 1916

Vernon Greaves

Captain Vernon Greaves, 6th Duke of Wellington's Regiment: I have had quite a long time here now – fifteen months and am quite a hardened old 'sweat'. I have seen one or two OEs. Once I had a mild shock when I took over some trenches from M. A. Prismall, and found Tillson in the same lot. Then I met C. E. Bodle in a town near here, and had a chat with him. I was awfully pleased to get *The Portcullis*, as there is nothing on earth like reading about the old School.

I see S. A. G. Harvey writes of a dog in the trenches. I'll beat him. We used to keep a goat and milk her twice daily.

2nd Lt. William Morgan: My address is 28th Siege Battery RGA. In passing, I may mention that it is the Siege Battery, however. This war is starting again. You know I'm at war don't you?

Terrible times we're having. Awake 16 hours per day and only four meals during that 16 hours. Shot and shell all around us, as well as blooming Frenchmen. My word! Aspen leaves are not in it. The weather is fine, which lessens our considerable and abundant discomforts.

Of course we have moved. I arrived back to find the battery preparing to flit once again. This was most sickening after two months digging and preparing our position. Our 'funk-hole' was the cutest little thing. Beat 'Hitchy-Koo' hollow. That 'funk-hole' was my effort. I drove a tunnel (at least the men did under my supervision) 40 feet under ground. I always do the 'funk-holes', because cold-feeted people always do that job well. I hope this war will end soon. I'm looking forward to the day when I return home, a battle scared – I mean scarred hero.

2nd Lt. C. H. V. Chewter, writing from Salisbury Plain: I was glad to have the School magazine and *Pro Patria* – a splendid list the latter is. This place will probably be my home for a while until I go out again, at a date which I think will be in the near future. When you toast absent friends please give one to Harvey for me.

2nd Lt. Albert A. Pine Worcester Regiment who is in Mesopotamia writes: I have had a very interesting time as a whole, having been in camp at Alexandria and Port Said for some time before leaving for the Persian Gulf. Here we were in camp at Busra [Basra] for a short time and went up the river to Sheikh Saad on a steamer. It's not a bad trip if the weather is fine and there is a good view of the Persian Hills. Unfortunately for me, colitis laid hold of me and I am now (April) back in Busra in hospital. I am getting fit again slowly and hope to take part in an advance on Baghdad, if they make one. I hope they'll relieve Kut soon, but I may get in for the attack on the last position necessary for that.

Pine was killed on the night of 16 January 1917 whilst preparing trenches for the offensive on the Hai Salient, which was part of the British strategy in their war with the Ottoman Empire. Pine's battalion (9th Worcestershire) were at the forefront of capturing the Salient, as the British forces planned to drive the Ottoman forces further up the Tigris with the intention of eventually capturing Baghdad, via the recapture of Kut.

G. E. Hopwood RAMC: Oh, it is difficult, very difficult at times to believe that this, futile squabbling life of ours is part of a great destiny, that an Infinite Wisdom watches compassionately over us all...I am still in good health and contented, waiting patiently for the war to end this year.

The Portcullis No. 69 Christmas 1916

Sydney Hare (Bedfordshires): During the early summer I was down on the Somme and saw a good deal of scrapping. My chief anxiety there was to exercise a sort of Sherlock Holmes instinct, which every infantry officer ought to possess. For example, the CO gives one a map showing the large and prosperous town of X and remarks, "I want you to guide the battalion in tonight; you go as far as the Post Office, turn to the right past the church and you will come to the billets." Off you toddle and on arrival there you find (a) six bricks, three damaged; (b) remains of a tombstone; (c) half a dozen whiskey bottles (empty) and (d) a tin of bully beef. From these articles you deduce (a) you have arrived at X; (b) that you have passed the church; (c) that you are near Brigade Headquarters and (d) that you are near the billets themselves. The strain of this sort of thing is, of course, enormous, but it has its advantages, since after three months of it, trigonometry or mechanics would seem child's play.

Reginald Chamberlain: Generally speaking, the warfare in this sector is limited to trench mortar 'strafing', with occasional shelling by both sides. In this, however, our own artillery is much more active than the Boche's, who sometimes leave us severely alone for days and then shell our lines like blazes for a couple of days, when, having apparently fired all their ammunition, they wait a week or more for further supplies.

It is interesting to note that the percentage of 'dud' Boche shells is very high and now and again it is as high as 50 per cent, when he throws over his medium heavies. We have made a good number of bombing raids and the Boche get very nervy at times. It is no uncommon thing to see his Very lights going up in almost broad daylight and the other night I was very much amused to see what must have been eight Boche on a front of about 50 yards, doing 'rapid' with their star shell pistols. This went on for over half an hour, when the firework display concluded.

An interesting feature is the predominance of our aircraft. There are always some of our aeroplanes about, but a Boche plane is a very rare sight and if he does venture over our lines it is at an enormous altitude and for a very short space of time. The weather now is getting very wintry and this morning we had to break the ice before we could drum up to tea.

Pte. H. Luckham writes from Gharial Spur, North West Frontier Province, India: We are situated up in the hills at an altitude of nearly 8000 feet and amidst the most magnificent scenery. In the far distance, on a clear day, can be seen the snow clad peaks of the Hindu-Kush Mountains... One part of our training is very interesting and exciting – miniature hill warfare. This is the stiffest training we have. All our training is done between 5.30am and 1pm and we never work in the afternoons.

The Portcullis No. 70 Spring 1917

QM Sergeant A. Bowyer, who has returned to England from Western Australia writes: My life in the Army, now extending over fourteen months, has been varied. I was first a clerk in Perth recruiting office, then a Corporal in a reinforcement of Engineers, then Sergeant in the Miners and last of all this job as Quartermaster Sergeant in the 5th Pioneer Co. Whilst at the recruiting office I met an Old Emanuel boy. My word! It was like a breeze from Old England to have a good chat with him. Let me be remembered to all old friends.

N. C. Kearney: I had previously been told off to take a message back to Battalion Headquarters, reporting that the Company had gone over the top, so that when we arrived in the front line I had to stand on the parapet and see that everyone had gone over before returning and reporting the same. It was a curious sensation to stand up there with bullets and shrapnel flying all around me, but I was not hit until I turned to get back into the trench – or what was left of it; I then got one in the back as I turned to speak to one of our fellows who had been hit, but this did no damage beyond tearing my coat and bruising me. However, I received two bullets in my left foot, one passing right through without touching my foot, the other inflicting a small wound and incidentally giving me a Blighty one.

H. S. Royffe 18 Squadron RFC writes: I have been shot down once by Huns, but had a lucky escape from personal injury; however, in a recent encounter between seven English and twenty Huns at 8000 feet and five miles over 'Hunland' I succeeded in bringing one machine down in flames and crippled another. Our squadron have also been doing a good deal of night bombing raids in which I was once lucky enough to wreck a troop train by means of bombs and machine gun fire.

Herbert Holgate: I looked up N. S. Mills at Athlone Hotel, Sliema, Malta, where he is engaged on the Eastern Telegraph Service. We had many happy hours together and saw the countryside on horseback.

There was a sketch on and I saw a figure which was familiar in a garb (which was also familiar – being that of a student); also familiar cigarette, in an unfamiliar make-up. The voice was altered and on the whole I was thoroughly perplexed as to whom it was. My programme said Pte. F. Moore. Then I knew. I called an orderly and said: "Go and ask Pte. F. H. B. Moore (and be sure to say F.H.B.) that I would like a few words with him." This he did, but didn't get the shock I thought he would, as he had already recognised me in the audience. He was quite fit, but fed-up with Malta.

C. H. Valentine Chewter quotes the line 'sic itur ad astra' and writes: I presume it refers to trench mortars; as a literal translation 'The stars descended and smote me'. I've thought several times today that they have, by the way, for I've had a deuce of a dose of minenwerfen lobbed at me, thumping great things, this variety, too! Some have greatness thrust upon them! My share this morning was four sandbags approximately in the neck and a cut on the arm. Now the evening has descended and all should be peace. I seem to have incensed his machine gunners beyond endurance, judging by the way they've been trying not to 'miss me in the long field.' After knowing them for two years, I'm forced to the conclusion at last that they're not nice fellows.

I cheered myself up this afternoon by rifle grenading him to fair effect – that was when he responded with 'Minnies' and I decided – somewhat hurriedly – that I could be more comfortable elsewhere! The first 'Minnie' had the situation well in hand, for she blew me into a shell-hole full of water, I needn't add, and I'm not dry yet! Playing boats is all very well in its place, but for a moment I wondered if the subsequent proceedings would interest me any more. However, a limp and bedraggled object succeeded in summoning up courage to move and the second one made me a present of four fine, bouncing sandbags and a bit... With a highly outraged sense of decency I hared off to happier hunting grounds.

The Portcullis No. 71 Summer 1917

Awards:

Captain A. W. Bird, with an Italian distinction already to his credit, has added to that the... Distinguished Service Order. What's in a name? Bird was the only flying man who braved the snow and hail on the day that Vimy Ridge was won. On the way back from his little trip, above the Boche 'territory', he dropped a few mementoes on some Germans retiring in close order. Bird began his career as an airman at an early age. When he was one of the wingless cherubims in the School choir, he ventured in a swing at the 'treat', attained some height and celerity and fell out!

August Wieland Bird's DSO was announced in *The London Gazette*:

For conspicuous gallantry and devotion to duty on many occasions. When on artillery patrol he succeeded in reporting thirteen active batteries, observing fire on and silencing several of them. On another occasion he attacked and scattered with machine-gun fire two parties of the enemy which were seen forming up. This operation was carried out for a period of 2½ hours in very adverse weather conditions.

Reports on injuries received by OEs:

There are some who have received not less honourable but much less desirable, decorations – so undesirable, indeed, that we wish them a speedy riddance. These include Fuller, who was wounded in the shoulder and has been discharged from the Army. Urquhart, who has been in hospital at Hampstead, found a bullet in the elbow far from 'humerus', but fortunately, he is regaining the use of his arm and looks very fit. H. White is suffering from trench feet, having been 'out' through a period of very bad weather. H. While has now recovered from a similar attack and has appeared at School several times lately. A. B. Elson is out of hospital and is convalescent. Urquhart, a confirmed teetotaller, has an amusing story to relate. The funny part is that he was fetching the rum rations. The Boche snipers spotted him and callously put a bullet through the jar. Urquhart didn't mind until they got him in the arm! But even that was a blessing in disguise, because it got him home for Sports Day.

The Portcullis No. 72 Winter 1917

Christmas 1917 was perhaps the most sobering in terms of news received about OEs in the war. After three years of fighting the War's impact was fully felt at Emanuel as one letter after another arrived on the Headmaster's desk with news of another Emanuel fallen.

'Captain Dancer was only married last year...'

A. C. Dancer, another of Emanuel's straightest sons, who had received the Military Cross for his services, fell on October 4th... The summer of 1916 found him on the Western Front, in the thick of the Somme battles and his MC was won at Mouquet Farm... "He was a born soldier", says his CO, "He did not know what fear meant." "He was a great leader of men", writes another officer, "a jolly good fellow, a very hard worker and absolutely fearless of danger." Captain Dancer was only married last year. A keen rugby player while at School and a First Fifteen, he was a notable member of the Old Emanuel Rugby Union Football Club.

Alfred Christopher Dancer enlisted as a trooper in the Surrey Yeomanry at the outbreak of the First World War. He saw action in Gallipoli in addition to the Somme and was gazetted to the 5th Battalion Dorset Regiment.

'Collins was all that could be desired as a soldier, a Christian and a gentleman.'

A. E. Collins, an NCO in the RGA, died on 21 July, from injuries received through the bursting of a gas shell which penetrated the roof of his dug-out. "He was all that could be desired as a soldier, a Christian and a gentleman; an excellent NCO, as he had complete control of his men and loved by officers and men alike." Collins visited the School in the autumn of 1916, his apology for not having turned up before, being that he thought the masters would be only too glad to forget him. He seemed very much struck at the kind reception accorded a 'black lamb', forgetting that the former suppression of his rather quaint humour was in the interests of discipline only.

The Portcullis No. 73 Lent 1918

An Old Emanuel writes: Sir – dashing back to billet after breakfast one morning for a hurried shave, I found a hefty-looking chap sweeping out my suite of rooms-(unfurnished)-and eyeing with disapproval my untidy kit. He said, "Hullo!" I said, "Hullo!" Then he said, "How's the *Portcullis* getting on?" It is difficult to shave when our deepest feelings are awakened. I nearly severed my jugular vein. Without recognising him by name as an Old Emanuel, I had piloted him through reclassification of trade and COs Orderly Room, where investigations were made into the loss of a pair of spectacles which he had never received. I have since seen him, wearing a mild look ill befitting the serious duty, escorting prisoners into detention. And every time I see him I am reminded that the British Army is held together by an intricate network of associations such as the freemasonry of Old Emanuels.

From France comes the news of the death of William Alexander Nichol, who was killed on 23 June 1917. Nichol resigned the post of Headmaster of the Grammar Public School, New South Wales, in 1916, to enlist as a private in the Australian Infantry. [William was killed on Messines Ridge. Eyewitnesses in the 35th AIF reported seeing him hit in the mouth by a shell fragment. He lived but only for a few minutes before he bled to death from the impact of the shrapnel which had gone down his throat. Private Swadling reported seeing the shell fragment come out of the back of William's neck. He was 27 years old.]

W. E. Curram writes: Poor Nichol was one of the School's most popular men... like myself, he was a 'Marlborough' man and it recently fell to my lot to discover his grave in a small British Military Cemetery, behind one of the much debated ridges of the Western Front.

Guy Cassie writes about the death of his brother Leith who succumbed to wounds received in fighting near Ypres:

He served 18 months abroad with the London Scottish until wounded on the Somme. He was then commissioned and had been three months abroad again. You may remember him as being one of the team that shot for the School the first year they entered for the Ashburton Shield.

Hugh Vaughan

Hugh Vaughan has been released from 'duresse vile' in Germany and writes from Sutton, Surrey to say that R. S. Gilbert turned up at Karlsruhe about the middle of October.

While on patrol he and his pilot were attacked by six German machines and were driven down. Gilbert was not wounded or hurt in any way. At the end of October, he, with other RFC Officers were moved from Karlsruhe to another camp.

Second Lieutenant R. S. Gilbert failed to return from a patrol on 11 October 1917. *The Portcullis* reported in Christmas 1917 that the weather was cloudy and it was presumed he and his patrol had lost their way and landed in hostile territory. There was no initial evidence he had been shot down. Gilbert had written many letters to the OEA, describing himself as 'doing famously, in a fighting squadron. Our duty merely consists of escorts to bombing formations and offensive patrols. We are usually detailed for patrol a long way over the Huns lines, but don't go very far before finding trouble.'

John Hopkins sends news of George Banting, who was in Italy: Banting is "having a pretty warm time of it from all accounts. He says the air is so thick with Huns that you can hardly see the sky or ground for them, while the concussion from 'Archie' shatters your triplex goggles and loosens your front teeth. He says that he has got another Hun down."

The Portcullis No. 74 Trinity 1918

John Collier F. Hopkins

J. C. F. Hopkins: How newsy the Mag seems now that I am away from the old school, compared with the days when we used to consider it – well, just a lot of hot air that had to be censored about umpteen times... Did I tell you that I was coming out on night bombing? Last week I was flying from about 8pm to 5.30am every night... Such things as a slight crash through to my engine cutting out are not worth mentioning when I didn't even kill my observer!

2nd Lt. James Whitehead (staff): I see the *Portcullis* has promoted me to full Lieutenant. I am still 2nd Lieutenant, so I must ask the editor to 'furnish authority' and then I can draw the increment in pay.

John Hopkins & Hugh Vaughan (third row from right) in an Emanuel classroom c.1913

J. L. P. Tremlett: After three months' training in Yorkshire, I get a month's leave and then sail for India... It will be some years before I see England again... I heard yesterday that Thew's adjutant at Reading is Waghorn. Lucky man! He ought to be able to play in any Old Boys' games.

James Jennings: It is only through the magazine that one hears what is going on at Emanuel.

Robert Urquhart: I met Johnny Walker, now in the 20th London Regiment and also Hopkins, in my own regiment (London Scottish). I met another OE here in the same hut as myself. He was one of the old boarders and left in 1911. He was contemporary with Morgan, Hirst, Camm, Horswell, Booth, Beath etc. His name is MacDuff... I don't think he is on our *Pro Patria* list. He would like to join the OEA. I propose him. Who seconds? I met Martin last night. He tells me that Camm went out again two or three weeks ago.

Reggie R. Turner: We spend most of our afternoons at football and my section has got as far as the semi-final in the inter-section competition, so we live in great hopes for the final. Must finish now as I have to change for a friendly game of soccer.

Reggie Turner

On 29 February 1964, Robert Urquhart, Reggie Turner and 'Johnny' Walker were on the touchline at Blagdons, the Old Emanuel ground in Raynes Park supporting the OEA First Fifteen who were facing the Old Bancroftians, formidable opponents who had lost only once that season before meeting the OEA. In need of support the Club called on its old members and as the OE Notes in *The Portcullis* put it, 'The old warhorses responded magnificently. It was heartening to see and hear on the touchline such heroes of the past as 'Molly' Urquhart, 'Johnny' Walker and Reggie Turner.' Their presence seemed to do the trick; these veterans of the Great War inspired the Old Boys to win the match by 11 points to 6.

The Portcullis No. 75 Christmas 1918

Wilfrid Giles (C. W. Scott-Giles) in his introduction to the OE Notes writes: Peace came to us in many places. To me it came when the editorial sanctum was a corner of a hospital ward, in sight of the School. I heard the sound of many explosions. A great cheer floated across from Emanuel as the Union Jack broke from the tower and lifted on the breeze. Hundreds of us have looked forward to the time

When the hurly-burly's done,

When the battle's lost and won,

As a port whence we can embark upon fresh enterprises and set out upon the voyage of life with high hopes. Now that the hour has come we may surely rejoice in peace with victory, but let us not overlook the solemnity of the time, remembering how many of our brothers, whose hopes were as great as ours and whose desires were as dear, have fallen in the fight.

News was received that Norman Charles Kearney, who had earlier written to the School, had been killed in a flying accident. The Editor noted:

N. C. Kearney, Lieutenant in the RAF was killed at Andover on 27 April. A first class pilot, he was the victim of an accident, due to engine trouble, which caused his machine to nose-dive to earth. Kearney, who was a member of a family well-known at Emanuel, after being rejected several times in the early days of the war, was accepted by the East Surreys in February, 1916 and saw service in France. He was wounded on the Somme in September and on recovery joined the RAF, where his skill as a pilot gained him recommendation to the post of pilot-instructor. He was the son of the Rev. Alan Wells Kearney, late Acting Chaplain of Battersea and the brother of Mr. E. W. Chalmers Kearney, the well-known inventor of the Kearney High Speed Railway.

Brothers who fell within one week of each other:

Two of the brothers Villis have fallen – Tom and Archibald – the former on October 11th, from wounds received from the explosion of a stray shell and the latter in action, seven days later. Tom was a second Air Mechanic in the RAF. Before joining the army he was a regular attendant of OEA meetings and though not a prominent member, always showed keen interest in the affairs of the School. Archibald was of a slightly later period. He also participated actively in School life. We are indebted to Frank Villis, the surviving brother, for the information.

Frank Villis attended Battersea Grammar School and was killed whilst disembarking from a troop ship on its way to North Africa in the Second World War.

The Portcullis noted that 2nd Lt. E. M. S. Kearney took a great interest in other OEs and mentioned quite a few in this extract from one of his letters which was published after his death:

Stephens, of Lyons was rammed by an Austrian destroyer in the Adriatic, but is going on fine. Hann (Howe) is in the Welsh Guards at Caterham. Halford (Howe) has been in Egypt for four years. Randall is out here (France) in some London Regiment. Gearing is a pilot at New Romney; he has been at it since 1915 and looks pretty sick. Paton (Wellington) is an A.M. [Air Mechanic] in the same squadron. These are a few that I have met in my travels.

Percy H. Ruffle, BEF 14 August: I am in France again with the Tank Corps and am now having a course in the latest type. They are the real thing in tanks and there are better to follow. Most people are beginning to love the tanks a little more than they used. At least, they ought to after the work they have been doing lately. So far, I have only met R. R. Turner from the old School. When I saw him, at Merlimont, he seemed in quite good spirits and I spent an evening with him.

J. Raworth Hill, Kilburn 22 Oct: I am now at Stonehenge as a Map Reading Instructor, but expect to be moving very shortly. I am going to be OC Map Reading at a new school in Norfolk.

Jack Toogood, Aeroplane Experimental Station, Woodbridge, Suffolk, 14 Oct: I have had a rather interesting tour, including Germany and Switzerland. Quelle vie! Am winning the war again now in a rather interesting way, but I wish I could remember more physics!

Jack Toogood joined 56 Squadron RFC in late April 1917. On 26 May Jack was engaged over Gouy-sous-Bellone with a formation of four two-seaters, with a larger formation of enemy scouts flying above him, and other members of 56 Squadron. Jack was later posted as missing by his squadron, having last been seen attacking an enemy aircraft. Five months later and Jack's father had written to the Squadron Commander to let him know that Jack had been made a POW. After engaging the two-seaters he had been hit by an anti-aircraft shell which had caused severe damage to his leg. Losing blood rapidly he almost fainted but managed to land and was captured by the Germans. His leg was later amputated. Imprisoned in Bavaria he was later repatriated via Switzerland and arrived back in England on 2 April 1918.

A. S. Feacey: I am now on the Army Reserve back at the bank. It's a jolly sight better than the trenches, I can tell you... I managed to get a good bit of cricket this year, and the loss of my eye has not made much difference to my bowling, although batting is rather difficult. In nine matches I managed to get 50 wickets for 170 runs.

F. A. Walker, also known as 'Johnny Walker', writing on 21 August describes his impressions on the opening day of The Battle of Amiens. Although Walker had placed the date as 7 August we can safely assume he actually meant 8 August 1918, the day on which the Fourth Army turned the tide of war on the Western Front. The Battle opened in the early hours. Walker attributes the over 400 tanks as the infantry's saving grace on that day. The Battle of Amiens is regarded as the first day of what British historians regard as the last 'hundred days', a series of Allied offensives which brought the First World War to an end:

I'm very pleased to be able to write, as I was in the stunt of August 7th and our Brigade had a rough time. In our Company alone, we had three figure casualties – all from bullets. If the tanks hadn't gone over with us I bet we would have been cut up.

Walker wrote again on 30 September:

I am now in Blighty after seven months' stay in 'sunny' France. I was hit on the 18th, just by Epehy. Fortunately, I was able to get away unaided, but I have been on my back ever since. (Written with the left hand).

Alfred Reginald Jackson

A. R. Jackson, No. 1 School of Navigation and Bombing, Stonehenge 3 September writes: J. F. Bates, of Clyde, is now observing in Salonika. He went to Egypt with me. I also met my namesake, C. J. Jackson, in Ismalia. He had transferred from the infantry and was training as a pilot and ought to be qualified by now. C. A. Stevens, of course, is a Flight Commander and instructor at Cranwell. I'm down here on a five weeks' course – mostly night flying – after which comes France at last.

Johnny Walker was hit on September 18th in the right hand, knee and left shoulder and came to England on the 21st. His sister tells me it is nothing serious, although they have not been able to see him yet, as he is in the 2nd Western General Hospital, Alfred Street, Harpurney, Manchester. If he hasn't paid his sub, now's the time to catch him! Reggie Turner is now in the Whippets [Tanks]. 'Skinny' Cox had recovered from diphtheria and then got jaundice.

R. A. Pleace: I am suffering from gas. I am feeling pretty fit now except for my eyes. When on a course at the Third Army Musketry Camp at Fort Mahon I saw Arnold, who is an instructor. I also saw Randall, who is now in the Borderers, being unfit for flying.

S. H. Thornton, Great Yarmouth, 27 September: I returned from France where I was flying land machines, last May, and transferred to seaplanes as I had rather a bad smash out there. I am now doing submarine patrols over the North Sea, but haven't had the luck to bag one up to the present and live in hope of doing so... I heard news of Underwood this morning. He is on the Furious flying-deck Camels, lucky beggar! Billy Boorne, as far as I know, is in Scotland.

HMS *Furious* was a Courageous Class battlecruiser converted to an aircraft carrier in the First World War. Frederick Underwood who was mentioned in Thornton's letter attended Emanuel School 1911–1916 and played in the First Eleven captained by Alfred Titley. On leaving School 'he entered the service of the Bank of Montreal in the Waterloo Place branch in London in September 1916. In November 1917, he enlisted for overseas service. He received his commission as 2nd Lieutenant in the Royal Air Force. He was detailed for service with the Grand Fleet and for some months he was engaged on scout duty, flying over the North Sea. He was on board the *Campania* when she was sunk in collision and at the surrender of the German Fleet he was on the *Princess Royal*. Later he was transferred to the *Furious* on duty at Scapa Flow in the Orkney Islands.' He died while still on service on 2 July 1919.

L. J. Mayrick, B.E.F: It is nearly three years since I came to France, but I have never forgotten 'Alma Mater.' They were glorious days, only one doesn't realise it until after. I am on the wireless staff of the 56th Division.

The Portcullis No. 76 Lent 1919

[Issued as No. 79]

I have to record the death of S. E. Roper, whose contemporaries will receive the news with real sorrow. His brother writes:

From the moment of his going out at the beginning of April, just before his nineteenth birthday, to the day of his death, no one at home had an inkling of what he was doing — not that he did not write; he wrote most regularly, always saying the same thing: "he was in the pink and hoped all at home were well." Yet from fellows in the same section we have learned that they were continuously in action from the date of arrival to the conclusion of hostilities. He seems to have been very well liked and was, on account of his invariable politeness, known as 'Monsieur'.

It was characteristic of Roper that he should serve "with quiet fortitude and uncomplaining calm". Those who knew him well at School knew him as one who thought deeply, was sincere and conscientious and a capable worker. He was a keen supporter of Drake and was in the House First Fifteen and Eleven.

The Portcullis No. 77 Trinity 1919

C. H. Valentine Chewter: Enquiries were made by several as to the whereabouts of S. Belder and it is regretted that no news is known to date, but I was with him for a spell at Festubert in early 1915 and he was wounded then in a manner that may interest readers. Early one morning Belder was unduly curious over the activities of a Boche 'stand-to' sniper, mounted the parapet and simply because the sun was strong, shielded his eyes with his hand. Considering that he was head and shoulders above the breastwork, it was not surprising that he duly received attention from the sniper and the bullet, which might have hit Belder in the head, struck his knuckles and shattered one or two fingers. With a coolness that never deserted him, he stood to have the hand roughly dressed and then walked to the Dressing Station.

A father's letter to the Headmaster – Mr. J. W. Jenkins writes to Shirley Goodwin with news of his son:

Doubtless you will remember my son leaving Emanuel in July 1916 and be interested to learn his army career. It is with much sorrow I have to inform you that he was killed in June of last year.

After a holiday in the Isle of Wight, he spent a month on the land with a gentleman farmer at Didcot. In November he was called up under the Derby Scheme and joined the 4th OCB at Oxford. In the following March he was gazetted to the 2/5th Gloucesters and joined his regiment in France. He was wounded in August in an engagement in which his platoon captured a Pill Box and about thirty Germans.

After further service in the trenches he was accepted in January 1918 for the RFC and training at Hythe, returned as an observer to France.

On Sunday, June 16th his machine was with a patrol of four and encountered a similar number of enemy planes. They took the offensive, but were surprised by a vastly superior force above them.

The pilots of the two machines who were left to guard the machines attacking, returned to the aerodrome some 100 miles away. The leader of the patrol, realising the great danger in which the two machines were in, signalled to break off the engagement, but, unfortunately, this was not seen, or it was impossible for this to be done. It is presumed that the machine was brought down, as information was dropped over the French lines some three weeks later, stating that my son and his pilot died of wounds the same day.

This occurred at Popincourt, between Mondidier and Noyon. Although this information also came from the Red Cross Society at Geneva and at Copenhagen, where his disc was received, the War Office will not accept his death as being official.

He was promoted to 1st Lieutenant just before his death.

Maurice Jenkins was flying as an observer with pilot Lt. J. M. Goller on the day he was killed. Jasta 57 Ltn H. Viebig claimed to have shot the Bristol Fighter F.2B they were in.

The Portcullis No. 78 Christmas 1919

News of OEs:

F. S. Pashley is about again. After a long spell in France ... he went to Salonica, was wounded and the adverse conditions there so affected the wounds that he came home minus one leg. After a long time in hospitals at home and abroad, he has been fitted with an artificial limb and has resumed business.

The Editor wrote: 'I am so grateful to the father of C. H. Chittock, whose death has already been announced, for the following particulars supplied by a member of the 12th Battalion London Regiment, in which our OE was a Rifleman':

At one o'clock on November 27th, 1917, a bombing raid took place... in which all four companies were engaged. We drove the Germans to the end of the trench, where they had a strong point which held us up... We barricaded the trench and retired to our own line. Very soon after, they counter-attacked and for about four hours, there was practically hand-to-hand fighting. Several men were killed on the parados of the trench while throwing bombs.

G. Steer writes from Rugely Camp Staffs: I am no longer in the Artists, but am now 5th KRRC. There are a good few OEs in this Battalion – Mackness, Perrett and one or two others... Bird, late of Drake, is here with the RW Surreys; I must look him up one day, but as the camp is miles in circumference... I shall have to take a few rations.

H. W. Broome writes from Lady Wantage's hospital, Welford Park, near Newbury: I was sent down here by the Pensions Committee for further convalescence after being discharged from hospital in February... I'm afraid I shall always feel the effects of the knocks I got across the other side. However, I mustn't grumble, I've got all my limbs and can get about and that's more than was expected of me a year ago.

News was received that C. W. Bing was suffering from what we assume was 'shell shock', he was with the Royal Flying Corps: C. W. Bing was invalided from the RAF, Army of Occupation, with a serious nervous breakdown and is lying in a very serious condition in the Lord Derby Hospital, Warrington. His father writes, "He is much too ill to communicate with you at present... but I think he is making slow progress towards recovery."

Sub. Lt. George E. Tustain RN writes from HMS *PC 61*, c/o HMS *Tyne*, Nervik, Stord, Norway: Have found my way out here in pursuit of mines, having helped to complete the Irish barrages. In our little portion of the Norwegian coast we have 10,000 mines to sweep, so you can imagine what fun it has been dodging mines: at times they were like young peas floating around.

F. O. Dougan is back in London after serving from August 4th 1914. An argument with a 10.4 resulted in his discharge, but he is playing rugger again now.

Frank Dougan joined the London Irish Rifles and was the sole survivor when the shell crater in which a number of soldiers were sheltering, was hit by a shell. He was taken to hospital in Wimereux Hospital suffering from shell shock and effects of gas. On returning to England he spent some time in the 3rd General London Hospital and Springfield Hospital.

The Portcullis No. 79 Lent 1920

J. D. Bradly, after serving in France, was attached to the Royal Flying Corps. He wrote from Lewisham: I am afraid I have little news of myself of interest, as I unfortunately managed to pile a 'Camel' [type of First World War aircraft] on the bank of the Thames near Dartford, returning from a night flight at 3am on April 28th 1918 and have had a long rest-cure in hospital and was only discharged on the 17th of last December, after a stay of 19 months... While out for a ramble in Kent about three weeks ago I met G. G. Banting and had lunch with him at his squadron, as is probably known, he is at the Instrument Design Establishment (RAF), Biggin Hill.

Joseph Dunstan Bradly was awarded the Croix de Guerre with Palm (a Belgian military decoration instituted in 1915 and awarded for various acts of bravery) in 1917 as *The Portcullis* Summer Term 1917 reported:

J. D. Bradly, after a career of excitement which would suffice most people for a life-time, has achieved the Croix de Guerre. Bradly was a civilian in the Railway Transport in the early days of the war and was wounded. That riled him, so he joined the East Kent Regiment and was wounded a second time. His training for his third expedition was delayed by an accidental bayonet jab, but eventually he went out again, was wounded (that makes three!) and captured...he was recaptured by the British and packed home to recuperate.

The Editor corrects a previous mistake: I regret that in the last notes I referred to Captain G. F. Hollands, being Mentioned in Despatches for services rendered in India. This is incorrect – it should have read Lieutenant F. R. Hollands, 1/21st London Regiment, was Mentioned in Despatches by F. M. Earl Haig, for gallant and distinguished conduct in the field.

F. R. Hollands writing on 13 October, 1919 from 1/10th Gurkha Rifles, Maymyo, Burma: Having got through four years of the old war in France and finding myself, by some miraculous chance, still alive, I applied for a transfer to the Indian Army... I consider myself very lucky to get a Gurkha Regiment, for they are unquestionably the finest in the Indian Army... I am always an OE and my mind often travels back to the old building and the playing fields.

The Portcullis No. 80 Trinity 1920

F. W. Borders had written to the School in 1918 on hearing of the death of three former Emanuel masters in the war, namely, the Reverend H. Buchanan Ryley, Mr. Chavetois and Mr. Elder, although the letter was only published two years later:

> My own part in the war has been a very humble though busy one. After I left the old School I tried for several regiments but was rejected each time. In October 1914, I managed to slip into the RE's, as a despatch rider and came to France. I was drafted back to England in July 1915, owing to illness and was discharged in a week. At the end of September 1915, after several more rejections, I was able to join the Motor Transport and came back here in February 1916. Ever since then I have been driving a motor-bus, used for rushing troops up to places where they are needed most urgently and in quiet intervals I have brought wounded through to safe hospitals from advanced Field Dressing Stations. I have seen the rear line work in every great push, both ours and the enemy's, from the Somme in 1916 to the Lys in 1918...
>
> I was married out here at Lillers to a French maiden on March 18th 1918... My only regret is that I could not go arm in arm with those OEs whom I have driven up to the 'last village before the line'.

Joseph Dunstan Bradly in RFC flying kit

A Portrait of John Burns by Harold Speed, National Liberal Club

The Colossus of Battersea and the Sorrow of War

John Burns MP and his son Edgar Burns *(Emanuel 1907–1910)*

There have been many notable Emanuel parents in the School's history and John Burns was one of the most prominent. A giant of late nineteenth century radical politics, his public image dimmed when the lights went out all over Europe in 1914. But his personal sorrow, as he saw his son go to war, tells us much about how fathers dealt with their emotions as they became disconnected and largely helpless as they stood watching the train carriages take their sons into battle. John Burns's war is one that has long been publically forgotten. Before we get to the fraught days of August 1914 we must first ask who was John Burns?

In 1909 the satirical magazine *Punch* published a cartoon titled 'The Colossus of Battersea.' It showed the MP John Burns towering above the borough shaking his fist. It was in response to a speech he had given warning that Battersea 'would never recover from the indelible stigma of rejecting him.' The words give the measure of the man, who dominated Battersea's politics for over 25 years. From a working-class family, John Burns rose to be appointed the first of that class in English history up until the early twentieth century to become a member of the Cabinet.[1] His fame even warranted a model in Madame Tussauds.

John Burns was a 'rebel with a cause' but his rebellious nature was channelled into improving the lives of those less fortunate and he steered away from class warfare for its own sake. Not afraid of stirring up a crowd he had run-ins with the law on more than one occasion and in 1888 received a six week jail term, spent at Pentonville Prison, for his part in what became known as 'Bloody Sunday', a demonstration organised by the Metropolitan Radical Federation in protest against the arrest of the Irish Nationalist William O'Brien, MP. But more fortuitously, Burns led the successful London Dockers' Strike of 1889 and in the same year won a seat on the London County Council. A few years later in 1892 he was elected as MP for Battersea. He was considered a Socialist but although he won his first Parliamentary Campaign as a member of the Independent Labour Party, he never joined the Labour Party.

When the second Boer War broke out he vehemently opposed it but one interesting side of Burns' character was his economic anti-Semitism as seen in a speech given to his constituents in Battersea Park on Sunday 13 May 1900, an opinion which characterised Burns' complex outlook on life.

> Patriotism was the last refuge of the scoundrel. The Union Jack, once regarded as the embodiment of liberty and freedom was becoming, in the language of Mr Rhodes, the greatest commercial asset in the world. Yes, a commercial rag, to be hawked about in the markets of the world for the benefit of a lot of Jews...[2]

In 1905 he was made President of the Local Government Board and on being so became a minister in the Liberal Government. In 1909 he oversaw the Housing and Town Planning Act, a significant piece of legislation to improve the quality of house building in Britain. In February 1914 Burns was made President of the Board of Trade but before the storm clouds across Europe appear our attention must focus on his son John Edgar, known as Edgar to his family.

Edgar was born on 16 August 1895, the Burnses' only child.

Edgar Burns

On Christmas Day 1900 when Edgar was five, John Burns confided to his diary:

> Boy not very well. Improved however as day wore on. Stimulated by his numerous presents and his mother's care he enjoyed himself very well. I read him the wolves' chapter out of his new *Robinson Crusoe*. Flushed, delighted and beautiful, after his undressing, (like one of Reynolds' three angels heads) he put his little face and kissed me many times ere he went in his mother's arms to bed. And what a pair as I looked at them with their faces together. He like her in many phases; what will he be twenty years hence? I know not; I hope much. I trust a great man with all his mother's virtues and none of his father's faults.

It was said of Burns that he worshipped Edgar and his diary extracts pay testament to this sentiment, for wherever John went Edgar would follow and vice versa. In 1907 Edgar won

Edgar Burns (third from right back row), Emanuel School, Marlborough House Second XI 1908

a Scholarship to Emanuel but the local press were critical that a boy from such a wealthy home should be a competitor. John wrote to his wife for Edgar's first day at School, 'Tell him to command his temper, behave well and above all he must not be arrogant or vindictive if the boys chaff him as they will.'[3] Edgar excelled at Emanuel and on several occasions he appeared in the national press for having won School prizes. Like his father, Edgar enjoyed cricket and can be seen in a Marlborough House Cricket photo of 1908.

One of Burns's biographers suggests that he became disappointed with Edgar as his hopes of him emulating his father diminished. A lack of the same energies and oratory were cited by the biographer, but what Burns may have confided in private he never expressed in his letters and diaries.[4]

Within four years of Edgar leaving School the general European crisis broke out in the summer of 1914. In July 1914 John Burns was resolute and did not believe Britain should warn Germany against attacking the French Coast as he thought it was an act of provocation that would draw Britain into a continental war that they need not fight. On the evening of 2 August 1914 at 6.30pm the Cabinet met. Burns, as he had done earlier in the day, told the Prime Minister Herbert Asquith that he, Burns, must resign. In his resignation letter to Asquith Burns wrote:

> Dear Mr Asquith,
>
> The decision of the Cabinet to intervene in a European war is an act with which I profoundly disagree.
>
> I therefore place in your hands my resignation of my office as President of the Board of Trade.
>
> With deep respect, cordial sympathy and best wishes,
>
> Yours sincerely,
>
> John Burns

Burns was one of two members of the Cabinet to resign, the other being Lord [John] Morley, Lord President of the Council.

Praise and derision for Burns's decision filled the comments pages of newspapers and Burns's letter box. The local newspaper the *South Western Star* commented:

We believe he has done this for conscience sake, though we are all well aware that it is perfectly possible for any man to mistake his own obstinacy and pride for the dictates of his conscience. Mr Burns may be blamed for resigning. His resignation may cost him his seat in Parliament, but when the present tyranny is overpast and Europe is again calm, Mr Burns will doubtless be honoured for the sacrifice he has made, though that sacrifice be a mistaken one.[5]

Burns's views were anathema to the *zeitgeist* prevailing in Britain at this time but the over seventy letters he received pay testament to the fact that many prominent individuals, albeit with Liberal and Socialist sympathies, admired his principled stand. The Foreign Secretary, Sir Edward Grey, wrote to Burns on 5 August expressing his sadness, 'I can't tell you how much I grieve to see your vacant place. Friendship remains now and ever.'[6] Clementina Black, the Deputy Treasurer of the Women's Trade Union Association wrote on the day war was declared, 4 August 1914, 'I do congratulate you upon your resignation. It is too horrible that England should be going to fight for Russia and wicked that we should go to fight at all.'[7] Welfare campaigner Emily Hobhouse implored Burns to join the Labour Party, 'Resign and join the ranks of Labour the only party likely to save us now. The Trades Unions alone can avert war if this weak cabinet proclaims it – we look to you.'[8]

Anthony Dell, Old Emanuel and the brother of two OEs, Michael and Roger Dell, also wrote to Burns. Interestingly Anthony had made headline news in June 1914. Anthony was a member of the editorial staff of *The Daily Citizen* newspaper and had travelled to Albania to learn more about the country when he was kidnapped by Albanian insurgents who apparently had grievances against the Mpret (King) William. He had been mistaken for a Dutch officer. The Mpret had at this time had in his pay a force of Dutch gendarmerie with Dutch officers. Anthony's plight was discussed by the Foreign Secretary in Parliament and in early July his release was negotiated. Coming from a Quaker family he was a Liberal supporter. On 6 August he wrote to Burns:

I wish to add my word of thanks to those which I am sure you must be receiving from Liberals all over the country for your stand for true Liberal principles.

It is a comfort to us to know that we have still one or two leaders whom we can follow. The present Cabinet has no longer any claim on Liberal support and sincerely hope it will get none at the next election.[9]

John Burns whilst President of the Local Government Board

The reason for Burns's resignation was a matter which individuals from all quarters pressed him to explain in the years after he left the Cabinet. Describing one exchange with Lord 'Jacky' Fisher, (First Sea Lord between 1904–10 and1914–1915 before he resigned after the failure of the Gallipoli Campaign) in September 1915 Burns confided to his diary his reasoning:

On the way to Commons in Whitehall was met by Lord Fisher who in most cordial way greeted us with a grand salute... He asked me why I resigned. I told him. Splendid Isolation. No Balance of Power. No Incorporation in Continental System. If you want a war for war's sake with Germany, the best, cheapest and only certain way on the sea alone, and through her £500,000,000 overseas trade bring her to her senses without the disability of continental entanglements and the other burdens of men, material and money which your Allies will demand. He agreed and was emphatic about the criminal folly of the Dardanelles adventure. He asked what I thought would happen. 3,000 millions. Half a millon dead men; two years and a draw as I predicted a year ago. He listened, as I thought, with a serious face and not a dissenting countenance.

During the war years high profile figures persuaded Burns to throw his energies into helping in some capacity with the war effort. Field Marshal Kitchener wrote to him requesting that Burns become the Chairman of the Control Board to administer Army canteens in the UK. He had requests to speak on army recruitment and at anti-conscription meetings but whether for the war effort or in speeches for or against the war, Burns eschewed all such offers, even from Lloyd George who asked him to help with the munitions programme.

Despite all his efforts to avoid the War after he had resigned it nevertheless happened to penetrate his life in a most personal way. In 1908 the recruiting officer of the London Scottish Volunteers had written to Burns asking that Edgar should join the Army, as his height and physique were just what the Army needed but Burns replied, 'My son is only twelve years of age and though 5ft 6in in height and at times of a warlike disposition, he is not old enough to determine the question you put to him and me.' Despite outward appearances Edgar's fitness was put in doubt in October 1915 when Major Sir John Collie of the Royal Army Medical Corps, later a temporary Colonel, wrote to Burns about Edgar's medical examination:

> I went carefully into the boy's case today and I am satisfied that he should not be a soldier. He has plenty of pluck, but no one has any right to call upon him to expose himself to three or four times the danger that anyone else would [be exposed to].
>
> I cannot be responsible for what anyone else will do, for he comes fairly near the borderline, but with a very clear conscience I can say most emphatically that I would not pass him. I referred him to my friend Dr. Lumsden of South Eaton Place, my deputy in the LCC, who entirely agrees with me.
>
> I am very strongly in favour of the lad going into medicine, for the liberal education it would give him. As I pointed out to him, before he has been in politics many years there will be a Minister for Health.[10]

A depiction of John Burns in Punch magazine by Leonard Raven Hill, 1909

THE COLOSSUS OF BATTERSEA.

Interestingly a 'PS' reveals how Edgar viewed his personal progress in relation to his father's lack of Cabinet position, for Collie noted, 'He, I gather, would go to the university if he had a chance but does not think he ought to now you are not in the Cabinet.' Not only was Edgar considered not fit enough to go to war but his own feelings about status and his father's social standing after resigning from the government led him to conclude that a university education would not be appropriate.

A few months later the actuality that Burns privately dreaded became fact. On 19 January 1916 Burns wrote in his diary:

> Early in the morning Edgar came into my room and said, "Father, I enlisted yesterday — Garrison Artillery. Will you kindly let me have some money at once?" I said, "Certainly, my son" and at once gave him what he wanted. Natural that he should do what he has done "when silken dalliance in the wardrobe lies." But I immediately felt keenly the need for the appeal to chivalrous youth the cause and wisdom and expediency I challenged at great cost, but that this the greatest sacrifice, my only child, cut me to the quick, but for the boy's sake I did my best to hide it. To Battersea Town Hall with him to catch the tramway for Whitehall. From this spot, monumenting many popular and personal achievements, I saw him

> leave our parish by his birthplace for where? Unknown to him I followed the Horse Guards Parade and there for two hours watched him and his companions till the two hundred of recruits, fine fellows all, with pipers at their head and band as well, they marched to Waterloo by way of Charing Cross. From there to County Hall, scene of my long labours for London. Her gallant sons pass by. Pride and passion, hatred of the cause, admiration of the misdirected devotion, surged within me as these lads of London went to their respective fates. I asked Edgar in the Last Rank where he was going and he told me with evident satisfaction, 'Dover.' I saw him off in the train, one and not the last of many millions that the ambition of kings, the craft of class, the temper of Ministers and the imprudence of diplomats have consigned to the Moloch of War.

Edgar served with the 105th Siege Battery Royal Garrison Artillery in France from May to November 1916. He also served in Italy and in the 204th Calcutta Battery in Egypt being discharged on 1 September 1920. The Heavy Siege Batteries were equipped with heavy howitzers and were employed to destroy enemy artillery and strategic positions. It would have been exhausting, grinding and above all else, noisy work for Edgar. Edgar was initially a Corporal and was later promoted to the rank of Sergeant.

Sadly the letters Edgar sent home whilst serving abroad don't appear to be in the surviving Burns papers but fortunately, due to John Burns requesting that Edgar send home all the letters his parents sent him, the parental correspondence survives.

Burns sent his son tens of letters over the course of Edgar's service experience. One letter sent on 9 July 1916 is also mentioned in his diary. Burns wrote: 'The garden is now resplendent with the roses you selected and mother in your absence has tended them with loving care and I am afraid has quietly admired them through a mist of anxious tears. Spartan though she is.'[11]

It was a Sunday when Burns wrote his letter and he had just visited Lord Morley, the only other member of Asquith's Cabinet to resign at the outbreak of the First World War. Burns mused in his diary:

> Both of us were all the better for exchange of news. He [Morley] was pleased at my letter to D.H. [Douglas Haig] and Edgar. The latter touched the old man to tears as it did myself when I wrote it. The mother in the garden, looking at her son's roses through a mist of tears when her heart was with her son fighting in a war his father and her husband resigned to avert.[12]

Lord Morley wrote to Burns that evening:

> My Dear Burns,
>
> I shall not soon, nor ever, forget your visit here tonight.
>
> I am more melted than for many a long long day past. The breadth of social survey and foresight — the angry vision of this hideous war — the tender pathos of the garden and the empty room — it all makes me proud that I hold the hand of such a comrade in a great piece of history.[13]

Throughout the war both Edgar and his own resignation were never far from Burns's mind. He detested the war as expressed in his diary entry of 24 August 1916:

> What I saw yesterday of war films marvellous as pictures but ghastly in that they reveal futile waste... misspent labours, unnecessary savagery but above all the waste of the wrong men's health and lives. It is kings, emperors, noblemen and diplomats that should be enduring the price their urchins the soldiers are paying for other men's stupidity and crimes.[14]

On 14 August 1916 Burns wrote a letter for Edgar's birthday two days later. The letter is revealing of the anguish Burns was feeling at this time as he and his wife were dislocated from their only child as he expressed in his letter:

> Dear Edgar,
>
> Yesterday your mother and myself had tea in the garden... Naturally our thoughts turned to you and all your comrades away from home. There was a particular interest in you today, because when this letter reaches your station on the battle field you will have entered man's estate in point of age; with war around you, fighting in front of you and amidst all the panoply or purgatory of war.
>
> This is [a] tragic environment for your 21st Birthday which we had hoped might have been celebrated in happier state. It is not our fault that you are away from home, it is less like home because of your absence and until you return there can never be that complete happiness which your absence deprives of us.[15]

Burns often sent news of home and in September 1916 notified Edgar that he been to see the film about the Somme in addition to observing a Zeppelin raid on London which he witnessed from Clapham Common on 2 September:

> We were up early on Sunday morning to see the Zeppelin Raid and from the Common got a good view of the attack and the repulse. So far as we could gather

they seem to come from Woolwich via Greenwich and Black Heath way and then turned NW over London and our aeroplanes tackled them NW over Hampstead en route for Enfield... The guns, the search lights and the aeroplanes seemed to work well together and did very well considering the cloudy night.

There was a roar of cheering everywhere, when the captured Zepp came down in a ruddy glow due north from Common near Town Hall to Hampstead.[16]

General Douglas Haig had been keeping contact with Burns since the latter wrote to him at the time of the opening of the Somme Offensive. Haig invited Burns out to the Front to inspect the troops but his letter arrived at the same time as news of Edgar's ill health. Burns politely refused the General's invitation and wrote to Edgar expressing his concerns for his health. Edgar had contracted dysentery. In fact he suffered a great deal in the war. One note in Burns's papers is marked with a list of illnesses connected with his war experiences. Edgar had been gassed and wounded, and all these combined experiences had weakened his heart. At some point he had also suffered from shell shock which periodically returned to haunt him.

In January 1917 Mrs Burns received a letter from Bournville. It was from George Cadbury, of Cadbury's Chocolate, to whom she had recently written. Neighbours, friends and acquaintances would often drop their home at 110 North Side, Clapham Common or send letters to enquire about Edgar. In his letter Cadbury wrote:

Dear Mrs Burns,

I was interested to get a letter from you, speaking of your son. I was wondering what he was doing.

Like Mrs. Cadbury, you must be an anxious Mother, for the risk is great to our boys. Our youngest son brought down a Zeppelin and is a daring aviator, so that he is constantly testing new machines, taking trial trips etc. and the risk is very great.

I am sending with pleasure a dozen 1 lb. tins of Cocoa and Milk Powder with best wishes from Mrs. Cadbury and myself.

These are difficult and troublous times. I am sending a small parcel for your own use, in addition to the supply of Cocoa and Milk Powder for sending abroad.

In the one letter that survives written by Edgar to his father while he was stationed in Larkhill before he was sent to Egypt, he displays all the firebrand elements that his father displayed when leading strikes in the nineteenth century. The letter is also revealing in that his father's resignation at the outbreak of war may very well have affected Edgar's abilities to obtain a commission in the Army. He detests the officers and his experiences appear to have left him jaded about the social structures apparent in the Army at this time. Edgar wrote:

I have resigned myself to the ranks. I do not expect a commission but by heaven the war has gone on and I hate every officer. I shall remember it all my days. I was proud of my social position, fond of being the son of the Rt. Hon. John Burns far above the common crowd whether working class or middle class. The son of one of the most important men in England... Well Dad if I ever get on in Parliament and I am anything to do with the War Office I shall do everything I can to hurt the Army. But in any case I never take any notice of the officers. I always remember that in civil life I am far above that. The war will not last forever and that after the war I shall not even look at them. I shall remember.[17]

The war ended and Burns noted in his diary on Armistice Day 1918:

A fine bright morning, but the news was brighter. The traditional historical good fortune of the British people brought them the triumph of an overwhelming victory. Armistice, Peace, Victory after four years of war, were celebrated with quiet elation and sober joy by the people in the streets. Everywhere soldiers, sailors, civilians, children and above all the mothers, wives and sweethearts, were solemnly glad the war was over and their dear ones safe from further dangers. In Whitehall and West End great yet decorous crowds filled the streets with flags, mottoes and other decorations. The massed bands of the Guards, the King's Ministers and MPs were in the streets and enjoying the occasion. I went to H of C [House of Commons] L-G [Lloyd George] read Armistice. House went to St Margaret's and apart from excusable personal elation of the chief figures, we were glad that the end had so auspiciously and successfully come. I found that, given my view, the people were kindly and considerate to me, the soldiers particularly so... I wired to Edgar in Palestine or Egypt and with the end of this act my reticence ends and a new chapter begins. What will it be? In doing my duty I have forfeited much popularity but kept the mastery of my own soul. The rich have made up their mind to succeed royalties in their ascendancy. The people's war against them now begins.[18]

With the ending of war came the end of Burns's political career. Edgar was demobbed in 1920 but in 1922 tragedy struck. Edgar and his father's relationship had already broken down considerably before Edgar succumbed to the after effects of shell shock. Edgar had been working with a firm of chartered accountants in France. This job ended in March 1921 and he subsequently took up a position as a clerk/typist with the Imperial War Graves Commission. In a revealing letter to his father it appears that a financial arrangement was made so that Edgar was to leave England. It is presumed that an argument broke out between them on Edgar's return from Palestine. It would appear he found it difficult to settle into post-war life and still resented his father's decision to leave the Cabinet in 1914. In a letter dated 19 February 1921 Edgar wrote of his disappointment at the late payment of an allowance his father had organised:

> I have no desire to be tipped like a schoolboy and in addition have to ask for it. Before I left it was understood that I was to receive a regular allowance of £5 per month for staying away from England...

Edgar then goes on to berate his father, asking if the reason he did not receive the money on time was due to his father's inability to pay. Edgar blames his father if this indeed was to be the case for he felt that the consequence of his father's actions at the outbreak of the war had disenfranchised him in addition to leaving him with fewer choices and being forced into a life he resented, as he angrily expressed in his letter:

> If you had continued as a Cabinet Minister you would have saved sufficient for me to have taken up my rightful position, not with the middle class whom I loathe and hold in contempt... That dream is spoilt. I am forced into the company of people I despise.

Edgar signed his letter, 'I remain, yours truly.' The love between father and son of earlier years had been broken by war. Families, like the Burnses, were dislocated by the conflict. In a letter sent on 21 March Edgar had moderated his tone but was still somewhat frustrated that his father handled their financial arrangement as if he were a schoolboy.

Just over a year later and at 6.30pm on 22 June 1922 Edgar collapsed in the Hotel-Dieu (hospital), Rouen. Burns travelled to France immediately and sent a telegram to his wife on the 23rd, 'I have seen Edgar he has passed away. I am bringing him home short illness heart.'

The shell shock Edgar had suffered during the War had afflicted him again a week before he died. The dates for the Great War are given as 1914–1918, but for combatants, the War lasted all their lives and long after 1918 millions of families across the world felt its impact. Edgar was 26 years old when he died and he was buried at three o'clock in the afternoon on 27 July 1922 at St Mary's Cemetery, Battersea Rise, a short distance from Emanuel School. One can only imagine the thoughts going through his parents' minds that afternoon. Burns had stood his ground against a war he profoundly disagreed with, giving up his Cabinet position, leading to a deterioration in his relationship with Edgar and ultimately through the effects of that war, losing his only child at such an early age.

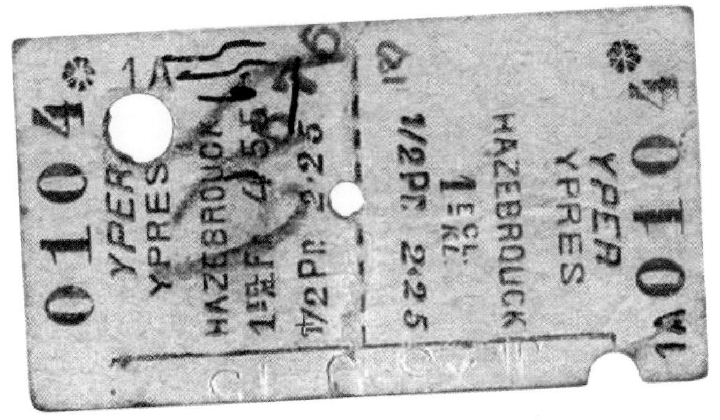

Edgar Burns's train ticket to Ypres

In 1936 Edgar's mother, Martha Charlotte 'Pattie' Burns, died with her husband at her side in Bolingbroke Hospital, a mere two minutes walk from Edgar's grave. She was buried in the same grave. Ill health plagued John Burns in his last years. On his 84th birthday he was sent a telegram from the Prime Minister, Winston Churchill saying, 'I think much of you.' This was accompanied by flowers from both Mr and Mrs Churchill. Having had to be carried to Bolingbroke Hospital, Burns died on 24 January 1943 aged 84. With son and wife, Burns now rests in the family grave.

References

1 Henry Broadhurst was the first man from a working-class background to reach a ministerial position. He became Under Secretary of State in the Home Department in Gladstone's Liberal Government. John Burns was the first man form a working-class background to be offered a Cabinet position.

2 William Kent, *John Burns: Labour's Lost Leader*, 1950, p. 102.

3 Letter to Pattie, 1907, BL Add MS 74261, f. 42.

4 Kent, *John Burns*, p. 225.

5 Ibid. p. 240.

6 BL Add MS 46303 f. 19 Sir Edward Grey, Letters to J. Burns: 1898–1914.

7 BL Add MS 46303 f. 12 Clementina Black, Letters to J. Burns: 1891–1914.

8 BL Add MS 46303 f. 15 Emily Hobhouse, Letters to J. Burns: 1900–1914.

9 BL Add MS 46303 f. 60 Anthony W. Dell, of Wandsworth, Letter to J Burns: 1914.

10 BL Add MS 74261 f. 144 Letter from John Collie to John Burns 21 October 1915.

11 BL Add MS 74261 f. 78 Letter to John Edgar Burns, 9 July 1916.

12 BL Add MS 46338, Diaries of John Burns 1916, entry for 9 July 1916.

13 John Viscount Morley, *Memorandum on Resignation: August 1914* (1928), p. xi.

14 BL Add MS 46338 Diaries of John Burns 1916, entry for 24 August 1916.

15 BL Add MS 74261 f. 83 Letter to John Edgar Burns, 14 August 1916.

16 BL Add MS 74261 f. 87 Letter to John Edgar Burns, 3 September 1916.

17 BL Add MS 74261 f. 112 Letter from John Edgar Burns to John Burns, 5 August 1917.

18 Kent, *John Burns*, p. 255.

A JUMP THAT WOULD BE USEFUL WHEN RUSHING THE TRENCHES.

E. Fisher (Emmanuel School) winning the long jump at the Public Schools Sports held at Stamford Bridge yesterday. Despite the croakers' attack on sport, the young men of England keep themselves fit by strenuous exercise, for they know that a sound body is the essential foundation for the good soldier. — *Daily Sketch*

Edmund 'Sir Edmund Tintacks' Fisher

Athletics star and boy soldier *(Emanuel 1908–1915)*

Edmund, more commonly known as Eddie, Fisher captained the Emanuel First Fifteen in the autumn of 1915. His character profile in *The Portcullis* reads, 'In zeal and energy he set a good example, which was well followed, and as a result the team, as a whole, played with considerable spirit.'[1] Not only was Eddie Captain of the Fifteen at the age of sixteen, he was also one of the most talented all round athletes of his generation.

In 1915 Eddie won the School's Athletics Challenge Cup after winning the 220 yards; Hurdle Race; High Jump; Long Jump and the 440 yards. His excellent form gained Emanuel the Challenge Cup at the Public Schools' Athletic Sports. *The Portcullis* recorded that Fisher won:

Eddie Fisher, First XV Captain, 1915

> The 120 yards Open Hurdles, the Long Jump Open, the High Jump Open and the High Jump Under 16... E. Fisher won the Hurdles in fine style by about two hurdles in 17 4/5 seconds. His time might have been better if he had been hard pressed. His High Jump and Long Jump were not the best he had done, for at the School Sports his High Jump was 5ft. 3½ in., and his Long Jump 19ft. 5½ in. At the Public Schools' Sports his High Jump was 5ft. 2ins. (tied) and Long Jump 19ft. 3¼ ins. This was undoubtedly owing to an accident which happened... about a week before the sports, which prevented him from training.[2]

The accident mentioned in the notes involved Eddie putting his head through the window of a railway carriage but no further details of how he managed it have come to light.

Eddie's long jump was reported in the press and the caption that went with a photograph of him flying through the air was ominous: 'A Jump That Would Be Useful When Rushing the Trenches.' The by-line kept up the theme of war: ... 'the young men of England keep themselves fit by strenuous exercise, for they know that a sound body is the essential foundation for the good soldier.'

Eddie rose to the position of Cadet Lieutenant in the OTC and on a night march in 1915 he rescued a party of exhausted boys: 'After a while Fisher, who had gone on with the others, returned triumphantly, driving a wagon and two horses, which he had commandeered to pull us out of the "miry fastnesses."'

On 3 December 1915 young Eddie Fisher, at the age of sixteen, lying about his age, joined the King's Forces. The date of birth given on Eddie's service papers is 1897 but it was in fact 1899. The material legacy relating to Eddie's war experiences does not exist and so we can only glean cursory information about him in 1916. What we do know is that he was as good a sportsman in the East Lancashire Regiment as he had been at School, for the regimental history notes:

> [2nd] Lieutenant Fisher was a real 'tearer' at the quarter-mile and sprints. At the brigade sports at Dieval, Fisher won the 100 yards, 220 yards and a gruelling ¼ mile; almost on the top of that he had to take part in a relay race, which he won for us by making up a deficit of at least a third of a lap – a wonderful performance.

We can only assume that Eddie might have gone on to become an Olympic athlete but for the Somme. On 16 November 1916 2nd Lt. Fisher, aged seventeen and attached to the 8th Battalion East Lancashire Regiment, was killed as his battalion were attempting to take German trenches in what became known as the Battle of the Ancre. There had been thick fog the previous day and so Eddie took a leap of faith into the unknown. He had only been in France since August 1916. His Commanding Officer noted that Eddie was a promising young officer who was popular with all ranks.

Eddie's father received a telegram on 23 November notifying him that Eddie had been killed. *The Portcullis* printed 'An Appreciation' in its Christmas 1916 edition. The author wrote:

> Do you remember how, when we were in Shell I, he was nicknamed 'Sir Edmund Tintacks'? 'Sir Edmund' – in truth he was a very perfect knight and like the knights of old, he made the supreme sacrifice in the cause of honour for King and Country.
>
> We of Emanuel are proud to belong to a School which can turn out such chaps as he. May we all, in whatever walk of life we may be called in the future, be aided, by the memory of E. Fisher and those other fellows who have left such splendid examples behind them, to be an honour to the old School.

His death made headlines in the local papers: 'Another Emanuel School Hero' and in the *New York Herald* Eddie's death was reported under the sub-heading: 'Athletes Famous for their Skill and Endurance Give Lives in War.'

Today Eddie's grave is situated off the beaten track in the middle of a field in Waggon Road Cemetery, Beaumont-Hamel.

Old Emanuel Joseph Deeks remembered years later, 'We felt the tragedy of war every week, for at daily service in the School Chapel we heard of the death of some Emanuelite serving in the front line... Perhaps the most tragic was the fate of Eddie Fisher.'

References

1 *The Portcullis*, Spring Term, 1916, p. 22.

2 *The Portcullis*, Summer Term, 1915, p. 21.

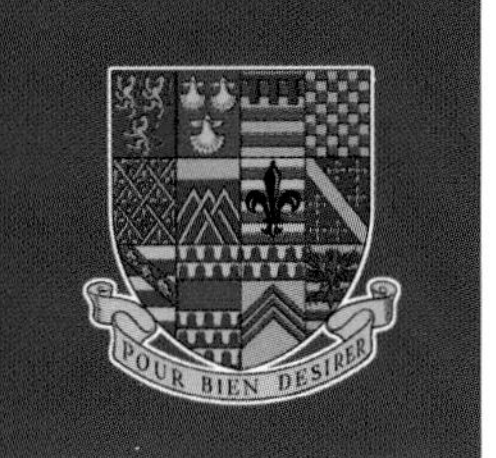

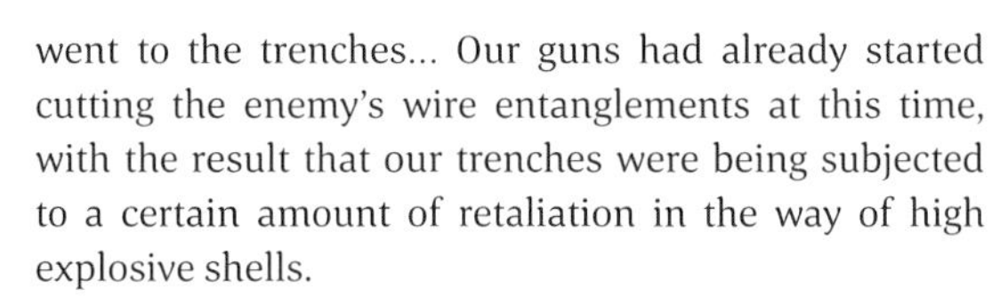

Leslie Stuart Clinton MC

(Emanuel 1906–1912)

Emanuel's first recipient of the Military Cross

The taking of the Trenches

'A promising player with plenty of pluck, but requires more experience.' This was how Leslie Stuart Clinton was described in the 1912 Emanuel rugby critiques. It was probably that extra pluck shown on the rugger field that won Leslie the Military Cross three years later. In the 1911–12 season he was in the three-quarter line, winning his School Half Colours. He was awarded the status of Prefect and became Captain of Wellington House and was a Sergeant in the OTC.

Leslie received a commission in the 23rd Battalion, The London Regiment and as 2nd Lt. Clinton travelled to France with the British Expeditionary Force. In May 1915 Leslie was based in the trenches at Givenchy. On 24 May the Battalion War Diary records: 'Battalion left at 2pm by Companies and relieved 22nd Battalion London Regiment in the trenches at GIVENCHY.'[1] The scene Leslie would have witnessed at Givenchy was of half-bombed-out ruins and ghost-like trees scattered across a vast network of sandbags marking out the trenches which sliced through the French countryside.

Leslie's Battalion were soon ordered to take the German trenches and we know in some detail what occurred due to an Officer's description sent to Battalion Headquarters and reported in the local South London newspaper the *South Western Star*.[2] Extracts of that account follow:

> We first heard that the battalion was to participate in an attack on the German trenches on the evening of Friday, May 21, and on Saturday morning the adjutant and I... went to the trenches... Our guns had already started cutting the enemy's wire entanglements at this time, with the result that our trenches were being subjected to a certain amount of retaliation in the way of high explosive shells.
>
> The attack... had to be postponed until the night of Tuesday, May 25... we were therefore put into the trenches on the evening of the 24th... We had a comparatively quiet night, but wire-cutting operations were resumed by our guns at daybreak which evoked the customary retaliating shelling on the part of the Germans.
>
> The extent of German trench we were to go for was about 500 yards in length and the depth of ground to be covered varied between 350 yards on the left and 100 yards on the right.

The Battalions came under enfilading fire as they attempted to secure the captured trenches and this was where Leslie Clinton with that 'plenty of pluck', as shown on the rugger field a few years earlier, came into action. The 23rd Battalion Officer continued:

> The machine guns had been sent up to the captured trench rather before midnight on the 25th, and, as you will expect, did extraordinary [sic] well, Lt. Clinton was wounded in the knee during the night, but after having his wound dressed returned to his guns and when it was decided to withdraw them, I believe carried one out himself.

A report reprinted in *The Portcullis* from a private in the 23rd provides further details:

> Lt. Clinton and a double company, with two machine guns, were ordered up to consolidate the captured trenches, which they found, however, to be untenable owing to an enfilading fire which the enemy were able to bring to bear upon them. They held out for a long time, however, and when a mere handful of men were left, Lt. Clinton continued to work the guns until the order came to fall back. Even at this point Lt. Clinton stayed to see the wounded taken in. Owing to this work the machine gun had to be left in the evacuated trench, but Clinton, returning under heavy fire alone, destroyed one and brought the other back in safety. He was slightly wounded in the knee while doing this.[3]

For this action Leslie was awarded the Military Cross (MC), an award newly instituted by Royal Warrant at the beginning of 1915. Mistakenly the *South Western Star* reported on 11 June, 'Emanuel School and the War. An Old Boy Recommended for the VC.' This was an easy mistake to make and probably based on rumour but the awarding of the MC to the nineteen year old Leslie was no less impressive than if he had been awarded a Victoria Cross. It was customary for the awards and announcements to be printed in the *London Gazette* and on 3 July 1915 Leslie's MC citation read:

> Lieutenant Leslie Stuart Clinton, 23rd (County of London) Battalion, The London Regiment (Blackheath and Woolwich), Territorial Force.
>
> At Givenchy, on 25th and 26th May, 1915, showed extreme gallantry in working his machine guns under very heavy fire in the captured German trench. After being wounded in the leg he returned to the trench after the wound had been dressed and carried out his gun himself when it was ordered to be withdrawn. In doing this he was again wounded.[4]

The School reported the news of Leslie's award with great pride:

> We are proud to record the fact that Lt. L. S. Clinton, 23 Batt. County of London Regt., has been awarded the Military Cross for conspicuous bravery at the Front.

The School notes continued:

> Remarkable scenes were witnessed at the School when Clinton made his first appearance after we had received the news. After carrying him shoulder high down the drive, the School was on the point of escorting him back to the 23rd Headquarters, when authority intervened.

Leslie's old house, Wellington also reported on the news:

Leslie Clinton

> The breast of every true son of Emanuel swells with pride when the name of Lt. L. Clinton is mentioned, who, as we all know, has been awarded the Military Cross for valour in the field, and still more should all Wellingtonites be proud since Clinton was in the House during his whole stay at Emanuel, and during his last term was House Captain.[5]

Later in 1915 Leslie gave a trophy to the School:

> The Clinton Cup, awarded since 1915–16 to the winning House in Rugby League, is a silver cup bearing an inscription stating that it was "presented by Lt. LESLIE CLINTON, MILITARY CROSS, 23rd Bn. County of London Regiment, T. F., as a Perpetual Challenge Cup for House Football, December, 1915." Above the inscription are the School Arms and the badge of the Regiment.[6]

Leslie fought with the London Regiment for the rest of 1915, before transferring to the 20th Hussars towards the end of that year. He had a career in the Colonial Police Force in Nigeria in post-war years reaching the rank of Commandant.

References

1 The War Diary of 23 Battalion, The London Regiment May 1915.
2 The *South Western Star*, June 25, 1915, p. 5.
3 *The Portcullis*, Summer Term, 1915, p. 60.
4 6536 Supplement To *The London Gazette*, 3 July, 1915.
5 *The Portcullis*, Summer Term, p. 15.
6 *The History of Emanuel School*, p. 285.

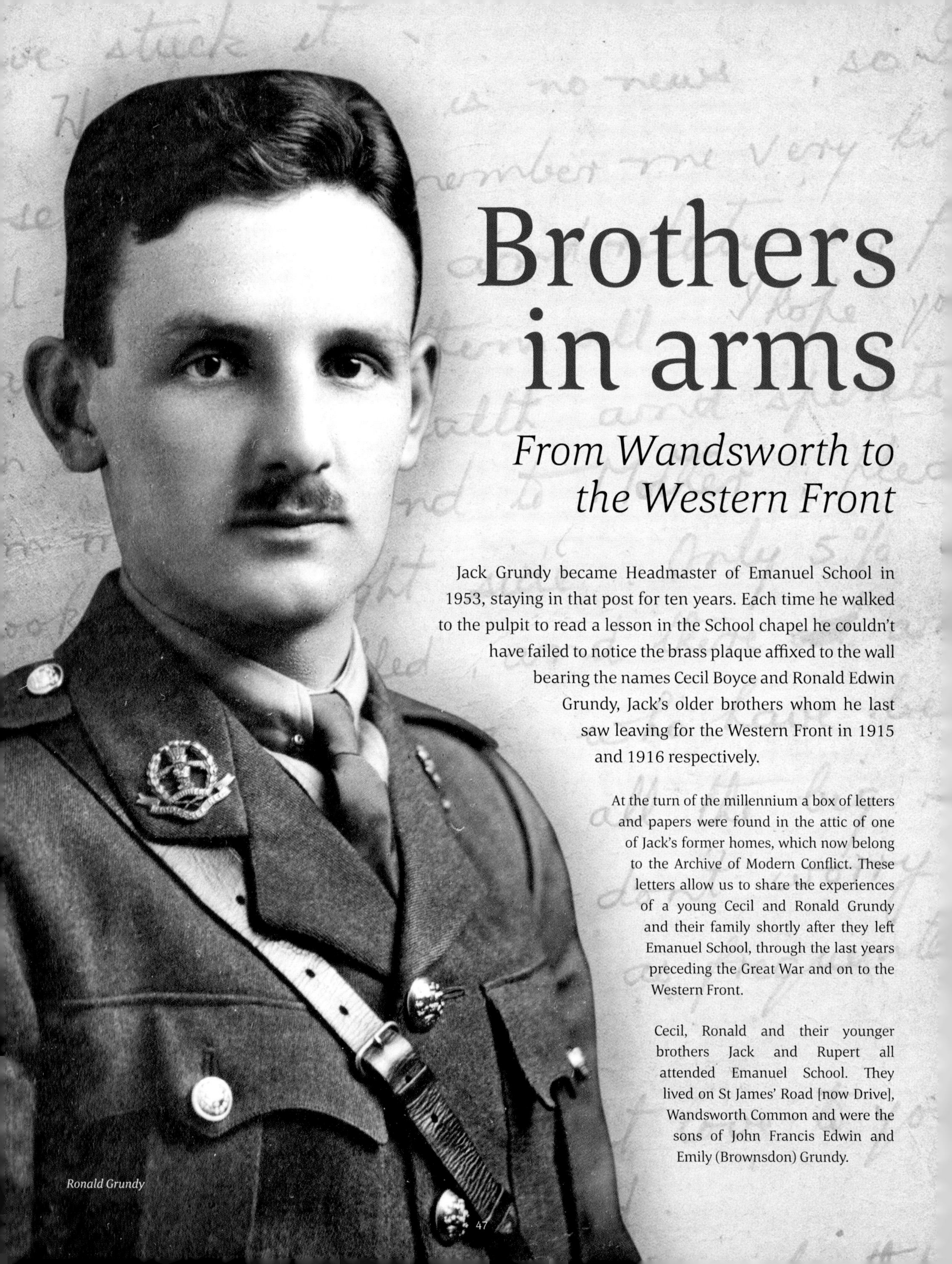

Brothers in arms

From Wandsworth to the Western Front

Jack Grundy became Headmaster of Emanuel School in 1953, staying in that post for ten years. Each time he walked to the pulpit to read a lesson in the School chapel he couldn't have failed to notice the brass plaque affixed to the wall bearing the names Cecil Boyce and Ronald Edwin Grundy, Jack's older brothers whom he last saw leaving for the Western Front in 1915 and 1916 respectively.

At the turn of the millennium a box of letters and papers were found in the attic of one of Jack's former homes, which now belong to the Archive of Modern Conflict. These letters allow us to share the experiences of a young Cecil and Ronald Grundy and their family shortly after they left Emanuel School, through the last years preceding the Great War and on to the Western Front.

Cecil, Ronald and their younger brothers Jack and Rupert all attended Emanuel School. They lived on St James' Road [now Drive], Wandsworth Common and were the sons of John Francis Edwin and Emily (Brownsdon) Grundy.

Ronald Grundy

John was a printer, publisher and one time President of the Fine Art Trade Guild, who persuaded the then Prime Minister Lloyd George to sit for his portrait in 1916.[1]

At Emanuel Cecil was a gifted young man, a recipient of prizes, a soldier boy in the cadets, a sports player and Prefect. Within a year of leaving Emanuel he worked at Burberry and travelled to Argentina to work in that Company's branch before returning to England in 1914. Ronald too was a keen sportsman; he was one of the School's first members to take up rowing when a few boys from the School started doing it at Putney in 1913. He also became Captain of Howe House. He wrote the following lines in the House notes in *The Portcullis* of 1913:

> At last we have gained our correct position in the School, that of leaders in the 'Rugger' competition. Although Fate has once more been against us (that perverse deity has always borne us a grudge) by twice crocking our best men just before a match, yet by means of a splendid start last term and a strong revival this term we have secured first place. The finish was very close, leaving us champions by one point only, but a miss is as good as a mile. The coveted position reached, all Howeites are hereby exhorted to see that we occupy it permanently.[2]

Whilst Ronald was searching for a career, Cecil, wrote home to his parents on the evening of 31 July 1914, at the end of a month known in history as the 'July Crisis', '...in any case I join with you all in sincerely hoping that England may not be drawn into the conflict.'[3] In the next few days as Europe went to war Cecil continued to write home. In a letter written on the day Britain declared war on Germany, he wrote, 'Although we are so very securely away from the war it has already caused several startling and unlooked for changes in our Republic. As was to be expected there was a big run on all the banks the first day that things began to look at all serious, and in reply the government at once ordered them to remain closed for the following week.'[4] Cecil continued writing his letter over a two day period and on 5 August wrote, 'News was received that England had declared war late last night and no sooner was it thrown upon the screen at the 'Prensa' newspaper building than the crowd went mad with delight, for the Latins are anti-German to a man and any little success on the part of the 'entente' provokes the greatest enthusiasm.'[5]

John Grundy wrote to Cecil at the end of August 1914 and from the letter we can glean Ronald's efforts in attempting to join the forces:

> Ronald is trying to do his little bit against the Teutons and has spent hours getting about making enquiries, all the recruiting places being jammed with candidates. First he went to Cornford (our next door Captain) at headquarters opposite the station near the 'Empire' Clapham Junction. Personally, I don't think much of that crowd so advised Ronald to apply to the Honourable Artillery Company which he has done, and they sent for him. He says there were hundreds there, nearly all men of the public school type. His turn has not yet come to be examined but is due on Monday and if they pass his spectacles I have no doubt but that he will get in.[6]

Cecil Grundy

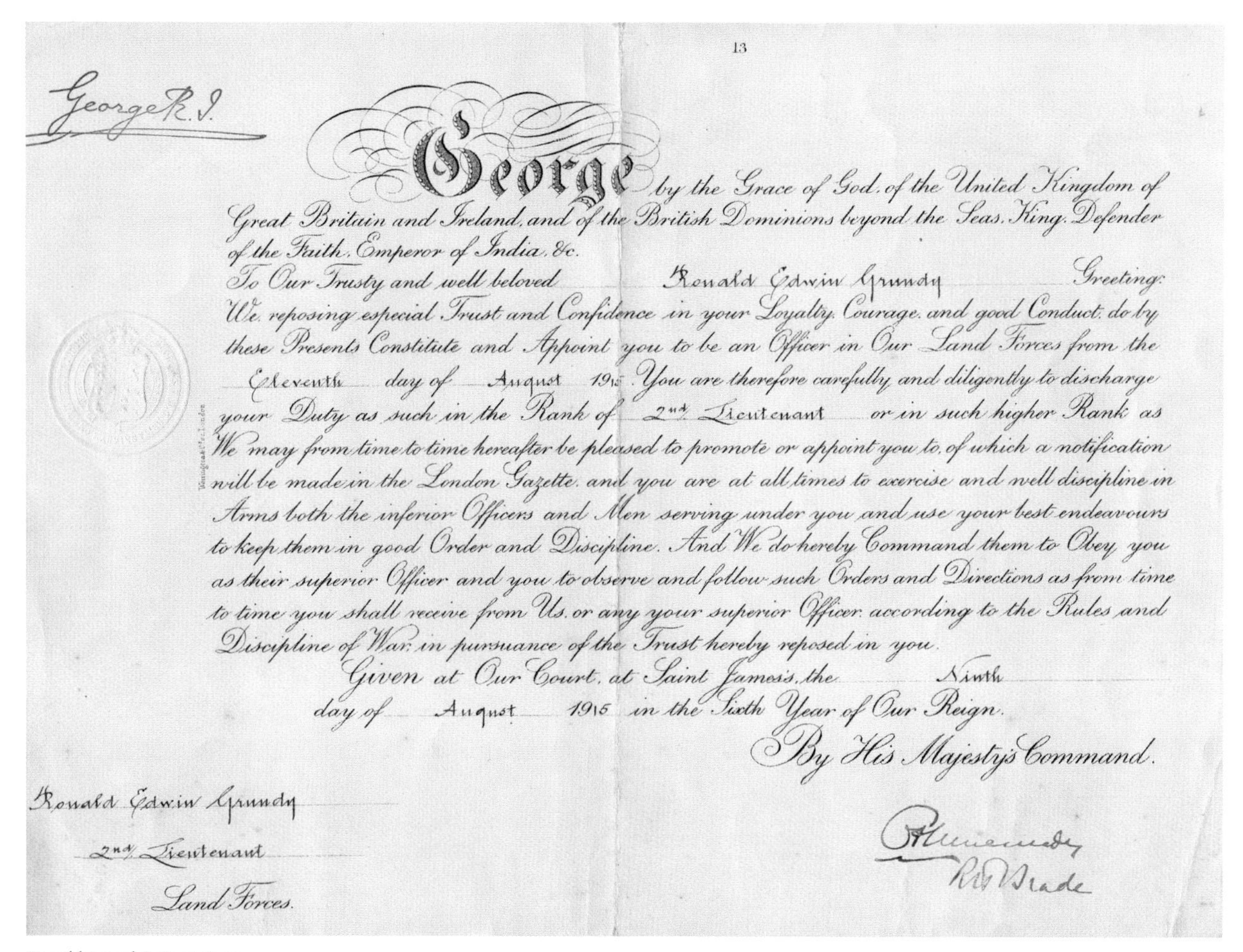

13

George R. I.

George by the Grace of God, of the United Kingdom of Great Britain and Ireland, and of the British Dominions beyond the Seas, King, Defender of the Faith, Emperor of India, &c.

To Our Trusty and well beloved Ronald Edwin Grundy Greeting:

We, reposing especial Trust and Confidence in your Loyalty, Courage, and good Conduct, do by these Presents Constitute and Appoint you to be an Officer in Our Land Forces from the Eleventh day of August 1915. You are therefore carefully and diligently to discharge your Duty as such in the Rank of 2nd Lieutenant or in such higher Rank as We may from time to time hereafter be pleased to promote or appoint you to, of which a notification will be made in the London Gazette, and you are at all times to exercise and well discipline in Arms both the inferior Officers and Men serving under you and use your best endeavours to keep them in good Order and Discipline. And We do hereby Command them to Obey you as their superior Officer and you to observe and follow such Orders and Directions as from time to time you shall receive from Us, or any your superior Officer, according to the Rules and Discipline of War, in pursuance of the Trust hereby reposed in you.

Given at Our Court, at Saint James's, the Ninth day of August 1915 in the Sixth Year of Our Reign.

By His Majesty's Command.

Ronald Edwin Grundy
2nd Lieutenant
Land Forces.

Ronald Grundy's Commission

Ronald replied to Cecil, addressing him as Bill, describing his experiences of the tests he had to complete as part of determining whether men were 'fit' enough to join the armed forces. It is a revealing letter and shows the viewpoint of a young man upon an older generation of men who were in charge of recruitment.

> On Monday last, after several hours waiting, I was examined by the doctor of the Honourable Artillery Company, and passed as a fit person, including eyesight (I passed this test by learning the bottom lines of the test by heart before I was questioned). Then I appeared before the Court of the Regiment, with a lot of other recruits...The Court is composed of rather old jossers who I suppose were once officers... The Court are a very particular set of old fogies, and keep the Regiment very select and exclusive... The Standard of efficiency is very high, and a fellow stands little chance of getting in unless he has been to a public school. The fact that I have been in the OTC will give me a good leg up, I hope.[7]

Ronald passed out as Private Grundy Honourable Artillery Company (HAC) on the afternoon of 7 September 1914 at the age of 17. Cecil too enlisted with the HAC on 23 October 1914.

Mrs Grundy wrote to Cecil on 1 September 1914 expressing her wishes, 'that the battle will be short and decisive not long drawn out.' With those sentiments went a chorus of a million voices but as days turned into weeks so, in turn, weeks became months and both Cecil and Ronald were fully engaged in their army training.

Cecil was 20 years old standing at 5ft. 11in tall with a 35in chest. He spent four months with the HAC before entering Sandhurst and being appointed to a commission in the Duke of Cambridge's Own, The Middlesex Regiment commencing on 14 July 1915. Ronald too received a commission commencing on 11 August 1915. By the summer of 1915 they were both Second Lieutenants in The Middlesex Regiment.

Between late 1914 and the summer of 1915 both brothers would have undertaken various training and exams on the

Trench digging in Gillingham, summer 1915

road to becoming officers. Their daily routines would have consisted of kit inspections, route marches, lectures and practical field exercises. We know from one of Cecil's letters what the lighter moments of a soldier's life could be like. It would be the last summer that both Cecil and Ronald spent together. On Saturday 29 August Cecil wrote of their activities the previous day, 'Ron and I took the motor bus to Maidstone yesterday afternoon and there took a boat on the Medway and rowed to a little place called Teesew, some five miles upstream. We had tea there in a quaint little garden served by a [sic] old man and his wife...'

The revolver range butts at Camberley

Cecil sailed for France in late September 1915 at a time when the British were engaged in the Battle of Loos. He wrote home to his parents 2 October 1915 saying he had arrived safely and indicating that his 'stuttering French' carried him along well. On 7 October he wrote to his mother as he was sitting in a train carriage. Including news of trips from Le Havre to Rouen with other soldiers he revealed the duties which had occupied him since landing in France. On 6 October we know that he was busy with 'machine gun and bombing demonstrations in the morning and a visit to the ordnance dept to complete one or two minor items of kit in the afternoon.'[8] He continues his letter with an account of his first day in France, 'But I think the day I arrived took the biscuit for hard work, as that evening we practised manning and relieving trenches from 5 to 9 o'clock all in the pouring rain on the blackest of inky nights. It was too realistic for me!'[9] He continued with news from the evening of 6 October, 'Last night I got my marching orders and was given a draft of 100 men to entrain and hand over to their own regiment on arriving at billets...they are

2nd Battalion HAC paraded for General inspection
Belhus Park, Aveley, Essex - 14 October 1914

Painting of Cecil Grundy

the dickens of a trouble to keep in or get back into their carriages whenever we stop at any station!' Cecil gave his address at this time as 1st Middlesex, 19th Brigade, 2nd Division BEF.

During the course of October 1915 Cecil was not involved in any battle but life in the trenches was arduous as snipers and shells were a regular occurrence in the waiting game being played out by both sides. Cecil wrote several letters home that month from which we gain insights into his life on the Front:

On Saturday 10 October he wrote:

> I was posted to A Coy... we have our work cut out and I get more responsibility that I wanted for a start off, having two platoons Nos 3 and 4 all on my own... The fellows are a nice lot but terribly raw so I hope for a peaceful first bout to give them and myself a chance to settle down somewhat.

On Tuesday 12 October he wrote wishing his father a happy birthday and penned, 'the best of luck for the next year!' He also wrote:

> Nothing much doing, we are still in billets, with ordinary parades and manoeuvres just as at home. The afternoons are free and we often get in some revolver practice then. I'm not half a bad shot. I got a horse from the transport officer this afternoon and set out, unfortunately I seem to have forgotten all I have ever learnt and was never so bumped about in my life. It's quite painful to sit down this evening!... by sheer bad luck the Colonel (Rowley by name) rode past, out for a ride himself, and witnessed my most interesting display.

On Monday 18 October Cecil headed the letter address with 'Really There' and recounted his first impressions of being in the trenches.

> We came down here – which is the firing line trenches – on Saturday so we've already had two days of it.
>
> It was some march down here, everyman being loaded to his utmost capacity and carrying all manner of things 'for use in the trenches.' In consequence we fairly staggered along and although it was only a six mile march in a dead straight line to the trenches a lot of the men were quite fagged out with it.
>
> My first impressions was being lost in an interminable maze, an impression which still holds good, for though I have learnt my way about in my own company lines I should be absolutely lost elsewhere. Somehow or other I had always imagined that one had to kill time and would while away the time by reading and playing cards in a dug out, but that's all wrong for I've never been so busy in my life, and sleep is to be sought after like gold! Of course we are short handed, but then everybody seems to be out here – all except one Scotch – Reg which turned out with 30 officers and 200 men.
>
> The Bombardment or 'Gunning' as it is called absolutely incessant, never leaving off for ten seconds but thank heaven it has all been on our part so far. However I'm not sure that it means that we have entire superiority of fire for friend Bosche is a wily bird and is doubtless safe in deep dugouts to reappear when he feels inclined and I guess when he wants he can bombard as much as we can.
>
> Our servants are marvels! Even here we get quite a good mess including porridge in the morning so we don't do so badly and our Coy is as cheery as ever.[10]

In his next letter to the family Cecil gives further details of life in the trenches and in particular his experiences with a German sniper:

> Most of the men never saw a German the whole time, and it was only when searching for a particular sniper that I sighted one – three of them in fact – and in the very act. We forthwith set out to snipe the sniper, but unfortunately missed and of course once shot at he did not appear again. Still he was quite a sport about it, for he signalled back my first shot a 'miss' and then turned to look for me, in which time I got in another, and by the time I'd looked up to see the result (in another place) there was nothing to see. Another time I shall have an observer with a periscope.

Cecil went on to describe daily life in the trenches and the types of duties they were expected to carry out.

> The day is pretty well occupied with various working parties on all sorts of jobs – building 'fire steps', 'dugouts', filling sand bags, drawing stores from the RE or preparing wire to put out at night, so our Company being somewhat short of officers we get no time to ourselves. As soon as it gets dark everyone has to be on the alert, one in every third man is posted as sentry and an officer has always to be on duty on the spot; so as everyone has to 'stand-to'

(or turn out) for half an hour or so at dusk and dawn we get precious little time to study our dugouts.

We are rather short of wire in front of our particular bit of line and so we are busy rigging up another row. Our little party sallies forth an hour or so after dark and carries on, but it usually isn't long before Bosche thinks something's up and starts sending up star shells. These are nothing more than first class Roman candles which give a regular blaze of light all around so there is nothing for it but to drop flat if you've seen it in time or remain dead still if you are caught in the act.[11]

Five days later on 28 October Cecil wrote to his mother:

We are now in the very thick of it – the mud I mean! When we took over there was quite six inches of water in half the trenches and a soft thick base of mud below that again.

The water we managed to bale out more or less – rather less perhaps – but that mud still remains and nowadays every step is a laborious task, for you've sunk in so that it requires quite an effort to move it; so there you go Squelsh! Splosh! Squelsh! along miles and miles of slimy trenches.

Cecil went on to describe the heavy task of travelling through the trenches to billets whilst the men had to carry 'full packs, rifles, ammunition and shovels', but on a lighter note he also asked his parents to send two more mouth organs before signing off, 'In best of health. Love to all. Cecil.'

The next morning 29 October, 2nd Lt. Athelstan Douglas Dempster Bonnor of "A" Company, Middlesex Regiment, wrote a letter to Mrs. Grundy:

Dear Madam,

I am sorry to say that your son was slightly wounded last night in the right thigh, but it is nothing to worry about and he is quite as well as can be expected under the circumstances.

A German sniper had hit Cecil as he was inspecting the trenches and on 30 October Cecil dictated a letter to his mother from the 6th Field Ambulance.

Dear Mother,

Have been unlucky enough to stop some German lead, and now here with a broken thigh bone in right leg. I don't think there is anything very complicated about the affair, the only trouble is that it is likely to be rather long and tedious, as they say it may be close on six months before I am hopping around again.

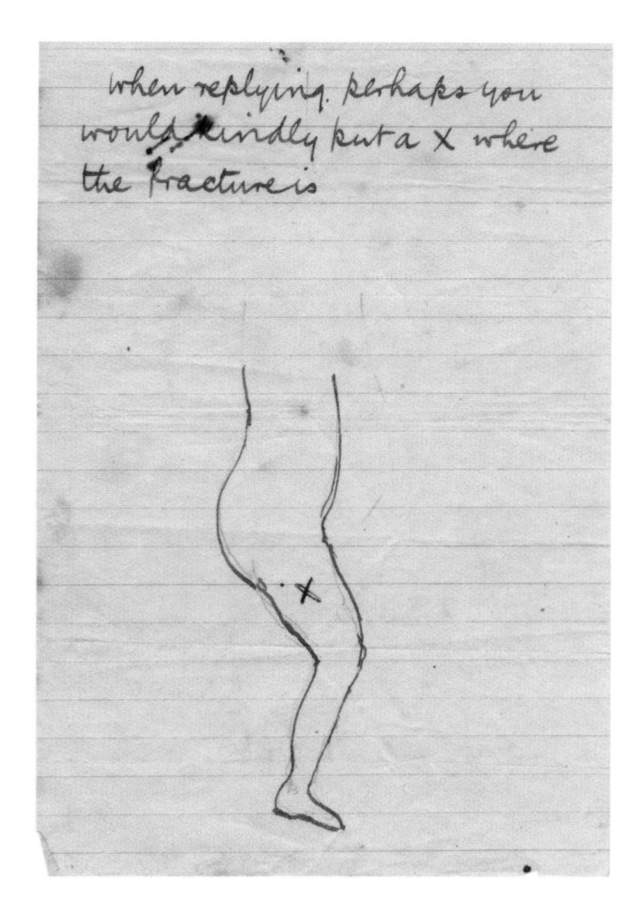

when replying, perhaps you would kindly put a X where the fracture is

A letter sent by John Grundy to Field Ambulance nurses asking them to indicate the position of Cecil's fracture

In the next two weeks Cecil dictated letters home, as well as writing a couple himself. Unknown to him the nurses who were looking after him also corresponded with the Grundy family. On 2 November his night Sister, Margaret Donnellan wrote to Mrs Grundy:

Dear Madam,

enclosed you will find a letter from your son Lt. Grundy – written by me but I could not possibly send it to you without letting you know how dangerously ill is he and how very anxious his medical advisers are about him – you know from previous letters he has a compound fracture of the thigh and... gangrene... We are all anxious to pull him through we cannot bear to lose one of our brave men.

Letters came nearly every other day with news on Cecil's condition. From his bed he wrote and dictated letters home. Mostly penned by the day Sister, nurse Catherine Elston, who in the summer of 1915 had been awarded the Royal Red Cross by King George V,[12] in addition to her own personal correspondence with Emily Grundy. On 14 November

No 6 Fld Amb Hospital
BEF
Monday Nov 8th

Dear Mother

I received your letter of Saturday afternoon first thing this morning which is quite quick work. But how is it that this is the first letter I have received at all? Did you never write between the last letter I got in the trenches & Sat last?

The nurses were the most anxious for they were so afraid they had written too much & though of course they've never said anything I think a personal acknowledgement from you or Father would be very acceptable to them.

Of course Father & the boys can't come out here; we are only 6 miles from the firing line so our mute friend Kitchener might intervene, & besides I can't stick talking to anyone beyond 3 minutes so there would not be very much

(2)

in it after all & Dad could not really help at all

No really I'm very glad things are panning out like this for it is quite probable that after another week or so here they may send me through practically straight to England i.e. instead of keeping me at the Base for the serious part they may keep me here.

9PM Nurse Donnellan tells me she has just had letter from Dad & I guess the other nurse (I know her just as well but I don't know her name – She is in charge) will get one to-morrow.

Owing to pending operations all the "slight" cases from upstairs have been put in our ward temporarily.

It does annoy me! Then I must be terribly cross sometimes now.

To-morrow I will tell you all about the wound & the dressings

Original letter written by Cecil Grundy from the BEF's No. 6 Field Ambulance Hospital, 8 November 1915

Catherine wrote a letter on Cecil's behalf in which he relayed an operation he had undergone. The tone was upbeat with news of his condition but the following day Catherine wrote to Mrs Grundy notifying her that Cecil's condition had worsened. At some time after 11pm on 16 November 1915 Margaret Donnellan penned the following lines:

> Dear Mrs Grundy
>
> It is my very painful duty to write and tell you of your son's death at 11pm tonight. I was with him when he died and I am glad to say his end was happy and peaceful and he died like the hero he was. He knew he was dying and regretted not seeing any of you – He spoke of you all. His mother and father particularly and also mentioned Vera several times.

In addition to correspondence between the family and Cecil's nurses, letters of condolence came from John Grundy's acquaintances who had read the news in *The Times*; Cecil's former servant in the Middlesex Regiment; and Lt-Col F. G. M. Rowley, the Commanding Officer (CO) of Cecil's battalion the 1st Middlesex.

Ronald, who was still training in England, received a letter from an Old Wellingtonian boy who was serving as a Lieutenant in Cecil's battalion. William Hugh David De Pass wrote on 20 November:

> My dear Grundy,
>
> It was very great grief that I saw in the papers this morning the sad news about your brother. I had hoped from your letter that he would recover, so it came as a terrible shock to me. I only trust that he did not suffer much pain. He has given his life, as I know he himself would have wished, in the service of his country and this at any rate must be a small consolation to you.
>
> Harris and I were only talking of him the other day, and were saying what a good officer he made.

Painting of Ronald Grundy

Please accept my deepest sympathy, which I feel for you, and express my great regret to your people.

On 22 November Ronald wrote to his mother from Belvedere Camp in Rochester where he was stationed and wrote the following to comfort her regarding Cecil's loss:

> Bear up, Mother dear, and find a little comfort in the fact that in 21 years he had made himself more loved and respected than most people do in a lifetime; and that he died the finest death there is. As Macaulay says: How can man die better, than fighting fearful odds. For the ashes of his fathers, And the temples of his gods.
>
> With Love to you all, Your affectionate son, Ronald.

During December 1915 Ronald wrote home with news of the signalling work he had been carrying out. Although he spent Christmas Day with his family, he spent the rest of late December occupied with theory and practical tests in signalling which included reading and sending messages by flags and lamps and laying wires between an imaginary battalion and brigade headquarters over an area of three miles, all exercises which were essential to Front Line combat. At this time he was also pre-occupied with finding himself a motorbike.

On 21 March 1916 Ronald wrote to his mother about being confirmed with his elder brother never far from his mind, 'Isn't it a coincidence that I am to be confirmed on the day that dear Cecil, had he lived, would have been 22. I am trying to be like him and in some way to make up for his loss.' Cecil continued to occupy Ronald's thoughts when he too was sent to France. In a letter on 6 June he wrote:

> I wish dear old Cecil were with me now. We could have helped each other a lot, or rather he could have helped me. When he was alive, he did lots of things for me which I never appreciated. I used to look upon him as slow and priggish; in fact at times I was almost ashamed of being his brother. That was because I wanted to be thought as well, and he tried to curb me. And now I am absolutely thankful that he was with me, and did check me; or else I might have gone to the devil. I wish I had been kinder to him and backed him up more. Out here I meet fellows who were in the 6th Middlesex and when they hear my name, they ask me whether I am brother to the Grundy who was killed with the 1st. And although he was only with the 6th about 2½ months they all say how much liked he was, and what a good fellow he was. And they mean it too: men in the Army never flatter or compliment each other without good cause. If I come back I shall try to be as good a brother to Jack and Rups as Cecil was to me.

On 4 June Ronald writes about the Battle of Jutland, the most significant naval battle of the War which began on 31 May:

> The Naval Battle seems to have been very even, I was afraid it was a victory for the Germans, but it is more in favour of us. At any rate, it will affect their fleet more than it will ours. What a terrible fight it must have been! But nothing to what the Army will be going through shortly.

Ronald alludes here to the offensive, which the British and French High Commands had been planning since late 1915 and what we know as the Battle of the Somme. On 5 June he wrote to his father:

> It is somewhat of a coincidence that I should be going up to the firing line on my birthday. I can't say I am at all sorry to go; it has been my chief ambition for a long time and I want to get it over. I don't suppose for a moment that, should I get the opportunity, I shall ever want to come out again. But it is a wonderful experience and one I would not miss for worlds. I used to be afraid my eyesight would stop me coming out, or that the doctors would find some hidden physical defect. But I have got out here at last, and it's up to me to make the most of my opportunities. I hope and pray I shall come back to you all again, to be a help and comfort to you and Mother. But if I don't, you will know I've died quite happy. I have had a happy life – the best parents a boy could wish for, and the best home.

Ronald left for the Front on the afternoon of Tuesday 6 June at 4.10pm and considered himself rather lucky as 'most people going up the line leave here at 4.10am.' He joined his battalion the next day on 7 June.[13] On the same day he left for the Front Ronald left instructions for how his property should be divided in the event of death. In the letter, in which he asked his father to dispose of his goods should the worst happen, he requested that money be left among others to family members, Emanuel School and Dr Barnardo's Homes. His gold ring was to be left to Janet who we presume was his girlfriend who is mentioned on more than one occasion in his letters.

Letters sent home from the front lines were censored to avoid information getting into the wrong hands but Ronald devised ways around the censors several times. Writing on the day he joined his battalion he ended his letter, 'P.S. I wrote Albert today, but am not sure of his address. Ask father about it.' We know through what he described in his letter that Ronald was stationed in the town of Albert, which sat a few miles from the British Front Line. He also asked his parents to tell him if any of his letters were ever censored.

The letter details the scenes he witnessed on that first day, being full of descriptions of landscape, life and the minutiae of army life at the Front such as the wearing of tin helmets.

> The town in which we are billeted is only just behind the firing line, and is always being shelled. The Bosch must know I've arrived for he has put several over this afternoon, quite near this house. No one takes any notice of them, and people walk about the streets quite unconcernedly. The Cathedral has had a good knocking about and the statue of the Virgin on the tower has been knocked over and is only hanging by a few threads of iron. They say when it falls, the war will be over...I am posted to "D" Company...We all have to wear these tin hats, like pudding basins, they look most picturesque.[14]

On 10 June Ronald writes home describing trench life and writes of his dislikes being, 'artillery fire, and rain.'

> At the moment I'm off duty, or should not be writing this. These trenches are very muddy, and have suffered considerably through artillery fire. It rained all Thursday and throughout the night and on Friday things were awfully messy – up to your ankles all the time, and of course covered with mud from head to foot. The trench coat and boots are unrecognisable; the boots are comfortable, but after 24 hours in the rain my feet were wet, which was hardly to be wondered at... Trench life is rather boring after the first day or two, especially when it rains (it has started again today). This bit of line is quite a hot bit – there is generally something on the move, especially at night. Consequently we get very little sleep at night...

On 12 June Ronald describes the life of an officer in the trenches, 'An officer has a tremendous lot of walking about to do, up and down the trenches, seeing that sentries are alert, and everything is all right. The men are splendid – of course they grouse amongst themselves, but they stand an awful lot – rain and cold, and mud and lots of hard work.' He continues his letter with what life was like for him being so close to bursting shells, 'the first time I was near it was one night, when I was trying to sleep in a little shelter, about 18 shells came flying over and burst about 20 yds away. I could see the flash from the door and didn't know what on earth to do – there was a terrific noise, and if I moved out, I might walk into it; on the other hand, I might get it if I stayed where I was.' Ronald also mentions his brother and Howe House, which he had once captained and now his younger brother Jack is a member of it, 'Tell Jack I'm very glad to hear that Howe are doing so well – I hope they continue their success... is he training for the sports?' Ronald was looking forward to returning to his family and as he put it, 'I want to enjoy the delights of civilisation again.'

On 15 June Ronald wrote to his mother describing the 20-miles march he and his fatigue party had to complete as

Officers of the 6th Battalion Middlesex Regiment, Gillingham, August 1915. Cecil Grundy standing second from right.

Soldier's Hymnal

Event	Hymn
Reveille.	Christians Awake
Rouse Parade	Art thou weary, Art thou languid
Breakfast	Meekly wait & murmur not
C.O's parade	When he cometh
Manoeuvres	Fight the good fight.
Disposal of accused.	Oft in danger, oft in woe
Kit Inspection.	All things bright & beautiful
Swedish Drill.	Here we suffer grief & pain
Dinner.	Come ye thankful people come
Rifle Drill.	Go, labour on
Lecture by officer.	Tell me the old, old, story.
Dismiss	Praise God from whom all blessings flow
Tea.	What means this eager, anxious throng
Last Post.	All are safely gathered in.
Lightsout.	Peace, perfect peace.
Zep raid drill	We plough the fields & scatter
Night Ops.	The day thou gavest Lord, is ended
Route March.	Onward, Christian Soldiers.

Soldier's Hymnal written by Ronald Grundy and intended for publication in The Portcullis

part of their training. Interestingly he also mentions putting his watch forward due to the French Daylight Saving Bill which reminds us that even though one hundred years have passed since he wound his watch, Ronald's world was very much, in this respect, the world we still live in – the twenty-first century. He also makes reference to his battalion:

> My servant is quite a nice fellow. Very polite and attentive. The battalion is one to be proud of, as far as the NCOs and men are concerned. They are thorough soldiers, ready for anything. They stand any amount of hardship and fatigue, and though, like all tommies, they grouse, they aren't really disconcerted. Their humour is of the type that can only be found in the British Army... to appreciate it really you want to be with them in the trenches during a bombardment – I will tell you some funny stories when I get back to 'Blighty' (Tommies name for England). My platoon is a good one; the fellow who had it before me was very popular. He got the military cross and a wound in a successful little raiding affair last month, in which 'Fritz' was severely strafed and is now in England recovering.

On 16 June Ronald took the extraordinary decision to send a letter home with one of the men who was returning to England. It certainly would never have passed the censor if it had been ordinarily posted, a fact Ronald was all too aware of. The letter to Ronald's father detailed British plans for what became known as the 'Big Push' or 'Great Advance'. Since Christmas 1915 Allied Commanders had been planning to break through the German lines in what was hoped would break the stalemate on the Western Front. As 1916 developed the plans evolved, with several strategies being contemplated. By June 1916 the plans would see an artillery bombardment attempt to destroy the German defences, the preparation for which is noted in Ronald's letter. It was hoped that such a heavy bombardment would cut the German wires and reduce the capacity of the Germans to attack when the 'Big Push' was to be launched on 1 July. Ronald wrote:

> My Dear Father,
>
> I am taking the opportunity offered by a man going home on leave of getting a letter posted England, where one can avoid the censor. I enclose some postcards of places in this neighbourhood; they will tell you exactly where I have been... In a week or two we shall be involved in about the biggest attack that has happened along this front. The whole 4th Army will be going for the Bosch and I can tell you from the preparations made that we are going to give him worse hell than he has ever given us. Whether the rest of the British line will advance, I cannot say. But I feel sure, if our affair realises expectations, Mr. Bosch will be feeling very sick. Several days artillery bombardment, followed by all sorts of things. Then the advance – 2nd Devons and our regiment will be first over the parapet in this division, attacking on quite a small front; but with other divisions on our right and left. Of course we go into battle light – all our kits will be left behind. I shall wear my body shield, and carry revolver, glasses, compass, one or two necessaries, and some food. We look to the artillery to do a lot of the dirty work, and I'm sure they will, for there are simply heaps of huge guns and unlimited ammunition. Some of our officers will be left behind as a reserve to replace casualties; but I'm glad to say I shall be one of the first over the top.

Ronald went on to list the contents of his two kits bags and then continued:

> Well, Dad, I won't go into further details, as I have told you enough to let you understand what is about to happen. As it is information that would be useful to the enemy keep it to yourself at least till the show has started. I should advise you not to tell Mother, until it is over, as it would only make her more anxious.

I'm not dreading; but if I don't come back – Goodbye, and God Bless you All. However I'm full of hope, and trust to come through with nothing worse than a wound. Perhaps in a month's time I shall be with you all once again – I hope so. Well, let's hope the fellow remembers to post this.

Love to all,

Ronald.

On 18 June Ronald tells his mother about the few luxuries he enjoyed at the Front, 'Just think of this. Yesterday I had strawberries and cream for tea – pretty good for a place as near to the firing line as this! And we always get bacon and eggs for breakfast in the trenches! This evening I have been over to the local village and had another hot bath – about four inches of warm water in an ancient slipper bath in an old stable. Still, it was greatly appreciated.'[15]

Ronald wrote home on the weekend before the opening of the Battle of the Somme. His letter contains both personal and general information and from it we can almost be transported back to his own times as he mentions the song he was listening to on the gramophone:

> Sometimes you get a good deal of time for writing in the trenches, but this last trip there was such a crowd of us in one little dug out, that there wasn't much opportunity for writing a decent letter...we were up all night and did a long march across country.
>
> Our billet is a French farm house. I don't think much farming is done by the inhabitants just now, but there are still some people living in the house. The barns and outhouses are full of men and I share a room with 3 other officers on the ground floor. Two others sleep in the garden in a bell tent. It is something to have a roof over one's head and to be able to stand upright. The men are simply wonderful. I admire them more every day. It poured with rain last night, and we had a most gruelling march, heavily laden, across country, over our ankles in mud. Not one of my platoon fell out, and this afternoon, after a few hours sleep, they are as chirpy as anything, busy scraping the mud off their clothes and cleaning their rifles. It is a hard life for them, with few comforts, and only an ultimate return to England to look forward to.

Once again, Ronald went on to give his appreciation that Howe, his old House at School, were doing so well and he suggested that his younger brother Jack should practise batting with patience if he was to get into a School team. He wrote that the memory of the ruined cathedral at Albert would always remain with him and paints the scene of life in the garden of the farmhouse in the last week before one of the most tragic and significant moments of the twentieth century. The juxtaposition between the garden scene and what was to follow is almost unbelievable, yet we can survey this panoramic scene on the Somme, sweeping from the comedy of a popular song to the tragedy of an artillery chorus through Ronald's experiences:

> Well, here I am, seated in the garden of my farmhouse, smoking the pipe of peace. With our gramophone a few yards away playing a comic song, 'Another little drink wouldn't do us any harm.' We've got heaps of very good records, but are running short of needles, so you might send me two boxes of medium 'His Master's Voice' needles in your next parcel.
>
> It is very peaceful in this garden... In the distance we can see the firing line and the artillery of both sides blazing away. Our people are fairly handing it out to Fritz. I should imagine he is strengthening his dugout feverishly!

His letter gives us an insight into what life was like for the inhabitants on whose country this war was largely being fought:

> The French are extraordinary people. Only old men and children and women are to be seen. The women are mostly old farmers' wives, and have a splendid spirit. They have all got sons; husbands or brothers fighting and most of them have had near relations killed. And yet they carry on a few miles from the firing line, resigned to everything. "C'est la Guerre" they say and after that there is nothing more to be said. Our landlady has lost a son at Verdun and told me all about it. She said to me, "Pauvres enfant et pauvres parents".

The next letter Ronald sent was to wish his mother a happy birthday for 5 July, expressing his desire for the war to be ended and to be home with his family. He also observed the peculiar uses to which Tommies put their tin hats, 'A universal thing out here nowdays is the tin hat. Every regiment that goes into front line trenches is equipped with them and they have to be worn as soon as you get within reach of enemy shellfire. To the Tommy they are invaluable, apart from their protective properties, for he makes tea in them, or soup, or uses them for washing purposes as every man has to wash when in the trenches, and no basins are supplied.'[16]

On 28 June Ronald writes a short letter to accompany the one he sent the day before which mentions that he has a document called, *The Soldier's Hymnal* which his younger brother Jack might use for the *The Portcullis*. It was never used in the School magazine but for the first time is reproduced here, almost a century after Ronald sent it.[17] Ronald wrote in

No. 23 (3).

than any of us have done before. & he must be in very good condition to have stuck it.

Well, there is no news, so I will close now. Remember me very kindly to all my friends and relations, for I can't write to them all. I hope you are all in the best of health and spirits, as I am myself. And to Mother, please always look on the bright side. Only 5% of the Army are killed, and there are lots of fellows over here who have been out 20 months & in all the big scraps. So cheer up, & don't worry: for I can't always write as frequently as I have done.

Goodbye & best love to you all.

Ronald.

P.S. A very happy birthday to you

Ronald Grundy's last letter home, 30 June 1916

the previous letter that it was 'a hymn for all the important events of a soldier's life.' Essentially it is a list of hymns to be used at various moments in a soldier's life, from 'Christians Awake' at Reveille to 'All Things Bright and Beautiful' at kit inspection to 'Onward Christian Soldiers' on route march.

On Thursday 29 June Ronald's mind was on his old House and the part his brothers were playing in its fortunes, 'I was sorry to hear of the defeat of Howe by Clyde, but there is no reason why you should not win the championship even now. When Howe won the Rugby championship 3 or 4 years ago, we won the first 5 matches straight off, lost the next 3, won the fourth and drew the fifth. Result – champions by 1 point.'

When one looks at the next letter one can see written in ink, 'recvd July 4 1st post'; a day before Emily Grundy's birthday and three days after the opening day of the Battle of the Somme. The letter was written on Friday 30 June. He mentions men in the services he has known, family news, the weather and the fact that he hasn't long to wait, which is an allusion to the Battle of the following day. The last page of that letter is a plea to his mother not to worry, 'Please always look on the bright side. Only 5% of the Army are killed, and there are lots of fellows over here who have been out 20 months and in all the big scraps. So cheer up and don't worry: for I can't always write as frequently as I have done.' The last words Ronald Grundy was to write were birthday wishes to his mother.

Saturday 1 July 1916

We can imagine that Ronald Grundy rose early this morning: his mind on preparing his platoon, number 14 2nd Battalion Middlesex Regiment. The evening before he had stayed with a team of machine gunners in one of four dugouts occupied by number 14 platoon in Ryecroft Street. That morning his thoughts may have causally drifted to Wandsworth Common and the walks along the railway line from home to school and back or those long cycle rides with Cecil to the coast, but chiefly his thoughts would have been on those men whom he thought so much of and on doing his best for them.

Ronald would have heard the roaring thunder of the artillery as the guns opened and shells flew furiously across No Man's Land towards the German trenches. A rising mist covered the void between the belligerents' positions, while smoke from shellfire covered the ominous and unknowing landscape ahead.

We have a fairly accurate description of Ronald's last moments. A friend in the Middlesex Regiment asked Ronald's servant, Lance Corporal W. Noyes, who was three feet behind him as they left the trenches, to write to the Grundys. In turn they asked Noyes several questions about their son's last moments and from Noyes's replies we can piece together Ronald's journey across No Man's Land.

Ronald had left his trench shortly after 7.20am. Leading his platoon he was waving a yellow swagger stick and had covered roughly 900 yards when at a distance of 100 yards from the German lines, all of a sudden he just crumpled without making a sound. Noyes thought that it was most likely that Ronald had been hit by a German sniper for, 'He was killed by a bullet which went in about a quarter of an inch above the collarbone close up to the neck on the left side and came out through the spine between the shoulderblades.' Noyes dragged Ronald to their advanced sap but he had to leave Ronald where he was so he took Ronald's jacket and covered his body. Ronald was later buried, Noyes having left his identification disc around his neck for this purpose and having removed any valuable items to be returned to his family. Due to the continued fighting Ronald's original grave was lost and so the headstone which bears his name in Ovillers Military Cemetery is a memorial rather than a final resting place but his body is believed to be buried nearby.

On that fatal day over 19,000 British servicemen lost their lives among a total of nearly 60,000 casualties. Over 40,000 received wounds, were taken prisoner or were recorded as missing. It was the worst day in British military history, but perhaps we should say British history, for the military aspect was only one part of the tragic story that encompasses the lives of the families and friends of those lost. Ronald was one, as far as it has been possible to ascertain, of four Emanuel boys who lost their lives on the first day of the Somme.

Jack Grundy described the scene when the family received the news of Ronald's death:

> I happened to be at home when...the telegram came about Ronald. My mother was resting in the early afternoon and I knew that this was no hour for a telegram. Moreover the bearer was not a boy but a man. For the first time in my life I opened what was clearly parental correspondence and learned that Ronald had died instantly in the battle of the Somme on 1st July 1916. He had waved not a sword, but the yellow-knobbed swagger-stick that British officers now carried.[18]

Ronald, as already noted, left money to the Emanuel School chapel and also requested that a trophy be purchased to, 'foster the Inter House spirit'. Ronald allocated the sum of twenty pounds to Emanuel and it was his father who carried out the bequest.

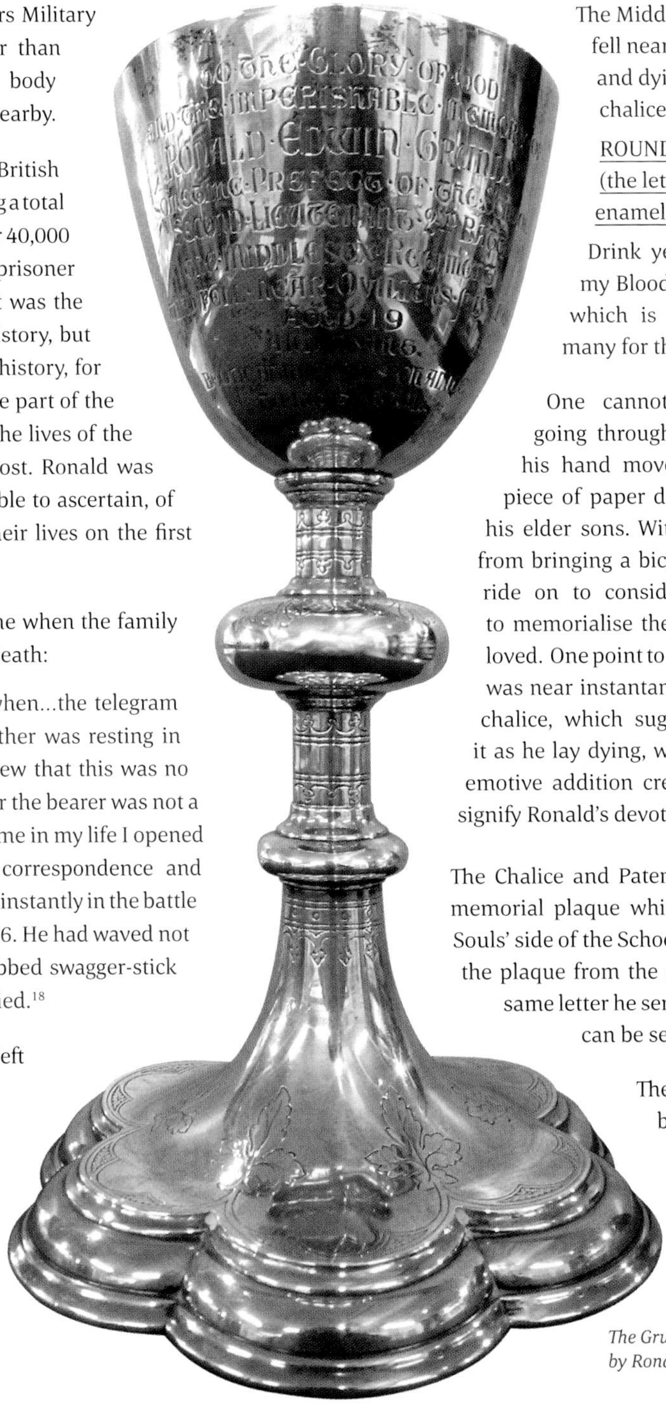

The following instructions were given to the engravers,

> Dear Mr. Hayco
>
> Thanks for yours of the 4th and 8th. Will you please tell me the cost of Chalice 8¾" no 21 in catalogue solid silver with paten plate inscribed round base:
>
> To the glory of God and the imperishable memory of Ronald Edwin Grundy sometime Prefect of the School, Second Lieutenant 2nd Bn The Middlesex Regiment, who fell near Ovillers July 1 1916 and dying bequeathed this chalice to his School.
>
> ROUND THE RIM INSIDE (the letters to be filled in with enamel)
>
> Drink ye all of this; for this is my Blood of the New Testament, which is shed for you and for many for the remission of sins.[19]

One cannot imagine the thoughts going through John Grundy's mind as his hand moved the pencil across the piece of paper detailing the memorials to his elder sons. Within a few years he went from bringing a bicycle home for his sons to ride on to considering appropriate words to memorialise them for the School they so loved. One point to note is that Ronald's death was near instantaneous so the words on the chalice, which suggest that he bequeathed it as he lay dying, were, we could assume, an emotive addition created by John perhaps to signify Ronald's devotion to Emanuel.

The Chalice and Paten were accompanied by a memorial plaque which was placed in the 'All Souls' side of the School chapel.[20] John requested the plaque from the same engraver and in the same letter he sent to Mr. Hayco. The plaque can be seen on the following page.

The Grundy Cup, as it became known, was the last memorial given to Emanuel in Ronald's memory. Again, John Grundy noted the details of the words to

The Grundy Chalice, bequeathed by Ronald Grundy

be engraved on the cup, which was to be instituted as a trophy for shooting competitions. It was 'a silver covered–cup surmounted by the figure of a private soldier in the time of the Great War, 1914–18, in full kit with rifle at the slope. It bears the School Arms and the inscription':

THIS CUP WAS BEQUEATHED TO HIS SCHOOL BY RONALD EDWIN GRUNDY (SOMETIME PREFECT OF THE SCHOOL) 2ND LIEUTENANT IN THE 2ND B'N THE MIDDLESEX REGIMENT WHO FELL NEAR OVILLERS, JULY 1ST, 1916, AS A PERPETUAL TROPHY FOR HOUSE COMPETITIONS IN MARCHING AND SHOOTING. 'STAND FAST, BRAVE HEARTS; WHAT WILL THEY SAY OF THIS IN ENGLAND.' [21]

It was fitting that the first House to win this cup was Howe, Ronald's old House.[22] In 1935 Mrs Grundy, in the presence of Emanuel School pupils, staff and Mr. John Grundy, presented the cup to Richard Kemp Wildey, who was a Company Sergeant Major in the OTC and also Captain of Nelson House. Interestingly Richard lived in St James' Road, the same road on which the Grundys had lived. Richard lost his life when the Halifax he was piloting crashed on the night of 15 October 1942 on a bombing operation on Cologne.

The significance of Ronald's death can be gleaned from the fact that his name appears in the Emanuel School Prayer, alongside that of the School's Elizabethan Founders.

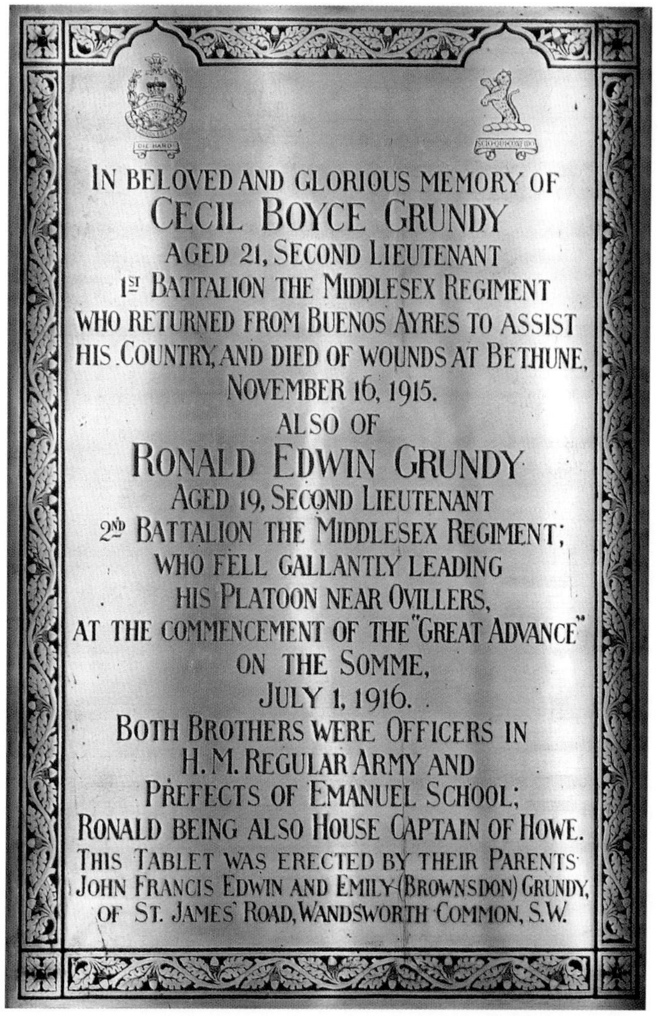

The Grundy Plaque

The Grundy family in happier times. Ronald seated centre and Cecil seated right

References

1 This was made into a coloured lithograph, copies of which can be found in the National Portrait Gallery.
2 *The Portcullis*, No. 58, Spring Term 1913, pp. 9–10.
3 Letter 81 from Cecil to parents dated 31 July 1914.
4 Letter 82 from Cecil dated 4 August 1914.
5 Ibid.
6 Letter 90 from John Grundy to Cecil, 29 August 1914, pp. 3–4.
7 Letter from Ronald to Cecil, Wednesday 2 September 1914.
8 Letter from Cecil to Mrs Grundy 7 October 1915 p. 5.
9 Ibid.
10 Letter from Cecil to family 18 October 1915.
11 Letter from Cecil 23 October 1915.
12 *The British Journal of Nursing*, July 3, p. 8. A photo of Catherine Elston can be found in the same edition on p. 9.
13 War Diary of 2nd Battalion The Middlesex Regiment, June 1916, see 7 June.
14 Letter from Ronald to his parents No. 10, June 7 1916.
15 Letter from Ronald to Mrs Grundy, No. 15, 18 June, p. 3.
16 Letter from Ronald to Mrs Grundy, No. 21, 27 June 1916.
17 Letter from Ronald, No. 21 A.
18 J. B. C. Grundy, *Life's Five Windows*, (1968), quoted, pp. 20–21.
19 Letter from John Grundy to Mr. Hayco dated 16 August, no year date.
20 *The Portcullis*, Spring Term 1917, No. 70, p. 5.
21 Scott-Giles, *History of Emanuel*, pp. 287–288.
22 Ibid. p. 202.

Cyril John Chamberlain

(Emanuel 1908–1911)

'He gave inspiration to all around from his own dauntless spirit.'

Cyril Chamberlain was considered to be 'a scholar and a sportsman' at Emanuel. After leaving Emanuel he entered the Islington Day Training College and also studied Arts and Sciences at the King's College London Evening Department after which he obtained a post at St Andrew's School. He enlisted with the London Rifle Brigade and received a commission, attaining the rank of Second Lieutenant.

Aspects of Cyril's First World War experiences can be viewed through the letters he sent to the School which were reproduced in *The Portcullis* 1916–1917. He described life in and behind the trenches but also provided a personal commentary upon the opinions of those who were far behind the lines. In his first letter he refutes the remarks of a reporter who thought that Tommies appreciated 'signs of activity' on their front after a long winter and his comments show us how those experiencing war at first hand regarded those who felt they could comment upon matters they experienced indirectly. We can glean from Cyril's response that waiting for 'signs of activity' was far from the minds of battle-wearied individuals who daily gazed at the shadow cast by the Grim Reaper's scythe sweeping across the trenches.

Letter from Cyril, Spring Term 1916

'Granted that those whose lot it is to hold the trenches know something about the conditions appertaining thereto, you can imagine our feelings when we read the fatuous remark of a special correspondent of a London daily to the effect that "the Tommies in the trenches greatly appreciate the signs of activity on their front, and indeed, welcome the change after the monotony of winter warfare." From personal experience, I can assure you that after twelve hours bombardment the only change which one is inclined to welcome is a place of rest as far away from the line as possible.

There can be no doubt whatever that the Bosches have livened up considerably during the past fortnight, and if they hoped to surprise us with an unexpected offensive, they have this time learned a lesson which should cause them pain and anxiety, for, with our infantry as magnificent as ever, our artillery has found its voice in no uncertain manner. You can imagine with what satisfaction I compare the conditions existing in May with those of today. Then, when by means of a surprise in the form of gas, an enormously superior massing of artillery, and a gap in our line which opened out possibilities for pushing home a success, his infantry had the chance of a lifetime to 'up boys and at 'em', we found that a cool head and clean rifle made them marvellously respectful, and now conditions have changed so completely that misgivings as regards defence are absolutely unwarranted...

'It seemed that nothing living could survive in such a shell-swept spot'

In the small hours of one morning I was detailed to go with a party on a bomb-carrying fatigue to a point about two miles away. Under the bright light of a full moon I set off cheerfully enough, and on account of the amount of shrapnel being lavished on all roads, railways, known routes &c. I immediately decided to essay a cross country trip, and, as events turned out, this was entirely satisfactory. At one of the halts, where they whiz-banged just short of us, we were treated to a panoramic view of the whole show. Away on the right spurts of flame seemed to leap from every bush and tree as our guns thundered incessantly, while overhead we could hear the whistles and screams peculiar to shrapnel, howitzers, 'heavies' and field guns. Over the Bosche lines, where we could see and hear the shells bursting, there slowly rolled a cloud of dense smoke, which was clearly discerned when the flares cast their incandescent light on the scene. It seemed that nothing living could survive in such a shell-swept spot, but the fact that flares of various hues and intermittent rifle shots were proceeding from the enemy's trench left no doubt that he was expecting and was ready to counter an attack.'[1]

Letter From Cyril Summer Term 1916

'My life has been one of contrasts lately... In one short trek, made at dead of night, we transferred ourselves, with all baggage, from the neighbourhood of the trenches, where 'a certain liveliness' was distinctly apparent, to the heart of France, where the sweet smell of bean flowers, the fields of rapidly growing hops, the chime of church bells from the neighbouring village mingling with the songs of delight of the birds, and finally the hops turned to good account, all combine to delight several senses. No longer do we gaze day after day at the rents in the roof where fragments of shrapnel have forced an entry, nor do we turn pale and start up when a battery, dead in rear, opens fire and all but deafens us. No, ours is a happier lot, for we are the privileged few who are taken far back for a rest. I don't know why it is, but one feels miles away from the front, when as a matter of fact we are closer up than many a town which has been strafed almost to ruins. I rather think it must be the atmosphere of the district which suggests nothing but peace and prosperity. The people here have been fortunate to live behind a quiet portion of the line and have never been the victims of the evening 'hate.'

Late in the day is the time for long range firing, when 'Lazy Lizzie' finds her voice and fills the air with a concord of sweet sounds. Assisted by a couple of smart monoplanes which patrol backwards and forwards for 'spotting' purposes, 'Lazy Lizzie' is able to do splendid work. Generally about six pip emma, when one feels inclined to settle down to a pipe and quiet read and glance around to search out the beauties of nature, 'Lizzie' will give her valuable assistance. Two thunderous crashes will be heard, followed almost immediately fast upwards towards the mouth, hitting the pipe and causing it to go to earth. The convulsion to the system is manifest by glaring eyes, jaws firmly set, hands tightly clenched, and the contraction of all muscles. Gradually this state of tension is relaxed, and the loud and persistent purring noise caused by the rapid passage of the 'souvenir' through the upper air induces a seraphic beam of pleasure to overspread the countenance. The shrillness and pitch of the note decline together, but one's attention is completely arrested until the long-looked-for crash, reverberating for several seconds, proclaims the fact far and wide that a dent has been made somewhere. Precisely at this moment one is permitted to remark sententiously 'Well, that wasn't a dud!' Without receiving a snub in reply, merely because that is precisely what everyone is thinking. Perhaps I should have told you before that 'Lazy Lizzie' is the pet name for a twelve inch naval gun which is accustomed to frolic with enemy 'strong points.'

Some weeks ago, the Bosche desired to make a closer acquaintance with Liz and to this end sent forward two stalwarts in a Fokker to find the address. They commenced their journey at about seven o'clock in the evening, when the bright rays of the declining sun threw all aircraft into vivid relief. I counted no less than fourteen of our planes up at this time and when the hostile craft crossed our lines a second time after being driven back by our 'Archies', I applied my eye to a telescope and awaited events. The Fokker, flying along beautifully at a high altitude in a clear blue sky, made a perfect picture when the light caught its wings and made them seem on fire. Incidentally our gunners were given a splendid target to aim at, and right gallantly they set to work. At first only one battery close behind our line was engaged, but as the plane penetrated further behind our lines, batteries from all points of the compass began to open fire. The pilot did not swerve at all and even when shrapnel barrages were put ahead of him he went straight on. Soon there was a thick trail of smoke in the sky, clearly indicating the course of the aeroplane, around which shells were bursting. Nothing daunted, he maintained his direction and having penetrated nearly four miles behind our lines, turned and made for home, hotly pursued by two of our planes. It must have been his lucky day, for time and again I thought the end had come only to see him draw clear of danger. Good luck to him, for he must have been one of the best. But he failed to locate our 'Liz'.'[2]

In July 1916 Cyril had the solemn duty of writing to the parents of one of his dear friends, 2nd Lt. George Latter of the 3rd Battalion London Rifle Brigade whom he had served with. These letters must have been so difficult to write and though they could not extinguish grief they would have assisted the healing of broken hearts at the loss of loved ones.

'As an intimate friend of your son and one who has served with him for more than a year, I feel it is my duty to write to tell you that he was most unfortunately killed on the night of July 10th. Both of us were former members of the LRB, and we first met when the battalion was doing work on lines of communication last summer. First at Aire and later at St Omer we were together and I think it is due to the fact that he wished to be among friends that induced him to apply for a commission in the Rifle Brigade. A few days ago it was decided to carry out a raid on the German trenches on our front. Volunteers were called for and a list of names more than three times the number required was sent in. Your son expressed a keen desire to be one of the party and eventually, when the scheme had been prepared, was put in command of one of the bombing squads whose duty it was to enter the enemy's trench, clear it of Germans and hold the ground until a search party had secured necessary identification. The actual operation was entirely successful and your son, one of the first to enter the trench with his party, worked his way along the trench in accordance with the scheme. Alone, he entered one of the dugouts in the trench and secured important documents which were safely brought back and when the order to return was passed along he worked his way clear with his party, regaining our trenches without loss. At this stage some difficulty arose because it was not known whether one of the party which should have returned earlier was back or not. Your son immediately volunteered to go out in front and render assistance, but was prevailed upon to remain until a messenger went down the trench to find if the missing party had re-entered at another point. It was then that a trench mortar bomb landed quite close to the parade, killing your son almost instantaneously. A stretcher-bearer was standing beside him at the time and in spite of his immediate assistance he quickly realised that the help he could render was unavailing. All the members of the party, as well as all the officers and men of the battalion, were much upset when they heard that your son had been a victim to such an unlucky accident, but the memory of his recent achievement, his coolness and courageous display, must comfort you as it does us. Your part is to suffer the loss bravely, while it is ours to pay the sacrifice if called upon. Bear in mind that your son died bravely while calmly waiting to go forward and help his comrades. When quietness was restored he was brought by stretcher-bearers to a small village some distance behind the lines, where he was buried yesterday by the Regimental Chaplain. Rest assured that everything was done for him and that his name and fame will ever be remembered.'[3]

The last letter to be reprinted in *The Portcullis* was one of Cyril's amusing and very satirical takes on life behind the front lines. One can easily imagine that this young man's life would have been the inspiration for a *Monty Python* film if they had written one based upon the odd moments of life on the Western Front.

Back to Front or The Trench Jigsaw

In the Field, BEF, France

'If, perchance, the thought that I have been 'too proud' or 'too busy Hun strafing' during the past five weeks has on one or more occasions flashed upon you, allow me to pronounce it entirely unfounded and wide of the mark. It is with a deep blush of shame that a confession to the following effect is drawn from me and yet what else can a body do, when you consider he belongs heart, soul, and all to the mysterious 'authorities' who unceasingly govern his destiny?

When I landed at the base and bowled along swiftly one fine morning to the reinforcement camp, my heart was filled with the hope that I should be posted, with a friend, to my old battalion, which I suspected was holding the trenches in a quiet part of the 'line.' However, after having reported, it was made abundantly [clear] that this was a snare and delusion, much too practicable and sensible in fact to meet official approval! My friend was drafted to the Second Battalion and I came here, although absolute strangers were sent to the unit in which we had both served for several months.

You can readily imagine the general appearance of horror, the raising of the eyebrows, the gasp of despair and complete bewilderment which followed hard upon a rapid perusal of a 'chit' ordering me to proceed and join my unit, before the base had been my home for twelve hours!

Wind up? Vivid pictures of fifteen inches bursting bombs, rifle fire, attacks and counter-attacks and the clashing of steel on steel succeeding one another with startling rapidity, but after swilling two whiskies, I sought out my steward and in a tone which spoke volumes for a state of self-possession ordered him to pack the valise by 8.30am and see it dispatched to the station. The railway journey lasting 18 hours, the skilful way in which the engine drivers slow down from 50 to 5 miles per hour whenever a fly or other serious obstruction is observed on the metals, the alternating periods of wakefulness when tinned salmon and fruits are cunningly hoisted on a knife to the aperture '6 o'clock from the nose', and troubled slumber which terminates 'tout de suite' when a pack or water bottle is jolted from the rack and impinges on the cranium, or when 'the other fellow' is hurled forcibly on top of you, the ten minutes halt at a station where 1d. cups of cold, unappetising coffee are obtained after a terrific struggle from a charming modest, young lady, keen as mustard on 'doing her bit', but gloriously incompetent when it comes to simulating a grocer's assistant and lastly the final scene where the military police come along one minute before the train continues its journey and tell you to "get out here" – before the completion of which you are hurling all your worldly possessions on to the permanent way, utterly regardless of the consequences. Who shall describe these and similar scenes which take place daily?

At the railhead, one reports to the RTO [Rail Transport Officer] and he issues further instructions. It is a recognised thing that if the train arrives before 10am the RTO cannot be seen personally – eggs, bacon, and coffee are probably absorbing all his attention – so one deferentially approaches

Reconnaissance photo of trenches on the Western Front taken by OE George Banting on 1 May 1917 in RE8 No. 85

his underling. RTOs, it is universally admitted, wield huge power second only to that of the commander in chief and woe betide the unfortunate individual who dares to question their authority, or allows less than half an hour for the preparation of a 'movement order.'

This explains the reason for the subdued voice and humble demeanour which lent an aspect of becoming humility, when I stated my division and hinted a desire to learn their present loyalty.

"Your battalion is at X, ten miles away. Go out of the station, take the first turning to the right. This road leads straight to X!" Oh! I thought of the glorious sunshine and the weight of my equipment and pack and, although my knees sagged a little and my heart sank, I determined to risk life and limb in the attempt to save boot leather.

"But isn't there a station at X?" A look of consternation and surprise manifests itself and the clerk is taken aback by the astounding impertinence of the question.

"Yes, that's so." "And don't any trains run there?" "Yes, there's a train this afternoon, but we have orders to direct all reinforcements for your division by road."

(This is unmistakeably the 'last' word, because the clerk turns away and continues his game of noughts and crosses). I give my friend a look of blank despair, which he clearly interprets as signifying "it's all up."

Suddenly, holy powers, a familiar face appears in the office and using all my available 'tact' I explain in a "hail fellow well met" tone, "Hullo! Weren't you clerk to the RTO at Aire, two years ago. Surely your name is Wilson?" "Well I never! Remember you quite well. You are Chamberlain". (How I envy the Indians their privilege of letting forth an occasional 'war whoop') Hearty handshakes and mutual greetings ensue.

"Have you any news of the old regiment?" "Yes, they're in the line now..." – and a general exchange of items of interest takes place.

Finally the moment to be 'tactful' arrives. "Awful journey from the base, jolted all the way. It's no joke having to march ten miles in the blazing sun!" "Where are you going to?" "X." "Well, I'll tell you what. There's a passenger train at 2.30. Why not go by that? I'll attend to your valise. In the meantime, I'll show you an officers' rest house, where you can get a wash and a good lunch. How will that do?"

"That will suit us splendidly." Very good of you indeed." "No trouble at all. Pleased to do all I can. Drop in here before the train goes and I'll have the movement ready. Good luck to you; goodbye, Sir."

Need more be said?

From that moment to this, fortune has never ceased to smile on me and the climax was reached three days ago, when, quite by accident, I smashed a mirror, thereby entitling myself to seven years' bad luck, which means I shall survive the first ten years of this great 'World Conflict.' Happy thought! I stand a chance of having a second 'pip' by that time, too!

More than a month has elapsed since I left the base and so far I have not been within ten miles of the line.

Best of luck, Yours sincerely,

Chamberlain.'[4]

A few months after the 'Trench Jigsaw' was published the Old Emanuel notes reported:

> The news that C. J. Chamberlain had been killed came as a shock to many of us. We had grown so used to his cheery letters, which appeared from time to time in *The Portcullis*, that it did not seem possible that we might have to record his death in these pages.[5]

On 7 October 1917 Cyril, with Ronald Townshend Fellowes, commanding the 1st Battalion, The Rifle Brigade, were reconnoitring new posts gained for a forthcoming attack on German lines at Poelcapelle at around 3.30am when from fifty yards away Cyril was killed by a sniper, thus extinguishing the flame of a bright light. A brother officer remarked of Cyril, 'We have lost a man indeed, and as one who has been with him under the best, as under the worst conditions, I can but add that his cheery smile, apt remarks, and fearless courage were of the greatest value to all who were with him. He gave inspiration to all around from his own dauntless spirit.'[6]

Cyril had been previously wounded in an action at Delville Wood but after recuperation he returned to the Front. He is remembered on the Tyne Cot Memorial.

References

1 *The Portcullis*, No. 67, Spring Term, 1916, pp. 42–43.
2 *The Portcullis*, No. 68, Summer Term, 1916, pp. 55–57.
3 Reprinted here http://www.roll-of-honour.com/Essex/Epping.html.
4 *The Portcullis*, No. 71, Summer Term, 1917, pp. 58–62.
5 *The Portcullis*, No. 72, Christmas Term, 1917, p. 49.
6 Ibid.

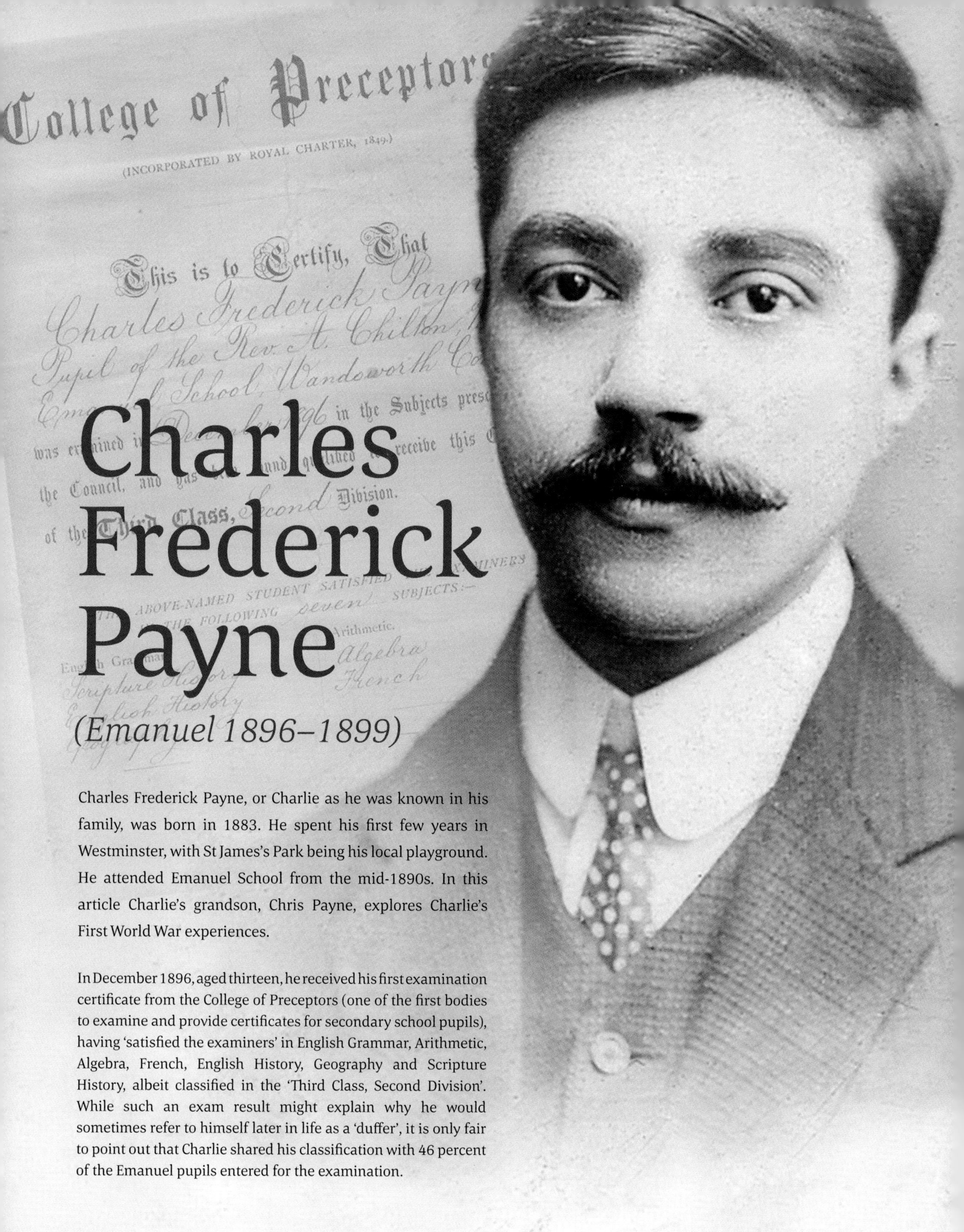

Charles Frederick Payne

(Emanuel 1896–1899)

Charles Frederick Payne, or Charlie as he was known in his family, was born in 1883. He spent his first few years in Westminster, with St James's Park being his local playground. He attended Emanuel School from the mid-1890s. In this article Charlie's grandson, Chris Payne, explores Charlie's First World War experiences.

In December 1896, aged thirteen, he received his first examination certificate from the College of Preceptors (one of the first bodies to examine and provide certificates for secondary school pupils), having 'satisfied the examiners' in English Grammar, Arithmetic, Algebra, French, English History, Geography and Scripture History, albeit classified in the 'Third Class, Second Division'. While such an exam result might explain why he would sometimes refer to himself later in life as a 'duffer', it is only fair to point out that Charlie shared his classification with 46 percent of the Emanuel pupils entered for the examination.

By May 1899, and heading towards his sixteenth birthday, Charlie found a job. In line with School expectations at that time, he became a clerk in the City of London. If he read the Christmas 1898 issue of the *School Magazine* before leaving, he may have noted some words of advice written by the Chairman of Emanuel's Board of Governors, Sir Sydney Waterlow (a Victorian philanthropist and politician) in 'A Letter to Young Men':

> You young men must not think that you have been born into the world too late, and that all the great deeds have been done, all the noble services rendered. You must not suppose that all the mighty acts of heroism have been performed, and that in your time there will be no more marching of heroes to victory, and defeat – for heroes march to defeat as well as to victory. Do not dream that in your time there will be no more saints and martyrs, and that the world has been robbed of its ancient grandeur and nobility. You must not think this. You have not been born into the world too late....You are the heirs of all the past ages; be of good courage, do not be cast down by failure or defeat, or by any sense of unworthiness. All the great men of the past sprang from youths such as you are, and the men of the future who will spring from you will do as great deeds as ever were done in the past, and they will live lives that will shine with a lustre not less than the lustre that now shines from the lives of the great and mighty dead.

Stirring stuff but, as Charlie headed off for his first job in the City, performing mighty acts of heroism was probably not at the forefront of his mind.

Between 1899 and 1905, Charlie worked for a financial agent who operated in international trade, specialising in metals and their associated commercial mining operations. London at that time was the largest port in the world and, through the trade contacts available across the British Empire and more widely in developing continents like Africa and South America, the business was well-placed to take advantage of the City's involvement in the trade and finance of emerging industries. By 1907, more adventurous than some, Charlie had moved to the American Express Company and left England in March that year to take up a post as a shorthand clerk at their office in Genoa. Among his friends and work colleagues in Italy, there was a good selection of nationalities, including several Germans, and Charlie mentioned in his 1907 diary some discussion of the respective merits of the British and German navies and armies.

By the time that war was declared in August 1914, Charlie had returned to the UK and had married his second cousin, Ida Payne. He was now living in Tooting and was the proud father of three sons. With his family commitments it is not surprising that Charlie did not rush to volunteer but, in November 1915, he formally attested (under the 'Derby Scheme') that he would be prepared to serve in the armed forces if and when the supply of single men dried up. When insufficient men volunteered, conscription was introduced for the first time in Britain, in

Army Form W. 3194.

11367—4426 500,000 10/15 H W V(P 467)

Name Charles Frederick Payne No. 38/59.

Address 30 Coverton Rd Tooting SW.

Group Number 38

Date of Attestation November 23rd 1915

The above-named man has been attested and transferred to the Army Reserve, until required for service, when he will be sent a Notice Paper, informing him as to the date, time and place at which he is to report himself. Fourteen days' notice will be given.

N.B.—Any change of address should be immediately notified to the Recruiting Officer Town Hall Wandsworth. Station.

Edmund Everett Signature.

Hon. Recruiting Officer Rank.

Nov 23rd 1915 Date.

Charlie Payne's attestation card

March 1916. By October that year, as the latter stages of the Battle of the Somme were being fought, the need for men had reached the point that older men with dependents, like Charlie, were being called up.

On medical grounds, Charlie was initially classified as B: 'not fit for general service' and therefore had reason to expect that he would be serving the Army in some supporting capacity either in the UK or overseas but would be unlikely to serve in the front line. However, that proved not to be the case. On 14 November 1916, Charlie and 69 other conscripted men assembled at the Kingston recruitment office of the East Surrey Regiment and were sent off to Clacton-on-Sea to start their training. As conscripts, any opportunity of selecting a regiment had disappeared. Men were now sent where they were needed and Charlie found himself attached to a provisional battalion of the Yorkshire Regiment (the Green Howards) which would remain his home until he was sent to France in August 1917.

By the date of his conscription, and to save money, Ida and the boys (now four in number) had moved from their rented house, into the ground floor of her parents' home next door. Allowances for soldiers' wives with dependants were not generous. The income for Ida and their children was about 30 shillings a week which compared unfavourably with Charlie's civilian pay as a clerk of 40 shillings. It is therefore not surprising that Charlie's first letter to Ida from Clacton emphasised the topic of money:

> **28 November 1916, part 1:** My dear wife, It was indeed good to read that you had got the ring paper and had been paid in full. How much did you draw? You ask me about pay, dear. Well, since the 1/- at Kingston I have received 2/- Friday week and another 2/- last Friday. I take it you received 2/6 per week as allocated by me? The ways of the Army are strange, and how and why we only record. 2/- is puzzling us all. Yes dear, I shall be in the Yorkshire Regiment but have not yet received definite number etc. We have not yet been served out with uniform and kit, but yesterday I got a splendid pair of boots – heavy of course but quite soft and comfortable. As you may guess there is not much left of my old ones but they will serve me for a rest. Pleased to hear better news of Bill and note Fred is well. Hope Mike will have the best of luck when he leaves the red country on the great adventure.

'Bill, Fred and Mike' were Ida's three brothers. Mike was a conscript in the Machine Gun Corps. Fred and Bill had volunteered; Bill was in France with the 13th East Surreys and Fred, being deaf, had ended up in the Labour Corps.

Ida and the four boys: (from the left), John, Rupert, Dick, and Ted (1918)

Charlie's letter continued, displaying his further annoyance about the lack of uniform, his concern about German bombing raids on London, but a positive response to Army food:

> The Zepps were about last night but we saw nothing of them here. Just heard the news that two have been brought down which is very good. I trust they will never again be allowed to reach London. We have had a thick day at drill (both 'physical jerks' and squad) but beyond feeling tired I thoroughly enjoy it. The grub continues to be good. Today: – Bully and sauce for breakfast; Baked muffin and spuds and currant duff (really good) for dinner; Bread and butter with a bun for tea. Sometimes we get sausages for breakfast and bacon and what do you think – tripe and onions and sometimes steak. Cheese for tea twice a week and jam. Jam rolly for dinner once. I miss your homemade bread and cakes, dear, but when I have a kit bag, and always provided your funds will allow I should much like to receive a parcel from you – but that's for the future. You may guess my coat and shirt are somewhat dirty, but do not send me any fresh as I hope to receive some kit soon. I think our little squad of 70 must have been overlooked

Charlie Payne (far right) and his billet colleagues (Christmas 1916)

by the War Office and it almost amounts to a scandal. A fortnight in our own clothes and I don't suppose we shall get any money for wear and tear. We get on very well with the Yorkshiremen – some of whom seem to be very ignorant and others very smart. Their brogue amuses me. "Aay laad" for instance. We went to church on Sunday and must say I liked it. Saturday morning is spent in scrubbing out our billets and bed boards. Can you picture us? Roughly we now do 6½ hrs. drill per day. I sleep very well o'nights but sometimes wake up a bit cold and wonder where I am. Generally shave overnight and of course we heat our water over the fire. We call it 'shaving parade.' Kiss all the dear boys for me and tell them all that you can about me. I cannot tell you how much I miss them and your own dear self, but to know that you are all well is good. When I have a kit bag I'll get you to send the photos down. Most of the others have their wives and kiddies in their pockets and are very proud of showing them. Seven in the billet and five married. 'Single men first.' Just heard you have had bombs dropped in London but I hope nowhere near you. Your loving husband, Charlie.

At Christmas, after a day or so's celebrations, it was back to training. However a photograph, taken on Christmas Eve, confirms that uniforms had now arrived.

28 December 1916: Well, dear, I expect your next letter will tell me how you spent Christmas – I trust you all had a most enjoyable time. We had a very good time indeed. Sunday evening four of us went to church to hear the carols and to feel 'free men' for a change. Our billet (Seven of us) were photographed in the morning and they will be ready on Friday. I had a slice of pork and some goose with stuffing, peas, potatoes; a pint of ale, Christmas pudding with sauce (very good), two packets Woodbines, Chocolates, two apples and two oranges so you see did not do badly. The sergeants waited on us and all the officers were present. Tea we had cake. In the evening our billet played Speculation till about midnight and unfortunately my luck was out and I lost nine pence. Never mind, old girl, unlucky at cards lucky in love. Boxing Day we paraded till dinner and were then free, so watched a football match. Wednesday we were back at full drill and this afternoon I have been on bayonet drill

and partook in my first charge. Like so many devils from hell. You may guess, dear, I am very tired as the ground was very muddy and the boots are heavy for running. We are having very frosty mornings but when the sun gets power it thaws, leaving our parade ground very sloppy so that we always seem to be wrestling with Napoleon's '4th element.' I am quite well but get a bit tired when marching in full pack. We have all our equipment now and it wants a lot of keeping clean I can tell you. Next week, I think we go in for firing at the ranges, — so shall soon be a fully-trained soldier.

During March 1917, Charlie's unit was moved from their relatively comfortable seaside-town billets to the nearby rifle range at Jay Wick where they were accommodated in wooden huts. Meanwhile, Ida had obtained a job as a post-woman to improve the family finances:

9 April 1917: Today has been my most exciting day since I became a soldier as I have thrown no less than five live bombs and I can tell you they are no joke. We had to throw them from a trench on to the beach and then duck down quickly to avoid being hit by flying pieces – rather more exciting than coconut shi-ing. We wore steel helmets for the occasion so you can just imagine how I looked. I am still at Jay Wick and likely to be until the move comes off. We had no coal all last week either for heating or cooking and I think it was the most wretched time I have ever spent. Men who have been to France said the food was never so bad out there. Once we had no tea and another day we got it at 7 o'clock instead of 4.30. However I am in splendid health and well able to rough it a bit and today the coal has arrived so things should improve.

Overall, it seems that Charlie coped pretty well with his initial experiences of training, including the physical demands, and he clearly took some pride in the fact that he was now 'in splendid health'. However, there were consequences. When he was medically re-examined he was upgraded and transferred, on 14 May, to another battalion of the Yorkshire Regiment based at West Hartlepool, whose role was to train men for the Front. Whether or not the knowledge that he would now be sent on active service influenced Charlie's thinking, he certainly found this new environment much less to his liking. In West Hartlepool he found himself living in a cramped hall, 'The Armoury', in squalid circumstances...and worse still, he felt that he was due for more leave.

22 May 1917: The Leave: I am putting in a written application on Thursday but really, my darling, there are little hopes of it being granted. If they do not give me one soon I'll give up 'soldiering' and turn 'scallywag' as I consider the way I have been treated is scandalous and there are thousands likewise. In coming to this place we have not struck oil and the conditions under which we are now living are bad. Fancy 300 men in one hall (not very large); and our food is dished out to us like pigs and there are not enough mugs etc. for the men, and worse than all you cannot leave a thing out of your sight for a moment – it vanishes. I have only lost up to now the old pair of boots and a boot brush; White had a razor 'pinched' this morning and every day something goes. My opinion of north countrymen is not great. It is indeed hard luck after being in a decent battalion to get into a 'mob' like this. I do hope to get into a southern regiment before going to France.

Charlie did have a brief break from 'The Black Hole of Calcutta' (as he re-named The Armoury), at a musketry camp in the Durham countryside, but all good things come to an end and, on 31 July 1917, he was sent to France.

There is some uncertainty about Charlie's initial movements on arrival in France, as some of his letters have not survived. Almost certainly, he spent some time at a Base Camp near Boulogne, probably Étaples. He was also transferred to another regiment in which he would see out the war; becoming a member of "B" Company, 2/5th Duke of Wellington's (West Riding) Regiment, one of four Yorkshire -recruited battalions in 186th Brigade, part of 62nd Division, which was then in the British Third Army. In addition, during August, Charlie was hospitalised for a week, whether through injury or infection is not certain. However, by 25 August he had joined his new battalion at a camp just north of Bapaume and reported home to Ida in reflective mood:

25 August 1917: Since leaving hospital I have been on camp fatigues etc. It is a very lonely place here far from any town or inhabitable village – in fact all is ruins and desolation. The big guns are nearly always busy and the air buzzing with aeroplanes. Just opposite our camp here is a small cemetery where the Germans have buried some of their dead, marking the graves with wooden crosses facing towards their own country and nearby are six French graves – it is all very sad. I seem to be the only southerner in my particular draft now and I shall be glad to meet some Londoners again – although the Yorkshire men are all very good fellows. Still as you may suppose I cannot help feeling somewhat lonely. I am the only one now who joined up at Kingston to find myself out here.

Fortunately, Charlie's loneliness was soon alleviated by discovering a few Cockneys in his Company, and by mid-September he had been sent for training as a Lewis gunner. It was in mid-October that he received his first experience of the Front-line trenches, in the Third Army sector between Bullecourt and Noreuil (south-east of Arras).

> 14 October 1917: I have had my baptism of fire (both shell and bullets). I went 'up the line' as a Lewis gunner. The Germans 'strafed' us dreadfully and my first impression was how poor a chance Man has against such infernal weapons as modern artillery, but I kept calm and cool and at times you, my darling, seemed to be very near me as we crouched down in the trench. Fortunately, our Regiment suffered few casualties. The weather has been bad lately so have had several issues of rum as of course we have no fires. Tell Dolce and Marg [Ida's younger sisters] I have had one or two 'come round the corners after me' and also heard them ringing through the air – all kinds of songs in all keys. We have had a church parade today and just where we are resting is out of reach of the guns and also out of hearing so you may guess, dear, it is a real rest for all our nerves. I am very fit just now. We are still in wooden huts and now have a blanket to sleep on which with our great coats and ground sheet makes a fairly warm bed.

The next few weeks would also prove rather stressful as, the day before Charlie wrote his letter to Ida, Douglas Haig had approved the plans for the British Expeditionary Force's next major 'stunt', the Battle of Cambrai, and 62nd Division would be participating in it. The Battle of Cambrai has been described as the beginning of the 'Modern Style of Warfare'. Its essential elements were a surprise attack that (unlike the Battles of the Somme and Passchendaele) included no preliminary artillery barrage, but involved the sophisticated targeting of enemy artillery positions by reconnaissance, sound-ranging and flash-spotting technology. The attack demanded close co-operation between artillery, tanks, and infantry with a lifting artillery barrage followed closely by tanks. The tanks were deployed to flatten and create gaps in the extensive wire defences of the German defensive position, the Hindenburg line, allowing the infantry to follow through. The attack was also supported by considerable numbers of aircraft to provide intelligence, air-cover, and to attack enemy infantry and artillery positions. In its 'All-Arms' approach, it became the form of warfare that conscripts such as Charlie encountered for much of the rest of the war.

On 8 November, Charlie and his battalion trained alongside tanks at the training ground at Wailly, just west of Arras. Further training took place over the next two days involving tanks, aeroplanes and practice attacks through gas. On 13 November the 2/5th Dukes started their march towards the battle zone, arriving three days later after marching only at night to avoid detection by enemy aircraft. On the night of 19 November they moved into position in Havrincourt Wood, together with tanks and artillery, ready for the attack the following day.

Havrincourt village was just north of the wood in which Charlie's Division was waiting. It was one of the most-strongly defended sections of the Hindenburg line (which ran through the village and slightly to the west) with the trenches well-protected by very substantial barbed wire defences. About 800-1500 yards behind the German front line was a second series of trenches, the Support Line. In addition to the trench systems, the German defences included a number of well-defended strong-points, containing machine guns.

At 6.20am on 20 November the British attack started with an intensive artillery barrage, lifting at a pre-determined rate, so that the tanks and the following infantry could quickly start moving forward. Havrincourt village, was the first objective for 62nd Division. The initial attack was led by other brigades, with Charlie's Brigade, the 186th, being held in reserve. With the tanks successfully flattening the barbed wire defences, the infantry were able to follow through quickly. The Germans were completely unprepared for what was happening and substantial numbers of Germans and weapons were quickly captured. The progress made was so positive that Charlie's battalion were ordered to advance much earlier than planned. They advanced west of Havrincourt, supported by surviving tanks from the earlier attack. Their final objective was north of the Bapaume-Cambrai road. As they approached Havrincourt they immediately encountered heavy machine gun and sniper fire from a German strong-point that had not been dealt with earlier. The battalion's Commanding Officer and several others were killed. Belatedly, the strong-point was successfully dealt with and 59 Germans and two machine guns were captured. Despite these early problems, the battalion's objective for the day was nonetheless achieved when Charlie's Company moved through to capture a German trench north of the Bapaume-Cambrai road, an advance of four and a half miles from the British Front Line; and at that time a record advance in a single day.

The following day was less successful, without the element of surprise and with many tanks out of action. The original plan was for tanks to lead a further thrust through the German defences towards Bourlon Wood. However, no tanks arrived to assist Charlie's battalion, and that attack was cancelled. New orders were issued for the battalion to use grenades to clear Germans from the Hindenburg support line trenches. "B" Company was charged with mopping up the rear support trenches. Problems were soon encountered, including an enemy strong-point, and strong German reinforcements that were moving down the trenches from the North West.

Training group at Jay Wick; Charlie Payne is in the second row from front, third from the left (March 1917)

However, one tank eventually arrived and helped to halt a German counter-attack. At midnight the battalion was relieved. Charlie reported back to Ida two days later:

> **24 November 1917:** Well, my darling, you will see from the papers we have been in some heavy fighting and some good pals of mine have made the great sacrifice. I thank God I am safe and sound. Our CO was killed. I must not say more, but I know the Germans have gone back a long way. At the moment we are out of the line, but for how long I don't know. Glad to learn the boys are well. Please excuse this short letter, dear, but I am very tired and we have to get to 'kip'. God bless you, dear and keep you in good health, is my constant prayer as I know what a fight you are making for me and the boys.

By now the Battle of Cambrai had lost its momentum, with German reinforcements arriving and the fighting was changing from rapidly-moving open warfare to a more familiar attritional confrontation. But Haig was determined not to lose the strategic opportunity to gain high ground overlooking Cambrai.

62nd Division were thrown once more into battle to complete the capture of Bourlon Wood and Bourlon. By this stage, the situation was very confused. Bourlon Wood had been partly captured by 40th Division (which unbeknown to Charlie included Ida's brother, Bill). It had been heavily shelled by the Germans and gas had been used which was lingering in the woodland. It was also snowing, and the conditions were awful. At 6.20am on 27 November, in pitch dark, Charlie's battalion were ordered to attack, aided by a small number of tanks, in an attempt to force the Germans out of the Wood and move the British front line to the railway at the northern edge of the Wood, overlooking Cambrai. Almost immediately, the entire wood came under a heavy enemy artillery barrage. In addition, "B" and "A" Companies had only advanced 50 yards when they came under heavy machine gun fire from an enemy strong-point and further advance proved impossible. "C" and "D" Companies were also unable to reach their objectives. The battalion was relieved at 11pm. Overall, it had not given ground to the Germans, but neither had it been able to achieve a significant advance.

Ultimately, the Battle of Cambrai failed to deliver its objectives for a number of reasons, including inadequate reserves of infantry Divisions and tanks. However, having learnt the lessons of Cambrai, adequate momentum in attack was delivered in the allied advances that ended the war, as we shall see later. In the meantime, Charlie and his Division moved into reserve, west of Arras and were transferred to First Army. Over Christmas, Charlie and others were deployed on working parties. In Charlie's case he was briefly moved to the 63rd Sanitary Section where he spent a happy few days as a carpenter, producing ablution benches! But by mid-January he was back in the trenches, in the Oppy-Gavrelle sector and shortly afterwards wrote to Ida congratulating her on the Christmas tips she had collected on her postal round and mentioning a problem with his feet.

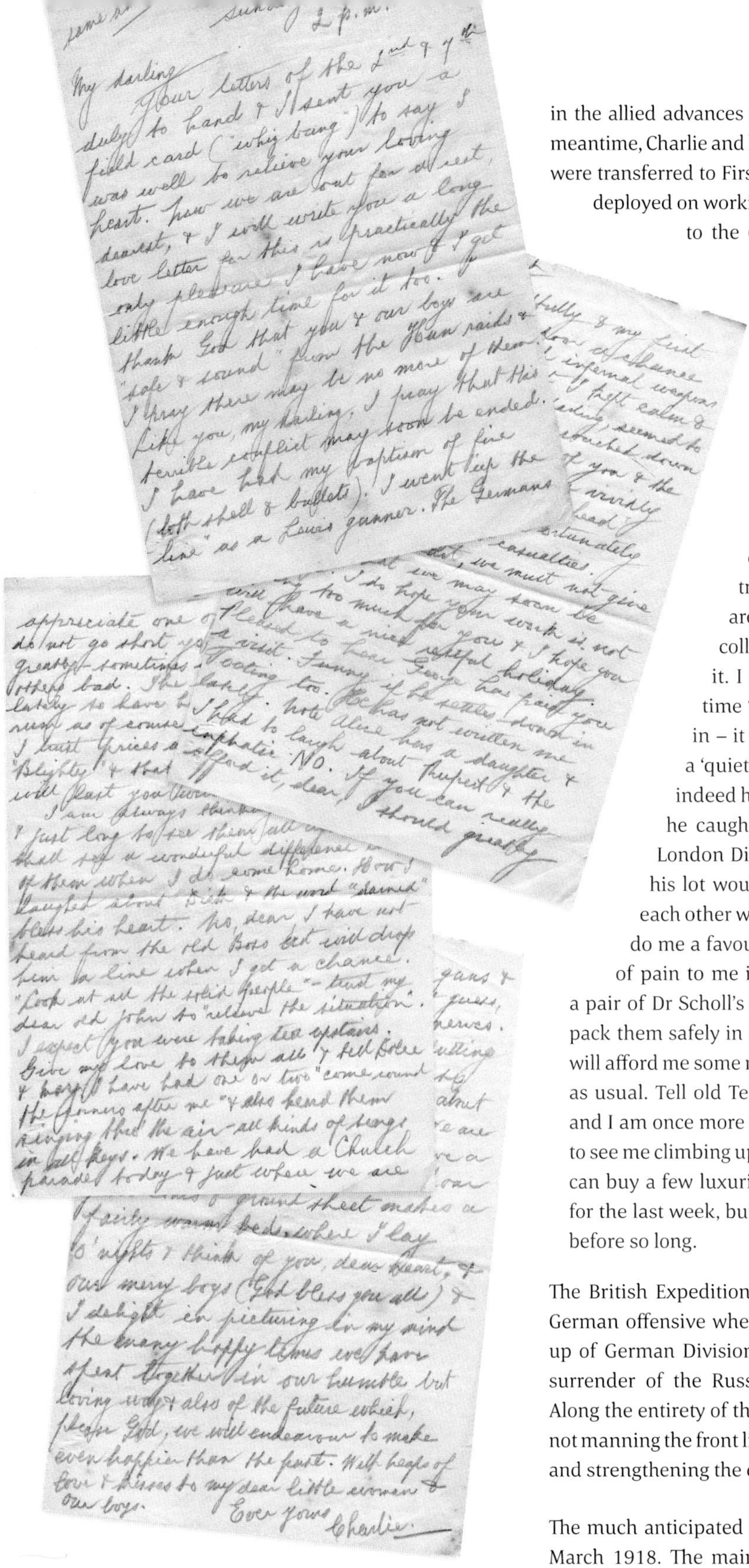

24 January 1918: I duly received your two letters, but as you will have guessed, dear, could not write sooner owing to being in the trenches. It cheers me greatly to learn that you are able to manage so well, dear, and that you collected £3 in Christmas boxes – you deserve it. I am fairly fit although we had rather a rough time 'up the line' this time owing to a thaw setting in – it was terribly muddy, but on the whole we had a 'quiet' time. Pleased to hear Bill is on leave – it was indeed hard luck he could not get to speak to me when he caught sight of me in November – I knew that a London Division were in our vicinity and I wondered if his lot would be there. What tales we shall have to tell each other when next we meet. Now, darling, I want you to do me a favour. My hammer toes have been a great source of pain to me in the heavy ground so I want you to get me a pair of Dr Scholl's Toe-Flex. Get them as soon as possible, dear, pack them safely in a little box and register them and I trust they will afford me some relief. We are in a village now, billeted in barns as usual. Tell old Ted we are sleeping one above the other again and I am once more on the top shelf – I guess you would all laugh to see me climbing up. There are several inns and shops open so we can buy a few luxuries. The weather has been fine and very mild for the last week, but expect we shall have another dose of winter before so long.

The British Expeditionary Force was now preparing for an expected German offensive when the weather improved, prompted by a build-up of German Divisions transferred from the Eastern Front after the surrender of the Russian forces following the Russian Revolution. Along the entirety of the Western Front, when the British infantry were not manning the front line, they were busy in working parties modifying and strengthening the defences.

The much anticipated German Offensive finally started at 5am on 21 March 1918. The main attack focused on British Army positions to the south of the 5th Dukes' position. That morning Charlie's battalion (now renamed the 5th Battalion) was in the front line of the Acheville

Letters written by Charlie Payne while on active service

sector still in First Army's area, but was relieved, as planned, later that day. On 23 March he reported back to Ida; his first concern being a missing food parcel.

> 23 March 1918: I have your letters of the 10th and 15th, but regret to say, dear, the parcel never reached my hands – it must have gone astray owing to being along with the RE's – hard luck – Was there a letter in it? I have now been returned to the battalion. Expect to be on the move a good deal now, but will endeavour to write as often as possible, dear, but must ask you to excuse brevity. At the moment we are out of the line. Now that spring is here, of course, dear, there must be some fighting – in fact, you will see by today's paper 'Johnny' is making an attack – he will catch a cold though, I have no doubt.

By 25 and 26 March the front lines of Third Army and particularly Fifth Army were savaged by the German onslaught, with serious gaps appearing. On 25 March, 62nd Division was transferred to Third Army and ordered down to Bucquoy to help blunt the German advance. Leaving the Arras area in the early morning, the men marched about thirteen miles to Bucquoy, before being ordered to establish a line on the railway South-East of Achiet le Petit. Charlie was again involved in open warfare, but this time in defence rather than attack. Later, orders were issued for the men to make a fighting withdrawal, first to a line in front of Puisieux and then finally to an old enemy trench system between Puisieux and Rossignol Wood.

At Rossignol Wood, the 5th Dukes were in a hazardous position as their right flank was completely 'in the air'. In addition, the Third Army Commander, Julian Byng, had issued an order that '...no retirement is to take place unless the tactical situation imperatively demands it.' Over the next few days, the battalion fought off numerous German attacks over open ground and by bombing up the trenches. A three mile gap on their right flank was plugged, after 24 hours, by the arrival of New Zealand and Australian forces. The battalion and Division essentially held their positions and the German attack finally ran out of steam. Charlie's battalion was not relieved until 2 April, having suffered 215 casualties by that stage. He reported back to Ida:

> 3 April 1918 [a partly censored letter]: You will see by the papers that the Germans have started their great offensive – but do not be downhearted, dear, — I cannot believe they will meet with success in the end — their losses must be terrible. We are now out of the line, but of course not for long these days. I note all your other news, dear, but have a lot of cleaning up etc. to do, so please excuse brevity. How pleased I feel that you keep so well, and I pray God that you may not have a recurrence of your old complaint. Keep up a good heart, dear. We cannot do more than that and just leave the rest to God.

Over the next two to three months, Charlie's battalion was intermittently in and out of the new front line near Bucquoy. However, on 22 May, Charlie mentioned to Ida that 'I am still in the water job and having a very comfortable time. Had I been with the Battalion. I should be in the trenches.' He was probably operating as a Water Point Warden, tasked with rationing the use of water, which was in limited supply. As Charlie would have been one of the older members of the Poor Bloody Infantry, perhaps a sympathetic officer had decided to give him an easier life for a while. But by early July, that task had come to an end and he was shortly to find himself in Champagne country.

At the height of the German Spring Offensive, Field Marshal Ferdinand Foch had been appointed Supreme Allied Commander on 26 March. This appointment had been prompted by the need for better coordination of British and French forces, In July, Foch anticipated a German attack in the Marne area and requested that four British Divisions be sent down to help repulse any such attack. 62nd Division was one of the Divisions sent, arriving in the area the day after the Germans had attacked. Their task was to counter-attack the Germans, up the valley of the River Ardre. There was no organised trench system in this open countryside of hills, woods, villages, and fields so, once again, it was open warfare. On 22 July, Charlie's battalion received orders to clear the Bois du Petit Champs, which contained two battalions of German troops, including many well-hidden machine gun positions, several of which overlooked the River Ardre and were preventing progress up the valley.

The wood was filled with dense undergrowth and the Germans were well-concealed. Working methodically, the 5th Dukes surrounded and rushed several German strong-points and by the day's end most of the wood had been secured, although "C" Company was almost annihilated in the process. Charlie in "B" Company was operating on the southern edge of the wood. He reported home to Ida.

> 2 August 1918 [a partly-censored letter]: You will see from the papers that our battalion has been in action again (wood fighting similar to last November). We have come through very creditably and succeeded in driving back the Huns to some extent. Of course once more I have lost some very good pals. I may soon be fortunate enough to get my leave – I have now completed twelve months out here – needless of course to remind you. How relieved I was to hear that little Rupert's fit was

Charlie and Ida Payne, September 1918

nothing serious, but still it must have upset you. The weather has been glorious here lately – a little too hot – fitter for picnics than for the devilish work going on out here. God grant it may now soon be over.

When they were relieved on 29 July, the Battalion War Diary records that morale was high but the men were physically exhausted after eight days fighting. On 1 August they marched past General Berthelot the officer commanding the 5th French Army under whose orders the successful advances had been made. By then the Germans were in rapid retreat from the Marne salient. The German Field Marshal, Hindenberg, later commented in his memoirs that 'It was of the greatest and most fateful importance that we had lost the initiative to the enemy.' However, the 5th Dukes had suffered considerable casualties in the process. To bring the battalion back to strength, during August it received reinforcements totalling almost 50 percent of the battalion's manpower.

On 8 August, the British Fourth Army delivered a successful attack near Amiens advancing up to eight miles on the first day, and starting what has become known as 'The Last Hundred Days' of the war. To capitalise on this, Third Army organised another major attack to the North, towards Bapaume. Charlie's Division was involved and between 25 August and 2 September, the 62nd Division pushed the German forces back another three miles.

The British advance was now developing considerable momentum. Charlie, however, was granted his first Home Leave since arriving in France thirteen months before. It is almost impossible to comprehend what it must have been like for Charlie and, of course many others, to be dragged off the battlefield one moment, returned briefly to friends and family for ten to fourteen days and then thrown back into the maelstrom of war. Something of what he did while in London is mentioned in his next letter, written when he had returned to France.

> 23 September 1918: It is good of you, dear, to write me so often as your letters cheer me wonderfully. However, I am fast settling down to the old routine, and today has been fine and bright which is good. I am pleased to learn that Dolce and little Rupert are having a good time and trust he will be quite well on his return home; also that the boys are well and good. A fortnight ago today we took them to the zoo; what a day we had and then to get home only to find the gas cut off and the workers on strike. I remember cursing a bit, but what would I give to be having dinner by candlelight now in 'Blighty.' It is odd how little things soon upset one in civil life after what we have to put up with cheerfully out here.

By 25 September the battalion was preparing for battle once more. The next target was to cross the St Quentin Canal at Marcoing. On the morning of 29 September the men arrived at Marcoing at 9am and passed through the battalion that had led the initial attack. They were already exhausted by a long night-time march which had involved carrying Lewis guns and other equipment through previously-captured enemy trenches. In Marcoing, the canal bridges had been severely damaged by the enemy and the canal bank was very deep, making it a very real obstacle. With great difficulty "B" and "D" companies managed (using planks) to dribble their Companies across the canal from about 11am. As the troops crossed the canal, they were subjected to heavy enemy machine gun fire. The enemy fire was reduced by putting Lewis guns into the attics of houses on the Canal-side to keep the enemy machine guns engaged whilst the troops dribbled across. A line was then established along the railway, east of the canal, which was heavily shelled by the enemy all day. The enemy was then seen massing for a counter-attack and orders were received that the battalion should pre-empt the counter-attack by attacking the enemy trenches at 6pm, aided by an artillery barrage.

The attack was chaotic. The initial phase secured some sections of the enemy trenches capturing 300 prisoners and nine machine guns. However, groups of men found themselves isolated, with Germans on either side and they had to retreat or charge the enemy. At one point, Charlie's Company found itself under fire from front and rear. Some of the German prisoners captured earlier had been inadequately escorted and had picked up rifles and opened fire on the British troops from behind. Fortunately, some reserve platoons who had been kept on the line of the railway restored the situation. As the divisional history puts it 'The treacherous prisoners were adequately dealt with.' The battalion then held their new positions overnight until they were relieved and moved into reserve. From a bivvy-hole alongside the Canal du Nord, Charlie wrote to Ida:

> 1 October 1918: Just a few lines my darling to let you know that I am well and safe. You will have seen from the papers that our battalion has been in action and again come through with great credit. I thank God I am safe, and as before when 'going over the top' you, my sweetheart, and our dear boys are very near me. You must not worry, little woman, if my letters are irregular for we get no opportunity of sending them off now when 'up the line.' We are now out for a few hours. As you know we are going for the 'Huns' hammer and tongs and I pray and believe the end is not far off. Tell Ted I am using his pencil to write this letter in a little earth 'shack' which I have just finished digging and which I have lined with some hay and straw like a little bird's nest – it is the snuggest 'kip' I have had since leaving home.

For Charlie there was to be only one more battle and he wrote home just before it started.

> 19 October 1918: I cannot say very much at this time, dear, but so far as I know the Huns are still more or less on the run all along the line and our artillery are always at him – they must be having a hellish time of it. You will know better than I how the line runs now and I trust they will not stop retreating until they reach their own country. The weather is very fair and the 'going' not so bad. I am pretty fit and billeting in the villages deserted by the Huns. We have been able to have decent fires and to boil a few spuds, carrots etc – we have also found decent beds in some of the cottages. I have seen a few French people left behind by 'Jerry' mostly poor old women – I often wonder what has become of the rest. Tell 'Nanny' I still have the piece of coal in my pocket and I hope she, Dad and the girls are all quite well.

Armed with his piece of coal as a good-luck charm, Charlie had an early start the next morning, as the battalion had been ordered to attack at 2am. Their task was to cross the Selle river, to clear the village of St Python and to capture the German defensive position of La Pigeon Blanc Farm. The river was about 25 ft wide with a depth of 1ft to 6ft. At 1.30am Royal Engineers started putting up light wooden bridges over the river. At the same time "A" Company forded the river, at the shallowest point. It was a moonlit night but with ground mist. The whole battalion crossed the river by two minutes before zero hour. The presence of civilians in the village precluded an artillery barrage and, although the earliness of the attack provided a significant measure of surprise, some stiff street fighting took place. Once the village was cleared, "B" and "D" Companies moved through to the eastern side of St Python towards La Pigeon Blanc Farm. The Germans put up a fight but their machine guns were knocked out of action by Lewis gun fire and the objective was gained and many prisoners taken. By 4.10am all the battalion objectives had been achieved.

After this encounter, and possibly to give an older soldier a bit of a rest, Charlie missed the Battalion's last fighting. According to his letters, he was sent on another Lewis gun course. However, he rejoined the 5th Dukes shortly before the 11 November at Maubeuge, from where he wrote to Ida several days after the Armistice.

> 16 November 1918: What a glorious thing is Peace. Out here we cannot yet realise it. I cannot now express in words the glorious feeling we have on rising and going to 'kip' and not to hear the awful roar of big guns – to know that we can sleep in security without fear of bombs and shells and above all to know that we shall not again have to go 'over the top.' Let us be thankful, dear heart, that soon we shall again be reunited in happiness with our own boys once more. I was not in the last fighting my battalion was in, but I have now rejoined and we are billeted in a town near the Belgian frontier and I fancy our Division will have to go to Germany – but I do not know definitely. I am quite well, dear, and supremely happy and thankful – longing for the day when I land in dear old England. So rapid has been our advance that letters etc. have not reached us yet, but I expect they will eventually reach us. The poor French people whom we have released in the towns and villages are mad with joy and make a great fuss of us. How I should have liked to have been in London the night you received news of the armistice – I guess people almost cried with joy. Peace must surely follow as the German soldiers are utterly demoralised and beaten. I hope to learn that Bill and Leo [Dolce's husband] are both safe and well and that all upstairs are likewise. We have still a lot of work before us, darling, so we must be patient. It will be a long march

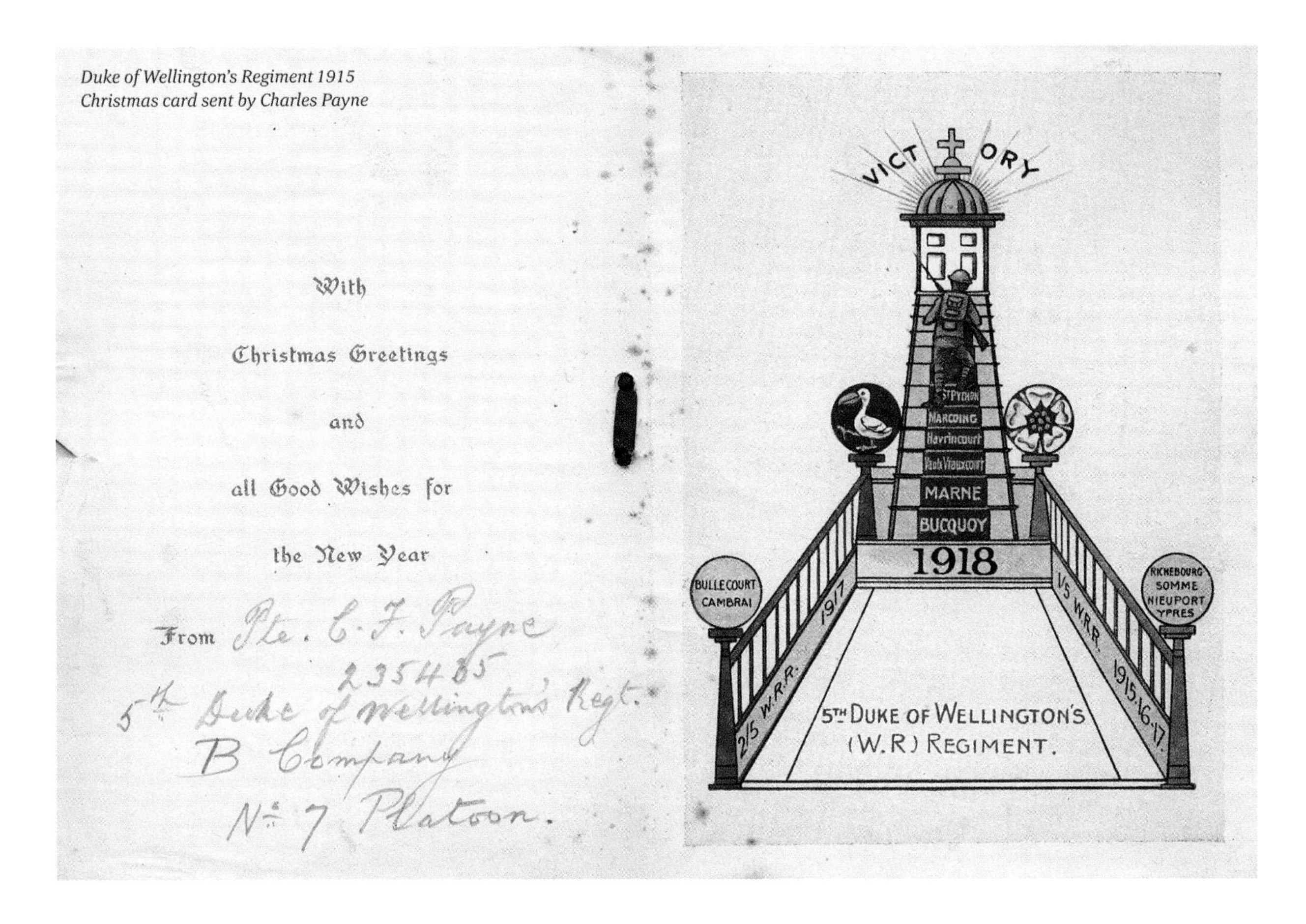

Duke of Wellington's Regiment 1915 Christmas card sent by Charles Payne

> through Belgium to Germany. Still continue to read the papers dear, and write to me as often as you can – it will make the time pass quicker. Think of me now, little woman, as being happy and comfortable. It is beyond belief almost that we shall spend no more awful days and nights in trenches and God be thanked for it.

As Charlie anticipated, 62nd Division marched to the Rhineland, arriving on Christmas Day. In January 1919, Charlie was promoted to Sergeant when he became an instructor in shorthand at the Brigade School that was set up to help the men acquire new skills prior to demobilisation. With the smattering of German he had acquired from colleagues during his time working in Genoa, he also acted as Company interpreter.

If one were writing a novel about 'Charlie's War' it would have a happy ending. Sadly, this true story does not. On 10 February 1919 Ida received a telegram, indicating that Charlie was dangerously ill in a military hospital in Boulogne, with pneumonia (probably brought on by infection with the 'Spanish Flu' virus). Charlie died the following day. Like those who died during the fighting, Charlie's body was not repatriated. His headstone at Terlincthun Cemetery records his substantive rank as Lance-Corporal, though the scroll that Ida received from the King refers to Charlie as a Sergeant. Ida paid for the additional words 'Ever in our thoughts' to be carved on his headstone and visited the cemetery in 1923. She never remarried and brought up her four sons on a War Widow's pension and by undertaking various part-time jobs. By the time that I was old enough to have a conversation with her, she was stone-deaf and I only became aware of her early life well after she died in 1980 aged 94. I am indebted to Ida and my father, Rupert (who had been too young to remember his father), for retaining Charlie's letters and for the opportunity to understand why I was christened Christopher 'Charles' Payne.

Sources

Emanuel School Magazine (1898) p.138.
Payne, C. F., diaries, and letters written to his wife Ida Muriel Payne between November 1916 and February 1919. (From the collection of C. C. Payne).
TNA: WO95/3084 and 3085. War Diaries of the 186th Infantry Brigade Headquarters (1917–1919).
TNA: WO95/3086. War Diary of the 2/5th (later the 5th) Battalion of the Duke of Wellington's (West Riding) Regiment (1914–1919).
TNA: WO153/747. War Diary of XXII Corps. Operations whilst employed with French Army (July–August 1918)
Hammond, B. *Cambrai 1917: The Myth of the First Great Tank Battle.* Weidenfeld & Nicolson, (London, 2008).
Wyrall, E. *The History of the 62nd (West Riding) Division.* (2 Volumes). The Naval and Military Press (2003). (Originally published by John Lane The Bodley Head Ltd in 1924/1925) Acknowledgements: Several photographs included in this section were expertly restored, from the originals, by Neville Sisson.

Alec Reader (standing)

Bertram Alec Reader

(Emanuel 1909–1913)

'A promising long-distance runner'

Early Life

Bertram Alec Reader, known as Alec, was born in Queen Victoria's Diamond Jubilee year, on 8 December 1897 to Fred and Rose. The eldest of five children Alec attended Lavender Hill School before joining Emanuel on 14 September 1909. The family lived at 4 North Side, Wandsworth Common, opposite Spencer Park and from their house the Reader family would have been able to see Emanuel School's spire. The children would have seen horses being watered in the horse trough opposite the house in addition to seeing plumes of whitish grey smoke rising from the railway lines as trains passed through Clapham Junction which at the time was one of the busiest railway junctions in the world.

In 1911 Alec won a School prize receiving a copy of *Stories from Shakespeare*. Alec was athletic, being described in *The Portcullis* as 'a promising long-distance runner.' Alec was also a soloist at St Peter's, Eaton Square.

Recruitment and Training

On leaving Emanuel Alec became a clerk with the Telephones Department of the Post Office on the west side of Wandsworth Common. Alec was fifteen when he left school and sixteen at the outbreak of the First World War. He would have seen many young men join the ranks at various recruiting stations around Wandsworth. A year passed by and in the summer of 1915 Alec made a trip to Somerset House, where recruits could join the 15th Battalion London Regiment, Prince of Wales' Own, Civil Service Rifles (CSR). Alec did just this, but he wasn't quite eighteen years old and so theoretically was under the official age at which you were allowed to join the Regular Army, but this did not deter thousands of Alec's generation and so at seventeen, Alec, lying about his age, became a 'boy soldier.' Having passed the medical inspection he left Somerset House as Private B. A. Reader 3623.

The choice of the CSR was quite possibly determined by Alec's job in the Post Office, for a number of Post Office workers, being part of the expanding Civil Service, joined the CSR. It is likely that recruitment posters were displayed in Alec's office in addition to copies of the CSR's booklet encouraging young men to fight with its recruiting call 'Come and Join the Regiment. Don't wait for Conscription.' Perhaps these sparked young Alec's interest or it may have been at the suggestion of a work colleague.

In August 1915 we find Alec training with the 3rd Battalion, 15th London Regiment, CSR in Richmond Park, writing home to his mother (known as Ma to Alec) on 12 August:

> Hope all at home are better than I am as I have poisoned my heel and am in a bad way. I can't walk 20 yards without my foot throbbing painfully. We are going strong down here, eggs yesterday and a kipper each today for breakfast.[1]

Alec spent the next few months in learning the rudiments of army life. Whilst training he was billeted with the Dubois family in Gerard Road, Barnes, who like many other families wanted to 'do their bit' for the war effort.

In November 1915 we find Alec at a Musketry Camp in Rainham, Essex, telling his mother that without his mittens he 'messed up the firing.' In January 1916 Alec is at Hazely Down camp near Winchester. Alec writes to his brother Arthur:

> We are in a very large camp (one mile long) and at present there are Canadians, Welsh, A.S.C... But more Regiments are expected daily and when we get full up it will be some camp.

Training was arduous as Alec explained in a letter home in February: 'Last Monday we went to the trenches and had to dig solid chalk to a depth of eight feet. Some war!' A few days before writing this letter Alec had his photo taken, 'To relieve the monotony I had my photo taken last Sat... note the new hat (2s/6d).' Alec had also been photographed with his family and many years later it sparked the curiosity of Alec's nephews, to whom we shall return.

Alec was hoping to get three days leave in February but his battalion had been put on Draft, which meant they could be called to the Front at a moment's notice with a shorter amount of leave. On 10 February he wrote to his Ma:

Postcard sent by Alec showing Musketry Camp in Rainham, 1915

> Am working very hard at present, trench digging, bomb throwing, bayonet fighting etc. and we do all our work in full war kit (Everything you take out with you)... I am quite ready for the end of the day.

By mid-February German Measles had broken out in the camp so they were to stay a little longer but within a few days those not infected were removed to a different hut. At this time Alec received a parcel from May Dubois, whom he had stayed with in Barnes and asked his mother to thank her when she visited. He also asked for some socks, a request that became a regular occurrence over the next few months.

Alec did not even get the 24 hours leave he had hoped for and on 24 February wrote to his Ma:

> We were told last night at 10 o'clock that we were to leave Winchester for Southampton by the 9.20am train this morning and so here we are...

Alec continues writing about the opinions of some of the other men who thought, 'the heavy fighting which is going to take place in March will finish the war one way or the other.' Alec gives his Ma hope by noting that he would be entitled to seven days leave in six months, writing 'So all being well, you will see me home before I reach the age of nineteen.'

In France

Alec's journey to France was delayed by a few days, for having embarked on a P&O liner they were all marched off again and sent back to camp in what Alec said was an 'official secret', but soon enough he made the journey across the Channel and sailed to Le Havre from where on 2 March he wrote:

> Hope you received my card alright. I wasn't allowed to write letters from there and you have to be careful not to say anything of importance. It was very rough indeed when we crossed, in fact there were only three chaps in the boat who were not sick... Another experience of mine has been a railway journey of 180 miles in 21 hours. We started at 10am and arrived at 7am the next morning. Owing to the fact that the railways here are like some tramways in England (a single line with doubles at intervals). The journey was somewhat tedious. We had to sleep eight in a carriage and were accordingly rather cramped. Since I left England I haven't seen any bread and have been living on bully and dog biscuits since I landed. I drew five Francs today, the first money I have had for the last four days. If you haven't already sent the money along, please do so as I need it badly.

March was spent settling in. Alec discusses the amenable conditions in the camp compared to the 'filthy condition' of Le Havre, which they were not allowed to visit. On 25 March his home sickness comes through in the following lines to his Ma.

> We work all day and every day here. (No half day off on Saturday). But as when I am not working I start thinking of home, which is the worst thing to do out here, I am glad to have mind occupied.

Alec saw his first real scenes of the war on what he noted on his letter as 'Fools Day', 1 April 1916.

> Last night's affair was a wash-out. We were taken up the line in lorries and dumped in a ruined village. There we drew picks and shovels and marched up to reserve trenches for digging. We started out at 7pm and got back at 3am. Reveille at 7.30am this morning... several large shells burst on our left and machine guns were very active at first, but towards midnight things quietened down and it seemed if hostilities had ceased for the night.

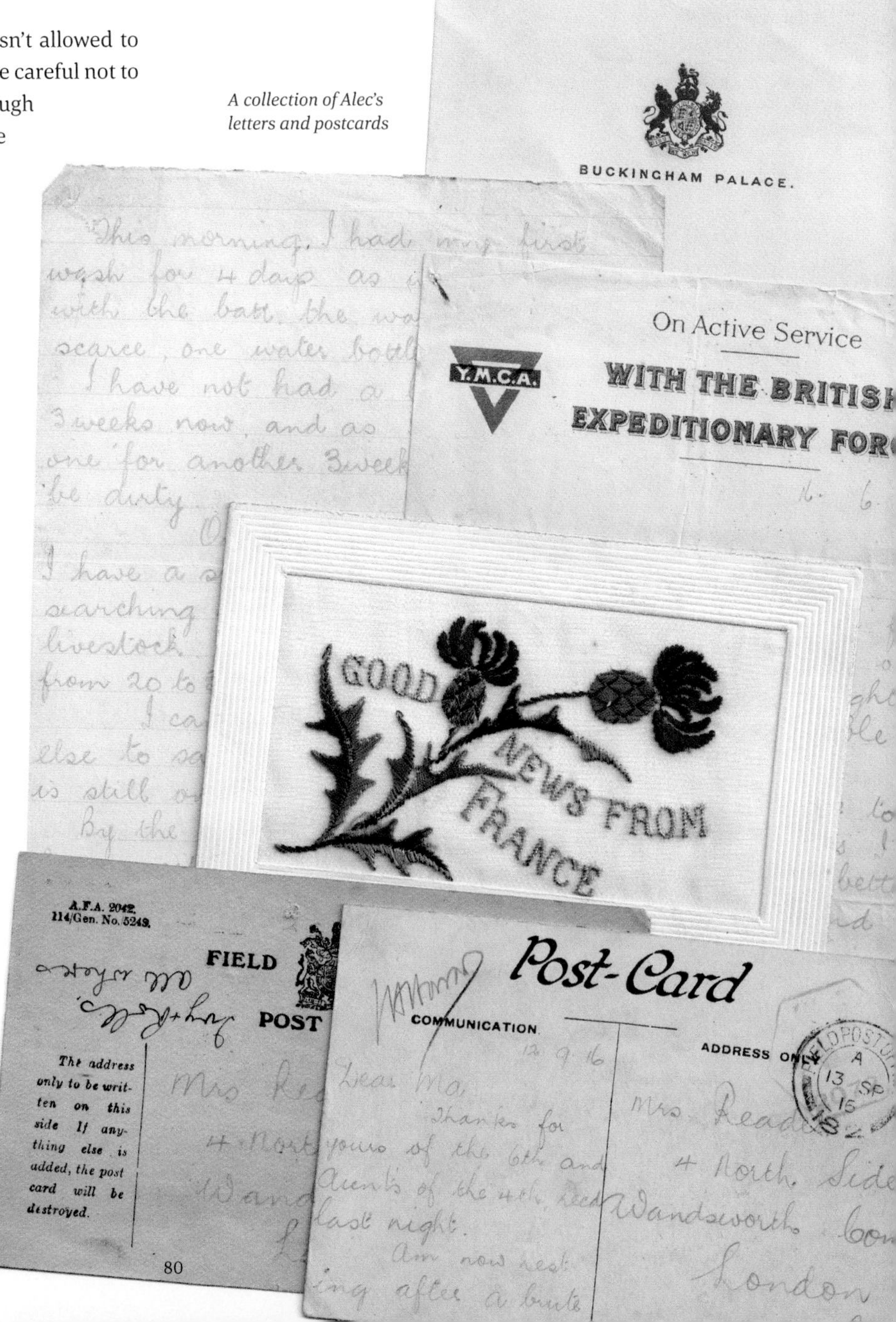

A collection of Alec's letters and postcards

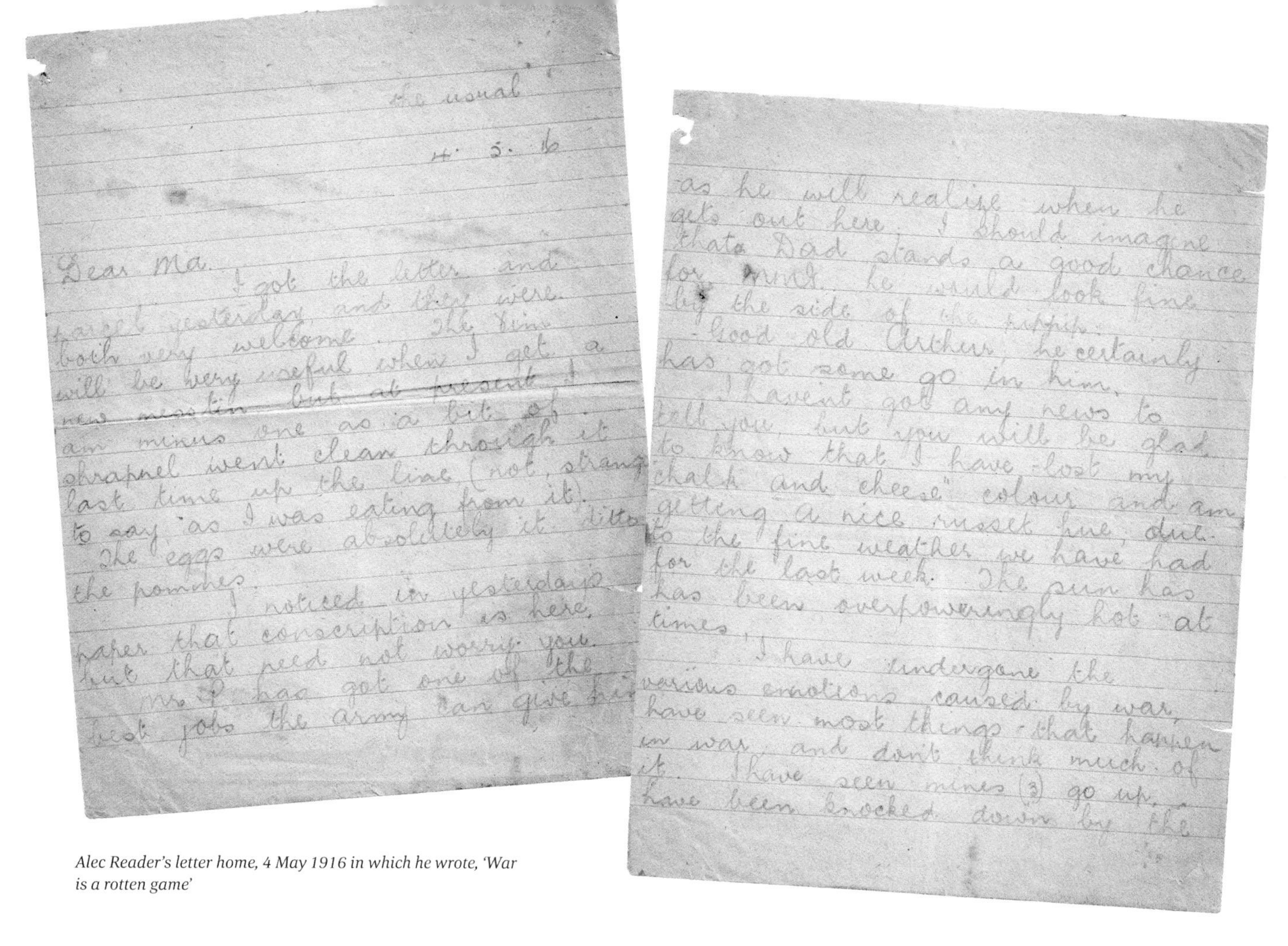
the usual

4. 5. 6

Dear Ma.
I got the letter and parcel yesterday and they were both very welcome. The tin will be very useful when I get a new mess tin but at present I am minus one as a bit of shrapnel went clean through it last time up the line (not strange to say as I was eating from it). The eggs were absolutely it ditto the [illegible].
I noticed in yesterday's paper that conscription is here, but that need not worry you. [illegible] has got one of the best jobs the army can give him

as he will realise when he gets out here. I should imagine that Dad stands a good chance for [illegible] he would look fine by the side of the [illegible].
Good old Arthur, he certainly has got some go in him.
I haven't got any news to tell you but you will be glad to know that I have lost my "chalk and cheese" colour and am getting a nice russet hue, due to the fine weather we have had for the last week. The sun has been overpoweringly hot at times.
I have undergone the various emotions caused by war, have seen most things that happen in war, and don't think much of it. I have seen mines (3) go up, have been knocked down by the

Alec Reader's letter home, 4 May 1916 in which he wrote, 'War is a rotten game'

Alec took the opportunity of a chap going home on leave to write a short note on 5 April to let his Ma know he was in Fresnicourt, mentioning that three mines had gone up in his last day in the line. The next day he explained that measles had meant confinement in an isolation camp and wrote about his daily routine:

> Our soft time consists of the following: –
>
> Reveille at 6am
>
> Breakfast (bread, bacon and tea) at 7
>
> Medical inspection at 8
>
> Parade at 10am
>
> 10 –12.30 – camp fatigues
>
> 12.30 dinner (kipper)
>
> Afternoon we rest
>
> 7pm – 2 – 3am working party (Digging trenches in reserve carrying trench boards etc.)
>
> Next morning reveille at 6am and so on

The battalion were camping in tents but the woods they were in were under observation as Alec explains:

> Shells, come fairly close, as there are two or three of our batteries near by and the Germans keep trying to find them but so far no shells have landed in the wood.

Life in the Trenches

On 7 April Alec gives a full description of what he saw whilst digging on the front lines. What thoughts must have gone through Rose Reader's mind after reading these powerful lines?

> Re: The working party. We marched up to a trench about 30 yards behind the front line and started deepening it. As there was heavy fighting in this part of the line last autumn we kept digging up tunics, trousers, bones, etc. In fact it was quite a ghastly job. We had no sooner started than a battery opened fire only 100 yards behind (they make the earth shake) and kept it up for two hours. After the first ¼ hour the Germans tried to find it, the first shells burst ¼ mile away and then they gradually got nearer, until they burst not 20 yards in front. Then it got exciting, every time we heard a whiz down we had to go among the aforementioned tunics etc. in order to dodge the splinters. This state of affairs lasted about

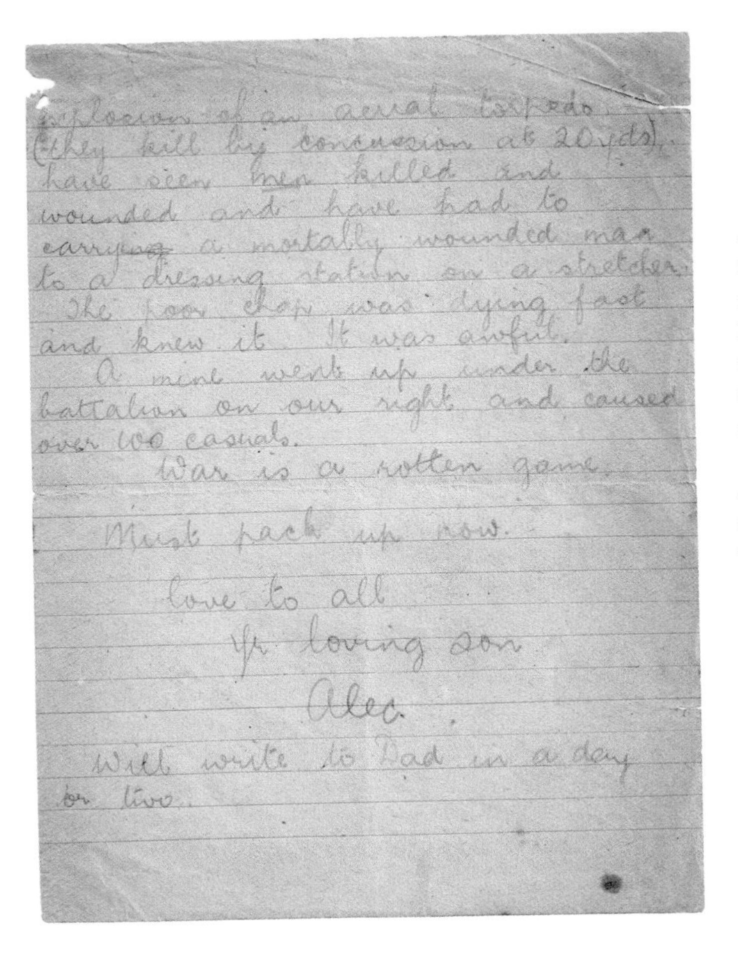

explosion of an aerial torpedo (they kill by concussion at 20 yds). have seen men killed and wounded and have had to carrying a mortally wounded man to a dressing station on a stretcher. The poor chap was dying fast and knew it. It was awful.

A mine went up under the battalion on our right and caused over 100 casuals.

War is a rotten game.

Must pack up now.

Love to all

Yr loving son

Alec

Will write to Dad in a day or two.

¾ hr, although it seemed a lot longer and then our battery had to give up and clear out. Soon after this it started raining and after working for 2hrs, in the downpour we came back soaked to the skin, covered with slush, faces and all (for of course when shells burst near you you get down as low as poss. In fact, at first I was so nervy that I buried my head in the mud and I was not the only one either).

Alec wrote affectionately to his younger brother Arthur and these letters show us Alec's light heartedness and gentle humour even though he was witnessing horrific scenes. In a letter on 8 April he writes to Arthur:

> You ask me to get the VC, well let me tell you a secret the only men out here who get distinction are those who lose their heads or have too many rum rations. The sensible ones get down into the bottom of the trench when things get a bit hot and they are the men who 'live to fight another day.'

That same sense of humour is seen in a letter to his father the following day, 9 April. Alec paints a picture of his 'garden', a satirical sketch of life in the trenches.

> I write from on an improvised table made from two trench boards and sundry stakes. The sun shines, the aeroplanes buzz, the guns bark and my unique collection of livestock bite. In fact everything in the garden's lovely.

Alec described how hard the work was and longed for the good old days when he was told to be in bed by 10pm rather than coming back from a night's work at 2 – 3am. He also suggests that swearing was a common occurrence amongst the men, 'Shell holes abound and coming back from a 'night out' the language they cause is to say the least unparliamentary.'

Alec wasn't afraid of giving graphic descriptions of what he experienced. His mother, Rose, must have been a very strong woman indeed, reading lines such as these:

> I enjoyed Easter muchly. I spent it in the front line; the Germans sent a mine up about 300 yards on our right and also sent a lot of rifle grenades, trench mortars 'Minnies' etc. over just to celebrate the occasion. They also strafed us for an hour and the old chaps say that it was the worst bombardment they had ever been in. I was on sentry during the strafe and of course I had to stand upright. Afterwards I was told that I had stood it very well. One of the chaps, about 25 years old who came out on our draft lost his nerve and laid in the mud groaning and crying the whole time.
>
> We were in a barricade about 5ft high and the only shelter we had was a sheet of corrugated iron (some trench). When the mine went up it threw us all over and nearly shook the parapet down. On the whole it was quite an exciting time.

The quintessential Alec humour is best illustrated in his response to the since much publicised war poster of a young girl asking her father what he did in the war. Its intention was to persuade men into joining the armed forces by appealing to their sense of shame so that one day they could tell their little girl that they played their part. Alec's amusing reply, after telling his mother of the unceasing digging of trenches was: 'In fact my answer to the question what did you do in the Great War Daddy? Will be "Dug up half France, Sonny".'

Thoughts on war

Humour was not the only facet to this young man, for simply reading his words without foreknowledge of his age would suggest a man much older, battle worn with a full life of experience having written them. Alec was only eighteen, yet his philosophy on the meaning of war, though written in layman's terms as addressed to his Ma, is nonetheless powerful as in this extract from his letter on 4 May 1916:

Alec Reader (left) with friends from the Civil Service Rifles

> I have undergone the various emotions caused by war, have seen most things that happen in war and don't think much of it. I have seen mines (three) go up, have been knocked down by the explosion of an aerial torpedo (they kill by concussion at twenty yards), have seen men killed and wounded and have had to carry a mortally wounded man to a dressing station on a stretcher. The poor chap was dying fast and knew it, it was awful. A mine went up under the battalion on our right and caused over one hundred casualties. War is a rotten game.

On 6 May Alec describes the treacherous course they had to navigate at night:

> The journey back was a farce; we had to hang on to each other's coat tails, it was too dark to see; when one chap went down he pulled about a dozen with him; I saved myself once by catching hold of someone's leg, but in doing so I pulled him down and when we had stopped rolling he was sitting in eighteen inches of water and I was on top of him and so had a dry seat. The guide kept losing the path and once we found that the rear had lost touch; we found them half an hour later in a swamp, they were up to their knees in the slime.

> This is a ragtime war! We get 'Minnies' high explosives and mines galore and yet in the front line we get our post and stuff from the canteen (tinned fruit, fags, sausages etc.) every evening.

Alec's resilience is quite remarkable, as it was for so many of his generation, but he casually brushes off expressing what is easily recognised as signs of deep distress with these candid thoughts to his mother on 13 May:

> My last letter to you was 'written' shortly after we came out of the line and of course I was feeling whacked, fed up, miserable etc. which is only natural after six days of nervous tension. You don't want to take any notice of that sort of letter, as we all have our rotten moments.

In the same letter Alec tells his Ma that he had to go on a bombing course and just over a week later wrote:

> Dropped you a card yesterday to let you know I am alright. We have had a pretty rotten time lately, but it's no use my telling you as you must have read the papers. We have been [letter then censored but readable] over the top and lost [letter then censored again] Please send me some socks as soon as poss as all my stuff has been blown to bits. Also a small sponge for washing.

Alec was cut short by the censor when he wrote of 'lost', but he was in all likelihood referring to heavy losses incurred in the counter offensive of 23 May by the 21st and 24th Battalions, 47th London Division.[2] In a letter next day Alec explains how his letter concerning the attack was destroyed by the censor:

> We went 'over the top.' A most unpleasant job. Yesterday I wrote to you but the regimental censor was so annoyed with the amount of verboten matter in my letter that he destroyed it. Please send me some socks as soon as you can as I lost all my stuff last time up. A shell apparently landed right on my pack, all I could find of it afterwards was one of the buckles. I have now got a casualty's stuff but he was very careless with his socks, they have all got holes in them.

The losses incurred at Vimy Ridge in May 1916 were over two thousand and even the authors of the official history of the 47th Division in the post-war years questioned the strategy employed. We can assume Alec had expressed similar sentiments in his letter which sadly the censor destroyed:

> It seems doubtful now whether our risky position near the crest of the ridge was worth holding at such cost, when a strong position on the high ground near Cabaret Rouge, with the same observation from the Lorette

> Heights, was available. The magnificent spirit which refuses to yield to the enemy any ground, however useless, is worth much; but were the Higher Command justified in incurring the resulting losses?[3]

In June Alec spent two spells in hospital, the first due to a bout of the flu and the next due to being gassed, but as he explained the latter illness struck him after he went into a mine shaft for some sleep only to be awoken by two men pumping oxygen into him after he had suffered from inhaling fumes caused by a mine explosion.

Alec's father, Fred, had joined No. 2 Balloon Training School, which trained in Richmond Park. These Balloon Units were used on the Western Front for observation of enemy positions. In late June Alec wrote to his Ma:

> You need not worry about Dad even if he does come out here because the nearest balloon is five miles from the line and the Germans leave it severely alone. In fact my job in the next war will be Dad's.

Alec concluded his letter with a P.S. 'Re: Ivy's remarks. If Dad shoots as many Germans as I have he will do well. I have not fired a shot since I have been out here.'

The Somme offensive began on 1 July but Alec retained his cheerfulness in his letter on 6 July:

> We have been in the line for seven days now; the first four were spent in the 'line of resistance' and had a fairly rotten time, but now we are in nice deep dugouts and if it would only stop raining all would be well. As it is the water drips through the dugout incessantly, everything is soaked but our spirits which apparently can't be drowned and it is a case of water, water everywhere but not a drop to drink. Still it's not a bad war at present.

He reassured his mother two days later that 'our part of the line is comparatively quiet.' Alec then faced a predicament, because as he was only eighteen years old he could choose to return home. He wrote to his Ma on 8 July:

> I have been placed in a very awkward position: An army order has been issued to the effect that "Men between the ages of 18 and 19 are to be sent back, but any who choose can volunteer to stay with their battalion." The temptation to get out of this ghastly business is far greater than you can possibly conceive, but of course there's only one decent thing for me to do, that is to stay here, but oh! it's going to be very hard.

Alec, as you will expect having read his extracts to this point, did not take the opportunity of going back and explained his reasons more fully in a letter to his father on 14 July. Fred had suggested that Alec transfer to the balloon section, in which he was serving, which would be out of the firing line but Alec believed it wasn't the done thing, writing to him:

> That transferring idea of yours is a jolly good thing, but it would be hardly the thing to leave the batt. now; It would look rather like running away from the advance, don't you think... To resume I have decided to stick out here until I get knocked out as that is, in my opinion, the only thing to do.

The tone of Alec's letter is reassuring and his enthusiasm that his father was a fellow 'brother in arms' suggests that he felt much more secure in this knowledge. However, it appears that Alec was putting a brave face on when he suggested that he wanted to stay and not be seen to be running away from the advance for Alec wrote another letter to his Ma on the same day and we now see a very different Alec:

> I wish you wouldn't take all that bosh about bravery. This ought to show you what a 'brave' boy I am – I am very glad that Dad has asked for me, as I am horribly fed up with this game. I could never have applied myself, but am only too pleased to shelve the responsibility (compris bravery). You must excuse the writing as at present I am up a sap about 40 yards from the Hun, and there are no facilities for letter writing. I am keeping fairly fit and am living in hopes... Did Dad state my age?

This was a boy who must have been scared to his core and yet his dear Ma was the only one he could truly confide in and tell the truth. He had watched men much older than him break down and cry in the trenches but at eighteen years of age Alec showed a brave face both to the men he was fighting alongside and to his father but all the while letting his Ma know how he was truly feeling.

By mid-July he was certain that the War would be over by Christmas and requested his Ma to 'make a lot of puddings this year.' He expressed how tiredness put him in no mood to write letters but asked his Ma to pull him up if he got too lax.

By the end of July 1916 Alec's battalion were on a march that would take them twelve days and illness amongst the men was rife. Alec painted a picture of the landscape:

> The heat just now is terrific; yesterday we marched ten miles. Only ten but two chaps have died of it, several are seriously ill [censored]... The dust on the road is 3 inches deep in a lot of places and water carts are unheard of in our part of the country, so you can guess our marches are a bit different from the Sunday morning appetiser.

The marching took its toll on Alec for on 7 August he wrote:

> I am in hospital once again; septic feet this time. I hope to stay here a day or two longer and then 'Back to the land.' The 'hospital' is situated in a meadow, we live under canvas or in the open as we choose. We do nothing, eat plenty and fully carry out the sentiment expressed by that well known poster, 'He's happy etc.' The only drawback is that they cut my feet about three times a day, causing me a small ration of pain but it's worth it.

A few days later and Alec was hopeful that he should be home within a few months:

> You remember that I got gassed a short time ago, well, the only lasting effect of it is to keep my face as white as the proverbial sheet, so when I come home look out for someone who is 'pale and distinguished looking!' ... What do you think of the news? Quite the 'Johnnie Walker' spirit about it I think. In my humble opinion Fritz is practically 'napood' and I put down the month of my return as October.

He expressed the same optimism in his letter to his young brother:

> If the war's not over before I shall be home next February on leave, but I hope to see you all in October. Of course, I shall stand a very good chance of a 'Blighty one' during the next three weeks, so don't be surprised to wake up one morning and find me at the Third London General Hospital.

By the middle of August it was clear that Alec longed to return home but on 15 August he made clear that even men who had been out for twelve months had not been allowed any leave so he encouraged his Ma and Dad to write to the Commanding Officer, 'It couldn't hurt me and it might do some good.' Rose had noted that Alec's tone had changed to which Alec replied in the same letter, 'You say that my letters are not so hopeful now; well when I get back I will explain all the whys and wherefores of the case. Still if I am not home for good by the end of October, well...'

By the end of August Alec was back marching and wrote on 24 August of the hard conditions his battalion were facing:

> When on the march an officer yells out, "We're being – shelled", upon which we all run into the fields and wait until the 'Heads' decide that the shelling has stopped. It's a great game, playing at soldiers. Tonight we are going to die as they have decided that we don't know how to use a spade – this after six months of 'shifting France' ...
>
> Once I get home I'm going to stick there like glue.

The Somme

Alec's transfer was delayed on the desks of bureaucrats, one piece of paper was never enough and it seemed that another form always had to be signed. This bureaucratic tardiness would have fatal consequences, although Alec remained ever hopeful that it would only take a month.

> The transfer is going on alright and another month ought to see it through. Thanks very much for the photos. Dad looks a proper soldier, more than I did when I first joined, or do now for that matter ... You seem very optimistic re my prospects, but, peculiar as it may seem, everybody hopes for a 'Blighty One,' more or less. It is one of the few things we have to hope for ... By the way there are about 50 Balloons in our part of the line, so I do stand a slight chance of meeting my 'Brother in Arms.' [His Dad].

The CSR soon learnt that they were to attack High Wood. The authors of the 47th London Division wrote, 'But we never saw anything quite like High Wood.'[4] To get to this place the Division had to pass through the town of Albert with its Basilica damaged in heavy fighting. By September 1916 the surroundings were like a medieval painting of Hell, with the Golden Virgin and her Child atop the Basilica balancing precariously, staring at the ruins below and the soldiers marching to the sounds of war. The 47th London Division history noted, 'We walked into a new world of war.'

Alec may not have been aware that between 31 August and 9 September, three of his contemporaries at Emanuel, Godfrey, Ryley and While had all been killed in the Somme region. They had been involved in actions to clear the enemy from various vantage points, but the Germans still held High Wood, which was strategically important for the Allies' key objectives of taking Bapaume.

Leading up to the main attack on 15 September Alec was still writing letters home, still hoping that his transfer would arrive within the fortnight but it would certainly not occur before the opening of the Battle of Flers-Courcelette, the name given to the Allied offensive on 15 September.

Alec's last letters home

> 7 September 1916 to Ma: Sorry to have kept you waiting so long for a letter; I wrote yesterday but had it destroyed by our Platoon Officer ... We are having a pretty strenuous time still, had an attack this morning ... Re the transfer; it appears that a special form is necessary and as it is a very unusual application from men nobody had got the

SP form and it is being sent up from the base. It will only delay matters a fortnight or so ... PS Ferrier (the chap I was billeted with) has got to Blighty with a SEPTIC FOOT. He didn't come out till June.

9 September 1916 to Ma: ... I am sorry to have to disappoint you, but the transfer has had another check. You see, after I had filled the form they found out that it wasn't the correct one ... If you don't hear from me for a day or two you must understand that the postal facilities will be very poor and it is quite possible that our letters won't be collected for a week ... We are billeted in a farm and the lady of the house is skinning a rabbit for her Sunday's dinner. In a minute she will clean out the cow shed next door to us so I must pack up, as when she does start the air turns very blue and we have to wear our gas helmets. Yes! Here she comes pitchfork in hand.

12 September 1916 Postcard to Ma: ... We are in 'bivouacs' which were made for 20 and hold 40, so we take it in turns, half in at a time. For amusement, having no money, we do some small game hunting, attended with marked success as this place unusually 'cutey'. Now for a sleep, we were up at 1.45am and have been on my feet ever since. Now 2pm. Bon eh!

The last thing Alec ever sent home was a Field Postcard just to signal that he was alive on 14 September. The next morning Alec's Company (A) of the 15th Battalion were ordered to take the German front line trenches and then advance on various positions which the commanders hoped would force the Germans out of High Wood.

This attack was the first in which tanks were employed, but it soon became evident on the morning of the 15th that these new land ships weren't quite developed enough to navigate the scarred landscapes in which the infantry were fighting.

Alec's experiences the day before the battle can be viewed through an unpublished diary of a friend in the 15th London, Private L. W. Vern Wilkinson; Vern gives a detailed description of the 15th London's movements on14 September:

We moved off at last on the great adventure heavily laden with ammunition, bombs, coloured flares, two gas helmets each and spades, we passed several places en route where villages had once been, but only heaps of bricks and rubble remained, the names of those little hamlets will always be famous, Fricourt, Thiepval, Mametz etc. We saw for the first time Delville Wood commonly known as 'Devilswood', the country seemed very difficult for fighting over and the ground was in a terrible condition showing everywhere the thoroughness of our wonderful artillery barrage, shell hole joined shell hole for miles around. The road was packed with troops and transport all moving up for the 'strafe' all in broad daylight too. No doubt our airmen had received instructions to keep Jerry out of the way whilst these reinforcements were on the road, otherwise there would have been some heavy shellings. On nearing the line the ground became rather difficult. We saw two horses shot because of their wounds, not a very cheery start for us.

Further on we passed a 'caterpillar' (later known as a tank) for the first time and gazed in wonderment at the cumbersome object, hoping too that the weird outfit would turn up all right when required. Dead horses were numerous now, some very badly hit with half their insides lying about the ground covered with clouds of flies. We entered the communication trench at last, this was badly battered in parts and many of our dead could be seen over the top of the trench where they had been pushed over to keep the trench clear.

We were in 'High Wood' (correct name Foureaux Wood) at last, the trench had been cut through tree roots in places, the majority of the trees were just scarred stumps, various trenches ran through the wood the major portion being held by Jerry. The wood lay on top of a ridge and Jerry had held us there for two months, consolidating his position with concrete machine gun emplacements and deep dugouts attempting to hold at all cost this last point of vantage overlooking our occupied territory. Various attacks had been made by us but all unsuccessful.

That we were 'in for it', we could plainly see. It was still daylight when we relieved the 21st. London Regt., our artillery was very active pounding away at the German positions, the weather was glorious, a great thing during an attack.

We hung about the trench wishing the attack would start right away, the hours dragged by, we heard about midnight that we were to go over at 6.20am.[5]

High Wood 15 September 1916

It was in late 2013, that the family of Vern Wilkinson got in touch with the author Neil Hanson who had written about Alec a few years previously. They had a piece of information that completed Alec's family's long quest to find out what had happened. Alec's family knew he was killed at High Wood on 15 September 1916, a fateful day for the CSR and the 15th London. What follows is Vern Wilkinson's description of the morning of the 15th.

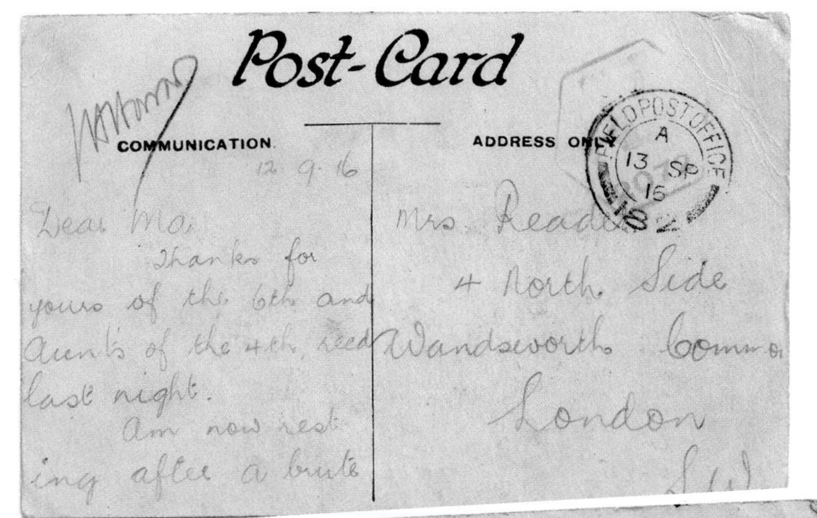

Post-Card

COMMUNICATION

12.9.16

Dear Ma

Thanks for yours of the 6th and Aunt's of the 4th, recd last night.

Am now resting after a brute of a 'constitutional' this morning. We are in 'bivouacs' which were made for 20 and hold 40, so we take it in turns, half in at a time. For amusement, having no money, we do 'small game hunting', attended with marked success as this place is unusually 'cutey'. Now for a sleep, we were up at 1.45 am and have been on my feet ever since. (Now 2 pm.) Bon ch!

Au revoir & Loving son Alec.

ADDRESS ONLY

Mrs Reader
4 North Side
Wandsworth Common
London
S.W.

Alec Reader's final postcard, sent home 12 September 1916. Three days later he was killed in action at High Wood

We were happy when we knew definitely what time the 'kick off' was, uncertainty made one nervous and irritable. We attempted a little breakfast in the early hours but the jam tasted of paraffin so we gave it up. A substantial rum ration however soon satisfied us, there was actually some rum to spare as some of the lads would not participate as they wished to have all their senses about them when the great time came. Others were quite merry and personally I had consumed plenty to make me feel like killing Jerry. We examined our rifles, bombs etc., time after time making sure all was in order. At last 'zero' came (6.20am) and the guns that had quietened towards the dawn broke out with a terrible clatter as they put down one of the terrible barrages that made advancing much easier for the infantry.

We clambered over the top of the parapet and were immediately met with a murderous machine gun fire, some of my pals falling at once. The din was terrific, the bark of our 18 pounders was heard above everything else and the shells themselves seemed to just skim over our heads almost scorching us. The rattle of dozens of Jerry machine guns made it seem impossible for us to live a second under the hail of bullets that showered by us, yet we pushed on.

Vern Wilkinson then explains Alec's last moments:

Young Reader fell at the side of me with a groan and blood rushed from a wound in the head. I just turned to glance at him and could see that death was instantaneous and so passed that cheerful spirited lad to whom everything was 'very cosy.'

The Times described 15 September as 'a great day for the cause of civilisation', but it seems hard now to see it as no more than a great waste of life.

Alec would not have known that another Emanuel boy was in the same region on the day he lost his life. Frederick Crosslé was a stretcher bearer with the RAMC who was bringing in the wounded after the taking of High Wood and was badly wounded in the thigh by a shell fragment. Frederick sadly died of influenza in October 1918.[6]

Condolences

Alec's Commanding Officer George Gordon Bates sat down to write two letters, one to Alec's brother and one to Alec's father. Captain Bates's letter to Arthur follows:

It is with extreme sorrow that I write to say that your brother 3623 Pte. Reader B. A. has been killed in action. During the time he was with my company, he proved himself a good soldier and will be greatly missed.

Please accept my sincere sympathy and regrets at being unable to write more at present. I have been unable to write before.

G Bates. Captain. OC "A" Company

P.S. His body was found and properly buried and the grave registered by the Graves Registration Committee.

Sadly Alec's burial could not be identified later when the Imperial War Graves Commission was carrying out its work to rebury the bodies of fallen soldiers, so Alec's name is now carved into a memorial panel on the Thiepval Memorial to the Missing along with 73,000 other names and ten other Old Emanuel boys who have no known identified grave.

Letters of condolence followed, one of Rose's friends writing, 'There are so many suffering the same sorrow, one has not to go far to find others that the war has robbed of their loved ones.' Rose's friend summed up the situation of the war aptly in another line when she wrote, 'It seems one great horror from beginning to end.'

The Headmaster of Lavender Hill School expressed his sorrow writing, 'Alec was a splendid boy at school and gave promise of a bright future.' Mrs Dubois whom Alec had stayed with in Barnes wrote, 'In such an awful time one cannot say anything that comforts but you must be very proud to have had such a good son and know that he died a noble and brave death.'

One can only imagine now what Rose and Fred must have gone through. They had five children, but as any one who has lost a child will know it is like losing part of yourself, but this cheerful boy continues to be remembered by his family and the Emanuel community.

The Next Generation

On 15 September 2016, Alec's nephew Doug and other members of Alec's family will visit High Wood to remember Alec's death a century before but it will be the culmination of a long journey. Alec's family toured the memorials and cemeteries of Northern France in 1928 but not until a few decades later was Alec's life so well remembered. Doug and Roger Goodman, Alec's nephews and both OEs themselves have been indefatigable in their quest in telling Alec's story. They travelled to High Wood in 1991 placing a message on a tree marking the spot where Alec died. They have deposited Alec's letters with the Imperial War Museum and have helped a number of researchers who have written about Alec.[7] Sadly Roger died an untimely death but Doug has continued the family's long journey and there isn't a day when Alec is not far from Doug's mind.

Doug Goodman, who provided all the information on Alec Reader, recalls the research his late brother Roger did to resurrect the young soldier's life:

Alec's nephews Roger (left) and Doug (right) Goodman

Alec's sister Minnie Goodman reading her brother's letters 70 years later

Roger Goodman was born in 1933 so grew up during the war. He did National Service and his first job was producing maps in the former SHAEF WW2 HQ in Bushy Park. Perhaps these experiences are what set him on the road to retracing Alec Reader's life. Roger was meticulous in his fifteen years' research: gathered every possible item of information on Alec; on 15 September 1916 battle; visited High Wood many times and interviewed many people. All this was on our mother's side — The Reader family. He even traced the Goodmans

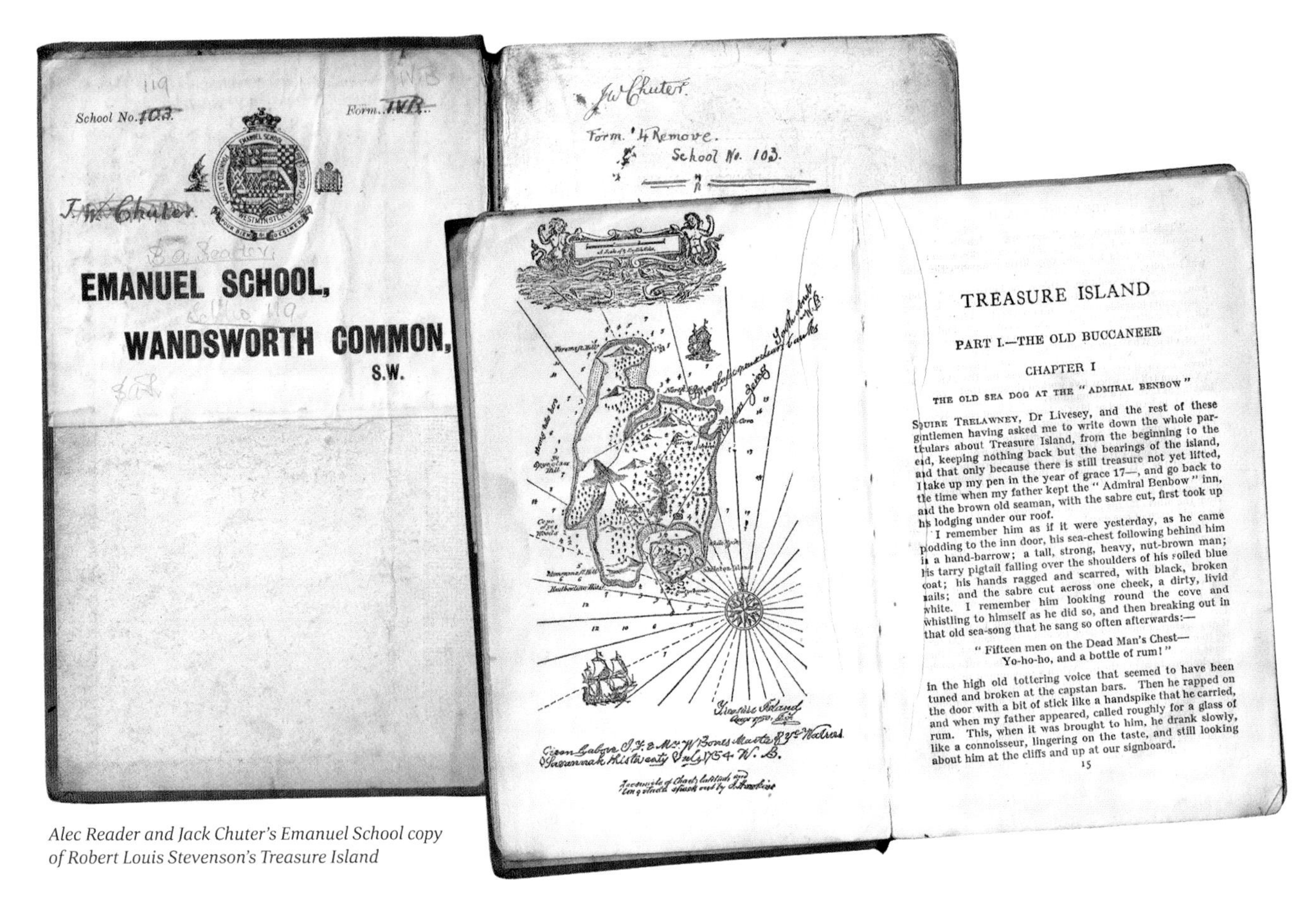

TREASURE ISLAND

PART I.—THE OLD BUCCANEER

CHAPTER I

THE OLD SEA DOG AT THE "ADMIRAL BENBOW"

Squire Trelawney, Dr Livesey, and the rest of these gentlemen having asked me to write down the whole particulars about Treasure Island, from the beginning to the end, keeping nothing back but the bearings of the island, and that only because there is still treasure not yet lifted, I take up my pen in the year of grace 17—, and go back to the time when my father kept the "Admiral Benbow" inn, and the brown old seaman, with the sabre cut, first took up his lodging under our roof.

I remember him as if it were yesterday, as he came plodding to the inn door, his sea-chest following behind him in a hand-barrow; a tall, strong, heavy, nut-brown man; his tarry pigtail falling over the shoulders of his soiled blue coat; his hands ragged and scarred, with black, broken nails; and the sabre cut across one cheek, a dirty, livid white. I remember him looking round the cove and whistling to himself as he did so, and then breaking out in that old sea-song that he sang so often afterwards:—

"Fifteen men on the Dead Man's Chest—
Yo-ho-ho, and a bottle of rum!"

in the high old tottering voice that seemed to have been tuned and broken at the capstan bars. Then he rapped on the door with a bit of stick like a handspike that he carried, and when my father appeared, called roughly for a glass of rum. This, when it was brought to him, he drank slowly, like a connoisseur, lingering on the taste, and still looking about him at the cliffs and up at our signboard.

15

Alec Reader and Jack Chuter's Emanuel School copy of Robert Louis Stevenson's Treasure Island

back to the early 1700s. And almost all his work was done before we had the Internet to make life easy. It's through Roger's magnificent effort that a massive file of historic information now exists on our uncle. This was given to the IWM so that others could share the story of Alec Reader and to date six books as well as countless press articles carry his letters and pictures.

Doug and Roger had made friends with Alec's Commanding Officer's daughter Ione Bates and in 2005 attended a memorial service at Somerset House for the 90th anniversary of the 1st Battalion Civil Service Rifles going on active service to France. Ione's uncle, Frank Dougan was also an Emanuel boy and so the links between the extended Emanuel family have been further strengthened.

Treasure Island – a book with a poignant tale

John 'Jack' William Chuter

(Emanuel 1911–1915)

In 2013 sitting with Doug in his house going through Alec's papers Daniel Kirmatzis noticed a red book and enquired what it was. As Doug opened it they saw a pasted down sticker on the inside cover with the words Emanuel School Wandsworth Common and the name B. A. Reader written in pencil, but there was also another name in the book, J. W. Chuter. Books get passed around from one form to another and we can assume that this copy of Robert Louis Stevenson's *Treasure Island* and *Kidnapped* was passed from John William Chuter to Alec, for a line had been drawn through John's name and Alec's name written in. The book is now in the Emanuel School archive but who was John William Chuter?

John, known as Jack, played rugby and also rowed at School. He appears in the earliest known photo of an Emanuel rowing team that was taken outside the main School building in 1915. On leaving Emanuel he went to Cranwell to become a pilot. His father wrote to the School in 1917:

> Our thanks are due to Mr. Chuter for kindly forwarding the following concerning his son, J. W. Chuter. "He has made rapid progress, taking his pilot's certificate a month after joining and passing through Cranwell with honours, thus graduating as a 'Scout' pilot. He is very keen on it and his letters are very interesting; he often refers to the Old School and says his training in the rugger team has been of service to him in this dangerous and nerve trying game, as he says in one of his letters, "when you

Jack Chuter in an Emanuel classroom (first from right)

> are between three and four miles above the earth and a long way above the clouds, which roll on and on like a sea, you have time to think of things that are past; it is fearfully cold and fearfully lonely and one gets so utterly fed up with the vast loneliness that you turn her nose down and rush through the clouds at about 120 miles an hour and the sight of mother earth is very agreeable after that huge vault that people call the 'heavens' and if you make a 'stunt' landing, you are overjoyed with the flight, but mighty glad to once again tread terra firma."[8]

Jack was attached to the RNAS and interestingly his flying record notes that he was a 'Good pilot. As an officer he has improved, but does not altogether appreciate the importance of setting a good example on duty as regards attention etc. Shows fair ability in command of men.'[9]

In the Clyde House notes of Summer Term 1917 we read:

> We are very sorry to have to relate the death of another old Clydeite, namely, Jack Chuter, who was accidentally killed while flying at Mudros, Isle of Lemnos. He was a Flight Sub-Lieutenant in the RNAS and whilst at school was a member of the First Fifteen and School Rowing Four. Always heart and soul in the doings of the House, we all mourn his loss very much.

When Jack was killed he was flying with Sub Lt. Aubrey Henton in a Nieuport Fighter on photo-reconnaissance. They died on impact on 9 June 1917.

Alec and Jack were both cruelly cut down in youth but their memories will grow as old as those who hold their lives dear and who never forget their sacrifices.

References

1 Daniel Kirmatzis would like to thank Old Emanuel Doug Goodman for his permission to reproduce Alec's letters. The collection of letters can be found in the Imperial War Museum. Catalogue number – Documents 4127.

2 A. H. Maude (Ed.) *The History of the 47th London Division 1914–1919* (1922), pp. 55–56.

3 Ibid. p. 57.

4 Ibid. p. 62.

5 The unpublished diary of Private L. W. V. Wilkinson 531606, 1921. With thanks to the Wilkinson family for permission to use extracts.

6 *The Portcullis*, Trinity Term, 1920, p. 43.

7 See Jill Knight, *The Civil Service Rifles in the Great War* (Pen and Sword, 1996); Malcolm Brown, *The IWM book of The Somme* (Sidgwick & Jackson, 1996); Neil Hanson, *The Unknown Soldier* (Doubleday, 2005); Anthony Fletcher, *Life, Death and Growing up on The Western Front* (Yale, 2013); Mark Tanner, *In Memoriam 1914–1918* (not yet published); Ione Bates, *Out of a Long Silence*, (An account of Capt. G. G. Bates MC during WW1 in the Civil Service Rifles) (Private publication 2006). Duncan Barrett, *Men of Letters* (AA Publishing, 2014).

8 *The Portcullis*, Spring Term, 1917, p. 43.

9 TNA, ADM/273/9/111.

Michael Dell

The Dell Family

The Dell brothers, Anthony Warner, Louis Michael and Montague Roger, (the last two known by their second names, Michael and Roger), were born in the late nineteenth century to Louis and Isabella Dell. The Dell family were corn merchants by trade, in a family business which started in the eighteenth century, and Quakers in their religious affiliation. In the 1890s the boys attended Emanuel for their preparatory education. Anthony and Michael went on to St Paul's School and Roger to University College School.

Anthony Warner Dell

Both Michael and Roger served in the First World War. Anthony was a conscientious objector. In Albania in June 1914 he was kidnapped by insurgents who believed him to have been a Dutch officer, a story that was widely reported in the press and warranted discussion in Parliament. He was a correspondent for the *Daily Citizen* during the First World War and was later sub-editor of the *Morning Post* and editor of *Reynold's News*. During the course of the war he worked in Serbia with The Religious Society of Friends' (Quakers) relief service.

Montague Roger Dell

Roger was the youngest of the three Dell brothers. Born in March 1892 he joined the East Surrey Regiment from the Royal Naval Volunteer Reserve. His service was mainly spent in Salonika although he also saw action in Macedonia. Sadly no letters exist of his time in the war but we do know that he was awarded both the Military Cross and the Serbian Order of the White Eagle, 5th Class with Swords.

Louis Michael Dell

Louis Michael Dell born on 11 August 1890. In 1913 he had just completed his studies at the Surveyors' Institute, where he had won the Galsworthy Prize, when the war broke out. He served with the 7th Battalion King's Shropshire Light Infantry. Michael arrived in France on 27 September 1915 and regularly wrote home to his family. Michael also edited the first edition of and contributed to, the 7th Battalion's own trench magazine, *The Dud*. He also contributed two pieces of original writing for the *Saturday Westminster Gazette* under the alias Richard Hagen for many officers chose to submit such works anonymously. One of the articles related an amusing situation of life in the trenches but more interesting are the footnotes explaining the specific language that would have been known to soldiers in France during the war.

Michael was killed at Montauban on 14 July 1916, aged 25 and is commemorated on the Thiepval Memorial.

The following extracts are from Michael's letters and detail his experiences between December 1915 and July 1916 on the Western Front, from the Ypres Salient in the winter of 1915–16 to the first fortnight at the Somme in July 1916. They portray what life was like in the trenches; discussing issues of trench construction, supply issues and the ubiquitous rats which ate almost anything they could sink their teeth into. The letters also discuss how men dealt with their emotions in the firing line. In one letter Michael refutes the idea of the newspapers' portrayals of fighting men as being made heroes by their experiences and illustrates the reality of the situation, 'What is so pathetic out here is to see the men who have fought the great fights not as the papers make out ennobled and made heroes in the process, but with their nerve gone and unable to keep a steady face during shelling.' The letters offer sobering thoughts on the realities of warfare.[1]

Letters Home

Mid-December 1915, Wednesday – to Mother: We are back here again and having a more comfortable time. Three weeks' determined work by ourselves and the battalion we share with has altered things a lot ...

Yesterday afternoon I went round most of the line to have a look round... In parts the mud was half-way up to our thighs.

Can you please send me in place of the usual Nugent boxes, a fortnightly box with one tin of biscuits (such as Huntley and Palmer's rich mixed) candles, matches and bulls-eyes. The tinned meats I am not so much in need of here, as we are in a good mess. But biscuits are handy as you can offer them round. A tin of anchovy paste or something tasty also, to put on at tea.

The Dell brothers and friend. Note Anthony and Michael wearing their Emanuel School caps

Christmas Day 1915 – to Mother: I have run out of writing paper. The mails have been very irregular lately, I have not heard from you for several days. They say there are submarines in the Channel, but I expect it is the pressure of Christmas posts. Today is windy and rainy. The Army in its wisdom issued mutton and so the men have had mutton stew and Christmas pudding (half a pound each, and very good stuff) ...

The artillery have so far been very quiet today.

Although we have had so few casualties you can see from their faces that the senior officers are already feeling the strain. In the four regiments that came out here together two commanding officers have already been invalided, (really through worry). ... It impresses you to think that these men who imagine ridiculous things such as mines going off and Germans in the next trench and who duck when our own guns fire are the men who have held the line so thinly that it seems incredible they could have resisted a serious attack.

... Now if the Germans put a shell over as a matter of principle we put five back. The consequence is they are afraid to fire at all. Our artillery is ordered to fire a very large minimum of shells a day whether they want to or not and whether they have targets or not.

A post has just come, with '*Punch*' from you, he is very good and spicy.

Boxing Day 1915 – to Aunt Rose: Thank you for your long letter which came yesterday. It is sunny today. There is always a strong wind blowing over the hill where we are ... I am trying to make a toboggan. The idea is that if a man is hit in front of the line while patrolling, you probably can't

The Dell brothers playing c. late 1890s

carry him in on a stretcher. We hope to make our sledge, put him on, and pull him in from the trench with a rope. The ridiculous part is that of course we can't get a rope for this from the Army, but that we can get a picketing rope for picketing horses, so we ask for it under that heading. The Army have all sorts of schemes to check waste but... most of them fail to do anything except hamper your operations. Last time I was back the pioneers made some wooden boxes and padded the sides with blankets. They make soup every night in the camp, the transport carries it up and it reaches the firing line boiling hot. We think it has saved us a lot of 'trench foot' cases.

I gave my pioneers 20 francs for their Christmas dinner. ... none of them said 'thank you.'

27 December 1915 – to Mother: It is showery today, sunny in between and a tremendous gale blowing from the west. We have to send in a wind report three times a day in the trenches and it is curious how difficult it seems to be. No two companies ever report the wind the same ...

From what I can see the war will be over before I get my leave. We shall be starting leave soon, two every ten days and I am about 24 on the list. I know nothing out here that you don't know and probably less, but things do seem to point at last to Germany feeling the breaking strain. The gas attack is reported a complete failure, so complete that people were wondering what it was done for, but it gave us an excellent rehearsal in resisting it. I can only suppose it was meant to be a real one and that our preparations were too perfect and smashed it at the start.

Our division is known as the Ironsides. The regiment has been getting a very good name the last fortnight, I hope we live up to it. It is always rather an ominous remark when a general calls you a fine body of men, at the present time the staff can't do too much for us. It is largely due to our keeping quite calm during the gas attack and not doing anything silly such as asking for artillery help when nothing was happening in front of us. We can thank Major Negus for a lot.

6 January 1916 – to Mother: I am very tired. This rest camp is as strenuous work for me and the pioneers as the trenches are. I got up at seven and have been on the go all the time. This evening I hope to finish a map of the trenches. Coming home from the trenches I had a thick time. We are eight miles from them. They can only get the buses to three miles from home. I had to march the light duty men to the buses and started at five ... To cut a long story short I got the last on board at 1.30, got on and went five yards when the bus went into the mud. The men walked, I had to wait with one sick man till I could get a waggon for him and walked home arriving 2.30.

Monday, early January – to Mother: I must say that I never expected to last a winter campaign in the trenches, but with reasonable luck I ought to, now we are half through. The first two times in this place always depressed me, but since Christmas jollifications we all seemed to have bucked up considerably. Most of us are adding weight, although the senior officers are feeling the strain a bit. After all, in the time we have been in we have improved the trenches wonderfully and they are quite different now from what they were in the first few dreadful days.

Mid-January – to Mother: We are working hard every night on our CT [Communication Trench] and getting about 20 yards forward each night. We wall the sides of the trench with hurdles and metal, held in by stout pickets and floor it with duckboards on little piles. It is difficult to keep to the same work when other things of vital importance turn up but we know that unless we keep steadily pegging away at our one small job we shall never really do anything.

I think we are leaving our mark on these trenches. They can't be compared to what they were when we came in, in spite of the fact that it has been wet most of the time and one or two frosts, they are drier and safer and very much stronger.

Things go much smoother when a garrison knows its trenches and all about them. We feel quite happy here now.

Experiences at the Front

In this letter Michael explains to his father his personal experiences of life in the trenches in early 1916. It is an eyewitness account of the conditions faced by the men and the problems they confronted such as being under fire, loneliness and the supply of dry socks:

January 1916 – Letter to Father:

'I have just been for duty in another part of our front line, attached to a company there and will describe my personal experiences.

I got to the line about 10 o'clock, walking across the open in the moonlight. The communication trench is a long way off this part. They had been a little worried in the line by snipers who could see into our trench from high ground on two sides. Two officers and three men had already been hit there. The OC firing trench took me along and we arranged the work necessary to meet the case and got a party working.

I inspected the whole line with the OC and we discussed various pieces of work necessary – draining, heightening and thickening parapets, building a dugout, making a fire step, etc. After we had got parties to work we got out and had a look at our wire.

The moon was nearly full, but the sky cloudy, a perfect night for us as there was enough light and no shadows. Fritz was 200 yards off, he was feeling comfortable owing to the moon and not firing or sending up lights. We walked along the wire and decided where it needed strengthening.

Roger Dell (fifth from left on the ground) in an Emanuel School class photo, 1899

Roger Dell in uniform, c.1914

The shelling however must not interfere with the serious business of life. As the shells were whistling overhead the NCO on duty came up, saluted and reported, "All the men have rubbed their feet, Sir, and changed their socks." It strikes you as funny at first, but the question of shells is really not the thing that worries a commander now. The problem, which Divisional Generals are not above tackling, the urgent question that is the bane of our lives, is how to keep the men supplied with changes of dry socks.

Presently the Germans increased their range and went away to our right. On our right flank was a piece of trench which owing to bombardment and the weather, was temporarily thinly garrisoned as it was very much commanded both by the Germans and ourselves. When the fire had swept along to the right some way a runner came in. He had run, scrambled and crawled through the muddy ditch that was where the trench had been. He brought news of the garrison in the middle of the gap. Two bays blown in, three men wounded, signal wire cut, could we telephone HQ, please. We got our guns on to the front line opposite and the firing stopped at once. Within a quarter of an hour our linesmen had got across the gap and the telephone was working again.

At one part of the sector there is a listening post a good way out. We went to this to cheer the men up as they feel lonely right out in front. There were two men sitting there in an old shell hole and certainly their job is not a lively one. We sat there and chatted to them for a short time and then came back.

As I had no routine trench duties to do I went to sleep in the dugout till six next morning. The two officers were on duty in turn.

On Sunday we were having breakfast about 8.30 when a shell came flying over and burst some 40 yards off. The German gunners were trying to get our trench but as we are on the slope they either hit their own trenches or go 40 yards beyond ours.

They plunked about 30 whizz-bangs over us feeling all along our sector but did not manage to score a hit.

I thought they might be feeling lonely in the next trench so putting a bottle of whiskey in my pocket I ran across to look them up. They were all as perky as could be, especially the wounded who were collecting souvenirs to take back to Blighty. The wounded had to wait for night to be got away. The trench as I found it consisted of one bay occupied, two bays blown in which you had to run round quickly and three bays intact, but partly enfiladed. There was just room for the garrison to sit where they couldn't be seen. On the right was another little gap, but close enough to shout across. Beyond that our strong line went on again.

The officer in charge, with his little garrison of seven men, three wounded men and three men along at the other bay was feeling quite happy, his only trouble was to conceal the fact that as I had come without rations, his resources would be strained to give me lunch.

We spent the afternoon sitting under the sandbag he called his headquarters watching a delightful strafe. It being Sunday the afternoon service of the hymn of hate commenced at two sharp. Ten big crumps landed on what the Hun fondly thought was our second line entanglement. They were beautiful hits, we had put the target where he could hardly miss it, our real second line he could neither see or hit.

He then carefully searched a little ditch where we had been filling sand bags burrowing our earth to make it look like a trench. When he had got that off his mind we just put four shells into his front line and shut him up.

As soon as it was dark enough I ran back across the gap, said goodbye to the OC there and came back here.'

Mid-January – to Father: We are having a wet spell here which interferes a good deal with the work. We are now working from 6pm to 6am, but last night it rained so hard about 12–2 that I sent the party back. Soon after we were back it came on fine. Major Negus and I were shelled earlier in the day looking along the trench. They were not falling too near us, about 30 yards off, but we noted with interest several direct hits on the trench scored on previous mornings and also a dugout where two of our men were killed last time.

18 January 1916 – to Mother: There were a lot of bullets coming over last night. I went out to have a look at our wire last night with a wiring party. They had a very nasty bit to do on a little crest, so that they stood out against the skyline. The German sentries kept firing at us, it was the first time I had seen the flash of a German's rifle, fairly close too. One man got hit in the leg, he was one of my scouts. He called out to me when hit in a joyful whisper, "I shall be in Blighty before you Mr Dell." Their joy at a Blighty wound is quite indecent.

Late January – to Mother: ... I went up to the fire trench with an orderly with about 60 notice boards, numbering different portions of the trench. I don't know what our neighbours thought we were doing, probably their intelligence reports states, "Sounds of hammering were heard from the British trench, sentries were doubled and the usual precautions taken." It is funny how we listen to each other and make mountains out of molehills. If they tap, or cough, or sing, or dig, full reports are collected of the suspicious circumstance. If some German sentry for a joke sends up about three more lights than usual, or none at all, or lets off his rifle in a suspicious manner, details, time, map reference etc., are all entered up in the log.

No doubt they do the same and we do various little stunts to frighten them and make them think something is going to happen.

To the FOO

(Forward Observation Officer)

Hate the Hun only with your lips
And I'll reply with mine
But keep your guns from going off
Until I leave this line.
Trenches that are so close as ours
Do need an aim divine
And when you strafe the Dutchman's trench
You drop your hate on mine.

I sent thee late a signal test
Requiring naught of thee
But just to see the wire was right
That runs from thee to me.
You sent me quick a dozen shells
And all dropped short but three,
Since when my feet much colder are
Not from the Hun but thee.

Fresh every morning is the fear
The shells and bullets give us here
Through their bombardment safely brought
And with our own dud fuses caught.

New perils each returning day
Hover around us while we pray.
New orders for patrolling given,
New hopes of leave, new fears of heaven.

When HQ concentrate their mind
On dangers of a South East wind,
New comforts still of countless price
(To us) they gladly sacrifice.

The daily round, the common task
Gives all the thrills we need to ask
Room to expose oneself, a road
That lays you underneath the sod.

21 January 1916 – to Father: This time I am having a much better time. I have got a good lot of materials for working on and we are getting on very well with numerous small jobs, such as enlarging latrines and wash-houses, making more duck-walks, making a better type of cross for our fellows and other little odd things to add to our comfort.

I have usually too much to do to be homesick but when I meet... people who have been home twice since I came out, it makes you feel a bit sick.

Roger Dell in Salonika, 1918

Late January – to Mother: I have just come off a tour of duty in a trench. The trench was only just dug in a new place and we had to be careful not to show ourselves. We were not allowed fires and we had no shelters or dugouts, or communication by day with our own line. Cold water (especially when purified by adding chloride of lime) is not entirely satisfactory as a drink for breakfast or tea when you have been sleeping in the open.

20 February 1916 – to brother Roger: I don't know whether this will reach you for your birthday.

My pioneering work is largely humdrum really, as everyone pioneers for three-quarters of his time, and I have only twenty men to look after whilst most 2nd lieutenants have half a company.

We have been out here five months. The leave is working slowly down, my turn should be in three weeks unless it's stopped. I hope I shall get it just when we get back and miss a tour of duty ...

Sir Douglas Haig came round the other day. He inspected Headquarter details, shook hands with the CO and with me and chatted for five minutes. He is a magnificent looking man, looked very much like Kitchener. He had rather a showy turnout with a flag and trumpeters and lancers. The CO's pony kicked his charger, precisely the thing that would happen.

Speaking of your pantomime, we run a jolly good little variety turn here, called the 'Mud Larks.' The fellows dressed as girls are priceless, but they are two wooden dummies. It is divisional. At present the craze here is caricature. We all caricature each other and we're filling an album with them.

Late February – to Father: We are getting along very nicely this time. The Hun is very quiet, except that he has been dropping a few more shells round, but with no damage. It is a wonderful thing to see a regular 'strafe' with shells dropping all about and no damage done. They say you never get used to shell fire, but it is less frightening when you know from experience that you have 999 chances out of 1000 ...

The Major last night was out wiring. I feel sure that, although it is very interesting, that that does not require the presence of field officers because it is after all rather dangerous work and very tiring to be out till four. The less work an officer can do, the more sleep and food he can get hold of, the more likely he is to do his job properly.

Late February – to Father: I have had an exciting evening. We have been repairing a bridge in the path across the open which we have to use for rations and water and trench building stores. The path leads across many old trenches some of which are bridged, and there are shell holes all the way. Yesterday we bridged a few trenches and brought a dead man back. It was a terrible journey struggling along with him in the mud, but fortunately there was no firing.

Late February/Early March – to Mother: The trenches are very narrow and you brush round corners, your equipment catching in something every few yards. You painfully lift your boots out of the mud at every step. Here and there at dangerous corners you have to crouch. The men are sleeping or working everywhere and perhaps you meet a ration party in a narrow bit coming the other way.

I have never heard such appalling language as they use. From some way off you hear a confused murmur like the sea. Gradually you can distinguish the twelve oaths most in use here and you squeeze to one side as they pass.

Each man is weighted down nearly double and his load keeps sticking in the side of the trench. At every hole in the flooring several fall down as they can't see at all, and pick themselves up painfully out of the mud. Every man keeps up a monologue of sighs, oaths and grumbles. "Remember Belgium. I'll — well never forget it", is a favourite remark. Everything here is so uncomfortable – that sums it up.

5 March 1916 – to Father: This afternoon I am burying the corpses that are in the trenches. The Germans made three counter attacks. They consisted of members of the Prussian Imperial Guard and Wurtemburgers coming across (evidently under pressure from the rear) holding up their hands, getting into our trenches and going down to Havre in droves. The artillery was very severe. The attack went down like clockwork, the only error in judgment was in thinking the Germans might show fight. The Germans, when they came across a soldier immediately pressed money and flash lamps on him to spare their lives. There seems to have been no animosity. Terror on the part of the Germans and amused contempt on the part of our men, eight of our men got into a trench with fifty Germans in it. There was a difference of opinion as to which side was captured, but there was no fighting.

8 March 1916 – to Mother: What the Germans are suffering around Verdun I can't imagine. They can't possibly have accommodation for all these extra men, rations also must get muddled. Even in our little advance, wounded were out in the snow for 48 hours before being found. When found they always asked for a cigarette. Pure swank, of course, but they had sufficient spirit left.

The barrage of fire the Germans put on us was exactly as if a line of country had been surveyed and ploughed. On each side untouched fields and hedges, and for a belt of 50 yards the earth ripped up and flattened. Our fellows carried bombs and ammunition through it continually.

9 March 1916 – to Father: When I got to Battalion HQ I went round the trenches to take over. All the stores had been blown to blazes, there was nothing to take over. Everyone's nerves were on edge ...

I am too tired to write a purple description but the patient endurance of these men is beyond belief. They swear a good deal of course, but there is no serious grumbling. Every few yards a man would fall down, partly through exhaustion, partly through the holes in the boards. I went down half a dozen times. Men were wet to the waist through falling into shell holes, cut and bruised through falling on the rails.

If you only look at Bairnsfather, every picture is true. When we are out, we laugh at it, when we are in we swear at it. I would change the definition, 'War is intolerable monotony varied by moments of intense fear', by substituting 'fatigue' for 'monotony.'

10 March 1916 – to Father: We left the town next day early, on the march to the new camp. On the way a car came up and myself and two others were sent to the trenches. The guns were going continually, but we were not troubled by anything till we reached the support dugouts. Here things were much changed. The whole place bursting with men, the Brigade HQ, living up in the ordinary Battalion HQ, all the old landmarks blown up, everyone happy but tired out. They had had 26 hours' continual intensive bombardment; several of them weren't far off mad. We were told that we should be taking over two redoubts, and an officer took us to them. On our way there across the open we had several big shells near enough to be unpleasant, and one just over our path soon after we had passed ... When we got back we looked at the dugouts. There was room for about half our battalion. We then walked to the road to meet our people. It snowed steadily all the time. There was a block on the roads – you can't conceive the amount of traffic that has to go through the roads – and the battalion got through about 3am, having taken ten hours to go six miles.

16 March 1916 – to Father: Did I explain my new job? I am now responsible for the arrival at the firing line of rations, water, ammunition etc, during quiet times and unquiet times. The pioneer's usual job is communication trenches so the thing works together. It is at present a matter of organisation more than anything. There are 72 bags of rations, 30 tins of water, bags of socks, pea-soup, baked beans, coke, charcoal, firewood, mail, whale-oil, Jey's fluid, rum, engineering stores, ammunition, grenades, candles and oddments. Some of these have to be divided equally, others in certain proportions as required, among the different sections of the line and in the dark it is difficult until you get a system.

18 March 1916 – to Father: Last night I was on the scene of a recent 'nibble', repairing trenches with 200 men as a fatigue.

We went there in lorries. The drivers had never been near the line before and were very windy. We took care to point out all the shell holes to them.

The place is a scene of terrible desolation as our guns were on it before the show and their guns after. The whole place is wet sticky sludge, mixed up with bits of wire, corrugated iron, timber and sandbags. Digging in it is fearful work. You can hardly conceive what a terrible place it looks, trenches gone, a few of the stronger dugouts are recognisable though shattered. In many of them are men who were wounded and crawled in for safety and could not be got out. The soil is foul and stinks beyond words and everywhere there are huge rats... It is policy I think, to keep the people who have to decide on these things away from the actual sights.

20 March 1916 – to Mother: My ration job has so far proved the safest job in the regiment and has consisted of standing in safety at HQ dividing up the stores among the different people ... I am tantalised till I itch all over with rumours of leave.

22 March 1916 – to Father: I went on patrol last night with Townsend, a jolly good chap and he was killed. We went out at about 10 o'clock. He was in charge as it was my first serious patrol. He has done any amount. We went all round the German wire in front (about 100 yards of it), round an advanced post of theirs. We got back safely and were just crossing our wire when they spotted us and sent over a rifle grenade which burst just in front. It killed him and peppered us with stones. He was hit in the head and still living but we could do nothing for him. I put on a bandage as well as I could but we could really do nothing for him. We got the stretcher bearers out of the trench and got him in with no further incident.

He was a fine chap, very quiet and no show, but the coolest man in the battalion. The night before last he refused to sleep in a dugout with a damp floor because it was 'dangerous to health' ...

Somehow the more of my friends are killed, the more it bucks me up. When you get used to seeing them go across, the less serious a matter it seems to be. I hate sitting still under shell fire and I can't carry on as if nothing is happening...

This is the first officer we have had killed in the battalion ...

I am more than ever convinced that if you want to live happily out here you have got to force yourself to care nothing for risks. The CO goes on patrol now and again as he says to keep his nerves in good order. He also says, that once you begin thinking 'My life is valuable, I can't go there' your usefulness ends.

23 March 1916 – to Mother: It is a very nervy business taking a large column of horse transport along under shell fire. The horses don't take much notice, the mules calmly stop (probably holding up a mile of transport), twist up their heads and gaze at the shell bursts. Still there is always the chance of a horse being hit and making confusion or a block; and the drivers don't like to leave their horses.

Animals don't seem to mind the fighting. There are singing birds on the trees by the front line, most battalions and batteries have one or more cats and last time a dog turned up from nowhere and lived with us till we went back. As for rats!

24 March 1916 – to Mother: Rum is a difficult problem. No NCOs apparently can be trusted to look after it. I am sure one was tight yesterday. It causes a lot of difficulty, if you give a man rum and it makes him drunk, you can't reasonably try him for it.

3.45am 27 March 1916 – to Mother: I just wanted to drop you a line. We have been having a strenuous time... I am in an old dugout. Major Rangecroft is snoring in the corner, Bowie, who is now Adjutant and I are having some tea. We have had a phone rigged up in the room.

27 March 1916 – to Mother: We are at last in the middle of an actual battle. When I wrote my last letter we were waiting for some mines to go up under the Bosch trenches. They have gone up now and our men are over the parapet. The mines shook the whole earth.

I was sent to an artillery observation post where I now am to observe our line. It was rotten coming here. The shells were bursting a good bit, not very near. The ground, very sticky and I did not know where the post was to 100 yards. I got into an old dugout halfway along and got my breath. Afterwards I saw a man move and made for him and got here.

We are as usual just on the edge and getting very little. The noise is tremendous. Every now and then there is a sudden pause like when everyone stops talking in a room.

We have just seen the CO walk across the open to another observation post. People keep streaming down over it. I suppose they are wounded, walking cases.

27 March 1916 – to Mother: We have just come through part of a battle... It started 4am this morning with our sending up mines...

The Germans bombarded the captured positions heavily this afternoon... I have never seen anything like today's bombardment. The landscape going up in great fogs of smoke, huge bits going up like mines, bursts along the ground, trees falling, ruins smoking, black, green, blue, yellow and white smoke in the air.

So far I am very perky.

29 March 1916 – to Mother: I think my best work for this battalion has been done in getting material to which we weren't entitled. There was the lorry I got hold of in the first rest when I collared ten tons of stuff and went about 70 miles. Also, the three lorry loads of timber in our camp when we were just going to the trenches in November.

2 April 1916 – to Mother: We are still in and having rather a rough time, but so far I am all right ...

We have just had 2,000 shells dropped here in ¾ hour, a new experience which we are not anxious to repeat. The dugout rocked from side to side with explosives, fortunately not hit direct it will stand anything else.

We are still inside. They keep sending shrapnel over to catch our stretcher squads, so we can only wait. We don't know what damage or casualties we have had. I am not keen on going down for rations tonight.

Bowie has gone out now to find out the damage; they keep sending them over.

A General was in at the time.

Sirsh, crack, thud, bump, bang, whistle.

We are now timing the intervals between the shells. A shell is now due – its come – 20 seconds late. They are coming every two and a quarter minutes. We have had five since I wrote the above ...

It is curious to speak on the telephone to people who are quite safe. They ring us up every few minutes to ask how we are.

On 4 April 1916 – he writes a telegram home saying he is coming home on leave. The next sequence of letters begin on 21 June 1916.

21 June 1916 – to Mother: Arrived at the port. Have got to go to the base before going to battalion.

21 June 1916 – to Mother: This is a big wilderness of tents where we wait for orders ... I seem to have made the usual mess over my packing. I have left my air pillow behind, I think it is on Roger's bed. That boot was in my valise, I am sending it back. I am orderly officer on Friday so I shall have plenty of time then to write home.

30 June 1916 – to Mother: It has been raining today so we have had a much needed day to devote to Company matters such as boots, hair cutting, greasing the tools etc. It wants constant attention to keep all these things up to date. I gave them lectures for about an hour but they can't sit and absorb knowledge indefinitely.

We have a kitten here CO rescued from a dug-out partly destroyed when we were in the line. No one knows its parentage, it was about four weeks old when found. He is very fond of animals.

He is getting very tired I think. I am sorry for him. He is always working and comes in at night quite exhausted.

2 July 1916 – to Mother: The Colonel is sleeping in a beautiful house in the middle of a rose garden. He has an ante room and a dressing room. He says, he sees, I imagine – as I do – that as long as the CO is comfortable he won't worry too much about the battalion.

4 July 1916 – to Mother: I have not had time to write you a long letter before as I have two new jobs. Captain Marey has got a job in England and I am in command of HQ Company. This is not quite the same as an ordinary company command as it is not a company but consists of bombers, pioneers, snipers, signallers, orderlies, clerks, police and all the oddments. It has more men than any other company and is really I think more difficult. We have no travelling cooker and have to borrow the other companies' dixies. Also, they are always widely separated and as it includes Battalion HQ, we are not so independent.

Secondly, I am now Battalion Billeting Officer. Yesterday we had no cycles available and I got a message when the brigade was on the march to go forward. The column is over two miles long so it was pretty hot catching the head of it up. When there I borrowed a cycle and got into this village about twenty minutes ahead of this brigade.

12 July 1916 – to Father: I want some more batteries please for the lamp. We are living in the middle of the guns. I find it rather trying when walking along a road to have a really big gun belch out apparently straight for you. It is not very comforting to know that the rise of the shell has been calculated to clear a mounted man. Apart from the bang, the flame is very alarming.

For the next week I shall be acting as a sort of Orderly Officer to the Second in Command so that if for any reason it was needed the Second could take command with me as his Adjutant. I have been round several Hun lines, the trenches

Michael Dell in uniform, c.1915

are beautiful especially their dugouts. The noise has been practically continuous since we came here nearly a week ago. Several times a day (and chiefly at night) it suddenly increases till it is quite deafening.

On 13 July 1916 Michael Dell wrote his last letter home to his Mother. The letter was received on 18 July.

'Enclosed please forward. We are just going off for the big thing. I am glad to have come through to see it. Don't worry, I shall do my best and feel sure I shall come through. Everyone is happy. We have a glorious chance in front of us. It is a fine evening, rain has threatened a lot but has fortunately held off. We are all in Tommy's tunics. All your parcels have just come, Froissart from the aunts, ointment, etc.

Goodbye, L Michael Dell'

14 July 1916 – The Battle of Bazentin Ridge

On Friday 14 July 1916, just thirteen days after the opening of the Somme Offensive, the British Fourth Army launched an attack on the German front and second lines along the Bazentin Ridge which comprised a number of woods. In the early hours of the 14th the attack was launched, but this is where Louis Michael Dell's war ended. On 17 July P. Erskine Lee of the 7th Battalion KSLI, wrote to Michael's mother:

'Dear Mrs Dell,

In the great attack of last Friday morning I lost a great friend, and you, a son. Your loss is infinitely greater than mine and I beg you to accept my sincere sympathy. Your son was brilliant in every way and he was always ready at every emergency. He took over the Headquarters' Company a few days before the attack and no detail was missed by him in the organisation of a company of specialists.

He was my tent companion for a long time and I saw a lot of him, so that you may understand how I feel. The wire before the trenches we had to take was not cut and in the attempt to get round he was killed instantaneously. His body was found and he was buried on the field of battle. I am sorry to say that a large number of old friends have been killed or seriously wounded, but their sacrifice has not been in vain. The trenches were taken, we have been able to let the cavalry go through and so start what looks like the final phase of the war. The men loved your son, his life has not been in vain; but we miss him and will still more do so. Please accept on behalf of those who remain our heartfelt sympathy.

From, Yours very faithfully, P. Erskine Lee C.F.'

References

1 The letters of Louis Michael Dell are reproduced with the kind permission of David Dell, son of Montague Roger Dell. The letters are deposited in the National Army Museum, Chelsea accession number 2002-02-1372: 01-04 consecutively.

'Soliloquy in Flanders II'

By Richard Hagen (aka Michael Dell)

The *Saturday Westminster Gazette*, 29 January 1916

[The scene is Flanders, fire trench Z 56 Bay 40[1], which an intelligent general officer will recognise as Sheet 101 W95 A1–4[2]. Private Smith is discovered toasting cheese on a brazier. He is wearing gum-boots, thigh[3], a greatcoat cut off round the hips and a steel helmet.]

Private Smith: Remember Belgium! When you've put the place, the whole of blooming Belgium into sandbags, Oo's likely to forget it? Kept awake all night by silent Sue[4]. With Grandmother[5], Mother[6] and Percy[7] giving you cold feet. For fear they'd drop some short. A gas wind, too

Enter Sergeant Jones: He puts out the Brazier as it is making too much smoke. Exit Sergeant Jones. Private Smith makes no comment but commences eating warm cheese and biscuit.

Continues: No milk today. Hardly enough fresh meat for two platoons among the company. Bully again. Bread damp and these damn baths.[8] Sending me socks with holes in. Charcoal short, No AFB[9] to cook with. What's the jam? Apricot! Strewth. Four days on apricot.

[He skilfully builds the apricot and bully beef tins into the fire step, which is built solid of unopened tins of bully beef and apricot jam.]

Now that's a puckha[10] fire step, I don't think. I wish these sappers[11] knew enough to lay a duckboard[12] – takes a soldier to do that. Old Fritz[13] has got the wind[14] up properly, what with his lights and rapid and MG, he can't make out why we don't say a word. Here's a stripe going for the first live Hun. And all the Dutchmen sit tight in their trench and loose off rapid. Why the suicides.[15] Have had no luck this week, not reached their wire. 'Ullo, 'ullo, the Purple Emperor.[16]

The GOC Brigade and staff pass through the bay. Private Smith 'sits to attention.'

Sporting old boy, I wish he'd change his hat, or keep his head down as he goes along. We'll have no ordinary strafe[17] just now.

I shall be glad when we get back to rest,* though what's the use? The beer so watery, you can't get drunk as these ere testaments.[18] O Gosh, I'm tired; my feet so soft and all with these old boots. Wonder if we shall have some empties,[19] or if we shall have to march. I can't march with these blame verocious[20] veins. We've had a cushy[21] time considering the trenches are so cutcha.[22]

[Shelling commences on the right] Morning hate.

Good job it's only on D Company. That was a lovely burst that whiz-bang[23] made right over the CT and woolly bears,[24] by jove and swelp me there's a proper crump.[25] Oo-er, that's near. The swine, I always thought they couldn't touch us here.

[A sharp whistle, followed by a loud bang. The parapet is blown in and the bay filled with smoke. As it clears Private Smith is picking himself up. He thoughtfully regards his forearm, which is sticking out of his sleeve.]

I'm blowed, A Blighty[26] one. Thank God for that. [Exit towards Stretcher Bearer's dugout.]

* Rest – A term applied to a period of fatigues between two tours of duty in the trenches. Derivation unknown unless from association of opposites (Staff dialect).

References

1 Method of labelling trenches.
2 Map reference of same place.
3 Sewer boots – AOC. dialect.
4 Silent Sue – Long Range Gun. When near the target no sound is heard until the shell suddenly bursts. When between gun and target noise made like a Tube Train.
5 Grandmother – The largest size gun. Derivation unknown.
6 Mother – Smaller ditto.
7 Percy – Naval Gun. After Admiral Sir Percy Scott.
8 The Divisional baths supply every soldier with dry socks daily.
9 AFB Anti-Frost Bite grease supplied by Medical Service. An excellent substitute for a Tommy's Cooker.
10 Puckha – Hindustani: well built.
11 Sappers – Infantry divide the fighting arms into Gunners, Sappers and Soldiers.
12 Duckboard – Wooden grating walk laid in the trenches.
13 Names of our neighbours; N.B. This also applies to 'Hun' and 'Dutchmen'
14 Wind – Frightened men pant, hence are windy.
15 Suicides – The Grenadier and Sniping officers.
16 Purple Emperor – GOC – Brigade. (Number censored).
17 Strafe – German 'punish' Slight bombardment.
18 Testaments–Fr. 'Estaminets,' small wine shop.
19 MT – Mechanical Transport. Invariably found empty, especially by troops marching.
20 Verocious veins – self diagnosis often advanced as reason for not marching.
21 Cushy – Easy, soft.
22 Cutcha – Hindustani: shoddy.
23 Whizz-Bang. – Light field-gun shell. Onomatopoeic.
24 Woolly bears. – Shell bursting with thick woolly yellow smoke.
25 Crump. – Large high-explosive shell.
26 Blighty. – Bolighty: Hindustani: Europe, hence England.

William Frank Godfrey

(Emanuel 1909–1914)

'By his example he made life easier for others'

William Frank Godfrey lived at 32 Bramfield Road, Battersea, a short distance from Emanuel School where he attended between 1909 and 1914.

In the last summer of peace before the outbreak of war we read in the Howe House cricket notes from *The Portcullis* that, 'Some good hard hitting was done by Godfrey...' He also gained special praise 'for the hard work in which he worked for the House in the team race' during the House athletics competition. He also took the young platoon of 'budding warriors' under his command as a Company Sergeant Major in the Emanuel OTC.

On 21 September 1914 young Frank made an application to the War Office writing, 'I desire to be considered for appointment to a temporary commission in the Regular Army.'[1] He was recommended for the Royal West Surrey Regiment but received a Commission in the 4th Battalion The North Staffordshire Regiment. Like so many of his contemporaries Frank had walked out of the Emanuel School gates and within a few weeks straight into the army. A local newspaper noted, 'From the outset he perceived the struggle would be severe and prolonged, and realised that it would require each and all to give of their best. He could not resist the call of Empire in its hour of peril and grave anxiety...'

Frank's letters were reprinted in *The Portcullis* during his time on the Western Front. All the original First World War letters have since been lost and so we owe a debt of gratitude to those OEs who reprinted OE correspondence

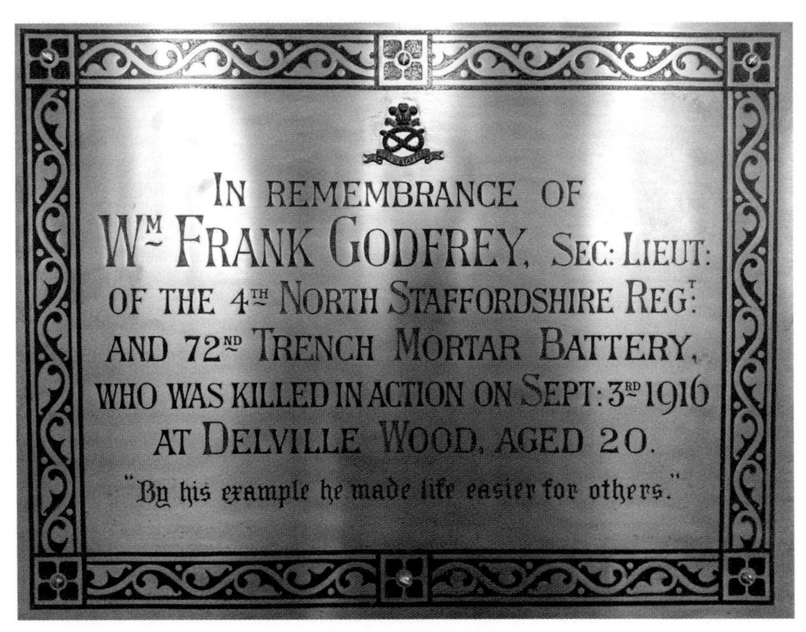

W. F. Godfrey's Memorial Plaque in the Emanuel School Chapel

in the School magazine, for without them we wouldn't have these precious vignettes of how Emanuel boys saw their experiences. Although letters were censored they still offer important information on the experiences of the war.

Letter: Summer Term 1915

W. F. Godfrey, Esq.,
"B" Coy. 1st Nth. Staffs. Regt.,
17th Brigade, 8th Div. B.E.F.

I was first under rifle fire when in charge of a fatigue party making a communication trench, but nobody was hit. The starlights which are thrown in order to see what the enemy are up to, produce very pretty effects at night, and it is entirely by means of these that the fire is directed.

My first two days were in the support trenches, but since then I have been in the fire trenches and so far have only lost two men out of my platoon, both wounded by snipers.

On the whole the work out here is very interesting and one cannot help being fascinated with it.

Regarding aircraft the activity is entirely on one side, only once have I seen a German aeroplane and he made off rapidly when one of ours came in sight. Our men are extremely daring in the way they utterly disregard the German anti-aircraft guns.

We are billeted in the sixth line of trenches, which is on the bank of a canal. Even that is a perfect heaven to where I am now, as my company occupies a very advanced part of the line round a small village, which has been shelled until it is little more than a heap of bricks and a few walls, the mud is nearly knee deep in places. There are very few dugouts and those there are, are of a very inferior quality. Mine measures two feet high by three feet square.[2]

Frank's next letter discusses the issue of not having had rest and his tone has changed in the course of a few months showing the effects of what long spells at the Front could do to morale.

Letter: Christmas Term 1915

For some time past the rumour has gone round each time that we came out of the trenches that we were going well back for a three weeks' rest, but so far this rumour has never materialised, and now we are about the only division at the Front that has not been to a rest camp since it has been here. For some reason best known to higher authorities, we are leaving the trenches tonight, instead of Sunday next, by which time our twelve days would have been completed. Needless to say, rumours are rampant. Suggestions are that Arras, Hooge, Archangel, India, or our three weeks' rest are in sight – nobody knows. Anyway, it is a wet night, and I would far rather be going out of than into the trenches, even if we go to a bivouac of leaky tents in a wood.

I am pleased to say that I. A. While and H. B. Ryley are still going strong, in fact are thriving on the air of Flanders. I wish Emanuel all good luck when next term commences.

By the time Frank was fighting on the Somme in the summer of 1916 he was with the 4th Battalion The North Staffordshire Regiment and was attached to the 72nd Trench Mortar Battery. The tone of the second letter suggests that he was battle weary and work with the Mortar Battery would no doubt have added to this feeling. We next hear of him in the Christmas Term *Portcullis* where in the Howe House notes we read, 'It was with the deepest regret, that we heard of the death in action of Second Lt. W. F. Godfrey. He was a Company-Sergt.-Major to the Corps, and in that position, as in all others, he worked untiringly for his School and House. To his bereaved parents we all offer our sincere sympathy, knowing that their loss is his great gain.'[3]

Within the space of one week, Frank, Harold Buchanan Ryley Junior and Ivor Austin While, all OEs and all in The North Staffordshire Regiment, had been killed in action in the Battle of the Somme. Frank was killed by the explosion of a shell on 3 September 1916 a few weeks after his twentieth birthday.[4] He was in action at Delville Wood on the last day of the battle of the same name. Frank would have seen Delville Wood as a desolate landscape, having been scarred by heavy shelling in the previous months.

Frank's Captain remembered him, 'He was always cheerful, even under the most adverse conditions, and was recognised by his senior officers as very plucky indeed.'[5] His Chaplain noted, 'He was one of those who, by his example, made life easier for others.'[6]

The *South Western Star* article continued its commentary:

> A truer epitaph of his life cannot be written, as he never spared himself in his unselfish devotion to everything worthy and inspiring. He will be sadly missed by all who knew him, and the memory of his splendid character and really lovable disposition will long remain.[7]

Frank wouldn't walk through the doors of 32 Bramfield again but his parents and elder sister had to and one can only imagine the sense of loss they must have felt. The *South Western Star* put it just right with these lines:

> The debt that is owing to those young lives who answered the first call, can never be measured. They gave themselves ungrudgingly, and sacrificed all to ensure the eventual triumph of Right over Might. Among that gallant company of heroes, Second-Lieut. W. F. Godfrey truly earned an honoured place.

Today when one visits Frank's grave there is nothing but silence, but his memory is full of the life of a young man who was cruelly cut down in youth, having known only the serene surroundings of Emanuel School and the hellish French landscapes during war time on the Western Front. He is now remembered in the Emanuel School Chapel, at St Michael's Church, Bolingbroke Grove in addition to his name being inscribed on the St Mary Magdalene memorial, Trinity Road, Wandsworth Common.

References

1 Letter 21 September 1914 to the War Office, TNA, WO 339/27429 Lt. William Frank Godfrey
2 *The Portcullis*, No. 65, Summer Term, 1915, pp. 49-50
3 *The Portcullis*, No. 69, Christmas Term, 1916, p. 15
4 *The Portcullis*, No. 80, Trinity Term, 1920, p. 45
5 The *South Western Star*, 15 September, 1916, p. 5
6 Ibid.
7 Ibid.

War

The glowing orb, whose gleaming, golden rays
Light this dark earth, and measure all our days,
Arose one morn and ordered a review
Of all the worlds, to pay their homage due
To him, the Sun, for light and heat bestowed;
And, as he watched, his golden visage glowed
With love, until our own sphere passed his eyes,
And then in tones, whose sorrow shook the skies,
He spoke: "Oh, wretched earth!
Upon whose breast the Son of Man had birth,
Upon whose beauty He Himself hath smiled,
He loved it, when He dwelt there as a Child.
Oh, wretched Earth! Thy peoples, made to bless
The lands where only now dark wars oppress;
Through men, whose lust for power has made run red
With blood the streets where peaceful lives were led;
Cry out to God in agonies of sorrow,
And pray each night, "Let peace come with the morrow."
They little thought to hear of war's alarms,
Or live, as now, amid the clash of arms,
The roar of guns, the heralding of hate,
Or in surrounding ether meet their fate!"

Then, as the Earth its faces turned round again,
Shewing the battle-fields with all their slain,
The very angels, who in heaven did sing
Their praises to the great eternal King,
Came to the gates in all their countless throng,
And, shocked to silence, quite forgot their song.
Hoarser with anguish, almost like a moan,
The Sun's voice spoke again, – yet scarce a groan
Came through the space to listening earth below.
And still the tide of war did onward flow;
And the Angels wept!

A.W.S.

The Portcullis, Christmas 1917, p. 13

George Aubrey Lyward *(Emanuel 1905–1912)* and Geoffrey Cholerton Smith *(Emanuel 1906–1913)*

'And those our brothers – we shall not forget them'

'I can hardly write of those times. I lost one friend after another.'[1] So George Aubrey Lyward described the First World War. The War brought friendships to a sudden halt and for many, like George Lyward, they would last see best friends leaving for the Front, never to return. He wrote, 'Then came the first Great War – why does it have to be called that? The holidays were on and I always spent days at my old school with friends who had been there with me. We played fives and sat and talked. One day we found ourselves called upon to put on our OTC uniforms and guard the railway line against spies. It was not many months before most of those I was with then were dead and buried – more poppies.'[2] Lyward described the impact it had upon him, 'In other words I lost many of my friends within months of those days when we sat together in school. I managed to make suitable comments until the day when one of the dearest of them was reported killed. A common friend came to our front door with the news and I burst into sobbing and was comforted by my mother who must have wondered how I had managed to weep – it may well have been the first and last time for many years.'[3] The impact upon George was strong for he wrote two poems about war. From a humble background George Lyward became a revolutionary educationalist, gaining a choral scholarship to St John's College, Cambridge. In the 1930s he founded Finchden Manor, a school for troubled teenage boys, which featured in BBC Radio Four's *Great Lives* series in 2012.[4] He was awarded the OBE in 1970, a short time before his death. Attending Emanuel before the war he knew many of those who were killed in action and when Harold Buchanan Ryley was killed in Palestine, Lyward wrote his obituary notice in *The Portcullis*.

George Aubrey Lyward

He went from Emanuel into teaching and then returned to Emanuel twice as a master. The Old Emanuel Association had suspended its activities in 1914 but with Lyward's assistance as Joint Secretary the Old Emanuel 1915 Society was established with OEs attending on leave from the Front. Lyward was a member of the Emanuel OTC and continued in the corps at other establishments. However, he did not serve in the war for as he described in his autobiography, 'Then conscription came. I was called up for medical examination at Kingston's cold, dreary public swimming baths. I remember going down on my knees and praying for courage – not in the baths, but the night before! They rejected me because of the foot I had injured in 1912 and they gave me a khaki armlet to show that I had attested.'[5] The death of one Emanuel friend, Geoffrey Cholerton Smith, stirred Lyward to write a poem in his memory titled ***G.C.S.***

G.C.S.

'Of Such is the Kingdom'

So young he was, yet dare we call him boy
Who himself dared so greatly, yearned to climb,
Higher, to taste all unalloyed the joy,
Of self forgot In faithfulness sublime?
We blamed him, praised him, for that mighty longing
That burning thirst which bade him drink so deep –
Still on his course he kept, and thronging, thronging,
The visions came, he followed, shall we weep?
Because he followed – mourn a faith that shone
Clear and unshaken? He who ne'er could tell,
The half of all he felt, now calls us on,
With no uncertain voice, a man he fell,
And falling rose to heights of finer joy,
A leader still and therefore still a boy.[6]

Geoffrey Cholerton Smith (seated centre)

Lt. Geoffrey Cholerton Smith

Geoffrey was a keen cricketer at School and from the Summer Term *Portcullis* of 1913 we learn that he was, 'A hard-working Vice-Captain and secretary. As a player his strong defence has been invaluable to the side...'[7]

Lt. Geoffrey Cholerton Smith obtained his commission in the Army Service Corps, before being attached to the Royal Flying Corps in which he was an observer. Living at 11 Magdalene Road, Wandsworth Common, both he and his brother attended Emanuel. Geoffrey was a member of the Emanuel OTC, entering Sandhurst in 1915. In September 1915 he made the journey to the Front where, being attached to the trench mortars of the Second Division, he saw action in the Battle of the Somme and won a Military Cross for gallant conduct at Delville Wood. His citation in the *London Gazette* reads:

> For conspicuous gallantry during operations. He assisted another officer with the guns in a very exposed position, until all the ammunition was expended. Together they then tended the wounded, and arranged carrying parties under very heavy shell fire.[8]

Geoffrey transferred to 6 Squadron RFC in April 1917, the squadron's motto being, 'The eyes of the Army'. The motto was appropriate for Geoffrey was an observer in which capacity he would have had various duties dependent on his squadron's briefing. Generally observers located the position of German batteries and reported back to either headquarters or the artillery in order for them to fire upon these locations. An observer would also have had to have taken command of a machine gun, typically a Lewis gun in RE8s, (Reconnaissance Experimental No. 8), a two seater aircraft which 6 Squadron were flying in the summer of 1917. On 31 July 1917, the opening of The Third Battle of Ypres, otherwise known as the first day of the Battle of Passchendaele, the weather was against observation due to low lying cloud and rain but flying in an RE8, Serial No A111, twenty-year-old Geoffrey and his pilot H. J. Snowden, also aged twenty, were first up. Having to fly low due to the weather conditions, both were wounded when hit by ground machine gun fire over German lines at Messines. *The Portcullis* later reported that, 'He managed to reach headquarters, and give his information, but the severity of his injuries overcame him and he died.'[9] He died of gun shot wounds to the chest in No. 3 Canadian Casualty Clearing Station and is buried in Lijssenthoek Military Cemetery, grave reference XIV – A – 10. Geoffrey's pilot was taken back to England for treatment but died eleven days later and is buried in Hampstead Cemetery grave reference WB. 567.

Descriptions of the Battle of Passchendaele are similar to those of the biblical Hell and it was an Emanuel boy who had a panoramic view of its opening day. A year earlier Lyward had been stirred by the Battle of the Somme to write an *In Memoriam* to Emanuel's fallen. Full of classical imagery it tells a story of a war that, although modern, was as old as any conflict and could easily be taken as referring to the battles of ancient Greece and Rome.

In Memoriam

"Now is it Rome indeed, and room enough"
Light of heart they who bounded up the field,
And we who watched them said the pace was killing.
Few they who found it theirs to give – or yield
(Save to a better man, and then not willing).
Men in the making, what had the game to give
To you, that made it ever worth the fighting;
Made all the story of those days to live
Though never a note of song, nor word of writing?
Full many a joy there was, but best of all,
A sense of room enough to breathe, to slay
Fear, and to laugh outright and scorn the fall
And rising dash like mad into the fray.

Many of those then with you since have caught
A glimpse of the self-same joy, when from the pages
Whereon were scribed the best of human thought,
They found the power and freedom of the sages
Who came, by trial and frequent bitter strife,
To lofty heights whence, with a vision clear,
And room enough to scan the whole of life,
They might defy the tyrant and hold dear
To truth. These many, one by one, recall
The days when blind obedience was their chance,
'Ere they had strength to scale the mountain tall,
And looked on life with trembling, all askance.

"No room to breathe, to pour out of our best!"
To call this peace was but to give the lie
To man's divinest longings, and to rest
Upon the mere material things, and die.
"Life is so cramped," we heard the millions cry,
Yet we were powerless too – and passed them by.

Man ever strives his chains to burst asunder,
Restless for room enough; his deepest shame,
Falseness to infinite self; then, Mother wonder
Not that thy sons bear part in this grim game
Of war; for those who thus have sought with duty
Freedom indeed to stand by an ideal
Grieve not, for they it is who know the beauty
Of days without the false, intensely real.
And those our brothers – we shall not forget them
Who sighed for room enough and earned it well;
Free now from all that here so sorely let them,
Still are they thine to love, Emanuel.[10]

by G.A.L. (George Lyward),
The Portcullis, Summer Term 1916, pp.8–9.

George Lyward (second from left) with other Emanuel Prefects 1911–1912

George Lyward's Coat of Arms

References

1 G. A. Lyward, *George Lyward: His Autobiography*, (2009), p. 54.
2 Ibid. pp. 41–42.
3 Ibid. p. 35.
4 http://www.bbc.co.uk/programmes/b01gg7g0.
5 *Lyward: His Autobiography*, p. 49.
6 *The Portcullis*, No. 72, Christmas Term, 1917, p. 55.
7 *The Portcullis*, No. 59, Summer Term, 1913, p. 42.
8 Supplement to the *London Gazette*, 20 October 1916, 10191.
9 *The Portcullis*, No. 72, Christmas Term, 1917, pp. 50–51.
10 Scott-Giles, *History of Emanuel*, pp. 214–215.

Hitting them for Six

Alfred Eric 'Titus' Titley *(Emanuel 1909–1916)*

Eric Titley was a master batsman at Emanuel. His legendary status warranted mention in a poem in *The Portcullis*:

> Not far behind strolls Titus, all aglow,
> His sunny visage wreathed in merry smiles
> From scoring centuries against the foe
> He now returns to snooze beneath the tiles

At School he was Captain of Boxing, Cricket and Fives. But it was cricket in which his talents shone through. In 1915 he won two records for the School, the first by scoring 979 runs in the season and the second winning the highest individual score by an Emanuel boy to that date with 157. His cricket critique eulogised his abilities, 'He has done more brilliantly than was ever anticipated from last season. His style is free and he has cultivated since the beginning of the season a good 'forward glide' on the leg side which makes his batting yet more attractive.' With the stresses of being Captain, his 1916 season was not as good as 1915. Aside from his sporting prowess he inspired younger Emanuel boys, and one in particular, Jack Grundy, who later became Headmaster, remembered in his autobiography:

> Now the climacteric of a boy's life does not perforce fall in the final years of privilege and prizes, but often at an earlier moment when he first feels minutely part of something larger than himself or his family, catches the first whispers of the place around him and takes root. The revelation may take a term or a year or an instant; it may be seen or missed. To me it came from Eric Titley and giant Edmund Fisher, already heroes of the public schools' athletics and rugby contests. To minnows like me they were Tritons and I never forgot how each of these great men sought me out with a word of condolence after my eldest brother (Cecil Grundy) was killed in France.

Eric at the crease on the Emanuel School pitch

Jack Grundy, who never forgot his boyhood hero, named the School's Fives Courts in honour of Eric. By the time the courts were opened in the summer of 1963 Eric had recently succumbed to cancer and they were unveiled by his widow on Flannels Day. After his death a plaque was erected in the School chapel in his memory.

Even gifted sportsmen have their faults and Eric was remembered, somewhat dubiously, for hitting a six through the chapel window. This fine cricket player was also a great academic and he won a scholarship to St John's College

Cambridge to study science, but after war service he decided to study French and German instead.

Eric left School in 1916 and was commissioned as a second lieutenant in the 2nd Battalion, the Devonshire Regiment. In 1917 he saw action in the Battle of Passchendaele but a few days before the opening of that battle he was involved in a raid on a German trench as the Devonshire Regimental history records:

Emanuel School prefects, 1915. Back Row (left to right) A.E. Titley, C. Delaforce, E. Fisher, J.C. Hopkins Front Row (left to right) H.O. While, (Sergt.), S.J.H. Balchin (Capt.), F. Shirley Goodwin (Headmaster), P.G. Page, (Lieut.), F.T. Pope (Sergt.)

> On the evening of July 26th, the battalion carried out a small enterprise: 2nd Lieut. Titley and two sections raiding Identity Trench just North of the Bellewaerde Farm. They entered the front line successfully, but found it unoccupied and little more than knee-deep. The Germans however, were holding their second line, Identity Support, in considerable strength and opened a brisk fire. The raiders replied, apparently with effect, but 2nd-Lieut. Titley, rightly considering that to push on would be useless, withdrew his men with only two casualties.

Eric subsequently saw action at Third Ypres, (Battle of Passchendaele). There is no surviving documentation recording Eric's personal experiences during the battle.

In 1918 Eric saw action during the German Offensive in March and was awarded the Military Cross. The description of this action was described in a certificate for Gallant Conduct and Devotion to Duty:

> At Moreuil Wood on 31st March, the enemy broke through the troops on the left of the 2nd Devonshire Regt and turned the flank of the battalion.
>
> Captain Titley, although his company was heavily engaged with the enemy, held his ground and formed a defensive pivot upon which the remainder of the battalion was able to form up and to be established intact in a strong position.
>
> This officer commanded his company under very heavy shell fire with the utmost bravery, going from post to post, keeping the enemy back and covering the movements of the other companies.

Eric was subsequently wounded on 25 April 1918 at Villers-Bretonneaux, a manufacturing town of some five thousand inhabitants who, except for one old lady, had fled the oncoming German troops. The 2nd Battalion Devonshire Regiment with other County Regiments and Australian Brigades successfully defeated the German troops but during fierce fighting Eric was shot in the elbow and was hospitalised. A few weeks later Eric's mother received a letter from a friend who thought Eric had been killed. They wrote, '...we must firmly believe that the promise of his youth is being fulfilled in the world beyond.' Indeed the 'promise of his youth' was being fulfilled but the world beyond was a cricket pitch! Eric wrote to the School from Eastbourne on 27 August 1918:

> My old arm is getting much stronger, but it is still rather crooked. I can still get some runs though. My highest, as yet, was 111 'not' a fortnight ago against a Canadian Battalion. I managed to get 52 today against Hastings RAF Cadet Wing.

After the war Eric became a House Master and English teacher at Marlborough College for 28 years, influencing a young John Betjeman, who later became the Poet Laureate. Years after leaving Marlborough, Betjeman visited Eric when he was ill and brought with him a packet of Spangles, a popular variety of boiled sweets made between the 1950s and the 1980s.

In the 1930s Eric was in charge of the OTC at Marlborough. He influenced many of the young officers who trained under him and who later joined various regiments during the Second World War. Eric and his wife Betty despaired at the waste of the young lives, of those they had cared for, as they were killed during the war.

Interior of a barracks in which Eric lived

Eric took charge of the South-West travelling wing of the War Office Home Guard School leaving his wife Betty to look after a house of sixty schoolboys. One Marlborough boy later remembered Betty was, 'a tremendous solace to so many boys and stood out like a beacon in the dark days of the war.' As part of his work in the travelling wing Eric gave lectures and demonstrations to various Home Guard units, including making and detonating bombs.

Eric left Marlborough in 1950 joining the Ministry of Education but in 1953 was diagnosed with cancer. After his death in 1961, he was awarded the Chevalier de la Legion d'Honneur for services to Franco-British education. The medal was presented to his wife Betty.

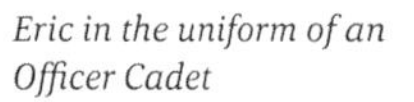

Eric in the uniform of an Officer Cadet

Eric (back row, first from left) with Officers of the Devonshire Regiment 1917

With the East Surreys

Frank Glover MC and Bar

(Emanuel 1910–1915)

Frank Glover was a Sergeant in the Emanuel OTC. A few months after leaving Emanuel he enlisted in the East Surrey Regiment. He and his family at this time lived in 'Athelstan', 37 Lavender Gardens, Clapham Common and interestingly this was the house occupied by John Burns MP and his OE son Edgar before Frank's family bought the house.

Frank served for three years on both the Western Front and in Italy. Initially joining the 4th Battalion between 14 December 1915 and 30 September 1916 Frank transferred to the 1st Battalion East Surrey Regiment from 30 September 1916 to 28 August 1918. Whilst serving Frank wrote nine manuscript diaries expressing his personal thoughts about the battles he fought in, the places he visited and the people he met. His surviving diaries, intelligence reports and documents provide a rich source for understanding the varied experiences of an infantry officer in the First World War.

Frank's brothers also served in the First World War. In a letter addressed to Frank on 14 December 1915 his brother Horace wrote:

> My Dear brother Frank,
>
> Thanks so very much for your cheery letter which reached me tonight. I was awfully pleased to hear that you were enjoying your training and glad to note your enthusiasm.
>
> No old man, there is nothing I am in need of but I very much

appreciate the thought. Found your marching song highly amusing. One takes many of that type even out here, for when one gets away from the firing line, a 'yell' helps things along.

Forgive so short a note and I have only a minute or two to spare. Very best wishes, your affectionate brother. Horace.[1]

Horace was killed in action five days after writing this letter. It was another 21 months before Frank got the opportunity of visiting his brother's grave. He confided to his diary:

'I found Horace's grave in the little shell-swept cemetery 50 yards from the ruins of the village which borders the main Ypres Road. He is buried among many others of his regiment in about the only corner of the cemetery which has not been destroyed by shells and over his grave is a plain wooden cross with a metal tablet affixed bearing the badge, a portcullis, at the top and underneath RFM H. A. Glover 3910 19th Dec 1915 Dulce Et Decorum Est Pro Patria Mori RIP. A major of his battalion (N.B. Tyrwhitt) killed on 28th Dec 15 is buried in the next grave but one. Along the road is the never ending stream of traffic toward the line. The call of the 'push."[2]

Between April and May 1917 Frank wrote of his impressions as the Allies launched the Battle of Arras. He describes the scenes on Vimy Ridge a few days after the Canadians had captured it, giving an eye witness account of the horrific scenes and the inclement weather the soldiers were fighting in. He also paints the scene of destruction wrought on the town of Arras. It is to be noted that in his diaries Frank misspells Mont St Eloi, the region North West of Arras but this has been corrected for the purposes of this book.

The Battle of Arras from the Reserve Lines

A note in Frank's diary: Vimy Ridge was taken on the 9th but we heard little or nothing of it. Zero hour was 5.30am.

8 and 9 April: A quiet morning and after lunch we fell in to continue our journey passing the starting point at 3.40pm. The march was very interesting and mostly along the main road to Mont St Eloi and in view of the forthcoming 'push' the traffic was tremendous and the road in parts much the worse for wear.

We arrived at our destination Bois Des Alleux (on the outskirts of Mont St Eloi about 9pm and our quarters huts in wood might have been worse. After a supper of sardines we all turned in and slept well until about 5am when the noise of the barrage on the Ridge (Vimy) woke us up. The wind was due west and so most of the noise was carried away from us. At 9am I had reconnoitred the road to La Targette and this took me through Mont St Eloi. I passed one batch of Bosche prisoners and several wounded. For the rest of the day there were streams of prisoners wounded and otherwise, our own casualties, motor ambulances and waggons. The Huns were in a bad state, covered with mud and looking very dejected. In all about 2,000 passed through. The batt. is expecting notice to move to the line at any moment.

It is rather cold but constant streams of traffic along the road and the many prisoners is very inspiring.

Mont St Eloi Church or rather the remains of it stand on a hill among the trees, a very pathetic sight.

This morning too, I saw one of our captive balloons break away, the observers descending in parachutes while the balloon disappeared into the clouds.

Tuesday 10 April: A quiet day. The weather is bad, snow and rain at intervals. We are still in the wood and passed the day at our ease expecting orders to move at any moment. The 13th Bde KOSBs, West Kents and Warwicks have taken a great part in the 'push' while we, as Corps reserve have yet our time to come. Our division is the only non-Canadian one in this corps.

Wednesday 11 April: Parades this morning and we endeavoured to do a little observation at La Motte Farm but the weather was unfavourable. Arras can be seen and many points on Vimy Ridge but these are not easily recognisable from the map. Plenty of snow and sleet while last night was frightfully cold in fact the weather has been anything but good for the fellows in the line.

Thursday 12 April: Parades as usual this morning. The weather is still very bad, much snow and rain.

Friday 13 April: Orders and counter-orders poured on us this morning but we eventually left Mont St Eloi for Cabaret Rouge. I came along with the details and our march was quite interesting. There were many dead horses by the roadside, victims of the frightful weather we have been having of late.

We occupied dug-outs which were quite comfortable though as usual full of rats and mice.

Saturday 14 April to Monday 16 April: Days spent in Cabaret Rouge dug-outs. During this time I tramped over the captured ground on Vimy Ridge. The earth was churned up in an incredible manner, the shell holes by the million, joining up and overlapping until not an inch of it was left untouched. There were not a tremendous number of 'stiffs' about an equal number Canadians and Huns. The front line trench I struck was not tremendously knocked in but was lined with dead 'cuffys.'

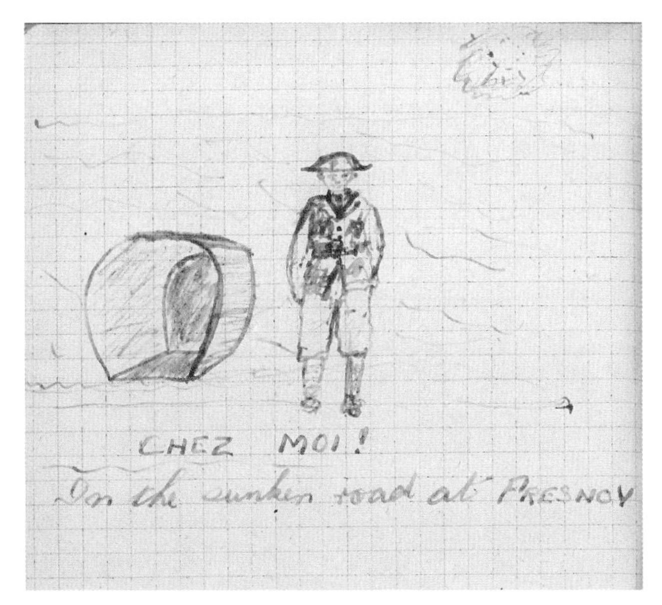

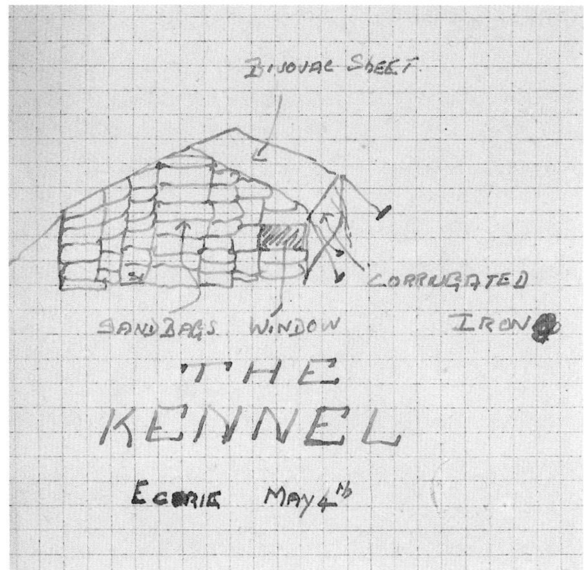

Sketches made by Frank Glover in his second diary

Tuesday 17 April: Had a fatigue starting at 5am at Souchez Dump and after standing about in the rain for four hours the whole thing was cancelled and we returned thoroughly wet without having done a stroke. Such is life!

On our way back the Huns put a few 4.2s across the road ahead and later at mess (lunch) one dropped on the roof of H.Q. and shook everything up. One also damaged the wheel of one of [the] cookers.

The battalion moved to the Quarries this afternoon and after waiting about for some time (during which it snowed furiously) all 'excess' officers were ordered to the transport Carency owing to the lack of accommodation. We arrived there, unexpectedly of course and then had to wait about until tents were procured which we pitched on ground sodden by months of rain. However we slept and in the morning I found the water had soaked through the straw on the ground and also the valise. What hopes!

Impressions of Arras

Monday 7 May: I visited Arras today. The town which has been a fine one is badly battered, the cathedral being but a huge mass of shattered masonry though one or two finely sculptured pillars and some of the finer walls still stand gaunt and pathetic to the sky. Quite a number of civilians still remain in the cellars of the town and numerous small shops are opened in the lower floors of the better preserved houses which an E.F.C. and a fine Pharmacy add to the interest of the place.

On 8 May 1917 the Germans attacked the British held positions at Fresnoy, North East of Saint-Quentin. Frank was in a reserve position but later that evening he heard of the loss of close friends. In his diary he describes the episode which proved catastrophic for the 1st Battalion East Surreys as, 'our glorious disaster.' [3]

Tuesday 8 May: Rumours of a big counter attack against our battalion and the 'Glosters' this morning and we went to the advanced Dressing Station to endeavour to gain some news from the wounded.

The battalion is to be relieved tonight and resting at Nine Elms until tomorrow two officers per Coy going up then to meet them.

[...] HQ Staff arrived about 10pm and then we learnt the full details of our glorious disaster.

Only one officer and about a hundred men (officers on HQ Staff excepted) came out of the show our casualties being about 550, all but one Lt. being lost.

Our line was in front of Fresnoy and the attack first took place at 3am, but this and the next one was beaten off with great enthusiasm. Then our fellows were faced with the greatest of all disasters. The Huns having broken through a battalion on our left they were on all sides and though our fellows fought and died like the heroes they were – they were simply swamped by sheer weight of numbers and practically annihilated. A few men escaped to the support line not many. They were great.

Of the officers one knows but little. Blackman, the finest fellow I ever knew was killed rallying his men, Sullivan was killed and of the others there is no news, though some were seen fighting to the last.

Summary of Snipers Reports

As an intelligence officer Frank had to report on enemy movements. He had to make detailed reports on any activity occurring in the German lines. What follows is one of his sniper's reports from 26 February 1917:

Enemy Movement

7.10am a man in a grey uniform soft cap with badge passing along a trench at A10c 30.07 was hit by our snipers.

7.15am a man in soft cap, with his rifle slung and using a stick was seen walking in the open towards the Canal examining telephone wires about A17c.

7.30am a German in a shrapnel helmet, who looked over Canal Trench at A16a 75.20 was hit.

7.45am Two men with a Dixie left a shelter at A10c 75.80 apparently a cookhouse as smoke was seen coming from it.

8.10am a man in grey uniform walked across the open and jumped into Canteleux Alley South about A17a 8.10.

8.30am Another man seen in the open about A17a.

9.15am a man in a grey uniform and soft cap appeared behind front parados of Bill Extension at A10c 30.12 exposed from his knees upwards. He was hit and toppled over.

2.15pm a man in peaked cap passed along Canal Trench (A16a 75.20).

2.30pm Hun with a white band to his cap seen in Canal Trench (A16a 75.20) walking up and down.

Seen again at 3.40pm.

4.15pm at (A16a 75.30) another German looked over.

Another seen at 5.30pm.

There is a day post at A10c 28.07 and a periscope is in use. Glimpses were seen throughout the day of the sentry's shrapnel helmet. At 5.10pm. he stood on the fire step... and our snipers fired hitting him in the helmet. He collapsed into the trench. Several of the enemy were seen in the mirror of the periscope round the spot, the periscope itself not being used for a quarter of an hour afterwards.

Smoke seen from front line trench at A16a 60.55.

An axe was in use in trench at A10c 35.02 at 4.40pm.

Third Battle of Ypres

On 1 October 1917 Frank describes the scenes a few days before the Battle of Broodseinde, which itself was part of the Third Battle of Ypres that opened on 31 July 1917:

95th Infantry Brigade Christmas card, 1916

'We arrived at brigade headquarters after a very nerve wracking journey through our guns which were all firing hard. There was scarcely a yard of ground which did not contain either a gun or an ammunition dump. Sanctuary Wood we found uncomfortable for the Bosche strafed it freely as we passed through. While waiting at brigade an aeroplane fight took place and a German plane with both wings shot off on one side and the engine still roaring came rushing down and burst into a vivid sheet of orange flame as it struck the ground where it continued to burn for the next half hour. The two detached wings floated down some five minutes after the machine itself had crashed. Battalion headquarters was eventually reached and proved to be a concrete structure just below the ground. While waiting for the CO to arrive the Bosche scored no fewer than seven direct hits on it with fairly heavy shells – but the place was so admirably constructed that beyond blowing out the candles and causing the roof to 'cushion' no damage was done.'

As so often the case death hung over the trenches but as Frank describes in one instance on 4 October it came upon captured prisoners:

Two Huns carrying down one of our men on a stretcher were knocked out by a shell which killed the man just outside Battalion Headquarters. The Bosche, both of whom were mortally wounded, we carried to shell holes and they were both dead next morning.

Summer 1918 – Military Cross and Bar

During the winter of 1917–1918 Frank spent five months in Italy in support of the Italians in the war against Austro-Hungarian forces, before returning to France in April 1918. In May 1918 Frank was awarded the Military Cross for intelligence work carried out in an attack on German trenches north of Merville by the River Bourre.[4] The citation reads:

> For conspicuous gallantry and devotion to duty. This officer, acting as intelligence officer before an attack worked day and night to secure information vital to its success. During the attack he advanced to the objective with the first wave, making a complete tour of the captured line and returned under heavy fire with a report to battalion headquarters. Later he several times crossed the danger zone to and from battalion headquarters, keeping them in touch with the situation. The next day he took over from the adjutant, who had become a casualty and most efficiently carried out his duties.

Frank spent his last week on the Western Front between the 20th and 27th of August 1918, but far from being restful it included what he described as, 'one of my most interesting days during the war.' Frank wrote about this week in his diary with the events of 21 August written in a separate account:

'Number 9 A rough diary while serving with the BEF. Written up on 23rd August 18 in the depths of a 60 foot Bosche dugout captured on the morning of the 21st on the outskirts of Achiet Le Petit.

Have reached 'Blighty' since penning the above so the closing pages of this diary are written in [the] comfort of 'Athelstan."

Sunday 18 August 1918: Rode into Doullens on a horse in the afternoon and had some inspiring cross-country counters 'en route'. While splashing about in my bath after tea I received news that the Bn is to move tonight and shortly after 8pm I was speeding to Doullens once more, this time on a cycle at the head of a billeting party.

The whole BDE is billeted in Doullens citadel so quarters are rather cramped. Officers are sleeping on the floor of an empty house though it was about 2am before the troops got settled in.

Monday 19 August 1918: All our marching is to be done after dark so in the evening I was once more on a cycle at the head of a billeting party making for Coigneux. This proved to be a somewhat battered village with but few inhabitants left and in a drizzling rain I fixed up the billets mainly due to the efforts of a veteran sergeant who had been billet-warden there for nearly three years.

Troops did not arrive until after 3am and it was dawn before any of us could get any sleep.

Tuesday 20 August 1918: On the move again at dusk after a very busy day of conferences and issuing maps. Our march took us right into assembly positions in front of Biezi Wood near Bucquoy which at zero we left to 'leap-frog' forward well into Bosche territory. The morning was terribly misty and though I did leave not HQRS until z+90 I soon found myself mixed up in the battle though the events of one of my most interesting days during the war is written in a separate account.

The Attack of 21 August 1918

'The artillery barrage commenced at 4.55am and Zero + 90. I left Bn HQRS (Keane Trench) and went forward with some snipers to gain touch with the attacking companies. A thick mist, however, made it impossible to see more than a few yards and when I reached the trench at L10C63 I found the Devon Bn HQRS and also "B" Coy of the East Surreys both completely lost. As it was impossible to find one's way across country I told Lt. Wilson (Commanding "B" Coy) to follow the wire of the trench running from L10A 5.0 to L17B 4.4 with his company, as this represented approximately the Right Boundary of the Bn. Sector. At the same time I sent back a message to Bn. HQRS (Appendix 1 attached) explaining the situation. No news could be gained of the front line companies as I went forward with "B" Coy to endeavour to get in touch with them.

At 9am we had reached L17B 0.7 where we came across Capt. Newington with two platoons of his company ("C") and four tanks of the 10th Bn, The Tanks Corps. There appeared to be no troops on our flanks, but the mist made it impossible to be certain of this, while apart from occasional bursts of MG fire there was no sign of the enemy. We therefore decided to push forward to the road W18C 1.8 to L1MD 3.1 and a message was sent back to Bn. HQRS to this effect. (App. 2) In order to prevent loss of direction the left tank was to follow the trench forming the left Bn ... the remainder being formed up in line with an interval as large as the poor visibility would permit (about 200 yds). As there was no sign of "A" Coy who were to have been the right attacking Coy of the E. Surreys I asked Lt. Wilson to get his company to follow the left tanks while Capt. D. Newington said he would follow with his

Coy ("C") the tanks on the right. The artillery barrage by this time had ceased so the success of the whole operation depended upon us getting forward with the tanks. The line was carried forward with little opposition until the sunken road in L17D was reached, but here the MG and rifle fire from the enemy about W18c 5.3 and also from the outskirts of Achiet Le Petit was rather intense for a short while, until the tanks had pushed forward to deal with these points.

The mist was beginning to lift by this time and a small party of Warwicks [were] on the left, so after a short pause in the advance to 'mop up' the Regimental HQRS and Wireless Station at L18c 7.3, the advance was continued down the hill and through the Nuts towards the final crest before the valley, in which the railway (Red Line) was situated was rushed. Unfortunately owing to the sudden clearing of the mist the Tanks came under direct fire from enemy Field Guns on the ridge SE of the Railway and in consequence could no longer keep a straight course. "B" and "C" companies therefore wandered off rather too much to the Right and were soon out of touch but a party of about thirty Devons, the East Surrey Snipers and a MKV Tank (J4) reached the crest overlooking the Railway, though the tank was immediately put out of action and MG fire across the valley from the enemy was particularly accurate. Further advance to the Red Line was impossible. The troops on our immediate left appeared well forward, but beyond the small party of the Devons referred to, none appeared to be up on our Right Flank.

Postcard showing the launch of a German observation balloon, 1916

A German Postcard 21 June 1917 in Frank's collection

I accordingly left some of my snipers on the ridge and went back to report to Bn HQRS which I found moving forward to the Wireless Station L18c 7.3.

Throughout the entire operation nothing was seen of either "A" or "D" Coys, who apparently lost direction during the first stage of the advance, eventually digging in about L23 Central.'

The Regimental history records Frank's role on 21 August:

'At noon, Lieut. F. P. J. Glover, the Battalion Intelligence Officer, returned to Battalion Headquarters and reported that six platoons had reached a line just short of their objective, the Arras–Albert railway north of Irles, that the enemy was still offering a stiff resistance and that a further advance without the aid of artillery or fresh tanks would be difficult. Most of the Tanks allotted to the Division had by this time broken down or been wrecked and the enemy was now beyond the range of the British field guns. At dusk strong patrols were pushed forward to the railway, but found it strongly held, and though they reached the embankment they could not establish themselves thereon. The patrols were therefore withdrawn and the Battalion threw out an outpost line for the night just short of the railway. During the day it had captured

95th Infantry Brigade Christmas Card, 1916

70 prisoners, nine machine guns, three trench mortars and one field gun.'[5]

For this action Frank won a Bar to his Military Cross. The citation reads:

> For conspicuous gallantry and initiative. As intelligence officer he went forward with the leading waves of an attack and when it was held up he organised flanking parties, which he moved at the same time as he delivered a frontal attack, capturing twelve machine guns and 70 prisoners. His personal courage, initiative and resource largely contributed to the success of the operation.

Frank continued his diary sitting at home in Battersea recollecting his last few days in France.

Wednesday 22 August 1918: A day of reorganisation in our newly won positions.

Thursday 23 August 1918: An early morning conference in the depths of the dugout and at 11am once more 'over the top', followed by a morning of quite thrilling battle. The 13th BDE exploited our initial success by carrying on through us.

What Frank does not describe in his own diary about the 'quite thrilling battle' is however recounted in the Regimental history:

'At 11 o'clock on the 23rd August the artillery barrage commenced and the Battalion advanced, "B" and "C" Companies leading, with "D" in support and "A" in reserve. The companies made rapid progress and soon reached the railway embankment, from which they drove back the enemy. A little later, "B" Company encountered strong opposition from a trench across its line of advance and was checked. Its rifles and Lewis guns, however, quickly established superiority of fire and led by Lieut. Glover and 2nd Lt. Wilson, the company rushed the trench and after a stiff bayonet fight overcame its numerous defenders. Nineteen machine guns were found in the trench, which was full of German dead.

By 11.35am the objective on the spur north-east of Irles had been taken and the companies were consolidating the captured trenches. It was a remarkable achievement and one that will be remembered with pride in the Regiment. In a little more than half an hour of hard fighting the Battalion had driven the enemy back 1000 yards and had captured 200 prisoners and 25 machine guns.'

Frank's diary continues:

Friday 24 August: A quiet day, though sounds of strife from Woupart Wood indicate the 13th are enjoying themselves. I wandered round our companies to say farewell to all the fellows for my transfer papers for the RAF have come through and I leave in the morning.

Saturday 25 August 1918: Said goodbye to the CO for the Bn. is moving forward again and with my servant and some loot (carried by a sniper) I made my way through swarms of traffic, along roads thick with dust to our transport lines at

An envelope addressed to Bryan Scurfield returned to Frank because Bryan had died in Greece

Bucquoy quite near our jumping off position on the morning of 21st. Had a wash and changed and then saying farewell to Pope and Poole I together with my servant and kit departed rearwards in the mess cart. Deserting later I eventually reached Authie, a village occupied by the dumped personnel of the whole division. Passed the night there.

Sunday 26 August: Boarded a lorry with my servant and kit about 9am and reached the railhead in good time for the leave train. Here I said farewell to Scriven my servant and made myself comfortable on the train (station was Authieul just before Doullens) which reached Boulogne in the afternoon. I put up at the Hotel De Paris.

Monday 27 August 1918: My efforts to get across by the morning boat were unsuccessful but I eventually reached London about 9.30pm and home soon after 10pm.

After two years of experiencing some of the toughest climates, witnessing death and destruction on unprecedented scales, Frank ended his diary in a cheerful tone, 'Thus ends the DIARY so far as it concerns the BEF a period filled with many happy memories during which I have met some of the best fellows in the world.' It is telling that despite the horrors of war it was the friendships forged under fire that mattered most to the men who fought the war.

Frank's experiences were religiously documented but it is the lighter side of his experiences which provide some interesting glimpses into leisure time activities in which he partook. Here are a few extracts from Frank's diary:

Friday 17 August 1917: ... Spent the afternoon in Boulogne having both dinner and tea there. There are some fine shops while the crowd is tremendously interesting consisting as it does of American 'Sammies', French, Australians, Canadians, Portugese, Tommies and [a] good sprinkling of French civilians.

Monday 20 August: Blighty is plainly visible from here this morning the jolly old white cliffs of Dover showing up through the heat haze. The weather remains simply splendid.

Tuesday 21 August: ... another fine day spent lazily. Left camp by bus at 2pm. Saw Banting (an OE) along the plage at Wimereux and left later for Boulogne.

Saturday 20 Oct 1917: Spent the morning on the summit of Mont Noir teaching the troops how to use a compass. Played in a 'Rugger' match in the afternoon BDE HQS v MGC. We were beaten 12–6 but I thoroughly enjoyed the game. [Next day Glover notes, 'I am still a little stiff after yesterday's game.']

Frank was transferred to the RAF on his return to England and remained with them until 1919. In the Second World War he was involved in the Home Guard and elsewhere in this book you can read one of his night duty reports during the Blitz.

'Be good darling – with love and kisses.': Bryan Scurfield *(Emanuel 1909–1915)*

Amongst Frank Glover's papers are two letters. The first is signed 'Be good darling –with love and kisses', but this was not from some sweetheart waiting at home. Instead it was written by Frank's Emanuel School friend, Bryan Scurfield. The teasing and gentle ribbing is apparent in both letters which were written with friendly affection. Like Frank, Bryan was a Sergeant in the Emanuel OTC. He also played football and cricket for his house and was a keen supporter of the OEA.

Bryan wrote to Frank in September 1916.

Letter from B. S. Scurfield 'Somewhere at Sea' 12/9/16

Dear F. P. J.

Just a line to tell you I am alive and kicking. I am having a jolly good time and enjoying myself immensely. The only flaw was when I had to sit down this morning and censor 200 letters which the men of my draft had written – still they were very amusing. It is getting very warm now...

We have had topping weather and I haven't felt a bit sick yet, so everything in the garden is lovely (why there isn't a garden here).

Well, I hope you are keeping away from Plymouth and generally leading a virtuous life. I don't know who will lead you in the way you should go now but I hope for the best.

The OC troops here is a priceless B.F. He wears an eyeglass...

We feed awfully well and I am sending a menu card to Capt. G. J. Y. S. but perhaps I will spare him.

I can't tell you any news because, for one thing, there isn't much to tell and for another I'm not allowed to tell it so – voila.

Well, having written all this bunkum with much labour and honest sweat I think it's about time I gave myself a holiday so I will lay aside my pen (some pen it is, too!)

Be good darling – with love and kisses from B. S.

p.s. Give my respects to the Macfadjeans when you see them.

Bryan served with the 2nd Battalion the East Surrey Regiment in Salonika. In September 1918 we learn that:

Lieuts. C. T. Wheeler and B. Scurfield and six other ranks commenced a course of training under the XVI Corps Intelligence Officer. These officers and men reconnoitred very carefully the ground in front of the Battalion, in order to take over the duty guiding the Cretan Division to the position from which it was to deliver an attack.[6]

It was during one of these reconnaissances that Bryan and Sergeant Powell captured a Bulgarian patrol of six men under a German officer. For this action Bryan won both the Military Cross and the Greek Military Medal, 4th Class. His MC citation reads:

He entered a house alone and found five enemy asleep in a room. Two of his patrol then came up and the enemy, after first showing fight, surrendered; but as they were being marched away, two more enemy appeared in the road and rushed at their captors. Lieut. Scurfield and a sergeant covered them and they also surrendered. The seven prisoners were then taken back to our lines.

'Athelstan'
37, Lavender Gdns.,
Clapham Common
S.W.11

8 IX 18.

My dear Scurfield,
I am certain I wrote the last letter, but refuse to argue on the subject. After all these years the only vision of you I can conjure up is that of a scraggy-bearded apparition, haunting the hills of Salonica, with a delapitated Sam Browne holding together a moth-eaten uniform, mainly composed of goat-skins. Is this but a dream and are you still the comely, well-dressed youth we knew of yore?
Anyway you might write and tell me.
Holgate, by this time, has probably told you all about his being tranferred to France, and of his first Blighty leave corresponding with my third, of the touching reunion, and

In the following week, British and French troops attacked Bulgarian positions in the Hills North of Salonika. The 2nd Battalion East Surreys, as part of the 28th Division, were in support of the Cretan Division which was to carry out a secondary surprise attack to the east and north shores of Lake Doiran, whilst the main British attack occurred to the west of the lake. The battalion were fighting in extreme conditions; death filled the air, which was made worse by the intense heat of a late Greek summer. Malaria and broncho-pneumonia were rife and Bryan, described as a 'gallant young officer' in the regimental history, succumbed to illness and died on 30 September.

A letter amongst Frank Glover's papers in the Imperial War Museum was intended for Bryan's hands. Frank wrote on 8 September 1918:

My dear Scurfield,

I am certain I wrote the last letter, but refuse to argue on the subject. After all these years the only vision of you I can conjure up is that of a scraggy-bearded apparition, haunting the hills of Salonica, with a dilapidated Sam Browne holding together a moth-eaten uniform, mainly the subsequent quiet 'blind.'

This was all about a month ago and within a few days of each other we returned to France.

I led the quiet life of trench warfare for a short time after my return but then, after a short rest, got mixed up with the battalion in the opening stages of this offensive which commenced in the dewy dawn of August 21st. On the first day we did several miles in the direction of Bapaume, paused for breath on the 22nd; and then went over the top once more on August 23rd, when we again mopped up a good many miles of Hunland in great style. After this particularly hectic day of slaughter a paper was thrust into my hand, according to which I should have left for England on the 19th, before the strife ever started!

I was not long filling my valise with souvenirs and making a hurried exit, and eventually arrived in 'Blighty' on August 27th.

Next day I reported to the Headquarters of the Royal Air Force at the 'Hotel Cecil' (for which reason I had been sent home) and they, after a very stiff Medical Board, passed me fit for a Pilot or Observer and gave me leave until September 20th (over three weeks).

At the moment therefore I am thoroughly enjoying the war, and have just returned from Brighton, where I have been doing the heavy for the last week.

When my leave expires I am having an operation for adenoids, after which I commence training 'somewhere in England,' though at present know not where.

If you are really ill enough to write a letter, send it to my home address which should find me, at anyrate for the next four months.

Cheerio, Scurf, and dont ruin your eyesight by writing too often.

Keep smiling!

Yours ever,

Glover.

A letter written by Frank to Bryan Scurfield but returned due to Bryan's death in Greece

composed of goat-skins. Is this but a dream and are you still the comely, well-dressed youth we knew of yore? Anyway you might write and tell me.

Holgate, by this time has probably told you about his being transferred to France and of his first Blighty leave corresponding with my third of the touching reunion and the subsequent quiet 'blind'.

This was all about a month ago and within a few days of each other we returned to France. I led the quiet life of trench warfare for a short time after my return but then, after a short rest, got mixed up with the battalion in the opening stages of this offensive which commenced in the dewy dawn of August 21st. On the first day we did several miles in the direction of Bapaume, paused for breath on the 22nd and then went over the top once more on August 23rd, when we again mopped up a good many miles of Hunland in great style. After this particularly hectic day of slaughter a paper was thrust into my hand, according to which I should have left for England on the 19th, before the strife ever started.

I was not long filling my valise with souvenirs and making a hurried exit and eventually arrived in 'Blighty' on August 27th.

Next day I reported to the Headquarters of the Royal Air Force at the Hotel Cecil (for which reason I had been sent home) and they, after a very stiff Medical Board, passed me fit for a pilot or observer and gave me leave until September 20th (over three weeks).

At the moment therefore I am thoroughly enjoying the war and have just returned from Brighton, where I have been doing the heavy for the last week.

When my leave expires I am having an operation for adenoids, after which I commence training 'somewhere in England' though at present know not where.

If you are really ill enough to write a letter, send it to my home address which should find me, at any rate for the next four months.

Cheerio, Scurf and don't ruin your eyesight by writing too often.

Keep smiling,

Yours ever,

Glover

The envelope this letter was sent in is attached to the original letter and across the top, written in pencil, reads, 'Deceased'. This letter never reached Bryan's hand. He had died just before it reached Greece.

References

1 Papers of F.P.J. Glover, IWM, Accession No. 78/10/1.
2 Diary Number 4 19/9/17 – 20/10/17 in the papers of F.P.J. Glover, IWM, Accession No. 78/10/1.
3 For an account of the attack see Col. H. W. Pearse D.S.O., & Brigadier H. S. Sloman, CMG, DSO, *History of the East Surrey Regiment: Volume III (1917–1919)*, (1924), pp. 5–11.
4 Ibid. pp. 116–118.
5 Ibid. p. 167.
6 Ibid. p. 180.

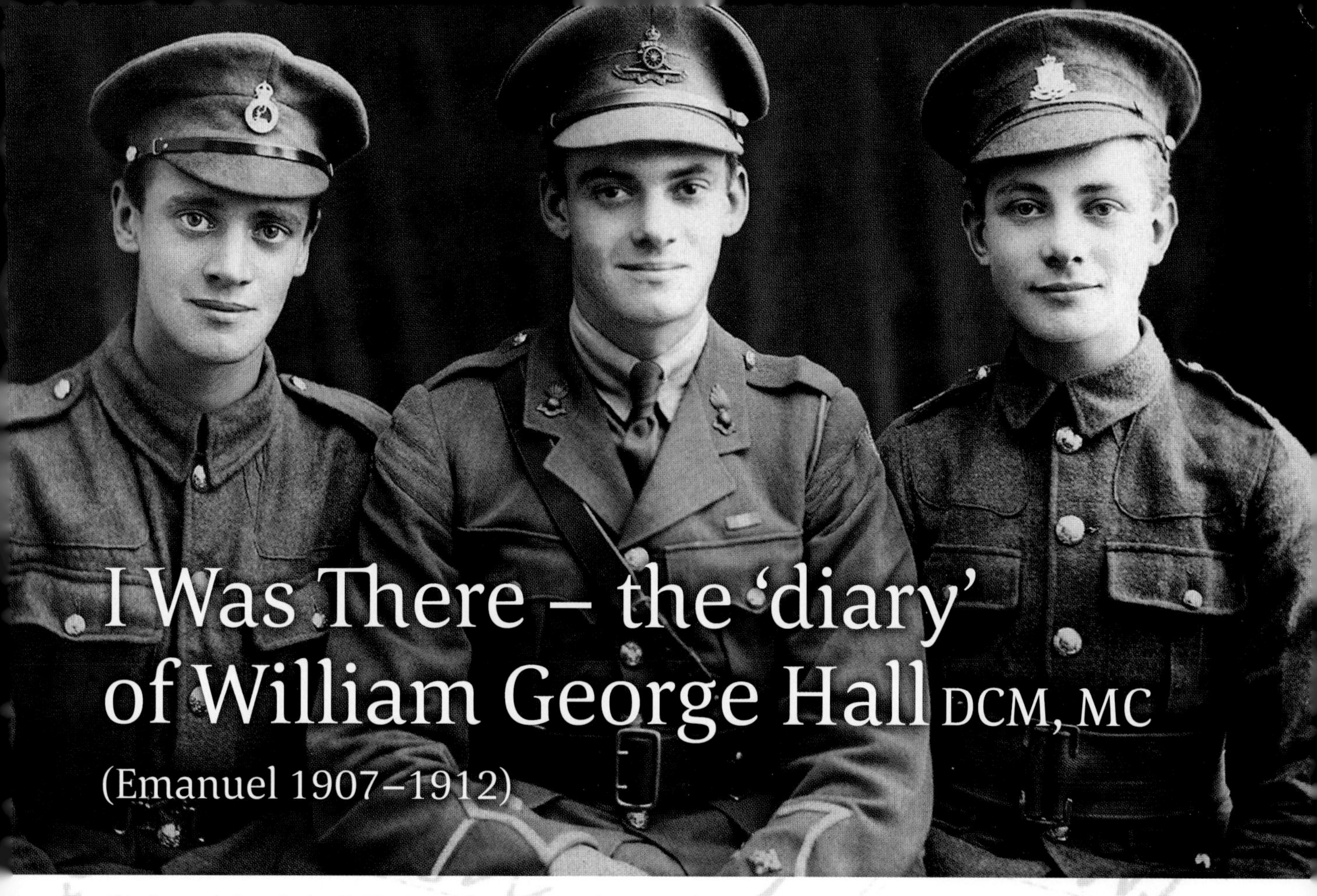

I Was There – the 'diary' of William George Hall DCM, MC

(Emanuel 1907–1912)

This photograph shows the three Hall brothers. William George is in the centre, Herbert Lionel Douglas who can be seen wearing his Emanuel School OTC uniform is on the right in the photo. The third brother, Arthur Edward Hall, on the left, served in the Machine Gun Corps in the First World War but didn't attend Emanuel.

Lt. William George Hall of "C" Battery, 64th Brigade, Royal Field Artillery won the Distinguished Conduct Medal in the First World War for: 'Conspicuous gallantry; he re-established telephonic communication during heavy rifle and machine-gun fire. The night was very dark and the ground much exposed to the fire.' He was also congratulated in the Spring Term edition of *The Portcullis* 1916:

> We heartily congratulate him on his achievement and wish him well, [for] bravery in repairing telegraphic wires under heavy fire.

In the Christmas edition of *The Portcullis* 1916, Gunner William Hall wrote home to the School:

> I am very grateful for the opportunity of being able to meet some of the old faces that I knew and have often thought of since I left. I have been fortunate enough to have seen practically every school magazine, but that is hardly the same as being able to come to School again. I very much regret to see that some of the fellows I have played rugger with have fallen in a much less sporting fight.

William kept a fascinating document which he titled a 'Diary of Lt. W. G. Hall RFA European War.' It takes the format of a log-book, listing in chronological order the major events at the start of the war, his drafting in September 1914 and the significant number of actions he was involved in including the Battle for the Hohenzollern Redoubt and the Somme Battles of 1916 and 1918. It also notes courses he attended, marches he undertook and lists places he visited including a walk around the Waterloo Battlefield on 15 December 1918.

In 1919 William was awarded the Military Cross.

Herbert Lionel Douglas Hall (Emanuel 1913–1917), William's brother, was a fine all round athlete playing for both the First Fifteen and First Eleven. He served in the RAF during the Second World War. He worked in banking until his retirement in 1961. Herbert's son Colin also attended Emanuel, and was a major figure in the history of the Curzon Club, the Old Boy society for ex-pupils of Howe House.

CHAPTER 4 – PART II OE POWS AND REFUGEES IN THE FIRST WORLD WAR

Old Emanuel POWs in the First World War

'Our blue and yellow rugger shirt is seen here on our football field'

25 Emanuel boys were made POWs in either Germany or the Ottoman Empire in the First World War. Records are more extensive on Emanuel boys made POWs in Germany, and the figure of 25 is based only on individuals Daniel Kirmatzis has been able to confirm were made POWs.

Owing to the nature of incomplete records on those OEs who served in the War this figure may well be higher. The focus here is mainly on OEs who were made POWs in Germany but the following story was reproduced in *The Portcullis* in 1920 and recounts a chance meeting which took place earlier in the war.

> During that part of the war that was in Mesopotamia – I refer, of course, to the last war, not the present eruption, Mr. Editor – a commissioned OE was wounded and taken prisoner. In course of time, his captors bethought themselves of his wounds and gave him attention at the hands of a German medical officer whose features seemed familiar to our OE. Subsequent conversation elicited the fact that the MO had also been at school in England – at Emanuel – and *pour bien desirer* his best skill and attention were devoted to the British Officer OE during the time he was under the care of the Germans.[1]

It was not unusual for OEs to meet each other in POW camps but it may well be unique that two OEs who were on opposite sides met, as the contributor to *The Portcullis* noted:

> I think it is a very interesting and significant episode and I am endeavouring to obtain full particulars. I do not imagine it came to the lot of many in the war to fall into the hands of an enemy who had shared company in the same form and playing fields of the same School a few years previously, and it would be vastly interesting to know the feelings of one who had that unique experience. We all know the form of enthusiastic greeting we extend on meeting again some Old Boy whom we have not seen for years, especially if he was a 'special crony' at School, but what a *mise-en-scène* for such an encounter![2]

Unfortunately the particulars of this event were never relayed but the significance of this episode is that the bonds of friendship, forged at Emanuel, didn't break in the course of war. In fact the spirit of Emanuel went with OEs wherever they were as evidenced in a letter from Edwin Dilnutt,

> Offizier-Gefangen-Lager, Holzminden, 17 Sept.
>
> I met a fellow gefangener here, E. L. Thompson by name, and he has lent me this *Portcullis* to read. I was captured in an aeroplane. April 25th, 1917, after spending since Jan. 15th in the Infantry. I met young Ginger Vaughan at

Claude Edgar Wallis (first from left) with other POWs in the Citadel, Mainz, Germany

> this camp last November — almost a year ago. You speak of Macduff in the London Scottish. Can you let him know where I am, or send me his address? Urquhart speaks of him. Of course you know of my young brother's death at Loos in 1916. *The Portcullis* does bring back memories to me, especially the names of Puggy Booth, George Hirst, Jimmy Morgan, Camm, Beath, etc. Do you remember Eric While? I crossed to England to join the RFC in the same boat in April, 1917. You will be pleased to hear that our blue and yellow rugger shirt is seen here on our football field.[3]

Edwin's letter shows the importance of how the School became an extended family for the majority of Emanuel boys. Memories and current news of the School and friends kept many an Old Boy in high spirits in what were otherwise alien surroundings. However, one letter expressing positive news cannot disguise the fact that many found captivity an isolating experience in which they suffered many privations including varying levels of violence and inhumane treatment.

During the First World War it has been estimated that around 175,624 British servicemen were made POWs in Germany but this figure is based on incomplete records so the actual number is higher.[4] The experiences of POWs varied for a number of reasons, for example those captured in 1918 after the German Spring Offensive were more likely to die of their wounds than had they been captured in an earlier phase of the War.

Months and years of training were meaningless in the microcosm that was camp life except for those who attempted to escape. Men who were captured during the early phases of the War were often transported to several camps during the course of their imprisonment. The 'Camp' in the twentieth century took on a new meaning; it became a way of life for millions. Public memory, particularly in Britain, has been shaped by the Hollywood image of the film *The Great Escape* based on true life experiences of POWs in the Second World War displacing our knowledge of POW experiences in the First World War with its public façade of a war spent in the trenches and the muddy fields of Flanders where poppies now grow. However, recent publications in the last few years are now challenging our perceptions, showing for example, that First World War POW experiences could often be far more brutal, on occasion, than the experiences of soldiers in the trenches.

Claude Edgar Wallis *(Emanuel 1899–1902)*

In August 1914 OE Claude Edgar Wallis travelled to France with the 1st Battalion, The Loyal North Lancashire Regiment. Within a few weeks he had been captured on 15 September and spent the next two years as a prisoner of war. In 1917 he gave a report about his experiences to the Committee on the Treatment of British Prisoners of War.[5] The interview reveals the myriad experiences of a POW from the rough treatment meted out at the beginning of his captivity to the more agreeable nature of one of his later camp's Commandants and the camp's censor.

Report by Lieut. C. E. Wallis 1st Loyal North Lancs

Capture: 15 Sept 1914

About 9am on the 15th September 1914, a party of Germans searched the ruined home in which I had been lying the previous morning. The NCO in charge spoke a little English. He asked me if I could walk. On my replying that I was too weak, owing to loss of blood, he replied that he would return in half an hour with a stretcher party. He then left, taking with him any who could walk. He appeared to treat them with consideration.

About a quarter of an hour after he had left, another party of Germans entered and threatened us with bayonets and made signs to us that if we did not get outside we should be bayoneted. I crawled out of the house on hands and knees, together with a few men who were also able to do this. The remainder – about ten – stayed in the house, being unable to move, and I do not know what happened to them. Outside two Germans lifted me to my feet, while one stood behind with a bayonet, with which he prodded me and shouted "March."

Treatment

I took two or three steps forward, but collapsed from weakness and in doing so the bandage and tourniquet round my arm became loose, and the blood commenced to flow very badly. Eventually a stretcher was found and I was put on it and carried about a mile. There were also two men of the Cameron Highlanders walking beside me – one wounded through the throat and the other through the shoulder. During this mile I was kicked by passing Germans several times and also struck in the face by a NCO. The man wounded in the throat was clubbed with a rifle-butt knocking him down, while the other one was several times struck.

Medical attention in the field

Our guards seemed to think it very amusing. Eventually we reached a dressing station. I was taken in and my wound examined, but nothing was done to it there and I was again taken out and carried about two or three hundred yards to another station and there put on a table and examined by a doctor, the first I had seen. He spoke a little English and was quite good, cleaning and dressing the wound and also giving me some food and a little wine. I was then taken out and put in an empty cottage, in which there were about 20 British soldiers, all wounded the day before, and had had no attention as yet to their wounds. Late in the afternoon the doctor who had dressed my wound looked in the room and I asked him if he could attend to some of the men. He refused, saying he had no time, but would attend to them tomorrow.

Food

No food had been given to any of the men since they had been taken, but in the evening some French villagers brought us large dishes of potatoes and rabbit which they were allowed by the sentries to give us. There were no sanitary arrangements and everyone had to relieve themselves in a corner of the room, on the floor at first, but later a Frenchman brought us a pail.

During the night one man who had been shot in the head went mad and eventually died in the early morning in delirium. A second, wounded in the stomach, died quietly.

In the morning we were all taken out and put in another house, also empty; the men were given straw to lie on and I received a mattress and a blanket. About midday Major Nicholson of the Cameron Highlanders was brought in, wounded in two places, and was given a mattress on the floor beside me. Later in the day his mattress was taken away and we shared the one I had during two days. We were fed twice a day with the same stew that the German soldiers had, but the quantity was insufficient. The sanitary arrangements were the same as in the previous house. The same doctor came in each day and attended to Major Nicholson and myself.

Major Nicholson, who spoke German, complained to the doctor about his lack of attention to the men and eventually got him to attend to two or three of the worst cases, but he absolutely refused to do more.

During the time we were in this house parties of German soldiers came in continually, night and day, to look at us. Some were abusive and several times we had to be protected by a medical orderly who was in the house. This orderly was very good to all of us, but he had had no medical training whatever and told us that he was a volunteer and that as he had never done any military service he had been given a Red Cross badge and told to look after the prisoners.

Journey to hospital

About midnight on the third night (18th) the doctor came in and said he had a place for me in an ambulance which was going to a proper hospital and that he was sending me before Major Nicholson as my wound was serious. He injected a dose of morphia and I was put in the ambulance, a 'lying-down' one, [with a] private in the Grenadier Guards who was seriously wounded.

Hospital at Laon: 18 Sept–26 Oct 1914

We were driven to Laon, a distance of about 17 Kilometres, where we arrived about 4am. Here we were lifted out and put into a hall in the Lycee buildings. Our rugs, which the doctor had given us, were taken away, but we were given mattresses but no coverings and as the night was very cold and the hall very damp, with the doors nearly always open, we suffered considerably from the cold. In the morning I had fever and had turns of deliriousness and unconsciousness. About 11am a French corporal, with the Red Cross badge, came into the hall and told me there was a French part of the hospital and that he would get permission from the Germans to have me taken into that part. He came back some time later with two other Frenchmen, one of whom was a doctor and took me into the French part of the hospital.

I told them that Major Nicholson would probably be coming during the day and they kept a look-out for him and on his arrival brought him into the same part of the hospital.

I remained six weeks in this hospital, tended by French doctors and nurses and receiving every care and attention. The food was good and sufficient and the Germans appeared to furnish the French with everything necessary for the carrying on of their work. The German Commandant visited all the wards every day and examined prisoners and sent away all those sufficiently well to be moved.

When I was strong enough to walk I visited some of the other wards where there were English wounded and found two or three of the men who had been in the room with me in the empty cottage. They said they had been there over a week after Major Nicholson and I had left and that during the whole of that time they had received no medical attention whatever. As a consequence one man's leg was in a terrible state from neglect and the French doctors had little hopes of saving it. Another man of the Welsh Regiment had been shot through the throat and the French doctors assured me that the man could have been easily saved if he had had medical treatment at the proper time. As it was the man died three days after he arrived at hospital.

Claude Edgar Wallis (right)

Examination by Germans

On 26 October I was warned to be ready to leave the hospital in the afternoon. I was the last English officer to leave it; Major Nicholson having left about two weeks before and two officers of the West Yorkshire about a week before. Two French officers also left at the same time with me. We were taken to the Kommandantur in Laon, where we were examined by a staff officer. I replied to his questions asking for my regiment, brigade and division but refused to answer a question about where we got our ammunition supply from Belgium.

The two French officers and myself were then told that we would wait about three days for a train to Germany and that the two French officers would be given a room in a house where there were German officers, but that the 'Englishman' could wait at the barracks with the soldiers and 'nigger prisoners' and that I should be given every opportunity of making the close acquaintance of my 'coloured allies.' Accordingly I was marched alone to the old French infantry barracks and locked in a room which was indescribably dirty and in which there was no furniture. In the room there were some Senegalese, Zouaves, French Tommies and three English soldiers. Practically all were wounded and had just come out of hospital; some of them were not fit to be moved. I was here three days during which time we were fed twice a day with most disgusting soup, which the Germans never had themselves.

Journey to Germany: 29 Oct–2 Nov 1914

On the third day I was taken out and put in a motor bus which was already full of Senegalese. There was an enormous crowd of German soldiers of all ranks, including officers, standing round and when I was put in the bus they all seemed greatly pleased and amused. The bus was then taken to the station and there I again met the two French officers who had been in the hospital with me. They told me they had been treated very well during the three days since I last saw them.

We were now all put in the train, which was an ambulance one. The two French officers were put in a compartment with some French NCOs and I was put in a compartment which had twelve berths, with nine Senegalese [and] two British soldiers. The arrangements on the train were good, but the food, although of good quality, was altogether insufficient and we felt very hungry during the whole three days we were in the train. The train did not start for another twenty-four hours and during this time we were left in peace, but when the journey commenced at every station we were a spectacle for the German soldiers. When we crossed the frontier into Germany we were mobbed at each station. Someone had written 'International Wagon' on the carriage and it appeared to be a source of great satisfaction to all.

At Saarbrucken we were all taken out of the hospital train and the two British soldiers with six of the Senegalese were put, with myself, into an ordinary third-class compartment for sixteen hours without getting out. During the time food was twice brought, but each time the Senegalese were given the food and told that they could give some of it to the English swine if they liked. If it had not been that the blacks were very decent fellows we should have had absolutely no food the whole time.

One of the two men, a corporal in the Berkshire Regiment I think, was so weak that he fainted several times. Finally we had to lay him down on the floor of the carriage and rest our feet on him. There was no room to do anything else, as there were eleven in the compartment. I may mention that during the whole of this part of the journey the two French officers had a first-class compartment to themselves and were allowed to send for any food or drink they required to the buffets at the various stations we stopped at. On several occasions they tried to send food to me, but were not allowed to do so. Two or three times during the journey German officers came and swore at us, one in fluent English.

At Darmstadt the men were taken out and I was then put with the French officers and we were taken to Mainz Citadel.

Mainz: 2 Nov 1914–10 June 1915

Here I was shut up in an attic for three days, being visited several times during the day and night by the officer commanding the barrack and by the guard. This officer was Major De Raadt. He treated all the officers in his barrack like convicts of the worst type.

Exercise

At this time (November 1914) there were two buildings on opposite sides of a court about 150 yards square. A portion about 75 yards square was divided off with wire netting and this was the only exercise ground for about 300 officers for over three months. The hours of exercise were 9 to 10.30am and 1 to 2.30pm for barrack II. This meant that the people in barrack I were indoors from 2.30 every day until 9 the following morning.

Treatment

During the exercise all games of any sort or description were prohibited and Major De Raadt would often stand in the centre of the exercise ground and shout at anyone who stopped walking or who appeared to be trying to play any game. He would also stand at one spot and make everyone salute him as they came round. In the rooms in his barrack no two Englishmen were allowed to be in the same room. Visits were allowed to other rooms on the same floor, but only until 6 o'clock, when a bell rang and everyone was expected to be in their own rooms. Lights out were at 9 o'clock and no talking was allowed after that hour.

Major De Raadt was found on several occasions to be listening at keyholes, both during the daytime and during the night. We were paraded at meal times in the corridors and marched across to the dining hall by tables. There, also, two Englishman were not allowed to sit together. Towards the end of December the canteen was closed and we were not allowed to buy anything at all of any description.

Letters and parcels

We were allowed to write letters when we arrived, but during the whole month of November we were not allowed to write letters. In December and January we were allowed two letters per month only. After that, two letters and four post-cards per month. During January and February we received practically no letters, as we were told that the censor at Mainz was too busy with other work to attend to our letters. During March and April we often received letters which we knew to have been in the office at Mainz since January. Parcels came through fairly well. I omitted to say that no one was allowed to write from a hospital in France, so that the letters I wrote from Mainz were the first I had been able to write since being taken prisoner.

Rooms

We had the ordinary rooms in the barracks, but very crowded and the beds either touched or were put one on top of another, bunk fashion. Other furniture consisted of one stool and one cupboard for each officer and one small table between four officers. One small washingstand with a jug and basin for about every six officers. There were absolutely no arrangements for baths during the first four months although there was a properly fitted douche except once a fortnight, when the whole barrack (about 200) were expected to have their bath within about two hours.

Sanitary arrangements

The latrines were of a most primitive kind and not kept clean. They were about ten yards away from one wall of the barrack and it was practically impossible to have the windows of the rooms open on that side of the building.

Heating

There were good stoves in each room and the supply of coal was sufficient.

Food

This was quite good in the earlier times but deteriorated very much about Christmas 1914. The quantity was just sufficient.

Medical attention

There was a special room when I first arrived at Mainz for officers who still required special treatment and after three days locked in the attic, I was put in this room, as my wound was still open and gave me a lot of trouble. The medical attention was good and a doctor attended every morning. Two medical orderlies who knew their work were always in attendance. Officers in the sick ward received the same diet as the others with the addition of wine if sanctioned by the doctor. At this time wine or beer was strictly prohibited for all.

Changes for the better

During the month of February, a representative from the Spanish Embassy visited the camp and after much trouble with the Commandant, some of us managed to speak to him. We complained of the treatment by Major De Raadt and about the hours of exercise, baths etc. Shortly after his visit, Major De Raadt was removed and a new commandant, whose name I forget, came in his place. The whole of the court was now thrown open to us instead of the 75 yards piece and we were allowed out at all hours between sunrise and sunset, allowed to visit the other barracks on the other side of the court, to play games, make a tennis court etc. In short, we were now practically free within the citadel and in addition we were treated with a certain amount of politeness when we had any dealings with the officials.

The douche was also opened every morning and also in the afternoons after games. The arrival of letters became more regular.

Parades

In the early days at Mainz there were several times during the day when we were counted, at the parade at 9 o'clock, at the parade for dinner, at the parade at 4 and at the parade for supper. We were also counted in bed at lights out. As the parades for dinner and supper were discontinued and we were allowed to walk over to meals, we were only counted at the morning parade, the 4 o'clock parade and in bed at lights out which was now at 10 o'clock.

Two or more English were now allowed in a room and it seemed that from about the month of April the English were treated, if anything, better than the other nationalities instead of worse.

Journey to Stralsund: 10–12 June 1915

On the 8th June we were warned to leave Mainz for an unknown destination on the 10th. We entrained in the morning and were in the train until the evening of the 11th when we arrived at Stralsund. The journey was most comfortable, the carriages being 2nd class and corridor. We had the same carriages right through to Stralsund via Halle and Berlin. Feeding arrangements were, however, bad and those who had not taken the precaution to bring provisions with them were very hungry for practically the whole of the trip. A very noticeable feature of the journey was the difference in the attitude of the civil population at the various stations we stopped at en route, as well as the almost polite bearing of the military and railway officials. We saw no sign of any demonstration by any civilians whatever, simply mild curiosity and the various officials were quite considerate.

Stralsund: 12 June, 1915–29 May 1916

We arrived on the island of Stralsund about midnight on the 11–12 May and found supper waiting for us.

In the morning we were paraded by the Commandant and then had a look round our new quarters. The camp consisted of a part of two small islands in the Baltic, lying between the mainland and the large island of Rugen. The part which was wired off for the prisoners was about two kilometres in circumference and consisted of gardens, woods and there was a channel of the sea between the two islands in which we could fish. The English (about 26 officers) were installed in a new building in the two best rooms, eighteen in one and eight in the other.

Sanitary arrangements

Although the building was quite new and had electric light, there were no bathing or washing arrangements at all and the latrines were a primitive type and always smelt very bad.

Rooms

The rooms were very crowded. The room which I was in was about 30 feet by 25 feet. There were eighteen of us in it, which meant eighteen beds, eighteen cupboards, eighteen stools, three washing tables, two stoves. It was necessary to pile the beds two deep. There was a canteen in the building where we had our meals, but the food here was very bad and was not fit to touch most days. This necessitated living on our parcels entirely. We accordingly had to cook (on spirit stoves) and wash up in our room, in addition to washing, bathing (in one tin bath), eating sleeping and reading, or amusing ourselves there.

Treatment

The camp was, however, generally considered to be one of the best in Germany, for in spite of the cramped quarters and bad food, the treatment otherwise was all that could be desired. We were always absolutely free on the islands and the size of the camp made this a great advantage. In addition, the Commandant allowed us to make a football field, cricket pitch and small golf course outside the camp and which we were allowed to use every afternoon. (In the mornings this extra ground formed part of the training ground for German troops.)

Officials

The censor, Baron Von Heyking, did everything in his power to make our captivity as agreeable as possible. He allowed us to write practically unlimited letters and would always execute commissions for anyone in the town. At Christmas 1915, he obtained a hamper for each English officer, containing a turkey, a goose, two bottles of whisky and a bottle of brandy and all at a quite reasonable price. In fact, I cannot speak too highly of his kindness. He lived for many years as a child in India, I believe, where his father was German Chargé d'Affaires. Another official was Unteroffizier Bluhm, who was in charge of the parcel office and who was very obliging and never made any fuss about any papers that he found in parcels, but used to ask you if you would mind lending them to him when you had finished.

Medical attention

A doctor visited the camp three times a week and, in addition to which, permission was always granted to consult a specialist or to go to the dentists.

Money exchange

Until about the month of March 1916, we had always been given the current rate of exchange on money sent from England, but about this time we were only given 102 marks for five English pounds, even when the proper amount was written on the slip with 127 mark on it, being the current rate of exchange for five pounds.

Life in general at Stralsund

I was just over a year at Stralsund and during the whole time had no unpleasantness with the Germans...They [the officials] never visited us in our rooms and left us entirely alone. The great drawbacks to the camp were the overcrowding in rooms, the food and the lack of bathing and washing facilities. However, the treatment made up for all this.

As I had been having trouble with my ear (for which I had been visiting an ear specialist Dr Karrer, who charged me nothing for several visits) and my right hand was partially paralysed from my wound, the camp doctor put my name down for the Swiss Commission. Orders came that all those who wished to see the Commission were to be sent to Mainz.

Journey: 29—30 May 1916

Accordingly, on 29 May, 1916, I left Stralsund together with two other English officers. We were accompanied by Baron Von Heyking. We had a very comfortable journey, the baron allowing us to have dinner on the dining car going to Berlin. At Berlin we had a two-hour wait and the Baron drove us round the city in a taxi and showed us the various places of interest.

Mainz again: 30 May–20 June 1916

We arrived at Mainz on the morning of 30 May. We went to the Citadel again. We found the conditions somewhat improved since we had been there over a year before. There was a billiard-room added and various privileges. The greatest of these was the walks in the country. At Stralsund, owing to the large extent of the camp itself, we had not been going out for walks in the country, but at Mainz, where the only exercise ground was 150 yds. square, it was the greatest imaginable treat to get outside twice a week.

Many of the officers and officials had also been changed and all the present ones seemed very considerate and polite, especially to the English. About 40 English officers were examined by the Swiss Commission on 19 June, of whom 25 were told a week after that they had been accepted and that they would leave the day after for Heidelberg, where they would have to pass another Commission.

Heidelberg: 25 June–11 Aug 1916

We arrived at Heidelberg on 25 June and were examined by the final Commission on 12 July.

At this camp the food was better than at the others I had been to, although about this time the meat ration for prisoners was reduced to about 250 grammes per week. By this time too, butter, eggs, sugar, bread and any form of meat was quite unpurchasable.

The rooms here were good, not too crowded and the washing arrangements excellent, there being a fine douche open all day. Postal arrangements were also good and the officials very courteous. The exercise ground is rather small, being about 100 by 30 yds. but as there were walks nearly everyday this was not so noticeable.

I asked to see an ear specialist and was sent to the University Hospital, where I was treated by Professor Beck. I visited the hospital several times per week during my stay at Heidelberg and always received every care and attention from Dr. Beck, who performed a small operation and wanted to perform a mastoid operation, but there was not time before my departure for Switzerland.

The medical attention in the camp, however, was very poor. The doctor only came about twice a week and at uncertain times, while the only medical orderly was nearly always in the town or feeding [a] large stock of rabbits they had on the premises for food. And this in a camp which was supposed to be full of invalided people who were waiting for the Swiss Commission.

Claude Edgar Wallis (first from right) overseeing his motor engineering class in Switzerland

Swiss Commission

Those who had been passed by the Commission were told so on 9 August, a month after the last examination and already two months after the first one.

Leaving Germany

We left Germany on 11 August, starting from Heidelberg at 3am; we arrived at Constance at 5pm after a very comfortable journey during which we had two meals with meat at each meal. We were taken over by the Swiss officials the same evening and crossed the frontier.

After his release from Germany Claude set up motor engineering classes in Switzerland for interned British prisoners. These POWs were interned in Switzerland, after being interned in Germany, under the terms of agreements made by Britain, France and Germany with the Swiss Government to neutralise a certain number of belligerent POWs who needed specialist medical treatment. These types of POWs recuperated in Switzerland and returned to their home nations when hostilities ceased.[6]

Lionel Strachan *(Emanuel 1885–1889)*

Servicemen were not the only ones to be made POWs in the War for thousands of civilians were considered enemy aliens and as such were imprisoned in the early months of the War's outbreak. One aspect of internment, especially for those who spent lengthy periods as prisoners was the monotony of camp life. To relieve this many POWs became students of what is commonly known as the 'Barbed-Wire University.' One OE who played his part in this 'University' was Lionel Richard Mortimer Strachan who attended Emanuel from 1885 to 1889.[7] At Emanuel Lionel Strachan was an editor of the *Emanuel Gazette* which pre-dated *The Portcullis* as the School's magazine. From Emanuel Lionel went to Merchant Taylors' School where he became an Exhibitioner to St John's College, Oxford in 1894. From 1901 to September 1914 Lionel was a Lector in English at Heidelberg University being dismissed by the German authorities in September 1914 before he was sent to Ruhleben, which was a POW camp for civilians.[8] English travellers, those who worked in Germany and English merchant seamen were all sent to such civilian camps in the early months of the war, being imprisoned as enemy aliens. Ruhleben was previously a racecourse and at the outbreak of the War its stables were hastily made into a concentration camp where up to four thousand English civilian POWs were imprisoned.

Lionel Strachan gave lectures to fellow inmates whilst interned in Ruhleben. His lecture titles included, 'The Town Life of Shakespeare' and 'English Sonneteers.' Lionel also spent his time translating the fourth edition of his friend, Adolf Deissmann's book *Licht Vom Osten* (*Light from the Ancient East: The New Testament Illustrated by Recently Discovered Texts of the Graeco-Roman World*). In his Translator's Preface to the fourth edition of *Licht Vom Osten* Lionel explains under which circumstances he translated the revised version:

> I should like to add that between 22 Nov 1914 and 23 April 1918 a certain portion of the time given to 'fostering Christian solidarity' was spent in tedious journeys half-way round Berlin to visit his [Adolf Deissmann's] English translator in internment either at Plötzensee Prison or at Ruhleben. Every two months or so a long, weary journey was undertaken just for the sake of cheering an enemy alien by half an hour's talk under the eye of soldiers in a guard-room; 21 visits were paid in all, permission having to be obtained for each, not without difficulty, from the military authorities. Rare indeed was the privilege. And the visitor never came empty-handed, but brought with him mental pabulum and always some creature comforts, even when the pinch was being felt in the homes of Germany.

After the war Lionel Strachan became Lecturer in German at the University of Birmingham until his death in 1942.

Leonard Marthews

Leonard Marthews *(1898–1918)*

When a son went missing it was a worrying time for his family for no immediate news of his fate could mean either that he had been made a POW or he had died. Letters would be exchanged between the young man's family and the War Office as they determined what had happened to him.

Leonard Gordon Marthews was a Cadet Officer in the Emanuel OTC and in the 1915 Christmas Term *Portcullis* we learn that he had built the Corps its own machine gun:

> On Thursday, November 4th, the Corps was presented with a machine gun by Cadet Officer Marthews. We are all very grateful to him for this, especially as he has made it entirely himself, and has taken utmost pains to render it as serviceable as possible. We look forward to the next Field Day, when we shall be able to include a new feature in our attack. The Machine Gun Section is now up to full strength and is working hard with its new drill.
>
> We are sorry to have to announce that Cadet Officer Marthews leaves us on November 25th to go to the Royal Military College, Sandhurst, but we send our best wishes with him and trust that we shall have him with us again after the war is over.[9]

Leonard went on to gain a commission as a Lieutenant in "C" Company, 2nd Battalion, South Lancashire Regiment and was involved in fighting during the opening days of the German Spring Offensive of 1918 but communication between himself and his parents was lost when he was reported missing on 22 March 1918. Leonard's parents spent several weeks trying to find out what had happened to him.

Leonard's father Walter asked his sister Mrs R. Kelly for her assistance in finding out what had happened and she duly wrote a letter to the Earl of Derby, Minister of War, on 7 April 1918:

> Sir, may I trouble you, my nephew has been reported missing since the 22nd March and his parents are unable to glean any news whatever. They are distracted and they beg me to assist. I am quite helpless, but would like to do anything I could to assist in relieving their anxiety. The young fellow was sent up here to Crosby after leaving Sandhurst with distinction and [has] been in France over a year...I should feel my Lord most grateful for any information.[10]

Mrs Kelly received a letter from the War Office reassuring her that if Leonard had been made a POW his parents...'will probably receive the earliest intimation of the fact from their son himself, either in the form of a postcard or a telegram sent through the Geneva Red Cross, as each captured officer as soon as he reaches his internment camp is given a postcard to send to his relatives notifying the fact that he is a prisoner or war wounded or unwounded as the case may be.'

On 26 May 1918 Leonard's father Walter Marthews was informed that his son had died of wounds whilst a POW. Lt. Arthur Watson who was a repatriated POW provided a statement about Leonard's death:

> I witnessed the death of the above officer and also his burial at Aix-La-Chapelle (Aachen) Germany – I cannot be sure as to the exact date of his death for all notes etc were taken from me by the Germans before I left Germany. But before leaving I was in possession of the diary of the above officer and from this diary he died on the same date as his own father's birthday of this year.[11]

Leonard died on 22 April 1918. Arthur Watson provided further details:

> His wounds were on the left shoulder and left arm and a very serious one on the right thigh – the latter being broken – All were caused by machine gun bullets – the latter wound was septic and he burst an artery in the right thigh before he died.

The German death certificate noted that Leonard had died at 9.15pm from heart failure due to a shattered thigh and severe haemorrhage. He died in the 2nd reserve hospital in Aix. He had been captured on 24 March 1918 in Monchy, south-east of Arras, two days after being reported missing. Leonard is now buried in Cologne Southern Cemetery and is remembered on the First World War memorial outside the main doors of the Holy Trinity Church on Clapham Common, South London where he was baptised on 11 June 1899.

Frederick White *(Emanuel 1912–1917)*

A talented boy at Emanuel, Frederick Richard White won prizes for English, Maths and Science. Few details are known about his war experiences except that he was made a POW in the days after 21 March 1918. Frederick was a Private (No. G/54297) in the 21st Battalion, Middlesex Regiment. The Battalion saw action in the neighbourhood of Croisilles, St Léger, Mory and Ervillers, south of Arras between the 21 and 26 March and it is presumed that Frederick was made a POW during this time.[12] *The Portcullis* reported 'F. R. White is wounded and a prisoner and doubtless he is scheming how to put his exceptional talents to account after the war to get his own back on the Hun, to whom he owes the loss of a leg.'[13]

Frederick died on 9 June 1918. His nephew Roger remembers that even after the Second World War Frederick's parents had preserved his study area in their home.

References

1 *The Portcullis*, Trinity Term, No. 80, 1920, p. 39.
2 Ibid.
3 *The Portcullis*, Christmas Term, No. 75, 1918, pp. 31–32.
4 See H. A. Jones, *Violence against Prisoners of War in the First World War: Britain, France and Germany, 1914–1920* (Cambridge, 2011), pp. 19–23.
5 Report by Lt. C E Wallis, 1st Loyal North Lancs, TNA, WO/161/95/61.
6 See Lt.-Col. H.P. Picot, *The British Interned in Switzerland* (1919). Wallis is mentioned on pp. 146, 148 and 152–156.
7 L.R.M. Strachan was imprisoned in Ruhleben, a camp for civilian prisoners which Bishop Bury described to the *Daily Telegraph* as the 'University of Ruhleben', due to the amount of studying which took place there. See Douglas Sladen, (ed.), *In Ruhleben: Letters from a Prisoner to his Mother* (1917), p.1.
8 For further details on L.R.M. Strachan see Husbands, Christopher T., *German-/Austrian-origin professors of German in British universities during the First World War: the lessons of four case studies*, (2013), n.8
9 *The Portcullis*, Christmas Term, 1915, p. 30. Marthews left Emanuel in 1914 but we can assume that he continued to help with the OTC for his younger brother who also attended the School would have only been 12 years old in 1915.
10 Letter to Lord Derby from Mrs Kelly, TNA, WO 339/66981 2/Lieutenant Leonard Gordon Marthews, The Prince of Wales's Volunteers (South Lancashire Regiment). These letters were answered by administrators rather than those in charge like the Earl of Derby.
11 Letter written by Lt. Arthur Watson, 19 June 1918, TNA, WO 339/66981 2/ Lieutenant Leonard Gordon Marthews.
12 For a description of the actions in which 21st Battn Middlesex were involved during the opening days of the Spring Offensive see TNA WO 95/2606/3 21 Battalion Middlesex Regiment, Appendix 1: Narrative of events during operations in the neighbourhood of Croisilles, St Léger, Mory and Ervillers, from the 21 to 26 March 1918.
13 *The Portcullis*, Trinity Term 1918, p. 32.

Refugee Journeys
Constantine Havery
(1902–1969)

In an article from the Lent Term 1919 *Portcullis* a new arrival to Emanuel describes the journey he made from Russia to England, via German POW camps in 1918.

Although we do not know the reason[s] why Constantine Havery and his mother and sister left Russia we do know that a civil war had broken out after the 1917 revolutions, between the 'Reds' and 'Whites', which ended in the Reds', or Bolshevik, victory in 1922 and we can assume with a Christian name like Constantine that the family were Russian Orthodox Christians. It is likely that Constantine's family wanted to escape the Bolsheviks as well as the civil war. Constantine and his family were therefore refugees as a result of civil war and his article offers a rich source on a refugee's journey during the last year of the First World War.

Constantine explores his time in German POW camps, discussing conditions and the lifestyle, such as the little food available in addition to what conditions were like for Russian POWs in German camps. Constantine also describes conditions in Ruhleben, the POW camp for English civilians, where he spent a number of months in 1918.

> On Friday 22 February 1918 I left Russia with my mother and sister by the 6 o'clock train to Beloostroff, a town on the frontier between Russia and Finland. Every member of our party hoped to be in England at the end of a fortnight. At Beloostroff we were compelled to leave our carriage and proceed to the station office where our passports had to be made out. At this time, the town was in the hands of the Bolsheviks, hence we had to answer numberless questions. At 10pm we were allowed to continue our journey and at 12 o'clock next morning we arrived at Helsingfors, the capital of Finland. Everybody was in the best of spirits, for we believed that very shortly we should be conveyed by boat to Stockholm. We put up at a hotel and after lunch went for a walk along some of the principal thoroughfares of the town. It is very large and clean, the roads are steep, the houses are big and the general appearance is extremely pretty. In the evening, we learnt that no boat would be able to leave Helsingfors for some time because the bay was frozen over and so next morning the English consul sent us to Mahtuluto which was not ice-bound, saying that in a few days a boat would leave there for Stockholm. At Mahtuluto the hotel was full, so we decided to go to Bjorneborg and wait for the train there. After a week's stay we heard that the vessel had struck an iceberg and had foundered!
>
> There was nothing for it but to go to Abo, where we remained for a fortnight. The only thing we could do now was to cross to the Aaland Islands on sledges. This took three days and three nights. On the second day we were met by a German patrol-boat. We had our passports taken away and were ordered to go to Eckero, the largest island of the group, where they had their headquarters. We arrived there on 16 March and were immediately put on board a German transport vessel, which was to sail in three days. I was put in the hold, which was full of sand, with an old gentleman and five Russian prisoners. All the food we got was small pieces of bread given us by the soldiers. We had to sleep on the wet sand. On the 20th, we left for Danzig at 5am. At 6 o'clock, all of us who were sleeping below were awakened by a sudden jar and crash. On rushing to the deck, we found that the ship had struck a mine. She was badly damaged forward and was down by the head. I asked one of the sailors if she

could float long enough to reach Danzig. He replied that the ship was stout and that the mine was only a Russian one. At 4pm we arrived at Danzig. We were escorted by a party of soldiers to the railway station, where we entrained for Tuchel.

Tuchel was a camp for Russian prisoners and was not really meant for civilians, so we were very uncomfortable there. On the first morning, the Germans came and examined our luggage. They gave us some food but it was so bad that we could not eat it. We lived for a fortnight on some tins of meat and some condensed milk that we happened to have. We had three so-called meals every day: watery coffee in the morning and soup composed of bad meat, frogs or fish, for dinner and tea. There was no soap and all we had in the way of a wash was a shower-bath once a month. This, although absolutely inadequate, was quite an event. We were awakened at 6 o'clock in the morning and were marched to the baths, which were some miles off. Our hair was clipped short and our clothes were put in steam to disinfect them. We were allowed a few glorious minutes under the shower-bath and then we had to dress again as quickly as possible and return to the camp. The food was so bad that the Russians were dying like flies. If they were too ill to work they were beaten. After a few days I became very weak. I used to get dizzy if I walked for long. We slept in small dugouts with little windows. They were very stuffy, and our beds were full of vermin.

On 19 April we were transferred from Tuchel to Ruhleben, the camp for English civilians. Everything was better here. We were treated well, lived in huts and had plenty of food sent by the English Red Cross. This camp was composed of 23 sets of buildings: eighteen for Germans, two hospitals, a school, a parcels office and one for the German guards. There were three grand-stands – for Ruhleben is a race-course – which served as our theatre, cinema and library. There were also a barber's shop and extensive kitchens. A big field was set apart, half for a market garden and half for games. In summer, we had vegetables twice a week from our garden. Berlin newspapers were sent to us daily and we were allowed to have maps of different frontiers. Every morning there was roll-call at 8 o'clock, and after that, school till twelve. In the afternoon, I prepared my lessons, or worked in the garden. We had special lessons twice a week for book-binding and leather-work. In the evening, we often went to the theatre and on Sundays to the cinema.

When the German revolution broke out, a Soldiers' Council was set up in the camp and we were allowed to go to Berlin if we had a pass from the Council. I went to the German capital twice. On 11 November, the Armistice was signed and on the 22nd, we left Ruhleben in the first party of 1500 people. At Sassritz, where we arrived next day, were two boats waiting to take us to Copenhagen. There, the liner *Frederick VIII* was awaiting our arrival and in three days we were at Hull. On the way across the North Sea, we saw the German Fleet going to surrender. Near Grimsby, we met some English vessels. From Hull we went to Ripon and from Ripon to London, where we arrived on 28 November 1918, having taken nine months to come from Petrograd.

C Havery

A contemporary postcard depicting the German siege of Namur

Belgian Refugees join the School

In the December 1914 issue of *The Portcullis* we find evidence of one of the earliest instances of how the First World War affected the School. Emanuel welcomed to its numbers refugees fleeing from the crisis in mainland Europe. Victor Rapalli wrote about the circumstances in which he and his brother joined Emanuel. The Rapallis were in Namur when the Germans started their bombardment. The article was originally published in French:

> During the first night of the bombing of Namur no one slept, not with all the firing making such a noise, we even thought a bomb had landed on a nearby hotel, because we were only 300 metres away from the local citadel. At 7am, two men from the civil guard arrived, armed with revolvers, and asked for our papers. After this they searched the whole hotel, because in previous days they thought there had been spies sending signals. The spy was the hotel manager. In the distance we saw wisps of smoke and the great bombs falling and landing on the houses and in the roads, making large holes. I stop here, because I do not know any more.

CHAPTER 4 – PART III

FOR THE MOTHER COUNTRY

Emanuel Commonwealth Soldiers

A number of Emanuel boys left England for new opportunities in Australia and Canada but when war was declared they fought with various Australian and Canadian units in France and the Mediterranean. The youngest OE was sixteen and the oldest was 41 when they enlisted. They saw action in some of the fiercest battles of the war. These are the stories of three of them, all of whom served on the Western Front.

Lieutenant Frank William Skinner *(1892–1916)* 7th (British Columbia) Battalion CEF

(Emanuel 1904–1908)

Frank attended both Honeywell Junior School and Emanuel. He passed the Cambridge Senior Local Examinations and went to work as a banker for the London City and Midland Bank Limited. Frank subsequently travelled to Canada in 1912 to take up an appointment at the Bank of British North America at their Head Office in Montreal, Quebec. He was subsequently transferred to the St John branch in the province of New Brunswick.

Frank enlisted into the 1st Divisional Signalling Company (DSC) in August 1914 shortly after war was announced. The small signalling unit was moved to Valcartier, Quebec where the rest of the Canadian Expeditionary Force was organising for active service. A huge camp of some 12,428 acres was established at Valcartier to accommodate 30,000 men.

The 1st DSC sailed for England in convoy with the rest of the 1st Canadian Contingent on 2 October 1914 and the crossing lasted twelve days. Whilst in England Frank completed his training on Salisbury Plain. Conditions in October worsened as heavy rain turned the ground to mud and the construction of promised huts was delayed due to the contractors not meeting their obligations so troops had to live in bell tents for longer than anticipated. The official history of the Canadian Expeditionary Force described training as a 'drudgery.'[1]

Frank sailed for France on 20 March 1915 and was set to work in the Ypres Salient. He was at the 2nd Battle of Ypres starting on 22 April, which not only saw the first major gas attack by German forces but was also the first major operation the

Frank W. Skinner

Canadians were involved in. The 1st DSC were busy restoring communications in the next few days where cables and wires had been destroyed by German artillery fire. Unfortunately we lack specific details of Frank's experiences during both this engagement and in the following days in which the Canadian battalions played their part in holding Ypres against the Germans.

Frank wrote to Emanuel in the Summer of 1915, 'We are all very optimistic as to the final result of the war. My training with the OTC proved very beneficial to me.'[2] *The Portcullis* noted that he was 'very anxious to obtain news of the School.'

In September 1915 Frank was admitted to hospital in St Omer suffering from boils but by November 1915 he was at a Cadet School and gained a temporary commission in the 7th (British Columbia) Battalion on 7 November 1915. This unit saw much front line action in the following months through to the summer of 1916 when Frank was wounded on 3 May 1916. He was hit by shell fire while the battalion was holding trenches in the Ypres Salient. He received what was described as a GSW (gunshot wound) to the abdomen and was taken to No. 10 Casualty Clearing Station. Two days later on 5 May young Frank, who only a decade before had been playing cricket for Marlborough House at Emanuel, died of his wounds.

Frank Skinner was buried at Lijssenthoek Military Cemetery Belgium. He was 24 years of age when he died.

Corporal Percy Alexander Connew, 3rd Canadian Mounted Rifles *(1876–1915)*

(Emanuel 1889–1891)

At the start of the War Percy was a farmer in Canada and enlisted in the Canadian Infantry at Vegreville, Alberta on 1 February 1915. He sailed with the regiment for England on 12 June 1915 and arrived as part of the 1st Canadian Mounted Rifles Brigade, then deployed to France on 22 September 1915. The 3rd Canadian Mounted Rifles war diary records that he was killed by a German high explosive shell while in trenches near dugouts south of Irish Farm, south-west of Messines on 1 December 1915. Lance Corporal Herbert Cecil Macintyre recorded that fateful day in a letter to his brother who lived in San Francisco. In his letter Herbert described what he and Percy experienced that day and ultimately Percy's fate:

> I will tell you briefly the whole fearful story of our first real taste of modern warfare ...
>
> Well, we started the day in the trench, which was mud and water varying from six inches to two and half feet in depth. God, I was cold and tired! We had some bread and jam and water and as we were not allowed to go in the dugouts, as an attack was expected, we laid down on the firing platforms and tried to sleep, but I was too cold, having had no gum boots. I had to cross a creek every hour on the way out to the listening post and got wet to the waist, besides the rain. So I wandered miserably around until noon when we had some bully beef, bread, cheese, jam etc. and some hot tea and we all got a good shot of rum. It tasted like nectar for the gods.
>
> **Place is Jammed:** I went down to the cooks and the place was jammed with fellows with their dixies full of water waiting their turn to use the brazier, so I went away and at 2pm Corporal Connew and myself went down again and at last managed to get our dixies on the fire. Connew was a huge, splendid fellow, English and every inch a soldier and a man. We walked up and down the trench, waiting for our tea to steep, but alas! Poor Con was destined never to drink anything again.
>
> Suddenly the whine of a shell arrested our attention and we saw a puff of white smoke above a group of houses half a mile in our rear which were used by the army for tools, engineers' stores etc. We knew them at once for shrapnel shells. Then a number burst simultaneously over them. We watched it idly then 'all hell broke loose.' The air was filled with terrible sounds and immediately the heavens seemed to vomit shells of all description on our luckless heads.
>
> We could hardly realise for a minute that it was all meant for us, but we were not long kept in doubt. A huge shell suddenly burst on the inner side of the parapet and we were deluged with flying debris. If I were Daniel Webster I could not begin to explain to you the inferno of sounds that followed. If there is a hell then the lid was certainly taken off. It was absolutely fiendish and altogether unlike any other sounds on earth.
>
> **Great variety in shells:** The shells, they were shrapnel, high explosive, French mortars, six and eight-inch shells, aerial torpedoes, 'whiz bangs' and 'coal boxes' (a coal box, next in size to a Jack Johnson makes a hole about ten feet across and from six to eight feet deep), shrieked, whistled, roared, hissed and moaned in a medley of sounds that was awful.
>
> The 'whiz bang' is well named and comes by you and explodes faster than you can say the two words. The 'coal box' comes fairly slow, but they always let you know when they arrive. Ha! Ha!
>
> The trench mortars seem to go a mile in the air above you and you can hear them coming down in a hurricane of sound. They land with a 'whump' and the whole trench seems to rock and sway. One shell – what it is I do not know – sounds like a gigantic frying pan full of fiercely frying bacon going by you with fearful velocity.
>
> We crouched down and waited for the death which was so soon to come for many of our comrades. There were bursting shells everywhere – in front, behind and overhead – and the air was filled with flying shrapnel. ...

In a Storm of Shells: All this time the shells were coming in a constant rain of shrieking iron and some landed in the trench and on the parapet and gaping holes showed here and there. I figured my time to die had come and I might just as well have a smoke first. I lit my pipe and as I had no matches asked an Irishman nearby for one and when I saw his long face I couldn't help laughing. He said, "It's a hell of a toime to be thinking of smoking", but he handed me his box and lit her up.

A piece of shrapnel came a second later, knocking the pipe clean out of my mouth. A moment later came a terrific roar and in came our parapet on top of us as if it had been pushed in by a giant hand. The firing platform gripped one of my legs and I was half covered with clay and mud, but I managed to twist out my legs before the weight settled on me.

Poor Connew was buried under seven or eight feet of debris and his head under the firing platform. I yelled up the line for an axe and one came down at once and I cut away three sections of platform cutting through nails, sheetiron, etc. I felt I had the strength of two men. I got his head clear and one shoulder and started to dig him out. He was not hurt much and perfectly conscious and I talked and joshed with him. A post had gripped him above the hip, but I had put in several braces before I dared to cut it away.

Just then there was another roar right by my head and something warm splashed over my face. I was thrown down and the accursed shell took a helper's head off from the eyes up. I was between Connew and another man not two feet away and they were both instantly killed. A big piece of shell tore into Connew's head and shoulder and then, merciful God, I was buried under tons of mud and timbers.

... I staggered to my feet and found I was on top of a piece of clay where the trench had been. I was dazed and deaf and half blind and it was just like an evil nightmare. I felt I was in the dark as I went along helping myself by my hands. I put my left hand into poor McGarry's head and will never forget my horror when I saw what I did and then fell over and rolled down the bank luckily into a part of the trench which had not been broken up.

... In my wildest dreams I never thought to go through such an adventure and sure hope I never have to do so again, but I guess I have seen my last glimpse of old Canada for I guess the war is good for another year and if so there will be very few of us to see the finish. But a man couldn't go in a better way.[3]

Herbert, who had tried so hard to rescue Percy that day was right in his prediction about both the War lasting into another year and not seeing Canada again for he was killed on 2 June 1916 and is remembered on the Menin Gate.

Percy was 40 years old when he died and is interred in the Berkshire Cemetery Extension, Comines-Warneton, Hainaut, Belgium.

Alan 'Jim' Pearman 41st Battalion Australian Imperial Force

(Emanuel 1914–1916)

Alan, known as Jim to the family, served in the Emanuel OTC but his father William, who later became General Manager of the London Power Company, did not want his son to fight in the First World War and so, when Alan was sixteen, he sent him to Australia, where Alan worked as a farm hand at Springhill, Queensland. Alan was both a good rugby footballer and swimmer.[4]

Despite his father's wishes, Alan joined the Australian forces still at the age of sixteen, enlisting with the 31st Battalion, 14th Reinforcement on 5 June 1917, and embarked to Britain on HMAT A20 *Hororata* on 14 June. He returned to visit the School whilst in training, but was soon drafted to France.

He was noted as a 'fearless and capable rugger forward' for Marlborough House and 'carried his football qualities into all his activities.' *The Portcullis* noted, 'he would take a request, but spurned an order.'

Alan was described by his comrades as 'rare good stuff' but sadly his life was cut short on 29 September 1918. The 41st Battalion which Alan was now fighting with, were part of the Allied armies that were attempting to break the three mile deep Hindenburg Line, the strongest of the German reinforcement positions which they had developed after 1916. This young man certainly carried the sporting mentality with him as he died trying to save the life of another. A few days after Alan was killed the Hindenburg Line was broken and within a few short weeks the war was over.

References

1. Col. G.W.L. Nicholson, *Official History of the Canadian Army in the First World War: Canadian Expeditionary Force 1914–1919* (Ottawa, 1962), p. 37.
2. *The Portcullis*, Summer Term, 1915, p. 51.
3. H.C. McIntyre, letter to his brother E.T. McIntyre, reprinted in the *San Francisco Chronicle* 9 April 1916, p. 48.
4. Our thanks to Alan's nephew Nicholas Pearman for additional information about Alan's father.

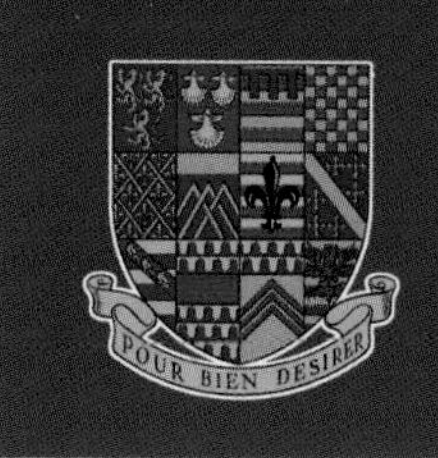

Brief portraits of OEs who fought in Gallipoli and in the Mediterranean

The Gallipoli Campaign of 1915 is perhaps one of the greatest mistakes in military history. By the time it ended in January 1916 the combined force of British, Australian, New Zealand and Indian troops had achieved little advantage and it appears justified to conclude, as one historian has recently argued, that 'the campaign was fought in vain.'[1]

The campaign was initially conceived as a naval one to knock out the Turkish guns which lined the route of the Dardanelles and thereby allow free passage for British ships to open up the Bosphorus and relieve Russia on the Eastern Front, fighting a two-pronged attack from Germany on its Eastern borders and the Ottoman Empire in the Caucasus. However some within the British military and political establishment argued that a naval attack could only achieve its aims if supported by infantry landings along the Gallipoli coast. The Allied troops attempted to force the Ottoman troops to retreat on several occasions during 1915 from the initial landings in April through to the Suvla Bay landings in August but the overwhelming problem was that the Ottoman troops held the high ground which proved deadly to any advance the Allied troops made. The campaign's aims appear chimerical not least in that its greatest proponents never quite seem to have grasped the realities of the situation on the ground.

A number of Old Emanuels fought in the Gallipoli Campaign and later in the wider Mediterranean campaign. The British and French established a base in Salonika, in northern Greece. Although Greece was neutral the Greek government acquiesced to Allied troops being established in the country. They were there to support Serbia but once they had arrived Serbian forces had already been forced out of Serbia as Austrian and German forces took Belgrade. The entry of Bulgaria on the side of the Central Powers in 1915 put further pressure on the Allies who were forced out of Macedonia. From April 1915 to September 1918 the Allies fought a war against the Central Powers in southern Europe until Bulgaria surrendered in September 1918.

Richard George Gabb *(Emanuel 1905–1909)*

Richard joined the OTC whilst at Emanuel. After leaving School he worked for an engineering firm and lived in Dalston. He was commissioned in November 1914 as a 2nd Lieutenant and landed in the Dardanelles in May 1915. Richard was killed in action on 6 August 1915. After his death the local paper reported, 'He was frequently in the thickest of fights and had several narrow escapes. He was, in fact, once wounded in a fight with a German officer, whom he succeeded in killing but the injury he got did not keep him out of active work. His letters home were always full of good cheer, though the hardships which he, in common with others, suffered were many.'[2]

Richard's father was landlord of the Windsor Castle Public House in Carshalton and just over a year later in December 1916, lost his second son, Richard's brother Stanley, who died whilst serving with the Machine Gun Corps.

Frederick John Sheppee alias Frederick Johnson *(Emanuel 1885–88)*

Frederick Sheppee was one of the earliest pupils at Emanuel School when it moved to Wandsworth Common in 1883. Born in 1873 he later became a labourer and when war broke out in 1914 he was in New Zealand and tried to enlist at the age of 41 but was refused because he was over age. He returned to Australia and enlisted in New South Wales giving the name Frederick Johnson and age 36. He became Private 1371, "C" Company, 2nd Battalion 1st Infantry Brigade, Australian Imperial Forces. He left for Egypt with the second reinforcements and was part of the first landing at the

Dardanelles on 25 April 1915 where he was wounded in the thigh. He spent time recovering from his wound in a hospital in Egypt but returned to duty and was killed in Gallipoli between 7 and 14 August 1915.

Charles Ernest Turner *(Emanuel 1904–1910)*

Charles Turner served in the School OTC and when war broke out was appointed a Temporary 2nd Lieutenant in the 11th Battalion Worcestershire Regiment and was eventually promoted to Captain in 1917.

The history of the Worcestershire Regiment records the 11th Battalion's move to France in September 1915:

> The 11th Worcestershire, with the other battalions of the 78th Brigade, left its Wiltshire training ground on September 21st, entrained at Warminster for Southampton and thence crossed to Boulogne. After a short stay in the rest camp at Ostrohove, near Amiens, whence they marched to billets at Foudrinoy. Two days later the battalion marched by Ferriers to Pont de Metz and thence, with the other battalions of the 78th Brigade tramped forward through Amiens and Lanueau, along the banks of the River Somme, through Aubigny to billets at Fouilloy.[3]

Charles at this time was with "A" Company, 11th Battalion. After a period of training and a short period of front line service on the Western Front, the battalion was transferred to Salonika, leaving Marseilles in November aboard the pre-dreadnoughts *Mars* and *Magnificent*. The regimental history records the action for which Charles was awarded the Croix de Guerre whilst the battalion operated in the hills north of Salonika:

> On October 9th orders were received to make a small raid against the 'Mamelon' (a Bulgarian held hill), with the object of capturing a prisoner and thus identifying the troops in front. At about 4.30pm while still daylight the raiding party – Captain P. A. Leicester, Lt. C. E. Turner and 30 other ranks pushed forward, up the Doldzeli ravine to the slopes of the 'Mamelon.' The party got within a short distance from a trench held by the enemy and charged. They were met by fierce fire from about 70 rifles and by many bombs. One bomb killed Private J. W. Rudd, another wounded Captain Leicester and two of his men. After a short fight it was realised that success was impossible and the raiders fell back behind cover. Then it was found that Private Rudd was missing. Believing him to have been wounded and left behind, Lieutenant C. E. Turner, accompanied by Private W. Hartland bravely went back. They found Private Rudd dead within a few yards of the enemy's trench. After running the gauntlet of a sharp fire they rejoined the rest of the Party. For their gallant conduct in this affair Captain Leicester was awarded the Italian Silver Medal 'for valour', Lieutenant. Turner the French Croix de Guerre and Private. W. Hartland the MM.[4]

Charles was wounded by shell fire to his right arm when the 11th Worcesters did another tour in the front line between 8 and 15 November 1916 in the vicinity of Doiran. As a result he was invalided to England. He resigned his commission on appointment to the Royal Air Force in 1918.

Arthur Collen *(Emanuel 1904–1912)*

In 1912 Arthur played Sergeant McDonald RA in an Emanuel School production of Arthur Conan Doyle's *Waterloo*. Starring alongside him was Dennis Furlong, who later became a Brigadier, winning the Distinguished Service Order for the part he played in the evacuation of troops from Dunkirk in 1940. Arthur was also a keen rugby player and is pictured in the Emanuel First Fifteen of 1912 with a number of boys who subsequently lost their lives in the First World War.

Arthur's nephews Richard and Rodney Freeman remember their uncle Arthur:

> Like so many at the time our uncle Arthur believed that the First World War would be a very short conflict. He was keen to serve his country and on the outbreak of war jumped on his motorcycle and went to the nearest military establishment to volunteer, only to be told by the sentry at the gate to 'push off.' He was however soon given a Commission in the Royal Marine Artillery. He used to say that an NCO working at the War Office at the time, who had been the School Sergeant at Emanuel, helped to obtain this for him quickly.
>
> In those days many young officers had private means and Arthur struggled to survive on his pay. On one occasion he had to pawn his sword in order to pay his mess bill. We don't know much about his training, but he did tell us that he and other young officers had sessions with the Regimental Sergeant Major, when they were instructed in how to use their voices when giving orders on parade.
>
> Arthur was sent to France, where he spent some time flying as an observer with the Royal Naval Air Service. On one occasion his plane 'ditched' in Dunkirk harbour.

This incident was recorded in a letter by Harold Rosher, the pilot of the plane, to his sister:

> I was sent with an observer this morning in a Vickers Gunbus (a pusher machine) and all went well until

coming home, when the engine petered out, when I was only 400 feet over the town... I pancaked (flattened out) as much as possible, but hit the water with a bit of a biff... I remember seeing my observer shot out into the water about twenty yards ahead and the next thing I knew was that I was under the water... I was relieved 'some' when I bobbed up to the surface... On arrival at the surface, I found my observer hanging on to the machine... We were only about 40 yards from the side of the dock, but didn't venture to swim, as the sides were twenty feet high and the ladders only just reached to the water... After a bit some life belts were thrown out and two men came out on a little raft. I swam to a life belt and my observer (Lt. A. R. Collen, RMA) got on the raft. We both had to be hauled up out of the dock with ropes and by the time we got to terra firma, it was as much as we could do to stand up. We were in the water about 20 minutes and I don't think I have ever been so cold before.

We walked rapidly off to the aerodrome, half a mile away and there had a stiff rum and milk and stripped in front of a fire and had a good rub down. We had lunch wrapped up in towels and were then rigged out in blue jerseys and blue serge trousers. This afternoon we have both had a hot bath and are feeling none the worse. The CO was very amused about the whole proceeding and laughed heartily at us.[5]

The Freemans continue their story on Arthur's service:

Later he was posted to the island of Bozcaada off the coast of Turkey (also known as Tenedos, and made famous by Virgil as the place from which the Greeks set sail to attack Troy). There he commanded an artillery unit. He and his men enjoyed swimming in the warm water of the Aegean, but Arthur had little company. His girlfriend Doris did what she could to help by sending him books to keep him occupied.

Arthur left the Marines at the end of the war, although he remained on the Reserve for some years. He married Doris and later became the manager of the galvanising department at an engineering firm known as Painter Brothers. During the Second World War this company helped to manufacture, 'Pluto', the 'Pipe Line Under the Ocean' which supplied fuel to the Allied Forces in Europe following D-Day.

Richard and Rodney were evacuated from Ipswich to stay with their uncle Arthur and aunt Doris in the Second World War.

The following photos are from Arthur Collen's collection taken at the British base in Mudros on the isle of Lemnos between 1917 and 1918.

References

1 Robin Prior, *Gallipoli: The End of the Myth* (2010), p. 252.
2 Our thanks to Andrew Arnold who has researched the individuals on the Carshalton War Memorial who died in the First World War. Richard Gabb's death was reported in the *Carshalton & Wallington Advertiser*.
3 Captain H. Fitzm Stacke, MC, *The Worcestershire Regiment in the Great War*, p. 121.
4 Ibid. p. 139.
5 Harold Rosher, *In the Royal Naval Air Service: Being the War Letters of the Late Harold Rosher to his Family* (1916), pp. 83–85.

Arthur Collen (seated centre with stick) with the unit football team

Gun crew relaxing

The British Fleet moored off Mudros, Lemnos

Gun crew with camouflaged gun

The old fort on Tenedos

Gnr. Cook (Arthur's servant)

Happy Valley gun and crew

Sgt. Miller & Bdr. McKeon

A fascinating collection of equipment without any explanation. It appears to include very early radio equipment, telescopes and possibly surveying equipment

Arthur Collen with his dog

No. 1 Gun's crew

Sir Alfred Butt

(Emanuel 1891–1893)

Theatre Entrepreneur, Politician, Racehorse-Owner & -Breeder

Sir Alfred Butt

Sir Alfred Butt attended Emanuel School in the 1890s. He built a theatre empire in the Edwardian period, becoming managing director of the Adelphi Theatre, the Empire Theatre and the Gaiety Theatre.

During the First World War he became Director of Food Rationing at the Ministry of Food. In 1918 he was knighted for both this role and work with war charities. Later, Mrs C. S. Peel remembered Alfred making a trip to the Westminster Bridge Kitchen, 'where I was greatly struck with his evident love for children, his interest in those who were buying their dinners, and his delight that instead of being obliged to dine off pieces of bread they could now go to the public kitchen and buy for a few pence a nourishing substantial meal.' [1]

He was a generous benefactor to Emanuel's Scholarships and War Memorial Fund and was elected MP for Balham and Tooting in 1922. Between 1924 and 1931 he was Managing Director of the Theatre Royal, Drury Lane.

In the 1930s his political career ended after he benefited from leaked Budget proposals. While playing golf with J. H. Thomas, the Colonial Secretary. Thomas is reported to have said to Butt 'Tee up', which was code for an increase in the tax on tea. With this Butt insured himself at Lloyds against such an actuality. Thomas subsequently resigned from the Cabinet.

Alfred is particularly significant in the history of the First World War for financing the only known film footage of parts of the Gallipoli Campaign of 1915. The film, which was shot by the British war correspondent, Ellis Ashmead-Bartlett, known as *With the Dardanelles Expedition: heroes of Gallipoli*, or more commonly as *Heroes* is the most culturally significant footage with regards to modern Australian identity. The Australian War Memorial acquired Alfred's copy of the film (a 35mm positive) in 1919 and it has been suggested that it is perhaps, 'the single most important film footage in the Australian War Memorial's collection' for the fact that parts of it show Australian and New Zealand troops in action around ANZAC Cove between July and September 1915. The film also depicts British, Turkish and Irish troops. *Lord of The Rings*-director, Peter Jackson, digitally restored the film in 2005.

A scene from the film Heroes

In 1919 the Commander of American Forces in Europe, General John Pershing thanked Alfred Butt and two others as leaders in organising entertainment for American troops stationed in London in the First World War. [2]

In addition to the theatre, Alfred's other passion was horses, and he had thousands of winners as both owner and breeder in a career stretching more than 50 years. After he retired from politics he purchased the Brook Stud near Newmarket, from where his career flourished. His two biggest winners came in 1946, winning both the Epsom Oaks and the Ascot New Stakes.

References

1 Mrs. C. S. Peel, *A Year In Public Life* (Constable, 1919).
2 'Entertaining the Troops', *The Times*, Monday 21 July, 1919, p. 10.

CHAPTER 6
LIFE ABOVE THE TRENCHES

Per Ardua ad Astra

George Banting CB, CBE Air Vice-Marshal

(Emanuel 1909–1915)

George Banting had a remarkable sporting career at Emanuel. He played in the First Fifteen, was a swimmer of considerable prowess and was also an Emanuel oarsman. In 1915 he was a member of the Emanuel OTC side, which won the British Shield, a short-lived shooting competition between Emanuel and Glasgow High School. On leaving Emanuel he entered the Royal Military College Sandhurst and was gazetted to the 1st Battalion the East Surrey Regiment. A short time later George became attached to the Royal Flying Corps, graduating on 20 March 1917. Being qualified to fly at this time meant being part of revolutionary technological advances. George's log books show that he flew a large variety of new aircraft including Avros, FE2bs, RE8s and Camels. Within less than two years of walking down the Emanuel drive George was fully engaged in one of military history's most dynamic periods. It must be remembered that flight was in its infancy having only been around for eleven years when the First World War broke out.

George trained at both the School of Military Aeronautics at Reading and No. 24 Reserve Squadron at Netheravon where he took his first practical flying training. In March 1917 he transferred to No. 34 Squadron and worked on aerial reconnaissance for the next year. The RFC had displaced the cavalry's traditional role of being the eyes of the army during the course of the First World War and for the first time in history, war was captured from a bird's eye view. On several occasions during reconnaissance flights George came under German machine gun fire and remembered anti-aircraft guns being, 'active, accurate, and persistent.' [1] George's log books from this time detail near misses and close escapes, for professional flying was still very much at the experimental stage which itself was being worked out during the course of a 'Total War.' Reconnaissance was dangerous work as George describes in his account, but work which proved of vital importance to understanding German movements on the Western Front.

In October 1917 George's Squadron were moved to the Italian Front where he carried out further reconnaissance work. He often flew twin-seated aircraft and in his account of his war experiences he illuminates his views as a pilot upon one of his notable observers who flew with him on the Italian Front, 'About this time Captain Wedgwood Benn, MP, DSO at present Secretary of State for India, was posted to my flight as an observer. He had no previous experience with the RFC...He proved to be very efficient, especially on long reconnaissance, when nothing on the ground seemed to escape his notice. From a pilot's point of view he was not so satisfactory, as enemy aircraft did not seem to interest him in the slightest degree, apart from the fact that his shooting was very bad indeed.' [2]

George Banting at the controls of his RE8 reconnaissance aircraft

George returned to England in early 1918 and worked in the instrument design establishment. He resigned his Commission in the East Surrey Regiment and was granted a Permanent Commission in the newly established Royal Air Force in the summer of 1919. In the inter-war period he continued his RAF career, qualifying as a flying instructor (Category A1), in 1927 and was at the RAF Staff College in the early 1930s before being appointed to the special duty list while employed as Chief Flying Instructor at the Point Cook training school for airmen of the Royal Australian Air Force in 1934. In 1940 he was posted to the staff of the Mission to Canada as part of the Joint Air Training Plan and was described in a recommendation for an award as, 'Highly qualified on all aspects of flying training and whole-heartedly devoted in giving his last ounce of energy to make things progress. He is popular with everyone in Canada. He has put in a tremendous amount of hard work and has helped the Royal Canadian Air Force considerably in furthering the Joint Air Training Plan.' George can be seen in a wings parade in a British Pathé News footage short film titled *PER ARDUA AD ASTRA*, which shows him awarding wings to Canadian pilots of the Commonwealth Training Plan. [3]

In the post-war years Banting rose to the rank of Air Vice-Marshal, having in the Second World War been appointed a CBE and Companion of the Order of the Bath. On Saturday 23 July 1949 he unveiled the Emanuel School Second World War Memorial in the School chapel. He continued to serve with the RAF, being posted to the Rhodesian Air Training Group in 1946 until retirement in the early 1950s. Banting's brother, John, also attended Emanuel and was a famous surrealist painter who knew many notable literary figures of the inter-war years including Ernest Hemingway whom he met whilst in Spain during the Civil War. In 1938 John accepted an invitation from Marcel Duchamp to contribute to the '*Exposition Internationale du Surréalisme*', held in Paris. In the Second World War John worked with Dylan Thomas as an art director for the Ministry of Information's Strand Films.

The following are extracts taken from the 1931 account of a 33-year-old George Banting recalling his service experiences as a reconnaissance pilot in the Royal Flying Corps during the First World War.

Banting recalls his time in France:

In March 1917, I was posted to No. 34 Squadron, stationed at Villers-Bretonneux. The Squadron was equipped with RE8s, and performed normal army co-operation duties. A quantity of photography was being done about this time, with a view of obtaining accurate information on the Hindenburg Line. One of the first tasks allotted to me in the Squadron was the taking of some of these photographs, and on photographic work I remained for the next year.

From a personal point of view, I thought photographic work had several attractions. Firstly, there was no question of rendering reports upon which important decisions were dependent. The camera did the reporting, and left no doubt as to the degree of reliability. Secondly, a good impression of the situation was given by studying prints and noting various work carried out by the enemy. Thirdly, the ground organisation of the photographic section was very interesting.

All instructions which I had been given in England on the subject of taking photographs had accentuated the importance of flying on a straight course, keeping the aeroplane level laterally, and maintaining a constant height. I found that if these instructions were carried out enemy anti-aircraft guns had every opportunity to range very accurately, and make excellent shooting. By flying in a zigzag course all over the area to be covered, and exposing a plate every time the aircraft was level, good results were produced, in spite of the fact that the overlap was irregular and many plates were wasted.

During the period of the Somme front, the squadron occupied several different aerodromes...on July 2nd 1917 the squadron moved to Bray Dunes, on the Belgian coast. The fine summer weather was ideal, and the call for photographs of the counter-battery area was great. The German anti-aircraft batteries situated in the dunes were more accurate than those in the Somme area.

One battery at Middelkerke of heavier calibre than the normal 77mm, was particularly efficient. The bursts of its shells were grey in colour, and very like shrapnel in effect. Such a menace did this battery prove when taking photographs, that it was necessary for my observer to watch the gun pits, and warn me the moment the gun flashes appeared so that I could change course quickly. The guns were mounted in concrete pits behind the village, and were a very difficult target for bombs or artillery.

On the morning of the 11th, I carried out a contact patrol, and succeeded in marking the British front line on the trench map.

In addition to the normal counter-battery photography with the standard L-type camera, there was a quantity of interesting photographic work on this front... made possible by the use of a 20-inch focal length camera, which, I believe, had a captured German lens... With this camera I was sent out to take oblique photographs of Middelkerke from 500 feet. The view required was of the sea front and therefore entailed flying parallel to the German beach for about ten miles, approximately a quarter of a mile out to sea. I do not think a single shot was fired at me on the way to my objective, but the moment I turned out to sea to return having taken the photograph, there was intense fire from the guns mounted in the dunes and, in spite of the fact that I was now about a mile from the shore at about ten to fifteen feet from the water, they made very good shooting. I presumed that the guns which did this shooting had been mounted with a view to dealing with any attempted landing on that part of the coast.

George Banting

> On a photograph taken a few miles south of Nieuport short straight trenches were observed radiating from the bank of the Yser... These trenches puzzled the intelligence staff for a long time. Eventually the 20-inch camera revealed that the enemy were attempting to dam the river under the bridge... If completed the dam would have caused flooding in the Belgian front line. Although the dam was within range of 12-inch naval guns at Adinkerke, it was not destroyed until about three weeks had elapsed. During this period it was photographed in every possible way.
>
> All this aerial activity must have made it perfectly obvious to the enemy that their work was observed and that no further secrecy was possible, but they continued their task and placed machine guns in the borrow pits to deal with low flying aircraft. A bullet from one of these guns wounded my observer, the shot passing through both his lungs. When it was seen that the dam was near completion it was destroyed by the naval 12-inch battery.

The Italian Front:

> At the end of October the squadron received orders to move to the Italian Front. The aerodrome at Milano, situated on the outskirts of the city, was used to house the squadron whilst the aircraft were erected and tested. Milano had a peace-time atmosphere and the Italians appearing uninterested in the war.

Soon the squadron would start work on the Front.

> The British troops occupied the Western bank of the Piave river... and the Austrians occupied the opposite bank. No man's land varied in width from approx 1000 yards to 200 yards. Prior to the arrival of the British forces the Italian Flying Corps had, in twelve months fighting, shot down 50 Austrian aircraft, but lost 100 themselves... In the first month of operations, Nos. 28 and 45 squadrons accounted for 88 enemy aircraft, and lost one Camel.
>
> Photographic work in Italy was somewhat different from that in France, as there were no fighter reconnaissance types to work in the enemy back areas. Photographs of enemy aerodromes showed they were badly laid out and exceedingly vulnerable to air attack. Advantage was taken by our Camel Squadrons who inflicted considerable damage by low bombing.
>
> The following day [26 December 1917] a bomb raid was carried out by the Austrians on Fossalunga aerodrome... 23 aircraft appeared over the aerodrome... and proceeded to drop bombs.

A Mark IV training tank, possibly photographed by Banting at Biggin Hill

In the dogfight that took place... eleven Austrian aircraft were shot down, or forced to land. Subsequent examination of the prisoners showed that they were all very drunk.

Later the same morning I proceeded over the line escorted by five Camels to photograph the aerodrome which we attacked. We intercepted a second Austrian raid... The leader... was shot down in flames... and the other two aircraft... escaped over their own lines. Better single seater tactics would undoubtedly have resulted in the destruction of all three raiders.

Flying on the Italian Front proved on the whole, to be both interesting and instructive. Neither the Italians nor the Austrians made good use of their aircraft. The Italians were almost entirely lacking in offensive spirit and never carried out offensive patrols. The Austrians had good aircraft which were badly flown and, like the Italians, seldom acted offensively. The example set by the British squadrons seemed to improve the standard of flying and aerial fighting. The Italians commenced to do aerobatics and improved in their fighting tactics, while German units were sent to augment the Austrian formations.

Reconnaissance photo taken by Banting over the Western Front

On his return to England:

In February of 1918 I returned to Home Establishment and was posted to the Wireless Experimental Establishment at Biggin Hill... [which] was concerned with the design... of wireless instruments. It consisted of an aircraft section... with an experimental staff of technical experts.

Having just returned from the war area, I could not help thinking that so much work of an experimental nature was unnecessary at the time. To me and many other pilots, it appeared that, even if perfect wireless instruments were evolved... they would not make any difference to the efficiency of the RFC, and I considered that an unnecessarily large number of pilots and aircraft were kept in England which could have been better employed in France.

There was also lavish expenditure on other instruments including 'navigational and night flying aids, acoustical devices, fog flying instruments and numerous miscellaneous 'gadgets' both useful and useless.'

But I still wonder if it was justifiable to carry out so much research at a time when every effort was necessary on the fighting front.

From a pilot's point of view, the work became increasingly more interesting and instructive. Long flights were frequently made by day and night, navigating either by wireless, or by sextant observation... the aeroplane became flying laboratories laden with instruments.

Only one night flying device is worthy of mention, namely the Davis Lamp. It was in the form of a powerful headlamp, which could be fitted beneath the forward portion of the fuselage of twin engined types and was a most efficient aid to landing.

I feel that, in writing about events which took place fourteen years ago, there is an inclination to lay stress on points which, in the light of later experience, seem trivial and uninteresting. At the age of nineteen it is not normal to look for the intention governing the issue of orders, but to be more concerned in their execution. It is only now, when attempting to find interesting data from which to draw logical deductions, that I realise how little, as a junior officer, I actually knew about the function of the service to which I belonged.

References

1 Service Experiences by Flight Lieutenant G. Banting, RAF Staff College, Andover, 11 March 1931, NA, Air1/2392/228/11/186 C554385, p. 4.

2 Ibid. p. 11.

3 http://www.britishpathe.com/video/per-ardua-ad-astra-1.

Dr John Collier Hopkins CMG

(Emanuel 1912–1916)

From oars to wings: The First Captain of Boats as an RFC night bomber

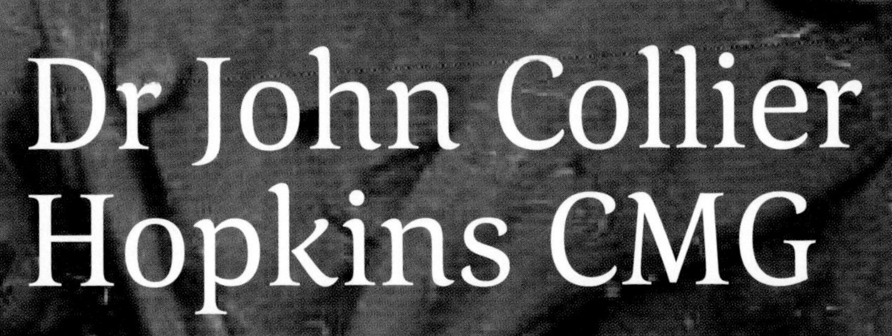

The striking contrast of the First World War lies in the experiences of those young men who were at one moment leading an ordinary life in the middle years of the War and the next playing a full part in its struggle.

On 24 July 1916 John Hopkins was stroking the Emanuel Four to victory over Kingston Grammar School in a race between Barnes Bridge and Hammersmith Bridge. The sight of a clinker four gliding across the surface of the river Thames on a summer's day is idyllic but within less than two years John, who was the first joint Captain of Boats at Emanuel, was diving out of the sky in night bombing operations on the Western Front in a two-seater fighter, the FE (Farman Experimental) 2b. A stroke of any rowing crew must be able to keep time, be a natural leader and possess the acumen to make a quick decision which makes the difference between winning or losing a tight race. All these skills would have aided John in those hair-raising moments coming under fire just a few hundred feet above enemy lines.

At school John was in the First Fifteen in addition to being a rower. In the Spring Term *Portcullis* we learn that he was 'A willing forward, who has not learnt to scrum properly. He gets his feet too far forward and does not pack tight enough in the front row. He has used his pace well and has not been afraid to tackle. Considering the short time he has played rugger, he has done very well indeed.'[1] A number of this Fifteen did not survive the greater tests of war, young men, whose last game was played out on Flanders Fields or across the wider Front stretching down into the Mediterranean.

John's true athleticism shone through in a boat but he was just as sharp with the pen being firstly sub-editor and then editor of *The Portcullis* in his last year at School. As editor also of the Rowing Notes he informed readers that, 'Great difficulty was experienced this year in obtaining dressing rooms and boats, our former boathouse being used as a workshop for munitions.'[2] He was also a School Prefect. Interestingly he played in the same Fifteen as George Banting in the winter of 1915. Both were better rowers than rugger players and both skilful airmen in the Royal Flying Corps.

John first joined the Honourable Artillery Company in October 1916 and was a Private in the Reserve Battalion, but within a few months transferred to the Royal Flying Corps on gaining a Commission. In 1972 John was interviewed about his time in the RFC which offers us a window onto his experiences during the First World War from the various training courses he undertook to the night bombing operations during the German Offensive in Spring 1918.

During the summer of 1917 John obtained his wings and rose to the rank of Flying Officer. Previous to this he trained on a number of different aircraft including the Maurice Farman Shorthorn, Avros, Sopwith Pups and Camels.[3]

Emanuel First Rowing IV, 1916. John Hopkins is seated first from right

John spent the autumn of 1917 with the Home Defence, providing air cover against German attacks on London.

An aspect of the world wars that some may take for granted is that the majority of young men who fought were just ordinary individuals thrown into the most extraordinary of circumstances. With all the derring-do and gallantry there is a tendency to overlook the nature of the individual but often, in interviews conducted many years after the events, they reveal to us this aspect of the individual behind the uniform or operation. In one instance the interviewer asks John to what extent pilot fatigue was an operational problem to which John replied:

> As far as I was concerned it was. When I was young I was very bad at waking up and if I got into a sleep I was just dead. And I nearly always had to be dragged out of my bed when it was time to go – on the second or third show say if I had tried to get a bit of sleep.[4]

There is nothing extraordinary in finding a young man having difficulty getting out of bed perhaps, but this is placed in context when we learn that this was his third operation across enemy territory that night. Here the difference lies between the general and the remarkable for, although he may have found it hard to wake from his sleep, John faced with each mission the prospect of eternal sleep yet still undertook his duties without complaint and with great fortitude.

RFC Night Flying Training

After obtaining his wings John was sent on night flying training at Marham in Norfolk and remembered, 'When it came to night-flying I must admit to feeling somewhat nervous in my first flight.' Different technical knowledge was required for night flying. For example in day flying one could see the horizon as the pilot was preparing the aircraft for take-off but at night as John describes, 'there was no horizon at all; it was just like flying into a black blanket.'

Although technological advancements accelerated in the first decades of the twentieth century, flying equipment was still very primitive as John remembered when discussing navigation instruments:

> We had practically no instruction in navigation; we had a compass and that's about all. And the compass was a very primitive affair; it used to swing round in all directions and – particularly if the weather was at all bumpy – it was almost impossible to keep your compass card on the course that you were flying. So we relied very largely on landmarks to find our destination.

One story John related best illustrates the 'crude' methods with which RFC pilots had to operate. John was transferred to Retford as a Flying Instructor and whilst there the Air Ministry had sent an Australian airman whose brief was to put the anxious pilots waiting to go overseas through a navigation course to test their readiness. John would pilot the instructor who sat as John's observer in a FE2b. During the course of the flight they encountered a snowstorm. As they descended through the clouds on their way to Grimsby, the land below was covered in a white blanket and there was a lack of clear natural markers to navigate a course so John decided to head back to Retford. The rules of the course were that the pilot was not allowed to have the map as they had already navigated a course at their base but the situation necessitated the instructor handing John the map. Realising they had been blown off course John found a big house to land by. As John says, 'Well there was one piece of gospel which was preached to all Flying Corps pilots in those days – "If you've got to have a forced landing, pick out a big house and land beside that" – because you're sure to get good entertainment.'

Before the forced landing they had flown over Gainsborough and John was annoyed that the instructor had not spotted this landmark because it would have only been ten minutes flight from Retford but as it turned out the Australian had indeed spotted the town, as John remembers:

> Soon as I got him on one side I said "Look" I said "Why didn't we spot that town we passed over; it was an obvious landmark. There was a railway going through it...and there was a river running right through the middle of the town. He said "River?" I said "Yes, the River Trent". Now you've got to remember he was an Australian; he said "That's no bloody river, that's just a creek!"

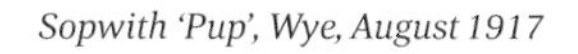

Sopwith 'Pup', Wye, August 1917

John joined No. 83 Squadron based in Narborough and in March 1918 flew from there via Lyme to St Omer. The snowstorm, crude technology and an Australian confusing rivers for creeks were nothing compared to the storm John was about to fly into.

Night Bombing and the German Offensive

Whilst Emanuel boys were losing their lives on the ground during the German Offensive of 1918, John was playing his part in stemming the tide of German troops as they broke through Allied lines. John was not the only OE in the skies over the Western Front during the German Offensive. William Sholto Douglas, later to head Fighter Command after Hugh Dowding in the Second World War, was commanding No. 84 Squadron RFC at this time. He remembered in the first volume of his autobiography: 'The build up by the Germans for the offensive against us in March 1918, was of proportions that were well-nigh fantastic and from the air we could see, for all the efforts that they made to hide what they were doing, that it was going to be a very big affair.'[5]

Sholto Douglas gives us his impression of what he felt at the time of the 'March Retreat':

> When I look back on it now and recall what it was like to be right in the thick of it, I know that I was not particularly scared. I was anxious, as we all were, and we would have been stupid if we had felt otherwise. But we had on our side the resilience of our youth and it enabled us to face that very serious set-back with a determination that was at least buoyant.[6]

Once John landed at St Omer his squadron was directed to go to Auchel as he explains: 'Auchel was quite a small aerodrome near a little mining village and it was behind Merville in the Armentières area. Not too far behind the lines but far enough to be reasonably safe; we were away from shellfire or anything like that.'

John was on night bombing operations during the March Offensive. He recalls what his duties involved:

> We were given an objective; we had to bomb it as accurately as we possibly could; we had to cross the lines and when we were over the lines of course we were subject to enemy gunfire, anti-aircraft; and at the height that we flew in those days, which was not much over two or three thousand feet, we were within machine gun range – and sometimes machine guns could be very troublesome. But we had definite objectives and we had to get there, we had to bomb as accurately as we could and we had to get back. So it was something quite different from what we'd been used to.

John Collier F. Hopkins in the new RAF uniform, 1918

John received bomb training whilst stationed in Marham as he explains:

> They had – I think they were called Carcass bombs. They were incendiaries. And some kind of a target was laid out on the ground and we used to fly over and drop these incendiary bombs on to the target.
>
> Well we had bomb sights – or what were called bomb sights. They were gadgets fixed up on the front of the nacelle of the machine – that is the front part where the observer sat. And he squinted down one of these things and he guessed what altitude – or I as a pilot could tell him what altitude we were at by reading my altimeter – and he'd adjust this bomb sight and then he'd squint down it and at the bottom of the nacelle, whichever was the arrangement – and pull a toggle on a Bowden cable which would release a bomb...we dropped one bomb at a time.

Avro 504 above Dover, 1917

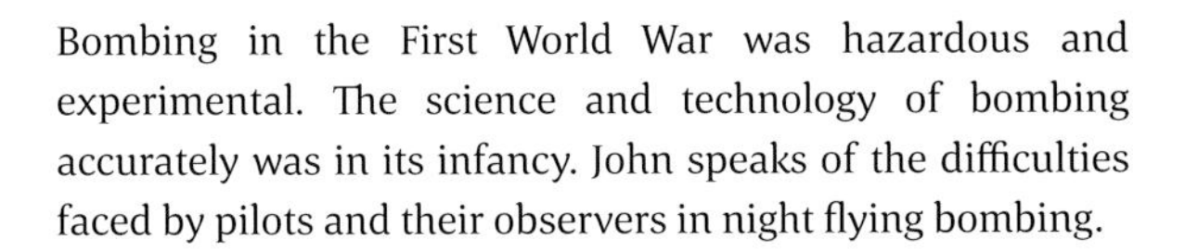

Bombing in the First World War was hazardous and experimental. The science and technology of bombing accurately was in its infancy. John speaks of the difficulties faced by pilots and their observers in night flying bombing.

> There were no proper bomb sights so one can understand it was rather hit or miss. In fact there are times when the pilot hung the bomb over the side and dropped it from his hands.

Sopwith Camel from John Hopkins's photograph collection

Targets included factories, buildings, crossroads, rail and road junctions and other strategic targets. John remembers the wind direction being another factor which they had to contend with and which could cause unforeseen results by causing the aircraft to drift thereby putting them off course. This meant that instead of bombing 'directly into the wind or down-wind' they bombed across-wind:

> I remember on one occasion we were somewhere out near Courtrai – I think – somewhere up that way and we were given a group of buildings to bomb. There was a railway there too and there was a lake – a small lake of some kind. A beautiful spot to pinpoint.
>
> Well, you see when we bombed we could see where our bombs hit: we could see the explosions. And I shall never forget the awful dismay with which I released my big bomb – which was 112-pound high explosive – on what I thought was going to be a direct hit on this big building and it must have dropped at least three-quarters of a mile or a mile away – even from a matter of about three thousand feet. It was an awful shock to me to think one could be so inaccurate.

Bombing strategy was changed as a result of the German Offensive as John explains:

> There was a distinct change because the operations were very much intensified. Instead of going into a map room, say, at dusk and getting our orders to do one particular operation – say a bombing operation on a junction – we were assembled earlier; we were given

FE2b Night Bomber, No. 199 Squadron, Harpswell, Lincolnshire, where John was an instructor from August 1918 to March 1919

It was hard to determine what damage had been done as John explains:

I think it was almost impossible to evaluate what damage we did to actual troops – columns of troops. The fact that we dropped some bombs and then the troops disappeared didn't mean to say we'd blown them up it simply meant they'd scattered to the side of the road.

Pilots like John could be flying for four hours an evening and when reloading and refuelling is factored in, an evening's work could last for up to eight hours. John describes how they felt:

We felt…like having a couple of scotches in the mess – although that wasn't encouraged. Cocoa was much more popular, a good hot cocoa; it was pretty cold just then. They were bright moonlight nights but very frosty.

an immediate objective. For the first few days this consisted almost entirely of attacks on roads which the enemy were using to bring their forces through in the push.

We took off earlier than usual while it was still somewhat light but we daren't cross the lines because of the danger from fighters and anti-aircraft guns in the daylight with those old machines flying so low. We waited till it was dark and went over.

We attacked – usually roads sometimes railways – anything where we saw troop movement. But the principal target for attack just for the first few days was the Albert–Bapaume Road – or rather the Bapaume–Albert Road – on which the Germans were advancing rapidly and we simply concentrated on that.

The weather, it so happened, was very fine; bright moonlight nights – we could see almost individual vehicles on the road and troops. And we just went straight out there; dropped as many bombs as we could. Most of the bombs we used then were anti-personnel bombs as against the larger high explosives we used to use for buildings. We'd return as quickly as we could to our aerodrome and there'd be intense activity, loading up the machine, filling up with petrol, oil, getting ready for the next show.

In addition to bombing John had to carry out reconnaissance and destruction of searchlights. He describes the type of work involved in reconnaissance:

This was accomplished by flying at about four thousand feet over a particular area that had been indicated and then dropping what were known as parachute flares. These were magnesium flares suspended on a parachute. They were rather like a bomb; they were launched through a tube and as they went through the tube an electrical contact fired the magnesium compound and the bomb-like thing dropped a certain distance, say, about five hundred feet or less and the parachute opened and at the same time the flare caught light.

Well, if we were observing a railway, for instance looking for traffic on the railway, we would fly along the railway, drop these parachute flares in a line and then turn round and come back over the top of the flares to observe anything that we could see underneath.

Reconnaissance work had its own dangers as John explains:

This was not a pleasant business at all because it was quite obvious to the Germans that having dropped the flares we were going to come back over the top of them again – and they were waiting for us. Well at the height we flew – which as I say was about three thousand feet – we were within machine-gun range and they had machine-guns there all right.

Then they had these things they called Flaming Onions which were balls of fire on wires and these things were shot into the air; they looked like enormous Roman Candles. They were quite terrifying but as far as I know they never did any damage at all – except to put the wind up you. But the machine-gun was definitely a danger.

Reconnaissance work was as John remembered, 'rewarding for the authorities', for 'people would find something that had never been observed before or reported – concentrations of troops for instance or some batteries opening fire.'[7]

Another dangerous but crucial task that John had to undertake was the destruction of searchlights.

...the Germans had their searchlights in barrages; three, four, five together. And each of these searchlights was armed with machine-guns and the searchlight used to sweep the air looking for a target and as soon as they buttoned on to a machine, the machine-guns would open fire.

One particular incident stood out in John's mind, showing us the realities faced by these pilots on the Western Front:

...going along quite cheerfully at about the usual height of two thousand five hundred, something like that, when quite suddenly and unexpectedly three searchlights opened up and they caught me – all three together – and we were surrounded with red tracer machine-gun fire coming up all round the place.

Well, I took evading action by just turning the machine away as hard as I could and I got out of the beam for a short time; then one of the searchlights picked me up again.

Well, the FE2B...was a machine with a big lattice-work tail; it had no body except a little thing in front. So that if you canted the machine – banked it – so that you were looking horizontally along the wings from the side it was, to a large extent, difficult to see. So one of the moves if you're caught in a searchlight was to slip down – side-slip down – the searchlight beam which I did and I got out of their searchlights. And no sooner had I done that than another one picked me up so I tried the same business with him, you see.

In the meantime I yelled to my observer "Joe" I said "For God's sake use your gun." And I don't know whether he was terrified or petrified or what but he didn't, you see, because one way to put a searchlight out was to fire at it – and I couldn't get him to use the gun. And I couldn't get a straight enough run onto these searchlights, because of the machine-gun fire, to drop the bomb.

So I did another side-slip. Well I must remind you we only started off at about two thousand five-hundred feet and by this side-slipping we lost an enormous lot of height. The next thing I knew, I saw Joe get up and I thought he was going to use the gun. Instead of that he just waved his hands up in the air for me to go up, you see. I looked over the side, I hadn't looked at the ground for a long time, was too busy dodging the searchlights – and found that we were skimming over the roofs of a whole lot of buildings. What they were to this day I don't know – but it looked like a factory or something like that.

So I yanked the machine up and giving it a terrific zoom we got out of the searchlight for a few seconds. As soon as I got high enough – you see to drop a bomb you've got to be over five hundred feet or else the safety mechanism won't have been unwound and they won't explode – so I got up to a sufficient height – luckily out of the searchlight – and as I turned round it came on me again. So I let him have four bombs. Well that put them all out for a little while.

So I rapidly climbed away and tried to get a bit of height and got up to about two thousand feet again – still circling round this place which I thought by having so many searchlights there must be of some importance. But I tried to tally this up with my route and my objective and I came to the conclusion that I'd lost my way and come across this nest of searchlights quite unexpectedly.

However I'd still got the big bomb on hand and I circled round for a bit waiting for them to open up but they delayed for a long time. In fact I don't think the searchlights came on again but the machine-guns did, they were firing at the sound of the machine. Well that was enough for me because with red tracer you could see where they were coming from, so I let them have the hundred and twelve pounder. I saw it explode – somewhere near the machine guns anyway – but it was sufficient to silence them.

No. 83 Squadron were forced to leave Auchel as the Germans advanced. John's Western Front experiences came to an end shortly afterwards. The Squadron found a new home with No. 101 Squadron and operated from their base but owing to a run in with poles in long grass John's aircraft became unserviceable for two nights in which time the rest of the Squadron were instructed on 101's drill for taking off which differed from 83's drill. John was unaware of the new drill:

I hadn't had these instructions and nobody seemed to realise I hadn't been told. So I went to take off just as we did in 83.

When it came to my turn to take off, I was waiting for the searchlight to go down to illuminate the flarepath – and nothing happened. Nothing happened and I was waiting with a whole line of machines behind me; engines ticking over and plugs oiling up – which is sometimes fatal in a take-off. And I thought, well I can't wait any longer, I don't know what's gone wrong with the searchlight.

So having seen the machine in front of me take off and saw the direction in which it went I thought, oh to hell with the searchlight, I'll go off now in the dark, I can see the way all right. I could see the faint horizon in front of me, so I took off but what went wrong, I don't know. I obviously went in the wrong direction and I veered to the right and I got off the flarepath.

Well unbeknown to me there was a haystack in the edge of this aerodrome and the first thing I knew that things were wrong was Joe, my observer, jumping in the front and waving his hands in the air as he'd done when we were in the search-lights, to go up – get up you see.

Well I hadn't reached full flying speed – having had a full load of bombs on – and to my horror the navigation light picked out this haystack on my right wing. Well I tried to bounce the machine over the haystack but it was no good. She hadn't got flying speed and we hit it with the wing and the whole machine cartwheeled – two or three times as far as I can gather, from what people told me – and there we were. And that was the end of my active service career in France. I subsequently spent three months of very inactive service in hospital.

The aircraft was covered in petrol but fortunately the safety devices on the bombs stopped them from exploding.

Between August 1918 and March 1919 John was a night-bomber instructor at No. 199 Squadron RFC at Harpswell in Lincolnshire. After the war John studied first at King's College London, leaving in 1922 to do a year's course in Mycology at Imperial College, London. He continued his rowing career, rowing for King's College and Auriol Kensington, the latter he represented at Henley Royal Regatta as Bowman in the Club's Four entered in the Wyfolds Challenge Cup in 1921. After Imperial, John was awarded an Empire Cotton Growing Corporation's Senior Studentship. He worked in Southern Rhodesia from 1927 to 1953. His mycological work saw him breaking new ground in the study of tobacco diseases. His research was published in 1966. In the Second World War John served as an instructor in the Rhodesian Territorial Force.

References

1 *The Portcullis*, Spring Term, 1915, p. 28.
2 *The Portcullis*, Summer Term, 1916, p. 48.
3 For a brief explanation of the operational roles of First World War aircraft see John Lloyd, *Aircraft of World War One*, (Ian Allan, 1958).
4 British Aviation of the First World War Period: Dr. J. C. F. Hopkins CMG: Experience of a night-flying pilot from home bases, 1917–18; and from Auchel, 1918, IWM Accession No. 000021 / 06. The collection is held in the Documents and Sound Section of the Imperial War Museum. Thanks are due to Trustees of the Imperial War Museum for allowing access to the collection.
5 Sholto Douglas, *Years of Combat: The First Volume of the Autobiography of Sholto Douglas, Marshal of the Royal Air Force, Lord Douglas of Kirtleside, GCB, MC, DFC*, p.261.
6 Ibid. p. 275.
7 Experience of a night-flying pilot, p. 28, Reel 4.

Emanuel OTC pre-First World War

The OTC and the Home Front in the First World War

When the First World War started few realised the life-expectancy of many Junior Officers would be so savagely short. Many OEs were quickly commissioned and promoted due to the military experience they had gained in the OTC. Emanuel, like many schools, had an OTC which dominated school life.

The sabre-rattling rhetoric which preceded the outbreak of hostilities led to a significant increase in the number of boys joining the organisation, and the powerful speeches of Headmaster Buchanan Ryley were a potent driving force.

The Scott-Giles *History of Emanuel School* reveals that over the course of 1914 the number of volunteers rose from 104 to 310. This meant that over 50 per cent of the School population served in the OTC. There were also School House events that promoted the OTC and *The Portcullis* 'House Notes' section frequently demanded more boys represent their House in these numerous drill and marching competitions. Participant numbers were meticulously noted and Houses with low turnouts shamed in the magazine reports. Boys who didn't join up were scorned and were seen as bad sports or worse.

Headmaster Harold Buchanan Ryley took great pride in his Corps and his successor as Headmaster Shirley Goodwin quickly realised that there was a great opportunity to take OTC activities to even greater heights. With long-serving teacher Captain Burnett as his Second in Command, the Corps was soon reorganised as a double company of four platoons, with the sections organised on a House basis. Machine gun and signalling sections were formed and a band was started. The parades took place every Friday at 4.30pm and, although numbers were initially low, it picked up and the drill made rapid progress. Indeed, in 1916, the Inspecting Officer, Viscount Churchill, told the Corps that its drill was 'Worthy of the Guards.'

On 28 July 1915 members of the Emanuel OTC organised a route march to the little village of Hartley, south of Gravesend. The marching was carried out at night. Having left Emanuel at 8.45pm their first stop was Streatham Common, which they reached at 9.50pm. They went through Crystal Palace, Bromley, Chislehurst Common, Fawkham and eventually arrived at Hartley at 8.45am the next morning. The scene was poetic; 'our route lay through pleasant undulating country, looking mysterious and fantastic in the semi-light before dawn.' Although their feet must have been blistered, these young boys, some only fifteen, showed real initiative and determination. Those who participated, including Banting, Fisher, Mott and Titley, all saw action on the Western Front within two years of this summer march.[1]

In *The Portcullis* published in the Spring of 1915, the editor of the OTC section was in good cheer and felt that: 'The School has realised what benefits can be derived from being in the Corps and recruits are coming in steadily.' The route the boys marched was impressive and was often very varied. The most common marching route snaked through Wandsworth, Wimbledon Common and back through Putney. Occasionally they ventured as far as Richmond Park. There was known to be plenty of singing, banter and whistling on these marches. Emanuel School also had its own OTC 'Corps Song' which has survived.

On 8 October 1915 the officers and NCOs of the Emanuel OTC inspected trenches in Richmond Park:

> We arrived at about 11.30am and spent the first half hour inspecting some firing-line trenches which had been made by a platoon digging itself in, in the shortest possible time. In spite of the water that had got in and undermined them, Lt. Daniel gave us some very useful instruction from them. We then went into the next field, in which were some very elaborate third-line trenches nearing completion and with the aid of the officer commanding the trenches, we were able to see and understand the building of some of the most perfect and serviceable trenches in use today. At the kind invitation of Colonel Shipley we then adjourned to lunch in the Officers' Mess of the 102nd Provisional Battalion, after which the Colonel obtained permission for us to see some trenches which the HAC [Honourable Artillery Company] had dug in two hours. These afforded us additional instruction, in that they gave us an idea of what a long line of trenches looks like.[2]

Emanuel OTC, winners of the British Shield shooting trophy, 1915

The OTC had many features and shooting was one of the most important. It was practised frequently throughout the course of the war, and in 1916 the School took second place in the competition for the Country Life Cup, behind Charterhouse. The School did very well in many shooting competitions and made excellent use of its rifle range which used to be located close to the current Sixth Form Centre. The Grundy Cup, a trophy for shooting, marching and drill squad also helped push up the general standards. The School was to remain a major force at shooting well into the 1950s.

Records indicate that the School Captains, Prefects and Lieutenants changed surprisingly frequently in the war years. This was often because boys joined up as soon as they were old enough to serve. This also led to joyous reunions as 'Old Boys' came 'back down the Drive'. These returnees were actually very young themselves and were simply returning to the School to visit their old friends and classmates. Being good for morale, they were welcomed with open arms. Leslie Clinton, Emanuel's first Military Cross winner, was hoisted on the shoulders of excited schoolboys when he returned to his old alma mater. Harold Buchanan Ryley Junior became Emanuel's first School Captain in 1913 and was later killed. His name can still be seen on the Captains' honours board in the School refectory. In 1916 OE George Lyward returned to Emanuel to start a teaching appointment but he also found time to become 'an officer of the Corps and Commander of the Subsidiary Corps.'[3]

A postcard depicting the pre-war workshop at Emanuel School

The School workshop played a crucial part in the home front effort and was a great morale booster for those involved. The basic plant consisted of three lathes, one screw-cutting tool and two heavier screw-cutting lathes. Staff and in particular 'Messrs Spark, Daniel, Appleyard and Williams', often gave up evening after evening of their leisure time to make the workshop function and help meet government requests to undertake munition and metal work. The School lacked the money to purchase machinery but help was at hand in the form of Mrs. Hunt, one of the School's benefactors who contributed £50 in addition to a £50 donation from the governors. The School community jumped at this chance to help the war effort. Pupils and Old Boys worked in shifts to create ball-bearings, bullet punches and other simple objects. The School felt great pride when it sent away its first batch of 'punches' to Woolwich Arsenal and received a very encouraging letter stating that extremely few had been rejected.[4]

As the War continued new Non-Commissioned Officers paraded almost daily and were taught the OTC basics. This included how to execute simple movements and commands. Learning timing was just as important as figuring out what to do and what not to do with the right foot! Most parades reinforced these simple practices and were devoted to the passing on of this hard-earned, but basic, knowledge. Of course, this was also interspersed with some new movements in company drill, with older boys bringing newer recruits up to speed. In reality, there was no real preparation for the trenches but many Old Boys felt that skills learnt in the Corps put them way ahead of the rest of the soldiers they were recruited with and were justifiably proud of their time in the Emanuel School OTC.

The Corps quickly volunteered to help protect the local area. This included patrolling the areas surrounding the twin railway lines in and out of Clapham Junction close to the School. Air raids were limited, but they did happen. A War Office telegram, dated 7 August 1914, also gave the Corps authority to guard the railways against possible wreckage and sabotage by spies. Emanuel boys took their jobs seriously, and as the Scott-Giles *History of Emanuel* humorously notes about a report in an edition of *The Portcullis*: 'One cannot get away from the fact that a big, burly man, the father of one of our own boys, being marched down the Drive between two small boys with bayonets fixed, does look ridiculous, and it is uncanny, when walking down the Drive, to be met by a dark form (the Headmaster Shirley Goodwin) and to find oneself looking down the barrels of two revolvers.' Whether they ever found any German spies was never revealed, but their hearts were certainly in the right place. In 1917 and 1918 the School sent over 100 boys to work under the Public Schools National Service Scheme during the summer holidays.

Leonard Edwin Fry in OTC uniform

However, the only firearms which were used to deadly effect were against the rats in the main building. Numerous School Sergeants were famous for their vermin shooting skills, but whether it was on the job-description is unknown. The Corps did keep a night and day guard going for a short while. It never amounted to very much, mainly because the boys could not be supplied with ball ammunition and when the long stalemate of the trench war went on, every sensible person knew there was no longer any danger to the School. From time to time there were also OTC church parades. This coincided with the resurrection of Sunday evening chapel services (previously stopped in 1909) when the names of fallen OEs were often read out. The School suffered relatively light casualties until the full horrors of the Somme were unleashed in 1916.

As the War struggled on the School started a War Fund. Its goal was to ensure those who stayed at home, 'endeavoured to do their share by supporting various funds in aid of those at the front, wounded at home and dependants in distress', as outlined in the Winter 1914 *Portcullis*. Originally the Fund was instituted to supply stamps and to enable concerts to be given to the wounded at the Royal Victoria Patriotic, adjacent to the School. It became the 3rd General London Hospital in the First World War and ironically a number of OEs spent time recuperating from injuries and illness on its wards. The Fund was expanded to make grants to the Red Cross Fund in addition to making goodwill gestures such as supplying a company of the Queen's Westminsters with Christmas puddings. Money was also raised by passing the Red Cross box at the School's rugby fixtures on Saturdays.

The Allotments

When the war started the School was still highly self-sufficient with home-grown produce. Its boarding school days may have been a thing of the past but many gardens, pastures and pupils with green fingers remained or were keen to muck in. By the spring of 1917 much of the green space around had become a veritable bee-hive of agriculture since the Headmaster called for a push to resurrect many of the old allotments. However, he drew the line at having his beloved lawn tennis courts dug up for potato growing as noted in this humorous creative writing piece which is rumoured to be based on fact:

> A crowd of small boys, with pride and self-consciousness stamped all over their faces, eagerly entered that awful sanctum, known as the Headmaster's study. "Well?" said the Head, looking up and surveying the invaders?
>
> "Please, Sir." said Smith, their ringleader (spokesman, I mean), "we've come to ask you if we could do something to help with the war. We wanted to work in the munition shop, but were told that at present they couldn't afford to have the School blown up, as schools were too expensive, but that they'd let us know later if they wanted anyone to wreck the lathes, or ruin the gas engine. So, please Sir, we came to you to know if we could take up allotments. We could first supply the School with our produce, and, on meatless days, go out with a barrow to sell the surplus. And then, Sir, we might build and support a large hospital with the money, for all our Old Boys from the Front."
>
> As, in his glowing efforts to be explicit, Smith appeared to be getting out of breath, the Head kindly interrupted him, saying, "Well, Smith, I see no reason why you and your friends shouldn't do so, provided you take all risks of injury from attacks by ferocious snails. But as to selling from a barrow in the streets; well, really, you know – it isn't done."

An Emanuel OTC Cap Badge, 1915

EMANUEL CORPS SONG.

March 1st 1915. By Arthur Cohen.

When o'er the hill and down the dale there comes the Bugle call,
"Fall in! Fall in! Ye who stand for liberty;
And ye who fight for truth and Right come fall in!
One and All."
What will then your answer be?
What will then your answer be?
When to her aid your country calls you,
Ready to face what e'er befalls you
This be your reply
This your battle cry,
"Emanuel! Emanuel! Emanuel! Emanuel!"
And then, when the clouds of war have parted,
And duty no longer weaves her spell,
This be your reward,
As you sheathe your sword:
"Well tried Emanuel!"

The Emanuel School Corps Song, 1915

"Thank you, Sir," cried Smith, adding an afterthought – "Shall we begin on your tennis-court, or the masters' Sir?" If he hadn't actually seen the transformation, he wouldn't have believed it possible for the Head to take a smile off his face so quickly and say,

> "If you think I'm going to permit a set of hooligans to hack up the tennis-courts for the sake of a few stalky potato-plants, you're greatly mistaken! The only place you can be allowed to lay waste is the remotest corner of the shrubbery where the eyes of the public will not be offended by the sight of you with your coats off. Now go!"

This included many vegetable plots around 'Gag's Corner' close to the Fives Courts and along the back walls from where cricket and rugby were watched. Although they are reported to have been well maintained, at various times the interest of small boys waned and weeds took over. There were also competitions between classes, run along similar lines to the modern House competitions of today. Staff, and the Sergeant, had also to keep a keen eye on the seasons to make sure seeds were planted at the appropriate times. Arguments also frequently broke out between pupils, as gardening styles often varied. *The Portcullis* kept a humorous eye on such shenanigans:

> Each boy had a different interpretation of 'Lying fallow', and as a result, in some cases, relations were rather strained between some of the parties concerned. For instance, Smith, thinking it meant 'to cleanse', inundated his plot daily with buckets of water, whilst his neighbour, thinking it meant 'to air', had already dug large holes to let the air percolate, and was therefore considerably annoyed when, each morning, he found his holes full of water, and likewise Smith when he found his plot nearly dry: this state of affairs led to a muddy warfare, which only ended when the former fell into a hole, pulling his adversary after him. It had to end then, as both were laid up with bad attacks of influenza for several weeks.

On a more positive note *The Portcullis* of Summer 1917 revealed that: 'One of the plots has already yielded to the kitchens a large enough amount to supply the School with dinner for two days, the vegetables in question being turnip-tops.' Apart from the odd argument pupils were encouraged to take great pride in their allotments and they were often allocated to School forms. Regular crops included spinach, carrots, cabbages, turnips, Brussels-sprouts and broccoli. The corner of the School which now has the tennis and Fives Courts was the location for the wheat-fields which produced the home-produced bread which was to become the norm in the dining hall.

In 1919 the School was presented with two huge guns for its contribution to the war effort, and in particular for its heavy losses on the Somme. *The Portcullis* noted 'OEs are now familiar with the two guns standing on the lawn in front of the porch and some may be in sympathy with the suggestion that they should be turned from their menacing attitude towards the Tower, to survey the covered approach from Spencer Park via the railway cutting. In support thereof, I may mention that one OE never leaves after a late session of the Committee without a mild occurrence of shell shock at the sudden encounter with 'two blinkin', winkin' muzzles' in position by the Drive.'

A German field gun given to Emanuel as a prize in 1919, later melted down in the Second World War

When the War ended, the interest in the OTC diminished for a time. This was the case across the country, even for the great military public schools. Although the appetite for war was gone, in ten years' time Cyril Broom would appoint Charles Hill to revitalise the movement in a command that lasted decades. Meanwhile in 1919, the government cautioned against schools neglecting their OTCs, stating that they should remain vital forces within their local school communities. At Emanuel the OTC took another hit when Shirley Goodwin resigned his command, after providing strong leadership throughout the War years. *The Portcullis* Trinity Term 1919 (No. 77) notes: 'It is with great regret that we heard on July 1st that Major Goodwin was obliged to resign his command. Yet it was singularly appropriate that his last parade should have been an Annual Inspection, which was certainly one of our best. We thank him for all the help he has given us during the last five and a half years, and we will assure him that we will maintain, and even improve upon, our already high standard of efficiency and that we shall give our utmost support to Captain Burnett, whom we heartily welcome as our new Commanding Officer.' Goodwin put everything he had into Emanuel School and died in the late 1920s.

After the War, compliments to the School continued to flood in for the way it, its OTC and its Old Boys had served the country. *The Portcullis,* No. 80, Trinity, 1920 commented with just pride: 'The War Office has again honoured the School for its signal services during the war and all OEs heartily congratulate the School on the presentation of another German gun.'

We can certainly sympathise with the visiting OEs who served in the war commenting that the guns made them 'jittery' but we'll never know whether the direction of these guns was ever turned around towards Spencer Park. The guns were eventually melted down for the Second World War effort. Amazingly there is only one known surviving clear photo of one of the guns, although the keener eye can sometimes find them lurking in the background of official rugby and cricket photos from the 1920s and 1930s.

Lieut. Colonel Turner DSO, GSO, who was the Inspecting Officer of the Annual Inspection in 1919, summed up the importance of the OTC to the war effort:

> You know that in Sir Douglas Haig's despatch, he paid great tribute to the part the public schools have played in the war. What we should have done without the OTC at the beginning of the war, I do not know. It supplied us with all the officers of our new army, and Emanuel did its share. Eight hundred of your number served and,

unfortunately, your casualties were very heavy – fifteen per cent having been killed. You have won three DSOs, six MCs, and Bar, twenty MCs, six Foreign Decorations, and one Meritorious Medal. Ninety per cent of those who served were commissioned. Of your officers who were accepted for Imperial Service, one died. Two Masters, who did not belong to the Corps, joined up and both were killed. I think this is a record of which any school can be extremely proud.

Among Emanuel's casualties in the war were two members of the pre-war OTC, Gerald William West and Cecil Boyce Grundy. When both died less than two months apart whilst serving on the Western Front the pre-war Headmaster Harold Buchanan Ryley was moved to write a poem dedicated to the boys whom he had spent many hours training in the ways of young soldiers.

A recovering soldier in front of the 3rd General London Hospital, Royal Victoria Patriotic Building, adjacent to the Emanuel School grounds

In Memoriam G.W.W. and C.B.G.

by Rev. H. B. Ryley
(Headmaster 1905–1913)

Dear lads, whom years ago I knew,
Ere yet your lives to manhood grew;
Dear lads who shared with me afar
The training of our mimic war,
The camp, the range, the march, the drill:
And now that blood-soaked Flemish hill
Has put you to the final test.
Thank God, thank God you gave your best!
God rest you, gallant gentlemen,
And keep you, as He held you then!
Sleep on in peace, O valiant dead,
Longed for, beloved, remembered,
We will not fail you: She for whom
You gave your hope, and light, and bloom,
England, the Mother of the strong,
England, the Righter of the wrong –
She will not rest until the price,
The measure of your sacrifice,
Be paid in full, and once again,
After the war-clouds' bloody rain,
Peace smiles upon a world set free
From all that Hunnish devilry
You fought, when not in vain you fell!
Dear dead, farewell, a long farewell!
We will remember to the end.
Farewell, dear friend! Farewell, dear friend!

The History of Emanuel School, p. 199

References

1 *The Portcullis*, Christmas Term, 1915, pp. 30–33.
2 Ibid. pp. 29–30.
3 *The Portcullis*, Summer Term, 1916, p. 48.
4 *The Portcullis*, Spring Term 1916, p. 33.

Minutes to the Governors

A Headmaster's wartime role

In Shirley Goodwin's 1914–1918 minutes to the Governors we discover the realities faced by a headmaster during the First World War: staff and money shortages, boys leaving mid-term, a dwindling school roll and a steady stream of sad news as OEs, most of whom were very young, died with alarming frequency.

Shirley Goodwin with the 1917 Emanuel Cricket Team

James Vaughan

Alfred Eric Titley

During the course of the War his predecessor Harold Buchanan Ryley was killed in action, the first School Captain (Harold Buchanan Ryley Jr) was also killed and what promised to be a short war became anything but. So the Headmaster bore the strains of a school in wartime, but remained upbeat and often reported medal successes and citations on the battlefield as well as the sad losses, along with the things that needed fixing in the daily existence of the School. These minutes provide a fascinating snapshot of those dark days.

The effect of the war begins to show in the minutes. In 1915 James Sims, a handyman, enlists in The Middlesex Regiment and the Headmaster found him very difficult to replace. Many 'support staff' joined the services but details are scant. He also notes that the school was doing very well with OTC manoeuvres, and that 'Mr Howard, an old boy of the school, was awarded the DSO in the holidays.' [It is now believed that William George Howard was not awarded the DSO]. On many occasions it is reported that losses had been heavy over the period of the conflict. One imagines there were too many names for him to name individually. Goodwin continues by noting that James Vaughan was also honoured:

> The School has gained another MC. This was awarded to Temporary 2nd Lieutenant James Vaughan 8th Battalion of the Buffs for "conspicuous gallantry and ability near Hulluch on Sept 26th 1915. When all his senior officers had become casualties he took command of his battalion, and brought it out of action safely and in good order." Lieutenant Vaughan was promoted Captain on the field as well. The same feat was performed by Lieutenant J. H. S. Richards also of this school who left in July 1914. Lieutenant Richards and Captain Vaughan are now senior officers of their battalion. Lieutenant Richards was badly hit but is recovering.

One consequence of the war was staff shortages, many having left at short notice to join regiments. Those connected with the OTC were also given further military support duties. Goodwin found it difficult to replace some staff, and reading between the lines, it is obvious that on some occasions he simply had to hire what was available. Indeed, on more than one occasion he voices his displeasure at the performance of several staff.

By mid-1916 Goodwin was in more upbeat mood. He noted that having little to say was indeed 'good news' and that attendance for the next school year was looking healthy and, as a result, he would be recruiting staff once again. He also proudly announced that three old boys won MCs on the same day for acts of conspicuous gallantry. The OEs in question were Captain R. G. Smithard, Lieutenant G. C. Smith (later killed) and Lieutenant G. N. Dolby.

Money was never far from the agenda. Goodwin frequently had to go to the Governors with delicate financial requests, more often than not, for staff salary increases; some of which were war-related. In regard to Sergeant Major Meacher, the Headmaster writes: 'You will remember that Meacher who has been in the Gymnasium, left during October to re-join the colours, and is now in France. He has a wife and a family of small children dependent upon him, and he has asked me whether I would approach you to see if you would make up the difference between his army pay and his salary here.' Meacher later returned home as a qualified drill instructor and began instruction of pupils.

Goodwin also informed the Governors that Mrs Godfrey – mother of Frank Godfrey, Prefect of the School, Company Sergeant Major and Cadet Officer of the Corps who was killed at Delville Wood, applied for permission to put up a tablet in the chapel to commemorate her son.

The war time Governor minutes conclude with a flourish of good news: 'J. R. Bradley [sic] has had perhaps the most adventurous career of any of our boys who have been fighting — has been awarded the Croix de Guerre with Palms, and created Chevalier of the Legion of Honour — has been granted the MC, and as his injuries have rendered him incapable of work on land has gone into the Royal Flying Corp.'

Further honours are also reported: 'A. E. Titley awarded MC and has also been recommended for further distinction, and also declined the Order of Danilo of Montenegro.' Captain Stevens has the last reference to the War when it is reported that he has been awarded a bar to his MC and has been made a Staff Officer in the RAF.

CHAPTER 8
DEADLY SPRING

'Dear old Emanuel, what a treasure house of happy memories!'

'SAG' Stanley Arthur George Harvey

(Emanuel 1902–1911)

A photograph from 1911 (seen on page 170) shows a young man standing with the Emanuel First Fifteen. His gaze is somewhat mournful, his arms are folded, but in fact this young man was full of life and love for his School. In his striped Emanuel rugby top, Stanley Arthur George Harvey, more popularly known as 'Sag', played a full part in School life.

In the Whitsun Term, 1911 *Portcullis*, we get a flavour of 'Sag's' character on the rugger field, 'Full Back. Has steadily improved throughout the season: his kicking is accurate: his tackling, though weak at times, is much better than it was.' He also played in the School Dramatic Society, in 1912 playing the role of Mr. Tinkler in *Vice Versa*.

After leaving Emanuel he had an active role in the Old Emanuel Association (OEA) and was known to frequently visit the School, having a great rapport with the younger boys. His war story can be traced through letters and articles reprinted in *The Portcullis*, which detail his movements and his rather amusing character sketch of a Tommy.

'Sag's' story as told in *The Portcullis*

Christmas 1915 – the Editor writes: ... at the time of writing Second Lieutenant S. A. G Harvey, of the Royal Berkshires, is on the eve of his departure, though he does not yet know where his duties will take him...

Spring 1916 – the Editor writes: ... Sag Harvey is in France and I'm sure he'll forgive me if I add 'at last.' The poor chap was so worried lest the war would be over before he got there, that it was almost a relief to his friends to learn by means of cryptic field post-cards that he was safely in the trenches...

In the Spring of 1916 'Sag' sent some 'first impressions' of life on the Front.

Spring 1916 – 'Sag' writes: Your good French housewife has one wise and jolly custom. Upon wires stretched across her best bedroom she hangs a goodly store of vegetables, dried 'au naturel.' Imagine the feeling of supreme happiness engendered when, on arrival at your billet late at night, dog-tired and with nerves on edge, you open the door and cannon into a bunch of onions, rebound into a pound or so of turnips, step hurriedly back to avoid a bundle of carrots, and bang your head against the wall! However it all adds to the gaiety of nations!

They are fond of their little joke, these good French folk. A British 'sub' squirming at the end of a door handle affords them the very acme of amusement. I will explain. Almost all the houses in the district are furnished with electric light and in almost every house is to be found a loose live wire. It is the particular joy of the fair daughter of the house to attach this wire to the door handle. Deep in his duty the platoon officer dashes from billet to billet, until, at length, he grasps a handle to which a wire has been attached and then – oh, curtain! curtain! For I've had some.

And then the trenches. They also provide their quota of amusement, for even war has its funny side. You would not expect to see a dog in the trenches, would you? Yet there are dogs, real dogs and no 'kid' (at least, I haven't seen one yet). For have I not the evidence of my own eyes and the lack of my own tea as proof? It happened in this way. I was sitting at breakfast in my 'dug-out' one morning (shall I say that I live in the pampered lap of luxury and that my 'dug-out' is a cellar and boasts a bed, a table, three chairs and a real stove), when in strolled a large and very muddy dog, of the hound persuasion. We gave him bread; he devoured it. We gave him water; he drank it. We gave him chopped up bacon, eggs and bread; he wolfed it. We gave him more bread; he ignored it. He was an insolent hound. He squatted down in front of our good stove and hid it from view. He scorned our caresses, likewise our bread, but he twigged upon our hearth the vessel (polite word for saucepan) containing our fresh brewed tea. He lapped with horrid sounds of relish. We stretched out eager hands for revolvers, rifles, bayonets, bombs – anything wherewith to fall upon and rend him, but he turned not a hair and calmly sat himself down to war once more. As for us, we forgave him and just laughed.

So from day to day one rubs along, making the best of one's surroundings, laughing when one may. But sometimes one thinks of home and of Emanuel. Dear old Emanuel, what a treasure house of happy memories! There are no Sundays out here, but sometimes one suddenly realises that this twenty-four hours is Sunday and that this Emanuel gathers together in her chapel. And it is all so easy to picture – our mellow light, the choir, the old familiar faces in the old familiar pews and Sergeant, good old Sergeant, tucked away in his corner, ready to lower the lights when the sermon begins. To us Emanuel is something more than just a thing of bricks and mortar.

Thus one dreams, but the crackle of the M.G. brings one back to earth, to remember that this is war, that just over there is the Hun and that between us there is but fifty yards of good French soil! But, begorra! he's for it and not us – which may be ungrammatical, but is most certainly true.

Summer 1916 – the Editor writes: S. A. G. Harvey has been home on leave, and an interesting article by him appears in this issue:

Tommy: A Character Sketch

The Portcullis, No. 68 Summer Term, 1916 pp. 58–60

The 'interesting article' was 'Sag's' impression of the atypical soldier more popularly known as Mr. Thomas Atkins or 'Tommy':

'Tommy is a creature of many parts and most alarming characteristics. He will burden himself like an elephantine Christmas tree, stagger down a muddy communication trench, fall, with the most precise and reassuring accuracy into every hole and swear horribly but impartially at them all. He will bang his toe on a trench board and moan for half an hour; yet he will get a shrapnel bullet through his arm and grin like a number one size Cheshire cat. He will offer himself with gusto for a bombing raid, but will not round a traverse at the sight of a rat. He simply loves to take off his gas helmet in the middle of an attack to get, as he says, a breath of fresh air. He will stick his head over the top when he shouldn't, he will roost in the bomb store and he will stand in all the places under observation; but if he can only manage to suffocate himself with the fumes from a coke-brazier, then he feels that he has done himself justice, that he has attained the acme of perfection.

But when Tommy gets an idea he becomes almost a public danger and certainly a personal danger – to himself. I know of one poor chap who conceived a great idea of firing five rounds rapid at the Bosch trenches, less than fifty yards away. He only fired three. Ah, Tommy, you are a great responsibility, but you are a wonderful man.

I remember one incident where Tommy came to my assistance in a situation of some peril. In my very best French I had endeavoured, for the space of half an hour, to make a good dame understand that I wanted to fix up a billet for one officer for one night. Apparently my French and her 'patois' were not on a basis of equality – certainly not on speaking terms. Of course, I blame her 'patois'! So for some thirty minutes we went at it hammer and tongs; I was the tongs. She was going 'some', about two hundred and fifty revolutions to the minute I should think, whilst I chipped in now and again on the low octaves. About the twenty-ninth minute she had speeded up to about three hundred and I was on the verge of brain fever. But at that moment a mess servant observed my predicament and dashed to the rescue.

He simply said, "Bong jewer, missus. Officer cushy, one night, compree?" pointing to the bed and holding up one finger. In a moment all was peace. Madame ceased to revolve and a glorious light of knowledge appeared in her face. I weakly mopped my brow and searched stealthily for brandy, but, finding none, staggered slowly away.

He is a bit of a wit, too is Tommy – quite a wag in his own way. One of the billets in the village has most of the front wall of the house blown away; above, Tommy has placed a placard – 'The Ever-open Door.' Another house bears the inscription – 'This is not an Estaminet. We do not sell eggs, nor do we know the way to the canteen.' Quite cute when you tumble to it, isn't it? Or shall I point to the immortal ballad sung by my own good troops in England, as they scrubbed their billet floors –

I wish I was 'civvy' again, ha! ha!
I wish I was 'civvy' again.
For when I was 'civvy'
I wasn't a 'skivvy,'
I wish I was 'civvy' again, ha! ha!
HA!

– sung mournfully, the brushes keeping time, to the tune of 'I wish I was single again.'

Missing, believed killed – Royal Blankshire Regiment No 1983, Pte. J. Smith (Aberdeen). How often have you casually glanced at such a line as that and what it has meant to you, I wonder.

Listen! He was one of your bombers, just such a one as any of the others, care-free, always hopeful, always faithful. And with the others he did his tour of duty at the end of that sap which thrust itself forward from your line. There, day and night, wet and fine, he sat out his spell, waiting ready.

It came so quietly; just a soft, sighing hiss heralded its approach, but when it landed beside him it woke to devastating, rending thunder. Thank God he never knew.

Presently your Sergeant came to you. "Aerial-torpedo landed in Sap H, Sir", said he "Wiped out the two men on duty, Sir. Mears and Smith, Sir." A pause. He continued. "Managed to collect most of Mears, Sir, but can't find no trace o' Smith, sir – but we knew he was there, Sir."

"Thank you, Sergeant. Put up Brown and Stokes to replace them."

"Very good, Sir."

It happens every day somewhere. But remember that five minutes ago he was a man, a laughing, grousing, 'stick-it' Tommy. And now – why he's just gone. Witness his obituary – 'Missing, believed killed.' That's all.'

Christmas 1916 – the Editor writes: We have welcomed with much pleasure the visits of a number of Old Emanuels to School this term, though our pleasure should, I suppose, be modified when wounds or sickness has been the cause of their return to 'Blighty'. S. A. G. Harvey, who was wounded in August, has devoted much attention to the affairs of the

OEA and many of us have enjoyable recollections of the dramatic talent he displayed at one of the 'socials.' 'Sag' and C. J. Chamberlain, – comrades in arms in slings – met at Southampton immediately upon their return from France and would have proceeded to paint the town red had they been 'in the pink.'

Summer 1917 – the Editor writes: At the time of writing S. A. G. Harvey is on the point of returning to France. We wish him all good fortune and congratulate him upon his engagement to Miss Norah Payne.

Christmas 1917 – the Editor writes: Satisfactory news has been received from S. A. G. Harvey...

Spring 1918 – the Editor writes: More of our Old Boys have paid the toll of the German Offensive with their lives and Emanuel wishes to express her sympathy with the relatives and friends of S. A. G. Harvey.

Summer 1918 – Wilfrid Scott-Giles started the Old Emanuel Notes in the Summer edition of *The Portcullis* with the following: 'I may, perhaps be forgiven if I place first in the term's Roll of Honour the name of one who has been my friend ever since we were together in Form 1, sixteen years ago. S. A. G. Harvey is dead – dear old 'Sag', who was for all of us a pattern of upright manliness and true friendship. Prominent in the corporate life of Emanuel during his schooldays, he took a keen interest in the affairs after he left and even when military matters claimed a large share of his attention, he would visit the old place on every opportunity and was very popular both among Old Boys and members of the present School, who will long remember the enormous success of an entertainment which he organised and which he took a leading part. Readers of *The Portcullis* will remember him, too, as the writer of one or two clever articles on war topics – notably his character sketch of 'Tommy,' which displayed that keen understanding of the private solider that made 'Sag' so successful and popular an officer. This article, indeed, formed the basis of at least one sermon. Soon after war broke out 'Sag' joined the Army and after serving for several months in the ranks, took a commission in the Berkshire Regiment and went out to France. He was wounded and home for a long spell, during which we often saw him and were glad because of his golden dreams for the future. But we knew that the near prospect of a second venture overseas filled him with an apprehension which he, perhaps, believed to be fateful. Nevertheless, he displayed the calm courage so characteristic of him. Emanuel in general will remember 'Sag' as one who typified all that was best in our School life, while his intimate friends will also cherish his memory as that of a brother.'

Emanuel First XV, 1911–1912

Back row (left to right) - F.S. Pashley, W.J. Hastings, S. Vaughan, F. Wingrove, W.W. Parkinson (V.P.), N. McKnight, T. Villis, S.A.G. Harvey, H.F. Booth, G.F. Camm
Middle row - P.J. Bate, A.C. Dancer (Vice-Capt.), W.F. Morgan (Capt.), F.J. Bilcliffe, A.R. Collen
Front row - F.R. Noel, R. Hedgeland

We can picture 'Sag' standing on the Emanuel rugger pitch anticipating the opposition's charge, but the cost of the opposition's victory was no more than frustration at losing and perhaps, one or two bruises. On the morning of 21 March 1918 the stakes were much higher and the cost far greater. The imposing classical red brick building overlooking the rugger pitch was replaced with the sight of a cloud of creeping gas and earth shattering explosions as the German Spring Offensive was launched. We know 'Sag's' fate through a short extract written by Lt. J. W. Randall, serving with "C" Company 8th Battalion, Royal Berkshires, whilst recovering from wounds in September 1918. Randall describes the fate of "C" Company as the Germans attacked:

> The attacking force was being continually re-inforced and, as the position had become quite untenable, Col. Dewing ordered a retirement by way of the communication trench to the battle zone. This meant moving in single file and we had not proceeded many yards before we encountered another large bombing party who had evidently been posted to cut off our retreat and to try to force us out of the trench. Some of them were actually in the trench and others lining either side. Lt. Harvey, the works officer, was leading the retirement at the time and he showed wonderful pluck in dashing straight at this party and shooting the first one he met at point blank range. Unfortunately he was shot by another of the enemy at almost the same second...

'Sag' was attempting to lead the men to safety from the advancing Germans and as with his rugger days he charged at the attacking force. Within a split second that dash became his last and with that moment fell a young man whose short life was devoted to his old School, in 'Sag's' words, 'a treasure house of happy memories!' Today 'Sag' is remembered on Panel 56 of the Pozieres Memorial, in addition to the Emanuel Archive. 'Sag's' body remains somewhere unknown but through his letters and his amusing sketches of life on the Front he lives on.

Wilfrid Scott-Giles wrote a poem in memory of 'Sag.' Simply titled 'SAGH', it reveals the raw emotion of losing a close friend and is full of references to the ways in which this generation of Emanuel pupils viewed the School not as being a place where one learnt a curriculum nor as merely bricks and mortar, but instead viewed it as a home from home, where friendships were eternally forged and where they always felt happy to return.

SAGH

"Weep for a fallen friend: dead, and forever dead; mourn for him." Thus the Thief
Speaks in our darkest hour, set upon stealing
The lantern of our faith, looking to send us reeling
Blindly, blindly down to the depth of unbelief.
"He that is fallen is dead," whispers the Thief.
Call him not dead, who dared so gloriously
Hell's every terror to face. Armed in the splendid strength
"God with us", - firmly held, but rarely spoken –
Gave (for his body, not his faith was broken),
His soul, came to its heritage at length,
Call him not dead who died victoriously.
And mourn him not. What does he know of grief,
Who stands beyond the limits of human feeling?
Joy after pain is his: after sorrow, healing.
Can earth afford that perfect joy, and that sweet relief?
"Weep: you have lost a friend," whispers the Thief.
Call him not lost to us. In friendship bounded
By earth's small prospects? Was the tie so little
That such a little thing as death can sever?
Friends we have been , and are, and shall be ever.
God made us so. And can the bonds be brittle
That He Who forged Eternity has founded?
Lift up your hearts. Of blessings his the chief,
In earth's mean trafficking no longer dealing,
Down from high Heaven, hear the bells pealing, pealing,
"Emmanuel" Emmanuel! Hold the belief.
...................................Silence the Thief.[1]

References

1 *SAGH* by CWG (Charles Wilfrid [Scott] Giles), *The Portcullis*, Lent Term, 1919, pp.35–36

Harry John Gustave Wyborn

(1877–1918)

On a Pozieres Memorial panel is inscribed the name Wyborn, H. J. G. It is not far from a panel bearing the name Harvey, S. A. G., but whereas Stanley was a young man fresh out of School when the War started, Harry had left Emanuel in 1891 and was in his late thirties in 1914.

An Easter card sent by Harry to his sister

The public conception of combatants is often projected through youthful images, of young men cut down in their prime but what is often overlooked is the fact that older men also fought and it was they who left behind young children to grow up without fathers in the post-war era. In this context our understanding of the term 'Lost-Generation' is extended.

Harry's aunt Jane Gallopin paid for his education at Emanuel. Jane and her husband, Olisine Gustave Gallopin owned a restaurant in Paris called the 'Brasserie Gallopin' until tragedy struck and Jane died, at which point Harry was apprenticed to a plumber. At the age of 24 in 1901 Harry was a plumber fitter and lived at home with his mother. Harry married Annie Clarissa Ellen Hughes on 26 October 1901 and the couple had four children.

Little is known about Harry's movements during the war. We know that he enlisted in the Royal Sussex Regiment in June 1916 as Private Wyborn G/12989, crossing to France in September of that year. In 1917 he was recuperating at Bath War Hospital after an injury, in which time he assisted in embroidering his new Regiment's badge on to cloth. When he returned to France in January 1918 Harry was Private G/40458 in "D" Company The Middlesex Regiment but when he wrote to his wife in March 1918 he had been transferred to "B" Company. On 19 March 1918 Harry wrote a letter to his wife:

'My darling

Just a line dearest to let you know I am quite all right and in good health and spirits and we are still resting as they call it. We are away from the line and in training, physical exercise, drill, musketry and running. I do not have to do the latter as I am too old, thank goodness. I am at present attached to headquarters but address my letters as before dear, don't forget B.Coy. I suppose you have got so used to D.Coy that it becomes quite natural.

Dear, about your allotment – I meant remittance and I cannot understand it at all. I am signing another one and hope you will get it this time, dear. Tell Marjorie I have not any money to send for the tank, we don't get much here; suppose they are saving it up for us.

I see from your rations you do not get too much allowed dear, but I suppose it is quite, if not more, than you can purchase with your money. I wish I could help you dearest, as you know, it is a great worry to me to think you are so short.

Tell little Harry he shall have some trousers and boots soon.

I hope the allotment at Minster Road will be a success for the Wharton Road School. Will Longley is indeed very lucky to be still employed in England and especially so near home.

What are you going to plant in the garden this year dear?

My darling France
March 14th 18
Just a line dearest to let you k
am quite allright & in good health & spirits
e are still resting as they call it
e line & in training, Physical Exercise, drill, muske
unning I do not have to do the letter as I am
d, thank goodness I am at present attached to he
arters but address my letters
boy. I suppose you have

I wish I were handy to dig it up then you could easily do it as far as the seeds go, especially with your handy-man. I have not seen a flower this year out here, except a little piece of palm. The weather now has changed and it is raining hard making everything, of course, wretched.

I am sorry Maj. Harman broke his umbrella in a gun on the tank. I should have thought that with his years he should have known it would have gone off. Remember me to him, please, and tell him we still carry on.

Dearest, I hope you all keep in the very best of health. God bless you my darlings and keep you under the shadow of his almighty arms until I come home to you again to love and cherish while this earthly life shall last. Goodnight my pet, your loving husband, Harry.'

One week after writing this letter, the 1918 German Spring Offensive began. Harry was killed in action, along with many others from "B" Company of 2nd Battalion, Middlesex Regiment engaged in defending the trenches at Eterpigny, on the River Somme.[1] 'Little Harry', his son never saw his father again.

Harry Wyborn

References

1 Everard Wyrall, *The Die Hards in The Great War*, Vol. Two: 1916–1919, p. 206.

Frank Henry White

(Emanuel 1911–1915)

Eye witness to 'Operation Michael' (The German Offensive of March 1918)

Frank White was a member of the Emanuel Second Eleven and was also in the OTC. He left School in 1915. Whilst the OTC would have prepared him for tactical operations, little could have prepared him for witnessing the great German offensive, 'Operation Michael', launched on the morning of Thursday 21 March 1918.

It is thought that Frank served with the Royal Fusiliers in the First World War. Frank's father who was editor of a parish magazine for Cobham in Kent reproduced in 1930 Frank's account of his experiences during the German Offensive which was originally written in a letter home to his parents shortly after the Armistice of 1918. It is unclear why the article omitted Frank's service details.

An eyewitness account of the German Offensive of March 1918:

'First of all, you will want to know how it came about that I was captured and I will give you a brief history of what happened. We went into the trenches from 'rest' on the night of March 20th in nice time for the opening performance of 'Fritz's' much talked about offensive, which was particularly severe on the morning of the 21st, when he shelled us and gassed us for five hours continually. Our Company was in the support line and after the bombardment finished we all 'stood to' and had to remain on the 'qui vive' all day. Meanwhile the two Companies in the front line were having a warm time of it, but were successfully sending Jerry back to his own lines when he attempted to get into our trenches. Our boys suffered badly in the fighting, but the losses of the —th London on our left flank had been even more severe, and in the evening we were sent to reinforce them. We took up our positions in their support trenches which subsequently became the front line as the —th London evacuated at midnight.

The next day was an exciting one for us and we could see the Germans pouring down the communication trenches to their new advanced positions, literally in thousands, and you may guess we derived little comfort from the fact that they were allowed to do so without being molested by our artillery. In addition to this, we were under heavy shellfire the whole time and had had no food or sleep for two days. Of course we all knew we were 'in for it' and it came as a relief rather than otherwise when the enemy came over on a bombing 'stunt' that evening. Things were really exciting for a while and we were successful in driving Fritz out again with the exception of a few whom we took prisoners.

At midnight we evacuated and retired quite a long way back arriving at our new positions about 5am – this was now Saturday 23rd. Apparently, however, our flanks had gone still further back as there was no sign of them and so rapid had the German advance been that we were practically surrounded; and incidentally the transport had not been able to get to us with our much delayed and badly needed rations. After a short rest the Colonel, who had collected together all the REs etc in the neighbourhood then took us up a ridge in artillery formation and when we arrived at the crest dashed down the slope on the other side under heavy machine gun fire to a trench manned by the survivors of two other battalions of the London Regiment.

Now I want you to try and visualise the scene that morning. The trench had been hastily, insufficiently and incompletely dug, eg. 6ft deep in one place, perhaps only 3ft in another and in places scarcely dug at all. At one end of the trench a bombing 'block' had been hastily built and a lively bombing duel was going on between our boys and the Germans who were on the other side of the block. The other end of the trench was open and presented the only means of escape from this death trap, though practically everyone who tried that means of getting away was shot down by machine gun fire. Have you got the picture all right? A single trench with no supporting flanks – the enemy being kept back by bombs at one end and the machine guns effectively barring the way out at the other. In addition, we were terribly overcrowded in the trench, which afforded very poor protection. There were probably 2000 of us almost shoulder to shoulder and inevitably getting in each other's way. The casualties were very heavy and due mostly to machine gun fire from one particular point. In a desperate case we were sent 'over the top' to capture this machine gun position. The odds, however were too great and after losing a great many of our men we were forced to retire back to our trench. I don't want to dwell more than I can help on the horrors of war and will leave you to imagine the state of the trench – already overcrowded when men were able to stand – filled with dead, dying and wounded. None of the casualties were fit for more fighting as the enemy used explosive bullets and the poor chaps suffered terribly in consequence.

By this time the end was practically in sight – the enemy had completely surrounded us. We had no more bombs, no ammunition for the Lewis guns, our rifle ammunition had gone to fill the empty panniers, less than 100 remained out of 2000 who manned the trench only a few hours before and we were not fit for very much after three days without food or sleep. At 3 o'clock in the afternoon the enemy 'came over' and took us prisoners. I think the exact number of us was 94 – the only survivors of 2000 – representing three battalions.'

Frank was made a POW but later escaped before the end of the war.

References

1 This letter was originally written by Frank White to his parents just after the Armistice, and published in a Kent church parish magazine, *The Record*, Vol 7, Nos 6 and 7 in 1930. He died in 1955.

Frederick Harry Bedloe Moore

(Emanuel 1908–1914)

Frederick was the only son of Ethel Moore née Goddard (daughter of John Bedloe), and Frederick Charles Hicks Moore, Ethel's cousin. He was born in Brixton. Frederick was a talented musician at Emanuel and played solos in the last Annual Concert to be held on 17 June 1914 in Battersea Town Hall, before the outbreak of war.

The Portcullis recorded: 'F. H. B. Moore and W. Lovelock were much applauded for their Pianoforte Solos and moreover, both did yeoman service in other departments, the former taking the Bass Drum in the Orchestra...'[1] Frederick played Grieg's 'Peer Gynt' Suite No. 1, op. 46 *Morning* piano concerto, a piece of music which conjures up dew drops on wet spring mornings with plush green grass and birds stirring in tree-tops and hedgerows. Frederick played this in the heart of Battersea merely a few weeks before the guns of August 1914 thundered across European skies.

At the time he joined up he was working as a motor engineer. Four days before his seventeenth birthday he volunteered to join the Territorial Force in May 1915 at Wandsworth. He commenced his military career as a Private with the Royal Army Medical Corp, 3rd London General Hospital. In December that year he volunteered for Malta where he was attached to St Andrew's Malta Hospital, No. 3 Malta Company RAMC, TF.

In March 1917, whilst still in Malta, Frederick applied for admission to an officer cadet unit with a view to a temporary commission in the Regular Army. He was accepted for an Officer Cadet Battalion in May and travelled back to England in June. By early July he was on his way to RAMC Blackpool. In October he joined No. 14 O.C. Battalion, Berkhampstead. On completion of his training he was assessed at Warwick Camp and accepted for a commission. The commanding officer considered him: 'A very nice type and is very keen. He should get on as an officer provided he keeps up his studies.' He joined the 9th (County of London) Battalion, The London Regiment, (Queen Victoria's Rifles) as a 2nd Lieutenant on 27 February 1918. He left England for France on 18 September 1918 and joined his unit on the front line near the village of Sauchy Cauchy on 22 September. He was killed in action at Sebourg on 4 November just seven days before the Armistice was signed and peace was declared. His battalion with other London Regiment battalions had advanced into the village of Saultain under heavy artillery fire. An order was received to attack at midnight.

The commanding officer records in his War Diary:

> Company Commanders assembled at Battalion HQ for their orders as this was the only place in which a light was shewn. The battalion was to move forward without a barrage as it was possible that the enemy were not holding the ground in front. A cavalry screen was to precede the Infantry and the 168th Infantry Brigade were attacking on the left and the 11th Division on the right.
>
> At 0600 hours the Infantry advanced and immediately came under distant MG fire, when the cavalry dismounted. What became of the cavalry later is not known as they were not seen again. The battalion advanced through Sebourg under intermittent shell fire and with slight casualties to the first objective (1500 yards beyond the village and 400 yards from assembly area). The troops were met by the civilians in Sebourg with the greatest enthusiasm and a number of prisoners, estimated at about 50 were captured before arrival at the first objective. The escort became a casualty on the way down and no receipt was obtained for the prisoners. As the rear companies passed through the village the enemy put down a very heavy barrage on it and the road approaching it from the west. As the companies crossed the River Aunelle the hostile machine gun fire became intense. As the average strength of our Platoons was twelve, the ground could not be searched and the leading companies must have passed over hostile machine guns during their advance.
>
> As "A" Company (on left) and "C" Company (on right) reached their first objective they came under an annihilating machine gun fire from the left which forced them into the junction of two sunken roads on the right of the battalion front. The enemy worked up this junction and enfiladed them badly. As Lewis Gunners got their guns into action on the top of the banks of the road they were almost immediately knocked out. Enemy jumped into the sunken road at the junction and hit the Sergeant Major of "A" Company. Sergeant Stinchcombe was killed attempting to charge them and 2nd Lieutenant F. H.B. Moore of "D" Company, who had come up to reinforce, was also killed. Lewis Gunners returned the enemy fire and fired many rounds. Many empty magazines and cartridge cases and two smashed Lewis Guns were found among the dead, at the spot later. Both roads, enfiladed by Machine Guns, were untenable. "A" Company was forced back to the North and "C" and "B" Companies to the South. A stand was made at the rear portions of these roads (each on the extreme flanks of the Battalion front).
>
> Battalion casualties that day: Killed 1 officer F. H. B. Moore and 20 other ranks, Wounded one officer and 52 other ranks.

There was much correspondence between Frederick's father and the army authorities dealing with the 'formalities' following a death in action. His death was reported to the War Office on 16 November and by December they were writing to his father about a possible will and where his effects should be sent. After a number of letters to the War Office his father received a cheque for £71-19-5d. in September 1919 representing monies due to his son. This comprised his pay as an officer £65-2s., his pay in the ranks £16, lodging, fuel and light and field allowance £4-10-5d. less pay overissued £13-13s.[2]

References

1 *The Portcullis*, Summer Term, 1914, p. 56.

2 Thanks due to Tim Goddard, relative of F. H. B. Moore for information he originally published on the Goddard family history website.

Emanuel School showing the OTC assault course

C. W. Scott-Giles OBE, MA

(Emanuel 1902–1911)

Charles 'Wilfrid' Scott-Giles devoted innumerable hours in service to his alma mater. His name is perpetuated in the most authoritative account of Emanuel School's history, originally published in 1935 and updated subsequently.

C.W. Scott-Giles

In 1916 at a gathering of Old Boys on Founder's Day, Wilfrid wrote a poem which became the School Song set to music by Mr. Hedley J. Evans, School music master at that time. Wilfrid also took centre stage as Dacre Herald Extraordinary, wearing a 'tabard of the School Arms over Elizabethan costume' in the ancient custom of beating the bounds. This ceremony, as the man himself wrote, served as, 'a useful purpose in stimulating interest in the School's history and pride in its traditions.' [1] It was this role which perhaps prepared him for one more significant when in 1957, he was appointed Fitzalan Pursuivant of Arms Extraordinary. It was in this capacity that on 30 January 1965 Wilfrid was on the steps of St Paul's, with other Heralds, to greet dignitaries attending the State Funeral of Britain's wartime leader, Sir Winston Churchill.

During the First World War he served in the Army Service Corps. He was also involved in the Emanuel War Memorial Fund. After the War he read history at Sidney Sussex College, Cambridge. He was a prolific author on his favourite subject of heraldry and Emanuel was always close at heart for in his first major book, *The Romance of Heraldry*, published in 1929, he sketched the Emanuel School Coat of Arms.[2]

Charles was largely responsible for keeping the Old Emanuel Association (OEA) afloat during the War. He handled many of the letters sent by OEs on active service and was editor of the OE Section of *The Portcullis*. In addition to his poem, *Pour Bien Desirer* – the School Song – sung in the School chapel well into the 1970s, he also penned other war poems. *Pour Bien Desirer* is without doubt a war poem, for not only does it use the symbolism of medieval battles, common in patriotic war poetry of the time, but it is also complete with notions of honour and duty as in these lines, 'Thus armed in spirit, naught shall shake/ Thy sons' resolve on stricken battle-field/ Stainless to keep/ and yet more glorious make/ Thy venerable shield.'

He started his career as a journalist, and was Chairman of the Parliamentary Press Gallery. He later became Secretary of the Institution of Municipal and County Engineers, and for his services he was appointed an Officer of the Order of the British Empire (OBE) in the Coronation Honours list of June 1953.

Charles was indefatigable in his approach to all aspects of Emanuel life. He is owed a huge debt of honour for writing such an authoritative history of the School and also for his noble efforts in keeping up correspondence with Emanuel boys serving in the First World War.

Scott–Giles War Poetry

Nobiscum Deus

When you're playing bagatelle with bombs in Flanders,
Or starting a shimozzle at Bapaume;
When the shrapnel falls on Yepper like a giant dose of pepper,
And you long for peace and butterscotch at home:
When you're Jehu in a Juggernaut joy-riding,
Or you're fighting lonely battles in the sky,
Or from London to Barbadoes you dodge the Hun torpedoes,
And sink, perhaps a U-boat if you're spry;

When the outlook's mostly bully-beef and Johnsons,
Your nerve the strain begins to tell upon.
And you feel you must go under – but you'll stick it out, by Thunder!
While your will can drive your weary body on;
There's a magic in the watchword that I'll give you,
A talisman in peril or the pip;
When you're fretting yester sorrow, or you're fearing for the morrow,
'Twill bring you ease, so get it in your grip!

Emanuel, the name you learned in boyhood;
The watchword with a subtle craft appeals;
As familiar, my brother, as the sacred name of Mother;
"God with us" both our faith and School reveals.
"Emanuel!" 'Tis but to speak to see it –
The tower, drive and field you knew of yore –
Where youth and honour flourished, and a brotherhood was nourished,
Which took its sporting instincts into war.

Emanuel, the School, will stand beside you
When you're feeling friendless, homesick and forlorn;
And Emanuel, the tidings, will in spite of all deridings,
Give you the heart to treat your fears with scorn.
There's comfort to the weary in the watchword,
There's solace to the anxious and bereaved;
"God with you" in your startings, your toilings and your partings,
"God with you" till your venture is achieved.

And when you've won the game, and tidied Europe,
And on the scrap-heap tossed the broken thrones;
When you've rooted out the culture of the trebly-crowned Vulture,
And devoured Turkey, legs and beak and bones;
And when you land again in dear old Blighty,
To share the peace and butterscotch you've won,
They'll distribute medals grossly, but what'll please you mostly,
Will be – "EMANUEL, Well Done!"

C.W.G.

Pour Bien Desirer

EMANUEL! For the noble aim
That marked in days of old thy great design,
For present merit and unsullied fame,
Honour and love be thine.
The love and reverence we give
To those who gave us life and early care,
Mother of Mothers, thou dost share,
Who taught us how to live.

Great relict of a knightly race and rule,
Thy Founders' tenderness in thought and deed
Lives in the spirit of the School
Which, passing, they decreed;
Spirit of chivalrous intent,
Spirit of duty, scorning pain,
Of Loyal service, freely spent,
So DACRE lives again.
Spirit of knowledge and of truth,
Spirit of friendship, strong and pure,
And love of country, learned in youth,
So SACKVILLE doth endure.

Thus armed in spirit, naught shall shake
Thy sons' resolve on stricken battle-field,
Stainless to keep, and yet more glorious make
Thy venerable shield;
Memorial of old affrays,
Of knightly deeds, and honour bravely won,
That telleth yet of peaceful days,
And simple duty done.

C.W.G. Founders' Day 1916

References

1 C. W. Scott-Giles, *The History of Emanuel School* (1948), p. 236.
2 C. W. Scott-Giles, *The Romance of Heraldry* (1929), p. 10.

Remembrance and the First World War

The First World War united an entire nation in grief. Every community felt its impact and every community mourned its dead. Emanuel similarly felt the loss of so many who were killed and also for those injured, many of whom were left with life-changing scars.

OE and famous educationalist George Lyward, who returned to Emanuel to teach in 1918, wrote in his autobiography many years later, 'I can hardly write of those times. I lost one friend after another. We were boys, just boys.'[1] The 'Lost Generation' was a generation of mainly boys, who as the poet Laurence Binyon so aptly penned, 'They shall grow not old, as we that are left grow old.' These boys were forever encapsulated in a single moment in time. They were not wearied by old age but the guardians of their memory were. The boys' existences were all too brief as they transformed from schoolboys to soldiers in a few weeks and within a few months they joined the ranks of the memorialised. Imagine a typical scene as an Emanuel boy was bounding up the field to score a victorious try winning the game for the School Fifteen whilst his parents, standing on the edge of the field, looked on proudly. Within a short time the same boy had his name carved on the School memorial and although his parents pride was no less diminished it was now accompanied by silent prayer as they sat at a remembrance service mourning the loss of their son. Sitting beside them at the same service may have been his friend who passed him the ball which led to the victorious try but as his friend sat remembering his school chum's moment of glory he too would have felt the loss of one so young who played the game for school and country on fields at home and abroad but who paid the ultimate sacrifice, never to play again.

At Speech Day in 1919 the Headmaster, Shirley Goodwin, after reading the School Roll of Honour, declared that the War Office could confirm that to Emanuel belonged the distinction of having had the highest percentage of casualties (not highest number) of all the schools in the country – a somewhat sad distinction to hold. The total number of those who were either killed or died as a consequence of the war was in excess of one hundred and fifty. No concrete number can be given because of the fact that many of those who left the School prior to 1906 simply lost touch with the School.

In the Christmas Term *Portcullis* 1919 we read of the first memorial service 'in memory of Old Boys who fell in the war'

EMANUEL SCHOOL

WAR MEMORIAL

Unveiling and Dedication Service

January 26th, 1923,

at 3.0 p.m.

From left to right Clifford Raymond Bodle, Cyril Robert Wightman Mountain, The grave of Roland Walter Bullivant, Lawrence John Maynard Allen, Charles Burleigh Sach, Stanley Macbeth, Gerald William West

held on Sunday 20 July.[2] It notes that the service opened with the Old Boys' hymn, 'From many ways and wide apart.' The fourth verse of this hymn by Frederick Hosmer reads:

Fair visions rise from out the years,
And fast the memories throng,
Till eyes are filled with happy tears,
And hearts with grateful song.

These lines set the tone of that first memorial service. We are told the Headmaster Shirley Goodwin impressed on the attendees not a time for mourning, which had its place, but for 'the greatness and glory of the occasion' and in his sermon he emphasised this point by reading from II Timothy IV: verse 7 'I have fought a good fight, I have finished my course, I have kept the faith.'

Amongst the attendees that day were a number of Old Boys as well as the father of 'Sag', Stanley Alfred George Harvey, who lost his life in the German Offensive of March 1918 and who has no known grave. One can only imagine the thoughts which Mr. Harvey must have had sitting in the School chapel that day.

Jack Grundy, Emanuel School Captain and later Headmaster, whose brothers Cecil and Ronald lost their lives only eight months apart on the Western Front, reminds us of the impact of the loss of sons on families. In his autobiography, Jack wrote, 'It is hard to measure now this setback to family life. For some years we lived withdrawn from the outer world. Gradually my father's cheerfulness returned, my mother's never. Naturally enough both had made the elder boys their special care and concern, and now, as the parents approached the age of sixty, they had not the strength to set about the younger in the same way. Not until I produced for them a grandson in 1940 – when I too was in khaki – did my mother's interest in the family revive.'[3]

On Friday 26 January 1923, the First World War Memorial was unveiled in the School's chapel by Earl Howe, father of Viscount Howe, MP for Battersea South 1918–1929. Bishop Ryle dedicated the memorial. The memorial is carved of wood and consists of the figure of St George standing under a canopy between tablets bearing the names of the School's fallen.[4] Beneath the memorial is the inscription:

GIVING THANKS TO GOD, REMEMBER YE WITH HONOUR ALL THOSE WHO GAVE THEIR LIVES FOR KING AND COUNTRY IN THE GREAT WAR 1914–1918, AND ESPECIALLY THOSE OF THIS SCHOOL WHOSE NAMES ARE HERE RECORDED.

Unveiling of the First World War Memorial in the Emanuel School chapel, 1923

In 1916 Shirley Goodwin had decided to remove extra pews behind the pulpit for the purpose of creating a Chapel of All Souls where OEs who fell in the War were to be remembered. During the course of the War and afterwards one plaque after another was erected in the All Souls corner of the chapel. [5] Plaques and names of OEs who fell were also erected and inscribed in churches and institutions across London and elsewhere. Lt. Gordon Marthews is remembered on the memorial boards of Holy Trinity Church, Clapham Common. The Grundy brothers and several others are included on the memorial screen in St Margaret's Church, Trinity Road, Wandsworth, whereas Lt. William Frank Godfrey has a brass plaque in St Michael's Church, Bolingbroke Grove.

Emanuel OTC boys stand guard at the War Memorial unveiling ceremony

The names of eleven OEs and possibly more, are included in the thousands of individuals commemorated on the Thiepval Memorial to the missing, a monumental structure which overlooks the fields of the Somme under which those names find their last resting place; where they fell and were never recovered. Their brief lives on this earth have also been eternalised in the Commonwealth War Grave Commission cemeteries across the world, the white headstones suggesting the innocence with which this generation is associated but somehow denying the true experience of war. Their families would have had to choose the inscriptions which accompany these headstones. Usually the inscriptions are religious or classical in tone but the parents of Roland Walter Bullivant wished that their son be remembered for being a 'Scholar of Emmanuel [sic] School, Wandsworth.

An Emanuel School War Memorial Fund was established with the original intention of establishing a memorial window in the chapel but the fund's purpose evolved and money was raised for both a war memorial and scholarships for as one notice in *The Portcullis* put it, 'Those who have passed were men, and leaders of men, and it is felt that any memorial to their achievement would be inadequate, did it not, beyond wood and stone and glass, take some form which would be as living as their deeds.' [6]

A War Memorial Fund Bazaar was organised in 1920 at which OE and entertainer Leslie Henson and his company performed a musical sketch, 'The Disorderly Room.'[7] It is interesting that there appear in *The Portcullis* several appeals to OEs, parents and others associated with the School to be more generous in giving to the Fund. Its target was to raise £10,000 but by 1921 it had raised £1000, and the treasurer repeated his disappointment that compared with other schools, a School with such traditions could not manage to raise greater funds and at a faster rate. Despite this, the first scholarship was awarded to a former Captain of the School, Francis A. Ollett, to attend St John's College, Cambridge.

The War was also remembered as being a victory and fight for a greater cause and in this tone the War Office awarded Emanuel a number of trophies as *The Portcullis* of Trinity Term 1920 put it:

> The War Office has again honoured the School for its signal services during the war, and all OEs heartily congratulate the School on the presentation of another German gun. The Head tells me that amongst war trophies now held by the School are: one 77m.m. German Field Gun; one 4in. German High Velocity Howitzer; one German Minenwerfer; one German Trench Mortar; five German Helmets; six German and Austrian Rifles and Bayonets. [8]

These trophies were short lived for when war approached again in less than twenty years they were melted down for use in the Second World War.

The First World War had its greatest impact upon the families and friends of those who lost their lives and also of those scarred both mentally and physically by its experiences. Young wives who lost husbands; mothers and fathers who lost sons; and sisters and brothers who lost siblings were all affected. To look at the names on the Emanuel School memorial is to look at once living, breathing, human beings who once shared in life's many experiences, all of whom were united by playing their part in one of history's most tragic episodes.

References

1 George Lyward, *His Autobiography*, published by John Lyward (2009), p. 54.
2 Memorial Service, *The Portcullis*, No. 78, Christmas Term, 1919, pp. 27–28.
3 J. B. C. Grundy, *Life's Five Windows* (J. M. Dent & Sons, 1968), p. 21.
4 A considerable number of individuals have now been found who were not included on the original memorial because their families may not have been in contact with the School after they left.
5 *The Portcullis*, No. 67, Spring Term, 1916, p. 46. In 2012 the memorial tablets were removed to a more prominent position in the School chapel.
6 *The Portcullis*, No. 78, Christmas Term, 1919, p. 28.
7 *The Portcullis*, No. 81, Christmas Term, 1920, p. 29.
8 *The Portcullis*, No. 80, Trinity Term, 1920, p. 35.

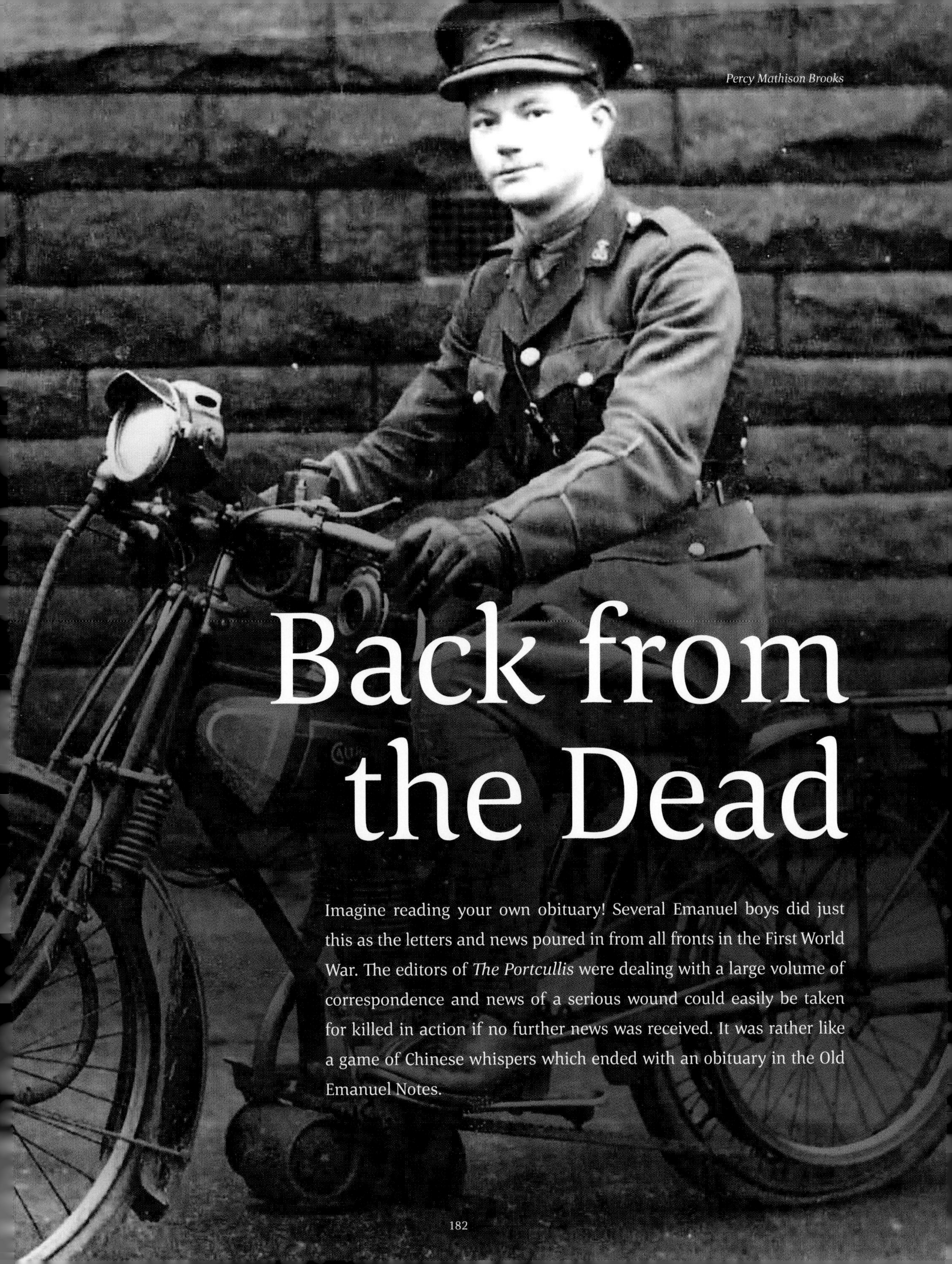

Percy Mathison Brooks

Back from the Dead

Imagine reading your own obituary! Several Emanuel boys did just this as the letters and news poured in from all fronts in the First World War. The editors of *The Portcullis* were dealing with a large volume of correspondence and news of a serious wound could easily be taken for killed in action if no further news was received. It was rather like a game of Chinese whispers which ended with an obituary in the Old Emanuel Notes.

3, CAUTLE
CLAP
L
22nd

My dear Inkster,
I beg to offer you my sinc
but I'm very glad to find that
has erred again. The news was so
so circumstantial, that it was f
by many of your old school friend
it is obviously unwise to verify eve
casualty by reference to bereaved re
and in cases of error such a cou
intensify existing anxiety – I offer
my excuse. I am putting mat
the forthcoming issue of the "Po
Emanuel has a right
its part in the war. We hav
that is "showy", but by Jov
sound to a man.
Hoping to see you aga
(I dimly remember you as a
very far above me)
I remain,
Under the Rose +
fraternally
O Wilf

AMERICAN RED CROSS NURSES AT WORK

AMERICAN RED CROSS HOSPITAL.
A group of American nurses a nd some of the convalescent British officers at the American Red Cross hospital at St. Catherine's Lodge, Rezgent's aPrk, London. The wonder ful work of the American nurse in England and France has been great ly appreciated by both governments.

Lawrence Inkster (right), circled recovering at the American Red Cross hospital and, (above), standing with his wife

In the Trinity Term 1918 *Portcullis* we read, 'The deaths are also announced of...Lawrence Inkster, who will be remembered by older Emanuels for his scholastic successes...'[1] In the Christmas issue a correction was published, 'It is now my duty to offer apologies and congratulations to Capt. Lawrence Inkster, who has had the unusual privilege of reading the announcement of his own death in *The Portcullis.* Capt. Inkster writes to tell us that he is alive and well. "I was wounded on September 20th, 1917, and am at present with my reserve battalion at Sittingbourne."' The story behind the Notes is revealed in a letter sent by Wilfrid Scott-Giles to Lawrence on 22 November 1918:

My dear Inkster

I beg to offer you my sincere apologies, but I am very glad to find that *The Portcullis* has erred again. The news was so general and so circumstantial, that it was firmly believed by many of your old School, and as it is obviously unwise to verify every reported casualty by reference to bereaved relatives – and in cases in error such a course might intensify existing anxiety – I offer this as my excuse...

Lawrence received another letter in December from a master at Emanuel F. P. Rudkins who commented:

> ...we thought you had to be counted, in our deep sorrow, among those in whom we had the glory by reason of thin manliness and devotion in sacrificing their dearest possession in England's cause. Now we rejoice on the strength of Giles' news that you are saved to us and that you will still take your part among the OEs.

Stanley Vaughan was also presumed killed, but as *The Portcullis* notes explain:

> Readers of *The Portcullis* will note with joy that the black cross against the name of S. Vaughan in the *Pro Patria* list should be removed. Vaughan, who was incorrectly reported to have died of wounds, is, we now understand, a prisoner of war. We wish him good health and a speedy release.[2]

In the Summer Term 1917 *Portcullis* the following announcement was made:

> Can anyone give us news of S. W. Lund, of the RAMC? He went out to Serbia with the Medical Mission in the early days, and we have received no news of him once.[3]

If you look at the First World War memorial in the School chapel today you will see a name scrubbed out. That name was S. W. Lund for it had been decided to include his name amongst the dead but the reason the name was covered becomes obvious when reading the Summer Term *Portcullis* in 1943 for we are told:

> An OE named Lund has written in mild protest to say that he is included in the War Memorial in the chapel!

Inkster and Lund were not the only individuals who were 'brought back to life', Alwyn Kerfoot Hughes was also included on the Roll of Honour. Alwyn's son Nicholas, who attended Emanuel in the 1950s had not realised that the A. Hughes on the memorial was his very much alive father. In 1915 Alwyn joined up – in the 3rd Queen's Westminsters. He was sent to France and on the Somme was wounded and taken prisoner. As a private he did not enjoy the comparatively easy-going conditions of the officer camps. After about three months in a German hospital he was sent to a POW camp at Minden. Then he was sent to work in coal mines at a place called Buer near Wesel in the Rhineland. This lasted for over two years; then he was sent to Friedrichsfeld where he spent the greater part of a year until the end of the war. The work in the mines on an unappetising and inadequate diet took a toll on his health, and he was in pretty poor shape when he was repatriated. Alwyn's sister said that some well-meaning person shook him by the hand at Victoria Station and he passed out. It was several years before he completely got over the effects of those lean POW years.

Those names are joined by three more, Entwistle, Hammett and Brooks, the last of whom had perhaps the most interesting resurrection.

Percy Mathison Brooks with Duke Ellington

'Hello Satchmo'

Percy Mathison Brooks attended Emanuel in the years 1907–1912. He was a keen rugby player at School, playing for the Second Fifteen. In the Christmas Term *Portcullis* we read:

> P. M. Brooks, Sec-Lieut. in the North Staffordshire Regt., who has also been killed, displayed in the Army the dogged characteristics for which he is remembered at Emanuel. He was a member of the Second Fifteen, and boxed for the School against Wilson's, winning what was practically a punching match by sheer endurance.[4]

Few details are known about Percy's war service. What is known is that he enlisted in the 2nd (City of London) Battalion

(Royal Fusiliers) on 4 November 1912 at the age of seventeen and three months. He was appointed a temporary 2nd Lt. before being promoted to Lieutenant on 30 March 1917. We know he served with the BEF in France and Flanders and also served in Salonika. At some point during his service he was wounded. He attended an Old Emanuel gathering in the summer of 1916 but a year later the School presumed he had been killed and so his name was included on the School's First World War memorial. The reason for this remains a mystery.

Percy's two brothers, neither of whom attended Emanuel, also served in the First World War. Sydney won the Military Medal but was severely wounded in the Somme Offensive and Charles was killed on the Somme and is remembered on the Thiepval Memorial.

Far from dying during the war Percy returned to England and during the 1920s lived in Bedford Road, Clapham. In the early 1930s he started a brief spell as Editor of *Melody Maker*, a British music magazine. During his editorship he interviewed two of the biggest names in twentieth century jazz history, Duke Ellington and Louis Armstrong.

At one point in Percy's interview with Duke Ellington Percy asks Duke, 'Which of your own compositions is your favourite?' to which Duke replies, 'That's a difficult one to answer, the things I've liked best I have often left on the shelf but of my published and recorded numbers I think I like Mood Indigo best.' [5]

If interviewing Duke Ellington wasn't enough of a claim to fame then perhaps being the individual responsible for shortening Louis Armstrong's nickname comes close to ensuring Percy is remembered for as long as jazz is being played. In July 1932 Percy greeted Louis Armstrong when he arrived with his band at Plymouth. At this time Louis was known by the sobriquet 'Satchelmouth' but as Louis told interviewers years later, when Percy greeted him he and his band members heard Percy say, 'Hello Satchmo.' The exact nature of how Percy came to call Louis 'Satchmo' is unclear but it is a story that originated with Louis which gives it added validity, even though some refute it. In a number interviews in the 1950s and 1960s Louis claimed that one of his band members thought Percy had called him 'Satchmo' because he thought Louis had more 'mouth.'

Percy served with the RAF on Barrage Balloon duties in the Second World War. These great silver-coloured balloons half-filled with hydrogen were stationed across London with the aim of deflecting the German bombers. Percy, who led a most interesting life, died in 1945.

Richard Clifford Montford with wife and children

In 2013 the grandson of Richard Clifford Montford contacted the School to donate a 1901 edition of the Charles Dickens novel *David Copperfield* his grandfather had been awarded as a School prize in July 1902 for his performance in his 1901 exams. The Lent Term 1918 *Portcullis* noted 'Mander tells of hearing the death of Montford in the Machine Gun Corps.' Obviously this was never verified and Richard was added to the list of Fallen names on the chapel memorial, a fact that surprised his grandson as Richard had survived the war.

Born on 29 June 1886, Richard was the fourth of eleven children and one of his brothers, who didn't attend Emanuel, was killed in the First World War. He had two daughters born in 1914 and 1916 and after the war lived in Wimbledon, working in sales. He died on 9 August 1966. Considering he attended Emanuel around 115 years ago it is surprising that some records still remain of Richard's time in the School, being noted in all the prize lists 1900–1902 and for passing the Cambridge Local Exam Certificate. He also participated in the 440-yard race in the 1901 Sports Day.

References

1 *The Portcullis*, Trinity Term, 1918, p.32.
2 *The Portcullis*, Christmas Term, 1916, p. 41.
3 *The Portcullis*, Summer Term, 1917, p. 57.
4 *The Portcullis*, Christmas Term, 1917, p. 51.
5 Duke Ellington talking to Percy Mathison Brooks, available to download from a number of albums online.

The Emanuel OTC being inspected in Wandsworth in 1936 for Speech Day

A photo of Hitler inspecting the Hitler Youth in the late 1930s taken by the sister of Old Emanuel brothers John and Richard Blackburn

CHAPTER 10
EVACUATION AND LIFE ON THE HOME FRONT IN THE SECOND WORLD WAR

Lt-Col. Charles Hill
OBE, MM, TD, BA

At the age of 29, in 1928, Charles Hill walked down the Emanuel School drive and into the Headmaster's office. On leaving after interview, he had little inkling that he would spend the next fifty years dedicated to the education of generations of Emanuel boys.

Charles Hill (centre) at an OTC camp c.1934

Charles Hill was one of those rarities in education, for in addition to teaching Geography he commanded the OTC and later CCF, was Rowing Master in the late 1940s and early 1950s, helped organise the fund-raising for the building of Emanuel's Boat House and in 1943 became Headmaster of Emanuel's tutorial classes which opened in London, whilst Cyril Broom was Headmaster of Emanuel in Petersfield. Charles was Housemaster of Marlborough at Emanuel for 34 years, founded the Geographical Society and produced Christmas 'rag' plays, akin to staff revues of later years. He also organised trips to Wales and the Tyrol for his Geographical Society. In the course of the Second World War he kept in contact with OEs serving across the world and assembled a collection of photographs of those who had fallen in the war.

He was later elected President of the OEA, a position usually reserved for Headmasters or OEs. Charles was also on the governing boards of several schools.

In 1980 Charles wrote a piece for *The Portcullis* titled 'Fifty Years Back' recalling his early impressions of Emanuel and the somewhat dilapidated state of the School. He discusses the situation of meals when the School opened for tutorial classes in 1943:

> The kitchen where the meals were cooked on a large coal stove was even more antiquated. An inspector looking around in 1943 when the LCC took over the meals remarked, "Did you say this was the Museum?"

Above all his commitments to Emanuel it was perhaps his involvement with the OTC, which later became the JTC [Junior Training Corps] and after 1945 the CCF [Combined Cadet Force], for which Charles will be most fondly remembered. His role in training young Emanuel pupils in the arts of soldiering became essential to a new officer class in the Second World War as he saw many of those he had trained become Captains and Majors in a number of British Regiments and who led their platoons into some of the greatest battles of the war. Charles was particularly affected by the loss of Alan Skillern who was killed in January 1944 during the course of the Italian Campaign, but also by the many others whom he had spent many hours with practising drill and route marches throughout the 1930s.

When Charles died in 1980 Jack 'Charles' Cuddon, a master at Emanuel for over 30 years, wrote an obituary in *The Portcullis*. It is from this that we learn the great contribution Charles Hill made to Emanuel during the Second World War:

'In 1939 Charles Hill was promoted to the rank of Brevet Major, an unusual distinction for an OTC officer (the term brevet dates from 1689 and denotes the conferring of a nominal rank on an officer, but giving no right to extra pay). The promotion was, in part, a reward for his study of military tactics. With another world war imminent it was a timely recognition of his soldierly interests.

Charles Hill, August 1918

In 1939 there began perhaps the strangest and most challenging period in Charles Hill's life. In that year the School was evacuated to Churcher's College, Petersfield. At about the time the evacuation was to take place Hill received a telegram from the War Office to report to Colchester Barracks for duty and potential war service. The WO, then thought better and displaying unusual perspicacity, decided that Hill would be more useful as a master at the School and more especially as a training officer for cadets in the JTC. Within a matter of months huge numbers of fighting men were going to be needed.

At Petersfield he organised and trained his schoolboy 'troops' with zeal and efficiency. There were commando-type training courses, night manoeuvres, cliff-climbing exercises, forced marches and two-day marches from Churcher's to Emanuel

Charles Hill leading in the Emanuel OTC. (above) and Charles Hill in relaxed mood with members of the Emanuel OTC and his wife (below)

(52 miles). Major Hill himself took part in these and also attended Army courses in Weapon Training, PT and Military Tactics. He also went twice to the Battle Training School at Llanberis. The JTC and its CO were well known in Petersfield and its band took a leading part in many local functions sponsored to aid Britain. Hill was also a member of the Home Guard (which in the early stages of the War had to train with wooden rifles) and the Civil Defence Corps. Numerous boys whom Hill trained afterwards fought in many different theatres of war.

In 1943 it was decided to re-open an emergency school at Emanuel, whilst the main body of the school stayed at Churcher's. Hill was put in charge of the London 'detachment' which numbered fewer than 100 boys. Quite soon the school expanded to 350. Charles Hill was Headmaster and did all the secretarial work. His unflagging energy and enterprise enabled him to run an official Cadet Corps, a debating society and a club for older boys on Friday evenings. He was also, of course, doing a full teaching programme. Your obituarist, who played rugby and cricket against Emanuel at Churcher's and Emanuel in the period 1941–43, has vivid recollections of Hill as a forceful personality who imparted his enthusiasm with a boyish gusto.

In 1955 the Queen invested him with the OBE (Order of the British Empire, Military Division). He was cited as the longest serving commanding officer of a Combined Cadet Force in Britain, and the award was recognition of a man who had given outstanding service to thousands of cadets and also to the Imperial Cadet Association, the Commonwealth Shooting Committee and the County of London TA Association Schools' Committee.'[1]

The character of an individual is shaped by their formative years and this is clearly seen in Charles Hill's case. To understand the unbounded energy which characterised Charles Hill's service to Emanuel we need only to read his First World War memoir that until now has remained unpublished. What follows is an edited account of Charles Hill's First World War experiences as a Private in the 2nd Battalion, The Bedfordshire Regiment.

'My War' 1914–1918 by Colonel Charles Hill

'Back at school for the autumn term we were caught up in the war fever. I joined the school cadet corps (3rd Cadet Battalion of The Middlesex Regiment). And mainly because of my loud parade voice was soon made a full corporal. I passed the London Matriculation in 1915 and was made a Prefect at the end of the Summer term ... I became Head Boy of the Kilburn Grammar School in September 1916. This was an office elected by the senior school from nominations made by the Headmaster in consultation with the staff. As I had been off games for a considerable period owing to my illness I had no popular appeal but a factor which helped to gain support for me was that I was a scholarly boy and the other three candidates were not. The other part I acquired was that of Headmaster's Secretary. The forces had taken not only masters, but the school Sergeant and the Secretary. I was rather surprised that I was asked to take on this for I was rather shy and a little uncertain of myself. I could hardly refuse the Headmaster's request, especially as it carried the handsome remuneration of ten shillings a week!

Joining the army filled our minds very much ... We even did a machine gun course with a detachment in the city. We knew the war wouldn't be a pleasant experience, but we all wanted to do 'our bit.' Under the 'duty scheme' one could attest after the age of seventeen, receive the King's Shilling, swear to obey him, his heirs and successors and then await call up at anytime after the age of eighteen. I reached that age on 1 July 1917 and received notice to report to Hill Barracks at the end of the month. Knowing that I would not be able to attend to Speech Day in the autumn, on the last assembly of the term with a lump in my throat I went up to receive the Head Boy's gold medal and the Donegall bronze medal for shooting.

Charles Hill with Urwin Thornburn, Colin and Kenneth Fowle, Mrs Dorothy Hill and friend on holiday in Wales

I reported at the barracks wearing my Head Boy's cap and immediately made friends with a fellow from Smithgate Grammar School who recognised the school badge ... We were allowed to go home for the night and after yet another tearful farewell from my mother reported back to be posted in Luton. I now found that my number was 72510 in the 25th Training Reserve Battalion consisting of some thousand men and run by a mixed crowd of Officers and NCOs, mainly Hertfordshire Regiment, many of whom had seen service overseas, others too old or unfit for active service. There were fifteen in our bell tent and a very mixed bag. There were two public schoolboys, the chap that had slept next to me had gone around with a circus as an odd job man mixing with house thieves and petty pilferers. The training was boring in the extreme especially as I felt I knew more than some of the instructors. We all attended school for instruction in the three Rs and when the Warrant Officer in charge realised that I had passed matric, I helped with instructors.

With the onset of winter the camp, never very comfortable became uninhabitable and we were billeted in the town. Four of us were in a very small house ... I had applied for a commission during the first month. It was approved by my Company Officer and I was given a stripe, but nothing further could be done until I passed on to a more regular training Battalion ... This happened before Christmas when a large number of us were posted to the Bedfordshire Regiment at Crowborough ... Training here was much more rigorous and realistic and the instructors really efficient. Even so, when I finally went to France, I had never taken part in a proper field exercise or been on night operations. We had never done any field cooking or slept in bivouacs. On joining the Battalion at Crowborough I had seen my Company Officer with my commission papers but apparently a very sombre order had been issued that no commission should be granted unless a man had seen active service. Many young lives may have been saved had this order been made before.

... Our turn for draft came on 22 April preceded by 48 hours leave during which I visited the Headmistress of the elementary school I had attended. She was a great character and I had been a great favourite of hers and had kept touch since leaving her school at thirteen. Religion was a very real thing to us in those days; indeed I had thoughts of going into the Church. On this occasion in her study, we knelt as she prayed for my safe return.

... We crossed from Dover next morning in convoy with destroyers circling round us, for there was always the danger from German submarines. On the boat was a large draft of American troops (Doughboys) who were mostly as excited as we were. Some older Tommies returning to the Front for the second or third time had no such feelings. "You kids will soon learn." We were under canvas for a short time at Calais before heading for an unknown destination – literally unknown – for things were still disorganised after the great withdrawal and the various units of the disbanded 5th Army were very scattered ... From then on it was a slow retreat back over the old battlefields of the Somme where the Division had fought in 1916. From time to time desperate counter attacks were made which had not only held up the enemy for a while, but often drove him back. The vicious onslaught was finally halted in front of Amiens and the Division became part of the 4th Army under General Rawlinson.

It should be mentioned that an Officer went into action in full uniform with brightly polished Sam Browns, wearing kid gloves and usually carrying swagger sticks. They were each armed with a revolver. Our Brigadier L de V Sadler Jackson, a former Cavalry officer, wore a canary coloured cravat and jodhpurs with bright red gorgets on his tunic lapels. He made a wonderful target for snipers, but lived a charmed life. He was wounded twice, for in any attack he was always with the leading troops.

... We were taken up the line by buses (most of them formerly in the London service) and deposited as far forward as it was safe to go. Just before dark we moved up to a position in reserve. My section (six men and a boy) was taken to a piece of trench about fifteen yards long, completely isolated and left there. The weather was wretched, it rained all the night and the floor was thick chalky mud. There were no dugouts and the only cover were holes dug lengthwise in the side of the trench ... It seemed a long night and it came as a relief at 4am when ordered to 'stand to' which was a routine procedure. In the line just before dawn and again at dusk, every man was on the fire step, equipment on and bayonet fixed ready for anything which might happen.

... In these first few days there were a number of false rumours of a new Gerry offensive which never materialised. There was intermittent shelling, most of which passed overhead, and we soon came to recognise the type of shell from the noise it made as it came over. The 'whizzybangs' were the worst, a high velocity shell which travelled so fast that it exploded almost immediately after being fired. The heavy 'jackjohnsons' lumbered over with a noise like a train. When occasionally a shell dropped in our vicinity our heads would pop up to see where it had landed, much to the amusement of the old hands ... A top level 'wind-up' involving trench foot

Charles Hill with an Emanuel OTC Shooting scoreboard; Bisley Park 1934 (above) and leading the OTC in a march (below)

gave us the first opportunity to leave our wretched trench. One night we were marched back to an old barn where our feet were bathed in whale oil and we were issued with a clean pair of socks. The order was obeyed, but as the bathing was never repeated I cannot think it was of much use.

... The nightly routine in support was to be digging fresh trenches or slits (to take two or three men), stretcher carrying parties or even wiring in the front line. The last job was hellish as it involved carrying heavy rolls of barbed wire and stakes for long distances in the dark, stumbling over broken ground pitted with shell holes. I was very tired and felt quite ill at times. I seemed to have a permanent backache. On one or two occasions I had a whiff of poison gas but apart from a headache and wretched feeling there was nothing serious.

... On 25 May we had our first official rest in a village well behind the line. This meant a dry and relatively comfortable barn and regular meals and a hot bath! There were drills, inspections etc, all rather boring, but we were away from the continual noise of shellfire and the squalor of the trenches.

... On 31 May we left our pleasant village and were back in the trenches in reserve and back to the old routine carrying, digging and backache. [... later] I found something which could be really interesting again. I was particularly good at map reading and earned the commendation of officer I/C. It was the first officer with whom I had had much contact since coming to France, so short of officers had we been.

... I struck up an acquaintance with an elderly French lady from Paris who was living in her summer residence in Mesnil Valle. Apparently I reminded her of a son killed in action and we became very friendly. She gave me her Paris address with an invitation to visit her after the war. We did correspond for a while but I never did meet her again.

... An attack was imminent and we were rushed up to the line and began digging ourselves in. The Platoon had no officers and our section had no NCOs. We went over the top the next morning but the resistance was only half hearted and we captured Trones Wood (one of the 1916 battlefields) and dug in again. By midday it was decided that there had been a complete withdrawal by the Germans and there was a general advance ... At dawn the next morning we again advanced through the wood, somewhat right of our former positions and came under shell and machine gunfire. Our recently acquired officer was wounded and the attack soon petered out. A small party of us took refuge in a large shell hole where we spent a hot and thirsty day. Any attempt to leave our refuge brought a hail of bullets and as no one seemed to worry about us we stayed where we were until night fall when we got to a small trench ahead ... Because of the shortage of officers for their casualty rate was heavy, we never had a Platoon Commander long enough to know him. In the intelligence section one had a good idea of the situation and one also got to know the officers better. There was plenty of opportunity to employ one's brain and I particularly enjoyed the map reading and tactical schemes where we were functioning for the whole Brigade which was now in reserve absorbing and training reinforcements.

... When we found "B" Company HQ we were further horrified. A distraught officer minus his tin hat was obviously suffering from shell shock. Two of his men were just sitting with that strained look and complete apathy which one so often saw in times of great stress. An NCO was more alert and acting as a lookout man. When I asked the officer for the whereabouts of "B" Company he just waved his revolver and in a hysterical voice shouted "This is all that's left of poor bloody "B" Company" and started to weep. As usual officer casualties were heavy. One Company we visited had no officers left. A cook, formerly a Sergeant, who had lost his stripes for various offences of which drunkenness was the chief one, had found his way up to his old Company from the transport lines. When we saw him, he had no equipment, a crime in itself, a rifle on his shoulders and a bandolier of ammunition. He was fairly full of rum but quite in charge of the situation. He led a charmed life and was decorated for his gallantry in this action.

[... later] Our turn came for the line again. We had received a large draft from the Lincolnshire Regiment to make up our depleted numbers and a number of them came to the intelligence section. Our troops had advanced a considerable distance since the Hindenberg line had been broken and we first had a long march to a railway station. On the way we saw a terrible sight where the cavalry had tried to break through. Almost to the end of the war the high command, containing many cavalry officers, had the idea that horses might help to win the war. In this particular case the ground was just littered with their corpses. Cavalry stands no chance against machine guns.

... The following morning two of us were detached to an observation post with orders to keep watch on this mill and the country between it and our front line. We also tried our sniper sights for the first time. Each sniper rifle had special sights adjusted to a particular rifle. During the March retreat some had been lost and the remaining ones fixed to any old rifle. Until now there had been no testing of these although why it could not have been done when we were out of the line I do not know. The most obvious target was a dead Gerry some six or seven hundred yards away and this was the only occasion I had actually taken aim at a German although I had blazed away indiscriminately on occasions to keep enemy heads down.

... The attack started at dawn preceded by a heavy barrage some of which seemed to be coming down amongst our own troops as did sometimes happen. ... Not far from the tape I came across what had been a German machine gun post – why they had not heard us the previous night I do not know. It had obviously suffered from the barrage and there were some dead men lying around. A wounded German soldier was propped up against a bank with a white handkerchief tied to his rifle. He looked very young, pale and scared. He looked most relieved when I spoke to him in German and gave him a drink from my water bottle. I comforted him with the suggestion that the war was over for him and that we treated our prisoners well.

... The war seemed to have eased up a bit. Our front line was so far ahead of base that there were transport difficulties in getting supplies up and a great deal of reorganisation was going on in preparation for a big push. The main job of the section for a while was manning observation posts. One such I remember was on a roof taking cover behind a chimney whilst another was in a church belfry. We had a lot of time on our hands and it was very closed country so we could wander round quite close to the enemy lines without being observed.

... About this time there was quite a lot of gas shelling. I had what my diary describes as a rotten dose and two days later one of the sections was sent down the line – gassed. Apart from this things were quiet and some civilians, mostly old men and women, were managing to get back. We found one couple in a cellar dead – gassed we surmised. The Pioneer Sergeant who did all the odd jobs, made a cross for us. I suggested that we should bury them in the garden. I said the Lord's Prayer whilst the rest of the section stood around, bare headed.

... Preux was captured (4 November) and apart from odd jobs, active service was over for the 2nd Bedfords. Looking into an empty house in the village I was horrified to see an old French man lying on his bed, fully clothed and dead. One was used to seeing dead soldiers, but I could never get used to seeing a dead civilian

On 6 November in pouring rain we made the long march back to Le Cateau which had come to life again for the population was slowly returning. Our section took over a deserted furnished house [two days later...] An apologetic and rather frightened old lady came home. She explained to me that she had been the housekeeper but did not know where the owners were. They had been separated when the Germans overran Le Cateau in 1914. She seemed surprised at her welcome for she was taken 'on the strength' at once, shared our rations and treated with great respect. In spite of her protests one of the bedrooms was handed over to her – she became Granny to all of us and she was delighted when I translated the word for her. When we finally left she was in tears and kissed us all – we had been such 'bon garcons.'

... There was also a visit by the Corps Commander and on another occasion King George V and the Prince of Wales came and informally walked between the lines of cheering men, but it was all so much a waste of time and I was rather bored with no particular job or incident ... The Battalion had been ordered to provide a guard for a large and growing ammunition dump some distance away. A map reference had been given for its position but looking at the map we decided that it was an unlikely spot for such a dump. We dare not doubt openly the Brigade Major's map reading, so the suggestion was made that I should take one of the section bicycles and make an unobtrusive reconnaissance on my own.

Highly elated I set off. It was rather eerie riding across a deserted and in most cases desolate countryside. At one point I did see a Company of the Chinese Labour Corps in the distance scanning the fields for salvage.

To cut the story short the dump was not there and I returned in triumph to BHQ. After an acrimonious discussion on the telephone a new map reference was found and a few days later I had the joy of escorting the guard to the dump, I riding my bicycle, while an envious Sergeant marched with the men. When I reported back to Tyso his "Good show young Hill" was very pleasing, but even more so when the information that the recommendation for the Military Medal had been approved by the Divisional Commander General Lee. It was the only Military Medal won by the Intelligence Section which I was with although three others were wearing the ribbon when I gained it.

... My last night in France was a sleepless one. I spent it with another Sergeant in a leaking tent at Dunkirk ... We left for Folkestone the next morning where on the quay we were met by some rather elderly ladies who gave us a bun and a bar of chocolate ... One dear old lady came up to me and clasped my hand "You dear brave boy, and I know you would do it all again for your country, wouldn't you?" I wasn't so sure.

I banged on the front door early in the morning shouting "Wake up I've come home." I was home but I was already beginning to miss the chaps.'[2]

References

1 *The Portcullis*, 1981, pp. 6–9.

2 Charles Hill, *My War 1914–1918*, unpublished, with thanks to Dr. Charles Tony Hill for permission to republish extracts of his father's memoir.

Emanuel OTC camp at Tidworth, 1932

The OTC and the Home Front
in the Second World War

The OTC slowly recovered from the heavy losses of the First World War and recruitment numbers began to rise in the mid to late 1920s. The Shirley Goodwin era ended and the long and hugely successful reign of legendary Headmaster Cyril Broom began.

In 1931 Charles Hill, one of Emanuel's most influential figures, became the Commander of the Corps, and retained the command until 1961. Hill was held in awe by many boys. His leadership and motivation was the major driving force behind the Corps as they hurtled towards the Second World War.

In 1932 Charles Hill had the Subsidiary Corps reformed and this led to an increase in numbers that continued throughout the remainder of the decade. Both the Headmaster and the Chairman of Governors supported new competitions such as the Warren Cup which saw Subsidiary Corps have House competitions for marching and shooting. Browsing through the surviving OTC albums stored in the School Archive you will see a 'Who's Who' of boys who went on to serve in the Second World War. These 'Soldier Boys', as Bob Deeks called them in his 2012 interview with Daniel Kirmatzis included many Old Boys featured elsewhere in these pages such as, Urwin Thornburn, Alan Skillern, Bertie Mann and Richard 'Dick' Wildey. They cut their teeth in the OTC and many went to war a short period after leaving School. Indeed, there were a significant number who used their OTC experience as a springboard to commissions in the services.

By the mid-1930s the Corps stood on shakier ground. Even though Hitler had already begun his sabre rattling, 1935 saw the London County Council decide to abolish the Cadet Corps in its maintained schools. Luckily Emanuel didn't buy into this philosophy, but it was certainly suggested that the Emanuel OTC contingent be abolished and replaced by a Boy Scout troop. However, it is unlikely that Charles Hill would ever have allowed that to happen. Across the country there was negative talk that the OTC had excessive levels of militarism and others believed its training methods were out of date. But views expressed in *The Portcullis* and reproduced in the School History argued against this:

> The Corps taught boys to be tidy, methodical and orderly and to assume leadership. The week at camp was thoroughly enjoyed, where dozens of contingents from all over the country met and worked together. The spirit of good fellowship and keenness bred friendly inter-school rivalry, broadened the outlook and inspired a desire to work for the common good.

We do not have to rewrite history and pretend the Corps was everybody's cup of tea – it was not. Old Boys have frequently commented that they felt there was far too much pressure put on pupils to join the organisation and that those who didn't join were unlikely to gain senior positions such as Prefect, Lieutenant or School Captain. To some Old Boys avoiding the OTC was a badge of honour in itself. Whichever way you look at it the OTC was a powerful movement at Emanuel School and it remained that way until it was replaced by the Duke of Edinburgh Award scheme.

Many Old Boys joined the Territorial Army after leaving School. This was a common route many graduates of the OTC system followed before joining the services when the War broke out. Others attended short-term university courses which were connected to the RAF or other army units. The Scott-Giles *History of Emanuel* reveals that in 1936 Old Boys were encouraged to join either the Queen's Westminster Rifles or the Civil Service Rifles as the original School OTC had been founded and trained in connection with these regiments with full members visiting the School to help with training and, as a by-product, further recruitment. Others joined regiments their father or grandfather had been in such as Eric Botting who was killed in North Africa. For others it was entirely random. When William Jeffrey turned up at the registration office ready to join the Navy, there was a hitch. He quipped in his 2012 interview with Daniel Kirmatzis "Bugger the Navy" and joined a tank regiment instead. The local battalion, the 9th Royal Fusiliers (City of London Regiment) was very popular and a lasting connection was established between the School and this battalion.

Meanwhile in School the 1930s also saw the annual Grundy Cup Supper turn into a successful reunion of Old Boys and cadets meeting and competing. These were big events and regularly had high-profile features in the local newspapers. A visiting inspector noted in April of 1938:

> I saw a great deal of this contingent both on and off parade. I also saw a large number of ex-cadets who are now in the Territorial Army or in the senior division of the OTC. There can be no doubt as to the interest displayed by present and past members. These facts speak for themselves, and it is certain that Emanuel School OTC is performing its duty to the country in no uncertain manner.

In 1935 Headmaster Cyril Broom speculated about the future: 'Perhaps the OTC may be transformed into an air scout corps and the tower have a new lease of utility as a beacon to aviators, whilst future boys may land their planes on our precious playing-field.' These were prophetic words from the Headmaster the boys knew as 'the beak' as within fifteen years the CCF would have a glider bunny-hopping across the playing field. But first the OTC would have to negotiate almost six long years in Petersfield.

The OTC becomes the JTC in Petersfield

Petersfield gave the OTC, now known as the Junior Training Corps (JTC) to avoid confusion with the full adult OTC, a completely new dimension and lease of life. Countryside dominated the landscape and manoeuvres, drills, field exercises and the early threat of a German invasion occupied the minds of many boys as the war rumbled in the background. Once routines which were as normal as they were ever going to be were established, JTC parades were held on Thursday mornings. Although the JTC had its own church parades it also took its place in local events such as Victory parades and National Savings events. Before long

Emanuel OTC at Tadworth Field Day, 1936

OTC cadets receive field dressing instruction, 1933

Emanuel drums and bugles marching along the High Street became a familiar feature of life in Petersfield and the School was fully integrated into the life of the town.

The escape from London was to lead to many benefits for the JTC. One of the most exciting was night operations, a form of training rare in London. These were practised in Petersfield by platoons and companies of schoolboys with adult reservists. 'Night treks' also became popular with some Corps, as they tried to navigate themselves over tricky terrain in the dark. A special 'tough' platoon was also organised and an assault course was constructed under the instruction of Charles Hill. It provided a sturdy test for cadets and drew the attention of the Guards Division who inspected it for Army purposes. *The Portcullis* No. 143 stated that this 'tough' platoon contained those who attended the majority of the voluntary parades and was distinguished by white lanyards, formerly worn by those who had attended annual camps. Special training such as climbing cliffs, swimming in drill uniform and bayonet fighting took place. Not to be outdone by the 'tough' platoon, JTC marches often got longer and longer. The Spring Term 1942 *Portcullis* outlined the timed route march. This wisely gave different age groups varying distances to run with a standard time in which to perform the march. For those over seventeen, had six hours to complete a 20-mile march, with thirty minutes break for lunch. The longest march noted was one of 40 miles to Chichester and back. Many extra voluntary route marches also took place on Saturday afternoons, and were often as long as eighteen miles.

There were also several marches from Petersfield to London and to the School in Battersea. There was night training to build up the stamina required and an overnight stay in tents in the Guildford area. Most of the marches took place at the end of term so that the cadets could spend time with their families and friends in London. *The Portcullis* recalls one of the successful marches:

> At the end of term, as a climax to this training, it was arranged to march to London. The happy little band triumphantly marched down the familiar Drive on the evening of the second day. Everyone suffered blistered feet, but were all in good spirits. A special word of commendation should be given to CQMS Haydock, who came on the march although he was joining the Army the next day to be greeted by Mrs Broom, a few parents and some of the smaller fry of the School.

As the War progressed the activity of the Corps increased and tougher tests were often set for its contingent. *The Portcullis* dropped down to a slim volume that appeared infrequently due to a paper shortage, but it still noted some of the more exciting JTC activities. One of these was 'The First Guard.' Emanuel supplied guards on one of the local railway tunnels on the London–Portsmouth line for three days in succession for the local Churcher's College boys were exhausted. They were also asked to take over for two days as a relief guarding places of strategic importance. The guard consisted of sixteen boys, under Stafford Hipkins. Each member of the guard did about three stretches of sentry duty, each of two hours' duration. These various guard duties were initially regarded as exciting. However, as they became more organised the excitement dwindled and monotony set in.

As the war continued pupils left the School and went straight into the services. A large number of boys who attended Emanuel in Battersea were then evacuated to Petersfield and subsequently joined up, never to see the School in Battersea again. As in the First World War many returned to visit or sent news of their exploits, exciting or otherwise. 'Otherwise' in the case of this letter from Ralph J. Firmin who writes about being bored on the Home Front:

> As you may know, I'm still on active service in this country. We are still in —, but I wish we were not, for a bleaker and draughtier part of country you're not likely to find. There are ten of us stuck in a field miles from anywhere (including pubs) with a searchlight, waiting. We've been waiting now for the best part of six months and it looks like we're going to wait for six or seven years. We've seen absolutely nothing of the enemy, and would welcome the sight of anything, even a submarine. I rejoice in the exalted rank of Sapper and work for 26 hours a day for fourteen bob a week. Life is one round of sleep and guards.

By 1941 there were 180 boys in the JTC. In the summer of 1942 we learn that the JTC became 'affiliated to a battalion of the Royal Fusiliers for training purposes and on the recommendation of the officer commanding our local TA battalion in London Lieut-Col E. Harcourt Hillersdon...we were given permission to wear the Royal Fusiliers' badge by the Colonel of the regiment, Major-General W. P. H. Hill, CB, CMG, DSO.'

Later in the War Cadets and NCOs attended weapons training and field tactics courses in Dorset. All boys over the age of seventeen joined the Home Guard in addition to their voluntary service in the Corps. They were involved in duties such as fire services, fire watching and helping in the report centre in the Town Hall. Although there was already much going on, the Home Guard continued to flourish and appealed to teenage boys as it enticed them in with techniques such as 'street fighting' and hand-to-hand combat.

The Portcullis published in the summer of 1943 highlighted some of the wider activities the evacuated schoolboys were involved in. The Spotters' Club was one of the most popular of these. It was formed towards the end of 1942 and was affiliated to the National Association of Spotters' Clubs and by autumn of 1943 there were over fifty members. There were frequent talks on aircraft recognition, films were shown and visits to local aerodromes took place. They also had their own library of more than 150 books run by David W. Palmer. Brian W. Haydock was responsible for club training, and K. W. Bouch arranged the competitions and tests. The club even entered the Hampshire Division of the Southern Region NASC Air League Trophy Contest and won other events. Mr Spafford helped run the club until he left the School in 1944. By autumn 1944 the Spotters' Club had expanded and also included train spotting. Not surprisingly, though the club died not long after the War ended, it resurfaced some years later when the School had returned to Battersea.

OTC annual inspection, 1936

Emanuel OTC c1936 featuring Michael Jeffery (second from left), Ken Richardson (third from left) and Bill Page (behind Ken)

Emanuel OTC cadets at Epsom Downs Racecourse

Mrs Grundy presenting the Grundy Cup to CSM Wildey, 1935

Many boys who attended the Spotters' Club also joined the Petersfield squadron of the Air Training Corps, which at one stage of the war was given priority over all other forms of preparatory training. ATC members were often leading lights in the Spotters' Club.

In each of the years 1940–1944 there were farming camps run by H. B. 'Dolly' Mearns, often taking up much of the summer holidays. A by-product was boys frequently helping in the local farms and the resurrection of allotments, similar to those of the First World War, in the School grounds. Work on the allotments was an alternative to games and captured the enthusiasm of a certain number of boys. Eventually though; farmers required considerably more help and boys continued to work in two-hour shifts, often as many as three times a week. Indeed, although it was hard work, many regarded the allotments as one of the most pleasant aspects of the evacuation. *The Portcullis* regularly updated the development of the allotments. In issue 140, published in 1940, it reveals: 'Where there was a jungle of nettles and weeds there now grows really opulent vegetable marrows, and in place of rough grasses a very fine crop of potatoes, and we have had beans and peas in good quantities.' Practically, the staff helped organise the boys in lessening the gardeners'

OTC annual inspection, 1936

heavy workloads. There were even bouts of theft, with the leeks all being uprooted and stolen one night. As the years rolled by the following crop was planned on a grander scale and basic produce such as potatoes were always in high demand.

As the War stretched beyond 1943 many boys longed to go home. Indeed, many of the younger boys had never attended the Battersea site of the School. Many began to see light at the end of the tunnel when the School reopened in September of 1943 for Emergency Tutorial Classes. These classes were opened for those juniors of Emanuel, Sir Walter St John's School who had remained in London, or for those who wished to return from evacuation. A few boys from the Battersea Grammar School were also included. The original number of pupils was under 100, with the oldest boy being fourteen. Because of their ages, the curriculum was based on

Epsom Downs, featuring (left to right): Cdt. Dean, Cdt. Firmin, Cdt. Surridge, Cdt. Elmes, Sgt. Galsworthy, Cpl. Wildey, Cdt. Hillier, Cdt. Yorke, Cdt. Wilson, Cdt. Jeffery

Emanuel OTC in the mid-1930s

the first three years of the school course. Emanuel boy R. J. Payton was appointed Captain of the School. Other Emanuel Prefects included: D. G. Burton, R. M. Barrett, J. Greenough, M. J. Skerritt, E. A. Duff and R. L. Miller. At one point in the winter of 1943, numbers fell to only sixty pupils and the boys spent a lot of the time in the shelters, but the School battled on.

Soccer was the winter sport and cricket was played in the summer. Flying bomb activity interrupted the cricket season and limited athletics. The Subsidiary Corps was restarted under the Headmaster Major Charles Hill who had returned from Petersfield to lead it and R. M. Barrett, E. A. Page and M. J. Burton had prominent positions.

The reopened School tried to provide as full a programme as it could. The Sackville Club for debates was revived and dramatic productions returned. There was a steady increase in numbers and by the summer of 1944 there were 208 boys on the roll, 159 of whom were Emanuel pupils. This grew to over 300 boys by the summer of 1945. Conditions were not ideal for working but the School steadily found its feet. In winter there was either little or no heat and the accommodation was inadequate. Doors and windows were blown in, ceilings came down and the chapel was damaged to such a degree it was considered unwise to use it. For large periods of time only the ground floor classrooms were used as the upper floors were unsafe, had broken windows and were infested with birds. But it was home and the rest of the School population longed to join these 300 boys, but they would have to wait until July 1945 for the majority of the School population to return from exile.

LESLIE HENSON REVIEWS THE SITUATION, AND

The General Outlook

"The situation as I see it is such that every effort should be made, by all who have any kind of interest at heart or elsewhere, to secure the evolution of those fructifying forces which tend to exercise a beneficent rather than a retrograde influence on the progress of events."

Foreign Affairs

"Casting our eyes abroad, what do we see, if indeed we can be said to see anything at all, and not rather to be gazing with horrifying uncertainty at a maelstrom of conflicting impulses tending towards an ever-more-possible—if not absolutely inevitable—dissolution."

Finance

"I foresee a difficult time for financial experts. There is little money in the money-market, and people tend more and more to take out what little there is."

Sport

"In sport, 1939 will be a remarkable year, filled with a number of spectacular successes. It is hard to foresee at this early date exactly by whom the successes will be won."

Love

"I am happy to be able to report a most beneficent confluence of congenialities for those in love. They will remain in love—not, in all cases, with the same partners."

FORECASTS THE COURSE OF EVENTS IN 1939

Home Affairs

"Turn rather to events at home. Here we are fortunate in the possession of a multitude of prophets, able to forecast from the increasing number of bicycle sprockets employed by the crofters of the Western Isles, an ever-growing demand for more of everything, everywhere."

Personal Affairs

"And so in a cloud of uncertainty the year goes out. Fortunately, in our private lives we are on firmer ground. We can be sure that we shall be genial, large-hearted and progressive—and that everyone with whom we come in contact will be mean, narrow-minded and depraved."

The Open Air

"Open the air of Britain has always been. Open it will remain during the ensuing twelve months. In some quarters it will be, if anything, more open than before."

Disarmament

"It will be illegal to carry a revolver or a life-preserver. But to carry a rifle may at any time become compulsory, particularly in the civilised countries."

. . . For The Future

"1939 will be succeeded at a rapidly-decreasing interval by 1940, the first year of a new decade—which in turn will give way to a further twelve-month period, 1941."

The School Prepares for the Evacuation

EMANUEL SCHOOL, S.W. 11.

A.I.

TO ALL BOYS TAKING PART IN EMANUEL EVACUATION SCHEME.

This notice should be shown to your parents so that they can know what must be done and help you.

1. You are attached to group : your group leader is

2. If an emergency arises during term, I shall tell you if evacuation is going to take place and give you a letter to your parents. We are to go on the morning of the 2nd day of evacuation. If your parents wish you to come, you should be at school on the 1st day of evacuation to receive any notices. In a crisis look carefully at newspapers and listen to wireless: you might be ordered by the Government to come to school on a Saturday or Sunday.

3. If an emergency arises during holidays and you are in London, you should come to school as ordered by press or wireless. Evacuation will be arranged for all who come to school on the day.

4. If an emergency arises during holidays and you are out of London, do not try to return to London. Your parents will ask advice from an official of the local authority of the town in which you are staying. They can discover from the Sergeant Major at the school where our party has gone and you might be able to join us later.

T A K E Y O U R G A S M A S K on your holiday.

5. On the day of evacuation if you live some way from the school, start from home earlier than usual. Wear school uniform dress with mackintosh or overcoat, and stout boots or shoes. You should bring a complete change of clothing - vest, pants, shirts with collars, sports jacket or blazer, trousers (or knickers) pullover, spare boots or shoes, handkerchiefs, several pairs of socks or stockings, with night attire, soap, towel, comb, tooth brush, face cloth, some toilet paper, cotton wool and plimsolls. You must also bring your gas mask, with your name written on the webbing, in a carrier. It is best to carry your luggage in a rucksack or haversack so that your arms can be free. You should have 2 linen labels supplied with string, one worn loosely round your neck and tucked in, the other fixed to your luggage. On one side of each label write your name and Emanuel School, London, S.W.11: on the other side 'L.C.C. H 56 '.

(THE SCHOOL NUMBER FOR EVACUATION IS H 56)

6. You should bring with you food for at least one day, but nothing that will easily melt or crush. The following are suggested -

Sandwiches (egg or cheese)
packets of nuts or seedless raisins
dry biscuits (with little packets of cheese)
Barley sugar (rather than chocolate)
apple : orange.

7. Bring with you some money and a small reading book. A ticket will be provided for you which will take you to your destination and secure you a billet. A master in each group will be asked to act as treasurer for your money, if you wish.

not a member of the school, coming
ing what is mentioned in 5,6, 7.
s are being sent to your parents.
group as any brother(s) of sister(s)

area, you will be settled in billets.
first pay for your board and lodging
parents or guardians to pay a part
I shall send the address
ce to the Sergeant Major who will
on the dining-hall door.
icial paid post cards and give them
postal address so that you can write

y in billets, let your group leader

cheerful. We want to reach
a casualty and we must win.

A I. and this number should be

G. M. Broom,

Headmaster.

25. 7. 39

A letter was sent to Emanuel boys' parents at the end of the school year, July 1939, notifying them of what measures to take in the event of evacuation. After the Munich Crisis in September 1938 the Government became increasingly aware that, in the event of another European war, the most

Letter sent by Headmaster Cyril Broom to Emanuel parents on 25 July 1939 regarding evacuation procedure

vulnerable in society, including children, the elderly and infirm would need to be evacuated from the most at-risk areas in a war anticipated to include aerial bombing of cities as had occurred in the Spanish Civil War. Evacuation had an adverse effect on pupil numbers for between January 1939 and January 1940 the School roll fell from 578 to 431 and the Headmaster was all too aware that, 'the problem of obtaining new boys will soon become acute.'

EMANUEL SCHOOL
POSTE RESTANTE
POST OFFICE
P E T E R S F I E L D
Hants.

September 8th 1939

Dear Sir or Madam,

I have to inform you that the school is now established at Petersfield, and arrangements are being made to carry on our work between the excellent accommodation provided by two well-known schools - Bedales School and Churcher's College. We have been very kindly welcomed by the Headmasters of the schools and the local authorities, and, though our usual programme of work may be slightly modified, there will be compensations in the opportunities afforded by the delightful country surroundings.

If you wish your son(s) to attend the school next term, you must make arrangements to send the boy(s) not later than TUESDAY NEXT, SEPTEMBER 12th. This is of the greatest importance as the billetting committee wish to complete the provision of accommodation for members of schools. The Board of Education in a recent circular has stipulated that fees will be payable as usual, and any fees to which you are liable should be paid to the Clerk to the Governors at 53 Palace Street, Westminster, S. W.I. until further notice. I hope that your son(s) will be able to join the school. If you do not propose to send him(them) I should be grateful if you would kindly notify me in writing to that effect so that I can in due course inform the Governors. It is desirable that all boys should bring, besides gas masks, a supply of clothing to cover as long a period as possible so as to diminish the necessity of sending further supplies. Our ladies' committee is making suggestions about laundry etc. and is carrying out periodical visits to the boys in their billets. I think that this change of environment will provide valuable stimulus to the general education of our boys.

With compliments,

Yours very truly,

C.G.M.BROOM

Headmaster.

Churcher's College, Petersfield (above) and Letter from Cyril Broom to Emanuel parents 8 September 1939 notifying them that the School was established in Petersfield

Emanuel School in Petersfield 1939–1945

By Local Petersfield Historian Vaughan Clarke

Part 1: The Arrival

In 1939 Petersfield and the neighbouring village Sheet with a population of some 6000 received a number of schools into the area, of which by far the largest was Emanuel School, which arrived with no fewer than 560 people mainly evacuated from London before the Blitz – and shared Churcher's College for some six years.

Emanuel's Michaelmas Term in 1939 started on Saturday 26 August, when the boys arrived back, but unfortunately the buildings were out of bounds because of redecoration, so games of cricket or lazing in deckchairs were the order of the day. The situation continued for the following week, and a member of the school stated 'This week will surely live in our minds forever. Never had the grounds looked more attractive; we could enjoy our leisure without the thoughts of 'prep' the weather was perfect. Moreover, a general spirit of happiness pervaded everyone.'

On Friday 1 September Emanuel evacuated. The train left Clapham Junction at 11.15am for an unknown destination. When they were well on their journey, they were told the final destination was Petersfield.

On arrival they were escorted to St Peter's Church to await instructions, then to the centre building in the elementary school and from there they were divided into parties and taken by billeting officials to various quarters of the town. Whilst they were waiting about in the streets offers of hot tea and cakes were showered on them.

THE PETERSFIELD SQUARE.

Sketch of the King William III statue in Petersfield Town Square by artist Flora Twort

Emanuel evacuees filling sandbags in Petersfield

The party from London was made up of some 450 boys (a further 100 had been left behind because their parents had made other arrangements, or did not wish them to leave London) about 45 brothers and sisters and some 65 adults, masters, their wives and parents.

The boys' foster-parents were referred to as their hosts and hostesses. Certain hostesses mothered as many as six Emanuel boys at a time, and there is a true story of one who, having generously volunteered to take in eight small girls, instead found eight burly members of the upper school at her door! Some of the billetings were very successful with some boys staying with their hosts over the whole period, though obviously there were others whose idiosyncrasies caused frequent changes and a few whose problems could only be solved by a return to their London homes.

Billets were visited by masters, who did their best to straighten out early difficulties, while liaison with the billeting authorities was maintained by Mr Hipkins, who took over the handling of all the billeting problems on behalf of the School, a task he fulfilled for the duration of the war.

The whole evacuation itself seems to have been somewhat chaotic, to put it mildly, for London County Council delegated its authority to Hampshire County Council, who were not equipped to cope with the situation, having more interest in those being evacuated from Portsmouth and Southampton after they suffered severe bombings. The result was that Emanuel had to negotiate for space and was responsible for bringing all its books and equipment from London.

Mr A. H. G. Hoggarth, the Headmaster of Churcher's College, promptly offered to share the college premises by means of shifts, so that the college would have lessons in the mornings, Emanuel in the afternoons. It was impossible for Churcher's to provide all the accommodation required, for its own numbers were fewer than those of Emanuel's, while the presence of boarders prevented the surrender of all its rooms, even during the afternoons.

Emanuel First XV, 1940

The School's week regularly began with a service at 9.30am at St Peter's, usually with an address by the Chaplain, with the lesson being read by a Prefect – and the service proved to be an impressive and valuable religious experience. Notices for the week were given out at the service, as it was the one time during the week when the whole school was together in one place.

Sport took place most mornings, with different groups using the facilities on different days and with the JTC parades held on a Thursday morning. When double summer time was introduced it meant that some cricket matches were started as early as 7.30am, on what could be called a very dewy wicket. Lessons took place between 1.30pm and 5.30pm, being five periods of 45 minutes with a fifteen-minute break. This usually meant hoards of cyclists, laden with books, heading in all directions around the town every 45 minutes.

Part 2: Early days in Petersfield

OE and Petersfield evacuee, Dennis Geen, gave us a personal insight into the early days at Petersfield. He was a fourth former at the time and can vividly remember arriving at Clapham Junction with the rest of the School, where he met a family friend who worked on Southern Railways and who informed him their destination would be Petersfield and that 'he would tell his mother where he was going.'

As the only member of the school, apart from the Headmaster, who knew the destination of the journey, this was his moment of glory and so armed with his knowledge he and his friends rushed onto the train to consult the map that was a feature of every train compartment at that time. Unfortunately, although they soon discovered the whereabouts of Petersfield, it meant absolutely nothing, as nobody had ever heard of the place.

One of Miss Bedford's Raglan House classes

Interior of Saint Peter's Church by Brian Stuart Turner (Emanuel 1932–1942)

The outlying rooms the School used, with the exception of the rooms in the Blue Anchor Inn, were some distance away, so staff really required bicycles, a lot of energy and waterproof garments to get around. It also meant the lessons were shortened and classes were left to their own devices for intervals between lessons. Difficulties pupils had to overcome included a lack of facilities in the form of teaching aids in the outlying rooms such as blackboards, chalk and paper. Staff had to expend a lot of effort in overcoming this.

Part 3: The Winter of 1940

OE Dennis Geen tells us the first three winters in Petersfield were bitterly cold. He remembers the deep snow and frozen Heath Lake with its skating. He doesn't remember feeling particularly cold, but those were the days when standing on cold lino was the norm and getting dressed and undressed under the bedclothes were nothing unusual! Not unnaturally there was frenzied rushing hither and thither about the prospect of skating and all the available skates were immediately brought out and used. Large numbers of the School and a few more valiant members of the staff turned out to make the best of the ice and amazed spectators with their skill.

The best skaters were immediately attracted by the prospect of ice hockey, so sticks of all shapes and sizes were procured and many vigorous matches, with Messrs Nussey and Spafford [both teachers] playing, were fought out. The School's best players were Johnson, Neubert, Bailey and Dixon. An inexperienced Emanuel team played a Churcher's side who were much better 'armed', but despite great efforts they were beaten.

Despite the distance, a few boys on occasion cycled back to London for the day, setting off early from Petersfield and arriving home by about midday, then setting off again four hours later for the long return journey. The illogical, but redeeming feature of the evacuation scheme was the almost general practice of returning home for the holidays. Despite all this to-ing and fro-ing to London no member of the School was killed or injured by enemy action.

The remarkable high standard of health bore further testimony to the suitability of evacuation conditions. Boys who fell sick were nursed in Heath House and eventually a hostel was set up to relieve hostesses of their sick charges. Some boys remained in Petersfield during the holidays and so the staff took their holidays in rotation in order to ensure that boys always had some members of staff available.

Emanuel Cricket Team, 1940

Emanuel Sevens rugby team

Part 4: Work and Play

The senior School uniform of black jacket and junior School uniform of grey jacket and dark navy cap soon became a regular sight on the streets of Petersfield. This uniform was only obtainable from Harrods and, despite it being wartime, a representative from the shop often came to visit the town at regular intervals for orders.

Games were a major feature in the life of Emanuel, but whereas Churcher's was able, at the cost of double wear, to supply practice pitches and facilities for some of the morning games, they did not have the facilities to allow the School use of the pitches in the afternoon for inter-school matches. For two seasons one of the fields of Lord's Farm was used, thanks to the generosity of the farmer. The first inter-school game of the war was played by Emanuel versus Churcher's and Emanuel went on to win. Emanuel went on to field a strong team for the rest of the war. The friendly spirit between the two schools was exemplified by holding mixed rugby practices each season.

One would have thought that with restricted wartime travel, there would have been a cessation of sports fixtures between schools that were a long distance apart, but this was not the case. All that happened was that the fixture list for the School was rearranged, fixtures that were further from Petersfield (eg Bedford) were dropped and new fixtures, closer, were added in Leatherhead, Reading and Salisbury. Members of Emanuel School teams in those days became hardened travellers, for the limited facilities in the town caused most fixtures to be arranged away. Saturday's games often meant a return to billets at about 10pm. In the cricket season it became later still. Wartime made people very resourceful.

In the summer of 1940 the School started an allotment of some three quarters of an acre on the Sheet allotment area and this produced crops throughout the war. The allotment, which was cultivated first under the direction of Mr Appleyard, who taught metalwork, and then of Mr V. D. Norris (woodwork master), was a task that was an alternative to games and captured the enthusiasm of a certain number of boys. It provided a quantity of produce that was sold. One of the houses (Raglan) was fiercely independent and farmed its own allotment, stoutly asserting its supremacy.

School activities were dominated by the Corps. This was run by Major Hill who had volunteered for active service but was told that his service to the Corps was too highly valued to permit this. At first it seemed that there might be a definite role for it to play, especially when invasion was expected in June and several cadets formed platoons for the emergency duty of guarding the Butser railway tunnel on the London–Portsmouth line, each platoon manning the guard for a 24 hour shift. The signals section fixed up communications between the units at the two ends of the tunnel. However these duties were discontinued because of the disruption to

CHURCHER'S PREP. SCHOOL

ATHLETIC SPORTS, JUNE 19th, 1941.

PROGRAMME OF EVENTS.

EVENT No. 1—80 Yds. Over 10.
Killick, Blagg — Stratford, Notley — Pratt, Gales — Knox, Vince

EVENT No. 2—80 Yards. 9 Years.
Cutler, Cross — Lindsey, Harwood — Dryland, Cuff — Rainbow, Bradshaw-Jones

EVENT No. 3—80 Yards. Under 9.
Lock, Fry — Luttrell, Money-Chappelle — Levy, Willmott — Payne, Gammon i

EVENT No. 4—Three-legged Race. Over 10.
Pratt, Matthews — Griffin, Notley — Gales, Stratford — McMichael, Day — Killick, Knox — Blagg, Pullen
Poore, Vince — Procter, Steelsmith — Wimshurst, Harvey i — Cheesman, Bray — Broadway i, Stein

EVENT No. 5—Three-legged Race. Under 10.
Cuff, Robb — Rainbow, Pellow — Broadway ii, Privett — Lindsey, Burley — Suthers, Harwood — Greenburgh, Harvey ii
Ward, Urquhart — Lock, Fry — Sykes, Money-Chappelle — Luttrell, Willmott — Levy, Gammon i — Isaac, Bray ii
Payne, Duffett — Gammon ii, Bradshaw-Jones

EVENT No. 6—Hurdles (Heats).
1st Heat: Stratford — Killick — Cross
2nd Heat: Pratt — McMichael — Notley
3rd Heat: Knox — Cuff — Blagg

EVENT No. 7—High Jump. Under 10.
Dryland, Cuff — Cutler, Bradshaw-Jones — Broadway ii, Suthers

EVENT No. 8—High Jump. Over 10.
Stratford, Blagg — Knox, Killick — Pratt, Broadway i

EVENT No. 9—80 Yards, Emanuel Prep. School. Under 9½ (Heats).

EVENT No. 10—200 Yards, Emanuel Prep. School. Over 9½ (Heats).

Churcher's Prep School sports programme which illustrates how the Emanuel Prep classes were integrated into the host School's activities

A campaign poster for Salute the Soldier Week - urging the public to save for the war effort

the boys' education. Some pupils actually sat their Higher Schools exam (the equivalent of A-levels) after a night guarding the tunnel.

A little later, Emanuel manned an observation post at Heath farm nightly by means of a five-night rota, four Corps sections each commanded by an officer and a section of eight masters, all of whom were newly enrolled in the Local Defence Volunteers undertaking duty for one night each.

Part 5: The Bomb Drops

The war passed over Petersfield for the most part, often literally in the form of German night and day bombers. The enemy, therefore, dropped but few bombs in the neighbourhood. Nevertheless, careful instructions were issued about precautions in air-raids and for some months boys carried their gas masks wherever they went. When day attacks were frequent, in 1940, most sat in silent contemplation in the Roman Catholic Church, a solid structure which gave more protection than the more modestly designed Methodist schoolroom nearby. Games of cricket were interrupted whilst players took cover in neighbouring houses or hedges.

The Battle of the Atlantic is being lost!

The reasons why:

1. German U-boats, German bombers and the German fleet sink and seriously damage between them every month a total of 700 000 to 1 million tons of British and allied shipping.
2. All attempts at finding a satisfactory means of defence against the German U-boats or the German bombers have failed disastrously.
3. Even President Roosevelt has openly stated that for every five ships sunk by Germany, Britain and America between them can only build two new ones. All attempts to launch a larger shipbuilding programme in America have failed.
4. Britain is no longer in a position to secure her avenues of supply. The population of Britain has to do with about half the ration that the population of Germany gets. Britain, herself, can only support 40 % of her population from her own resources in spite of the attempts made to increase the amount of land under cultivation. If the war is continued until 1942, 60 % of the population of Britain will starve!

All this means that starvation in Britain is not to be staved off. At the most it can be postponed, but whether starvation comes this year or at the beginning of next doesn't make a ha'porth of difference. Britain must starve because she is being cut off from her supplies.

Britain's losing the Battle of the Atlantic means Britain's losing the war!

A German propaganda leaflet dropped over Petersfield

November 1940 brought the one serious incident in Petersfield, when a single German raider dropped a bomb on the Poor Law Institution, possibly because it looked like a barracks from the air, killing seven people. Senior members of the JTC, which had just come off parade, helped to remove the survivors and were publically thanked for their work.

When Portsmouth was heavily bombed and refugees came flooding into Petersfield, Emanuel working parties prepared rest centres, in which Mr Hughes (biology master) served as medical officer.

Part 6: Wartime Activities

It is not well known that in 1940 the evacuation authorities had made a decision to move Emanuel from Petersfield and relocate it in Basingstoke where there was better school accommodation, but this was strongly resisted by the Headmaster who estimated that there were not enough billets for all the pupils and staff involved. It was thus decided to stay in Petersfield.

Despite being evacuated, it was extremely important to ensure that the School operated a full range of out of school activities to suit all tastes and to keep pupils occupied. Not only were the expected clubs such as photographic, music, field naturalist, school crusaders etc organised within the School itself, there were also links with other local schools. Some keen debates took place with Churcher's College, Midhurst Grammar School and Portsmouth High School for Girls who, at that time, were resident at Adhurst House on the outskirts of Sheet. These contacts grew into an inter-sixth form discussion group with the addition of seniors from Bedales and the Petersfield Girls' High School.

The School was able to make a noteworthy contribution to the cultural life of the town, with school plays being performed in the large well-equipped Town Hall and some of the other performances, reinforced by some introduction of Petersfield talent, raised considerable sums of money for charity, in addition to being well received by the local population. Later in the war the School formed its own dance band which was much in demand.

Part 7: Problems with Numbers

By 1942 Emanuel had become an established part of the town, taking part in the life of the area. The problems of a school which has been evacuated some distance from its natural home did not really become apparent for some considerable time. The main problem such schools suffered from was the recruitment of new pupils, since the natural base was miles away from where they had been evacuated – and in Emanuel's case, as their recruitment was mainly from winners of places in the London County Council exams, these were boys who were already evacuated from London. School numbers consequently fell and by 1942 the intake had fallen from three forms to two forms. This situation could not continue without drastic consequences and so a decision was made to restart part of the school back in Wandsworth.

Emanuel School Prefects in Petersfield, 1945. From left to right: Anthony Parry Pritchard, I. M. Pritchard, Robert Thomas, P. K. Skinner

Part 8: Victory in Europe

On VE Day, 8 May 1945, an assembly was held at 9.30am outside the pavilion and everyone was dismissed for the next two days. The crowd surged out of the gates of Churcher's and down Ramshill. By the time they had reached the bottom of the High Street they were strung out across the road, arm-in-arm as they marched up a flag bedecked High Street, followed by marching along most of the streets and eventually finishing back in the Square. Everyone then dispersed to celebrate in their own way.

In the afternoon many pupils arrived back in the Square dressed in original, if somewhat loud, costumes which at times verged on fancy dress. In the meantime the statue of William of Orange had been variously decorated with ties, scarves and caps. Mass celebrations seem to have occurred and there were many photographs taken of the event.

Drawing of Emanuel JTC exercises on Butser Hill which originally featured in The Portcullis, No. 145, Spring 1942, p. 40

GOINGS-ON ON BUTSER.

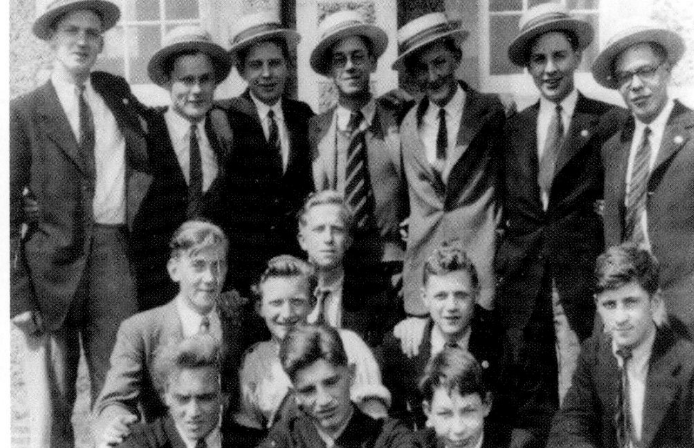

Modern Sixth friends in Petersfield, Summer 1944

One of the sixth formers, David Palmer, dressed as a French gipsy girl, was borne up the High Street on a stretcher, which apparently was no mean task as he was somewhat large!

The School's greatest service to Petersfield that day was the appearance of the 'Windsor Rhythm Kings', this time on top of the shelter in the Square. Lights had been fitted up during the day and the band were able to play until midnight. As Petersfield's own official celebrations were not until the following evening, the band proved a great attraction. A large crowd of people were obviously extremely grateful for its efforts and £15 was collected for the local hospital. The crowd danced to its music for over four hours.

Part 9: Farewell to Petersfield

It was known when the summer term opened in 1945 that it would be the last in exile and the closing days of the term were occupied in the considerable task of packing up. The pile of items gradually diminished as lorry after lorry left Petersfield on the way back to London. Then, suddenly for those still remaining, the farewell gathering was upon them, their last night in Petersfield.

This gathering of hostesses and friends took place at the town hall on Wednesday 18 July. After the reception the Headmaster, Mr Broom, and his wife met with hosts, hostesses and numerous friends of the School and there was a light-hearted concert, including a sketch dealing with the seamy side of evacuation (from a hostess's point of view). To the relief of the players a wholesale exodus of hostesses did not occur at the rowdiest point – possibly because they had become hardened to that sort of thing.

Speeches followed from the Headmaster, Governors, the Headmaster of Churcher's and Mr Gammon, who spoke for the residents of Petersfield. This in turn was followed by refreshments and a dance until midnight, with the School band once again providing the music.

As a recognition of local debt to the town and in expression of its gratitude the School raised a fund of £500 as a gift to the hospital. This sum was subscribed to by members of the School, Old Boys and parents of boys who were in Petersfield. It is commemorated by a plaque in the hospital. A sum of money was also given to Churcher's College to endow an annual prize to commemorate Emanuel's long stay and to express gratitude for the friendly hospitality the pupils and staff of Emanuel had enjoyed. Personal gifts were also made to others who assisted the School during the war years.

VE Day musical celebrations featuring 'The Windsor Rhythm Kings'

Memories from Petersfield

Emanuel boys remember their time as evacuees

Clive Barnes *(Emanuel 1938–1945)*

Six Years in Petersfield

The renowned theatre critic, author and ballet expert Clive Barnes who was an Emanuel evacuee wrote the following account of life for Emanuel boys in Petersfield. It appeared in the Summer Term 1945 *Portcullis* but aspects of the account are not all as they seem. In 2009 a large contingent of OEs returned to Petersfield for the 70th anniversary of the evacuation and whilst they were being led around Churcher's College, several of them told Archivist Tony Jones that on the day of the evacuation Barnes had flu and was driven to Petersfield some days later by his parents! This was perhaps the first time Barnes used what is known as 'artistic licence' to stress a point, a useful skill for a journalist. True or not, we'll never know for sure.

Clive Barnes wrote:

'In September 1939, I was twelve years old. Old enough to remember, with the fuddled clarity of youth, Abyssinia, Spain and the other wars and rumours of war from my early life. That late August was hot. On Saturday, 26 August, the School assembled ready for evacuation.

Clive Barnes

The School buildings were being re-decorated and the synthetic stink of paint and varnish hung in the hot air. The cricket square was a strange technicolor green and everyone was gay and noisy like a vast garden party waiting for the arrival of the expected conjurer.

On Friday, 1 September we evacuated. Our train left Clapham Junction at 11.15am for an unknown destination. All I remember of the journey was heat, noise, near-molten chocolate and a mouth organ playing 'South of the Border.' The country was still uneasily at peace.

On arrival at Petersfield we were escorted to the Parish Church. It seemed a very large church, but then, as I realise now, it was a time of superlatives. Billeting started almost at once. It seemed great fun and most of us, at least the younger of us, felt a guilty sense of shame that we should be enjoying it. The next day we met at the Council School.

For two weeks things bustled. Pantechnicons journeyed to London to return with vast cargoes of books and other necessary school equipment. When School started there was the slow realisation that Petersfield had most of the same things we had in London. The first year was a time of waiting – few thought the war would last beyond Christmas. It did and we waited to go home.

In the October, rugger started. Eddie Page scored our first war-time try. This was the first of our derby matches against Churcher's. We won, but they were the first to score. We had a very successful season, ably led by Gurling.

The next term started. Emanuel were settled. The black caps had become as much a feature of the town as khaki. Mr Appleyard and Mr Mearns and later Mr Norris led the school allotment drive and we also had our first war-time sports day. Both the school javelin and discus records were broken.

When the Battle of Britain started everyone was tense. It was a common occurrence to see tanks roll past the School. Invasion was expected. Many masters and seniors joined the Home Guard. They waited for the enemy who never came. By the time the Battle of Britain ended, about a quarter of Emanuel boys had never seen the School in Wandsworth.

It was this term that Petersfield was bombed. Seniors were able to help in the rescue work. In the third year, where I was, the prevailing emotion was sensation rather than fear. It seems to be an observed fact that the fear of sudden death promotes a kind of shallow hilarity.

Masters had left to go to war and our first mistress joined the staff. Mr Appleyard was also to retire. I, personally, will long remember the ovation he received at his last 'hall.' He was and, happily is, a great personality and much loved by many generations at Emanuel.

A sign of the times this term was the amalgamation of the eight Houses into four for the purpose of house rugger. The number of societies continued to increase including the Sixth Form Society, the Dorset Club and the Philatelic Society amongst others.

The Monday services continued and from our first arrival with a short service at 9.30am at the start of the week.

Back in London the night raids started in earnest. The School chapel was hit and the playing fields were wrecked. The number of homeless evacuees increased due to the steady flow of people leaving Portsmouth, which was being heavily bombed. The mood was dark for school leavers, there was little prospect of work and a much bigger possibility of the imminent call-up made 'carpe diem' the order of the day.

A cloud of futility and frustration – the war seemed unending. At Christmas the Dramatic Society put on 'The Rivals.' The 'Streets of London' was to follow and from then on Emanuel regularly put on dramatic productions.

Towards the end of the term a night operation was held in conjunction with Winchester College. I, a very junior cadet, remember getting very wet. It rained almost all night. I also had the somewhat dubious distinction of being Winchester's first captive. In the autumn of 1942 there came another march to London, this one was completed in a week. Around this time the *Portcullis* became erratic and a rival production appeared called The Independent. It was to disappear after a few issues however.

Before he left in the summer of 1942, the School Captain, David P. Bowler, suggested the formation of a Music Club for the School. The Dorset Club also went from strength to strength and had over 35 meetings in a single school year, quite comfortably a school record for any society. Meanwhile, the Science Sixth made the second of its three abortive attempts to form a Scientific Society. A Spotters' Club was formed at the end of the term. The two Haydocks pushed it along and if membership and longevity are any criterion, it must have been very successful.

By the summer of 1943, the war situation looked far more hopeful. Peace was now something to look forward to. We were now at the end of the beginning, if not yet at the beginning of the end.

In the Autumn of 1943 emergency classes started up in the London school, under the headmastership of Major Hill. It was by then an unfortunate fact that only a small proportion of the School at Petersfield remembered the London buildings so much had we become accustomed to our surroundings.

This was the great season of Emanuel rugger. All through the war, the standard of the School had been very high. Thanks for this are due very largely to Mr Shaw, to whom, since Mr Neath went into the RAF in 1940, all the rugger coaching has fallen. This Fifteen of 1943–44 contained three full colours and three half-colours. They were defeated once and then only once by a penalty goal.

Since 1941, the School has regularly entered Sevens for the Rosslyn Park Sevens. In 1944, the School fought its way to the fourth round. After the sevens both A. L. C. Thompson and A. P. Prichard were selected to play for the Public Schools.

By Easter 1944 Emanuel had cemented its reputation for dramatics in Petersfield after another excellent Mr Mearns production. This was also my first year in the VI and I was slowly initiated into the VI Form pleasure of coffee in 'The Punch and Judy' and of browsing among books and records in No 1 The Square and the Music Studio respectively.

As D-Day approached tension was here again, extensive traffic on the roads kicking up dust. As rumours of a return to London persisted Mr Mearns ran his fourth farming camp in succession. This was, perhaps, the most successful.

There was no customary play in the Christmas holidays of 1944 as Mr Crowther had returned to London for the Tutorial Classes. Soon peace was inevitable. People did not seem to be any happier and that annoyed me. I myself did not seem to be any happier and that annoyed me more.

When peace did come I was in London with a large part of Sixth Science. I should rather have liked to have been in Petersfield with the main body of the School. Of the present Sixth Year, approximately a third of our lives has been spent in Petersfield. It does not seem so long in retrospective. A jumble of years, like goldfish in a bowl, occasionally rising to the top to be inspected.

One of my most vivid memories of school life in Petersfield is a recent one – after the declaration of peace. It is of D. P. Bowler, now a medical student, talking to the Sixth Form about his experiences at Belsen.

The technicolored cricket squares of 1939 are now leading to Beveridge; they could so easily have led to Belsen.'

Charles James Sammonds
(Emanuel 1940–1943)

After being evacuated with Battersea Central School to the Petersfield area, Sammonds was encouraged to sit the Emanuel School entrance exam. He was quickly promoted in the JTC and joined the Home Guard. In 1943 he was badly injured when down a mine. However, he was determined to join the Army despite the disability and ended up working with Military Intelligence (MI8, the field security department), before joining the Intelligence Corps and ultimately the Royal Artillery until 1948. After the war he became a lecturer in business studies and when he retired was Head of Post Graduate and Professional Studies at a further education college.

Charles Sammonds

Here Charles Sammonds discusses the difficult transition from Battersea Central School to Emanuel, at Petersfield:

'So, the transition from Battersea Central School and its strong cockney working class culture to Emanuel School with its mainly middle class culture proved to be yet a further element of confusion in my mind. I learned to modify my strong Battersea accent, in fact to speak with a touch of Hampshire burr without taking the mickey out of my local country friends. The masters of the School seemed so different as well and I was rather afraid of them to begin with, although I came to like and respect them all later. It was decided, and it lowered my already low morale, that I would join the Science form, 3Sc, with boys who were a year younger than I and that I had to face up to doing the equivalent of five years' work in two and a half years before taking the General Schools Certificate in 1943. Another problem was school clothing. The boys in my year were expected to wear long grey trousers and I had only short ones! At the start of each school year a representative from Harrods visited the School to take measurements for the clothing and equipment required by the new boys and the fact that the School had been evacuated made no difference to this tradition. When my turn came to be measured by the 'Harrod's Man', I asked what the cost of the black jacket would be and was horrified to be told it was eight guineas - "But of course your parents will be invoiced." [Sammonds's father managed to pay the Harrods' invoice by borrowing the money from the Tallyman and repaying a half-crown a week for the next eighteen months!]

My first term at Emanuel was almost horrific in so many ways: to start with I had to ride my bike seven and a half miles to Churcher's College by nine o'clock each morning including Saturdays, then the ride back to Empshott after school finished at half past five, in the rain, snow and ice. Then, many of the lessons were unintelligible to me during the initial few weeks, until I was able to borrow books from the masters. The amount of homework I had to cope with was unbelievable, but the masters were most considerate once they realised how conscientious I was in wanting to catch up.

My period at Emanuel was exceptionally hard work, with little or no leisure time and virtually no socialising. In fact some lads used to think, and occasionally comment, that they thought I was 'queer' because I had no girlfriends. Whereas many of my class mates were able to go to evening dances with girls, play tennis or other recreational activities, I was either slogging away at homework or extra study, or doing a bit of gardening or farming work to bring in a little more cash. I realised, as early as 1940 and not yet fifteen, that a social life was important to any human being, but also that it was critical to decide on one's priorities in life – where did one wish to go in the future and how to get there.

In the early days of evacuation, both the School and its teachers and the organising elements of the villages, tried hard to ensure that we had plenty to do after school hours. In Hawkley the Social Club provided outlets for youthful energies and in Empshott the Village Hut was opened to

Painting of the Market Square in Petersfield in the 1930s by Flora Twort

us for games, reading, homework and play-acting in the evenings. We became quite expert at monopoly, billiards and chess and, if no masters were present, then some of the lads showed their maturity (and ignorance!) and attitudes to authority by smoking cigarettes. I still wonder where they got them from and how they afforded them, but the sheer acrid smell put me off, as well as my conscience telling me it was wrong, even if I did not know why other than our ages.

Unfortunately, or otherwise, the pressure of schoolwork and the need to take examinations earlier than normally scheduled demanded more and more study in the evenings and weekends. Financial pressure also required me to obtain part-time work to cope with the costs of clothing and sports equipment. The latter became critical when I ran for the House cross-country team and did well, although I had to run in normal school clothing and consequently ruined my shoes. I was selected to run for the School team against local colleges and Southampton University, so not only did I need a new pair of school shoes, but also proper cross-country kit.'

Dick Raine *(Emanuel 1940–1947)* *Destination Unknown*

[Originally published in 'Been There, Done That', by Petersfield U3A]

'In 1939, like hundreds of other children, wearing a label and carrying a gas mask, I was put on a train at Clapham Junction for an unknown destination, which turned out to be Petersfield. I remember sitting in anticipation in St Peter's Church, waiting for the billeting decisions.

The families of teachers went with the evacuated schools and this was how I came to live in Hawkley. My father was the Second Master from Battersea Central School in London, and he led the contingent of older boys from the School to Hawkley and some of the surrounding villages. My family was billeted with the Vicar, the Reverend Scott, for five months, after which we moved to Parson's Place, a thatched cottage next door where we remained for the rest of the war.

... For youngsters from Battersea, country ways came as a shock. The following experiences were all new: walking up to two miles along country lanes to school; outside WCs; 'Pussy' Whittington, the night-soil man, whose fields grew acres of tomato seedlings; and cob cottages in Snailing Lane. The very low noise level and absence of lights at night made many newcomers uneasy and adjustment was difficult, although by Christmas most had settled into their new life.

Emanuel School had been near my home in London, so a transfer was possible for me. I began a school timetable of 9.00am–5.30pm with morning classes taken in rooms behind a number of pubs in Petersfield, including The Sun Inn and The Blue Anchor. Also used were church halls and the small town hall. In the afternoons we used the labs, workshops and classrooms in Churcher's College. I soon became familiar with animals in the Square and the bustle of market day, together with the specialist shops in town – Bassetts for tools and Caplin's in the High Street. I used to leave my bike behind Caplin's, where my father bought his bee-keeping equipment.

Leaving at 8.00am for the six mile journey to School on my heavy Rudge Whitworth three-speed bike, I often started in bright sunshine and freewheeled at high speed down Hawkley Hill. Then, depending on the season, I might find myself suddenly plunging into thick valley fog with only sounds to warn me of any other traffic – however infrequent. At other times the reverse occurred. At Hawkley there would be thick mist and dripping trees and hedges and the prospect of an unappealing wet journey, and then, halfway down the hill, I would burst out of the heavy cloud into the maximum visibility of the dry Rother Valley.

I have uncomfortable memories of wet neck, socks and shoes, French lessons, unfinished homeworks and, of course, the plod uphill, pulling my bike, at the end of each day at School. These were compensated for at other times by watching the seasonal activities: ploughing, sowing, and the Italian POWs working at harvest time. Other rewards included gathering mushrooms, hazelnuts and blackberries and, while cycling or walking, watching the activities of the birds. I also fed pigs and helped at harvest and other times on the farms.

Although adequately fed at breakfast, my most abiding memory is of always being hungry by midday. Most boys went home to their billets for lunch. However, four or five of us living outside the town had to frequent the British Restaurant behind the town hall, as it was the only place to eat. I remember that once it was closed for alterations and two of us were sent to the Battersea Girls' School canteen... What a contrast! Home-cooked food and, for us boys, second helpings. For fourteen year olds from a boys' school, mixing with girls was a treat, but it only lasted a fortnight!

... I'm sure cyclists will remember how tailgating behind a tractor or slow-moving lorry helped the weary legs up a hill. This I did whenever possible. During D-Day preparations American troops bivouacked along the foot of the hangers as they progressively moved down to the coast. The heavier vehicles travelled by day along the main roads and my tailgating got me to school more quickly. However, the scariest near-death experience occurred when I found myself struggling to keep up my own top speed to get in behind a heavy lorry's slip-stream, only to discover I was trapped behind the lorry and a low-loading tank-transporter it was towing. The road was so narrow I couldn't get out. I don't know how long I pedalled furiously before the road widened enough and I could escape.

Many other tales could be told: the bombing of the workhouse; making pennies out of halfpennies by placing them on the rails close by Rams Hill bridge for the train wheels to squash; the music of the School group, the Windsor Rhythm Kings; dances in Steep Village Hall; and experimenting by firing 303 armour-piercing bullets through a six inch square fence-post to see if they really worked.

We have all had problems with homework, but how about this? Before 1944 during their last years at School, the senior boys belonging to the Cadet Corps were stationed with a Home Guard detail at Butser. They stood guard at the Petersfield end of the railway tunnel throughout the night and attended School as normal the next day, without any dispensation for homework. This excuse couldn't be used today!'

James 'Jim' William Cleverley
(Emanuel 1939–1946)

Recalls the School characters and teachers in Petersfield

'So what of the School? The staff were a wonderful collection of characters who, despite the difficulties of scattered classrooms and wartime restrictions kept up the academic standard and gave us a first class education.

The Headmaster – known as 'The Beak' – was Cyril G. M. Broom, who was held in awe by most junior pupils. The Deputy-Head was himself an Old Boy of the School, Stafford-Hipkins, known as 'Pump' after Hipkins Bicycle Pumps, he taught English and tried to maintain good manners and appearance among the boys. Nail inspections were frequent and could evoke cries of "You could grow a crop of potatoes under those nails! Go back and wallow in the gutter where you came from."

The craft teachers were 'Duke' Appleyard (metalwork) and Vic Norris. The 'Duke' was a real Londoner with a heart of gold and a nose that suggested a love of pints. When dealing with a mischief maker he would yell, "Come on! Own up! I know

K.J. Gurling

Peter Downs

J.G. Worth

the boy what done it." He was the member of staff responsible for ARP matters and spoke in short phases interspersed with pauses. Lecturing the School on the subject he said, "Any problems go to your local" – pause – cheers from the sixth form – "ARP warden."

Another real character was Claude 'Taffy' Neath who, along with Bill Hyde and George Worth taught Latin. Taffy would correct a grammatical error by standing behind the miscreant with his signet ring turned so that the flat side was on the palm side of his hand and clip the culprit across the back of the head, chanting, "The adjective must agree with the noun in number, gender and case, boy!" He volunteered for the RAF and was awarded the DFC as bomb aimer on the aircraft which sunk the German battleship *Tirpitz* in a Norwegian fjord. I played rugby with him at Blagdons after the war when at past forty he could still show a burst of speed over five yards playing stand off.

Then there were the quartet who lived at The Crown Inn, now no longer in existence, George Worth (Classics), Tommy Hughes (Biology), Louis Spafford (Physics) and Colin 'Crowbar' Crowther (History and English). On another occasion 'Spaff' got fined for drinking after hours to the delight of the boys.

'Crowbar' directed the annual students' play in Petersfield Town Hall. In December 1942 it was George Bernard Shaw's *The Devil's Disciple* in which I played Mrs Dudgeon, mother of Dick, played by A. L. C. 'Elsie' Thompson, with his pretty wife Judith – John Dewdney. The illegitimate daughter, Effie was played by Brian Longfellow and Colin Bell playing General Burgoyne.

The following year the play was *Richard of Bordeaux* by Gordon Daviot. I had taken my School Certificate after one term in the fifth form in order to be able to take Higher School Certificate before I was called up. Forty-eight hours before the play opened, Doug Wright, went down with chicken pox. Crowbar sent for me as I had just finished my last exam and made me take over the part. Brian Haydock played Richard and still remembers the production which was not without some glitches.

The Maths staff were A. C. Rogers (another Welshman), Dr Allan, Ben Shaw and occasionally 'Dolly' Mearns whose main subject was Economics, but who also taught English and Maths – he was a great all-rounder.

The other history teacher was Joe Hunt, known as 'Holy Joe', who could make the most exciting periods of European History boring. He was also in charge of cricket. Hubert Harry Hirst was the Chemistry master, known as 'Tubey Hooby' because he was rarely without a cigarette, tube being slang for a cigarette. He also had a tolerant sense of humour for those who only took General Science.

Ralph Lee taught Higher School English and had a fine analytical mind which he applied to our literature essays. He was nicknamed 'Goofy' because of a cast in one eye, but was nobody's fool. The Modern Languages staff were Oswald Owen Ginn, known as 'Boozer' and Miss Chaplin who taught French, and Miss Wilkinson or 'Frau Kaiser' who was a lovely blue eyed blonde with a bad leg, which was the result of an accident; who took German. There were also Harry Dixon (Art), 'Doc' Newell (Music), 'Twanky' Toyne (Religious Instruction), Mr Nussey (Physical Education), and Major Charles Hill (Geography and the Junior Training Corps). No doubt I have forgotten someone, but it is 63 years since I left.

What can I say about my peers? I could go on for hours but must restrain myself. The Head Boy when I arrived was Ken Gurling. Immaculately dressed with a slight lisp, he was a fearsome and fearless wing forward on the rugby field. It was rugby that was an important aspect of my social life, both in providing role models and later colleagues. Tom Manley, Austin Wheatley, Bob 'Bass' Younger, Spray Lawrence, Ginger Waldrom, 'Sue' Palmer, Ian Pickwell, Tony Pritchard, Arthur Haddon, Viv Higgs, Johnny Lampden, Roy Maxwell, David Haydock, Bill Brommige were my contemporaries, whilst Ken Rogers, Dave Cameron and A. L. C. 'Elsie' Thompson were my heroes, ahead of me.

There were, of course, some notable characters; Mitchell who gained fleeting fame for being the first person across the new Waterloo Bridge on his bike, also played an April Fool's joke on the Headmaster. He borrowed an umbrella to escort the lady members of a staff production of *A Month in the Country* from the changing room to the stage door of the Town Hall on 31 March. He returned it the next day, neatly rolled, but filled with cigarette ends and bottle tops which showered down on Mr Broom when he opened it. Called to account for this he was told "Mitchell, my umbrella may be old and dilapidated, but that is no reason to turn it into a rubbish tip!"

Ned Edwards was a very bright lad who took his School Certificate at fourteen and therefore spent a long time in the Sixth Form, much of it in the French set. On one occasion Miss Chaplin was absent for the last two periods and her students decided to go home. 'Boozer' Ginn, remembering her absence, sent some work by the hand of Edwards who returned saying no one was there. "Go and tell the Headmaster that Miss Chaplin's class are playing truant!" yelled Ginn. "Do your own dirty work" replied Edwards and sat down.

Then there were the dances in Petersfield Town Hall to the music of the Windsor Rhythm Kings – Bass Younger (trumpet), Pete Dudley (trombone), Viv Higgs and Mike Sutters (saxophones), 'Dicky' Goodchild (clarinet), Tom Manley (bass) and Eggy Ley (drums), and which naturally involved girls and what a delightful group of young ladies there were: Betty Thomas, June Gander, Sonia Ingram, Teresa Warren, Anne Broadway, Bridget Leale, Jean Urquhart, Christine Legg, Rita Passingham, Maureen Ventham, Barbara Surrey, Audrey Hawkins, Molly Dwen and more. Of these I know Sonia Ingram married David 'Sue' Palmer, Rita Passingham is now my wife and we are in touch with others.

When the School left Petersfield at the end of July 1945 several tearful girls stood at the level crossing to wave us farewell – all part of the kaleidoscope of memories that made up six years as an evacuee in Petersfield.'

Ronald Horlock *(Emanuel 1933–1942)*

'I was evacuated to Petersfield, with the rest of Emanuel School, on 1 September 1939 - a memorable birthday for me. We had a sort of dress rehearsal in 1938, but after Neville Chamberlain brought back his piece of paper promising 'peace in our time' Emanuel was able to continue on its twelve acre site in Battersea for another year.

1 September 1939 was the day the Government gave the go ahead to evacuate the children of London and other big cities to less dangerous areas of England. In our case 450 boys, each equipped with a gas mask and other items of kit, set out from the School assembly hall to walk to Clapham Junction and board a train to an undisclosed destination. Petersfield it was and few of us had a clue where we were. From the station we walked through the town to the parish church to await further instructions and then on to the playground of a primary school. There we were met by the billeting officials who were ready to take us to the homes of apprehensive householders. It was early evening when I was on the doorstep of a pleasant looking house waiting to see who would open the door. I was very fortunate as my host was a schoolmaster at Bedales School and his wife had been a school matron. During my three year stay at Petersfield I had five billets because my hosts either moved house or their relatives came to stay. All of my hosts (schoolmaster, postman, civil engineer, general's widow and bank cashier) and their wives, were agreeable and patient people who put up with their evacuee with good grace. We shared with Churcher's College their classrooms; they worked in the mornings and we in the afternoons. Our morning lessons (when not playing games) took place in the backrooms of The Sun Inn, The Blue Anchor, The Weslyan Chapel and The Working Mens' Institute. We sheltered when there were air raid alerts in the nearby Roman Catholic Church because it had stout walls.

There were times of joy and woe. The Petersfield lake froze over in the very cold winter in 1940 and the ice was thick enough for ice hockey. We discovered, walked and cycled over and around the majestic and wonderful South Downs –Butser Hill, War Down and Harting Downs.

We watched the convoys of exhausted men coming back along the A3 from Dunkirk and we mourned for our friends who were just a few years older than us and who were killed 'On Active Service' only a year or two after leaving School. We were bombed by a lone raider whilst on JTC parade – the bomb missed us but sadly there were fatal casualties nearby. There were 'field days' that sometimes extended into nights and for a short period we mounted guard at Buriton railway tunnel. Academically the School did surprisingly well and we certainly grew up fast and became more self-reliant.

The Petersfield saga is now no more than a 'blip' in the long history of the School and it is a sobering thought that the 'Petersfield Boy' will soon become an endangered species and dare I say it – extinct.

In 1943 I volunteered to be a PNB (pilot, navigator, bomb aimer) in the RAF and after medicals and interviews was placed on deferred service waiting to be called up. In the autumn of 1944 RAF casualties were tailing off and I and many other RAF volunteers were 'invited' to join the Army. Living in southern England, it was hardly surprising that I and all the other bods should start our Army life as far away as possible. Fort George was where we went in north Scotland on the banks of the Moray Firth. On 1 September 1945 – my twentieth birthday - I sailed on a troopship down the Clyde bound for Bombay. In due course I became a sergeant in the RAOC and served without distinction on a 'Cook's Tour' of Asia until I returned to the UK to be demobbed in Aldershot in December 1947.'

The Sun Inn was used for temporary classrooms. Picture originally published in The Portcullis, No. 142, Spring 1941

Roy Maxwell *(Emanuel 1939–1944)*

Here Roy Maxwell remembers his Petersfield experiences:

'I didn't go down with the main body on that fateful 1 September, we had relatives in Cornwall and my mother took me down there. After three weeks my mother said, "You can't sit down there doing nothing, you should go and join the School."

My billet was a semi-detached house. It had a bath which I never had before. The man of the house had been the signalman up at Petersfield station and had been in the Army... and was the cook. He lived at home pretty well the whole time. He had two daughters who were older than me. It was a little three bedroom semi-detached, I had the smallest room for my bedroom. There was a long garden which went right down to the fields. They accepted me as one of the family.

Every now and then you would see a battle going on in the air... I saw a 109 shot down and it fell in Ditchum Park, we all cycled up there madly to find bits of it, we were always collecting bits of shells and cannon shells when they fell to earth. We had the gory tale that this pilot had come down and hit a cow and the whole thing had blown up and they only found 5lb of his body, oh God, it was gory but you know you had to accept that sort of thing when you are thirteen or fourteen.

We had one bomb, which came out of the blue one day. I was walking along the road by the Town Hall and this aircraft came over and my mother who was very nervous about this said "Oh dear is it a German?" and by then we boys knew our aircraft recognition, we could spot what it was from a small dot. I said "You'll soon know if it's got black crosses on it", being facetious...I looked and it was a Heinkel 111 and over it came right over our heads and turned and went towards London and the next thing there was a great whistling noise... my father and I ducked behind a wall... my mother was left standing there and when the bang came she turned round and wondered where we'd gone. It was a tragic day as the bomb had gone through to the cellar where the old people actually were taking shelter and they were one of the few groups who actually took shelter when there was a warning and six of them were killed. Our boys were out doing their OTC work... they were helping to get the bodies out. That must have been a bit traumatic for some of the seniors who got involved with that.'

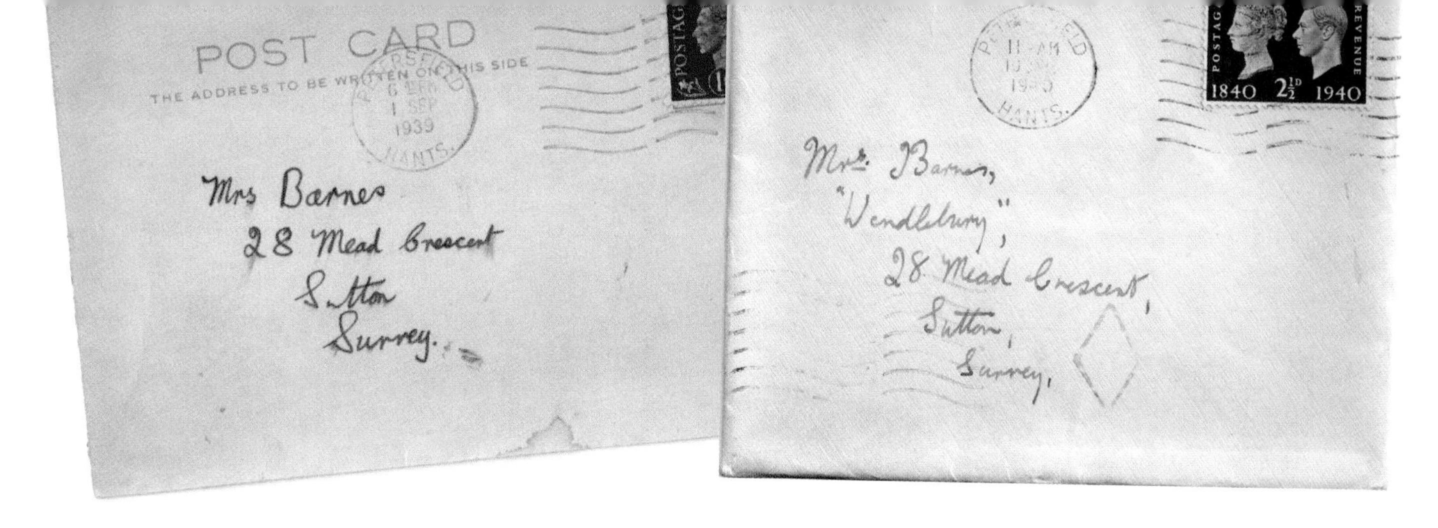

'Send some stamps'

The story of Allan Barnes's evacuee experiences

Allan Barnes was evacuated with other Emanuel boys on 1 September 1939. In 2011 Daniel Kirmatzis had the opportunity of interviewing Allan. They struck up a friendship which sadly ended when Allan died in 2013. On a summer's day in 2012 when Daniel went to visit him Allan revealed that he had kept all the letters he had sent to his parents as an evacuee. The 58 letters offer a unique insight into the concerns, feelings and thoughts of a young Emanuel evacuee between 1 September 1939 and the summer of 1942. Allan was an avid stamp collector and his letters often request that his father Arthur send him some new stamps.

Presented here are extracts from Allan's evacuee letters between 1939 and 1941:

1 September 1939

When we got here we were divided out with rations we got ... a large tin of Nestles sweetened, a tin of corned beef (12oz), two half pound packets of biscuits and a ¼ lb slab of Cadburys chocolate. Pretty good eh!

There is a Woolworths (wonderful) and a whole picture palace (ten seats!) We have been going round together today to see the town. This evening I did my bit of national service by filling sandbags.

Mrs Blackman has just told me to tell you that she will do all she can to make me comfortable and happy. She thought this would stop you worrying about me. I hope you got my card I sent, I sent it as soon as I got here. Write after it, will make me feel nearer you and more at home.

7 September 1939

The Head came down with us but Mrs Broom and brush (little broom) are coming down afterwards.

I filled a lot more sandbags on Saturday. Altogether on Saturday we filled about 300 bags round at the police station and made pals with one of the cops (bobbies) known to you as Peelers. They (cops) are all wearing their tin hats.

10 September 1939

P.S. Don't forget to send me stamps off parcels as I am trying to get a complete set of them.

21 January 1940

The pond down here has frozen over and we often go skating. I have been several times.

11 February 1940

A stamp club had been formed down here with Major Hill (Charlie) as boss. We had some good fun but of course we didn't do much as it was only the first meeting.

19 February 1940

Charlie Hill took us over for a while at OTC. We had some good fun. He suddenly said, "Enemy over by the railway line, get down by that hedge and fire at them." So we all rushed over to the hedge and started firing at them (the enemy that wasn't there)...

I counted my stamps yesterday and discovered that I had 1901.

15 September 1940

I have just come back from church. We had a warning while I was in there and the all clear went before we came out.

What road was the house damaged which Dad said was 200 yds from you?

16 October 1940

A few weeks ago some bombs were dropped the other side of the heath, about ¾ mile away. We got up and came downstairs when we heard them.

27 October 1940

I got Dad's letter last Wednesday. Has any damage been done to the house, or has Jerry bombed up any of my onions?

10 November 1940

We went on field-day last Thursday. We were issued with ten blanks. In the (our) attack I didn't fire a single shot, as we didn't see any of the enemy as we attacked down their flank. So when the enemy counter-attacked I had all my blanks to fire. I reckon we licked them up. Minnie had a shot fired at him at point-blank range and so his arm was cut and it had to be bandaged up before we went home.

24 November 1940

I didn't know that Dad's office had been bombed twice. I only knew of one bombing. I'm glad I wasn't still in the Balham flat, as it probably is now (flat). I had heard about Balham tube station being flooded from a boy who was there at half term. Over a 100 dead weren't there?

Now here's a bit of news... Last Thursday as we were being dismissed a plane came over, not very high... Bull/Major Hill said "It's a Jerry seater"... I laid in some long grass. The store keeper rushed into the armoury and brought out clips of 'live.' This was issued to the officers and NCOs. The plane had disappeared into the clouds. We heard it turn and come back then a 'Boomp', it went overhead into the clouds and then when it came out they 'potted' at it to no avail. We were then rushed into the shelter but it had gone for good as we came out and came home and discovered that the bomb had hit the Poor Law Institution about 200–300 yds from our house...I was in uniform and so I went and helped. One man was behind a chimney pot.

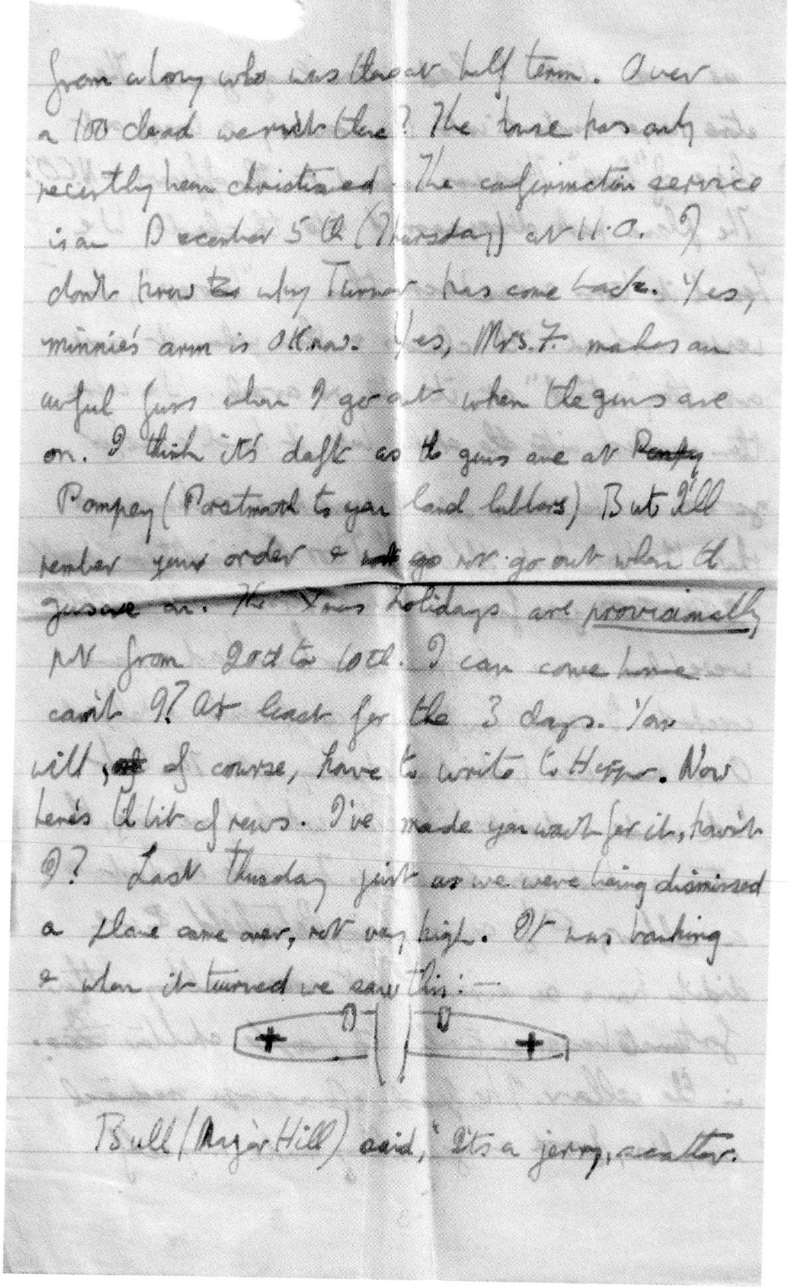

from a boy who was there at half term. Over a 100 dead weren't there? The house has only recently been christened. The confirmation service is on December 5th (Thursday) at 11.0. I don't know why Turner has come back. Yes, Minnie's arm is OK now. Yes, Mrs. F. makes an awful fuss when I go out when the guns are on. I think it's daft as the guns are at Pompey (Portsmouth to you land lubbers) But I'll remember your order & not go out when the guns are on. The Xmas holidays are provisionally put from 20th to 10th. I can come home can't I? At least for the 3 days. You will, of course, have to write to Hopper. Now here's the bit of news. I've made you wait for it, haven't I? Last Thursday just as we were being dismissed a plane came over, not very high. It was banking & when it turned we saw this:—

Bull (Major Hill) said, "It's a jerry seater."

Letter sent by Allan Barnes to his parents 24 November 1940

2 December 1940

I told you about the bombed institute didn't I? Well we had a bit more 'fun' on Saturday. At 8.55 we heard a swishhh and Mr. F said, "Bomb", "Get down flat." So we did and we heard a 'Boomp.' Then at 2.20 (I was asleep) there was another 'Boomp.' This woke me up and I must have sat up in bed before I awoke because when I woke I was sitting up. I must have woken a second after the bomb had gone off because the window was still rattling. That was a time bomb going off. They said that there were more and there must have been because today (this afternoon) we've heard another four 'Boomps' They must have been small bombs (by the way they were in the fields) because a house fifty yards away didn't have its windows broken. The Jerries seem to be concentrating on certain towns each night.

4 April 1941

I'm b-----well fed up with being back. I've been shoved into the small room again because Mrs. F wants the big room for people for bread and breakfast.

30 April 1941

The seeds in my garden have come up. I have some of each. The broad beans are 3-inches high and the first onions I put in 2-inches. Ask Dad not to forget to send me some tomato plants when he gets them.

20 May 1941

Petersfield war weapons week started on Saturday. Our JTC marched in a grand procession through the streets. There is a front-page picture of our company in the Portsmouth evening news. I'm there but you can only see the top of my hat as I'm on the other side of the picture. In the procession there were: Royal Marines, two JTC's, RAOC., Royal Navy, WRNS, light and heavy guns, A.A. guns, searchlights, bren gun carriers, N. Zealanders, RAF, Home Guard, ARP, AFS fire brigade, Red Cross rescue parties etc.

23 June 1941

P.S. The Head in church gave announcements about holiday farming. I said I was going, didn't I? Well, after the exams there is... training for boys to drive tractors. The training, as far as I know, is to be given in the neighbourhood and then in the holidays the boys would work on tractors at various farms because there is a shortage of tractor drivers.

1 October 1941

I have good news: I have been elected secretary of the Philatelic Society. We had a meeting yesterday – my first as secretary, it went off all right.

8th WONDER OF THE WORLD

Paper stained with genuine orange juice

Stupendous !!!!!!!

Gigantic !!!!!!

Amazing !!!!!!

Wonderful !!! !!!

A letter stained with orange juice sent by Allan Barnes to his parents (above) and Allan Barnes in discussion with Lt.-Col Sir John McClure, Bt., inspecting the Emanuel JTC in Petersfield, 24 July 1941

Five French Boys Cross the English Channel in Canoes

A colourful tale of brief friendships in Petersfield

As Europe lay under the weight of Nazi occupation in 1941, five French boys were planning their escape to join General De Gaulle and the Free French Forces in Britain, but several obstacles lay in their way, not least of all the English Channel!

Under the cover of darkness on 16 September 1941, the boys, Pierre Lavoix, nineteen – the leader, and his brother Jean Lavoix, sixteen; Reynolde Lefebvre, seventeen; Christian Richard, seventeen, and his brother Guy Richard, sixteen, escaped from France in two wooden Canadian canoes, crossing the English Channel in an episode that reads straight from a Boy's Own Paper adventure story.

The boys took months planning this amazing voyage. A full report in *Life Magazine* revealed that a friendly German motorboat crew actually helped repair one of the canoes they used in their escape![1] They diligently collected food, much of it stolen from German stores and hid it in the sand close to their boats. On the night of the escape, after curfew, each of the boys left a note for their parents on their pillows: 'Chers Parents – I have gone to join General de Gaulle.'

The escape itself would have made an entertaining action film. On 16 September they started their journey from Fort-Mahon-Plage beach located 60 kilometres south of Boulogne. They had two sources of inspiration. The first was a speech

Winston Churchill and wife Clementine toast five French boys, who escaped from France in canoes, in the grounds of 10 Downing Street, September 1941

Memorial plaque showing the journey of the five French boys, on the Watch Tower, Beachy Head

made by General De Gaulle on 18 June 1940 as he implored Frenchmen to join him in England to keep up the struggle against Nazi Germany as France was preparing to surrender to Nazi invasion. The second, as Jean and Pierre later explained in 1952, was the historic struggle between France and Germany. They saw this escape as, 'their turn to keep up the fight' that their father had begun in 1914 and before him their grandfather in the 1870 Franco-Prussian War.

Avoiding Nazi patrols they headed out to sea armed with, '20lb of bread, 75 soldier's ration biscuits, a homemade French flag, a service rifle and 40 rounds of ammunition 'borrowed' from a surrendered arms dump at Nazi HQ.' They kept course by Pierre's grandfather's compass; time by Christian's alarm clock and we presume faith by the Bible they carried. After several hours of paddling they were almost spotted by a German E-boat, 'Suddenly their searchlight picked us out. But a few seconds later the light flashed off and the sounds of their engines died away.'

Due to navigational errors, what they thought was a one night trip quickly became two. Eventually, after choppy seas, sickness and restless nights sleeping in three inches of sea water, they were spotted by a Spitfire which circled within 50 feet but although it had called for a motorboat to search them out the boys had gone some 10km off course. As the sea got rougher, their food and books got wetter and wetter, but they began to see outlines of the English coastline. Although they were overjoyed, they were also fearful of mines. As they approached shore Pierre recalls an amusing incident: '...clutching our French flag, we scrambled exhaustedly over the rocks. Suddenly a gruff voice shouted "Halt!" We gaped at a woman in a very short skirt holding a rifle. I knew the British were expecting an invasion but I didn't think the coast guard would be kept by tough women in short skirts. We approached and I shouted back to the others: "It's a kilted Scotsman."'

Luckily for the boys the Scotsman spoke perfect French and they were taken to a cottage for some hot tea before the police came and gave them shelter, a hot bath and new clothes.

A few days later the boys met Winston Churchill and his wife Clementine in 10 Downing Street. The moment was captured on film by several news agencies including British Pathé and was widely reported in the world's press. Churchill exclaimed that the boys represented the 'true face of France' and they enjoyed a toast in the gardens of Number 10. On one film one of the boys says to the camera in English, 'We came from France in 30 hours and we are very glad to be here and to see the first Minister, Mr Churchill.' The boys also met General De Gaulle and in an amusing episode we learn how Pierre related to the General that Christian had hoped to take his baccalaureate in France but his books had been damaged in the crossing, but the General told him that he could take the 'Baccho' in England after which Christian's 'face fell.'

Four of the boys joined the Free French Cadet School in Malvern, where a number of other 'Free French' were training in General De Gaulle's Free French Army. Pierre went to the Naval College to train to become a Naval Officer. Four survived the Second World War but Reynolde Lefebvre was killed on 17 January 1945 in the plains of Alsace, near Obernai during the liberation of his homeland.[2]

So what is the connection with Emanuel School? The day after the boys had met Churchill they were sent for a holiday in the south and after this were guests of Emanuel at Petersfield. Emanuel boys had won numerous French language prizes in the 1930s and in 1941 the Emanuel Grand Concours team carried off the *Objet d' Art*, which was a magnificent bronze lion presented by General De Gaulle. So Emanuel had strong French connections and we can assume this is why the School was chosen to host the boys for a short while in the autumn of 1941. *The Portcullis* reported:[3]

> First, the Headmaster welcomed them in his study and then they were shown round the School. After that they were received by Form VI Modern, to whom one of the boys gave a talk on his trip. In assembly that afternoon the Headmaster welcomed them officially in the name of the School and the School, led by Bowler, the School Captain, gave them three resounding cheers. Later in the afternoon they were entertained to tea by Mr. Ginn and some of the senior boys. In the evening they were guests of the Captain and Lieutenant of the School, some of the Prefects and Mr and Mrs Keith Gammon.

[The French boys] were much in the company of our boys during the next few weeks. A group of five presented a wide variety of tastes and a wide variety of tastes were catered for by Emanuel. Among other things, Christian did some practical chemistry experiments under the supervision of Mr Hirst, in preparation for his bachot (Higher School Certificate), which he was able to take at the Institut Français in London. Pierre, who was highly popular with everybody, gave a number of very interesting talks to various forms. In the first and second year Sixth Forms he spoke on 'La France sous l'occupation allemande', to the 5th, 4th, and 3rd Forms he spoke on the geography of France and 'La Vie française.' Members of Form 2a, with whom he had the best time of all, discussed enthusiastically with him whether there were farms in France, what animals you found on a French farm, whether they had four legs and a tail like English animals, the ranks of the French fighting services, the adventures of his crossing and numerous questions about the Boches. Nor were Form 2a to be outdone in the generosity of their hospitality. Each form inviting Pierre had asked to be allowed to make a little present to him, and 2a, headed by N. Abbott, though only eighteen in number, subscribed no less than six shillings. Pierre was greatly touched by the warmth of the welcome accorded by this form and when he left them they mobbed him with their handshakes and autograph books. He later paid them a further visit, but on the condition of no more autographs and no further 'bêtises' like presents. A delightful incident happened with one of the members of this form. He met Pierre in the street and Pierre said to him "Qu'est-ce que vous faites maintenant?" He answered, "Je vais faire une promenade avec vous," and without more ado walked Pierre round the countryside for three hours and talked French all the time. During the past year he [Pierre] has been a frequent visitor to Petersfield to renew his friendship with Emanuel.

References

1 *Life Magazine*, 27 October 1941.
2 *Journal of Free France*, No. 53, December 1952.
3 *The Portcullis*, Autumn Term, 1942, pp. 9–10.

Emanuel JTC inspection in Petersfield, 24 July 1941

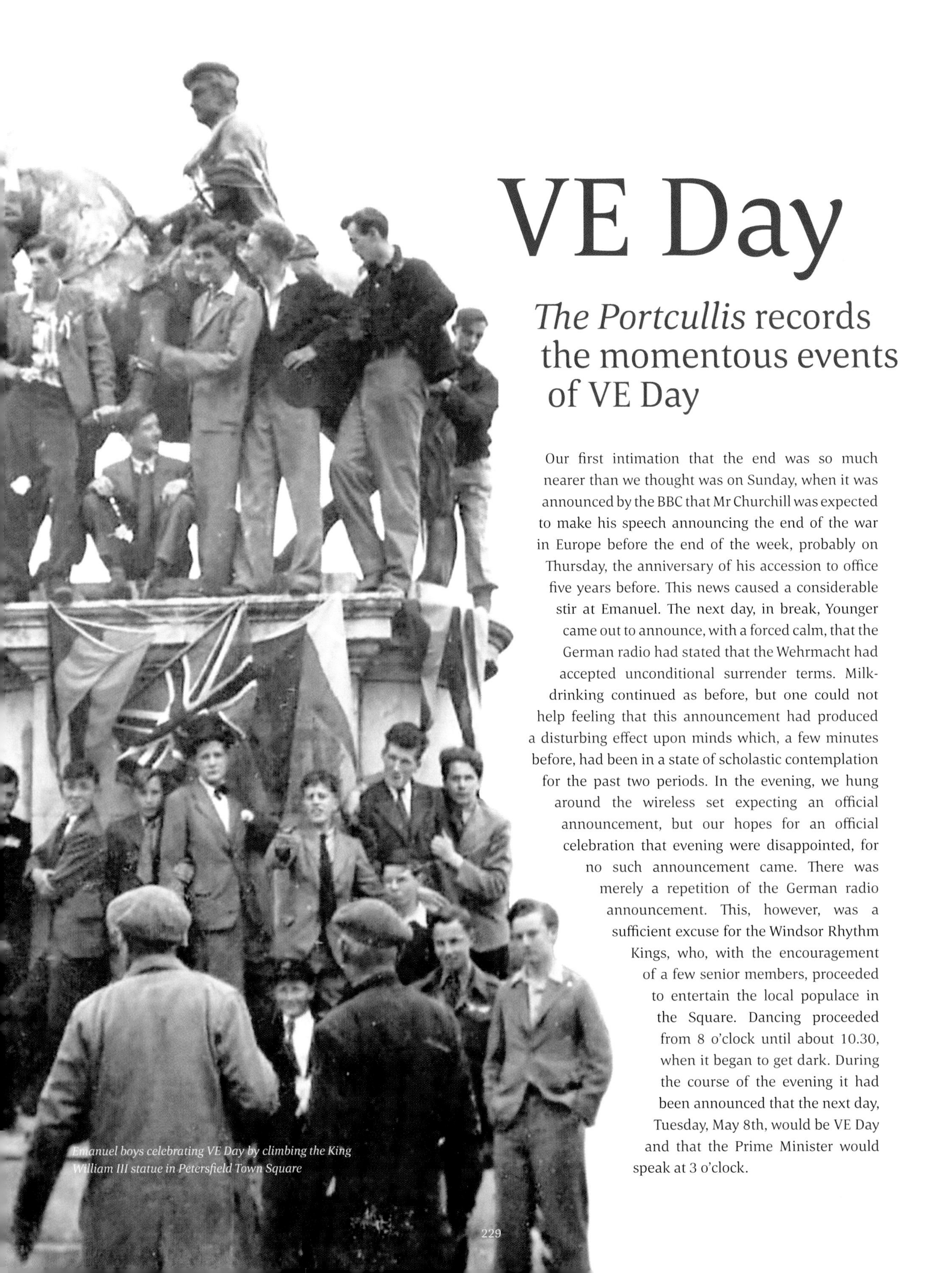

Emanuel boys celebrating VE Day by climbing the King William III statue in Petersfield Town Square

VE Day

The Portcullis records the momentous events of VE Day

Our first intimation that the end was so much nearer than we thought was on Sunday, when it was announced by the BBC that Mr Churchill was expected to make his speech announcing the end of the war in Europe before the end of the week, probably on Thursday, the anniversary of his accession to office five years before. This news caused a considerable stir at Emanuel. The next day, in break, Younger came out to announce, with a forced calm, that the German radio had stated that the Wehrmacht had accepted unconditional surrender terms. Milk-drinking continued as before, but one could not help feeling that this announcement had produced a disturbing effect upon minds which, a few minutes before, had been in a state of scholastic contemplation for the past two periods. In the evening, we hung around the wireless set expecting an official announcement, but our hopes for an official celebration that evening were disappointed, for no such announcement came. There was merely a repetition of the German radio announcement. This, however, was a sufficient excuse for the Windsor Rhythm Kings, who, with the encouragement of a few senior members, proceeded to entertain the local populace in the Square. Dancing proceeded from 8 o'clock until about 10.30, when it began to get dark. During the course of the evening it had been announced that the next day, Tuesday, May 8th, would be VE Day and that the Prime Minister would speak at 3 o'clock.

8th June, 1946

TO-DAY, AS WE CELEBRATE VICTORY, I send this personal message to you and all other boys and girls at school. For you have shared in the hardships and dangers of a total war and you have shared no less in the triumph of the Allied Nations.

I know you will always feel proud to belong to a country which was capable of such supreme effort; proud, too, of parents and elder brothers and sisters who by their courage, endurance and enterprise brought victory. May these qualities be yours as you grow up and join in the common effort to establish among the nations of the world unity and peace.

Letter sent to school children across the UK in 1946

The next morning a spirit of gaiety prevailed. An assembly was held at 9.30 outside the pavilion, and we were dismissed for the next two days. The crowd surged out of the gates of Churcher's and down Ramshill. By the time we had reached the bottom of the High Street, we were strung out across the road, and, arm-in-arm, we marched up the flag-bedecked High Street singing. The march continued round the town and back to the Square, where it broke up, and we all dispersed to our various occupations, the Sixth Form mainly to imbibe coffee.

The afternoon saw many Emanuel seniors arrayed in original if somewhat loud costumes, which at times verged on the fancy-dress. Some idea of these may be gathered from the photographs which were taken by Hardcastle that afternoon and afterwards printed en masse and sold to the School. The chef d'oeuvre was a snap of the Headmaster standing at the foot of the statue, in the centre of a mob of gesticulating Emanuels, all obviously enjoying themselves immensely. Many of those now at the School will cherish this photograph in after-years as typical of the spirit of Emanuel on VE Day. In the meantime, the equestrian statue of William of Orange had been variously decorated with School ties and scarves, and a certain well-known type of black headgear.

The School's greatest service to Petersfield that day was the re-appearance that evening of the Windsor Rhythm Kings, this time on top of the shelter in the Square. Lights had been fitted up during the day by Manley, and the band was able to play until midnight. Petersfield's own official celebrations were not until the following evening, so the band proved a great attraction. A large crowd of people were obviously extremely grateful for its efforts, and £15 was collected for the Hospital. The crowd danced to its music for over four hours. The band that evening consisted of Younger, Higgs, Sutters, Rassell and Ley, the regular members, augmented by Goodchild and Dudley. To all of them we owe our thanks for an extremely happy time that night. Without the band there could have been no dancing or general jollifications such as took place, and without the School the town would not have been enlivened or amused during the day.

J.K.W. *The Portcullis*, Commemoration Number, 1945

Ron Williamson recalls VE Day:

How strange it was to be standing close to the Headmaster in such a relaxed and informal setting – in contrast to the awe in which he was held in his school study, or in the main hall during Assembly.

The boys living in Petersfield fell into one of three groups – Emanuel School, Churcher's College, or the 'townies'. I have never understood how Emanuel seemingly took over the Square on VE Day, to the exclusion of the other two groups – but we did. Perhaps it was because the 6th Form jazz band – the Windsor Rhythm Kings – had taken up position on top of the air raid shelter in front of St Peter's church, and played well into the night.

VE Day celebrations – (above) Headmaster Cyril Broom with Emanuel boys in Petersfield Town Square (below) Emanuel boys celebrating the end of war

(Left) The 1989 50th Petersfield Reunion (Right) The 2009 70th Petersfield Reunion

As Time Goes By – Petersfield Reunions

On 23 September 2009 Emanuel School pupils from the period 1939–1945 gathered to mark the seventieth anniversary of their evacuation from Emanuel to Petersfield. Even after seventy years a few Emanuel 'boys' had remained in contact with the families who had hosted them. Several settled in the local area and others met their future wives whilst in 'exile' from Battersea. Leaving the smog of London for the countryside was a revelation for many boys. Maurice Rowdon who became a philosopher of some note stated that his spell in Petersfield was amongst the happiest periods of his life and had a major impact on both his future writing and life-style.

Emanuel Headmaster Mark Hanley-Browne commented in his letter to those who attended the 2009 event 'I can scarcely imagine what it must have been like to travel on that train, with my predecessor Mr. Broom, to an unknown destination on the first day of term in September 1939.' In reality most OEs the archivist Tony Jones spoke to about this took the excitement of the move in their stride and when they discovered they were going to Petersfield had no idea where it was. Simon Williams, Headmaster of Churcher's College which hosted Emanuel, also noted, 'It must have been a difficult time for many, especially for those of you who had to de-camp from Clapham to semi-rural Petersfield, but the very fact that the Old Emanuels are venturing down the A3 once again is testament to the efforts that the staff and pupils of both schools gave to make the experience a pleasant one.'

Since the 1980s, reunions have been held every five or ten years. There have been dances, speeches, letters read out, gifts exchanged, tears shed, chance meetings with old friends and memories swapped. Emanuel's Headmaster from 1984–1994, Peter Thomson, who made an unannounced visit to the 1985 event, recalled, 'A fine and sunny afternoon in which many OEs had returned to Churcher's for the unveiling of the memorial gates. Ron Dear, Roy Maxwell and Ron Williamson were particularly hospitable. I have often chuckled over the gems from the Williamson photo album and VE Day in the Town Square.' The OEA Secretary was warm in his praise of the Churcherians' hospitality, 'Forty years on we all took the opportunity of revisiting those Petersfield landmarks that meant so much to us all in our formative years and there was scarcely a dry eye in the house.'

The 1989 50th Anniversary brought together 50 members of the original evacuation party and a further 50 who joined the School during the War. Influential staff also attended, including the popular maths teacher Aeron Rogers who masterminded the School timetable and its multiple locations around the town. Aeron was known for his often quoted phrase 'We've got to have schemes boys.' Roy Maxwell organised an event in the town hall which was attended by the local mayor, and a dance was held at Churcher's College in the evening. The event was even attended by eight locals who had hosted Emanuel boys and the OEA gave the town hall a new clock as a thank-you gift.

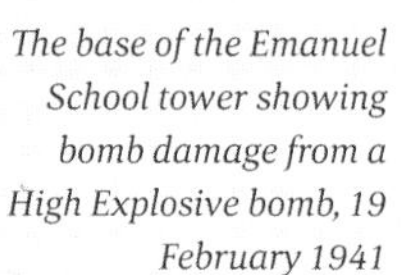

The base of the Emanuel School tower showing bomb damage from a High Explosive bomb, 19 February 1941

Bombings and Civilians

The Second World War was materially the most destructive in human history. Millions of tonnes of bombs were used in this 'Total War' where civilians were targeted as much as combatants. Homes, businesses, factories, infrastructure and lives were lost in six years of warfare. The greatest periods of destruction in Britain were during the Battle of Britain, the Blitz and later in 1944–1945 during the V1 and V2 Rocket attacks.

Hundreds of bombs fell on Wandsworth during the course of the Second World War, including 738 High Explosive bombs between October of 1940 and June 1941. A strategic target was Clapham Junction, which was the busiest railway line in Britain, and its proximity to Emanuel meant that the School unintentionally became a target.

Bombing of the School

When the School tower was bombed on 19 February 1941 the chapel was also damaged, but although it was debris-covered, the main loss was the stained-glass windows on the east wall. Of all the School buildings the chapel was by far the worst affected. One of the upper floor form rooms lost its roof and some of the science rooms and the old rifle range were also damaged.

Over the course of the war there were many Air Raid Damage Reports filled out noting that several incendiary bombs dropped in the School playing fields. There were crater marks spread across the playing fields and one particular bomb was rumoured to have uncovered the original foundations of the old School hospital which had been demolished before the First World War. There was also considerable damage recorded to the School Drive and some of the gas streetlights were damaged beyond repair.

When the School was evacuated to Petersfield Alfred Eade remained in London as School Caretaker and Sergeant. His obituary notes that he was almost hit by rubble when the bomb hit the tower. Another of Eade's responsibilities was reporting any unexploded bombs to the authorities. There is enough surviving paperwork to show he was very busy. Interestingly enough, although not noted in any of the School histories, there is evidence to show that the bomb that damaged the tower injured a maintenance worker who may have died, at a later date, as a consequence of his injuries.

Unexploded bombs were a serious problem and the School grounds had to be regularly searched after air raids in the local area.

Chris Banwell (Emanuel 1943–1953) remembers the V1 Rocket attacks:

> My most vivid memory was the arrival of the V1 flying bombs. The first one landed in London on 14 June 1944. This pilotless plane's main feature was when the engine cut out it went into a spiral descent, eventually crashing and destroying buildings, unless it landed on an empty space.
>
> It was on 17 June 1944 that a few of us were playing on the cricket field behind the School when the next wave of V1s arrived. Horror of horrors, one of the engines cut out right overhead and it started to spiral downwards. Whoever was in charge shouted at us to spread out and lie down. We watched in fascination and youthful ignorance as it spun downwards. We were lucky as it eventually landed somewhere near Clapham Junction. [This V1 destroyed two shops and houses at 84–86 St John's Hill.] The frequency of these attacks over the next few months and, subsequently the more destructive V2s, contributed to a very frightening period.

The Headmaster's wife, Mrs Daphne Broom, was travelling on a bus when it was hit by a flying bomb. She was the sole survivor but sustained severe spinal injuries from which she later recovered.

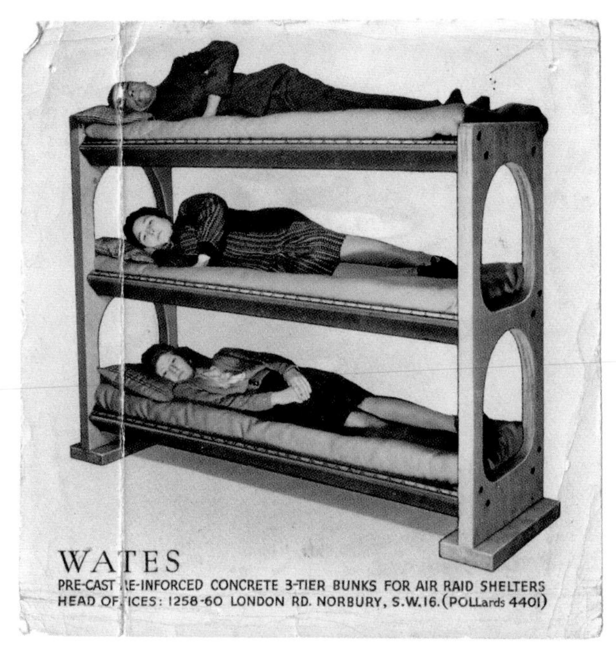

Pre-cast reinforced concrete bunkers built for air-raid shelters by Wates Ltd. Three Old Emanuel brothers, Allan, Norman and Ronald Wates, ran the Company

Wartime Nocturne

The Portcullis is full of articles with Emanuel boys' impressions on the war and in particular Norman Francis Bartlett wrote about the atmosphere in London during a night-time bombing raid, first published in 1942.

> There is a sickly glow in the sky over London. The indescribable beauty of the night is somehow enhanced by the questioning fingers of the searchlights. A shadow passes across the moon and then a green and orange light streaks across the sky. A flare is descending slowly to the roof-tops and its ghostly iridescent glare discovers a new city, white and clean. A factory chimney silhouetted sharply against a low bank of red clouds, stark and black, takes on the symmetry and grace of an ancient monument.

The cold, impersonal light of the stars is dimmed by the artificial brilliance of a new, presumptuous glare. Below, the nebulous shadows flicker across the canyon-like streets. They are deserted and lonely, but the very fear of their inhabitants seems to have transposed itself upon the inanimate buildings. The houses huddle closer for protection; they cower together in endless rows, stretching towards the bright horizon.

The earth shakes and one waits, expecting to see the roads split and spew up a host of primeval monsters, but the thundering roar dies away in the distance and a cloud of dust ascends slowly from the tortured city, mingling with the smoke from the burning buildings and hangs in the sky, a dense, funeral pall.

Slowly, unobtrusively, the night slips past and the roseate fingers of the dawn compete with the garish flush of the night. O, the beauty of that morning! The city is shrouded in a sepulchral veil of quietness. One by one the houses appear through the mist, their shuttered eyes look out upon the same old, unchanged vista of drab concrete, but somehow they seemed astonished, for a new ethereal beauty exudes from the dusty streets and quiet squares; beauty out of Armageddon, life out of death.

OEs killed in bombing raids

News was received by the School in 1943 that Old Boys A. C. Ashburner and Eric Holland had been killed in bombing raids. The former was killed in May 1941 and the latter in 1940.

Another OE, John Henry Mills, was killed on 19 April 1941 as he, his wife and daughter were having a drink in the Lugard Public House in Lugard Road, Peckham. One of the bombs that fell was a direct hit on the pub. Seventeen people were killed including John Henry, with many more being injured. All the dead are buried in a mass grave in Camberwell New Cemetery and after the war, a memorial stone was placed to mark the spot. Mills's wife and daughter both survived the attack, the daughter with minor injuries.

John Henry Mills

On 28 April 1941, Allan Earlsman Frederick Wheeler who attended Emanuel between 1925 and 1932, was killed with 43 other sailors and 21 Royal Engineers when the shelter they were in at the Royal Navy base camp HMS *Raleigh* received a direct hit from a German bomb. Allan joined the Royal Navy in 1941 and briefly saw his newly born son, Michael, before being killed the following month. Tragically he was killed the night before he was to go on his first home leave.

At School Allan was a Sergeant in the OTC and gained his War Office Certificate 'A' in March 1931. He was a member of the Dramatic Society; played for the First Fifteen and also rowed. As a rugby player he was a good all-round forward who was equally aggressive in the scrum as he was in open play. He was also a member of the Modern Sixth class.

On 2 May, the Prime Minister, Winston Churchill, visited the scene of the bombing. Churchill's Assistant Private Secretary, John Colville recorded what they saw:

> We reached the Royal Navy barracks where bombs had killed a number of sailors. There was a gruesome sight in the gymnasium: beds in which some forty slightly injured men lay, separated only by a low curtain from some coffins which were being nailed down. The hammering must

Allan Earlsman Frederick Wheeler by Flora Twort

> have been horrible to the injured men, but such has been the damage that there was nowhere else it could be done.[1]

After Allan's death his family commissioned the artist Flora Twort to paint a picture of him based upon previous photographs. The completed work was bequeathed to the Hampshire County Council Museum Service, which operates the Flora Twort Gallery.

Derek William Cadman (Emanuel 1932–1940) was killed when the RAF station he was in was attacked in May 1941. *The Portcullis* noted:

> He evacuated with the School to Petersfield, where he entered the Modern Sixth and was soon appointed a House Prefect of Howe. He was prominent in every branch of School life. He was a member of the First Fifteen, ran for the Athletics team, acted for the Dramatic Society and was a Sgt in the JTC. He gained London University General Schools Certificate in the summer of 1939. His cheerfulness made him universally popular and everyone was sorry when he left at Christmas 1940. After a short time he joined the Royal Air Force and was still in training when he was killed during the course of a bombing raid on his station.

Bombing of Emanuel's Founders

Not even Lord and Lady Dacre, Emanuel School's sixteenth century founders, were excluded from German bombing. Their monument rests in Chelsea Old Church, Old Church Street, Chelsea, which was severely damaged in a raid on 16/17 April 1941 but fortunately the Dacre monument survived, even if a little shaken.

Photo showing damage to the Dacre monument in Chelsea Old Church

The Dacre monument as it stands today

Night Guard duty during the Battle of Britain

Although most OEs who had fought in the First World War were too old to be combatants in the Second, many played their part in other roles such as in the Home Guard, on barrage balloons, fire watching, manning anti-aircraft batteries, as well as numerous other roles essential to the war effort.

Frank P. J. Glover, who had fought at both Arras and Passchendaele, was a Sergeant in "D" Company Belmont Home Guard and was a night guard in Sutton on the evening of 26/27 August 1940, during the Battle of Britain. His report that evening shows us the typical duties the Home Guard had to carry out during bombing raids:

> 20:15 / 20:30 Guard Mounted.
>
> 21:00 Sgt. Carson lecture on 'Bombing – Hand Grenades'.
>
> 21:30 Air Raid Siren Sounded – 'Takes Cover.'
>
> 21:30 Enemy aircraft active in many directions but no incidents in our immediate vicinity.
>
> 00:10 Stick of bombs (6) fell some miles distant in SW direction.
>
> 00:30 Sentries withdrawn from railway cutting and Belmont Bridge.
>
> 01:40 Sound of bomb explosion (distant) in Northerly direction A.A. (Anti-Aircraft) fire observed some miles away to East.
>
> 02:25 Stick of bombs dropped by enemy aircraft a few miles to North. Plane held by searchlight for about five minutes and subjected to A.A. fire. Passed overhead at about 3000 feet and disappeared in southerly direction.
>
> 02:30 Pom Pom fire and tracer bullets observed in direction taken by above enemy aircraft which, sentries report, appeared to bring it down as burst of flame followed from what seemed to be the explosion of petrol tanks as it hit the ground in direction of Caterham.
>
> A round of 303 ammunition was accidentally discharged by Mr. Funneil in the Hall, fortunately without causing a casualty.
>
> 02:45 Relief of two men despatched to Sutton and Cheam Hospital under Cpl Milward.
>
> 02:50 Further enemy aircraft activity in immediate vicinity but nothing seen of hostile machine.
>
> 03:40 Sirens sounded, raiders passed. Runner was sent to withdraw Sutton and Cheam Hospital patrol.
>
> 03:50 Hospital patrol returns.
>
> 03:55 Mr Fletcher passed on instructions for Alarm Reserve to 'stand down' and left HQ.
>
> Nothing further to report.
>
> 07:00 Handed over to Day Guard.[2]

J.B. Phillips

Influential Theologian recalls the impact of the Second World War on his local church

J. B. Phillips *(Emanuel 1918–1924)*

John Bertram Phillips spent all of the Second World War preaching in churches and bomb-shelters in South London. He also conducted a large number of funerals particularly during the Blitz.

Phillips recalls in his autobiography:

> As many will remember, the declaration of war came on a sunny day in September 1939. The first sirens blew their eerie warnings and I was sharply told to 'take cover' by a passing Air Raid Warden on a bicycle. I remember this because I was in fact putting the finishing touches to one of my gas-proof almshouses, before taking the morning service. Well, the 'all clear' sounded soon afterwards and no further raids, real or imaginary, happened for nearly a year. It was the period called by the Americans 'The Phony War.'

> The declaration of war made quite a difference to me. Quite often this meant 40–50 funerals per week in the Borough of Lewisham and led me to spend many a day at the Hither Green Cemetery with sandwiches and flask.
>
> Suddenly on a glorious September day there appeared to be hundreds of German Bombers hell-bent on the destruction of London. I, as it happened, had just finished conducting a funeral and was on my way home on my bicycle. It seems ridiculous now. But I put my head down and pedalled furiously to get home. I supposed the bombers were travelling around 250 miles an hour and my bicycle speed was scarcely a tenth of that.[3]

After the war Phillips wrote a number of Christian books, being one of the few Christian authors to sell more than one million copies of a single title. His modern translations of Biblical texts were regarded as influential in bringing Christianity to the younger generation in post-war Britain.

Night Bombing

Out of the darkness can be heard a low
And distant roar. Another night has come
To London, and the busy, bustling hum
That marked the city is no more.

A siren wails its warning, low and long,
The bombers, laden with their gory load
Throb overhead. Their seed of death is sown,
While guns below roar out their deadly song.

The noise of battle lessens – dies away,
Down in the city gleams the ruddy glow
Of fires. But soon the sweet, protecting day
Will come, and London, gazing at this show,
Will comb the dust from out her hair, and pay
Tribute to those the morrow will not know.

D.A.S. *The Portcullis,* Autumn Term 1941 p. 40

Derek Cadman

References

1 Diary extract reprinted in M. Gilbert, *Finest Hour: Winston S. Churchill 1939–1941* (1989), p. 1077.
2 The Collection of Lt. F. P. J. Glover, IWM 78/10/1.
3 J. B. Phillips, *The Price of Success* (1984).

A voice against war – Conscientious Objection

In both world wars there were individuals whose strong convictions rejected warfare at all costs. OE Philip Dransfield in correspondence with Daniel Kirmatzis explains his decisions for being a conscientious objector in the Second World War.

'I held pacifist convictions whilst still at School and for that reason never joined the OTC. This did not make me very popular, especially with one militaristic master Charles Hill. He was my geography teacher and went out of his way to try and get me to join the OTC. My brother Stephen did join it, but we respected each other's views. My father left us to make our own decisions, but I can say that my mother supported my pacifism.

Coming back to myself, when the time came for me to register in 1940 under the Military Service Act I registered as a 'conscientious objector' which meant that I was treading a very unpopular and despised route. But I would like to make it clear that I have never regretted that decision and on the whole my family were supportive, especially my mother.

At the time of my registration I was a medical student and therefore in a reserved occupation, but I wanted to be known as an objector to military service. As I saw it, soldiers and doctors had very little in common. I proceeded with studies at St George's Hospital, London, until I gained my degree at the London University in November of 1943. I think my qualification was reported in the School magazine in 1943.

After qualification I had to attend a tribunal to decide whether I was a 'genuine C.O.' and this was held at Fulham Town Hall before Judge Hargreaves who was rather a 'hawk.' He was Chairman with four assessors and they came to the decision that I was 'genuine' and my name was placed on the list of conscientious objectors. They asked me if I would be willing to serve in the Royal Army Medical Corps and I said that I was. I worked in two London hospitals, treating air-raid casualties, including victims from both the Blitz and flying bombs in areas such as Kensington and Plumstead.

The dropping of the atom bomb was a terrible happening which began a new era in human history and created problems with which the world is still struggling. Clearly I contributed nothing to military actions and I was averse to military prowess and killing on any scale. I simply tried to apply the Christian principles with which I had been inculcated.

By a comedy of errors I was drafted into the RAMC in 1946 for two years' service. I served in Italy, Libya and Egypt and had an interesting and instructive time and was glad when the war was over.'

The following extracts are from Philip Dransfield's pamphlet *Christians and War: a Christian Pacifist Reply*. First published in 1996, by the Anglican Pacifist Fellowship the document deals with pacifist answers to questions they are often asked:

Pacifism is starry eyed idealism. It is not practicable.

Reply: Any militarist who takes the view that the world can be improved by resorting to war and using today's weapons of vast destruction must be 'starry eyed' to the point of self-deception. As a method of solving the world's international and social problems war must be regarded as the least

Grave of William Leonard Page, who was originally a conscientious objector at the outbreak of the Second World War but was later killed while serving with the Royal Fusiliers in the Italian Campaign

Aftermath

A gentle breeze blows o'er the land
Which Man once called his own.
A pile of stones where once did stand
His pride.
And he is dust.

The cannons now have sung their song
Of blood and death and hate;
And they their maker have destroyed
In war.
And he is dust.

And Nature's wrong is now aright,
For Man himself has killed.
The world has now a chance to live,
To live.
For he is dust.

A.V.R., 5 Sci. *The Portcullis*,
Lent Term, 1940, p. 22

practicable that man can achieve. It is also worth recalling that during the nineteenth century it was considered 'starry eyed idealism' to abolish slavery. Wilberforce with a few Christian friends accepted the challenge. He was convinced that what was morally wrong was never expedient and had to be got rid of, whatever the cost. We know that the campaign succeeded. In the same way, having at long last realised the wickedness of war, we have to take the necessary steps to renounce it. The alternative to pacifism could be world destruction.

You must have armed forces to deter aggression. You can only negotiate from a position of strength.

Reply: Those who use this argument presumably concede to others the rights they claim for themselves. So all other countries can act on the same conviction that they must have armed force to deter aggressors and they must amass sufficient armaments to be able to negotiate from strength! Taking the argument further, each country must be stronger than any of the others before it feels able to negotiate at all! What an absurdity and what a succession of errors and fallacies underlie this mode of thinking. It is a matter for comment that men, apparently intelligent in other things, cannot see the folly and stupidity of insisting that we all negotiate from strength. It is a situation for Alice in Wonderland. After all if a country feels stronger than its neighbours it would see little or no point in negotiation. The point must be made that armed forces do not always deter 'aggressors.' A country can become so embittered and desperate through oppression and injustice that it may choose to wage war against heavy odds. The deterrent effect of armed forces then counts for very little and the outcome of the war may be determined by the state of morale of the fighting armies.

Boy Racer on the Home Front

Leonard Mitchell *(Emanuel 1937–1944)*

One of the most colourful stories from the Home Front era is that of Leonard Mitchell and his maiden voyage across the newly opened Waterloo Bridge in August 1942. Although we were aware of the story it was verified when Leonard's son sent us this iconic photograph.

Amongst the boys who were evacuated to Petersfield, Leonard attained a certain level of fame and the story was retold in OE circles. At the time it made the front page of many daily newspapers and Leonard had his fifteen minutes of fame. Indeed, if you search for 'Mitchell' and 'Opening Waterloo Bridge' you'll find the whole story on the Internet.

In 1942 the story was reported in the *Evening News*:

> Sixteen year old Leonard Mitchell, Oakmead Road, Balham, beat other cyclists, buses, cabs and cars to be first across the New Waterloo Bridge today. As Big Ben struck ten this morning barriers were thrown across the ends of the temporary bridge and policemen beckoned to waiting vehicles to take the smooth, new roadway across the five span bridge. Although there was no official ceremony, hundreds of people collected to see the new bridge brought into use.
>
> Eight cyclists shot ahead of the first vehicle – a cab – but Leonard Mitchell, a scholar at Emanuel School, beat them all ... A horse-drawn four-wheel cab, with an elderly man and a schoolboy as passengers, attempted to gate-crash, but the driver was directed back to the main traffic stream over the temporary bridge. The removal by workmen engaged on the construction of the new bridge of red flags in the approach was the signal for the 'go.' The cyclists got a flying start, followed closely by a taxicab, a car, and a bus loaded with passengers. As the field raced across the bridge the workmen, who were lining the balustrade cheered.

This colourful incident goes to show that although times were lean on the Home Front teenagers would always find ways of having fun. In April of 1944, at the earliest possible opportunity, Leonard signed up and trained to be a pilot on Tiger Moths but because of his poor eyesight he became a navigator. Most of his training took place in Canada and he was then based in Northern Ireland. Leonard never saw active service and was discharged in November 1947 before attending university.

The Second World War

'The fire was persistent, causing casualties since the men were only in shallow scrapes having had no time to dig in, and we were unable to respond. When you have command it is necessary to give a steady example.'

H. J. HUTCHINS

Old Emanuel Rugby Football Club

1st XV 1938–1939

D.S. Hoare *POW*	D.J. Warren *DSO, MC*	D.G. Morrill *KIA*	K.M. Millist *DFC, KIA*	A.R.J. Skillern *KIA*	S.J. Ayers *Unknown*

W.C. Neath *DFC*	F.H.S. Palmer *POW*	H.J. Hutchins *MC*	E.F. Clinton *Served*	J.D. Royal *KIA*

E.D. Page *Served*	K.J. Gurling *Served*	C.M. Harris *Served*	K. Horseman *POW*

John Frederick Banting

(Emanuel 1913–1920)

John Banting, brother of OE George Banting, is shown here pulling a disparaging face at the Swastika flag flying over Innsbruck in March 1938. The image was captured by the artist and photographer Humphrey Spender, famous for his photographs of working-class life in Bolton and for his work for the social research organisation – Mass Observation. Many of Spender's photos were reproduced in the weekly magazine Picture Post.

John Banting was a well-known surrealist artist. In March 1938 he was in Austria with Spender and, according to Spender's annotation on the photograph, John was arrested for throwing himself in front of Nazi troops as he tried single-handedly to prevent them annexing Austria. Spender had to bail him out.

The Nazis marched into Innsbruck as part of the Anschluss [union] with Austria on 12 March 1938. According to Spender, Heinrich Himmler, [leader of the SS] was in the same hotel. By 1938, and after the Spanish Civil War, John was a politically active member of the left-wing Surrealist group and wrote a piece in the group's last edition of their magazine, the London Bulletin, in June 1940 titled 'The Careless have Inherited the Earth.'

Leslie Lincoln Henson

1891–1957 (Emanuel 1903–1906)

Wartime and peacetime entertainer to Kings, Generals, Admirals and a legion of adoring fans

Leslie Henson was one of the most popular entertainers of the early 20th Century. His star shone brightly in theatre land in the inter-war period and during both world wars he entertained the troops and both Kings George V and VI.

Born in Notting Hill he attended Cliftonville College before entering Emanuel at the age of twelve in 1903. In addition to being the touch judge for Emanuel's first Rugby team of 1906, he also got his first taste of theatre at Emanuel as he remembers, 'theatricals were frowned upon by our very strict headmaster, but encouraged by everyone else –

Leslie Henson, Emanuel 1906 First XV touch judge (first from right standing)

particularly on Sunday afternoons after scripture. There was a platform in what was known as the New Hall, and on this I used to give a concert party programme.' [1]

He continues:

> We had a boy keeping cave at the door to give warning of the headmaster's approach. This was necessary, for he often did come. Directly we heard the cry of 'Cave!' we performers went into hiding under the platform because of our costumes and make-up, and our audience, including some of the younger masters, split up into groups and the hall had the appearance of a normal Sunday afternoon. [2]

Known as 'Troutie' at school for as he writes his 'piscatorial features', Leslie took an interest in both cricket and football.[3] One can imagine he was rather an amusing school boy as the Emanuel School history explains:

> While we regard it as generally unfair to refer to school reports, we have, with Mr. Henson's consent, made an exception...he made good progress in music under Mr. Evans, and that his strongest point in classwork was English composition. But probably a more valuable clue to the talents and personality which have resulted in a series of brilliant theatrical successes is a red ink note on one of his reports: 'General behaviour, N[ot] S[atisfactory]–S.T.W.' Apparently the fund of humour and high spirits which made 'Trouty' so popular in dormitory and classroom was not always appreciated by Mr. Whitaker, who was unable to see the real genius which underlay them. [4]

After leaving School he worked for a firm of hide, skin and tallow merchants in Dundee before becoming an apprentice butcher with the family business, but his heart was in the theatre and after amateur roles in *Aladdin*, where he first learnt to contort his facial features for which he would later become famous, his mother encouraged him to become a drama student. He got his first break in 1910 with The Tatlers concert party but tragedy soon struck with the early death of his father. Minor roles and tours followed until he made his first appearance in the West End in 1912 in *Nicely, Thanks*, although he and the rest of the party almost never performed again. When they went to take a bow at the end of the first part of their programme the act drop, which was a solid curtain, came crashing down on their necks.

In 1913 he made a lifelong friend of the comedian Stanley Holloway, with whom he later recorded a Second World War comedy song called 'Careless Talk', which had a serious message for the wartime population of Britain that they shouldn't talk about wartime related news in public because they never knew who was listening and any such news could be used to the enemy's advantage.

A small part followed in the musical comedy *To-night's the Night* and at his first audition at the Gaiety Theatre was Old Emanuel and theatre impresario, Alfred Butt. The show opened in New York and Leslie's ship sailed in November 1914.The German raider *Karlsruhe* chased it part of the way but none of its passengers knew this at the time.

Whilst in New York Leslie was offered a contract for three pictures but had already accepted an offer to open at the Gaiety Theatre in London. Leslie thought at the time that moving pictures wouldn't 'last any longer than roller-skating' and so a Hollywood career never materialised. Theatre work during the First World War was not without its perils as Zeppelins bombed London. Leslie remembered:

> One of the Zeppelin raids on London occurred while we were actually playing, and a bomb fell so near the theatre that the door of the scene-dock was blown in and shrapnel rattled on to the stage. Our messenger boy was killed and the call boy was seriously injured.

Leslie was quick to act and calmed the audience by jumping up on a couch and moving in time to the music of the orchestra being directed by the conductor who had jumped up into a seat. The audience proceeded to take their seats again.[5]

Leslie played in a sketch called *In the Trenches* at a charity matinée at the Gaiety in 1916. Leslie suggests that the war had been a taboo subject on the stage up to 1916. The sketch which was about a lonely soldier who never got a letter and asked to read a bit of another's soldier's letter went down well with an audience of injured soldiers on its first night and continued to run 'for successive weeks at Hackney, Chiswick and the Coliseum'.

In 1916 Leslie joined the Royal Flying Corps and qualified as a first-class motor driver and second class air mechanic. He soon took charge of the RFC's technical reference library and quickly became frustrated with red tape when technical books which were needed urgently were not ordered immediately because he was told an order from the Treasury was required. Leslie recalls that he could have got them within less than a week but six months later and after landing in France those books still had not been ordered. At this time Leslie had just finished playing in *Yes, Uncle*.

Leslie reported to an officer in Farnborough but immediately recognised the Posting Major as Lawrence Legge who had played in *The Chocolate Soldier*. Thanks to Lawrence, Leslie was transferred from quarters under canvas to Salamanca Barracks, Aldershot. He also benefited from being recognised by the Corporal in charge of the cookhouse who had worked with his father for fifteen years in Smithfield Market. He soon left for France after doing several entertaining stints at Farnborough. When in France he had a couple of hair raising journeys, one of which could have seen the early end of Leslie as he was climbing underneath a train to join his friend on another that was about to leave on an adjacent platform. He missed the train and was carried away on an empty one in a story that reads straight out of a comedy. The initial hiccup was soon over and he received a commission because General Sir Hubert Gough wanted him to organise shows for the troops.

Leslie remembers organising his first show:

> I got busy at once, and in a week had a concert party of twelve in pierrot costume and make-up. Our theatre was a barn, but we had good lighting. I called the party 'The Gaieties', for what then seemed old times to me.

Leslie Henson (far left) with 'The Gaieties'

Leslie Henson theatre posters and book cover

Leslie was in France at the time of the German offensive of March 1918 when he describes walking back after a show one evening with his friend Major Dennis Critchley-Salmonson:

> ... we walked back together about midnight to our billet in a creepy, ghost-like farmhouse, and I remember him saying solemnly: "Matey ('Matey' was his name for me), the big offensive starts this morning." So when at 4am or thereabouts we were wakened by a soul-shaking, terrifying sense of sound that vibrated and quivered through the night, I knew what Critchley-Salmonson meant when he said: "Matey, here they are!" The great German offensive of March 1918, had begun.
>
> After breakfast we made our way back to Nesle, amid the sound of gunfire and resounding crashes, while ambulances came tearing down the road...things were bad and going from bad to worse. The Fifth Army was in retreat. We retired from Nesle, soon to be smashed up, and went from one uncomfortable spot to another. At last, in Amiens, we began to take root again, and I raced round trying to get hold of people to make up a show – never more needed than in those black days of the retreat.

His show performed in 'barns, in schools and in tents.' The Tanks Corps built them a theatre with Chinese labour in a day, with an audience of around a thousand officers and men at one point. Leslie's job after the German evacuation of Lille in October 1918 was to find a theatre. The Germans had completed the building of Lille's theatre after they occupied it in 1914. Leslie was tasked with getting this theatre in to shape and to organise shows as soon as possible. An interesting coincidence occurred some years after the war when Leslie adapted a play by the German authors Arnold and Bach. Arnold travelled from Berlin to see Leslie in England. Arnold's play, *Nice Goings On*, was the fourth Leslie had adapted and in his dressing room the two spoke about the war, which had been, by this stage, over by fifteen years. Leslie takes up the story:

> We began to reminisce, and naturally the Great War was mentioned. I told him the story of my tenure of the Lille Opera House, and threw a compliment to whoever the German director was who had run the theatre so beautifully during the four and half years' occupation.

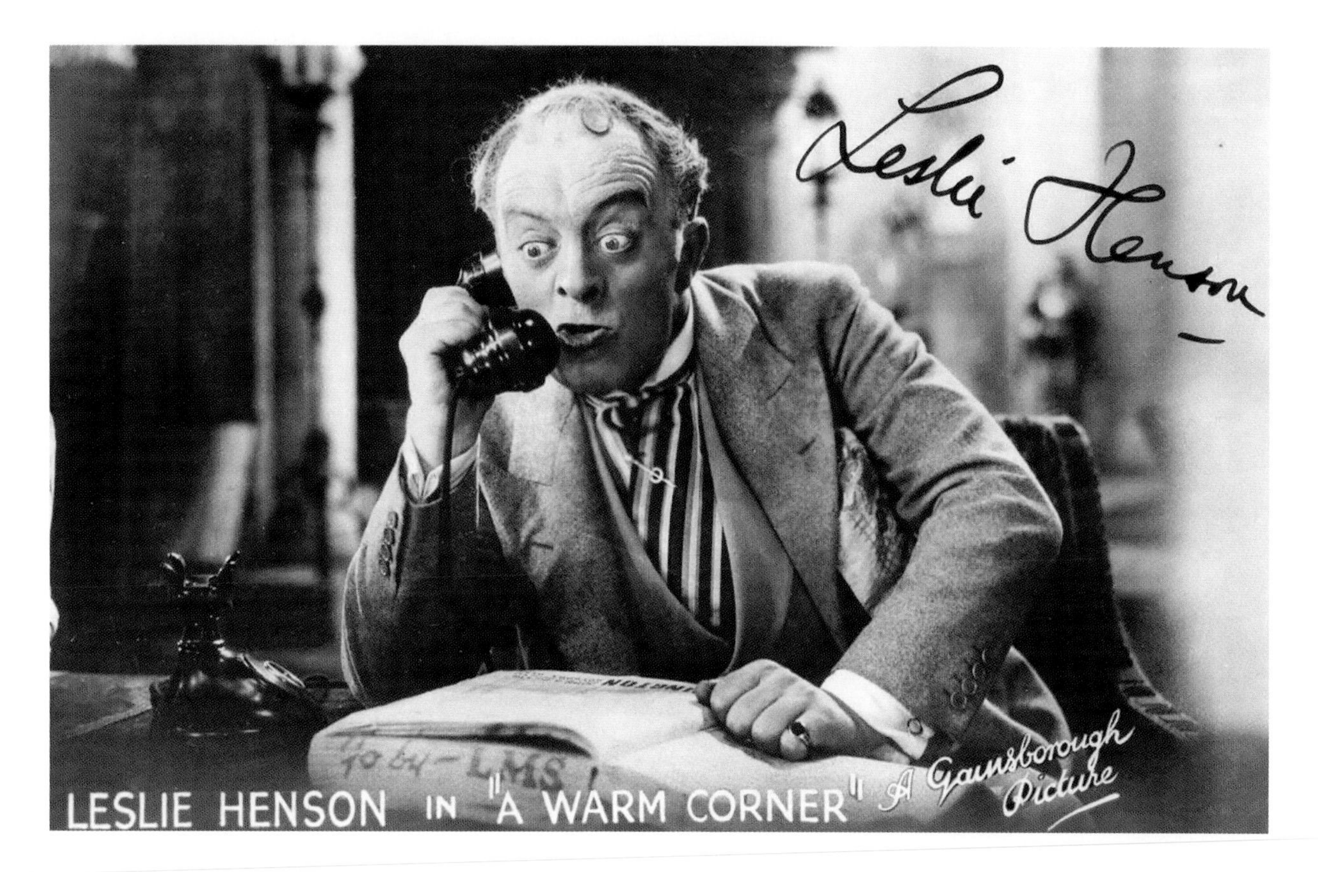

Arnold's eyes lit up. "Herr Henson, I was that director. I walked out as you walked in."

The Theatre was up and running in a week. Leslie's 'Gaieties' was very much an 'Allied revue' for it included French artistes. Leslie paints the scene of the show's grand finale:

> It began with a series of tableaux, Number one was 'The Angelus' –interrupted by the 'Fall in!'...Number two was 'Au Revoir' – a *poilu* saying goodbye to his girl... Number three was 'The Enemy' – a German officer appeared, seized the girl and put chains round her wrists and ankles. I was the German officer, and I was very proud of that make-up. No laughs here. Hisses galore, but no laughs – an artistic triumph. Number four was 'Occupation'...Number five was 'Liberation' – the German officer explaining in dumb show that all was over...strains of 'Tipperary' from the orchestra, and finally a Tommy rushing on to help take the chains off the girl. Then the black cloth behind them went up revealing the full stage set as a palace scene, with a hundred convent children (marvellously stage-managed by the nuns) grouped on stairs at the back. All they had to do was...sing the Marseillaise...the audience rose to their feet.
>
> A Scottish pipe band was heard in the distance: they were in a scene dock three floors below the stage. Nearer and nearer they came until they appeared, marching on to the stage...slowly down the steps walked Bert Errol... draped in a gigantic French flag. On one side was a Tommy, on the other a *poilu*, who...duly embraced his sweetheart.[6]

The show was a huge success being packed out with soldiers and civilians but on one special occasion they played to King George V who occupied the Royal Box with his sons, the Prince of Wales, later King Edward VIII and the Duke of York, later King George VI. When King George VI visited the start of Leslie's entertainment show at the beginning of the Second World War he reminded Leslie that he had been with his brother watching him in Lille in 1918, a moment Leslie recalls, 'Thus I had played for three Kings of England in one night, and that in a foreign country, viz. – George V, Edward VIII and George VI.'[7]

Leslie was sure that what the family called 'the Henson Luck' had brought his friends back safe from the war as his mother had given him and 29 others a lucky bead to carry with them on their journeys.

The war ended for Leslie when he was demobbed in February 1919 and he set upon a golden inter-war career being one of the most recognisable faces in show business by the time of the next conflict in 1939. In quick succession Leslie performed in three successful productions, *Kissing Time, A Night Out* and the silent movies, *Alf's Button* and *Tons of Money*.

When Emanuel was collecting money for a war memorial Leslie brought his Company to the School for the War Memorial Bazaar to perform the musical comedy sketch, *The Disorderly Room*.[8] Emanuel remained very close to his thoughts throughout his career and one Old Emanuel, Vernon Greaves wrote to the School after the war to say he dined with Leslie in France.[9]

In 1928 Leslie played with Fred and Adèle Astaire in the smash hit play, *Funny Face*. It was during this run that a large gas explosion took place outside the theatre in Holborn in December 1928 and an iconic photo was taken of Leslie with the Astaires outside the theatre. Leslie's career went from strength to strength throughout the inter-war period and his friends during this time read like a Who's Who of early twentieth century theatre and comedy. His talents were endless, being an actor, producer, director and interviewer having on one occasion interviewed George Bernard Shaw. He was also passionate about filming and his home movie collection is a unique document, now held by the British Film Institute, including colour footage of Second World War scenes of Mountbatten, Prince Philip, scenes on a troop ship, bomb damaged buildings in Berlin and the Victory Parade through London in 1946.

Leslie Henson with Fred and Adèle Astaire after a gas explosion in Holborn where they were performing in the play Funny Face

Leslie was in Capetown at the outbreak of the Second World War. He returned to England with a large convoy escorted by HMS *Neptune*. Leslie described his return:

> Arriving in London in the black-out and miseries of war, was an immense contrast to the happiness and sunshine of what is most inappropriately termed 'Darkest Africa'. Most theatres had closed, and I, as an old campaigner in wartime entertainment, immediately went to Drury Lane...[10]

Leslie felt a sense of duty to do his part in the War as he explains, '...for the whole six years of pain and distress I was only too anxious to devote myself to the service man who was doing so far greater a job than I could ever do. An actor is the servant of the public.'

Leslie met with Basil Dean and Sir Seymour Hicks in order to organise a national entertainment organisation and Leslie came up with the name ENSA, which stood for Entertainments National Service Association. King George VI and Queen Elizabeth visited his concert group, the 'Gaieties', at a final rehearsal before they set off for France in late November 1939. He did two tours in France, one in 1939 and the other in 1940 before returning to England to appear in his first Revue. Soon the Battle of Britain was upon them at which time all theatres were closed. In 1941, London's Saville Theatre, where Leslie had been playing, was hit by four bombs, and a photo depicts the damage with a sign reading 'Les Hen', the other half of the sign having been blown away.

Being a popular figure, Leslie appeared in a National Savings Week film where he urged the population of Britain to save so that arms could be bought for servicemen. As he exclaimed, 'We cannot let these gallant gentlemen down.' He encouraged the population to save in order 'to supply the munitions which will help to protect these men's lives'. He finished with a stirring appeal, 'So save and lend to defend the right to be free.'[11]

Before-and-after shots of King George VI taken during his visit to the Home Fleet at Scapa Flow in March 1943 where he watched an ENSA show organised by Leslie Henson. The King can be seen before the show starts and during the performance laughing at one of Leslie Henson's jokes. On the right is Admiral Sir John Tovey, Commander in Chief, Home Fleet, and on the left is Captain E. D. S. McCarthy, Captain of the Fleet

Leslie entertained the troops across the entire globe during the course of the Second World War. He went to France, Scotland, Gibraltar, North Africa, Italy, Northern Europe and the Far East. At the Navy station in Scapa Flow Leslie once again entertained King George VI and a photo of the performance shows the King being more than amused by one of Leslie's jokes. After the show he dined with the King on board the battleship *King George V*. Sitting opposite the King, Leslie placed a bet of half a crown with His Majesty about a scene in the Noël Coward war film *In Which We Serve*. Some months later and after Leslie had taken up the issue with Noel Coward, the bet was lost and when meeting the King again in Hammamet, North Africa he duly paid him 25 Francs, which was roughly equivalent of half a crown. [12]

After a spell in Gibraltar Leslie was touring in North Africa when, after a long day in which he performed three shows, he was entertained at a reception by General Eisenhower, Leslie noted, 'I don't know which was the bigger pleasure. To meet him or drink his beautiful cool American concoctions.' A little while later and he was performing before the Eighth Army. As he explains:

> Monty himself came on to the stage after our first night. (What a reception he got as he walked into his box...) He made a charming speech of welcome to us telling us we were appearing to 'His Soldiers, the Finest Soldiers in the World' – that we were doing good work for their morale, that indeed he considered us 'a battle winning potential.' What a personality! [13]

The audiences were very large as Leslie recalls playing to 16,000 Desert Rats, in a Roman Amphitheatre. Leslie notes one moment from the show, 'Back of me were the only two remaining pillars standing among the ruins...These were two beautifully fluted pillars with flat tops. I look back at them, sigh, and say, "Good old Battersea Power Station".'

Leslie was an advocate of Sunday Opening for the Theatre, an issue he championed both in the 1930s and again in the Second World War. He argued that thousands of pounds had been lost by the Red Cross and Prisoners of War Fund because the authorities had refused to change the law and allow theatres to open on a Sunday. The genesis of the issue was both established on religious grounds of Sunday being a day of rest but also for fear that no one should work seven days in one week, which was a spurious argument as Leslie suggested theatres could choose to close on another night in a week. Despite Leslie's efforts the law did not change for a number of years.

In January 1944 Leslie entertained the troops in Italy at Campobasso. Malta, Sicily, Belgium and Holland followed that year. In 1945 he toured the Far East where he played to ex-POWs:

> For the first time we played to ex-prisoners of war, and later had an opportunity of talking to some of these poor fellows. All the gaiety of our tour was completely damped for the time being by the pathetic abnormality of the tortured men, and the work took to itself a much more serious turn. [14]

Whilst in the Far East he entertained troops aboard the aircraft carrier HMS *Colossus* and dined with Lord Louis Mountbatten, Supreme Allied Commander, South East Asia

The bomb-damaged Saville Theatre, 1941

Command. Leslie took the opportunity to film the time he spent with Mountbatten and also photographed the surrender of the Japanese Imperial Army at the Singapore Municipal Building in Singapore on 12 September 1945.

Leslie's contribution to entertaining the troops in both wars was a remarkable achievement and it must be emphasised that he was still carrying out a busy schedule as a performer, producer and director of revue shows.

In December 1951 Leslie attended the 350th anniversary commemorating the granting of the Charter of Incorporation by Queen Elizabeth in 1601 of Emanuel Hospital held at St Margaret's, Westminster, and at a celebration luncheon in the Rembrandt Hotel, Kensington he gave the toast of 'The School.' Sadly in 1957 Leslie passed away at the age of 66 but he left behind an extraordinary legacy never more so than in the thousands of laughing servicemen in two world wars. He made the cruel and savage experience of war a little lighter. A friend who attended Cliftonville with Leslie wrote to the *Wandsworth Borough News* after Leslie died and felt Leslie never received the recognition he deserved for the immense journeys he made in both wars to entertain the troops. Perhaps a statue of the great man is long overdue!

Leslie's eldest son Joe started the Cotswold Farm Park in 1971 and Joe's son Adam is a regular presenter on the BBC's *Country File*. Leslie's youngest son Nicky Henson followed his father's footsteps into film and theatre, including appearances in a host of television dramas, the most recent of which has been as Charles Grigg in ITV's *Downton Abbey*. Nicky also appeared as Mr. Johnson in an episode of John Cleese's *Fawlty Towers* in addition to appearances in the cutting edge 1960s programme *The Frost Report*, presented by the late Sir David Frost.

References

1 Leslie Henson, *Yours Faithfully*, John Long Limited, p. 15.
2 Ibid.
3 The Emanuel School history by Scott-Giles uses the spelling "Trouty".
4 *The History of Emanuel School*, p. 182.
5 *Yours Faithfully*, p. 53.
6 A Poilu was an informal name for a French Infantryman in the First World War.
7 *Yours Faithfully*, p. 116.
8 *The Portcullis*, Christmas Term, 1920, p.29.
9 *The Portcullis*, Lent Term, 1920, pp. 39-40.
10 Drury Lane became the headquarters of ENSA.
11 National Savings Week – Leslie Henson – British Pathé Collection.
12 *Yours Faithfully*, p. 118 and 134.
13 Ibid. pp. 134-135.
14 Ibid. p. 162.

Roland Leonard Hastings McNish DSO *(Emanuel 1897–1899)*

The Perils of the Sea

By the time Roland McNish retired from the Merchant Navy, a day before the D-Day landings, he had travelled thousands of miles across the world's oceans. His career stretched over two world wars with some hell-raising moments.

The role of the Merchant Navy was pivotal to keeping the British, their Empire and Allies, stocked with precious foodstuffs and materials during two world wars. By the early twentieth century the lines drawn across maps showing the world's oceans in reality represented the veins and arteries of the British Empire and it was the Merchant Navy's role to transport supplies through these channels. Goods such as exotic fruits, tea, coffee, wool, rubber and cocoa were transported to Britain. The merchantmen landed these supplies at the many docks and ports where they were unloaded waiting to be transported on to their journey of transformation into commodities for the market economy and then sold out to the world. The journey had its dangers in peace time but take into account mines, submarine warfare, attacks by dive bombers and raiders and one begins to build up a picture that peace time operations were pleasurable in comparison to the conditions faced by the merchantmen in times of 'Total War'.

At the end of 1915 the German Auxiliary Crusier *Moewe* made it through the British Naval blockade and into open waters where it proceeded to lay mines before embarking on a journey in which it destroyed a not inconsiderable number of merchant vessels.[1] Film footage exists of the *Moewe* in late 1916 delivering prisoners to Germany and her Captain Korvetten-Kapitän Burggraf Graf Nikolaus Zu Dohna-Schlodien being congratulated for his efforts by Admiral Reinhard von Scheer.[2] Interestingly it was Old Emanuel, Bernard Evelyn Relleen, who encountered the *Moewe* when she captured the ship he was serving in. The ship in question was the British steamship *Appam*. In the early afternoon of 15 January 1916 as she was making her way from Freetown to Plymouth she was encountered by the German raider which ultimately sent its latest prize to a neutral port, where Bernard Relleen's war ended due to being landed on American shores, at this time a neutral country.[3]

Roland's First World War experiences took a dramatic turn on 10 March 1917 when he also encountered the *Moewe*. He related the story of the New Zealand Shipping Company's ship, the *Otaki,* to a reporter in April 1919. Roland was the ship's first officer who was at the centre of the action on the afternoon of 10 March. It was at about 2.30pm, when the *Otaki* was roughly 350 miles east of St Miguel, when she spotted the *Moewe*, but as Roland related, 'There was nothing particular about her appearance to give rise to suspicion. She was going into a heavy head sea, while we were in ballast, and going our full speed.'[4]

The situation soon changed when the *Moewe* signalled the *Otaki* to stop but the *Otaki's* Captain, Archibald Bisset Smith, refused to do so. The *Otaki* was outgunned having as it did only one 4.7-inch stern gun, whereas the *Moewe* was fitted with four 5.9-inch, one 4.1-inch, and two 22-pounder guns. McNish described what happened next:

> The truth was brought home to us with dramatic force when the overtaking vessel was within a mile of us, for we heard the report of a gun and a shell ploughed up the water near us. That fixed her identity beyond all doubt, and all hands were called to the boats, while the gun was manned. Within a few seconds we had opened firing, and the gunners did excellent work, for, in spite of the heavy swell, out of twelve rounds, fired, eight hits were registered.[5]

K. T. Roussell's 'Sinking of the SS Otaki by the German Raider Moewe'

The *Otaki's* gunners had caused a fire to be started on the *Moewe*, which was put out with some difficulty. They also killed five of the *Moewe's* crew and wounded ten others. The fight put up by the *Otaki's* crew might very well have succeeded but she was simply outgunned and in the ensuing combat lost four of her crew. Captain Smith ordered the crew to lower the boats so that they might have a chance of survival. The ship was heavily on fire and with a combination of rough seas the situation did not bode well for her crew. Two of the five boats had been smashed and so the crew's chances of survival looked slim. The last boat was instructed to wait in case of any more survivors.

Roland, Captain Smith and the carpenter waited with the vessel for a further half an hour as Roland noted:

> There was a huge hole in the vessel abreast of No. 4 hatch on the port side large enough for a motor car to pass through and as the last boat was in danger of being caught by the suction, she was let go and drifted astern.

At this point, the last boat waiting for surviving crew members was valiantly trying to keep up with the *Otaki* but was being left behind. Roland explains what happened next:

> Thereupon I went down below to try to ascertain the extent of the casualties. I took one or two hatches off and found the water up to between decks. Here I came across the ship's carpenter. As we were about to undertake a search for the Captain he appeared along the starboard alleyway. He informed us that there was a trimmer on the foredeck with his leg shot away, and asked us to render assistance. The man was in a semi delirious condition, and as the ship was getting well down, the only thing that could be done for him was to put a lifebelt and buoy around him and drop him into the sea in the hope of one of the boats picking him up.

After they lowered the trimmer, Roland and the carpenter consulted with Captain Smith as to what action to take next and it was decided to lash three lifebuoys together and attach them via the rail so that all three could lower themselves into the water with the last man releasing the line. However only Roland and the carpenter were to escape for as Roland relayed in his interview, 'Within a very short time the ship got practically under water by the stern and we decided that it was time to go.'

Captain Smith, with his Gieve's life saving waistcoat on told both men to make their way off the ship whilst he let go of the line. This unselfish act from a devoted Captain was the last time anyone saw him as Roland witnessed:

> Up to that time the captain had indicated every intention of going with us...the last sight we got of the captain was as he stood by the rail.

Roland believed that Captain Smith had gone down with the ship and for his 'conspicuous gallantry and devotion' Smith was awarded a posthumous Victoria Cross, which was one of only two to be awarded to the Merchant Service during the war. His family donated the medal to his old college, 'Robert Gordon's' in Aberdeen, the Otaki Shield to be presented to a boy who showed exceptional character. In addition to the awarding of the Shield the recipient received a travel scholarship and every year, except those of the Second World War, the Otaki Shield recipient has travelled in New Zealand, a country closely associated with Captain Smith.

As for Roland and the carpenter, they found themselves drifting astern after, 'narrowly escaping being sucked down by the powerful suction from the shell hole...' and shortly afterwards, 'the Otaki disappeared beneath the waves.' Witnessing one's small rowing craft capsize on the Thames is enough to set the heart beating a little faster so one can only imagine the extra adrenaline pumping through Roland's veins that afternoon as he saw this towering vessel being swallowed up by the open sea. Roland explains what happened next:

> Three quarters of an hour afterwards we were picked up by the *Moewe*, where an attempt by the prisoners from other ships to mutiny when we fought the raider had been quelled, and we found her to be in pretty bad condition. She had been hit by seven shells, and was badly on fire. It took thirty-six hours to extinguish the flames. We were given shocking accommodation while we were on the way to Kiel...

Nothing more was heard of Roland until July 1917 when he sent a postcard from his prisoner of war camp to the New Zealand Shipping Company:

> I beg to state that the *Otaki* was sunk on 10 March by a German cruiser. I regret to report the following casualties:
>
> Captain SMITH went down with his ship.
> Chief Steward WILLIS was drowned.
> KILNER and MARTIN, apprentices and KEWSTON, seaman and A H LITTLE, third engineer, were killed.
> GLITZ, trimmer, had a leg amputated
> JACKSON, seaman, PAYNE, apprentice, LANCASTER, RANDALL and GROVES, firemen, were wounded but not seriously.
>
> Several others were slightly wounded. All hands lost every stitch they had except what they stood up in. Please excuse postcard, as it is all I am allowed to write.[6]

Roland spent time in six different POW camps until his release in December 1918 from the German POW camp, Karlsruhe. Unfortunately we know nothing about his experiences as a POW. For his part in the *Otaki* action Roland was awarded the Distinguished Service Order (DSO), being gazetted on 24 May 1919.

Roland's career at sea continued until the day before the D-Day landings when he reached the age of retirement. During the course of the Second World War he commanded the Merchant Ship *Suffolk*, which landed crated aircraft and other supplies at Diego Suarez during October 1942.[7] He was also in command of a number of voyages in convoy travelling thousands of miles across the oceans with cargoes of cheese, meat and various supplies for civilians and soldiers at home in Britain and to various British bases such as the one in Malta.

References

1 A. Hurd, The Merchant Navy, Vol. II (John Murray, 1924) pp. 380-381.

2 http://www.criticalpast.com/video/65675049917_Count-Dohna_SMS-Moewe_fishing-steamer_Fleet-Admiral-greets.

3 For more on the *Appam's* fate and the Maritime legal issues which surrounded her status as a Prize see A. Hurd, *The Merchant Navy, Vol. II*, pp. 386-387 and pp. 390-391 Also see *The Portcullis*, Christmas Term, 1916, p. 39 for mention of Relleen, N.B. Spelt wrong in *The Portcullis*.

4 'Story of the *Otaki's* Doom', *Auckland Star* Vol L Issue 84, 8 April 1919, p. 2.

5 Ibid.

6 'Sinking of the SS *Otaki*', URL: http://www.nzhistory.net.nz/media/photo/sinking-ss-otaki, (Ministry for Culture and Heritage), updated 15-Jul-2013.

7 S. D. Waters, *Ordeal By Sea: The New Zealand Shipping Company in The Second World War 1939-1945* (1949), p. 171 and p. 222.

The Mascot of the Battersea Battalion

Lawrence Inkster MC *(Emanuel 1900—1906)*

Lawrence (addressed by family members as 'Lawrie') Inskter was born in a room above Battersea Library on Lavender Hill on 2 May 1891. His father was Battersea's first Borough Librarian. At Emanuel Lawrence was a member of the School choir. After leaving Emanuel Lawrence became a bank clerk with the London and South Western Bank.

In 1909 he enlisted in the Territorial Army with the 14th Battalion County of London Regiment (London Scottish). In 1914, being part of the reserves, Lawrence was called up and sailed to France with the 1st Battalion, London Scottish. Within a few weeks Lawrence's regiment saw action at Messines in fighting which became part of the First Battle of Ypres. The 31st of October 1914 was a fateful day for the London Scottish. The 1st Battalion were ordered to Ypres. Their mode of transport was 45 London buses. On the morning of the 31st the battalion saw action at Wytschaete (known to the British as Whitesheet) where they lost 190 men. They were disadvantaged by the fact that their rifles were incapable of taking the ammunition they were provided with thereby causing them to jam. Lawrence wrote to his sister Gladys on 5 November, 'You have no doubt heard about our being in action, and hope that I have been lucky enough to come out of it safely. In my last I said I had not seen Fletcher, he has turned up all right since.' In his next letter on the 7th Lawrence described the intensity of the battle:

> By the time you get this you will have heard all about our performance here. I had plenty of thrills on Saturday afternoon 31st October...
>
> We were in a trench and comparatively safe from shells that went past us and burst behind, but if one of them had landed into the trench nothing on earth could have saved us. After a time we got used to the noise they made (like an express train) and we sat tight until they went by, but sometimes they were terribly close.

Lawrence Inkster

Lawrence Inkster c.1915

> By the way, we went into the trenches in daylight, a very unusual proceeding and we were followed by aeroplanes all the time and were shelled in a village in the morning before we got into the trenches. It was there that I was knocked over by the concussion of one of them, but I was not hurt. But three or four of our chaps were wounded before we even got into action.
>
> Then after this shelling all day we had the infantry attack at night.... By some extraordinary miracle I am still alive and out of it, but I lost many of my friends, I am sorry to say.

By late November Lawrence writes about the effect of the cold weather at night-time, writing on the 24th, 'We seem likely to stay at this farm for some little time yet. It is quite a decent little show. It is not quite so cold this morning, but last night our water bottles were frozen hard. We can get hot milk and coffee several times a day and we manage to get various little luxuries with our meals.'

In January 1915 Lawrence wrote to his sister outlining his experiences in reserve during German attacks, 'The day before yesterday there was a big attack by the Germans and we were rushed up from the village where we were having 48 hours rest. Fortunately for us we were only required ... in reserve and our casualties were not heavy, but some of the other regiments had a bad time, but as usual the result was satisfactory, the Germans being slaughtered as they advanced in large numbers.' On the next day 28 January, Lawrence continued his letter explaining how the lot of a soldier meant having to prepare to move at any given moment:

> Last night we had some excitement. We have lights out here at 8.30 and about 10 o'clock last night the order came round for all the blankets to be rolled and packed on the cart and a few minutes afterwards the order followed to put on equipment and be ready to move at a moment's notice as the firing up where we had been the other day was very heavy. We rather expected it as it was the Kaiser's birthday, in fact the attack the other day was probably with a view to giving him some good news on his birthday. However, soon after we were informed that it was a washout, nothing doing, so we went and recovered our blankets and went to bed again, more cheerfully than when we got up. These are the commonplaces of a soldier's life. One always has to be prepared to do anything at any moment.

In his time with the London Scottish Lawrence wrote to his sister on a variety of topics, from the death of colleagues, the layout of the trenches and the need to keep secret any information he had written in case it fell into the enemy's hands.

Death at the Front – Letter 02.03.1915:

> Just a quick few lines to let you know that I am going on all right. We are back in action again rather sooner than expected. But for my part I find it rather a relief, as the firing line in some ways is more restful than a rest camp. ...
>
> We have nearly been here two days now and we have only had two casualties so far. One poor chap in my company was killed last night by an unlucky stray bullet and we buried him this morning in a nice little graveyard. Well looked after, some little distance from here. It is satisfactory to know that we are able to give our fallen comrades a better burial.

The Trenches – Letter 19.05.1915:

> We are in action again, as you have probably heard. I was up in the trenches 48 hours ago, and now I believe we are going to have three days on and three days out, half the battalion at a time. It seems pretty decent up here and we can go nearly all the way by a very long communication trench, which makes it fairly safe, but it is an ordeal going through it, as it is very narrow and winds a great deal. ... The trenches and dugouts are very well made, for instance the dugout I share with four others is almost high enough to stand upright in, and it has a fireplace and a front door. ... It is like a small town almost, with back streets etc. Several times when I set out to get to another part of the trenches, owing to the weird winding nature thereof I walked for some-time and found myself back where I started.

The same letter is revealing for the insight it affords us of how soldiers fighting on the front viewed public perceptions at home and the frustrations Lawrence felt at those who played down the seriousness of the war:

> Yes, the *Lusitania* business was abominable, but to us out here we hope things like this will bring the war home to the public at home. It seems to us that the general public will never realise the seriousness of the war and the fact that we shall need every ounce of effort there is in the country. The fact that so many of the young men of the country have nothing else to do than attend to sport and pleasure is, at a time like this, wicked and while some of our press continue their cheap nastiness I cannot imagine recruiting progressing as it should.

Local inhabitants – Letter 25.05.1915:

> I have been for a walk to a part of the town where a few inhabitants still hang on and where we can still buy various things, chiefly bread, butter and eggs. These people tell us that in the early part of the war they stood at their doors and watched the French and Germans fighting with bayonets at a little distance. There is evidence of very fierce fighting in the town.

Maintaining Secrecy – Letter 28.06.1915:

> By the way be careful even among friends about mentioning anything I may have said in any of my letters. People talk, the Germans overlook nothing in their efforts to get the best of it. I don't think I have ever said anything that they don't know already, but you never know. Did I ever mention the fact that we have actually had Germans dressed in British uniforms giving orders to our men. They have usually been done in afterwards.

On 4 August 1915, which marked the first year anniversary of the outbreak of war, Lawrence reflected on his position noting the lighter side of his experience:

> Well, we have reached the anniversary of the declaration of war without any undue excitement. There was a certain amount of windup about a possible celebration. By the time this reaches you, it will be twelve months since I left your place.
>
> My company was relieved this morning and we have come down to the village at the back. We are going out digging tonight ... We had many cups of tea at the little stall, that has been set up lately, this afternoon, with cheerful tunes going on the gramophone and the scene reminded me very much of school sports with the music, al fresco tea and a large gun ... to represent the pistol starting the races, rather a powerful substitute by the way.

A local south London newspaper *The South Western Star* reported on a lucky escape during Lawrence's time with the London Scottish, 'An instance of the good fortune that attended him was that one night he and a number of others were sleeping on the floor of a room. A shell dropped through the roof and burst. The splinters mostly flew upwards, like the sparks, but the roof came down, as also did some of the brickwork. No-one was killed, though several were severely injured. Lieut. Inkster escaped without a scratch.'[1] By the time the report was printed Lawrence was in another regiment and the paper hoped that, '[Lawrence] will prove the mascot of the Battersea Battalion.'

In September 1915 Lawrence was in England for officer training and received a commission as a 2nd Lt. in the 10th (Service) Battalion, The Queen's Royal West Surrey Regiment. In February 1916 Lawrence married his fiancée Elsa. Lawrence's best man was William Archer 'Joe' Pope who also attended Emanuel before completing his education at Christ's Hospital. Joe Pope was working at Bilbrough and Co. shipbrokers at the outbreak of the war before he volunteered for service joining the Queen Victoria Rifles. Joe went with the first contingent of Territorials to France in September 1914. He served throughout the winter of 1914 and whilst engaged in action at Ypres in March 1915 was wounded by a bullet which passed through his foot. Joe was evacuated to England and during his recovery the Mayor of Battersea, Mr. Simmons, recommended him for a Commission. Joe became a 2nd Lt. in The Queen's Royal West Surrey Regiment, later being promoted to Captain.[2]

The contrast between celebrating a wedding in February 1916 and manning machine guns and scrambling to put gas helmets on in June 1916 couldn't be greater, but this was the life millions of men experienced. Lawrence wrote to Gladys on 19 June:

> I was on the go so much last night that I was unable to open a parcel from Elsa which arrived at dinnertime last night until about 4.30 this morning. Soon after dinner last night both Hoggett and Bretherton (my company commander) were hit by a machine gun, Hoggett having a useful one in the shoulder and Bretherton getting it badly in the lungs. We had not much hope for Bretherton last night, but he is reported to have improved this morning. Soon after that we had a gas alarm, which is a nuisance as the gas helmets hamper one so. Fortunately we had got Hoggett and Bretherton dressed before that began and anyhow no gas came over our way. So there

Lawrence Inkster (second from right, seated) with men of the 10th (Service) Battalion, The Queen's Royal West Surrey Regiment

was Hopkinson ... and myself to run the company. Pope had the machine guns to look after.

Lawrence wrote shortly after his regiment carried out a raid on German trenches on the 26th to the 27th of July 1916 in which he had manned the machine guns.[3]

> We have had our first important show since I wrote to you last and it went off well. The five officers who played leading parts all got wounded and only Ranson got there and carried him through and covered himself with glory. Since then we have shifted our position in the line back to our old spot and after a rather long spell in, we are back in our old billets again.
>
> Some of my platoon acquitted themselves very well in the Hun trenches and I was rather bucked when they told me afterwards that they wished I had been with them. Did I mention that Ranson was hit while carrying in his fourth wounded man?

Interestingly Lawrence also relates a rather daring story about one of the men in his company which wouldn't have gone a miss in one of the satirical magazines produced by the regiments, 'One of our fellows took a bundle of English newspapers over to the Hun lines last night, but he was unable to leave them there, as there were too many patrols about.' A little later in his letter Lawrence writes, 'I have just heard the fellow did leave the newspapers last night, but it was a good distance from the Hun trenches. They are flopping about there today, so possibly Mr. Hun will come out and fetch them tonight.' One should imagine the 'fellow' in question didn't approach the German lines shouting, 'Extra! Extra! Read all about it!', but the episode does illustrate the sometimes surreal nature of trench life, for surrounded by so much death were lighter moments.

By September 1916 Lawrence was promoted to the rank of Lieutenant. On 4 October Lawrence mentions that he was sending 'Joe' Pope, who was further up the line, some items, 'I am sending my burberry up as he hasn't got one and various articles of food and drink, including something hot in a thermos.' On that very same day, 'Joe' Pope, who had been by this time promoted to the rank of Captain, was badly wounded. Having been evacuated to the 36th Casualty Clearing Station he died four days later aged 24. The commander of the regiment, Lieutenant Colonel Oakley, himself at home recovering from a wound, wrote to Joe's parents, 'It is a great blow to me and the regiment, for officers like him are few and far between nowadays. A better officer in every way never wore the King's uniform. He has always been the greatest help to me, hardworking, clever, trustworthy and beloved by officers and men.' Lawrence was moved by his best man's death writing to his sister, 'Isn't it perfectly sickening about poor old Pope? He was my oldest friend in the regiment along with poor old Hoggett. It is curious that it only struck me this afternoon (I have been too busy to think before) that I have been over the ground where poor Joe was killed lately, but of course I never had the opportunity to look for his grave.'

Lawrence organised concert parties during his time with The Queen's but in a letter to his sister in November 1916 he also conceived of a Grand Opera based upon life in the trenches but questioned being able to construct such a show:

> The difficulty is that there is so much of the commonplace in war and the only time such stirring moments could arise would be in the middle of a strafe and then I am afraid it would not be very convincing to have all the principals and chorus standing up and shrieking. That was all very well in the old days but it requires a greater brain than mine to conceive the necessary musical accompaniment to, 17, 15, 12, 10, 9, 6, 4, 2, in 3, 18 pounder shells, heavy, medium and big trench mortars,

Lawrence Inkster's Battalion Concert Party first performed in May 1916

> hand grenades and machine Lewis guns. Tchaikovsky is the boy for that. ... I am very much afraid that modern war does not fit in with opera somehow. Farce is the thing for it.

In early 1917 life at the Front was arduous as Lawrence describes in a letter on 7 January:

> The last night's wiring I did was very near to the Huns' lines and the moon was not sufficiently down and I had my first casualty on that job. I only had five men out there, but one of them caught it in the foot. He did rather wonderfully, rushing back fell into a shell hole full of water, scrambled out and fell into the trench before I could get at him. I got rather excited trying to dress him as he was raving very wildly, but I got it done and persuaded him he was very lucky and by that time the stretcher bearers were up and took him away.

In a letter from 17 January Lawrence describes the Herculean efforts of his men who were battling the elements in the front line:

> It is snowing hard now and both last night and the night before it snowed practically all the time I was out with my working party. I am out every night for six hours work. I am officer in charge night work in the front line. Wonderful feats of engineering are required there beyond your wildest dreams and a heavy fall of snow each night knocks over the results of several hours' strenuousity [sic]. I am perfectly amazed at the spirit of the men. Imagine, dear, if you can working six hours with shovels covered with snow, frozen sandbags and in water anything from your ankles to the knees and if you slip, up to your waist or further. Yet these fellows keep slogging away. Of course they grouse a bit, but they really are wonderfully willing. Of course where I am working at night is absolutely exposed to the Hun in daytime and I can only think he is waiting until we have got well on with it and then he will knock it over and we start again.

On 24 February, Lawrence led "B" Company 10th The Queen's Royal West Surreys on a raid of the German trenches in the Hollandscheschuur Salient, near Vierstraat for which he won the Military Cross. Among the objectives the battalion were to take prisoners and destroy enemy positions. In the late afternoon of 24 February the attack was launched. After less than two hours the Battalion achieved their objectives but at a heavy cost.[4] The men of his company wrote him a note expressing their admiration, 'In remembrance to you on your great courage and bravery, also devotion to the N.C.O.s (Non-Commissioned Officers) and men under your command.' His MC citation gazetted 17 April 1917 read:

> For conspicuous gallantry and devotion to duty during a raid on the enemy's trenches. He handled his company with marked ability and carried out the task allotted to him with conspicuous success. He subsequently reorganised the defence of the front line.

Of this action Lawrence wrote to his sister on 24 March:

> As regards my coming through unscathed some of my friends, one in particular, told me beforehand, that I was bound to be all right. No engine of frightfulness capable of strafing me having yet been invented. Some of the lads did get a bit restive about me, as I was about the last of the battalion to return and wild rumours got about. A sergeant in my company is another weirdly lucky man, one of our own 18 pounders going into the parapet beside him, where he was standing just before going over, but it didn't explode.

During the Battle of Passchendaele (Third Ypres) Lawrence

was responsible for saving his Commanding Officer's life. The 10th Battalion were engaged in the early hours of the first of August 1917 in clearing enemy positions east of Battle Wood near Hollebeke. Lieutenant-Colonel Roland Gwynne decided to move forward into No-Man's Land to assess whether it was possible to attack the German positions without the covering Allied barrage which by 4.40am he realised would be of little help. Unfortunately Gwynne was hit twice in the thigh by machine gun bullets shattering his thigh bone into twelve pieces. As he lay in the dark, his men not knowing his position, Gwynne decided to blow gently on his whistle. Fortunately Lawrence heard him and at once arranged for a party of stretcher bearers to accompany him to Gwynne's position. They managed to get Gwynne onto the stretcher and get him back to the trenches. It was later revealed that had he lain out any longer it is likely Gwynne would have bled to death as an artery had been cut. On 17 August Gwynne wrote to Lawrence from B Ward, 20 General Hospital, 'I shall never forget your kindness to me the morning I was hit and your unselfish bravery fetching that stretcher. I can never be thankful enough to you.' Lawrence and Roland Gwynne remained friends for years after the war.

On 20 September 1917 Lawrence, now promoted to the rank of acting Captain, was wounded by a bullet to the right shoulder during the Battle of the Menin Road near Ridge Wood.[5] The early morning raid had been devastating with the Battalion only being able to advance 50 yards before two German machine guns opened fire killing two officers. Lawrence later returned to England and spent a long period recovering from his wounds. His recovery was spent in several hospitals and places of recuperation for wounded servicemen. By March 1918 he expressed his frustrations of not being at the Front, writing on 23 March from Torquay:

> It seems perhaps that I am wasting time here, to be living in comfort and luxury when there is work to be done over there, but after all it is undeniably true that I am not yet in a fit state for any prolonged strain, though in my clear moments I was never better equipped mentally than I am now for my work and I should probably find were I suddenly transported into action that I should be equal to all possible requirements. But the reaction afterwards would be too strong and we have no time for the weaknesses of the human machine over there.

Lawrence returned to France in late 1918 but shortly before he embarked on 20 October he wrote to his sister about his experiences in a manner which was not perhaps untypical of many men, 'Such is the human heart, when over there one wants to get home and when here one wants to go back there.' By November Lawrence was back there and on 24 November wrote:

> I was at Etaples when the armistice was signed. There was very little excitement there. It seems to have been very lively in London. Fighting went on pretty fiercely until the actual moment the armistice began. Our boys have had a very strenuous time for the last few months. The civilians showered flowers on most of the first troops to arrive and everywhere overwhelmed us with kindness.

Flight Lieutenant Lawrence Inkster c.1942

Lawrence spent November 1918 to February 1919 on various official duties such as officiating Courts Martial but on the lighter side he continued arranging concert parties. Lawrence travelled through Belgium with the 10th Battalion which as part of the 41st Division was to be part of the Army of Occupation in Germany but in February 1919 he was demobilised. In May 1932 Lawrence made a battlefield pilgrimage along with hundreds of men of the 41st Division to pay their respects to the fallen. He laid a wreath with Colonel Oakley on behalf of the 10th Battalion at the unveiling of the 41st Division memorial in the village of Flers on the Somme.

In the Second World War Lawrence was appointed commander of the Battersea Air Training Corps with the rank of Flight Lieutenant. Lawrence's sons all attended Emanuel School and all served in the Second World War. Alan (Emanuel 1934–1939) joined the RAF and for much of the war was based with the ground crew at the R.A.F. station Mildenhall in Suffolk. Donald (Emanuel 1934–1942) joined the Royal Engineers but owing to an accident served with the Royal Army Pay Corps. His story is told in a later chapter. Lawrence Junior (Emanuel 1934–1937) was a Captain in the London Scottish Regiment and served in the Indian Army as part of the 51st Frontier Force in the Burma Campaigns.

References

1 *The South Western Star*, 3rd December, 1915, p. 5.
2 William Archer 'Joe' Pope's obituary appears in *The South Western Star*, 20 October, 1916, p. 5.
3 For further details on the raid see Paul McCue, *Wandsworth & Battersea Battalions in the Great War* (2010), pp. 184-186.
4 For further details on the raid see McCue, *Wandsworth and Battersea Battalions*, pp. 199-200.
5 Ibid. pp. 212-213.

Major Sholto Douglas, Commanding Officer No. 84 Squadron RAF, 1918

William Sholto Douglas

1st Baron Douglas of Kirtleside, Marshal of the Royal Air Force GCB, MC, DFC *(Emanuel 1904—1905)*

Sholto Douglas attended Emanuel for one year between 1904 and 1905. In the first volume of his autobiography he wrote, 'The elementary education I received at St Mary's School in Balham was a sound one, and when I left it at the age of about eleven and went on to Emmanuel School [sic], in Wandsworth, I found that I could easily hold my own with the other boys of my own age in everything but Latin, which was a subject new to me.'[1] After leaving Emanuel Sholto continued his education at Tonbridge School from where he won an exhibition to Lincoln College, Oxford.

In the First World War Sholto Douglas was awarded both the MC and DFC. He remembered being naïve as to the realities of war in 1914, 'I find it a little touching to recall that I went into action mounted on a horse with a sword dangling at my saddle-bow. My views then about war were quite unrealistic and far from serious.'[2] He summed up the innocence of a generation in this reflection, 'We who were in our late teens and our early twenties in 1914 did not know that war could produce a depth of misery to which even death would be preferable; and we did not know then anything about the horror that was to be inflicted upon what came to be so well known as the Western Front. The names of the Somme and Ypres were merely those of a river in northern France and of an ancient town in Belgium.'[3]

On applying for a commission in the artillery he was nearly rejected because the medical officer at his examination failed him for flat feet, an observation rejected by Sholto who argued his case and went on to serve in the Fifth Brigade, Royal Horse Artillery in France. After two months in France he transferred to No. 2 Squadron RFC as an observer and on doing so he began a career in the air force which shaped the rest of his life. Interestingly his father joined the Army Service Corps and served in France in 1915 and 1916. Qualifying as a pilot Sholto joined No. 8 Squadron RFC in the summer of 1915 and whilst with No. 8 in January 1916 he was awarded the MC and for an action that was reported in *The Times* under the headline, 'A Risky Air Dive. British Pilot's Fine Exploit. Six Machines to Two.' On 29 December 1915 and Flying in a B.E.2c aircraft Sholto was 'ordered to do an extensive reconnaissance as far as Cambrai and St Quentin.' Sholto, his observer, James Child and escort pilot David Glen met six German Fokkers [First World War German aircraft].

Glen and two Fokkers were shot down and the remaining four set upon Sholto and his observer.[4] Child shot one Fokker down and a battle commenced between Sholto's B.E.2c and the remaining three. A mile from the lines the Fokkers turned back and Sholto landed among French heavy batteries south of Arras with what he reported was about 100 holes in the aircraft from enemy bullets. Sholto was to learn later that two of the Fokker pilots were the famous German flying aces, Oswald Boelcke and Max Immelmann. Boelcke wrote about this action in his book the English title of which is *Knight of Germany*.[5]

During the First World War Sholto served with and commanded a number of RFC squadrons, including Nos. 43 and 84 [from 1918 No. 84 RAF], in addition to being engaged in most of the major battles on the Western Front.

Over the Western Front in August 1918 Sholto encountered Hermann Göring, who was a fighter pilot in the First World War and a leading figure in the Third Reich, becoming, among other appointments, head of the Luftwaffe, the German Air Force, in the Second. Sholto remembered, 'I have wondered many times about the extent to which the course of history might have changed if, in one of our encounters in the air at this time, I had managed to draw a bead on him long enough to finish him off. It would have saved the world, and me, a lot of trouble many years later.'[6]

In 1918 Sholto was awarded the DFC for leadership of his squadron and 'successful reconnaissances of the enemy front at exceptionally low altitudes in face of intense hostile rifle and machine-gun fire.'[7]

In the Second World War Sholto was appointed as Commander of Coastal-, Fighter-, and Middle East Command but was overlooked in favour of Lord Louis Mountbatten for the position of Supreme Commander, South East Asia Command.[8] During the Battle of Britain Sholto was Deputy Chief of the Air Staff and was involved in what became known as the 'Big Wings Controversy' which was a tactical difference in the way fighter squadrons should approach enemy attack. Sholto deals with the issue rather diplomatically in the second volume of his autobiography, *Years of Command*.[9] In November 1940 he was appointed Air Officer Commanding-in-Chief of Fighter Command, an appointment that he recalled being overawed 'by the importance of such high command.' He wrote in his autobiography, 'To a large extent the fate of the British people would be resting in my hands.'[10] Being in such a strategically important role meant that Sholto spent time with Winston Churchill at the Prime Minister's retreat at Chequers and remembered, 'There were moments while we talked when Churchill would suddenly electrify us with something that he would say, and quite often he would start composing some part of what would later become one of his famous speeches.'[11] But Sholto was balanced in the account he gave of the Prime Minister noting that, 'All of

(from left to right) General Sir Alan Brooke, ACM Sir Sholto Douglas, R.G. Casey, Winston Churchill, Sir Miles Lampson and Major Randolph Churchill at the Minister of State's house, Cairo, January 1943

us who ever had any dealings with the PM could not help but become vexed at times with the way in which he would fly mercurially off on those tangents to which he was so addicated', but, summing up, Sholto concluded that a huge debt was owed by so many to Churchill for rallying a nation at its lowest ebb.[12]

At the end of 1942 Sholto was appointed Air Officer Commanding-in-Chief Middle East. In 1943 he was heavily involved in the, later, controversial operations to take the Dodecanese islands including Leros, where OE Bill Taylor fought and was made a POW. Sholto maintained that supporters of the campaign had been let down and in assessing its overall failure he made his feelings known: 'I believed at the time, and I believe now that it was the disregard by the Americans in general and the indifference of Mediterranean Air Command in particular which left us in the difficult position in which we found ourselves.'[13]

In 1944 Sholto was appointed Commander-in-Chief of Coastal Command and stayed in the post through the Allied invasion of Europe in June 1944 to the end of the War in Europe. His task during the invasion was to work 'with the Royal Navy in clearing the seas of enemy ships and submarines.'[14]

For Sholto's post-war career see the features section.

References

1 Sholto Douglas, *Years of Combat:* The First Volume of the Autobiography of Marshal of the Royal Air Force Lord Douglas of Kirtleside GCB, MC, DFC (1963), p. 28.
2 Ibid. p. 40.
3 Ibid. p. 41.
4 *Years of Combat*, pp. 117-124.
5 Ibid. p. 121.
6 Ibid. p. 326.
7 Ibid. p. 335.
8 Michael Howard, *Grand Strategy Volume IV: August 1942 – September 1943*, History of the Second World War United Kingdom Military Series (1972), p. 578 and *Years of Command*, pp. 225-226.
9 Sholto Douglas with Robert Wright, *Years of Command* (1966), pp. 88-90.
10 Ibid. p. 91.
11 Ibid. p. 146.
12 Ibid. p. 172.
13 Ibid. p. 223.
14 Sholto Douglas's despatch on Coastal Command's ops No. 38111 Supplement to the *London Gazette* 28 October 1947

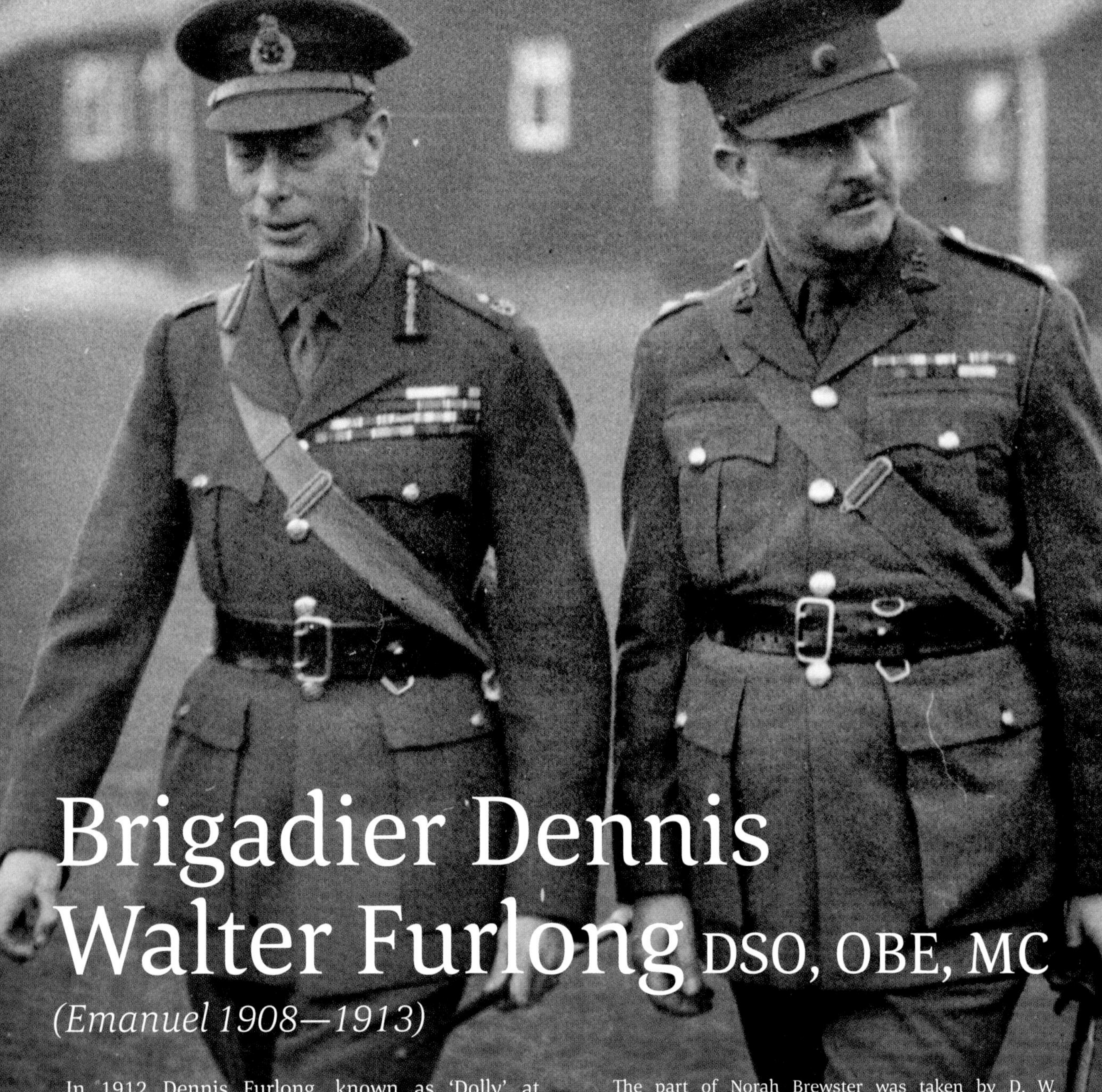

Brigadier Dennis Walter Furlong DSO, OBE, MC

(Emanuel 1908—1913)

In 1912 Dennis Furlong, known as 'Dolly' at Emanuel, played the part of Norah Brewster in a School performance of Sir Arthur Conan Doyle's play, *Waterloo*. The review in *The Portcullis* noted:

The part of Norah Brewster was taken by D. W. Furlong, who presided over the sergeant's domestic arrangements in a very fascinating way. Perhaps it might have been objected that she knew a little more of the 'sidelong glance' effect than was proper for a lass fresh from the country but the whole character was unquestionably well realised and Furlong deserves our heartiest congratulations.[1]

Colonel Dennis Furlong (right) with King George VI (left) on the King's visit to the Infantry Training Centre at Brock Barracks, Oxford Road, Reading, Berkshire, 23 October 1939

Dennis Furlong c.1917

Although acting remained a passion for Dennis throughout his life, he joined the Army and obtained his first commission in the Royal Berkshire Regiment in 1915. For his services in the First World War he was twice Mentioned in Despatches in addition to being awarded the Military Cross and the OBE. Dennis's MC was for reconnaissance work carried out at Boom Ravine in February 1917 when the 1st Battalion Royal Berkshires were carrying out raids on German positions. It was gazetted on 27 March 1917 and reads:

> For conspicuous gallantry and devotion to duty. He made a dangerous reconnaissance under very heavy fire, and sent in an invaluable report. Later, he moved up some men to fill a gap and placed several machine guns in a favourable position.

Dennis's father worked in the War Office and received congratulations for his son's MC from no lesser figure than the Foreign Secretary, Sir Edward Grey, himself, who wrote on 7 March 1917:

Scenes of devastation after the evacuation of Dunkirk, June 1940

> I need not tell you how pleased I am for I know, although you won't say much about it, you will be non-the-less bucked. And rightly so – it is great and gratifying news. When you are writing to the boy tell him how glad I am to know of it, first for his sake and then for yours. He has done you proud.[2]

Dennis had a very distinguished service career, serving as a staff officer in the Supreme War Council in Versailles from March 1918 to April 1919. Positions as a staff officer in the Rhine Army and also with the Allied Army in North Russia followed. In the inter-war period he served overseas in Iraq, Waziristan and Palestine. From 1932 to 1934 he was a staff officer at the War Office and on 15 October 1934 was appointed Brigade Major, Aldershot Command. In the late 1930s appointments in Palestine and the Transjordan were followed by promotion to Brevet Lieutenant Colonel on 1 July 1938. On 24 December 1939 Dennis took command of the 1st Battalion Royal Berkshire Regiment.

The Evacuation of Dunkirk

Far from being a deskman Dennis led from the front during the crucial month of May 1940 when the fate of the BEF hung in the balance. At first Dennis was still in command of 1st Battalion Royal Berkshire Regiment. When the Germans launched their attack on 10 May 1940 Dennis noted in his diary, 'Air raids and then Plan "D", so we are off!' The pace of the withdrawal can be likened to running a marathon every day for several weeks. Being in command meant being responsible for men's lives, not a duty to be taken lightly when confusion permeates everywhere. The 1st Battalion's long withdrawal from France was arduous but even under extreme circumstances relief was at hand, not from artillery support, or anti-tank guns but as Dennis noted on 17 May,

'Thanks due to DLI (Durham Light Infantry) for cup of tea.' Tea aside, 17 May was gruelling as the history of the Royal Berkshire Regiment recounts:

> The 1st Battalion's move was extremely long and exhausting. Their buses did not arrive and beneath a cloudless sky the sweating and weary men continued their march. After a further seventeen miles they arrived at Den Hoek, where the brigade was concentrated.[3]

Absence of B Echelon transport which carried the cooks and the food necessitated foraging with light relief being supplied as already mentioned with the DLI's cups of tea. They started off again at 8.45pm in the direction of Moerbeke. During the early hours of 18 May Dennis billeted his men at Gammarages. They had covered forty miles since fleeing the rivers Dyle and Lasne 28 hours previously. The following day, under enemy fire and having to navigate the Belgian roads congested with hundreds of refugees fleeing the German advance, the Battalion arrived at Tournai.[4]

On 20 May 1940 Dennis handed over command of 1st Battalion Royal Berkshires to Major F. N. Elliott and thereafter assumed temporary command of Sixth Infantry Brigade during the rest of the evacuation. One day in particular during this period proved extremely demanding. A strategic error had led to two companies of the Brigade being on the wrong side of the Lys Canal. Dennis made the decision to cross the bridge over the Canal to inform Lieutenant Harrison of the Royal Welch Fusiliers and the 2nd Durham Light Infantry, its sister company in Sixth Brigade, that they should retire as German tanks rained down fire on their positions. This course of events, so historian Hugh Sebag–Montefiore has argued, may have been due either to feelings of guilt, on Dennis's part, over the strategic error which led to this occurrence or Dennis being an exceptionally brave man.[5] The latter observation, when one considers Dennis's actions with the Royal Berkshires, seems justly appropriate.

On his return to England Dennis was awarded the Distinguished Service Order for his part in the evacuation of Dunkirk. His citation noted:

> Assuming command of Sixth Infantry Brigade in the period of its withdrawal from Belgium, Brigadier Furlong proved himself by personal bearing and example a leader to be trusted. On arrival in the Aire–La Bassee canal sector it was found that the sector of the front allotted to the brigade was in fact in enemy hands. When ordered to retake the line of the canal the brigade proceeded with utmost courage and determination, and although the complete success of their efforts was denied them, the brigade devoted itself to its task thereby holding the enemy during 48 critical hours notwithstanding the very heavy casualties that they suffered. Finally surrounded but indomitable, the remnants of the brigade were led back to our lines by the gallant leadership and example of Brigadier Furlong. Although decimated, the period 26–28 May must be regarded as epic days by Sixth Infantry Brigade, of which they will be deservedly proud.[6]

Dennis's wife Nancy Furlong, also made a narrow escape from France as the press reported a few weeks later, 'She was

Dennis (third from left, seated) with the Drums of the 1st Battalion (49th) Princess Charlotte of Wales's, The Royal Berkshire Regiment c.1920s

Brigadier Furlong and Mrs Nancy Furlong outside Buckingham Palace, July 1940

a driver for the French Headquarters staff and just got out in the last sardine boat from Bordeaux.' Nancy served with the Women's Mechanised Transport Corps.

On 5 September 1940 whilst inspecting coastal defences along the Yorkshire coast Dennis and his intelligence officer Lieutenant M. D. P. Magill were accidentally killed by a mushroom mine.[7] It was a great tragedy that someone who had shown such gallantry only a few months previously should have lost his life in an accident such as this. Dennis was buried in Kilham Cemetery in Yorkshire.

After his death a fellow officer in the Royal Berkshire Regiment wrote a eulogy for Dennis which was published in *The Times*:

> The death in action of Brigadier Furlong, DSO., OBE., MC., is a severe loss to the Army, which loses a very brave and capable commander. His brother officers in The Royal Berkshire Regiment have lost an old comrade whose best years were devoted to service abroad with the first battalion. He will always be remembered by the happy band of warriors who served with the 49th at Hillah in Mesopotamia and at Kasvin in NW Persia. Later at Bareilly, and on the NW Frontier, when he was adjutant of the battalion, he was responsible for a large share in the efficiency of a very good battalion. His quiet humour and his talent for seeing the amusing side of the occasional reverses which fell to our lot, led him to play leading parts in the regimental concert party for many years, while his contributions to the China Dragon were invariably welcomed by an editor to whom such material came all too seldom. The care which he lavished on his particular hobby, the drums of the 49th exemplified the attention to detail applied to everything Dennis undertook. Although not naturally athletic he was a keen tennis player, represented his company at hockey, and was always ready to turn out for the officers in their frequent contests with the sergeants at every sort of game.
>
> After several hot weathers in the plains, shared with the same few comrades, the writer got to know Dennis better than most others. His natural wit and powers of repartee added to the pleasure of dining in mess after a long Indian day, which never failed to supply him with incidents lending themselves to humorous description. In later years the Staff College claimed him, and a succession of Staff appointments prevented him from serving with the regiment. Occasional meetings in the hunting field and joyous reunions at the regimental dinner showed that Dennis had not lost the entertaining insouciance of Bareilly days. His gallantry in the recent operations in France was rewarded with the DSO. Had he lived he would have gone far in his profession.[8]

References

1 *The Portcullis*, Easter Term 1912, p. 16.
2 Letter from Sir Edward Grey to Mr. Furlong, 7 March 1917. A digital copy can be found in the Emanuel School Archive.
3 Brigadier Gordon Blight, *The History of the Royal Berkshire Regiment, 1920-1947*, (1953), p.195.
4 For an overview of the 1st Battalion during the evacuation see Gordon Blight, *Royal Berkshire Regiment*, Ch.5.
5 Hugh Sebag–Montefiore, *Dunkirk: Fight to the Last Man* , (2006), p. 294.
6 Reprinted in *The Portcullis*, Spring Term 1941, pp. 7-8.
7 For a description of what happened see Reel 13 from Harry Moses interview with Paul Armstrong, IWM Catalogue No. 14974 from 26 mins to 32 mins.
8 *The Times*, Wednesday 11 September 1940.

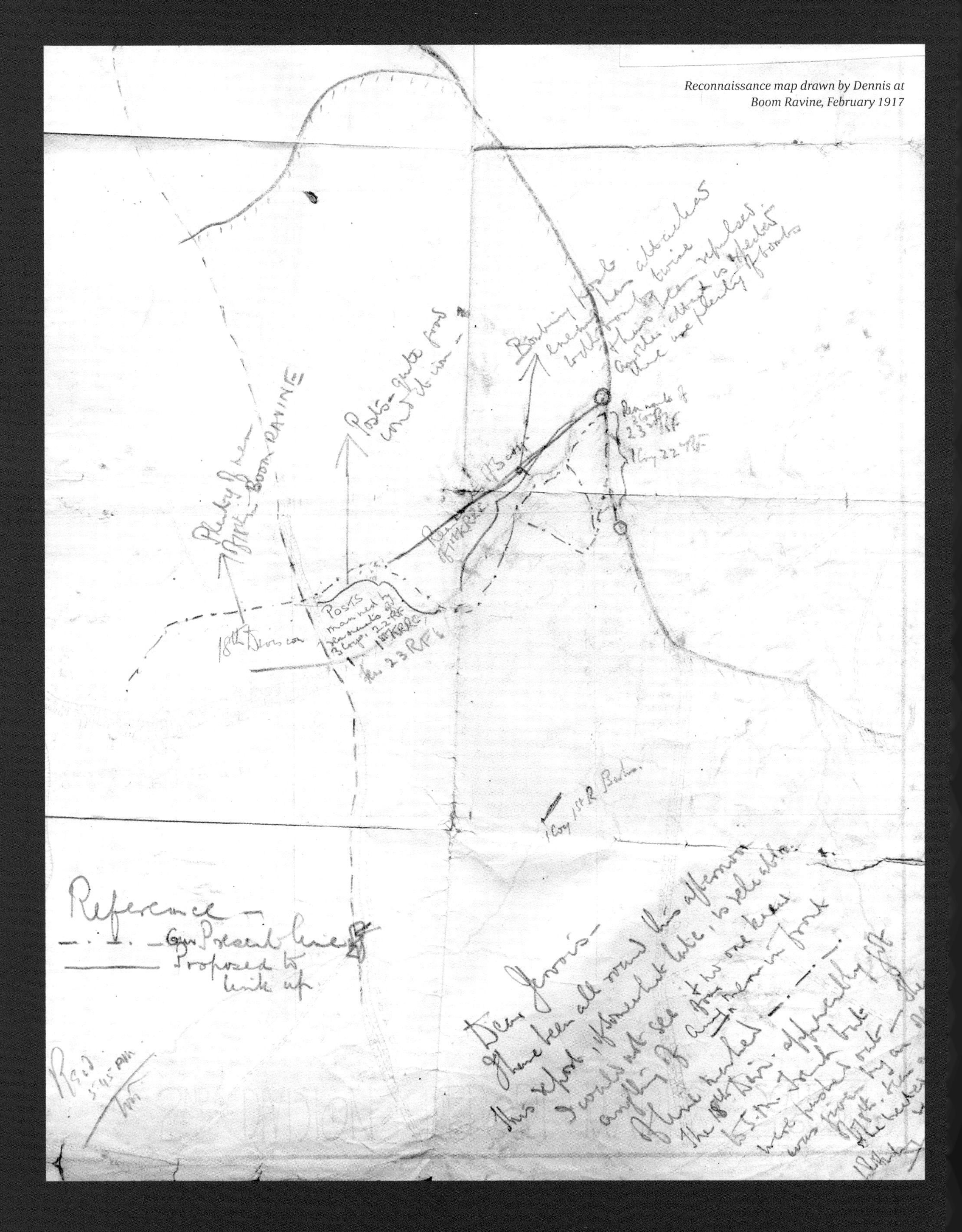

Reconnaissance map drawn by Dennis at Boom Ravine, February 1917

Leader of the First Air Raid on Mannheim, Christmas Eve 1917

Air-Vice Marshal Cecil Alfred Stevens, CB, CBE, MC and Bar, DL *(Emanuel 1908–1914)*

At Emanuel Cecil Stevens was a member of the OTC. He also once played a housemaid in a School adaptation of *Vice Versa*, a novel by F. Anstey. After leaving Emanuel Cecil entered Sandhurst and in 1916 he was commissioned in the Duke of Wellington's (West Riding) Regiment. He transferred to the RFC in early 1917. On Christmas Eve 1917 he led the first British raid of ten De Hallivand DH-4 (nicknamed 'The Flaming Coffin') aircraft over Mannheim which was reportedly the longest duration bombing raid up to that point in the First World War.

The War Office reported on 30 December 1917:

> Two of our formations, totalling ten machines, crossed the line at a height of 9,000 feet between 10 and 10.15a.m. The two formations arrived over the objective almost simultaneously and in spite of heavy and accurate anti-aircraft fire, dropped their bombs from a height of over 13,000 feet.
>
> Sixteen 112lb bombs and two 230lb bombs were dropped in all, four bursts being observed in the main station, several in the Lanz works, two in Ludwigshafen and several in the munitions factory between Mundenheim and Rheingonnheim, bursts being partially confirmed by photographs taken at the time.
>
> Two formations of enemy aeroplanes were encountered, totalling eleven machines, of which, however, only five reached the height of the bombing machines and these did not attempt to attack at close range.
>
> The anti-aircraft defences around Mannheim appeared strong and brought down one of our machines which was last seen descending under control. In addition, one of our observers was wounded, but reached home safely.
>
> Haze and mist added to the difficulties of the operation, some towns in the Rhine valley being completely covered.[1]

According to the official British history of the war in the air, the attack resulted in the deaths of two civilians and the wounding of twelve others whilst official German reports claimed that no military damage was incurred.[2] British bombing raids of German industrial targets started in October 1917 as a 'reprisal' for German aerial night attacks on London in September 1917.[3] But the Mannheim raid has an interesting 'What If' scenario associated with it. According to a newspaper report originating with a reporter in Switzerland at the time, the raid could have changed the course of history if only it had been scheduled to take place a little earlier than it did. The article suggests that less than one hour before the raid the Kaiser and his Staff had been returning from the Verdun front on their way to Berlin when they stopped at Mannheim Station. Their train was reportedly the last to leave the station before the British raid which partially destroyed it.[4]

Cecil was awarded the Military Cross and a Bar to his MC. The citation for the MC states:

> For conspicuous gallantry and devotion to duty. He took part in over 30 successful operations over enemy lines, including long distance photographic reconnaissance and bombing raids. On one occasion he was heavily attacked by enemy aeroplanes, one of which he destroyed and returned with excellent photographs and with his machine badly shot about. On another occasion, when leading a bombing raid, the formation was heavily attacked by enemy aeroplanes. He skilfully kept the formation together and led it back to the aerodrome. He consistently set a fine example by his skill and determination.

The citation of a Bar to his MC noted:

> For conspicuous gallantry and devotion to duty as a leader, of numerous bombing raids. On one occasion he led ten machines a distance of 130 miles from his aerodrome, obtaining good results. During all the raids in which he acted as leader he has lost only one machine and he has invariably given a splendid example of skill and courage. His skill and determination have had an admirable influence in his squadron.

After the First World War he remained in the air force and was stationed in India between 1924 and1930 in addition to other posts. According to his obituary, as a Wing Commander at Air Staff HQ No. 11 Group in 1936, he was involved in the early application of radar in addition to his involvement in the layout of the group underground operations room which was later the command centre for the RAF's operations during the Battle of Britain. At the outbreak of the Second World War he was a Senior Air Staff Officer (SASO) at the HQ of the British Forces in Aden. In 1941 he returned to England to become a S.A.S.O. at the HQ of Balloon Command. He was also SASO, of No. 9 Group, Fighter Command, which was responsible for the defence of North West England and for one month in November 1943 Cecil was temporarily appointed AOC (Air Officer in Command) of the Group. In 1944 he was appointed Air Officer in charge of Administration, 3rd Tactical Air Force which supported Allied air operations in Burma. Cecil had further appointments at Air HQ Burma and as A.O.C. Allied Air Forces in the Dutch East Indies. His last appointment was as S.A.S.O., Home Command from 1951 to 1954. He retired shortly after this. In 1955 he inspected the Emanuel Combined Cadet Force (CCF) and on Saturday 29 November 1958 he was on his way to an Old Emanuel Association dinner when in the afternoon he was taken ill. He died later that day.[5] Cecil Stevens had previously been President of the Old Emanuel Association.

Cecil Stevens second from left in discussion with Air Commander-in-Chief, South East Asia Air Marshal Sir Keith Park in the War Room at Headquarters Strategic Air Force, Eastern Air Command in Calcutta, India

Cecil Stevens by Walter Stoneman, 1951

References

1. Leonard Miller, *The Chronicles of 55 Squadron RFC and RAF* (1919) pp. 55-56.
2. H. A. Jones, *The War in the Air: Being the Story of the Part Played in the Great War by the Royal Air Force, Vol. VI* (Oxford, 1937), pp. 126-7.
3. For an interesting discussion on the term 'reprisal' as associated with the British bombing raids see H. A. Jones, *The War in the Air: Vol. VI*, pp. 125-126.
4. Miller, *Chronicles of 55 Squadron*, p. 54.
5. *The Portcullis*, No. 202, December 1958, pp. 3-4.

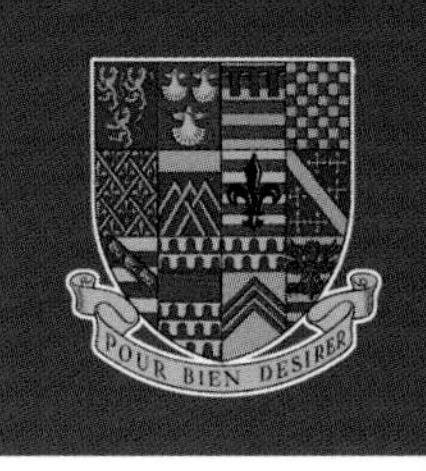

The First Casualties of 1939

Flt Lt Frederick Ernest Royston King

(Emanuel 1926–1930)

On leaving School Frederick joined the RAF following a brief period in the Merchant Navy. He was commissioned as a regular officer from RAF Uxbridge in the mid-1930s. He learned to fly at No. 4 Flying Training School. Abu Suier, Egypt. Frederick then converted to Sunderland flying boats at 204 Squadron RAF, Calshot, Southampton Water and served with 204 Squadron successively at RAF Bircham Newton, Norfolk, at Felixstowe, Suffolk and finally at RAF Invergordon.

Frederick King in Emanuel OTC uniform

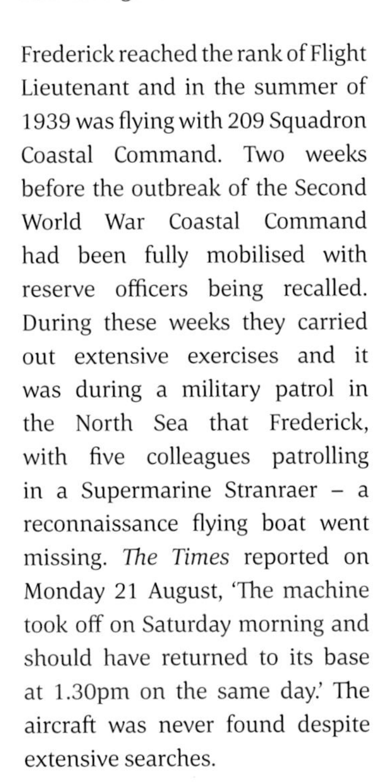

Frederick reached the rank of Flight Lieutenant and in the summer of 1939 was flying with 209 Squadron Coastal Command. Two weeks before the outbreak of the Second World War Coastal Command had been fully mobilised with reserve officers being recalled. During these weeks they carried out extensive exercises and it was during a military patrol in the North Sea that Frederick, with five colleagues patrolling in a Supermarine Stranraer – a reconnaissance flying boat went missing. *The Times* reported on Monday 21 August, 'The machine took off on Saturday morning and should have returned to its base at 1.30pm on the same day.' The aircraft was never found despite extensive searches.

Herbert Brian Lightoller

(Emanuel 1928–1929)

Herbert Brian, known as Brian, Lightoller was the son of Charles Lightoller, the most senior surviving officer of the sinking of the *Titanic*. Brian was a pilot of a Blenheim Bomber, serial number N6189, part of 107 Squadron Bomber Command. In the opening salvo of the Second World War, Bomber Command sent out fifteen Blenheims and fourteen Wellington Bombers to attack German warships. Brian's crew left for Wilhelmshaven, on the afternoon of 4 September in the second wave of bombers, where the German cruiser *Emden* had been spotted during reconnaissance operations. It is believed that Brian's crew didn't get a chance of firing upon the *Emden* and instead was shot down by anti-aircraft (flak) fire. 107 Squadron lost four of its five planes on the raid. Brian was among the first British casualties of the Second World War.[1]

At first, details were sketchy and it was hoped that Brian had survived but official German reports were received two months later confirming that Brian and his crew had all been killed. They were initially buried with full military honours in the Naval Garrison Cemetery in Wilhelmshaven but Brian and his crew were later exhumed and reburied in the British Military Cemetery at Oldenburg (Sage).[2]

Nine months later on 31 May 1940, Charles Lightoller with his son Roger, left Cubitt's Yacht Basin in Chiswick for Ramsgate. On his yacht *Sundowner* they made their way to Ramsgate. At 10am on 1 June he sailed for Dunkirk. The resulting story of the rescue of 130 men, without loss, from the beaches of Dunkirk is one Charles Lightoller attributed in large part to Brian. The following account by Charles details how young Brian through conversations with his father before he was killed, contributed to saving men of the British Expeditionary Force:

During the whole embarkation we had quite a lot of attention from enemy planes, but derived an amazing degree of comfort from the fact that the Worcester's Anti-Aircraft guns kept up an everlasting bark overhead.

Casting off and backing out we entered the Roads again, there it was continuous and unmitigated hell. The troops were just splendid and of their own initiative detailed look-outs ahead, astern and abeam for inquisitive planes as my attention was pretty wholly occupied watching the steering and passing orders to Roger at the wheel. Any time an aircraft seemed inclined to try its hand on us, one of the look-outs would just call quietly, "Look out for this bloke, skipper", at the same time pointing. One bomber that had been particularly offensive, itself came under the notice of one of our fighters and suddenly plunged vertically into the sea just about fifty yards astern of us. It was the only time any man ever raised his voice above a conversational tone, but as that big black bomber hit the water they raised an echoing cheer.

Herbert Brian Lightoller

My youngest son, Pilot Officer H. B. Lightoller (lost at the outbreak of war in the first raid on Wilhelmshaven) flew a Blenheim and had at different times given me a whole lot of useful information about attack, defence and evasive tactics (at which he was apparently particularly good) and I attribute, in a great measure, our success in getting across without a single casualty to his unwitting help.

NAME Lightoller, Herbert Brian, SCHOOL No. 184
BORN 19.1.18 AT 3059.
PARENT'S NAME C.H. Lightoller. OCCUPATION Retired
ADDRESS 60. Upper Richmond Rd, Putney S.W.15.
ENTERED SCHOOL Jan. 16th 19 28. LEFT 11. 4. 19 29
PREVIOUS EDUCATION Westminster City
ON LEAVING ENTERED
SCHOOL RECORD

Herbert Brian Lightoller's Emanuel School index card

On one occasion an enemy machine came astern at about 100 feet with the obvious intention of raking our decks. He was coming down in a gliding dive and I knew that he must elevate some 10 to 15 degrees before his guns would bear. Telling my son "Stand by", I waited till as near as I could judge, he was just on the point of pulling up and then "Hard a-port". (She turns 180 degrees in exactly her own length). This threw his aim completely off. He banked and tried again. Then "Hard a-starboard", with the same result. After a third attempt he gave it up in disgust. Had I had a machine gun of any sort, he was a sitter – in fact there were at least three that I am confident we could have accounted for during the trip.[3]

Late on the evening of 1 June the *Sundowner* returned to Ramsgate with all 130 men, crew included, safely delivered.

References

1 For details on the Operation see: Capt. S. W. Roskill, D.S.C., R.N., *The War at Sea: 1939-1945, Volume 1* (1954) p. 66; Sir C. Webster & N. Frankland, *The Strategic Air Offensive Against Germany, Volume 1: Preparation* (1961), pp. 191-192; M. Middlebrook & C. Everitt, *The Bomber Command War Diaries: An Operational Reference Book 1939-1945* (2011), p. 22; G. Warner, *The Bristol Belenheim: A Complete History* (2005), pp. 139-40.

2 See TNA, AIR 81/1 Accidents to Blenheims for correspondence with families of those killed in the raid of 4 September 1939.

3 The whole story is recounted in A. D. Divine, DSM, *Dunkirk*, (1945), pp. 201-203.

Tragedy in France

Graham Eric Richardson *(Emanuel 1929–1936)*

Graham Richardson was remembered for being an outstanding soloist in School concerts. Captain of Lyons, he was also member of the OTC. But no OTC training could have prepared young Graham for what faced the British Expeditionary Force in May and June 1940.[1]

Graham served as a Private with the 2/6th Battalion the East Surrey Regiment. Strikingly blunt, the Regiment's history records that, 'The story of the 2/6th in France in 1940 is a tragic one.' The history notes the reason why, 'Within three weeks of their landing ... these partially trained and incompletely equipped troops were put in the line to try to stem the tremendous onslaught of the German divisions, to fight desperately amid the chaos of the Blitzkrieg.'[2] They were woefully unprepared for the swift German advance into France which drove the BEF into the sea. The Battalion sailed from Southampton for Le Havre on 21 April 1940. For the first few weeks they carried out their duties, such as the guarding of ammunition supply points and were unaware of the catastrophe that lay ahead of them. From 18 May the Regiment was constantly on the move and by late May the 2/6th, with conflicting orders being given as a result of the rapid German advance, were eventually ordered into position west of Rouen. As the Germans advanced into Abbeville and Amiens the 2/6th Surreys received orders 'to take up defensive positions to cover the river crossings on the Bresle between Le Transloy and Gamaches' but before they could gain a footing they had to fall back to the Le Tréport area. Shortly afterwards the Battalion established defensive positions on the River Béthune, where they remained for the next nine days. By 3 June the Battalion moved south east of Béthune with the two-pounder anti-tank guns of the 1st Armoured Division's Support Group covering the left flank of the 51st Highland Division. On a thinly spread 20 mile front the Battalion held its position under intense air attacks especially around the Forges-Aumale area on 7 June. Bitter fighting broke out in the following days and by the early hours of 10 June leading elements of the German 5th Panzer Division were bearing down upon an orchard south of Aumale where Graham and others from his company had rested in hastily dug trenches the previous night.

Graham Eric Richardson

We know of Graham's fate on that day due to Private Peter Janes, who was later captured but managed to escape. Having spent over a year in France and trying to avoid the Germans, Peter Janes reached Spain via what became known as the Pat O'Leary escape line. Imprisoned in Spain he was later repatriated to the UK. Peter's son Keith Janes wrote a book based on his father's diaries from which the following extracts are taken:

> 09.06.1940: We all slept in the orchard in hastily dug trenches, which was done in the night. At four in the morning a French officer rushed round to us and

Kenneth Richardson (far right) with 107 MU RAF

shouted 'Les Allemands, Les Boches'. Then all hell broke loose. We were bombed by planes, shelled by artillery and bombed by trench mortars. And the machine-gun fire was incessant. Two Allied posts were firing over our heads into the valley and the Germans absolutely plastered us with bullets. Then three of us, Mr Naylor, another of the Heywoods and myself took the front post. We had only our rifles and grenades. The bombs fell all of the time, some of them ten yards away. Naylor was scared but was sticking it well. Heywood was panicky but he also did his best to keep cool. I was actually happy and got out of the trench and got a couple of blankets to make it more comfortable. I did not see a German at all and did not fire a single shot. The French machine-guns were firing continuously in bursts of about twenty rounds. They have a beautiful crack crack crack sound to them and it is very easy to distinguish from the Brens roaring chatter or the big Vickers bellow. Then things got too hot and we got the order to retreat. Naylor and Heywood went like scared rabbits at the double, I stayed and collected all [the] ammo and Mills bombs in the various trenches, also all of my kit and overcoat. At this time I was the last man left in the line and was last from the field. ... Outside of the orchard was a fearful sight, the 12th Division of the French Army and our lads were in full retreat.

In his diary and continued on a loose sheet of paper tucked into the back of it, Peter Janes described what happened to Graham:

> Just inside of the field was Richardson, the best looking lad of the Army class, his whole face below his forehead was blown away and his scalp was hanging over a log like a ghastly lid. His whole head was one awful pool of brain specked blood. I looked at his rifle. Called up for Service he had never fired a shot, never in practice and never in war. He was in the front line with [a] clean gun.[3]

Graham was killed fifteen days short of his 21st birthday. Graham is buried in Lannoy Cuillere Communal Cemetery. Graham's death deeply affected his family and one thinks of how his brother Kenneth (Emanuel 1932—1939) must have received the news. Kenneth was a member of the OTC at Emanuel and in the Second World War served with 107 Maintenance Unit RAF in North Africa.

References

1 For an overall account of the evacuation of France see Hugh Sebag-Montefiore, *Dunkirk: Fight to the Last Man* (2006).

2 David Scott Daniell, *History of the East Surrey Regiment: Volume IV 1920–1952*, (1957), p. 89.

3 Our thanks to Keith Janes for his permission to reproduce extracts from his father's diary. For the full diary see Peter Scott Janes and Keith Janes (eds), *Conscript Heroes* (2004).

CHAPTER 13

FIVE OF THE FEW

The Battle of Britain

What General Weygand called the Battle of France is over. I expect that the battle of Britain is about to begin. Upon this battle depends the survival of Christian civilisation. Upon it depends our own British life and the long continuity of our institutions and our Empire. The whole fury and might of the enemy must very soon be turned on us...

Winston S. Churchill 18 June 1940 'Their Finest Hour'

Picture the scene, it is June 1940, thousands of exhausted men of the British Expeditionary Force are waiting on the beaches and harbour at Dunkirk. They come under fire from Luftwaffe pilots and in the sea awaits an armada of all sized ships, from cruisers to motor boats, standing ready to pick them up and return them to 'Blighty'. The German Blitzkrieg which started in May has left the British hugging the French coast with nowhere to turn but home. Over 190,000 BEF men make it home and are welcomed as heroes but in fact they have been part of a gigantic military defeat. With France about to fall, Britain sits alone nervously anticipating the one thing they fear most of all – an invasion.

The one major strategic obstacle for the Germans, except the English Channel, was the Royal Air Force. Any planned invasion of Britain, known operationally as Operation Sea Lion, could only be achieved with air superiority. If the RAF could be knocked out then a sea-borne invasion could be attempted. So from August to September 1940 the Germans, having secured the entire length of coast facing Britain from Norway to the Atlantic, set about destroying aircraft, airfields and ultimately British morale in the hope they would lose the stomach for continuing the war. The period between 10 July and 31 October 1940 is known as the Battle of Britain and five Emanuel boys, all of whom left the School in the 1930s, played their part in defending their country during this most dangerous time.

Still taken from George Darley's gun camera on a Supermarine Spitfire Mark I as he opens fire on a formation of Heinkel He 111s of KG 55 which had just attacked the Supermarine aircraft works at Woolston, Southampton

Horace Stanley 'George' Darley DSO

(Emanuel 1926–1932)

Horace, known as George, was one of Emanuel's shining lights. He was Captain of both the Boat Club and Swimming, a Sergeant in the OTC and a House Lieutenant of Howe House. When he left School the House notes remarked: 'I can only express my own personal gratitude for the staunch and vigorous support which he always gave me and gave readily in all matters connected with the House.' The previous term's Rugger notes commented: 'A forward who takes his share of the hard work.'[1] George's character had been forged in the Emanuel corridors. Here George described what he did next:

> As a member of the Officers' Training Corps I obtained a Certificate 'A' and so applied for a commission in the RAF which was granted in August 1932, when I was 18 years old. I was awarded my wings a year later after being trained on Avro 504 Ks and Ns and Atlas aircraft. In September 1933 I was posted to 207 Bomber Squadron at Bircham Newton, Norfolk, flying Fairey Gordons as an operational pilot aged 19.[2]

George Darley by Cuthbert Orde

The mid 1930s were spent in Aden and British Somaliland mostly on border patrols as tensions heightened after the Italians invaded Abyssinia, thereby putting British interests in the Middle East at risk.

In the late 1930s Darley was back in the UK and became an instructor in a role that would prove vital to his Battle of Britain experiences.

> May 1938 saw my first, but lasting, introduction to the Royal Auxiliary Air Force by being posted as Adjutant/ flying instructor to 602(B) Squadron at Abbotsinch, Glasgow. I was required to train new pilots from ab initio on Tutors, advanced training on dual Harts and thence up to squadron training on Hart bombers.

Soon George was introduced to the Spitfire but without accompanying notes he decided to make his own for his pilots as he explained:

> After several landings and aerobatics I was duly impressed but typed out my own Spitfire notes for my pilots to study. Then a converted Battle arrived, intended to introduce pilots to the Spitfire, the rear cockpit confined to a throttle, control column and rudder and an airspeed indicator, but no instruction notes. So after some handling sorties and issue of my own notes the trainees became used to things which went up and down. Operational training for my converted Spitfire pilots was then provided at Digby, Lincs, during weekends. I was promoted to Sqn.Ldr. on 1 April 1939, age 25.

The Second World War broke out in September 1939 and George soon found himself being moved through several positions:

> When the Second World War was declared I was posted to Catterick Ops. Room, Yorks, for a short stay before moving south to Debden, Essex to take over their Fighter Ops. Room. In late April 1940 I was posted to No. 63 Wing, Air Component, BEF France at Merville, until we lost all our communications during the retreat. We finally evacuated via Boulogne, and I was subsequently given a mention in Despatches.
>
> On return to the UK in June 1940 I was posted supernumerary to a Spitfire squadron operating from Hornchurch, Essex. After 3 sorties I had discovered how NOT to command a fighter squadron (never having flown before in a regular fighter squadron) and on 28 June was pleased to be given command of No. 609 Spitfire Squadron based at Northolt, London.

Not all was well with 609 Squadron when George

arrived as the pilot John Bisdee later explained:

> George Darley... really pulled the squadron together, we'd lost all these experienced pilots, they had probably been lost because [of a] lack of training [so] a lot of them never saw what hit them... under George Darley we were sent to Middle Wallop, this fellow Darley was an absolute first class chap and he worked at us and did a very good job at getting the squadron re-established and trained and then of course the Battle of Britain was on us...

Supermarine Spitfire Mk.Ia R.6915 flown by George Darley during the Battle of Britain – now displayed in the Imperial War Museum, London

The Squadron's personnel ranged in ages from thirty to nineteen and George became concerned that the younger recruits might soon start to lose morale as many of the older men's best friends had been killed. George was worried this negativity would filter down, so he had to think quickly and come up with a solution, as he explains:

> This squadron had suffered casualties at Dunkirk, and I closely questioned the pilots on how the losses were incurred. To me it was apparent that the main causes were too rigid a formation and no knowledge of deflection shooting. With my flying instructor background I considered these and other causes as yet another flying problem which eventually led me to examine all aspects of a fighter sortie from take off to landing. The squadron was then moved in July from Northolt to Middle Wallop in Hampshire where I put my unproven theories into practice.

One of the most striking things about George's command was his age, as he was only 26 when he took command of 609 Squadron. But with a wise and experienced head upon his shoulders and after assessing all the evidence, he soon challenged the convention of how pilots were taking off and facing enemy aircraft:

> Having reversed the accepted order of take-off i.e. Commanding Officer last instead of first, I put my 4 sections (each of 3) into loose line astern, stepped below their leaders. This allowed eleven pairs of eyes to seek for bandits, with an occasional glance to their leaders. I always detailed one section to maintain some 500 ft up sun from us to give warning of any imminent Me 109 attacks from down sun, and they maintained this position by guidance from me whenever I changed course. I always led with a section of three, and by changing these pilots with other members of the squadron, I was able to train them all in my tactics. With the remaining two sections above me on each side, I was able to concentrate on map reading, to consider our courses given by our Operations Room, and to adjust them as I decided upon the probable target. Accounting for cloud cover, I would then adopt a sweeping curve of pursuit, if possible down sun, to bring us above and behind the bombers thereby arriving there 'firstest with the mostest' instead of a squadron shamble. As the leader I regarded my primary role as that of breaking up the bombers before they reached their probable target. Spreading my section out, I took it straight through the whole formation from astern to ahead, firing as we went. Invariably we threw it into confusion, thereby splitting it into separate targets for the rest of my squadron.
>
> By detailing my section daily from all the pilots in the squadron, they assimilated my tactics. The resultant squadron debriefing after a sortie ensured that my instructor background reaped results.

George's pilots recognised his efforts as John Bisdee later remembered:

> The great contribution of people like this chap George Darley to us was that he flew as a target and trained us to attack from out of the sun to do quarter attacks to do head on attacks and so on...

George Darley, 1940

George Darley and wife Majorie outside Buckingham Palace after George received his DSO

George Darley drinking tea at RAF Warmwell, c.1940

George was conscious of wanting to train the pilots himself and disregarded textbook flight formations. Here was a commander who knew what he wanted and put it into practice.

On 8 August George found himself in combat with a number of enemy aircraft (E/A) and his first claim. The squadron had been ordered to patrol a convoy off the Needles. What follows is the combat report George gave that day:

> B flight were ordered to patrol Pewit at 10,000ft. After taking off I climbed through cloud from 1-4000ft. and after climbing to 7000ft. I could not see the objective owing to a layer of cloud to 3,500ft. north of the convoy. I then saw a balloon coming down in flames and turned towards convoy. I saw E/A diving on convoy and as I approached 5 Me 110s [Messerschmitts] had just finished a dive and were climbing up below us and in the opposite direction. I gave the order to attack independently and turned right about and dived down on the ME 110s and after that lost contact with the remainder of my flight. I was not in a good position for the ME 110s so I climbed up again and saw one ME 110 a mile ahead, heading due south. I flew in and out of cloud and then dived down and opened fire in one half second burst at 250 yards and another ¾ second burst, closing in to 75 yds. As I turned away I saw the ME A/C bank steeply to port, then I broke away to right and turned back left and saw E/A hitting the sea. My attack was a quarter attack aiming at starboard engine and pilot's cabin. Return fire at first from rear gunner T then circled the neighbourhood and made a full deflection attack on a ME 110 at 200 yds with no apparent result; and also did a head on attack on a JU 87 at 200 yds. Giving half second bursts in each case. No apparent result. I also attacked another JU 87 coming straight towards me 300ft above me. I gave an extremely short burst; again without apparent result. I again circled the vicinity and I saw one single seater A/C unidentified pursued by another single seater A/C. The target A/C burst into flames, took half roll and went straight into sea. Also saw a parachute coming down into the sea about 10 miles S of convoy. Position reported to Bandy.
>
> Most of my action was spent 5–10 miles south of convoy where there was a clear patch of sky. As I could no longer see any more E/A in my neighbourhood I returned to base.
>
> Rounds fired 130 rounds each gun. Ranges. Maximum 250-yds. Minimum 75-yds.[3]

The Battle of Britain began in earnest for the Germans on the day they marked out as *Adlertag* or 'Eagle Day' 13 August 1940, the day on which they would begin to attempt the destruction of the Royal Air Force. It became 609's 'lucky day' as one of the squadron's pilots, David Crooks, recalled in his book *Spitfire Pilot*:

> At about 4pm we were ordered to patrol Weymouth at 15,000 feet. We took off, thirteen machines in all, with the C.O. (Darley) leading and climbed over Weymouth. After a few minutes I began to hear a German voice talking on the RT, faintly at first and then growing in volume. By a curious chance this German raid had a wave-length almost identical with our own and the voice we heard was that of the German Commander talking to his formation as they approached us across the Channel. About a quarter of an hour later we saw a large German formation approaching below us. There were a number of Junkers 87 dive-bombers escorted by Me. 109s above and also some Me. 110s about two miles behind, some sixty machines in all...Meanwhile the bombers with their fighter escort still circling above them, passed beneath us. We were up at almost 20,000 feet in the sun and I don't think they ever saw us till the very last moment. The CO (Darley) gave a terrific 'Tally ho' and led us round in a big semi-circle so that we were now behind them and we prepared to attack.[4]

George describes 609's operations on the 13 and 14 August:

> On 13 August, for example, 52 Ju 87s escorted by Me l09s and Me 110s were briefed to make a landfall near Portland (according to post-war German Air Force (GAF) records). 609 were scrambled, and, having decided (correctly) what was to be the likely target, I manoeuvred the squadron so as to attack from the sun, below the escort, which I left to my section top cover. As usual I flew my section right through the Ju 87s from stern to bow, firing as we went, thus creating the desired chaos. The net result was 9 Ju 87s destroyed and 6 damaged and 2 Me l09s destroyed and 4 damaged without loss to us. In his book 'Eagle Day', Collier states that this debacle was witnessed by Churchill and Generals Brooke, Auchinlech and Montgomery, who were then inspecting coastal defences around Portland. I hope that they were impressed and joined in the many congratulatory signals which we received.
>
> However, the next day 14 August being cloudy, I recognised it as being 'Ju 88 weather', i.e. ideal for 3–4 Ju 88s to attack airfields through broken cloud and to escape thereby. So I, as usual, ordered sections of three aircraft at a time to maintain patrols around our airfield, and to expect a raid because of our regular punishment

of Ju 87s trying to bomb our South and SW coastal regions during the past few days. As I expected a Ju 88 group arrived, destroyed my hangar (1 of 5) but sadly also killing two of my gallant airmen. Apparently, this raid was witnessed by three very senior German Air Force officers in a nearby Heinkel, but they were unable to testify because less than one minute afterwards their aircraft was shot down by my only Sgt. Pilot, Feary: all its occupants were killed. Thus 609 received more black marks in the GAF diaries. Indeed after the war research defined 609 Squadron by number and location as a definite target.

From 8 August to the end of September George was responsible for destroying three enemy aircraft, took credit for three 'probable' destroyed and damaged a further two aircraft.

On 5 September, later designated as Battle of Britain Day in the UK, the Luftwaffe launched heavy attacks. George recorded in his combat report:

Ordered squadron to attack by sections from beam and quarters. Selected last two stragglers and opened fire from starboard quarter, closing from 250–150 yds, with 4 sec burst at starboard aircraft. As I broke away saw white fumes appearing from Port engine. As these two began to dive and were being engaged by the rest of the squadron I chased the rest of the formation...I attacked from starboard quarter, opening fire at extreme range as I had difficulty in closing quickly.[5]

As a squadron leader George had to keep his men in order, which wasn't so easy in the heat of battle as he remembered when interviewed in 1989 about pilots actively seeking dogfights:

I remember one particular chap, real 'Boy's Own' stuff. You have to remember we were often heavily outnumbered to begin with, odds of 10–1 or worse. So as Commander I was against chaps going in on their own ... I used to fly right into the enemy bombers to split them up so that the individual pilots could pick their targets and finish them off. Some wanted to be 'fighter to fighter' an 'Ace', more 'Boy's Own' stuff and I had to tell them this was not what I expected in my Squadron. The pilot I mentioned earlier who wouldn't follow instruction, shot down a German 'Ace' in a dogfight. He was then shot down himself by the 'Ace's' number two pilot and his own number two was also shot down. This was all because he wouldn't listen to instruction ... Much of our tactics was to lure the fighters away from the larger bombers whom they were escorting and this left the bombers as easier meat.

During George's period of command 609 Squadron shot down 85 aircraft. His impact upon 609 is best summed up by David Crooks DFC.

...a very great deal of the credit for our changed fortunes was due to the CO. He came to command the squadron at the beginning of July when, owing to lack of experience, we were not a particularly efficient fighting unit. He was with us all through the bad times when we lost more than we shot down and when morale of the squadron might have suffered. But he flew as much as anybody else, led us skilfully and throughout remained so imperturbable, so confident and so cheerful that he held us together by his example.

And so the end of August found us with a very satisfactory and solid background of success and victory and we now faced the future with an ample confidence that whatever the Germans might do, we could do it far better.[6]

Another 609 Squadron pilot John Bisdee remembered: 'I think I said once that when we had this farewell parade... and he had been given his DSO and so on there was rarely hardly a dry eye in the squadron.'

For his command in the Battle of Britain George was awarded the Distinguished Service Order on 22 October 1940. His citation read:

This officer has led his squadron in a brilliant manner during its recent successful operations against superior numbers of enemy formations. He has displayed determination and coolness and, by his skill in action, he has contributed largely to the great successes obtained by his squadron.

George was posted to RAF Exeter after the Battle of Britain as he explains:

On 5 October I was promoted to Wing Commander to command RAF Exeter with two day fighter squadrons and one night squadron, still at the tender age of 26. During my command of 609 from 28 June to 5 October we were credited with 85 victories, but lost 7 pilots killed. Added to the previous score of 7 victories this became 92. On 22 October I was most gratified to be awarded the DSO for leadership with the appointment signed by HM George VI. I was amused later to hear that 609 groundcrews had dubbed me as the John Wayne of the RAF.

Exeter activities were mainly directed towards night raids against Midland cities, and involved most interesting experiments in directing radar equipped

Colin Francis

fighters from newly developed mobile radar warning units. But the station operations room was merely two tables in a corner of a hangar and was almost useless. I promptly had an empty house a mile away requisitioned and with the usual Trojan work of the GPO quickly converted it into an efficient 24 hour centre.

George spent most of the rest of the Second World War in the Far East and this aspect of his career can be viewed in a later chapter.

Colin Dunstone Francis *(Emanuel 1933—1937)*

Colin joined the R.A.F. on a short service commission in April 1939 and in the summer of 1940 was a pilot officer in 253 Squadron which had moved from Prestwick to Kenley.

At School Colin was in the OTC but little is known of his movements until the Battle of Britain. What is known is that he took part in No. 253 Squadron's first action of the Battle of Britain on 30 August 1940. The 'A' Flight Emergency Section Squadron Leader, Tom Gleave noted in his combat report:

> I was leader of Emergency Section with Fl/Lt. Brown as No. 2 and P/O Francis as No. 3. At approx 11.30 hours we were ordered off to patrol base at 2000ft. At 1,700ft we were ordered to climb to 20,000ft. in a South Easterly direction. At 17,500ft large formation of 109's sighted travelling S.S.E. Attacked from sun into E/A's flank...No sign of No. 2 or No. 3.[7]

Funeral service for Colin Francis, 29 September 1981

Fl/Lt Brown had been shot down and badly injured but Colin, flying a Hurricane, serial number L. 1965, had been posted as missing, later presumed killed. He was 19 years old.

In 1981 excavation work was being done at Wrotham Hill in Kent. Unknown individuals had been digging at a farm which belonged to a Mr. Percival in 1940 but it had since changed hands. Then Bill Blundell a local enthusiast sought permission to dig at the farm and it wasn't long before he and others helping him discovered uniform and parachute material. The Ministry of Defence were called in and a pilot and the remaining aircraft were recovered from fourteen feet of clay. The identification of the serial number confirmed that this was the Hurricane Colin was flying when he had crashed forty-one years previously. In addition to the wreckage a wrist watch was found with Colin's name engraved on it.

Colin was buried at Brookwood Military Cemetery on 29 September 1981 and in attendance that day were George Brown who had been shot down on the 30th and the Squadron Leader of Colin's flight that day, Tom Gleave, who commented of Colin, 'He was a damned fine kid with lots of guts.'[8]

Colin, along with a Canadian Pilot Officer by the name of Carthew, were known to the Squadron as Tweedledum and Tweedledee and Colin's death moved Carthew so much that he never flew again.

Kenneth Milton Millist *(Emanuel 1931—1935)*

Kenneth Millist

Ken Millist had a very successful school career. He was Captain of Rugby, a member of the successful 1935 rowing Four and a Lieutenant Corporal in the OTC. He was also a regular in the pre-war Old Emanuel Rugby sides. Ken joined the RAF on a short service commission just before the outbreak of war. In the summer of 1940 he was transferred from 98 Squadron to No. 4 Ferry Pilot Pool and then No. 5 Operational Training Unit, which was part of No. 12 Group Fighter Command and was a unit for training fighter pilots in the last stages of their training. In September Ken joined No. 615 Squadron at Prestwick. It was while stationed here that Ken practised air to air firing at West Frough before being posted to No. 73 Squadron where on his first flight with the Squadron he made a heavy landing, smashing his propeller and damaging his port wing in the process. Ken went to the Middle East with 73 Squadron in November 1940, the story of which is told in a later chapter.

Brian Robert Noble *(Emanuel 1927—1933)*

Brian was a talented sportsman at Emanuel, gaining his First Fifteen Colours in addition to being part of the rowing Four which won the Reading Regatta Public School Fours trophy in 1933. On leaving School Brian worked as a trainee company secretary for The London Scottish American Trust Ltd.

Brian joined the Royal Air Force Volunteer Reserve on 4 June 1938 as a Sergeant Pilot; he received his commission on 14 June 1940 as a Pilot Officer and joined No. 79 Squadron at Biggin Hill on 1 July of that year. Throughout the Battle of Britain period Brian flew Hurricanes and carried out a number of patrols throughout August 1940. On 28 August Brian was in action over Hawkinge with Heinkel 59 Floatplanes which were escorted by three Messerschmitt 110s. He claimed a share in shooting down one of the Heinkels that day.

By the end of August Brian had already flown 70 sorties, a remarkable testament to the sheer mental and physical strength these pilots possessed. Then on Sunday 1 September the Squadron were scrambled in the early afternoon to engage roughly 20 bombers and one hundred enemy fighters at 20,000 feet.

In the early 1980s Brian recalled what happened on that day:

> I remember being recalled from the officers' mess after a vain attempt to eat a hurried luncheon and being 'scrambled' immediately on arriving back at dispersal. Subsequently, during the climb we intercepted a large Luftwaffe bomber formation (height 12–15,000 feet) and surrounded by enemy aircraft and tracer and cannon fire,

Pilot Officer B. R. Noble

Brian Noble in an Emanuel classroom, early 1930s

whilst turning left to run through the formation I felt a dull thud and simultaneously saw a burst of flame below my feet indicating a hit in the main fuel tank behind the instrument panel. My remaining memory is of releasing the locking pin on my harness, pushing the stick hard forward to convert the left turn into a 'bunt', the effect of which was to project me out of the cockpit (fortunately the preamble to an attack was to slide the canopy back to allow for just such a hurried exit!) I recall having some trouble pulling the parachute ripcord – my hands having been burned – and I lost some nails on both hands. I recall only two brief moments whilst parachuting down – one of being close to another parachuting airman at one time, whilst both of us were 'investigated' by a friendly fighter and secondly of being over water into which I fell almost immediately. This in fact was the Marley sand/gravel pit at Riverhead, Sevenoaks and from which I was promptly rescued by the Local Defence Volunteer, one of whom took me to the local hospital at Sevenoaks, where I was to spend the next month in company with F/O (later G/Capt) Trevor Bryant-Fenn of 79 Squadron, my section leader on that sortie.

After one month in Sevenoaks I moved away to Torquay and later went to the burns unit at Queen Victoria Hospital at East Grinstead and never did find out what happened to my Hurricane P2062.

The front page of *Sevenoaks News* for 5 September also described the scene that day:

On Sunday morning, at a great height, British fighters engaged the enemy. With a bright blue sky as a background and amid puffs of white smoke, a white line curled downwards, decreasing in intensity. Then a machine was seen on a horizontal course with darker smoke issuing from it until the airplane burst into flames and began falling.

"	"	P3100	"	"	TO HAWKINGE
"	"	P3100	"	"	PATROL
"	"	P3100	"	"	FROM HAWKINGE
29	"	P3100	"	"	BIGGIN HILL TO HAWKINGE
"	"	P3100	"	"	PATROL
"	"	P3659	"	"	PATROL
31	"	P3659	"	"	PATROL
"	"	P3659	"	"	PATROL
"	"	P3659	"	"	CROYDON TO BIGGIN HILL.
"	"	P3659	"	"	PATROL
SEPTEMBER 1	"	L P2062	"	"	PATROL
"	"	L P2062	"	"	PATROL. SHOT DOWN

S/LDR O.C. 79 Squadron. 23.4.41.

S/ F/O. O.C. "A" Fl

GRAND TOTAL [Cols. (1) to (10)] 262 Hrs 20 Mins.

TOTALS CARRIED FORWA

A page of Brian's RAF Log Book showing the entry of his shooting down 1 September 1940

Brian Noble (third from left) during a period of recovery at Palace Hotel, Torquay, 1941. Also in the photo is James B. Nicholson (first from right) the only RAF Fighter Command Pilot to receive the Victoria Cross in the Second World War

Brian (first from left) at the Battle of Britain film première, Cardiff 1969

Brian was badly burned and underwent a series of skin graft operations being one of the first members of the Guinea Pig Club, an association founded in July 1941 for pilots who had had treatment for their burns.

Interestingly Brian's nurse at Sevenoaks, a Mrs Muriel Harrison, related that people had thought Brian was either Polish or German when he landed at Marley. It was only the fact that someone spotted the makers label, Irving, on Brian's parachute that they realised he was an English pilot. Due to the pain of his injuries people couldn't understand him for his speech was stilted.

In October 1940 Brian received a letter from his old boss in the City. He expressed his admiration, which was shared among thousands, for the bravery airmen like Brian had shown during Britain's darkest hours, 'There is a soft spot in my heart for all you young knights of the sky who fight for our country with so much daring and skill.'

Whilst resting at Torquay Brian befriended James Nicholson who had been injured during the Battle of Britain when he was shot down but before bailing out managed to shoot down a Messerschmitt. James was the only Fighter Command pilot in the Second World War to be awarded the Victoria Cross. Two photographs show Brian and James together playing golf, one is signed by James who, sadly, was killed in May 1945 when the aircraft he was flying in, as an observer, caught fire and crashed in the Bay of Bengal.

Brian returned to non-operational flying duties in May 1941. In April 1942 he was posted to India as a member of a ground control unit. Returning to England in April 1944 he had a brief spell with a training unit for air gunners and was second in command of a cadet training school. His last flight took place on 7 May 1945 and his log book records he piloted fifteen different types of aircraft in a period of 7 years. For his war service he was Mentioned in Despatches in June 1944.

He left the RAF in 1946 but later rejoined in the Fighter Control Branch reaching the rank of Wing Commander and retiring in 1969. In the same year as he retired Brian attended the première of the Harry Saltzman production, *Battle of Britain*. Brian died at the age of 73 in 1990.

Harry Prowse c.1940

Harry Arthur Robin Prowse

(Emanuel 1932—1939)

At School Harry was a scholar, musician and actor, his final performance being in *Saint Joan* in the winter of 1938. He was also a Lance Corporal in the Emanuel OTC gaining his War Certificate 'A' and on leaving School in 1939 he joined the RAF on a short service commission. He spent the rest of 1939 training and on 6 January 1939 he was posted to 9BGS, Penrhos, as a staff pilot.

In June 1940 Harry was flying with No. 4 Ferry Pilots Pool. This meant that Harry would deliver aircraft to various locations, from the factory to various squadrons based in their different locations either in Britain or abroad.

Several accounts written over the years suggest that he was shot down by flak in a field near Lille in June 1940, but the evidence suggests otherwise and it is believed that he crashed on 8 June at Marseilles-Marignane, before making his way back to England shortly before the fall of France.

On his return to England Harry joined a training unit before converting to flying Spitfires and transferring to 266 Squadron before eventually joining 603 Squadron on 20 October.

On 11 November 1940 Harry saw action five miles east of Foulness Island where five Messerschmitt 109s had been spotted. Harry, by now a Pilot Officer wrote in his combat report:

> When on patrol as Red 2 with 603 Squadron, I attacked an Me 109 which had left four other Me 109s. Directly the Squadron caught up with them. I chased him down from 20,000 feet to 2,000 feet and when he flattened out fired a three second burst from dead astern at a range of 300 yds. Immediately a trail of white vapour came from the undersurface of his port wing root. He began to twist and turn and I was only able to fire an occasional short burst at him. By this time I had closed to 100 yds. He straightened out and began to climb. I fired a three second burst from dead astern. He did a half roll and dived towards the sea. He pulled out at 500 feet and immediately executed another half roll from which he dived into the sea.[9]

Harry Prowse (centre) shortly after capture. Luftwaffe pilot Josef Priller is first from right

Harry saw a period of intensive action in the summer of 1941. After damaging a Messerschmitt on 14 June he destroyed an Me 109E on the 30th. He wrote in his combat report:

> On being attacked by 6 Me 109s from behind I turned to starboard followed by the rest of my section and climbed to 22,000ft, where we were joined by Red 3. I then patrolled between Audruicq and Cassel awaiting the return of the bombers. Over Cassel I saw 6 Me. 109Es at about 12,000ft. I dived towards them and 2 of them turned towards me. I half rolled and dived underneath them. On pulling out at 6,000ft. I saw an Me. 109 about 300 yds ahead. I closed to 150 yds and gave him an 8 sec burst, closing to 50 yds. Dense clouds of black smoke came from E/A which turned onto his back and dived down. I circled above losing height awaiting results and saw E/A crash into a wood and explode. Blue 3 saw E/A going down with dense black smoke.
>
> On the return journey I fired a 4 sec burst at a Me. 109 from 300 yds which was attacking 54 Squadron. E/A rolled onto his back and dived down being engaged by a member of 54 Squadron.[10]

On 4 July 1941 Harry's Squadron was flying in support of a bombing raid on a power station and the Kuhlmann chemical plant at Chocques. The Squadron was received by the Luftwaffe. I and III Gruppen of JG26, with a JG2 Gruppe scrambled in response. Dogfights broke out across the Channel but the bombers reached their target. However, by now Flight Officer Prowse found himself in combat with one of the Luftwaffe's most skilful pilots, Josef Priller, who by the end of the war claimed over one hundred victories against the Allied air forces.

Pilot Officer Falconer saw Harry diving over the airfield at St Omer. Falconer called Harry up on the R/T and Harry replied that he was ok but no more was heard of Harry until 16 July when another pilot had been listening to the German propaganda broadcasts of William Joyce, known by the sobriquet 'Lord Haw-Haw', who announced that Harry was now a prisoner.

Years later in retirement in Brazil Harry reflected on that day:

> My departure from 603 was somewhat similar to the start, but in a small field near St Omer. The damage was even greater both to the Spitfire and me. However, before hitting the ground I had remembered to turn off my ignition switches (magneto switches) as well as blow up the IFF unit, all in accordance with standard regulations. This particular Blenheim bomber escort flight had all the premonitions of disaster from the start. Squadron Leader Smith was leading the Squadron at the time, I was acting A Flight Commander. From the time we took off to the time I was shot down we saw neither the rest of the Hornchurch Wing nor the Blenheims we and the rest of the Wing were supposed to be escorting. Milling around in the air above Galland's airfields was not the healthiest place to be at that time. 603, according to my log book, lost four pilots including me during the ten days prior to my farewell on July 4th 1941. A date never to be forgotten by me.[11]

Harry had in fact set his Spitfire alight with his Very pistol. Shortly afterwards he was captured and interestingly was photographed with the man who claimed to have shot him down, none other than Josef Priller, standing with another Luftwaffe pilot Rolf Pringel. In the photo all men are smiling but soon Harry would find himself a POW. Harry was eventually sent to Stalag Luft III as prisoner 1626.

In an early letter home he assured his family that he was being treated like one of the Germans but on 15 July he expressed his frustrations:

> Well, I've now been twelve days in captivity and it seems like twelve years. The time goes so very slowly with nothing to do all day but read and think. The food isn't so hot, but is nevertheless always welcome as it breaks the monotony somewhat. The weather has been very hot which is a good thing until some clothes arrive.

On the 29th Harry wrote:

> GEFANGENENNUMMER: 1626.
> ZIMMER – NR. 1 7.
> LAGER-BEZEICHNUNG: OFLAG VIIc.
> DEUTCHSLAND.
>
> Here we are again! Not much news but enough to fill this miserable piece of monthly ration. I'm just dying to receive a letter from home. Another three weeks should see the first roll in. The days are going by faster now and things aren't so bad as my first letter and cards written in violent fits of depression made them out to be. I'm in the orchestra now and rehearsals take up half the day. There is a good library and I've started to learn some more Spanish. Much of the day is spent in washing out dirty clothing and washing up dirty dishes (I'm becoming quite an expert). I've sent off a card to Capt. Skinner and another to the Dutch Red Cross with the possibility of being 'adopted' by some kind-hearted Dutchman. We RAF types are still hounded out by the Army for news of home and there are several Army officers here who know people in the RAF I am acquainted with. One Scots captain is a great friend of my old CO [George Denholm] many an hour has passed in swapping yarns, and some of the stories they have to tell of their capture and first few months of imprisonment are very interesting. They had a terrible time at the beginning. There is more to tell but no more room for it.

Harry's time in captivity wasn't a happy one overall. When Harry died in 2010 his nephew John Neale, who attended Emanuel in the 1960s and later became a design and technology master at Emanuel, wrote in Harry's obituary:

> It took many decades for Harry to talk freely of the camp, but during his retirement, enjoying the wide vistas from the veranda of his wood cabin on the banks of the Rio Grande in Brazil, he described cold, hunger, boredom and horror... While Harry had nothing good to say about the prison guards – and what he did say in the rare letters that reached home was scrubbed out by censors – he spoke warmly of the German doctors who treated him with compassion.

As the Red Army closed in on Germany in 1945, Harry, and around ten thousand other Allied airmen, were ordered to leave Stalag Luft III as their captors put them on a forced march deeper into German territory. They walked out into a light snowstorm in the early hours of 28 January 1945. The march was arduous and conditions unpleasant with many of the men feeling the effects of malnutrition.

Eventually Harry was freed on 2 May 1945 and returned to England on Victory in Europe (VE) Day, 8 May.

Of his time with 603 Squadron Harry later remembered:

> I was very young and found life exciting. I hated the transfer or loss of friends from the Squadron but life in general was good with little to worry about, for me at any rate. In particular I recall with nostalgia the period between Dec 17th 1940 and May 16th 1941, during the Squadron's 'rest period' at Drem and Turnhouse. Even a Sassenach like myself seemed to receive the same generous treatment from the people of Edinburgh as any other member of the Squadron.

On his return to England Harry started a refresher flying course in October 1945 and stayed in the RAF for a further two years. Finding it hard to settle back into life in post-war Britain Harry, 'accepted a job growing oranges in São Paulo state, sailed to Brazil with his young wife, the former Windmill dancer Margaret Harris, who had waited for him to return from the war, and made his life there. He flew light planes and learned to speak fluent Portuguese.' In recognition for a great man the Brazilian Air Force arranged a fly past at Harry's funeral.

George, Colin, Kenneth, Brian and Harry were just five young men who showed extraordinary fortitude in the face of an invasion in the summer of 1940. They spent hours learning the technical skills for operating various aircraft and flying high above the skies over Britain, the Channel and France and played no small part in the Battle for Britain and by doing so kept the hopes of a nation alive.

Tom Morriss Priestley

An eyewitness account of the Battle of Britain

In February 1941 Old Emanuel Tom Morriss Priestley wrote to a friend in Bogota explaining how he had lived through the Battle of Britain. Tom attended Emanuel before the Great War. Being refused for the Army because of a heart condition he worked at the Board of Trade and organised the national distribution of yeast in the 1914–1918 war. Directorships followed including a seat on the Board of the Baranquilla Railway Company. In the Second World War he was living in a house named White Friars in Kent until a bomb hit it. Tom starts his letter by explaining that his letters in the previous months had not alluded to events in England because of the censor but hoped that now the Battle of Britain was over he could write more freely as he explained:

> Dear Mr. Koppel,
>
> ... It cannot possibly help the enemy to know, if this letter should go astray, that in October last he blew up White Friars in the middle of the night and that this is the reason why I have left Kent and am now living in Oxfordshire.
>
> You know as well as I do that Kent has been the battle area

OE Sir Sholto Douglas and Winston Churchill during the Prime Minister's visit to 609 Squadron, 1941

for our RAF against the German Air Force since the latter opened its first great air attack in September last.

Throughout the 24 hours hundreds of planes, bombers and fighters, swept over our home on their way to London and other objectives. By day we were able to watch them through our glasses. I personally witnessed many tremendous battles and memorable scenes. At night the whole sky was ablaze with searchlights and AA Fire. When bombs and shells fell near we were forced underground into a concrete shelter which I had had constructed away from the house.

Finally in October last White Friars was blown up by a high-explosive bomb which scored a direct hit in the middle of the night. Fortunately, we, with our household, had gone to cover and so escaped all bodily harm. When we came out of our dug-out we found a high explosive crater distant but 20 feet.

Throughout September, October and November by day our Hurricanes and Spitfires put up a tremendous defence and at night our AA guns threw a screen-barrage of millions of shells around our London.

I could tell of many great fights and of one early morning in September when I saw a formation of twelve Heinkels shot to pieces. Parts of the blazing wreckage fell in my own gardens.

... I am now with part of my home at Goring in Oxfordshire, where fortunately I had another house...

The fall of France and the trial of Dunkirk were hard blows. But they resulted in a tremendous revival of effort and decision in this country. The threat of invasion acted like magic. Every man and woman seemed to spring to action... Throughout June, July and August we spent anxious days in preparation and waiting. The Germans never came. If they did make an attempt they failed hopelessly even before they left the coast of France. They may try again. But they will be beaten and smashed. They will never conquer England now, if they ever had a chance in June 1940. Not all the soldiers in the Third Reich would be enough to gain a foothold. They would be decimated before they could reach even the outskirts of London.

References

1 *The Portcullis*, Lent Term, 1932, p. 14.
2 The Memoirs of Group Captain H S 'George' Darley (unpublished), 17pp.
3 609 Squadron Combat Report, TNA AIR/50/171 pp. 87-88.
4 D. M. Crook, *Spitfire Pilot* (1942), pp. 46-47.
5 609 Squadron Combat Report, TNA AIR/50/171 pp. 99-100.
6 *Spitfire Pilot*, p.62.
7 253 Squadron Combat Report, TNA AIR/50/97 pp. 117-118.
8 Andy Saunders, *Finding the Few* (2010), pp. 53-55.
9 TNA AIR/50/167 Harry Prowse Combat Report, p. 344.
10 Ibid. p. 349.
11 David Ross, Bruce Blanche and William Simpson, *The Greatest Squadron of them All: The definitive history of 603 (City of Edinburgh) Squadron, RAUXAF* (Grub Street, 2003), p. 27.

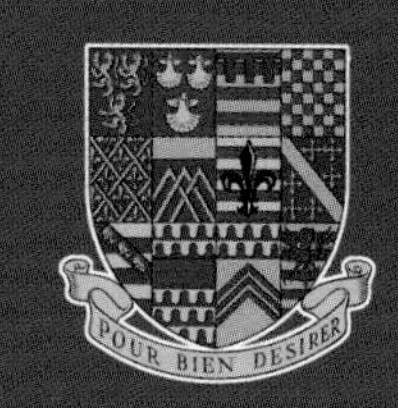

R.K. Wildey's DFC

'He was a Grand Young Fellow' – The Life and times of an Exceptional Squadron Leader

Richard 'Dick' Kemp Wildey DFC *(Emanuel 1926–1935)*

Dick Wildey was a young man with a zest for life. Photographs of his time at Emanuel and later in the RAF show him with a broad beaming smile. This energetic young man had a full and colourful School career, with appointments as a School Prefect and Nelson House Captain. He played for the Second Fifteen and rowed in the First Eight. He was remembered for being an exceptional Cadet Sergeant Major in the Emanuel OTC gaining his War Certificate 'A' and was known for 'his charming and unassuming manner.' He enjoyed spending his time in the School workshop and being behind the scenes in School plays but also appeared on stage several times and was fondly remembered for his talent for mimicry.

R.K. Wildey, 1934

On leaving School Dick took a Short Service Commission in the RAF in 1935. His RAF career can be explored through his three RAF Pilot's Log Books which Dick's son Peter has kindly donated to the Emanuel School Archive. These log books provide a wealth of information detailing the training Dick undertook, the types of aircraft he flew (for how long and with whom), his progress registered by various commanding officers in addition to the notes he made in relation to the many operations in which he participated. Dick trained to become a Bomber Command pilot. Training was intense and by October 1935, only a few months after leaving Emanuel, Dick had already notched up 50 hours of flying in 46 days. Flying a variety of aircraft, learning his craft inside and out, from changing fuel supplies to undertaking heart-stopping manoeuvres, from loops to turns, gliding into the wind and flying low. It was the stuff of Boys' Own magazines but with an impending European crisis looming over their heads in the late 1930s, it was a serious business not to be taken light-heartedly. Dick sailed through the flying training schools (FTS). The Officer Commanding 'C' Flight No. 11 FTS RAF Wittering noted that Dick's proficiency by May 1936 was 'Above average.' He undertook intensive training in the next three years and then a note added to his second log book appeared under 3 September 1939, 'England declares war on Germany at 1100 hours.'

By December 1939 Dick was impatient to see action as he wrote to his fiancée Eileen, 'I must say I'm getting browned off with this inactivity and wish they would let the night bombers have a crack at something.'[1] Dick was a Captain in No. 78 Squadron RAF based at Dishforth and led the Squadron's first bombing operation on 19 July 1940, less than a month after the squadron became fully operational. But before this Dick had flown sorties with No. 51 Squadron during May 1940, bombing industrial targets such as chemical works in Leverkusen on 24 May and a railway marshalling yard in Duisburg on 25 May. On the same day as the raid on Leverkusen Dick wrote to Eileen, 'As you will have gathered I've had my first crack at the enemy. All I can say about it is that its good fun, now I have a crew of my own. The other night I went as navigator and in spite of my efforts we got back to England!'[2] In his first engagements Dick relayed his excitement as in a letter on 27 May, 'This squadron's much more fun than 78. I've had three cracks at the enemy now and the queerest part of all is, when the news from the BBC comes on the next day, you hear what you took part in.'

Dick's fiancée's twin brother was OE Douglas Hoare. On 29 May 1940 news was received that he was missing in France. Dick wrote to Eileen later that day, 'Tonight I'm going to avenge this. I can now continue my part in this war with a clear mind.'[3] On 5 June with still no news of Doug's fate Dick wrote to reassure Eileen, 'I feel a bit down since there's still no news of Doug. There isn't a thing I can do to find out anything ... but just because they haven't paid him this month doesn't mean much at all, you see they stop paying on the same day as a person is reported missing. We had a Flight Commander who had been missing for three weeks and has now been reported in Germany, so don't start giving up hope yet, after all news comes through very slowly.' A week later relief came with the news that Doug was safe and had been made a POW.

Like everyone else Dick had an opinion of general developments in the War and on 17 June 1940 he wrote to Eileen after the news that France had surrendered:

> Boy we are up the creek are we not, of course we knew two days ago this was bound to happen but what a shock now the rats [French] have just given in, it's much too early to see what our country will do but I hope we will go on.
>
> I wonder how USA feels about things now, just a little late to offer help.

Bomber pilots were under extreme pressures and this is also evident form Dick's letters to his fiancée, noting in one, '... I've found that the operational flying I'm doing makes me smoke...' In addition to his flying duties Dick was responsible for overseeing the operations of the crews under his command, which consisted of sitting up through the early hours in the operations room, checking on the progress of the squadron as they flew over Germany and greeting them on their return. But it was the loss of colleagues that put them to far greater emotional tests, and which they had to block out in order to carry on with their daily tasks. On 10 July Dick wrote to Eileen, 'The worst news of all has come in today. Tony was shot down last night so I'm afraid you will never meet him. This one has shaken the whole group more than all the others, you see he was the most popular member of all the Whitley Squadrons, but as I said once before one mustn't think about it, doesn't get you anywhere if you do.'

Life on a bomber station was characterised by hard work but also light relief in the occasional beer and game of darts or snooker. Between operations and thinking about all the technical elements of being a part of a Bomber Squadron there were moments of much-needed relaxation and Dick's letters to Eileen are full of anecdotes about life between his duties as a Squadron Leader.

On 14 September Dick wrote to Eileen to tell her that the journalist Godfrey Winn had been to see him for an article which appeared on 15 September 1940 with the headline, 'I Bombed Berlin'.[4] Dick tells Eileen that Godfrey based the article on what he had told him. We know from No. 78 Squadron's Operations Record Book that on 11 September a Whitley Bomber Mk. V, P. 4958, did bomb targets in Berlin but Dick's name does not appear in the crew list, although he flew a number of times with this crew and they are the same one referred to in the *Sunday Express* article. The operation is not recorded in his Pilot's Log Book either.[5] Dick may have been a replacement on the flight at the last minute or he may have based the article on what the crew told him when they returned. The article should be read in the context of the Battle of Britain and the frustration Dick felt knowing members of his family and Eileen were in London which is referred to in the article, 'the certain knowledge that we have done something to revenge what our own folk, especially in London, have been going through the last few days...' The article refers to their target:

> ...we let them have it good and strong. The Potsdam railway station and all its sidings was our main objective. One, two, three, four, five, six, seven, eight ...[space in original] we made three runs across the city before we had released our whole load, and the fellows who come after us, when they got back to our airfield, gave a swell report about the fires we had lit.
>
> As we turned, we could see the wide road they call the East-West Axis, amazingly clear in the moonlight, and the Tiergarten spread out below. Now our navigator sets us a course for home – and, oh, boy, are we off quickly!

In October 1940 Richard and Eileen got married. Leading up to the wedding Dick was bombing targets in northern Europe by night and planning his wedding by day. 1940 ended with a marriage to the woman he loved and the news that he was to be awarded the DFC. One newspaper questioned whether he was the youngest squadron leader in the RAF, being as he was only 24 years old. The DFC citation in the *London Gazette* on 22 November 1940 stated:

> This Officer has captained an aircraft on 23 sorties at night over enemy territory. He was appointed a Flight Commander when this unit became operational and has consistently set a high standard of leadership and morale. By his personal example of devotion to duty and resolution in the face of difficulties he has materially contributed in inculcating an excellent spirit in his squadron.

In April 1941 Dick transferred to the headquarters of No. 4 Group Bomber Command, York, where he trained pilots until 26 July 1942. He was then posted as Officer Commanding No. 10 Squadron Bomber Command based at Leeming and then, from August 1942, in Melbourne, Yorkshire. September 1942 proved to be a busy month with operations to bomb

Eileen and Dick Wildey c1941

Saarbrücken. A photo of the German searchlights which were beamed onto bombers for the purposes of directing anti-aircraft fire can be seen here. A raid on 4 October 1942 gives an indication of just what these bomber crews were flying into. Dick noted in his Log Book, 'Operations Bombing town of Aachen.[6] Held in searchlights. Bad weather on route – icing and electrical storms. Bombed target from 9000 feet – heavy flak.'[7]

German searchlights during a raid over Saarbrücken, 1 September 1942

On 15 October 1942, and by now promoted to Wing Commander, Dick piloted a Halifax, serial number W1058 'S' on an operation which included eight aircraft from No. 10 Squadron and 289 planes overall, to bomb Cologne. The Hailfax took off from its base at 18.33. The Operations Record Book noted, 'Seven crews attacked the primary target over thick ground haze, reporting fires in the target area and considerable flak and searchlight opposition. One crew

No.78 crew (left to right) Sgt. T.W. Donoghue (wireless operator); F/O Robertson; S/Ldr Wildey (first pilot); P/O N.W. McLeod (tail gunner);

Captained by W/C R. K. Wildey DFC OC 10 Sqn failed to return from this mission, no messages being received from the aircraft after it left base.'

Dick's wife Eileen held out hope for nearly a year that Dick may have been made a prisoner of war but in August 1943 she received the news of what happened on that fateful night from her OE brother Douglas who had been a POW for three years by then. Douglas had met a fellow internee who knew Flight Sergeant Sanderson Miller who was with Dick on the night the Halifax crashed. A full report of Dick's last moments on 15 October 1942 were provided by Flight Lieutenant Michael Davis who was the navigator that evening. Michael wrote to Eileen after the war:

> I will give you the story to the best of my memory and I don't think I am wrong over any important matters, even though the confusion at the time and the long interval may have casued me to forget some of the minor details.
>
> We first got into difficulties at a height of about 14,000 feet and with a very fine effort Dick regained level flight at about 5000. Unfortunately our aircraft caught fire at this point and after a short time it was clear that we could not control the fire: the inter-communication system, too, was out of use. Therefore Dick gave the order, by word of mouth to abandon aircraft. I received the order from the second pilot [Pilot Officer James Wilfred Murphy] and relayed it to the wireless operator and Bomb Aimer in the nose of the aircraft with me and then left the aircraft (if you remember the front escape hatch in the Halifax is in the navigation position).
>
> I heard later from the Bomb Aimer, who said that [he] left the aircraft last at a height of about 1000[ft] that Dick stayed with the aircraft all the time, trying to get in touch with the two gunners by the system of inter-communicating lights and giving them a chance to leave the aircraft. I myself am very grateful to him for his fine feat of flying in regaining control and it was certainly a great deed to stay in the aircraft as he did to improve the slim chance that the gunners had.
>
> The Bomb Aimer said that he heard the aircraft strike the ground shortly after he baled out and while I believe that none of us has any definite information I could not advise you to keep very much hope that Dick might be alive. If he had lost his memory he would have been almost certain to have been captured and identified from his disks.
>
> I shall always remember your husband with gratitude and I know the other members of the crew could say the same.

The Mid-Gunner, Sergeant Dubroy and Tail-Gunner, Flight Lieutenant Brindley were also killed in the crash whilst the remaining five members of the crew were made POWs.[8]

At the time of the crash Dick and Eileen were expecting their first child. Peter was born in April 1943. The Emanuel connection with the Wildey name was re-established in the 1980s when Peter sent his son Richard to Emanuel.

References

1 Letter 14 December 1939, p. 3. Richard Kemp Wildey's letters are held in the Emanuel School Archive.
2 Letter 24 May 1940.
3 Letter 29 May 1940.
4 'I Bombed Berlin' *The Sunday Express*, 15 September, 1940, p. 9. Also Richard Wildey's Letters to Eileen, 14 and 15 September 1940.
5 Operations Record Book, No. 78 Squadron, TNA, AIR/27/660 entry for 11 September Whitley Mk. V, P. 4958. Also Richard Wildey, RAF Pilot's Flying Log Book, 3rd, entries for September 1940, in Emanuel School Archive.
6 Dick spelt the town 'Archen', in the Log Book.
7 Richard Wildey, RAF Pilot's Flying Log Book, 3rd, entry for 4 October 1942.
8 Interetingly the ORB records the Mid-Gunner's name as Sgt. N. D. Dubrey, but a photo depicting a grave marker with the names of the three crewman, including Dick, killed in the crash, refers to a Sgt. J. W. Dubroy of the Royal Canadian Air Force.

The Last Flight of Halifax DK203

Maurice Gordon Sheerman *(Emanuel 1931–1933)*

Little is known about Maurice Sheerman's School career except that he was in the OTC and that his brother Eric also attended the School. However, Maurice's fate in the Second World War is well documented.

By October 1943 Maurice was on operations with No.76 Squadron RAF.[1] On 3 October its target was to bomb the Henschel works at Mittelfeld on the north-west outskirts of Kassel which sits on the river Fulda. Kassel was an old medieval German town that in the nineteenth century had been home to the Brothers Grimm who wrote many of their fairy tales there. But in the Second World War Kassel became a target for Bomber Command because of the Henschel works, which produced railway materials and locomotives as well as trucks and aircraft engines.[2]

On 3 October 1943 Flying Officer Maurice Sheerman was a tail gunner on the operation to bomb the works. The crew flew in a Handley Page Halifax V Serial No. DK203 'A'. The crew were:

Pilot – 2nd Lt. N. S. D. Eckhoff *(Norwegian)*
Tail Gunner – F/O M. G. Sheerman
Bomb Aimer – Sgt. R. Coupe
Navigator – Sgt. S. Meieran *(Norwegian)*
Wireless Operator/Air Gunner – Sgt. J. Skjelanger *(Norwegian)*
Mid-Upper Gunner – Sgt. C. H. E. Coster
Flight Engineer – Fl/Sgt. A. Hayes

At 6.13pm the Halifax took off from its base at Holme-on-Spalding Moor, in the East Riding of Yorkshire.[3] It was 50 miles from the target area when it received a 'blow of considerable force.' A hole in the metal cladding of the Halifax's forward fuselage appeared and the bomb aimer was sucked out of the aircraft along with the majority of the navigator's equipment. The bomb aimer was lucky to have

Halifax V Serial No. DK203 'A'

Maurice Sheerman (second from right) with the crew of Halifax DK203

survived; using his parachute he landed and was made a POW. The crew however, continued their journey. Lightening the load of the Halifax by jettisoning bombs and reducing altitude to maintain flying speed they decided to head home, navigating by the stars. As they approached the Dutch coast the Halifax was intercepted by a lone Luftwaffe night-fighter pilot, Lt. Heinz Vinke. The navigator Sigmund Meieran recalled what happened:

> The rear-gunner called 'fighter, fighter' and in that same second the flight engineer, who was standing next to me, yelled out in pain from being hit in his left leg. The entire rear section of the aircraft was ablaze. Hayes, despite the wound to his leg, and I grabbed some fire extinguishers and attempted to fight the fire, but it was to no avail. All extinguishing fluid gone, I turned around and saw the pilot directing me to get out. All the others had by then abandoned the aircraft and in the rush the flight engineer had taken my parachute. However, it did not take me long to find his and a few minutes later I landed in the sea.[4]

Reconstruction drawing by Willem de Jong depicting the removal of Maurice Sheerman's body from Halifax crash site

Maurice was killed and his body remained in the crashed aircraft, the shell of which had crashed on a sandbank east of Terschelling island. Maurice's remains were later recovered from the aircraft by the Germans and today he is buried in West Terschelling General Cemetery. A family, whose uncle adopted Maurice's grave at the end of the war, lays flowers on his grave each Dodenherdenking 4 May – a Dutch commemoration day.

The pilot Nils Eckhoff was killed whilst trying to escape the aircraft. The engineer Albert Hayes died of his wounds on 6 October. The wireless operator Jens Skjelanger as well as Sergeants Coupe and Coster were made POWs, but one of the most tragic stories is that of the navigator, Sigmund Meieran. Having escaped from Norway before it fell to the Germans in June 1940, Sigmund made his way to Sweden, Russia and Japan from where he sailed on a Norwegian merchant ship to Canada. Having joined the Royal Norwegian Air Force in Canada it was from here that Sigmund was transferred to England in 1943 and began operations with 76 Squadron. After he escaped from the Halifax Sigmund was made a POW. He made several escape attempts. Whilst in Canada Sigmund had changed his name Meieranovksi to Meieran to disguise his Jewish faith and also to protect his family in Norway in the event of his capture. After one escape attempt Sigmund was interrogated by a Gestapo Colonel who believed Sigmund to be Jewish because he 'had a big nose' but Sigmund suggested to the Colonel that he too must be Jewish because he also had a big nose. Sigmund survived this interrogation and was liberated from Stalag XI-B at Fallingbostel, Lower Saxony, on 16 April 1945 by British forces. But Sigmund's ordeal was not over. When he returned to Oslo to be reunited with his brother John he discovered that their parents, along with his brothers Jack and Charles and his five-year-old niece Elinor, had all been murdered by the Nazis in Auschwitz.[5]

The story of this Halifax crew was meticulously researched by a local Dutch historian, Willem de Jong, who went to great lengths in remembering their lives and due to his research work young men like Maurice and the crew of DK203 will rightly be remembered as individuals.[6]

References

1 For the history of 76 Squadron and its two revivals in the 1930s and 1940s see W. R. Chorley, *To See The Dawn Breaking* (Reprinted 1996), pp.7-15.
2 For the priorities of Bomber Command in 1943 see Sir Charles Webster and Noble Frankland, *History of the Second World War: The Strategic Air Offensive against Germany 1939–1945, Volume II: Endeavour* (HMSO, 1961).
3 TNA AIR/27/651 Operations Record Book 76 Squadron October 1943, p. 1.
4 W. R. Chorley, *To See The Dawn Breaking*, p. 92.
5 Our thanks to the Meieran family for supplying information about Sigmund's war experiences.
6 Willem de Jong's research is available on Tom Bint's website remembering 626 Squadron.

A Life in the Royal Air Force 1940–1946

Flight Lieutenant Gordon Eric Victor Townsend DFC

(Emanuel 1930–1936)

Vic Townsend was a member of the Emanuel OTC and played for the Second Fifteen. His elder brother Cyril attended Emanuel in the 1920s. In the Second World War Vic was awarded the Distinguished Flying Cross for his role as a navigator on operational tours to Germany, Italy and the Far East.

Fl/Lt Gordon Townsend

His DFC Citation notes, Flight Lieutenant Townsend 'participated in many attacks against heavily defended targets in Germany, Italy and the Far East. He has proved himself a most efficient navigator and his determination and fearlessness have played a large part in the successful completion of many missions.'

Vic wrote about his wartime experiences and the following is an edited account of his memoir.

Joining Up

In October 1940 I was interviewed for Air Crew. Later I was 'attested' into the RAF with a number of others, clutching a very tattered Bible. Under the orders of an old-sweat sergeant, we swore 'to defend King George, his heirs and successors.'

Initial Training

It was rumoured that we might be sent to bases near our homes. We didn't believe it, but amazingly I landed up in Kenley, a Battle of Britain base in 11 group. The first words I hear on arrival were on the tannoy. 'Red Section, Swannee Squadron, Scramble!' followed by the roar of Merlins.

We spent our time on Ground defence, learning about the Vickers Gas Operated Gun, filling sandbags and chipping ice off the runway at night by the light of a 'chance' floodlight, turned off without warning if enemy aircraft were thought to be in the area.

Gordon (fourth from left) with his crew

Gordon in a navigation class

I managed to visit my fiancée if I had a pass, returning by bus. Sometimes during an alert the conductor would hang out and ring the bell for the driver not to stop if no one was waiting. In 1941 I was sent down to Shoreham, to defend it with a 22mm Hispano Cannon in a gun pit on the bank of a canal on the east side of the drome. We did get attacked by some low flying ME's [Messerschmitts] one morning when I had come off duty and was having breakfast. The bods on the cannon let fly with their pathetic thirty rounds and because of the nature of the frying pan shape of the drome, succeeded in putting a few shells through a Commer truck parked on the other side of the drome!

Canada

We finally finished this stage of training and were sent to Blackpool to await shipment to Canada. We couldn't officially know it was Canada. But it seems someone in authority wasn't too sure either, for when we arrived at Halifax Harbour no one knew who we were! The RCAF had taken over the grounds of the Canadian National Exhibition, which was very large. This was the intake area for new recruits to the RCAF. Our flying training took place at Crumlin airport. Our class had a F/O Halperin, a brilliant maths man and a hard taskmaster when it came to classroom work on navigation, but when he came on the occasional flight to monitor our practical work in the air, he sat on the floor of the A/C looking green and was utterly unable to monitor anything.

When our course at Crumlin finished, we were shifted to Fingal Base for Bombing and Gunnery training. We were on Lake Erie, about 60 miles south of London. We flew in old Fairey Battles, even then obsolete, though they had been to France as the Advanced Striking Force in 1939. The Observer sat behind the Pilot, separated from him so that the only communication with him was through a small diameter tube. You had to crawl under the pilot to the bombing position, where there was a primitive bombsight. You slid back a hatch and slid the sight down into space. There was no glass and nothing between you and the waters of the lake.

On my first bombing trip, I dropped the last 7lb practice bomb. 'Bomb gone, exercise completed.' I don't remember if the pilot gave any 'hang on' warnings, but I do remember being pressed to the floor and seeing the sun through the open hatch. It was my first and only loop!

Leaving Canada

We sat in Halifax Harbour for about a week, with ice on the rigging and rumours of U-Boats waiting outside. When we did sail it wasn't in convoy. The troopships were escorted by a destroyer and a corvette, which made circles round us. We had a single gun in the stern. We had one or two emergencies and deck musters before one night we were called on deck again, heard the sound of depth charges being fired and our solitary gun produced its one and only bang.

The next morning – no destroyer. It had been sunk and we were told it had put itself in the path of the torpedo meant for us. We collected for the relatives of the 100 crew. We were glad to see an old Stranraer flying boat come out to meet us off the coast of Ireland. After landing we were sent down to Bournemouth.

Posting

We finally got into the real training at the Operational Training Unit (OTU) at Finningley Yorkshire, where we crewed up with Jack Cockshott, our Pilot, and our Wireless Operator Ted Roberts and Jack (killer) Liddell (called 'killer' by us on 61 because he never got a chance to fire his guns in anger). We knew absolutely nothing about each other,

Gordon in a training aircraft – Crumlin airfield, London, Ontario

so I was lucky with Jack. He finished up on 617 (the 'Dam Busters') as a Squadron Leader Flight Commander and DFC and Bar. We were all Sergeants at this stage.

We converted on to Wellingtons at OTU. It was here that my good friend Harry Jelleyman, a Welsh school teacher, was killed on night circuits and landings. I was also on these exercises and started about an hour after Harry. When I came into the room I shared with Harry and another fellow I saw his bed was empty. 'Where's Harry?' I said, – 'Haven't you heard? He's just got the chop', replied my roommate. Harry had got the trophy for the best navigator on the course in Canada.

Operations

Our first op to Genoa was not an auspicious beginning. We took off late due to a change to the reserve aircraft, so we arrived at the target late not helped by the fact that Jack did not believe the height of the Alps! Still the Italian gunners were quite hopeless. I discovered over Europe on the way to the target that I had left my parachute in our original aircraft. I didn't dare tell Jack for fear of worrying him. Italian trips were known as 'white glove trips' meaning that they had a lesser degree of risk.

Sleep patterns did not exist for the aircrew. Although we were on night ops, the time of take-off would vary from about four o'clock in the afternoon to midnight. The time of landing therefore varied from 10pm to 4 or 5 in the morning. It took about a couple of hours to stash our flying gear, go to the debriefing, have a traditional egg and bacon breakfast and cycle back to the farmhouse.

Pathfinder Force had its teething problems. On the first Berlin raid for about 18 months, we were given strict instructions not to bomb visually, but only on the ground markers. It was a very clear night and the ground was covered with snow, largely obscuring the normal topography. We waited – and waited. No indicators. We circled, in flak and searchlights. With few identifying marks on the ground we drifted downwind, save for a few rebels who did bomb visually. Eventually the target indicators did appear and we bombed, nowhere near the real target. English newspapers the next morning announced that 'The RAF were careful to bomb only the industrial portion of the city.' The first casualty of war is truth.

Some crews, not too keen on the target area, dropped their bombs short, in the countryside, or even in the Channel. So a megapower photoflash was automatically dropped when the Bomb Aimer pressed his button. The camera magazine, locked in place, was very quickly removed by the photo technicians as soon as the aircraft stopped rolling. Each squadron amassed points on a Photographic Ladder at Group HQ. If the photo showed an impact fairly near the aiming point, each of the crew was given a print of a Lancaster with all the crew members' names on it, signed by the Group Captain, in our case, Gus Walker. Closer still to the aiming point and you got a much larger print signed by the Group Commander, in our case Air Vice Marshal Cochrane.

A Commission and Instructing

My commission came through when I had been sent to 1654 Conversion Unit at Wigsley. Later, when I had my new uniform on, it took me a fraction of a second to realise I was being saluted for the first time! The Lancaster was a fine aircraft as we got more used to it, when the initial teething problems such as dodgy oil pressure, icing and the lack of heat for the gunners were either overcome or tolerated.

Probably the most enjoyable op we did was early in the tour. A low flying daylight trip to Milan through France, returning as dusk was falling to be past the German fighter bases in the dark. Another image forever in my memory is scraping over tree tops and lowering over the farm paddocks scaring a poor old French farmer at his plough.

Next I was posted to Hampstead Norris, in Berkshire, where I became a Flight Navigational Officer and had an assistant.

Off to India

We spent a week in Bombay, then attended a jungle training course and we didn't know what was going to happen to us. We spent D-Day on an airfield near Poona. We were very fed up. We were sent between Bangalore and Madras. I volunteered to work as a bomb aimer, just to get on a crew. I soon returned to navigating, but there wasn't much going on, as there was very little Japanese fighter activity any more.

We now flew in a Liberator which was a heavy aircraft and our trips were a fair bit longer than in Europe.

A satirical drawing from Gordon's Log Book listing his crew's names on a raid on Wilhelmshaven

Typhus and a Crash Landing

Between December 1944 and June 1945 we operated in Bengal. Whilst we were still working the squadron up I contracted 'Scrub Typhus', a high fever with a splitting headache. I was taken to hospital in Calcutta. When I was able to sit up, I had a sack of 'air letters' to read. They were dumped on my bed from other ranks in the R.A.F. to be censored, bits to be cut out that might be of use to the enemy. Many letters were semi-literate and it made me consider becoming a teacher of English. My first trip to Darjeeling was a really good pick me up. I ate well and taught myself to ride one of the ponies. There is a gap in my logbook between 27.09.44 and 09.12.44, so I must have been in hospital for some time. I began ops again on 13.12.44. We bombed bridges on the infamous Burma–Siam Railway. It was thought that only low level bombing would be accurate enough, especially as we knew that there were British, Aussie and New Zealand POWs in huts along the lines. We had no bombsight for low level but practised, with 7lb bombs, putting chinagraph marks on the glass panel in front of the bomb-aimer until we got some sort of reasonable result. Of course with a 250lb bomb it would all be different.

On our first attempt we charged along the line spraying gunfire to keep the Japs' heads down. Attacking at right angles was obviously not an option. Unfortunately the bomb bounced off the line, not being vertical enough to penetrate. It travelled along underneath the rear gunner with a 10 second delay. The rear gunner was counting off the seconds and yelling blue murder. We made a few attempts like this but were finally told that the Japs had alternative bridges already built should one bridge be destroyed.

We then moved 70 miles north of Calcutta. On 26 January 1945 we went over to a nearby drome to pick up another aircraft, manhandling a lot of pyrotechnics and ammo out. It had been used for Air Sea Rescue. Returning to base around dusk we must have undershot by a few feet. As far as I could make out from skid marks on the concrete the nose wheel hit the proud edge of the runway, where the paddy field stopped and burst its tyre. At close to 140mph the nose undercart went, then the main undercarts, one after the other and we sank onto our belly, slewing round fiercely. Fortunately we were all in our braced landing positions, myself against the main spar facing rearwards.

I had arranged with my wife to send her a coded letter, telling her I had 'heard from auntie' so that she would know that I had started ops. I hadn't written to her when I was sick, so she phoned the Air Ministry.

The Japanese were eventually turned back from the Indian Border and were on the run. Opposition on the ground was not very fierce and although we had two aircraft shot down over Moulmein, our greatest hazard was the weather. In non-monsoon weather we did long flights of between 10 – 15 hours, but we had virtually no nav-aids. Monsoon weather was a different matter. Torrential rain, thunder and lightning and heavy turbulence forced us to fly over the sea, attacking coastal targets. The only option was to fly below the cloud in the rain, where the turbulence was less, probably at fifty to one hundred feet. By the time this tour finished we had 34 ops, totalling 347.48 op hours.

Gordon in later years photographed in front of the Lancaster at East Kirkby

When the tour was finished I visited the Grand Hotel in Cal where I met my brother Cyril. We had a drink together then as I left him I was stopped by another Army Captain who said he recognised me from Emanuel School. I did not recognise him but when he told me his name, Simendinger [whose story is told in another article], I remembered, though I had never really known him, his name came immediately before mine on House Roll Call on Friday. I guess it had been eight or nine years since I had left school, so I was surprised at being recognised. Perhaps I had had a slightly higher profile than some as I had played rugby for the school and had appeared in several school plays.

The end of the war and Asmara

After some confusion I was posted to Egypt to instruct on a Liberator Conversion Unit. I flew across from Calcutta to Karachi to await an onward flight. Then, with no warning, we heard the news that the atom bomb had been dropped and the war was over. After a while in Cairo I was finally called to go to HQ. When I arrived at the Conversion Unit the Group Captain told me that they thought I had got lost in Tibet because it had taken me a few weeks to arrive!

Home

I finally got a plane to start my journey home, via Khartoum. And I began to wonder what the future really held for me. I was talking to a W/Cdr pilot, after we had reported to Group HQ. He said 'I can't go back to my old job.' – 'Why not Sir?' – 'I was a bus driver.' That was the problem for many men leaving the service. After travelling across Europe, we arrived in England and took the train to London and were bussed across to, I believe, King's Cross. The buses were manned by redundant aircrew.

Winning the DFC

My gong had come through whilst I was in Asmara, via my wife, who had seen an article in the local newspaper with the citation, also saying that I had been Mentioned in Despatches which was news to me. The official bumph eventually came through the channels and I got one of the DC3 pilots to get me ribbons in Karachi. This too got me extra status with the army wallahs and the Americans, most of whom were really desk men who had probably not seen much in the way of action. I was demobbed appropriately on 1 April 1946, given my grotty demob suit and was on my way home.

I could have stayed in the RAF and applied for a permanent commission but they couldn't tell me when I might get such a commission and couldn't even tell me when they could tell me when I might![1]

References

1 The memoir of Fl. Lt. Gordon E. V. Townsend 'A Life in the Royal Air Force 1940–1946.' The full memoir is available to read in the Emanuel School Archive.

Harold Bertram Hale

(Emanuel 1930—1937)

Harold lived in Allfarthing Lane, Wandsworth. During the Second World War he was a wireless operator and Air Gunner in both Coastal and Bomber Commands. His Observer's and Air Gunner's Flying Log Book survives and its detailed entries allow us to follow this young man's path through the war.

Harold Hale

After attending 9 Aircrew Selection Board on 25 August 1940 Harold was recommended for the two-year training as a wireless operator/air gunner (W/Op/AG). After training via a number of courses at Stratford-upon-Avon, Farnborough, Scarborough and Yatebury he qualified as a W/Op/AG at 8 Air Gunnery School at Evanton in May 1941.

Harold arrived for the last stage of his training at 10 OTU at Abingdon on 2 June 1941. Here Harold flew most of his flights as a wireless operator and three as an air gunner, flying on the Armstrong-Whitworth Whitely. His tours involved convoy patrols and anti-submarine sweeps along the Cornish coast. On 4 September 1942 Harold was flying as a wireless operator on a Whitley (6985) (R) which was on convoy patrol when they were attacked by two Ju (Junker) 88s, but the attack broke off and the Whitley escaped with minor damage. Then on 9 September he was on a Whitley piloted by Harry Gumbrell when on an anti-submarine sweep they were attacked by three Arado seaplanes (the standard aircraft of the German Navy in the Second World War). They didn't sustain any damage but instead managed to shoot down one of the seaplanes.

In October 1942 Harold was with 1654 Heavy Conversion Unit (HCU) at Wigsely in Nottinghamshire. Continuing his training on Manchesters and Lancasters he flew a number of training flights under Flight Officer Henry Maudslay, who later lost his life on the Dam Busters Raid. Rejoining 101 Squadron based at Holme-on-Spalding Moor, from where Harold had transferred to the 1654 HCU, Harold underwent a period of intense operational tours in the first half of 1943 with both 101 and 12 squadrons. Harold's Log Book attests to the dangers faced by bomber crews and not only from enemy fire for on 4 January 1943 Harold records that the Lancaster in which he was a wireless operator was hit by a British vessel. On 27 January 1943 he records that the pilot blacked out 50 miles from the Dutch coast.

Harold finished his first operational tour on 25 June 1943 and was commissioned as a Pilot Officer after a total of 26 ops. Between the middle of 1943 and late 1944 he was on rest tours being based with operational training units. In late 1944 he moved to 1699 HCU before becoming operational again in February 1945 with 223 Squadron at Oulton.

223 Squadron – Liberator, serial number TS526 (T)

In March 1945 the Allies were making their advance across the Rhineland and Bomber Command was still targeting industrial positions within Germany. On 21 March Flight Officer Norman Ayres's crew, of which Harold Hale was wireless operator, was scheduled for leave, but on 20 March 1945 they were assigned for an operation in support of the bombing of the synthetic oil producing plant at Böhlen near Leipzig and the Heide oil refinery at Hemmingstedt. The crew flew in a Liberator, serial number TS526 (T). They became

Date	Hour	Aircraft Type and No.	Pilot	Duty	Remarks (including results of bombing, gunnery, exercises, etc.)	Flying Times Day	Flying Times Night
					Time carried forward :—	319·50	273·10
5.3.45	1910	Liberator 42/50744-P	P/O Ayres	Wireless Op	Operations; S.D patrol Mannheim		6·35
8.3.45	1820	TS 519-S	P/O Ayres	—do—	Operations; S.D. patrol Hamburg.		7·05
12.3.45	1505	TS524	F/O AYRES	—do—	AIR FIRING.	1:10.	
14.3.45	1725	BV -P	P/O Ayres	—do—	Operations; S.D Patrol Wiesbaden		6·15.
20.3.45	2330	TS 526	F/O AYRES	—do—	OPS. MISSING.		
		Summary for MARCH 1945 / Unit 223 SQUAD. / Date / Signature		1. LIBERATOR		1:10	20·00
		A E L Morris F/Lt		o/c B Flt.			
					Total Time ...		

Harold Hale's Flight Log showing his final operations

part of the western Window (an anti-radar counter measure) force leading a feint attack on Kassel. The Germans believed that Kassel was a genuine target and moved at least five night fighters to counter the threat. As the Liberator turned away from Kassel it was hit. The evidence assembled by Squadron Leader Richard Forder and Steve Bond's book, *Special Ops Liberators: 223 (Bomber Support) Squadron, 100 Group, and the Electronic War*, suggests that it was hit by Hauptmann Johannes Hager flying in a Messerschmit (Me 110 G4). The Liberator spun out of control and most parts were on fire. The pilot Norman Ayres attempted to keep it under control, evidenced by the crew's efforts to lighten the aircraft and thereby keep it in the air. Unfortunately it faced wooded rising ground on a hill named Opferberg. Breaking in two and with one of its engines tearing off, it hit the ground. The only survivor from the crew was Alfred Cole.[1]

Harold had married his girlfriend Doris Sands at St Paul's church, Hammersmith during the war and we can only imagine how Doris must have received the news of Harold's loss, especially so near the end of the war. Similarly Harold's cousin Bob Lewis, serving at the time in the Far East, describes receiving the news as 'earth-shattering.' Harry Gumbrell, the pilot on many of Harold's operational tours with 101 Squadron, remembered him as a 'quiet, reserved, man.'[2] Interestingly the news of Harold's death did not reach the School immediately and it was only much later that they were notified. This fact is evidenced in Harold's name being added at the end of the list of names in the Roll of Honour book and the School's Second World War memorial.

References

1 For a full account of Liberator TS526 (T) operations and fate see Dr. Steve Bond and Richard Forder, *Special Ops Liberators: 223 (Bomber Support) Squadron, 100 Group, and the Electronic War* (2011), pp. 140-162.

2 Ibid. p. 237.

Into the Storm

Eric John McMillan *(Emanuel 1933—1938)*

After leaving Emanuel Eric, known as 'Jack', worked for the London and Lancashire Insurance Company in Fleet Street, where he met his sweetheart and later wife Doris. The offices were bombed during the war and the staff were relocated to a mansion in Surrey. At the time Jack spoke about volunteering for air crew services. His work colleagues teased him, calling him Biggles and Brylcreem boy but Jack was serious and on 11 June 1941 he enlisted at Weston-Super-Mare. The No. 3 Aviation Candidates Selection Board recommended him for training as a wireless operator/air gunner.

Doris had misgivings about Jack entering the services but remembered the feeling of pride she had when he put his uniform on for the first time. Jack has been described thus, 'He cut a dashing figure, tall with wavy, brown hair and the most wonderful sparkling blue eyes that matched his keen sense of humour ... By nature he was a responsible young man who was mature beyond his years and very popular among his circle of friends. He was a competent rower and keen on all sports.'[1]

Eric McMillan

After training at No. 10 (Signals) Recruits Centre in Blackpool, in late 1941 Jack was posted to Yatesbury in Wiltshire where he was one of forty-five u/t (under-training) wireless operators at No. 2 Signals School. Here Jack continued to learn Morse Code signalling. From Yatesbury he was posted to 24 Squadron at RAF Hendon. In April 1943 he was learning to shoot on an Emergency Air Gunner's course at No. 1 Air Armament School, situated at Manby in Lincolnshire. This was followed by training at No. 100 Advanced Wireless Training course where 'the emphasis of the course was on cross-country exercises' and where 'the wireless operators were able to practise making contact with airfields around the country' with 'exercises becoming longer and including more night flying.'[2] Jack passed this course in June 1943.

In May 1943 Jack married his sweetheart Doris in the parish church at Burgh Heath in Surrey. Wartime rationing meant food was limited but their families and the community chipped in to make the day a memorable one. They spent a week together, first stop London, staying at the Strand Palace Hotel in the West End for two nights and then on to Maidenhead to stay at the Riviera Hotel. It was in Maidenhead that Jack rowed his bride up and down the Thames. After a week filled with memories wartime realities returned and Jack was posted to 12 Operational Training Unit (OTU) at Chipping Warden on 15 June 1943 where he became part of a regular crew for the first time. It was at the 12 OTU where Jack received further specialised training on the latest equipment of its time including the Harwell Box, fitted with radio telephony and direction finding equipment. These training compartments were the forerunner of the computerised flight simulators of later generations.

Eric McMillan's wedding day

It was while based at 12 OTU that Jack became part of a crew that was transferred to a Heavy Conversion Unit at Stradishall in early September 1943. On 3 October Jack was involved in an accident when the Stirling he was flying in swung off the runway and crashed on to rough ground resulting in the undercarriage collapsing. At the time Jack didn't tell Doris about this. He expected to receive a commission soon and looked forward to joining a squadron.

Jack would often visit Doris in London, obtaining a 48 hour pass. The last time they saw each other was at Liverpool Street Station as Jack returned to Stradishall. In the early evening of 22 October 1943 he was with his crew preparing for a 'Night Special' exercise which was to consist of a long cross-country run over the route Stradishall – York – Mull of Galloway – Ludlow – Leighton Buzzard – Stradishall. At approximately 21.40 hours Stirling EF352 crashed six miles NNE of Hereford at Rosemaund Farm, Preston Wynne, killing Jack and eight other crew members. The findings of the Court of Inquiry into the cause of the crash were inconclusive, although both adverse weather in the form of a thunderstorm and icing have been offered as possibilities. The latter could have caused blockages to the carburetors or oil coolers which could have led to a loss of power. The Court of Inquiry concluded that the aircraft had hit the ground vertically and at high speed, exploding on impact.

Doris's daughter from her second marriage decided to write about her mother's first husband and the crew of Stirling EF352 and in 1998 published *Into the Storm: The Making of a Bomber Crew* with Dennis Williams. Sue was moved by Jack's story from an early age and in 1996 started making enquiries about the accident and location of the crash site which until 1996 her mother Doris had not known. Doris and Sue visited the crash site that year and what follows is Sue's account of what happened that day:

> 53 years later Doris stood at the site of the aircraft crash for the first time in her life. There was now nothing remarkable about this place, the corner of a field like so many others on the farm. The sun was shining and it was hard to envisage the scene of destruction in the field on the night of the accident. Then, great craters had been made by the Stirling's engines as they bored deep into the heavy clay soil. Many trees had been mutilated as the aircraft cut through them and others were destroyed by fires which followed the massive explosion as hundreds of gallons of fuel detonated on impact. Wreckage was scattered as far as two miles away and for weeks small pieces were being found in the pastures and ploughed fields of the surrounding undulating countryside which typifies Herefordshire. For the local inhabitants this was a horror story, the tragedy of war having been brought to a part of the country which mercifully had escaped serious action until that time.
>
> It was difficult for Doris, at last knowing that this was the place where her young husband of almost a lifetime ago had drawn his final breath. Her thoughts, as always, that this accident should never have happened, were made so much more confusing by the lack of any evidence which might have revealed its cause. Had Jack been aware that the aircraft was crashing? Did he suffer? For these and many other questions there were no answers which would make sense of the waste of life.
>
> Over more than half a century Doris has never forgotten her love for Jack. It was as a remnant of that love that she visited Rosemaund Farm in 1996 at the age of seventy-six, and laid roses, one red and eight white, at the spot where nine young men died together. She could still cry for Jack down all those years of lost opportunities and unrealised dreams. As she gazed across the field she wished with all her heart that Jack could be walking towards her once more.[3]

A memorial service was held and a plaque unveiled to the nine young men at Holy Trinity Church, Preston Wynne on Sunday 8 June 1997 and so these brave young souls are forever remembered.

References

1 D. Williams & S. Mintram-Mason, *Into the Storm: The Making of a Bomber Crew* (1998), p. 52.
2 Ibid. p. 53.
3 Ibid. p. 8.

Recipients of the Distinguished Flying Medal

These Old Emanuels were recipients of the Distinguished Flying Medal. In each case their citation has been recorded.

Richard Frost

Ronald Cuthbert Besant *(Emanuel 1922—1930)*
580838 Acting Sergeant, No. 51 Squadron

L.G. 22/11/1940, Air Observer, Air28856.

> This NCO has shown courage and zeal well above average. He has completed 28 operational flights and his good work has contributed largely to the successful sorties of the crews with whom he has been flying.
>
> 20 September, 1940.

Remarks by AOC:

> The efficiency, courage and enthusiasm of the Air Observer has been a great factor during 28 operational flights which he has completed over enemy territory, producing most successful results. Recommended for an award of the Distinguished Flying Medal.

Ronald's name did not appear on Emanuel's original Roll of Honour or Second World War memorial in the School Chapel. His death was discovered during the course of research for this book and so his name will appear on a new memorial in the Emanuel School chapel which will commemorate all those OEs who were not originally included. At Emanuel Ronald was a member of the Dramatic Society. Ronald went missing over the Bay of Biscay, later confirmed killed, on 11 August 1943 whilst flying as an observer in a de Havilland Mosquito FB.Mk.IV.

Richard Charles Frost *(Emanuel 1935—1938)*
905118 Flight Sergeant, No. 55 Squadron

L.G. 5/2/1943, Sorties 78, Flying hours 248, W.Op/Air Gnr, Air2/8933.

> This NCO Wireless Operator/Air Gunner, on his second operational tour, has been a member of Sqn. Ldr. Plinston's crew since June, 1942. Between 1st and 22nd July, 1942, he made 15 sorties against the enemy's troop positions and landing grounds. His keenness, efficiency and devotion to duty have set a very fine example to both experienced and inexperienced members of aircrews in the squadron. He has now completed a total of 78 operational sorties against the enemy involving 248 hours operational flying. He is recommended for the award of Distinguished Flying Medal.
>
> 21 December, 1942.

At Emanuel Richard was a member of both the Cross Country and Tennis teams. Richard's sister married Old Emanuel Alan Skillern who was killed during the Italian Campaign. In his letters home Alan Skillern often asked after his brother-in-law Richard who was known as 'Dickie.'

In the Christmas Term 1939 edition of *The Portcullis* Richard wrote about his experiences as an RAF recruit:

Diary of an RAF Recruit

Like many of my contemporaries I found, at the outbreak of war, that to try and join up was extremely difficult. The Army and Navy were not taking any more recruits and so I tried for the RAF. To my intense satisfaction I was accepted and began the hectic life of a recruit. The idea seemed to be that we must be rushed through a very extensive and thorough training in the shortest possible time.

On enlistment I found myself, with many others, waiting in a cold room for a medical examination – to fail in it meant rejection. Fortunately, or perhaps because of a need for recruits in the branch I was entering, most of us passed through successfully and awaited with some trepidation our fate.

In common with many others I imagined that every man in a RAF uniform was a potential flier, such is the folly of youth. How soon were we to be deceived. The electricians, mechanics, fitters, armourers, ground staff and wireless operators may never leave terra firma, but they are a very essential part of the youngest fighting force. If a recruit does not possess [War Office] Certificate 'A' or 'B' he is sent to a 'receiving depot.' Here he is given a short test in his civilian occupation and if the examiner can be convinced he is proficient, he may not be sent to a training school. Such a course, however, is the exception rather than the rule.

At the training school we are taught to apply our particular knowledge to aircraft. The next event in the life of a recruit is something with the prepossessing title of a 'Disciplinary Course.' For this course we are transferred to an RAF station. Here previous training as an OTC is invaluable. The disciplinary course consists of rifle and foot drill. Such a course to an OE presents few difficulties.

Life in an RAF depot is somewhat similar to Corps Camp. At 6am, with the usual curses, we hear reveille. Beds have to be made, kit cleaned and at 7am we are ready for breakfast. The difference between Corps Camp now becomes apparent – our food is excellent. After breakfast from 8am until 9am we have a hour's physical training, then from nine until three with an hour and a half break for lunch, drill. At 3pm we are given a lecture, corresponding to a demonstration at camp.

On being passed out one is either sent to a squadron to commence duty, or to an RAF school for technical training. It was the fate of the writer to be sent to such a technical school. The recruit stage is over and the specialist training just beginning. Hard work mentally as well as physically.

Here the writer boggles; at the present time he is, he believes, working really hard to obtain a technical certificate. Life in the RAF is clean, healthy, and exciting. Civilian life, without regret is left far behind.

On 12 February 1943 Richard's DFM and experiences in the North African Campaign were reported in *The Streatham News*:

Twenty-one in April, he [Richard] was educated at Streatham Hill College and then Emanuel School, Wandsworth and developed a love for rugger and tennis. On leaving school he became apprenticed to a local firm of bookbinders ... When war broke out he volunteered as an observer and in July, 1940, was posted to the Middle East. There is no doubt that the knowledge of wireless he derived from a transmitter which he operated at home was no small factor in his rapid promotion. He has had many adventures abroad and on one occasion extinguished a fire which took hold of an aircraft by beating it out with his hands and the logbook.

During the Abyssinian Campaign he operated with his squadron from airfields in the Sudan, and last spring was detailed for special duties. So attached has he become to his squadron – a crack squadron which has broken two records – that he refused two offers of an instructor's job in Kenya.

In his letters home appear some vivid accounts of the air war in the Middle East. An extract from a letter he wrote last September detailed the opening stages of Montgomery's victory drive to Tripoli: "I was in the first formation that brought back the news of the full-scale retreat and from the air it appears a ghastly shambles. Trucks were three or four abreast, moving at speed along tracks made for single lines of transport. Fires were burning where oil and petrol had had to be destroyed. The air was full of our own aircraft on harrying duties. All this indicated the enormously superior forces at our disposal. Return tickets have definitely been issued this time – we go to stay!"

Alan Patrick Savage *(Emanuel 1921—1929)*
546368 Flight Sergeant, No. 254 Squadron

L.G. 26/9/1941, Sorties 76, Flying hours 267, W.Op/Air Gnr, Air2/9257.

This NCO has been a member of this unit since its formation in October, 1939, and has been the Wireless Operator/Air Gunner on 76 operational sorties totalling 267 hours. He has always been an example to the other aircrews and has taken part in the majority of this unit's operations over Norway. By his accurate fire, he has driven off enemy aircraft in many engagements and with careful instructions to the pilot as to the avoiding action to be taken has enabled the aircraft to escape under cover of cloud. On 6 July, 1940, his section of two Blenheims was acting as an escort to our Naval force 100 miles east of Stavanger and was engaged by four enemy craft. Both Blenheims were shot down after a hot fight and though the aircraft in which Flight Sergeant Savage was Air Gunner was in flames, he continued firing until it struck the sea. He was picked up by one of our cruisers and returned safely.

18 July, 1941

At school Alan was a member of the Emanuel OTC.

(left) Ronald Simedinger's DFM and (right) Ronald Simendinger

Ronald Charles Simendinger

(Emanuel 1932—1938) **P./O., No. 78 Squadron**

At Emanuel Ron played for the Second Fifteen and was a member of the OTC. Ron joined the RAF in late 1941 at the age of 20. After training in the Isle of Man and other locations his first operational sortie was in November 1942, where he was bomb-aimer on a raid over Turin. By March 1943 he had completed his first tour – 30 Ops – as bomb-aimer with 78 Squadron, based at Linton-upon-Ouse in Yorkshire, flying Halifax bombers. He was awarded the DFM and became a commissioned officer. His DFM citation stated, 'A very efficient bomb aimer, has completed a tour of operational duty during which he has maintained a very high standard of efficiency.'

His second tour of bombing operations as navigator was between April and December 1944 with 76 Squadron based at Holme-on-Spalding Moor in Yorkshire and then with 192 Squadron at Foulsham in Norfolk, again flying Halifax bombers. In the summer of 1944 before and after the D-Day landings he undertook a dozen Ops supporting the ground offensive in northern France.

He continued flying at the end of the war on duties round the world, and remained with the RAF reserve until 1952.

Ronald Simendinger (second from left) and crew at Holme-on-Spalding Moor

Ron remained very proud of the Halifax bomber – aggrieved that it never enjoyed the heroic standing of the Lancaster. Nevertheless it brought him back safely time and time again, much to the relief of his wife Joy.

In Memoriam - Emanuel's RAF & RAFVR losses

The following Old Emanuels lost their lives in either aircraft accidents or on operations. The youngest was nineteen and the oldest 26 when they were killed.

Anthony Elger

Anthony Charles Elger, RAF, F./Sgt.

(Emanuel 1935–1939)

Anthony was killed when two Lancaster Bombers were involved in a mid-air collision on 20 December 1942. Anthony was flying in Lancaster W4269 of No. 44 Squadron when shortly after it took off from Waddington it crashed into an Avro Lancaster W4182 WS-B. Both bombers fell from the sky out of control and crashed on Bracebridge Heath, about two miles south of Lincoln. All fourteen airmen on board both aircraft lost their lives. Anthony had only completed his training a few months previously but had taken part in numerous successful bombing raids.

At school Anthony had a love for music and a remarkable memory for cricket statistics. He was known to organise school trips to the West End and on one occasion more than 60 boys accompanied him to the theatre. He was also a leading member of the School Gramophone Club. The Portcullis noted, 'Elger was a person of great charm, full in interests, which he followed with keen study. He was one of those who would have done much to make the world a better and brighter place.'

Raymond Fitzgerald

Douglas John Fitzgerald, RAFVR, F./Sgt.

(Emanuel 1933–1939)

and Raymond C Fitzgerald, RAFVR, F./Sgt.

(Emanuel 1934–1939)

Douglas Fitzgerald was a pilot of a Beaufighter X (Serial number NE778) aircraft of 236 Squadron which crashed into the sea two to three miles from its base of North Coates on 30 August 1944. At the time of the crash he had been part of a 'Recce in Force' which consisted of 50 Beaufighter and twelve Mustang aircraft which were searching for enemy ships. A patrol found parts of the main plane, three aircraft wheels and an empty dinghy attached to the main plane but no survivors.

By a tragic coincidence Raymond C. Fitzgerald, another Old Emanuel who was flying as Navigator on the same aircraft, was also killed. They were not related.

As a schoolboy Douglas had been a member of the Modern Sixth class and had passed his London Matriculation exams. He played for both the First Fifteen rugby team and the Second Eleven cricket squad.

The Commanding Officer of 236 Squadron wrote to Douglas's parents about the two Fitzgerald boys:

Douglas Fitzgerald

Jack Royal

> Your son has been on my squadron for just over four months and he and his navigator gave every promise of becoming an outstanding operational crew. They were both very popular amongst the air crew and ground crew alike and their loss is felt very keenly not only by me personally, but by the whole squadron.

Douglas had married a Miss E. M. Adams only a few weeks before his death. At Emanuel Douglas was great friends with G. 'Eric' Richardson (Emanuel 1929–1936) who was killed at Dunkirk in 1940. After Eric was killed Douglas wrote the following epitaph on the back of a photo he had of Eric:

He loved the birds and green places,
And the wind of the heath;
And saw the brightness of the skirts of God.

Jack Douglas Royal, RAFVR, F./Lt., Mentioned in Despatches

(Emanuel 1926–1934)

As a schoolboy Jack Royal was a great athlete and was a member of the First Fifteen and the First Eleven and was remembered in particular for being a fantastic and stylish runner. He played the three-quarter position on the rugby field and was noted for his speed and skill in opening up the game. As a cricketer he was a very reliable batsman. He was also a House Prefect and a member of the OTC. Jack joined the RAFVR as a Sergeant Pilot in 1936 and was a Wellington Bomber Captain who made many raids over Germany. He was also Mentioned in Despatches. In 1942 Jack was a Flight Lieutenant operating from 20 OTU but on 18 May that year he was killed whilst flying a Wellington (Serial Number P2516) in a training flight. Shortly after taking off the aircraft flung off the runway and crashed into an excavator killing Jack and two members of his crew as well as the operator of the excavator.

In 2014 Jack Royal's granddaughter contacted the School. After Jack had been killed in the aircraft accident his son was adopted. It wasn't until his son who was searching on the internet in 2014 discovered his father's name appearing in a list published on the Emanuel School website that he and his family knew where his father had attended school. Furthermore the family were given a number of photos of Jack's school days and also photos of him in Old Emanuel Rugby teams. Jack's son had never seen a photo of his father until this time. From an Emanuel rugby photo Daniel Kirmatzis recognised that an Old Emanuel Second World veteran Bill Taylor had played Rugby with Jack Royal in the early 1930s and so Jack's family were put in contact with Bill who was able to illuminate the family about the talented athlete he remembered at School.

(above) Rodney Young (third from right)

Back row (left to right), K.C. Bloore, F.W. Harris, D.L. Roddis, N.S. Fairman, L.W. Shaw, M.E. Vincer, B.F.T. Johnson, G.P. Warren, W.C. Neath
Centre (left to right), M.W. Knight, A.F. Fox, W.L. Page, C.G.M. Broom (Headmaster), K.J. Gurling, H.S. Page, E.D. Page
On ground (left to right), F.G. Burrett, R.P. Smith

Rodney Young

Rodney Frederick Harding Young, RAFVR, W/O, Winner of DFM

Emanuel (1926–1934)

Rodney was described in *The Portcullis* as 'outstanding for his quiet manner and his steady application to school work.' He was a School Prefect, Captain of Raglan House, and a Sergeant in the Corps. He was also awarded School Colours for rugby. He left school in 1934 and joined the RAFVR in 1938 being called up when war broke out. He was awarded the Distinguished Flying Medal in 1941.

> Young, Rodney Frederick Harding. 741708 Sergeant, No 144 Squadron.
>
> L.G. 6/6/1941. Sorties 31, Flying hours 198.25. Pilot. Air2/9333.
>
> For continuous gallantry and devotion to duty during raids into enemy territory including four flights to Berlin. This NCO has carried out 31 operational trips, making a total of 198.25 hours operational flying. During this time, his work has been of the very highest order and he has never hesitated if necessary to bring his aircraft to a low altitude to locate and attack the target. All Sergeant Young's flying has been carried out during the winter months, generally under very severe weather conditions and there is no doubt that his coolness has many times been responsible for the safe return of his aircraft to base.
>
> 25 April, 1941

Rodney was reported missing after a raid on Frankfurt on 25 August 1942 and is believed to have drowned.

The Commander of his Squadron, in a letter to his family wrote:

> Your son had been with my squadron since March and he had maintained the reputation with which he came and continued to display the same gallantry and skill in the performance of his hazardous duties, which deservedly won him the DFM some time ago. He has taken part in a further twenty raids including the 'Thousand Raids' and the daylight attack on Danzig and he was, without doubt, one of my outstanding pilots. He was well known and liked by all and we are most sorry to lose him.

Bramwell Frederick Thomas Johnson, RAF, Sgt./P. *(Emanuel 1933–1939)*

Bramwell visited Emanuel, in Petersfield, only two weeks before his death. He was an exceptional athlete and was crowned Victor Ludorum in 1940 after leading the School Athletics Team. He also played for the First Fifteen and had the reputation of playing an energetic game with endless stamina. He was also a House Prefect, Captain of Howe, Captain of Fives, Second Eleven cricket player and was a Corporal in the JTC where he gained his War Office Certificate 'A' qualification. Bramwell was a true all-rounder and was a member of both the School Shooting VIII and Surrey Colts Shooting Team. Bramwell left School and went into the world of business but soon volunteered for flying duties with the RAF. He had reached the rank of Sergeant Pilot but on the evening of 16 July 1941 whilst flying in a Wellington bomber (Serial Number IC X9630 BL-J), which was returning from a bombing raid over Hamburg, he lost his life. The Wellington's crew had radioed routinely as it crossed the Dutch Coast on its return but it crashed into the sea. Bramwell's body and that of another crew member were never recovered. Three other crew members' bodies were recovered and buried and one crew member survived the crash and was made a prisoner of war. Bramwell was only nineteen when he died.

Bramwell Johnson

An Artist's War

Cecil Keeling *(Emanuel 1923–1928)*
Artist, etcher and war illustrator

Cecil Keeling was a book illustrator and engraver of international repute. He illustrated several books including two which recount his early service experiences. In *Pictures from Persia* he explored his time in Baghdad and Persia (modern Iran) describing and illustrating his take on the peoples and places he visited. This account includes descriptions of how British soldiers intermingled with the populations and provides an interesting perspective on everyday life in the markets, shops and alleyways of the Middle East during wartime.

Cecil also published another war-related book *Modicum of Leave* a humorous account of a soldier's leave from camp life whilst stationed in the UK. He served with the Royal Artillery but details of his service are as yet not in the public domain. However whilst stationed in Italy he painted on his tent canvas, the variety of uniforms worn by different nationalities. This is now part of the Fire Power Museum's collection. After the war he illustrated a number of books including being a contributory illustrator for the publication *The Queen's Beasts* which depicts the Heraldic animals which stood at the entrance of Westminster Abbey on the occasion of Queen Elizabeth II's Coronation in 1953. Cecil died in the 1970s.

Reproduced here are eight of Cecil Keeling's illustrations with descriptions from his two wartime related works.

1

1. Baghdad – Here along the colonnaded pavement, the crowd swam towards us, out of the shadow into the light, faces catching a ray of green or violet or orange light from the shop windows and into shadow again. Goya faces, Daumier faces, Gillray faces. Faces of young men that looked curiously ashen and dead, only the eyes were brilliant and alive. Faces pitted by smallpox or ravaged by hereditary disease. Perfect faces, like terra-cotta masks with eyes, eye-brows that seemed to have been painted upon them with Indian ink. Enormous black eyes that shone beneath the shadow of the kuffieh, or, more startlingly, blue eyes fringed with heavy black lashes. Eyes that were not eyes at all, but hideous fixed red and white globes.

3

2

4

2. Persian Faces – As we halted, with the flat, mud-coloured roofs of Kermanshah lying before us in the distance, the lads of the fields came out to greet us, appearing in [a] satisfying variety of rustic Persian costume...

3. Charity – At the car park, picking its way from puddle to puddle like a lame frog, was a dreadful child beggar. His face was withered like a monkey's and his eyes were surrounded by flies. His hands and feet were so ingrained with filth that they had become seamed and coarsened like the skin of a tortoise. He was naked save for a pair of tattered pantaloons and a soiled strip of rag knotted about his shoulders, his flesh was a dead grey-brown. With his paws tucked beneath his armpits he stood shivering and whimpering before a group of British soldiers, who stared down at this apparition in shocked embarrassment, sucking at their pipes.

4. The Voice of Authority – Near the bridge was a little encampment. A staff car drew up on the road and a Brigadier stepped out, with the calm deliberation of one who never has cause to be flurried and made his way to the first tent. A soldier appeared at its entrance, yawning and carrying a towel upon his arm. He saw the formidable, emblazoned figure descending upon him, leaped to attention and appeared to mutter some swift, panic-stricken warning to the tents' occupant and a little, humble, distraught figure emerged, damp as from a bath, fumbling with a cap in one hand and clutching a towel about his naked loins with the other. Officer disturbed while bathing. The Brigadier appeared to enjoy the discomfiture of this underling with a sour relish. The Batman enjoyed it. I enjoyed it, maliciously and then realised how small our mental world had become.

5. Corner of my Tent – I had always regarded a tent as the flimsiest and least inviting of all temporary abodes. But our tent, erected over the pit, became an inviting cavern. We bought hurricane lamps and made ingenious little illuminations out of tobacco tins, filled with paraffin and wicks made from pieces of tent rope ... As time passed, a lively Persian note crept into the decoration of my particular corner in the hut. I bought a small china horse, a couple of pots and a china cat with a sweeping moustache that constantly reminded me of the late Mr. Neville Chamberlain. I bought a wall hanging and draped it upon the tent wall. I liked my notes of naïf colour amid the chaos that my bed space almost always presented – not untidiness, I protested, at each successive rebuke, but picturesque disorder.

6. Frost – Two of our men, returning by car to the camp at night, lit up with their headlights a frightful withered figure that stood by the roadside with snowflakes whirling round it. The following morning they found the creature lying upon the road, frozen to death, the powdery snow drifting lightly across his hollow features and wasted limbs.

7. A Modicum of Leave – The first leave! Who doesn't know the thrill of it, the excitement of those last fumblings with one's wayward kit-bag, the grand feeling of having a leave-pass in one's pocket! Even the grotesque difficulties which beset the equipment-laden warrior as he gets wedged on the escalator are borne with blissful patience. Then the joy of meeting old friends on the way – then home, the pride of the family!

8. A selection of uniforms as worn by various Allied soldiers in Italy, painted on Cecil Keeling's tent canvas.

6

7

8

A Queen's Man

Derek Harrington *(Emanuel 1926–1933)*

The following account is based on an article written by Old Emanuel Peter Harrington about his father's experiences in the Second World War.

Derek Harrington was an outstanding schoolboy. He hooked for the First Fifteen, rowed for the First Eight, was Captain of Boats, House Prefect of Clyde and a School Prefect. He was awarded his full rowing colours in 1932. He was also a very committed member of the OTC where he was a Lance Sergeant and passed his War Office Certificate 'A' in March of 1932. Derek was a member of the Dramatic Society and was a member of the Modern Sixth class. He often wrote to the Old Emanuel Association during the war years.

Clyde Grundy Cup Squad 1930 Derek Harrington (first from right)

Peter Harrington recalls that his father's saying, 'Hitler took away the best years of my life', was said more as a statement of fact than one of deep resentment. His interest in the army started in the OTC, and he became a Lance Corporal and commanded the Clyde Grundy Cup Squad. In 1932 he enjoyed attending a camp at Tidworth Park where Emanuel were crowned champions. After passing the OTC Certificate 'A' examination he was eligible for consideration for a commission in one of the reserve forces and had been promoted to sergeant by the time he left the school in 1933. After school, during teacher training, he joined the Queen's Royal Regiment, upon receiving a commission.

Captain Derek Harrington, King's African Rifles

When war began he was called up to the Queen's Royal Regiment and spent the very early stages of the war defending the Kent and Sussex coasts. Not much information exists from this period except the excitement of arresting and detaining a French submarine and its crew to ascertain they were not German 'invaders.' Derek transferred to RAF Brize Norton in Oxfordshire where he gained his pilot's licence and 'wings', training on the Airspeed Oxford A10. Although he remained in the RAF until 1942, Derek said that 'the RAF trained too many pilots' so he returned to the Army on 3 October 1942.

Derek (centre) at Brize Norton 1941–42 during the Secondary Flying Training Course (flying Oxfords)

In 1943 he was posted to East Africa as War Substantive Lieutenant on 24 June 1943 and was initially attached to East Africa Command, 55 (SR) GT Company. For most of his service he was attached to the 1/1st King's African Rifles (KAR), who were based in Jinja, Uganda during the Second World War. He was involved in running convoys of supplies.

This was an exceptionally busy and adventurous time for Derek who travelled extensively and had a wide range of duties. He also enjoyed the varieties of wildlife he encountered whilst in Africa. He journeyed to Jinja as well as a number of other places, including Nairobi, Mombasa and Gil Gil in Kenya; Juba in Sudan and Mwanza in Tanganyika. The convoys of supplies ran from Juba in Sudan to Mombasa on the coast but it is unclear what they were for as the East African Campaign, which occurred mainly to the north in Somaliland, Eritrea and Ethiopia, had finished with the fall of the Italian East African Forces just before his arrival in 1943.

Derek and wife Muriel on their wedding day, 23 September 1939

There is a reference to Derek's time in Africa in *The Portcullis*, Autumn Term, 1943, which reads: 'D. J. Harrington is finding life in Kenya most exhilarating. His last airgraph spoke of skinning a python to send home to his young son Peter.'

In 1944 things took a turn for the worse when he broke his leg whilst undergoing training on an assault course. If the break hadn't occurred he may have been transferred to Burma. Later in 1944 and 1945 he was promoted to Acting Captain and then Temporary Captain. He returned home to the UK after the end of the war once he was able to get a ship from Mombasa. He had a very successful career as a teacher becoming headmaster in schools in both Reigate and Carshalton.

Geoffrey Victor Smith

(Emanuel 1935–1939)

At Emanuel Geoffrey was in the Air Training Corps (ATC) and also rowed for the School. In the summer of 1939 he took his matriculation exams but he did not do well enough in French to matriculate. In September 1939 he was evacuated with the School to Petersfield where the boys were delighted to find some of their lessons were to be held in a local pub. In January 1940 he retook his exams and matriculated. He had the rare, if not unique, distinction of achieving 100% in maths on both occasions.

Geoffrey Victor Smith

Geoffrey in later years on a birthday Tiger Moth flight at White Waltham

For a short time after leaving school he worked for his father in his publishing business in Battersea. He applied to join the RAF as a pilot but was too young and his father told him that in the meantime he had to get a proper job, so he then joined the Westminster Bank. A regular customer told him of a special scheme set up during the war for those who had matriculated who had applied to joined the armed forces and were waiting to be called up. The scheme allowed them to study at the top universities, completing an academic year in one continuous six month period, and at the same time do basic training for the armed forces.

Geoffrey successfully applied to Cambridge to read arts having specialised in sciences at school, thinking that would round off his education. 'Arts' included an array of subjects such as British Geography, Political and Economic History and American History and Politics. One of the geography classes was taken by Professor Debenham who was the meteorologist on Captain Scott's ill-fated expedition to the South Pole. Like others, Professor Debenham was persuaded to come out of retirement to make this scheme work.

Geoffrey went to Cambridge with just a suitcase and his bicycle. During the six month period there, Geoffrey and the others on this scheme had just two days off for Christmas. Nonetheless he found time to row for his college Peterhouse and they bumped four times in three days.

After coming down from Cambridge, having completed his basic training for the RAF, he was sent to Dallas, Texas, to get his wings as a pilot. Many pilots were trained in Dallas or Phoenix because of the fine weather and because there was no risk of attack from the Luftwaffe. They completed 70 hours elementary instruction initially on P.T. 17 Stearman biplanes and then AT6A Harvards. On returning to England Geoffrey became a flight instructor teaching other pilots how to fly Tiger Moth training aircraft.[1] They were given six weeks training instead of six months. Many of them went on to to serve as bomber pilots and sadly many would not return, having been killed during operations. He was stationed at various airfields, eventually serving at the Central Flying School. He was promoted to Flight Lieutenant a few months before being demobbed in 1946. As a result of hours of flying training Geoffrey developed hearing problems and suffered with hearing loss. After the war he returned to the Westminster Bank where he worked until his retirement. He died in 2010.[2]

References

1 For Tiger Moth training see Ch. 6 in Alan Bramson and Neville Birch, *The Tiger Moth Story* (1964).

2 The article is based on an account by Geoffrey Smith's family.

Supporting the Infantry – Making the Army Function

Vitally important to wartime operations was how the Army was supported from behind the front lines. In the Second World War soldiers were transported across vast distances to a wide variety of environments which required a large support network both in operational and rest conditions. Considerations such as the control and distribution of money, the provision of building supplies and the smooth running of equipment all had to be taken into account.

There was a whole network of corps, supporting front line troops, such as the Royal Army Pay Corps, the Royal Army Service Corps, and the Corps of Royal Electrical and Mechanical Engineers. A large number of Emanuel boys found themselves involved in these.

Joseph Clement Deeks *(Emanuel 1913–1920)*

Joseph Deeks played for the First Eleven at Emanuel in addition to being a Lance-Corporal in the OTC. He was awarded both the MBE and the US Legion of Merit (Degree of Officer) for his work in the Royal Army Pay Corps in the Second World War. His citations read:

Award of MBE 18 February 1943

Captain T/Major Joseph Clement Deeks RAPC has been in charge of all cash and banking transactions in connection with the provision of funds for Middle East Forces since 1.6.41 In this capacity he has had important contacts with Senior Civil and Military Officials of all nationalities in negotiating contracts to ensure the supply of local currencies by tender and by exchange. He is responsible for the supply of funds in bulk and for the administration and organisation of all Field cashiers and thereby the direct supply of cash in the field. All these duties he has performed with the greatest zeal and efficiency. His services are worthy of the highest praise.

Award of the Legion of Merit 16 January 1948

Lieutenant Colonel Joseph Clement Deeks, Pay Branch, British Army. For exceptionally meritorious conduct in the performance of outstanding service in connection with activities of the United States Army Forces in the Middle East from June 1942 to December 1943. Through his untiring efforts and initiative he successfully arranged for British Paymasters to furnish funds to disbursing finance officers of the United States Army Forces in places where banks did not exist, thus eliminating the risk involved in shipping large amounts of currency and facilitating the prompt payment of United States Ninth Air Force troops at all times during the drive of the British Army across the Western Desert. Where it was not possible for security reasons to contact local banking institutions he negotiated arrangements whereby United States Army Agent Finance Officers were enabled to cash official checks [sic] with British Army cashiers in numerous foreign countries, thus allowing our government to benefit by exchange rates enjoyed by British Forces. His cooperation and acceptance of responsibilities far beyond the ordinary call of duty has been an outstanding factor in the successful functioning of United States Army Finance activities in the Middle East.

Peter Herbert Mason *(Emanuel 1922–1933)*

Peter had a successful School career having been a Prefect, Captain of Drake house, Captain of Athletics, Captain of Fives and a Cadet Sergeant Major (CSM) in the OTC. In the Second World War he reached the rank of Captain in the 46th Recce Regiment, Royal Armoured Corps and was awarded a Military Cross for services during the Italian Campaign. Peter's MC citation states:

Award of MC 8 June 1944

During September and October 1943 and again during part of January and February 1944, Capt. P. H. Mason was in temporary command of 'B' squadron. On both occasions he took over command at very short notice. On the first occasion he led the Squadron on their successful advance from Vietri to Naples and on the second he was responsible for holding a comparatively large portion of a difficult front on the r iver Garigliano in the area of Cocuruzzo with great success. For a prolonged period on the Garigliano he had to contend with extremely inclement weather and very difficult supply problems. No movement could be carried out during daylight owing to direct enemy observation. The role was not one for which he or his squadron had been trained. In the face of all difficulties he proved himself to be possessed of outstanding tenacity, courage, initiative and resource. The successful exploits of his squadron were in great measure due to his leadership, cheerfulness and powers of organisation. Under prolonged hardship and danger in the face of all difficulties he was an inspiration to all those under his command.

Donald Russell Naylor
(Emanuel 1927–1934)

Donald Naylor was a high achieving athlete at Emanuel. A Captain of Rugby, a rower, a Captain of Shooting in addition to being a School Lieutenant, Captain of Drake house and a CSM in the OTC. In 1945 he was awarded an M.B.E. for his role as Deputy Assistant Director of Electrical and Mechanical Engineering (DADME) in REME Directorate at Allied Force Headquarters (AFHQ). The award stated:

Award of MBE 13 December 1945

During the last eight months Major Naylor has been DADME in REME Directorate AFHQ, where he has been responsible for the acquisition and allocation of all Plant and Machinery and for the development and maintenance of premises and accommodation vital to the operation of the REME Base in CMF.

Circumstances have been such that a large proportion of the plant and machinery required has had to be extracted from existing Italian resources. In selecting and acquiring this plant it has been necessary to maintain the very delicate balance between types and quantities which is necessitated by a continually fluctuating workshop task. This problem has been accentuated by the fact that the vast bulk of workshop premises available to REME have had to be planned for operation under conditions of only partial re-instatement.

The high technical ability and devoted energy of Major Naylor in handling intricate matters with skill far above the average, have contributed in large measure to the maintenance of the operational fitness of the mechanical equipment of the Armies.

John Arthur Solkhon *(Emanuel 1929–1936)*

John Solkhon was an outstanding Greek and Latin scholar at Emanuel. He was a towering figure who was Captain of Swimming and a Lance Corporal in the OTC. In the Second World War he rose to the rank of Major in the Royal Army Service Corps and was awarded an MBE when he was in the rank of temporary Captain for his role as Chief Stores Officer. The citation states:

John Arthur Solkhon in Rome, 1944

This officer has been quite outstanding in carrying out his duties as Chief Stores Officer. By coupling extreme energy with all round capability, he is largely responsible for the particularly successful operation of the Unit.

His services have been specially valuable throughout the Campaign in Sicily and Italy and he has at all times been an example to those serving with him.

George Oliver Cowles *(Emanuel 1930–1936)*

George Cowles was a Library Prefect and a member of the OTC. In 1945 he was awarded the MBE for his role as Warrant Officer in the REME. Telecom Section as his citation states:

Award of MBE 13 December 1945

This Warrant Officer has for some time been in charge of the REME Telecom Section of this Regt and has given consistently outstanding service, both in his own work and in supervision of the Section.

During the period under review a large quantity of Radar equipment in addition to the Regt holding had to be serviced, involving many modifications and some experimental work. During the whole period AQMS Cowles worked untiringly and it is mainly due to his outstanding efforts that the Regt's state of operational efficiency was maintained during the closing phases of the period of hostilities.

Medicine Men

These men saw at first hand some of the most shocking scenes of warfare. They were responsible for repairing the devastating effects brought about by mechanised warfare, from mines, shells, bullet wounds and the psychological impact of being prisoners of war. Their experiences were so harrowing that some chose not to elaborate on them, but for Professor Robert Ivy his experiences in the First World War became essential to his pioneering work in plastic surgery.

Professor Robert Ivy *(Emanuel 1891–1897)*

A pioneer of Plastic Surgery

Professor Robert Ivy was a pioneering plastic surgeon who served in the Medical Corps of the United States Army in both World Wars. He was an internationally acclaimed surgeon because of his pioneering work on the lip and cleft palate deformity. He was also highly skilled at reconstructing the jaw and teeth, an area he specialised in during both conflicts.

Robert Ivy attended Emanuel as a boarder in the 1890s. He remembered in his autobiography that, 'The boarders regarded themselves as superior in every way to the day boys and had very little use for them except as smugglers of sweets and other delicacies from the outside.'[1] He also remembered seeing Wandsworth Prison from the dormitory windows and on gruesome occasions he would see, 'the black flag...signalising the hanging of a murderer.' Robert was a member of the choir and was also confirmed in the School chapel in 1894. He fondly remembered playing Fives and being appointed a school monitor, a precursor to the prefect system. He also played cricket and football and remembered the great West Indian athletes Hagley and Keny at Emanuel at this time. Robert was also awarded a number of prizes for his school work which in those days were copies of famous literary works or subject specific text books. Robert returned to Emanuel in the 1920s and again in 1955 and stayed in close contact with the School becoming a member of the Old Emanuel Association. In 1959 he attended Flannels Day where cricket and tennis matches were put on for Old Boys and met the Headmaster Jack Grundy.

On leaving Emanuel Robert entered the University of Pennsylvania Dental School. He lived with his uncle Dr. Matthew Cryer who became Professor of Oral Surgery at the Dental School and who had a great influence on him and his future career. His uncle taught him much about the anatomy of facial bones as Dr. Cryer's photographs of carved human heads for medical research was pioneering. Robert matriculated from the School of Medicine of the University of Pennsylvania in 1905 and later received the recognition of being the first dental intern in the Philadelphia General Hospital and in the United States.

Professor Robert Ivy

America entered the First World War in 1917 and Robert accepted a commission as a Captain in the Army Medical Reserve. Originally being a member of Base Hospital No. 22 which was being organised for service in France he instead was put on active duty and told to report to 'the Office of the Surgeon General in Washington to assist Major Vilray P. Blair in organisation of the Sub-Section of Plastic and Oral Surgery, where plans were to be formulated for the care of war injuries of the face and jaws.' For one year between 1917 and 1918 Robert worked in the Office of the Surgeon General. In February 1918 Robert was promoted to Major. Major Blair, who was by this time stationed in France, sent for Robert, 'for assignment as maxillofacial consultant in the Vichy and Clermont-Ferrand areas, with operating HQ at Base Hospital 115 at Vichy.' Robert sailed to France as part of 'Surgical Unit Number 1' which was made up of ten medical corps lieutenants. He sailed on board the *Wilhelmina* and being the senior medical officer he was made responsible for the health of the troops. Unfortunately an influenza outbreak resulted in the deaths of fourteen men. Robert was responsible for writing the report into the outbreak which is reproduced in full in his autobiography. The men were ill prepared before embarking and 'for several days prior to arrival at the Port of Embarkation, had been subjected to severe exposure to wet and cold and lack of rest and sleep.' Of the report Robert wrote:

> It affords a good idea of the urgent need for troops to carry on the last few months of the fighting in France. The situation was so critical, that practically no time could be spared for training a seasoning of replacements and many of the men who had just been inducted into the service were rushed to the front as rapidly as possible. As a matter of fact, I later saw one or two soldiers who had sailed to France on our transport late in September, in the hospital with wounds before the November 11 Armistice.[2]

Surgical Unit Number 1 disbanded in France and Robert was given orders to proceed to the Hospital Centre in Vichy as Consultant in Maxillofacial Surgery and was consultant to all five Base Hospitals at Vichy.

While in France Robert was influenced by the work of Major Fernand Lemaitre who was director of a large French Army Centre Maxillo-Faciale. Robert remembered, 'What I learned there watching his methods of treatment proved invaluable to me in the care of our own cases, both at Vichy and later on my return to the United States.' Robert was with Lemaitre in his operating room on the day peace was declared and remembered, 'Never did I see anyone show so much relief and joy. Every few minutes he would pause in the operation and murmur the word "Armistice!" savouring it like a delicious morsel of food.'

Of his work in France Robert wrote, 'In our hospitals in France, the primary object of treatment of maxillofacial cases was to get the severe ones into as good condition as possible for transfer back to the United States where definitive treatment could be carried out...Many of the less severely injured were returned to duty.'

Robert returned to the United States where he was ordered to report to the Office of the Surgeon General where he found he was to be made Consultant in Maxillofacial Surgery and Chief of the Maxillofacial Service at the Walter Reed General Hospital. Awaiting him at the hospital were a sizable number of face and jaw casualties. In June 1919 an exhibit of Robert's work was shown at the Atlantic City Meeting of the American Medical Association where he met Varaztad H. Kazanjian, another pioneer of plastic surgery. He was promoted to Lieutenant Colonel in August 1919 and when the stream of casualties from overseas began to slacken he was discharged from his duties but applied for a commission in the Medical Reserve in the same rank.

In 1940 Robert was invited to be a member of a Committee on Surgery, set up by the Division of Medical Sciences of the National Research Council, to represent maxillofacial surgery. He was later made Chairman of a sub-committee on Plastic and Maxillofacial Surgery. He served for two periods as Colonel of Medical Corps, United States Army Reserve. He wanted to be considered for active duty for the 'duration' of the war but because he was not on active duty when the Japanese launched their attack on Pearl Harbor and also because of a policy of excluding reserve officers who had reached the age of sixty, this was refused. The authorities considered that Robert's services were of greater use in teaching and so he remained at the University of Pennsylvania. Robert lectured and organised courses for medical and dental officers on plastic and maxillofacial surgery and in 1945 he was appointed as a Civilian Consultant to the Secretary of War which required visits to inspect the nine Army General Hospitals designated as centres for plastic surgery. Robert also contributed to a number of scholarly papers during the Second World War on treatment for war injuries with his work warranting a mention in *Time* magazine.

For his civilian services in the Second World War Robert Ivy received a Certificate of Appreciation from the War Department which read, 'As Consultant to the Secretary of War he gave lectures on plastic and maxillofacial surgery to the classes at the Army Medical School. By his superior knowledge of the subject and his extensive teaching experience he contributed in an outstanding degree to the success of the courses and to the war effort.' In 1947 he was also awarded the Dr I. P. Strittmatter gold medal for 'extraordinary meritorious service.'

During his long and distinguished career he was Professor of Plastic Surgery at Penn's Graduate School of Medicine, Professor of Clinical Facial Surgery at the University's Dental School and Chief Plastic Surgeon at Graduate Hospital. He was a founder of the American Board of Plastic Surgery and was made an honorary member of the British Association of Plastic Surgeons. His lasting legacy is to be found in the Robert H. Ivy Society of Plastic Surgeons founded in 1954. He was 93 when he died.

Frederick A. Walker FDS, RCS

(Emanuel 1909–1915)

Frederick Walker

Frederick Walker in Emanuel OTC uniform

Frederick 'Johnnie' Walker was a keen sportsman who was both the Vice Captain of the First Fifteen and rowed for the School. He was also a School Prefect and academically a very bright pupil. As a boy he was interested in medicine and when he left School registered to be a dentist in August of 1916. However, because of the war he deferred studying and instead joined the Royal Fusiliers and fought in France and Belgium. He was badly wounded by shrapnel and was sent home to a hospital in Manchester. After the war he eventually studied dentistry at Guy's Hospital and had a very successful career which included working in Harley Street. His love for 'rugger' (as he always called it) never diminished and he continued to play the sport for the Old Emanuel rugby teams. He also captained Old Emanuel teams and in the 1960s was the President of Old Emanuel Rugby Club.

In the Second World War he specialised in emergency dental surgery and was a highly skilled expert who published many papers on the subject. He worked in the same team as Sir Harold Gillies in the Emergency Medical Unit at Rooksdown House, Basingstoke. Patients, mainly from the army, arrived with severe facial injuries. Many spent several years having their faces remodelled or spent months being operated on.

David Bowler

Johnnie Walker's son, John Walker, in a letter exchange with Tony Jones, noted that: 'After D-Day train loads of patients arrived at Basingstoke Hospital. There was a line of ambulances to and from the hospital of over three miles. The workload for surgeons was enormous and some operated in the theatre for over seventeen hours a day. Patients included prisoners of war and air raid civilians. There was a wonderful team spirit amongst the surgeons, the matron, sisters and nurses.'

Dr David Philip Bowler *(Emanuel 1935–1942)* Bergen Belsen Medical Relief Staff

David Bowler was an outstanding pupil and was Captain of the School, Captain of Drake, Captain of Hampden, rowed for the School, and played for the First Fifteen in both 1941 and 1942. He had the reputation of being an aggressive front row forward with excellent hooking skills. He was also a S./Sergt. Instructor in the JTC and passed his War Office Certificate 'A' in 1940. David was a superb academic who was a member of the Science Sixth class, passing both his London Matriculation and London Higher School Certificate. He was Captain of the School when Emanuel was based in Petersfield. This was a period of great change for the School and the senior pupils played a significant role in helping the younger, home-sick, boys settle down in strange surroundings.

After leaving School David studied to be a doctor and was a medical student at Westminster Hospital Medical School. In the course of his studies he had periods abroad and was a member of the relief staff which supported former prisoners of the concentration camp Bergen Belsen which was liberated by the British on 15 April 1945. He returned to give a talk to the School's pupils in 1945 about his work at Bergen Belsen and the non-military and humanitarian aspects of the end of the war. Emanuel pupil Clive Barnes wrote in *The Portcullis* that David's talk was one of his most vivid memories of all his experiences of being evacuated in Petersfield.[3] David would have witnessed some horrific scenes at Bergen Belsen of emaciated bodies that were contorted by diseases such as typhus, TB, gastroenteritis and enteritis in addition to patients being severely dehydrated and suffering from starvation.[4] Apart from his initial talk to the School it was a subject that in later years he became reticent to mention.

In the 1950s David took up an appointment as Paediatrician/Administrator at Batu Gajah in Malaya. He arrived in Malaya during the 'Emergency' when British forces were fighting Communist insurgents. David looked after sick children but in emergencies he also undertook surgery on those afflicted by gun shot wounds among other types of operations. In 1956 he took over the position of State Paediatrician Penang where he worked around the clock in the care of the sick as a young colleague remembered, 'Daily morning and night rounds, visits to children in district hospitals, visits to the orphans at the Penang Convent, not forgetting a daily packed outpatient clinic. On his way home in the evening, if he found the General Outpatient Clinic crowded, he would sit with the out-patient doctors clearing the paediatric crowd.'[5] David later moved to Australia continuing his work in a place called Broken Hill and for his work he was awarded the Advance Australia Award.

Major Allan Forsyth Wallace MC *(Emanuel 1924–1933)* Royal Army Medical Corps

Allan Wallace enjoyed a successful career. He was a School prefect, Captain of Rodney, a member of the First Fifteen and Lance Sergeant in the OTC. In the Lent Term 1933 *Portcullis* Allan's rugby critique read, 'He has often been able to start an unexpected attacking movement.' It was perhaps this quality which led to Allan's distinguished service in the Second Word War. Allan commanded a company of 175 Highland Ambulance. During the period of 1944–1945 his company was responsible for evacuating casualties from 152 Infantry Brigade Group. During November 1944 operations in North Holland carried out by the Brigade included three assault crossings undertaken in darkness over the Aftwatering and Neder Canals, attacking obstacles defended by minefields and being subject to machine gun and artillery fire. During the assault casualties had to be evacuated in assault boats from collecting posts established on the far side of the canals. Major Allan Wallace personally undertook these duties and was awarded the Military Cross. The citation noted:

> An operation rendered extremely difficult in the darkness by the irregular and high sloping banks of the canals and by enemy interference by intermittent and often heavy shell fire. Success depended on careful preliminary arrangements, detailed reconnaissance, the exact siting and constant supervision of the collecting posts and the maintenance of close contact between the Regimental Medical Officers and the collecting posts.

The citation continued:

> Both in the preparatory stages and throughout the operations he worked tirelessly and without sparing himself, and by frequent personal visits to the RAPs and collecting posts during the course of the assaults ensured that the evacuation of wounded proceeded smoothly and without delay. It was undoubtedly due to his boundless energy and devotion to duty day and night that all casualties from his brigade were evacuated without delay and without mishap in circumstances of considerable difficulty. Throughout all the operations in which he has been engaged Major Wallace has shown exceptional powers of leadership and his high sense of duty and the outstanding example he set to his officers and men have resulted in a material reduction in the suffering of the wounded.

Dr Malcolm Sinclair Campbell
(Emanuel 1926–1931)

Malcolm excelled at Emanuel School and was a House Prefect for Marlborough. He also played for three seasons in the First Eleven and was a highly accomplished cricketer who may have been skilful enough to play the sport professionally. After leaving School Malcolm studied Medicine at the University of London and qualified as a doctor in 1937. In 1941 he became a Fellow of the Royal College of Surgeons of Edinburgh.

In 1940 Malcolm volunteered for the Royal Army Medical Corps Territorial Reserve. Leaving his pregnant wife Muriel behind, Malcolm, holding the rank of Major, was sent to India as part of the 114 British Military Hospital in 1944 and remained there until he was demobbed in 1947. He arrived in Bombay in December 1944. His base was the so called 'hospital town' at Jalahalli, ten miles outside Bangalore in the state of Mysore, which had an astonishing 10,026 beds over nine hospitals. Malcolm played a pivotal role in the development of the surgical section of this facility during his time in Bangalore. His final rank was Lieutenant Colonel. Officer in Charge Surgical Division. A newspaper report at the time noted of this huge medical facility, 'In an incredibly short space of time the rocky, scrubby, territory has been transformed into a field of spacious white or cream brick buildings with red-tiled roofs which will combine to make a huge base general hospital for the final treatment of war casualties, including men suffering from disease.'

Malcolm Campbell

Malcolm was also one of the senior medical staff leading the surgical teams on board HMHS (His Majesty's Hospital Ship) *Karapara*. The ship was the first into Rangoon to pick up prisoners of war who had been liberated from Rangoon Jail. The men were from all nationalities including British, Chinese, Indian, Australian and American. The newspaper *The Sunday Statesman* noted that the men were in high spirits when they arrived on board but their condition and appearance told a story of hardship, 'They were, however,

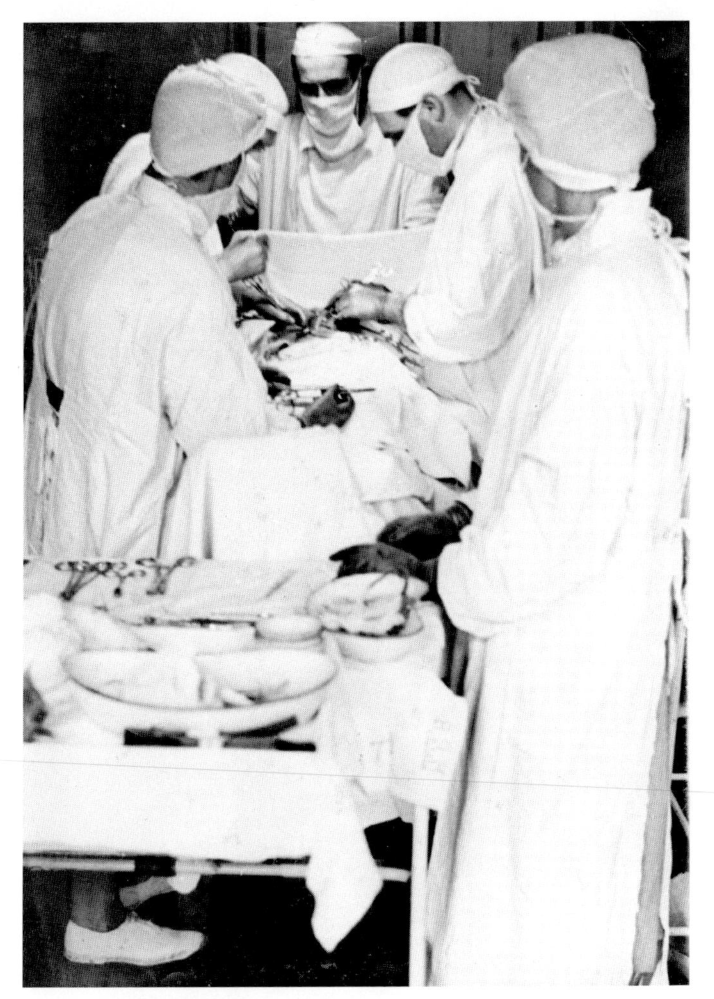

Malcolm Campbell in an operating theatre

HMHS Karapara at Rangoon taking on PoWs, 1945

in rags. Their clothes were torn and verminous. Every man had lice or scabies. In prison the men had been allowed two mess tins of water each week for all washing purposes. They were without any personal possessions.' The paper noted that to the men the smallest gift was an 'immense treat' and this was also something Malcolm remembered about peeling an orange for a POW who was finding this task difficult. After giving the orange back to the man he was told 'Thank you – that is the kindest thing anyone has done for me in a long time.'

Towards the end of the war and after VJ Day he continued to work at the British Military Hospital throughout the rest of his time in India. He treated many survivors of the Burma Campaigns of different nationalities. His earlier skills training in casualty and orthopaedic work would have provided helpful and valuable experience to draw upon throughout his time in India. The development of the large hospital town at Jalahalli, together with its role in the final treatment for the military personnel involved in Burma, explains his posting in India lasting until early 1947.

Once back in England Malcolm worked as a surgeon for the NHS in Hull. When he retired in 1978 he was a highly respected surgeon and was awarded the Queen's Silver Jubilee medal. He was a founder member of both the Hull Medical Society in the early 1950s and the Hull League of Hospital Friends in the 1960s. He also had a successful tenure as President of the Hull Medical Society besides being Chairman of the League of Hospital Friends. He died in 2002 aged 89.[6]

References

1 R. H. Ivy, *A Link with the Past* (1962), p. 4.
2 Ibid. p. 42.
3 *The Portcullis*, No. 155, Summer Term 1945, p. 8.
4 For more on the medical aspects and conditions at Bergen Belsen see Col. E. E. Vella, 'Belsen: Medical Aspects of a World War II Concentration Camp' in *Journal of the Royal Army Medical Corps*, 1984, 130, pp. 34-59.
5 N. Paramaesvaran, 'Dr. David Bowler 1924-1990', in *Berita MPA Newsletter, The Malaysian Paediatric Association* (October 2010) pp. 8-9 .
6 Daniel Kirmatzis would like to thank Malcolm Campbell's daughter Helen Rowell for providing a wealth of information about her father's experiences in the war.

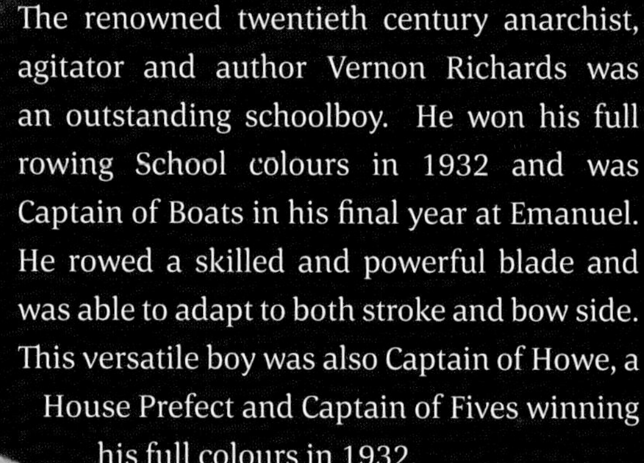

The renowned twentieth century anarchist, agitator and author Vernon Richards was an outstanding schoolboy. He won his full rowing School colours in 1932 and was Captain of Boats in his final year at Emanuel. He rowed a skilled and powerful blade and was able to adapt to both stroke and bow side. This versatile boy was also Captain of Howe, a House Prefect and Captain of Fives winning his full colours in 1932.

Not surprisingly Vernon (known at Emanuel as Vero Recchioni) was also an outstanding academic and was a member of the Science Sixth class before he left School for King's College London to study Engineering. He was also a member of the Howe House Old Boy Society The Curzon Club.

Vernon Richards

Anarchist and Revolutionary *(Emanuel 1925—1932)*

His early anarchist activities began by helping his father with propaganda work against Mussolini and as a result he was arrested in Paris in January 1935 and extradited from France because he had been suspected of being associated with anti-Fascist refugees. In 1936, he published in collaboration with Camillo Berneri a bilingual anarchist and antifascist paper *Italia Libera/ Free Italy*. Although it was not proven, his father was rumoured to be involved in plots to overthrow Mussolini and had been a political prisoner in Italy for five years.

Vernon Richards self-portrait

As Richards grew older he became more involved in the struggle against Fascism in Spain, founding and editing *Spain and the World*, and *Freedom* newspaper from 1945. These were early examples of a huge range of politically driven anarchist publications which Richards was to be involved with for the remainder of his life. He also edited some of the longest surviving anarchist newspapers.

Because of his civil engineer training he avoided the Second World War draft and was employed during the war by a private company as an engineer. At the outbreak of the war he was registered, under protest, as a political conscientious objector and was imprisoned in 1945 for nine months for inciting agitation among soldiers between the period of November 1943 and December 1944. The prosecution believed that Richards and two others had 'conspired to endeavour to seduce from their duty in the forces, and to cause among them disaffection likely to lead to breaches of their duty.' (Richards had also had a poem called 'Fight? For What?' seized by the police).

Vero Recchioni (aka Vernon Richards) as an Emanuel boy

This was a high profile trial and raised major questions about freedom of speech in the UK during the war. Despite a high profile defence campaign backed by the likes of George Orwell, T. S. Eliot, E. M. Forster and Benjamin Britten which defended freedom of speech Richards and his co-defendants were convicted. Leading publishing houses also expressed their concerns against what were seen as both harsh sentences and freedom of speech being limited. Many believed the sentences would have been much harsher had it not been for the high profile nature of the trial.

This trial of 'disaffection' as the media called it, took place in the Old Bailey. Richards, aged 29 at the time, was featured in the newspapers nearly every day with his wife who was accused as a co-conspirator. The evidence against Richards included the document *War Commentary*, of which nineteen copies were found in his home. Journalist Reginald Reynolds sarcastically challenged the validity of the trial in the *Forward* newspaper on Saturday 5 May: 'Copies of War Commentary have been passed round. I remember once seeing a court absorbed like this with a dirty book, in an obscenity charge, as though it had been a public play-reading. Today it is a left-wing paper, a paper rarely seen or read except among people of "extreme" views; and there is something ludicrous in the sight of it here.' The convictions led to fierce debate amongst the world's leading anarchist thinkers about the lengths democratic governments would go to restrict the privileges of freedom of speech.

On the bright side prison gave Richards the chance to resume playing the violin from his childhood and he even formed a band with other jailed musicians and regularly entertained the other inmates and wardens. Friends regretted that he never played again after his release. Although there were a few OEs who were conscientious objectors, Vernon Richards is the only known OE who was sent to prison for activities which were deemed anti-British. He was never to work as a civil engineer again either, saying that the one thing he learned in prison was the folly of pursuing a 'career.' This was ironic, as he seemed to have several careers in his colourful life.

Following prison he returned to the family business in Soho until it was sold in the 1950s. Richards was also a highly accomplished photographer, something he often kept on the back-burner. Without doubt his most famous sequence of photos were those of George Orwell from the 1940s. They showed very simple images of Orwell working and playing with his young son. Although Orwell wasn't an anarchist, the men were friends and these photos gave a rare insight into the life of a very private man. They have all been republished in the last few years by Freedom Press. He also produced incredibly striking self-portraits. His correspondence with George Orwell included the final years of Orwell's life when he lived on the Isle of Jura.

Freedom Press remains one of the biggest and longest running publishers of anarchist literature and Vernon continued to edit the magazine *Freedom* until 1964 and managed Freedom Press for many further years until his death in 2001.

So I Joined the Royal Army Pay Corps... A story of delays!

Donald Inkster *(Emanuel 1934–1942)* recollects his Second World War experiences

I left Emanuel School in 1942 when I was 17 years old knowing that I would be called up as soon as I was 18. As a keen railway enthusiast I was able to take a job at Waterloo Station for a few months. The hours were on early and late shifts six days a week plus an occasional Sunday but I enjoyed it.

Donald Inkster

My call-up notice duly arrived and after six weeks of primary training at Chichester they must have assumed I was a true railwayman and posted me to the Royal Engineers Transport Depot at Longmoor, Hants, home of the Longmoor Military Railway – which was wonderful!! All those vintage steam locomotives and ancient wooden-bodied carriages to ride in, north to Bordon or south to Liss and the connecting Southern Railway service to Petersfield, the town to which Emanuel had been evacuated in 1939. I was able to make a short visit occasionally and see how things were going at Emanuel.

After the standard Sapper training course (field works, use of explosives etc.) and having won a prize for art and studied pure and applied maths in the 6th Form at school I took the course for Railway Draftsmanship, resulting in a useful pay increase.

At Longmoor I was suddenly called in for interview and asked if I had thought of applying for a commission. ... I passed the tests and was posted to the large Pre-OCTU establishment at Wrotham, Kent. Most of it ranged along the nearby lengthy escarpment, with several training fields down below. Everything was 'at the double' and running down the hill and hopefully up it as well - twice a day! We were also required to learn to drive an army truck and ride a motor-bicycle. I mastered the Bedford truck with its crash gearbox in five days and passed the test driving

The Inskter brothers, (from left to right) Donald, Alan and Lawrence with their mother

round Maidstone on a busy Saturday morning! I managed it without hitting anything and that was that. The motor-bike took me a bit longer. I suppose I preferred four wheels to two! It included some rough riding in the gravel pits near Dartford.

My next move was to the Infantry OCTU in Morecambe. The training programme continued on much the same lines as before but with a few additional items such as 'How to escape if taken prisoner by the enemy' – given by an officer who had done it and followed it with a successful run home ... For many of us the high point of the weekly programme was the Regimental Sergeant Major's Drill Parade on Saturday mornings. His drill parades were memorable and I enjoyed them no end.

My time at Morecambe ended abruptly early one morning when I suffered a bad fall during an exercise on the moors a few miles away. I could not stand without passing out, so I was taken to a farmhouse nearby and left there for a jeep to be sent to pick me up later ... I was told that I had been downgraded medically from A1 to B7 and thus of no further use to the infantry and I should await further orders. I spent much of the time in the reading room, a place full of maps, campaign records and so forth. I thought to myself 'This is ridiculous. There has to be other work in the army where I could seek a commission even with a low medical grade.' The war was ended, I had already been in the army for over two years I had not really achieved anything useful.

... Eventually I received my posting orders to the RAPC OCTU in the Isle of Man, sailing from Fleetwood to Douglas and catching the quaint old narrow gauge steam train down to Port St Mary ... The training sessions were many and varied, with system lectures and many references to the massive binders known to us all as 'The Precis'. But we had to remember that we were still soldiers and had rifle drills and some field exercises ... On Saturday afternoons we all took the train into Douglas where a number of well-known tailors from the mainland had set up shop to produce officer's uniforms, always made to measure, and make regular visits for fittings etc. After that we were at liberty to enjoy our leisure time in the town. Having successfully completed the course we were all commissioned on 21 August 1945 and posted to the units allocated to us. Two of us reported to RPO Oldham, 49th Bn. RAPC. This was actually situated in an old cotton mill in Hollinwood on the road from Oldham to Manchester. We took up our duties and settled in quickly.

Our work at the RPO was largely carried out during normal office hours so that evenings were generally free. One could catch a tram into Oldham or Manchester and I did this fairly often, but there were various social activities sponsored

Donald Inkster at Emanuel School 2013

locally by the Corps, including occasional dances which took place in a hall in nearby Failsworth. There was also a flourishing dramatic society which soon attracted my attention. In due course we put on a production of Noel Coward's comedy *Hay Fever* in which the female roles were taken by ATS members and civilian colleagues ... After six months I attained war-substantive Lieutenant status and put up my second pip. I thought I might be posted away somewhere and did not have long to wait.

... It transpired that I would be going to the Middle East. A large contingent of officers and men would travel by what was known as the MEDLOC route: ferry Dover – Calais, train to Toulon, troopship to Alexandria and train to Cairo. ... For some unexplained reason I was appointed Security Officer for the Jerusalem United Services Horse Show in the autumn. I was apprehensive, but was told not to worry as Warrant Officers and Sergeants did it every year and would deal with any trouble; thankfully there was none.

... Concert parties appeared at Schneller, staying there for a few days while performing for other units in the area. Their leader had honorary Lieutenant rank and stayed in the Officers' Mess, where he proved to be a red-hot table tennis player. The top of the bill comic, a tall chap who wore a fez and did conjuring tricks rather badly but always getting the last one right, went into the Sergeants' Mess. Yes, his name was Tommy Cooper. The others occupied rooms in the married quarters. One evening they invited me to go out with them to watch the show at another venue. On the way I sat next to Gwen who was the pianist and she said to me "That fellow is going to go right to the top" as indeed he did – and she became his wife.

I was then posted to the Cash Office in Sarafand, a huge permanent encampment on the coastal plain east of Jaffa, where I took up duty as a field cashier during the summer months. It was a busy office requiring two cashiers, the other being a Captain, so evidently I was sent to replace an officer who had departed, perhaps to be demobbed ... It was in the Officers' Club at Sarafand that I met my French master at Emanuel, Cornelius Prinsl, now a Captain in the Intelligence Corps. I have always remembered him as one of the best language teachers I ever had.

I was called back to Schneller to be told that I was being posted to Greece to join the Cash Office in Athens. ... The cash office was located on the ground floor of the Bank of Greece close to Constitution Square and was once again a busy place needing two cashiers. ... This posting proved to be the most memorable, although demobilisation continued apace and our numbers were steadily reducing. The CO moved away, leaving the unit in the hands of our Major, then my fellow-cashier left and I carried on by myself. Eventually the Major called me and said "I see your demob is coming up, but there is no-one to take over, so would you be prepared to stay on until we find a replacement?" I was quite happy to do so and in fact continued for another six weeks. I had twice been invited to sign on for a permanent commission and had given it some consideration, but I felt the time had come to leave. The usual delays took place including a change to a smaller ship, from the liner *Empress of Australia* to another Empire class vessel which took no less than nine days to reach Liverpool – yet another delay! From there I went by train to York where the formal demobilisation took place. Thus ended my four plus years of military service.

I am proud to have served in the Royal Army Pay Corps at home and overseas and am now a life member of the Regimental Association. I attended many reunions of the Schneller Orphans and took over as Treasurer, for a few years until shrinking numbers led to its formal closure as a separate organisation in 2002.

Richard (centre) and Jack Blackburn (right)

Desert Rats

Percival John 'Jack' Blackburn *(Emanuel 1923–1932)* and his brother Richard *(Emanuel 1923–1929)*

Jack and his brother Richard attended Emanuel in the late 1920s with Jack leaving in 1932. Both brothers were mechanics professionally and in 1937 they joined the Middlesex Yeomanry TA which became two regiments at the outbreak of the Second World War. Jack and Richard served initially with the 2nd (Middlesex Yeomanry) Armoured Divisional Signals (a unit of the Royal Corps of Signals) during the evacuation of Greece in 1941 and in the Western Desert (North African) campaign. Later they served in the 7th Armoured Division (The Desert Rats) part of 30 Corps 8th Army, during the battle of El Alamein.[1] Both also served in Italy and during the North-West Europe Campaign. Their tasks included supporting the armoured divisions they served in by ensuring that engines, generators and other mechanical instruments functioned in the theatres in which they operated.

This series of photos depicts a variety of scenes as witnessed by Jack and Richard during their service in North Africa.

References

1 For a history of the 7th Armoured Division see Major-General G. L. Verney, *The Desert Rats: The History of the 7th Armoured Division 1938 to 1945* (1954).

(above) A Stuka shot down in the desert (below) Pulling together – a typical desert scene

(above) A 25pdr field gun undergoing maintenance (below left) Richard Blackburn (first from right) and (below right) Jack Blackburn

(above) A break in fighting – a Grant Tank's crew takes a rest (below) Jack Blackburn shakes Field Marshal Montgomery's hand at the launch of Monty's memoir in 1958

Major Colin Fowle, c1942

Kenneth Fowle, 1934

Band of Brothers – OE Brothers in the Second World War

Kenneth Geoffrey Fowle *(Emanuel 1928–1934)* and Colin Arthur Armstrong Fowle *(Emanuel 1933–1939)*

Colin and Kenneth Fowle were athletic brothers, Colin was in the School athletics team and Kenneth was in the School Cross Country team. They were both sergeants in the School OTC and both were in Clyde House. Kenneth was Captain of Clyde and Colin became a House Prefect. Kenneth was Captain of shooting at School and both brothers gained their War Office Certificate 'A.' In an earlier chapter they are seen with Ned Thornburn and Charles Hill larking about on a holiday in the early 1930s.

In 1935 Kenneth joined the Artists Rifles TA and won a number of prizes at shooting competitions in the late 1930s. Kenneth was called up at the outbreak of war and served with The King's (Liverpool) Regiment. Kenneth spent most of his war in England becoming an intelligence officer in 1941, promoted to Adjutant in the 5th Battalion King's in the same year. He was later Motor Liaison Contact Officer with 115 Brigade and later Brigade Transport Officer moving across northern Europe after the invasion of Normandy.

Colin Fowle volunteered with the Rifle Brigade (Artists Rifles) on 11 October 1939 later being called up on 12 September 1940 joining The Middlesex Regiment. After OCTU Colin was commissioned into 1/8th Battalion The Middlesex Regiment (Machine Guns). Colin wanted to join the Commandos but was later grateful that instead he was transferred to the Royal Artillery missing out on the dangerous and somewhat suicidal missions the Commandos were designated during the war. On 18 December 1941 until the end of the war Colin served with the 57th (East Surrey) Anti-Tank Regiment, RA. He went through the North African Campaign where in 1943 he became an intelligence officer with 30 Corps and landed at Salerno on D+3 in September 1943 during the Italian Campaign. After the war Colin was promoted to Temporary Major. He joined the Territorial Army commanding 'Q' Battery 381st Anti-Tank Regiment RA.

General Sir Bernard Law Montgomery talking with with General Sir Harold Alexander (left) and CIGS, General Sir Alan Brooke talking with Major Finlayson. General Sir Oliver Leese (behind, wearing plus fours)

The Page Brothers

The Page brothers in 1938 – (left to right) John, Bill, Frank and Eddie with John's wife Cynthia

Frank Page *(Emanuel 1928–1930)*

The Page brothers were exceptionally talented members of Emanuel in the 1930s. The eldest was Frank Page. A member of the Emanuel First Eleven of 1930 Frank was also in the OTC. In the Second World War Frank was an armourer in the Royal Air Force. Armourers' duties included maintaining bombing equipment and required a good degree of mechanical knowledge. He spent several periods at the Royal Navy shore establishment, HMS *Vernon*, and after the heavy bombing of Portsmouth most departments of *Vernon* were established in Roedean School for Girls, Brighton in spring 1941. HMS *Vernon* was the Royal Navy's torpedo, mining and electrical training establishment and Frank would have been given all the latest information on fusing the mines and torpedoes that the bombers from his base would have deployed. After initial training at an Operational Training Unit Frank was mainly based from February 1943 to the end of the War at No. 33 Base – Waterbeach, Cambridgeshire. No. 33 Base became home to No. 514 Squadron Bomber Command which was part of No. 3 Group Bomber Command, in November 1943. No. 514 flew Avro Lancaster B.I, B.II and B.III types and undertook 3,675 operational sorties during its time at Waterbeach. Frank's job was demanding and the emotional strain would have been great, having seen hundreds of young men fly off into the night sky never to return.

Frank Page

Sir John Joseph Joffre Page OBE
(Emanuel 1926–1933)

John Page was an all-round talented pupil, winning a scholarship to Emanuel in 1926. He was a Prefect, Captain of Drake House and Captain of Boxing; a member of the School Athletics and Rugby teams; a Sergeant in the OTC and obtained his War Certificate 'A' which was the OTC certificate of proficiency which assisted many boys at the time when they enlisted in the armed forces. John was the second eldest of the Pages. Their father had served in the First World War and was a milkman and an insurance agent after the war, dying of pneumonia in 1935.

John joined the RAF in 1933 and was posted to an armoured car company at Habbaniyah in Iraq where he served supporting bombing actions against various warring factions. He was a skilled administrator and was appointed ADC to the Air Officer Commanding. In 1939 he joined Iraq Petroleum but at the

John reading to his son

outbreak of war rejoined the RAF serving in the Middle East and North Africa in a liaison role with Montgomery's staff. In 1943 he was Mentioned in Despatches and rose to the rank of Group Captain. He commanded the RAF training station at Halton in Buckinghamshire before being demobilised in 1946. John had a distinguished post-war career as a manager in the Iraq Petroleum Company in addition to appointments as Chairman of the Mersey Docks and Harbour Company in the 1970s and 1980s retiring as Chairman in 1984, and as Chairman of the National Ports Authority. He was appointed OBE in 1959 and was knighted in 1979.

William Leonard Page *(Emanuel 1931–1939)*

Bill Page in East Surrey Regiment uniform

William known as 'Bill' was a talented athlete at Emanuel. He was also a Prefect and Captain of Drake. *The Portcullis* recorded some of his many sporting achievements:

> There have been few in recent years who could rival Bill Page's achievement in games. In both Rugger and Cricket he received Colours in five successive seasons, from 1935 to 1939. Tall and powerfully built, he was a fine forward and a successful captain in his last two seasons. In the Cricket XI he was a valuable bowler, slow left-hand with a nice variation of pace and flight and a forceful bat. He proved a skilful captain in the 1939 season. What one admired most, however, in his sports activities was the tireless devotion with which he coached younger boys in junior team rugger practices, in the nets, or on the fives courts. His all-round excellence, together with his seriousness and depth of character, won him general respect and made his name something of a legend.

Bill (first from left) jumping the hurdles on the Emanuel School field, c1935

Bill Page was politically aware in an era when international politics was critical to the lives of ordinary citizens everywhere, and was selected to take part in a Youth Group discussion which was broadcast on the BBC. He was originally a Conscientious Objector but enlisted in the East Surrey Regiment, first serving in a pioneer unit, then in the Royal Engineers and, finally gaining a Commission as a Lieutenant, he was attached to the 9th Battalion, Royal Fusiliers (City of London Regiment). Bill was killed in action around 5.20pm on 26 December 1944 during bitter fighting on the north-east coast of Italy as his company was ordered to hold the via Mazzolana, south-east of Ferrara. The Allied advance up the north-east coast had been fiercely contested by German forces during the Christmas period.[1]

Edwin Douglas Page *(Emanuel 1933–1939)*

To anyone who knew him Eddie Page was an Emanuel stalwart, regularly attending Old Emanuel functions. Like his brothers he was a talented sportsman, being Captain of Cricket in addition to being a talented First Fifteen player. Eddie spent one term with Emanuel in Petersfield before leaving School in December 1939. On leaving Eddie worked as a bank clerk before enlisting on 17 July 1941 and being assigned to the Royal Fusiliers. He was recommended for an Officer Cadet Training Unit and received his Commission on 26 November 1942. On the same day Second Lieutenant Page was granted an emergency commission in the Indian Army, 1st King George V's Own Gurkha Rifles. Eddie spent three years in the Far East undergoing intense training in India and

Eddie Page (second from left) on the Emanuel School field in a match against Rosslyn Park, 1938

Burma, including in the Himalayas, on a diet of long marches through all weathers and terrain. By May 1943 he had been promoted to Lieutenant and in June 1945 he was appointed a temporary Captain.

The 1st Battalion 1st Gurkha Rifles were part of the 20th Indian Division which fought with the 14th Army in the Burma Campaign.

In April 1945 Eddie wrote to the OEA allaying concerns that he was having an easy war now that he was a liaison officer at 20th Indian Division HQ. He wrote:

Eddie Page

> Of myself I should like to correct a false impression which might have been gathered from *The Portcullis*. The point in question is .... "and we hear that E. D. Page is also on the staff in India." This, to my mind, conjures up visions of Delhi, electric fans, iced drinks, palatial quarters, etc., whereas the truth is that I am writing this letter under a dilapidated piece of tarpaulin in the very hot, dusty and acrid Central Burma Plain. I admit that at the moment I am on the staff in Div. HQ, but I was with my regiment, the 1st Gurkha Rifles, during the Japanese offensive on India last year.
>
> My present job is Liaison Officer to one of the brigades and I find it quite interesting, and it saves me from having to stick around in Div HQ all the time.
>
> You will have heard all about the activities of the 14th Army, so I will not waste paper by repeating it. Suffice to say that the Japanese have received a sound thrashing, from which they have no hope of recovery, and, in my humble opinion, the whole of Burma will be ours before the end of the year.[2]

Eddie saw action during the Japanese siege of Imphal and Kohima in Assam, India between March and July 1944. Sadly no detailed memoir of Eddie's experiences exists except for a collection of photos showing him with the 1st Gurkhas in training during the course of 1942–1943.

Eddie concluded his service career in French Indo-China before being demobbed in 1946 with the honorary rank of Captain. In post-war years he joined the Civil Service where he remained until retiring in 1981. He was also a Samaritan councillor for a number of years. Eddie was devoted to his family and to Emanuel and died in July 2011.

References

1 War Diary of 9th Battalion Royal Fusiliers, 26 December 1944, p. 17
2 Letter from E. D. Page, 4 April 1945 reprinted in *The Portcullis*, Spring Term 1945, pp. 13-14.

Once a Gunner

John Howard Neale *(Emanuel 1931–1937)*

John Neale was a Prefect, Captain of his House, a member of the Second Fifteen, editor of *The Portcullis*, a corporal in the OTC and an oarsman. Shortly before he died in 2009 he wrote about his rowing experiences on the Thames. He painted an idyllic picture of a summer spent rowing in a pair with an Emanuel friend, replacing the weight of the cox with sandwiches and beer.

After the war he was made a Colonel of the Territorial Army and was awarded an OBE in addition to working as a manager of several steel firms in Sheffield where he lived for most of his life. His brother Bruce was also at Emanuel (1934–1940) and like John served in the Royal Artillery. After the war Bruce won an England rugby cap playing for the national side for most of one season including against Ireland.

In the last month of war in Europe John was awarded a Military Cross for his part in disabling German tanks and in the disorganisation of enemy infantry leading to the taking of a number of prisoners. His MC citation notes:

> Capt. Neale, who is a Troop Commander, was in support of an Indian battalion attacking to the north west of Ferrara. On the night of the 23/24 Apr. he established an OP (Observation Post) in a block of flats in I Gorghi. The next morning it was found that the enemy were still in possession of part of the town. During the morning snipers killed two runners to the OP and spasmodic bursts of machine gun fire were directed through all the windows which were suitable for observation.
>
> During the morning Capt. Neale saw six German tanks leave a hide. Apparently a signal had been sent to the German troops north of Ferrara to withdraw and for three hours targets of infantry and tanks presented themselves. During this time Capt. Neale at great risk to himself, used binoculars instead of his periscope for the sake of speed; he broke up repeated attemps of the enemy to counter attack to cover this retreat.

John Neale (centre, standing) with Emanuel Prefects and Headmaster Cyril Broom (seated right), 1936

Emanuel School Boat Club 1936 – Back row (left to right): LW.F. Stubbings, J.H. Neale, A.F. Harris, H.S. Page
Middle row: A.F.S. Fox, A.R.J. Skillern (Captain), Mr J.G. Worth, J.B. Slowman, P. Elliott; Front row: R.F. Naylor, C.R.E. Legg

> At the same time his O.P. which had apparently been discovered, was being subjected to accurate small arms and mortar fire in an attempt to neutralise it.
>
> By his courage and devotion to duty in the face of this fire, Capt. Neale knocked out one enemy tank, with two other 'probables', caused many casualties to a group of sixty enemy infantry and so disorganised their attempts to withdraw that our infantry were able to take a large number of prisoners.

60 years after serving in the Second World War John sat down to write his memoirs which cover some 68 pages. The following are extracts from John's Neale's memoir, 'Once a Gunner.'

This memoir, written nearly 60 years after its events, cannot be a detailed history and far less a diary of all that happened to me over six years in the Army. During that time I learnt enough about the technical and tactical practice of field artillery to use it and even to teach it, as well as picking up more than a little of general military duty and of the structure and systems of the army overall, especially of the Royal Artillery ...

1939–1942

When war was declared in 1939 it was hardly unexpected, but like many others of my age I had done nothing about it personally. So it was not until 19 September that I was sworn in as a Gunner recruit in the Honourable Artillery Company (HAC), where in fact there were so many that we were sent away to await call up training ... I am not clear why I opted to be a gunner, unless it was a distaste for walking and I was equally vague about whatever else would be involved. I set off to find out on 19 July 1940, by train to Bordon with a group obviously bound for the same destination and became 931008 Gunner Neale ... We were by no means the first intake and the staff, regulars in the main, knew exactly what they needed to do with us, however unhandy or unwilling, to turn us into basic gunners acceptable in service regiments ... The squad NCOs, all sergeants, were a mixed bunch of regulars, all capable of pushing us hard especially if we deserved it. ... And then, at last, we were off to Larkhill to fire guns for the very first time. Our equipment were 4.5-inch howitzers of First World War vintage. We came home very pleased with ourselves and subsequently carried on a much more varied training programme.

John Neale during the Italian Campaign

... I was sent to 121 OCTU, the senior field artillery unit formed on the basis of the HAC. ... The unit was organised in three batteries, one of which took in cadets from every sort of source and for a month ran a hard programme to confirm our general basic standards, whether we came from training regiments or service units. ... Our training became more and more interesting, starting with lectures and moving onto field exercises of every sort, from drill orders with guns to tactical exercises. ... In retrospect it may look hard to see this as war service, but it was in fact making a fairly homogeneous breed of us, with the habits of thought and responses of young officers, whilst not turning us into automata. More than that we were becoming gunners and that is by way of being branded for life. ... A posting in mid April 1942 put an end to that cosy existence and I set off to join 58th (Suffolk) Medium Regiment, with little idea where this would take me.

1942–1943

Joining 58 Medium was something of a muddle, since I arrived in Christchurch to find them packed up ready to move the next morning at 06.00 and on arrival at Cheriton there was more to do than worry much about me. ... I was in 230 Battery, who were mainly from Bury and its surrounding villages, mainly consisted of senior NCOs of regulars, and a wide mixture of others from all over the UK. ... Embarkation leave done with, we set about preparing to go abroad. All our vehicles and equipment were prepared and loaded with everything we could think of, since this would all leave early and shipped separately with a small advanced party of drivers. ... Our main occupations were playing endless card games and listening to our US companions singing sentimental songs. But we certainly ate well on five courses, even at breakfast. ... Approaching Algiers we met for the first time the typical sweetish smell of Northern African agriculture. ... In this atmosphere we marched for twenty or more miles to our first billets in a winery and I fell for the duty of bringing up a rearguard to collect the not inconsiderable number who found such an effort hard on their feet. It would be a day or two before our vehicles and equipment arrived after unloading from their other ship.

... It was steep and hilly country, so that while we travelled by day in shirt sleeves I rode a motorbike much of the way for convoy control, stopping to buy oranges, unseen at home for years, and throwing them in the back of trucks in passing.

... As always there was a lot to learn. Living permanently on what we had with us and in a rough country and climate, we soon acquired and with little or no movement for a while, comfort that was not too hard to find.

... Still with little activity, I recall clearly the day when the local Luftwaffe nuisances handed over to Italians and overflew the extensive gun area to show them the local scene, while we all kept our heads down and avoided movement. That was until the Italians came back on their own, flying too low and had six of their formation shot down. ... During this period the Eighth Army had been fighting its way into Tunisia, bringing pressure to bear on Rommel and the threat of being pinched between the 1st and 8th Armies. This led to an attack to the west aimed at the extreme south of our line in Tunisia, which was manned by Americans, amongst whom it caused serious problems and 6th Armoured was despatched to stabilise the position, taking us with them.

... The German's rapid movement northward up the coast reinforced their formations already in Tunisia, with the defensive aim to hold off the 8th Army. This led to a major re-planning of the business of pushing the Germans out of North Africa. This was clearly in the minds of those who now set about a combined assault from Medjez el-bab at the capture of Tunis, which would frustrate the possibility of a German or Italian evacuation on any scale. Our part in this was to move northwards again to join the rest of 1st Army Group Royal Artillery (AGRA) and to prepare for what was foreseeably the last big North African battle.

... Our attack was a little delayed, but the capture of Grich-el-oued and its heavy defences was anything but easy. We were busy, although much pressed by the CO of 19 Field to put at his disposal all of our Ops, which was hardly possible in the light of our other commitments. It was not long, however, before we were able to move forward and to prepare for the formal attack which was shortly to follow ...

The big effort was to be supported by a huge gun area, comprising the field regiments of several divisions, as well as medium and heavy regiments from our AGRAs. ... The planned attack, astride the Tunis Road, was to break out from the heavily defended Medjez position, contested by 1st Army for many months. It was aimed at deep penetration to Tunis and Bizerta and was not to wait upon any cautious blind up the flanks. ... The artillery effort was reputed to be on the scale of Alamein and I have never forgotten the sight and sound of the gun area that night. Not a moment passed without rounds of gunfire, much of it obviously on timed programmes and the volume and duration of fire so heated up the guns that the muzzles of 5.5-inch and 7.2-inch could be seen glowing red hot in the darkness. Having suitably admired that, it was back to the command post to deal with our programmes and ammunition supply and to ensure that we were fresh enough and ready to go when we were called for. The main infantry attack went off according to plan, followed by us in our direct support role which proved to be mobile and variable in every way. For the first recce I set off with a warning that there might be a Tiger tank on the way but it was, mercifully, untrue.

... Here we had sad casualties on the gun position, when a gun drill mistake led to one of the guns being double loaded. Crushing the fuse of the second shell, it exploded in the open breech. Sergeant Johnson and Bombardier Statham were the untimely victims. ... Firing was diminished, but our Ops could still see many targets as the Germans, cramped for space and not always under orders sometimes attempted to fight although soon white flags began to appear. ... Our ultimatum invited an early total surrender before heavy gunfire was directed at their now exposed positions. And so Von Arnim surrendered. Many of his troops did not look as if they were beaten, bringing their equipment and singing as they came. But not for long.

... Tunisia and Algeria were full of troops and were geographically well placed as a base from which to launch and support operations in Sicily and eventually in Italy on a considerable scale. This included establishing a school of artillery, including a firing range, together with a reinforcement centre to hold and train the intake of gunners from the UK. ... There was even a short leave at a coastal camp for a few days on a very hot beach with lovely meals from a friendly French family who seem to have adopted us. ... All well and good, but perhaps too good for one's conscience. Following Allied landings in Sicily and despite some US successes, the Germans still managed to evacuate most of their men across the narrow straits to Italy. Our landings there followed without heavy fighting and progress was made northwards. There was also an influx of regular officers from the UK, who had as little battle experience as we had when we first landed. They disapproved of what they regarded as our relaxed habits of discipline so I was not sorry, therefore, to find myself back to 230 Battery in Italy.

The Italian Campaign – 1944–1945

... I was to go back to 230 Battery, still as a Captain, to replace a wounded Troop Commander. Up to this point in time, my work had been mostly at the gun position, with a share of general responsibility for a troop of men and their vehicles and equipment. Less obvious, but sometimes more difficult, was dealing with the performance and personal affairs of one's men, including sorting out occasional domestic issues, however far away. One had a share of Observation Post [OP] duty too, which was now to be my major occupation. ...

We settled when things became static near Lanciano, after taking over a gun position from another medium regiment, the Duke of Lancasters Own Yeomanry. They had built enormous gun-pits dug into a hillside, refitted with steel ammunition boxes filled with soil, which even included fireplaces. It was while straightening up one of these that we found some boxes still full of live charges which was not a comfortable thought. Here we carried out counter battery and harassing tasks and some shoots for the Air OP. Our rounds were observed by gunnery officers flying light aircraft which was an effective way of working.

... My job was to harass the Germans in their occupied villages – Lama di Pelligni, and Palena if we could reach them. This involved finding gun positions in what amounted to a narrow gorge, which we eventually did, by lowering the guns down its steep slopes by winch to find platforms with a subtle arc of fire. All of this was done by night. Then to find OPs we climbed two or three hundred feet, escorted by a mixed squad of Dogra infantry and Italian partigeani. We may well have been seen, but hardly ever stayed very long in one position. Climbing up was arduous but not difficult, despite the signal tackle that we had to carry, but coming down was quite another story and we had to learn to glissade down the long shale slides which were a feature of this landscape.

... One has often heard discussions about why we never used our heavy anti-aircraft guns in a field role. We did so occasionally, not as anti-tank weapons, but making use of their excellent clockwork time fuses which worked on a powder ring system for airbursts, which proved to be very accurate. The local battery was commanded by a Colonel known as Mad Mac who was happy to put his guns at our disposal since they now had very few German aircraft to engage.

Next, and in awful weather, we were summoned to the West coast and while the lighter vehicles eventually made it through the snow on the mountain roads, the main column of the regiment was stuck for several days. So steep were the roads that they called for care even in good weather. The wreckage of a heavy gun tractor like ours had been left embedded in the ruins of a house on Dentecane hill where an unfortunate driver had tried to change gear while going downhill and had run away in neutral. Italy is not always for summer holidays.

We headed for the valley of the Garigliano, where there had been serious fighting and slow progress during January 1944, along the Gustav Line, a carefully planned defensive position hinged upon Monte Cassino of evil memory. We called for orders at HQ 15 Army Group at Caserta and at HQ 5 Corps at Sessa Auranca, before preparing gun positions near the villages of Lauro and Catrese, ready for the regiment to arrive. ... When the guns did arrive we were soon busy again with harassing and counter battery tasks, as well as occasional fire plans in support of the Cassino fighting when we could reach that area.

... The regiment's last two phases of activity, although separated by the breadth of Italy, had not involved any direct part in major operations, but nevertheless there had been plenty. The serious losses incurred at Cassino had involved many divisions and nationalities and even after the monastery fell there was heavy fighting to clear the way into the Liri Valley through which ran the road to Rome. At the same time, the landing at Anzio, meant to get behind the Gustav line and force a withdrawal from Cassino, had been less successful than hoped and it was not until the end of May 1944 that we really broke through and the whole front moved North.

We had time, therefore, to learn a new pattern of activity quite different from Africa. For a start, we were no longer so close to 6th Armoured for direct support as we had once been. We were often deployed with a divisional artillery in direct support and were often busy with a variety of fire plans and counter battery and harassing fire. We followed the retreating units northwards, eventually supporting 4th Indian Division up to Chieti and the Pescara river. Here the whole 5th Corps was rested so we moved south again on a long and spectacular journey to Campobasso to get ourselves in better order for the next job. ...

... A period of rest like this gave us a chance to review our varied experiences and to learn more of the conditions under which we were expected to operate, sometimes leading to specific training in new techniques. It must have been about this time that Colin McQueen, of 229 Battery, produced a graphical method of calculating the range and bearing for every gun in a battery to produce a STONK. This was not, as was (and still is) often wrongly thought to be a concentration of gunfire, but was in fact a way to produce a linear distribution of fire from a battery of eight guns, rather like a line of a barrage, which could be aligned with a feature or a defended position of that form – we found this easy and quick once mastered.

... We had learned, as well, a useful technique to try to ensure good gun areas and accommodation in areas to which our guns might have to move. Units all bore, on their vehicles for example, a number for recognition and we would mark useful looking places with the figures 40, which was in fact Divisional HQ, as a deterrent to keep them available for the battery if it should move there ...

In mid August we were placed under command of the 4th Indian Division, given the task of an approach to make contact with the Tedeschi. We found ourselves sent to work with a field regiment, who were not entirely happy to lose their previous medium support, but we did not find it hard to settle down with them. Their route forward, working as always closely with their affiliated infantry, was well away from any but poor hill tracks and I had been offered two mules with Cypriot drivers, to carry my OP radios and heavy tackle. At first this seemed to be a good idea, but it was not long before we found this full of snags. The mules were no doubt fine, but the drivers were most unhappy about where we were going and despite the language difficulties made it very clear that they expected to be fed to their tastes rather than to ours, so I found the first opportunity to lose them. ...

... We met little resistance as we approached the river Foglia, where we knew that the real work would start, despite one small hold up which was briskly dealt with by the infantry with the help of Shermans which had joined us, before tentative plans for a fire plan were completed. That was probably the first time that I really met the enemy face to face, when as the only wheels available I carried two wounded German prisoners back to battalion HQ. One was only a youngster and in pain from heavily bleeding leg wounds, while his companion, much older and with a nasty chest wound, berated him harshly for letting us see and hear his weaknesses.

John Neale's medals including his MC (second from left)

... Pressing on, we were shortly overlooking the river which we needed to cross and I was able to find a quite magnificent OP commanding the river valley and the ground over which our units would have to attack shortly. This was a house on the forward slope, standing in a patch of thin woodland which prevented detailed observation by the Tedeschi [Germans], but where I could see all that I needed – although one did not go in or out in daylight. It had... been recently occupied by the enemy.

On 30 August 1944, when our attack went in, it may have been that we had managed to surprise the enemy by the speed of our approach and the river was crossed without too much trouble. It was another story when heavily defended towns and villages were tackled and I was given the particular task of dealing with one trouble spot – Monte Calvo.

... The Gothic line, although incomplete in some sectors, still offered many defended villages and features to be tackled by infantry and armour and we were involved in a number of such contests which almost always meant a river crossing well covered by gun and mortar fire, with a crest to follow from which dour infantry resistance could be expected. Considerable casualties were often incurred. This meant that not only were battalions often changed, but brigades, and divisions were fed into the battle. ...

April 1945

... Then, after a lot of scuffling along the embanked rivers, we were finally involved in a set piece attack across the river Senio. The artillery preparations were said to be the biggest effort ever put on by the 8th Army. There was an elaborate fire plan with guns, flame throwers and ground strikes by aircraft used in succession and in three successive phases. With this exception – that on the third run the aircraft went through the motions of attacking but did not open fire. The idea was that the Germans, following the pattern of the attacks, would keep their heads down for long enough for the infantry to assault the embankments, and to seize positions over the river. This was successful enough to allow the embankments to be bulldozed down at bridging sites where tanks carrying bridge sections were driven into the rivers to permit armour and other supporting arms to cross. It worked, although not without tough fighting, and we were soon able to press on to treat the river Santerno in much the same way ...

Despite Hitler's orders, surrender was the order of the day for many of the formations now facing us and we found little to do while plans were laid to move into Austria. This was a matter of urgency because the Russians were already showing signs of ignoring the limits set in Yalta. Some German units stayed where they were awaiting orders, more set off through the

Alpine passes on their own initiative, and some few deployed to continue to impede us as long as possible. ...

1945–1946

While we waited and wondered outside Udine, 5th Corps hatched a scheme which was offered to people like us with little to do. Officers with a modicum of German were to be placed with German units in surrender in order to maintain some degree of control over their movements. Brian Rowe and I both felt suitably qualified to cope and were promptly attached to Corps HQ for this duty. There was only one snag, in that the Tedeschi were disinclined to accept us on this footing and had their own ideas on how they should behave and be treated. Most of the volunteers were returned to their units, but five of us, including Brian and myself, remained as liaison officers for the general who thought we could be useful seeing what was going on in the country at large ... This phase did not last very long and 5th Corps moved on shortly into Austria, settling in handsome holiday houses on the north shore of the Worthersee just short of Klagenfurt, while we were quartered in small houses round about and were quite well received. ...

By now, my regiment had reached Klagenfurt and occupied a German barracks. I still saw little of them since my job turned out in the end to be quite hard work. The Austrians were puzzled by what they saw of us, especially the daily ceremony of changing guard in the town square of Klagenfurt ... Our work was to travel the countryside to see what movements of troops were going on. The formal armistice terms, strictly applied, required the Germans to surrender to the Allied forces they happened to be facing – logically enough, it seemed. But the Germans did not want to surrender to the loosely organised units whom they called the 'Titobanditen', as the said Yugoslavs only wanted to strip them of their weapons, food and personal items of any value before turning them loose on the roads for us to worry about. It had the makings of a muddle as can be imagined ...

The need for us scanning the countryside clearly got less and before long I was on my way to rejoin our battery ... the battery was in the nearby village of Pider, only by a concession from the Russians, who did not like British units too close to the line they chose to occupy despite the fact that they were far past the Yalta limits. This meant that when we put our guns on display in the little village square, all at the same elevation, they installed an OP manned night and day about half a mile away to keep an eye on us. We did manage to get on slightly better terms than that later ...

It was in this area that we found unexpected contact with the Russians. It seemed that a few deserters had taken to the woods and were terrorising some of the remote hamlets and our neighbours contacted us with the idea of making an infantry sweep to catch them. This agreed, they offered us their success in the form of the offenders' graves, but they had certainly trespassed over the official frontiers and had quite a large contingent out in roadless country nearer to our tracks than to any they might have had and asked if we could help by transporting them back home. ...

We got on very well with most of the Austrians although there were a few reputed Nazis to be found. We sometimes had the problem of picking them up, often on night raids, and handing them over to intelligence for at least interrogation. We wondered if they were very important, since most of them only seemed to have served in German rather than Austrian units and often were sent home again shortly after their arrest ... Austria was, in many ways, rather like England must have been before the first war, or perhaps earlier. Riding across country, farmers would stop their work and open gates for us and seemed happy to be rewarded with a few cigarettes for the courtesy. ... Even the winter months offered enough interest for both leisure and work to keep one busy, despite the decline in our numbers and the falling number of friends. Eventually we had to close down the regimental mess and live in a transit hotel where there was always a changing population of people who provided good and amusing company.

Sweethearts meet in Austria

John had a month's leave at home before returning to Austria and finding a job as Staff Captain at Sub-District HQ in Klagenfurt. At the same time a Junior Commander in the Auxiliary Territorial Service (ATS). by the name of Mollie Cordiner arrived at the same HQ to do the same job John had just taken. Their Commander invited Mollie to stay with the HQ while he found her another job. John and Mollie became good friends and were soon engaged.

[After getting married...] Going home seemed simple when the date was finally given and we knew enough to arrange for some ATS girls going home to be put on the MEDLOC train by which we would travel while Mollie's status as draft conducting officer ensured us a carriage to travel home in privacy by ourselves.

So it all ended, with our surprised parents facing us on our return. We had left as little more than school children in their eyes but returned in the guise of a married couple. But that is another story altogether.

The Emanuel 1935 First IV, from left to right, Alan Skillern, Kenneth Millist, Cornelius Legg, Henry Duffield and Howard Cross

A Four at War

The story of the 1935 Emanuel First rowing crew and their fates in the Second World War

There is an old black and white photo in the Emanuel School archive of the 1935 First Four. They were the most successful crew Emanuel had produced to that date. They won several up-river regattas including Staines Regatta where, after the race, standing in their white Boat Club flannels, they triumphantly displayed their tankards. They were five athletic, smart and determined boys.[1] Many of the crew also played rugby and were members of the Emanuel OTC. Their wartime stories include those of many of their Emanuel contemporaries, especially those who served in the territorial battalions of the Royal Fusiliers. In 1935 the rowing master James Worth gave the following critiques of the crew:

The 1935 First IV upriver of Barnes Bridge opposite the White Hart

Bow: Skillern, A. He has fitted in well with the rest of the Four and acquired a good style which he uses with characteristic vigour.

2: Cross, H.G. When at his best is quite a useful member of the crew.

3: Millist, K. By intelligent application he has overcome a tendency to shortness which was a serious drawback in consideration of his weight. He now pulls a strong blade with good length.

Stroke: Duffield, H. C. His previous experience in the School Boat has been most valuable and in addition to his great keenness has made him a very competent Captain and Stroke. Success this season is largely due to his energy and ability.

Cox: Legg, C. R. E. Has realised the first duty of a cox, so easily forgotten in the excitement of racing: to keep his boat straight. His work has been first class.

Bow: Major Alan Reginald John Skillern *(Emanuel 1928–1937)* and the 9th Battalion Royal Fusiliers

As *The Portcullis* noted, Alan 'had a brilliant school career.' The Headmaster, Cyril Broom, wrote Alan a letter of recommendation after he left School in which he said:

> He is a gentleman of the highest character and attractive personality and has a record of outstanding service in the School. He has been Captain of Rowing, the most successful Captain of Rugby Football in recent years, an unusually efficient NCO in the OTC in which he has recently become an Under-Officer and a member of the Shooting Eight and Tennis Team. Since January he has been Captain of the School and has exercised an admirable influence by his own high standards and the force of his personality.

On leaving School Alan joined the City of London Regiment, Royal Fusiliers, gazetted to the 9th (Territorial) Battalion on 12 May 1938. At the time of mobilisation Alan was commanding a Carrier Platoon. He then spent time as Brigade Liaison Officer and Battalion Weapon Training Officer before being promoted to Captain in 1941.

The 9th Battalion trained in England for the first two years of the war, carrying out various duties such as guarding the beaches along the eastern seaboard. In 1942 the 9th embarked at Liverpool on board the *New Holland*, escorted by a cruiser and five destroyers on its way to Basra, via the Cape and Bombay. The 9th Battalion were part of the 167th Brigade, 56th (London) Division and once they arrived in Iraq they were incorporated into PAIFORCE (Persia and Iraq Command) which had been established in response to initial German success in the Caucasus in early 1942. By the end of 1942 the threat to British interests in this region had diminished due to the Germans being held in Southern Russia and the British counter-offensive at El Alamein. Following this victory the focus of British strategy changed

Alan Skillern

and preparations were made for an assault on Italy, via Sicily, planned for the summer of 1943. Before this the 8th and 9th Battalions, Royal Fusiliers, started on a two-and-a-half thousand mile journey from Kirkuk to Enfidaville in Tunisia to join the British 8th Army arriving in time for the final weeks of the war against Axis forces in North Africa.

Kenneth Baker

At Enfidaville, on 9 May, the 8th and 9th battalions mounted an attack west and north-west on an area known as the 'Humps.' In heavy fighting the 9th Battalion's Commanding Officer was badly wounded and Major John Gould Coleman *(Emanuel 1922–1930)* took command. Four Emanuel boys in the battalion were involved in this action – Alan Skillern, John Coleman, Kenneth Baker *(Emanuel 1930–1936)* and Stanley Charles Warner *(Emanuel 1932–1937)*. An account by a Sergeant Myall whose mortar carrier supported "D" Company commanded by Alan Skillern, recounts what these Emanuel boys faced that day:

> The enemy started to shell the battalion right from the start and I saw one chap killed almost before he'd gone a hundred yards...We advanced out of the olive groves completely into the open and I've never seen the battalion so grand. They advanced in their section formations just as if it was a manoeuvre... There were shells dropping amongst them right from the start. I've always been proud of my battalion and knew they would uphold themselves in action, but they towered miles above even my expectations... When we topped the ridge, there was a vast open plain in front of us with not a scrap of cover and beyond this the hills – mountains you might call them – which were the enemy's positions. I gave up all hope then, because I thought we'd never be able to cross this and survive, but on they pressed, completely undaunted. Now we were actually in view and the fire increased tremendously – shells, mortar bombs, bullets, everything he had.[2]

Interestingly this action was also described in a subaltern's letter to Old Emanuel Kenneth Baker who was commanding "B" Company at the time:

> You may be interested, if you haven't heard already, in an account of the closing stages of the battle so far as "B" Company was concerned. Just as that machine-gun fire started playing ducks and drakes with us from three sides, we came to the edge of a minefield (it was about fifty yards in front of where you were hit)... I crawled forward to try and find a path through the minefield because I knew it would be no good to put in an attack if we lost any more men by pushing straight across it. I was lying looking over the anti-tank ditch that ran across the centre of the minefield when the enemy started pounding the hell out of us again, so I crawled back and told the blokes to go to the ridge we had just left. At the ridge we found Harding and a tank, got on to battalion headquarters on the tank's wireless and received orders to retire further... You will be pleased to hear that 'B' Company was quite a distance farther forward than anyone else... If you don't think there was anything particularly good about the show you put up, I can assure you that everyone else does... Your presence with us was a great source of moral courage and steadiness and you were hit about fifty yards behind the front man in the battalion. Nice going, Ken![3]

Fusilier E. Wright also wrote to Ken Baker, 'I have heard a lot of what you did in the attack, sir. "You should have seen old Ken," someone said, "walking up and down with his map just as if he were on a scheme".' Ken's wounds were severe and after returning to England he later died from them on 1 December 1943.

British and US troops, including 9th Battalion, Royal Fusiliers at 'Roger Amber' beach, Salerno, September 1943

The Fusilier battalions received high praise for the battles in which they engaged at Enfidaville. As Cyril Northcote Parkinson so aptly wrote, '... they were splendid fighting soldiers and quick to learn.'[4]

With the war in North Africa drawing to a close Alan and other Old Emanuels of the 9th Battlion carried out 'dryshod' exercises and practised amphibious assaults in Tripoli in preparation for the invasion of Italy.

The decision to invade Italy evolved over the course of three Allied conferences in 1943: Casablanca, Washington and Quebec. The Allied conquest of Sicily was complete by mid August 1943 and eventually it was decided that two landings on the Italian mainland would be attempted in September 1943. The one that concerns us here was codenamed *Avalanche* which was a beach assault by the US 5th Army on the Bay of Salerno. The 9th Battalion Royal Fusiliers as part of 167th Brigade, 56th Division, formed part of the 10th Corps under command of the US 5th Army led by General Mark W. Clark. The Italian surrender was announced the evening before the 9th Battalion were to land on the Salerno beaches but this wouldn't affect the opposition they faced as German troops were reinforced in Italy. A few days after the Salerno landings Alan Skillern wrote down how he felt the evening before the invasion – 8 September 1943. The note reveals the anxieties of a Company Commander leading his men into battle and the checks and double-checks which plagued his thoughts as he visualised what lay ahead.

The Landing – a pencil-written note by A. R. J. Skillern

The atmosphere in the ship was different, it had altered perceptibly during the day and now, only a few hours before Z, there was an air of gaiety, forced gaiety perhaps; but good humour prevailed. In the ward-room there was much badinage and leg-pulling and little thought appeared to be given to the task that was before us.

After dinner most of us went to our own cabins where, in the privacy of them, we studied our maps and mosaics for the hundredth time. As a Company Commander – I did. I remember asking myself, 'what haven't I done?' – 'Did I explain that?' – 'God, that road looks different' – If '-----------' goes, can I have Sergeant '-----------' to take over the Platoon? – and so on unceasingly. Finally and almost in desperation, I tried to sleep but, like the others, I only turned restlessly; waiting for the loudspeakers to announce TROOPS PREPARE TROOPS PREPARE. It came and the reaction was in the pit of my stomach which momentarily experienced a sudden sensation of – nausea was it? I don't know!

There was much to be done. Life-belts to be adjusted, equipment, cape, haversack and respirator to be fitted. A touch to check my pistol, yes, it was loaded, compass, glasses round neck, map-case, torch and, of course, a helmet.

TROOPS TO EMBARKATION STATIONS TROOPS TO EMBARKATION STATIONS. Already? I hope the Platoons are ready.

On my way to my own L.C. I passed quiet orderly lines of heavily laden soldiers moving to their stations and I realised here was the result of so much practice and rehearsal.

The ship's lights were completely extinguished, it was uncomfortably hot below deck. We were to embark from the sally-ports and I hoped there would be little waiting.

There wasn't, for very shortly came the order EMBARK EMBARK and every Platoon, every Section and every individual quietly followed into place until all were embarked. I remember quickly checking the three craft which held my Company before I climbed in myself. I remember the refreshing breeze.

9th Battalion, Royal Fusiliers on the road to Battipaglia. Major Alan Skillern circled

The boats were gently lowered into the water and Z was only an hour away. We were to land at Z plus 20. The troops were very silent in their seats. There was little moon and I could only see, dimly, set faces staring ahead from beneath their helmets. Some of the bayonets shone. I could see, only dully, the mountains which loomed over us rather menacingly. There was the almost silent throb of our craft as we glided towards the beach.

Z minus 30, Z minus 20, Z minus 10. I couldn't see anything.

Then the naval bombardment of the beach commenced – the operation was on.

In the light of the bursting shells, I clearly saw the beach and the outline of the coast was easily distinguishable. The first craft must be nearly on the shore. Were the enemy waiting for us? Were they? Were they? Were they?

At this stage we were at very high pitch and the answer to that question meant almost everything. I was buoyed up with a tremendous hope – anticipating the glorious relief an unopposed landing would afford – if they weren't.

I had a few minutes in which to reconcile myself to the inevitable bloodiness which must follow – if they were.

We knew some of his positions, but --------?

I was not really surprised when I saw the enemy tracer criss-crossing the beaches and heard his wretched mortar-bombs bursting on the beach, but was possessed by a feeling of depression. I realised that we were to pay a high price for success. I realised only too well that I might be part of it. There was nothing to be done about it – we were all afraid – but a task had been set us and we were determined to carry it out. And it was with this feeling in our hearts that the landing was made. And the troops moved inland exactly as if it had been another exercise. I then thought of the morning and the inevitable counter-stroke – it came and our battle started.

The 9th Battalion achieved their first two objectives with greater ease than their third which was the capture of the town of Battipaglia. Initially they captured the town but they then faced a counter attack which started on the morning of 10 September. In the next few days fierce fighting broke out around Battipaglia and down towards St Lucia, south-west of the town. Fusilier Captain Carter recounted the Battalion's experiences that week:

Captain Stanley Warner (second from left) being briefed by Cedric Delforce (second from right, sitting) in St Lucia

> They stayed there all day and then in the late afternoon the Germans stormed each entrance with tanks and infantry. The troops fought on and on until each anti-tank gun was knocked out. As many as four different crews manned some guns, each being knocked out one after another, only to be mown down. In the end, men came out into the street (they had been posted in the houses) firing Brens, from the shoulder, at the slits in the tanks to make them close down – until they, too, fell. ... The remnants of that gallant force fought their way out and continued to fight with terrific determination and courage during the rest of the battle...[5]

Old Emanuel Captain Stanley Warner was recommended for, and duly won the Military Cross for his actions at St Lucia on 16 September. Stanley's MC citation reads:

> At S.Lucia on 16 September Capt. Warner was commanding a forward coy [Company]. At first light the coy was heavily attacked by infantry supported by tanks. At about eleven o'clock a determined effort was made by the enemy tanks to penetrate our F.D.L.'s [Forward Lines]. Although under heavy MG fire Capt. Warner with complete disregard for his personal safety went across the open to our own A/Tk [Anti-Tank] guns and tanks

Major John Coleman

> and directed their fire onto the enemy. As a result of this and of his visits under fire to his forward platoon, 2 enemy tanks were destroyed and a large number of casualties inflicted on the enemy infantry.
>
> The gallant conduct of this officer, his determination and fine leadership, was a great inspiration to all and resulted in the enemy being successfully and decisively defeated in his efforts to penetrate our position.

On 16 September Old Emanuel Major John Coleman took over command of the 9th Battalion until late November 1943, whilst Alan Skillern spent six weeks in hospital. During the period of John's command the battalion as part of the US 5th Army pushed northwards in a series of bitterly fought struggles. One of the most bitter before the close of 1943 was the taking of Monte Camino. This mountain feature of almost three thousand feet was essential to Allied strategists if they were to reach the road to Rome. The 8th and 9th Battalions, Royal Fusiliers, were tasked with taking the summit known as point 819. One factor against the attacking forces was the weather, which from November onwards had caused many problems; not least was the mud as a result of continuous rainfall.

The 9th Battalion were to start their assault at 1715 hours on 2 December. We get a sense of what they took into battle from Cyril Northcote Parkinson's history:

> Each man carried either a Bergen pack or his large pack, containing a blanket, a cardigan, a pair of socks, a groundsheet and compo rations (with burners) for forty-eight hours. Each carried, in addition to his weapons, an entrenching pick or shovel and such items as '69' Grenades and a hundred rounds of ammunition. Each man wore over his battledress a leather jerkin.[6]

A programme of 'Terror Stonks' had hit enemy positions hard. Heavy rounds of fire were sent across their positions. Despite artillery assistance the 9th Battalion faced a treacherous climb on 'steep, rocky and wet ground.' The climb to the forming up position took eight hours and by the time the men neared the top most were exhausted; it was indeed a feat of incredible physical strength.

The assault was scheduled for 0600 hours but it was soon realised that apart from "Y" Company of the 8th Battalion, the greater part of the attack would have to be carried out by companies of the 9th Battalion. Both Stanley Warner and Alan Skillern played vital parts that day as the history of the Fusiliers in the Second World War tells us:

> Again the nature of the boulder-strewn slopes prevented full deployment, but "B" Company of the 9th (under Major Stanley Warner) went round the left corner of the wood and dealt with a series of spandau posts "with the greatest vigour, determination and bad language." Three Germans were shot and fourteen captured. The objective was taken by the third platoon under covering fire from the two platoons which, until then, had been leading. "D" Company under Major Alan Skillern, was equally successful on the left...[7]

Monte Camino was secured by mid December and the 9th Battalion patrolled positions along the river Garigliano until late December. German forces had retreated across the river and now sat facing Allied troops.

The Allied Command had decided that a crossing of the Garigliano was to be made in January 1944. The date was set for the evening of 17 January. Both the 8th and 9th Battalions Royal Fusiliers were to be part of the attack.[8] Alan Skillern led "D" Company on the evening of 17 January. They started to cross the river at 2100 hours and made their advance at 2250 hours but soon met stiff opposition from enemy machine gunners. It was during this attack that Alan Skillern lost his life. One of Alan's best friends, Captain John Canty, an old boy of Dulwich College and member of the 1st Battalion Royal Fusiliers wrote to Alan's wife Peggy in March 1944 detailing how Alan was killed:

> Evidently Alan and his Coy were going to attack by night along a railway line. After laying everything on Alan spent the afternoon with Stanley lying in the sun talking about his usual topic of yourself and Dickie. The time for the attack arrived and Alan and his Coy moved off through Stan's Coy, who were holding the bridgehead. Up until that time there had been the normal amount of enemy activity with the odd burst of machine gun fire, which you soon get used to. The Boche is not like us he fires his machine guns every so often even if there is no target. Anyway Stan got his Coy moving forward when he suddenly came upon Douglas Bannerman, who was a bit dazed and who told him that Alan had been killed. So Stan told him to carry on with Alan's Coy and he himself went forward to see if it was true. Evidently poor old Alan was killed – a burst of machine gun fire. There is certainly no doubt that he knew nothing about it. Father Hardy buried him later where he was killed on the railway. My C.O. has told me that in about a fortnight's time I may go over and find his grave. I will take my camera with me and take some photos of it for you and I will then be able to explain to you where it is.

John Skillern visiting his father's grave in 1980

> George Hollings told me that when he sorted Alan's kit he came across a letter addressed to him telling him what Alan would've done with all his kit and ending up with the words, "I hope that you never read this." I wonder if he wrote a similar letter before each battle or whether that is the first one he wrote. Unfortunately we shall never know.

John Canty was godfather to Alan's son John. John, who never knew his father, has written about his experiences of visiting his father's grave for the first time in 1980:

Influenced no doubt by knowledge of my father's love of the Army, on leaving school I followed him into the Armed Forces and joined the Royal Marines to enable me to fulfil my wish to become a commando, the Royal Marines being the only regiment after the Second World War to have commando forces.

My last operational tour before I left the Royal Marines was in the 23,000 ton Helicopter/Commando Carrier (formerly a Fixed Wing Aircraft Carrier) HMS *Bulwark* [1979–1981], where I held the appointment of 'Amphibious Operations Officer' (responsible for coordinating all amphibious operations from the ship) in the rank of Major RM.

It was during an unscheduled visit by HMS *Bulwark* to Naples in Autumn 1980 that I decided to take the opportunity to find and visit my father's grave which I knew was in the Minturno War Cemetery near the river Garigliano (where he was killed during the river crossing in January 1944) approximately 50 miles north west of Naples. Because my being in Naples at the time was unexpected I was not prepared for a full 'battlefield tour' as such so I decided to take pot luck and see what I could find. I was accompanied by a close colleague of mine Commander 'Bushy' Shrubb RN who held the appointment of 'Commander Air ['Wings'] on board (responsible for co-ordinating all flying operations from the ship).

We decided to make a day of it, grabbed our nominated ship's landrover and firstly headed off south east via the A3 highway to look at the landing beaches at Salerno which we found after a very picturesque drive around the Gulf of Naples. We went to the shoreline and imagined what it must have been like to land there under heavy fire in an area which was dominated by the enemy-held high ground overlooking the bay from the north. A daunting and no doubt frightening experience for those involved in the assault in September 1943.

From Salerno we returned to the main highway and headed north west again around the Gulf of Naples following initially the A56 and then the more scenic coastal road via Castel Volturno, Mondragone to the Garigliano river and the Minturno War Cemetery.

The cemetery entrance by the road was impressive and after a short walk up a well-manicured drive we consulted the Graves Register situated in a small enclosure called the Register Box at the entrance to the cemetery itself. Having established the details it didn't take long to find my father's grave [Plot: 7, Row: G, Grave: 16] amongst the hundreds of immaculately laid out graves. Once there Bushy kindly took the pictures of me by it. It was an emotional moment, surprisingly enough for both of us but especially me, and one that I will always remember particularly as no one from the family had ever been able to visit father's grave before. It was given more poignancy by the evidence of bullet and shrapnel scarred structures still standing near to the cemetery and the actual river Garigliano flowing past nearby. It reminded me that my father, sadly, was just one of several thousands to make the ultimate sacrifice in the battle for Italy!

Stanley Warner

Bushy and I returned to Naples and HMS *Bulwark* having experienced a very interesting and thought-provoking day out.

Alan's Colonel said he, 'was by far the best and finest of all my Company Commanders.'[9] Charles Hill, who commanded the Emanuel OTC when Alan was at School, was particularly moved by Alan's death and wrote of OEs' fond memories of Alan when he met Alan's wife in 1960, offering also his congratulations that Alan's son had been accepted for the Royal Marines.

Stanley Warner, Alan's Emanuel School friend, who had the unpleasant task of discovering Alan's body, continued with the 9th Battalion in its advance through Italy. Being promoted Major he later reverted to the rank of Captain on an appointment to the staff of the 56th London Division. He was home on leave in May 1945 but sadly on his return to Italy he died of Infantile Paralysis on 19 July 1945 and is buried in Udine Cemetery. *The Portcullis* reported:

> His Commanding Officer says of him – "Stanley was everything that a regular officer should be: fearless in battle, energetic and a born leader with a wonderful sense of humour." To this we would add – "With a charm of manner equalled by few." He was a very fine young man; his regiment and the Service has sustained a great loss by his death, as have all who came in contact with his pleasing personality.[10]

2: Howard Gordon Cross
(Emanuel 1932–1935)

The passage of time and the fact that Howard was an only child have left little record of this young man's life. We know he was a member of the Emanuel OTC and in addition to rowing also played for the First Fifteen. His rugby critique for the year 1935 read, 'Has weight and strength, but at present is too often tempted to hang about on the edge of the scrum instead of getting his head down at once.' Forward to 1940 and young Howard was caught in a far greater scrum in the evacuation of Dunkirk. He was a Lance Corporal in 3 Corps Signals (Royal Corps of Signals) and lost his life on 31 May 1940 in the retreat from Dunkirk. The War Diary for the month of May 1940 for the 3 Corps was written from memory and there is no surviving evidence thus far found which gives details of Howard's last moments. We do know that he was Mentioned in Despatches for his part in the evacuation but apart from the mention in the *London Gazette* no concrete details of his efforts have been found.[11]

At the base of his grave in Dunkirk Town Cemetery we read that Howard's father was killed at Arras in 1918 at the end of the First World War. We can only imagine the pain Howard's mother must have felt, losing her husband at the end of the First World War and her son at the beginning of the Second.

3: Kenneth Milton Millist
(Emanuel 1931–1935)

Kenneth's experiences up until 1940 have been told in an earlier chapter on the Battle of Britain. What remains to be explored are his experiences after 1940. In 1941 Kenneth was flying with 73 Squadron RAF in North Africa. The Allied air forces at this stage were in combat with both German and Italian forces in the battle to gain supremacy in the desert. Squadrons would often patrol over their areas and on 4 April 1941 Kenneth was flying a Hurricane when he and two other pilots intercepted the Italian pilots who had set out to rescue one of their own pilots, Serg Ezio Masenti. The leading Italian aircraft, which was shot down by another 73 Squadron pilot, was escorted by three CR. 42 Biplanes. It was one of these CR 42s, flown by Serg Antonio Camerini of 366a Squadriglia, which Kenneth intercepted head-on. Kenneth had been hit in the engine and landed ten miles north-east of Benina.[12]

Kenneth 'Tiny' Millist (fourth from left) with No. 73 Squadron in North Africa, 1941

The other 73 Squadron pilots were unaware of his fate and Kenneth was posted missing. The next part of his journey could be a scene out of any 1950s war film.

After crash landing Kenneth ran away from his aircraft and for two days, without food or water and evading an Italian motorcyclist on one occasion, he made his way to safety, meeting on 6 April an Australian Army sergeant who gave him food and water before giving him a lift to Derna from where he made his way to Gazala and back to his squadron. Kenneth was known as 'Tiny' Millist because of his height of over six feet, towering above many of his colleagues. A fellow pilot remembered when he heard the news of what had happened, '...when he was shot down by the vintage biplane everyone laughed their bloody heads off. He went at it head-on... We were told not to tackle them head-on, but Tiny did and got hit in the radiator for his pains.' The Italian biplane theoretically could not match a Hurricane but their manoeuvrability and the fact Kenneth went for a head-on attack meant that the biplane got the upper hand.

By April 1941 the Italians were joined by their German partners with the arrival of Erwin Rommel in the desert theatre. That month Kenneth saw action against Luftwaffe aircraft and shot down a Ju 87 with another one damaged. The Allied forces were on the retreat in the face of a German thrust across North Africa and Kenneth as part of 73 Squadron was defending the skies above Tobruk. He and another Hurricane pilot took off at 1400 on 7 April 1941 but this time failed to return, being shot down by ground fire. He is remembered on the Alamein memorial.

Just before his death Kenneth had been notified that he was to be awarded the DFC, which was gazetted in November 1941. This was for his brave actions in March 1941. The citation states:

> On the night of 12 March, enemy aircraft attacked the aerodrome at El Adem, hitting the officers' mess and killing one Italian prisoner and trapping several others. Pilot-Officer Millist, who was sleeping in a nearby house, which was itself machine-gunned, immediately went to the scene and with other officers, assisted in rescuing the wounded, refusing to take cover from the repeated bombing and machine-gun attacks until all prisoners had been rescued. Pilot-Officer Millist was then driven to his aircraft and without a flare path or knowledge of the position of bomb craters, took off and patrolled over the aerodrome for an hour, giving great encouragement to those on the ground. He attacked an enemy aircraft and drove it off, landing after the raid without exterior aids. Pilot-Officer Millist displayed exceptional courage, initiative and devotion to duty throughout the whole of the raid and showed complete disregard for his own safety.[13]

Stroke: Henry Clive Duffield *(Emanuel 1932–1935)*

Having had an exceptional School career, Henry joined the RAF in the war. His log books still survive but sadly, at the time of writing it has not been possible to provide further information on Henry's war service. His brother Ronald (Emanuel 1932–1935) managed to return from Dunkirk in the summer of 1940 before losing his life in a flying accident on 30 November 1942.

Henry survived the war, becoming a Chief Magistrate in what was then Rhodesia. He died in 1999.

Cox: Cornelius Legg *(Emanuel 1931–1937)*

Cornelius Legg's war experiences remain unknown.

Coach: James Gabriel Worth

James Gabriel Worth

James Worth joined Emanuel in 1920. He was born in Tasmania and came to England to further his education at Exeter College, Oxford. He taught at Emanuel until 1945, rising to the position of Head of Classics. He was a scholar of the highest order having had two books published by the Cambridge University Press. He was in charge of rowing from 1929 to 1937. Having been an experienced oarsman, in a career which included rowing for Thames Rowing Club at Henley Royal Regatta, he took Emanuel to their most successful season by coaching the 1935 crew to their up-river regatta triumphs.

In the First World War James, served as a Captain in the RASC. He was also a friend of the Oxford poet Rex Freston, who, serving with the Royal Berkshire Regiment, was killed in France on 24 January 1916.

James died on 22 November 1945 in Bolingbroke Hospital, a building which faces Emanuel from across Wandsworth Common. A measure of the affection people felt for him is in the fact that there appeared three obituaries and appreciations for him in the School magazine.

The Emanuel 1935 IV warming up before a race *(inset) Chelsea Pensioner Albert Marle laying a wreath on Alan Skillern's grave, 2011*

There is one paragraph which sums up how James felt about the Second World War and there is no doubt he must have thought about all those boys he had coached on the river and who went to fight. Writing of his feelings someone noted, 'The tragedy of the war oppressed his sensitive soul with an impatient exasperation at the bestiality and stupidity of the human race. He was profoundly distressed by the collapse of France and the extinguishing of the light of spiritual things.'[14]

It may be fitting to end with a verse James wrote for a fellow Exeter College friend and which could so easily apply to the sense of loss so many felt at the early and tragic deaths of three fine young men from the 1935 Four.

Sometimes it seems to me the red rose weeps
That it must fall and die;
The red rose knows no waking once it sleeps,
But we know – you and I.

References

1 To read of their rowing triumphs refer to D. Kirmatzis, *Biblicarta: The History of Emanuel School Boat Club* (2009), p. 18.

2 C. Northcote Parkinson, *Always A Fusilier: The War History of The Royal Fusiliers (City of London Regiment) 1939–45* (1949), p. 110.

3 Ibid. pp. 110-111.

4 Ibid. p. 112.

5 Ibid. p. 138.

6 Ibid. p. 146.

7 Ibid. p. 147.

8 For the geographical features see Brig. C. J. C. Molony, *The Mediterranean and Middle East: Volume 5: The Campaign in Sicily 1943 and The Campaign in Italy 3rd September 1943 to 31st March 1944* (1973), pp. 598-599.

9 Alan Skillern's obituary in *The Portcullis*, No. 151, Spring Term 1944, p. 5.

10 *The Portcullis*, No. 156, Autumn Term 1945, pp. 6-7.

11 *The London Gazette*, Tuesday 29 April, 1941.

12 Christopher Shores, Giovanni Massimello with Russel Guest, *A History of the Mediterranean Air War 1940–1945: Volume One: North Africa June 1940 – January 1942* (2012), p. 124.

13 *The Portcullis*, No. 144, Autumn Term 1941, p. 6.

14 *The Portcullis*, No. 158, Summer Term 1946, p. 6.

With 'The Elephant Boys'

William Robert 'Bob' Deeks *(Emanuel 1930–1935)*

Bob Deeks served throughout the whole of the Second World War, serving from May 1939 to June 1946. He had won a scholarship to Emanuel in 1930 and enjoyed playing rugby and cricket but was never a member of the OTC the members of which he described in an interview in 2012 as, 'the soldier boys', in which he showed no interest. One overriding memory Bob had was of Headmaster Cyril Broom (Headmaster 1928–1953):

> I found him a frightening man; absolutely frightening. He didn't often appear but when he did appear in the corridor he used to walk terribly quickly and that gown of his would be sort of flapping in the breeze but the crowds used to just scatter down these little side alleys to get away from him. And then his cry would go, 'Boy!'[1]

On leaving School in 1935 he was employed as an underwriter's clerk at Lloyds. But the political situation in Europe in the late 1930s was darkening and so Bob joined the Territorial Army in Offord Road, Islington on 5 May 1939, which was the headquarters of the 53rd Medium Regiment, Royal Artillery (RA) which in 1939 was the parent of 64th Medium Regiment RA which became Bob's regiment throughout the War.[2] He officially served with "C" Troop of 212 Battery, 64th Medium Regiment, Royal Artillery.

Bob initially trained and served as a signaller with the 64th Medium Regiment, having to learn Morse code, flash light signals and the laying of signal cables in addition to using radio equipment. He embarked for the Middle East in November 1940. Within a few months Bob saw his first action when his regiment was engaged on 23 February 1941 at the Battle of Keren in Eritrea, East Africa against Italian forces. Bob was in charge of his regiment's signals at Keren. The battle was over in a few months but this part of the East Africa Campaign was a gruelling trial, as Bob remembered when asked what the most striking feature of the battle was:

> Well I think to climb up that hill to the observation posts, great boulders the height of tea chests, that was awful. The stink of dead men jammed between the rocks and you couldn't get them out. And last of all, but actually should be first of all, the flies. I'd never known flies like them and it was impossible to have a cup of tea without waving your hand over the cup all the time. Before you got it to your mouth they were all sitting around again. We were there with an Indian division, very good guys ... but even they were suffering; they thought it was terrible. Hot, hot, hot.[3]

Bob Deeks (circled) in North Africa

The North African Campaign was fought with troops from across the British Empire and one of the most feared regiments was the Gurkhas. Bob remembered them being both determined and fierce fighters:

> This time the guns weren't commissioned and the Ghurkhas went in at night and they went in without any artillery support, absolutely quiet. So there you have a situation all very peaceful, I mean war is not sort of 24-hours bang, bang, bang, bang, bang. People have all sorts of things to do to get ready for the next thing. And the Gurkhas went up, and these poor ruddy Germans looking out over their night watchmen [when] suddenly this knife would sort of whizz through the air and cut the head off; they just attacked without any barrage.

Bob served throughout the North African and Desert Campaigns including in Syria supporting the 7th Australian Division against the Vichy French, and in Bardia Second Battle of El Alamein where he supported any unit requiring assistance with general loading and offloading of equipment in preparation for the battle.

An illustration depicting 64th's elephant emblem in the Second World War

Bob Deeks (first from right) with 'Confusion', the name given to 'C' troop's 5.5 inch medium gun – Germany, April 1945

He attended OCTU but did not become an officer, instead he remained a Sergeant but as the North Africa Campaign came to a close and the Italian opened up Bob became number one gun commander on 5.5-inch howitzers. Landing in Sicily after the Allied invasion in July 1943 Bob's regiment fired a barrage across the Messina Straits in support of the Allied assault on mainland Italy.

Operating the gun:

So how exactly did a gun crew operate? Bob describes the process they went through during an average action:

> The instructions come from the command post. You have a tannoy system and it tells you angle, slight and the range and all the details required to fire the gun and then if they say ten rounds gunfire, fire, then it's up to the gun commander so he fires as quickly as he can, or sometimes it will be wait for further instructions. So if it were ten rounds gunfire it's just a question of banging the shell in, pulling the lanyard and making sure all the settings are right, but as a number one you had to check that the layer had done his job and that the charge is the correct charge and the ammunition is there, and then you fire.

By Christmas 1943 Bob was back in England after two years in North Africa but rest and celebration were short-lived as preparations got underway for the invasion of Normandy in June 1944.

North West Europe

The 64th Medium Regiment as part of 30 Corps landed on Gold Beach, Normandy on 7 June 1944. They fought across northern France and into Belgium. At Arnhem they provided gun support for the 1st Airborne Division for which they were granted the right to wear the Pegasus badge on their lower right sleeve. It was noted by a member of the regiment that there was nothing 'in all their fine record of which the 64th gunners' were 'prouder than the time they were friends in need to the men [of the 1st Airborne] whose courage thrilled the world.'[4] After fighting all the way through to Germany Bob was demobbed in 1946. He died in August 2014 but this 'Elephant Boy' will be long remembered for his long war service.

References

1 Interview W. R. 'Bob' Deeks, by Daniel Kirmatzis 2012.
2 For an account of the 64th Medium Regiment RA read Denis Falvey, *A Well-Known Excellence: British Artillery and an Artilleryman in World War Two* (2002).
3 Interview Deeks, 2012.
4 'With Our Forces Overseas: Gunner's Splendid Record', *Warminster Journal*, 30 March 1945, p. 2.

Col. William 'Michael' Squire Jeffery

(Emanuel 1932–1938)

At Emanuel Michael was a gifted sportsman, being both a Forward in the First Fifteen and rowed two in the School Eight described in the Trinity Term Portcullis as being effective but with a 'somewhat rugged style.' Michael was also Captain of Shooting, a Prefect, member of the Swimming Team and a Sergeant in the OTC being awarded his War Certificate 'A.'

After leaving Emanuel in 1938 William 'Michael' Jeffery joined the Port of London Authority. As war approached in 1939 he signed up with the Territorial Army in Clapham Junction on 8 May, exactly six years before VE Day. Michael joined the 2nd London, 48th Battalion, Royal Tank Regiment. He remembers being excited at the outbreak of war. Michael became the Company Officer's tank driver. Being moved up to Sanderstead, he trained in Mark II medium tanks. A move to Colchester meant the task of defending the coast between Felixstowe and Harwich during the Dunkirk evacuations. After Dunkirk, Michael was moved again, down to Salisbury Plain in August 1940. He was approaching his 19th birthday. He applied for a commission and after going to the Officer Cadet Training Unit he joined the 2nd Royal Gloucestershire Hussars Yeomanry (RGH), Royal Armoured Corps. He received his Commission in January 1941.

Sgt. Michael Jeffery, Emanuel Shooting VIII, 1938

Sailing out to North Africa on the P&O liner *Strathmore*, he arrived at Port Tawfiq on the Suez Canal on 1 October 1941. On Friday 13 December 1941 Michael saw his first action during Operation Crusader. At this time he was a second Lieutenant in 'G' Squadron RGH. He saw action in several desert campaigns in 1942 including at the Battle of Gazala and the First Battle of Alamein against Axis forces led by Erwin Rommel who was making solid progress towards his target of Egypt between May and June 1942.

One of the most intense periods for Michael in North Africa was during July 1942. On 2 July 1942 'G' Squadron, 2nd Gloucesters, joined the 22nd Armoured Brigade. On 12 July 1942 during the First Battle of Alamein Michael and his troop captured a Panzer II and its crew. The intensity and strain on tank commanders and their crews during the summer months of 1942 is best illustrated from a report by the Medical Research Section at General Headquarters MEF from July 1942 which highlights the pressures and extreme climates under which tank crews were expected to operate including widespread fatigue being one of the major problems facing the them.[1] So how did these men find the courage to continue leading others under such extreme conditions? Michael's answer to this question when Daniel Kirmatzis interviewed him in 2011 was:

> There were two things basically. One is, what you're frightened of most is letting your soldiers down and that keeps you busy and then once you've made yourself busy you don't have bloody time to worry. It's as simple as that really. But your one fear is to let your soldiers down. I never knew of anybody who failed on that.

On 16 July 1942 Michael was injured when under anti-tank gunfire the glass of his Crusader tank shattered onto his face and he spent several weeks in hospital recovering.

For his actions in the battles of Gazala and the First of Alamein Michael was Mentioned in Despatches which was announced in *The London Gazette* on 24 June 1943.

Photos of Michael Jeffery during the North African campaign c1942

Michael Jeffery post-war

When interviewed in 2011 Michael reflected on how, as he saw it, the British and Germans viewed each other during the war. He recalled, 'There was a distinct sense of chivalry between the Afrika Korps and the 8th Armoured Division. There were a number of instances of it. We often said if we were to be captured it would have to be by the Italians because it would be easier to escape.'

After the North African Campaign Michael served in Italy in support of the 78th Division and also served with the 51st (Leeds Rifles) Royal Tank Division which played a significant part in the reconquest of central Italy from May to August 1944.

At the age of 90 Michael had one very personal and vivid memory that for him stood out among all his war experiences: It was during the Italian Campaign that he recalled:

> This friend, David ... got his troop up a mountain and was coming back down the hill at the end of the day to replenish and so on. Going down the hill he noticed there was quite a steep drop on one side and that his driver was getting near the edge. So he picked up his microphone and said driver left. Now he'd got his box on the roof and his other two tanks heard him and not the driver. Over they went, he was sitting on top, the rest of the crew was alright but he was killed. And you know there was an absolute conspiracy, I spent part of my honeymoon with his parents. He was an only child, a lovely, lovely man and they never knew that it was his own fault. They never knew, as far as they knew he was killed in action. It would have been cruel had they known so nobody ever told them unless the mother found it out as mothers do, but such a tragic loss of life. I visited his grave one time when we were in Italy on holiday. I stood there and said "You bloody fool you could have been here now." That was the worst thing to me.

At the end of his interview in 2011 Michael made a point that he wanted remembered by future generations and which encapsulates the spirit of the war-generation:

> I think I would like to finish by saying I was privileged to be part of it, and at the start of the war the country was absolutely united. My grandparents, my parents and my generation – we all realised that it had to be, you couldn't back away from it. I wish sometimes we could be as united as that now. Maybe we will one day.[2]

Before the end of the war Michael has contracted jaundice and returned to England in March 1945. After the war he took a regular Commission in the Royal Tank Regiment in addition to being an instructor at a Cadet School and in 1966 Regimental Colonel, Royal Tank Regiment. Michael died in May 2014.

References

1 Report of the Medical Research Section at GHQ, MEF, July 1942 reproduced in Captain B. H. Liddell Hart, *The Tanks: The History of the Royal Tank Regiment, Volume II, 1939–1945* (1959), pp. 210-212.

2 Interview Michael Jeffery, by Daniel Kirmatzis, December 2011.

'His Heart was in Soldiering'
Eric Harold Botting *(Emanuel 1932–1937)*

Eric's School career was described as 'uneventful', but it was noted that when his interest was aroused in a particular topic he showed an 'unusual intelligence.' He was a keen member of the OTC achieving his War Certificate 'A'. His passions were natural history and stamp collecting and he would often lead people on bird-nesting tours.

Eric's ambition was to emulate his father and grandfather who had both been in the London Rifle Brigade (LRB). In 1941 Eric married Margaret Snow but married life, for so many of that generation, was interrupted by the War. Eric served with the 7th Battalion (1st Battalion The London Rifle Brigade) Rifle Brigade. Sgt. Botting 6968254 travelled with the battalion to North Africa, arriving in Egypt in July 1942. According to John Longstaff, another member of the battalion, the conditions on the troopship travelling from the UK to Egypt were appalling.[1] By the time of their arrival the war in the Western Desert was in the Axis's favour with the Allies in retreat. By June Erwin Rommel's forces had driven the Allies back to a defensive position at El Alamein. Rommel's target was the Suez Canal – control of which meant access to the vast oil fields in the Middle East which may well have been decisive to an Axis, rather than and Allied, victory. In September 1942, the tide turned at the Battle of Alam Halfa where Rommel's thrust was halted and in the weeks following plans were made for an Allies assault at El Alamein – Operation Lightfoot.

The Second Battle of El Alamein opened on the night of 23 October 1942 with a massive artillery barrage of around 900 guns. The opening offensive was a surprise but individual armoured corps commanders in the field lacked the bite the GOC of 8th Army – Lieutenant-General Montgomery – had wished for and so the first days of the Battle were not as successful as hoped, even though the overall battle was decisive, in Churchill's phrase being the 'end of the beginning', with Axis forces eventually being defeated in the Western Desert in May 1943.[2]

The 7th Battalion formed part of the British 7th Motor Brigade which provided infantry support for the 1st Armoured Division's armoured units. In fierce fighting in El Wishka, Matruh – Egypt, just two days into the battle on 25 October

Eric Botting, Emanuel Shooting VIII, 1936

Eric was killed whilst gallantly attempting to save the life of another man. His Commanding Officer wrote:

> Botting, learning there was a wounded officer and man in no-man's land, some 400 yards out, jumped into his truck and drove towards them. He had got almost half-way when a shell hit it and then machine guns opened on it. His death must have been instantaneous – tragic, but a very great show nevertheless and it must have been an inspiration to his Company, because they put paid to a number of Jerry tanks afterwards.

Eric is commemorated on the Alamein Memorial.

References

1 John Edward Longstaff, IWM Interview 14/09/1988 by Conrad Wood Catalogue Number 10382 – Reel 5.

2 See Nigel Hamilton, *The Full Monty: Montgomery of Alamein 1887–1942* (2002), Chs. 21–23.

The 70th Anniversary of the Second Battle of El Alamein

On Saturday 27 October 2012 OEs Bob Deeks and Michael Jeffery met for the first time at an Evensong at Westminster Abbey to commemorate the 70th anniversary of the Second Battle of El Alamein. Although their School careers overlapped, Bob was three years older than Michael and they hadn't know each other whilst at Emanuel. Daniel Kirmatzis, who had interviewed both men several months previously, introduced the OEs to each other. Having spoken with Michael Jeffery a week before the Evensong, Daniel was made aware of the service and so contacted Bob's son, Richard, and arrangements were then made for everyone to attend. Afterwards Bob and Michael met in a reception in the Church House Conference Centre, Westminster. When they first met they sang one of the School's House songs with remarkable energy and laughed through shared memories of masters and famous School characters.

Michael had fought in several desert campaigns including in the Battle of Gazala but Bob was at the Second Battle of El Alamein. When interviewed in 2012 Bob remembered the opening evening of the Battle – 23 October 1942: '... it wasn't sort of one lot on and then the other, they [the artillery] all opened up, all pulled the chain at [9.40pm] and the sky, you've never seen anything like it. ... what the Germans thought about that I can't think. They must have gone absolutely mad.'

Both men were introduced to General Sir Peter Wall, Chief of the General Staff (2010–2014) and General Sir David Richards, Chief of the Defence Staff (2010–2013). Bob and General Sir David Richards in particular discussed the role of artillery having both been gunners.

Bob Deeks (left) and Michael Jeffery (right)

General Sir Peter Wall (left), Bob Deeks (centre) and Michael Jeffery (right)

From North Africa to Normandy

Harold Stanley Page *(Emanuel 1931–1939)*

During the Second World War Harold served with the 58th Field Regiment, Royal Artillery, in both the North African and North West Europe Campaigns. In a series of letters he wrote home he discussed a variety of topics, including leisure time, desert conditions and the reactions of liberated Belgians as the Allies moved through North West Europe in late 1944. He finished the war with the rank of Captain.

28.07.1942: On board en route for North Africa – They've given me the job of Gunnery Officer – that is looking after the anti-aircraft machine guns. This gets me out of lots of other duties but won't be so good when things get going.

Today I was leaning on the side watching the sea gulls when a sailor nearby whistled the first line of a familiar tune. I thought hard and decided that I had last heard it with the words 'Emanuel for the noble aim' attached so I repeated it and we met. I only remember him vaguely as a little boy but he remembers me very well. He's been in the Navy four months. Still no news of our ultimate destination...

31.07.1942: en route North Africa: The rest of the impediments in the cabin consist of wash stand – cold fresh water for two separate hours daily – a dressing table with a fair number of drawers (all quite adequate for one or two people but not for five) and also three tin trunks and a couple of suitcases sticking out from under the beds.

Ventilation is difficult. The port hole is permanently blacked out but allows the air to come in. We have two electric fans which at least move the air if they don't purify it.

Most of the ship is blacked out in this way and we are under electric light a good deal of the time. Food is still good. Breakfast: tea or coffee, porridge, cereal or fruit, bacon and whatnot – toast and marmalade. Lunch:– soup, fish, meat, veg or curry, pudding, cheese and lettuce. Dinner:– soup meat & veg, pudding & apple. Meat is often pork and sometimes chicken. Service good...

Harold Page (third from left), with service friends

18.08.1942: en Route North Africa: If anything life on the ship has improved. We do four hours training a day; often lecturing the men with information that we ourselves have gathered only 5 minutes before. It gave me great pleasure to take Bren Gun classes – a thing I have not done since Reading. These classes, although in themselves valueless are valuable in that they keep the men distracted and not thinking continually of home.

24.10.1942: Egypt: I am quite whole & have not suffered in any way from the journey. I can't say I am delighted with this station. There really is an awful lot of sand here. The curse of Egypt seems to be the fly – just the ordinary fly. If you remain still for a moment, and probably if you don't, you have about 50 flies crawling and bussing over you. I hate them.

06.01.1943: We have just had a sandstorm which has kept us with our bellies to the ground for two days the wind which carried it was the worst gale I have ever felt even at sea. Heavy tins were lifted up and carried quite a long way. The air was brown with sand which got in everywhere. In an hour pockets were bulging with sand if ever you were foolish enough to remain unsheltered that long.

Today I shook out most of the sand from my kit & transferred it from the case which was on the point of collapse to a cartridge box which should stand up to most things. I am still quite fit and we still get food although the water has turned salt again and makes tea unbearable.

Mind is being slowly warped by conditions. Can no longer think in any great depth for any great length of time. I hope this will pass. I must learn to transcend. People you read about always do but I find thought and comfort go hand in hand and asceticism produces no results. The sooner we can wallow in comfort and luxury the better.

It is unlikely in my opinion that an early victory out here necessarily means an early return home. I think we would stay in this part of the world for sometime afterward.

Apart from the pleasure of getting to England I don't think it would be desirable to return too soon because they will have a lot of work for us in Europe before too long.

Nevertheless, I hope so much that I will be with you and Carol soon...

06.02.1943: For some days now we have been in country which is not all rock and sand. True it is sand underneath but a great part of it is cultivated & grass grows freely. The weather has been lovely (except today when it has rained) & we have been enjoying a short rest. Water comes from any of several wells operated by wind-pumps probably installed originally by the Italian government and in consequence have been able to get myself & my hoarded dirty laundry clean. There are lots of bright coloured wild flowers & also groves of almonds lemons and olives.

I have been in to Tripoli. It looks as though it was a pleasant enough city although at the moment there is little life in it. What shops there are selling nothing but razor blades, soap, sweets and a whole lot of trash that they pass off as souvenirs.

The other day we had a visit by Winston Churchill – I expect you heard all about it at home. We lined either side of the road and he drove down very slowly in a car. To me it looked all the world like Movietime News. He did all his usual tricks and we shouted all the usual things. He must be very tired of it. He looked very pale and I was surprised to hear on the English News that he returned 'bronzed by the sun.' I expect we are all very brown but we don't notice it.

Winston Churchill sitting in Montgomery's Staff Car, Tripoli, 1942

09.05.1943: As you have heard, Tunis and Bizerte have gone but we still have a lot to do. Naturally speculation about our future is even wilder now but general rumour seems to damn all chances of return. But nevertheless we are all looking forward to cessation of bangs even if we only return to the Delta....

12.05.1943: 58th Field Regiment. MEF: At last it's over. As Mr Eliot would say, not with a bang but a whimper. For the last few days our guns have only paused in their firing for very short periods. We heard of the fall of Tunis and Bizerta & of people surrendering here and there & predictions of the collapse but still we went on firing. Eventually with my voice gone through shouting I had to use telephones to each gun from my Command Post.

This morning we were told that it was unlikely we would fire up to 12.30 because a temporary Armistice had been called on part of the front in order that terms might be discussed. Our observation post was reporting scores of white flags & hordes of prisoners coming in. We could see these ourselves in all sorts of transport and on foot coming down the road, the Italian sometimes pleased sometimes dejected, the Germans prevalently cocky. But nevertheless all fighting hadn't ceased & Jerry had a last fling with a minerwerfer – a rocket gun which fires half a dozen shells at a time. These things are pretty lethal and kept us in our holes when we were not firing back. About an hour from the end one of them landed slap in a slit trench and killed two. This is about a record for bad luck. And then at last about lunch time I had the pleasure of shouting 'Cease Firing.' We moved out of action about four in the afternoon. We went back through Enfidaville which seemed a pleasant little village that had been knocked about instead of the dreaded hot spot to be avoided. So here we are now just south of Enfidaville.

It is difficult to describe our feelings about it all. Possibly in England you too felt that the conclusion was so foregone

& the whole thing so protracted that there could be no hilarious release of victory feeling. At present it is hard to get used to the idea that we haven't to dig or duck. It is difficult to realise that we are not moving off into action somewhere else.

Our plans are indefinite but they say we are going to rest here for a few days. In the past few months we have been continually in action – Medemine where we shot a lot of tanks – the Mareth line – Wadi Akarit at the Gabes Gap position – finally about four different positions in the last show. We have supported anybody and everybody when and how they wanted it. In this last we supported Indians, Highlanders, New Zealanders, French & the 56th Division at different times. We remained in the south with one foot on the foothills putting in attack after attack as a feint while our armour got around to take Tunis and Bizerte and cut off Cap Bon.

Of course, Jerry knew that it would all end sometime and merely planned to make it last as long as he could. As it was he was taken by surprise and lasted six weeks (at least) less than he expected. On our part of the front the suspension of hostilities while terms was [sic] discussed gave him time to destroy his equipment but in the north a lot of M/T. and other equipment was captured.

And now to relax as ordered.

13.05.1943: The first day of my relaxation was spent on a rather harrowing tour round the battlefield. The chief object of this was looting, the other object was to have a look at the enemy gun positions, etc. Certainly he had dug himself deep in but in several places our artillery had obviously been very effective. On the whole I was depressed by the whole business. Everything looked so desolate. Smashed and burnt equipment was lying about and everything gave the impression that nobody lived here anymore. As far as looting goes I did not do very well. I found this writing paper and that's about all. Other loot included plenty of food (very good too) two three ton trucks & new gadgets. I am certainly very glad that it was unnecessary for us to take these positions in the hills. It is good country for defence & very dangerous to attack.

Rumours say that we return to Tripoli for intensive training. Second Front? It seems very unlikely that anything better than this will happen.

Letters from late May to June sent from Tripoli area

28.05.1943: 58th Field Regiment: Here we are at Tripoli again. Not quite so near this time but pleasantly enough situated in sandy orchards. We can eat tiny bitter sweet apples and ripe apricots to our stomachs' discontent. We are neatly laid out in a peacetime fashion and we have allowed ourselves the luxury of officers' lines. Snob alley I have christened it. Magnificent tents & wigwams have sprung up, most of them looted from the battlefield.

We saw *Desert Victory* by means of mobile cinema that came around one evening. I was impressed by the way they put it over. It looks worse than it is, darling. They leave out the quiet moments. I should think the rest of the campaign will make an even better film. The country was certainly more interesting.

As I forecast I left the regiment to go to a Mines Course in Tripoli on the 20th. Owing to the King's visit the course did not start till today. Not only did we have a free day in consequence but we missed the regimental parade. For this parade they rose at 4.20 a.m. and did not expect to get back until tea time.

On the course with me was a captain from the other battery & we devised quite a different program. After breakfast we got a lift into town which we found deserted except for the troops lining the main streets. No shops were open because all civilians had been confined to their houses on pain of a twelve pound fine. This left us rather at a loss so we drifted along to the main square and waited developments. Before long George arrived & inspected troops in the square – I expect you saw this on the films.

ENSA actresses (from left to right) Kay Young, Bea Lillie, Dorothy Dickson and Vivien Leigh

27.06.1943: The chief event of the last few days was a visit to the show that has been in town this week. It was the best show that I have seen for ages. Beatrice Lillie, Dorothy Dixon & Vivien Leigh. Vivien Leigh was very decorative if nothing else and the other two – both of them must be well over 50 – were magnificent.

It was so different to the other ENSA shows where someone comes on to do a 'turn'. These people held the audience. We laughed for two hours.

September 1943: Here we had our suspicions about the Italian situation before the Armistice. It didn't seem as though we were trying very hard at first and the news of the peace seemed to fit in very well. Of course there is quite a change in Tripoli. The Italian prisoners now go about unguarded and some of them that live locally have been sent to their homes. I am afraid my Italian is not sufficiently advanced to sound their opinions about the situation but as far as I can make out the Tripolitalian colonists have never been great fascists.

Sickening to observe the change of policy in the *Tripoli Times*. Before the armistice the leaders were urging the full penalty for the Italian army's crimes, but now, of course, they are plugging the 'new allies' line of talk. No doubt English papers are the same...

I think that this is about the most difficult part of the war out here. Static on peaceful program without the attractions of England we are by now getting very niggly and very homesick. If we were in action this wouldn't be half so bad. But then you can't have it both ways.

We do our best to amuse ourselves with cricket, football, basketball and swimming so far as the heat will allow.

During the morning somebody discovered a mine in a spot of ground where we do our training. General dismay. In the afternoon Page & other heroes were conscripted from his troop and went and lifted it and a dozen others that I found in a belt. I had also taken a couple of Bren guns with me that needed adjustment. During the firing of these a ricochet skidded on to an old Italian ammunition dump & then the fun started.

The explosions lasted an hour and a half and were accompanied by columns of smoke of different colours as high as Nelson's column. Big bangs and little bangs. It spread over half a mile and was watched by my party (after we had withdrawn to a safe distance) in much the same spirit at a November the fifth party.

Later I was thanked by a major in the REG (regiment) who said that he had been waiting for it to explode of its own free will for some time.

02.11.1943: We are still on the move. They are making the journey excessively tedious by travelling very little distance each day.

The mornings are quite cold. We get up in the middle of the night for breakfast in a cold gloom and don't warm up till midday travelling as we are over ground we know so well it is disconcerting to see how deserted it is. Places which to us were full of life now have desert with only tracks to show how transitory an occupation it was. It was like travelling through a cemetery and it impressed on us that war in the desert is a back number – indeed as we are too.

The natives are quite conscious of the change. It is obvious that they have lost interest in troops now that they can cultivate the desert unmolested & apart from the begging boys shouting 'backsheesh' we pass unremarked.

Perhaps the more farsighted of them still watch with a wary eye the course of the war. If the Germans win it means more disorganising change for them & everyone out here – even those who are European – wants to be left alone more than anything else. I move nearer to you but I have some misgivings as to the outcome of this journey. Cross your fingers we may be lucky.

Harold was on leave in January 1944 and then he was stationed in Yorkshire on training manoeuvres.

Harold Page shortly before action at Bremen

The Normandy Campaign

England, D+2 1944: I left England on D+2 and arrived in France D+3. My last few days in England were spent in a cage of barbed wire – very similar to a concentration camp in appearance and restrictions – from which we were not allowed to emerge or have any contact with the outside world. It was a fairly uncomfortable few days. Well the voyage to France was not exactly a pleasure cruise but fair enough. You have read about the thousands of ships, the immunity from attack (except at night), the organised beaches – if I endorse the newspapers it is enough.

It was lovely in France. The same green fields that we had left. The villages of course look rather different especially the churches which are boxy buildings of no great dignity. Three coloured flags & Jacks everywhere and two fingered grinning civilians lining the roadside. All this you have read. I had little time to observe or record impressions of the countryside. We were on the job as soon as we were ashore. I had my guns in action within a few hours of landing and have not stopped yet. Seems my stand-in hasn't left England and consequently I have had no relief. The days are so long now, there is little sleep time & this is disturbed by the telephone, fire orders and the Boche. But to make up for all this is the weather which is really lovely.

During the day we are unmolested as far as Jerry is concerned even though we throw an awful lot of stuff at him (touch some wood). But at night we have quite a bit of trouble from aircraft.

We have sampled local produce – Camembert – but wine is very scarce although there is cider about.

29.06.1944: The war is not too bad but rather noisy... I am drinking plenty of fresh milk and eating Camembert. Progress here seems to be reasonably satisfactory.

03.09.1944: We have been very much on the move and on this anniversary of the war we are enjoying something like a Victory march. We are all very much excited by the intensity of the welcome we receive as we go forward. I wish I could tell you more details but I am afraid I will have to wait a few days before I do. I would like to have stayed at some of the places through which we passed...

In one town in which we stayed for a little while the local radio broadcast that the War was finished. Naturally all the civilians dashed out of their houses shrieking the news & started wassailing. Fortunately our chaps accepted their statements with some reserve and after listening for the news from the BBC & not getting it we decided it was a canard. But the civilians didn't mind. After all the war is finished for them anyway.

12.09.1944: Things have moved very quickly and the war of Normandy seems very far distant. Since then we have travelled a long way in a very short time often in an atmosphere of pageantry which really turned the war into a crusade. Indeed being at the very front of the advance and receiving the full impact of the welcome of the inhabitants before it had time to cool we felt that we really were liberators.

Across France we found everyone pleased to see us and cheering & giving us fruit, etc. On the whole they looked smart but not well fed. One and all hated the Germans & the Maquis did some good work in rounding up Germans which we had not time to do.

But the trip across France had nothing on the gallop to Brussels. Here was the real welcome. Everybody went mad. From hiding places came bottles of brandy, wine, and even whisky saved from before the war. I like the Belgians. As one of them said to me 'We are sympathetic to you.'

Harold Page (left)

We were fortunate enough to stay there for a day or two. Brussels I think must have the loveliest girls in the world. They continue to look incredibly smart and groomed with very little material & it was indeed rare to see a plain one & they were all so friendly!

They crowded round us helping us when we were working and begging us to go to parties. Theoretically we weren't allowed but it was impossible to disappoint such charming people.

While we were there an armistice rumour started. A woman rushed out of her house screaming that Germany had capitulated. She had heard it on the radio. This was soon confirmed by lots of others and soon there were celebrations.

But the British – tradition and all that – remained calm. While they screamed it to the roof tops we said 'Oh yes, we will wait until we get it officially', an attitude which was later justified since the BBC made no mention of it at all. I suppose it was some fool or knave on Brussels radio.

Belgian troops arrived & received a great welcome. In an address by the Major he said that it was hard to distinguish them from British troops since they were battle class and

Harold Page in khaki

were washed and shaved – I think this is a double edged compliment and don't quite know how it was meant.

On the whole a lovely time. The Belgians seem to be Anglophiles and so many of them speak English. Nevertheless my French was exercised & is improving.

On the whole I do not think they have had as bad a time as the French. Practically anything was obtainable in the capital if you had sufficient money. Far more hatred than for the German army was for the Belgian SS. Most of these cleared out to Germany before the Germans left but not all escaped. The houses of these and other collaborators were looted and burned.

Well it was a wonderful experience for us and the first time I felt proud of being in the Army. I wonder if the welcome home will be as good?

Some of our fellows who have been wounded & are back in England tell us when they write that people at home think that the war is all over and out here we have only got to finish it off. This isn't very cheering for us here because people are still dying round us and we look forward to quite a tough period ahead. It is not good to hear of the premature suppositions of peace made by comfortable people at home. For us here there is no peace until Germany packs in and then if necessary.

10.11.1944: We have been dodging about a lot lately and the general idea seems to be that we are maids of all work. As soon as it becomes quiet anywhere we are whisked off to somewhere noisy.

Of course the weather is not playing very fair at the moment and there is a terrible amount of mud and water about. We even had some sleety snow yesterday. Wherever possible we get into barns or even houses but since the guns are always in action and need plenty of room we rarely find ourselves in built up areas.

Our substitute is a hole in the ground with a sheet of canvas over the top, but most of the ground is so damp that a hole a foot deep will fill up with water in no time. At the moment my Command Post is a large hole three feet deep. The water started to come in so we put down some concrete paving stones which so far have done the trick. But the tour de force is a stove, yes, a fire. We took a stove from an old German barracks and it has become part of our equipment. Usually we burn wood but at the moment there is plenty of coal handy.

25.11.1944: I feel I must bring you a little more up to date on my movements. From Brussels we went with the armour to Nijmegen – a most exciting journey during which we were turning our guns in all directions – behind us as well. It is unusual for a medium regiment to work with tanks but we must have done pretty well because the same division has been asking for us ever since. Nijmegen wasn't any picnic. It was there that we had bomb trouble. We were also disappointed with the Arnhem failure.

We went a wee bit west along the Woal to finish off an attempt by Jerry to re-cross it & then went back to Nijmegen to prepare for the next lot. But before this happened they sent for us to help the Canadians clear the Scheldt. Pretty hard there. We could see the vapour trails of rockets going to England & heard flying bombs on their way to Antwerp.

Well that finished up OK and now we are here. Our chief concern at the moment is to make ourselves comfortable with limited materials. The other day we shot a few pigs and had a pork feast for a few days. Last night we had duck.

Captain Stanley 'George' Holliman

The Holliman Brothers

The young Holliman brothers – George, Ken, Peter and John

Four Holliman brothers attended Emanuel. The eldest brothers, Stanley 'George' and Kenneth 'Ken' saw active overseas service in the Second World War. Peter the second youngest left Emanuel in 1941 and worked for the London Midland and Scottish Railway in the offices at Euston House, London before starting an engineering cadetship. He later joined REME and did National Service in Kenya. John, the youngest Holliman brother, was an evacuee, like his three brothers, with the School in Petersfield, leaving Emanuel in 1946 and started a career in banking. Their father had served in the First World War and their grandfather served in the Second Boer War.

Stanley 'George' Holliman MC

(Emanuel 1933–1941)

Stanley (known as George) was an exceptionally bright pupil at Emanuel. He was Captain of the School, Athletics, Boxing, and Tennis. He played rugby for the Second Fifteen and cricket for the Second Eleven. He was a CSM in the School and was awarded his War Certificate 'A.' However the sporting life did not handicap George's academic abilities, in fact they complimented them for George was an outstanding scholar who won a Travel Scholarship to France in 1939 and for three years, 1938/39/40 was a Grand Concours Prizewinner, a French language competition established by the French Republic for English schools. George believed that the OTC

George Holliman (centre) in Hammam-Lif, Tunisia, 1943

[later JTC] prepared him for his Army experiences in that it taught him discipline and teamwork but it didn't prepare him later on when he was surprised to learn that individuals he trained with in the army couldn't read or write. Unlike today many people didn't always attend secondary school for five to six years and the necessity of helping to provide support for their families meant they were required to leave school early and find a job.

George was in France at the outbreak of the Second World War on a London County Council travel scholarship but remembered, when interviewed in 2013, that there appeared no imminent threat to France and so people were not too concerned. He returned to England in October 1939 and joined his brothers who had been evacuated with the School to Petersfield. George was billeted in Steep Village near Petersfield.

George left Emanuel in February 1941 and worked for a few months in the income tax department of the Civil Service before being called up, joining the Queen's Royal West Surrey Regiment. In 1942, after attending an OCTU, George was commissioned into the Royal Engineers. He remembered a discussion with the selection board:

> So they said, "What would you think about joining the Royal Engineers"? I didn't know what the Royal Engineers were or what they did. I said, "Well, look, I joined the Army to fight. Will I get into a fight"? And they said, "Oh yes, we can promise you that". I still remember those words, they said, "Yes, we can promise you that".[1]

During his training with the engineers George learnt a lesson from the corporal or sergeant training him about leading by example:

> We had to dig trenches in the winter without shirts on. Then we had to fill the trenches up again. The corporal or sergeant, whoever was in charge said, "No good moaning about it. One day you're going to ask your men to do it and you should be able to say you've done it", which is fair enough.[2]

George started sapper training, where, between digging trenches and physical exercise, he learnt about explosives including how they were fused and detonated. But George also remembered recruits playing pranks on each other; even in wartime there was amusement to be had.

Among the most important lessons were understanding the different types of mines, as George recalled:

> We were taught what the German mines looked like and they produced one or two, how you went about clearing a minefield, and if you were laying [a] minefield, how you plotted it so that if you had to come and lift it, you knew where the mines were.

Postcards depicting Royal Engineers building bridges during the Italian campaign

In the summer of 1942 Lieutenant S. G. Holliman was posted to his company, 564 Field Company, Royal Engineers with whom he served through the North African and Italian Campaigns. After further training in Monkton in Scotland the Company sailed in convoy in two ships; George was on the Polish cruise ship *Sobieski*. As part of an Anglo-American Assault Group supporting 168 Combat Team 564 RE were given the task of getting all the arms ashore at the unopposed landing at Vichy French-controlled Algiers as part of Operation Torch on 8 November 1942. A few weeks later, as the Allies were advancing on Tunis, George, serving with 3 Platoon 564 RE, was involved in an action to blow three small railway bridges on a line from the town of Medjez el Bab in northern Tunisia to Bizerta on the coast.[3] The Germans made an advance on Medjez and George with 3 Platoon was given the task of preventing the enemy forces using the bridges. Originally George was on a lone patrol whilst his platoon were sent to blow the bridges. George disobeyed orders that day in order to find what was happening to his platoon. It could have ended in a court martial but instead it ended with the award of a Military Cross. George related what happened:

> So I disobeyed orders and I put various slabs of explosive and fuse, short fuse and igniters and detonators in my pack and I got on my motorbike and I rode north until I found the first bridge hadn't blown and they had no transport and they didn't know what to do. They didn't have an officer with them, or I think the highest was probably a lance corporal. So I gave them some more gun cotton and fuse, detonators, and told them to go down and do it again. We went up to the next one and they had blown...the second one had blown.
>
> I went up to the third one. There were a few troops who were on their way back, walking down. I went up to the third one, which hadn't blown, and the troops were hiding under the bridge because there was an advancing tank and not far away there was fighting going on and they were a bit worried. So I got them out and we blew

up the bridge. Then I sent them back, walking, marching, running or whatever, and just then a German flame-throwing tank came across the plain, not very far away firing jets of fuel.[4]

The official citation reads:

> On 10 December 1942 this officer was in charge of certain demolitions on the railway north of Medjez el Bab. Owing to faulty fuze [*sic*] two of the demolitions failed. In spite of machine gun fire on the demolitions this officer went out and placed five different pieces of fuze [*sic*] in position in an attempt to carry out the demolition.
>
> He subsequently again under direct enemy fire remained behind in order to lay anti-tank mines to delay enemy tanks which were then advancing.
>
> On other occasions he has shown great coolness and disregard of danger in the disposal and removal of bombs and booby traps. He has at all times set an excellent example.

An OE, John Peters, wrote to George's parents after the award of the MC writing to congratulate them for having such a fine son but also to make a point about the Old Boy network, 'Some people try to "fade out" and ridicule the Old School Tie, but, happily for this Country of ours they fail, and the Tie keeps bobbing up as proudly and as virile as ever, all over the world. Floreat Emanuel!'[5]

From January to May 1943 George served right through to the end of the Tunisian Campaign when the Allies won a final victory over Axis forces. 564 Company were ordered to support the Eighth Army in their operations up the east coast, on the Adriatic side, of Italy. George described his experiences of the Italian Campaign thus, 'it was just road and bridges, road and bridges, road and bridges.' The Italian landscape wasn't conducive for two highly mechanised armies fighting across Renaissance bridges, fast flowing rivers and steep hills and mountains. The engineers played a vital part in overall operations in keeping the armoured and infantry divisions moving.

In his interview in 2013 George described his experiences during the Italian Campaign, but two incidences stood out for him in particular. Near the river Sangro on 23 November 1943 George and two of his platoon, Sergeant Lynn and Corporal Duncombe were clearing a minefield. They created a preliminary pathway through the minefield marking it out with white tape. Corporal Duncombe was in charge of the mine-clearing party when he accidentally stepped outside the white tape and was killed. Sergeant Lynn had to recover Corporal Duncombe's body which had been shattered by the mine. No amount of training could have prepared these men for such circumstances but they had to get through it with 'black humour.' When Sergeant Lynn gathered the Corporal's body in a blanket, he lifted it up and said, 'well, duncy, you don't weigh as much now as you did a few minutes ago!' To those who haven't experienced this it may appear callous but, as George explained, they had to get on with a job, they didn't have time to grieve when they were still at war. That came later, when they had time to reflect.

In another incident on the morning of 1 September 1944 George was on a forward recce in support of 138 Brigade with the task of opening the road ahead near the Apsa stream. The road went up a steep hill and he was asked to check to make sure the road was clear of mines. On the way he came across a badly wounded infantryman lying at the bottom of a tree who begged George to shoot him because his injuries were so severe, but George instead sent his batman back to see if he could get medical assistance. George proceeded up the hill and at the top there were two houses one on each side of the road. He went into one of the houses where there were German backpacks in the room. George saw two machine gun nests outside the window. He fired the Tommy gun at one nest and the other machine gun nest saw him so he threw his gun away and ran back down the hill, at that moment he recalled the cowboy films from his youth when they would roll in the fields away from flying axes. George got through the field, managed to find a bicycle and pedalled furiously back to his lines.

George was later promoted to Captain before his war experiences ended in Austria. He remembered the diverse working backgrounds of his platoon and remembered that 'As a team they were fantastic.' George was demobbed in 1946. In the post-war years he had a distinguished career in banking working for Barclays Bank, becoming a Fellow of the Institute of Bankers and working in West Africa for fifteen years during a turbulent time for the continent including in Nigeria and the Congo. He was later appointed General Manager of Barclays Bank. George believed that his years in the Army were important to his post-war career and said that he entered the Army as a boy and exited it as a man in the sense that he learnt a lot about life.

References

1 Interview Stanley George Holliman by Daniel Kirmatzis, May 2013. The transcript is available to consult in the Emanuel School Archive.
2 Ibid.
3 See *564 Field Company Royal Engineers: A Brief Account of the activities of the Company during the years 1940 to 1945*, n.d., pp. 6-7.
4 Interview Stanley George Holliman.
5 Letter from John Peters to the Mr and Mrs Holliman, 1 October 1943, Holliman family collection.

Kenneth 'Ken' Harold Holliman

(Emanuel 1934–1940)

Ken Holliman was a member of the School OTC but his main passion, even throughout the Second World War, was playing rugby. He was evacuated to Petersfield but was only there briefly before leaving Emanuel in 1940. In January 1942 at the age of 18 Ken enlisted in the Royal Naval Volunteer Reserve. He trained at the Royal Navy shore establishment, HMS *Royal Arthur*, Skegness. In August 1942 he transferred to another shore establishment, HMS *Vincent*, in Portsmouth which trained officers of the Fleet Air Arm. Further training took place overseas in Trinidad before Ken qualified as an observer and received a Commission as Sub Lieutenant Holliman RNVR, joining 826 Squadron, Fleet Air Arm. Ken was flying as an Observer during Operation Mascot – the fleet carrier attack on the German battleship *Tirpitz* on Monday 17 July 1944. The Admiralty were planning on restarting the Arctic Convoys post the invasion of Normandy in June 1944 and estimated that by July 1944 the *Tirpitz*, based in Altenfjord – Kaafjord, Norway, would have had sufficient time to repair from earlier attacks in September 1943 and April 1944 and be ready to carry out limited attacks on any new Arctic convoys. Ken was an Observer on a Barracuda torpedo-bomber carrying a 1600lb bomb and accelerated from HMS *Indefatigable* in the early hours of 17 July. This unsuccessful attack on the Tirpitz was due to the type of aircraft being used. The Barracuda was too slow on its approach, giving the German defence systems ample warning of an attack. This afforded the Germans not only enough time to create a smokescreen to shield Tirpitz, but also reduced visibility for the attacking force. Ken's Barracuda was part of 9 Wing and on its return from the attack it ditched in the sea 'having just "made" the ship.'[1] The Barracuda's engine had been hit by flak. Ken and the other two crew members, Sub Lieutenant Falwasser and Leading Airman Weller were picked up by HMS *Scourge*. Ken became a member of the Goldfish Club, an exclusive group founded by Lt-Col F. Baden-Powell of the firm P.B. Cow & Co, who made the dinghies and sea-rescue apparatus that saved many an airman's life. The original idea for the club, which later encompassed all Allied airmen who found themselves in the sea after combat and were saved by their dinghies, was the brainchild of P.B. & Cow's chief designer Charles Robertson whose signature can be seen on Ken's membership card which notifies us that he escaped 'death by the use of his emergency dinghy...' Ken continued to fly a significant number of operations and in January 1945 took part in the strike force for Operation Meridian with the task of bombing the Pladjoe oil refinery on Sumatra, which was vital to the Japanese war effort. It was a dangerous operation resulting in the loss of a number of aircraft.[2]

Ken worked at Barclays Bank before the war and after it had a career with Shell. He died in 2007.

Membership Card

This is to Certify that S/Lt. (A) K. Holliman, R.N.V.R has qualified as a member of the Goldfish Club by escaping death by the use of his Emergency Dinghy on 17th July, 1944.

Signed CHARLES A. ROBERTSON Hon. Secretary

Sub. Lt. Ken Holliman, RNVR

(left) Ken Holliman's Goldfish Club membership card and (right) Ken in flying kit

References

1 TNA, 826 Squadron Diary, ADM 207/25, 01 December 1943 to 31 October 1944, entry for 17 July 1944.

2 For a post-war account of Operation Meridian see Supplement to *The London Gazette*, 3 April 1951, pp. 1803-1811.to *The London Gazette*, 3 April 1951, pp. 1803-1811.

‘Rome indeed’

Brief Portraits of OEs who served in Italy

Walter Beyer

(Emanuel 1923–1930)

Walter was a talented all-rounder. He was a Prefect of the School, Captain of Drake, a member of the Second Fifteen and was a Corporal in the OTC in which he gained his War Office Certificate ‘A’ and became skilled in dismantling a Lee Enfield rifle. This very talented musician was also a member of the School Orchestral Society. He left School after passing his General School Certificate and was a member of the Modern Sixth class. Coming from a musical family, he learnt to play the violin when he was a boy and eventually joined the Wandsworth Memorial Hall Orchestra and played in many social events at Battersea Town Hall. Music was a constant feature throughout his long life.

In 1940 Walter enrolled in the Local Defence Volunteers and years later wrote about his own military career in the magazine ‘Blackfriars Sinfonia’ and it is obvious he never forgot his time in the Emanuel School Orchestra or the influence music had in his life:

> I was called up for duty in the Second World War and went to the Searchlight Training Regiment in Oswestry, Shropshire. I was asked to play in a dance band which was formed by Cyril Harling – I was also playing saxophone at the time – and I got leave to go home to fetch the sax and violin. We played in the Garrison Theatre there as well as the Officers’ and Sergeants’ Mess and various local town halls where all the local girls were also invited.
>
> After an edict from the War Office stating that all A1 men in training camps were to be posted to active regiments I went to the Royal Artillery and was trained as a Radar Operator (frightfully secret in those days) and saw service in Algeria and Tunis, over to Italy and up into Austria. One of my jobs was to operate early RADAR systems to identify enemy aircraft. The Americans had set up a rest camp in Rome and when we got there, we were given a week’s leave in the rest camp and went to the Vatican City to meet the Pope, who blessed us. I finished up in Graz, was eventually demobbed and eventually returned to my job in the electricity industry.

Walter Beyer

Walter continued to play the violin until he was 97 but his failing eyesight meant he could no longer read music. On his 100th birthday St Bartholomew’s Orchestra had a party to celebrate the occasion and the Mayor of Lambeth gave him a bottle of champagne. Walter died in 2013.

Frank Abbott and his wife christening a boat named after him at Emanuel School Boat Club, 3 May 1981

Frank Louis Abbott

(Emanuel 1921–1933)

Frank was a superb school sportsman. He became Captain of Rodney, Fives, Cricket and ultimately School Captain in his final year. As a cricketer he was noted as a fine wicket keeper and an attacking batsman with a wide variety of strokes who could play dogged innings when his back was against the wall. He also played for the Richmond Public School Eleven in 1932–1933. He was an equally accomplished rugby centre three-quarter who was a fast and clever player with solid tackling and good kicking. Frank was also a member of the School Athletics Team and attained the rank of Sergeant in the OTC by the time he left School, obtaining his War Office Certificate 'A' in March of 1933.

When the war broke out he entered the Army, attaining the rank of Captain. He served with 9 Platoon, No. 3 Company (Machine Guns), `B´ Support Group, 2nd/7th Middlesex which in January 1944 took part in the Allied amphibious landing at Anzio on the west coast of Italy. John McLoughlin, who has studied the part played by the Middlesex Regiment at Anzio writes:

> During the landings at Anzio on 22nd January 1944 Lieutenant Francis Abbott commanded No. 9 Platoon, No. 3 Company, 'B' Support Group of the 2nd/7th Middlesex. He was evacuated from the Beachhead on 25th January, as he had caught a very bad chill. His replacement was killed barely two weeks later. Lt. Abbott returned to Anzio on 8th February, joining a mortar platoon of 'A' Support Group. He also saw action on the breakout from Anzio and in the subsequent battles to liberate Rome in June 1944 and Florence two months later. He fought in the mountains north of Florence, seeing action along the Arrow Route and in the Monte Grande area just south of Bologna. The latter sector was the Battalion´s last action in Italy, but they served in the Middle East for most of 1945 as part of the British security force in the burgeoning crisis between the Jews and Arabs. By this stage he had been promoted to Captain. Francis Abbott remained with the Battalion until it was disbanded in December 1945.

It speaks volumes that over a year after Lieutenant Abbott had commanded them on the Beachhead, men of 9 Platoon still sought both his advice and company, even though he was now serving in a different platoon and had little to do with them. When speaking of Francis Abbott the soldier, mention has often been made of his kindness and generosity, but also of the importance of sport in his life. Only recently, his cricketing prowess was recalled, when ex-Private 'Jimmy' Plumbridge spoke in May 2014 of the times he played cricket in the Middle East with 'Bud' Abbott. One old soldier by the name of Harry Dopson, from Bow, East London, perhaps summed it up best in 1987, forty-one years after 'Bud' had given his last military order, when he described him fondly as 'a good officer and a proper gent.'

Frank Abbott (circled) with men of 9 Platoon, No. 3 Company (Machine Guns), 'B' Support Group, 2nd/7th Middlesex

Frank regularly wrote to the editor of the Old Emanuel notes in *The Portcullis* and was known to meet other Old Emanuels in far-flung and distant places. The Summer Term 1943 edition of *The Portcullis* reported, 'Capt. Frank Abbott has managed to get a cricket pitch rolled out near camp in N. Africa, but complains that it is very dangerous and sighs for Blagdons.'

Frank's good natured character was praised some years after the war by a Private in Frank's platoon. The said Private and another man had been charged for not being with their platoon when it left Naples, the resulting judgment being that they lost 2000 lira in pay. The Private in question remembered:

> We had a platoon officer named Abbott. He was a lawyer in Civvy Street and when he heard of our punishment he was dumbfounded. He told us not to tell anyone and he gave us 2000 lira each. We were reluctant, but he said "Take it. I can afford it." We took it and thanked him. That was a proper gent, for at one time, both hands bandaged, he wrote to all our wives with reports of us. He was on sick, hands bandaged to the wrist, in pain and taking the trouble to write to our wives was magnificent.

Even later when the judgment on the two men was revoked Frank refused to take the money back.

Frank lived and breathed Emanuel School. He was on the school governing body from 1950–1992, and chairman from 1964–1985. He must have loved meetings as he was on the local council for thirty years and Chairman of the Greater London Council from 1972–1973. This Emanuel legend was a perfect gentleman who, as the story goes, used to deliberately get bowled out whilst scoring in the 90s when playing cricket as it was 'not apparently the done thing' to score a century. In the years after leaving Emanuel School Frank played both rugby and cricket for many OE teams both before and after his time in the war.

Frederick Gordon Burrett CBE
(Emanuel 1933–40)

Gordon was a House Prefect and Captain of Clyde, sub-editor of *The Portcullis* and played in the First Fifteen from 1938–1940. He was noted to be a powerful tackler, with good dribbling skills who was a very accomplished front row forward. This outstanding pupil was also a Lance Corporal in the OTC and was awarded his War Office Certificate 'A'. He was a superb academic who had won a plethora of scholarships by the time he completed the Modern Sixth including a LCC Travel Scholarship in 1939, a State Scholarship in 1940 and a Senior County Scholarship also in 1940 before winning an Exhibition in Modern Languages to St Catherine's College, Cambridge.

Gordon served in 579 Army Field Company, Royal Engineers in the Second World War and was Mentioned in Despatches in 1945. Gordon's Company were in action during the Salerno landings on 9 September 1943 and throughout the Italian Campaign. In Italy Gordon met Old Emanuels Frank Abbott and Maurice Rowdon and one of his letters was quoted in the Summer Term, 1944 edition of *The Portcullis*. It is reminiscent of so many letters that were sent home in the First World War showing the parallels between the experiences of servicemen in both world wars, in particular how Emanuel represented much more than an educational institution to them. It came to symbolise the very essence of a world before the wars and a time that many longed for again. Gordon wrote, 'If it is at all possible, I would be very grateful to receive a copy of *The Portcullis* now and again, as a reminder of better and happier things. I think there are few OEs on active service who do not at times look back to the School as something of a symbol of a more agreeable and saner existence and I, for one, would like to feel I was in touch.'

The RE's aim was to keep the army moving. They carried out dangerous jobs such as mine clearing and demolition as well as repairing roads and railways, and perhaps the most important element of their operations during the Italian Campaign was bridge building. In late 1944 and early 1945 Gordon was in action in Niksic in Montenegro and Dubrovnic on the Adriatic as German troops, having been forced out by Albanian partisans, were attempting to make a way back to Germany. Between 11 to 13 of December 1944 Gordon was supervising the removal of booby traps which the unit itself had laid along the road between Niksic and Danilovgrad but which were no longer required. Gordon stayed in Dubrovnik until January 1945. His duties were recorded in the Company's War Diary, 'A rearguard in Dubrovnik under Lieut. Burrett stood by to load engineer stores for shipping to the mainland of Italy and spent most of its time on training in anticipation of a Spring offensive in Italy. A training programme shows that Lieut. Burrett gave hour long lectures.' These lectures were on a variety of topics including German and Italian mines, mine laying, recording of minefields by the Indian rope method, booby traps, building Bailey bridges and ended with a quiz on mines. By the end of January 1945 Gordon, accompanied by a corporal and a batman, travelled across liberated Italy collecting samples of German mines and booby traps for training purposes.

After the war Gordon had a distinguished career in the Civil and Foreign Services working in numerous departments and countries. He worked for HM Foreign, subsequently Diplomatic, Service, HM Treasury and the Cabinet Office.

Gordon Burrett (third from right) at OCTU training, Kent 1942

Among his appointments Gordon was Third Secretary in Budapest 1946–1949, Vice Consul for New York 1951–1954 and First Secretary in Rome 1957–1960. Gordon worked on a large number of government reviews throughout his career. He was also Chairman of the Redundant Churches Fund, later Churches Conservation Trust from 1982–1985. Before retiring he was Deputy Secretary of the Civil Service Department, 1972–1981. He was awarded the CBE for services to the Foreign and Civil Services in 1974.

John Pritchard

John Pritchard

(aka O'Callaghan Wylde)

(Emanuel 1933–1936)

At Emanuel John was in the OTC and was in the shooting team that competed for the Ashburton Shield at Bisley. He attained the rank of Captain in the Cheshire Regiment in the Second World War serving in both the North African and Italian Campaigns. In April 1943 he saw action in the Battle of Wadi Akarit in which he was wounded. Whilst convalescing in Palestine he wrote to his brother and sister who were evacuees in Somerset that a piece of 88m shell had gone through his right elbow during the battle.

(above) Bridge at Castellamare near Salerno built by Gordon's platoon October 1943

(left) Gordon Burrett (front row right) in Yugoslavia, 1944

Gordon's platoon building a bridge under fire, Yugoslavia, Spring 1945

Jack Halligan (second from left) in Italy, May 1945

Memories of Italy

John 'Jack' Edward Halligan

(Emanuel 1931–1937)

Jack Halligan was described as, 'a keen and efficient fielder' in the Emanuel Cricket critiques of 1937. A few years later in 1940 he was using that keen fielding technique in the defence of the south coast against the threat of Nazi invasion.

Jack started his army career as a Lance Corporal in the East Surrey Regiment, based at Dover Harbour in 1940. By 1941 he was a Lieutenant in the 85th Heavy Anti-Aircraft Regiment in Algeria, Tunisia and Italy. Between 1944 and 1946 he was a Captain in the 1st Regiment Royal Horse Artillery in Italy. These are Captain Jack Halligan's notes on incidents and different experiences in the six years he spent in the army:

Emanuel Cricket First XI, 1937 – Back row (left to right): L.W. Spafford Esq., T. Barnes, F.G. Thompson, J.F.B. Embleton, J.E. Halligan, R.V. Pinkham Middle row: J.P. Kirk, W.L. Page, The Headmaster, S.F. Gandar, J.W. St Hill Davies; Front row: E.D. Page, K.C. Bloore

I was called up for army service soon after my twentieth birthday in March of 1940. After four months infantry training I joined the East Surrey Regiment at Pevensey Bay where we lived in beach bungalows. When our army was evacuated from France most of its equipment was left behind. Because of this our only weapons with which to face an enemy landing were rifles, bayonets and light machine guns but the beach was covered with land mines as a first defence. Later we moved to Dover to guard the harbour and the headquarters in the castle. Here we lived in caves in the cliffs with concrete floors and electric lights. The caves were a very safe place to be when the Germans fired shells across the Channel from long-range guns in France.

After an interview in the castle I was sent to an Officer Training Unit in Wales to learn anti-aircraft gunnery, radar predictors and aircraft recognition. My first appointment as an officer was with the 85th Heavy Anti-Aircraft Regiment on the Isle of Sheppey. We left Sheppey and went to York to equip for a move overseas. Two weeks later, at Greenock in Scotland, we loaded our guns and vehicles on to a cargo ship and joined hundreds of other troops on a liner with blacked out port holes. We had now joined the 1st Army, but going where, nobody knew.

During our days at sea we were joined by many other ships all sailing in a zig zag course to avoid submarine torpedoes. I was one of a team stationed at positions on deck watching for the wake made by submarine periscopes. We knew that if our ship sank no other ship could stop to help us because it would become a stationary target. But we were not attacked. Years later I learned that we had cracked the code used by the Germans when radioing orders to their submarines. One morning, on watch, I spied land and when it came nearer I recognised it as the Rock of Gibraltar. We sailed through the Straits and landed at Algeria.

General De Gaulle's Free French Army controlled parts of Algeria and our task was to advance along the coast of Algeria to Tunisia where our 8th Army was fighting the German African Corps, having driven them out of the Libyan desert. As anti-aircraft gunners we had to defend forward ports where supply ships from England and America were unloading.

We arrived at one forward port as daylight was fading. The lining up of guns, instruments and radar had just been completed when a message was received 'HOSTILE 20 PLUS APPROACHING.' As the gunners and command post soldiers ran to their positions a plane flew overhead releasing a line of parachute flares which lit up the port. Without waiting for the enemy bombers to arrive all 1st Army anti-aircraft guns in the area together with Free French rocket batteries created a circle of air bursts over the port. Faced with such a concentration of fire ahead of them only two planes dropped bombs setting a harbour fuel store ablaze. No ships were damaged and our first action overseas was successful.

Shortly after arriving at the Tunisian border we heard the loud noise of approaching vehicles. It was the sound of tanks on transporters, vehicles pulling guns and troop carriers filled with American soldiers. The German African Corps fighting the 8th British Army would now also be attacked by the British 1st Army and the American 5th Army. They retreated northwards until they became the first Germans to surrender to Allied armies. In the victory march through the city of Tunis we followed a Scottish regiment with bagpipes playing. It made marching a pleasure.

Our next order was to defend an American bomber aerodrome on a huge flat salt lake in Tunisia. One day 20 planes began taking off in pairs forming a circle, then close formation. They were going on a long flight to bomb petroleum wells which were supplying the German armies. Many hours later they returned in small groups of planes showing damage to wings and fuselage.

We then returned to Algeria to prepare for the landings in Sicily and Italy. Churchill had called this 'attacking the soft underbelly of the Axis power.' It was to be more difficult than that. After Sicily had been taken the main Allied and American attack was to be on the western side of Southern Italy. As our four ton anti-aircraft guns could not land on beaches we unloaded in the captured port of Taranto on the eastern side. But then came the bad news, our regiment was to be disbanded and most of the soldiers would be sent to infantry regiments. The officers were interviewed and to my surprise, I was to remain in the artillery.

When I arrived at a base reinforcement unit, a Royal Artillery Officer was interviewing for a replacement and I joined the Chestnut Troop of the 1st Regiment Royal Horse Artillery, a regular army unit. My new regiment had self-propelled armoured guns mounted on tank chassis. Although we were in the British 6th Armoured Division we supported tanks of the 2nd New Zealand Division. Pushing the retreating Germans northwards was slowed down by the many Italian ruins which provided them with natural defence protection.

During one long pause we heard that Rome had been declared 'an open city.' It would not be attacked or defended because the Pope lived there in the Vatican City. With another officer I drove quickly to the Holy City. We arrived and joined hundreds of soldiers walking towards the Vatican. The Pope appeared on a balcony and blessed us, as probably he had blessed the departing German soldiers the previous day.

We were preparing our guns to fire a barrage the next day to support the crossing of the river Senio. Suddenly a German plane flew over our gun positions showering us with leaflets. On one side was a colour picture of a young lady holding a basket full of fruit and flowers beside a river. Beneath were the words: 'British soldier the river Po welcomes you.' On the other side of the leaflet was the same picture in black and white, but instead of a young lady was a skeleton and the basket it held contained the bodies of dead soldiers. But the words below were the same: 'British soldier the river Po welcomes you.'

The next morning, in darkness, we fired a two hour drag net barrage combing the enemy's positions on the other side of the river Senio, followed by opening lines of fire behind which our infantry advanced. The enemy retreated quickly which suggested a regrouping and determined stand at the wider river Po. We drove behind the New Zealanders' tanks into the fields bordering this river expecting to be met with gun fire. But the Germans in our sector had departed and were probably on their way back to Austria.

The next day the German High Command surrendered and the war in Italy was over. It took two days to cross the river because the bridges had been blown up, but the engineers built pontoon crossings 620 feet long in record time! Our final destination was the Italian city and port of Trieste, very close to the border with Yugoslavia. We arrived in the hills overlooking Trieste and set up our gun position. A band of Tito's partisan soldiers suddenly emerged from a nearby wood, some were women and all carried sub-machine guns.

Our artillery men hurried to greet these brave fighters but we were met with stony faces. We were to learn that Tito wanted Trieste to be given to Yugoslavia as retribution for the Italian invasion of his country. But Churchill and Roosevelt were opposed to a Communist country having a strategic position on Europe's borders. The partisans showed their anger by lighting large fires on other hills above Trieste, in the shape of two letters 'Z' and 'T' (standing for Zivio Tito – long live Tito). We responded by making our victory parade in Trieste a column of tanks and armoured guns instead of the usual marching soldiers.

An Allied Military Government was set up to decide Trieste's future and my regiment, the Royal Horse Artillery, was stationed near the city. Because of this situation I remained in the army, in Italy, for another year during which time I met my future wife of 63+ years, Maria Bianca.

Maurice Rowdon

(Emanuel 1933–1941)

Maurice Rowdon in Petersfield, c.1940

> "You'll be all right when you are out there with the others", the Major told him. "My boys never let me down. I'm not going to let them say that anybody in "A" company let them down.
>
> And at last, wiping his eyes, the young soldier went out with the corporal into the naked open air and the white cottage was waiting.
>
> He was killed. Someone told me that he was found by a hedge without a mark on his body. It was said that two patrolling Germans had suddenly looked over the hedge, they had shouted and run away and then he was found dead. They believed he died of terror. The vision was too great for this child.[1]

From an early age Maurice Rowdon was bright, thoughtful and intelligent. He wrote poetry, starred in School plays including the 1938 Emanuel adaptation of George Bernard Shaw's *Saint Joan* in the part of Gilles de Rais (Bluebeard) and spent time rowing on the Thames in Emanuel crews. Maurice had an insatiable passion for knowledge, spending time working for Mass Observation – a movement that recorded the everyday lives of the nation from the late 1930s and throughout the Second World War – during his summer holidays. Maurice's older brothers, John and Leslie, also attended Emanuel and encouraged Maurice's interests in the arts and politics. John's interests included the arts and film and shortly before the Second World War broke out he moved to India and worked on short government films and scripts for radio plays in addition to broadcasting educational talks for Indian children. Leslie became an accountant and at the outbreak of war joined the Royal Artillery on an Anti-Aircraft (AA) battery, serving on the Orkney Islands in Scotland, on the Isle of Wight and on the Solent forts in the English Channel. Leslie was responsible for calculating the position of enemy air and sea craft in order to direct the fire of the AA guns. He reached the rank of Captain and was part of the invasion force assembled to re-take Guernsey but fortunately the German surrender in May 1945 made this unnecessary.

Maurice was evacuated with Emanuel to Petersfield in 1939 and spent two years gaining what he later regarded as some of his happiest memories among the Hampshire hills which gave him time to explore his interests. It was at this time and later that he came into contact with Norbert Elias, one of the most famous sociologists of the twentieth century. For many years they exchanged letters on the nature of civilisation. On leaving Emanuel Maurice was awarded a scholarship to study history at Keble College, Oxford. In September 1941 he enlisted with the Queen's Royal Regiment and was placed on the reserve list whilst he completed a short war degree for one year at Keble. He later returned after the war to study philosophy. In 1942 he was made a Second Lieutenant after completing his training at 123 Officer Cadet Training Unit (OCTU) Royal Artillery.

After a year of training Maurice was posted to 71 Field Regiment, Royal Artillery, landing at Salerno in Italy on 16 September 1943. Apart from one period of rest between March and July 1944 when Maurice was removed to Egypt and Palestine, he spent the majority of his war service as a Forward Observation Officer (FOO) in the Italian Campaign. It was his war experiences which led Maurice on a life-long quest to understand what it is to be human. In 1955 his account of those experiences was published under the title *Of Sins and Winter*, in which Maurice explored not detailed battle movements but instead his thoughts on war, its destructive nature upon those who fight it and how the effects of war exaggerated an individual's nature which turned some into 'killing machines.' It is also a book of self-exploration in that Maurice assesses his own actions during the war in order to understand how the exigencies of war lead an individual to make certain decisions.

Maurice Rowdon (first from right) in Greece, c.1945

Maurice spent much of his life trying to understand how one could achieve rehabilitation from the effects of war and unnatural environments, dedicating years of research to a breathing technique he called Oxygenesis. Maurice spent the last years of his life on a second edition of his war memoirs in addition to what he considered was his most important work, *The Ape of Sorrows*. In his last ten years Maurice was seriously ill and so his writing took on an added urgency. When he died in 2009 he left a unique collection of writings, plays, unpublished books and more, all of which are a testament to one of the twentieth century's most gifted scholars. He was an author, philosopher, healer, director of his own plays, and presenter of a television programme on Venice in the Silver Age. He wrote widely on such topics as Leonardo Da Vinci, Italy and animal intelligence as well as writing a number of works of fiction which were critically acclaimed.

The most appropriate way to illustrate Maurice's experiences and his thoughts on them is to provide examples of some of the situations he found himself in as a FOO and his reflections upon them afterwards. As a FOO Maurice was tasked with moving ahead of the infantry and reporting on enemy movements. Essentially this meant having a front row seat in the action. A FOO had to make calculations and where necessary was required to call down fire support from the artillery in order to target enemy positions.

Interestingly Maurice found that the war constricted his ability to write about his experiences and so he eschewed mention of them in his letters home to his parents who lived in Earlsfield, south west London. Fortunately a newspaper report published in April 1944 gave an account of Maurice's extraordinary bravery and calm *in extremis* during operations in the mountains and ridges along the river Garigliano where Maurice was in action in February 1944. His unit was part of X Corps, 46th Division under the US 5th Army. The article reported:

> In the dusk through a narrow valley beneath the barren heights in which a British division of the Fifth Army is now fighting in Italy, walked a young officer and two gunners – Lieut. Rowdon of 49 Waldron Road, Earlsfield, Gunner J. Walton of Newcastle-on-Tyne and Gunner Asbury of Burton-on-Trent. They were on their way to the assembly area of an infantry regiment which was about to go into the line. Their wireless and equipment necessary to set up an observation post were carried on two mules. The next three days were spent in the assembly area – three days of rain and sleet, extreme discomfort and boredom only enlivened by occasional shell-fire.
>
> On the night of February 10 they moved up to the forward crest of Mount Cerasola, a bleak, shell-swept rock mass from which they were to direct the fire of the Field Regiment R.A. The two gunners set about the vital business of communication at once. They installed their wireless on the reverse slopes of the crest with the mast bent away from the enemy to avoid giving away the post.

British trucks on the move during the Italian Campaign, c.1944–1945

Subjected to Shell-Fire

Lieut. Rowdon built himself a 'sangar' or stone shelter on the crest. All that night they were subjected to shell-fire to which mortar fire was added in the early hours of the morning. Just before dawn the enemy counter-attacked, venturing within 30 yards of the post. Lieut. Rowdon coolly continued to observe, giving his fire orders to one of the gunners who scribbled them down on a scrap of paper for the other to send over the air. The infantry sent them grenades for self-defence and these were used with telling effect.

The next three days were spent under much the same conditions. Counter-attack after counter-attack was put in by the Hun, only to be driven off by a combination of infantry dash and the devastating effect of the fire directed by Lieut. Rowdon. On one occasion shell-fire became so heavy that the post had to be moved further east along the crest. Shortly afterwards, Gunner Walton had to crawl up the crest with a message for Lieut. Rowdon which had come over the air. He reached the 'sangar' without being seen by the enemy 60 yards away but as he raised his hand to give the message to his officer it was spotted.

A rain of grenades

At once a rain of 'lolly grenades' – German grenades on the end of sticks – came down upon them. The infantry on Cerasola replied and there was a short sharp battle at the end of which the Hun retreated further down the slopes. The gunners played their part in this action, flinging grenades at the retreating enemy.

The post remained in action until the battalion whom they were supporting was relieved on the night of February 13. They were never out of wireless communication and were constantly able to engage the enemy throughout this period. The conditions under which they fought were almost indescribable – rain, sleet and snow during the day, fog at dusk which enabled the enemy to creep close to them, severe frost at night which left their hands numb with frost bite and perhaps most trying of all, a never ceasing strain from being under constant fire.

By the time they were relieved they were stiff and aching from exposure, almost deafened by shell bursts. They were infinitely glad to get out and they went with the knowledge that they had done their job and done it extremely well.[2]

It was on Cerasola that Maurice's signallers believed he had died. Cerasola became more than just an episode in the timeline of war; it became part of Maurice's soul and haunted him for the rest of his life. In his first war memoir he explored the meaning of those experiences on Cerasola and how they and the war in general had affected his attitude to war, the Germans and most importantly himself. When he was writing his first memoir Maurice was in his early thirties, writing about being at war at the age of only 21. Like so many of his generation, Maurice had been made old by war, it stole his youth like a thief in the night. Throughout his writings Maurice distances himself from his own fortitude and what to a later generation are clearly acts of incredible bravery. But it is clear by reading his volumes of notes on his experiences that he was deeply disturbed by notions of bravery or heroism. Instead he was disgusted by war and how it transformed a human being into an abstract murderer. Here Maurice explores some of these themes through the experiences at Cerasola:

I remember how at Monte Cerasola a group of men stopped along the white mountain path and stared at me with horror. I particularly remember the horror in their eyes as they stared at me, refusing to believe in my existence. Among these peaks there were legions of ghosts. One of the men said, "But we saw you lying dead lower down by the path. We were sure it was you. And they reported you dead." Monte Cerasola is listening in my flesh because it was the scene of my first helpless capitulation to terror.

At Cerasola I brought my signallers away from the path and we found a tall boulder behind which we could sleep, protected against the shells. It had been raining since morning and it was winter. We were frozen, sodden to the skin and our clothes were quite useless in the icy wind, so we stripped naked and huddled close together, five of us, under two blankets through which the water streamed like a shallow brook. ... At dawn we saw that we were half way up a slope, overlooking a flat ravine. ... We wrung out our clothes and put them on again bitterly. ... Cerasola was white. It had legions of white ghosts. This was because we were starving and all things real became ghostly and the mountain pebbles shone blinding in the light. ... I made my bed of pebbles among the legions of white ghosts, scooping out the stones to make a place like the bottom of a bath for my blanket. Then I took my ground-sheet and laid it down, a thin old man in my folly, my hands trembling and gaunt as they used the heavy stones to stop it flapping, an old fool alone in his burrow piling his silly stones, beyond the serious things of life. And I watched the shivering old man at my side, a year younger than myself, who was now twenty-one.

Shells fell, but then they were not German shells and someone touched me on the shoulder. In everything I failed. The ghosts blinded me. I was the very plaything of terror. He said to me, "These are your guns," and I heard the other men grumbling behind the wall of my handmade house, asking if Jerry was not enough without their own fellows. The splinters hit my wall and I took up the mouthpiece of my wireless and said, "Stop firing, stop firing!" But the shells ran their ordained length because the wireless was dead.

I remember how at Cerasola I passed a German prisoner coming along one of the mountain paths. I stopped to let him pass, because the path was narrow. He was young. He was wet and exhausted. I stared rudely into his face as he passed. I gathered the saliva in my mouth ready to spit at him, but swallowed it again. I tried to make my eyes as hard as possible and I saw him flinch back from my gaze. I looked into his eyes, drilling and drilling into him, blaming him for the shells which hit the boulders, for the pebbles near the peaks which yielded under the feet like beaches, for the lack of food and fires in the English lines, for the decimation of English troops day after day in a battle for ground it was useless to win and for the absence of cover from the sky. I wished to lay this at his door and I told him this in my stare. I hated with my gaze. It was the first time I had looked at a man in this way and I now knew that the child had been raised up and that I could not turn back. And I was conscious of having committed foulness, because the boy flinched and turned away.

You cannot make an abstraction real. I could not realise the Enemy in this fair-haired boy, nor could I get an answer back from the fine, round, frightened eyes.

For the truth was that I had failed as a scholar of war and I could not forgive myself for this. I made one green attempt at heroism, the empty gesture of a novice, when a tall signaller said to me in a terrified voice, "I can't go along that path." In the early afternoon it had begun once more to rain and the Guardsmen stood about in a dreadful white hollow under the mountain buckling on their belts and ammunition pouches. Then we moved forward, in single file into the thick of the shells along the narrow path. We crouched, tried to draw in closer to the uncaring mountain-side. Suddenly my signaller ran off the path to a tree nearby and lay there, trembling.

I followed him down and hooked him by the shoulders. He was very pale and the skin of his face seemed strangely loose, for his terror was an astonishing discovery to him. I pulled him to his feet with a show of brutality. He was my terror; I was dominating myself. I think I was frowning as I took him by the belt and drew him nearer to me. His head was bent forward. His body was without will and I could pull it about as I wished. I unbuttoned my revolver case, took out my charged revolver and showed it to him at the end of the white lanyard, with my chin up, looking at him as though I despised him. I laid the weapon in the palm of my hand and looked into his eyes, showing it to him very privately, with my back turned to the other soldiers on the path. I kept hold of him and murmured at last, "You're going to follow me. Do you understand that?"

I looked him calmly in the eyes, my chin up and told him to come away from the tree. The hidden oracle was failing to speak to me, giving me no signs and I wanted to delay joining the silent Guardsmen in their slow walk towards the peak called Cerasola. I wanted him to refuse because I myself was useless without him. It gave me an

> excuse to stay behind. I could point to him and say, "He is my wireless signaller. I am no use without him. His cowardice held me up." That would be an answer to the cold magisterial gaze of the inward scholar of murder, on his daily round of soul recruitment.

Maurice was self-effacing about his role as a Forward Observation Officer but with the utmost sincerity, for the war had penetrated his innocence and writing after the war he could never quite come to terms with what he witnessed, as is related in the following lines he wrote in summing up the Cerasola episode:

> I was no use to the infantry. I merely hung back with my men under the shelter of boulders. I gave help only when it was asked for. I had advanced only as far as the credo of battle, 'I believe in the flowing of blood and the screaming of men. I believe in the death of children.' But that was not enough.

The lines are powerful and evocative and when Maurice wrote about the 'death of children' he was discussing the death of young men in war, who, like himself, at times resembled frightened children, scared by the darkness of war. The following description of an incident at Cerasola is one horrific scene these 'children' witnessed:

> We passed a Guardsman sitting close to a corpse. He was staring in front of him. The dead soldier, right by his ankles, had his genitals torn out. The blood was new, bright. The Guardsman didn't look to left or right. He had no fear of shells now that his best pal was gone. We passed him in his vigil...

Maurice's descriptions of death and destruction in the Italian Campaign coils round every line of his writing like a snake constricting its prey, making the reader gasp for breath at the incomprehension of it all. These are more than mere words – they are a life lived by a young officer tortured by the memories of men in their last moments, drawing for breath as shell wounds dragged them screaming to early graves.

These writings are intended for everyone, the scholar, the layman and perhaps most importantly the young soldier, for his writing bears witness to what to expect in war as in this observation, 'Yet killing somebody is remote from a soldier's mind. He simply defends himself. Faced by a strong enemy you quickly learn that the killing is reciprocal and the death in an enemy's last gaze is your death too. Not a stunning truth – but one that makes a soldier and is his real baptism of fire.'

Maurice wrote with purpose. He wrote not only to rehabilitate himself from nightmares forged in war, but also to make succeeding generations aware of war's true face that his generation stared at for six long years. One of the most powerful examples of Maurice's writing is his description of his signaller's death:

> I lost two men in that sacred green hollow. One was my own signaller, too badly hurt to scream. We got him into a hut and put him face down. He had two deep holes in his back, behind the lungs. One of the troopers asked him if he'd like a smoke and he managed to raise his head. The trooper put a cigarette between his lips and was about to light it when the man coughed blood into it so that it swelled up and fell with a plop to the cement floor. Then his head fell forward. And things were suddenly quiet and he was dead...

During the course of confronting German troops near a farmhouse at Faenza Maurice saved the life of the men in his Company by making a bold decision to call down artillery fire close to their position. It was a decision which should have won him the Military Cross but he didn't write up the action as requested because, as he wrote, 'For me it was just an ignominious thing to sit down and play the reporter with death.' Maurice wrote about what happened at that farmhouse in both his original memoir and later in life after sixty years of hindsight. Comparing the two accounts makes a fascinating study about the way Maurice viewed the same experience from the viewpoints of both a young and old man. His later account deals differently with the ways he saw things compared to when he wrote at 31, especially in the way he views the Major's collapse from terror. In his later writing he describes the Major as having had shell shock, not something Maurice committed openly to the page in the 1950s, but after a lifetime of trying to understand the war and its effects he wrote with a different voice. It is the original account of what happened at that farmhouse, with the rawness of a young man's thoughts untouched by a lifetime's reflection, that we draw upon here:

The Farmhouse at Faenza

> At dawn ... we moved again ... Went among shrubs and young trees, towards the fields where everything was particularly still, with that fatal immobility of the battlefield. We walked along a deep ditch, crouched down and made for a house at the foot of the hill. This house, like another to its left which was almost identical, overlooked numberless wide, flat fields. These fields were in enemy hands.
>
> The house was open to the enemy on three sides; moreover, since it stood on a hillock, it could easily be cut off from the rear and surrounded. One by one we jumped from the ditch up to the back-entrance. It meant running for a yard

or so across open ground, so we jumped at intervals, as the commander let us go. Then we walked through a barn where there were two Germans lying dead, their arms held stiffly up, to a great kitchen where we put down our packs and lit cigarettes. It was a sunny morning. We did not know whether the enemy had observed us coming in.

I set up my wireless by one of the flank windows, but if I wished to observe the enemy I had to go beyond the kitchen to a cattle-shed with long barred windows. This looked directly across the enemy line of advance. My task would be to bring down fire on that field if it were necessary.

I lost no time. Once my signaller had exchanged signals with the rear, I went into the barn and after looking briefly at my map, began calling out orders to him. A few minutes passed, then the first shell came over. I corrected it, ordered several more and at last registered the target in the very middle of the field before me. I did the same with the fields to the flank. Thus, after less than an hour, I had all the enemy's lines of approach covered by our guns. ...

We had a day of sporadic bombardment. When dusk came double sentries were posted at all the windows and at the great open doors of the barn. No movement could be seen in the dark fields outside, but suddenly there was an explosion, one of the men in the cattle-shed screamed out and part of the shed-wall collapsed. Brick-dust came drifting through into the kitchen. A large hole had been blown in the wall, either by a tank or a bazooka. Our sentries did not reply with Bren-gun fire. They wanted to give the impression that our house was unoccupied. ...

The German patrol did not come again. But all through the night we heard the jarring scream of their armoured vehicles very close by. We felt alone and exposed on our hillock. No tank could possibly come to defend us. But enemy tanks could come safely to the very windows of the cattle-shed and blow down our walls. We had nowhere to run, no trenches ... and no anti-tank weapons. The men knew soon enough that this was a most untactical position ...

After a day they were all lying about the floor with mute condemned faces. A bombardment had brought half the roof down and no one expected the walls to last much longer. There were forty or more men, lying on their backs and huddled together in silence, waiting for the second fatal dusk to fall ...

During the afternoon, there was a sudden shout from the cattle-shed and someone called me. I ran to the machine-gunner's side and looked out of the barred window. At the edge of the field before us I saw a terrifying spectacle.

It was exactly what we had feared most. The other men were looking at me helplessly, as if only I would know how to rescue them. For at the edge of the ploughed field there was a German tank, not more than a hundred yards away and slowly its gun-turret was turning, in the direction

The after effects of shelling during the Italian Campaign

of our house. It was too late for me to order gun-fire. My shells were in any case rather ineffectual against tanks and there would certainly be no time to order a bombardment by heavy guns. We were without trenches. If we ran out of the house we would be machine-gunned. The cannon-shells of this tank could pierce two thick walls. The slow turning of the gun-turret was our sentence of death and we all watched it in breathless silence, wide-eyed like children.

The farmhouse to our left, only a few yards from us, was now occupied by another company. Only a small valley of bushes separated us.

The tank was now quite still. Just to the right of it, at the end of the field among the furrows, I could now see a section of German infantry. I saw them throw themselves down. One of them was carrying a bazooka.

The gun-turret continued to turn slowly, then stopped. We were astonished. It was another reprieve. The muzzle of the tank-gun was trained on to the other farmhouse. We waited, to make sure. It did not move. It remained fixed on the house to our left, undergoing final adjustments for range.

I asked quietly, 'Can you see Jerry?' and the machine-gunner nodded. We agreed not to fire unless the enemy made a direct attack on us. The Germans were lying in the furrows quite conspicuously, making signs to each other, waiting for the tank to send out its first deadly sting.

It fired once, then paused. It sent forth a great puff of white smoke, while the long barrel recoiled. Then it fired again. This shell hit the farmhouse to our left, square on the front wall. A yellow shower of rubble went up and the Germans in the field ran forward, leaping over the furrows. The tank fired again and this time blew most of the wall down. Then we saw the back-door of this farmhouse burst open and the Englishmen there come running out, towards the cover of the trees and bushes further uphill. Some of them were hatless and covered with yellow dust. They left everything behind them – their armoured carrier in the back-yard, their maps and their wireless equipment. All this we could see clearly from the cattle-shed.

The Germans ran to within a few yards of the house. Gradually, man by man, the one giving covering fire to the other, they surrounded it and found it empty. The attack was swift and expert. One or two of them began examining the armoured carrier in the back-yard, turning over all its equipment with rapt curiosity. They seemed to have forgotten our farmhouse. We were quite sure now that they thought it unoccupied.

The tank's gun-turret began to move slowly away from us again. Then its great motor started up and it moved along the path, away from the field and finally out of sight.

Nevertheless, everyone began to feel that the Germans would come again at dusk, that they were only biding their time because they were not quite sure of our strength. So, as the dusk grew, every man was cowed down for the final blow. There was no worse monster to the infantryman then the enemy tank, with its huge grinding wheels and relentless gun. It could not be resisted.

Everyone spoke in a low voice now, lest the Germans in the other house should hear them. When the farmer went out to draw water a machine-gun instantly spoke from this house and he lost some flesh off a finger. Then blue tracer bullets came spraying all over the side wall, shattering our windows. It now seemed quite certain that they would come after dusk. Again the silence fell.

The commander had now capitulated entirely to his terror. Strangely, this gave me heart. His orders were absurd and he delivered them in a trembling voice which hid nothing from the others. He sat with a swollen, wan face under the chimney, his eyes moving about, while the sergeant-major, hitherto legendary for his courage, lay straight out under the stairs, everything in him sunk down to a doomed torpor. I stepped over his body and said something to him, but he hardly opened his eyes to reply. I remember feeling a quick flame of anger go through me, but I stopped myself making a scene. I wished to bide my time.

As the dusk grew the sound of tanks, grinding and whining, came weirdly from the German lines, so loud and ominous. A machine-gunner was crouching down underneath the window, alone with his fear, while the muzzle of his gun pointed uselessly to the sky. In the barn the wounded man lay grieving and people tried to quiet his persistent moans, lest the enemy should hear. Men sat with their heads bowed, or lay on the stone floor, or watched with quiet, unimpassioned curiosity the face of their commander in the hour of his capitulation. They watched the haunted shifting eyes as they might watch an experiment, with their sympathy disengaged and their hatred also.

In this room heroism had become an eccentricity. My cue was given to me quite unexpectedly. It came from one of my own men, whom I expected to be influenced by my counterfeit calmness, as in other battles. My terror rarely, if ever, showed in my face, my movements or my tone of voice. But this signaller had been sleepless too long. All afternoon he had been nursing his fear. He came murmuring to me in the dusk, trying to hide his voice from the others. It was as if he were deliberately co-operating with my wish. I was sitting on a black sofa next to the wireless-set, waiting to speak to my headquarters and he knelt down at my side, gripping my leg. He was trying to hold back his tears and I heard him say, "Please let me go back. It's no use. I can't go on."

He said this in quite a matter of fact way, as if he were asking me to be sensible. At first I did not understand, because it happened so suddenly. I kept asking, 'What? What?' Then I saw how he was kneeling, half-cringing at the edge of the sofa, speaking with his head bowed, as the tanks grated and whined outside and the wounded man cried out in the barn. The infantrymen in the room were all aware of what was going on. They were waiting for my verdict, to discover how far it was permissible for a man here to capitulate to his terror. I saw my opportunity. I spoke to my signaller loudly, no longer caring for the cautious silence everyone was preserving.

My feelings were quite cold, but I answered him in the manner of one who feels an unbearable contempt, a hot disgust.

I shouted, "Look at you grovelling and snivelling on the floor! You're just a worm. Do you dare to talk to me in that condition? You're disgusting to me. I don't want you near me. You're not human any more, you're something low...." I do not know that these were my precise words, but they are near to what I said. I think I spoke in a terrible castigating tone, like a punishing father, I shouted into the silence of the room, with all the other capitulators listening and feeling the sting of my rebuke on themselves.

As I turned back to the wireless my other men took the signaller by the shoulders and drew him away, whispering to him. For now everybody knew the capitulation was not permissible. My last words to the man were: "Come back to me when you're human."

The recovery was quick. This was the first stage of my success. When it was almost dark he returned to my side and said in a very clear voice, "I'm sorry sir. I'm all right now." I looked up at him grudgingly and quite deliberately gave him a kind of fierce, patriarchal look. Then I replied, my effect gained: "Very well. You may go back to your post."

I gave orders down the wireless for all guns to stand ready. The guns of the entire sector were put at my disposal and I asked that heavy guns should also be called on to my target, as many as possible. I prepared everything just before dusk fell. I had my plan ready.

I jumped up and began walking among the infantrymen. I felt a sudden triumphant abandon. I began pointing at them and ridiculing them, laughing at the way they were all lying down. I mimicked their terrified faces. I made little prancing steps across the room between their bodies. I did a mock trembling. Some of them turned away because I made them feel ashamed. In their own eyes they had ceased to be men.

I then addressed them, shouting at the top of my voice. I told them I could save them if they wanted me to. I told them I could do this by bringing down bombardments so near our house that our own lives would be in danger from them. Many of the shells would hit the house. Some of us might be killed. I therefore required their permission. It was our only chance. Would they risk it? There was no other means of survival. They had put themselves in my hands. If they did that, if they were prepared to leave everything to me, I would save them, I would get most of them out of here alive.

"You're good men," I told them, "you are worth saving, so for God's sake don't give up yet."

I threw out my voice like an actor, speaking with a kind of fierce rhetoric. My body was tensed, as if I were about to spring forward. I walked among them and even chucked one of them under the chin. They were suddenly children before me and men of forty looked back to me like embarrassed sons. I was utterly taken aback at the thought of my power over them. I stirred them to go back to their posts at the window and to fight again. I had acted my speech and my antics with no effort whatsoever.

It came as something quite natural and I moved swiftly and easily, as if I were predestined to do so, into this new mood of leadership. I think I had spoken to men like this before, but never with this absolutely sure calm. My calm was not at this moment counterfeit. I feel free and therefore fluent. I was free because I knew at last that I and no commanders, no headquarters behind us, controlled this battle and that perhaps on this battle depended the fate of our sector.

I had heard of a gunner who had brought down shells on himself to save a position; that act was spoken of as gallantry. And I was doing nothing less... I could have wept with gratitude, that this spirit should so suddenly have entered me.

They agreed to be bombarded. I had given them the chance to make a free heroic decision and in doing so I renewed their characters for them. As for my plan, I would have followed my plan in any case.

But I did not believe in our success. Perhaps, at this time I was the only man in the room who did not. I was sure that the bazookas would blow holes in the walls, that the Germans outside, lying among the furrows, would brave my shells and throw grenades in at the windows and surround the house and take us prisoner or shoot us in the dark. I became nervous as the night fell and the silence outside in the ploughed field pointed forward to the attack. But I knew at least that the men at the windows would now fight.

I gave my orders quickly over the wireless and the voice in the earphones asked me whether I would take responsibility for such a close target. I said, "Yes, I will take responsibility for the closeness of this target," announcing it not only to the rubber mouthpiece of the radio but to the infantrymen in the room, as they elected themselves heroes in the dusky silence. There would be hundreds upon hundreds of shells falling and I hoped that they would catch the enemy in the furrows. I waited for the guns of the Division to report *Ready*, then I gave the order, *Fire*; it was almost nightfall.

The men stood about in the dark room and the sentries at the window waited. They listened for the shells as they might for the steps of a saviour, with both awe and complacency. They passed the word to each other, speaking in low voices; *the shells are coming over now*.

There was a first whisper, then another whisper, a light singing in the sky and suddenly the first shell dived down and crashed close to the house. The second came, then they began to fly over in choirs, the noise immense now, the house shaking, the men all shouting at each other and thick pungent shell-smoke drifting through the windows and the open barn-door. The sentries were lying low to avoid the splinters which came whirring in.

A shell exploded near the mouth of the barn, then another inside the door and the wounded man lying out there with the dead Germans for company cried out again and again to be taken farther into the house, but it was not the time for wounded men, it was not their time of blessing. There was so much noise and so much moving about that his was only the faintest of cries, buried in thunder.

Maurice Rowdon in the 1980s

I was sitting on the black sofa, crouched down so that I would have as much protection as possible from the window behind me. The shells hit the walls, but being light did not break them down. The dust and shell-smoke was making everybody cough and there was the sound of rubble falling down from the walls outside and the slated roof.

A machine-gunner at one of the windows suddenly shouted, "They're outside!" I heard another man shout, "Fire, you silly bastard!"

At once the machine-guns sounded out, filling the room with a deafening metal clatter as they sprayed the black field from side to side. In answer to them, only a second or two later, came a long jet of blue tracer bullets from the enemy house, lighting up the room.

Someone called out to me and I jumped up, feeling my way across the floor. "Who wants me?" I shouted. A man caught hold of me in the darkness and told me that a German had just looked in at the window, had stared right down the muzzle of his gun. He thought he could make out at least a section of German infantry close to the house. He had seen nothing after he had opened fire. It was possible that they were scouting forward while the main Enemy body stayed behind in the flat of the field. It was among these other men, lying in the furrows, that I hoped my shells were falling.

The shell-fire was beginning to abate. The moment I realised this I rushed back to my wireless, pushing over the men who stood in my way and felt for the black sofa, then snatched the mouthpiece of the radio away from my signaller and shouted into it: "Repeat. Repeat."

The machine-gun paused, there was almost silence for a space, then gradually the sky began to fill again with the whirring of handfuls of shells and again the explosions echoed across the field. One, two, three fell together, then a pause, then a rain of dozens upon dozens. Splinters were hitting the ceiling and dropping to the stone floor, as the machine-guns began to fight out another long clattering battle.

At last, during one of the pauses, we heard the muffled cry from the field outside, quite close to the window: "Kamerad! Kamerad!"

A sentry called out, "They've got their hands up!" Somebody else shouted back, "Keep them covered. Make them stay there," as I took up the mouthpiece of the radio again. With a feeling of most blessed ease I spoke to the artillery lines: "Stop firing. Stop. Gun-fire successful."

When the field was silent again, the last spasmodic shells finished, one of the English sentries called to the men outside: "Comme zee here!"

Eight Germans rose out of the furrows, probably the first section of a company which had retired and walked around the house to the door of the barn. They came into the room in single file, still murmuring, "Kamerad, Kamerad," while the wounded man in the barn seemed to weep now rather than moan, in an aftermath of the deepest, most horrible misery.

After the war Maurice wrote a collection of war poems and one in particular encapsulates the feelings of the soldier who has been to war and is longing for home. It is simply titled 'England.'

England, hills, farms,
Lovely untouched bride
For whom we died,
Welcome our broken faces
Back to your shade,
Take us again, soft
Bride in the evening,
Time will lay down
Our wounds under lawns
And shade of elms
Where cattle go,
Oh, take us again!

References

1 Maurice Rowdon, *Of Sins and Winter* (1955), pp. 25-26
2 *The South Western Star*, 7 April 1944, p. 1.

'Certainly no boy ever loved the School more'

Lt. Peter Harold Jackson MC *(Emanuel 1932–1938)*

At Emanuel Peter was a House Prefect, Captain of Rodney, Captain of Athletics, Captain of Cross Country and a member of the First Fifteen and OTC. Peter was also a member of the Dominican Club, an association for members of Rodney House which began in the First World War period.[1] He was in the Science Sixth class and was awarded his General School Certificate.

Peter enlisted in the 42nd Royal Tank Regiment at the age of eighteen and became a Sgt. Major. He received an emergency commission and after attending the 102nd Officer Cadet Training Unit he transferred to the 1st Battalion Northamptonshire Yeomanry (Royal Armoured Corps), and was later selected by his Colonel for special attachment to the Queen's Bays (2nd Dragoon Guards).

Peter was awarded a Military Cross for the part he played in the last weeks of the Allied campaign in Tunisia in spring 1943.[2] The Allies were preparing to defeat the Axis forces which lay behind the Mareth Line, a pre-war French defensive system built to defend against an Italian attack from Libya. As part of the Battle of the Mareth Line the Queen's Bays supported the New Zealand Corps in an outflanking movement, of German forces, as they advanced on the town of El Hamma. In bitter fighting Peter led from the front as the official citation for his MC states:

> On 26th March 1943 during the advance of the 1st Armoured Division on El Hamma, Lt. Jackson was commanding the leading troops of the Queen's Bays. His troops were constantly under heavy anti-tank fire from the front and both flanks. By the fire of his troop he destroyed many anti-tank guns which were holding up the advance and enabled a steady forward movement to be continued. Just before last light his tank was hit and disabled. He immediately got into another tank of his troop and again led the advance when it recommenced at midnight. His tank was again hit by an 88mm at about 250 yards; in spite of this he continued to fight his tank and by accurate Browning fire forced the enemy to abandon the gun. On the morning of the next day, both the remaining tanks of his troops were hit by heavy artillery and caught fire. Regardless of the shelling he supervised the removal of the wounded from both tanks and collected morphine from another tank, finally shepherding both crews back to safety. His coolness, courage and determination throughout were an example to all who saw him.

After winning his MC he volunteered for the Special Air Service (SAS) and served in "D" Squadron, 2 SAS Regiment during the early phase of the Italian Campaign. "D" Squadron was one of five given the task of reconnaissance and defensive patrolling that went ahead of the bulk of Allied troops.[3] Peter carried out jeep patrols from Taranto to Bari from September to November 1943. The jeep was mounted with twin Vickers machine guns, which were known for their quick firing capabilities. Peter was involved in several hair-raising actions as described by Roy Farran of 2 SAS, in his book Winged Dagger. Peter's dogged determination is evident from Farran's account of an incident beside a blown bridge near the town of Grassano, southern Italy:

> A gully ran down the hillside across my path and I was able to walk up it without further fear of discovery. Peter Jackson, one of my troop leaders, was engaged in a fire fight with two Spandaus [British term for German machine guns] on the top of the crest. Both sides were just wasting ammunition although Peter claimed to have hit two Germans. ... He loved a fight and was very hurt when I told him to withdraw to the station.[4]

The next day Roy Farran sent Peter across a makeshift bridge, which had been built to replace the one blown by the Germans, in order to assess the strength of the German forces, 'It was just strong enough to take an unloaded jeep, so I pushed Peter Jackson across with his troop. He came back thirty minutes later with a broad smile on his face. Apparently the Germans had blocked the road with an anti-tank gun, but Peter had made hay of its crew before it could come into action.'[5]

Lighter moments were enjoyed during a lull in fighting as Roy Farran colourfully explains about one evening in Canosa:

> Peter and I went into the town in the evening to see if we could find some amusement. It was not long before we were surrounded by all the celebrities of the village who pressed us to go into their houses for a drink or something to eat. We could not possibly satisfy them all, so we compromised by accompanying the mayor to the café in the village square. It was great party. Bottle after bottle of wine was produced. ... All the belles arrived in their party frocks and we danced on the cobbled floor to the tune of a piano accordion. ... It must have been about eleven o'clock in the evening when Peter and I were sitting each with an arm round a girl, singing, 'The troopship was leaving Bombay.'[6]

The gaiety of that evening did not last. On the road to Castellerano a short while afterwards and approaching hilly ground Peter and Roy faced enemy fire again as Roy explains:

> The jeeps laboured up a stony track through a flock of sheep until we came to a steep precipice. Below I could see enemy trucks moving like dinky toys on the road. Peter Jackson, who was leading, beckoned me forward to a crest on the left. We were perhaps three hundred yards from a village perched on the top of a round knoll. Through my glasses I could see Germans running out of what appeared to be the school and we heard one or two rifle shots. It was clear that the alarm had been given.
>
> I had just given the order for the jeeps to turn round when Roach, Peter's Irish driver, spotted a German steel helmet in the bushes about fifty yards away. Almost immediately a tremendous hail of machine-gun fire was directed towards us. At least four Spandaus were firing simultaneously. My own jeep had not yet turned round. Leaping into the driver's seat, I set her nose at the wood of young saplings, charging them at top speed.
>
> We crashed down one tree after another in a desperate attempt to get under cover. One other jeep followed me but there was no sign of the others. My last view of Peter was of his crew still fighting the guns from a blazing jeep. It was a gallant attempt to cover our withdrawal ...
>
> We all returned to Brigade together, our hearts heavy at the almost certain death of Peter, Roach and Durban. After I had reported to the Brigadier, we leaguered for the night in one of those red *carabinieri* stations which one comes across at intervals all over Italy.
>
> I was just folding my maps for the next day's run when Peter walked in through the door. For some moments I could not speak. Then all I could say was, "I thought you were dead." He explained how they had avoided being hit, by a miracle. Durban had fought his guns until the flames reached the petrol tank. Then they had run under the cover of the black smoke into the woods, pursued by several Germans. They ran non-stop for over three miles until they came to a farm where they borrowed a pony trap to complete their journey. I poured out two glasses of brandy and we sat back, German cigars in our mouths, exchanging versions of the battle.[7]

Peter was involved in several such actions. In one incident on the road between Castelnuova and Torre Maggiore he pursued a motorcycle to a house in a village and after a skirmish he and his men captured four Germans. Roy Farran relates one amusing episode between Peter and one of the German prisoners, 'Peter's German was even more limited than mine. When a prisoner came up to him and said, "Ich bin krank" [I'm sick], he put out his hand and said, "Oh, how do you do. Ich bin Jackson."'[8]

Peter was also involved in the capture and defence of Termoli between 5 and 6 October 1943, until the enemy forces were driven back. But sadly on 10 November 1943, a day after his 23rd birthday, Peter was killed in an accident. Roy Farran wrote, 'Poor Peter Jackson was killed in a jeep accident on a wet road near Taranto when his vehicle skidded to avoid a cart. He was one of the few losses in the war which really affected me. He was such a reckless, gay person that it was impossible to realise he was dead.'[9] In a similar tone his obituary in *The Portcullis* noted that, 'Certainly no boy ever loved the School more.' Peter is buried in Bari War Cemetery.

References

1 See C. W. Scott-Giles, The History of Emanuel School (1947), pp. 227–228.
2 See Kenneth Macksey, Crucible of Power: The Fight For Tunisia 1942–1943 (1969) for a general history of the Tunisian campaigns. See Douglas Porch, Hitler's Mediterranean Gamble: The North African and the Mediterranean Campaigns in World War II (2005), for the best one-volume history of the Mediterranean Campaigns.
3 Anthony Kemp, The SAS at War 1941–1945 (1991), p. 103.
4 Roy Farran, Winged Dagger: Adventures on Special Service (1948), p.181
5 Ibid. p. 182.
6 Ibid. pp. 189-190.
7 Ibid. pp. 193-194.
8 Ibid. p. 198.
9 Ibid. p. 220.

A Disciplined Service

John Chiles MBE *(Emanuel 1934–1939)*

At School John Chiles joined the Subsidiary Corps which was for boys too young to join the OTC but when he was old enough he became a Corporal in the OTC. On leaving School in 1939 John joined the Local Defence Volunteers in Reigate with the rank of Sergeant.

After volunteering for the Royal Armoured Corps in 1941 John was posted overseas to the Indian Armoured Corps Tank School. He was then transferred to the Probyn's Horse Regiment, where he maintained the regiment's tanks during the gruelling Burma Campaign. John has written a short account of his experiences in the Second World War:

> It was not long after leaving school that I decided that tanks looked exciting and I volunteered to join the Royal Armoured Corps. I found myself in the 61st Training Regiment RAC at Assaye Barracks, Tidworth and facing discipline even greater than that at a pre-war school.
>
> Most of the officers and senior NCOs were 8th Hussars and expected the highest of standards in everything. I was in a barrack room with about twenty-five other Troopers. We slept in two-tier bunks around the room, where the floor in the centre had to be kept highly polished and never trodden on.
>
> I trained as a tank wireless operator, but I also had to be capable of driving tanks and operating their guns. We trained on Matilda and Valentine tanks. Our live firing was carried out at Castle Martin in Pembrokeshire, where we also undertook coastal defence. It was my turn. I aimed and fired the 2-pounder gun of the Valentine tank on the range, but as I did so the tank gave a huge lurch and the shell hit the nearby lighthouse, taking a lump out of its side!
>
> I was later interviewed as a possible candidate for a commission by the CO, an elderly cavalry colonel who had obviously been recalled at the outbreak of war. The first question he asked me was –'Do you have a private income?' I immediately replied 'Yes, sir.' Fortunately he did not seek details, or I would have had to own up that it was the few pence that I received in interest on my Post Office Savings account!

John Chiles

> I got through that interrogation and also the War Office Selection Board that I had to attend at an Oxford college. It was there that I was told that my services were required in the Indian Army. A kindly brigadier, who had obviously spent very many years out East, walked

me around the college grounds to give me advice as to what I should do when I became an Indian Army officer, such as 'Don't forget my boy, don't have your first noggin until after sundown!' (Sound advice when fighting the Japs).

We sailed from Glasgow on the *Stratheden* in a large convoy escorted by the aircraft carrier HMS *Eagle*, the battleship HMS *Malaya*, the cruiser HMS *Newcastle* and a considerable number of destroyers. We crossed a stormy north Atlantic in mid-winter to within 24 hours sailing of Canada to successfully avoid U-boats, before going south and then east into Freetown to refuel.

On gaining my Commission in the Guides Cavalry, I was sent to Lucknow and almost at once ordered to take a convoy of lorries, driven by Sowars under training, up to Raniket in the foothills of the Himalayas. I was just a 2nd Lieutenant and hardly able to speak any Urdu. In the Indian Army you were given a lot of responsibility at an early age. At Raniket we loaded all the lorries with large containers of resin from the pine forests and took them down to the railhead in the plains. The only good thing about this four-day trip was the Chevrolet limousine I was given, still in civilian maroon colour, with the driver.

The Indian Armoured Corps Tank School was being set up at Babina, a very hot place in the Central Provinces, where prickly heat was all too common. I was sent there with another young officer, as we had been with a UK training regiment, to set up the Driving and Maintenance Wing and organise the training of the first intake. At the same time I had to learn Urdu and pass, within six months, the oral and written examinations. Failure to do so would have meant I would have had to leave the Indian Army.

I was posted to Probyn's Horse (5th King Edward VII's Own Lancers), an outstanding regiment with whom I spent the rest of my army service. We fought the Japanese in Burma, where we were one of only four regiments equipped with Sherman tanks. We took part in the crossing of the Irrawaddy river, then seized and held Meiktila, the vital centre of communications of the Jap 15th Army. The Japs threw everything they had at us for three weeks until Mandalay, in the north, was taken.

A Japanese Officer's sword – acquired by John Chiles after the Japanese surrendered.

All our petrol (a Sherman does three gallons per mile!), ammunition, etc., was dropped to us from the air, as happened during our subsequent race to Rangoon, which we had to reach before the monsoon broke and air support would become impossible. We had many tough battles against suicidal Japs at many places en route. Some times we would by-pass a 'tough nut' and leave it to follow-up troops. We took a route west of Pyawbwe in order to attack this town from the South. We waited on a hillside, overlooking the main road, with 6/7th Rajputs, a company of 4/4th Bombay Grenadiers, a self-propelled gun battery and two armoured car squadrons of 16th Light Cavalry. The Japanese had no idea that we were there and during the night a convoy of Jap lorries came from the south and some Japanese tanks from the opposite direction. Every tank and artillery gun opened fire and the enemy was destroyed.

I knew nothing of this battle until I woke at dawn! I was the Technical Officer of 'C' Squadron responsible for 15 Sherman tanks always being fit for battle. This meant that I spent many nights, hidden from the Japs under a tarpaulin sheet, undertaking major replacements of suspension, etc., by torchlight, with my excellent Muslim fitters. On the night of the battle at Pyawbwe I had been able to stretch out in my slit trench, in front of the tanks and artillery and had been so tired that I did not hear a thing!

Of the original British officers in my Squadron I was the only one who was not killed or wounded. There were several occasions when I thought that I had run out of luck.

By the time we had fought our way to Rangoon most of us were showing signs of vitamin deficiency for we had been on half rations or less for several months and had not had any fresh food. It was due to the good discipline and training of the excellent soldiers of Probyn's Horse, that complete success was achieved by the Regiment in its demanding role in clearing the Japs out of Burma. I was also mentioned in Despatches for distinguished services.

When VJ (Victory in Japan) day came, we were waterproofing our tanks in readiness for the invasion of Malaya. That night all the officers, including the Commanding Officer, climbed on or into a Sherman tank and we drove into town to Government House which was being used as an Officers' club. We drove up the stone steps to the entrance, but did not actually drive through the entrance doors. When visiting Burma three years ago with my wife Pam, I wanted to see if the marks of the tank tracks were still on the steps but we found that Government House no longer existed!

In more recent years I was appointed MBE for service to Commonwealth ex-servicemen, women and their families.

John Chiles, (centre, front row) with men of Probyn's Horse (5th King Edward VII's Own Lancers)

The Interview

In 2013 Daniel Kirmatzis interviewed John Chiles in which he explored further John's encounter with Japanese forces during the Burma Campaign.

Daniel: Can you run me through your personal experiences on the road to Meiktila?

John Chiles: Well the first thing when we set off I put a tin helmet on and it was the only time in the campaign I ever wore a tin helmet. Forever after that I just wore my black beret and one of the first villages we had to capture was a place called Sittang.

Daniel: How were you travelling at this time, were you in a jeep?

John Chiles: I had a jeep and a T16 carrier. A carrier was rather like a Bren Gun carrier but it wasn't, it was a T16 carrier which had tillers to steer it rather than a wheel and my own wireless operator was a Indian Corps of Signals technician who was my mechanic for looking after all the wirelesses in my squadron. I had an electrician and two mechanical fitters. Sometimes I might travel in that and they would be in my jeep but those were my two vehicles. It was on that first day when we ran into Jap suicide people who would dive under a tank with picric acid to blow it up and we went through a village called Sittang and in 2005 my wife and I went back to Burma. We went along that same route and we stopped in Sittang and I asked the interpreter to ask the villagers where they were when we were fighting that battle. They replied that they were either hiding in the jungle or in temples and an elderly woman piped up and she said she was just a child at the time but she said she remembered our tanks going through their vegetable garden so I was able to apologise after all those years.

Daniel: Can you describe going through the village?

John Chiles: Well I wasn't with the leading vehicles but I always kept up very close to the tanks because I reckoned it was safer in an open vehicle like a jeep or a carrier to be fairly close to them rather than way back. Then of course we would harbour at night and that was where we had to do all the necessary repairs and maintenance and if tanks broke down through petrol or blockages or anything like that then we would have to deal with that and get them going again. I also at times had to command a troop of tanks so I had a fairly wide brief as far as an officer was concerned.

Daniel: When did you first engage the Japanese?

John Chiles: There was fighting all the way there but in relatively small pockets because I think the Japs began to realise what our target was, what our aim was and they brought in every possible man to defend Meiktila and it was quite a major battle to capture Meiktila, we went round to the North and came in from the North East and managed to capture the air strip.

Daniel: What was the terrain like?

John Chiles: By the time we got to there we were more or less on more open country, not so wooded. There were a fair amount of trees around but nothing like a jungle, more open and the Japs threw absolutely everything at us to try and get rid of us there but we managed to hang on. We were being shelled a lot – we would go out on armoured sweeps sometimes for a day, sometimes for two days, to find their guns and destroy them.

Daniel: What were your feelings at that time?

John Chiles: One had a lot of responsibility and that I think affected one's attitude. You've got a job to do and you had to get on with it. There was one morning when we were going off on one of these armoured sweeps when as soon as the tanks showed their noses just North of Meiktila they were very heavily shelled and then I arrived with my 6 wheel Dodge trucks loaded with ammunition and petrol and my fitters to go to the forming up point and immediately we were heavily shelled and I had to make a quick decision. My fitters you couldn't replace them easily so I decided to leave those behind and I asked for volunteers to drive these trucks of ammunition and petrol through this shelling to where we had to get and I had no problems with that all, I drove the first one myself with my head down with my foot flat down and when we got to where the tanks were forming up I got a tremendous rocket from the Colonel who said 'Where are your fitters?' I told him what had happened and I didn't want to risk losing them in the shell fire and he said shelling's nothing to worry about and I must say I rather laughed like a drain later that morning when I heard over the regimental wireless that he had been hit by shrapnel from a shell that had gone through his nose.

Daniel: Can you tell me what it was like capturing Meiktila?

John Chiles: Well we sat there for about a month going out on these armoured sweeps and being shelled and being bombed with them trying to recapture Meiktila but I think we were quite confident we would hang on and of course everything had to be dropped to us by air. We had no line of communications at all and that didn't worry us at all. We still had the air strip so planes could fly in with fuel and ammunition but then we lost that for a while.

Daniel: Can you take me through your experiences after Meiktila?

John Chiles: Well, as I said earlier, we were completely surrounded by the Japs. There were two lakes there. We were harboured by the southern lake because of all the shelling we had to dig in all our soft vehicles, you can imagine having to dig a huge hole in the ground with a ramp and drive a truck down into it, that was the only way we could shelter the vehicles from the shelling. If one wanted a wash, one went into the lake and it was quite amazing being in the lake with shells bursting in the lake. It was rather like being in a Jacuzzi.

Daniel: How did you get sleep?

John Chiles: Wherever we were through the whole campaign each officer had to dig his own slit trench so that you were just below the surface of the ground and then you had a bedding roll and you stretched that out which was a canvas bedding roll with a blanket inside and you stretched out just below the surface and hoped it didn't rain.

Daniel: When you were fixing tanks and doing them up, just run me through that process, what were conditions like, did you do that at a particular time of day?

John Chiles: The main problem was the suspension, particularly the bogey wheels on the tanks and they would break and we frequently had to spend nights replacing these and it was quite a job because you would have to jack up the arms which were under considerable spring pressure and then remove a large shaft, take out the damaged bogey wheel, put the fresh one in and then get that shaft back lined up with the two arms. It wasn't easy at all and we were having to work with torches under a sheet of canvas and then not far away you would hear the Japs calling out 'Hello Tommy, where are you Tommy?' and the odd firing going on and that sort of thing.

Daniel: How did you regard the Japanese soldiers?

John Chiles: They would come at you in a continuous scream like ants across a floor and you could stamp on them and then more would come and that's how they operated. I've spoken to Japanese since the war and they were acting under orders, the same way as we were acting under orders. The only thing is that their behaviour at that time was acceptable to them but wouldn't be acceptable I don't think now and certainly wasn't acceptable to us but they were soldiers and they were doing what they were told to do.

Daniel: You've been involved in lots of veteran activity over the years. Can you just tell me which Veteran Associations you've been involved with and why has that been important to you?

John Chiles: I've been very much involved with the Royal British Legion, I'm still on the County Committee and a Vice President of the Surrey Royal British Legion. I am Chairman of the Epsom Branch of the Burma Star Association and for the past twenty years I've been on the Commonwealth Council of the Royal Commonwealth Ex Services League representing the Ex Services Association of Pakistan. I have also given my services as a Borough Councillor and served as a Mayor of my borough but the reason I think behind this was, as I mentioned earlier, that although I am a pretty poor Christian, knowing all my faults and there are many of them, I've got a tremendous faith in God and a tremendous faith in prayer and in my own squadron in the war I was the only one who was not killed or wounded and I believe rightly or wrongly that I was saved to serve others and that is what I've tried to do and what, in spite of being 91, I am still trying to do.

Needham the Chindit

With the Chindits in Burma

Major Robin Needham *(Emanuel 1923–1929)*

A keen and talented ball player Robin represented the School in both the First Fifteen and First Eleven teams. Fifteen years after leaving Emanuel's well kept fields he was slogging his way through the dense Burmese jungle as one of Major General Orde Wingate's Chindits.

In 1939 Robin joined the Royal Artillery and initially commanded a searchlight battery on the Thames at Woolwich. Robin's wife was in charge of fire watch on the roof of Du Cane Court in Balham.

Between December 1941 and March 1942 Japanese forces swept across what was known as the British Empire's crescent, a number of strategically important garrisons which ran

Emanuel First XI, 1928 – Back row (left to right): F.E. Usher, K.R. Needham, T.F. Lynam Esq., W.R. Haining, F.L. Abbott, J.W. King; Middle Row: H.B. Deeks, C.N. Stephens (Capt.), C.G.M. Broom Esq., S.W. Stephens (Vice-Capt.), R.M.O. Williams; Front Row: F.W. Patten, E.N. Pinkham

Robin in Royal Artillery Service uniform

from Burma to Hong Kong. Throughout the first half of 1942 the Japanese forced what was left of the British forces to the Indian border having taken thousands of prisoners of war. In their conquest of Singapore in February 1942, the Japanese exacted on the British Army its worst military defeat in its history by attacking the British naval station from the north and taking an estimated 70,000 British Empire troops prisoner. It wasn't a surprise to Winston Churchill who was aware of the dire defences of Singapore in January 1942 but nonetheless it sent shockwaves across Britain with much criticism directed towards the Prime Minister. In the next few months the Japanese consolidated their early victories and gained control of Burma.

As a Lieutenant, later Major, in the 51st Field Regiment Royal Artillery, Robin was based in Bangalore as British strategists planned how to drive the Japanese out of Burma. It was September 1943, when as Robin writes, 'the officers of 16 I.B. were summoned to a lecture by Major General Wingate' and it was after this lecture that all officers, 'battery captains' and above were addressed by Wingate who said, 'Well gentlemen...how do you like your new job?' As Robin wrote, 'This was the manner in which the 51st heard that they were to become Chindits.' The name Chindits is a variation on the word Chinthé given to the mythical winged lion seen across Burma. Wingate's forces were officially known as the 77th Indian Infantry Brigade but the moniker Chindits allowed the legendary Orde Wingate to distinguish them and their long-range penetration operations from other infantry brigades. Robin fought in the second Chindit Expedition codenamed Operation Thursday. The aim of the brigade was to disrupt the less fortified areas of North West Burma under Japanese command. The Chindits fought in some of the harshest terrain and climates of the Second World War, fighting as they did across mountains, ravines and jungle.

Robin wrote a 27-page account of his experiences as an Intelligence Officer in the 51st Field Regiment during the Second Chindit Expedition which details the extraordinary strength that these men possessed.[1]

Professionally, Robin was a journalist. After the war he attended the Nuremberg Trials and reported their development for British newspapers. He also assisted Charles Hill in compiling the Emanuel School Second World War Roll of Service as well as being editor of the Old Emanuel newsletter for forty years, Chairman and President of the Old Emanuel Association and an Emanuel School governor. Robin's son Patrick also attended Emanuel in the 1960s.

The Second Chindit Expedition:

The 51st Field Regiment RA September 1943 to October 1944

Throughout December training went apace. The men licked their wounds, forgot their sorrow and got down to it. Men quickly learned to make themselves comfortable in the jungle. They learned to march all day carrying their entire wardrobe, their entire larder and all their bedding. The men quickly formed the impression that Mr Churchill's famous phrase 'sweat, toil and tears' must have been wrung from the lips of a dying Chindit.

On Jan 20th the unit was honoured by a visit from Lord Louis Mountbatten. In one of his famous soapbox speeches he thoroughly endeared himself to the men giving them encouraging news from home and, with complete candour, speaking of the epic job on which they were about to embark.

After a long and tiresome railway journey this column reached Linkha-pani, up beyond Ledo. Only allowed to leave the train in the dead of night, for the purposes of deception, it was driven by American-negro drivers. One of them amused us with the sombre reflection: "You's goin' the wrong way brothers!" The roads were quagmire. A squelching march followed and it was a desolate picture. The rum ration was as deserved as it was appreciated. Undoubtedly morale was extremely high and the good humour of the British soldier was never more emphatically shown in depressing conditions.

Meanwhile the long string of column mules was making its way by road to the camp. All the way they were cheered and sustained by American troops constructing the Ledo Road. At one place 40 of them were invited into an American mess, a spread put before them and cigarettes handed over. This is mentioned because of the foolish antagonism between British and American troops in other parts of the world where there was often open resentment. But to the 51st Column they were friends indeed.

Weight for weight, it must be remembered, men were carrying much more than the strongest mules. It was a task which called for gritted teeth, unflinching will power, and a stout heart. Men would make a few laborious yards only to slip on the greasy slope and be precipitated to a point below at which they took their last breather. Mules would make a prodigious effort only to lose their footing and go plunging backwards, head over heels, lashing wildly in all directions. The dangers were prodigious, the labours stupendous. Men soon revised their ideas about necessities for the journey. Some men even threw away their handkerchief to lighten their packs.

We saw very little of the Nagas. The route we took was chosen for – one might almost say – its impossibility. No Jap would ever think of an enemy sending a force through such country. Those we did see were friendly enough. Well they might be, having heard of our coming through what means of jungle telepathy one can only guess at. The approach to a Naga village was guarded by a large bamboo platform on which flowers, food, and water were placed. They were put there to welcome and propitiate any spirits which might happen to wander that way.

Still those dreadful hills. From 1000 up to 4000 feet. From 4000 down to two. Up... Up... Up and still up. We reach 5800 feet and curse the beauties of the primitive country around us. To the Column it represents only backbreaking work. Occasionally we notice a casualty from other Columns. A man from the Queens passes us in an attempt to find his way back to the Ledo Road. Someone has put a piece of bamboo on the fire, sealed by its joints...the bamboo explodes. A piece has hit him in the eye...He stumbles past us blindly in pain.

Books have appeared from heavens know where. One can picture the gratified smile on faces of certain authors if they can only see the soul-saving pleasure they are giving at this moment, to as hard-driven a band of men as ever went into bloody battle. Here is 'Pickwick Papers' and there is Charles Reade's 'Martyrdom of Men'. 'The Wallet of Kai Lung' is passed from hand to hand. A mule leader has one eye on Galsworthy's 'Country House' and one on his wicked charge. Another scares himself stiff with 'The Body in the Library'.

Another day of making our way along the bed of a stream. Most of us have been growing beards for the better part of a month. We all look somewhat Mid-Victorian, and we like it. Although we have been in Burma for some days – how many we cannot tell as the boundary between Assam and Burma is not a thing which anyone has seen fit to worry about it. The river is the natural defence line for the Japs' usurped positions in Burma. The thought of this river crossing has set many a heart beating during the past fortnight. We have learned in training to make 'sausages' of our kit wrapped up on a groundsheet. Weak swimmers will have to be towed across with stronger swimmers to give them a hand.

The following order of the day by Brigadier Fergusson is read to all men. "We are going into Burma to hit the Jap and to hit him hard. We are going to hunt him ruthlessly and without pity. We belong to what may well be the best brigade in the history of war; and we are making history with every step we take..."

As we made that fantastic crossing of the Chindwin – rather like Richmond on a regatta day – the aeroplanes were swooping down onto the opposite bank. General Wingate... talked in his jerky staccato fashion to the men as they left the boats. There is little doubt but that he fully realised the rigours of that appalling march. His manner reached the nearest heights to friendliness that one could imagine possible in one so remote from ordinary minds.

A small party of Japanese agents were captured just south of the river. In the scuffle that followed at least one got away, so they could tell their superiors they met with British troops in an unexpected quarter. Later a man was caught filching rations at a supply drop dump. If he had more than his share somebody else went short. It was a crime against the community. During the long halt at midday in the broiling sun he was tied to a tree. Rest and peace of mind were denied him. But justice was served.

On March 15th the columns made their way up a tortuous chaung towards Lonkin. It was a deceitful chaung. Any resemblance it showed to the one marked on the map was purely coincidental. All day we toiled up it. When we guessed we were within 6 miles of the village of Malam we had a council of war. It was decided that 51 column should attack the town from the West. But the jungle was thick, the Jap was well dug in, in cleverly concealed positions. It was difficult to locate him, let alone dislocate him. The platoon was pinned down until it could pinpoint the enemy. It took vigorous actions to expel the Japs from the west end of Lonkin. They disappeared like wraiths taking with them their dead, dying and wounded. At the cost of 2 dead and 2 wounded the column had taken the western half of Lonkin.

One night we are listening to the news on the RAF wireless. When laughs are few the operator tries to get a Japanese broadcast of news in English. He has got this programme tonight and we prick up our ears when we hear that British forces recently made an attack on Lonkin. Enthusiastically the announcer goes on to tell us that the British were driven from the town with heavy losses. Really?

The march goes on. The hills are gradually getting the better of us. As on that fearful trek through the Naga mountains the heights are so sheer that the track winds in funicular fashion up the face of the precipices. On April 10th the column reaches 'Aberdeen', the famous Chindit airstrip in the heart of Jap occupied territory [North of Indaw]. We are given nearly 3 days rest and the men revel in the joys of eggs and bacon for breakfast. The American K ration is good. But we have eaten nothing else for two months and we are beginning to hate the sight of it.

Later the column marches truculently into the midst of the Japanese positions west of Indaw Lake. There are some brisk skirmishes and the support platoon, patient for so long, have the satisfaction of bringing their mortar fire down on enemy positions. The column puts a chip on its shoulder and hangs about in the neighbourhood of Pebin and Thetkegyin. But the Jap is not to be drawn. He has more than a passing respect for these wild Chindits by now and nothing will draw him from the comparative safety of his business. The wounded are flown out and so is Lt. Needham, who is sick. The remainder make their way back to Aberdeen without further incident. The end of the journey is in sight and for the first time some of the doughtiest members of the column know fear. After having survived so much how terrible it would be to fall now. The column is told to stand by to be flown out. We are in first. It is only fitting that we should go out first.

The column marched over 500 weary miles. Words can only give but the vaguest idea of the hardships and tortures of that march. *The Times* referred to it as one of the greatest feats of human endurance so far performed in the Far East. No one could argue with that statement. Had not the doctor declared that men were at the peak of human endurance – but then they carried on for two months after that statement was made!

One had felt that each day was worse than the last – and nothing could transcend today in weariness and discomfort. We had thought that each day for three months. And yet – how proud each man could feel as he looked back on this expedition. There had been comradeship, heroism and humour of a high order, as we advanced the brigade into the very heart of enemy country and Brigadier Wingate said: "One day you will be proud to say you were there." How true were those words.

References

1 Major K. R. N. Needham – The 51st Field Regiment R.A. September 1943 to October 1944, Imperial War Museum accession number 80/49/1.

Dennis Victor Geen

(Emanuel 1936–1942)

Dennis came to Emanuel from Lavender Hill School in 1936, being attracted to Emanuel because the boys wore blue caps with gold braid zigzagged all the way round but when he eventually came to Emanuel they took away the caps. Dennis got his love of music from Emanuel's music department and has enjoyed singing all his life.

As a young boy growing up in the dark days of the late 1930s Dennis remembers slit trenches being dug on Clapham Common after the Munich Crisis of 1938. A year later in 1939 at the age of fourteen, Dennis was evacuated with Emanuel to Petersfield. Dennis remembered going up to Emanuel several times in August 1939 and just sitting waiting, until 31 August when they were told the next day they were to be evacuated. When he arrived in Petersfield the contrast with Battersea was 'quite amazing.' Later that day 1 September 1939 Dennis recollected, 'One of the masters, Hughes was his name, bought a copy of the Portsmouth Evening News and there it was "Germany Invades Poland" so we knew the war had started.'

Dennis was billeted with an elderly lady at first but after a month he was moved and on his second move he met another Old Emanuel, Peter Downs, and with Peter Dennis moved for a third time into new billets, remembering that his evacuation experience was a pleasant one. Dennis cycled from Petersfield to London twice during the war and in term time returned to see his family in Battersea.

Dennis Geen

A photo showing part of the Burma plain

On leaving School in 1942 Dennis spent six months working as a clerk in the War Office. After this he joined the Army at Preston and then spent six weeks in Northern Ireland on infantry training and six weeks on gunner training in Wales where he learnt how to fire 25 pounder guns. He then transferred to a course to study how to be a technical assistant in the Royal Artillery where he learnt how to plot gun positions on an artillery board. After his training Dennis was posted out to India and joined the 1st Field Battery Royal Artillery. Travelling in the SS *Otranto* in November 1944 they arrived in Bombay and then made their way to Dulali, where the HQ of the Indian Artillery was based. More training followed then Dennis moved through Bangladesh until being posted to the 1st Battery Royal Artillery (The Blazers) in Assam. He was taken with the journey as he remembered when interviewed in 2013, 'It was quite fascinating really, all these places had just been names in a book.'

In February 1945 Dennis was in action during the British advance on the Japanese garrison of Meiktila.[1] He was in the artillery command post plotting targets on the artillery board. He describes how this was achieved, 'You would have a Forward Observation Officer who would signal back, giving you a rough map reference which you would plot on the artillery board. We would have our gun position on the artillery board and the FOO's target position and with an arm which gave us the range and a segment which gave us the angle we would give it to the guns who would fire on the target.'

Dennis remembered being agitated during the Meiktila engagement and the trauma he experienced when a Forward Observation party were mortared and killed. They buried the men the same evening. When interviewed he said, 'It brought it all home to you.' As for many of those who fought in the war these experiences remained as vivid seventy years later as when they happened. Of driving into Meiktila Dennis remembered both sides of the road being lined with dead Japanese forces. He noted, 'the stench was awful.'

After Meiktila Dennis moved with British forces towards Mandalay. As people in Britain were celebrating victory in Europe on 8 May 1945, British forces in Burma were still fighting. But when victory in Japan was declared Dennis had a well-deserved bottle of beer. The realities of war soon returned when he had to take charge of one party of Japanese who had been made POWs, but before long he returned to India where he was held in reserve for anti-riot duties but he was never called upon. He returned to England in May 1947 on the MV *Georgic*. After being demobbed Dennis returned to the War Office, which later became the Ministry of Defence, until retiring in 1984. During his time with the Ministry Dennis travelled the world inspecting defence attaches.

References

1 For a brief overview of the taking of Meiktila see Louis Allen, *Burma: The Longest War 1941–1945* (1984), pp.425-458.

Escape from Singapore

Horace Stanley 'George' Darley DSO

(Emanuel 1926–1932)

After posting to RAF Exeter in October 1941 George's next move was to Singapore. His memoir recounts the chaos of evacuation as Japanese forces swept across south-east Asia.

In May 1941 I was posted to Air HQ Far East, Singapore. On arrival by sea, via Glasgow and Durban, I was informed that I had to introduce an air defence system for Malaya and Singapore, there being none – no operations room, no warning radar and no observer corps. At least there were anti-aircraft (AA) guns. We set up a fighter operations room in Singapore town using a large house, but incoming plots were scarce.

My parish embraced also Hong Kong and Burma, including conferences with the Americans in the Philippines and the Dutch in Sumatra. At the behest of the Governor of Hong Kong my Air Officer Commanding (AOC), Air Vice Marshal Pulford, gave me 'carte blanche' to convert its Kai Tak airfield into a fighter base. Having borrowed a Catalina and a Works Directorate officer, I arrived there to be kindly invited by the GOC to put me up. The next day we both attended a meeting with the Governor, who not only endorsed my AOC's directives but also required the GOC to establish and centralise air raid warnings. I borrowed a Vildebeeste from the local squadron, and, having warned the Chief of Police, I carried out different approaches to the airfield to the consternation of the office-bound tycoons in their cars. I finally decided that a police station and one hangar had to be demolished to provide an adequate approach lane and landing area.

Work began the same day and I understand that it was still under way when the Japanese took over: they approved its completion to my design.

My main interest then became the construction of a proper air defence operations room at Minlagdon near Rangoon in Burma and I wished the plotting table to be aligned with that of Alipore Air Ops. Room near Calcutta, so that aircraft plots could be exchanged. To my horror I found that the mapping experts of the border areas of India and Burma had never exchanged notes, so aircraft plots 'jumped' 50 miles or more north or south on crossing in or out of the two areas. On return to AHQ Singapore I consulted my old friend, the navigation staff officer and he recommended a review of the various 'trig' points upon which Burma maps were produced. We flew to Rangoon; I borrowed a Blenheim and off we went on a 3 day tour as far north as Lashio, including several airfields, and then south to Chittagong. The result was an amended plotting table in Burma and also in Alipore at Calcutta, which I eventually supervised.

My next job was to assist the so called 'Flying Tigers' a fighter squadron formed by the then Colonel Chennault from the US Army, Navy and Marine sources to assist China on a mercenary basis. Our AOC had provided them with an airfield at Toungoo in Burma, and as they arrived at Singapore, I directed them on to Rangoon. Since none of these pilots had combat experience they needed training in fighter tactics. My AOC had offered me to Chennault and I spent some fourteen days with them at Toungoo. I was astonished to see many of them making approaches to the runway at some 120 mph, a number of whom then disappeared into the jungle unable to slow down after landing. Aircraft and spares were at a premium, so I demonstrated that an approach at 85 and 90 mph was quite safe and less costly. After that they listened to me. It was no help that the three U.S. air arms had three different views on fighter tactics.

In December 1941 I was again in Burma inspecting progress on the Operations Room and in the early hours of Sunday 8th of December boarded an Imperial Airways flying boat for Singapore. Fellow passengers included the (then) Rt. Hon. and Mrs. Duff Cooper, and also General Gordon Bennet, GOC Australian Army in Malaya. The night stop was to be at Bangkok, but at mid-morning the captain announced that a Japanese invasion of Thailand precluded this and he would return to Rangoon: this disturbed us all. Following discussions over the urgent need of us all to reach Singapore, the captain discovered that the UK bound flying boat, which was due to land the same day at Rangoon, was a longer range version of ours and that he would change aircraft. So the next day we changed over, refuelled in the Andaman Islands, spending Tuesday night at Sabang in North Sumatra. Taking off early on Wednesday 10 December, we landed at Singapore at midday. I hastened to the Fighter Ops. Room, to find a Buffalo squadron taking off in response to a belated call for assistance from the battleships the *Prince of Wales* and *Repulse* off Kuantan. These had left Singapore on the afternoon of the 9th of December, without arranging for possible fighter assistance. After Japanese air detection, both ships turned south at 00.10 hrs on Wednesday the 10th of December. The first call for fighter protection was not received until 12.04 hrs from *Repulse*, although *Prince of Wales* was torpedoed at 11.44 hrs and *Repulse* at 12.23, sinking at 12.33 hrs. *Prince of Wales* was abandoned at 13.10 hrs. The fighter squadron took off at 12.26 hrs arriving at 13.20 hrs with little fuel. Naval radio silence and their lack of prior concerted plans frustrated earlier support from the RAF. Such was my introduction to the war in the Far East.

The Japanese, having established a strong foothold in southern Thailand and naval supremacy off eastern Malaya, then launched air and ground attacks on northern Malaya with heavy casualties to Australian and RAF squadrons. Within a few days I repacked my bags yet again and was ordered north to command Ipoh airfield, an Australian Air Force base, only to find a handful of serviceable Buffaloes, an American fighter aircraft, with little hope of repairing the remainder. We then had no option but to follow our ground forces' withdrawal south and settled at Kuala Lumpur with a mixture of Australian and RAF, but it had been bombed on 21 December; Army Corps HQ was in the town. At the same time, my few remaining Buffaloes

Group Captain Darley when CO of RAF West Malling c.1952–1954

were withdrawn to Singapore, because maximum air cover was required for arrival of sea transports carrying Army personnel diverted from the Middle East: all I could offer was an occasional PR sortie. On 10 January 1942 I made my usual morning visit to Corps HQ only to find that they had completely evacuated the area without any warning to me. Communications to AHQ at Singapore then being nil, I drove down there, some 200 miles, early in the morning of the 11th of January, and asked to be briefed on present and probable events, in particular when and how many Hurricanes were expected and their future location. This prompted me to advise my colleague in the Fighter Ops. Room to warn his civilian outposts of Observer Corps of an impending withdrawal to Singapore and returned to Kuala Lumpur that evening, after a round 400 mile journey. I heard that the Japanese had crossed the Slim River on 7 January 1942, with an open road to Kuala Lumpur. The next morning I informed my heads of sections of my withdrawal plan to Singapore, so all personnel left the next morning by our own transport, to spend the night en route. I retained a small group of armourers to attach

George Darley (first from right) on Field Marshal Montgomery's inspection of troops at RAF Middleton St George, 3 November 1955 and (right) in conversation with Montgomery

fuse wires to the pre-positioned drums of gelignite in holes in the airfield surface which we demolished. We blew up the fuel installations, and then saw a steam roller used by an excellent group of New Zealand Army engineers to construct aircraft shelters. However, its pace was well below that of the Japanese advance! So we crammed it full of gelignite and surplus ammunition, lit the fuses and retired. The result was spectacular – no engine left but pieces then began to descend upon us as thunderbolts! As a parting gift we left a booby trap attached to the chain of my private loo next to my office.

I made my way south calling at all the newly established Observer Corps centres. I briefed them on the general situation and assured them that as civilians they were free to decide their next step. I arrived at AHQ Singapore in mid-January 1942 to hear conflicting rumours as to the arrival of Hurricanes.

I had tested the Buffalo, used by the Australians, shortly after I arrived in Singapore. I found it to be a pretty useless heap of ironmongery to heave around the sky, with R/T limited to about 10 miles. In combat its guns were most unreliable, being operated by solenoids which were scarce. More often than not an aircraft which could fly had guns which could not fire. No wonder more were destroyed on the ground rather than in the air. The agile Japanese Navy Zero fighter and later its Air Force equivalent amply showed the Buffalo as a useless fighter.

On 13 January 1942 some 50 crated Hurricanes were unloaded in Singapore with 24 pilots. The former were sent to dispersed sites for erection, only to find that they were of the type designed for ground attack operations in the Western Desert complete with sand filters, desert survival equipment, de-rated engines and 12 guns all thoroughly greased up. Special assembly tool kits were few and of course were widely dispersed. Nonetheless the ground crews worked wonders and the first squadron was in operation on 20 January, flown by pilots new to the hot and humid climate and weather conditions. All the desert equipment and four guns were discarded in a forlorn hope to repel escorted bomber raids on Singapore which had begun in early January and of which we had only ten minutes warning. The bombers concentrated upon our airfields with light fragmentation bombs designed to damage aircraft on the ground but not the airfield surface. The few Buffaloes remaining gave cover for the withdrawal of our ground forces from the mainland.

On 16 January 225 (B) Group was formed in Singapore and transferred to Sumatra near Palembang (known as P. 2 airfield) two days later with the surviving bombers.

Towards the end of January 1942 we heard that 48 more Hurricanes were to be flown into Singapore from the aircraft carrier *Indomitable* and 39 more to be delivered in crates by sea. As the general withdrawal of our forces from Singapore began on 27 January, all these Hurricanes were diverted to Java, with resultant confusion among the air and ground crew originally allocated to them by squadrons. On 1 February 226 (F) Gp was formed at Palembang town and as the diverted Hurricanes became operational they flew in groups to this airfield (known as P. 1.) A few days later I was posted from Singapore to 226 Group arriving by sea and found as usual that I was expected to form a fighter operations centre for the third time from scratch, i.e. a house with one large empty room, no communications, no staff and in a foreign country. However, knowing that Palembang was a garrison town, I called upon the Dutch Army HQ for help which came at once. A vacated furnished house, trestle tables and maps, with telephones to my Group HQ and the fighter airfield (P. 1.). My urgent need was R/T communication with the few Hurricanes at airfield P. 1 which had been flown from Singapore, where they had been depleted by being outnumbered from six to one to fifteen to one. Our Dutch friends merely commandeered a civilian type receiver from the nearest shop. The transmitter was more of a problem until they realised that oil tanker convoys on the Moesi River, which connected Palembang oil refinery with the Banka Straits, some 50 miles north, were controlled to one way traffic by R/T at the refinery. I obtained our R/T aircraft frequencies, found that the refinery control room could accept them and connected a telephone to them from my Ops Room. When I wished to transmit to our fighters, all I had to do was to ask for 'transmit', receive confirmation from control and that is how we operated the air defence of the oil refinery urgently needed by the Japanese as part of their war objectives.

On the morning of the 14th of February, following reports of an invasion fleet, I ordered the Hurricanes at P. 1, then about 20, to patrol the Banka Straits, but low broken cloud prevented a sighting. However, whilst returning to P. 1 they were attacked by Navy Zero fighters obviously from an aircraft carrier. At this juncture I received reports of 200 paratroops descending on P. 1, and over the R/T I ordered all P. 1 aircraft not to land at base but at P. 2. In the middle of this fracas four more Hurricanes from Java tried to land at P. 1 without prior notice or correct R/T frequencies. The ground crews at P. 1, alert to the situation told the pilots to go to P. 2 but some of them required refuelling. So more Hurricanes were lost. My telephone contact with P. 1 was then cut and so I drove to HQ 226 Group in the town, collected another officer and two airmen with rifles (only one man in twelve had one due to an acute shortage) and we set off to P. 1 to ascertain the situation. Soon after turning off the hard road to the dirt track through rubber plantations to P. 1, we were fired on, plus grenades. To avoid this ambush we returned to the main road where we met a Dutch army unit. We warned them and returned to Group HQ where we were told that it was in retreat to P. 2, and where I was to organise the remaining fighters. Intending to retrieve some essential kit from my quarters, I had to pass by the ferry which was the only link across the river that split Palembang in half, linking it with southern Sumatra. There was absolute turmoil; lorries full of personal kit, crowds of airmen, but no officers. All P. 1 staff, except for some pilots, were, of course, ambushed there. I stopped, fired two revolver shots in the air and produced peace. I called all senior NCOs forward, told them to form squads of ten men each with rifles (again a shortage) and at once put them as guards on the ferry bridge, deck and engine room preventing the crew from deserting. Then, to my horror, ambulances began to arrive without warning, full of patients. I saw no doctors or other officers. (Some time later I realised that the Dutch must have provided the RAF with beds and medical care, because 225 Group HQ in Palembang town were mainly operations and technical staff. Hence no doctors available to escort RAF patients.) I ordered all lorries to be emptied, replaced by patients and for them to be ferried across and thence down the road to P. 2. I also told another armed guard to take over the rail terminus on the far side of the river serving the south to prevent any trains from leaving.

As the ambulances became empty I sent them back to the hospital for more patients including extra mattresses and pillows until each driver had confirmed with me that none were left. In the meantime I transferred the unarmed airmen to the far side, to make the patients as comfortable as they could and then to occupy vacant space themselves, and drive to P. 2. This process took 3 – 4 hours; unfortunately the railway station guard reported a deserted train there, but nobody who knew how to start and drive it, let alone operate the signals. So in the evening I, still a solitary officer and a handful of men, were left on the wrong side of the river by ourselves; we crossed by the ferry, thanked the crew for their help and the men joined a lorry whilst I sat in the front of an ambulance to direct the driver to P. 2. A few miles down the road one patient asked for his position on his stretcher to be altered so we stopped to help him. Whilst doing this a panic stricken Dutchman in a car hit us from behind; the patient was saved but the rest of us suffered minor injuries, mine being a sprained ankle. I explained to the driver in explicit English what I thought of him.

Having arrived at P. 2, I went to the Operations Room, then arranged as a bomber and recce basis. I took over a corner to brief and control our few remaining fighters, warning them of probable action the next day.

The next morning the 15th of February 1942 started dull but at dawn a recce took off during morning briefing and reported Japanese sea activity in the estuary of the

Moesi River some 50 miles from Palembang. Weather prevented our fighter sorties but as it cleared and as more reports came in, it was evident that a convoy of troop landing launches was on its way towards the town's oil refineries with the assistance of the previous day's paratroops. The convoy was bombed as the weather cleared and I followed this up by Hurricane sorties, although the weather was still unsettled with low cloud. The first sortie took off about 11.00 hrs, found open barges full of troops in a column some two miles long moving up river. They wreaked immense casualties with their eight guns without any Zero fighter opposition, probably due to the weather. On landing at P. 2 the Hurricanes were serviced, taken over by fresh pilots which resulted in another sortie of carnage without air opposition. It was of some satisfaction to all of us at P. 2 that we had in some small part avenged the surrender and capitulation of Singapore on those two days 14 and 15 February 1942.

Having been warned by the Dutch at this moment that Palembang town could not be defended it was decided to evacuate P. 2. All serviceable aircraft were flown to Java and personnel were moved by rail and road to (then) Oesthaven, a port in southern Sumatra, where the SS *Yoma* had arrived with now unwanted military supplies. Having embarked all personnel, she set sail north through the Soenda Straits between Sumatra and Java to (then) Batavia, where RAF reviews decided upon the numbers of aircrew and groundcrew required to maintain existing aircraft in Java, together with the Dutch forces. The remainder were allocated to ships in the harbour or sent to a port in south Java, all destined for Australia. We then heard that a British and a Dutch warship had been attacked and sunk in the Java Sea so a safe passage was doubtful. I was destined for Australia.

On re-embarking in the *Yoma* I found a motley collection of all three services, detachments of their Nursing services, elements of the BBC and many women with their children. The ship's 'trooping' officer who liaised between the captain and the troops told me that all the deck crew and part of the engine room staff had deserted, and asked for assistance. Scratch crews were soon forthcoming and just enough steam was raised for the ship to limp out of port, being barely able to maintain steerage way. We passed back through the Soenda Straits but then to my astonishment she turned to the west and not the east. In reply to my query the captain stressed that he and his crew had not seen Glasgow (his home port) for many a long year, and that going to Australia did not appeal to him (nor me, preferring the Middle East war). So that was that, and I turned my attention to creating some law and order among the passengers. Later I heard that many of the ships bound for Australia were sunk by Japanese naval action at the cost of many women and children.

Eventually all alone and chugging at 5 knots, we reached Colombo, which did not want us, except for the RN contingent who were to replace casualties following the sinking of an HMS cruiser during a recent Japanese aircraft carrier attack on the port. We were directed to Bombay and moored in the harbour from where I hired a launch to Ballard's Quay and then a taxi to the Bombay Army embarkation officer to discover our future, giving him details of my passenger list. He promised to send a party by launch at 09.00 hrs the next day to clear us medically and then to sort out my complicated problem. I was thus able to re-assure all passengers on my return.

The next day after two hours of embarkation staff indolence, I hired all launches around us, filled them with furious women, ushered them into taxis, drove to the Embarkation Office, ascended the stairs, poured them into the CO's office, shut the door and listened outside – most enlightening! The next morning the ship was medically cleared and a team interviewed the passengers and my committee whilst *Yoma* was being berthed to a quay. By noon everybody, civilian and service, except RAF personnel, had been disembarked and so, awaiting further instructions, I relaxed in company with the captain and his officers. At mid afternoon about twelve Army officers appeared, stating that they were ordered to Karachi.

So again we set sail, less crowded than usual; and docked in Karachi in mid-March 1942. So I finished my self-imposed task still aged 27. On the bridge of an empty ship the captain produced a bottle of Scotch, we toasted ourselves and as there was nobody else to whom we owed anything, we consumed a cold lunch toasting ourselves with another bottle. I regret that the captain and his *Yoma* were again utilised in the Mediterranean, resulting in their sinking. I and many others owe our lives to him and his crew. I do hope some reached their Glasgow.

Then having arrived at RAF Karachi, where we were settled in and sorted out, I was told that I had been posted to command RAF Colombo. It was clear to me that Colombo would not be bombed again and therefore any officer of my rank would suffice for this post. So, as I was qualified as a flying instructor and with fighter experience, I pressed for a more suitable post. I was then in April 1942 selected to command No. 151 Operational Training Unit (OTU) at Risalpur in North West Frontier Province, 30 miles east of Peshawar. Here the original Indian Air Force squadrons, some ten in all I think, were being converted from their Harts, via Harvards, to Hurricanes, just as I wanted. It also gave me an opportunity to make friends with the commanding officers and their flight commanders which stood me in good stead some six years later. Following this conversion programme we began to receive new Indian pilots from Ambala, with their wings, also for conversion to Hurricanes. So 151 OTU after my tuition, expanded to now require a CO in the form of a Group Captain in February 1943. Not pleased at becoming a No. 2 at my own developed station, I applied for a posting to Middle East, to actively re-enter the war. Instead I was posted to 221 Group, Calcutta, a mixed bomber and fighter group, operating over Burma and also defending India, based at Alipore, near Calcutta. So as Wing Commander Ops. I had an interesting job, detailing bomber operations whilst keeping an eye on providing radar warning stations for Calcutta. To my great satisfaction, I found that the discrepancies in mapping between India and Burma, which I had discovered in late 1941 by a navigational survey over Burma, had been rectified. I kept 'my hand in' by being invited by the OC Alipore, Fighter Station, to his weekly station conferences and also by taking his job over when he was on leave. In the meantime, I flew into all our bomber bases in Burma to discuss any snags in the pipeline.

My patience was rewarded in June 1943 when I was promoted to Group Captain and ordered to return to and command 151 OTU, Risalpur NWFP after five pleasant months in 221 Gp Calcutta.

In early 1944 I moved 151 OTU from Risalpur to Peshawar, some 30 miles west, which having a permanent runway, was much superior to our boggy grass airfield. To my pleasure I was invited to become a committee member of the prestigious Peshawar Club, possessed of a long military history. But good news came in early June when I was told that my three year tour overseas had ended and that a troopship was leaving Bombay in four days time. So out came my Anson; I piled in my chattles, warned my second pilot and two groundcrew and we took off for Agra, spending the night there and reaching Bombay at noon. I sorted myself out with the embarkation staff and sailed the next morning. What a relief it was knowing that at long last my wife Marjorie and I would be rejoined.

We arrived in Liverpool a month later, after an uneventful voyage, I telephoned Marjorie and caught a crowded night train for Exeter. Like so many thousands of wartime couples who had been separated for years with little or no letters, it was a touching experience for both of us. She had lived at a hotel in Exeter throughout my absence, had joined the Church Army in order to drive a mobile canteen every day, serving all the dispersed units scattered over Dartmoor and Exmoor.

Post-War RAF Career

George's RAF career continued into the post-war years with a number of commands. In August 1944 he was posted to command No. 62 OTU, Ouston, near Newcastle. Then he was made Senior Air Staff Officer to No. 12 Group of Fighter Command located at Watnall, Notts. Following this he was posted in October 1946 to command Wittering, near Stamford, with squadrons of Hornets and Spitfires as a Wing Commander. In February 1948 he was posted to command RAF Station West Malling.

He was invited to establish a Staff College in India, based at Wellington in the Nilgiri tea plantations in southern India near Ootacumund, 6,000 ft up in a hill station. Posted back to West Malling again he supervised the transition of the then three regular and one Royal Auxilary Air Force squadrons to jets, namely Vampire and Meteor night day fighters. George also became Controller of the Metropolitan Fighter Sector, operationally responsible for the performance of all fighter and radar stations in Kent and Essex. In July 1952 George was posted to the Air Ministry to initially devise and supervise air traffic control over SE England with Civil Aviation. After this he became deputy Director of Overseas Operations entailing constant visits to RAF Germany, the Middle East and Malaya during Communist uprisings. In June 1954 he was posted to supervise the tuition of young men into competent pilots of combat aircraft with command of No. 4 Flying Training School, Middleton St George, near Darlington. During his command, it converted to Meteors and latterly to Vampires. Later George was made Chief Intelligence Officer, Far East Air Force, Singapore. An appointment as Sub-Chairman of the Joint Intelligence Committee Far East (JICFE) and also the UK intelligence representative on the SE Asia Treaty Organisation followed. George officially resigned on 15 June 1959 completing 27 years service, during which he commanded no less than eleven stations. After looking at possibilities in the business world he later recalled his gladness to receive an invitation from the (then) Air Ministry to be considered for a new intelligence post in the Retired Officer category. He was accepted by the board and so began fourteen years as what he described as a 'Whitehall warrior', the Air Ministry later on being absorbed into the Ministry of Defence (MOD). He died on 9 November 1999.

Portrait of A. S. 'Bertie' Mann by artist William Dring, 1944

Albert 'Bertie' Sydney Mann DFC

(Emanuel 1927–1937)

Albert 'Bertie' Sydney Mann was an exceptional wartime photo-reconnaissance and fighter pilot. As an Emanuel schoolboy he also had an impressive resumé and was both Prefect of the School and Captain of Marlborough. His interest in shooting originated from his time in the School OTC where he reached the rank of CQMS. He was awarded his War Office Certificate 'A' in 1935. He was also Captain of Shooting and was awarded his full School colours in 1936. An excellent shot, he represented Surrey at Bisley. He was also a member of the Science Sixth class. Bertie took a Commission in the RAF soon after leaving School.

Pre-War Years

Bertie Mann's flying career started at the Bristol Flying School, Yatesbury in 1937. During his training Bertie encountered such characters on the course as David Tomlinson, who not only became a flying instructor during the Second World War but later found fame as an actor perhaps best remembered for playing George Banks in the Disney adaptation of P. L. Travers's 'Mary Poppins'. Bertie's next move was to the RAF Depot, Uxbridge, where young pilots were moulded into the Service learning everything from drill to how to behave in the public eye. Over the course of the next year, Bertie moved through various flying training schools. Interestingly, he had a different perspective on what many have seen as a British policy of 'appeasement' towards Hitler in 1938. Bertie believed that Neville Chamberlain's 'Peace in Our Time' diplomacy after the Munich crisis contributed in saving his life, as overseas trooping arrangements were resumed and Bertie was posted to India. In contrast the majority of new pilots on Bertie's course at Wittering who stayed in the West were killed in the first two years of war.

In India Bertie joined No. 31 Squadron flying Wapiti biplanes over South Waziristan. The North West Frontier Province was a dangerous place with intensive tribal activity. As war approached, Bertie was transferred to No. 28 Squadron flying Audaxes on proscription leaflet and bombing sorties. In mid June 1940 he went to Calcutta on appointment as the regular Adjutant to the newly formed No. 3 (Calcutta) Indian Air Force Volunteer Reserve (IAFVR) at Dum Dum. When Japan entered the war in late 1941, No. 28 moved to Lashio. A year later in October 1942, Bertie was given command of No. 28, now being equipped with the 'tank buster' Hurricane 2D. This was intended for close air support of Orde Wingate's first Chindit operation but it turned out to be impractical and Bertie concentrated its effort on photo-reconnaissance.

The following extracts are from Bertie Mann's account of his Second World War experiences before 1944.

Burma – 1942

It was unsettling, to say the least, that from thousands of miles away, the Japanese were already 'knocking on the door' of our southern frontiers only a matter of six weeks after the commencement of hostilities. We knew nothing about our new enemy other than the rumours of the last few months; and nothing of their advance after the defeat of Hong Kong, Malaya, then through Siam to the Burma border, until a sudden awakening on our arrival in the country. Previously, stories had been put around that 'they couldn't fight in the jungle', had antiquated equipment and flew paper aeroplanes which were underpowered and without armour-plate. So we had nothing to worry about!

Bertie Mann in Emanuel OTC uniform with the School Shooting VIII, 1934

I never had the chance to settle in at Lashio. I was sent at once to Rangoon with one of the other Flight Commanders to take the GOC 17th Division, Lt. Gen Tom Hutton and his ADC to a meeting with General Chiang Kai Shek in Chungking where they would discuss and arrange assistance in the defence of North Burma by the Nationalist Chinese Army. We took two Lysanders via He Ho and Toungoo, landing at Mingaladon on the evening of 30 January. On the following day, I went with Bill Tate, the other Flight Commander, to meet the General and his Staff Officer to be briefed on the timing and route of our journey to China. I would fly the General's ADC, Lt. Chancellor, Burma Rifles. The flights to Toungoo, then He Ho were uneventful except that there were long delays in refuelling by hand from cans. Notice of our flight had been sent by telegram, but the Burma Post Service seemed to have completely broken down! We did not arrive

Bertie Mann, (third from right, back row) in the County of Surrey Colts Team Shooting Squad at Bisley 1936 with OEs David Warren (fifth from left, back row) and Ernest 'Dixie' Dean (second from right, seated)

The wreckage of the Lysander

at He Ho until late afternoon, and after refuelling and a meal, it became clear that we could not get to Lashio until well after dark. After some discussion it was decided to carry on. The weather was 'gin clear' with little wind and a full moon was expected early in the night, so we had no qualms about continuing the journey. We took off with about half an hour of daylight remaining for the two hour flight to Lashio. After an hour, the moon rose and at once we had a problem. A thin haze had formed in the valleys which was hardly noticeable until the moon appeared; then they filled with 'milk' – the bright moonlight reflecting off the surface of the haze. We could not let down because of the mountainous high ground, and had something like 30 minutes fuel left with the GOC Burma (and his ADC) on board! We had to land. There was a very noticeable clearing on a tree covered hilltop below us which looked to be quite adequate for the Lysander in the bright moonlight. Tate flew low over it and was obviously satisfied, for he landed and ran for some way. His aeroplane then did a violent ground-loop and disintegrated. There was a small fire which lasted only a few moments, and no sign of movement thereafter. Overhead, we had great concern for the General, and while orbiting I suggested to the ADC that he should 'bale out' and help if he could. I climbed a bit to be sure he had about 1,500ft, and he went overboard bravely and in good style. I believe his parachute snagged on a tree but he was able to get to the ground quickly, and quickly get to the crash. I should have baled out too, but made a questionable decision to try a landing. I could see nothing wrong with the field until I was committed with my wheels on the ground. After rolling for about 50 yds, two substantial trees loomed up and I could do nothing but steer between them – they took the wings off and poor old N1274 fell to pieces on the spot. I found myself sitting beside her, dazed but otherwise unhurt. General Hutton was injured quite badly but was on his feet and the ADC was in one piece. I have never seen such a mess – the engine was behind the fuselage which had broken in half, and the wings were upside-down on the ground alongside. Things were not good with the other aircraft, for Tate was unconscious with serious head injuries and it was not

Bertie Mann pre-war

possible to move him. At that moment, thinking that we were alone on top of a hill in an unpopulated part of the Shan States, we three survivors were trying to decide what to do when we saw a light and heard loud shouting in English. We were escorted to the nearby Railway Institute where they were holding their weekly dance – quite unbelievable good fortune, for if the place had been deserted we would have been in very dire straits. Bill Tate was brought in on a stretcher. Meanwhile, our rescuers arranged a special train to take us on from the station at Manpwe to Lashio eighteen miles away. General Hutton left by train for Chungking with his brave ADC to arrive a day late for his meeting. Very sadly indeed, in spite of the ministrations of the Squadron MO and the staff of a small local hospital, Tate never regained consciousness and died the next day.

At that time, in late January 1942, when the threat to Burma became imminent, the air forces available to defend the country totalled less than 75 aircraft.

From 20 February, I was kept busy by the Army. At the beginning they needed any information they could get about the advance of the Japanese northward from Moulmein to the Sittang river crossing. This was a long straight road mostly out in the open along the coast of the estuary. There was traffic on it which consisted entirely of those escaping from further south. Most movement was by night, but I was able to report a few stragglers and an enormous build-up of vehicles in the town of Kyaikto at the eastern end of the Sittang Bridge (which was solely a railway bridge).

It was now obvious that we were involved in a large scale retreat. The Japanese advanced in strength from the east and south along roads leading towards the Sittang Bridge and their air forces occupied airfields near enough to maintain a continuous presence over the Rangoon area. Our land force which had remained to the east side of the Sittang gathered, increasing in size; but was under immediate threat of being over-run with no possibility of either holding out or withdrawing to the west of the river except by taking to the water or a difficult crossing by the railway bridge with no road. ... During the night of the 22 February our troops were at such a disadvantage that the fateful decision was taken to blow the bridge in the early hours, leaving two thirds of the British force on the wrong side of the river.

A Close Escape

On the eighth day after the blowing of the bridge, and the eighth successive early morning sortie over the same area at the same time, I was looking carefully under the trees overhanging the river from about 800ft, this time in a Hurricane. I had located a few local 'sampan' type craft tucked into the bank some miles north of Pegu. There was no other sign of movement so I went up to about 1,500 and in the fashion of the trained Army Co-op. pilot was noting the map reference and time on my knee-pad message form (with pencil sharpened at both ends and tethered on a string), straight and level and at about 240 mph., when I heard a couple of unusual 'clicks' in quick succession. Nothing dawned on me so I carried on writing – then it happened again accompanied by a snatching at my right shoe. This time I looked behind and saw three 'Army 97s' (little paper fighters with fixed undercarriages) taking it in turns to line up on me! There was no sense in mixing with them so I started to leg it back towards Mingaladon. A touch on the throttle and the Hurricane easily drew away, and after a few seconds we were a mile or so ahead. They must have seen a wisp of steam and continued to follow, for before a minute was up the Merlin engine was beginning to overheat. In seconds it seized solid and we landed wheels up in a large 'paddy field' without much trouble. Already this was not the proudest day of my wartime flying career! Somehow they had hit a coolant pipe, or the radiator itself, with one of their very few hits. I was out of my aeroplane in a brace of shakes, by which time the little men were overhead and doing copybook air to ground attacks on it. After dashing thirty or forty yards my right foot was excruciating and I could run no more, so I just stood and watched until they went away! I cannot believe that they didn't see me all this time and must conclude that they were surprisingly chivalrous. It is possible that they thought their ground troops were nearer than they were in fact and so felt sure I would be taken as a POW. On going back to the Hurricane I saw very few holes in it, and while watching them it had occurred to me that they weren't very good shots. It was clear after a couple of quick tries, that you cannot set fire to a Hurricane with a Colt .455 automatic pistol and a box of matches when you are in a tearing hurry so I retreated with my parachute which, of course, had an escape kit in the seat. It was a very large 'paddy field' but I could see some habitation in a clump of trees four or 500 yards away. Limping across I found a small village and was met by the head man who welcomed me in English and announced that he had been a labourer at Toungoo airfield before returning home recently. He said a small party of Japanese had been seen early that morning but they had gone away to the West. Not surprisingly I decided to leave as soon as possible. I asked if they could provide a bullock cart for transport which they cheerfully agreed to do when they saw the vast sum of money I was extracting from my escape kit. They also thoughtfully filled the cart with straw and piled it on top of me before we set off. The driver was a quiet smiling young man who thought the whole business was a joke. Short of an hour later we stopped and turned onto a main road; as it turned out, the road to Pegu and Rangoon. Not long afterwards I heard a lorry and my driver flagged it down. It was laden with a platoon of the Burma Rifles – at first I thought they might be Japs. I said goodbye to my happy friend and went on my way on the back of it complete with parachute, log-book and carrying my right shoe which had a bloody hole in it. A few miles further and a light tank met us, and after taking my leave of the Burma Rifles I was loaded on to the back and continued my journey with a rather 'boot faced' major of the 7th Royal Tank Brigade who showed all the signs of being unimpressed. Almost without a word I was taken to the battalion HQ of the 1st Cameronians near Pegu and debriefed by their Intelligence officer in a ditch.

Bertie took over command of No. 28 Squadron in late October 1942 and visited No. 6 Squadron at Shandur on the Suez Canal for a month where he learnt 'the technique used in the Western Desert to attack enemy tanks with the Hurricane 2D and its 40mm. Cannons.' He says 'it was elevating to meet veterans of the Desert War which, by then, was almost over'. He then returned to Burma where No 28. Squadron was already beginning to re-equip with 12-gun Hurricane IIBs.

Into Burma: The First Arakan Campaign

We had been joined by a number of new pilots straight from their operational training on the Hurricane, and one or two seasoned veterans from the Middle East. Nevertheless, we were pushed to have a Flight ready operationally for a detachment to the Arakan, by the end of the first week in January, to which the squadron had been committed. ... Our 'new blood' had made the squadron more cosmopolitan – we now had two Australian and three Canadian Sergeant Pilots with us who were a cheerful and very effective asset.

When 'A' Flight, under Colin Dunford-Wood, moved into its new home I went down with them to see the 'lie of the land', find out what was required and make my number with the army. Maungdaw was a newly laid strip on the edge of the jungle. It was a bare strip, formerly a 'paddy' field with a few recesses into the trees for dispersal. Flying distance from Ranchi via Chittagong was some 350 miles and required long range underwing tanks. During this short stay I also met Frank Carey again for he was in charge of the Fighter Wing now based there. ... This was close to the 14th (Indian) Division whom I visited to discuss Army Co-op. There was a mile wide flat coastal plain and any movement was overlooked by the enemy who, at this stage, did not have many troops on the ground. The aim of the operation therefore, was to clear the Mayu Peninsula of Japanese, and to secure both sides of the mountains, advancing to Donbeik at the southern tip, anticipating a later crossing of a narrow strait and on to Akyab. This operation proceeded successfully to a point some ten miles short of Donbeik, and on an early occasion, a Bren Gun Carrier on reconnaissance drove down to the tip of the peninsula without seeing any of the enemy. However, they had been observed by Japs who were hidden in jungle covered hillsides, so that a sizeable force of the opposition moved up by night and established strong defences in cleverly sited and impregnable bunkers. From here, the Japanese were able to repel any movement advancing down the coastal plain, and a long stalemate resulted which lasted until we were forced to withdraw at the onset of the heavy rain season in April 1943.

Visual Reconnaissance of the Mayu Peninsula

Daily operations commenced with almost continuous visual reconnaissance of both sides of the Mayu Peninsula, but little was seen – the enemy being clever at concealment, particularly in such jungly country. On two or three occasions in the early days, our sorties were intercepted by fighters operating in small numbers out of Akyab. By this time the Japanese were using the Zero (single-seat, low-wing monoplane) in Burma. Because of the lack of useful visual observation we used more photography, and produced a number of vertical overlaps and some mosaic cover of the peninsula, particularly of its southern tip. On one of these sorties we lost a most excellent and popular Sergeant Pilot who was 'jumped' by a Zero during a photographic run at 9,000ft. His 'Number Two' reported a sudden attack from above and gave a hair-raising account of the accuracy of the enemy pilot. One beam attack at full deflection on each of our aircraft shot the leader out of the sky in the middle of a photo run when he was necessarily flying 'straight and level'. The other Hurricane tried to engage the Jap but was unable to climb quickly enough. A few moments later his instrument panel and reflector sight disintegrated in a series of loud explosions. Our man dived away and was lucky to land safely at Bawli Bazar – a disused strip north of Maungdaw. He only had a scratch on his nose! It was clear by now that we had to be very watchful indeed, for the nearest hope of fighter cover for our operations was at Chittagong, a hundred miles to the north, where Frank Carey's squadrons were otherwise engaged. We did not enjoy very high priority! On another occasion I was flying with Dunford-Wood on a visual recce towards Akyab when we met a Blenheim haring along at low level chased by another Zero. The Jap broke off his attack when he saw us and, strangely, carried on flying northwards away from his base. We turned very quickly to try to catch him but lost all our speed. He was able to climb over the mountains and escape to the east. Although the 'Hurries' were fast enough to catch him up, we were a thousand feet below and I only managed an upward burst with no effect. We would have done better to climb at once without losing much speed – then we might have caught him on the way home. At least we helped the Blenheim! This was war in earnest again, and it had brought us quickly back to reality.

The Japanese maintain aggression

... On one or perhaps two days a week, the air over the Mayu Peninsula was full of very offensive Japanese in all kinds of fighters, bombers and reconnaissance 'what have you' aircraft, just looking for targets all day long. You could get away with this once, but I was sensitive to the danger of repeating the performance regularly; specially at the set hours at which lunch is eaten even in the front line. I had been caught napping myself at Rangoon and it was fresh in my memory that my regular daily 'first light' sorties over the Sittang had attracted the opposition with dire results.

My own private loo!

... A matter of less operational significance could have changed my war drastically. The flight commander and his trusty 'A' Flight team, with my comfort in mind at all times, had dug a private loo for me – the 'boss's Thunderbox'

No. 28 Squadron's delivery of their first five Lizzies, pre-war

which consisted of a deep hole, with polished seat above, surrounded by a cubicle of hessian duly supported by 'guy ropes'. It overlooked the mouth of the Naf River and out over the (thunderous) Bay of Bengal and was named 'Seaview' – (appropriately, with boarding house name-board), and was situated on a scrub covered hillock to the south of our camp – i.e. very exposed to any enemy incursions! There had been one or two minor skirmishes as night patrols by brave Japanese penetrated to the perimeter of the 14th Division HQ. encampment which was about half a mile to the north of us; so 'Seaview' was a veritable 'forward position'. It is little wonder that I suffered from a serious bout of lonely, claustrophobic apprehension at all times when 'communing with nature', and this was not conducive to proper completion of 'the necessary business'.

The Squadron is spread too thin

... Things got very busy; for in mid-January, 1943 we were ordered to send 'B' Flight (Flt Lt H.G.F. Larsen) to Imphal, on the border between Assam and Burma and now threatened by the Japanese. Imphal is some 300 miles north of Maungdaw. This spread us out even more and kept the Squadron Commander very busy; now that we had the Squadron Headquarters at Ranchi in Bihar province roughly 350 miles to the west of both operational detached flights, which were themselves 200 miles apart! ... So 28 Squadron truly became the front-line 'spearhead'; first to be back on Burmese soil and actively operating on two fronts, a year after the ignominious retreat from Rangoon. However, with the onset of the 'rainy season' in April, 1943, the 14th Division withdrew from the Arakan, and 'A' Flight returned to Ranchi.

'Why are you still here?'

Then came the blow that had to fall. Our busy one squadron station with its Wing Headquarters became a focus of attention and we received our first visit from the Commander-in-Chief, Sir Richard Pierse. During the proceedings he saw that I was wearing an India General Service Medal and asked how long I had been in the theatre, which by that time was a lot longer than most others. His words were ominous – 'Why are you still here?' – My answer was that I had been asked to stay, and the Group Commander, the popular Jack Hunter who was also present, confirmed this with some encouraging remarks. For reasons which are easily understood, the authorities newly arrived in the theatre were strongly of the opinion that pilots who had spent many years flying Wapitis and Audax on the Frontier were less likely to adapt to the demands of the deadly serious air war which had now descended upon us. ... A few weeks later on, a notice posting me to the Home Establishment arrived at Ranchi and my six months extension of tour was over. I was sad about this at the time for I had been with 28 for nearly four years!

The return journey to the UK

So it came to pass that I left India for the UK ... The voyage was in two parts. The first leg was aboard HT *Strathaird* of the Royal Mail Line which took us from Bombay to Durban. It sailed alone, not in convoy, and relied on speed and the tactical, variable 'zigzag' for safety from the submarine menace. There were occasional disturbing reports on the ship's News Sheet that we were being 'shadowed' but fortunately they came to nothing. I remember very little of note about this part of the journey, except that it got colder by the hour after we had been at sea for a day or two. We were still in our shorts and bush shirts with no warm clothes to wear, and there was an order out that we could not have access to our 'Wanted on Voyage' luggage until the end of the week. ... As we moved into seas where 'U' Boats were more prolific, there were many alerts and a 'boat drill' every day. ... We were lucky. After several sallies towards the South Pole the ship made its way northwards in its deliberately erratic fashion and arrived at the hot and sticky Freetown. We were moored outside the harbour and beset at once by crowds of ardent watermen in boats loaded down with fruit, unattractive wood carvings etc. They also took parties ashore. I have to say that I would not visit Freetown again unless obliged to do so, and am sure it hasn't changed much since that time. Last leg to Liverpool took us to the north and west up the Atlantic Ocean, approaching Liverpool via the near-Arctic through the Irish Sea from the north.

Home Again

On arriving at the capital, I remember being faced with navigating three trunks across London to the outer suburbs, and hailed a taxi for a four-mile ride from the nearest station to my home. 'Smog' happened at all times of the year in those times – it was dark, there was a 'black -out' and the visibility was five yards. The driver stopped after a mile-and-a-half, announced that he would drive no more and deposited my luggage on the pavement. There I was, abandoned with 200 lbs of trunks with a couple of miles to go, having come from Calcutta! Luckily, after a few choice comments about his 'war effort', I didn't have to wait long before a public spirited and friendly motorist delivered me all the way home, although it took the best part of two hours! My faith was restored.

In the next chapter you can read about Bertie's experiences at D-Day until the end of the Second World War in Europe.

Signals in the Far East

The following brief portraits are of Old Emanuels who served in various signals units in the Far East during the Second World War. Each would have had specific signalling training depending on the nature of the operations they were involved in. Signals units were required to keep lines of communications open between various sections of the Allied forces. It was a critical task during operations as headquarters were trying to map the situation on the ground especially during fast developing offensives.[1]

Horace James Cocks *(Emanuel 1925–1929)*

Horace, like many of his generation, had already felt the impact of the First World War due to the absence of his father who was killed on the Western Front in 1917. He joined the Middlesex Yeomanry at the outbreak of the Second World War and went to the Middle East in 1941 where he spent time with 8th OCTU (Officer Cadet Training Unit) Royal Corps of Signals. By March 1943 Horace held the rank of Captain. His two years in the Middle East had worn him down as is evident from a letter home where he wrote of the varied climate, mosquitoes, the ubiquitous sand and not being able to take leave in eight months. All this combined left him rather frustrated as he noted on 22 March 1943, 'This going home business seems to concern lots of people but me – quite a few are on their way – but I fear yours truly will not be one of the fortunates unless something wonderful happens. I can't even get leave – or a day off – so sometimes I think I shall go nuts...However although there is no bright side – imagine there is one and look at it. Have long forgotten the meaning of hearth and home.'[2]

Horace Cocks

By April 1943 Horace had arrived in India and, writing from HQ 1st Indian Air Formation Indian Command to his brother and sister-in-law, he described the obstacles he had to face in this new climate, such as learning Urdu and getting used to the humidity. Among other things he described these tasks as like 'working in a maze because everything is so new and different.' In a letter home to his mother on 24 May 1943 he wrote of his long voyage, 'The journey from Suez by boat took nearly 14 days. To Bombay was over 3000 miles. I spent a week in Bombay and then had a 1000 mile train journey to the other side of the country.' Being far from home and away for a number of years he wrote to reassure his mother, 'Keep smiling mother and don't worry – it's 3½ years out here now – time had passed quickly – so don't worry – it may be perhaps another two years – who knows?'

In November 1943 Horace wrote to his mother describing the conditions and environment he was working in including the disease and poverty he encountered but also his first encounter with the Japanese:

> Have been in the jungle areas and my company is now in a pleasant looking jungle glade. I say pleasant looking – because it isn't really. What with snakes, leeches and a host of various types of insects and river water which seem to cause everybody to have itch or ring-worm – it is not so good. Last night I was entertaining a leech – they do not hunt at all – but I found the thing this morning full of my blood – a grisly mess. Malaria seems to be common – but a new treatment and a daily tablet is making it less harmful. Monkeys abound about the place but do not come very near. The paddy fields (rice) are nearly ready for harvesting and the monsoon definitely has finished – so I suppose the fun and games will soon begin. The Jap has been over once or twice and bombed us – the damage being negligible. I saw several single dead beggar children – still clutching their beggars' cans – rather pitiful. I saw Jap equipment the other day – poor stuff compared with ours.

By July 1944 Horace wrote to his brother and sister-in-law expressing his displeasure at his location, '...my spirits will be at their best when I see Bombay from the blunt end of a ship...If I stay much longer...I shall probably go nuts and end up in front of a psychiatrist.' However Horace's frustrations were frequently levelled more at the Japanese than at his surroundings, providing revealing insights into the way men reacted to the daily proximity of death, 'Grub improves a great deal since the road was freed from "yellow bellies" but prospects of leave seem remote – Jap killing being the order of the day – burying of same being the order of some other day – a pity that vultures are not too common in these parts – but the crows put up a reasonably good show.'

Horace also wrote about the Bengal famine, the worst man-made disaster of Britain's rule in India. Due to administrative incompetence in not making adequate plans for the supply of food, in addition to what some historians have attributed as the 'racist' policies of the British Prime Minister, Winston Churchill, 1.5 million Bengalis were left to starve between 1943 and 1944 and the figure may well be in excess of 3 million once the figures of those who died as a result of famine-induced disease are included.[3] Horace wrote to his sister-in-law on 7 December 1944, 'Yes the famine in Calcutta was and is pretty awful – they used to put little red lamps at the heads of the corpses at night – the disposal squads had to be pretty slick to stop the jackals and vultures getting at them. It would not take long – I've known a colossal water buffalo be quite clean picked in a day.'

William Henry Attfield *(Emanuel 1936–1941)*

William played for the Second Eleven at Emanuel and was also a member of the JTC gaining his War Office Certificate 'A'.

William wrote this short account detailing his service record:

> I was called up in 1943 and after six weeks infantry training went to the Royal Corps of Signals. After training as a wireless and line operator I was posted to HMS *Dundonald*, a Royal Navy Combined Operations centre. Wireless communications were playing an important part in many of their naval landings. I went to the communication area for the landings in the South of France and after a short spell in Italy returned to Scotland on HMS *Royal Scotsman*.
>
> I was involved in training in the Royal Navy organisation of communications, in particular training in semaphore and lamp signalling. The ship's signal sections travelled to Falmouth and embarked on HMS *Persimmon*.

Defeated Japanese soldiers give a guard of honour for HMS Waveney at Saigon on 30 September 1945

> We then sailed to HMS *Braganza*, the Royal Navy depot at Bombay. After a short stay the unit joined HMS Waveney and landings in both Burma and Malaya were to follow. When the landings in Malaya were completed, the ship sailed to Saigon and HMS *Waveney* was the first British warship to dock at Saigon. A small unit of Royal Signals was attached to the Royal Naval Headquarters (RNHQ) to install and maintain a telephone exchange and internal telephone lines.
>
> Whilst in Saigon I witnessed the Japanese surrender. Being a Japanese navy garrison a Japanese admiral saluted and handed over his sword to the youngest sub-lieutenant at headquarters. With the arrival of French forces the Navy withdrew and I was posted to the 20th Indian Division Signals. This unit, soon after, returned to India and was disbanded. I then went to the 73 British Infantry Brigade where the Royal Signals were responsible for wireless communication for the four infantry battalions and the Calcutta police.

Bill Attfield at Emanuel in 2013

Landing Craft Assault (LCA) landing in Malaya

Allied Air-Drop of supplies, Operation Dracula, Rangoon

The brigade was engaged in anti-riot duties connected to Indian independence and partition. This was my last posting and I returned to Great Britain and was demobbed in 1947.

Bill Attfield in the Second World War

Dennis William Peck *(Emanuel 1934–1940)*

Dennis, who was a Signalman in the Royal Corps of Signals fought in some of the most vicious and significant battles of the Far East Campaign, including Kohima and Imphal. These battles, fought between March and July 1944, resulted in one of the largest defeats in the Japanese Army's history. The Allied victory had stopped Japanese forces holding the strategic positions of Imphal and Kohima which they had planned to use both as a spring-board for an attack on north-east India and to counter a British offensive to retake Burma. Dennis also spent time in Rangoon and was sent to Malaya when peace was declared before moving to Singapore, where he was the first English Officer to enter Changi Jail. He followed this by further communication work in Italy.

References

1 For more on the role of the Royal Corps of Signals in the Second World War see Major General R. F. H. Nalder, CB OBE, *The Royal Corps of Signals: A History of its Antecedents and Development (Circa 1800-1955)* (1958).

2 The Horace Cocks collection of letters is available from the Emanuel School Archive.

3 For a brief overview of the Bengal famine see Lizzie Collingham, *The Taste of War: World War Two and the Battle for Food* (2011), pp. 141-154.

In pursuit of Freedom D-Day 6 June 1944

Robert Edwin Fielder *(Emanuel 1935–1941)*

Robert Fielder came to Emanuel from Holden Street Boys' School in 1935. A talented musician he played the violin. Robert was also a member of Emanuel's Officers' Training Corps.

Robert was evacuated with the School to Petersfield at the outbreak of war and often wrote to his sister Margaret with news. From his early teens he was keen to do his bit for the war effort as is clear from a letter he sent on 4 January 1940 where he tells Margaret he had volunteered for fire fighting duties. In the same letter he discusses his experiences of being in the Emanuel OTC, 'So far I have got the trousers of my uniform. I have also been shooting on Churcher's range... The first five shots I missed the target altogether. I hit the target with four of the next five and three of the next five.' On leaving Emanuel he began training as a chartered accountant before being called up at the age of eighteen. He joined the Royal Army Service Corps (RASC). Normally four companies of the RASC supported a Division by keeping it supplied with ammunition, petrol and rations.

Robert Edwin Fielder

Robert was transferred to 716 Company (Airborne Light) which in 1943 became part of the 6th Airborne Division. It was soon designated for special operations in connection with Operation Overlord – the Allied invasion of Normandy in June 1944. It wasn't until the spring of 1944 that the commanders of the Airborne Division were given the code word Overlord. Lower ranks would have been kept in the dark until much nearer the time of the invasion. The Airborne element of the invasion had to be carried out in two parts for logistical reasons – one before the sea borne assault and the other for the evening of D-Day. Carried out in the early hours this was codenamed Operation Tonga which Robert would subsequently take part in.

Robert was in No. 1 Parachute Platoon 716 Airborne which jumped with the 5th Parachute Brigade. Robert had passed the required eight jumps in order to qualify for airborne operations.

On 30 May 1944, Robert wrote to his sister Margaret:

By the way, if and when the second front does start, will you please save the morning papers for me for the first fortnight or so and when you write again please send a couple of Penguin books, not too blood-thirsty.

We were inspected last week by the King and Queen and Princess Elizabeth...They looked like what I expected except Princess Elizabeth who was smaller than she seems to be in photographs.

I'm afraid that leave is out of the question for some time yet. I think however that it will be sooner than you will expect.

Robert Fielder in Airborne uniform

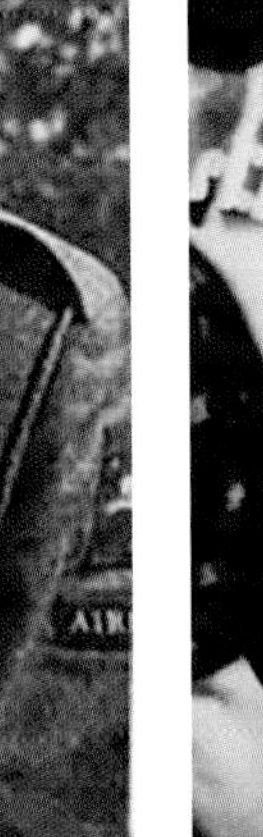

Robert's sister (far left) and mother meeting Montgomery in Normandy after the Second World War

In the early hours of 6 June No. 1 platoon took off in a Stirling aircraft from RAF Keevil. 5th Parachute Brigade's objective that day was to support Major Howard's Oxford and Buckinghamshire Light Infantry glider-borne assault team who were tasked with the capture of the Bénouville and Ranville Bridges which crossed the Caen Canal and the river Orne. 5th Parachute Brigade was also tasked with clearing German anti-airborne defences. Members of 716 Company RASC were tasked with gathering the various supplies being dropped by bombers and transport aircraft and distributing them to the fighting units.

However, on that fateful dark morning Robert, who was designated number twelve to jump, opened his parachute over Ranville but as he descended it caught on telephone wires. As he hung on the wall of the Chateau below he was shot by German troops. A French Countess recovered Robert's body and covered him with a shroud, an act for which she was later awarded the Croix de Guerre, a French military decoration. Robert was later buried in Ranville War Cemetery. He was only 19 years old when he was killed on D-Day. Robert's family made a number of pilgrimages to visit his grave after the war and met Richard Gale who commanded the 6th Airborne Division as well as Field Marshal Montgomery who commanded 21st Army Group and who developed the battleplan for the Normandy Campaign.

Robert's mother standing at Robert's grave in Ranville War Cemetery

---

References

1 For an overview of 6th Airborne's part in Operation Overlord see R. N. Gale, *With the 6th Airborne Division in Normandy* (1948).

David Warren wearing his medals including the DSO, MC and Second World War Campaign medals

Brigadier David Warren
DSO, OBE, MC *(Emanuel 1930–1937)*

David Warren had an exceptional school career being a Prefect, Captain of Wellington and former Captain of the Junior House Raglan. He was also a brilliant sportsman who won his full rugby colours in the 1936–1937 season and was Honorary Secretary of the Rugby Club.

Perhaps David was destined for the services as he had an outstanding record in the Emanuel School OTC in which he was awarded his War Office Certificate 'A' in November of 1935 and the rank of CQMS. He was also a brilliant marksman being Captain of Shooting. David competed in many Surrey events and was awarded his Surrey Shooting Colours in 1936 and Surrey Colts Shooting Colours in 1937 and was part of the London Public Schools Shooting VIII team. When he left School he was commissioned in the Supplementary Reserve of Officers, East Lancashire Regiment.

Later in the war and by 1943 promoted to the rank of Captain, David took part in beach landing assaults both during the Italian Campaign and on D-Day. David landed with the 1st Battalion Hampshire Regiment on the east coast of the Pachino Peninsula on 10 July 1943 as part of Operation Husky – the Allied assault to capture Sicily. Securing Sicily was essential to the Allied plans for the invasion of Italy. In July 1943 the Italians were still members of the Axis alliance and were guarding the beaches on which David landed. Of that landing he remembered:

> We were on the *Otranto* and sailed with this enormous convoy and were at sea for three or four days wondering whether we would be spotted by the Germans. We had the usual briefings in detail and models of where we were going to land. Everything went well except the wind seemed to increase as we got nearer to Sicily. On the night of the landing it was quite rough. We should have anchored about five miles off the coast of Sicily, off Cape Passero, and we were due to land at a little fishing village called Marsamemi, but the wind was blowing quite hard and so there's always something that goes wrong. The arrangements were that a submarine should go in at about last light and fix a position with a small buoy, a sonar buoy, so the ships would anchor in exactly the right place because they could pick up that buoy. In fact what happened is that we anchored two miles further out than we should have done and the significance of that was that we had an even longer run in the landing craft... battered around by the waves. I recollect we were wearing our usual khaki drill, but with the spray coming over one soon got quite cold and it was a long way in. People were being seasick and so on.
>
> But when we got to the beach I remember that the final part of the landing craft opened up and as the senior officer in charge I considered it my duty to go out first. Unfortunately when I got outside, I caught my foot in a pothole. The beach consisted of volcanic lava and I fell over and cut my knee quite badly. The soldiers behind me thought I had been shot and weren't anxious to get out. I was angry with them and shouted at them to get out and get on with it, which they did. We had to attack a position which was right on the beach. Incidentally, all the enemies on the beaches of Sicily were Italians and it wasn't expected that we would meet any Germans and we didn't. So we went off to attack this position and the Italians were not really full of fight because when we got to the position, I remember there was this sentry who was standing silhouetted against the skyline and was shot without any difficulty. When we got into position the Italians offered no defence whatsoever. They were anxious to get their hands up and get out of it.[1]

David Warren (third from left) with the Emanuel OTC Ashburton Team, 1935

The fighting in Sicily only lasted a few weeks but there were several bloody battles and one particular problem was booby traps as David recounted, 'The Germans booby-trapped the dead by putting an explosive charge behind the head with wire in front of the face. This was very grisly and greatly disliked by our soldiers. It was a very bloody battle.'

After the Allies secured Sicily David was involved in the invasion of Italy with "C" Company, 1st Battalion Hampshire Regiment. The 1st Hampshires, as part of 231st Brigade were to make an assault at Porto San Venere, with the idea that they could get behind the enemy as the 5th Division, who had landed further South, made their way up to meet them. The initial plans for a landing at Gioia had been cancelled due to the outbreak of a violent storm and by the time this passed the 5th Division's progress necessitated that the 231st Brigade land further North. So on the morning of 8 September 1943 David and the 1st Battalion Hampshires landed at Porto San Venere but not all went to plan. They were landed on the wrong beach and as soon as they landed the landing craft went astern off the beach and left before the Battalion had fully disembarked, leaving them without a full supply of mortars that David had been allocated for the landing. David later recalled what happened that morning:

> We used vessels called Landing Craft Infantry which was bigger than a landing craft and could not be transported on a ship, it had to go on its own. We got on board the landing craft... on the beaches of Sicily, near Messina and set sail in the dark for Pizzo and Porto San Venere. When we landed the following morning... we realised we weren't in the right place. So after landing we started off on the long walk towards the final objective and as we were getting nearer the road which ran from southern Italy up towards the north we heard vehicles approaching. This was quite early in the morning, six or seven am. We were under the cover of olive trees and could see the road, and we saw it was a German column of vehicles and they were blissfully unaware that we were there.
>
> We opened fire on the Germans, particularly with our hand held anti-tank weapons – a weapon called a PIAT. The Germans tried to dismount from their vehicles and became a very good target and we had a short, sharp battle with them and fortunately I had a mortar... and as they tried to go up the hill so we mortared them. We captured quite a lot of them on the road and I remembered that incident because my Company HQ was on the road... and one or two of [the captured Germans] were very truculent, they were spitting at us and using some filthy British language they had picked up and they were very insulting and I thought this was extraordinary because they must have realised that this wasn't the moment to antagonise the British because we might have turned on them and... one or two of the soldiers were inclined to do just that. We continued to climb up the hill – we had to get to the top of it – our objective and we had inflicted casualties on them because we found some bodies of the Germans up the hill that had been killed or wounded by our mortar. We got to the top of the hill at about nine or ten o'clock in the morning where we proceeded to dig in. We were overlooking the sea and looking forward... in the westerly direction we could see a cemetery. We were able to dig and prepare ourselves in a defensive position. Later in the day we had these unfortunate attacks that occur in war [a friendly fire attack]. We were attacked by American Warhawks who must have mistaken us. So after getting a strutting up from them we suddenly observed some movement in this cemetery and we could see German troops clearly getting ready for an attack.

At that point the Battalion had the advantage of higher ground and opened fire on the Germans. As a result they were able to break up the German troops before they were able to attack. The Germans withdrew and the Battalion never saw them again. The Division proceeded to make its way to Salerno to support the Allied Divisions who were fighting there but after two days the 231st Brigade was told they were to leave for Sicily before returning to England.

David was awarded an immediate Military Cross during the invasion of Italy in 1943. His MC Citation read:

> On 8 September 1943, at the landing at Porto San Venere, Capt. Warren commanded one of the assault Companies. Advancing with great speed up difficult hilly country, he cut the main road and surprised a column of enemy Army Fighting Vehicles. Taking command at once of the first available sections, he personally led an immediate attack. He was successful in killing a number of Germans and destroying several vehicles. By his promptness and eagerness for a fight he set a fine example and in his personal leadership showed a complete disregard for his own safety.

After serving in Italy David Warren returned to England in November 1943 with the 1st Battalion, Hampshire Regiment and by D-Day had been promoted to the rank of Major. The battalion did not expect to be part of the main assault on the continent but with changing circumstances came the news that the 1st Battalion as part of the 50th (Northumbrian) Division, having already completed two assault landings, in Sicily and in Italy, was now to be part of the main Allied invasion force. In the spring of 1944 the battalion practised seaborne operations at the Combined Training Centre at Inverary. They were finally stationed at a camp between Lyndhurst and Beaulieu. They practised embarkation exercises on their assault ship around the Isle of Wight and landing exercises at Studland Bay. When David was interviewed in 1993 he remembered that 'We had marvellous models – they were very good indeed, they had all the information and intelligence about the enemy.'

David Warren was awarded the Distinguished Service Order for the part he played in the invasion of Normandy. His citation records that he 'led his Company on to attack the defended houses and pillboxes covering the beach with great dash and determination' and 'throughout the operation ... showed the greatest courage and leadership.'

The experiences of David Warren on D-Day and the first few weeks in the Liberation of Europe

We up anchored at about 5.30pm in the afternoon in the Solent. Not too rough, you could see other ships moving. You could see the minesweepers which led to the convoy ahead.

I remember standing on deck admiring the scenery and it seemed unrealistic that we were going to war in the morning.

We got up at about three in the morning to get ready. It was difficult to get to sleep, one was a bit apprehensive. We hadn't got into the rhythm of war, though we had all been in that before. Once you get into it you can sleep quite easily, in fact you can sleep very easily because you are always very tired, but we weren't all that tired. I remember... going over in my mind again and again the various things I had to remember for tomorrow.

In the morning we were called up on the tannoy to get up and we got up and the ship had arranged for us to have a very good breakfast indeed probably the best they could produce. Then it was time to get down to the troop decks to join your serial for the embarkation and I remember going down there and checking through the equipment and stuff we had to carry up and put in the LCA the landing craft we used. We had put some of the heavier stuff in the LCA the previous day. People were curiously quiet that morning. The sea was distinctly rougher. It was a rather grey morning. We got into the landing craft at 5.30, because we had to get the landing craft lowered into the sea and then we would circle about while we formed up in our flotillas. It was just about first light and soon after first light suddenly this enormous armada of Naval ships... opened fire with a terrific noise, I think we passed the cruiser HMS *Ajax*, a six-inch gun cruiser and she let go just as we were near her, with a terrific noise. We bumped around in the landing craft while we formed up for the run in and I recollect that we had had tea and rum put in for people to drink going in but a lot of people were feeling seasick and I don't think tea and rum was the best thing for people feeling seasick, fortunately I don't suffer from it but we had to cope with it. Apart from our equipment... we had these Mae Wests which were blown up and were supposed to keep us afloat if we got hit and had to go into the sea.

We had the run-in in the rather grey light of the morning and a very noisy morning too and it was very impressive the number of ships which were formed up off the Normandy Coast. It was terrific, I had never seen anything like it before.

The next horror

We knew a great deal about the beach on which we were going to land. We had all sorts of air photographs taken so we knew what it was like. We had the model, but going in I suddenly realised that with the bombardment there was such a lot of dust and some fires and smoke... that it was difficult to see where we wanted to land exactly. We knew exactly where we wanted to land but to pick it out was difficult. We went on and we finally drew very near the beach. My landing craft bumped into a runnel – a small sandbank... the doors opened in the front and we were being shot at and there was the odd bit of mortar fire and stepping out you suddenly stepped into the water which came right up to your chest, very cold water that morning so we had to struggle through this although we didn't have any casualties from drowning on my landing craft. They did occur with shorter men because we were carrying a great deal in terms of ammunition, mortar bombs... far more than for a normal battle.

I went in up to my chest. One of the great things that is always impressed upon you about an amphibious landing is get up the beach as fast as you can, to get away from the landing craft... that is... what one did. I could see the beach and there was the odd specialist tank stuck on the beach. I think there was one on fire which had been sent in ahead. Their job was to make gaps through the mines and the wire at the top of the beach. One of the difficulties that we had was that we expected to find a gap on the beach to go through but it was not there. They had not been able to get up the beach. This particular beach was enfiladed, that is there was a German position at the end of it and they could rake the whole of the beach with fire and there was also a gun which appeared to be some form of anti-tank gun and that of course was in concrete and steel. This position at Le Hamel where we landed was to cause us a great deal of trouble... it had excellent fields of fire and the Germans... did not show much sign of giving up. When we got up the beach I realised that we should have to gap our way through ourselves – cut our way through the mines and the wire. Meanwhile the casualties were piling up because the fire was very strong from the Germans and it was raking along the top of the beach where people were trying to get. It was while we were trying to gap our way off the beach that I saw the Commanding Officer Colonel Nelson Smith limping rather badly. He had been hit by a piece of mortar bomb as he got out his landing craft and he obviously wasn't going to go very far. It was there that he told me to take over.

I was suddenly faced with this problem of coping with a very difficult situation because we wanted to get off the beach and our plan was rather geared to getting off the beach and getting round to the back of things.

David at this point knew that one Company which had been directed over a cliff top was proceeding well but "A" Company were not, as he remembered:

I learned that "A" Company... should have landed right on top of this position at Le Hamel. They would have scaled up the sea wall and silenced it. In fact they didn't and there were very heavy casualties... they really ceased to exist as a Company. We incorporated all the people we could find and told them to join up "C" Company and I decided that we must deal with this position overlooking Le Hamel.

By this time we had been able to gap our way off the beach and we got over the mines... and there I met a tank which was called an AVRE – a Royal Engineer assault tank specially equipped. This particular one had a mortar-like gun on it called a petard which fired a large bomb. I spoke to the commander of the tank and told him I wanted him to support the attack on Le Hamel. The tank came forward and it fired the bomb onto the building [an old hospital which had been reinforced] and when he did that we assaulted it and went inside and it was silenced and that was a great relief to all concerned because there were a lot of landing craft which were having difficulty on our beach. They could then come ashore and the beach masters could get things organised rather better. Meanwhile the fighting was going on just east of Arromanches and also at the back of Le Hamel. There were odd Germans everywhere. At Hamel west there was a position we had to capture. When we got there the Germans put up no fight at all, they came out with their hands up.

We continued on with the battle and once the position east of Arromanches was secured, I decided that we had better get into Arromanches. That was very important as we all now know the Mulberry [a floating temporary harbour] was going to be built there. So we went into Arromanches. There was no resistance in the town at all... so we secured that. Time passed incredibly quickly. It was somewhere near seven or eight o'clock in the evening and so I arranged to secure Arromanches from a counterattack and to keep an eye out for the Americans who were supposed to link up with us from their beaches further west. In fact we never saw them. We didn't connect with them for about two days.

I established the battalion quarters in Le Hamel in some outbuildings of a farm. By this time it was dark. It was necessary to give some orders out for the following day which I did which in particular concerned patrols at first light out from the area of Arromanches going west where there were some various little villages, Tracy-Sur-Mer was one and Saint-Côme-de-Fresné which we were supposed to clear. Then about two in the morning the Brigade Commander arrived and he gave out some orders and told us the next day we would be advancing on Bayeux. The following day the whole of the sea... was full of ships and ships coming in and out and the first bits and pieces of the Mulberry were coming in to Arromanches. We started off on the road to Bayeux... where we had practically no opposition. By the end of the day we were very nearly at Bayeux and we were told to stop which we did and we waited for further orders and they came along from the Brigade Commander. We were told to advance south of Bayeux and it was reported that there was little sign of the enemy in Bayeux. It was near there the next day when we bumped into the enemy. This is where we started very severe fighting south of Bayeux across the road between Bayeux and Tilly and we took up our positions there after a bit of a scrap with the Germans. We were settling down now to what I call battlefield routine – casualties were happening... everybody was getting acclimatised to living at war.

We were at a place called Bernières Bocage. It was being mortared and shelled. We took up positions there. We weren't quite sure where the Germans were – they were very active, particularly their mortars. We had to cope with digging-in there while the enemy shelled us and mortared us and made life as unpleasant as they could. We knew that we had to advance and sure enough we got our orders to advance on the following day to a crossroads which was straight ahead of us called La Senaudière. We had some reports from patrols that at the crossroads they had seen some Panther tanks. It was clearly defended, so we started off on this battle and we fought our way towards the crossroads at La Senaudière. In support of us we had a troop of what they called Crocodiles. That was a Churchill tank with a flame thrower

David Warren in later years

> on it. The troop commander of the Crocodile misread his map. He didn't come to the forming up position of the Hampshires but he proceeded to motor straight on to the crossroads and suddenly saw these Panther tanks and with some presence of mind he squirted them with his flame throwers and destroyed two of them. This didn't please the Brigadier very much... that he had lost his way... but as far as we were concerned we were quite glad to hear that two of the German tanks had gone. That battle was successful. We took up our positions around that crossroads at La Senaudière and we realised that the German Division we were fighting, by this time, was called the Panzer Lehr Division... filled with a number of young zealots for the Nazi cause. They fought with great determination and they proceeded to make everything very difficult and they laid mines and booby traps in a number of places.
>
> By this time the 50th Division was astride the road between Bayeux and Tilly and the next battle that we fought was for a place called Hottot which was south of that road. It was strongly held by the Germans. We started on this battle to get Hottot which was a very tough battle and we incurred a number of casualties including myself later in the day. On the evening of the first battle of Hottot I found myself going off under the orders of the Commanding Officer to show a company commander where he was to put his company. I remember crossing a track with him and suddenly there was a terrific flash, I didn't hear anything... the next thing I knew I was waking up as it were lying on the track that we had just crossed and I couldn't move and what's more I couldn't see and I couldn't hear and I was only conscious of one thing, I knew that the tanks were moving up on this track and that was at the forefront of my mind that I was hoping that someone was to pull me away. I didn't want to get run over by a tank. By this time it was half dark. All was well and somebody did pull me away. I was evacuated as a casualty and the next day I found myself in England flown out by a Dakota.

David was hit by a booby trap. He was temporarily blinded and had incurred a damaged ear, and several bits of shrapnel from the booby trap had lodged themselves into parts of his body and his head. David never returned to Europe as the Board would not pass him as fit due to his damaged ear.[2]

David's war ended there but his military career continued. In 1946 he went to Sudan as a Staff Officer with the Sudan Defence Force. In 1961 he was appointed to command 1st Royal Hampshires when they were in Jamaica and was on the first British aircraft to land on Honduras as part of a relief effort after it had been struck by a hurricane. In 1964 he was awarded an O.B.E. Appointments followed as an area commander in South Arabia; Commander of the Federal Regular Army in the Eastern Protectorate and Head of the British Military Mission in Libya in 1967 until his retirement in 1971 when he was appointed Colonel of The Royal Hampshire Regiment. David died in 2001.

References

1 The original interview conducted by Conrad Wood with David John Warren can be found in the IWM Collection, Catalogue Number 13041, 02/09/1993.

2 TS of an interview by Conrad Wood with David John Warren, IWM Catalogue Number 12962, 18/01/1993.

Major Urwin 'Ned' Thornburn MC, TD, MA

(Emanuel 1924–1933)

Urwin Thornburn (known as Ned) had an illustrious School career. His passions at Emanuel included cricket and acting. He was Lieutenant of the School which meant he was effectively Deputy Captain, Captain of Clyde House, a member of the Dramatic Society and Sub-Editor of *The Portcullis*.

He was awarded his First Eleven colours and was an active member of the OTC holding the rank of CQMS. In 1928 Emanuel's Dramatic Society performed Bernard Shaw's *Androcles and the Lion* and a commentator in *The Portcullis* noted, 'who would have thought Thornburn could be such a perfect shrew?'[1]

On leaving Emanuel Ned was awarded a choral scholarship to Corpus Christi, Cambridge where he was awarded an honours degree in history. His chosen profession was teaching which, apart from his wartime service, he remained in throughout his life. Before the Second World War broke out he taught at Rugby and as senior history master at Wrekin College. In post-war years he returned to Wrekin before being headmaster of Bridport Grammar School in Dorset where he oversaw the School's transition to a comprehensive school renamed Colfox School. Ned remained as headmaster for 23 years before retiring in 1979. Teaching young people after the War gave him pause for thought as he recalled in a volume of his trilogy of the 4th Battalion King's Shropshire Light Infantry (KSLI), 'As I got back to my peacetime job as a schoolmaster I always had a number of my Sixth Formers who were already over 18. When talking with them I used to think of Lieutenant Wilson, who was called on to shoulder the responsibility of leading men into battle at the same age as they are now.'[2] However, not every headmaster could claim to have played a pivotal role in the liberation of Europe but for Ned this was a true fact from a remarkable career. Ned was also a devout Christian who firmly believed in God's providence in every aspect of his life. Indeed, Ned wrote about it often as he reflected on the war years and on trying to answer one of the most searching questions during his battle experiences – 'Why was my life spared and my friend's taken?' Ned's answer was:

> There is no quick answer and no obvious one. For my own part I would say this: it is not for man to question the workings of God or Providence. God will call us to His presence when He is ready to receive us, and if He chooses to spare us for the time being, it can only be because He considers that there is some useful service which we can still render to mankind.[3]

Ned Thornburn

Ned commanded "D" Company, 4th Battalion, KSLI from 13 June 1944 to February 1945. In retirement he wrote a three-volume account of the part played by the 4th Battalion in the North-West Europe Campaign – *In Normandy, First into Antwerp*, and *After Antwerp*. Ned wrote the accounts with a clear intention to remember those who fell as they fought together:

Ned Thornburn playing the leading lady (third from left) in the Emanuel School production of Androcles and the Lion, 1929

> My own escape from assured death on the slopes at Aubusson, and the loss of Buster, Walford, Peter Garrett and so many other great-hearted companions has left me with the realisation that I owe it to them to preserve their memory for posterity.

In 1938 Ned accepted a Territorial Commission in the Wrekin College OTC and at the outbreak of the War he was mobilised serving with 4th Battalion of the KSLI, which was the regiment's senior Territorial battalion. It was initially part of 159th (Welsh Border) Brigade in 1939. The Brigade was transferred in 1942 to 11th Armoured Brigade which fought in North-West Europe from 1944 to 1945. But the men of the 4th Battalion were not career soldiers and this is an important distinction to which Ned alluded:

> The Territorial is a civilian citizen who abandoned his life's vocation, at which he was probably very efficient, to help his country in a crisis. He is therefore by definition dedicated, and when he applies himself to a new discipline he is likely to be pretty competent, and will learn quickly from experience.[4]

Ned saw action in some of the fiercest fighting in the Allied drive to defeat Germany between 1944 and 1945, including in the battles for Hill 112, Caen, Antwerp and Asten. "D" Company sailed for Normandy on 13 June 1944, a week after the D-Day landings. Ned remembers landing on the beaches the next morning, '...the most amazing sight – hundreds of craft of all shapes and sizes thronging the coastline as far as the eye could see ... No finer morale booster could have been conceived than this display of British command of the sea.'[5] One of the overriding problems for the Allied command was that Germany did not just surrender with their hands up. Hitler threw everything at the Allies as they fought, stage by stage, on their way to Germany, a fact Ned commented upon, 'it cannot be denied that our British Generals always seem to have been taken by surprise at the unexpected depth of the German defensive positions which had to breached.'[6]

Emanuel boys in the vanguard

Second in command of "D" Company 4th KSLI, until he commanded "A" Company in 1945, was OE Reginald John Harrison (Emanuel 1927–1935). He fought alongside Ned for most of the Campaign in North-West Europe a fact noted in the Autumn Term *Portcullis* of 1944:

> Major U. Thornburn and Capt. R. J. Harrison 4/KSLI, B.L.A., were well up with the forward troops in the sweep across Northern France, and it was their company which liberated Vimy Ridge, concerning which a paragraph appeared in several English papers, based on an interview Thornburn had with a Canadian war correspondent. Whilst on 48 hours' leave in Antwerp, Thornburn met Wing Commander A. S. [Bertie] Mann, DFC.[7]

Reginald Harrison, like Ned, was a Lieutenant of Emanuel. He was also Captain of Drake, Secretary of the Rugby and played with the First Fifteen in addition to being a Sergeant in the OTC achieving his War Certificate 'A.'

Ned remembered Reginald during Operation Epsom when the battalion were forming a bridgehead at the village of Baron after the crossing of the river Odon. Reginald came under artillery fire as Ned recalls:

Ned Thornburn (first from right) and Reg Harrison (circled), Speech Day 1932

Reg Harrison (left) and Ned Thornburn (right), 'D' Coy. 4th Battalion KSLI

> Reggie had set off in the direction of the Herefords for some reason or the other. On his way back he heard a Minnie [trench mortars] coming in his direction. He was a pretty cool customer and would normally have ignored it, but he reckoned that this one was going to be a bit close, so he decided to go flat. Just as well that he did! The six Minnie bombs exploded in a circle right round him – and he hadn't a scratch to show for it! 'Now', he said, when he got back to the Company, 'we know where we stand with these blighters. Go flat and you will probably get away with it.'

A year later and Commanding "A" Company, 4th Battalion KSLI, Reginald, now a Major, was killed in action during the Battle of the Rhineland as the Allies prepared to force a crossing of the Rhine. "A" Company were riding on the tanks of the Royal Scots Greys on 1 March 1945 heading for the hamlet of Maeshof. The ground was waterlogged and the leading tanks became bogged down. Ned explained Reginald's fate:

> "A" Company now dismounted and continued the advance on foot. The shell fire was now increasing in intensity. A group of farm buildings materialised and the leading platoon moved forward and cleared them, but immediately the enemy brought down heavy mortar fire augmented by intense and well-directed machine gun fire from well-prepared positions. Major Harrison, never one to look for cover, went forward to the platoon and was promptly killed outright. Only a week or two earlier he had heard that his wife had been killed in London by a V2 rocket.

For a full account of the pivotal role Ned Thornburn played in the North-West Europe Campaign one should refer to his magisterial three-volume account of his battalion, but two incidents stand out among Ned's many brave actions. The first was during the assault on Antwerp for which Ned was recommended for the award of the Military Cross. (Ned was in fact recommended twice for the MC and awarded once). Ned, leading "D" Company, played a crucial role in the capture of Antwerp's German Commander on 4 September 1944. Part of the MC recommendation reads:

> On 4 September 1944, during the attack on Antwerp, Thornburn's Company was ordered to capture the building used by the enemy as its Kommandantur. This building was strongly defended by enemy infantry. The enemy fought well, but this Officer led his Company with magnificent dash and got a platoon into the building. Eventually, after 80 minutes fighting, seven officers and 85 men surrendered to Major Thornburn. Throughout this action Major Thornburn was continually to the fore, leading and encouraging his men.[8]

Ned and Dora Thornburn on their wedding day in 1945

The second incident, for which Ned won his MC, was the part he played in the assault on the town of Asten, south-east of Eindhoven in the Netherlands, as the 4th Battalion supported the eastern flank of General Montgomery's plan to seize the bridges over the river Mass at Grave, the river Waal at Nijmegen and the river Neder Rhine at Arnhem (Operation Market Garden) in order to avoid crossing the Rhine – essentially a short-cut to defeating Germany by Christmas 1944. Operation Market Garden was unsuccessful, but the fighting was hard and Ned's part in it a significant one. His MC citation reads:

> On 22 September, 1944, his Company was the leading Company in the assault on Asten across the Bois-le-Duc canal. The bridgehead made during the night proved to be only fifty yards deep, and the exit from it was under considerable enemy small arms and mortar fire. The enemy were determined, and fighting stubbornly.
>
> The leading Platoon crossed the bridge but was held up by heavy fire from buildings on the far bank. Major Thornburn, with complete disregard for his personal safety, went forward and reorganised the attack so successfully that the momentum was restored. Out of these buildings this Company succeeded in capturing some fifty prisoners, in addition to inflicting numerous casualties.
>
> The advance continued, the Company's objective being the centre of Asten. As the leading Platoon reached the outskirts of the town, they were held up by heavy small arms fire and, by his outstanding example of personal bravery and leadership, he exhorted his men into the attack. The enemy opposition was overcome and the objective captured at great loss to the enemy.
>
> This operation was so successfully carried out that the remainder of the town was quickly cleared by the other Rifle Companies. Major Thornburn's Company was therefore virtually responsible for the capture of Asten, a vital road centre on the line of advance, and one which had been fiercely contested by the enemy. In this operation some seven officers and 150 other rank prisoners were taken, in addition to the numerous enemy killed and wounded.
>
> Major Thornburn's superb courage and leadership were an inspiration to all. He is always in the forefront of the battle, leading and encouraging his men.[9]

Ned was a humble man and noted that although he led his Company, 'they had to deliver the goods', but without a good Commander companies can so easily lose their way; "D" Company had one of the best in Ned Thornburn.

Whilst in a Brussels hospital with diphtheria in November 1944 Ned met Dora West, a senior member of the Queen Alexandra's Imperial Military Nursing Service, and they married in 1945 in Wrekin College's chapel. Dora was awarded four military medals in the War. She travelled to Normandy with 108 British General Hospital and nursed both casualties from Normandy and the North-West Europe Campaign in addition to 90 German prisoners of war and her future husband.

In February 1945 Ned was injured when he was hit by a shell fragment during the Battle of the Rhineland, but thankfully recovered.

Ned never forgot his experiences and returned many times to the places he had fought including on the 40th Anniversary of the liberation of Amiens and Antwerp. Ned died in 1994 and in 1998 his wife and family attended a ceremony held in the small town of Aubusson, Normandy which renamed its main square *Place Major Ned Thornburn*. Today Ned's uniforms can be seen in the Emanuel School Archive to which they were kindly donated by his family.

References

1 *The Portcullis*, Lent Term 1929, p. 52.
2 Major Ned Thornburn, *After Antwerp: The Long Haul to Victory – The Part Played by 4th Bn King's Shropshire Light Infantry in the Overthrow of the Third Reich, September 1944 to May 1945* (1993), p. 75.
3 From a Remembrance assembly given by Ned's grandson, Daniel Thornburn, to his pupils. A copy is available to consult in the Emanuel School Archive.
4 Major Ned Thornburn, *The 4th KSLI in Normandy* (1990), p. 8.
5 Ibid. p. 11.
6 Ibid. p. 22.
7 *The Portcullis*, Autumn Term 1944, p. 15. Also see Ned Thornburn's account of Vimy Ridge in Major Ned Thornburn, *First into Antwerp: The Part played by 4th Bn King's Shropshire Light Infantry in the Liberation of the City in September, 1944* (1987), p. 12.
8 *First into Antwerp*, p. 8. For a full account of Ned's role in Antwerp see his *First into Antwerp* (1987).
9 *After Antwerp* (1993), pp. 26-27.

A Bridge Too Far! The story of a Welsh Guardsman in North West Europe

Allan Francis Charles Barnes *(Emanuel 1935–1943)*

In 2011 Daniel Kirmatzis interviewed Allan Barnes about his experiences during the Second World War.[1] In an earlier chapter we learnt how Allan had been evacuated with the School to Petersfield. Allan left School in the summer of 1943 and instead of going straight to university he made the decision to join the Army. He enlisted in the Welsh Guards and served with the 1st Battalion during the North-West European Campaign from July 1944 to the end of the War in Europe.

Before leaving for the continent in July 1944 tragedy struck in England. Allan lost a number of friends in the Welsh Guards Training Battalion when a V1 [Vergeltungswaffe 1] rocket, which was a pilotless 'flying bomb' launched from the French and Dutch coasts, landed at the Metropolitan Police's Sports Ground at Imber Court, East Molesey on 30 June 1944, where the Guards were holding an athletics meeting. Nineteen Welsh Guardsmen lost their lives that day, an event Allan remembered vividly:

> So we had our sports day at the Metropolitan Training Ground at Imber Court and at the back of the building area there was a 440 yard track and we did all our normal sports activities on and around the track. At one end of the track was the high jump set-up and I went along there to do the high jump, along with a lot of other people. I was very good friends with a chap called Ian Glen and he in fact cleared the height on the high jump and I didn't, so I was banished and I walked off to the other end of the circuit, and he stayed there to take the next level of high jump. At that time a V1 came over and it dived and went straight into the middle of the high-jump area so he was killed along with about 20 people in the Welsh Guards. I had gone to the other end of the

Allan Barnes with the Welsh Guards Training Battalion c1944 – Allan's friend Ian Glen (second from left, back row)

circuit and I laid on the ground when I saw this plane coming in and I was completely uninjured so by beating me in the high jump he really saved my life.[2]

The Allied advance across Europe after D-Day was marked by a number of setbacks as the decisive victory, as hoped for by Bernard Law Montgomery [promoted to Field Marshal 1 September 1944], proved elusive in the last months of 1944. German resistance proved stronger than some Allied Commanders had anticipated. Field Marshal Montgomery's plan known as 'Operation Market Garden' aimed to secure a number of bridges across the Rhine and Maas rivers. Once the bridges were secured by airborne and infantry it was hoped they could turn in towards the Ruhr and defeat Germany by Christmas 1944 but this ambitious plan proved to be, in the now famous phrase attributed to Lieutenant General Browning, a 'bridge too far', and, at great cost, Montgomery's plan did not achieve its desired outcome. Historian John Buckley refers to the plan as 'poorly conceived, ill-considered and deeply flawed ... which stood little chance of success before it had even begun.'[3] Allan Barnes experienced it at close hand.

Interview

Daniel: Can you tell me what training you did when you joined?

Allan Barnes: The Guards Depot at Caterham was the starting point for all the Guards Regiments and there we trained in the usual weapons, mainly the rifle and an awful lot of arms drill and so on, which was largely a waste of time when it came to fighting against the German Army, but the Guards thought the Guards Drill was terribly important so we would have been very good at doing Trooping the Colour but that wouldn't have helped us much in fighting the German Army.

Daniel: So how long were you training for before you were sent out to France?

Allan Barnes: We did our initial training which I think was six weeks, it might have been two months. We were then transferred to the Welsh Guards Training Battalion and the Training Battalion had taken over the whole of Sandown Park Race Course and there we did much more training, we certainly did a lot of physical training because one thing that the army did to its recruits was to make everybody very very fit because we obviously had to walk for miles all day carrying a lot of equipment when we were in action so we needed to be very very fit. We certainly went to an open air swimming pool at Hampton Court and in the early part of the year it was a bit cool but we still had to swim one length of the pool because they said this was the equivalent of having to cross a river in winter so those of us who could swim well would dive in and take a few strokes and come out at the other end but those who couldn't swim had to climb in and then pull themselves along by the rails on the side of the pool and get out at the other end.

Daniel: When did you know you were going to be called out to France?

Allan Barnes: Originally I was drafted to go to Italy but at the last minute I had tonsillitis which only lasted a couple of days but they crossed my name off the list and put somebody else on so I was then available to go to Normandy instead of going to Italy where the Welsh Guards had their Third Battalion acting as purely infantry.

Daniel: You went across to Normandy in July 1944?

Allan Barnes: I went to Normandy the end of July 1944 because I went across as a replacement, the original Battalion had gone across about two weeks after D-Day with all the tanks and everything else you have in an armoured division and so I had to wait until enough people had been killed to make a vacancy in the Battalion for me.

Daniel: Can you remember the first time you actually saw the beaches of Normandy? Can you describe the scene for us?

Allan Barnes: We landed at Arromanches where they had built the Mulberry Harbour and this really struck me at that time – the tremendous effort that had to go in to putting the army ashore. The Mulberry Harbour was absolutely full of ships coming and going and loading and offloading. They were offloading all the military equipment that was necessary and loading with German Prisoners of War to be brought back to England but the collection of ships and the collection of anti-aircraft equipment around the area was very very impressive.

Daniel: Can you describe what it was like in those first few days and weeks in Normandy, what you were doing, what role you had at the time?

Allan Barnes: Well I was in a reinforcement unit and the thing I really remember first about Normandy are the dead cows. All the fields had a lot of dead cows which were highly bloated and of course very smelly, so we tended to avoid getting anywhere near them if we could, and then I was simply moved on as a member of the replacement unit waiting to join the Battalion.

Daniel: What happened after those first couple of weeks? You were in Normandy, can you tell me about joining the Battalion?

Allan Barnes: We joined the Battalion and we went on the breakout from Normandy and we went almost due North up through Northern France and then through Belgium and Holland. On the way we liberated Brussels on the 3rd September which was the anniversary of the start of the war of course and then we just carried on. By this time the German Resistance had become very very weak but every town and every village we came to did have a force of German troops defending it but usually quite a small force and we, as an armoured division, just went straight through without much trouble.

Daniel: You reached Brussels on the second day is that right?

Allan Barnes: Yes, for some reason or another I was one of the last ones to go in, the second day after the liberation on the 3rd September.

Daniel: Can you describe how the civilians were, how did they act towards you?

Allan Barnes: The civilians were absolutely berserk, as you would expect them to be because the Germans had been pushed out and the British Troops had arrived so they were liberated, they could do and say what they liked and every civilian, a bit of an exaggeration, but it seemed every civilian had a bottle of wine and a glass to offer to the soldiers.

Daniel: From Brussels where did you move on to?

Allan Barnes: We went through Holland, the only place I remember was Eindhoven, but we went through various towns in Holland. The objective was that we should reach the southern end of the bridge at Arnhem and take the southern end of the bridge and the airborne had taken the north end of the bridge and so they had more or less control of the north end, but not complete control, and it was our job to break through to the south end but we just couldn't make it because we reached a village called Elst and the road from Elst to Arnhem was just a pre-war main-ish road so it was quite narrow, it would just take two trucks, one each way, and then there was a slope down into flooded fields so we couldn't go through the fields and we couldn't get along the road because it was covered by anti-tank guns. The Irish Guards tried to get along the road but they lost eleven tanks over a distance of a very few hundred yards and then a group of the Welsh Guards went along the slope between the road and the flooded field and tried to get along that way but this slope was of course covered by machine guns from the Arnhem end and so they didn't stand a chance so they turned around and pulled back. Several were wounded. I don't think anybody was killed at that point.

Daniel: Can you describe to me what it was like seeing the airborne divisions come down?

Allan Barnes: It was absolutely incredible because they were dropping a few miles from us, not only the paratroopers but also the gliders and the fleet of planes that came over was absolutely incredible. These were all Dakotas carrying just a handful of men so there were hundreds of Dakotas that came over and dropped the paratroopers in this area, about seven miles away from the city centre - an absolutely incredible situation.

Daniel: How quickly had you realised that it wasn't going to be achievable to take the bridge?

Allan Barnes: I don't think that we as simple soldiers quite understood the severity of the situation. We knew it was a serious situation, almost everybody had dysentery or something like that but nobody went sick. We were hoping that we could do something but as simple soldiers we didn't really know what, if anything, we could do and of course in practice there was nothing we could do. The airborne withdrew a little west from the city of Arnhem, from the city centre, and then they came across at night and that was the end of the matter but they of course lost an enormous number of men, both as killed, wounded and prisoners.

Daniel: Where did you move on to from Arnhem?

Allan Barnes: After Arnhem we spent the next several months clearing the western part of Germany, west of the Rhine. It's a comparatively narrow strip of Germany to the west of the Rhine but it was Germany as opposed to Holland and it was our job for the next several months, so this would have been the rest of '44 and the early part of '45 and we were clearing the various towns and villages and so on, on the western side of the Rhine so that the final assault from the Rhine into Germany could take place.

Daniel: You were at Nijmegen and Namur. Can you tell me about the experiences there?

Allan Barnes: At Nijmegen I had the job of shooting at anything floating down the river from the German occupied part ... because there were reputed to be floating mines down the river with the hope that they could blow up the bridge support and so my job, because I had learned to shoot well at School ... was to shoot at anything coming down the river. Whether there were any mines or not I have no idea but I used to shoot at anything that happened to be passing, usually just old bits of logs and packing cases, this sort of thing.

Daniel: And then from Nijmegen where did you move on to?

Allan Barnes: From Nijmegen we then went to do this repeated taking of German positions to the west of the Rhine, except for Christmas time in '44 when the Germans broke out through the Ardennes and their idea was to go from the Ardennes straight west so that they isolated the British Army on the north of their thrust and the American Army on the south, but in fact the Germans eventually ran out of petrol which is really what stopped them. But in order to do this western advance they had to take the town of Namur in order to get across the river at that point. We were in reserve position somewhere and we were waiting for our Christmas meal on 25 December. On 24 December the orders

Allan Barnes in Palestine c1946

came through that we had to go to take hold of Namur so the Germans couldn't get through, so at 4 o'clock in the morning on Christmas Day we got into trucks and went to Namur and we got there fairly quickly so we couldn't have been very far away, a few hundred miles that's all. And then we occupied the road that the Germans would have come down had they advanced, and we held a position on either side of the road and a house on one side of the road, so we had a good field of fire up the road. On the other side of the road a group of Welsh Guards were in a local small café and at the back of the café there was a burial ground and, being a Roman Catholic cemetery, it had very large granite headstones and so these would have made ideal firing positions to defend the road if the Germans did come along but they didn't of course.

Daniel: Which guns or rifles did you use?

Allan Barnes: Originally we had the short magazine Lee-Enfield Mark III which was a standard rifle as used in the First World War and then we went to, I think it was the Mark IV, which was a similar rifle but had a flash eliminator at the end of the muzzle. And then finally we had the Mark V (but I can't remember whether this was during the war or after the end of the war), that was similar basically to the Mark III but without the wood and the wood of course on the Mark III was very good because you didn't burn your fingers on the barrel when you fired a few shots.

Daniel: Can you describe to me what it was like being shot at?

Allan Barnes: I was shot at twice and this was a bit unnerving when I realised what was happening, that that bullet should have hit me – it was just that the German soldier had not done enough arms training; that was the trouble for him. He shot at me from a cabbage patch a few hundred yards away so I went into the farmhouse that we had taken, but by the time we went out to look for him he had obviously departed back into the town. We were on the edge of the town – where this was I have no idea, this would probably be in the autumn of '44.

Daniel: If there was one significant event of all your experiences in France and Belgium and Holland, what would it be?

Allan Barnes: I think it's the memory that we didn't get through to the southern end of the bridge at Arnhem and that everybody was ill one way or the other but nobody went sick. We thought we were going to win the war. The atmosphere was quite incredible. We didn't even have any proper rations, we were living on German rations which had been captured by the army and we had black coffee made from acorns which of course was a German standard so the whole atmosphere was hopeful. We didn't realise what was going to happen, what had happened and why it was going to happen but we had hoped that we were taking part in the end of the war but in fact it wasn't to be.

Daniel: What do you do on Remembrance Sunday?

Allan Barnes: It's the only time in the year I really cast my mind back to the war and it makes me very very upset. Like I say, it's the only time in the year I remember it and I remember the various people. I remember this man called Ian Glen who was killed at the Metropolitan Training Ground and the various other people that I trained with and knew. I remember them, I've got photographs of groups of them but I can no longer remember their names or remember anything about them.

Daniel: Was the transition to civilian life an easy one? You say you came back to do your degree at Imperial College.

Allan Barnes: No. This was a very difficult transition and virtually all the students in my year, and there would only have been about 40 or 50 of us, all the students suffered in exactly the same way and of course we had people there who had been all over the world and so they had different wartime experiences but knuckling down to do academic work after a gap of 4 years was very very difficult.

After the Second World War Allan served in Palestine for two years as thousands of Jewish refugees scrambled to leave Europe. On his return to the UK in 1947 Allan studied at Imperial College, London, before working as a research scientist at Fry's Metals Foundry in Merton Abbey, where in 1955 with Vic Elliot and Ralph Strauss he revolutionised the electronics industry by developing the wave solder process which provided for the efficient and economical mass production of printed circuit boards.[4] Allan died in 2013.

References

1 Interview with Allan Barnes by Daniel Kirmatzis July 2011. A copy of the transcript is available in the Emanuel School Archive.
2 Interview Allan Barnes 2011.
3 John Buckley, *Monty's Men: The British Army and the Liberation of Europe, 1944-5* (2013), p. 208.
4 '50 Years of Wave Solder: How wave solder came to light' in *Technology* (Nov 2006), pp. 19-21. A copy is available from the Emanuel School Archive.

Albert 'Bertie' Sydney Mann DFC

(Emanuel 1927–1937)

In chapter seventeen we discovered the exceptional flying career of Bertie Mann who by 1944, as an Acting Squadron Leader, was given command of No. 268 Squadron. In the months leading up to D–Day Bertie's Squadron was tasked with crucial reconnaissance operations to photograph technical structures such as radar stations, airfields and launch sites for the V1 rockets that would end up killing thousands of UK civilians.

In the build up to D-Day Bertie flew an operation to photograph a heavily defended radar 'chimney' in Boulogne to confirm that it had been disabled by rocket firing Typhoons in an earlier raid. For this action Bertie and his No. 2 Flying Officer David Ashford were awarded the Distinguished Flying Cross. Bertie's award announced in the *London Gazette* stated:

> In May 1944, this officer was detailed to reconnoitre a heavily defended target in Northern France. In the face of considerable light anti-aircraft fire, Squadron Leader Mann executed a most successful run over the target and secured excellent results. His skill and coolness were beyond praise. This officer has completed a large number of sorties and has invariably displayed a high degree of determination and devotion to duty.[1]

The following is Bertie Mann's account of his experiences leading up to D-Day from his return to the UK from India in late 1943, and then until the end of the War in Europe.

The Command of No. 63 Squadron

All at once things started to move quickly. Nothing had changed much during nearly five years' absence. Both parents were well and my father's office was still in the City although there was much bomb damage round about. The trains and buses were still running on time, but there was a severe shortage of petrol and it was necessary to be an 'essential user' to get any at all. Within three weeks a telegram arrived from the Headquarters Air Defence of Great Britain at Bentley Priory summoning me to an interview with the C-in-C. In an easy-going five minutes Air Marshal Leigh-Mallory told me I had been selected to command No. 63 Squadron, a Mustang I Fighter Reconnaissance Squadron.

No. 63 Squadron was practicing naval gunnery spotting at Barry Budden ranges and sharing facilities with No. 603 Squadron at Edinburgh when I arrived on 8 November 1943. I took the squadron down to 123 Airfield at Thruxton to return to our operational mode. Two days later, as part of the preparation for our mobile future in the Second Tactical Air Force prior to the invasion of Europe, 123 Airfield moved to Sawbridgeworth in Herts, then on 30 November to North Weald where we started work in earnest. No. 63 Squadron formed part of No 84 (Tactical) Group and its associated Reconnaissance Wing were to be based along side the headquarters of 1st Canadian Army throughout the forthcoming advance.

Operations over Northern France

63 Squadron, now back and operating over northern France and the Low Countries, quickly found its feet again and became busily employed on the standard type of visual and photographic reconnaissance called for at that time which were known as 'Popular' operations. Pairs of aircraft would penetrate, perhaps as far into the enemy occupied countryside as Paris or Chartres to search for any German military activity, area by area, taking pictures of communication centres, marshalling yards and rail movement, radar installations and other known targets of interest. At this time the Luftwaffe was still active and there

were, of course, many fighter airfields in these parts. Evreux, Vitry and Beauvais were probably the most dangerous in our field of activity and planning and briefing took these seriously into account.

I remember my first operational sortie over enemy occupied France very well indeed. We were briefed to carry out an airfield photo-reconnaissance of Maupertus aerodrome on the north coast of the Cherbourg Peninsular which was a fairly straightforward task. We crossed the enemy coast on the west of the peninsular having flown at 0 feet from Selsey towards the Channel Islands with the intention of making a pass over the airfield at 3,000ft on the way north and then get on home at sea-level. We had avoided the town and docks which were obviously heavily defended and approached Maupertus which looked quite peaceful and almost deserted. As we flew round the perimeter steadily at 240 mph. with cameras running, the air filled with large black puffs, grey puffs and white puffs close in front and all around; sometimes you could hear the loud tearing crack. There was also a multiplicity of red and yellow balls which left the ground in a slow and graceful curve, not at all threatening until they speeded up with a vengeance engulfing our aircraft. Looking over the left wing, most of them seemed to me to flash over the wing-root to the left of the engine, and caused a sudden involuntary and extreme tightening of the anus. We left without ado and set off home over the sea. Just as a welcome sight of the south coast appeared, No. 2 climbed up very suddenly and discarded his canopy, announcing that his engine was 'creating' and he wanted to land on the Isle of Wight. This was inconvenient and 'dicey' for Tangmere was straight ahead and nearer – but he knew better! In the event he collided with some earth-moving equipment on a runway under construction at Somerton near Cowes. I pressed on taking the photos back; they were good, but after all that they only showed one light aircraft taxi ing on the landing area. The pilot must have been as surprised as I was at the fury of the reception we received and he, too, would have had just as big a fright – for sure! It was a good initiation, and provided a most powerful lesson. Up to that time my operational experience was against the Japanese whose stiff and very effective opposition was in the air. Their units on the ground were inclined to withhold firing on recce aircraft for fear of giving away their position and in any case their small arms fire had no tracer – what the eye doesn't see the heart doesn't grieve about!

Moving to No. 268 Squadron

I found that I was not to stay with 63 for very much longer. The squadron was not one of those selected to participate in the forthcoming invasion. OC 35 Wing (Peter Donkin) asked me how I felt about taking over No. 268 Squadron which had been one of the most successful 'outfits' in the earlier days of fighter reconnaissance. The Mustang was now well and truly in the role, and tactics had been properly developed to update the old fashioned concept of Army Co-op. 268 were destined for the 2nd TAF / 35 Wing Order of Battle and were at that time about to return from their 'rest' at Turnhouse. Who would refuse?!

I was on my way back to Scotland but was sad, in a lot of ways, to be leaving 63 Squadron – I had made many friends. They were conscientious and efficient and had given me a hearty welcome. In the event, they were not left out completely and shared the direction of naval bombardment with us during the early hours of D–Day.

No. 268 Squadron

This was another rousing reception! No. 268 was an amazingly cosmopolitan outfit – there were seven Canadians, two Australians, three Trinidadians, one Austrian (!), one Maltese, one Scot and a Welshman. We were joined later by two Polish ex-cavalry officers and an Indian Squadron Leader. Five of the squadron complement were already decorated. This was an awesome prospect for their new commander, particularly as they were highly boisterous and, seemingly, not just a bit unruly!

We entered a busy period at once. There were coastal photos to be taken of the Low Countries and France from the Dutch Islands in the north, to the north coast of the Brest Peninsula. Usually flying at between three and four thousand feet, we were to photograph radar stations, ports, airfields, railway marshalling yards; and by visual reconnaissance to obtain photographs of road and rail movement; also troop movement by day if any could be seen. By February 1944, preparations for the launching of Hitler's secret weapon, the V1 Flying Bomb, became evident. We began to watch over building operations at launching sites which appeared in a narrow coastal strip in the Pas de Calais and down about as far as Dieppe in the south – these operations were called 'No Balls'. Most others were 'Populars', the general term applied to all low level visual and photographic sorties to do with the plans for invasion – beaches, estuaries and bridges. The enjoyable 'Rhubarb' offensive recce during which any road rail or other war effort could be attacked at will by cannon fire became a thing of the past.

268 Squadron really was a first class fighting unit. The majority were old hands, men of high calibre who were able to take turns at leading the operational sections of two aircraft – this was particularly important as the Luftwaffe were still pretty attentive at the time. I was supported by two of the very best Flight Commanders I could wish for – Alec Brees DFC and Maurice Lissner, a British subject of Austrian

Flak wagons in action at a railway marshalling yard in Normandy

His task was 'hum-drum' compared with that of the air defence fighter pilot in the Battle of Britain; but none-the-less brave. The fighter-recce section-leader and his No. 2 felt lonely and vulnerable much of the time; particularly when the Luftwaffe was known to be active. Attention was directed 99% of the time to the task in hand, and towards the main aim of getting the reconnaissance report and/or photos back where they could be analysed as soon as possible. Flying low and loitering in a confined area of operations, they were the object of a sort of duck-shoot, and suffered the undivided attention of the guns on the ground; all the time keeping a very watchful eye out for the airborne hawks which might be about, preferably not on their tail! There was no time to be aggressive except by necessity, and then the recce section would be at a disadvantage, single-mindedly attending to their primary task. Not very often an exciting opportunity arose and we shot an enemy out of the sky – in the whole year I was with 268 we only managed a score of two downed.

descent (later decorated). I had the feeling that it could not go wrong! Sadly, after a couple of months, Alec Brees was posted to an 83 Group Typhoon squadron. He was later killed after the end of the war in Europe.

To start with, we certainly took our share of casualties. These were not all due to the Luftwaffe, although in March 1944 one of our sections disappeared over the Cherbourg Peninsula. Subsequently the controllers at Manston confirmed they had been intercepted. On one occasion I was with 'Smithy' my Canadian No. 2, flying near Chartres beneath a broken cloud layer at about 3,000ft, when we found ourselves passing, head-on, through a 'gruppe' of twelve 109s (German Messerschmitt aircraft) with a height separation of about five feet! I'm glad to be able to say that we popped, very quickly, up into the cloud and I think they flew straight on! Many casualties on these operations could be put down to 'bad luck'. When masses of black puffs and red balls came up, most of the time you were dodging about; but, while taking photos of a lengthy target like a beach, a road or railway line, it was like a deadly serious 'Aunt Sally' if you flew straight-and-level for long. The best operational altitude was well inside the most effective range of light ground fire (such as the railway 'flak wagon' or the defences of airfields, convoys, radar installations etc.). On these jobs you were lucky not to get hit somewhere, and many a damaged aircraft returned to base – some didn't! The Second World War reconnaissance pilot had to think. His was not the 'tear off the ground three times a day – 'Buster' – 'Tally Ho' – frenzied action with brief periods of intense fear – 'Bingo' – then arrive back at your airfield which had just been bombed' – type of engagement, followed hopefully by a 'victory roll'; but, quite often with a disastrous ending and a parachute descent or much worse.

In February, my squadron was sent to Llanbedr near Harlech in Cardigan Bay, and spent ten days at No. 13 Armament Practice Camp, air–air and air–ground firing with the four 20mil cannons of the Mustang 1A. The guns were remarkably accurate and well 'harmonised'. The aeroplane was a magnificent 'gun platform' and the squadron scores were a lot higher than I expected – a great confidence builder.

Towards D-Day

So the year moved ahead towards D-Day and we pressed on with our given tasks. Some were 'No Balls' to photograph the developing 'V' weapon sites, which incidentally, were very well defended. Most were 'Popular' Ops, 'overlaps' and 'pinpoint' photos of beaches all along the French coast from Calais to St Malo or thereabouts, cliff-top Radars and inland military routes and railways; all came up in a busy day, subject to the weather which luckily was usually fair. The sea crossings were made at wave-top height to avoid enemy radar. We 'crossed out' at briefed points on the South and East coast – Orfordness or Manston for the North Sea – Dungeness, Beachy Head, Selsey Bill and Portland Bill for the appropriate parts of the Channel. A landfall carefully selected for its negligible gun defences, and for its convenience to the target area, would be quickly identified and before crossing the enemy coastline, we would climb to our operating height, between three and four thousand feet, and 'cross in' strictly as briefed. The route to the target would be chosen to avoid such dangerous locations as airfields, defended townships, railway marshalling yards and known troop formations. We then commenced 'weaving' and watching each other's tails with understandable diligence while carrying out some demanding pilot navigation to reach a target which was often camouflaged or otherwise obscure and hard to locate from a lowish altitude. If all went well, we would return via a different 'crossing out' feature on the enemy coast, reducing height to sea level for the watery dash home.

An important aspect of pre-D-Day training was exercise in moving smoothly from base to base as a matter of habit. In the six months before the great day on 6 June 1944, 35 Wing moved with its Airfield from North Weald to Sawbridgeworth, to Thruxton then to Gatwick and lastly Odiham.

After Air Firing Practice Camp at Llanbedr in February, 268 continued operating from North Weald and Sawbridgeworth until the end of March when we set off for Dundonald in Ayrshire for training in the direction of naval bombardment from the air.

The Navy is 'different' to the Army in many ways – not least in the way it directs its gunfire! The Navy's concept required reports of the fall of shot relative to the target by 'clock code' which they 'computed' into sighting adjustments.

We were in a tented camp next to a steel plank runway on a field just to the east of Troon Golf Course, nicely comfortable with a hospitable clubhouse and a hostelry nearby. Our mentors of No. 1 Bombardment Unit were as friendly as you could expect and ran a short course of lectures. We were very quickly directing gunfire, firstly on land with a resident 25lbdr battery of the RA who familiarised us with the 'ins and outs' in preparation for our 'debut' with the 'big stuff' and the new procedures. The cruisers *Glasgow* and *Bellona* were off-shore waiting to loose off at a target on the island of Ailsa Craig with their 5.5in. guns. As well as the changes in R/T and observation procedures, our pattern of flying between ship and target required to be modified. The range was in excess of eight miles and the shell took time to get there. One disturbing feature was that you could see the missile in flight and the trajectory was uncomfortably near to our flight-path! On the cry of 'Fire' the directing aircraft would be behind the ship commencing a 'figure of eight' to arrive in the best position to observe the fall of shot at the end of the expected time of flight. Then, a voice from below would announce – 'Splash' – on the R/T. The observation would be reported and the aircraft complete its figure of eight, standing by for the next 'salvo.' We completed our course with happy success and flew back to Gatwick.

The busiest period of Overlord operations began at this time. We quickly lost four of our best men. 'Tubby' Bourne – downed by coastal ground fire while taking photos of the prospective beach-head; a very capable, decorated and engaging Canadian, Bill Conway – near Dreux south of Paris, a Luftwaffe stronghold; and Messrs. Sam Seddon and Eric Feldon while flying on visual reconnaissance over Normandy. All among the cream of the squadron.

Among the regular operations flown by 35 Wing prior to D-Day there were those which were part of a 'Cover Plan'; i.e. they were designed to mislead the enemy as to where and when the landings in occupied France were to be made. In addition to bombing and other offensive treatment, these required photographic and visual reconnaissance sorties over well defended beaches, radar and port installations etc. and over areas away from the Normandy beaches, from the borders of Belgium to the Cherbourg Peninsula. I can describe one such operation involving a large 'Chimney' type radar in the northern outskirts of the port of Boulogne. I was briefed with my No. 2, Flying Officer David Ashford, to take close-up pictures which would confirm that it had been disabled following an earlier raid by rocket firing Typhoons. As the defences of this target were likely to be formidable, I decided that we had to pass it at very high speed and at very low level with some degree of surprise. I would fly close in and take a one exposure 'pinpoint' photo as there was a danger that, at short range, the object would be missed between exposures in a high speed automatic 'overlap' run. Ashford would fly alongside, a hundred yards or so further out with his camera running to take an overlapping series of pictures, fast but in the normal way. Leaving Gatwick; a short trip over the Channel, and we crossed the French coast just on the northern outskirts of Boulogne at 5,000ft.; trying hard to look like a normal recce section heading for an inland task – hopefully of little interest to the Luftwaffe considering what else was going on to occupy them at the time. If we were lucky, this could also lull the ground gunners and delay their reaction. In the event, it didn't! There is an escarpment about half a mile inland behind the town; and as we passed over it, I made a brief R/T call to start the proceedings and rolled into a steep dive, back towards the sea (and home) with a lot of power and revolutions, aiming at a point a little short of the target. Ashford followed. Dives at high speed are necessarily in a straight line which makes it easy for the gunners, but the idea was to fox their aim by being very quick. I was expecting to reach about 500mph. In the dive and the elevator controls became very stiff so the 'pull-out' needed gentle and judicious

Single-Engine Aircraft				Multi-Engine Aircraft						Pass-enger	Instr/Cloud Flying [Incl. in cols. (1) to (10)]	
Day		Night		Day			Night					
Dual	Pilot	Dual	Pilot	Dual	1st Pilot	2nd Pilot	Dual	1st Pilot	2nd Pilot		Dual	Pilot
(1)	(2)	(3)	(4)	(5)	(6)	(7)	(8)	(9)	(10)	(11)	(12)	(13)
53·50	1061·45	1·55	32·20	1·45	·35	70·00			4·30	66·35	10·15	
	1·00											
	1·20											
	·50											
	·20											
	·20											
	·30											
	1·05											
	1·10											
	1·20											
	1·05											
53·50	1070·45	1·55	32·20	1·45	·35	70·00			4·30	66·35	10·15	
(1)	(2)	(3)	(4)	(5)	(6)	(7)	(8)	(9)	(10)	(11)	(12)	(13)

45. O.L.O. R.D.F. 'CHIMNEY' at CAP D'ANTIFER (BRUNEVAL) Very poor vis. Lost no 2, F/O NORMOYLE, over target, both returned independently mostly by instruments. Medium light flak S. of ETRETAT. Successful.

46 O.P.P. R.D.F. 'CHIMNEY' at BOULOGNE !! Dived from 7000' and passed target at 500 IAS. Unpleasant reception No 2 F/O ASHFORD hit and wounded in side but O.K. and carried on to take his pictures which were first class. Successful.

Self and David Ashford awarded D.F.C.

Bertie Mann's Log Book entry detailing the photographing of the radar chimney at Boulogne for which he won the DFC

use of the fore-and-aft trim wheel. It was like flying through a heavy snow-storm of flaming 'red balls' which got more and more vicious! By better luck than judgement, I found myself passing the target at the right height and distance, and adopted the School of Army Co-operation very old fashioned 'copy-book' method of taking a so-called Oblique Pin-Point – straight and level and watching the target pass the trailing edge of the left wing-tip. David was to the side and slightly behind taking his 'overlap'. Regrettably, he took a hit from an unfriendly 30mm. shell and a fragment entered his side causing internal injuries. These were not immediately incapacitating, but he flew on towards home in increasing pain. We got back to Gatwick and they met him on the runway with a waiting ambulance. He made a complete recovery. All the pictures were good, making the whole 'business' very worth-while.

The radar chimney at Boulogne

Following that description, it behoves me to emphasise that every pilot of the 35 Wing Mustang squadrons flew such sorties frequently, almost as routine, and often on a daily basis, for many months on end; and some were very much more demanding and dangerous!

Meanwhile, in early May, the news had broken that the whole fighter reconnaissance force (two Wings) were shortly going to run out of Mustangs. The timing was not brilliant with only a few weeks to go before D-Day, and 268 was to be the first to re-equip with Typhoons. I had a go at it with the two Flight Commanders and none of us were impressed; for after our beloved Mustangs it was like flying a London bus! I decided that no one was to fly the Typhoon on operations unless he had done a minimum of five hours on type at the discretion of the Flight Commander. The Typhoon was fast but very heavy on the controls, and the enormous Rolls Royce Sabre engine vibrated to the extent that we had a very poor 'camera platform.' Photographic sorties continued on Mustangs where possible.

Very sadly, the youngest member of the squadron was killed at this time. 'Sandy' Fraser was one of three young pilots from Trinidad who came over here eager to help. Sandy was a keen and happy lad, and even at his tender age he set us all a splendid example.

D-DAY – AT LAST!

At last it became obvious that preparations were at the most advanced stage – squadrons, army formations and ships were in position to launch the first assault and the congestion at ports, airfields and other base facilities could not be left in this state of readiness for very long. We were briefed in the afternoon of the 5th of June to position a section from each of the Mustang squadrons at Lee-on-Solent for a final briefing and take-off at 'sparrow-fart' on the 6th for the first naval bombardment sorties. I took a Canadian No. 2, Bill Tuele, and after we had landed at Lee, we were greeted and directed in a way which was unusually business-like and courteous. In an enormous briefing room set up in a hangar, we found we were present at a most historical gathering. Leading the 'stage' party was the Supreme Commander, General 'Ike' Eisenhower with Monty, a number of US and British Generals, Air Chief Marshal Leigh-Mallory and his Group Commanders. The 'small fry' sat well back in the audience for the 'pep' talk, then a weather briefing by Group Captain Stagg, before hiving off for the detailed briefing when we were to meet senior staffs from the ships whose gunfire we were to direct. I was lucky to be allocated to the battleship HMS *Warspite* – very big guns and very big shells! After a generous breakfast we were airborne at 06.00 and set off towards the action. Over the sea immediately an incredible sight spread out ahead of us. This was history indeed! Orderly lines of ships and landing craft, literally thousands, moving southwards in a most stately fashion as far as the eye could see; protected by destroyers, Motor Torpedo Boats, minesweepers etc. with enormous numbers of aircraft overhead. The bombardment force was already in position. We had been briefed to cross the Channel at 4000ft. instead of our usual wave top performance as a defence against any trigger happy 'Tars' not familiar with the Mustang (or perhaps prepared to shoot at anything in range that was coming towards them!) for the Luftwaffe had put quite a strong force in opposition. They were literally in a 'no win' situation, though, because there were 9,000 Allied aircraft in the air over the invasion area on this day. We truly had 'Air Supremacy'!

So we arrived over the bombardment group some ten miles off the beach-head and prepared to play our part in the shooting. *Warspite* was to engage targets near Villers to the west of Trouville at the eastern end of the beach-head area. These were 'casemates' (enemy heavy gun emplacements) and their associated buildings. It was the habit of the Royal Navy to fire single shots at the 'ranging' stage, then break into 'salvoes' once they got a hit or a very near miss. Flying a figure-of-eight pattern at 4,000ft. between ship and target, it was important to be in the right place at the right time. Radio communications were the key to the whole process. When you called 'Ready' the ship fired, and timed the shell to its estimated strike on (or near) the target. At which point the directing aircraft, having watched the shot leave the ship, would move into the leg of the 'eight' from which he would be able to observe the point of impact. When the time was up, the ship called 'Splash' (!). The directing pilot then reported the fall of shot by the 'clock' code. The process was repeated until the target was demolished, or the ship turned its attention elsewhere. Either by luck or otherwise, *Warspite* fired its first 'sighter' which fell about 30 yards short of the seaward side of the casemate. I was filled with admiration and wonder, and after formally reporting this amazing shot, I added – 'You've been practising!' The answer came back at once in a 'laid back' tone of voice – 'Hang-up 15 this is *Warspite* – Practice Makes Perfect'!! Things went swimmingly afterwards. In three 'shoots' we silenced and as good as destroyed two concrete emplacements and a reputed headquarters building. I remember being amazed at the performance of the Royal Navy, firing big guns over very long

D-Day+6 Banville, Normandy, June 1944

range from a moving, or at least a rocking platform! Then, after almost two hours with the ship, it was time to go home. We were back at Lee by 0845hrs from the most exciting and satisfying flight of my whole career!

On 6 and 7 June, most of my pilots got to engage the enemy during the bombardment programme, and all were impressed by the accuracy of the Navy and their response to directions from the air. After the first sorties, our Mustangs went direct to the beach-head after briefing at Gatwick without calling at Lee-on-Solent. We continued our 'normal' reconnaissance activities while waiting for the situation to permit the preparation and construction of tactical airstrips on the beach-head from which we could continue operations in support of the 1st Canadian Army.

Later in June, 35 Wing was to move to Odiham and continue operations before crossing to our first base in France. In the weeks before we went overseas across the Channel, the tasks became almost routine – visual and photo recce of the battlefield, the Normandy hinterland and the lines of communication from the north and east to the battle area. There was the occasional departure from the normal pattern to direct gunfire, or occasionally a 'contact' recce to locate our own forward troops when they would display coloured 'groundstrips' momentarily when they found time to do so as we were overhead and they had satisfied themselves that we were on their side! From mid-June, most of this work involved landings at a beach-head airstrip for briefing and de-briefing by Intelligence staff. Eventually, daily operations left Odiham to land at 'B3', 'B4' or 'B10' advanced landing grounds which were located close to 1Cdn. Army for briefing by our own Army Liaison Officers who were in position by that time.

The critical period following the D-Day landings was prolonged while sufficient forces of the US 3rd & 9th Armies and British 21st Army Group consolidated inland of the beach-head. Meanwhile, the enemy were able to call in considerable reinforcements. At this time the main tasks of the Recce Wings were to observe possible enemy reinforcement routes; to carry out special sorties for the army in the immediate battle area and provide artillery and photographic reconnaissance. In the first week of August, Main Headquarters 84 Group prepared to move to its location at Amblie alongside HQ 1st Canadian Army with the Group Control Centre nearby. At the same time, 35 Wing HQ were in position with all three squadrons at the newly prepared airstrip B10 (Plumetot) by 12th August. Operations were unaffected by these moves.

It is worthy of mention that just before 268 Squadron moved to Normandy, we were joined by two supernumerary Squadron Leaders and I was highly delighted to receive them both into the outfit. I was particularly pleased to welcome Squadron Leader Karen Krishna Majumdar DFC of the Indian Air Force [IAF]. We were well acquainted since my earlier days in India and Burma. He had commanded No. 1 Squadron IAF during the first Burma campaign and had asked to come to 268 because of our past association, being keen to get all the experience he could in Western Europe before returning to a senior position in India. He made a very earnest and considerable contribution, playing a full part in the programme of operations, and could be seen regularly hanging about the Operations Room on the off-chance of undertaking, out of turn, any unexpected demands which might arise! His award of a Bar to his DFC was very well earned. Our other senior visitor was Squadron Leader A. Golko of the Polish Air Force. A genial and willing officer who took his turn as a squadron pilot. He had brave history as a senior Polish army officer, driven out of his own country to take up the fight after escaping to the UK. This officer was in his late forties, over twice the age of most squadron pilots – he acquitted himself with quiet, impeccable but warlike efficiency, and deserved great credit.

From our airstrips across the Channel, we were able to respond more urgently to changes in the ground war and deal with requests from the army within minutes if necessary. In the absence of interference by the Luftwaffe, recce pilots obviously felt more secure and to some extent could do a better job. Great elation settled on us all now we were on French soil and in the business of liberation. Requests for immediate support in the form of special visual, low-level photo and artillery recce became much more frequent. As we were immediately available in France we were able to improve our performance; 1st Canadian Army got better service and was not slow to give credit when we were able to help their successes. Frequent messages of thanks were passed back to 35 Wing and announced at morning briefing. The squadron commanders took it in turn to attend the morning conferences held at HQ 1st Canadian Army and were able to involve their units by passing on a first-hand understanding of what was happening on the ground. The whole business of the war had taken a positive turn and I never heard a word of disappointment, frustration or dissent. If there was any it wasn't allowed to show; – real 'team' work!

Once across the Channel we spent only days on each of the beach-head airstrips at B10 & B4 where things were a bit primitive. However, we did get regular pilots' rations of orange juice, milk, chocolate, oranges (in fruit form) and vast quantities of free cigarettes in sealed Players 50 tins. There were no non-smokers!

So we were out of the beach-head and moving up towards the Pas de Calais. Next stop B27, then B31 and B43 St Omer/Fort

Rouge where we were to stay for about three weeks until 27 September. Ghent was our next location, and here we enjoyed comparatively great comfort. No longer under canvas, the wing moved in on a splendid Convent (unoccupied) on the edge of the airfield at B61 St Denis Westrem.

Although the daily missions in the battle for France and the Low Countries were usually similar, they were by no means routine or boring. Each mission, usually flown at between 2,500 and 4,000ft, braved a sustained curtain of AA fire from target areas ranging from the 30mm quad Oerlikon type weapons to medium and heavier calibre AA batteries near conurbations, enemy concentrations, and such likely targets as marshalling yards, etc. Every effective operation remained a feat of courage with a serious risk which could certainly not be 'shrugged off'. There were no 'drop-outs' or shirkers. It would, perhaps, be appropriate to include the transcript of a communication received from the Intelligence staff at 1st Canadian. Army in the terms it was written at the time:-

> The defeat of the German Armies in Normandy was an achievement in which all arms and services of all the Allied Forces can claim a share. Of these no-one can claim more than the recce pilots and no-one is better fitted to say so than the Intelligence Staffs who fed on their information.
>
> There are many reasons for that defeat and one is certainly that the enemy did not accurately estimate our strength and intentions but that we, in our turn, did get a clear picture of his. That we were able to do so was a result of many sources, and one of the most fruitful was Air Reconnaissance. It helped in three memorable ways. It gave us eyes to see what the enemy was doing behind his forward positions and in this way we detected his defences, his dumps, his reserves, his Headquarters and above all his movements. It gave us an accurate photographic picture of his positions and with these to hand every major land attack was made. Finally, it found us targets for the air attacks which broke his spirit as it shattered his plans.
>
> The army can do a great deal more with the aid of air reconnaissance. We have conclusively proved what we can do against an enemy without it!
>
> The Intelligence types of 1st Canadian Army, served by 35 Wing, R.A.F., take this opportunity to thank the Group Captain Commanding and all his men for what they did and how they did it!
>
> Lt Col (G1) Int 1st Canadian Army

Bertie (centre) standing between General Montgomery (far left) and King George VI inspecting Bertie's men, Antwerp, 1944

A Royal Visit

As we were about to move on to Antwerp (B70 – Antwerp Duerne) events got more exciting in a rather different way. 35 Wing were due to arrive there on 11 October, 1944, and on the 13th we were to be honoured by a Royal Visit when King George VI would inspect the squadrons. We were able to get up to our new base in advance to make preparations while still carrying on with the war. The day came, the weather was fine, and the whole Wing looked smart and efficient. 268 'stole' a bit of 'a march'! Recce pilots had been wearing somewhat scruffy khaki battledress in the air on operations for quite a while. We turned out on the day 100% clothed in smartly pressed blue uniform; unlike our colleagues whom we showed up as a mixed rabble! For this, and a special proud deportment for the occasion, we won great acclaim! Envy and disgust in Nos. 2 & 4! HM arrived with Monty the Army Group Commander, who sat on his 'shooting stick' through most of the proceedings. The Monarch's visit was a splendid encouragement and a great benefit to us all.

The War Continues

Hostilities then took a new turn. The liberation of France had seen off the threat of the 'Doodle Bug' V-1 weapon (although they came back in droves a little later). Now suddenly we were faced with the V-2 Rocket. The first to arrive on Antwerp-Duerne made a huge bang in the dispersals used by Typhoons of 146 Wing, who shared the airfield. It came without warning and was immediately followed by what turned out to be a sonic 'boom' and a threatening rushing noise as if something else was on the way! There were some casualties, a couple of aircraft destroyed, and we saw that they were fairly accurate used against airfields and urban areas, and were unpredictable. After this initial baptism we were on the alert and in fine weather at the time, we were able to watch these weapons ascending as they emitted a white, vertical trail which curved towards the target area at very high altitude. During this period they were launched from a point near The Hague well to the north of us but it seemed as if the launchers were mobile as they, indeed, were.

The Chief of the Air Staff, Sir Charles Portal, came to visit the Wing, and as things had warmed up a bit war-wise, he seemed to be quite impressed. He made a point of talking to many individual pilots. Gave us all a 'pep' talk and left quietly.

During successive weeks in September, the channel ports of Le Havre, Boulogne, Calais and Dunkirk had been cleared after fierce enemy resistance in spite of Hitler's order that they be held at all costs. Our lengthening lines of communication

Sir Charles Portal (left) talking with Bertie Mann (right), Antwerp, 1944

now made it increasingly important to open the major port of Antwerp; but this was not possible immediately because of the strong pockets of enemy holding the Breskens area of Belgium on the southern coast at the mouth of the Scheldt estuary, and the Dutch island of Walcheren and its well defended port of Flushing on the opposite coast: also, the Scheldt estuary was heavily mined and must be cleared. Many visual and photo sorties were flown over these areas and provided valuable information on which the Canadians depended to plan and execute their assault operations. Events were fast and furious on the ground, for in spite of these hold-ups, the forward troops of 1st Canadian Army were already fighting at Tilburg on the south bank of the river Maas over the border in Holland. I am reminded of one Artillery Recce sortie which I flew over Breskens at this time. I have already remarked on the greater accuracy of heavy guns in general, and on this occasion we were directing those of a Medium Regiment (I believe it was No. 4). We were pounding a large star-shaped fort overlooking the Scheldt. The first shot was not far off target, and after a correction easily applied from map features and distances, my No. 2 (and I) burst into shouts of astonishment when four shells fell in quick succession right on and about the only entrance portal. We had noticed that the open area inside the fortifications was packed with transport, and the dreaded Hun would have had a bother getting it all out! Another remarkable occurrence deserves mention. There was a large mansion type house in the line-of-fire about five miles from the fort. I was just turning towards the target on the last leg of a figure-of-eight which gave me a view of this house, and I happened to glance at it. At this moment one of its tall Elizabethan type chimney stacks was suddenly 'beheaded', and the top tumbled over the roof to the ground. I had always thought that shells from heavy guns achieved their range and accuracy by firing at high angles (i.e. watching the shells in flight during the naval bombardment on D-Day). I suppose this could have been some sort of misfire!

Bertie Mann in his Mustang, 1944

At Antwerp, we continued with our busy daily mixture of visual and artillery reconnaissance, oblique photography and other tasks passed back by the Canadians, who were by now advancing into south and west Holland. We were paying special attention to the defences north of the Maas and at Walcheren right up to 24 November when we moved to B77 Gilze-Rijen near Breda; in Holland and just south of the river Maas. 84 Group Headquarters moved to Tilburg close by, at the same time.

The pressure of operations increased, and we were getting satisfying results in meeting the needs of our army users who were, indeed, having a hard time establishing on Dutch soil to press on with their advance. November passed, and as December 1944 progressed two new 'threats' materialised. Firstly, Field Marshal von Rundstedt mounted an offensive in the Ardennes to cut off the Allied advance. The US Army Air Corps were largely providing air support to forces that were now on the defensive in that area. The USAAC did not have any dedicated fighter reconnaissance units. We were able to help, and to this end I was detailed to visit their base at Charleroi with the purpose of setting up and co-ordinating efforts on this front. Several sorties were flown but with limited success as enemy armour, guns etc were set in the abounding forest and we were having the same trouble seeing them either visually, or by photography, as I had experienced in the jungle of Burma in 1942.

The next threat which intensified our operations from Gilze was a plan to attack the right flank of our Canadians in the south of Holland and retake the port of Antwerp. By now, Antwerp was handling 20,000 tons of Allied supplies and was, of course, essential to our continued advance. Happily neither of these plans succeeded, but to add pressure and some distraction to our efforts the Luftwaffe re-appeared for what seemed to be a 'last fling'. The weather got steadily worse as December progressed – dank misty, some fog and with snow on the ground.

In spite of the weather, a positive feeling had spread among all ranks that the war was as good as won. In this atmosphere, I was not ready for the news that I was to be relieved and a new 'boss' would take over the splendid 268 in early January. I had no business to complain or be too disappointed. I had commanded the squadron for a whole year throughout the process of the biggest invasion in history including the whole period of preparation. I had a team and felt very much a fixture. It was sad but the war must still go on!

There were still some trials ahead, and to say the least, some moments of intense surprise – not to say fright! There was the odd moment of spontaneous humour and a bit of 'aggro', too.

One startling episode in my little 'Odyssey' happened during personal preparations for Christmas. I was to be away for four days and would be back for the New Year. I took my jeep into Antwerp with the intention of having a haircut, some lunch and buying a few presents; if I could. Parking the jeep and walking up the street towards the Excelsior Hotel which had been taken over as an Officers' Club, and where I could get shorn and have a meal, I was passing the Rex Cinema when there occurred a terrible, enormous, ear-splitting, God-awful 'BANG'. For minutes, you couldn't see for dust and I found myself lying face down clutching a small sapling rooted through a grille in the paving and trying to hide behind it! I looked up eventually, and realised that the large cinema had taken a direct hit from a V-2. The only signs of life were from the camera operators whose projectors were in a room above the entrance, and who were trying to climb out, waving feebly from windows behind the large 'REX' sign now dismally hanging down. Most of the audience must have been vaporised. Emergency services arrived and a small crowd gathered. There was nothing we could do to help, so I staggered up to the Excelsior to continue with my original plan. I sat down in the barber's chair still wearing my leather Irvine jacket and looked in the mirror. I was white with thick dust all over. The barber didn't turn a hair but carried on shampooing and hair-cutting with complete calm and not a word! You could hear the scissors grinding away on the grit! I still have the Irvine jacket which remains ingrained 60 years later! I completed my day's shopping, such as it was, and flew myself home the next day. Back on the 31st – nothing amiss. Then, strolling on my way to the Ops Tent early on New Year's Day, the air filled with unusual engine noises. 190s and 109s in large numbers tearing around firing off their guns and dropping 'things' – Whatever next! Our RAF Regt Bofors were quick to respond and as I was running past on the way to my destination, a swooping 190 was climbing away ahead of me. A Bofors on my right got off four shots and the third took the flap on the port mainplane clean off; I saw the tracer strike. Gilze-Rijen lost a Typhoon but no Mustangs, although one of mine was damaged. I saw the downed 190 pilot in the control tower where he had been taken. He was a teenager and scared out of his wits! This was to be the last appearance of the German Air Force in any strength. They called it 'Operation "Bodenschatz" (Base-plate)' in which their force lost well over 200 aircraft and pilots killed, wounded or POW. A Section of 268 led by Flight Lieutenant David Mercer accounted for a Ju.188 destroyed and an Me.109 damaged while on an early mission to Utrecht.

The fateful day arrived when I had to begin my hand-over of the beloved 268. It took a week officially, and then I hung on for a bit. Nobody seemed to notice, probably because they were used to seeing me around. I was able to keep flying by the good offices of my former flight commanders. Secretly, I had wanted to finish the war with my squadron; but this was not to be. On 18 January, I did an Arty/R sortie (abortive) in the morning and after de-briefing went to the Mess for lunch. Afterwards, I dozed off by the fire and awoke with the worst pain in my gut I ever had, and dragged myself to Sick Quarters literally on my hands and knees. Our Maltese doctor 'Baldy' Baldicchino did his duty and told me I had a serious problem with my appendix. He sent me at once, through the snow, to the nearest Mobile Field Hospital in tents at a monastery in Oudenbosch between Breda and Tilburg. A sad end to my wartime operational career! I went 'under the knife' in a freezing tent and, not surprisingly, caught pneumonia. A 'Cook's Tour' of hospitals followed; first to RAF Hospital, Brussels, from where I was evacuated by air to Wroughton near Swindon, then on to the RAF Chest Centre at King Edward VII Hospital at Midhurst in Sussex. They looked after me well, and eventually sent me home on sick leave.

Headquarters No. 84 Group – 2nd Tactical Air Force

Bertie Mann in post-war years

By now it was early April and a surprise telegram arrived from the OC 84 Group Support Unit at Lasham offering me promotion and a post at HQ 84 Group if I would forgo my sick leave and return to Holland where the headquarters was now located at Delden near Hengelo. Of course I did so without ado and found I was to take over as Wing Commander Operations. Having just come from 268, I had a good insight of the excellent system of operational co-operation and co-ordination. This was assisted greatly by frequent occasions when I had been deputed to attend General Crerar's briefings on progress and the latest army requirements for offensive and reconnaissance air support. I got a good run around my very friendly and efficient Canadian Army contacts, most of whom I already knew, and was quickly prepared for the job of accepting and allocating requests for all forms of Air Support that they needed. The AOC ran his Group like a family, and a very happy and effective one at that! My old squadron were nearby at B106 Twente. Everything went fast and furious and the days flew by. My office had been established in the rickety superstructure of a DIY caravan mounted on a one ton truck of doubtful serviceability – as a 'prime-mover' it was a sad failure and when required to move, it was usually towed. I had five telephones; one to G1 Ops 1 Cdn Army, one to Gp. Capt Ops., one to 84 GCC (the Group Control Centre) and two mostly for incoming calls and direct contact with the Wings. To start with it was pandemonium as compared to the placid life of a squadron commander, but after a few days the panic cleared and I was playing it like a 'Wurlitzer'! I had two experienced Flight Lieutenant Ops Officers, one Polish and one English (whom I could understand), and between us I think we made a pretty satisfactory 'fist' of it. 1st Canadian Army were going 'great guns' and it became clear that the war was as good as over 'bar the shouting'.

VE Day

Highly important signals arrived – the Instrument of Surrender was signed; then Hitler committed suicide – it was suddenly 8 May - 'VE' Day!

'VE' night is a hazy memory. I looked in at Twente airfield; it was eerily quiet – Mustangs Typhoons and Spitfires neatly lined up with no prospect of the usual busy day tomorrow – you would have sworn they knew that the job was done and the famed and essential war horses were left lonely while the men were out to celebrate.

Bertie Mann's post-war career included time as Chief Flying Instructor at RAF Valley and station commander of Kai Tak, Hong Kong, in 1962. He retired from the RAF in 1974. Bertie died in December 2009 at the age of 90.

References

1 Fifth Supplement to the *London Gazette*, Tuesday 20 June 1944, Published Friday 23 June 1944.

Back to France – From Dunkirk to D-Day

Phillip Russell Drew OBE

(Emanuel 1930–1932)

Phillip Drew

Phillip excelled at Emanuel as a Prefect and Captain of Boats where he was known to have an easy style and a powerful drive. He was also a member of the First Fifteen, known as a hardworking and reliable forward. An all-rounder Phillip was also Captain of Swimming. He was a Corporal in the OTC gaining his War Office Cert 'A' in March of 1931.

In 1933, shortly after Phillip's eighteenth birthday he was commissioned in the 6th Battalion of the East Surrey Regiment as a Territorial reserve officer. He was promoted to Lieutenant, then Captain in 1939. At the outbreak of war he was appointed as a Staff Captain at the headquarters of the 132nd Infantry Brigade. After training he went to France in early 1940 as part of the British Expeditionary Force. At Dunkirk he was among the men ordered to defend 'until the last', in order to give other troops maximum time to escape. Fortunately, just before the Germans closed in, the Brigadier to whom he was appointed was recalled and they both escaped on a paddle steamer. For his part in the evacuation of Dunkirk Phillip was Mentioned in Despatches.

Phillip Drew (centre) at a post-war Victory parade in Kingston-Upon-Thames

The citation reads:

> For continuous staff work of a high order and devotion to duty during the period of active operations in the advance into Belgium and in the subsequent operations at Audenarde, Courtrai and the Forest of Nieppe between 10 and 29 May 1944. This officer as Staff Captain of the Brigade was untiring in his efforts to serve the troops and succeed in no small measure in lightening their problems. He worked indefatigably to ensure that supplies of all descriptions were forth-coming at the right place and time and often improvised with marked success. He had often to deal with sudden adverse situations caused by hostile actions and always rose to the occasion. Kept his staff organisation going and maintained touch with higher formations at all times. He never spared himself or shirked duty under heavy shell fire. In the brief intervals between battles during this period he made valiant attempts to get the necessary replacements made good immediately. I found I could rely on him implicitly.

On his return to the UK he was posted to Dover Castle and then as an Instructor at the Combined Operations Centre in Inveraray, Scotland. Then he had a spell in the USA teaching the US forces in Combined Operations relevant to D-Day. On his return to England he was promoted to Major in 1943 and posted to the Headquarters of the British Army Corps where he took part in the planning and training for the invasion of France. On D-Day itself he landed at H-Hour plus 6 on Juno Beach. Phillip's grandson Nick Drew remembers his grandfather recounting how his driver drove their jeep into a German machine gun position. When asked what happened, and according to Nick in Phillip's rather understated way, he simply said, 'Well, we turned around and drove away pretty quickly!' At the end of the war he was given responsibility for movement control in an area of Germany. In January 1945 he was awarded his OBE and the next year promoted to Lieutenant Colonel. He became a full Colonel in 1949.

The citation for his award of OBE noted:

> I cannot speak too highly of the work carried out by Lieutenant Colonel Drew as AQMG (Assistant Quarter Master General), (Movements) 1 Corps between July 1943 and D-Day. Exercises, trials and experiments followed one another in quick succession up to the time final planning commenced and then towards the end of planning final exercises were necessary.
>
> Throughout this very trying period Lieutenant Colonel Drew carried out his work with quiet, conscientious efficiency. His work was invariably sound and practical. Nothing was too much trouble and all work; there was a very great deal of it; was coolly and calmly performed...
>
> After landing on D-Day, Lieutenant Colonel Drew continued to carry out his duties with distinction until he left Corps HQ.

Among many post-war activities Phillip enjoyed show jumping and, as well as many other prestigious appointments in this sport, he served as president of the British Show Jumping Association between 1996 and 2000.

References

1 Our thanks to Phillip's grandson, Nick Drew for supplying details of Phillip's service career.

From D-Day to Trumpton

Gordon Murray
(Emanuel 1929–1937)

Here is the clock, the Trumpton Clock. Telling the time steadily, sensibly, never too quickly, never too slowly, telling the time for Trumpton.

A generation of children in the 1960s and 70s grew up watching the *Trumptonshire* Trilogy. It was a gentle, nostalgic, children's animation, was ground breaking for its day, and was shot both in colour and using stop-motion animation techniques. Its creator was Gordon Murray who attended Emanuel School between 1929 and 1937 and was interviewed by Daniel Kirmatzis in 2014. Whilst at School Gordon was involved in the Dramatic Society playing a number of roles. On his love of drama Gordon said, 'It was built in as it were.' He made his debut playing a servant but later he says, 'I got quite good parts.' Gordon was also a member of the OTC.

Gordon's brothers, who were older than him, attended Emanuel in the 1920s. The family lived in St James's Drive, Wandsworth Common. On leaving School Gordon was learning the business of journalism, working as an office boy on *Home Gardening and the Smallholder* in the Strand. Whilst working for *Home Gardening* he joined the local Territorials, who were part-time soldiers. Gordon went once a week to the Territorial Head Quarters in Victoria taking part in their drills. He was in the Territorials when war broke out and on 2 September 1939 he received his call up papers from the London Scottish Regiment. Gordon's brother Norman was also called up in the London Scottish and both became full-time soldiers. At this time the eldest Murray brother, Richard, was

Gordon Murray in service uniform

Puppet master – Gordon at work in the 1960s

working for the Bank of India. He became the Adjutant in the local Territorials in Malaya rising to the rank of 2nd Lt. As the Japanese swept through the Pacific in 1942 Richard was made a POW and wasn't released until September 1945.

On 3 September 1939, Private G. Murray (Service Number 314644) was in Olympia and was told by the Territorial Officer that war had been declared. As the war progressed Gordon was trained as a Radio Mechanic in the London Scottish, receiving private instruction on electricity and radio. He trained with the Royal Electrical Mechanical Engineers and after three months found himself on a searchlight patrol, where he had responsibility for the radio controlled searchlight. Searchlights were used to light up German bombers over Britain's skies and assisted Fighter Command pilots and anti-aircraft guns at night as they made attacks on these bombers.

Gordon then applied for a commission into the Royal Corps of Signals. His war service had been carried out in England until 1944 when the Allies launched D-Day. As a platoon commander Gordon moved to Portsmouth as preparations were made for the crossing on 6 June 1944. Gordon described the atmosphere amongst the men as being 'quite ebullient.' He recalls, after landing at Gold Beach, sleeping in a ditch on the first day after D-Day.

The Royal Corps of Signals were tasked with keeping the lines of communication opened for the Allied advance. The RCS set to work repairing switchboards and cables and laying new cables in what was essentially the most important aspect of the Allied advance, for without their vital contribution, the advance would have been considerably hindered.

During a halt in the Allied push forward in the winter of 1944 Gordon organised a play in Belgium called *By Candlelight*, which was performed to the various Allied Units. Gordon both produced and took the leading part in the production. After the war ended Gordon also performed in a play called *Women Aren't Angels*, produced by Bill Fraser, who ran a repertory company in England.

Gordon's brother Norman was commissioned into the Royal Scots and also took part in operations to liberate North West Europe in 1944 and 1945. Aside from the business of war Gordon took the opportunity one day in 1945 to drive in a jeep to see Norman whose birthday it was. Norman was stationed on the banks of the Rhine at this time and no doubt was pleased to share the bottle of brandy Gordon had brought him.

With the conclusion of hostilities and after serving in the Regular Army for six years Gordon was soon demobbed. It wasn't long before his passion for drama was renewed. In the 1950s he was in a specially built tent on the sea front doing puppet shows. His love of puppets he describes as having been 'built in' and was ignited by his father who took him to theatres in London which had puppet shows playing, including ventriloquist acts.

Gordon had established a puppet company touring theatres around the UK when one day in the mid 1950s his talent was

Gordon Murray with some of his characters

recognised by BBC producer Freda Lingstrom whom he had invited to a performance. From this Gordon's career took off. He operated Spotty Dog in the BBC Children's show *The Woodentops* and oversaw the BBC's puppet theatre in the 1950s producing an adaptation of Hans Christian Andersen's *The Emperor's Nightingale* and thirty-three episodes of the Rubovia Legends. In the early 1960s Gordon was offered Head of Children's Television but he turned it down and decided to form his own production company. Gordon then created *Camberwick Green* which became the first series of the classic children's television trilogy, *Trumptonshire*, which included *Trumpton* and *Chigley*. In 2014 the character Windy Miller from Gordon's *Camberwick Green*, was made into a Royal Mail stamp for their Classic Children's Television collection. Millions of children in the 1960s and 1970s adored Gordon's programmes. They had a gentle and nostalgic feeling and a host of memorable characters. Perhaps most fondly remembered are the *Trumpton* Firemen, Pugh, Pugh, Barney McGrew, Cuthbert, Dibble and Grubb. Their names were given in a roll call given by their commander, Captain Flack and as with all of the *Trumptonshire* series there were memorable musical numbers or rhythms as in the opening titles of *Trumpton*: 'Here is the clock, the Trumpton Clock...'

Gordon Murray in 2012 with Trumptonshire characters, Windy Miller on the right

After the *Trumptonshire* series Gordon made new animations *Skip and Fuffy* and *The Gublins* which appeared during *Multi-Coloured Swap Shop*, another classic children's television show aired between 1976 and 1982.

In 2012 the original *Trumptonshire* series was restored by BBC Studios and Post Production and can now be enjoyed by a new generation.

The Wates Brothers in the Second World War

Allan Charles Wates *(Emanuel 1919–1927)*
Norman Edward Wates *(Emanuel 1917–1921)*
Sir Ronald Wallace Wates *(Emanuel 1917–1923)*

The Wates family have had an association with Emanuel for almost a century. Three brothers Allan, Norman and Ronald all attended the School between 1917 and 1927. The boys' father and uncle started building light, compactly built houses to replace uncomfortable Victorian houses in the early 1900s and by 1926 Norman had joined his father and uncle in the business.

Allan Wates

Two to three years later Allan and Ronald also joined the Company which by the 1930s had moved from Streatham to London Road, Mitcham and then to Norbury. By the 1930s Wates Ltd. was firmly on the map and in the twenty-first century Wates Ltd. still flourishes as one of the largest construction companies in the UK.

Up to the outbreak of the Second World War in 1939 the Company was constructing around 2000 houses per year. The Company's Contract Department was inaugurated under the direction of Allan Wates in 1936 allowing it to expand its business, initially securing deals for the building of fire stations, drill halls, libraries and a variety of public works. These included Kingston Drill Hall and Sutton Library.

The Munich Crisis of 1938 did little to assuage those who firmly believed Czechoslovakia would not be the last in Hitler's territorial ambitions and so by late 1938 Britain was preparing itself for a potential European conflict. At this time Wates Ltd. secured contracts from the War Office to erect camps and defence works in southern England. In collaboration with consulting engineers they also produced the designs and put into production precast concrete air raid shelters and trench linings in early 1939 including for

Ronald Wates (fourth from left, front row) standing next to King Haakon VII of Norway

the whole of the borough of Battersea.[1] The Company also supported its staff in any National Service they wished to undertake including providing an extra week's paid holiday to staff who were Territorials (reserve soldiers).[2] Once the war began they also provided pre-cast floor slabs for a London tube station which was converted into a shelter.

At the outbreak of war the Company was handling over one hundred contracts for the War Office. At this difficult time Wates Ltd. moved to reassure its employees, 'Each of us will find inconveniences, difficulties and hardships, but will tackle them cheerfully in the knowledge that each one overcome is a contribution to the national effort.'[3]

In October 1939 the War Office wrote to the Federation of Civil Engineering Contractors with a request for one hundred steel fixers and one hundred carpenters for urgent work overseas. The men were to be enlisted into a Corps of the Royal Engineers. At this time Wates Ltd. decided to offer their services to the War Office by forming the Wates Royal Engineers General Construction Company.[4] This was later designated as 687 Company, Royal Engineers.

At the height of the Battle of Britain Wates Ltd. sent Lord Beaverbrook, Minister of Aircraft Production, a cheque for £5,000 for the purchase of a Spitfire.[5] Contributions such as these were vital to the war effort. The Spitfire was named *Endeavour* and saw action in a fighter squadron at the end of 1941, being engaged in offensive sweeps and protecting convoys through to 1942 until it was withdrawn for special flying duties with the RAF.[6]

Norman Wates watching his wife Margot christen a Mulberry component

Allan Wates was a very active pupil at Emanuel. In sports he played for the First Fifteen and was captain of swimming. He was also a Prefect and Corporal in the OTC. Norman and Ronald were also members of the OTC and Norman played for the Second Fifteen.

Wates Company of Royal Engineers embarking for Norway

Once war was declared Norman and Ronald ran the Company whilst Allan led the Wates Company of Royal Engineers. Construction was a reserved occupation and was deemed of vital importance.

The 687 Company of Royal Engineers carried out defensive works in London in addition to serving in both Norway, before it fell to the Nazis in May 1940, and Iceland. Britain captured Reykjavik in May 1940 to establish air bases in the offensive against Axis submarines in the Battle of the Atlantic. Although the government of Iceland formally protested, the occupation became permanent until 1941 when the United States assumed responsibility for Iceland.

687 Company under Major Allan Wates built air strips and accommodation in Iceland and Allan captured this on camera in what is a unique collection of photos relating to the Company's time there. In one set of photos he captured Winston Churchill's visit to Iceland on 16 August 1941 after Churchill had returned from America where he and President Roosevelt had agreed the Atlantic Charter – a set of common principles and a blueprint on which the two nations agreed for the reconstruction of a post-war world.

Allan wrote a letter for the *Wates News Sheet* in February 1941 describing conditions in Iceland:

> Conditions out here are much improved and we now live quite well. It is, of course, very cold, but we get used to it and only feel cold in the hands and feet, etc. Of course the frost makes our sort of work very difficult and it requires a lot of thought to keep the jobs going. The days are now getting longer and I suppose in another six weeks or so we will be working 24 hours a day again.[7]

In 1942 Allan Wates, among others of the Iceland [C] Force, received certificates with the approval of King George VI for exceptional good service.

After the war Allan gave an account of 687 Company's wartime activities:

> The idea of forming an RE Company was first conceived in November 1939, when the Federation of Civil Engineers, at the request of the War Office, approached us with the suggestion that we form a Company out of the members of the firm ... it was decided that I should have the honour of commanding the Company ... I was able to go to the War Office at the end of December to tell them that we were ready to form an RE Company.
>
> About the end of January, 1940, instructions were received to report to Chatham on February 7th, so we all said our fond farewells to wives and sweethearts, as we all expected to be in France within a few days. The 250 of us duly arrived at Chatham on the appointed day and what a day it was, bitterly cold and about six inches of snow on the ground. Our billets were terrible, being in the basement of Brompton Barracks – they were damp, dark and smelt like stables. The next day we were all paraded and marched off to be vaccinated and inoculated for typhoid and tetanus. These were normally given over a period, but we all got the lot in one go. Within an hour or two we were all wishing we were dead and regretted the day we ever decided to go in the army. Our first parades were as funny as any West End farce; we all appeared partly dressed as civilians and partly as soldiers, some had battledress trousers with their ordinary jackets whilst others were the exact opposite ... we must have soon got the hang of things as 687 was selected to be the first Company on parade for His Majesty the King's inspection.
>
> On March the first, we received orders to move to Potters Bar. We were all disappointed as we had anticipated that we were going straight to France and I was called to the

Allan Wates's photo of HMS Bittern in Norway, April 1940, before she was attacked by Junkers JU 87 dive bombers on 30 April

War Office and told we had been kept back for a special job in April.

We moved to Scotland and by this time we had all guessed that we were bound for Norway. On arrival at Glasgow we at once went aboard the *Lancastria*, afterwards sunk in the withdrawal from France. We stayed aboard this ship for about two days, during which time we fed like fighting cocks. Every meal was up to the pre-war standard about seven or eight courses a meal and drinks were also very cheap ... we received orders to disembark, but our luck still held and we were put aboard the *Oronsay* (afterwards sunk). ... We had been on board about two days when I received orders to split the Company in two, as one party was to go before the other to prepare the way. Who to take and who to leave behind was a hard decision to make, as none of us knew what was to happen, my chief concern was to keep two halves as evenly balanced as possible. The decision made, I and two sections of the Company went aboard a Polish ship called the *Chorley*. We now knew that we were to form an advance party at a destination unknown and our role was to build a pier to enable larger ships than ours to unload, but as we subsequently sailed without tools I did not know how this object was to be achieved. We woke up one morning to find ourselves at sea, accompanied by two small destroyers. We sailed for about two-and-a-half days in a very calm sea, but had a number of submarine scares and depth charges were dropped on quite a number of occasions. The Officers' Mess was forward on the boat deck and whenever these depth charges went off, we were nearly bumped out of our chairs.

We arrived off Namsos early one morning and I must say, looking at the snow-covered landscape, it was hard to imagine that somewhere on those shores hell was being let loose. Everything looked so peaceful. Namsos itself was a little hamlet about 30 miles inland down a most beautiful fjord and as we steamed down we could almost imagine ourselves on a pleasure cruise. We arrived at Namsos about 10 o'clock and immediately started disembarkation operations. Everything went according to plan for 30 minutes when suddenly a German 'recce' plane appeared above us. As there was no room to take evasive action, we let go everything and shot for the open sea. We had just got to the sea when a German flying boat appeared and dropped a couple of bombs, the nearest one falling about 80 feet away on the starboard side. He circled us and was just coming in for another run (we did not like this at all as we only had one AA gun aboard manned by the crew) when suddenly there appeared from I do not know where, an AA ship which let fly with everything it had got. It was a very heartening sight and the Jerry changed his mind about taking another run. When things had got back to normal, we entered Namsos again and found that it was not quite so big as it was on our first visit and that one or two ships had been sunk. We again started disembarkation and again were observed by German 'recce' planes and again we shot for the open sea. This performance repeated itself three or four times and on the last attempt, when there was very little left in Namsos, we were informed that the withdrawal from the south of Norway had commenced and we were ordered south to pick up some of the survivors. After having picked up about 300 of them we went full steam ahead for Leith.

Construction of Wates's Camp, Sandskeid, Iceland

Allan Wates in Iceland

We met the other half of the Company at Gailes camp and I think this was one of the biggest thrills in the Company's history. You see, none of us knew what had happened to the other half and we, having seen the disaster off Norway, feared the worst. The whole Company was given 10 days' leave and ordered to return to Potters Bar at the end of the leave period.

Winston Churchill's visit to Iceland, 16 August 1941, after the Atlantic Charter meeting

After a further six weeks in Potters Bar, we moved to Iceland and this time sailed in the luxury liner *Georgic* (afterwards sunk at Suez) and fed and lived like lords. We arrived in Iceland about the end of July 1940. Our first job was to build huts to house some 2,500 troops scattered all over Iceland; on completion of that work, we started on an aerodrome. ... Conditions in Iceland were bad when we first arrived and everybody was housed in tents – we, in fact, stayed in them until the end of September. We built just over 900 huts in nine weeks – no mean achievement when you consider that all huts were built in isolated spots. There were no roads, no water supply, no builders' merchants and supplies of cement often had to be got to the site by sea, rafts and pack pony. Water supplies often had to be run from the mountains and sites were as far apart as 900 miles. ... Still, we all enjoyed our stay in Iceland and we worked hard and really earned our corn. The Company, as it was in Iceland, was the best RE Company I have ever met.[8]

The Company returned to England in 1941 and worked in Thame, in Oxfordshire for three years until moving to London in October 1944. The original 687 Company had started to break up by the time they moved and in January 1945 Allan was posted to India.[9]

687 Company on parade in Iceland, with newly built huts behind

Mulberry Harbour in action – Spud pierhead assembly with casualties being cleared (left) and Army vehicles being unloaded from Landing Craft (Tank), (right)

The Mulberry Harbours – 'The greatest engineering task of all time.'

Perhaps the most important project in the Wates Company's history was the contract they took on for building components of the pre-fabricated harbour, codenamed Mulberry, which assisted the supply of goods and military equipment in the wake of the Allied invasion of France in June 1944.[10] Eventually two harbours were established, Mulberry A, to support the beaches on which US troops landed and Mulberry B at Arromanches, in the British invasion area. Mulberry A was largely destroyed in a powerful storm on 19 to 20 June 1944.

Allied planners understood early in the war that once their forces landed in any planned invasion of the French coast they would need to be supplied with reinforcements. The disastrous results of the Dieppe Raid of 1942 led to a rethink of how the Allied forces could launch and carry out an amphibious assault of the French mainland. Their main obstacle was the lack of harbours along the stretch of coast that they eventually designated for the operation known from 1943 as Overlord. The solution to this problem required the best engineering minds available.

Prime Minister Winston Churchill wrote a memorandum headed, 'Piers for Use On Beaches', to Lord Mountbatten, the Chief of Combined Operations, on 30 May 1942, 'They must float up and down with the tide. The anchor problem

Superstructures being fitted to Mark I beetle pontoons

Mulberry ports in process of construction in UK before deployment to France

Mulberry dock a few hours before floating, 25 March 1944

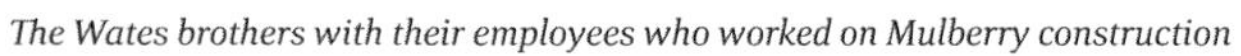

The Wates brothers with their employees who worked on Mulberry construction

Boat building at the Wates's Willow Lane site, Merton, South London

General view of Mulberry Harbour 'B', Arromanches, 1944

must be mastered. Let me have the best solution worked out. Don't argue the matter. The difficulties will argue for themselves.' With this order a team of engineers were called upon to work out ways in which this could be achieved.

Between 1943 and June 1944 Wates Ltd. became one of a number of companies which set about putting the idea of an artificial harbour into reality. Wates Ltd. carried out their work on the Mulberry components at yards and docks across the country including at Goat Road in Mitcham and the West India Docks.

Essentially the harbours consisted of a line of floating breakwaters three miles out from the coast and inside them, sunken concrete breakwaters. Connecting these to shore were floating pontoons and bridges. Hundreds of thousands of men and women of the Allied forces landed at the harbour in Arromaches as supplies were delivered to Allied forces as they set upon driving German forces out of France and the Low Countries. The historian Max Hastings raised doubts in his book, *Overlord: D-Day and the Battle for Normandy 1944*, whether the huge costs and man-power in constructing the Mulberries was commensurate with the results delivered i.e. Hastings and other researchers questioned if a smaller scale operation would have delivered similar results and more efficiently than ended up being the case with the problems which beset the Mulberries once established. But there is no doubt that the indefatigable energy of the Wates brothers and their workforce was of the highest order when one considers the huge scale of the operation, which ultimately played no small part in supporting the Allied advance, despite the difficulties it faced.

The following is the story of Wates' contribution to the Mulberry Harbour as retold in the *Wates News Sheet* in November 1944:

In recent weeks the story of the Prefabricated Port of Arromanches has been told and it is now possible for us as a Company to speak of the not inconsiderable part which we have played. Our connection started a very long time ago – back in the spring of 1942. Just previous

American troops on the Wates's beach landing mats, c. June 1944

to this Sir James Lithgow, the Controller of Merchant Shipbuilding, had asked us to help the Army with our experience of concrete barge building to solve some transport and constructional problems which were arising in Egypt and Persia. This put us in touch with the appropriate division of the War Office and from that time onwards we were always called upon to co-operate with them in some of the many problems with which they were grappling. We were able to be helpful in many ways – providing from Barrow floating crane pontoons and motor transport ferries and from London the beach landing mats from which and upon which, so many great operations took place – Dieppe, North Africa and

Normandy. These, however, were sidelines compared with the main long term problem which faced the War Office – that of providing the means of landing on the continental shore the millions of tons of heavy equipment required for the invasion of Europe. Looking back now, it is seen that the War Office seemed always to have had in mind just the sort of conditions found at Arromanches – long flat sloping beaches which are so suitable in many ways for tank landing craft, but so unsuitable for larger ships and even coasters. To make these beaches more useful to all sorts of ships, it was necessary to construct the means of landing vehicles and other equipment from ships lying in deep water which might be nearly a mile from the shore. Many schemes were thought of in 1942 and several experiments made. The scheme which was ultimately to prove successful – the War Office scheme – was the one for which we were asked to provide the pontoons. This was a pier scheme embodying flexible steel spans supported on our reinforced concrete floats. Like all the other details of the proposal, the mere statement 'reinforced concrete floats' conveys little of the complexity of the problem. These floats had the most difficult design conditions imaginable. They must be light, yet strong enough to support the weight of spans and tanks when aground. They must be of shallow draught. They could not be too beamy, otherwise they would foul the bridge in rough weather. It would be useful if they could tow as well broadside as bows on – and many other considerations. The responsibility for the reinforced concrete design was taken by Messrs. L. G. Mouchel and Partners, with whom we collaborated in order to ensure that the design should be as straightforward in production as possible, having regard to the complexity of the conditions.

Beetle pontoons being tested

Boat construction at Willow Lane

These were built at Barrow in conditions of great secrecy in the autumn of 1942 and delivered to a place in Scotland where the first experimental pier was built in the early part of 1943. It must be remembered that all this was going on when the U-Boat menace was at its height and the nation's whole shipbuilding resources were taxed to the uttermost and it is because of that fact that reinforced concrete was the material chosen, instead of steel, for the floating parts.

This pier was a great success from the outset and films of its performance were taken to Ottawa for the Prime Minister's conference in August 1943, where the

Mulberry dock being tested early 1944

final invasion plans were decided upon. There it was decided that whilst the pier scheme was to go ahead up to ten miles, there should also be about five miles of breakwaters constructed partly to protect the piers and partly to provide protection to the beaches.

Upon the War Office experts' return with this vast commitment – all to be completed in about five months – Brigadier Sir Bruce White, the Director of Ports and Inland Water Transport, set up two committees to give him certain advice concerning the breakwater scheme. The first was composed of many eminent engineers who were concerned with design. The second consisted of three contractors, Sir Malcolm McAlpine, Mr. Storey Wilson of Holloway Bros., and Mr. Norman Wates, whose job it was to say which designs were easiest to construct, what facilities and labour forces were required and how long the job would take. In less than a fortnight of continuous and intensive work by both committees, the report was submitted and the Ministry of Supply embarked upon their gigantic task.

The responsibilities with which we were entrusted were indeed heavy. Failure in quality or delivery in any of the various items would have had catastrophic results for the invasion. As an example, if our mooring shuttles had not been anchored in time. In all our production this was fully realised by everyone concerned and planning and production went ahead with a very keen sense of the momentousness of the task upon which we were engaged.

The Company's commitment consisted of the provision of all the pier pontoons, some 450 in all, 12 pierhead pontoons, 500 shuttles or mooring vessels and proto-type S.L.U.G. boats. The work was carried out at West India Docks, Southsea, Marchwood, Beaulieu, Balham, Bedfont, Willow Lane and the Goat Yard. Barrow, on geographical grounds, was ruled out, but the pioneer work they did was of inestimable service. Despite the magnitude of the task we can say with pride that in point of time and quality, economy of labour and construction generally, we reached complete success in all the various craft.[11]

One of the most pressing concerns for the post-war government was the issue of reconstruction. Bombing had devastated large areas of London and there was an urgent need to provide new homes for those displaced by the destruction. Wates Ltd. was heavily involved in this reconstruction as explained in a short history of the Company:

The specialised experience in precast concrete obtained on our marine contracts had already been applied in theory to civil needs and the summer of 1945 saw the erection of the prototype pair of 'Wates' Non-Traditional Houses at Sutton, Surrey. A pilot scheme of 60 modified houses of this type was carried out at Croydon for the Ministry of Works and by 1951 nearly 10,000 of these houses had been provided for Local Authorities throughout the country.

The Wates brothers also financed the majority of the costs that helped Emanuel School build a Boat Club adjacent to Barnes Bridge in 1958 and opened in 1960. A plaque remembering this generous gift adorns the walls of the School Boat Club.[12]

A 687 Coy RE Christmas Card with Polar Bear emblem

References

1 *Wates News Sheet*, No. 44, 17 February 1939.
2 *Wates News Sheet*, No. 49, 25 March 1939.
3 *Wates News Sheet*, No. 71, 9 September 1939.
4 *Wates News Sheet*, No. 9, 19 January 1940.
5 *Wates News Sheet*, War Time Economy Number, No. 25, 30 August 1940.
6 *Wates News Sheet*, No. 89, 18 May 1943.
7 *Wates News Sheet*,War Time Edition, No. 38, 28 February 1941.
8 *Wates News Sheet*, Vol. 4, Feb-March 1946, No. 2 pp. 6-7.
9 *Wates News Sheet*, Vol. 4, April 1946, No. 3, p. 6 Allan Wates also provides a fascinating account of aerodrome building in Iceland on page 7 of the following editions of *Wates News Sheet* – January, Feb-March and April 1947.
10 For a short account on the Mulberry Harbour see Sir Bruce White KBE, *The Artificial Invasion Harbours Called Mulberry: A Personal Story*.
11 *Wates News Sheet*, Vol. II, No. 10, November 1944. For a technical discussion of the types of crafts Wates Ltd built see Cyril Raymond James Wood, M.I.C.E., 'Reinforced-Concrete Pier Pontoons and Intermediate Pierhead Pontoons' in *The Civil Engineer in War: A Symposium of Papers on War-Time Engineering Problems Vol 2, Docks and Harbours* (1948), pp. 443-445.
12 For further details see Daniel Kirmatzis, *Biblicarta: The History of Emanuel School Boat Club* (2009), pp. 235-236.

An MC-Winning Rugger Captain

Major Harold John 'Ham' Hutchins MC, 5th East Lancs and 5DCLI

(Emanuel 1921–1928)

In this article Harold's son, Roger Hutchins, explores his father's service both to Emanuel and during the Second World War.

Harold John Hutchins (1910–1999), known to his Emanuel contemporaries as 'Ham', was born in Fulham, his parents' only child. His father was a Territorial who in 1914 at the age of 38 lost his collar and tie fighting his way in to the Recruiting Office; serving with the 12th County of London Bn. (The Rangers), he was one of their 53 survivors of one week in the Second Battle of Ypres in 1915.

At Emanuel from 1921 to 1928 Hutchins gained distinctions only in history and art. But he had been in the cadet force for six years, rising to CSM, then under-officer, had been a Prefect, Captain of Drake House and Captain of the First Fifteen. At 5 feet 8½ inches he was not big, but stocky and strong and played hooker. He also rowed in the First Eight.

Upon leaving Emanuel he became a clerk with Price & Pierce, a company of timber importers in the City and found the work congenial. He promptly joined the OERFC (Old Emanuel Rugby Football Club) and was Vice-Captain of their First Fifteen 1932–1933, Captain 1934–1935 and 1937–1939, and Fixtures Secretary 1936–1939. He was also a member of Vesta Rowing Club.

Joining the Territorials, in January 1929 he was commissioned 2nd Lieutenant in the Kensingtons (13th London Regiment). Thence his life pivoted on OE and TA weekday training evenings and weekend matches or training. Against his parents' wishes he acquired a motorbike to commute to those activities. His parents only discovered the illicit machine when failure to take a corner put him in hospital.

Hutchins recalled that Armistice Day each year was commemorated by the Kensingtons in their drill hall, by 'the First World War cohort returning to act out scenes from the trenches, to great approval. The beer flowed, and I was deeply impressed by their cheerfulness and loyalty to the Regiment.' He led his

Harold Hutchins in Emanuel Rugby kit

Harold Hutchins (third from left) in Emanuel OTC uniform

platoon in the *Daily Telegraph* Competition in 1932 and 1933 and also boxed for the Kensingtons. A keen shot at School, in 1935 he transferred as a private to the Artists Rifles 'because I saw that their training was more demanding, and with a club house at Bisley they did more shooting.' He won their Recruit's Prize that year, competed at Bisley each year 1936–1939 and was a member of the Artists' Bayonet Team at the 1939 Royal Tournament when they beat the Regular Army to win the All Services Championship.

A man of few words or visible emotions, he enjoyed his beer, the comradeship of rugby tours or TA camps, and was quick to enjoy a joke rather than make one so that his smile was more characteristic than laughter. His prolonged captaincy of the OE First Fifteen and recruiting a whole platoon of OEs into the Artists attests to his ability to inspire and motivate. The friendships he made at Blagdons and in the Artists, he treasured for the rest of his life.

As for so many others, the Second World War was a defining experience. 'We all knew it was coming. I didn't worry about it. I was a trained soldier, and we were confident that there would be no more Sommes, because the tactics were now based on mobility.' Later he saw it in terms of those who had had 'a good war', and those who had not. He explained that as 'those who had faced the experience of being under fire, survived without being maimed, and had behaved properly when put to the test.' Four of his OE First Fifteen were killed. In 1997 he was unusually keen for me to take him to an Open Day at the School, his first return for more than 20 years. He did not tell me why. Once there he struggled up the stairs to the chapel and asked me to find the Second World War memorial. From the centre aisle, unable to read the names himself after fifty years he asked 'Is Millist there, Morrill, Skillern and Royal?' Satisfied that they had been properly recorded, he was content to go home.

Commissioned 2nd Lieutenant in December 1939, he and three Artist friends managed to be posted together to the East Lancashire Regiment. The 4th Battalion was under orders for the Far East, so he was posted to "C" Coy of the new 5th Battalion which included 'undesirable elements'; time was spent between recruiting and training on the moor. There he met his future wife, Betty, who recalled that 'He had lived a very quiet life at home; the war, his commission, and the mixed social life in Lancashire which was new to him, brought him out.' They married in September 1940 while 5 East Lancashire Regiment were on coast defence in Yorkshire. Still a 2nd Lieutenant, Hutchins was given command of "C" Coy now 150 strong. At the end of 1940 he was promoted Captain and the Battalion moved to Newry in Ireland for two more years of training. In late 1942 he was promoted Major, the only Territorial company commander. He and Betty got to know many of the men, some of their wives and knew of their children.

Hutchins saw his responsibility as being to train his men so that they were as well prepared as they could be for the moment they came under fire. His men complained that the discipline was hard and never relaxed.

5 East Lancashire Regiment crossed to Normandy on 26 June 1944, D–Day+20. On 16 July Hutchins led "C" Coy as point company of the lead battalion of a brigade attack to capture the Caen to Villers Bocage road. They reached their objective, an orchard, but the battalion took 250 casualties that day. Despite the losses in his own company, the company clerk later recorded that 'He held us without any difficulty on the objective. He was badly wounded, not seriously, but nastily and painfully [by a mortar fragment in the shoulder], but he hadn't given up, and he was cheerful and energetic.' He was recommended by his CO for a DSO, but was awarded a MC. The citation read:

> During the attack and consolidation he controlled his platoons by direct personal contact despite heavy enemy mortar fire. He received wounds but declined to go back for attention, continuing to visit platoons and reporting information back with an inspiring disregard for the enemy small arms and mortar fire. The German counter attack outflanked the Coy on the right with tanks and leading elements of infantry, and threatened to outflank on the left. One Platoon on the right retired under cover of smoke from point blank machine gun fire from a tank and there appeared to be a danger of the position being overrun. Major Hutchins then rallied and reorganised his Coy. His personal example inspired the Coy to stand fast. During the critical period he shot one of a party of German infantry penetrating towards the centre of the Battalion position, and thus caused the withdrawal of the remainder. This was within 150

General Montgomery presenting Harold Hutchins with the MC

Weert. Hutchins was told that his company was to be one of the two lead companies – he had almost no time either to reconnoitre personally, or to assess his platoon commanders and the readiness of their men; "A" Coy was to capture De Polak and its Lock; "D" Coy would capture the canal crossings. The weather was fair, sometimes wet and stormy. The objectives were taken by 21.15, but there was difficulty clearing the enemy from the anti-tank ditch; "A" Coy took 14 prisoners from a Parachute Battalion. On 22 November "D" Coy was withdrawn to provide a garrison at Weert. The enemy shelled intermittently all day. On 23 November the Maas overflowed. "A" Coy was withdrawn from Weert, along with five more prisoners they had found hiding in the town. Next day most of the land around Weert and between Heugde and the Maas was under water. In the following days there was occasional shelling. On 29 November Lt-Col. Tedder was replaced, and on 30 November the battalion was withdrawn.

yards of a German tank. He also personally opened fire at infantry targets with a Bren, drawing counter fire from the tank. Later he acted as FOO [Forward Observation Officer] and succeeded in bringing down accurate artillery fire on the only tank remaining visible ... and then upon an infiltrating German section of infantry. This fire proved most effective. He then located the FOO with whom he arranged a medium artillery shoot on the tank. The whole of this offensive action was carried out under constant searching enemy mortar fire, and it is certain that but for Major Hutchins' determined and offensive leadership the German counter attack would have jeopardised the remainder of the Battalion position. During the whole of this time this officer was wounded and in considerable pain.

Having recuperated from his wound, and the remnants of 5 East Lancashire Regiment having been disbanded to reinforce other units mauled in the Battle for Normandy, Hutchins was posted on 20 November 1944 to 4th Battalion, Royal Welch Fusiliers, 71 Brigade, 53 Div., at Weert in Belgium.

There, Hutchins met Colonel H. J. Tedder and was immediately placed in command of "A" Company. The Battalion was under orders to attack at 19.30 hours next day, 21st, to capture

Hutchins had swiftly decided that Tedder, who had commanded since 22 July, was incompetent and the lack of training lamentable. Ordering an officer to take command of 120 men and within 24 hours lead them in a night attack across ground he had had no opportunity to see, displayed an extraordinary lack of regard for the Company. Hutchins later remarked 'I was as ready as the others to take my chance, but not to have my life carelessly jeopardised by my commander, nor be the means of his risking the lives of men he had not ensured were properly trained or led.'

He immediately visited Brigade HQ to seek a transfer to 1st East Lancs and was delighted to find that the Brigade Major was an OE whom he knew and that the brigadier had formerly been an East Lanc. There being no vacancy in the 1st Battalion for a company commander, they suggested he transfer immediately to 5th Duke of Cornwall's Light Infantry, where on the same day, 30 November, he took command of "B" Coy. Their regimental history later recorded Hutchins as being 'an outstanding company commander, and an asset to the battalion in every way.'

Meanwhile, Hutchins had been ordered to attend on 2 December a 53 Division Investiture at Weerte in Holland, where General Montgomery was to present awards. Hutchins stayed up late into the night helping his batman to remove all the new DCLI flashes and insignia that had just been put onto his best set of khakis, and sew on all the East Lancs insignia. He enjoyed relating that at the field parade: 'My name was called, "Major Hutchins, Royal Welch Fusiliers", and I marched

Harold Hutchins in service uniform

up to Montgomery, saluted, and reported: "Hutchins, 5th East Lancs, Sir!" There was some consternation and consulting of lists. He returned the salute and asked "What's this? Why are you wearing East Lancashire insignia?" I explained that I had won the MC while serving with 5th East Lancs under his command in Normandy, that my recent RWF post had been temporary, and that I wished to have the award officially gazetted for credit to my own men. His aide looked nonplussed. "Very well!" said Monty, and pinned the ribbon on. I had been determined to wear the East Lancs insignia on whatever occasion the award caught up with me, so had brought it out in my kit from England. It felt right.' Some 30 years later he was able to visit the beautiful little cemetery at Fontenay-le-Pesnil where his East Lancs comrades lay. He spent a long time walking the lines of headstones, reading and pausing at each one. Afterwards, standing back, and asked what he felt, he replied 'I see each one lying there, in his uniform as if on parade, fresh faced, just as if it was yesterday.'

After further action with 5DCLI, Hutchins was involved in the February 1945 battle for the Reichswald Forest and specifically for the key road junction at Goch. On the night of 16 February he was standing in the doorway of a farmhouse at Bergmannshof while his company area was subject to random artillery fire. An 88mm shell landed ten yards away in the yard. As he turned away a white hot shell splinter entered at the base of his neck, went across the spine, and exited at the top right hand side of the neck, fractionally missing the main artery. Many years later when asked why, when he had a wife and baby son, he was standing in a doorway watching shells burst, he said: 'The fire was persistent, causing casualties since the men were only in shallow scrapes having had no time to dig in, and we were unable to respond. When you have command it is necessary to give a steady example.'

Evacuated for treatment, Hutchins later rejoined 5DCLI as they entered Bremen. During house clearing, he entered an empty upstairs room where a stove was smoking vigorously. He opened a large cupboard and discovered a well fed man in his underclothes hiding there. An SS Colonel who had tried to burn his uniform, he was in mortal fear for his life. Hutchins simply told his corporal to take the man down to the street as he was to join other prisoners. For Hutchins the war was over. The atomic bombs prevented him being deployed to Japan as had been intended.

After the war, now with three sons, Ham needed to work an allotment to feed his family. Prevented by his wound from playing rugby, but concerned to revive the OERFC, he became Treasurer for 1946–1950 and colleagues credited his enthusiasm as being largely responsible for the club's swift revival. He became President for 1960–1961 and every year returned to watch at least a few of the home games and to have a beer in the Blagdons club house with old friends.

In December 1997 he manoeuvered his three sons to attend him at the Artists' Reunion at the Duke of York's HQ (his old drill hall), and in February 1998 he was the most senior member attending the OE Presidents' and Vice-Presidents' lunch at Blagdons. One or two OEs, a few years younger but with whom he had played rugby before the war, turned up. During the post-war decades it mattered very much to him to put on his blazer and appropriate tie, attend a function and listen to the CO's or Headmaster's reports. He came away reassured that his old institutions were functioning in the proper way, that all was well, and that he had had the chance to see old friends or contemporaries. Just days after the OE lunch an operation deprived him of his health and he died in July 1999 aged 88.

A Day Out (or so) to Minden

John Banbery *(Emanuel 1936–1942)*

At School John was a member of the Second Fifteen and was a Lance Corporal in the JTC. He was awarded his War Office Certificate 'A' in 1941 and was a member of the Classical Fifth class. He also played rugby in the School Sevens at Rosslyn Park.

John was evacuated with Emanuel to Petersfield in 1939. Leaving Emanuel John worked for a construction company. Being in a reserved occupation John volunteered for the Army and selected the Armoured Corps. He trained first with 30 Primary Training Wing followed by the 58th Training Regiment at Bovington in Dorset. John underwent a variety of training and drove Bren-gun carriers and Loyd carriers [small tracked vehicles]. He also spent time on a variety of tanks including Crusaders. At Bovington John learnt the theory of gunnery training and put this into practice at Lulworth on a range where they fired on stationary and imitation moving targets.

Michael Williams (left), Eddie Page (centre) and John Banbery (right), Petersfield 1939

John joined the Gloucester Hussars where he trained with 'D' Squadron. By the summer of 1944 John was a fully trained wireless operator. In September 1944 John joined 6th Airborne Armoured Reconnaissance Regiment and sailed for Belgium on Christmas Day 1944.

One of John's most vivid memories of his war experiences is of a hair-raising day around Minden in late April 1945 as the Allies advanced to the Baltic in the last fortnight of the war in Europe.

John Banbery (second from right) after Minden

This article, written by John, originally appeared in the Royal Gloucestershire Hussars Regimental Association newsletter.[1]

In September 1944, thirty members of the 1st Royal Gloucestershire Hussars (RGH) volunteered for the 6th Airborne Armoured Reconnaissance Regiment.

The regiment, having just returned from Normandy, had formed a heavy troop of four tanks in each of its two Sabre Squadrons. We had recently trained on Centaur tanks which also incorporated the four light airborne tanks.

At the time of this incident, three ex-RGH members crewed tanks in 'B' Squadron – Pete Talbot, Bob Arkell (yes, related to the brewers) and myself. It was apparently going to be an interesting day. Not only did we have a new tank commander, Bill Round (an aggressive, decisive commander), but the tank commanders had also drawn for leading vehicle, instead of taking it in turns. We drew the short straw again. Unusually, the Colonel and the Regimental Sergeant Major waved us off.

We travelled with Sergeant Johnston's carrier, driven by Mick Hood, directly behind. During the day our gunner Terry Lovewell had a field day shooting up a barge and an armoured car re-charging its batteries. I popped a 36 grenade in the top of a German self-propelled gun going in the same direction as us and we crossed three bridges, or was it four? Two had big holes in them and one had a couple of 1000lb aero-bombs wired for trouble. We discouraged the Jerries who were about to press the plunger and went on. We also ran over several cars that were parked badly in the road.

When the batteries came into sight Bill Round radioed for instructions and the Squadron Leader, Major Selwyn, told us to push on. We discovered later that the batteries were 12x88mm's manned by Germans and 8x88mm's manned by Italians put there for anti-aircraft protection of Minden. We went past the guns at speed firing a few rounds of Besa [Besa machine gun] but it was too dangerous to traverse the turret for fear of hitting telegraph poles etc. Past the batteries, we paused in a village whilst the battery guns fired airbursts at us. Unknown to us our support squadron was being shot off the road. Our troop commander led us into the outskirts of Minden and we stopped at another blown bridge for the night. I saw Steve Brown drive a jeep (with a German housewife acting as interpreter) carrying a badly wounded officer into a hospital in hostile Minden. That night Bill Jowett (our driver) and I were nearly scalped by two Panzerfausts (bazookas) that demolished an adjacent garden wall whilst we were on guard. The next morning we gingerly crossed the gap blown in the bridge and went to the main bridge in the centre of the town. The Squadron Leader took our tank up to the edge of the bridge under sniper fire to view the demolitions. The proceedings were enlivened by our Squadron Sergeant-Major Fred Murray arriving with a lorry and trailer full of fuel and ammo, well within sniper range. We left Minden after paying a visit to the big army stables for the benefit of our regular cavalrymen. We moved out and then paused to clean guns, have a wash and shave and watch one of our second drivers (hull gunners) have driving practice in which he managed to flatten a military police 15 cwt truck, making it two dimensional.

Three of the four tanks in the troop were 'battle weary' reconditioned Cromwells, supplied as battle replacements.

One had a jammed turret and the main gun had to be laid by the driver, one had a very unreliable 19 Set and our vehicle had no remote firing gear for the 75mm, so I fired the gun using a spanner.

We had only a four man crew as our second driver had joined the troop sergeant as a battle replacement for his driver. Our driver Corporal Bill Jowett was later awarded a much deserved Military Medal for this and other operations.[2]

References

1 For a full interview of John Banbery's experiences in the Second World War and after see Banbery, John Charles – IWM interview – Catalogue number 15205 – Production date 1995-01-21.

2 First published in *The Journal of the Royal Gloucestershire Hussars Yeomanry Association: The Donkey Walloper*, 2013.

CHAPTER 19

THE INTELLIGENCE WAR

A Translator's Life at Bletchley Park

Dr Ronald Gray *(Emanuel 1931–1938)*

Outstanding German scholar, academic, author and Bletchley Park translator

Dr Ronald Gray is a Life Fellow of Emmanuel College, Cambridge. For 33 years he lectured on German literature, thought and history until his official retirement in 1982, and has made a significant contribution to German studies, publishing widely in a variety of journals and national newspapers.

His books include *Goethe the Alchemist. A study of alchemical symbolism in Goethe's literary and scientific works* (Cambridge University Press, 1952) which was regarded as a major contribution to Goethe studies. His later work includes *Shakespeare on Love*, a copy of which Ronald Gray signed and donated to the Emanuel School archive and a second volume *All Triumphant Splendour. Shakespeare on Love II.*

At Emanuel School Ronald played for the First Fifteen and was a member of the OTC. The latter he resigned from as he regarded himself as a pacifist although as his recollections make clear he changed his mind after a trip to Germany in 1938. He won a major scholarship in French and German in 1938 to Emmanuel College, Cambridge where he returned after the War to take a PhD on Goethe and where subsequently he spent his teaching career. Ronald expressed his gratitude to his Emanuel French master Oswald Owen Ginn who encouraged him to apply for the scholarship. Ronald was an outstanding German scholar and in his correspondence with Daniel Kirmatzis in 2011 he made it clear that the teaching of German at Emanuel in the 1930s was exceptional.

Ronald's early war experiences included time in an Anti-Aircraft Unit in Portsmouth but in 1944 his language skills were commandeered for translation work at the Government Communication HQ at Bletchley Park, where he translated decoded German messages. The work carried out at Bletchley Park during the Second World War remained a closely guarded secret until the early 1970s. Today it is a museum dedicated to the men and women who played a vital part in the Allied victory over Nazi Germany.

Ronald Gray's war and Bletchley Park recollections

I resigned from the school OTC as I saw myself as a pacifist, but having been to Germany in 1938 I changed my mind and volunteered for the Army in September of 1939. I was called up in September 1940 and assigned to Anti-Aircraft Units of the Royal Artillery in Portsmouth, Bristol and Slough after being commissioned at Shrivenham near Swindon. There was little to do in the unit after Germany invaded Russia and I volunteered for Air Observation with the Field Artillery, but failed after some months to pass the flying test which required low flying over hedges and avoiding fighter aircraft. I would have been hopeless at that.

A year working at SE Command HQ Reigate was followed by a transfer to Government Communications HQ at Bletchley Park in July 1944. This was the one place where I felt I was doing something useful, translating a steady stream of decoded top secret German radio messages. I went back there a few months ago and was interested to hear that the UK had been reduced to six weeks' supply of food at one point. Thanks to our decoding the future whereabouts of U-boats became known and they were sunk in large numbers. But for that the War would have been over, Hitler would have won in a few short weeks.

EMANUEL SCHOOL.

1st XV. 1937-38.

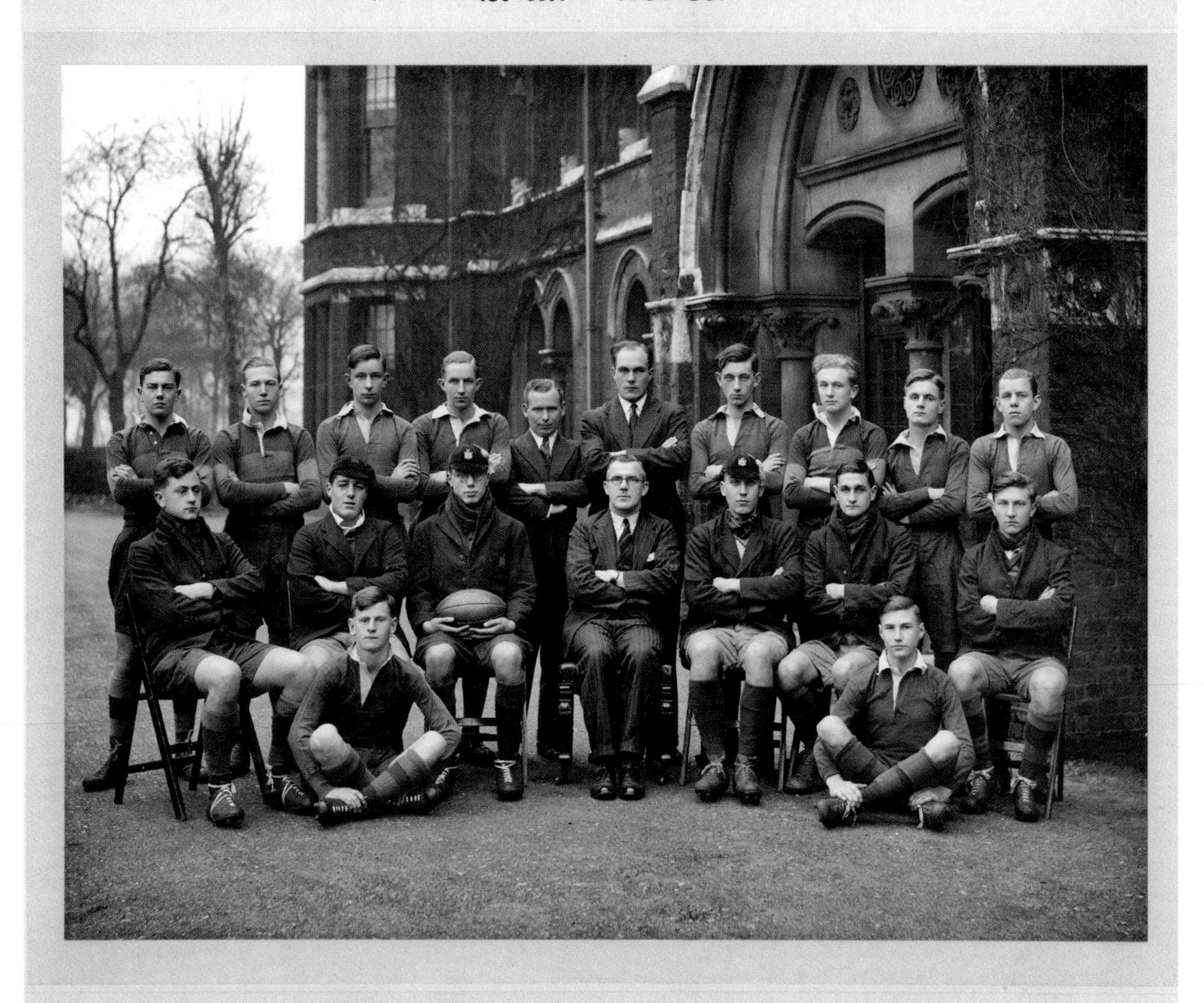

G.T. Thomas. K. Poole. M.W. Knight. S.A. Hill. W.C. Neath, Esq. L. Shaw, Esq. R.D. Gray. T.D. Olver. E.D. Page. B.F. Johnson.
A. F. Fox. K. J. Gurling. W. L. Page. The Headmaster. D. J. Warren. J. F. B. Embleton. H. S. Page.
M. H. Macdonnell. D. L. Roddis.

For four years, I suspect, the 'Colossus' decoder had begun to turn out a huge number of messages and 'the powers that be' raked the lists for people who knew German, as I did, having been taught German at Emanuel by Mr Cyril Bond and Mr Camfield and read German and French at Cambridge University from 1938 to 1939.

I was in barracks at Bletchley at first, but later was billeted on various people. The first was an Irish lady whom I tried to entertain by reading her fortune in tea leaves. One night she said I had made it all up and reported me. I wrote to tell my wife how I was getting on and she dropped her job as a teacher in Croydon and found one in Leighton Buzzard. We were then billeted on a Salvation Army family, who had to accept us even though we were total strangers and before long they gave us the push. There must have been thousands of homes like that one, stuck with people they had never met before. Pat and I lived for a few months in a car-breaker's yard, using a broken down furniture van and the cabin of a lorry for our 'Elsan' toilet. It had to be emptied in a hole which I dug once a week. We were not entitled to any waste collection either as we didn't pay taxes.

Bletchley was in use 24 hours a day. My shifts were either: nine – four, nine – six, six – midnight (twice) and midnight – nine in the morning in rotation, with 48 hours off in between. A daft idea!

There were army, navy and RAF people in uniform, along with ATS and civil servants, several hundred shipped in by bus twice a day from nearby villages and towns. I think we ate in the dining hall, part of the unique house still standing today. I took part in a play *The Late Christopher Bean*, and went to some concerts, but not many I think. There was no social life, I just got into my job and went home after work.

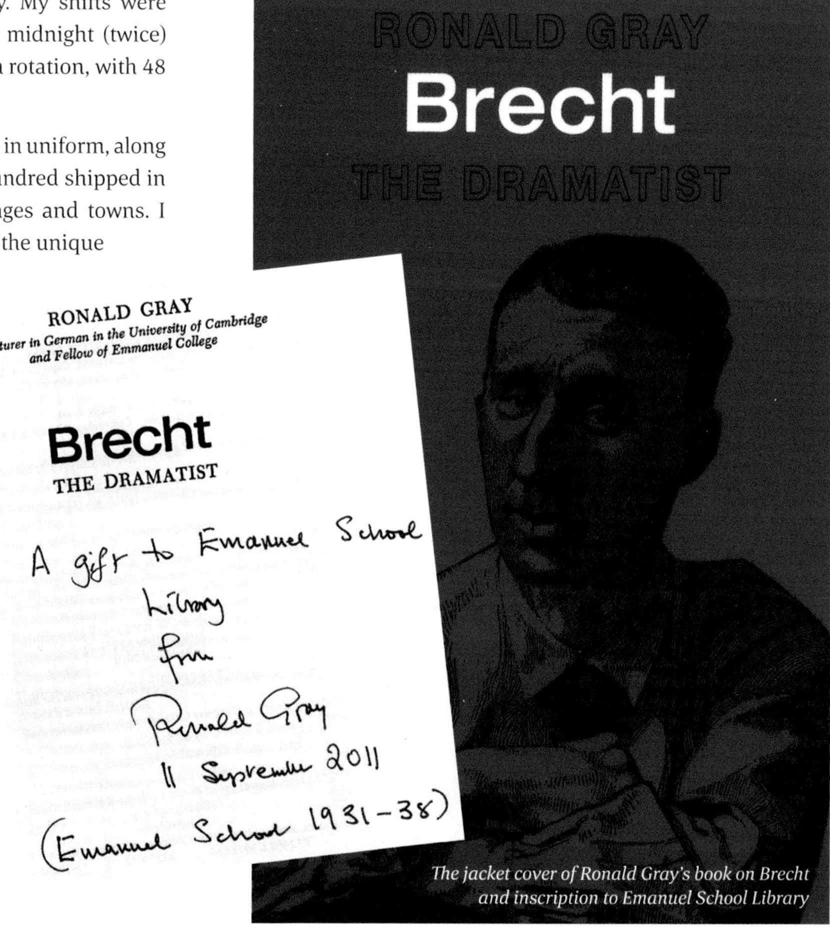

The jacket cover of Ronald Gray's book on Brecht and inscription to Emanuel School Library

I did no decoding and knew nobody who did. We were kept apart, no-one being allowed to know more than they had to and all sworn to secrecy under the Official Secrets Act. In my wooden hut we sat at a table curved on one side, straight on the other, about nine or ten altogether, in the German section. When I first arrived I was in the Yugoslav section, still translating German. I later found out there was also a Japanese section somewhere.

You received messages in the form of old fashioned telegrams, or strips of paper with capital letters all the way. You translated, consulting the card-index dictionaries for technical terms because you only saw a small tranche which made little sense. Secrecy was maintained by never revealing that the message came via radio.

The translations were vetted for accuracy by the head of the section who passed them to one or two evaluators, who would then decide who was most likely to be interested. Only the top brass were allowed to know if the messages were decoded from radio signals. That meant difficulties sometimes. I heard that we knew exactly which ships were loading in Italian ports to cross to Africa with supplies to Rommel. To have sunk them all would have been giving the game away so 'Top Brass No 1' would tell 'Top Brass No 2' who might just be 'in the know' and RAF planes would be sent out with one of them directed to a place where we knew he would find a ship and so the ships would assume they had been spotted. The pilot would report back and the ships would be sunk. Care was taken to sink only ships carrying arms. Those with food were spared because we had our POWs to care about.

The only dramatic message I remember was at the end of the war when I had something from Goebbels or Himmler, I can't remember which, saying 'Our shield and fuehrer, Adolf Hitler is dead.'

We danced all day in Leighton Buzzard Square when VE Day was announced. Well nearly all day. It was great. Then it was decided that I had lived a soft life for too long and so I was sent to Italy. There wasn't much to do, but I couldn't complain as some men had had a really tough time. I was back at Cambridge in December of 1945 and resumed my studies.

In recent years I met Major John Neale TD several times, a great friend from my schooldays. Another I was close with was Horace Page whom I met at an old boys' gathering. We were a trio.

Cunning wordsmith who was unrivalled with the pen

Norman Frederick 'Wally' Simpson

(Emanuel 1930–1937)

Lauded by Sir John Mortimer as 'really changing the course of comedy', Norman Frederick Simpson, known as 'Wally', for having the same surname as King Edward VIII's fiancée Wallis Simpson, was a comedic genius who influenced Peter Cook and Monty Python as well as being one of the most prominent playwrights in the early years of the Royal Court Theatre in the late 1950s.

N. F. Simpson's play – 'One Way Pendulum'

Wally was the master of the absurd and his plays were performed by the leading comedy lights of the 1960s including John Cleese, Peter Cook and Jonathan Miller. His three most well known plays were huge hits in the 1950s. *A Resounding Tinkle* (1957), *The Hole* (1958) and *One Way Pendulum* (1959). In *A Resounding Tinkle* we find a young couple disturbed by the presence of an elephant, which they had not ordered, in their front garden and in *One Way Pendulum,* adapted for screen starring Jonathan Miller, Peggy Mount and Eric Sykes, we see Jonathan Miller directing weight machines to sing. These examples of surreal situations, comedy and absurdity were a mark of Wally's style. Wally's works presented logical twists as well as twisted logic but his great gift was his ear for picking up the way people talk and in particular the ways people express themselves. A typical example of the way in which he transformed banal phrases into dialogue in his plays, for instance, is in *One Way Pendulum*, where the mother tells her daughter 'You should have thought of all this before you were born.'

Norman Simpson (first from right) swimming as part of basic training, 1943

Norman Simpson in Emanuel School uniform

Ian Greave, archivist to the N. F. Simpson collection writes that 'Wally played a significant part in BBC2's early satirical output' and indeed wrote several television productions, including *Charley's Grants* (written with John Wells and John Fortune) and a 1973 'Comedy Play House', *Elementary, My Dear Watson,* starring John Cleese.

Wally's fame was at its peak in the 1960s and 1970s but by the 1980s his style of comedy fell out of fashion and he decided to purchase a narrow boat and travel around the canals of England. His decision for doing so was influenced by a book he read at Emanuel, 'At school we read W. H. Davies's *Autobiography of a Super-Tramp* and fancied the nomadic life. The closest I could get was a narrow boat.'

In 2007, four years before Wally died, his work underwent a revival. There was a BBC Radio 4 documentary about his life, *Reality is an Illusion Caused by Lack of N. F. Simpson*, and also a film documentary of the same title with contributions from John Fortune, Jonathan Miller, John Mortimer and Eric Sykes. A full-length reading of *A Resounding Tinkle* was also performed for the Royal Court Theatre's 50th anniversary.[1]

On leaving Emanuel Wally worked both as a bank clerk and a teacher before the outbreak of the Second World War. His war experiences may never have come to light if during the course of research on the roles of Emanuel boys in the world wars, Wally had not been asked to write an original piece specifically for this publication. What follows is his brief account of his war.

Wally's War

Well ... 11400218 Gunner Simpson was stationed at Beckenham till 1943 manning a 3.7 anti-aircraft gun with only one memorable incident when someone (not me) dropped the bicycle lamp we used to see what we

Norman Simpson in Italy, 1945

A flyer for an evening with Norman Simpson c.1960s

were doing when setting fuses before firing. A German aircraft perfectly on cue dropped magnesium flares – which enabled us to dispense entirely with the bicycle lamp! I was laughing so much I nearly dropped the shell. In 1943 I transferred to the Intelligence Corps and was sent first to Italy where we cipher clerks were billeted in Settimio Soprani's piano accordion factory in Castelfidardo near Ancona. Then it was Palestine (now Israel) and after that Nicosia in Cyprus where, believe it or not, we went skiing one February on Mount Troodos. It was there that I achieved the distinction of rising to the rank of Lance-Sergeant. A highly distinguished war record if ever there was one! The only piece I can recall writing about it all was a short thing in Birkbeck College's student magazine *The Lodestone* called *The Grave My Silencer*. It was about our basic training for the Intelligence Corps which included being taught to ride motorbikes over rough terrain. I never mastered even the art of riding the things on smooth terrain and, although I was passed out, just, I was never let anywhere near a motorbike again. The stuff of legend![2]

The Grave my Silencer by N. F. Simpson

This is one of N. F. Simpson's earliest published works, for the *Lodestone Magazine*, Vol 45, No. 1, Spring 1954. It is also one of the very few occasions in which he wrote about the War.

Although Private Toomey had an easier time of it than I had when it came to getting the upper hand of a motor-cycle, it probably took more out of him in the end. Nothing Sergeant Broadrib ever had us all doing caused Toomey the same distress of mind as the things we might possibly be having to do next. With me it was quite the other way. The fear that tomorrow we might be riding single file round the rim of a blast furnace hardly troubled me at all as I went hurtling down one slagheap and up the next.

What Toomey experienced on the mental plane was more than matched by pretty nearly everything I went through on the physical. It generally got put down to my reflexes, though never by Sergeant Broadrib. As there was precious little the matter with Sergeant Broadrib's reflexes, he very likely looked on mine as a form of malingering.

It often seemed to me that Broadrib understood more about our machines than he did about us. Or than we did about either. In spite of that he was an excellent instructor who, so it was said, could be thoroughly caustic in his abuse without ever arousing rancour. Even those of us who had difficulty in telling where one ended and the other began had to agree that it was a fine gift to have. Or even to be thought of as having.

I can see now that I ought to have been far more disheartened than I was by his incredible feats of motor-cycling skill. Those who had the sense to be thoroughly disheartened by them on the first day out got off on the whole fairly lightly. At least he never got as nettled about their kick-starters as he did about mine. "It isn't on that side for crissake!"

In the end he more or less gave me up. We gave each other up in a way. Not that our relationship had done much except founder from the start.

"On the whole," I remarked once, smiling gingerly, "it's played a pretty minor part, all this sort of thing, in my way of life." Without taking his eyes off me, he put a cigarette between his lips and felt for his matches. "Till now," he said.

Shortly after that I got rid of my front brake. It was ripped off in one of the two or three quarries at the top of which I was supposed to have brought my machine to a halt. I shall not go so far as to pretend that I had no idea what the front brake was for, but it was obvious that the loss of it was going to make very little difference to me. Sergeant Broadrib seemed to see it in much the same light. He silently wound the trailing cable round my handlebar and waved me on. As I went I noticed him putting the brake lever into his pannier; perhaps to him it was a symbol of something or other.

At moments of crisis like that I have a fortunate knack of standing right outside myself and weighing my own reactions with cool detachment. No one else seemed to be able to do that, least of all Private Toomey. Perhaps he was afraid that once out he would never be able to get back in again. It would certainly have matched up well enough with some of his other fears, such as that Broadrib was out to humiliate him by having us all riding through the streets of Halifax in gasmasks. It was his native city.

We did, as it turned out, have to ride a couple of miles wearing gasmasks, though not in Halifax. It was not a very alarming experience for those whose eyepieces had been properly smeared with anti-dim beforehand. Mine, which had not, quickly began clouding over on the inside. Soon I was riding blind. It was a nasty enough situation even for one who to all intents and purposes had been riding blind since the course started; for anyone else it must almost certainly have ended in disaster.

Nothing, I suppose, could ever have got to be as distorted as some of these things obviously have, without having been pretty incredible to begin with. No less incredible in its own way is the fact that within three weeks I was passed out as a dispatch rider. One week more and I expect they would have made me an instructor. Fortunately I never had to go near a motor-cycle again.[3]

Norman Simpson in comedic mood, 2006

References

1 Obituary of N. F. Simpson, *The Times*, Thursday 1 September 2011, p. 54 and Letters, Ian Greaves, *The Times*, Thursday 20 October 2011, p. 62.
2 An original piece written by N. F. Simpson for Emanuel School at War.
3 Our thanks to Adrian Punacks of Birkbeck College, London for finding the *Lodestone* article.

‘Relentless search of wine…’
Life in Second World War Intelligence

Emanuel OTC Parade, Jack Grundy standing behind podium

John ‘Jack’ Brownsdon Clowes Grundy
(Emanuel 1912–1920) Emanuel Headmaster (1953–1963)

Born in 1902, Jack Grundy was Headmaster at Emanuel School from 1953 to 1963. He inherited a very successful School from Cyril Broom and continued to advance the high academic standards set by him, as well as develop the school buildings, including a new Boat House, rebuilding Hampden Hall and new Fives Courts.

The Boat House will be perhaps Jack’s lasting legacy as it helped Emanuel achieve both the first of eleven wins in the Schools’ Head of the River Race in 1962 and in 1966 the winning of the Princess Elizabeth Challenge Cup at Henley Royal Regatta, a moment Jack described in his autobiography, ‘Exhausted but exuberant, we were just in time to greet the victorious crew and I do not think I have known a moment of greater gladness in my life.’

Of course, Jack was also an Old Boy of the School himself, beginning in 1912 in IIA, in the form of ‘Flobby Edwards’ and his autobiography *Life’s Five Windows* indicated that he could be as mischievous as the next teenager and was known to drag his bike over the back wall behind the sports fields which was out of bounds, as means of a shortcut. Either way Jack was an outstanding scholar when he attended the School. He rose to Captain of the School, Captain of Howe, Captain of Rugby and Captain of Boats. He was also a Cadet Officer in the OTC. After Emanuel he attended Fitzwilliam Hall, Cambridge, following that with a modern languages doctorate at University College, London. He was an outstanding linguist and wrote *Brush up your German* which was a notable contribution to German teaching in the 1930s.

A very colourful and wide-ranging teaching career began at St Paul's School, followed by teaching English at Gottingen University. Between 1929 and 1939 he was modern language master at Shrewsbury School. His obituary, which was published in *The Times* noted: 'With typical enthusiasm he breathed new life into the modern side. He imparted to his pupils not only the importance of the style and traditions of the French and German classics but also the practical need for familiarity with the modern idiom.'

An earlier section has already recounted how both his elder brothers Cecil and Ronald were killed on the Western Front in the First World War. Jack, who was too young to serve in that war, seized the chance to play his part in the Second. Jack was a Territorial Reservist but it was his Cambridge connections, including Robin Ridgway, military private secretary of Hore-Belisha, the Secretary of State for War, that helped land him a place at a new intelligence school at Minley Manor. Enrolling in January 1940, Jack proceeded to have intensive instruction in everything from map reading to prisoner interrogation. However, because he spoke excellent French and German, in hindsight, he felt the Army had badly underused his linguistic ability.

His knowledge of languages led to a move to the Intelligence Services and a number of educational and back-staff roles. Although it remains very difficult to pinpoint exactly what many soldiers did in the Intelligence Services, one would have thought his excellent German would have been a major asset. Indeed, his autobiography recalls:

> Several scores of Germans were now in the Tower of London and we were to interrogate them there and on their way to a POW camp situated in a Lancashire cotton mill... We went down to the dungeons where the prisoners were housed.[1]

Without going into too much detail Jack explains how it was his job to try and entice every possible piece of information from a captured soldier. Everything from which airports they had flown from to what training they had received. He noted that often he 'found out remarkably little.'

After training at the intelligence school Jack was posted in the summer of 1940 as Intelligence Officer to the Third Division, situated in Frome, Somerset. The Division was commanded by Bernard Law Montgomery. Jack's autobiography recalls his first meeting with Montgomery:

> He met me at the hotel entrance, an envelope in his hand and dressed in grubby flannel trousers and an odd jacket. 'Your name Grundy?' – 'Yes, Sir.' – 'See this letter?' I thrilled with importance: secret orders? 'Now go out of the front door and turn left. Left, see?' – 'Yes, Sir.' – 'Walk a hundred yards and you come to a pillar box. Post this letter!' I went off somewhat dashed. But I knew that Monty's little green eyes had been sizing me up during the half-minute.

Jack Grundy in 1920 with Headmaster Shirley Goodwin

By Autumn 1942 Jack was still a Captain at the headquarters of Third Division and things remained slow 'repelling imaginary invasions from Kent to Somerset and Dorset.'[2] Grundy's next position held considerably more excitement. He was now based in the HQ of V Corps which housed 'a very hush hush upper room in which cross-Channel raids were planned.' Jack didn't remain long enough with V Corps to get acquainted with this room and was soon transferred again, this time to Whitehall, where he became No. 2 in the Intelligence Room at GHQ. It was whilst based here 'two storeys below the ground floor of a building in King Charles Street' that Jack met Winston Churchill on a number of occasions as the Prime Minister would often visit the rooms after long discussions with various ministers. Jack notes that spending so much time indoors and far from the enemy wasn't really what he had in mind when he joined the Army

An Emanuel assembly in the Hampden Hall. Jack Grundy on stage

Emanuel Headmaster, Jack Grundy in his study c. late 1950s

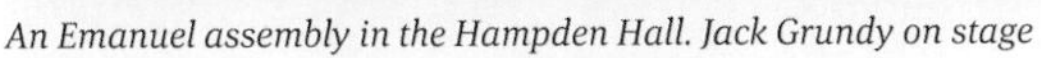

and in a rare moment when he mentions his elder brothers notes: 'I sometimes wondered what my elder brothers would have thought of this way of fighting a war?' Like many soldiers he was transferred many times and probably stayed in a post for an average of six months or less.

Jack's next posting was with HQ XII Corps which took him to Tunbridge Wells. He was involved in making German broadcasts for the BBC. The programmes were directed at enemy civilians and repackaged recent events from the German press which were narrated objectively. Jack recalls one broadcast when he was cut off in mid flow:

> ... the broadcast was in full swing when I felt that minute draught which told that the noise-less door had been opened. A hand reached out and we were off the air. At first I thought that I had made some howler. The real reason was that the number of aircraft engaged in the raid upon Kassel that I was about to describe had been exaggerated. Since this programme depended for its value upon the strictest truth the transmission must be stopped.

Over this period he was also involved in low-level intelligence discussions about pinpointing the best landing spots in France for an Allied invasion. He ironically points out that even to the lowest of Intelligence Officers, the invasion points were pretty obvious and so he noted 'It was difficult to understand why the German High Command, even up to the Autumn of 1944, expected the main allied invasion to come east of the Seine.'

By Spring 1944 Jack feared he would miss active service altogether as an order came from HQ stating that Intelligence Officers who had not already had active service abroad would sit the impending invasion out. Jack found this deeply disappointing and his autobiography notes that 'This was the sack' and that he 'might as well have stayed in Shrewsbury.' However, a new staff branch called Civil Affairs to be attached to every corps was soon formed and this ensured that he would make it to France after all. His autobiography makes no allusions to this being a front row role and he accepted being 'banished to the motley throng of Rear HQ.' This new branch were expected to deal with civil problems which might arise after the invasion. Jack was made No. 2 in the rank of Lt.-Col. in XII Corps. Jack describes both his journey across the Channel and how he spent the first few days:

> I forget how the wind sat on invasion day, but we all expected fireworks as soon as we should reach the downs – especially as every ship flew a captive balloon. Not a shell came our way and we recorded gratitude to the Navy and the Air Force for their efficient preliminaries on the other side. Everything went like clockwork as we drew near to the astonishing Mulberry Harbour at Arromanches. Offshore we trans-shipped into new

Jack Grundy in bowler hat at an Emanuel OTC inspection

The three Emanuel Headmasters – (from left to right), Cyril Broom, Charles Kuper and Jack Grundy

> American landing craft and everyone received a hot dog and cup of coffee before he reached the beach almost dry-shod, a kindly welcome which we appreciated.
>
> Soon the vehicles were landed too and we were off. I spent my first two or three nights in a comfortable dry ditch and during this time we lived on special rations which included the new self-heating tins of soup. Gradually the tents appeared, the notice-boards were put up, the field telephones installed; batmen arrived, the mess was opened and life became almost normal...

Whilst Jack's duties on his own account were less than taxing he did travel through a battle scarred Caen which the British-led forces took a month of bitter fighting to secure. Jack describes witnessing his first battlefield:

> Dead horses, abandoned stores and ammunition, human corpses, broken farm-carts and limbers littered the Norman roads and villages wherever a stand had been made or a unit caught by our tanks or artillery. In the warm weather the sickly smell of decomposing flesh was nauseous. Striking was the absence of enemy motor transport from the wreckage. It was known to be in short supply: I saw none.[3]

Being in Civil Affairs gave Jack time to explore interesting places in France. With Lynton Lamb, a camouflage officer who was also painter and lecturer at the Slade School, Jack made all manner of excursions including one to a private house where, as Jack explains, they went to 'investigate the alleged destruction of an 'important' library ... and found that it had consisted of a couple of hundred novels in half-leather.'

So these were activities far from the front-line, but which still had to be handled delicately. He was also the 'wine secretary for the mess' and had to try and acquire alcohol for the officers as they headed towards Belgium. Their advance continued towards the Dutch frontier, as did the search for alcohol. As they were now within forty miles of the German border Jack decided it was time to get a pocket book of basic German printed for the officers and NCOs.

As part of XII Corps, Jack witnessed a number of sights as he travelled across Northern Europe but one he recalls as, 'something to remember', was the build up to Allied Operations at Arnhem where Allied forces unsuccessfully attempted to take the bridges across the Rhine, 'The only incident in its slow progress north-east was the sight, on an afternoon in late September, of the great fleet of parachutists and airborne troops bound for their fruitless task in Arnhem. I had watched gliders being built near Wolverhampton, but had never seen hundreds of them on tow in the air.'

Yet another move saw Jack posted to a Reinforcement Unit. In his own words 'Here were gathered the misfits. Most of them were former professional people like me.' These included opera singers, classic scholars and insurance salesmen. This move was necessitated by what Jack describes as an 'adverse report' sent to the Military Secretary by Jack's Colonel, but the details of the report were never revealed. The report was later destroyed and no more was heard of it as Jack notes, '...I received an official buff envelope of which the contents touched me deeply. It was a crisp official letter from Monty to the effect that, as I had obtained further employment since my adverse report and was performing it satisfactorily, the report would by the provisions of Article something-or-other be destroyed forthwith.'

Jack only spent a short time with the Reinforcement Unit and was swiftly reposted to Civil Affairs probably because of an old contact and took over the translation section, whilst based in Brussels. A final surprise move to the Control Commission for Germany, based in London, saw Jack return to the UK now ranked as Colonel. For the remainder of the war he was embroiled in educational committees and with Foreign Office business. He was offered demobilisation not long after VE-Day and as he states in his autobiography 'seized it with both hands.' At the age of 43 it was time to go home.

But not quite England. In 1945 he returned to education and served as the first representative of the British Council in Helsinki and in 1949–1950 was head of the British Institute in Cairo. The call of the classroom returned in 1950 when Jack was appointed senior modern language master at Harrow School. It has long been suspected that working at this leading boarding school helped shape his ten year tenure at Emanuel. He had a vision of pulling Emanuel out of the Grammar School doldrums and aspired for something better.

In 1964 he moved to Sierre Leone where he was Senior Teaching Fellow at Fourah Bay College. His job consisted mainly of teaching prospective scientists the languages in which their textbooks were written.

Although Jack notes 'I enjoyed my war' there was definitely a sense of what might have been. A bomb dropping three tents away was the closest he got to the frontline. He also noted he never fired a shot in anger during the whole campaign. He states in black and white that his final rank of Colonel was an 'absurdity' and was a poor reflection on the fact that there were 28 men behind the frontline for every one man in front of it. Of course the Second Word War was fought in a completely different way from the first and the terrible deaths of his two brothers were a far cry from the pleasant years he, by his own admission, spent in the Home Counties.

Jack died in July 1987 at the age of 85.

References

1 J. B. C. Grundy, *Life's Five Windows* (1968), p. 133.
2 Ibid. p. 136.
3 Ibid. p. 152.

Jack Grundy overseeing an Emanuel OTC inspection

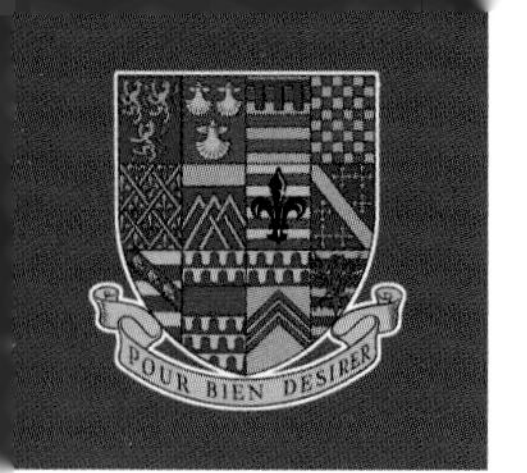

CHAPTER 20
OE POWS IN THE SECOND WORLD WAR

Almost 40 Old Emanuels were made prisoners of the Axis (German, Italian and Japanese) forces in the Second World War. Their experiences and chances of survival depended largely on where they spent their captivity. Those made prisoners of the Japanese and who were interned in various locations across the Far East suffered intolerable privations and fared far worse, in most cases, than those in European camps. Three OE Far East Prisoners of War (FEPOWs) never returned home whereas all those who were POWs in Europe survived.

Douglas Hoare, (second from right), at Oflag–XXIB, Schubin

Vernon Avery

The fact that those OE POWs interned in Europe all survived doesn't diminish the hardships they suffered or the torments that haunted them for the rest of their lives. One such example is that of Vernon Avery (Emanuel 1930–1937). Vernon was a Lance Corporal in the Royal Corps of Signals and had been captured in North Africa. At first he was sent to Prisoner of War Camp 73, Fossoli di Carpi, near Modena until 1943 before a move to Austria.[1] On the whole Vernon considered he was treated well by his Italian and German guards but, nonetheless, he did suffer being stripped to his underwear in sub zero conditions and being hosed with freezing cold water for three days after fellow POWs had attempted to escape from Stalag XVIII-A in Wolfsberg, Austria. Similarly towards the end of the war some OEs suffered intolerable freezing conditions, with little food, during the forced marches of 1945 in which POWs were moved west by the Germans to avoid the Russian approach from the east.

Generally, however, European prison camps followed the rules of the Geneva Convention. This comprised a series of treaties for the protection of, among others, POWs who were rendered incapable of combat, first signed by twelve states in 1864 and subsequently renewed. In practice this meant that, as a general rule, those in European camps were allowed to write home and receive their Red Cross parcels full of 'luxuries' that they were lacking in the normal course of camp life, such as foodstuffs which provided a much needed nutritional boost. Of course towards the end of the war when the tide turned against Germany the distribution of parcels became erratic in some cases.

Basic prisoner rights were set out in subsequent additions to the original Geneva Convention. One of these later additions was the '1929 Convention relative to the Treatment of Prisoners of War.' By signing this Convention Japan became a State Signatory, but they never ratified it and their failure to do so resulted in them ignoring the laws covering the treatment of prisoners. One consequence was that Red Cross parcels were distributed infrequently in the Far East. This wasn't only due to the fact that the International Committee of the Red Cross (ICRC) lacked the infrastructure to secure supplies but also to the actions of Japanese guards who often obstructed their delivery to prisoners. In addition to the lack of these basic rights Japanese forces were responsible for some of the most inhumane treatment suffered by combatant prisoners in the entire course of the Second World War and many of those who did survive were reticent in discussing their experiences. The post-war accounts of those who did recall what life was like in Japanese prison camps are chilling and full of innumerable atrocities. The nightmares which haunted so many attest to the unwillingness of many survivors to relive their experiences for post-war generations.

The general picture of life in a prison camp can be gleaned from how they have been referred to as 'Barbed Wired Universities.' Of course caveats apply depending on location, but similar to universities, individuals mainly in European camps but not exclusively had the chance to study for exams, play sports, put on shows and make innumerable friends. However the term 'Barbed Wired Universities' masks the reality that for many life in the camps was monotonous and frustrating in that being fighting men they felt hopeless in not being able to carry on the war effort. However, many did find ways to carry on their own war behind the wire. Many became members of escape committees and some OEs successfully escaped. These acts of resistance interrupted resources the Axis powers could have put to better use in fighting the war and although the overall impact on the Axis' defeat may have been negligible it provided a much needed morale boost for the individuals involved.[2]

Among those OEs who escaped was Gordon Pople who had been a member of the Emanuel OTC in the 1930s. *The Portcullis* reported in the Summer of 1944, 'Lt. Gordon Pople (Nelson), Prisoner of War No. 1929, Oflag VIII F, Germany, was previously in Italy, having been captured in N. Africa. He escaped and had walked over 400 miles, almost back to our lines, when he was re-captured.'[3] Another escapee was OE Douglas 'Sammy' Hoare who escaped from Oflag VIB Warburg in May 1942 for a whole week before being recaptured. One OE who made a successful escape was Peter Glendenning (Emanuel 1932–1939. Yorks & Lancs attached to 5th Green Howards). Originally captured in North Africa in January 1942, Peter was made a POW in Italy being interned in Campo 49, Fontanellato. When Italy surrendered Peter's camp was evacuated and he proceeded to make his way south only to be recaptured by the Germans at Roseto degli Abruzzi on the Adriatic coast, on 19 October 1943. He was then transferred to Sulmona via Chietti where he was put on a train for Aquila. Forcing open the window of the truck, he made his escape two hours after leaving Sulmona. Peter then made contact with British troops on 20 November 1943.

Gordon Pople in Emanuel OTC uniform, 1933

The following accounts from the experiences of OEs gives us an insight into what life was like for POWs. They explore the circumstances of their capture, the journeys they made as they were transported to various camps, the friendships that were forged and their daily routines. They also afford us a window onto their private thoughts through their letters home or log book notes written at the time, or their reminiscences written in memoirs or given in interviews afterwards. They are stories of frustration and hardship as well as courage and heroism. But most importantly they are the real life experiences of ordinary men who found themselves living through extraordinary times.

It will be noted that the European camps had different names depending on the type of prisoners held in them. Please refer to end note four for a key to these camps.[4]

References

1 After the Allied inmates were transferred to German run camps Camp 73 became a Jewish concentration camp where the author Primo Levi was interned before being deported to Auschwitz.
2 For an excellent account of the POW experience see Midge Gillies, *The Barbed-Wire University: The Real Lives of Allied Prisoners of War in the Second World War* (2011).
3 *The Portcullis*, Summer Term, 1944, p. 18.
4 *Oflag* (Officers' camp); *Stalag* is an abbreviation of 'Stammlager', (Base Camp); *Stalag Luft* (air-force base camp); *Dulag* (transfer camp); *Front Stalag* (camp in enemy occupied territory); *Kommando* (detachment or section of main camp); *Marlag* (naval camp); *Milag* (merchant seamen's camp).

William 'Bill' Henry Taylor

(Emanuel 1929–1935)

Bill was a talented rugby player at School being selected to play in the First Fifteen at the age of sixteen. Rugby has remained a passion throughout his life. During the Second World War Bill was involved in a far greater scrum with German troops on a little known Aegean island called Leros leaving him a POW from November 1943 to April 1945.

During his internment Bill, like most POWs, was given a log book by The War Prisoners' Aid of the YMCA in which he recorded his wartime experiences.[1] In 2011 Bill was the first OE Second World War veteran Daniel Kirmatzis interviewed as part of the Emanuel School at War project and so, in addition to the log book, a wealth of information now exists to tell the remarkable story of a young South London boy who, until 1939, had travelled no further than Jersey but who would, in the following years, be one of the men destined to spearhead what some call Winston Churchill's 'folly' of pursuing a strategy of defeating the Nazis' European Empire through what he termed the 'soft underbelly' of southern Europe. But as Bill and many others discovered the 'soft underbelly' turned out to be, in US General Mark Clark's words, 'a tough gut.'

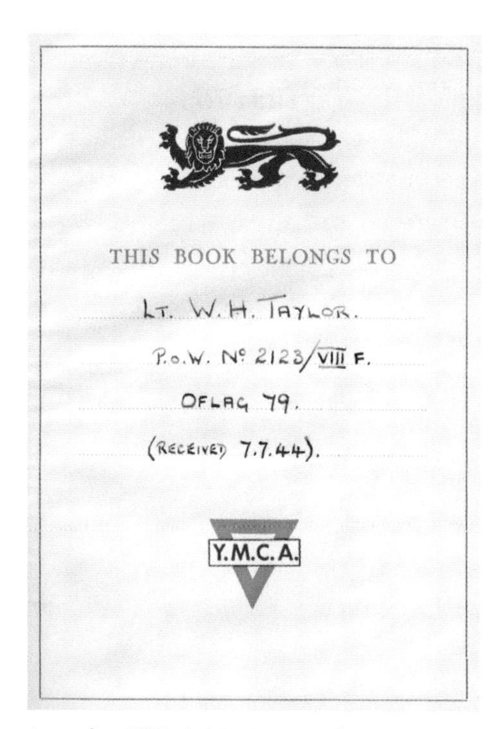
THIS BOOK BELONGS TO

LT. W. H. TAYLOR.

P.O.W. No 2123/VIII F.

OFLAG 79.

(RECEIVED 7.7.44).

Y.M.C.A.

A page from Bill Taylor's YMCA Log Book

After leaving School Bill worked as a clerk in the accounts department in the Head Office of British Associated Cinemas Ltd. In the summer of 1939 Bill and his fiancée Grace had holidayed in Jersey and on their return to Southampton on 2 September 1939 they experienced the first signs of a country preparing for war as Bill noted later in his POW log book:

> We steamed into Southampton Docks and we saw our first barrage balloon. It was only just above the housetops and was naturally an object of interest to all. We also noticed some business-like sandbag emplacements... When it became properly dark there were no lights, or at least only faint bluish glimmers in the station and the train in which we travelled to London was unlit throughout. This was our first experience of the blackout.

After the declaration of war on 3 September 1939 Bill noted that he had no overreaching desire to rush to the colours believing that the nations would come to their senses, but as the weeks passed any hopes of a resolution vanished and so Bill decided to join up. It had been his wish to become a pilot and so he made enquiries about joining the RAF but due to the thousands of applicants Bill never realised his dream. In January 1940 Bill was called upon for a medical examination and after passing as A1 fit he received his papers on 8 February 1940 to report to the East Surrey Regiment's barracks at Kingston-upon-Thames on 15 February 1940. Bill remained at Kingston for thirteen months during which time he received his Lance

Bill Taylor (first from right, standing) with the Emanuel First XV, 1934

Corporal stripe, a position which required assisting the Sergeant with the training of new recruits in various drills such a Bren-gun instruction, on occasion taking the lessons himself. In addition to the barracks, manoeuvres were carried out in a camp based in nearby Richmond Park. Training in Kingston didn't go without incident as Bill was based there during the Battle of Britain and noted down more than one occasion in his logbook of bombs dropping near the barracks during air-raids.

As his contemporaries, who were called up at the same time as Bill, started to receive commissions Bill decided it was time he should try for one, so he asked his company commander for an interview. After further interviews with an Officers Selection Board Bill was posted to an Officer Cadet Training Unit (OCTU) platoon at the depot. After two months Bill was transferred to 164th OCTU at Barmouth in North Wales.

At OCTU all previous ranks were relinquished and the men became privates with equal standing. As part of the training each cadet was given the chance of holding a different rank to test their commanding abilities. Bill later confided to his logbook that he felt at a disadvantage compared to some other cadets for not ever having been part of a battalion; but where he stood out was in knowing his weapons and drill back to front. The first month's training consisted of lectures where cadets were expected to take notes that were later inspected, drill exercises, arms training and PT (Physical Training). By the second month training included sand table exercises which included Q&As on various battlefield scenarios. In the third month it was learning how to ride a motorcycle and truck which for Bill at the time was a new experience. As he later remembered, 'I had never sat on a motorcycle before, my first attempt I shot straight over a wall in front of me and ruined the bike and didn't do myself any good. They immediately put me on another motorbike, which I proceeded to ride and got used to it.' In the fourth and last month at OCTU the cadets had to undertake night exercises, which were more intense than in previous months. They waded through streams up to their waists, trawled through mud knee-deep, scrambled through barbed-wire and cut themselves on gorse bushes; but at the end of the day Bill looked forward to a well-earned cup of tea at his billets. At the end of the course, dependent on passing out, they had to choose which regiment they wished to join. Bill had preferred to be commissioned into the East Surrey Regiment

Bill and Grace Taylor on their wedding day in December 1941

but with no vacancies at that time he was commissioned into the King's Own Royal Regiment (KORR) instead. Bill returned to London where his fiancée Grace, mum and Dad were all proud of the newly commissioned 2nd Lt. Taylor.

Bill was ordered to report to the KORR depot in Lancaster and soon found a change in lifestyle when after his first night he awoke to find a batman had been sent to polish his boots and the buttons on his tunic. A few days in Lancaster and Bill was on the move again this time to the 7th Battalion KORR in Banbridge, Co. Down, Northern Ireland. Bill spent six months on manoeuvres in Northern Ireland but by far the most important moment during this time was phoning his fiancée and asking her to marry him. Grace said yes and they were married in December 1941. Grace worked for the Queen's dressmaker Norman Hartnell in the 1930s and among the many dresses Grace worked on was Queen Elizabeth's (later the Queen Mother) mourning dress for the funeral of King George V.

On his return to Northern Ireland Bill was drafted overseas. He Spent Christmas Day 1941 at home, but on Boxing Day he was ordered to Chester from where he would prepare to go overseas. On leaving his wife and parents behind Bill wrote, 'I felt a lump in my throat, but at the same time had so much adventure and excitement to look forward to that my spirits were not so very low.' A short stay in Chester and Bill finally left England, via Liverpool and the Clyde, on 5 January 1942, sailing in the troop ship HMT *Laconia*. By March and after a difficult crossing for Bill who had experienced a violent bout of sea-sickness, the *Laconia* arrived first in Freetown and then Cape Town where Bill enjoyed the city lights in contrast to the Blackout in London.

After spending time training in the Middle East Bill was transferred to Malta. Following a bumpy ride across the desert he embarked on the *Breconshire* on 19 March 1942. He noted in his log book that the men looked for Malta on the map in relation to the German sphere of influence, 'Malta appeared to be a tiny spot, entirely surrounded by the enemy and almost inaccessible from either east or west.' The *Breconshire* set off as part of a convoy and for the first two days they sailed with ease until, as Bill describes in his diary, 'Hell was let loose.' The convoy came under attack. Bill describes what happened:

> There were about 20 of them, Stukas if I remember correctly, and for the next 20 minutes hell was let loose. All the ships opened up at the planes which had broken formation and were coming in from all directions. Bombs whistled down and great fountains of water shot up into the air.

This attack was repelled but the crew assured their passengers that another attack wouldn't be long coming and indeed the second attack followed shortly after as Bill explains:

> About half an hour later more planes were sighted. So it went on all day. I still cannot understand how the convoy escaped as it did but I think a great deal was due to the skipper who remained as cool as the proverbial cucumber and steered the ship on its zig-zag course.

These episodes were mild compared to the following days when Italian destroyers bore down on the convoy. They were repulsed by the cruisers and destroyers and by a smoke screen which was laid around the merchantmen, but on the fourth day as they approached Malta worse was to come. Thinking that two Allied fighter aircraft had come to meet them Bill and another officer were casually leaning on the rail of the ship watching them when, as Bill noted:

> They parted from one another and one came down low over the water and made for us in a straight line. We thought this rather peculiar but soon discovered the

Bill on a motorbike in Malta

> reason. When the plane was about three hundred yards away it suddenly opened up on us with machine guns. My companion and I threw ourselves on the deck and bullets spattered all over the side of the ship. Then we were literally lifted off the deck by a terrific jolt. Our guns had opened up by now and the plane, as it zoomed up over us fell away to one side and crashed into the sea. But it had found its mark with a small bomb which had penetrated into the engine room immediately below where I had been lying.

The ship drifted towards Malta the next day and although there was an air attack it passed over them. Attempts were made to tow her in but this was difficult due to rough seas and the loss of the destroyer *Southwold*, which had struck a mine. The *Breconshire* was finally towed by two paddle tugs and eventually arrived at Malta. Bill, unsurprisingly relieved, was to stay on Malta for the next eighteen months. He had looked forward to a good night's rest but his first night was interrupted by a bombing raid. On 27 March 1942 the *Breconshire* was sunk whilst in harbour. (Malta underwent relentless bombing in the Second World War and for the bravery of its people the island was awarded the George Cross in April 1942).

Having arrived on Malta Bill transferred to The Buffs (East Kent Regiment) as the 8th Battalion King's Own did not require officer reinforcement. Bill and his friend Gordon Guest joined "B" Company 4th Battalion.

Whilst stationed on Malta Bill continually managed to avoid the dangers of bombing but remembered one particular raid as, 'one of the most terrifying experiences' he had during the course of the war.

Bill became Motor Transport Officer (MTO) of his battalion. Duties as an MTO were varied but included organising transport for troops and supplies from convoys to store-dumps outside of the 'danger zone' of regular bombed areas. After a collision, in which Bill was lucky to have survived, he was relieved of his duties as MTO and rejoined "B" Company. His platoon was assigned as the protective platoon to the London Government, and whilst based at Verdala the London Government received a number of distinguished guests including George VI, General Eisenhower and Lord Louis Mountbatten.

On Malta Bill had the opportunity to meet up with his Old Emanuel School friend, Sidney James 'Jim' Barker, who was in the Fleet Air Arm. On one occasion they flew across an area that Bill and his battalion had camouflaged. Free and above an island in the sun it must have been hard that afternoon to imagine that they were in the middle of a war. But the reality of their situation was always at the forefront of their minds. In September 1943 Bill left Malta for North Africa. He returned briefly to see the Italian Fleet come into Malta after it had surrendered to the Allies but Bill was Alex (Alexandria) bound.

Arriving in Alex Bill started a week's leave and, from his wartime log book we can see that he enjoyed swimming and cinemas (which were like 'palaces' compared to London cinemas) and in the evenings he relaxed in clubs with bands and bars. But then Bill's leave was cut short a day early. The battalion was on the move, destination unknown. Route marches and weapons training started in earnest. After a short while Bill embarked on the Type-II Hunt-class destroyer, HMS *Dulverton* – destination Leros.[2]

Leros – November 1943

The Aegean campaigns in the autumn of 1943 placed significant strains on Allied relationships. Churchill dreamed of bringing Turkey into the war and of launching an assault on Nazi satellite states from southern Europe but Eisenhower, Commander-in-Chief, Mediterranean Theatre, was more concerned with plans for the Allied Offensive on Italy which was, in his mind, far more important to the overall endgame than fanciful forays into an idea which looked as if it was pulled out of a nineteenth century Imperial adventure story.[3] But Churchill was appeased and so men like Bill, being the pawns of their government's strategy, were sent to Leros.

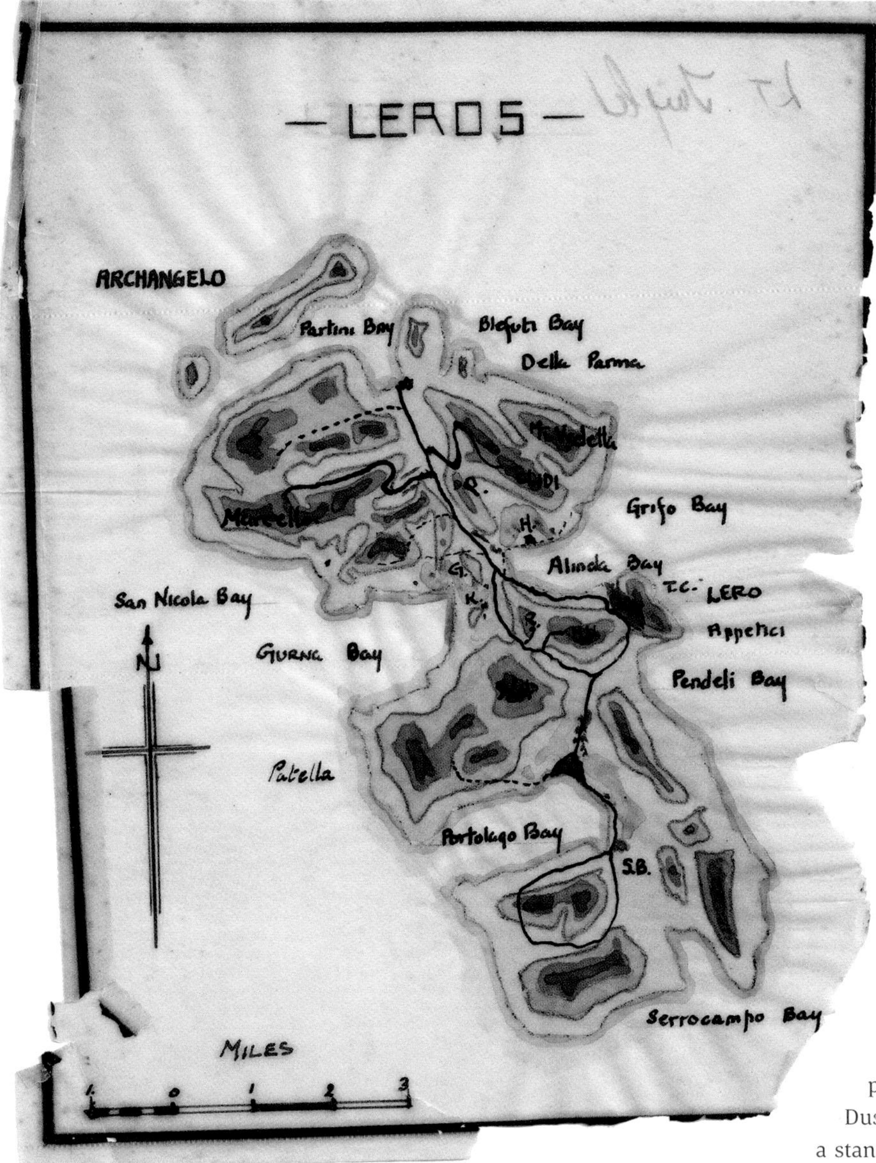

A map of Leros painted on rice paper by a fellow POW

"B" Company of the 4th Battalion, The Buffs, landed at Parteni Bay, north-east Leros on 26/27 October 1943. After unloading in some haste, Bill learnt of the fate of HMS *Eclipse* which was carrying "A" Company. It had struck a mine on the way to Leros with the loss of many of Bill's friends.

The first fortnight on Leros was spent digging-in and preparing their positions, essentially waiting for an expected German assault on the island. Digging-in was difficult due to the nature of the rocky ground. With two Vickers machine-guns they sat looking over the bay. But British positions were too far apart and weak. With a force of some 2,730 the German Eastern Battle Group landed on 12 November. Repulsed by The Buffs several times they managed to gain a foothold at Grifo Bay below Mount Clidi. "B" Company were ordered to recapture this position. Bill describes what happened:

In the attack on Clidi my platoon (No. 10) was left forward platoon. 2nd Lt. Morgan with 12 platoon was on the right, while Lt. Dusty Millar with 11 platoon gave us supporting fire from behind and slightly to our right. During the attack 2nd Lt. Morgan was fatally wounded and died within half an hour. One of my men was killed and several wounded including two of my section commanders.

On Pt. 292 our company commander, Major E. Hole was killed and I was in command of the company. When we withdrew to Clidi, Captain Tony Wood took over the company.

We remained in the Clidi area all that day and in the afternoon Dusty Millar was sent out with his platoon on a standing patrol in the Grifo Bay area. ...

The following morning I was to take my platoon out with the object of contacting Dusty Millar or, if unable to do so, to set as a standing patrol in his stead. But this order was cancelled and instead I was sent with my platoon to take up a position on Quirico, a piece of high ground overlooking Alinda Bay from the west.

We remained in this position all day and in the evening were ordered to move to the area of Bn. HQ. Here we were given a hot meal, the first we had had for three days and were told that the enemy had succeeded in dividing the island into two parts, the north being cut off from the south, the only means of communication being by wireless. It was proposed to concentrate all our troops in the north of the island into an area near the rock of land joining the north with the south and in a dawn attack the following morning to drive the enemy into a restricted area where they would then be wiped out. The position was a serious one and by appearances the proposed attack was to be a last effort which must

Two pages from Bill's Log Book describing the action on Leros

succeed if the invasion were to be crushed. The garrison by this time, after five days continuous fighting was fast becoming exhausted and the continuous bombing was an overwhelming element in the enemy's favour.

After a long march we reached our allotted positions just after midnight and by the time I had put my platoon in position it wanted two hours to down. Sentries had been posted and I ordered the remainder of the platoon to get some rest. I had been lying down myself for about half an hour when Jack Green came along and informed me that the island had capitulated. I was astounded at this information and could not believe it to be true. I went immediately to my company HQ to enquire about the situation and found that Tony Wood had been given the same information but had decided to wait for confirmation from Major Pike, our battalion second in charge. I returned to my platoon and was told that during my absence the commanding officer had visited the area and had told Corporal Bradley, one of my section commanders, that the information was correct and that we were to return to our original company areas by first light.

On Mount Clidy Bill was responsible for capturing over 40 prisoners. He and the men of the 4th Battalion, The Buffs, had shown great skill and fortitude but the German commitment to take the island was overwhelming as Bill wrote in his log book:

> Shortly after I got back a runner arrived from company HQ with a message to the effect that I was to bring my platoon to a certain rendezvous where the whole battalion was assembling prior to returning to its original position. The information had therefore been correct and I, together with what was left of the garrison, was made a Prisoner of War!

Bill listed the numbers who had been killed on Leros but among them one in particular affected him and was on his mind some 70 years later when Daniel Kirmatzis interviewed him. Bill noted:

> Among the other officers killed was Gordon Guest. The news of his death came as a shock to me as he had been a particularly great friend of mine. We had known each other for a long time – ever since N. Ireland days – and had spent many happy days together.

The numbers Bill lists in his logbook having died of wounds or being killed in action are sobering and 'Churchill's Folly' turned out to be a costly enterprise. Of the 4th Battalion, The Buffs, four officers and 25 other ranks either died of wounds or were killed and there were many other casualties.

Prisoner of War

Bill was a POW from November 1943 until April 1945. He was transported across Nazi-occupied territories, from Greece to Germany via Austria. Bill and other survivors from the Leros action were ordered to assemble and await their fates. In his log book Bill wrote extracts of a diary he kept in the three weeks immediately after his capture. On 20 November the POWs were put on board an Italian destroyer and transported to Greece. Arriving in the early hours of 21 November they landed at Piraeus before being removed to a POW camp in Athens. On the 22nd Bill wrote about what concerned him most, '... anxious about Gra[ce] worrying at no news from me.' For the next ten days Bill got a glimpse into what life would be like as a POW. It was a monotonous existence. There was lots of hanging around with nothing to do except waiting for meals, singing occasional hymns and brewing up. Bill's general impression of the rations they were given left him feeling 'bloody hungry' most of the time. However, one of the chief frustrations Bill experienced was not having news of what was happening in the outside world though once they were moved from Greece this did not pose a problem. A remarkable characteristic of this generation was their ingenuity. Bill remembered one man who built his own radio and cleverly disguised it from his captors:

> Some clever technician had built a wireless set into the head of a broom; they took the bristles out of the broom, built this thing into it and put semi-imitation bristles back. The Gerries could never understand why these fussy English stupid idiots wanted to take this brush with them to clear up when they got to the next place. So the brush went along containing a wireless. It got to Brunswick and when we were at Brunswick, a representative from each room of 20 to 25 men were having a history lesson and the history lesson was the report from the BBC. So we knew before the German guards knew where our men were. They had a big map on the wall outside where they were saying they were going to be next and bets to how far they were going to advance.[4]

On 3 December 1943 they were loaded onto cattle trucks at 16.30hrs, with around 20 men to each truck. Bill described conditions in the truck, 'There was no light in the wagon and as it was very cold we all went to bed. There was very little straw on the floor and we were very cramped. Devised a tin scoop for a 'latrine' which we stuck under the door.' They were taken from Athens to Salonika arriving at 18.00hrs on 5 December. The trip wasn't without incident with four more officers being put in Bill's truck after they had attempted to escape. On the 6th it was Bill's second wedding anniversary but as he noted, 'What a way to spend it! Dirty, unshaven, cold and hungry – good job Grace doesn't know what I'm doing. ... Thought of Grace all day, wondering what she was doing – am certain she was thinking of me.' Indeed, Grace had received a telegram from the War Office notifying her that Bill was missing in action. Then two weeks later a man, whose son was a POW, visited Grace's father to tell him that he had heard Bill had been made a POW. Names and addresses of POWs were given out on the radio and the man wanted to help others whose loved ones had been made POWs.

Bill and his friend Ron Hills in Oflag–79, Brunswick

As their journey proceeded Bill described the beauty of the scenery in juxtaposition to their captivity, passing as they did snow-peaked mountain tops and, as they crossed the Danube, everyone hummed the 'Blue Danube' waltz, 'at the tops of their voices.' Then on 15 December they arrived at Moosburg – in southern Germany – after a two-week journey Bill described as, 'the worst I have ever experienced.' They were marched to a transit camp – Stalag-VII A where Bill's kit was inspected and shortly afterwards they were shown to a sparsely furnished barracks, consisting of two stoves, several long tables and beds which became their living quarters. One blessing during his captivity was the regular distribution of Red Cross parcels which added variety to the otherwise basic diet of root vegetable-soups. The next three months were spent reading, attending lectures, and other such activities which were possible in a POW camp; but the most interesting experience from reading Bill's log book is his attendance at the funeral of a Black South African who was fighting for the British. It appears that other officers had declined to attend his funeral for reasons which are impossible to clarify now but 'race' could have been a factor. Bill was the orderly officer and did attend. They walked to a cemetery close to Moosburg where the South African's coffin was draped in the Union Jack and as he was lowered into a grave a German firing party provided a salute.

AQ/5286.

MAY 12 1944 P/4

BRITISH RED CROSS SOCIETY AND ORDER OF ST. JOHN

NEXT OF KIN PARCELS CENTRE.

CONTENTS ¼ lb. Gift Chocolate added

No.	Item	No.	Item
9	TOWELS	1	COMB
	PANTS	6	PRI LACES
	VESTS	6	PENCILS
	HOUSEWIFE		FACE CLOTH
	BRUSH		SCARF
	TOOTH BRUSH		PULLOVER
	RAZOR BLADES	6	HANDKERCHIEF
	SHIRTS		
	SHAVING SOAP		2 Soap
	FOOT POLISH		
	TOOTHPASTE		80

Please complete Particulars on back of page. [P.T.O.

(above) List of items sent in a British Red Cross next of kin parcel sent to Bill whilst a POW (left) Token money distributed to POWs in German captivity

On 14 March 1944 Bill was moved with a number of other officers on a five-day journey to a new camp – Oflag-VIIIF at Mährisch Trübau, 25 miles east of Prague. The behaviour of the German guards was cordial and towards the end of the journey Bill noted that they lent one POW a mouth organ to play during a sing-song. Bill arrived at Oflag-VIIIF on 19 March. He described the camp's features in his log book:

> We were accommodated in large 'chalets' consisting of a number of rooms. There were ten people in my particular room. We slept in two tier bunks and were given a locker between two. It was a fairly large camp, the majority of people being accommodated in a large factory-like building (nicknamed the Biscuit Factory) while the remainder were in chalets similar to our own. One building was set aside for a hospital while another was used as a theatre. There was a rugger/soccer pitch (which had a large telegraph or cable-bearing pole dead in its centre) a running track and a swimming pool. In the Biscuit Factory there was a fairly extensive library and many rooms were set aside for educational classes. Roll-call was held twice a day at 8.30 in the mornings and at 9 o'clock in the evenings. We had our photographs and fingerprints taken and were issued with a metal identity disc.

The luxurious setting of this camp wasn't to last long as five weeks later Bill was transported to what would be his last camp – Oflag-79 in Brunswick. Bill spent April 1944 to April 1945 in this camp. Life in Brunswick varied little from his earlier experiences. Long periods of boredom were the order of most days but Bill also made seats for shows put on in the camp and was part of escape committees, though owing to a hernia, he didn't attempt escape himself. Two instances remained vivid memories for Bill 70 years later. The first was the shooting of a Sikh officer who playing quoits [a traditional game for two players. Played with ring-like objects and thrown over or near two spikes] as Bill explained:

> They had a wire across the perimeter ... and about six feet away from the wire they had a trip wire and you weren't supposed to go anywhere near it. Let alone step over it. And there were two Indians, they wore turbans,

Dacre Day 2014 – Bill stands with members of Emanuel's First XV, 80 years after he played rugby at Emanuel

> and they were throwing this quoit back and forth and it went over, and he stepped over to pick it up and he was shot from the centre [and] on each corner of the camp and he was shot dead. Because he put his foot over the wire to retrieve this thing, which didn't go down very well of course. They refused to go on parade for a fortnight.[5]

The second was one of those unfortunate accidents which occur in war. The term 'friendly fire' seems to disguise the tragedies that can spring from the wrong target being pinpointed for attack but one such incident happened at Brunswick on 24 August 1944. American bombers landed several high-explosive bombs on the camp. A factory was adjacent to the camp and an aerodrome close by and so it was assumed that these were the intended targets. There were several fatalities in the camp and dozens of male and female slave labourers who were sheltering in the woods near the camp were also killed.[6]

Just after 9.30am on 9 April 1945 Brunswick was liberated by men of the US Ninth Army. After seventeen months as a POW Bill was finally free. Remembering that day years later Bill expressed his feeling, 'Euphoria – that's a big word isn't it? But thank goodness for that, now what? Let's get home. We wanted to get home as soon as possible.'

By 27 April Bill was back in England. He journeyed to Brussels by Dakota and returned to England in a Wellington Bomber, landing in Oxfordshire. Bill and Grace celebrated VE Day in Piccadilly, dancing the night away. After 95 days' leave Bill reported to No. 7 Civil Resettlement Unit where he worked to find employment for other ranks ex-POWs to help them return to civilian life. Bill and Grace celebrated their 70th wedding anniversary in 2011 and at the annual Dacre Day (held at Emanuel School each July), Bill was photographed with members of the Emanuel First Fifteen – some 80 years after he had played for Emanuel.

References

1 A digital copy of Bill's log book is available in the Emanuel School Archive.
2 For an account of the Leros action see Anthony Rogers, *Churchill's Folly: Leros and the Aegean*, (2004).
3 Martin Gilbert, *Road to Victory: Winston S. Churchill 1941–1945*, (Minerva, 1989), p. 546.
4 Bill Taylor interview by Daniel Kirmatzis July 2011. A copy of the transcript is available from the Emanuel School Archive.
5 Bill Taylor interview. For an illustration of the incident see Gordon Horner, *For You the War is Over*, (Privately published, 1948), under the page titled 'Two Ways of Escape.' N.B. Book not paginated.
6 For a description of what happened that day see James B. Chutter, *Captivity Captive*, (1954), pp. 176-179.

‘Has never failed to play a sound game’

Douglas Sydney ‘Sammy’ Hoare

(Emanuel 1929–1935)

Douglas ‘Sammy’ Hoare was an exceptionally talented rugby player at Emanuel. His rugby critique in the Lent term *Portcullis* noted, ‘A good full back who has never failed to play a sound game. A reliable tackler and a very fair kick.’

Douglas was also a Prefect, Captain of Wellington and a Lance Sergeant in the OTC and was awarded his War Certificate ‘A’. He played rugby for the OEA after leaving School and was in the 1938/1939 OEA team Captained by Harold Hutchins.

A year after leaving School Douglas joined the RAF. He trained on a number of different aircraft from 1937 to 1939 including the Tiger Moth, Hawker Hart, Hawker Audax, and the Glosters Gauntlet and Gladiator. His first flight for the RAF was on 16 November 1936 in a dual-controlled Tiger Moth, piloted by a Mr Corke and lasting ten minutes, at the Basic Training School in Perth, Scotland. After a year of introductory training in which he developed into a proficient pilot he was posted to No. 74 Fighter Squadron Hornchurch, Essex, on 1 September 1937.[1] He recorded his first impressions of RAF Hornchurch for a book by Richard Smith in which Douglas recalled:

> I remember reporting to the squadron office and there I was greeted by the squadron adjutant, Tom Rowland, who was very pleasant and began to tell me what a very good squadron I was about to join; he proceeded to show me around the place. It was very exciting for a youngster, but I was very disappointed when reaching the hangars to see mostly Gauntlets, but also a few Demons. The Gauntlet was only slightly faster than the Hawker Fury which I had been training on at Flying Training School.[2]

In the tense period of the Munich Crisis in September 1938, when the British Prime Minister Neville Chamberlain went to meet Hitler in order to avoid war, No. 74 Squadron were ordered to camouflage their aircraft as a preventative measure. Douglas remembered:

Douglas Hoare, Emanuel OEA rugby First XV

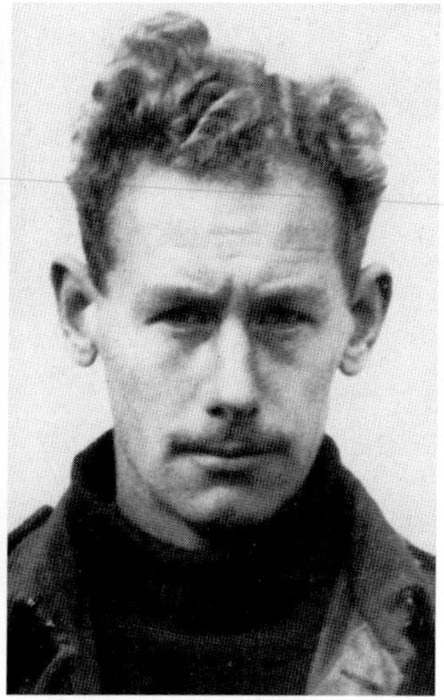

Douglas in Oflag-XXIV Schubin c1942-1943

> ...up until then [Munich] we’d had our Gauntlets all nicely silver painted with the squadron badge and the Tiger stripes painted along the Fuselage. ... We were then told to camouflage all the aircraft. This was fine but we did not have the required materials to do the job. We had various coloured paints ... but we didn’t have enough green; we mixed blue and yellow together. Not enough brown, so we mixed red and black; all sorts of mixtures to achieve or resemble green or brown camouflage. ... The aircraft looked terrible and stayed this way for two or three weeks until we received the right amount of proper ... paints. Of course, after we got rid of our Gauntlets we received Spitfires, but these were already camouflaged.[3]

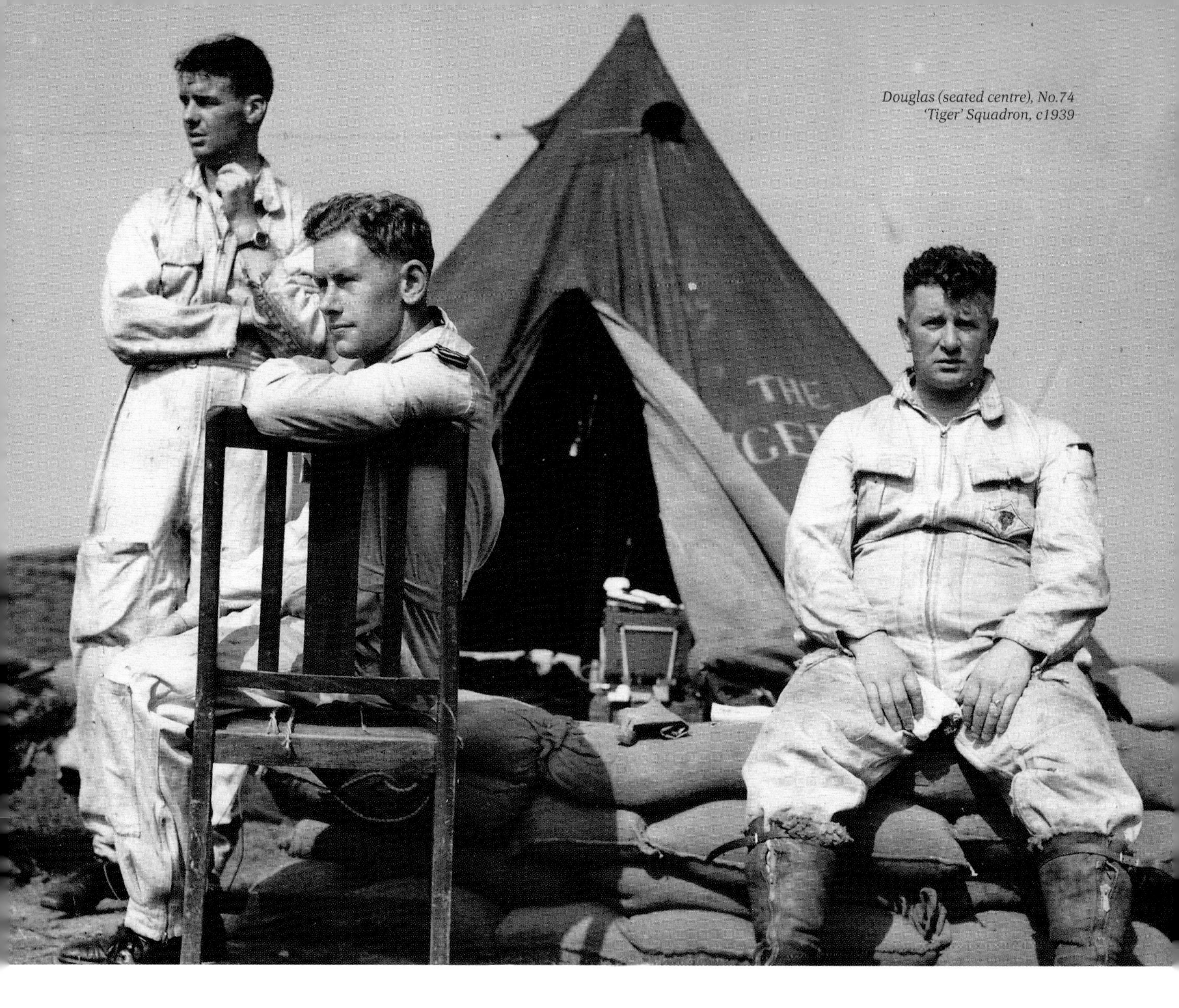

Douglas (seated centre), No.74 'Tiger' Squadron, c1939

On 20 February 1939 he flew his first Spitfire for 30 minutes on a sector-recco (reconnaissance). From February onwards he trained on Spitfires and also the fighter trainer, Miles Magister, building up experience on this type of aircraft. Spitfire training continued until he qualified on 12 June 1939. With 460 hours' experience he qualified as a fighter pilot, being above average with no faults.

Between June and September 1939 Douglas continued training until war was declared on 3 September. He made his first war patrol on 6 September lasting 50 minutes – no enemy aircraft (EA) sighted. On the same day he did a 25-minute flight for the making of the film *The Lion Has Wings* (starring Ralph Richardson and Merle Oberon – a propaganda war film by the Government). On 20 September he did a further 35-minute flight for the film. He later looked back on this experience:

> For about a week we had the film crew on the airfield who were taking lots and lots of shots of the tents we lived in, the aircraft pens and a few take-offs and landings. We were still wearing our smart white flying suits at the time and it was a very entertaining week. We had lots of beer flowing and we joined in with the film crew.[4]

Dunkirk – May 1940

During May 1940 Douglas, by now a Flying Officer, was contemplating the situation on the continent as the Germans launched their invasion of France and the Low Countries. On 10 May, the day the invasion was launched, Douglas was looking forward to some leave when he wrote to his mother, 'I was looking forward very much to the weekend at home and possibly a day at the coast. I expect Dick [Wildey] has been recalled also – it really is most annoying that the Blitzkrieg should have to start this weekend and just when my leave is starting too.'

On 21 May 1940 Douglas wrote again to his mother:

> I don't think I have written since you sent my *Portcullis* – thank you very much for it. It was very interesting reading through that list and seeing what some of the other fellows are doing.
>
> There is actually hardly anything to say as everything here is still just the same as before and there is very little real activity. We have had one or two more trips to the Dutch and Belgian coast but have not seen anything worth shooting at. There is absolutely no sign of life at all in any of the towns over there and we saw quite a number of large fires in Dunkirk which had been started by a raid the previous night. I hope that everyone is taking ARP [Air Raid Precaution] seriously now as it will not be very long before we get some raids over here – that is when we shall start really hard work. The situation in France seems pretty bad at present but perhaps we will bring off a really good counter-attack soon. We are also very proud of the RAF squadrons out there – and slightly envious, though we are all quite certain we shall get all the chance we want when it starts over here.[5]

In May 1940 No. 74 Squadron was engaged on operations over the French Coast during the German Blitzkrieg which forced the BEF to coastal waters in a bid to escape the ferocity and speed of the German advance. On 24 May Douglas noted,

Douglas Hoare (sitting, first from left) during Hawker Hart training

'I was leading the sub-section of B Flight 74 Squadron on an offensive patrol over the Channel Ports. (Intelligence at that [time] was almost non-existent and we had no idea where the German front line was).' He went on to describe what happened that day:

> We had on that occasion seen a Henschel 126, a German reconnaissance aircraft. Although our instructions were to patrol just the Channel coastline, we were told that we could go inland, if we were investigating any aircraft, or for some other reason; in this case we had seen this other aircraft. Paddy Treacy had seen it and I was leading the second section. We must have been somewhere around St Omer, about 15 miles inland. The Henschel was flying very low and in fact by the time I went into attack it with my section, it was down to about treetop height. It was in flames and just as I

Douglas Hoare (left) c1939

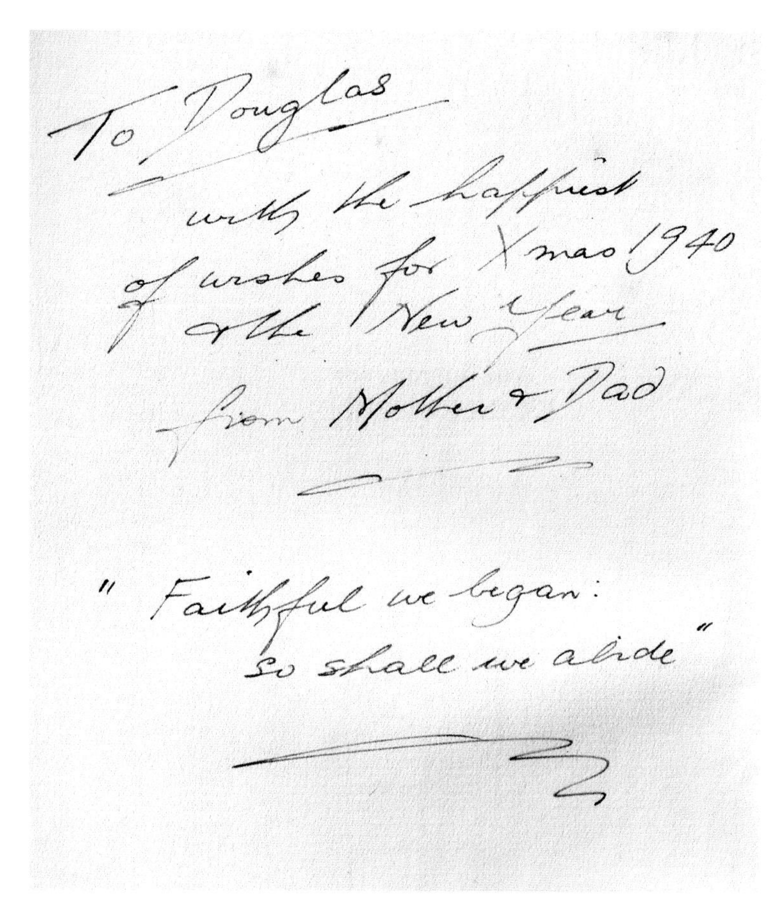

Inscription by Douglas' parents in his copy of 'The History of Emanuel School' sent to him whilst a POW, Christmas 1940

> pulled away, I saw it crash and go up in a pall of smoke. Anyway, I managed to collect a bullet from somewhere; it may have been a German infantryman or light flack. It may have been from our own troops on the ground, or even the Henschel we'd just shot down. Nevertheless I reformed and intended to go back to base, when Mungo-Park called me up and said I was streaming glycol; so I thought the sensible things to do was what Squadron Leader White had done the previous day and go into Calais-Marck airfield.
>
> I knew the previous day that we had sent two ground crew over to the airfield to service his aircraft and repair it. I thought if I can get in here, perhaps they can do a quick patch up and then I can get home. But it didn't work out that way, and I was too late.
>
> At that time the military intelligence just could not keep up with the speed of the German advance westwards. We were not told the disposition of British and French forces nor where the front line was (did anyone know!) and there was never any mention of an evacuation. In fact Calais had been reinforced only the previous day with a British armoured unit.
>
> When I landed on the airfield Corporal Higginbottom and Aircraftsman Cressay came out, and were beside the aircraft immediately; I told them what had happened. They saw a hole on the side of the engine cowling; ... We found quite a large hole in the pipe leading.... Before I had landed my radiator temperature gauge, my oil temparature and pressure gauges were all registering well above the limits.[6]

With German troops approaching the three men made their escape through the long grass. In a spirited but unsuccessful attempt Douglas and Corporal Higginbottom, (Aircraftsman Cressay had become separated from the two men and was later captured), made their way due north and on two 'borrowed' bicycles reached the coast, but they failed in their attempt to get any boat off the sand dunes and on the evening of 25 May, along with French civilians and some British Army officers they were surrounded on the beaches between Calais and Dunkirk by an SS Panzer unit.

Douglas explained what happened to him next:

> We did quite a bit of walking from the beach where I was first captured until reaching Germany in early June. The first organised POW camp I reached was Dulag Luft–III but this was only a transit and interrogation place and I moved a few days later.[7]

For the next four years Douglas was a POW. He spent time in eleven camps including the following, with dates:

- Spangenberg – Oflag IXA(H) (RAF Camp), Jun–Jul 40
- Barth – Stalag Luft–I, Jul 40–Feb 41
- Spangenberg – Oflag IXA(H), Feb–Mar 41
- Thorne (Poland) – Stalag Luft–XXA, Mar–May 41
- Spangenberg – Oflag IX(H), Jun–Oct 41
- Warburg – Oflag VIB, Oct 41–Aug 42
- Schubin (Poland) – Oflag XXIB, Aug 42–Apr 43
- Sagan – Stalag Luft–III, Apr 43–Aug 44
- Gross Tychow – Stalag Luft–IVD, Aug–Sep 44

Douglas's twin sister, Eileen, who in November 1940 married Douglas's School friend Dick Wildey, often wrote to him with news from home during Douglas's captivity. Emanuel's role as a focal point for pupils after they left is evident from one letter Eileen sent to Douglas on 28 August 1940 in which she wrote:

I sent a letter off to Kimber ... but have heard no reply yet. I asked him to see about sending the *Portcullis* home still, if he can arrange it, if for no other reason, you will be able to have a record of the School activities when you get back, and also we can keep an eye on the names therein, and in turn pass on the information to you.

Letters and cards both to and from Douglas initially arrived after several months delay but once the exchange began Douglas retold his experiences through his correspondence, albeit under the watchful eye of a German censor. Later letters and cards also could take many months to arrive home and likewise from England to Douglas.

By November 1940 we get an indication of Douglas's personal condition in captivity. He wrote to his mother from Stalag Luft–II on 23 November, although the letter wasn't received until February 1941:

Thanks again for the clothes parcel, you have really no idea how nice it was wearing really clean clothes again for the first time for 6 months. Unfortunately the cigarettes and chocolate did not arrive and the grey flannel were classed as civilian clothes and confiscated by the authorities, so I have still no uniform or jacket and trousers other than the rags I picked up in France. Neither have I any shoes – perhaps they will come in the next parcel.

As for many others, life in POW camps was monotonous for the most part, but monotony wasn't for Douglas so he got himself involved in escape plans and made an escape from Oflag VIB, Warburg, in May 1942 but was recaptured after one week. Friendship was also important during captivity and, although not officially established, there could have been an Old Emanuel Association POW society because a number of OEs met up in the various camps. Douglas wrote in one letter on 5 April 1942 of OE Allan Goodger (Emanuel 1923–1928) a Lieutenant in the Royal Army Service Corps who was also captured in 1940, 'Allan Goodger now bangs a double-bass and was in the last band-concert.'

By January 1943 Douglas's tone was downbeat about going into a third year of captivity. He wrote from Oflag XXIB, Schubin on 26 January:

I myself find it difficult to raise much enthusiasm over anything these days but no doubt I shall get over that when I get home. The third year of this life is ten times worse than either of the other two. I read a very interesting book the other day; I thought it was about the last war till I got half way through, then suddenly realised it was about the beginning of this one. It seems years ago now.

During his time in Stalag Luft–III Douglas took the University of London Intermediate Examination in Science

Princess Alexandra inspects a Vampire T.11 trainer with Douglas Hoare at the controls, Oakington, Cambridgeshire 1956

and passed in the following subjects: Pure Mathematics, Applied Mathematics and the written papers in Physics and Chemistry – with good reason POW camps were often referred to as 'barbed wire universities.'

In a letter to his parents from Stalag Luft–III on 27 September 1943 Douglas reveals his views on his POW experiences and the impact they had on both him and those around him. He wrote:

Although you have always been against it, you can realise how much I would love an hour or two in a pub some evenings. I'm amazed at the news of Donald being a father – it seems all wrong. I still refuse to be 26 and try and stick to 22, but most of the people I've been with all the time seem to grow very much older, so I suppose I have really changed a lot also.

Having been moved from Stalag Luft–III to Stalag Luft–IVD in August 1944 Douglas was repatriated to England in September 1944 due to mental health problems which he told his children he feigned. He didn't speak about the repatriation. By the end of the year on 6 December 1944 he was flying again on a dual-controlled Oxford trainer. Douglas continued flying in the post-war period and ended his career as a Group Captain. He died in 2007.

References

1 A full history of Douglas Hoare's flying career can be consulted in the Emanuel School Archive.
2 Richard C. Smith, *Hornchurch Scramble: The Definitive Account of the RAF Fighter Airfield, Its Pilots, Groundcrew and Staff, Volume One: 1915 to the End of the Battle of Britain* (2002), p. 30.
3 Ibid. pp. 39-40.
4 Ibid. pp. 55-56.
5 The letters of Douglas Hoare; copies are available to consult in the Emanuel School Archive.
6 Ibid. pp. 66-67.
7 From the introduction to the unpublished letters of Douglas Hoare, a copy of which is available to consult in the Emanuel School Archive.

The Cool and Fearless Captain

Douglas William Finlay

(Emanuel 1938–1940)

Douglas was an exceptional schoolboy. He held positions as Captain of the School, House Lieutenant of Wellington and Captain of Shooting. He played for the Second Fifteen in addition to rowing in the First Eight. Douglas was an excellent shot and represented the Surrey Colts on the rifle range. He was also a member of the Dramatic Society, the Carey Foster Society and Editor of *The Portcullis*.

Douglas William Finlay (centre, standing) with his Lancaster bomber crew, 103 Squadron, Bomber Command, Elsham Wolds, Lincs 1943

In 1938 he played the Earl of Warwick in Emanuel's production of Bernard Shaw's *Saint Joan*. Douglas held the rank of CQMS (Company Quartermaster Master Sergeant) in the JTC and was awarded his War Office Certificate 'A'. In 1938 he was awarded his General School Certificate and was a member of the Science Sixth class. Evacuated with Emanuel to Petersfield Douglas joined the Local Defence Volunteers. On leaving Emanuel Douglas took up a short course at Emmanuel College, Cambridge to read Engineering. After joining the University's Air Squadron Douglas soon enlisted in the RAFVR (Royal Air Force Volunteer Reserve). He went to Canada for flight training before a move to Florida, gaining his wings at No. 5 Flying Training School.

On his return to England Douglas completed his training at 1662 Heavy Conversion Unit at Blyton, Lincolnshire before being posted to 103 Squadron, Bomber Command based at Elsham Wolds, Lincolnshire on 16 April 1943. 103 Squadron was originally formed during the First World War as an RFC Squadron. It was disbanded in 1919 but was reformed in 1936. Each member of a bombing crew had a specific task, from the pilot, to the navigator and the bomb aimer. Douglas's crew was:

Flying Officer D. W. Finlay DFC RAFVR – British – Pilot

Pilot Officer R. H. J. Rowe DFM RAFVR – British – Flight Engineer

Sergeant J. H. Macfarlane RAFVR – British – Navigator

Sergeant I. D. Fletcher DFM RAFVR – British – Bomb Aimer

Sergeant H. S. Wheeler RAFVR – British – Wireless Operator

Pilot Officer R. J. F. Vivers RAAF – Australian – Air Gunner

Pilot Officer W. C. Gillespie RCAF – Canadian – Rear Gunner

Douglas and his crew were soon detailed for their first operation to bomb the Italian naval dockyard at La Spezia on the evening of 18/19 April 1943.[1] They carried out this and subsequent operations in Lancaster bombers. Their journey was to last nine hours and to a later generation only used to commercial flights it is hard to imagine being locked in a confined space, flying over enemy territory for so many hours with the mind concentrated on carrying out a mission. For all crew members these operations were exhausting but more so specifically for the pilot, who had the responsibility of not only getting his crew to the target, but also safely back to base in England.

Between April and August 1943 Douglas and his crew completed 25 operations (ops). The crew were designated to take part in the first of four attacks on Hamburg on the evening of 24/25 July 1943. Hamburg was home to Europe's largest port and was Germany's second largest city. The raid of 24/25 was carried out with 791 aircraft and resulted in widespread destruction. Douglas noted in his Pilot's Flying Log Book, 'Heavy Flak; Large numbers of searchlights – a Heavy Prang.' The Hamburg raids of late July 1943 have courted controversy for the firestorm which engulfed Hamburg on the raid of 27/28 July in which 40,000 people were killed. The bombing war on both sides was to many of that and later generations, a tragedy. But this was a 'Total war' that not only caused the deaths of millions, but also witnessed, on occasion, extreme strategies in the pursuit of victory. However, it must never be forgotten that the controversies associated with Bomber Command's strategy should not diminish the bravery and fortitude shown by the thousands of young men, like Douglas and his crew, who had to carry out these operations under the most difficult conditions and with the greatest stresses and strains that put the capabilities of the human mind and body to its limits.

On a moonlit night on 17 August 1943 Douglas and his crew took part in a raid on the German research establishment at Peenemünde on the Baltic coast where they were working on the production of V-2 rockets. The main targets of the raid were successfully bombed and a number of scientists and workers were also killed. Unfortunately this number included Polish workers being used as slave labour by the Nazis. Some have argued that the raid delayed the V-2 programme by at least two months and possibly reduced its impact later on in the war when V-2s wrought wide-scale damage on London. Douglas recorded in his log book, 'Good trip; Target hidden by smoke; Moderate Flak. Many fighters.'

The risks associated with Bomber Command operations were high and Douglas had more than one narrow escape. In one case as his crew were over the North Sea the oil pressure in one of their engines dropped. It was decided to return to base and so they released their 4000-lb high capacity (HC) bomb (known as a Cookie) into the sea. As they returned they were attempting to land at Kirmington but as they made their approach all the lights on the airfield suddenly went out. Douglas took evasive action and managed to lift the aircraft over high ground when they saw the lights of Elsham airfield and landed safely. If they had landed at Kirmington they would have collided with another aircraft on the runway and through the quick thinking of the airfield controller by switching the lights off he had saved the lives of two crews.[2] On another occasion on the evening of 23 August 1943 Douglas's Lancaster ED767 PM-H 'Harry' had just successfully completed its engine and equipment checks. They were given the green light to move for a raid on Berlin, when the engines of Lancaster PM-C 'Charlie', on the adjacent dispersal pad, started with its bomb doors still open. All of its bombs and incendiaries fell out and it burst into flames with Douglas's Lancaster only a short distance away. Douglas and Flight Engineer Rowe managed to get the two outer engines started. They started to taxi the aircraft but couldn't avoid having to pass the burning bombs. Then there was a huge explosion, with large chunks of shrapnel passing by and through the Lancaster. Most of the crew got out of the front hatch but Sergeant Harry Wheeler was killed when he was struck on the head by large lump of metal.[3]

On the night of 23/24 September 1943 Douglas and crew were detailed for ops over Mannheim. The objective that night was to destroy targets over the northern part of the city. However, their aircraft was shot down 20 miles N.N.W. of their target by a Messerschmitt 109. Douglas's brother Derek has written about what happened, 'The fuel tanks in the port wing were soon ablaze and the incendiaries in the bomb bay caught fire.'[4] Douglas ordered his crew to bail out but sadly two of them, Sergeant Macdonald and Pilot Officer Vivers were unable to escape and lost their lives. Douglas managed to hold the plane on a level course long enough for him to bail out. Douglas noted in his log book later, 'the port inner engine was u/s – tanks on fire – electrical system u/s – concentrated prang. Fighters very active.'

At first Douglas's family knew nothing of his fate, having only received a telegram from the Air Ministry stating that Douglas was 'missing on operations.' Six weeks later, Douglas's brother Derek recalls, 'The morning post was delivered. Suddenly my mother shrieked aloud, "Doug is safe!"' Douglas had been able to send a postcard to his family stating that he was alive and was a POW in Stalag Luft III, the camp for Allied aircrew officers in Sagan, Germany. Douglas spent the next sixteen months at Stalag Luft III.

It was while Douglas was a POW that news came through that he had been awarded the DFC. Douglas collected his DFC from King George VI on 22 June 1945, only a few weeks after he had landed back in England. The citation reads:

> Flight Lieutenant Finlay is a cool and fearless captain of aircraft who is one of the outstanding pilots in his squadron. He has completed many sorties the majority of which have been directed against industrial targets in the Ruhr. His skill and determination in action have helped to maintain a very high standard of morale in his squadron.

During the Second World War The War Prisoners' Aid of the YMCA provided prisoners with log books in which to record their experiences, thoughts and routines. These log books provide a wealth of information and Douglas's is of special interest for the fact that he passed his log book around fellow POWs to record a variety of experiences through art, poetry

Douglas Finlay's drawing of the memorial to the 50 RAF Officers of The Great Escape

and prose. Douglas's log book is replete with sketches, both amusing and reverent. In one Douglas himself sketched the memorial in żagań to the 50 RAF officers shot by the Nazis on Hitler's orders, after they, with 26 others, escaped on 24 March 1944. 73 of the 76 were recaptured and in order to deter other POWs from escaping 50 were selected to be executed in an act that turned the tide in prisoner relationships with their captors. The events were portrayed in the 1960s film *The Great Escape*. Douglas spent his time in room six which was in Block 123. This Block was adjacent to Block 122 where one of the tunnels for the 24 March escape, nicknamed 'Dick' was aborted. The log book details the names of all those in Block 123, around 80 men in all. In Douglas's room there were eight men, each given a moniker, Douglas's being 'Bishop' or 'Bish' for short.

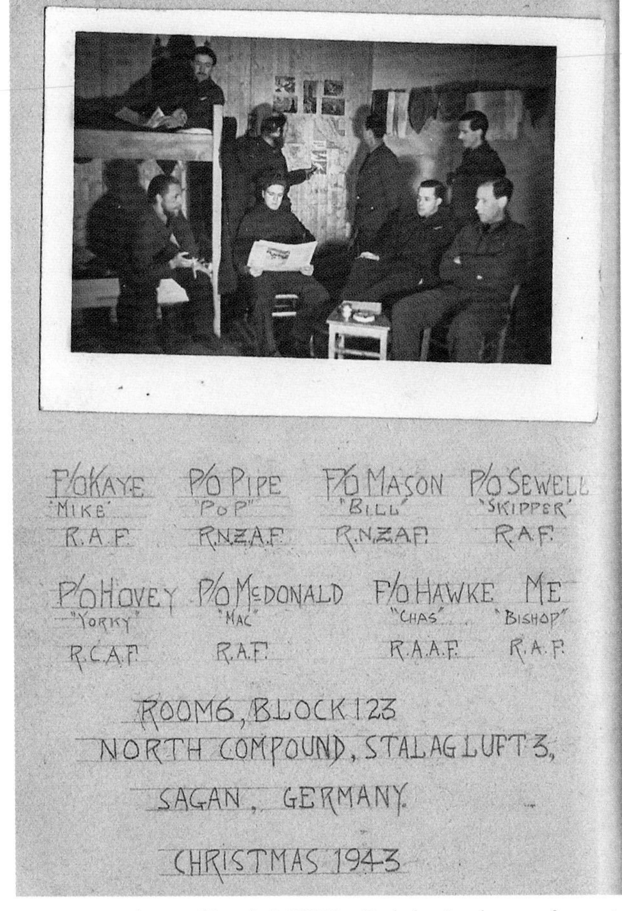

F/O KAYE "MIKE" R.A.F.
P/O PIPE "POP" R.N.Z.A.F.
F/O MASON "BILL" R.N.Z.A.F.
P/O SEWELL "SKIPPER" R.A.F.
P/O HOVEY "YORKY" R.C.A.F.
P/O McDONALD "MAC" R.A.F.
F/O HAWKE "CHAS" R.A.A.F.
ME "BISHOP" R.A.F.

ROOM 6, BLOCK 123
NORTH COMPOUND, STALAG LUFT 3,
SAGAN, GERMANY.
CHRISTMAS 1943

A page of Douglas's POW Log Book showing the men of room six Block 123, Stalag Luft–III

The log book also details the types of food and portions they received, excerpts from books such as *My Early Life* by Winston Churchill in which he discusses what it is like to be a POW from his own experiences during the Second Boer War and maps of the prison camp.

The deep affinity expressed by POWs for their fallen comrades is expressed through the several poems of remembrance recorded throughout the log book, such as Rupert Brooke's 'The Soldier' and the 14th Army's epitaph to the fallen in the Far East campaigns, 'When You Go Home', attributed to the English classicist John Maxwell Edmonds but often misquoted.

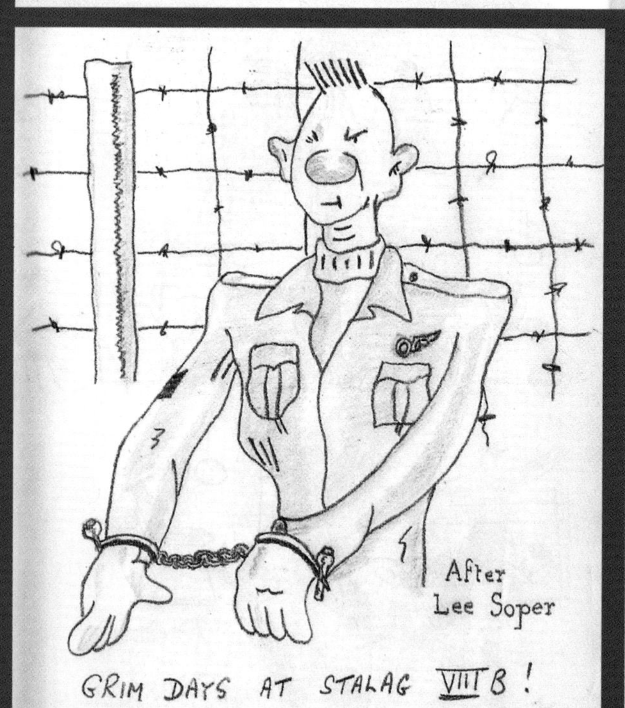

Satirical drawings of camp life in the form a holiday brochure from Douglas Finlay's POW Log Book

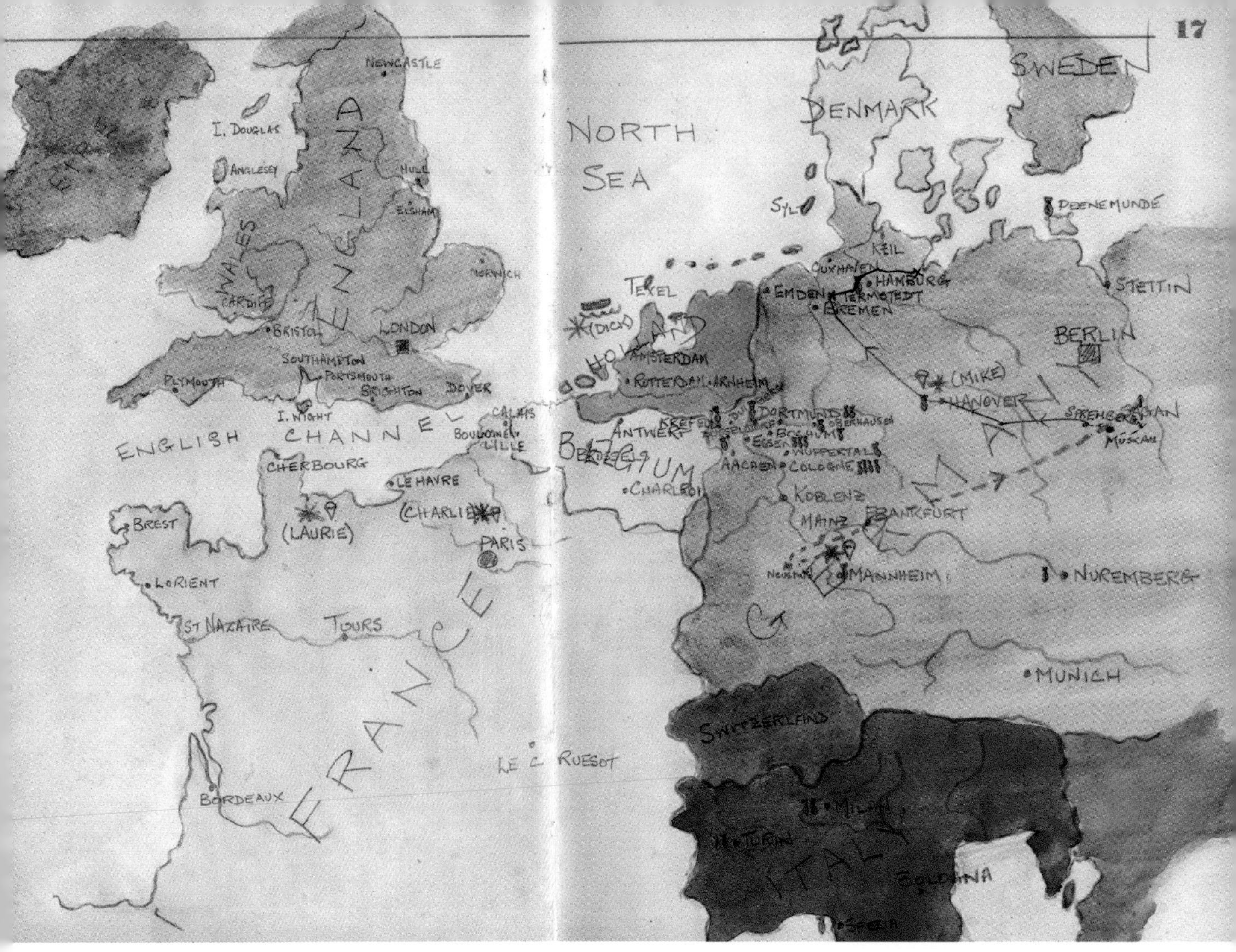

A map from Douglas Finlay's POW Log Book showing where he and fellow POWs landed after either being shot down or crashing in Nazi occupied Europe

By January 1945 the tide was turning against Nazi Germany. On the eastern front the Red Army launched their Vistula-Oder and East Prussian offensives on 12 and 13 January. In response to this advance the eastern-most German POW camps were evacuated. On 27 January over 10,000 prisoners from Stalag Luft III were forced out of the camp on a march ultimately destined for a Marlag in Tarmstadt near Bremen. The march took place during a bitterly cold winter and in appalling conditions.[5] Douglas's experiences were recorded in his log book under the title 'The Great Trek.'

27.01.1945: This afternoon there is tremendous excitement again in the Camp when the OKW (Oberkommando der Wehrmacht – Germans Supreme Command of the Armed Forces) states that the Russians have extended their Bridgehead across the Oder at Steinau and are fighting north of this point. Is freedom at hand or will the Germans move us before the Russian Armies can reach Sagan? In the evening Polly brings us rumours of Kriegies marching 150 km in six days in appalling weather. We poo-poo these but are all secretly rather worried. At 8.30 we have had supper and I am making toffee when 'Fagan' is told to stand by tonight for bigger work. He, Mike and I are discussing when and if the Russians will reach here when Deacon rushes in with news, "Pack your things, we're off in an hour!!" And so our trek began...

Packed and ate all we could, destroyed all clothing, cigarettes and food left: sat up waiting to move. Mild night, plenty of snow.

28.01.1945: Finally moved off 0400 hrs – collected food parcel each and set off on Gorlitz road. Halbau at 0830 and Friewaldau at 1400 – civilians quite friendly – marched on at 1530 reaching Springruh at dusk – bitterly cold. Paddy all in – Curly and I carry him – long wait for a barn – 12 hrs rest. Distance 35 km – worst day of all.

29.01.1945: Arose at 0700 and moved off at 0800, bought sledge for packet of prunes – bitterly cold and snowing – left Gorlitz Road after 2–3 km and turned NW – Prillbus at noon. Past Russian prison camp 1400. Paddy, Mike, Deacon and Johnny in bad way – Muskau at 1900 – quartered in Theatre – crowded but warm and dry – hot brew and a good wash – distance 30 km.

30.01.1945: Quiet day at Muskau – people friendly trading for cigs etc. Germans supply bread and marg at last.

31.01.1945: Dep. postponed – thawing rapidly – talk to survivors of Herman Goering Panzer unit from Litmanstadt, ordered to move at 1700 – departed with sledges at 2300.

02.02.1945: Sledges abandoned after 4km – packed up! Heavy going carrying food – reached Granstun at dawn, 3 hrs sleep in barn. 0730–1030 – marched on Spremberg – reached Military Barracks at 1400hrs – Germans supply hot meal – joined by East Camp – left 1400hrs on train 1730. Distance for day 30 km – 40 officers / cattle truck – departed about midnight.

03.02.1945: Hohenbock at 0830, Ruhland 1030 and Plessa 1120 – crossed Elbe 1520 at Jorgau – Halle 2030 hrs – long waits, but generally quick travel – hardly room to lie down at night.

04.02.1945: Hildeshum 0700 – fine and worried about air attacks on train – Hanover at 0800 – some bomb damage. Verden 1200–1500 – first water of trip – atrocious treatment – Tarmstadt at 1630 – left train and marched 3 km to Marlag – reach camp 1730, kept waiting in wet until midnight while 2000 POWs were searched – finally in bed about 0100 hrs and so to sleep.

After three months at the Marlag, Douglas and his fellow POWs were liberated on 2 May 1945 by the Cheshire Regiment, attached to the 11th Armoured Corps. Douglas penned a letter home to his family:

> Dears,
>
> The great moment came at 1 o'clock today when an armoured car with a real-live Tommy perched on it came rolling up. Boy oh Boy! What a sight. I've no idea how long it will take to get home but I guess fourteen days should do it...
>
> After sixteen months behind barbed wire at Sagan these last few months have certainly been exciting even if miserable at times.

Douglas's brother Derek remembers the day he returned home:

> On 8 May, our family was at home celebrating VE Day. With us were my uncle Peter, my father's eldest brother, his wife and my cousins. Just after lunch, one of us noticed the front gate open. A knock on the front door, opened by one us and standing there in a new RAF blue battledress was my brother – a moment I shall never forget as long as I live. I remember him drinking two pints of milk straight off and the still drawn face on him that reflected his own exhilaration at finally being free again – really the whole issue the war had been about for all of us.

Douglas was demobbed in 1946 and returned to Cambridge, this time to read Economics. He also rowed for Emmanuel College and rejoined the Cambridge University Air Squadron. In August 1948 while attending the Air Squadron's camp at Shoreham Flying Club, Douglas and another pilot, Gus Forder, were killed when their aircraft crashed into the garden of the writer and poet, Hilaire Belloc. Only four weeks earlier Douglas's mother had died through a coronary thrombosis. The Emanuel Headmaster Cyril Broom wrote offering his condolences to Douglas's father, 'Douglas had been outstanding as a Captain of the school by his charm and courtesy, his calm and dignified leadership and his versatile ability...His example is an inspiration to the school and his loss will be sorely felt in the Old Emanuel Association...' It seems such a tragedy that after so many dangerous operations across enemy territory, time spent as a POW and surviving the forced march that Douglas should have lost his life so soon after the war. However his memory lives on for, through the benefaction of Douglas's brother Derek, on 21 September 1995 His Royal Highness the Prince of Wales opened The Douglas Finlay Museum of College Life at Emmanuel College, Cambridge.

References

1 The raid on La Spezia ended with the bombing of public buildings as the centre of bombing was north-west of the aiming point. See Martine Middlebrook and Chris Everitt, *The Bomber Command War Diaries: An Operational Reference Book 1939–1945* (2011), p. 379. For an overview of the Bomber Command bombing campaign against Italy see Richard Overy, *The Bombing War: Europe 1939-1945*, (2013), pp. 510-546.

2 For further details see Andrew R. B. Simpson, *Ops: Victory at All Costs: On Operations over Hitler's Reich with the Crews of Bomber Command* (2012), p. 201.

3 See Simpson, *Ops*, pp.214-215 for further details.

4 R. Derek Finlay, *Ten to Take Her Home: The Life and Times of RDF* (2012), p. 9.

5 For a comprehensive account of the march Douglas and his fellow POWs undertook see Simpson, *Ops*, pp. 377-393.

Kenneth Horseman

(Emanuel 1929–1936)

At School Kenneth (known as Ken) was a House Prefect of Wellington House and a member of the First Fifteen. In the Christmas 1936 edition of *The Portcullis* his rugby critique concluded, 'Another winning forward and perhaps the outstanding member of the pack; very fast; a demon tackler with good hands and a deceptive side step; an excellent forward in every way.'

In the Second World War Ken was a rifleman serving in the 9th Battalion, the Rifle Brigade. After training in England he was sent to North Africa, where he became a truck driver and desert convoy navigator. He wrote a journal of his experiences for the period from the end of 1941 until the end of the war. It begins with his capture and relates his experiences in some detail.

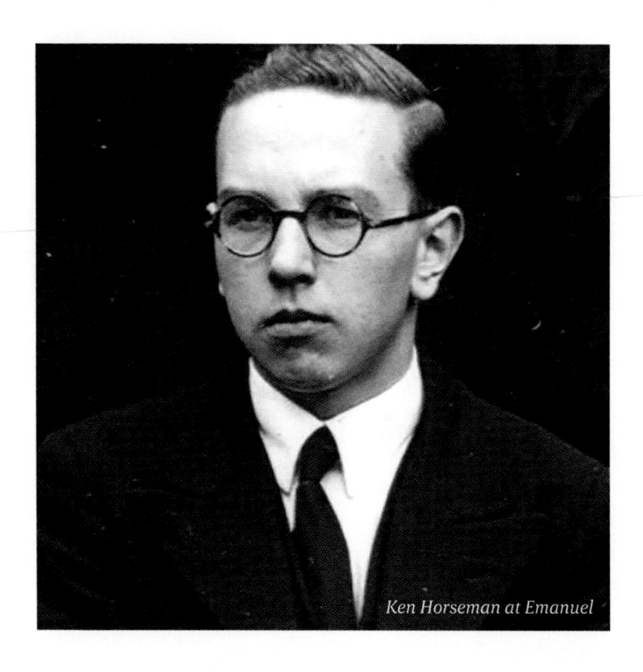

Ken Horseman at Emanuel

He had been in the desert for the whole of 1941 and rashly demonstrated a skill in desert navigation. His dubious reward was to be made lead driver and convoy navigator. As he said himself, 'if there were any mines lying about the place, I'd be the one to find them.'

The initial journal entry is dated 26 February 1942, at Capua, Italy and was written in retrospect:

Well, it really starts about Boxing Day 1941. We were attached to the 2nd Armoured Brigade – a most inefficient brigade which seemed to be commanded by half-wits. For the past week, supplies had been very few and far between and Christmas Day rations and petrol didn't arrive until four o'clock. The rations consisted of bully and biscuits, so we had a magnificent Christmas Dinner. Boxing Day we moved a few miles, west as far as I can remember without incident, but on the 27th after moving about ten miles (many trucks being stuck in sand banks) some enemy Mark IV tanks were sighted about eight miles away.

Our 25 pounders opened up on them, but as far as we could see without much effect. We could see a few vehicles on our extreme right (the tanks were on the left) but as they appeared stationary and about eight miles away, we didn't worry a great deal.

Night fell and we pulled into laager as usual and we saw the usual Jerry flares going up especially to the west, but also at one or two other points.

Morning came (the 28th and we broke laager as usual at first light and pulled about half-a-mile away from Brigade HQ. We breakfasted and Bert Land and I transferred my petrol reserve, approximately sixteen gallons, into Jerry containers and stowed it away in the back (I mention this for a reason). At this time we were on the right of Brigade HQ facing approximately south west. About 8.30am we could see vehicles moving in front on both sides. I drove Major Clayton round the platoon positions and en route we encountered

Ken at the wheel of a 8cwt truck and Bob Perkins (right), Egypt, July 1941

an armoured car of the 12th Lancers. We enquired of them whose the vehicles in front were, but they hadn't the least idea who they were and didn't seem very interested anyway.

We passed on to 2 Platoon's position and found that Parker and the sergeant had already gone out in a truck on a recce to investigate the vehicles in front. As we were talking to the section leaders, the 15 cwt [a Second World War truck] came in, Parker saying that he'd been fired on. From here I drove to Battalion HQ and the Major saw the Adjutant, who protested that he'd already spoken to Brigade twice, but had been more or less told to pipe down. However, he said he'd send the Intelligence Officer over in person to Brigade HQ to see if that would have any effect.

We drove back to our position and Bert and I started digging slit trenches. We'd dug one, when the rations and petrol and water arrived (water two pints per man for two days), time approximately 10.00am. We got back on the trenches and almost immediately about a dozen Stukas came over and dropped some bombs about 100 yards behind my truck.

Bert and I dived behind a bit of scrub in rather ostrich fashion, Bert clutching the Tommy gun while the major dived into the trench. We didn't get in with him as we were rather fed up with his orders for carrying the water: he wanted it all on our truck while we wanted it all on the trucks on which we ate and the canteen truck.

No one was hurt by the bombs in our mob, but I believe there were a couple of shrapnel casualties.

Soon after this the shelling began and the 'Honeys' [light tanks] began to trickle back through our lines. After a short while I saw a long string of trucks moving south east on our left, with shells bursting amongst them and before long one of them burst into flames. The shelling didn't affect us very much, most of the stuff appearing to pass over our heads. Every one else had retired and still we didn't get the order to move, so Bert and I continued with our trenches.

However, at last we got the order to move and the Major told the SM to take CHQ [Company HQ] back whilst he collected 3 Platoon and the Anti-Tank gunners. We collected 3 Platoon and also the driver and crew of a broken down Honey, (the AT gunners having moved already) and we began to retire. By this time the rest of CHQ were out of sight, all except the W/T truck with the 2nd in command on board.

Ken Horseman in khaki

Group photo on patrol – North Africa, June 1941

March 1941 'Kilo 843 – my old truck with Italian badge on the front'

Shells were dropping unpleasantly close as we caught him up, so we stopped for the Major and the Captain to confer for a while. We started up again and I picked my way as best I could between the sand banks, as the following 15cwts would have stuck and been an easy target for the gunners.

By this time shells were actually dropping amongst the 3 Platoon trucks and were coming from in front of us, so it appeared as though we were being fired upon by our own guns. I whacked up the pace to about 30mph, hoping to get to the guns which we could see on our left front before they could do us any great harm, but at that moment someone opened up on us with a Light Machine Gun (LMG) probably a Bren and bullets began zipping in front of the truck. I think I must have looked a bit apprehensive – I certainly felt it, as the Major leaned down (he was standing up) and shouted to me to keep going.

As I put my hand behind me and reached for my tin hat I remember comforting myself, probably rather callously, with the thought that if anyone's going to get hit, the Major will get it first. I hotted up the pace even more to about 40, the shells still falling pretty fast, but the machine gunning stopped as we pulled over to the right behind some big sand banks.

Almost immediately we came in sight of about half-a-dozen trucks, which looked rather like the Jerries', so we stopped again and I went round to the back and asked Bert how it felt to be shelled by our own guns. He said he didn't know they were ours and seemed quite comfortable and not at all worried. It was decided by the Big Shots to make a right handed detour to avoid the suspicious looking trucks, so we moved off again, at right angles to our former course, me in the lead again.

I'd just crested a big sand dune when I heard an explosion very near and caught a glimpse of something ahead. As we dipped down into the sort of valley between the sand-hills the Major bellowed at once to stop and I stood on everything. We both hopped out and I looked back and saw the W/T truck stop on top of the sand-hill and something explode underneath it. All the crew hopped out and scampered down into the valley and almost at once a second shell hit the truck and it blazed up furiously. The Major and I crawled forward to the front of the next sand-hill, he with the Tommy-gun, I with nothing.

We both peered up over the top and about 100 yards in front I saw a Jerry Anti-Tank (A/T) gun with its limber slightly to the left. I bobbed down a bit quick, while the Major let fly with the Tommy-gun, but it fired only one shot and then refused to function. Meanwhile 3 Platoon had made good their escape.

The Major threw the Tommy-gun down in disgust and went back to the truck for a rifle. He went round to the back and the next thing I knew was him saying that Bert had caught it. I remember repeating rather foolishly "What, old Bert dead?" and he said "Yes". I realised then that the first loud explosion I had heard was an A/T shell exploding in the back of the truck, having passed through the place where I had previously stored spare petrol.

The Major took my rifle from the front and came back to where I was. He popped up his head again and fired one shot. The Captain, the driver of the two signallers from the other truck had reached us by now and it was decided to crawl away to the right of the truck and to try to hide in the scrub until darkness fell when we'd make a break for it.

We crawled about 30 yards: I felt all the time that I could drink a barrel of water, although it was a cold day with a strong wind blowing. As we were crawling, a heavy machine gun opened up on us and I could hear the bullets smacking into the sand not far away. Of course, we flattened ourselves in the sand and out of the corner of my eye I saw a Dodge truck come up on our left with a chap standing on the roof with a heavy machine gun. It stopped near my truck and I heard Major Clayton say that we'd better give ourselves up, as he'd already stopped one in the arm – I think they must have spotted his white cloak and fired at it.

I got up and immediately about three Jerries came towards us, one with a revolver and the others with Tommy-guns.

They shouted "Hands up, hands up" and we had to explain that the Major was wounded and couldn't put his hands up. We got to the truck and the Jerries were already looting the back. I saw Bert for the first time and he wasn't a pretty sight, so we put some of the truck sheets over his head as he was lying on the ground near the tailboard.

The Jerries looked after the Major pretty well and bandaged up his arm right away, while we asked the Jerry sergeant if we could bury Bert. He seemed quite pleased that we had suggested it, so Shirley, one of the other signallers and I dug a shallow hole (all we had time for), wrapped Bert in a couple of blankets and covered him up.

The Captain made a small wooden cross and just wrote on it R.F.N.A. LAND R.I.P. We couldn't find his pay book or identity discs and we didn't know his number. The Jerries tried to start the truck (they changed the punctured wheel) but I had turned the petrol off, so it wouldn't start, so they left it.

The Jerries marched us away then (the Major rode in the Dodge) but I went back to the truck and collected my box of letters and toothbrush and toothpaste. We came to a Ford 8cwt. stuck in the sand and pushed it out, Williams in the process pushed an envelope of secret papers into the sand.

We were loaded into the back of the Ford and taken for almost a five mile drive. Eventually we came to a place where three of our 3 tonners were and from which petrol was being transferred to Jerry trucks. We got out of the Ford and just then about twenty Hurricanes went over and all the Jerries banged away merrily, but without effect.

We were loaded into one of the 3 tonners and about thirty other prisoners got in also, so there wasn't much room. After a short while we set off, with one guard on the back who for some reason refused to allow anyone to smoke. Someone found some biscuits and cheese at the back of the truck, for which we were jolly grateful, as we had had nothing to eat since breakfast and it must now have been around three or four in the afternoon. We passed quite a lot of Jerry vehicles and tracked stuff and at one point just before dusk their guns went into action and fired about five rounds at some vehicles which we could see on the sky line.

Just as it was getting dark we pulled into a sort of laager with all the soft skinned stuff in the middle and the guns and armoured stuff on the outskirts. It appeared that we were staying there the night and the guard gave us the remains of his stew (which didn't go far among forty of us) and also gave us four tins of pears and passed his water bottle filled with coffee or tea several times.

We spent a most uncomfortable night, especially as a most detestable pilot officer and our own Captain took up most of the floor space, with total disregard for anyone else.

Morning came and we all felt pretty stiff. The guard brought us about half-a-dozen loaves of black bread, already sliced and reputed to come wrapped in silver paper daily from Berlin. The bread was delicious and we were also given four small tins of some sort of red jam: inferior to ours, but good nevertheless.

After breakfast our truck went round the laager pulling other Jerry trucks to start them – many of their trucks seemed in a pretty decrepit state. On alighting I found we were with another crowd of prisoners, about 150 in total, amongst whom were most of our CHQ, whom I fully imagined had got away. I was pleased in a way to see Bob Perkins, Charlie Morton, Alan Duke, Tommy Luxford and one or two others. The Company Sergeant Major and the Company Sergeant were also there, but of the Major there was no sign.

I took a blanket from the 3 tonner as it was very cold and I had no overcoat or groundsheet. Bob had nothing either, so we shared the blanket. The other chaps had various stories to tell, but fortunately the only casualties had been on my truck and as far as we knew everyone else was unhurt. Most of the other prisoners were 'B' echelon men, mainly from the 12th Lancers.

We were marched a couple of miles to a collection of Jerry vehicles and stopped about 200 yards short of them. Several Jerries came out from the general mass of vehicles to inspect us and several brought cameras and took snaps of us, probably for propaganda purposes.

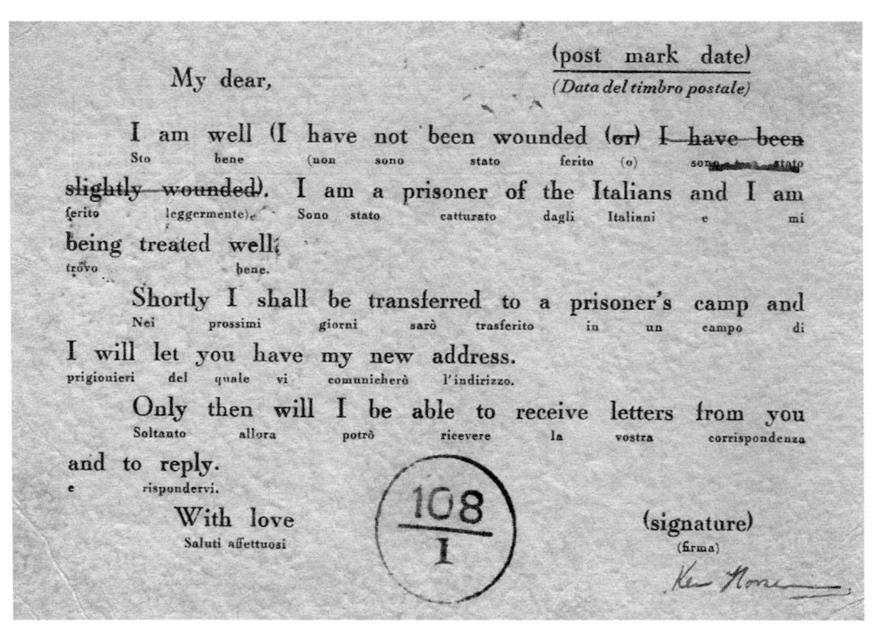

(post mark date)
(Data del timbro postale)

My dear,

I am well (I have not been wounded ~~(or) I have been slightly wounded~~). I am a prisoner of the Italians and I am being treated well.
Sto bene (non sono stato ferito (o) ~~sono stato ferito leggermente~~) e Sono stato catturato dagli Italiani e mi trovo bene.

Shortly I shall be transferred to a prisoner's camp and I will let you have my new address.
Nei prossimi giorni sarò trasferito in un campo di prigionieri del quale vi comunicherò l'indirizzo.

Only then will I be able to receive letters from you and to reply.
Soltanto allora potrò ricevere la vostra corrispondenza e rispondervi.

With love
Saluti affettuosi

108
I

(signature)
(firma)

Postcard from Ken stating that he is a prisoner of the Italians

Over the next day Ken and the men from his company were transported to El Agheila.

At length we pulled into the side of the road at a Medical Dressing Station, where most of the chaps who had desert sores had them dressed. We had a drink of lemonade here, but still nothing to eat. After about an hour, to our great surprise, the whole convoy turned round and went back up the road at great speed. We reached El Agheila again and after much parleying in the yard between the Italians and the Jerries we drove out again, back to the forward supply dump where we had breakfasted.

Between Agheila and this place one of the trucks broke down and the two officers, a sergeant and a trooper of the 12th Lancers made their escape – having no rations, water or maps! We were told we had to sleep outside the trucks that night, the first since we had been captured and we didn't feel very pleased as it was bitterly cold and Bob and I had only one blanket between the two of us. However, we scooped a hole in the sand and lay down, but were roused almost immediately by demands as to where the two officers were.

There was quite a to-do when it was discovered they had escaped and a search party was sent out immediately, while we were piled into the trucks and driven down to Agheila and handed over to the Italians. We were loaded into two of the diesel trucks and were so cramped that some people had to stand up all night. I doubt if anyone slept, that night – I know I didn't.

Ken was taken to Certi via Nufilla. In the afternoon of 1 January 1942 he was presented in front of an Italian officer:

I was the next one out and was taken across the courtyard to an office, where an Italian officer and two minions were waiting. Immediately they emptied my pockets and I was asked what Regiment I belonged to, whether I'd been in France, my name, rank and number and was told I'd been in Egypt almost exactly a year – which was obvious from my Pay Book. My letters, photographs and other belongings were all inspected and given back to me, the only thing they retained was my Jack knife.

After leaving the office I was directed to a sort of stable place with a stone floor, open on both sides, where Bob and one or two others who had already been searched were waiting. The searching process was so slow we saw it would probably take all night to finish everyone, so we decided to try and sleep. We put the overcoat on the ground and lay down with the blanket over us and I was so tired I went to sleep almost immediately.

When I woke up, just after daybreak, the last of the prisoners was just being searched, so we got up and waited to see what was going to happen. After about a couple of hours we were lined up and given two biscuits and one tin of bully. I think most of us ate a biscuit and the bully right away we were so hungry. We waited for about another hour and then were taken to a couple of diesel trucks, one of which was open and pulled a trailer. Bob and I were unfortunate enough to be loaded onto the open truck, it was very cold and windy. We followed the coast road all that day and it was the coldest ride I've ever had - we just huddled together as best we could and shivered.

They were taken to Misurata where they stayed for a night before setting off the next morning for their first prison camp near a village called Tarhuna, Libya.

At first sight it looked quite decent – not bad buildings, only about one strand of barbed wire round the place. We got down from the trucks and went through the wire barrier and I was picked to help issue blankets. The bloke – a broken down looking Italian soldier who spoke very good American and who acted as interpreter, apologised for only giving us four blankets and we thought that wasn't so bad. However, the blankets were tiny things, about five feet long and very thin.

The dormitory, or barrack room was about 150 yards long, paved with tiles (red) and had coat racks right down the middle. We were issued a sort of rush mat to lie on and that was all the furniture there was. We all bagged places against the wall, to sleep and hung about reading the names written on the white walls in pencil of all the other unfortunates who had spent time there.

The rest of the afternoon we spent having all our hair cut off – I thought he'd taken my scalp off when I saw all my hair on the ground – and filling in forms confirming our parents' names, where we were captured and suchlike details. About five o'clock we were given a biscuit and a tin of bully and then shut in our room for the night.

We did very little the next day, except clean the place out and fill in Red Cross cards, but we had our first taste of the Tarhuna so-called food. At about 8 o'clock we had about a quarter of a pint of luke-warm coffee, after standing about in the cold waiting to be counted for about an hour. This was a regular feature of coffee and soup time, at night and the old commandant seemed to be absolutely incapable of counting any more than ten and we were usually counted (about 200 of us) about four times and there were a lot of arguments between him and the NCOs before he was satisfied.

At half-past-eleven we were given two rolls (brown and very tasty) and a ladle of macaroni and beans, or just macaroni, or just beans – it varied. About 5 o'clock we had a ladle of so-called soup – just hot water with a little grease floating on the top and a piece of meat – or rather a scrap of meat sometimes absolutely uneatable.

We did nothing at Tarhuna but sit around in the sun when it was out, or walk around to keep warm when it wasn't.

After a few days the Jerries opened a sort of Ordnance depot in some of the buildings with the stuff they'd rescued from Benghazi and some of us used to go over and unload trucks or make shelves and such like odd jobs – it broke the monotony a bit. There were some pretty bad scenes over the food, people used to fight to get any scraps left over in the dixies – it made one absolutely disgusted. There were also a good many cases of people's bread being stolen, so we used to carry ours about with us.

After a month and with several false starts where Ken and the other prisoners were transported to and fro between the quayside and a holding camp they eventually sailed for Italy at the end of January 1942. Ken remembered arriving in Naples at lunchtime on 31 January, 'We entered the Bay of Naples escorted by a destroyer. It was a lovely sight - the black cloud of smoke above the snow covered Vesuvius - the sweeping curve of the harbour and Naples itself nestling up against the hills to the left of the volcano.'

Ken described what happened next:

We dropped anchor and the quarantine doctor came on board. He just ambled around, asking if anyone was sick and as no-one was, he just vanished again. We then collected our few belongings and went down the gangway, managing to collect a few small slices of brown bread from a steward along the way. About a third of us were loaded onto a small steam tender and ferried across to the other side of the docks, where there was a bath house and fumigation centre. There I had the first shower I'd had for about five months and gave my desert sores a good washing.

In the late afternoon we marched about 500 yards and then came to a sort of level crossing, where we boarded a train consisting of one coach (for the officers, poor little things) and cattle trucks with wooden seats inside for us.

Ken's son Brian continues his father's story after Ken was loaded onto the cattle truck:

Following arrival in Italy, Ken was transferred (via Milan jail), to Campo P.G 59, where he was by 14 March 1943. Life under an Italian regime seems to have been tolerable: both sides seem to have been convinced that the other was entirely barmy, leading to baffled amusement on both sides. Ken kept a diary during this period but written in pencil, on poor quality paper, in minuscule writing, so it is now all but impossible to decipher. In any event it relates mainly to the weather, parcel deliveries, the boredom of camp life and a focus on food.

He was moved subsequently to Campo P.G. 146/NX. In a postcard to his brother Arthur in August 1943 he describes it as not too bad – apart from the heat, flies and mosquitoes. This is only weeks before Italy signed an Armistice at which point all the camp guards promptly decided to go home, abandoning the prisoners.

The prisoners walked out too, but were now in German

controlled territory. They split up into small groups to try to make their way South, across the front line. Ken was with a small group of friends and they were aided by the very poor residents of a remote hamlet. As it was in the mountains and winter was drawing on, food and shelter were priorities. After about three weeks they were betrayed for a bounty and rounded up by the Germans.

By stages they were moved to Germany itself and by May 1944 he had reached Stalag IVF, a subsidiary of the largest of all the POW camps, where Ken spent the remainder of the war. Stalag IVF was mainly for French troops captured in the Battle of France and British troops captured in North Africa. Conditions in Germany were getting grim by this time and the supply of Red Cross parcels became erratic. The prisoners were also forced to work. In his letters Ken mentioned that after all the digging he had done he didn't even want to look at a window box when he got back, but that might have been a lesser evil than being forced into the coal mines. They did find some opportunities for casual sabotage, though. 'Forgetting' to put the reinforcing mesh into precast concrete panels was one example, or if they had to unload truck engines from the backs of lorries – each crate labelled 'this side up' in German – they would roll them end over end to drop off the tailboard – until a guard noticed. Or they might drop a handful of small screws into the cylinders of new engines if unobserved.

The camp was liberated by the Americans in March 1945. Ken's group of inmates were then processed and fed, before being flown back to England in a bomber, arriving on 22 April 1945.

On 29 May 1943 Ken's father received a letter from Major Mark Clayton who Ken last saw shortly after their capture in 1941. Major Clayton wrote wanting to find out what had happened to Ken but also to give his appreciation of Ken's service while under his command. He wrote:

I had been his Company Commander for about two years and for the last six months he had been my personal driver, a duty which he performed to perfection. He had a real flair for driving a truck over the desert and could find his way about without maps or compasses in a most miraculous fashion. Apart from this he kept the truck in excellent condition and was always helpful and cheerful.

I tried to persuade him to take promotion on many occasions, but he always refused. I am not writing this as a polite letter to his father, but quite sincerely to tell you that I appreciate all that he did for me in the time he was in my Company.

I should be most grateful for any information you can give me. I was lucky enough to be repatriated because of my wound, but am now quite fit again apart from a rather battered arm.

Alec Shoosmith

(Emanuel 1934–1936)

Alec Shoosmith standing in front of a Light Tank Mk VI

At School Alec was a member of the OTC but no training exercises on summer camps could have prepared him for his experiences during the Second World War. Alec was a Territorial soldier and on 1 September 1939 he was called up. He served as a Sergeant in the 3rd County of London Yeomanry (Sharpshooters). In August 1941 Alec's regiment sailed for Africa, passing Freetown, Cape Town and Aden before eventually arriving in Alexandria in late October. Alec kept a diary of part of that voyage from England to Cape Town where he noted which ships joined his in convoy and when they departed, the weather and hearing Churchill's speech after his Atlantic meeting with President Roosevelt.[1] Alec noted, 'It came over very well and I thought it was very good although his speeches are very much of a muchness.' Alec's impressions of the voyage were positive and his descriptions of Freetown harbour could be straight from a travel brochure, writing on 28 August 1941 of seeing 'Palms, beautiful sands and vegetation.' But within weeks Alec was in action at El Adem landing field, south of Tobruk during Operation Crusader. The contrast with the sea voyage couldn't have been greater. On 23 November 1941 Alec was captured and made a POW. In 1946 he wrote an account of his war experiences including details of his capture and the three-and-a-half years he spent as a POW which ended in Stalag IVB, via Greece and Italy.

The following is an edited version of Alec Shoosmith's account of being a POW.

Introduction

It is now nearly nine months since I arrived home from being a POW for three and a half years in Italy and Germany. My account is told entirely from memory and I would ask my readers to remember that it is my experiences as I saw them. Many other POWs had harder times, so any incidence that is omitted please forgive me. So please be patient and I sincerely hope that you will find it interesting. I would like to thank the British and International Red Cross whose work made it possible that we all came through fitter than we might have done.

Circumstances leading to Capture

This tale begins in November 1941 at a place about four miles south of Tobruk, the El Adem landing field. It was during the second push on the desert. My regiment, the London Yeomanry, had had several encounters with the enemy in which they had lost a number of tanks and crews.

We had been given orders to approach the rise on which the landing field was situated, when without warning our troops began to fall back. The next thing – we were moving onto the high ground and a battle started between our regiment and a German Armoured Division. The time was about 3.30 and the light was beginning to fade and with our much smaller guns we found it difficult to get the enemy's range and came under their fire before we could fire on them with any good effect. But our lads went in without a thought for themselves. Very soon tanks were on fire on both sides but we were the heavier losers.

I myself had to withdraw out of the action because my guns jammed. I had to pass through a smoke screen and on coming out the other side of it found myself silhouetted. The enemy infantry were immediately to my front, upon which I opened fire and succeeded in stopping their advance. But unknown to me there was also another section on my right flank, which managed to bring their anti-tank gun into action and put two shots through the side of the tank, one wounding my operator from which he later died and the other into my petrol tank and setting us on fire. I immediately ordered my crew out. My driver not knowing we were on fire was just changing gear in readiness to drive over the enemy in front. We managed to bail out lifting our operator as well. Our only remaining tank was nearby and the eight of us climbed on board and got out of the action.

Alec and his crew were ordered onto another tank but it broke down near the South African Artillery lines. Taking time for some tea and something to eat they managed to get some rest before an enemy barrage started early next morning. Walking east they encountered another barrage in the early afternoon. Alec continues the story:

One cannot imagine how naked one feels when you have been used to armour around you all the time and suddenly you find yourself in the open. The barrage had been going on for two hours when my driver told us to get up because there was an enemy Mk IV tank coming straight at us. Upon getting up it turned away and ordered us up to the rear. We all felt rather dazed. This attack and defeat by the enemy was made possible for the simple fact that all our tanks and anti-tank guns were out of ammunition. We could do nothing to repel the enemy.

We did not have to walk far before we could see a mass of our troops lined up and being searched. We were hustled into this queue. Presently we were ordered to drive some trucks so we did this in the hope that we might be able to get away and it was whilst we were doing this that our tanks came into attack. Unfortunately they put mine and my driver's lorry out of action. The attack did not succeed and a German soldier took us to another lorry. How he noticed us, I don't know, as we both were lying very low. We spent the rest of the night in a lorry surrounded with camouflage netting.

Early days as a POW

Alec was transported to Benghazi via a wadi where the Italians 'came out to spit and jeer' at them. After a three day journey they arrived at Benghazi where they stayed for five days before being loaded onto a ship, where 2000 prisoners were squeezed into holds. Whilst at sea the ship was torpedoed resulting in heavy casualties. Alec and the survivors eventually landed on the west coast of Greece. After initially being interned in a medieval castle the prisoners were moved after a week to a camp in the hills above the town of Patras. Disease was rife among the men as Alec remembered:

From here we were marched up into the hills where we were to make tents out of the ground sheets. This place was to become known as Dysentery Acre. For it was here that we had our worst bout of this terrible disease. Fellows used to have to lie by the side of a pit because they were too weak to walk there every few minutes and those not inflicted were just able to walk themselves.

Move to Italy

In the next few months conditions were pitiful with men being covered in lice and fleas. Then in March 1942 they were moved to Italy, arriving in Bari and soon being transported to a camp just outside Taranto. It was here that the men received their first Red Cross Parcel which was the first communication they had had from the UK in six months. Alec remembered how this changed the men, 'To see the difference on the fellows' faces was wonderful.' The next move was to a camp near Gravena where Alec would spend the next fifteen months. He gave his impressions of life in the camp:

At first the food was not too bad, but as time went on and more prisoners came in we got our rations cut. Having written to the Red Cross and with assistance from the Vatican City we began to get games and parcels here. It was through the Vatican City that many of our relations and dear ones heard of our safety for the first time. Very soon with the aid of the parcels and the basketball, deck tennis etc we got back on our feet again. Some more fitter fellows even took up boxing. Then came the bad news about Tobruk falling and we began to wonder if we would ever get out, but even then we used to tell the sentries that very soon we would have them out in Libya, just as we had in Abyssinia. Some of the fellows went out to work on farms and some on the quarry outside the camp itself. For this they got an extra loaf.

The fellows who did not go out to work, used to spend their time making various little things such as stoves, clocks and picture frames. These were made out of tin from the Red Cross parcels. Occasionally there would be an exhibition to which the Commandant would come. He was often amazed at the way the exhibits were made with us having so few tools but he didn't know that many of the tools had come from his workshops.

The day usually started with roll call and when this was over there would be one mad rush for the fire and wood on which we made our morning cup of tea. At about 11 a.m. bread and cheese would be issued but some of the loaves, if you could see them, were so small you could sometimes put them in your mouth all in one. This of course called for another brew. Then there was a wait until 4pm when the skilly was got. This was usually macaroni with a few onions and tomatoes in it. At this camp we were luckier than some for we were able to get quite a lot of fruit in the canteen including dried figs. But I must say they were not up to our standard, but they were very eatable. In fact there was always a large crowd for these.

On the move

In July 1943 the Allies invaded Sicily and Alec and the other prisoners were moved out of their camp, loaded onto cattle trucks and moved North to a new camp at Bologna. Interestingly Alec writes fondly of an Italian sentry who aided the men in fetching hot water at each stop so they could make tea as Alec explains:

One of our sentries squashed his hand in between the sliding doors of the carriage and none of his pals would do anything to help him so one of our fellows bandaged it up and we gave him some of our food when ever we had some. For this he used to run to the engine at every stop and get us hot water to make tea in a bucket.

Later Alec heard that the sentry was awaiting court martial.

Men had to work together in order to survive. Punitive punishments would see the men at their best as they 'mucked in' to help one another. These small acts of resistance were key to getting through the camp experience but occasionally their situation got the better of them as Alec explained:

Anyone who has never really had to go short of food and I mean short (No one need ever starve in this country) would understand the feeling we got sometimes. You could literally feel your sides of your stomach knocking against each other. I have seen fellows fight one another over a small piece of stale cabbage. It was at a time like this that one's temper would get the better of you and many fought over the silliest of things.

Italy surrenders

Italy surrendered on 8 September 1943 but far from enjoying freedom Alec was soon a prisoner of the Germans.

Well eventually we arrived at the time when Italy could take no more and we had a funny feeling that something was about to happen. But it was not until 8pm on 8 September that we got the good news. Everyone went mad, burning everything they could lay their hands on and making large bonfires. It died down by about 2am and we all got some sleep, but on waking the next morning we had a nasty shock. Armoured cars and infantry were out in the fields around us. These were our other enemy. The Hun. We were warned by the Commandant that these were about and that we were not to panic, but that he had sent out a patrol and these would let us know when they were anywhere near us and so give us time to get away. I suppose being behind the wire for such a time and getting this news we did not stop to think that all the Commandant said was a blind. Well anyway we were prisoners again after about ten hours of so called freedom.

Everyone's reaction to this was to find some way to get out. Some dug tunnels, others went out in rubbish carts and then again others would cut their way through the wire at night. It was this way that a pal of mine and I decided to have a go. But the night that we were going to cut the wire away we decided to try this gap. There were two fellows in front of me and when the fellow was crawling through the wire, the sentries twenty yards away talking to some other fellows turned around and saw this fellow crawling across the path. He opened fire immediately but not to hit which goes to show that even the Jerries have a little heart occasionally. We inside the wire scattered for we knew that the Breda guns would open up any minute. Which did happen in this case very quickly. We did not get another chance for the next day we were off to Deutschland.

Alec wrote of his preference for the Germans over the Italians after the latter surrendered for the fact that Red Cross parcels had been stored up for a week for what Alec claimed was the Italian officers' intention to use them personally, until the Germans distributed them among the prisoners. However, he also made clear that this was merely a preference between the devil and the deep blue sea as he wrote, 'Please don't think I like the Jerry, for I don't.'

Destination Germany

So in September 1943 Alec was moved again – destination Germany. On a stop at Innsbruck station Alec relates an interesting story about the reaction of school children to them, 'From these we had to take being spat and jeered at. But to their amazement we only laughed.' This episode was not the only rude awakening for a day or two later as they approached their new camp Alec witnessed the treatment being meted out to Russian prisoners:

Whilst walking to here we saw for the first time the German treatment of prisoners of war. There passed us about 20 Russian men all of about 50 years of age, but it is probably the treatment that had made them look so old. As they passed one of them collapsed and the guard immediately started to hit him with his rifle butt. Some of our fellows jeered at him and his reaction to this was to threaten us with his Luger... The fellow on the ground was bleeding on the face and just managed to get up before he was shot.

Camp Entertainment

Alec's new camp was Stalag IVB Mühlberg-am-Elbe. To break up the monotony of the daily routine men would organise games and shows. These would be a reprieve from the hours spent thinking of home or how to escape.

Later on games kits started to come in and football and basketball started. To make these sports become keen, there were international and knock out competitions held between huts. For this, each hut was named after a well known home team such as Chelsea and Everton, which was our hut...As to the international matches, they became very well supported, especially when one of the other nationals had beaten us and there was a return match. These were held on a Saturday and the Germans used to come in fairly big numbers, so they got some good entertainment for nothing. Some of the footballers well known in England were with us, there was Hanlon of Manchester, Steen of the Wolves and plenty more and in fact there were enough professionals to make up a team and these had many a tussle with the amateurs.

Another very good thing that was got going for our entertainment was the C.A.D.S., our theatrical society. The Germans allowed us to build our own theatre and put on shows such as Outward Bound, varieties and orchestral concerts. To make all this possible the fellows made the costumes out of old clothes and occasionally managed to hire proper costumes from a theatrical shop in Berlin. These were hired for cigarettes.

The all important thing that made life bearable was the fact that we had the news every night from the BBC. This was made possible by the fact that the Commandant's wireless went wrong and he sent for one of our fellows to repair it. This he did, but he took away a lot of the parts and with the aid of razor blades and tins made us a wireless. He kept it in the lavatory at night.

Liberation and home

After sixteen months imprisonment Stalag IVB was liberated on 23 April 1945, the Germans having fled the previous evening. The POWs were ordered to stay put and after a week marched to Risa. On this journey Alec saw, 'signs of battle and much destruction.' After weeks of waiting to be transferred to the American lines Alec and others decided to make their own way. Avoiding Russian guards, who were sending people back, they set off. After a few days travelling they crossed the river Molder. On 25 May Alec was flown by Dakota to Brussels and the next day arrived back in England, being flown back in a Lancaster. Alec thought the Dakota a more comfortable ride but he was relieved to be going home. His first stop was to see his sister in Worthing. He wrote about being back at home, 'The only difference I found in Blighty was that I felt closed in.' Like so many others Alec had to adjust to life back at home and to being free after years in captivity. The next day he had an emotional reunion as he remembered:

After leaving my kit at home I went to meet the most important person of all. Peggy, my wife. I met her at King's Cross and I am afraid I didn't know what to do. I felt like crying, but didn't and instead we kissed and set off back to my people's.

So I had come back, just like many others, but we will never forget the ones we left behind, our operator and the ones who could not face the life of imprisonment. I will be going into civvy street again very soon and I won't be sorry although it may be difficult. But with the help of Peggy, it will be much easier. God bless her.

References

1 Alec Shoosmith's papers are held in the Kent & Sharpshooters Museum, Hever Castle, Kent.

'Take Care of Christopher'

Arthur Daniel Willett *(Emanuel 1925–1933)*

Arthur Daniel Willett was a keen cricketer at Emanuel. He was also a House Prefect in Nelson, played in the First Eleven and was in the OTC being awarded his War Office Certificate 'A' in November 1932. He gained his full cricket colours in 1932 and was an excellent defensive batsman, a good fielder and valuable member of the team. Arthur was also a member of the Emanuel School Dramatic Society.

Details about his war service are currently sketchy but it is known that he was captured by the Japanese when Singapore fell in February 1942. On 7 January 1944 an article appeared in the local Battersea newspaper, the *South Western Star*, which announced that Arthur's father, Mr. Thomas Charles Willett (who was the Mayor of Wandsworth's secretary), and Arthur's wife, Betty Moira Bell Willett, had received information that he was alive and that he was in No. 4 POW Camp Thailand. In his letter to his wife Arthur wrote, 'Take care of Christopher.' Christopher was born after the fall of Singapore and never had the opportunity of seeing his father.

Emanuel School cricket First XI, 1932 – Back row (left to right): C.E. Crimp, P.T. Addison, S.G. Standing, W. Webber Esq., A.D. Willett, U. Thornburn; Middle row: W.J. Biles, F.L. Abbott, The Headmaster, A.E. Mills, V.S. Nargang; Front row: E. Matsuyama, D.E. Cheadle

The following year having had no further news of Arthur a second article appeared in the *South Western Star* on 19 January 1945. The headline announced, 'Mayor's Secretary Informed of Son's Death.' For a whole year his family thought he was alive, not knowing that shortly after he had sent news home in 1943 he had died.

Arthur was a private in the 5th Battalion Bedfordshire and Hertfordshire Regiment. We know that he was listed as prisoner 5955656. He was a POW for 22 months before dying through complications caused by ulcers on 8 December 1943. One can only imagine the inhumane conditions Arthur would have experienced in those 22 months and perhaps the thought of home, his wife and the son he never met gave him the strength to survive for so long. A mere decade before, he had been running across the Emanuel School cricket pitch on a summer's day. He was 28 when he died. Originally buried in the camp in which he was a POW, Tasao No. 2, his remains are now buried in Kanchanaburi War Cemetery. It is likely that Arthur was involved in the construction of the infamous Burma-Thai Railway.

Percy 'Peter' Coe *(Emanuel 1934–1935)*

Another Old Emanuel to make a daring escape was Percy 'Peter' Coe. After leaving Emanuel Peter studied mathematics and mechanical engineering at the Regent Street Polytechnic. At the outbreak of war in 1939 he joined the Merchant Navy.

TELEGRAMS:-
INLAND {MOORISH, FEN, LONDON. RUNCIMAN, NEWCASTLE-TYNE.
FOREIGN {MOORISH, LONDON. RUNCIMAN, NEWCASTLE-TYNE

TELEPHONES:-
LONDON, ROYAL 41
NEWCASTLE 233

RUNCIMAN (LONDON) LIMITED

SHIP & INSURANCE BROKERS, ETC.

AGENTS FOR
MOOR LINE LTD.
RUNCIMAN SHIPPING Cº LTD
WALTER RUNCIMAN & Cº LTD
NEWCASTLE UPON TYNE

52-54, LEADENHALL STREET,
LONDON, E.C.3

MANAGERS OF
ANCHOR LINE LI
GENERAL EUROPEAN AG
MOBILE OCEANIC

OUR REFERENCE WJB/LF.
YOUR REFERENCE

5th August 1941.

P. Coe Esq.,
1 Brecon Road,
FULHAM W. 6.

Dear Sir,

With reference to your Son, Mr. P.N.Coe who sailed on board the "A.D.HUFF", we have now received information that he is in Gibraltar. We regret we have no further details but should we receive same we will communicate with you immediately.

Yours truly,
FOR RUNCIMAN (LONDON) LIMITED

A letter from Runciman Ship and Insurance Brokers notifying Peter's family he was in Gibraltar

On 22 February 1941 Peter was serving in the Canadian Merchant Vessel *A. D. Huff*, which was making its voyage from England, where it had just unloaded a cargo of iron ingots, newsprint and pit props for Welsh coalmines, to Newfoundland. The *Huff* was 600 miles off Cape Race when a German seaplane dropped a surrender demand from the German battle cruiser, the *Gneisenau*. The *Huff's* Captain ignored the message and ordered the ship to continue at full speed. Unfortunately the *Huff's* full speed of around eight knots was not enough to outrun the *Gneisenau* which at a little after quarter to one in the afternoon opened fire with two shells landing in the *Huff's* wake. The *Huff* had been hit around just over thirty times when Captain McDowall ordered his crew to lifeboats. The *Gneisenau* proceeded to sink the *Huff*. Peter, with other survivors of the *Huff*, was transferred to the prison ship *Ermland* during the course of their journey across the Atlantic. Proceeding to France the prisoners were transported overland reaching La Rochelle in late March 1941. After ten days in La Rochelle where Peter and the others were imprisoned in St Médard en Jalles, an ex-Foreign Legion barracks renamed by the Germans as Frontstalag 221, the prisoners – including sailors and merchantmen from other ships sunk by the Germans – were loaded onto third class train carriages with the seats removed. They were to be transported to a new prison camp – Stalag XB at Sandbostel, near Bremen. During the course of their journey, 20 prisoners, including Peter and the Canadian bosun from the *Huff*, Ernest Shackleton, jumped from the train near Aachen. Whilst most of the escapees were recaptured, Peter and Ernest managed to travel across Vichy France. Ernest travelled south, via Marseille and Peter made for the Pyrenees where he crossed into Spain.

Emanuel Headmaster Mark Hanley-Browne with Lord Coe in the Emanuel Archive, 1 October 2013

Reaching Spain Peter was interned in Miranda de Ebro – the Spanish concentration camp for foreign prisoners. Peter's mother Violet, in all this time since the sinking of the *Huff*, had had no news of her son's fate. A visit by the Chaplain of the line which owned the *Huff* bringing news of Peter's presumed death and an arranged memorial service for the victims of the sinking did nothing to shake Violet's firm belief that her son had survived. That belief was vindicated when Peter was released after several months in Spain and returned via Gibraltar arriving at Greenock on the Clyde on 14 August 1941. Peter's return afforded the authorities the first news of what had happened to the *A. D. Huff*.

Before the war and after Peter was a keen cyclist. In his spare time he studied the science of endurance training and became particularly interested in middle-distance training which he spent much time reassessing. He applied this knowledge to coaching his son Sebastian who showed an early aptitude for running. The father and son partnership was a huge success with Peter ultimately coaching Sebastian to win a gold medal in the 1980 Moscow Olympics 1500m final as well as doing much in the preparation for Sebastian's second 1500m gold at the Los Angeles Olympics in 1984. In 2013 Lord Sebastian Coe visited Emanuel School to give a talk and afterwards he took time to visit the School archive where he was able to see his father's School reports and registration card.[1]

References

1 For more on Peter's life see Seb Coe, *Running My Life* (2012).

Peter and Seb Coe after a training session

Albert 'Bert' Edward Bumstead *(Emanuel 1933–1939)*

When Albert (known as 'Bert') attended Emanuel he was a member of the Dramatic Society and the OTC and had been awarded his War Office Certificate 'A' in 1938. He was a member of the Modern Sixth class and passed the London Matriculation exams.

After leaving School he trained to be an auditor before he joined the RAF and obtained his Air Navigator's certificate (2nd Class) in 1942. Bert spent much of his time lecturing on navigation but longed to become operational. Bert was sent on a course to gain experience as a navigator with 76 Squadron RAF when on the night of 4/5 May 1943 he joined an operational flight that technically he should never have been on! However he went with a crew on an operation to bomb targets in Dortmund. This was the first major attack on this city with over a thousand buildings destroyed. The Halifax, serial number DK134 took off from Linton-on-Ouse at 10.06pm on 4 May. On its return to England, as it flew across the Dutch coast, the Halifax was shot down. It is believed that the pilot responsible was Hauptmann Wilhelm Dorman of the 3rd Gruppe of Nachtjagdgeschwader 1.

Bert Bumstead

Bert's parents received news that he had been reported missing. Shortly afterwards, his commanding officer at No. 1 Elementary Flying Training School wrote to Bert's mother, 'It is the spirit of young men such as he which makes our air force the finest in the world.' But a few weeks later several letters arrived from complete strangers notifying Bert's parents that they had heard on the radio that Bert had been made a POW. From Cornwall a Miss Mary Downing wrote on 1 June 1943, 'Dear Mrs Bumstead, On listening to the German radio tonight Sgt. Bumstead's name was given, but no message could I pick up as it was not very clear and I thought you would be glad to hear that he was safe.' Letters such as these show us the camaraderie that was forged in wartime, not only between combatants but also between civilians who connected with perfect strangers during a time of national crisis.

Bert had indeed been made a POW. After being shot down the Halifax crashed at 0155 am near Kilder, some 5 km south west of Doetinchem, Holland. Bert and the other crew members all jumped from the aircraft. They were all

Bert Bumstead (second from left in group photo) and by himself (right)

eventually captured and made POWs. They were interrogated and later sent to POW camps. Bert was initially interned at Stalag Luft I near Barth, Germany then moved Stalag Luft VI located near Heydekrug in East Prussia and finally Stalag Luft IV in Gross Tychow, Pomerania. It was his experiences during a forced march from Stalag Luft VI to Stalag Luft IV in July 1944 that remained a vivid memory for Bert throughout his life. Russian advances in the East necessitated a move of POWs to a new camp. The journey was atrocious and on the road to their new camp POWs were pricked with bayonets and hit with rifle butts. Bert experienced another forced march in February 1945. Bert returned to England and his son Ian attended Emanuel in the 1970s.

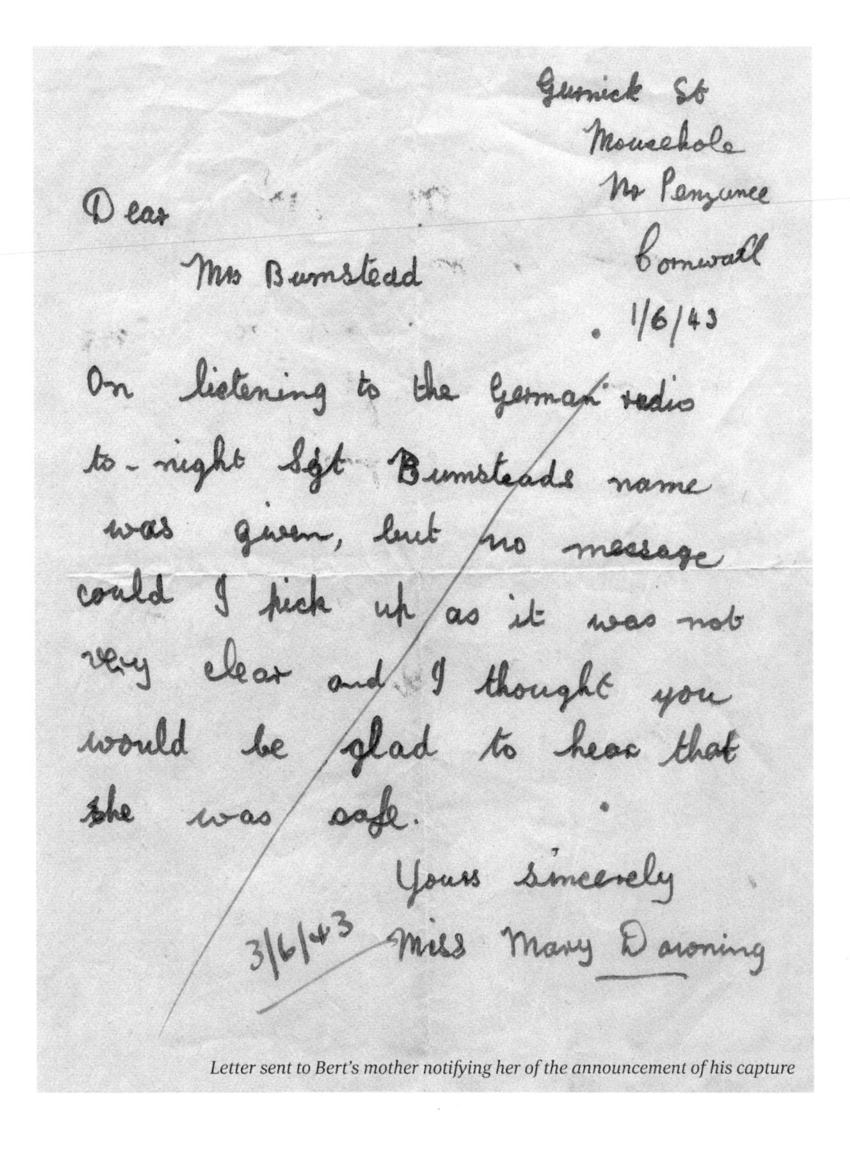

Gurnick St
Mousehole
Nr Penzance
Cornwall
1/6/43

Dear
Mrs Bumstead

On listening to the German radio to-night Sgt Bumsteads name was given, but no message could I pick up as it was not very clear and I thought you would be glad to hear that she was safe.

Yours Sincerely
Miss Mary Downing
3/6/43

Letter sent to Bert's mother notifying her of the announcement of his capture

References

1 For an account of the march see John Nichol and Tony Rennell, The Last Escape: The Untold Story of Allied Prisoners of War in Germany 1944–45 (2003), pp. 17-28.

'A one-man resistance movement'

Major Felix Harvey Spencer Palmer CBE

(Emanuel 1920–1928)

Felix had a colourful School career, being Captain of his House and Swimming. He also played for the School Second Fifteen in addition to being a member of the OTC. In later life Felix Palmer was at the time the only Englishman to chair the Timber Committee of the UN Economic Committee for Europe, advising the UK Government on the industry for sixteen years. This may sound like a modest profession for a soldier who had a remarkable war. In the Second World War he undertook military reconnaissance work in Norway, ending the war being moved around various prisoner of war camps, earning the moniker 'the one-man resistance movement.'

In 1929 he was commissioned into the TA – 6th East Surrey Regiment. Having boxed at School he also competed in the TA Inter Services tournament for five successive years. His father was keen for him to become a doctor like himself and his elder brother Geoffrey Blake Palmer (Emanuel 1919–1925), who was studying at Guy's Hospital. However medicine was not for Felix and instead he joined a firm of timber agents and stayed in the timber industry for fifty years.

Felix Palmer in OEA Rugby kit, 1938

Three days into his honeymoon on 22 August 1939 he was recalled as the key party of the TA was mobilised. By 1 September he was with his battalion at Chattadene Barracks in Kent. Its duty was to guard the Isle of Grain oil depots due to the insufficient numbers of the Royal West Kent TA to adequately protect all the points surrounding the area.

In the 1930s Felix had worked in Finland studying sawmilling and he also spent time learning the language. It was due to this skill that in February 1940, when Britain sent the 5th Army Corps to Finland, that Felix was sent as intelligence officer to the Corps. Felix was given the task of finding the quickest route from a base in Trondheim in Norway across Sweden via the railway and into Finland. He was sent to Trondheim as part of a British military reconnaissance unit in order to survey all the vulnerable points that needed guarding. Since 30 November 1939 the Russians had been fighting against the Finns as part of their plans to widen their defences. In addition the Germans coveted the rich supply of iron-ore that Sweden in particular could supply for their war efforts. British interests relied on securing Norway against any planned German attack and supporting the Finnish Government against Russia if the Finnish Government asked them for it. However on 13 March 1940 the Finns eventually capitulated, the Russian forces proving too strong.

By late March 1940 Felix was back in England and on the third day of four days leave he was called to the War Office. He had arranged to have lunch with his wife but the meeting ran over and he did not see her until much later in the afternoon. He couldn't at this stage tell Betty where he was being sent to but he said he hoped to return by 13 April 1940. As it turned out when he said goodbye to Betty at the station, later the same day, he wouldn't see her again for five years and one month.

Felix was sent on a mission to Trondheim to stop the Norwegians firing on planned British naval manoeuvres to stop Swedish iron-ore being transported to Germany. Britain had planned to occupy Narvik, Trondheim, Bergen and Stavanger in what was known as Plan R 4 after the *Altmark* incident in February 1940 when the then neutral Norwegians had failed to find British POWs during their searches of the German tanker *Altmark* in their waters. The POWs had been transferred from the German 'pocket battleship' *Admiral Graf Spee* in the South Atlantic before the *Graf Spee* was later scuttled at Montevideo. However, British and German plans for occupation in Norway were running simultaneously. On 9 April 1940 the Germans launched their Norwegian Campaign and Felix described the circumstances leading to his capture and internment:

> The consular shipping adviser rang my hotel at 5.30am to tell me to get out, alas the Germans had control of the main telephone exchange and before I was fully dressed two Germans burst into my room with drawn revolvers, so my war ended I thought. Next day I was flown down to Oslo and dumped in a cellar in the castle, with water running down the walls, occupied by numerous Norwegian soldiers, whose uniform the Germans had taken to camouflage their troops. Next morning I was taken to the airport – so much for the German promise that I should not leave Norway and would see the American consul next day. I was flown in a small 108 Junker cargo plane, with two German soldiers armed with rifles and wearing life jackets – I had neither. ... When we made land I could at least tell my guards that we were making for Hamburg as I saw the Alster lake through the porthole – the only German city I had ever been in. I was lodged in the police-holding/prison and thereafter began nearly seven months solitary while the Germans tried to establish an espionage charge. I was moved to two other prisons, each a stage worse, the next the remand prison the third the prison for sentenced people. I was questioned two or three times a week for a long while demanding to be sent back to Norway as I was arrested before Norway were at war. The boredom of the interviews was unbelievable, always started by recording my father's Christian names and my mother's maiden name and always ending asking me to sign the date in German and I awaiting the translation to be typed. I was perhaps lucky because quite early they asked me whether I had ever been in Germany before and I said yes, in 1929 when I came to Hamburg. They wanted to know the address, and I told them that I could not remember but if it were any help to them it was the third Alster lake boat after leaving the lake, I turned right at the exit, walked 500m and the people I stayed with were a Japanese family living on the left hand side.[1]

In November 1940 Felix was at his third prison and by this time the Germans had decided to treat him as a civilian internee but he was almost found out when the War Office in their wisdom had decided to print in the *London Gazette* that 'Major Felix Palmer, 6th East Surrey Regiment' was missing presumed POW. However Felix again devised a way to fool his captors as he explained:

> Luckily I knew there was an 'E' reserve which allowed late mobilisation for any special industrial experts, which I explained applied to me and was why I was buying timber in Norway for export to the UK, as I had originally told them. I could strengthen my story because my passport had the trip to Sweden as well

as to Finland stamped, both timber export countries – my uniform was only flown to Finland after my arrival from my attachment. They wanted to know where I went in these countries, luckily I knew enough sawmills to dazzle them with science. At least it made a change in the routine questioning as for quite a while they were excited, thinking that my explanation was rather a thin story.

Felix was sent to a camp in Nuremberg, initially he was looking forward to escaping solitary confinement but soon realised he preferred it compared with conditions in the camp where rooms held up to 72 people. To keep sane Felix threw himself into exercise, joining PT classes twice a day. During his internment he obtained a crystal wireless and when moved to other camps he managed to take it with him by stuffing it into a medicine ball.

On 1 December 1944 Felix was taken to his last camp Ilag VII located in Laufen castle in south-eastern Bavaria. He discusses his actions towards the end of the war:

I gathered together a group to plan what might occur at the end of hostilities since I felt there could possibly be complications. Our camp was on a small hill and from us the white flag was to be dropped to surrender to the allied forces on behalf of the village of Laufen. Our camp commandant was by then almost putty in our hands. He promised that he would not blow up the bridge over the Salzach leading to Saltzburg in return for us promising to put in a good word for him to the allies when they released us. Patton's [General George Patton] tanks liberated us in early May. I got the major commanding the tanks to dash down to the bridge and get the explosives off in case others thought differently from our tame commandant. Patton's tanks were running three days ahead of his infantry and I was left with looking after the bridge and village with fifteen soldiers and two tanks, until they came along.

The Americans drove Felix to the Ulm in Belgium where the main POW repatriation assembly was based and he returned to England on 12 May 1945. He was sent to a war officers' selection board camp for debriefing and after being put into a group of twelve for a general group talk he proceeded to spend an hour with a medical psychologist. To an audience at the Esher Branch of the Royal Legion Felix ended a talk on his experiences with this observation:

The group session at the start was unbelievably odd; the opening address that greeted us was the statement that all long-term prisoners would be 10 per cent subnormal for at least a year – what a way to build confidence! – even before they knew whether the officers were of a nervous disposition – anyhow they were pretty inaccurate with me many think for me the estimate for subnormality was far too low and the duration – already 50 years lasting – is normality may yet come!

Felix's brother and OE Geoffrey Blake Palmer served as a medical officer with the 5th Field Ambulance as part of the Second New Zealand Expeditionary Force during both the withdrawals of Allied forces from Greece in April 1941 and Crete in May 1941. For the part he played in the evacuation of Greece he was Mentioned in Despatches and awarded the Greek Silver Cross. He also served in North Africa and Italy and between 1944 and 1945 Geoffrey broadcast a series of talks on Italian towns for the New Zealand Forces,[2] which he then published in a book *Italian Journey* in 1945.[3]

Geoffrey Blake Palmer carrying out blood tests at Papakura Camp

References

1 Talk given by Felix Palmer to the Esher Branch of the Royal British Legion 5 March 1997. A digital copy is available in the Emanuel School Archive.
2 Consult The New Zealand Archive of Film, Television and Sound.
3 G. Blake Palmer, *Italian Journey* (1945).

CHAPTER 21

THE WAR AT SEA

HMS Manistee, commanded by OE Eric Haydn Smith, lost with all hands 24 February 1941

The battles fought on the oceans during the Second World War were some of the toughest experiences of all. Crews on a great variety of ships, from merchant vessels to cruisers and destroyers sailed under extreme conditions with adverse weather being just one obstacle to operations. A greater threat presented itself in the form of enemy U-Boats, submarines and aircraft all scouring the oceans for their prey. A number of Emanuel boys lost their lives during the sea battles of the War and presented here is a series of short biographies on ten of them.

Richard Frank Owens *(Emanuel 1931–1934)* was a Midshipman on the merchant cruiser HMS *Jervis Bay* which was sunk by the pocket-battleship *Admiral Scheer* on 5 November 1940 as she was escorting 37 ships of Halifax convoy H.X.84 returning to Britain. The gallant actions of the *Jervis Bay*'s Captain, Edward Fegen, saved all but five ships of the convoy. He ordered the *Jervis Bay* to engage the *Admiral Scheer*. It was a David and Goliath contest but Goliath got the better of David this time and despite a spirited attempt the *Admiral Scheer's* salvoes destroyed the *Jervis Bay*. Eyewitnesses talk of men on fire jumping overboard and the Captain's arm was severed before he was killed. The Captain was awarded a posthumous Victoria Cross. The *Portcullis* noted of Richard that, 'His death was a glorious one, and he and his fellows displayed the courage and tenacity of the British seaman.'

Eric Thomas Francis Brainwood *(Emanuel 1936–1937)* was a wireless operator on the Merchant British Vessel *Western Chief,* which was carrying a cargo of steel from New York to Newport when the Italian submarine *Emo* sank her in the Atlantic Ocean on 14 March 1941.

Ordinary Seaman, Cyril Alfred Leggett *(Emanuel 1922–1929)* lost his life when the British Battle Cruiser HMS *Hood* was sunk on 24 May 1941 by the German battleship Bismarck.

Frank David Bowles *(Emanuel 1931–1937)* also lost his life when serving as a leading stoker on the C-Class light cruiser HMS *Curacoa* which was sunk on 2 October 1942 after a collision with the ocean liner RMS *Queen Mary*, carrying American troops to Britain, which it had been escorting to Greenock.

Frederick Prigden Adams known as 'Dinky' *(Emanuel 1926–1931)* lost his life when HMS *Daffodil* was sunk by a mine off Dieppe on 18 March 1945. Dinky's nephew Robert remembered attending the memorial service to Emanuel's fallen in 1949 when OE George Banting unveiled the Second World War memorial.

Eric Haydn Smith, 1939

Eric Haydn Smith *(Emanuel 1918–1919)*

Eric Haydn Smith's name does not appear on the original Emanuel Second World War memorial or Pro Patria but through contact with his family, and research to establish that he attended the School, from 2014 his name now appears with three others on a new memorial board in the chapel.

Eric attended Liverpool College before entering Emanuel in 1918, staying for 20 months. After Emanuel he was indentured as a Cadet in the British India Steam Navigation Company completing his cadetship in 1923. He passed his Board of Trade Steamship Certificates in 1928 and throughout the 1930s rose through the ranks to become a Commander in the Royal Naval Reserve by 1940.

By 1931 he held the Rank of Chief Officer and for the rest of the 1930s he served in a number of ships including the cruiser HMS *Adventure*, destroyer HMS *Acasta* and Armed Merchant Cruiser HMS *Rawalpindi*. Following this Eric served in the Armed Merchant Cruiser HMS *Maloja*.

In the early stages of the War Eric steered HMS *Rawalpindi* from Aden to the UK. Eric was serving in HMS *Maloja* when on 13 March 1940 it intercepted the German Merchant Ship *La Coruna* which was flying a Japanese flag to disguise herself, south-east of Iceland. The *Maloja*'s Captain was suspicious and moved to intercept her when the *Coruna* scuttled. The *Maloja* proceeded to take her Captain and 50 crew prisoner.

The Sinking of HMS *Manistee*

At the outbreak of the Second World War the Merchant Navy was arranged into convoys. Basing their experiences on the First World War the Admiralty knew that there was a double threat from German Air and Sea power and in particular from U-Boats. By the first months of 1941 Winston Churchill minuted to the First Sea Lord, Admiral Sir Dudley Pound, 'I see that entrances of ships with cargo in January were less than half of what they were last January.'[1] Britain relied on imports of raw materials to feed its population and continue the war effort and if it lost the Battle of the Atlantic, it may very well have lost the War.[2]

In September 1940 Eric Haydn Smith became commander of HMS *Manistee* which was requisitioned by the Admiralty and commissioned in December 1940 as an Ocean Boarding Vessel (OBV) which patrolled the waters north-west of the British Isles. On 23 February 1941 the *Manistee* which had been escorting convoy OB-288, course set for North America was hit in the engine room at 2242hrs by a U-Boat – *U-107* – under Lieutenant-Commander Günter Hessler. *U-107* had fired a spread of two torpedoes and slowed the *Manistee* down. The *Manistee* had left the convoy at 0900hrs. The Italian submarine *Michele Bianchi* also claimed a hit on the Manistee at 2256hrs. The *Manistee* managed to avoid more from *U-107*. The *Michele Bianchi* broke off its attack and pursued the convoy. *U-107*, however, continued its attack on the *Manistee* firing more torpedoes before midnight and giving chase throughout the night. At 0758hrs on 24 February *U-107* fired two more torpedoes, one of which hit the *Manistee* in the stern. Eric had managed to steer his crew all through the night until that fateful morning. The *Manistee* sank with all 141 of her crew; there were no survivors despite a search for her by the Corvette HMS *Heather*, the destroyer HMS *Churchill* and the Free French destroyer *Leopard*. On the same day Adolf Hitler referred to the actions of the Kriegsmarine in a speech given on the 21st anniversary of the founding of the Nazi party.[3] Günter Hessler, Commander of *U-107* was the son-in-law of Vice-Admiral Karl Dönitz who at the time of the Manistee's sinking commanded Germany's U-Boat fleet. Hessler later wrote the official three-volume account *The U-Boat war in the Atlantic 1939–1945* at the request of the Admiralty. Eric is remembered on the Portsmouth naval memorial.

William 'Bill' Benjamin Bevis

(Emanuel 1918–1929)

Bill was Captain of the School, Captain of Boats, Vice Captain of the First Fifteen, and was an Under Officer in the OTC of which he remembered, rather amusingly, 'those awful breeches and itchy puttees'. He captained the winning Grundy Cup shooting competition for three years running. He was also House Captain of Wellington and Captain of both Shooting and Swimming. Incredibly he also found time to be a member of the Dramatic Society but recalls fluffing his lines, an incident which put him off acting. As rugby forward he had the reputation of a strong work ethic and versatility. As stroke in the First Eight he was incredibly skilful with excellent length – vital for a good rower.

Steve Fairbairn opening the Emanuel School rowing tank in 1929 – William Bevis (stroke), John Coleman (3), Jack Lee (2) and John Edwards (Bow)

In the era of the Great Depression Bill considered himself lucky to find a job with Shell on a starting salary of £1.25d per week. He continued to play rugby for the OEA and rowed for Shell's boat Club – Lensbury, winning Henley Royal Regatta three times. In 1935 Shell posted Bill to Malaya. He was back in the UK at the outbreak of war but was too old for pilot training and had his commission vetoed by the Colonial Office who required him to return to Malaya. On his return to Malaya he joined the Malayan Royal Naval Volunteer Reserve. He trained in HMS *Laburnam* where he learnt the rudiments of seamanship. Bill was appointed First Lieutenant in the minesweeper HMS *Malacca* which was posted to Penang. In November 1941 he married Gabrielle, whom he met in Malaya, but within just over a week of their happy day the Japanese attacked Pearl Harbor. He remembered, 'The honeymoon was interrupted in the early hours of 7 December by an urgent phone call from Penang Naval Office to say the Japs had invaded and we were to return forthwith.' Bill's best man was made a POW for four years and one of his ushers died of exposure after trying to escape from Singapore in a dinghy when the Japanese invaded the island in 1942.

A Narrow Escape

What happened next is told through extracts from Bill Bevis's 20-page memoir:

> [We managed to escape] after a heck of a struggle getting someone to unlock the petrol pump for our Hillman Mini Coupe. A week later Penang was evacuated, Gabrielle and her mother taking the last train from Butterworth to Singapore, leaving all they owned including our unopened wedding presents behind, never to be seen again. The wedding photographs were never developed.
>
> In the meantime, *Malacca* was 40 miles north of Penang rescuing British soldiers escaping in native canoes from the rapidly advancing Japs. On the way back we saw Jap planes expertly dive-bombing the Butterworth airfield and on the radio heard that HMS's *Prince of Wales* and *Repulse* had been sunk. All were omens of worse to come as we steamed south arriving at Singapore on 19 December 1941.

Bill met OE Reginald Dunkin once or twice who was serving with the Royal Army Service Corps but was captured when Singapore fell on 15 February 1942 and spent four years as a Japanese POW.

In January 1942 Bill drove his wife to the docks and both Gabrielle and his mother-in-law managed to get on board the troopship *West Point* and got back to the UK via Ceylon and South Africa.

Sir Alfred Butt presenting prizes to William Bevis, Emanuel Speech Day 1929

On 13 February Bill as skipper of HMS *Malacca* with a crew made up of survivors from the *Prince of Wales* and *Repulse*. He recalled leaving Singapore:

> With Singapore in flames and shells landing in the harbour we received orders from Admiral Spooner via Commander Alexander to embark senior HQ army personnel and proceed to Batavia, Java. *Malacca* was one of the last ships to leave, but the delay had proved to be a blessing in disguise as, unknown to the Admiral, due to the premature destruction of all codes books, the route through the Banka Straits had already been cut by the Jap navy and air forces. Thus of the 40 assorted vessels which left on or just before the 13th none got through. Whereas we got the news that the Japs had reached Palembang in time to change course.

The *Malacca's* journey after leaving Singapore is detailed in a report Bill wrote on Board SS *Khoen Hoea*. One particular eventful day was 14 February 1942, the day before Bill's 30th birthday:

> 0700hrs – Anchored off False Durian, camouflaged ship, and landed most of the troops. Eighty enemy aircraft passed overhead during the forenoon, so the camouflage seemed successful until the 'Tin Peng', together with a water boat and a 'Eureka' tied up astern. As somebody remarked disgustedly we looked like the 'last day of Henley week.' Sure enough at 1330, the next formation of nine twin-engined bombers came for us and dropped about nine bombs from approximately 3000 feet. They fell all around within 20 yards but missed. We staged a 'panic party' and after circling four times the planes made off. The Eureka went aground in the excitement and was abandoned high and dry. The only serious damage sustained was a broken steam tube in the engine room [later repaired] 1400hrs – We re-embarked the troops and got under way. At 2145 in

William (sitting centre) with members of the local Malay Defence Force

> the pitch dark we heard shouts to starboard, turned and picked up Sig. Finlay, a New Zealander, who had been drifting for hours on an Orepesa float. He reported that he was from HMS *Changteh* which had been sunk by aircraft the same afternoon. Hearing that Palembang was under attack from sea, being short of coal and the Army Officers' request to be put ashore at first opportunity, we decided to enter the River Indragiri.[4]

They put in at the Indragiri River and scuttled *Malacca*. Joining others who had made similar journeys they made their way overland across the Sumatran mountains to Padang, where they found a Dutch steamship, SS *Khoen Hoea*, previously engaged in livestock transportation. Bill recalled, 'We finally left Java just ahead of the Jap Army with about fifteen other vessels on 27 February.' They reached Fremantle, Australia on 9 March 1942. Bill stayed in Australia for two months before heading for the UK on 14 August 1942 after a long journey via New Zealand, the USA and Canada, returning in a convoy to Liverpool which lost two vessels.

On his return to the UK Bill started minesweeping operations in the English Channel and served in Motor Minesweeper (MMS) *30* as First Lieutenant and MMS *139* as Commanding Officer. Bill's wife Gabrielle searched for accommodation for them both in addition to her duties in a services canteen and air raid duty.

Operation Neptune – D-Day

Bill was at the forefront of the Allied assault on the Normandy Coast in June 1944. He was commanding MMS *139* during Operation Neptune, the naval element of Operation Overlord, and was Second Senior Officer of 115th Minesweeper Flotilla. The Channel had to be cleared of mines before the main bombarding forces could make their assault. MMS *139* was part of Force 'S' of the Eastern Task Force and was assigned to escort the 15-inch gun monitor HMS *Roberts*.

In his memoir Bill noted:

> After a false alarm when we were turned back by bad weather, we finally crossed the Channel on 5 June (D-1) ahead of the bombarding force, prepared for the worse ... but apart from nearly being run down by a battleship, I think HMS *Warspite*, in the dark, [and] a few odd shells and torpedoes, the enemy seemed to have been taken completely by surprise. Many magnetic and acoustic mines were dropped at night by German aircraft in the ensuing period. These kept us busy, but the storm force gale after about ten days nearly finished us and the invasion.

After D-Day and whilst Commanding Officer of HMS *Sapphire* Bill was Mentioned in Despatches for a particularly brave action during minesweeping. Bill's son recalls the story:

Bill was a strong swimmer. It was something of which he was inordinately proud, and this was his undoing when a German mine fouled his minesweeping gear in mid-channel. The only solution was for someone to swim to the mine, get a line onto it, and then it could be towed away, to be sunk with rifle fire. Bill, the skipper, who ought to stay aboard and remain in charge, also knew he was the strongest swimmer. Unfortunately his crew knew it as well and, there being an uncharacteristic lack of volunteers, he felt he had to take to the water himself. He confessed to it being the worst moment of his life; on arrival at the mine, he said, he was not so much frightened by the detonator horns as by the razor sharp barnacles which threatened to cut him open like a tin opener. He got the line on though, and got it safely back to the ship. But he missed the mine with his own rifle shots and it had to be blown up by someone else.

After the War Bill and his wife returned to Malaya and he spent the rest of his career with Shell travelling all over the world, returning to England in the 1960s. Bill died at the age of 91 in January 2004.

Jack and Pam McGregor on their wedding day

The McGregor brothers - Ken (circled top), Jack (left) and Roy (right)

John 'Jack' Harvey McGregor
(Emanuel 1916–1923)

At Emanuel John, known as 'Jack', was a House Prefect of Marlborough and played for both the Second Fifteen and Second Eleven. He was also a Lance Corporal in the OTC and passed his War Office Certificate 'A'.

Jack's father, Robert McGregor OBE, was an admiralty official. In 1924 Jack joined the Royal Navy as a cadet. After officer training he served in the battleship *Royal Sovereign* in the Atlantic Fleet and later in the cruiser *Lowestoft* on the Africa station. In 1931 he was appointed to the River Gun Boat HMS *Bee* – the flagship on the river Yangtze. The naval office was in Shanghai and it was whilst stationed in the city that he met his wife Pam whom he married on 22 September 1934. Further appointments followed to the cruiser HMS *Arethusa* and the battleship HMS *Royal Oak*. Whilst with the *Arethusa* he was involved in saving a woman from drowning and received a Life Saving Commendation.

In 1937 Jack was appointed to a position in the Admiralty. Before war broke out Jack and Pam's sons John and Richard were born. In early 1941 he was posted to the Leander Class Light Cruiser HMS *Neptune* as Acting Paymaster Commander. Jack was responsible for all the supply and secretarial functions of the ship and bartered in Kenyan markets for fresh fruit and vegetables to prevent scurvy among the 770 of the ship's company.

The sinking of HMS *Neptune*

The Mediterranean Sea routes in the Second World War were vital to both the Allies and Axis forces as they moved to reinforce their positions with troops, tanks, ammunition, fuel and food in the battle to control North Africa and ultimately the Suez Canal and the Middle Eastern oil fields.

On 18 December 1941 Force K, which HMS *Neptune* had joined on 17 December and after escorting the *Breconshire* safely to Malta on one of her numerous convoy runs, sailed to intercept an enemy convoy en route to Tripoli. The story of what happened next is written by Jack's sons John and Richard:

> The three cruisers *Neptune*, *Aurora* and *Penelope*, supported by four destroyers, were steaming south, in single line ahead on a dark, stormy night when at 1.06am *Neptune* struck a mine. Astern, *Aurora* hauled out to starboard, but only a minute later she too exploded a mine. Two minutes later, there was an explosion on *Penelope's* port side. *Neptune*, going full astern hit another mine, which wrecked her steering gear and propellers and brought her to a standstill. The cruiser force had run into a minefield, in a depth of water and at a distance from land, which made it utterly unexpected.
>
> Both *Aurora* and *Penelope* extracted themselves from the minefield. Although dawn would soon break and they were only fifteen miles from enemy-held Tripoli, the destroyers *Kandahar* and *Lively* were sent to assist *Neptune*. But at 3.18am *Kandahar* hit a mine. 45 minutes later *Neptune* hit another mine and sank.
>
> *Kandahar* was submerged from abaft the funnel. She gradually drifted clear of the minefield and at 4.00am the following day the destroyer *Jaguar* arrived from Malta and rescued 178 of her crew. With dawn breaking, *Jaguar* fired a torpedo into *Kandahar*, sinking her. *Jaguar* then started passage back to Malta.
>
> *Kandahar* lost 73 men and *Neptune* 764. Only one man survived from *Neptune*, Leading Seaman Norman Walton being rescued by the Italian Navy after five days in the water.[5]

Jack was one of 764 crew members to lose their lives on HMS *Neptune*. He is commemorated on the Plymouth Naval Memorial, Panel 45, Column one.

Eric Monkhouse in full dress uniform

Eric Carl Monkhouse *(Emanuel 1919–1928)*

Eric joined Lloyds Bank when he left Emanuel and then enlisted in the RNVR, returning to Lloyds after the War until he retired. He had the reputation for being a fantastic rugby player who also played for United Banks. Little is known about Eric's war service except that he served in HMS *Rodney* and was a Lieutenant Paymaster.

As a boy Eric was an exceptional all-round sportsman who was both a Prefect and Lieutenant of the School. He captained both the Rowing and Rugby teams. As Captain of Boats he was known for his drive to win, rowing a very strong, stylish, blade. As a rugby player he was an aggressive forward who worked hard both in the scrum and the open. Eric was also House Captain of Nelson, Captain of Swimming and an Under-Officer in the OTC and was awarded his War Office Certificate 'A'.

Eric was the first of three generations to attend Emanuel. His son, John Monkhouse, (Emanuel 1959–1967), was also both School Prefect and Captain of Rugby and Athletics. Sadly Eric died two years before John's son was born, but they named him after his grandfather Eric. Eric 'Junior' was at Emanuel from 1987–1994 and like his grandfather was Captain of Nelson. He also led the unbeaten rugby tour of Canada in 1994.

Time Witnesses Meet Each Other

David Linck *(Emanuel 1937–1939)*

In 2014 David Link's daughter contacted the School to find out further information about her father's time at Emanuel. Until she did the School was not aware of David's service in the War, as his name did not appear on the Second World War Pro Patria. At the age of fifteen David trained as a radio officer in the Merchant Navy. David served in the Ellerman Line's steam passenger ship SS *City of Nagpur*. On 29 April 1941 the *Nagpur* was sunk by U-Boat *U-75* around 600 miles west of Valentia Island, Ireland. David may have been the radio officer sending messages after the *Nagpur* was hit but when *U-75* opened machine gun fire the radio messages ceased. Around 470 survivors including 273 passengers were picked up by HMS *Hurricane*. Over 50 years later, in October 1993, David met one of the senior officers of *U-75*, Oblt.z.S. Horst Wilhelm Kessler, when David invited Horst and his wife to his house in Perth, Australia. David had become aware of Horst and his connection with the *U-75* through his brother's research. After the *Nagpur* sinking Horst Kessler was promoted to Commander and Captain of the U-Boats, *U-704* and *U-985*, being responsible for the sinking of two more ships, and being awarded both the Iron Cross second and first classes. Horst and his wife spent a week with David and his family. The meeting was recorded in a German magazine which noted, 'They were able to understand their differences and come to terms with their past.'[6] David was thankful that many German crews obeyed the 'unwritten rules' of the sea and did not just kill all survivors of sunken ships and wanted future generations to know that fact. Despite once being enemies in a different time they were able to achieve rapprochement in later life.

David Linck, 1942

References

1 Winston S. Churchill, *The Second World War: Volume III The Grand Alliance* (1950), p. 100.
2 The term 'The Battle of the Atlantic' was used in a Directive by Winston Churchill on 6 March 1941 in response to statements coming from the German High Command, in particular a speech given by Adolf Hitler on 24 February 1941.
3 Bulletin of International News, Vol. 18, No. 5 (8 March, 1941), pp. 267-269.
4 Report of W. B. Bevis, First Lieutenant HMS *Malacca* written on board SS *Khoen Hoea*. A copy is available to consult in the Emanuel School Archive.
5 With thanks to John and Richard McGregor for the information they supplied about their father and HMS *Neptune*.
6 By 'OWS', from the publication *Daheim at Home*, December 1993, p. 10. Note the article gives the wrong date for the sinking of the *City of Nagpur*.

Operation Chariot – ‘The Greatest Raid of All’

Seymour Charles ‘Peter’ Pike DSM *(Emanuel 1933–1937)*

At Emanuel Seymour Charles, known as Peter, coxed junior rowing crews. He is seen in a photograph of one Emanuel crew on the hard just outside Tom Green’s Boat House which was adjacent to Barnes Bridge in the mid-1930s. Peter was also a member of the Tooting Sea Cadet Corps. Both roles would have allowed Peter to gain a familiarity with the sea and rivers from an early age.

He was also interested in languages and Emanuel in the 1930s had excellent German language teachers which proved essential to Peter in the Second World War. His father, Roy Seymour Pike, also attended Emanuel and served as a mechanical engineer in the Royal Naval Volunteer Reserve during the First World War.

On leaving School Peter worked as a shipping clerk for the Anglo-Iranian Oil Company. As the impending European crisis unfolded he volunteered for the Royal Naval Volunteer Reserve on 10 May 1939.[2] After training in signals at the Royal Navy shore establishments, HMS *President* and HMS *Pembroke* between August 1939 and July 1940 Peter saw active service with the Dido-class light cruiser HMS *Naiad* which spent much of 1940 and 1941 on convoy protection in both home waters and on voyages to Freetown, Sierra Leone. Between April 1941 and March 1943 Peter served at various times in HMS *Eglinton*. However, it was his selection for a pivotal role in Operation Chariot – one of the most daring raids of the Second World War – that secured Peter’s name in the annals of that conflict’s history.

Peter (seated centre) with an Emanuel rowing crew, mid 1930s – also shown OE Michael Jeffery (seated first from left)

During the days of the British Expeditionary Force’s retreat from Dunkirk, Lieutenant-Colonel Dudley Clarke, a General Staff Officer who was military assistant to the then Chief of the Imperial General Staff, Sir John Dill, contemplated how Britain might make its return to the continent. His thoughts drifted to historic examples such as the Boer Commandos in the Second Boer War who had harried the much larger British forces with their use of raiding parties. Out of these musings was conceived the idea for Combined Operations and the beginning of the Commandos.[3]

In the summer of 1940 Britain’s war was defensive, with efforts concentrated in repelling a German invasion. However, Churchill and other like-minded individuals wanted to take the offensive at the earliest opportunity. If raids on the continent were to be carried out the infantry would need naval support to land them at designated targets, hence the term Combined Operations – a force which utilised all three main services. In early 1942 such a raid was planned by Combined Operations Headquarters (COHQ), to attack the Atlantic seaboard dry-dock in the port of St Nazaire.

The ‘Louis Joubert’ (*Forme Ecluse Louis Joubert*) lock/dry-dock, as it was officially known, was constructed to accommodate the building of the 83,000-ton super passenger liner SS *Normandie*, after which the dock’s name became popularly known.[4] It was a huge feat of engineering enclosed at either end by two gates or caissons. The ‘*Normandie* Dock’ could be used as either a lock or dry-dock, the latter requiring water to be pumped out by powerful machinery in the pump houses on the west side of the dock, where the hydraulic plants for operating the caissons were also situated. The caissons were structurally extremely strong, both to withstand the pressure of water from the outside and accidental ramming by ships, a fact that was critical in the planning of the raid on the dock.

Seymour 'Peter' Pike

St Nazaire, at the mouth of the river Loire could be reached by navigating the five-mile long Les Charpentier channel. Navigation of the channel required careful planning due to the features of shoals and mud-banks which could prove disastrous if the tides were misjudged. After the fall of France in June 1940, St Nazaire became one of five strategic positions for the German occupying forces along the country's Atlantic coast.

The destruction of the dry-dock would reduce the threat posed by the German battleship *Tirpitz* which, in the event of engaging Allied shipping in the Atlantic, would require the dock at St Nazaire for maintenance between patrols. But according to Captain John Hughes-Hallett, who was Lord Mountbatten's [Commodore Combined Operations] head naval planner at the Directorate of Combined Operations, the target's location was chosen for two main reasons: firstly, because it was the furthest target which a raiding force could reach within a window of only one period of daylight and secondly, during the spring tides, vessels could pass over the shoal water to the south of the Les Charpentier channel, getting within reach of the deepwater channel close to St Nazaire.[5] Central to the plan was the use of a ship packed with explosives, timed to go off after the Combined Forces attacked the dock area, escorted by a series of motor launches and machine gun boats. It was an audacious plan that relied on precision; timing was the key to the whole operation.

The Attacking Force

An ageing American destroyer, HMS *Campbeltown*, was chosen as the ship to carry the explosives with delaying fuses. Disguised as a German *Möwe* Class destroyer she was ultimately to be rammed into the *Normandie* dock gate. The base of operations was centred on Motor Gun Boat (MGB) *314* which, along with Motor Launches (ML) *270* and *160* would form the spearhead of the operation and it was in MGB *314* that Commander Robert Ryder directed the raiding force. In addition to MGB *314* there were sixteen motor launches, including *270* and *160*, one Motor Torpedo Boat (MTB) and two escorts, HMS *Atherstone* and HMS *Tynedale* that accompanied them for part of the journey.[6] A dress rehearsal for the raid took place at Devonport dockyard on the evening of 21 March 1942. Before and after the dress rehearsal the force assembled at Falmouth. At 1400 on 26 March 1942 the force sailed from Falmouth – destination St Nazaire.[7] The raid ran into difficulty on the morning of 27 March when the force encountered a German submarine *U-593* but fortunately the U-Boat, not realising that the force was heading for St Nazaire, signalled to German Group Command West that Ryder's fleet was on course for Gibraltar, this was due to Ryder's change of direction that the U-Boat mistook as their final destination.

Motor Gun Boat 314 at sea before the raid

'Assault on the Old Entrance at St Nazaire' – drawing by Commander Robert Ryder VC

Peter's role in the attack

The details of the raid have been well documented in a number of books but here it is important to reflect on Peter's role.[8] On the night of 27 March 1942 MGB *314* became operational when Cdr Ryder transferred to it from HMS *Atherstone*, accompanying him were Colonel Newman, who led the Commandos on the raid and Peter in addition to several others.[9] Being guided to the river Loire by the submarine HMS *Sturgeon*, the attacking force made its way up the river whilst the escorts *Atherstone* and *Tynedale* waited out at sea to cover the returning fleet after the raid. There was a diversionary attack planned by RAF Bomber Command over St. Nazaire for 2330hrs but it was unsuccessful due to low cloud. However whilst Peter was on the sea another Emanuel boy, Richard Ryder (Emanuel 1930–1935) was flying as an Observer on a Whitworth Whitley Mark V heavy bomber (Z9481) of 51 Squadron RAF, which, after returning from the diversionary operation over St. Nazaire, crashed at Great Whernside injuring the crew with Richard being thrown from the aircraft.[10]

The force proceeded up the Loire estuary over the shoals in the hour after midnight on 28 March. It had got within two miles of the harbour before they were illuminated by No. 3 Heavy Coastal Battery. If they were going to reach their target they needed a deception tactic to hold the German defences off long enough – enter Peter Pike. Cdr Robert Ryder continues the story:

> We were challenged from the shore, first by one of the coastal batteries and later from somewhere in the dockyard. It was for this moment that Leading Signalman Pike, who could send and receive morse, had been attached to my staff. The challenge was accompanied by sporadic flak, aimed indiscriminately at the force. It was 1.23am, we were a mile and a half from our objective; ten minutes at that speed. How long could we bluff? ... every minute still counted.
>
> We did not know the correct reply to the challenge, but we instructed them to 'wait' and then gave the call sign of one of the German torpedo-boats known to us. Without waiting for them to consider this Pike embarked on a long plain-language signal. With an 'urgent' prefix, the gist of this was, 'Two craft, damaged by enemy action, request permission to proceed up harbour without delay.' Firing ceased. Without finishing the first message we made the operating signal to 'wait' again. We had to reply to the second station. We were about to give them a similar message when we came under renewed fire from the north bank, heavier than the first ... Using our

Peter's mother Hilda collecting Peter's DSM at Buckingham Palace, 5 December 1944

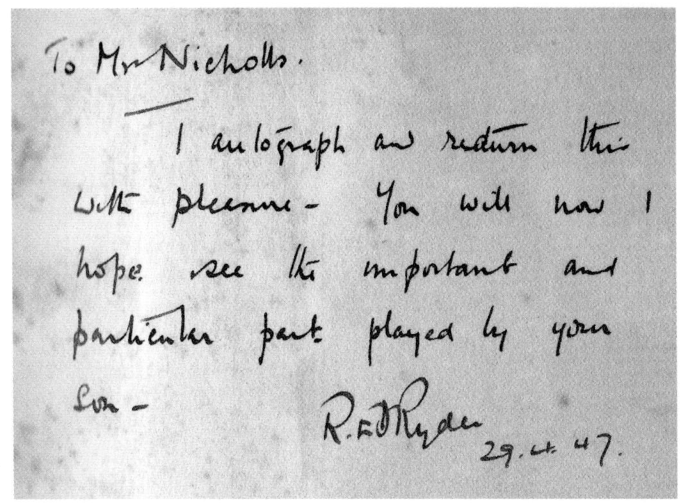

To Mr Nicholls.

I autograph and return this with pleasure - You will now I hope see the important and particular part played by your son -

R.E.D. Ryder 29.4.47.

Inscription by Robert Ryder VC to Peter's mother, written in his account of 'The Attack on St Nazaire'

> Aldis lamp, we made the international signal for ships or vessels being fired on by friendly forces. ... Our bluffing had practically achieved its object.[11]

In fact Peter had to deal with two German signals, one from the guard ship *Speerbrecher* and one on MGB *314*'s port beam. He gained the force vital minutes and Cdr Ryder noted in 1947, 'Information now available confirms the valuable part played by Pike in thus delaying the enemy's fire.' A little later, during the heated exchange of fire and lacking a sufficient report as to the *Campbeltown*'s placing and sinking Cdr Ryder disembarked from MGB *314* at the north side of the Old Entrance of the Bassin St Nazaire, at which point he later recalled, '...Pike, who, discarding his signalling apparatus for a broken bayonet which he had discovered, decided that a bodyguard was required.'[12] In a desperate situation and under heavy fire Cdr Ryder made the decision to evacuate, leaving the raid now in the hands of the Commandos who continued to fight onshore. As they made their escape with 40 extra men on board the MGB the scenes were distressing as Ryder recalled, 'The decks everywhere were slippery with blood, making it difficult to walk between the wounded lying crowded together.'[13] On the morning of 28 March the delaying fuses on the *Campbeltown* sparked and she blew up whilst being inspected by a large party of German officers. The explosion rendered the dry dock inoperable for the rest of the war and Operation Chariot was a success, although 169 men out of 611 lost their lives. For his integral part in the success of the raid Peter was awarded the Distinguished Service Medal.

Peter later served again in HMS *Eglinton* and was serving in HMS *Laforey* during Operation Husky – the invasion of Italy when the *Laforey* sunk the Italian submarine *Ascianghi*, and also during Operation Avalanche – the Salerno landings in September 1943. Peter was at sea off the coast of Salerno whilst those he would have known through rowing at Emanuel, like Alan Skillern, were landing on the beaches.

Peter had much to look forward to writing to his mother on 23 September 1943 with the happy news that he was to get married after the war as his girlfriend Marian had accepted his proposal. However fate was not kind and Peter lost his life when the *Laforey*, on anti-submarine patrols, was sunk by a U-Boat, the *U-223*, on the evening of 30 March 1944. The U-Boat was then sunk by other British destroyers who had been in company with *Laforey*.[14] Peter's mother received several letters of condolence from friends of the family and also a survivor from the *Laforey*, one individual remarking, 'I always shall remember Peter as one of the finest characters I came across in this country.' In December 1944 Peter's mother collected his DSM from Buckingham Palace.

References

1 Tom Green's Boat House no longer exists. Hounslow Council now owns the new Boat House and since the 1970s Thames Tradesmen's Rowing Club has rowed from it.
2 A digital copy of Seymour Charles 'Peter' Pike's Certificate of Service is available to view in the Emanuel School Archive. For a history of the RNVR see J. Lennox Kerr and Wilfred Granville, *The RNVR: A Record of Achievement* (1957).
3 Hilary St. George Saunders, *The Green Beret: The Story of the Commandos 1940–1945* (1949), p. 21.
4 The 'Normandie' (Louis Joubert) Dock was completed in 1934.
5 Richard Hopton, *A Reluctant Hero: The Life of Captain Robert Ryder, VC* (2011), p. 128-129.
6 See a full list in Commander R.E.D. Ryder, *The Attack on St. Nazaire* (1947), pp. 21-22.
7 For a map of the route taken by the naval force see Captain S. W. Roskill, DSC, RN, *The War at Sea 1939–1945: Volume III, The Period of Balance* (1956), p. 169.
8 See James G. Dorrian, *Storming St. Nazaire: The Dock Busting Raid of 1942* (2001) and an older account by C. E. Lucas Phillips, *The Greatest Raid of All* (originally published 1958, reprinted 2000).
9 The journalist Gordon Holman was also on MGB *314*.
10 Richard lost his life on 6 September 1942 when his aircraft of No. 51 Squadron went missing whilst attached to Coastal Command on anti-submarine patrol.
11 Ryder, *The Attack on St. Nazaire*, pp. 48-49.
12 Ibid. p. 56.
13 Ibid. p. 76.
14 Peter C. Smith, *Fighting Flotilla: HMS Laforey and her Sister ships* (1976), pp.168-169.

CHAPTER 22

POST-WAR

Dordrecht in Wartime

The following account of life in Dordrecht in wartime was reprinted in *The Portcullis* in 1945. Emanuel had sent a Dutch schoolboy a copy of the summer 1945 edition of *The Portcullis* with Clive Barnes's account of life in Petersfield in wartime and the boy replied, writing of his impressions of life under Nazi occupation. This included how, after the German forces surrendered, the inhabitants of Dordrecht exacted their revenge on girls who had fraternised with the occupying forces by cutting their hair in what was a common scene across Europe for those who were accused of collaborating with the occupying forces.

On 10th May, 1940, at four o'clock in the morning the German Ju 52 appeared over our town and airborne troops landed in the outskirts. We were awakened by the noise of the aeroplanes and the anti-aircraft guns. The soldiers fought five days but the Netherlands were lost. We were occupied and that occupation I shall never forget.

The Huns began to forbid all the National clubs and to transport all food to Germany. We had food enough for six years, but the result was, that in September 1940 the bread was rationed. We had tobacco for ten years but [by] the end of 1940 it was very hard to get any cigarettes. As time went on, we got deeper and deeper in the dumps. In 1942 the Germans stopped some factories, because they wouldn't work for the 'Wehrmacht' and they sent the labourers to Germany. That was the beginning of the end. Every man who could be spared was transported to Germany. In 1943 the Germans stole all radios, but they did not have ours. Till 1944 we had no bombs in Dordrecht, but in 1944 we saw bombs dropping on our town several times. It happened that there were some German generals in Dordrecht. The 'underground forces' knew that and reported it to England. The result was the house where they met each other was destroyed and three generals died but one bomb fell on a school and killed seven children and a teacher. One of my friends was helping near a house that was bombed; when he came home, he found his own house bombed and his mother killed. So we have had three bombings and our town is not so very much damaged.

Our town lies on an island and we had four very nice bridges; only one is left. One was blown up by accident and happily three Germans were killed. The other two were blown up when the Allied troops came nearer. Those were bridges of 1000 and 1400 metres. In the winter 1944–1945 the food situation was very bad. We only got 400 grams of bread and 1000 grams of potatoes a week; no butter or sugar. Several times we got bread and butter from the Red Cross. The bread and potatoes were mostly not to be had and were not eatable. When there were no potatoes we got sugarbeets, so you will understand it was terrible to eat. You saw everywhere, men, women and children asking for some potatoes or slices of bread or looking into the dustbins for something to eat. Many persons died or fell ill from hunger, got big legs and arms, could not eat and died after some days.

In September 1944 the Canadian and English troops were at Moerdijk before the river but because the two bridges were blown up they did not come across. So you will understand that was a great disappointment for us. At the same time many young men tried to cross the river but that was a very difficult and dangerous job, because the river has a width of one kilometre, that means $^2/_3$ mile. At last there were no boats any more and the Huns killed everybody they caught. In January 1945 we got a razzia for men from seventeen to forty years old. In the morning at seven o'clock, soldiers rang and put in the letter-box a paper on which had been written: You must assemble at a school before 11 o'clock and bring with you food for two days and blankets. Many men went without any food. But after eleven, the soldiers (Jerries) went from house to house, entered, and looked everywhere and found many men (they could not find me, because I was hidden between the ceiling). At five o'clock in the afternoon the razzia was finished.

In February men of the underground broke open the prison because the Germans had caught a girl and she knew too much about the underground. Sixty prisoners were set free again. In the same month they blew up the building of German S.D. (Sicherheitsdienst) and in March the office of the 'field-security' (Feldgendarmerie) was bombed and many papers about men who 'dived under or who had a radio in their house' were damaged. After they had broken open the prison, we had to stay at home after 1800 hours. You see, that was not so very nice. Every night we were sitting in the dark or by candle light. Nobody had electricity and there was not enough coal, or food and with an empty stomach we listened to the radio, generating electricity by cycling on a bike in the room. So you will understand, we were very glad when we heard over the radio that the German troops in Holland had surrendered. Next morning you saw flags everywhere and everybody was glad. The Germans stayed at their camps and everyone did what he liked and the boys began to cut off the hair of the Hun girls. In some streets you could walk over the hair, but of course, we had some nice days. When the allied troops entered the town everybody went mad with joy. I hope that I have given you a short impression of what happened during five years of terror in Dordrecht and I say goodbye now. Long live the Netherlands and the bond of friendship!

Your Dutch friend, W. V. D. STEENHOVEN.[1]

References

1 *The Portcullis*, Autumn Term 1945, pp. 19-20.

Japanese Surrender: Photo taken by Leslie Henson showing General Seishiro Itagaki signing the instruments of surrender of the Japanese armies in South-East Asia, Municipal Building, Singapore, 12 September 1945. Admiral Lord Louis Mountbatten can be seen in white at a desk signing on behalf of the Allies

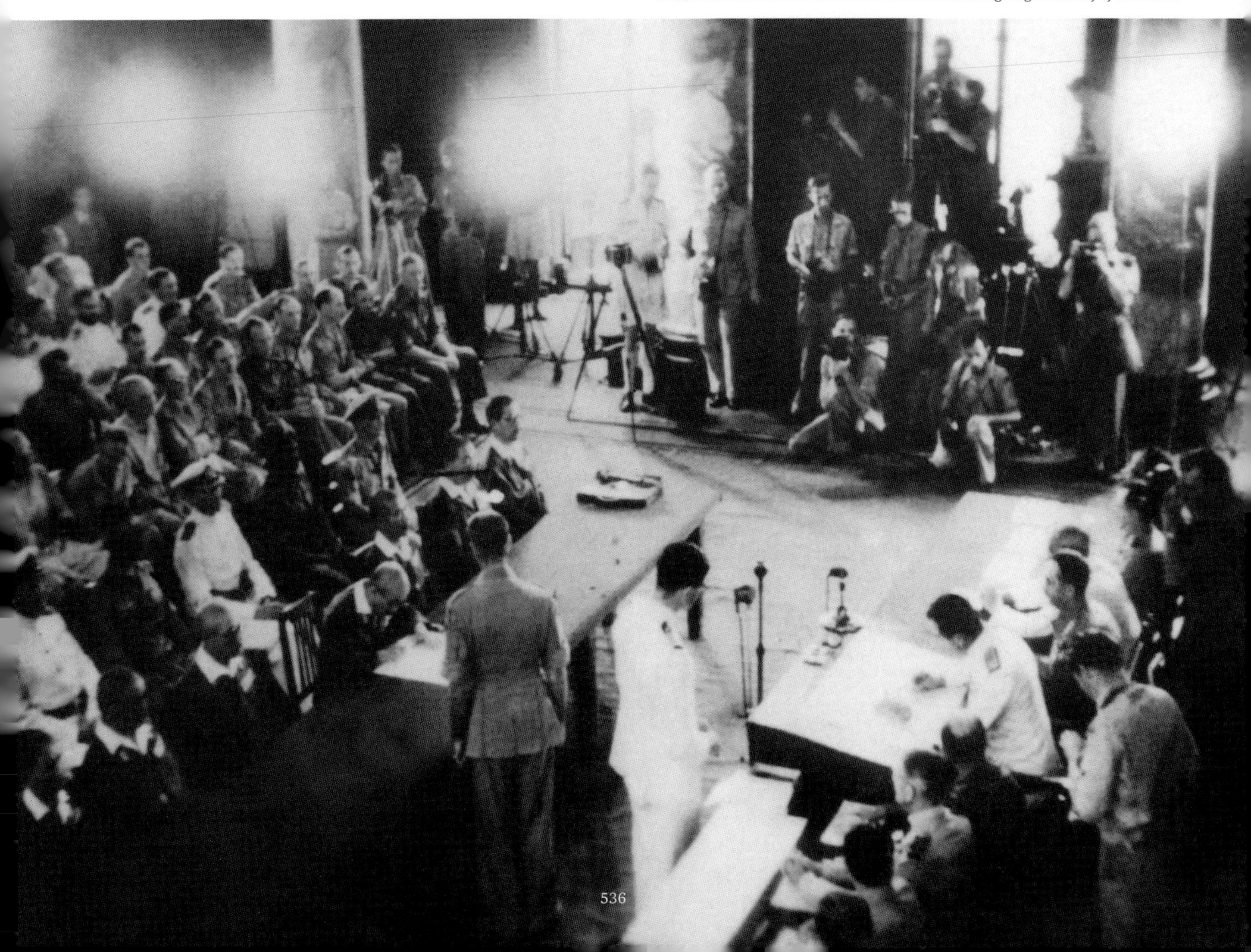

A piece of tiling masonry from Hitler's New Reich Chancellery designed by Hitler's architect Albert Speer.

A View of Berlin

Henry Carpenter *(Emanuel 1939–1946)* was an Emanuel evacuee in Petersfield who later forged Old Boys links in North America and Canada. Henry was a great friend of Emanuel School and although he emigrated to Canada decades ago, he found the time to visit Emanuel every few years and attend Petersfield evacuee reunions. He loved his time in Petersfield and spent his final school year at Emanuel in Battersea.

He was significant in the development of the Old Emanuel Association in Canada and North America, organising functions and frequently writing for the Old Emanuel Association Newsletter. Henry was slightly too young to serve in the Second World War but whilst he was doing his military service he spent some time in post Second World War Berlin and took a number of photographs which he has kindly donated to the Emanuel archive. He also collected a souvenir piece of masonry from the ruins of Hitler's New Reich Chancellery which may be a unique example of the interior decoration of this building.

A scene of destruction which shows the bitter battle which took place in Berlin during the course of 1945

The Brandenburg Gate in Berlin

The Soviet War Memorial (Tiergarten) which commemorates the 80,000 Soviet soldiers killed in the Battle for Berlin between April and May 1945

Emanuel Masters in the Second World War

Lt Col. Cyril Edgar Bond OBE

(Emanuel Modern Languages 1930–1936)

Cyril Bond in Emanuel OTC uniform

Cyril Bond joined Emanuel straight after university at Oxford. He was granted a commission in the Territorial Army to become an Officer in the Emanuel OTC. He was Housemaster of Lyons and helped coach rowing. When war broke out he joined the Royal Fusiliers (City of London Regiment) in which many OEs had taken commissions. He served in Italy and was promoted to Lieutenant Colonel, and was later awarded an OBE. After the war he worked at the City of London School for many years.

His citation for his OBE reads:

> Bond was involved with the civil authorities towards the end of the war in Greece. There were significant administration problems, which the British hadn't prepared for. Even though there was a very confused state of affairs Bond succeeded in making a reception plan whereby the Division was smoothly disembarked at Piraeus prior to moving to staging camps well planned and organised by Bond beforehand. In subsequent moves around Greece he was presented with similar problems but accomplished the schedules with maximum convenience of those concerned. Throughout the Division's stay in Greece Bond has laboured relentlessly for the welfare and administrative convenience of the camps. He proved himself to be a careful and skilled planner and the manner in which he has executed his duties has been an inspiration to all.

Paul Norman Craddock

(Emanuel Modern Languages 1949–1981)

Paul 'Joe' Craddock served in the RAF Intelligence Corps in West Africa, Italy and Germany. At the end of the war he was an official interpreter in Gottingen for British scientists of the Aerodynamic Research Institute, interviewing German scientists. Paul was a language genius and was known to speak over sixteen languages fluently. He worked at Emanuel for 32 years and continued to visit and teach the very brightest long after his retirement in return for a free school lunch! Many Emanuel schoolboy linguists credit Paul Craddock as their bedrock in languages. He was also leader of the Action Campaign in the 1970s when the ILEA

Paul Craddock (first from left) with Emanuel staff c.1970s

ran a long campaign to end Emanuel's status as a Grammar School. Paul died in 2003 and when OEs visit the School many invariably refer to 'Craddock', with a tremble in their voice. The late historian and twentieth century intellectual Tony Judt, who attended Emanuel in the late 1950s and early 1960s, remembered 'Joe' Craddock, ('Joe' after Joseph Stalin), in one of his last books, *The Memory Chalet*. As Tony lay paralysed by the degenerative motor neurone disorder, he dictated his memoir to an assistant and devoted an entire chapter to his language teacher at Emanuel. Tony remembered, 'If I recall 'Joe' Craddock with such affection and appreciation, it is not just because he put the fear of God in me or had me parsing German sentences at 1.00am lest I be dismissed the next day as "absolute rubbish!" It's because he was the best teacher I ever had; and being well taught is the only thing worth remembering from school.'[1]

Derek Drury – A Man for all Seasons

(Emanuel History and Rowing 1955–1966)

Derek Drury was educated at Whitgift and came to Emanuel from Chiswick Grammar School in 1955. For ten years Derek taught history, was a commander in the Naval Section of the Emanuel Combined Cadet Force and took the Emanuel School Boat Club to new heights when in his final year his crew won the much-coveted Princess Elizabeth Challenge Cup at Henley Royal Regatta.

Leaving Whitgift in 1944 Derek entered the Y-Scheme for the Royal Navy and got a place at New College Oxford before starting naval training in the summer of 1944. In the next year he trained at HMS *Ganges* and in HMS *Dauntless*, carrying out a number of duties including mast head look out for mines and enemy movement. From here he moved to *King Alfred* at Hove where he passed out – receiving his commission as a midshipman. At this time he volunteered for special operations and having signed the official secrets act in Baker Street he started training on the Welfreighters which were midget submarines developed by the Special Operations Executive. By the time Derek trained on them it had been intended to send troops to the Far East after the conclusion of hostilities in Europe, but the dropping of the atomic bombs on Japan meant these plans were abandoned. The Welfreighter project remained classified fifty years after the end of the Second World War. After the war Derek spent time on mine sweepers based at Cuxhaven from where he went out on sweeps into the North Sea. It was during this time that he learnt how to sail, a skill which he put to good use when he took Emanuel naval cadets on Baltic cruises in the late 1950s. After he left Emanuel, Derek moved to Shiplake College and ended his teaching career at Candford School. In the late 1960s he coached both Oxford and Cambridge crews in the Boat Race and was pivotal in the foundations of junior rowing in the UK.

Derek Drury in Naval uniform c.1945

Rowing Master Derek Drury as captured by Roger George Clark c.1962

Major Anthony Maycock
(Emanuel English 1972–1983)

Anthony Maycock saw active service in India, Japan and Burma in the Second World War with the Worcestershire Regiment. In 1945 he was seriously wounded in the leg during an attack on a Japanese stronghold at Pear Hill, Mandalay. This injury put paid to any career prospects in the military, post-war. Instead he entered Magdalen College as an undergraduate. Anthony was described as 'an exotic and colourful old soldier' and a character in the novel 'Venetian Cousins' by Stephen Carroll is rumoured to be based upon his friendship with Henry Upton. He worked at Emanuel for many years and in later life became an ordained priest and converted part of his flat into a private chapel.

Wilfrid Claude Neath *(Emanuel Classics & Modern Languages 1936–1972)*

Wilfrid Neath

Claude's long period of employment at Emanuel was broken up by the war. In 1940 Neath had been promoted to Pilot Officer in the Royal Air Force Volunteer Reserve and undertook duties as a radio operator in Bomber Command. He flew a large number of operations with No. 61 Squadron, gaining promotion to Flight Lieutenant and winning the DFC. When the war was over he returned to Emanuel where he volunteered to lead the new RAF section of the JTC. The exceptionally popular classics teacher was 67 when he died.

Howard John Roberts
(Emanuel Art 1974–1987)

Howard Roberts worked in the art department towards the end of his successful career in teaching and the art world. He was a well-known and respected artist and gallery proprietor, establishing Wales's first successful commercial art gallery. Before the Second World War he attended Cardiff College of Art, but his education was interrupted by gruelling war service in North Africa, as a wireless operator in the 57th Field Regiment, Royal Artillery. He eventually transferred to a camouflage unit in company with other artists. Towards the end of the war he taught art in Florence. On his death in 2001 the Howard Roberts Gallery left a large permanent legacy in public collections.

Jack Town (first from left) with Emanuel Staff. Lt-Col Charles Hill (centre)

Edwin John 'Jack' Town *(Emanuel 1927–1933) & (Emanuel History Master 1970–1981)*

Jack was a First Eight rower and Captain of Boats in 1933. He was also in the First Fifteen for three seasons and in the School Shooting Eight from 1930–33. He was a House Prefect of Drake and a Drum Major in the OTC. Jack was awarded his War Office Certificate 'A' March of 1932 and was a member of the Dramatic Society. After leaving School he joined the police force and played at a high level for the Metropolitan Police at rugby, as well as divisional cricket.

During the war Jack served in the RNVR. After the war he was promoted several times in the police force reaching the position of Superintendent before retiring in 1966. After retirement he took to refereeing both police and Old Emanuel rugby sides. Jack won a shooting national championship in the police VIIIs at Bisley in 1964. He was also awarded the Queen's Police Medal for Distinguished Service. He retrained as a teacher and returned to Emanuel to teach History. He was a Drake housemaster for eight years and helped in organising the CCF. He was one of Emanuel's most popular and highly respected teachers. His son Ian both attended and taught at Emanuel, overlapping with his father before his retirement and Ian's son Jeremy was also an Emanuel boy. Interestingly Jack shot for an Old Emanuel shooting team 51 years after first competing for the School in a similar competition.

Emanuel School Rowing Team, 1932
Back Row - D.J. Harrington, M.G. Jones, J.G. Worth Esq., L.G. Tucknott, K.A. Sheppard
Middle Row - E.J. Town, H.S. Darley (Captain), The Headmaster C.G.M. Broom, V. Recchioni, B.R. Noble
Front - C.E. Bird (Cox'n)

Charles Clifford Kuper

(Emanuel Headmaster 1964–1975)

Charles Kuper's Headmastership was met with a turbulent period in the School's history as he fought to save Emanuel from government intervention in the 1970s. It was largely due to his leadership that he steered the School towards independence and the fact that Emanuel has continued to provide a sound education forty-years later is a testament to his labours.

During the Second World War Charles Kuper rose through the ranks to command the castle class corvette – HMS *Hadleigh Castle* (K355) between 22 November 1944 and 19 May 1945. Before being appointed as Emanuel Headmaster Charles had previously worked as a history master at Wellington College and Haberdasher's Aske's School and had been Headmaster at Queen Mary's School, Basingstoke. Very few specific details exist of Charles Kuper's time at sea but mention of some of his experiences is recounted by Basil Mitchell's memoir – the former Nolloth Professor of the Philosophy of the Christian Religion at the University of Oxford.

Mitchell was in South Africa awaiting his next naval posting:

> In the Navy transitions always involved delay and I spent some days in Durban employed in censoring mail, together with officers awaiting return to the UK. Among them was Charles Kuper who had been an Intelligence Officer in the Middle East and was on his way back, like me, to discover his next job. He was a big man, somewhat older than me, an entertaining conversationalist, well read with an apt quotation for every occasion. He had been a history master at Wellington and hoped to return there after the war. It was good to know that I was assured of congenial company on the journey back however long that was to be.
>
> It was to be longer and less direct than either of us expected. On arrival at Cape Town, after a spectacular

railway journey through the Karoo and down into Cape Province through the Hex River Valley, we were transferred to the Royal Mail Liner, *Highland Chieftan*, now a troop ship ... Having crossed the South Atlantic and arrived in the River Plate, we were all put ashore at Montevideo ... Among the special treats prepared for us was an excursion into the country. We were taken in a fleet of buses for a long and attractive ride out of Montevideo to what at first appeared to be a large country house, but turned out in fact to be a brewery ...

Charles and I used to go regularly to the Anglo-Uruguayan Institute, run most effectively by the British Council. There was a great demand for English books and for lessons in English and teatime in particular offered a good opportunity to meet Uruguayans who could speak English ... It was at tea one afternoon at the British Council that Charles and I were given an unexpected assignment. A woman came along to our table and said to us 'I don't know what I am going to do. I have an English class of fourteen to sixteen year olds at 5pm and I have lost my voice!' There was nothing for it but for Charles and me to offer our services. "We are English", we said "and we should be able to keep them interested for a while. How long does the period last?" She said "three-quarters of an hour." So Charles and I presented ourselves to this mixed class of boys and girls and said, "Your teacher has lost her voice and cannot be with you so we are taking her place and will talk to you in English for the next period. What would you like us to talk about?" They replied, ... "The history and traditions of the Royal Navy." Charles was an experienced teacher and had some acquaintance with naval history. Between us we could remember, or invent, a reasonable collection of traditions. ... There is no doubt that the occasion was a great success. The bell was entirely ignored and the session went on for well over an hour.

After Mitchell returned to the UK:

The period at Tobermory was attended by one great blessing. I discovered that Charles Kuper had been sent for sea training to *Western Isles*. He told me that the plan was to put him for three months as an additional officer in one or other of the ships that were going through Tobermory. I had no difficulty in persuading him that he should join *Oxford Castle* and to this the Commodore and Holden readily agreed. Charles had found life in *Western Isles* less alarming than we all had feared ... Charles later had to escort a Vichy French Captain to lunch. The Frenchman had very little English and Charles spoke no French. After lunch the Frenchman remarked "It is very good of your Commodore to invite

Charles Kuper with Mary Davies, Headmaster's Secretary for 40 years at Emanuel

me to lunch like this." Charles realised he spoke very good English and not long afterwards an embarrassed Commodore came trotting along the deck: "Wrong Frenchman m'boy, wrong Frenchman." And Charles had to do it all over again! ... After three months or so it was judged that Charles Kuper had completed his training and to my great distress he left us.

Every Emanuel School boy knew Charles Kuper had served in the Royal Navy. Indeed, Old Emanuel Gary Dibden noted that when he did the entrance exam Charles Kuper had the boys take an extra exam. In addition to Maths, English and Verbal Reasoning, there was a special surprise. Gary recalls the Headmaster giving a long talk about navigation and lighting signals in the Royal Navy and then realised he would be answering questions on it in an extra exam! This may sound strange, but one wonders whether the Headmaster's talk wasn't inspired by his adventures in Uruguay. Old Emanuel Nigel Smith also remembers being questioned by Charles at interview. Charles asked Nigel his ambitions and Nigel replied that he wished to join the Royal Navy, an answer that Nigel maintains secured his place at Emanuel.

On a different note, Old Emanuel Peter Hain (Emanuel 1966–1968) MP and Secretary of State for Northern Ireland 2005–2007, remembered his first encounter with Charles Kuper:

The Headmaster, lugubrious and ruddy faced with whiskers, seemed rather a toff. "Would you like to write an essay, boy?" he asked, "No thank you very much, sir", I replied, putting a literal interpretation on the very English phrase, 'would you like', and not recognising it for the polite instruction it actually was.[2]

References

1 Tony Judt, *The Memory Chalet*, (2011), p. 90.

2 Peter Hain, *Outside In* (2012).

CHAPTER 24

Distinguished Old Emanuels
who Served in the First and Second World Wars

Lieutenant-Colonel Ernest Tristram Crutchley CB, CMG, CBE

(Emanuel 1890–1893) Civil Servant

Ernest Crutchley entered Emanuel in 1892 and rose to be appointed a School Prefect. His father was Commander William Caius Crutchley, 'a famous and forthright captain in the Merchant Navy' according to his grandson. His son wrote a short biography of Ernest in which he discussed his father's First World War service:

> He was an active volunteer in his younger days and when war broke out in August 1914, after he had been on the surveying staff at Exeter for three years, he hurried to London to rejoin the Civil Service Battalion of the London Regiment and organise a company of men of military age. In September, however, he was transferred to the Royal Engineers as Deputy Director of Army Postal Services, Home Forces and was given the rank of lieutenant-colonel, which clung to him, much against his wish, for the rest of his career.[1]

An obituary for Ernest appeared in the Michelmas Term Portcullis, 1940:

> Crutchley belonged to an older generation. He was made a Prefect at Emanuel in 1892 (or Monitor as it was then called), and did outstanding service to the School by founding, in 1893, with W. G. Murphy, the *Emanuel School Magazine*, which ran continuously until 1906 when its name was changed to *The Portcullis*.
>
> His lovable personality and his literary gift, which brought him distinction at Emanuel, were two qualities which helped him in his future career as a Civil Servant.
>
> During the last war he was appointed to organise the Army Postal Services for the forces in this country and was promoted to Lieutenant-Colonel. In 1921 he was on the Staff of the Chief Secretary for Ireland. In 1928 he was given a special mission connected with migration to Australia, and so successful was he in this particular task that in 1931 he was appointed Representative in the Commonwealth of Australia of His Majesty's Government in the United Kingdom. The Times speaks of his 'outstanding diplomatic ability and resourcefulness', and suggests that his work in Australia was the finest of his many achievements.

Ernest Crutchley

In 1935 he succeeded Sir Stephen Tallents as Public Relations Officer, and in 1936–37 became Assistant Under-Secretary of State at the Dominions Office. In 1938 Sir John Anderson asked for his services at the Home Office to explain to the public the new Civil Defence Measures.

Continued overwork at the Home Office, and later as liaison officer between the Ministry of Home Security and the Ministry of Information, undoubtedly led to his collapse and sudden death.

A penetrating and original mind combined with a magnetic personality were undoubtedly the secrets of his success. The Times says: 'Crutchley had fine dignified manners and a charming and lovable personality. No one had more friends in the Civil Service.'

We shall remember with pleasure his visit to the School a year or two ago, when he gave a stimulating talk on Australia.

Derek Davis *(Emanuel 1934–1938)* Artist

Derek Davis

Derek Davis was one of England's foremost potters and ceramicists and when he became too elderly for the heavy work associated with pottery he returned to painting, in which he was highly accomplished. Derek had a reputation as an imaginative and inventive potter and was widely regarded as one of the pioneers of post-war ceramics, pushing the boundaries of what could be done with clay. His education was interrupted by the war and in 1943 he joined the Kings Royal Rifle Corps but didn't see active service abroad.

Several original pottery pieces are on display in the Emanuel School Archive. His obituary noted:

> During the autumn of 1967 Derek was artist in residence at Sussex University, an experimental time culminating in a lecture and two exhibitions. Exhibitions worldwide followed as his reputation grew, and in 1976 Sir Roy Strong selected Derek and his fellow potter Mary Rogers to represent the 'Spirit of the 70s' for an exhibition at the V&A. Exhibiting in prestigious galleries such as Peter Dingley in Stratford-upon-Avon and Amalgam in London assured Derek a place alongside the likes of Lucie Rie and Ruth Duckworth as one of the most prominent potters of the decade.[2]

Examples of Derek Davis pottery

Sir Arthur Norman Galsworthy

(Emanuel 1924–1934) Diplomat

Arthur Galsworthy was the second of two Emanuel brothers to be knighted. As a boy he was Lieutenant of the School, Captain of Drake, a member of the School Athletics Team and a highly competitive winger in the First Fifteen. Sir Arthur was also a Lance Sergeant in the OTC and gained his War Office Certificate 'A' in November 1932. This highly

Arthur Galsworthy in service uniform

Arthur Galsworthy with Intelligence Officers, Sicily, 1943

academic member of the Classical Sixth was also Editor of *The Portcullis* and winner of several highly sought after university scholarships. These included a State Scholarship and the Dacre Exhibition Scholarship to Corpus Christi College, Cambridge.

After university he joined the Colonial Office in 1938, but at the outbreak of the Second World War he enlisted in the ranks of the Royal Fusiliers and was commissioned in the Duke of Cornwall's Light

Sir John Galsworthy c.1978

Infantry. He was attached to the Intelligence Corps and served in North Africa where he landed as part of Operation Torch. Later he was in Sicily and Italy, finishing the war as a Lieutenant-Colonel. After being demobbed he returned to the Colonial Office before a succession of high-profile promotions in the Foreign Office led to him being British High Commissioner in New Zealand 1969–1972 and Ambassador to the Republic of Ireland 1973–1976. His younger brother John, also an OE, was an Ambassador to Mexico. Sir Arthur died in 1986.

Sir John Edgar Galsworthy

(Emanuel 1928–1937) Diplomat

John Galsworthy was a Prefect of the School and former Lieutenant of Drake house. After gaining his Higher Schools Certificate he won a scholarship to study Modern Languages at Corpus Christi, Cambridge. John joined the Army at the beginning of the Second World War (Duke of Cornwall's Light Infantry) only to be invalided out after losing his right eye in a training exercise. His war wasn't over though as he then worked at Bletchley Park as a code breaker. In 1944 he moved to the Foreign Office as a Temporary Third Secretary in the Northern Department. A controversial incident in his career occurred when he was involved in the forced repatriation of Russians at the end of the Second World War as part of the

By the KING'S Order the name of
Captain (T/Major) A. N. Galsworthy,
Intelligence Corps,
was published in the London Gazette on
11 November, 1943,
s mentioned in a Despatch for distinguished service.
I am charged to record
His Majesty's high appreciation.

[signature]

Secretary of State for War

Arthur Galsworthy's Mention in Despatches

Yalta agreement. Although the Soviet Union was an ally in the defeat of Fascism, the British Government, and Anthony Eden in particular, pursued a policy of 'repatriation' that many later regarded as an inglorious episode in British Foreign Policy.[3] After the war he remained in the Foreign Office, ending as Ambassador to Mexico after a succession of promotions. He was knighted for his services to the British Empire and the diplomatic services.

Reginald Goddard *(Emanuel early 1900s)*

Founder of Chessington Zoo

Goddard with Chessington Zoo mug

Little is known of Reginald Goddard's time at Emanuel except that he competed in the School Sports Day which took place on 27 July 1901. In the First World War, he attained the rank of Lieutenant in the Royal Naval Air Service and qualified as a balloon pilot in Roehampton in 1917 and served on a number of Kite Balloon bases in England.

Reginald Goddard founded Chessington Zoo in the 1930s. He had managed his family's slate and slab firm in Battersea when in 1931 he drove past a mansion for sale which was ideal to house a collection of exotic animals. The zoo opened on 28 July 1931 and became a popular attraction in 1930s England. At the outbreak of the Second World War Reginald closed the zoo as the risk of London and the surrounding areas being bombed was high. An evacuation took place and his animals moved to Primley Zoo in Paignton, Devon. This move not only saved Primley, which was struggling financially, but also ensured the safety of Goddard's animals. In 1946 the animals were returned to Chessington and the Zoo brought some much needed colour to the grey post-war years of austerity London which, like the rest of the UK, still experienced rationing well into the 1950s. Reginald Goddard sadly didn't enjoy the post-war years long enough and died on Christmas Day 1946.[4]

Jack Chetwynd Western Heming

(Emanuel 1912–1917)

Children's Novelist and Journalist

Jack Heming got his first taste of adventure when he joined the Emanuel OTC and when he left in 1917 was well aware of the opportunities for travel which the First World War offered. Firstly, he joined the Royal Naval Air Service as a Probationary Flight Officer but whilst in France he suffered a serious crash which ended his career in the air. He promptly transferred to the Royal Naval Volunteer Reserve, as a Midshipman, serving in training and shore-based establishments in London and saw active service in several of His Majesty's Motor Launches including Nos. 100, 154, 272, 137 and 380. He also spent time at HMS *Colleen* in Ireland during the period of troubles in the immediate post-war years.

Jack Heming

Jack Heming on an adventure

In the inter-war years Jack and his first wife Eileen wrote a number of popular children's adventure stories and Eileen also wrote several novels and short stories. In 1943, Eileen portrayed Jack's war adventures in her book Commandos Raid at Dawn and when Eileen died in 1948 Jack completed several of her unfinished manuscripts. Jack met Eileen when he trained as a medical student at Guy's Hospital for a brief period after the First World War but his medical training was short-lived and it is not a career he pursued. Jack became a meteorologist with the Air Ministry before he embarked upon a career in journalism. At first he worked for a paper in Cardiff before being appointed editor of the *Egyptian Gazette* in Alexandria. Appointments with the *Evening News* and as an editor with *Encyclopaedia Britannica* followed before

Book jackets of Jack Heming adventure stories

joining the *Daily Telegraph* with which he was associated for almost 40 years. In the 1930s he wrote talks for the BBC and a play that was adapted for film and it was at this time that Jack, Eileen and his younger brother Bracebridge were inspired to write aviation adventure stories believing that they could improve the style of several authors publishing in the same genre. Jack's first air adventure was *The Air Treasure Hunt*, published by Sampson Low, Marston & Co Ltd, 1935.

A superb biography by Eric Bates makes it clear that Jack Heming was a born adventurer. Being an editor in the 1930s he kept a close eye on political events on the continent and having fought in the First World War he thought another conflict likely so a month after the annexation of Austria in 1938, Jack enrolled in the Royal Naval Volunteer Supplementary Reserve (RNVSR) attached to the London Division of the Royal Naval Volunteer Reserve. At this time, Jack and Eileen provided refuge in their Forest Hill home for several Jewish women and girls who had fled from Nazi Germany. The war interrupted Jack's writing career but Eileen's flourished and overall it was Eileen who became the more prolific author.

In late 1939 Jack was called up and reported to HMS *King Alfred*, a Royal Naval Volunteer Reserve training centre in Hove. By December 1939 and with a promotion to Lieutenant, Jack transferred to the Royal Navy training centre HMS *Raleigh* at Torpoint, Cornwall, where he remained as an instructor for a year. Another promotion to Lieutenant Commander followed, with a posting to the Royal Navy Coding School at Warrington, Lancashire where Jack remained for two years. From 1943 to April 1945 he was stationed at the Fleet Air Arm Training Centre at Risley (HMS *Gosling*), near Warrington. Jack then served for seven months as Acting Commander at HMS *Afrikander*, the Simon's Town Royal Navy base ship in South Africa, until December 1945. Up until 1956 Jack remained a member of the RNVSR, being recalled for training on six occasions. Two of Jack's children also served in the Second World War, daughter Elizabeth in the Women's Royal Naval Service (the Wrens) and son Jack Rupert Dempster in the Royal Armoured Corps and the Reconnaissance Corps.

The war ended Jack's career as an author of children's adventure stories, due in part to the fact that he lost his passion to write such works which now seemed misplaced. As the sun finally set on the British Empire so too did the backdrop to his once popular stories. The rapid societal changes resulting from the Second World War, the dismantling of the Empire and conditions in austerity Britain

Sidney Rowland Hudson as Emanuel First XV touch judge, 1914–1915

William Lovelock

called for a new form of escapism which was provided by the likes of Enid Blyton and C. S. Lewis, not daring aviators who were now the redundant poster boys of a crumbling empire.

In post-war years among jobs for the BBC World Service, Jack also worked for British Naval Intelligence and was appointed Temporary Acting Lieutenant Commander.

He was well into his 80s when he died and his ashes were scattered at sea, being accorded full military honours by the Royal Navy, at Dartmouth. For a while his children's adventure novels rivalled those of Biggles, but with the passage of time and changing tastes they have drifted into obscurity.[5]

Sidney Rowland Hudson

(Emanuel 1908–1915)

Headmaster Alleyn's School 1945–1963

Sidney appears in the First Fifteen rugby photograph of the season 1914–1915 which saw very heavy casualties. In his time at the School he was involved in a wide range of activities including three Sports Days from 1913 to 1915 and is featured on a number of School prize lists. Not long before he joined the army he participated in the Inter-House Swimming competition and in 1916 wrote to the School with the good news that he had been commissioned.

Sidney joined the Royal Fusiliers and after surviving the war used his experience in running the OTC at Alleyn's where he was Commanding Officer. This was the beginning of a remarkable career in education and Hudson was quickly promoted and remained Headmaster of Alleyn's School 1945–1963. In total he worked at the school for 37 years, first arriving in 1926 as an assistant master. As Headmaster he had a major role in the school achieving direct grant status in 1958.

He also played a pivotal role in the school's evacuation to Rossall in the Second World War, when he was a housemaster. He remained closely linked to the Alleyn's Old Boys' Club until his death and was President for many years.

William Lovelock *(Emanuel 1910–1916)*

Music Teacher, Author and Composer

William Lovelock was an outstanding music teacher, educationalist, composer and music critic who had learned to play the organ when he was twelve. At sixteen he won an organ scholarship to Trinity College of Music. He was a brilliant musician from a young age winning many school music prizes, county scholarships and organ sight-reading competitions. Little is known about his time in the First World War except that he served in the Royal Garrison Artillery on the Western Front. He returned to Trinity College after the

Owen Saunders

war. However, he was never far away from Emanuel and throughout the 1920s returned to play in Old Boy concerts and School events.

Between the wars Lovelock began to cultivate his reputation as an outstanding musician, but was also caught up in the Second World War when he was stranded in India examining for Trinity whilst his wife and son remained in England. He was commissioned in the Indian Army Ordnance Corps in March 1942 and rose to Temporary Major in 1944. He wrote a concerto for piano and orchestra while stationed at Benares (Varanasi) in 1945. When he returned to Britain in 1946, he rejoined the staff of Trinity College and wrote a sequence of highly successful music textbooks which became standards in music teaching for several decades. Later in life he concentrated on his composing. This ranged from teaching pieces for children to full-scale orchestral, choral, brass and military band works, including concertos for piano, wind instruments, harp and organ. The Sydney, Melbourne and Adelaide Symphony orchestras recorded several of his works. He was a very distinguished Old Emanuel who returned to the School many times to judge competitions and perform in the orchestra. Indeed, he even wrote music which was premiered at Emanuel School, and was known to be a regular at Old Boy dinners.

Sir Owen Saunders *(Emanuel 1913–1919)*

Scientist

Owen Saunders was a leading scientist concerned with applying mathematical and physical principles to the understanding of practical engineering problems. However, although he excelled in the field of science, he struggled at school because of a lack of interest in sport. Team sports were an important part in private education and, at the age of nine, Owen found himself attending Emanuel where he was to remain until 1919.

From an early age his mother realised he was gifted in the areas of maths and science. This created problems for Owen as the Emanuel Headmaster, Shirley Goodwin pressured him to study Classics. He did this under duress but continued to study chemistry and logic at home. Owen won school prizes in both these subjects, although he had not attended lessons in either. This was a great embarrassment to the Headmaster. He eventually left Emanuel after one term in the Classical Upper Sixth after a further dispute with the Headmaster over whether to continue on the Classics route of study or switch to the sciences.

Owen studied at Birkbeck College before gaining a scholarship to Trinity College, Cambridge where he qualified with an upper second-class degree in natural sciences in 1926.

In the 1920s and 1930s Owen was involved in research on industrial furnaces and applied heat transfer and co-wrote a highly influential book *The Calculation of Heat Transmission* with Margaret Fishenden, published in 1932. This led to him giving many new lectures on heat transfer and in related areas such as thermodynamics.

By the outbreak of the Second World War Owen was involved in the supercharging of aero-engines which led to an appointment as the Deputy Director of Turbine Research at the Ministry of Aircraft Production in 1942 where, in association with Harold Roxbee Cox, Hayne Constant and Dr. G. Feilden he worked on aspects of Frank Whittle's jet engine.

His war-time research applied his understanding of fuel flow to the fine tuning of the exhaust systems of aero-piston engines at high altitude. This helped to give British fighters a vital speed advantage over enemy aircraft during the War. Much of this was connected to the design of combustion chambers and aircraft propulsion. Owen was also widely involved in teaching many Polish escapees and servicemen who came to Britain. Many were already qualified and so required a place to finish their studies. To this end Owen help set up the Polish University College under the aegis of Imperial College, London. The results proved fruitful both for the war effort and in post-war research.

After the War Owen returned full-time to Imperial College and spent the remainder of his career in research and university life taking on a wide range of different duties including appointments as Chair of Mechanical Engineering and Head of Department. He was also involved in a plethora of government committees and scientific organisations such as the Air Ministry, the Aeronautical Research Council and was Chairman of the Propulsion Committee and the Rockets Committee in addition to other appointments. In 1958 he was made a Fellow of the Royal Society and in 1960 he was elected President of the Institution of Mechanical Engineers. In 1966 he was appointed to the Board of the London University Computer Centre. His colleagues never understood how he found time to be a member of so many committees in addition to his other highly demanding duties but Owen was also in fact a magician! Among his many accolades he was a member of the Magic Circle, finding time in his busy schedule for 'sleight of hand' tricks that were known to mystify his staff. Other prestigious appointments included being Rector of Imperial College from 1966–1967, Vice-Chancellor of the University of London 1967–1969 and Chairman of the first Council of the combined Royal Holloway and Bedford College. Among his many awards he was knighted in 1965.

After a distinguished scientific career he suffered with failing eyesight in later years and died in 1993.[6]

Professor David L. Stockton

(Emanuel 1937–1943)

Classical Historian and Author

David Stockton was one of the 550 boys evacuated to Petersfield and was billeted with the family of the retired Dr. Pankridge, who was a source of great encouragement to him. He excelled at school and was elected to the top demyship at Magdalen College, Oxford. In his final year at Emanuel he was made School Captain and Editor of *The Portcullis*. Before he could take up his place, however, he was called up and joined the Navy in 1943. Colour blindness kept him out of the Fleet Air Arm. After a year on the lower decks he volunteered for a crash course in Japanese and was sent to Bedford. He excelled at this and was promoted to sub-lieutenant and worked at Bletchley Park and with Naval Intelligence at Greenwich breaking Japanese codes.

He returned to Oxford as a student in 1946 and was awarded a First in Classical Moderations. He furthered his career in other academic institutions before becoming a highly respected Oxford don and leading classicist. His wide ranging body of work includes what is widely regarded as the leading study on Cicero published in the twentieth century.

David Stockton in his Emanuel days

He was a Governor of Emanuel School in the 1990s. David was exceptional at solving crosswords and it is believed he developed the logic for this whilst breaking Japanese codes at Bletchley.

A page from David Stockton's Emanuel Latin Vocabulary book showing war related drawings

References

1 Brooke Crutchley, *Ernest Tristram Crutchley: A Memoir* (Cambridge University Press, 1941), pp. 3-4.
2 The *Guardian*, Thursday 9 October 2008.
3 See Nikolai Tolstoy, *Victims of Yalta* (1977).
4 Further information can be found here by Peter Carroll: www.paigntonpeople.co.uk/Zoo-Evacuation/story-18306478-detail/story.html
5 Eric Bates, *Among Her Own People: Lives & Literature of Eileen Marsh, Jack Heming and Bracebridge Heming* (2005).
6 For a full biography see Hugh Ford, 'Sir Owen Saunders: 24 September 1904–10 October 1993' in *Biographical Memoirs of Fellows of the Royal Society*, Vol 41 (Nov., 1995), pp. 378-394.

Features

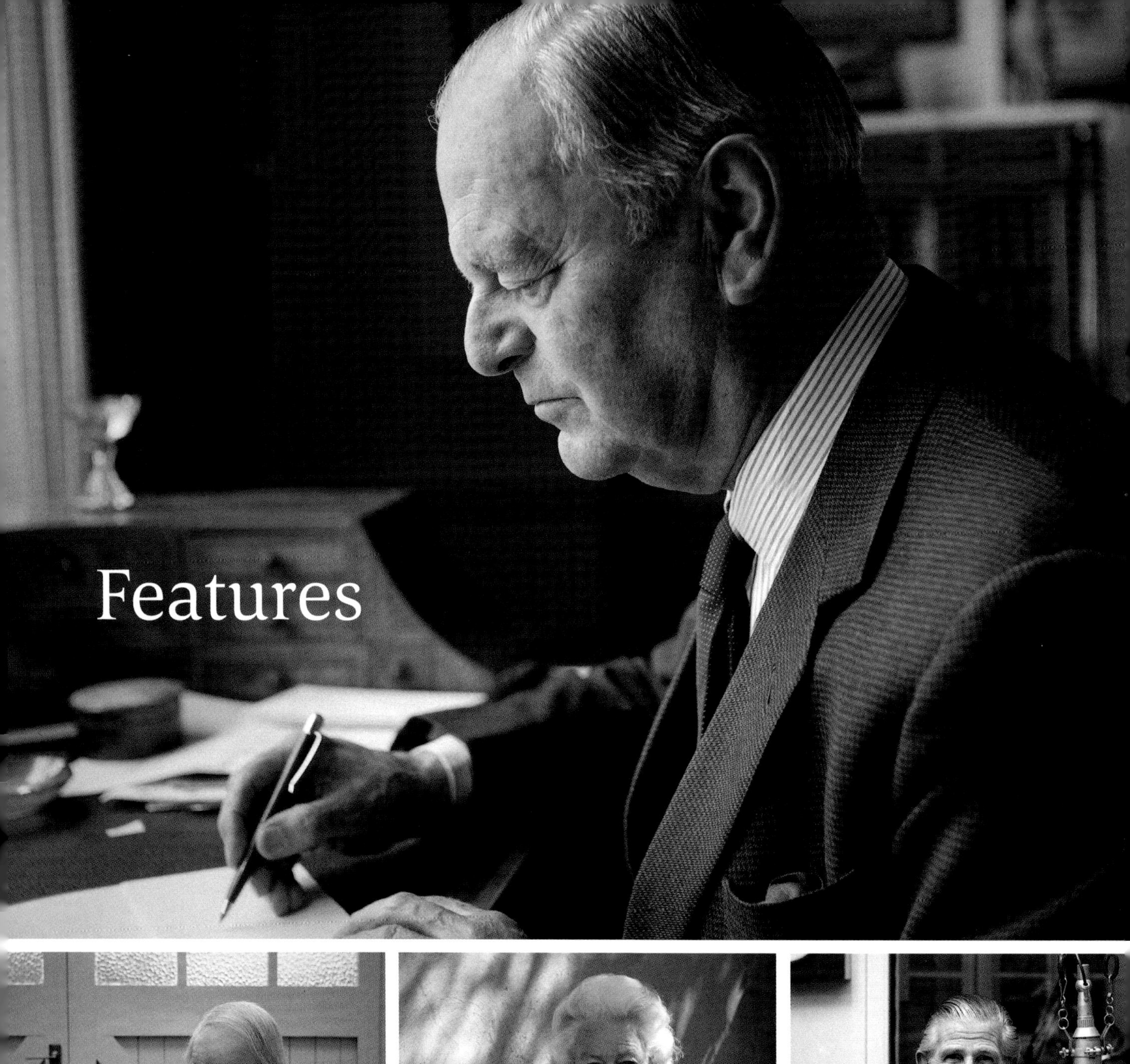

Previous page – Portraits by Roger George Clark (clockwise from top) Kenneth Clark (Director of the National Gallery in the Second World War and Chairman of the War Artists' Advisory Committee); Alvar Lidell (Radio announcer who introduced Neville Chamberlain at No. 10 Downing Street on the day the Second World War was declared, 3 September 1939); Gracie Fields (Wartime entertainer/singer famous for singing songs such as 'Wish me luck as you wave me goodbye'); and Henry Moore (Artist and sculptor who depicted life on London's underground during the Blitz)

Roger George Clark's Gallery of Second World War Personalities

Roger George Clark as an Emanuel boy

Presented here are a series of six photographs. Four of the individuals shown played a significant role in shaping the outcome of the Second World War, whilst the other two documented it. They were taken in the 1970s by Old Emanuel Roger George Clark *(Emanuel 1956–1963)*. They include Albert Speer and Earl Mountbatten, individuals whose decisions turned the course of human history.

Roger has worked as a producer and broadcaster in news and current affairs across BBC Radio, including BBC Radio London, Radio 4 and the World Service. Along with broadcasting, photography is his passion. Combining journalistic skills with photography he produced a series of portraits of some of the most influential people of the mid twentieth century. Roger has over 40 portraits in the National Portrait Gallery, London.

Some of the most intriguing portraits show Hitler's architect and Armaments and War Production minister Albert Speer. Roger interviewed him in 1979 at his Heidelberg home, recording three and a half hours of material for BBC Radio. He explored Speer's thoughts on everything from architecture to the Holocaust. During the interviews Roger asked Speer whether he felt guilty about the working conditions of slave labourers. The Nazis forced them to produce armaments in exhausting conditions and many died.

Speer's response provides a glimpse into a complex man's mind and reveals something about the ways men such as Speer operated in the Nazi regime during wartime, albeit a reflection of those experiences after twenty years in Spandau prison, Berlin.

> Well, I have to admit freely that at that time I didn't feel responsible for it. The responsibilities were shared by others and I had my own worries, a lot of worries, the whole day. I also had worries about the fighting and air attacks on German industrial towns. Of course I was shaken by seeing human beings in such a state but the next day I was in my office and occupied by other tasks, so it was not in my mind too long. Being a man on the desk and not a man who was executing orders leads to a situation where you put away such things and see problems only in figures. I wouldn't say that I am abnormal in my reactions towards human beings. When I see somebody suffering now, it hits me too, but there was a kind of numbness that shoved away the conscience.[1]

Roger has provided a short biographical sketch of each individual to accompany his photos.

Albert Speer, Hitler's architect, outside his front gate in Heidelberg

Albert Speer *(1905–1981)*

For ten years Speer was Hitler's architect designing his palace – the New Reich Chancellery, in Berlin - as well as the huge Zeppelin stadium in Nuremberg where the Nazis staged their rallies. His most spectacular architectural effect was the 'Cathedral of Ice' – luminous architecture produced by searchlights pointing up into the night sky. These created the illusion of a hall thousands of metres high with clouds drifting amongst the columns. In addition, Speer drew up plans for rebuilding Berlin with gigantic buildings – one of the boldest architectural schemes in modern times.

Because he worked for a reprehensible regime Speer's work has been shunned by many architectural critics, although it was central to twentieth century history. While he and his master rejected the excesses of Modernism they championed a modernised classicism – a style that was both old and new - as did many American, British, French, Italian and Russian architects.

In 1942 Hitler appointed Speer Minister of Armaments and War Production. He became the second most important person in the Third Reich, presiding over a vast slave empire. Despite allied attacks Germany's war production increased. Ultra efficient, Speer extended the war by a year.

At the Nuremberg trial Speer was sentenced to 20 years imprisonment for crimes against humanity. One writer called him 'the greatest slave-dealer since the Pharaohs.' Another pointed out that many famous architects worked for dictators and asked the question, 'Can a war criminal be a great artist?' as Speer's Berlin and other cities still bear the imprint of his vision.

Legendary naval commander, Earl Mountbatten of Burma

Earl Mountbatten of Burma *(1900–1979)*

When war broke out in 1939, he commanded the 5th Destroyer Flotilla aboard his ship *Kelly* which had a short, but dramatic, history. The vessel almost capsized in a high sea, collided with another destroyer, was mined once and torpedoed twice. German dive bombers finally sank the *Kelly* during the Battle of Crete in 1941. The ship's story inspired Noël Coward's film *In Which We Serve*. Coward, a personal friend of Mountbatten, copied some of his speeches in the film and wore his hat.

Churchill was captivated by Mountbatten's energy and drive and appointed him Chief of Combined Operations. Mountbatten's role was to organise raids against the European coast and prepare for an eventual invasion. After the disastrous attack on the German-occupied French port of Dieppe in 1942 Mountbatten realised that successful landings on a fortified enemy coast called for a large range of specialised equipment and skills. So he surrounded himself with a team of talented and maverick advisers. Together they came up with the idea of PLUTO – pipeline under the ocean – an underwater pipeline from England to Normandy. This supplied fuel for the allied armies in France after D–Day. They also championed the development of Mulberry – an artificial harbour constructed of concrete caissons and sunken ships – and developed amphibious tanks.

In 1943 Churchill appointed Mountbatten the Supreme Allied Commander of South East Asia Command (SEAC). He took over at a time when everything was going wrong. The Allies were losing. But under Mountbatten's leadership Burma was recaptured from the Japanese by General Slim and the Japanese surrendered at Singapore in 1945.

Douglas Bader, Battle of Britain fighter ace - one of 'The Few' - at the RAF Museum, Hendon.

Group Captain Sir Douglas Bader

(1910–1982)

Bader joined the RAF in 1928. Daring and hot-headed, he often risked his life in training by flying dangerous stunts. In 1931 he crashed while attempting low-level aerobatics and lost both legs. Although terribly injured he recovered, had artificial limbs fitted and retrained as a pilot. But the RAF refused to take him on and he was retired on medical grounds.

At the outbreak of the Second World War in 1939 Bader reapplied to the RAF. As they were short of fighter pilots he was allowed to rejoin. He scored his first victories over Dunkirk during the Battle of France in 1940. Later he took part in the Battle of Britain.

In 1941, Bader bailed out during an air battle over German-occupied France and was captured and imprisoned in a POW camp. He spent nearly three years in Colditz Castle from which he tried to escape many times – despite his lack of legs. He remained there until April 1945 when the camp was liberated by the Americans.

A film was made of his life – *Reach for the Skies* - and he was knighted by the Queen in 1976 for his services to amputees. Bader died in 1982 of a heart attack and one of the mourners at his funeral was the German fighter ace Adolf Galland.

Barnes Wallis – aeronautical designer and engineer

Sir Barnes Wallis *(1887–1979)*

Wallis is best known for developing the bouncing bombs. These skipped across the water and destroyed the Ruhr dams during the Dambuster raid in 1943. The attack was immortalised in Paul Brickhill's 1951 book *The Dam Busters* and the 1955 film of the same name.

Among Sir Barnes Wallis's other inventions were the R 100 airship, the Wellington bomber and earthquake bombs – the Tallboy (6 tonnes) and Grand Slam (10 tonnes). These bombs plunged into the earth at supersonic speed and exploded 20 metres underground. They destroyed V-2 rocket sites, submarine pens, viaducts and bridges and sank the German battleship *Tirpitz*.

After the Second World War Sir Barnes Wallis invented the swing-wing aircraft. He's seen here at his drawing board surrounded by his inventions.

Sir Cecil Beaton

Sir Cecil Beaton *(1904–1980)*

Although famous for royal and celebrity photos Beaton became a distinguished war photographer. The Ministry of Information asked him to document Britain's war effort. His brief was to avoid horrors and concentrate on taking positive images to combat propaganda photos pouring out from the enemy.

The war wrenched Beaton out of the artificial fantasy world of the studio and plunged him into real life. But Beaton brought all the skills he lavished on film stars and fashion models to bear on ordinary people. He could make a factory worker, shop assistant, soldier, or sailor look as glamorous as a movie star. He gave ordinary people style. Photographed in their work places, or on the battlefield, these pictures were pioneering examples of environmental portraiture.

Camera in hand, he set out to photograph the London Blitz. Travelling throughout England he pictured shipyards, munitions and aircraft factories, the RAF, and Churchill in 10 Downing Street. The French leader Charles de Gaulle agreed to be photographed. So did the Supreme Allied Commander and future US president Dwight D. Eisenhower.

One of Beaton's most famous pictures was his study of a bombed-out child, Eileen Dunne, sitting up in a hospital bed clutching a doll. This photo appeared on the front cover of *Life* magazine in September 1940 and was said to have influenced American feeling concerning the war more than any other picture. Beaton also travelled widely in the Middle East and north Africa photographing the desert army before the Battle of El Alamein.

Like most Allied photographers Beaton used a German camera – a Rolleiflex – throughout the war. Despite his flamboyant appearance he was surprisingly tough and resilient. Beaton never turned down a wartime assignment, however challenging – even after he was involved in a horrifying air crash. His pictures appeared in countless wartime magazines and newspapers and nine books.

John Snagge (first from left) with Roger George Clark (centre) recording a programme in Churchill's bedroom at the Cabinet War Rooms, 1975

John Snagge *(1904–1996)*

Snagge was the Voice of the BBC during the Second World War. As Presentation Director he was in charge of the radio announcers. He read many historic news bulletins, telling Britain and the world about the invasion of north Africa, the fall of Rome, Arnhem and VE-day. His most famous was the D-day announcement on 6 June 1944. 'This was the most dramatic announcement I had ever made,' he said. 'It had an electrifying effect.' After the invasion he presented the nightly programme *War Report*.

In addition, John read many of Churchill's speeches on air – Parliament wasn't broadcast at that time. Here we see John, on the left, sitting on Churchill's desk in the underground Cabinet War Rooms during a post-war recording in 1975. Churchill made some of his famous wartime broadcasts from this desk. BBC producer Roger George Clark is in the centre discussing the programme being made.

John was also renowned as the Voice of the Oxford and Cambridge Boat Race, which he commentated on for 50 years. He described numerous State occasions including the coronations of King George VI and Queen Elizabeth II, and Churchill's funeral in 1965.

He appeared in comedy programmes such as *ITMA*, *The Goon Show* and *Hancock's Half Hour*, as well as announcing the radio editions of *Dad's Army*.

References

1 Roger Clark, 'The man who kept the war going', in *The Listener*, 13 March 1980, Vol.103, No. 2653, pp. 322-323.

A View from the Other Side of the Hill

The experiences of a German artillery officer from Dunkirk to Monte Cassino

Dr. Henrik Langelüddecke was Head of History at Emanuel School from 2001 to 2006 after completing a DPhil in History at Oxford University and teaching for five years, at Alleyn's School and St Mary's Girls' School in Colchester. He has published a number of research articles on the Personal Rule of Charles I, but has always had a strong interest in the First and Second World Wars, topics that were integral parts of Emanuel's History curriculum. In this article, he describes the wartime experiences of his father, Kurt Langelüddecke, based on the stories he heard over the years from his father and his father's fellow officers. They are supported by details from his father's army file and further reading on the campaigns and units in which his father fought. His father provides a view of the War from what the English soldier and military historian Sir Basil Liddell Hart called 'the other side of the hill.' After the war Liddell Hart interviewed German generals for their accounts of the War and their view of the allies. Kurt Langelüddecke gives us the view from a lower ranking officer in the German army and what he thought of his opponents at the time.

Langelüddecke as Forward Observer in the Ukrainian steppe, 1941

Dr. Langelüddecke's father spoke openly about his youth in Berlin during the Weimar Republic, his national service and his wartime experiences. He had no sympathy for those of his generation who refused to tell their children about these times. He took a great interest in politics and discussed it often, drawing parallels with the times in which he grew up. After the War Kurt Langelüddecke travelled the world widely and visited Britain many times. He was an anglophile and admired the innate British small-c conservatism. He supported his son's decision to study, work and live in Britain. Despite, or perhaps because of, their father's experiences, all of his four sons became either professional or reserve officers in the German army. Dr. Langelüddecke's narrative of his father's experience benefits from the fact that he had the same training as an artillery officer although he never experienced combat himself. His acute interest in the wartime stories of his father's contemporaries also informed his teaching of these periods at Emanuel. After initial scepticism, his students appreciated the alternative interpretations Dr. Langelüddecke offered on the First World War, the Versailles Treaty, or interwar foreign politics. Each

October half-term he organised trips to the First World War battlefields to honour the OEs buried there. During a visit to Vimy Ridge, he related the strong emotions of his father many years earlier, when he and his father were standing at the graves of two Canadian soldiers who were killed in action on the day Kurt was born – 10 April 1917. Years later, Henrik married his Canadian wife and his father rocked his German-Canadian grandchildren on his knees.

'Kurt Langelüddecke's views on the War', Dr. Langelüddecke says, 'remained firm and unreconstructed throughout his life: he had done his job, like anyone else in the War and had committed no crime. Hitler was an evil man, but most Germans had not fought for Hitler, but for their country. Likewise, the Allies had not fought the Nazis, but Germany, to finish a job half-done in 1918. In 1945, Germany had not been liberated, but defeated.' Needless to say, these views that were once uniformly held by his generation after the war, soon became heresy in modern Germany.

This is Dr. Langelüddecke's account of his father's time in the German Army in the Second World War:

The war experience of my father Kurt Langelüddecke, who died in 2010, shaped his life like no other. It reinforced his natural resilience and optimistic outlook on the future, but also moulded his scepticism of human nature and fostered his disdain for political ideologies and self-righteous younger Germans who condemned his generation for fighting in the war. He was born in 1917 in to that small population of children whose low numbers were as a result of the impact of the First World War. My father grew up in a lower-middle class family in Berlin-Tempelhof. Politically, his parents supported Gustav Stresemann's *Deutsche Volkspartei* – economically liberal, socially conservative, and nationalist. My father always emphasized his schooling happened in the Weimar Republic, not Nazi Germany. While he approved of the revival of national unity under the Nazis and of their revision of the Versailles Treaty, as a fierce individualist he disliked their plebeian character and petty insistence on outward conformity. When he publicly spoke against the forceful merger of the *Christliche Pfadfinder* boy scouts, of which he was a senior leader in Greater Berlin, with the Hitler Youth in 1934, he was briefly arrested. Needless to say, he never joined the NSDAP [National Socialist Workers' Party] or any other party organization; indeed, he stressed that active army personnel were banned by law from joining *any* political party.

Gun crews practising after the Poland campaign, early 1940

In 1934, his older brother was accepted as a volunteer for a non-commissioned-officer career in the highly selective 100,000-men *Reichswehr*. As conscription was reintroduced a year later, Kurt was called up for national service in 1936 at the *Beobachtungsabteilung* 3, affiliated to *Artillerieregiment* 3 in Frankfurt on the Oder. The pre-war training and discipline in all branches of the *Wehrmacht* was extremely tough – comparable with that of modern special forces – and pushed soldiers to the limits of their physical and mental endurance. Leave was almost unknown for the first months; training and chores started at 5am and finished at 10pm. His instructors, long-serving NCOs from Bavaria, expressed their gratitude for their posting in Prussia with particular zeal and sadism.

Artillerieabteilung 602 on the march through a Belgian village, May 1940

After general training in a horse-drawn artillery unit from which the city boy developed a life-long fondness for horses, he was instructed in the counter-artillery technologies of sight and sound tracking that had been banned under the Versailles Treaty. In the second year of his national service, he extended his skills at the *Lehrstab* of the German Artillery School in Jüterbog, south of Berlin. Exercises at Grafenwöhr involved the fire of 120 artillery batteries (about 500 guns). At Malchin, the *Wehrmacht* demonstrated its might in front of Mussolini, and during the preparatory briefing for

2nd Battery moving into firing position minutes before being hit by own Stukas

Hitler, which was conducted by his commanding officer, my father was in charge of flipping over the situation maps. Since he had the *Mittlere Reife* school certificate and had completed his vocational training as a graphic designer and typesetter, Langelüddecke was entitled to apply to become a reserve officer. He was accepted and passed the officer cadet course. His report, however, stated that his 'conduct lacks seriousness and he tends to behave in an unmilitary way. Lack of leadership qualities and ambition.' Discharged in the rank of sergeant on 29 October 1938, Langelüddecke returned to his work as typesetter at the renowned Mosse publishing company in Berlin.

At the outbreak of war with Poland, my father was not drafted to his mobilization unit, *Artillerieregiment* 23 in Potsdam, but continued to work at Mosse. On 5 December 1939, he was finally called up to serve as an instructor of recruits in the *Schwere Artillerieersatzabteilung* 59 at Frankfurt/Oder. During the preparation for the campaign in the West, Langelüddecke, by now promoted to *Wachtmeister* (staff sergeant), was transferred to *Artillerieabteilung 602 (motorisiert)*, a battalion consisting of three firing batteries (a total of twelve guns) that had been formed on 28 August 1939 with other units in an impressive ceremony in the Berlin Olympic Stadium. The battalion, led by the sanguine Lieutenant-Colonel Bruhn, was not attached to a particular division, but was a *Heerestruppe* at the direct disposal of the OKH (*Oberkommando des Heeres*) and had distinguished itself in the tough battles for the Warsaw suburbs of Praga and Modlin. 602 attacked Belgium on 10 May 1940 crossing the river Meuse and the Albert Canal and providing fire support for the 18th Infantry Division. Breaking through the Dyle Line south of Brussels on 17 May, 2nd battery lost a dozen soldiers and a few guns to *Stuka* bombs at Nivelles, as the pilots had mistaken the columns for retreating French troops. Langelüddecke directed the fire of his *Abteilung* as forward observation officer accompanying one of the infantry companies of the division.

Breaking French and British resistance at Tournai, the division crossed the Schelde and Lys rivers and reached Ypres. One of Langelüddecke's observation posts was the Kemmel, a commanding height heavily contested in the First World War. By 31 May, 602 was supporting the 31st Infantry Division and reached Dunkirk where over half a million British and French troops were trapped. Three days later, 602 was allocated to the divisions breaking through the French positions into the south of France.

For his actions during the crossing of the Somme alongside assault engineers in rubber boats, Langelüddecke was awarded the Iron Cross 2nd class. The hasty pursuit of the French army across the Seine west of Paris was interrupted by a confusing battle near St Calais when the advance elements of 602 found themselves entangled with Senegalese infantry and were nearly captured. The *Abteilung* crossed the Loire, took the French Cavalry academy at Saumur and reached the Atlantic coast on 25 June. Firing over open land onto ships carrying the French government out of the Gironde at Royan, 602 met the fierce response of heavy naval artillery of the accompanying British warships. Then the War in the west was over.

After a four-week period, during which 602 was part of the occupation force in Southern France on the beaches of Arcachon, they made enjoyable sightseeing trips to Biarritz,

Guns of 602 pass burnt-out Kim Voroshilov tanks, Ukraine, July 1941

the Pyrenees and Paris. The *Abteilung* was transferred to Piaski, east of Lublin, in the *Generalgouvernement* near the demarcation line to Soviet-occupied Poland. In September my father was promoted to Second Lieutenant, and the command of 602 was handed over to the intrepid Lieutenant-Colonel Paul. In the meantime the situation in the Balkans had changed dramatically. Italy had attacked Greece in October 1940 and Slovakia, Hungary and Romania had joined the Axis in November. The Soviet Union's claims on Romania and Bulgaria the same month, and continuing reinforcements of British troops in Greece, increased Hitler's worries about Germany's access to Romanian oilfields. As a precaution, in February 1941, 602 was transferred to the *Heeresmission Rumänien*, a *Wehrmacht* command established in the autumn of 1940 at Constanca on the Black Sea in order to liaise with Romanian forces.

A *putsch* against King Paul of Yugoslavia in March 1941 prompted the transfer of the 12th Army to Bulgaria, which had joined the Axis earlier that month. My father was part of a delegation of the 5th Mountain Division that was invited to a banquet with Bulgarian King Boris III in order to coordinate actions with Bulgarian troops. He took comfort from the clairvoyance of the wife of a Bulgarian colonel that he would survive the war to have four sons, become very wealthy and live to the age of 92 – all predictions that came true. After a reconnaissance around Petrich – in Bulgarian uniforms to disguise the operational objective – Langelüddecke supported the attack of assault engineers on the Metaxas line (an imitation of the French Maginot line) with the artillery fire of 602 on 6 April and finally broke through the Greek positions along the rapid Struma river. On his birthday, 10 April, the division had reached Saloniki. While the bulk of the 12th Army engaged the remainder of the Greek and British forces on the Peloponnese, 602 was ordered to secure southern Yugoslavia, and on 5 May, transferred back to Cosel in Upper Silesia.

For his actions during the crossing of the Struma, my father was awarded the Assault Badge and the Royal Bulgarian Soldier's Cross For Courage.

Operation Barbarossa against the Soviet Union started on 22 June 1941. From 29 June *Artillerieabteilung* 602 was involved in the battles for Galicia and pushed past Tarnopol towards Shitomir. By now, my father was the Forward Observation Officer of 1st Battery. With artillery fire he supported the companies of the SS divisions *Leibstandarte* – Hitler's elite bodyguard – and *Wiking*. The latter entirely composed of Scandinavian volunteers. His instinctive anti-Communism was reinforced by the sight of hundreds of corpses lying in pools of blood in the local prisons – butchered by the retreating NKVD (the forerunner of the KGB). He was astonished not only by the welcome for the *Wehrmacht* by the local population offering the traditional bread and salt in every village, but by freshly constructed prisoner of war camps behind the demarcation line – clear evidence to him that Stalin's attack on Germany had been imminent. The poor living standard of the local population was appalling and even in large cities only the main road was paved and every other street was a mere dirt track. Langelüddecke was impressed by the death-defying fighting spirit of the SS infantry and amused by the reluctance of their officers, with whom he liaised, to offer the Nazi salute which usually resulted in a hybrid of the 'Heil Hitler' and the military salute. In hard battles, 602 pushed the Russian forces towards the Dnjepr [Dnieper] river and supported XIV (motorised) Corps in the encirclement of the 2nd and 6th Russian Armies at Uman in early August.

My father was horrified by the common tactic of the Red Army to ply their troops with alcohol and send them – often unarmed – in massive waves against the German positions, driven on by the Commissars. More than once, German commanders had to force their soldiers who cried 'but this is murder, *Herr Leutnant*', to fire on these attacking Russians. He witnessed the treks of thousands of Russian POWs and assisted in the impromptu amputations of gangrenous limbs of some of the prisoners who had been spotted in the columns by the *Stabsarzt* [Medical Officer] of 602.

Two weeks later, Langelüddecke crossed the Dnjepr at Kremenchug in assault boats for which he was awarded the Iron Cross 1st class. On 30 August he was appointed the *Artillerieverbindungskommando* (*AVKo*) of 602, in charge, as the tactical right hand of Colonel Paul, of coordinating the actions of all the *Abteilung's* Forward Observers and advising the commanders of the infantry and *Panzer* battalions and regiments in their deployment of artillery fire. Following 'SS Wiking' to the Sea of Azov in early October, the hazardous dust of the Ukrainian steppe wreaked havoc with the vehicles' engines. This was followed by quagmires of mud after heavy rainfalls, which seriously impeded the further advance. Swinging south from the Donetsk Basin, by November XIV *Panzer* Corps now crossed the Mius river and attacked the big industrial city of Rostov-on-Don. Mud had been replaced by bitter cold and snow and my father's photos show ill–equipped soldiers making the best out of their inadequate uniforms, some of them even wearing ladies' fur caps that had been hastily donated back home and sent to the front line.

On 25 November, Marshal Semyen Timoshenko organised a surprise Russian counter-offensive across the river Don. Over a thousand yards wide, the river was frozen in temperatures plummeting to minus 50 Celsius. Field Marshal von Rundstedt was forced to pull out of Rostov, a move which resulted in Hitler sacking him as commander of Army Group South. The Germans dug themselves in and for the next six months fended off Russian attacks from static positions. While my father had survived whizzing bullets and shrapnel every day for the last six months, he almost failed to make it into the new year. During a reconnaissance deep into Russian terrain on 31 December 1941, his *Kübelwagen* jeep was shot to pieces by seventeen *Polikarpov* I-16 Russian fighter planes. Stranded in a desert of ice and snow, he and his driver, *Gefreiter* Garbowski, struggled through breast-high snowdrifts, taking hours to travel a few hundred metres. When, by nightfall, Garbowski pleaded with his boss to shoot him, Langelüddecke kept shouting and beating him, finally piggy-backing him and reaching German infantry positions precisely at midnight. At that point German guns opened up – not to repulse a Russian attack, but to welcome the new year with 'fireworks', as is customary back home. My father retold this story to his family every New Year's Eve for the rest of his life.

During the defensive battles of the 'frozen-meat winter' of 1941/42 along the Mius river, 602 was billeted with friendly Ukrainian families in Taganrog. Colonel Paul, the popular '*Paulchen*', who had the habit of driving through eight-foot-tall maize fields riddled with Russian infantry standing upright in his jeep, had been replaced as commander by the first reservist Captain Söpp, who soon disappeared near the Volga German town of Gustavsburg. Söpp was either taken POW or may have deserted to the Russians. His replacement, Captain Rentrop, led the *Abteilung* for the next fifteen months. While the battery commanders in this unit had already been only First or even Second Lieutenants, from now on the entire *Abteilung* was led only by Captains. In late-June 1942, the spring offensive of Army Group South began, and 602 supported XIV *Panzer* Corps under General von Wietersheim, which retook Rostov and crossed the Don. Army Group South was now divided into Army Group 'A' pushing south towards the Caucasus to secure the oil fields of Azerbaijan and ultimately unite with Rommel's Africa Corps, while Army Group 'B' attacked Voronezh and Stalingrad. Wietersheim, whose dislike of the Nazis was widely known and who had lost two sons in the War, not only carried his Knight's Cross in his trouser pocket, but bluntly told Langelüddecke about Hitler: 'Der Kerl muss weg' (that scoundrel must go). My father seemed less pessimistic and by now had decided to apply to become a professional officer and stay in the army after the war was over. A positive evaluation from his unit endorsed this decision and while 602 switched to support the Slovak Mobile Division, he was sent to a selection course at the Artillery School at Jüterbog. His appraisal supported his career choice attesting to his dutiful and eager attitude and assertiveness, but criticised his inadequate knowledge of artillery theory and manuals. He was also promoted to *Oberleutnant*.

In late September my father rejoined 602, by now supporting the 198th Infantry Division and crossed the mighty Kuban river near Krasnodar. After heavy battles for Goryachy Klyuch in which the *Abteilung* lost sixteen men, 602 fought its way through the alpine terrain of the Caucasus Mountains. Russian troops, however, prevented the breakthrough to the Black Sea and another static position ensued from October 1942 to January 1943.

The defeat of the 6th Army at Stalingrad had now left Army Group 'A' in a precarious situation. Field Marshal von Kleist was ordered to break out south of the Kuban river towards the Kerch Peninsula where the Black Sea and the Sea of Azov linked.

In December, my father received the encouraging news that his application for professional officer status had been confirmed; he also was appointed deputy commander, 2nd battery. During the retreat towards Kerch, my father displayed particular *sangfroid* when he foiled the attack of a Russian battalion by ordering fire on his own position in a pig collective farm near Novorossiysk using ricochet firing. Unfortunately, he fell out with the temporary commander of 602, a Captain Bergmann, who replaced Rentrop, over a minor tactical decision. Bergmann, a former officer of the Tsarist army from the Baltic, was a fervent Nazi and in his civilian life had been mayor of the town of Jüterbog, the home of the Artillery School. He threatened Langelüddecke with court martial but when the situation on the Kuban got too hot, succumbed to a sudden fit of lumbago and left 602 with a sickness note. Having fought their way through the Kuban marshes, 602 escaped Russian encirclement leaving their heavy equipment on the Taman Peninsula and made it to Kerch and the Crimea. Henceforth, the *Wehrmacht* records classify the *Abteilung* as 'annihilated'. After he had been nursed for a couple of weeks through severe tonsillitis in a yurt [a nomadic tent] by Crimean Tartars, Langelüddecke and his men were flown out to Dzankoi. Trains took them home to Germany after two years on the Eastern Front.

602's 105 mm howitzers and Raupenschlepper Ost negotiating difficult terrain in Albania, 1943

Back in Germany, in April 1943, 602 found itself far away from its Prussian homeland in the Württemberg garrison town of Ulm on the Danube. It was refitted as a light artillery battalion with three batteries of 10.5 cm howitzers. These were pulled by the tracked *Raupenschlepper Ost* that replaced the *Sd.Kfz 11* half-track and the four 10 cm cannons and eight 15 cm howitzers that were abandoned at the Strait of Kerch. Reinforced by Swabian men and officers, 602 spent the next four months acquainting itself with the new weapons. My father was appointed commander of 3rd battery in May.

A few weeks earlier he had become engaged to Ilse Henkel. She was the 19-year old daughter of a colonel in the Frankfurt/Oder garrison. My father met her through a pen-pal arrangement set up by her school in 1941 to cheer up soldiers on the Eastern Front.

When Marshal Badoglio overthrew Mussolini in July, 602 received marching orders for Albania. They were to assist in the disarming of the Italian forces based in this Italian 'colony.' This was a prudent move as in September Badoglio declared Italy's neutrality and switched to the Allies side in October.

Captain Lüdecke, the new commander of 602 belatedly requested acknowledgement of my father's valiant conduct on the Kerch Peninsula. The commander of the 100th Rifle Division, which 602 now supported, submitted his name for the 'German Cross in Gold.' This, however, was turned down by the Commander of 2nd *Panzer* Army.

As soon as 602 had entered Albania, on 10 September 1943, my father received the order to persuade a 2000-strong unit of Italian troops to surrender – backed up by eight of his soldiers. The Italians did.

His next mission was to commandeer a fishing boat and take the island of Saseno with a small detachment of *Jäger* riflemen. Fortunately, the Italians had cleared the island just before his arrival with an armada of smaller boats. The resourceful German *Jäger* reactivated the 30.5 cm WW1 Krupp gun that was the main weapon of this little island fortress and sent a few rounds after them.

For the remainder of 1943, 602 secured the area between Tirana and Valona against partisans and used local labour and Italian POWs to build a number of bunkers along the coastline of the Ionian Sea. More than once, *Raupenschlepper Ost* [Caterpillar Tractor East – a lightweight vehicle] toppled down steep ravines along the hazardous Albanian roads killing entire gun crews.

In November, my father was called to Tirana to speak to General Utz, commander of the 5th Mountain Division.

Langelüddecke's field of fire from the top of Monte Cassino monastery, March 1944

Expecting to hear that he had been selected to attend the 17th General Staff Course, he was in fact told that the *Führer* had approved his marriage to Fräulein Henkel. On 25 November 1943, Kurt and Ilse married in the Gertraudenkirche in Frankfurt on the Oder and spent their brief honeymoon in Bad Reichenhall in the Alps.

On 17 December, Langelüddecke returned to Valona and was immediately involved in a patrol into the countryside. Heavy machine guns opened fire from both sides of the valley. His immediately thought 'partisans', but as it turned out, his detachment had been caught in the blood feud of two Albanian clans. Invited by one of the clans to a meal and surrounded by turbaned tribesmen armed to their teeth, the sheik pulled out the eyes of a boiled sheep skull and offered it to Colonel Weller, the commander of the infantry element and Langelüddecke as the guests of honour. Needless to say, they both swallowed this delicacy with lots of the local grape schnapps.

By September 1943, the Allies had, with great difficulties, taken Sicily and crossed to mainland Italy. The newly formed German 10th Army defended the hilly area south of Naples against the 5th US Army and the 8th British Army and then withdrew behind the heavily fortified Gustav Line. In February 1944, 602 left Albania for Italy to support the 1st Parachute Division that held the town and monastery hill of Monte Cassino, a key position between the Volturno, Liri and Rapido rivers. On his way, my father stopped in Rome for some sightseeing and persuaded a German guard to let him – illegally – slip into the Vatican. Once in, he asked one of the Swiss Guards for a private audience with the Pope, which was granted at short notice. After half an hour of jovial conversation with Pius XII, my father left the Vatican with a written blessing for his mother who had been excommunicated for having her two sons baptized Protestant. 602 reached Monte Cassino at the height of the Second Battle, during which 600 bombers obliterated the monastery on 15 February because the Allies – wrongly – claimed the building was fortified and used by paratroopers.

For the next twelve weeks, Allies from twenty nations attacked the town and surrounding hills, inching closer at an enormous cost of lives. The fiercest assault by Gurkhas and New Zealanders in late March nearly succeeded. My father was impressed by the chocolate and lemons the Kiwis threw into the German trenches during local ceasefires. German supply runners, who managed to survive five trips up the monastery hill, were automatically awarded the Iron Cross 1st class. The rubble created by the aerial bombardment provided perfect cover for the Germans. Langelüddecke's command post was in the crypt where St Benedict had lived

and founded this cradle of all monasteries - the only part of the building that survived the fighting intact.

On busy days, like 16 February 1944, nearly 200,000 shells were fired on the town and hill. Historians have referred to this struggle as the last First-World-War style of battle. When French troops finally broke through the Gustav Line on 16 May, and Polish troops began another assault on the hill, the German 3rd Parachute Regiment, down to a couple of hundred men, was given permission to withdraw. Langelüddecke (a captain since 1 April) argued against surrender with Captain Beyer (the last wounded Para officer and holder of the Knight's Cross), and persuaded 28 paratroopers to break through the lines of the enemy who by now had surrounded the hill. All but four men survived this adventure on 18 May, and when he reported back at his *Abteilung's* command post, one of his fellow officers who had spent the last three years with him, introduced himself to this unknown Captain – the stress of battle had changed Langelüddecke beyond recognition.

As Lüdecke had moved on to a new command, Langelüddecke now became Acting Commander of 602 during the months of fighting retreat along the Italian east coast. His final army evaluation praised his courage, toughness, decisiveness and organisational abilities and recommended him for further promotion and training. The assassination attempt on Hitler on 20 July was considered politically naive by the officers of 602, but when the order was read out to the entire *Abteilung* that the army from now on was to use the 'Heil Hitler' salute, a roar of sarcastic laughter went through the ranks – a clear show of defiance by an otherwise highly disciplined unit.

In October 1944, my father was summoned by General von Graffen, the Higher Artillery Commander of 10th Army. The General recommended him to attend the 18th General Staff Officer-training rather than formally be given the command of 602. This is because, Graffen argued, the War was lost and Langelüddecke was now the father of a little boy who had been born in August. My father accepted and began training at the Artillery School II in Groß-Born near Stettin as instructor of senior army administrators who were to be trained as artillery officers. He enjoyed being closer to his young family, but Russian troops crossed the Vistula and had pushed towards the Oder river by February 1945. This necessitated the relocation of Artillery School II to the former Czech garrison of Rokitzan near Pilsen. Once more my father was fortunate, since most of the school's personnel were subsequently formed into fighting units and met their end during the Russian offensive on Berlin in April 1945. As it was American forces led by General Patton that reached Pilsen on 4 May, and not the Russians, Langelüddecke also escaped the fate of breaking rocks in the Gulag after the war.

After two weeks of confinement in an open-air POW camp with hardly any food, the Americans loaded their prisoners on trucks and – unbelievably – drove them to their home towns along the way west. On 25 May, Langelüddecke was dropped off at the market square of Ilsenburg, the town where his wife and son had found refuge with relatives after Frankfurt/Oder had been declared a fortress during the Russian attack in April. The War was over.

Langelüddecke's adventures did not stop here. Two weeks after his arrival, he became involved in 'Operation Unthinkable' in which the British army created new German units and prepared them for a showdown with the Russians. He continued to live in Ilsenburg after it was transferred from British to Soviet occupation, worked as a lumberjack in the Harz Mountains and then as a self-taught gravestone engraver. Owing to his familiarity with the terrain, he helped countless people escape through the Iron Curtain via the mountains only a couple of miles away. When, in 1948, the Soviet administration started rounding up German ex-servicemen that had not yet paid their dues in Siberia, Langelüddecke fled to West Germany and started yet another new life, retraining as a master printer and later becoming the managing director of two well-known printing companies in Frankfurt/Main and in Stuttgart.

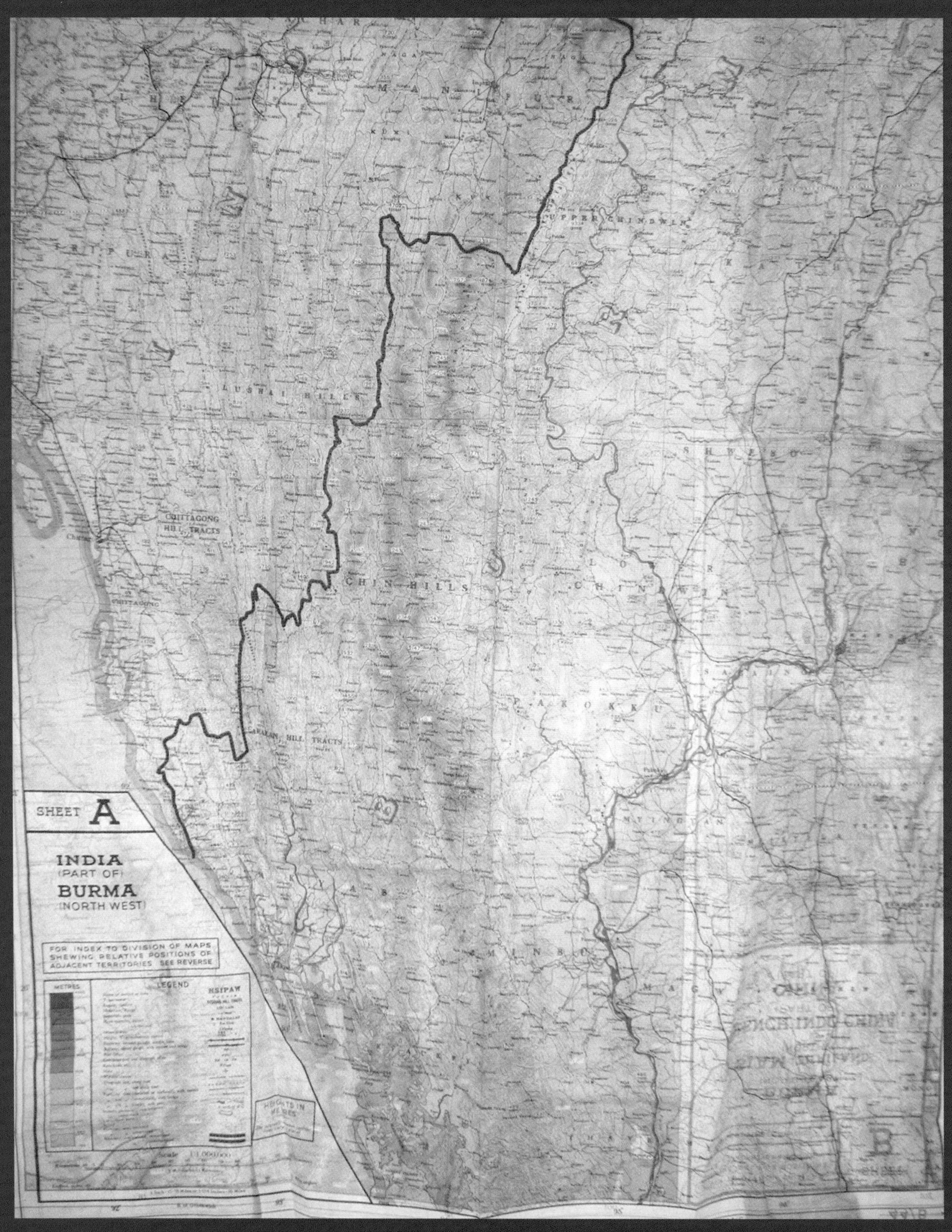

Eddie Page's silk map of India and Burma. Silk maps were distributed to servicemen to prevent the enemy hearing the rustling of the paper versions.

Eddie Page (second from right) Sainti trips, 1942

Tanda recruit boys

Eddie Page (circled) with Gurkha soldiers in Dharmsala, December 1942

Gurkhas at Tanda

Eddie in training, Dharmsala, December 1942

Sir Sholto Douglas (centre right) arrives at Gatow airfield, Berlin, 1946

William Sholto Douglas

Marshal of the Royal Air Force in Post-War Germany

In July 1945 OE Sholto Douglas took command of the British Air Forces of Occupation in Germany. Then in 1946 he took over from Montgomery as Commander-in-Chief of the Armed Forces and Military Governor of the British Zone of occupied Germany in addition to being appointed the British member of the four-power Allied Control Council in Berlin. The issues facing him were daunting, not least the food situation in Germany – a topic which he discusses in a 1946 British Pathé film titled *Germany's Food – The Truth*. But a far greater matter, which vexed Sholto during this period, was his direct involvement in the Nuremberg Trials of leading Nazi War Criminals. As one of four members of the Allied Control Council he was part responsible, in case of guilt, for the sentencing of Nazi War Criminals, which included decisions for the reduction and altering of such sentences in response to appeals for clemency. He was never entirely satisfied with the legality of the trials and, in particular, showed an aversion to being involved in the final decision to determine the method of execution for Hermann Göring, with whom he had once done battle in the skies over the Western Front. In his second autobiography he devotes an entire chapter to his involvement and displeasure vis-à-vis the Nuremberg Trials.[1] He noted, 'Twenty-eight years before, Goering and I, as young fighter pilots, had fought each other in the cleaner atmosphere of the air. As I spoke the words that meant for Goering an irrevocable death sentence I could not help feeling, for all my loathing of what he had become, the strongest revulsion that I should have to be one of those so directly concerned with it.'[2]

After Germany he was appointed a Director of the British Overseas Airways Corporation (BOAC) and Chairman of British European Airways. In 1948 he was made a Labour Peer. Lord Willam Sholto Douglas of Kirtleside died in 1969.

References

1 Sholto Douglas with Robert Wright, *Years of Command* (1966), Ch. 21, pp.329-347.
2 Ibid. p. 344.

A

Form $\frac{\text{S.D.}}{460}$

Officers Training Corps.

CERTIFICATE " A."

This is to Certify that

Mr. *Urwin Thornburn*

of the *Emanuel School* Contingent,

JUNIOR. Division, Officers Training Corps, has fulfilled the necessary conditions as to efficient service, and has qualified in the INFANTRY. syllabus of examination, as laid down in the Regulations for the Officers Training Corps. He is, therefore, eligible for consideration for a commission in the Supplementary Reserve, Territorial Army, Territorial Army Reserve of Officers or Active Militia of Canada.

In the event of a national emergency involving the mobilization of the Regular Army and the embodiment of the Territorial Army, he is requested to notify his address immediately to the Under Secretary of State, The War Office, S.W.1, with any offer of service he may wish to make.

On offering himself as a candidate for—

(1) Admission to the Royal Military Academy, Woolwich,
(2) " " " College, Sandhurst,
(3) " " Royal Air Force Cadet College, Cranwell,
(4) A commission in the Naval Medical Service,
(5) A commission in the Royal Army Medical Corps,
(6) " " Royal Army Veterinary Corps,
(7) A Paymaster Cadetship in the Royal Navy,
(8) A Naval Cadetship or supplementary first appointment to a commission in the Royal Marines.

he will be entitled to the privileges conferred on holders of this Certificate as set forth in the Regulations concerned, and to any further privileges that may be authorised after the date of this Certificate.

THE WAR OFFICE,

Date 10 MAR 1931 19 .

C Bonham Carter

Major-General,
Director of Staff Duties.

(52176X) Wt. W139/3519 6,000 5/31 *H. J. R. & L., Ltd.* Gp. 121 J.100.

Urwin 'Ned' Thornburn's War Certificate 'A' awarded on 10 March 1931. The War Certificate was for proficiency in the OTC and supported many Emanuel boys in their applications for commissions in the services.

Ned Thornburn (second from left) and Dora (fifth from left) at a veterans reunion in Overloon in the early 1990s

In October 1944 Ned Thornburn had been in action with the 4th Battalion King's Shropshire Light Infantry at Overloon, an action which he later noted, 'had finally loosened the German hold on Venray.' The battalion was called upon to carry out a flank-protection attack in support of the 3rd British Division which was engaged against the German First Parachute Army, and were exposed to heavy machine-gun fire. Ned returned to Overloon forty years later with his wife Dora and veterans of his battalion.

The Thornburn family at the renaming of Aubusson's main square to 'Place Major Ned Thornburn', May 1998

Left to right – Daniel (grandson), Hannah (granddaughter), Lt. Col. Tony Thornburn (son), Dora (widow), Elizabeth (daughter) and Hilary (daughter)

Bob Deeks OE (centre) with Emanuel students James Harvey (left) and Esme Nias (right) at a Thanksgiving service for the foundation of Emanuel at Westminster Abbey, Monday 21 November 2011

Appendices

Emanuel School

First World War
Pro Patria

The original Emanuel 'Pro Patria' lists from the First and Second World Wars have been updated for this book. The new lists contain the full names, regiments and ranks of Old Emanuels and masters who served in these conflicts. Whilst every effort has been made to correct mistakes, these lists may still contain errors because of the imperfect data from which the original lists were compiled. However, over 100 new names have been added to the First World War 'Pro Patria' list and so the number of Old Emanuels now believed to have served in both world wars exceeds 1700.

- A -

Addey, Herbert Edward (dob 1888) The Buffs (8th East Kent Regt). *[Also listed as 'H. Addey']*.

Aitken, Albert W. (EM1900–09 dob 09.08.1892) Notts. & Derby Regt., (Formerly 16th Middlesex Regt., Public Sch. Btn). *[Also listed as 'A. D. Aitken']* 2nd Lt.

Aland, A., R.F.C.

Allcock, Isaac John (EM09–14 dob 02.11.1897) R.G.A. *[Also listed as 'I. J. Allock']*.

Allen, Harold Alfred (EM09–14 dob 06.02.1898 dod 04.08.16) 5th Seaforth Highlanders, (Died of wounds). Pte. ✤

Allen, Henry Charles (EM08–13 dob 24.10.1896) The Buffs (The East Kent Regt). (Invalided out).

Allen, Lawrence John Maynard (EM08–14 dob 02.11.1896 dod 02.07.16) 8th Wiltshire Regt., (Formerly Royal Fusiliers). 2nd Lt. ✤

Allum, Sidney Edward (EM mid-1890s dob 13.09.1885) R.F.A.

Alsing, R., R.N.A.S.

Ambrose, C. G. (dob 18.05.1886) R.H.A. *[Also listed as 'C. C. Ambrose']*.

Ambrose, Harold Eastlake (EM05–11 dob 06.08.1895) Royal Fusiliers, 2nd Lt. (Invalided from Mediterranean).

Angold, Sydney Arthur (dob 02.10.1889) A.O.D., Lt.

Ansell, Eric Norman (EM13–16 dob 27.05.1900) R.A.M.C.

Arnall, Cyril John (EM08–13 dob 20.11.1895) 13th East Surrey Regt., 2nd Lt. (Wounded).

Arnell, Eric Warren Carstairs (EM07–11 dob 22.01.1896) R.F.A., (20th London Btn.). 2nd Lt. (Wounded & invalided from France). *[Also listed as 'E. W. Arnell']*.

Arnold, Reginald William (EM07–09 dob 25.04.1895) East Surrey Regt., Lt. *[Also listed as 'R. Arnold']*.

Arnold, Thomas Wallis (EM13–15 dob 20.12.1899) O.C.W., R.A.F., Cdt.

Arter, Henry Charles (EM1900–08 dob 17.10.1888) Australian Contingent *[Also listed as 'C. Arter']*.

Ash, Douglas John (dob 27.03.1893) 7th London Regt.

Ashenden, Edward James (EM05–09 dob 27.01.1896) London University, O.T.C.

Ashenden, Frederick Roy (EM02–12 dob 29.09.1894) R.N.V.R., (Interned POW in Holland).

Atkin, A. D., Public Sch. Btn.

Atlee, H (dob 23.09.1889) 25th London Regt. (Cyclist Section) *[Also listed as 'H. Atlee']*.

Austin, Robert Charles Edwin (EM11–19 dob 31.01.1900) O.C.B.

Ayles, Edgar Owen William (EM12–13 dob 10.11.1898) R.F.C., 2nd Lt., *[Also listed as 'C. O. W. Ayles']*.

- B -

Bacon, Percy Eldnet (EM06–10 dob 22.05.1893) 15th London Regt. (Civil Service Rifles).

Baker, Charles Gordon, R.F.C., (Formerly Army Air Corps Mechanical Transport), 2nd Lt., *[Also listed as 'C. J. Baker']*.

Baker, F., R.A.M.C.

Baker, Irvin Jas (dob 26.02.1892) R.N.A.S (Armoured Car Section).

Baker, Joseph S. (dob 30.06.1881) R.A.M.C. *[Also listed as 'J. Baker']*.

Baker, Philip Graham (dob 21.12.1889) Yeomanry (Wounded).

Baker, Victor Friend (dob 02.12.1896) R.A.M.C. *[Also listed as 'V. Baker' & 'U. F. Baker']*.

Balchin, Spencer James Harold (EM09–15 dob 24.12.1895) R.N.A.S., (Invalided out).

Balder, S., 21st London Regt. (1st Surrey Rifles).

Ballantyne, John Douglas (EM09–13 dob 17.02.1899) 25th London Regt. (Cyclist Section). Bedford Regt.

Banks, Harold Edward (dob 29.01.1885) R.E., Motor Despatch Carrier *[Also listed as 'H. C. Banks']*.

Banting, George Gaywood (EM09–15 dob 25.02.1898 dod 27.12.1973) Sandhurst, R.F.C., R.A.F., Capt.

Barber, Harry Mason (EM07–09 dob 08.04.1894 dod 08.08.18) East Surrey Regt., London Regt., 2nd Lt. *[Also listed as 'H. A. Barber']*. ✤

Barker, Laurence (dob 29.05.1889) Canadian Contingent.

Barnard, John Hobbs Furlong (EM09–12) 19th Royal Fusiliers, (Formerly Officers' Cdt Btn., R.W. Surrey Regt). 2nd Lt. *[Also listed as 'J. N. F. Barnard']*, (Wounded).

Barnet, Leonard Edward (EM15–16 dob 08.07.1900) R.N.A.S., Prob. F./O. *[Also listed as 'L. F. Barnet']*.

Barton, Percy William (EM07–11 dob 11.09.1895) R.F.A. *[Also listed as 'P. Barton']*.

Bartram, Cyril Goodwin (EM08–13 dob 19.12.1896) 10th South Staffordshire Regt., 2nd Lt.

Bastable, Francis John Norman (EM10–11 dob 24.05.1897) Royal Fusiliers, 2nd Lt. *[Also listed as 'F. J. Bastable']*, (Wounded).

Bate, Philip James (dob 03.05.1893) R.G.A., Lt.

Bates, Jessie Frank (EM10–15 dob 15.09.1898) R.A.F., London Regt. 2nd Lt.

Batstone, Donald Keith (EM1900–07 dob 07.12.1891) R.N.V.R. (Interned POW in Holland) *[Also listed as 'D. Bastable']*.

Batstone, F., 15th London Regt. (Civil Service Rifles).

Beadle, F., Regiment and rank unknown. ✤

Beard, Edmund Roland (EM16–18 dob 10.01.1902) Regiment and rank unknown.

Beard, Laurence George (EM10–15 dob 17.08.1899) H.A.C.

Beath, Kenneth Cameron (EM05–09 dob 08.11.1892) 2nd Dorset Regt.

Beaumont, Victor Charles (EM12–13 dob 19.04.1899) Regiment and rank unknown.

Beesley, G. F. (EM08–10 dob 03.01.1896) Canadian Contingent (Mounted) *[Also listed as 'G. Beesley']*.

Belden, Sidney (dob 15.11.1893) 21st London Regt., (1st Surrey Rifles). *[Also listed as 'S. Belder']*.

Bennett, Douglas George (EM03–08 dob 29.02.1894) K.R.R.C., (Formerly H.A.C.). 2nd Lt.

Bent, A. R. (EM07–12 dob 22.09.1895) A.S.C., R.A.M.C. *[Also listed as 'R. A. Bent']*.

Bernard, George Robert (dod 08.04.17) R.E., 2nd Lt. ✤

Best, Frank Percival (EM08–11 dob 06.01.1894) Royal Fusiliers., (Wounded & invalided out). *[Also listed as 'F. Best']*.

Bignall, Gerald Francis (dob 1885) Colour Sgt. *[Also listed as 'C. F. Bignall']*.

Bilcliffe, Edward Jocelyn (EM06–12 dob 13.05.1894) R.N.V.R. Surgeon.

Bing, Colin Wallis (EM12–16 dob 01.12.1898) R.F.C.

Bird, Augustus Wieland (EM06–14 dob 17.05.1897) 11th East Surrey Regt. (formerly H.A.C). R.F.C. Flying Officer, (Reported wounded & missing). Awarded D.S.O., & Italian Decoration. Capt.

Bishop, Charles Frederick (dod 04.04.18) Royal Fusiliers, 2nd Lt. ✤

Blackman, G. F. W. (EM c1895 dob 15.03.1881) L./Cpl., *[Also listed as both 'G. Blackman' and 'G. F. H. Blackman']*.

Blackmore, Vivian Charles (EM11–15 dob 01.08.1898.) Inns of Court, O.T.C., Dorset Regt., att. R.F.C., 2nd Lt.

Blogg, Ronald James (dob 1885) 16th London Regt, 2nd Lt. *[Also listed as 'R. G. Blogg']*.

Board, George William (EM10–12 dob 27.09.1897) 4th East Surrey Regt., 2nd Lt.

Bodle, Clifford Raymond (EM07–09 dob 24.05.1891 dod 07.09.16) 16th London Regt., (Queen's Westminsters). Rifleman. ✤

Bone, Frederick William (EM10–17 dob 12.12.1901) R.F.C., R.A.F.

Boorne, William Henry (EM11–17 dob 24.11.1899) R.N.A.S., P.F.O., R.A.F.

Booth, Harold Frank William (EM03–11 dob 16.08.1894) R.F.C. (1st Class Air Mechanic).

Borders, Frederick Wight (dob 15.11.1897) A.S.C., (Motor Transport).

Bosher, Albert Henry (EM04–08 dob 26.08.1892) 16th London Regt., (Queen's Westminsters) East Surrey Regt. and R.A.F. (Wounded).

Botting, Arnold John (EM11–16 dob 20.03.1900) London Regt., Artists' Rifles., Scottish Engineers.

Botting, George Alfred (dob 20.12.1898) 16th London Regt. (Queen's Westminsters) (Wounded & Invalided out).

Bourne, Frank Woodhouse (EM14–15 dob 17.09.1899) Royal Sussex Regt.

✤ = *Killed or died of wounds*

Bowell, William Arthur (EM09–14 dob 28.12.1897) R.F.C., R.F.A.

Bower, Anthony (EM08–12 dob 31.01.1897) Australian Engineers/Contingent (Sapper). Q.M. Sgt. *[Also listed as 'A. Bowyer']*.

Bowes, Stanley Ward (dod 29.09.15) 3rd Dorset Regt., 2nd Lt. ✤

Bowles, Christopher James (dob 1887) A.S.C.

Bradford, Frederick Clement Arthur (EM10–13 dob 16.01.1899) A.S.C.

Bradly, Joseph Dunstan (EM11–14 dob 19.04.1898) Suffolk Regt., att. R.F.C., 2nd Lt., (Formerly The Buffs., 5th East Kent Regt). Awarded Croix de Guerre, Belgian Order of Leopold. *[Also listed as 'Bradey']*. (Wounded).

Brain, Henry Alfred (EM11–17 dob 26.08.1898) O.C.B., O.C.T.U.

Branch, Alec John (dob 26.04.1889) Canadian Engineers *[Also listed as 'Brunch']*.

Braund, Edward Percy (EM10–15 dob 06.03.1899) London Regt., L./Cpl., 18th London Regt. The Queen's Royal West Surrey. Cpl. (London Irish) *[Also listed as 'E. B. Braund']*.

Bray, R.F.A.

Bray, Charles Henry (dob 1886) R.C.H.A., Capt. (Invalided from France).

Brewster, Robert William (EM10–16 dob 28.10.1898) London Regt.

Brinkler, Charles Henry (EM10–12 dob 29.06.1896) London Regt., Sgt.

Brinkler, Edward Hamilton (EM11–12 dob 14.07.1897) Argyll and Sutherland Highlanders, 2nd Lt.

Brinkler, W. D. (EM10–11 dob 08.05.1895) Cycle Corps., London Regt., L./Cpl. *[Probably 'William Pennant Brinkler']*.

Broadbridge, George Alan (dob 22.05.1899) R.A.F., Cdt.

Brooks, H., City (3rd County) of London Yeomanry. (Invalided out).

Brooks, Percy Mathison (EM07–12 dob 12.08.1895) 1st North Staffordshire Regt., 2nd Lt. (Wounded) *[Noted as KILLED and appears on First World War Memorial. Died 1945]*.

Brooks, Sydney George Alvercy (EM1900–09 dob 04.01.1893) 14th Middlesex Regt., 2nd Lt.

Broome, Harold William (EM08–13 dob 07.06.1897) London Regt., (Wounded).

Brown, Oscar Whitclock (dob 1889) Australian Contingent (Wounded).

Brown, Robert, Royal West Kent Regt., Awarded M.C. and Bar M.S.M. 2nd Lt. (Acting Captain and Acting Major) [Also listed as *'R. R. Brown']*.

Brown, Stanley George (EM09–14 dob 31.10.1897) 16th London Regt., (Queen's Westminsters).

Brown, Thomas Finch (EM07–12 dob 09.03.1896 dod 1983) H.A.C.

Brumfitt, Gilbert (EM08–12 dob 08.06.1898) Indian Police (Mounted).

Buck, Harold Arthur (EM10–14 dob 08.03.1899) London Regt.

Buckley, Clarence Wilbraham (EM09–13 dob 04.06.1896) 5th Royal Fusiliers, 2nd Lt.

Budd, John Ernest (EM10–15 dob 11.03.1896) R.G.A., 2nd Lt. *[Also listed as 'J. E. C. Budd']*.

Bullivant, Roland Walter (dob 21.08.1895 dod 01.05.17) Somerset Light Infantry., 2nd Lt. (Wounded) ✤

Burford, Gerald George (EM09–14 dob 22.08.1898) London Regt., M.G.C.

Burns, John Edgar (dob 16.08.1895) R.G.A., Bdr., *[Also listed as 'J. Burn' and 'E. Burns']*.

Burns, Robert (dob 22.04.1887 dod 01.12.17) London Regt. London Scottish. *[also listed as 'R. Burn']*. ✤

Butler, R.N.A.S., Sub./Lt *[Possibly 'Albert Edward' but impossible to verify]*.

- C -

Cahill, Albert Edward (dob 10.05.1887 dod 10.10.17) M.G.C. Pte. ✤

Cairns, William Harding (dod 01.07.16) (Public Sch. Btn.). Middlesex Regt, Sgt. ✤

Calder, F. W., R.G.A.

Calder, William John Percy (EM11–15 dob 16.07.1900) R.M.L.S., L./Cpl.

Callingham, Leslie George (dob 1888) R.F.C., Lt., Chevalier Legion d'Honneur.

Camm, George Frederick (EM07–13 dob 05.01.1895) 21st London Regt., (1st Surrey Rifles). Capt., (Wounded then invalided from France).

Cannon, Arthur Leslie (dob 24.12.1891) 14th London Regt. (London Scottish). Lt.

Capps, Frederick William (dob 09.06.1893) 13th London Regt., (Princess Louise's Own Kensington). Lt.

Carson, John Harold (EM10–14 dob 28.02.1897) 8th King's Shropshire Light Infantry, Lt. (Invalided from Salonika).

Carter, Charles Cecil (EM11–16 dob 31.05.1900) R.A.F., R.N.A.S.

Cartwright, George Herbert (EM06–10 dob 11.07.1893) 2nd Canadian Contingent.

Cass, Ernest Walter John (EM09–14 dob 14.07.1898) 4th East Surrey Regt., 2nd Lt.

Cassie, Guy (EM02–08) (dob 26.06.1892 dod 12.08.1960) Argyll and Sutherland Highlanders, Lt.

Cassie, Leith (dob 21.01.1890 dod 11.12.17) 14th London Regt. (London Scottish) later Argyll & Sutherland Highlanders. (Wounded) ✤

Caswell, Thomas (EM09–13 dob 24.10.1897 dod 02.01.17) Middlesex Regt., Lance Cpl. ✤

Cawte, Reginald George (EM09–13 dob 18.11.1897) R.E. (Field Coy). Cpl.

Chamberlain, Cyril John (EM08–11 dob 28.12.1892 dod 07.10.17) Rifle Brigade, 2nd Lt. (Wounded) ✤

Chamberlain, Reginald Arthur (EM08–11 dob 24.12.1894) 21st London Regt. (1st Surrey Rifles).

Chambers, William George Emanuel (EM06–08 dob 09.06.1894) A.S.C. (Motor Transport). *[Also listed as 'W. G. Chambers']*.

Chandler, Arthur Ernest (EM09–15 dob 18.08.1899 dod 27.04.18) London Regt., Rifleman. ✤

Chaplin, Charles Arthur (EM1900– dob 22.06.1889) R.F.A., (Formerly 5th London Regt, London Rifle Brigade). (Wounded at Ypres).

Chapman, Leslie E. G. (EM11–15 dob 05.07.1900) 16th London Regt., (Queen's Westminsters) *[Also listed as 'L. Chapman']*.

Charles, William George (EM04–08 dob 10.10.1889 dod 27.04.15) 5th London Regt., (London Rifle Brigade) Rifleman. ✤

Charlton, Leslie William J. (EM11–16 dob 19.09.1899.) London Regt. *[Also listed as 'L. W. Charlton']*.

Chester, Walter E. T. (dob 1885) Royal Fusiliers, Awarded D.C.M.

Chewter, C. H. Valentine, 12th Royal Warwickshire Regt., 2nd Lt. (Formerly 21st London Regt). (Wounded, invalided from France).

Chittock, Charles Henry (dob 04.06.1888 dod 27.11.17). London Regt., Prince of Wales's Own Civil Service Rifles, Pte. ✤

Christie, Cecil Murray (dob 30.01.1895) R.F.A.

Chown, John Emery James (dob 20.10.1884) A.S.C., Staff Officer, Lt. *[Also listed as 'J. F. J. Chown']*.

Chuter, John William 'Jack' (EM11–15 dod 09.06.17) Prob. Flight Sub./Lt., R.N., R.N.A.S., Lt. ✤

Clamp, Charles Gordon (EM11–16 dob 25.08.1899) R.N.A.S.

Clarke, Seaforth St. John (EM13–14 dob 13.09.1898 dod 26.03.18) Seaforth Highlanders, Pte. ✤

Clarke, S. (EM10–11) R.A.M.C. *[Presumed to be 'Sidney William Henry Clarke' dob 24.07.1895]*

Clarke, S., R.N., (Wounded).

Clarke, Walter Norman Parry (EM08–13 dob 29.09.1896) 19th London Regt., (St. Pancras Rifles). Cpl.

Clegg, Percival Douglas (EM11–12 dob 27.05.1895) A.S.C., R.N.A.S.

Clement, Frank (dob 1884) 18th London Regt. (London Irish). Lt.

Clement, Herbert (dob 1888) Royal Warwickshire Regt., Lt.

Clements, William George (EM06–10 dob 30.01.1895) Oxford & Bucks Light Infantry.

Cleeve, Stewart Montagu (dob 20.10.1894 dod 05.01.1993) Music Staff, R.G.A., Lt.

Clinton, Leslie Stuart (EM06–12 dob 03.04.1896 dod 1974) 20th Hussars, (Formerly 23rd London Regt). Awarded M.C., (Wounded twice). Lt.

Coates, Charles (EM04–11 dob 23.10.1894) King Edward's Horse, Yeomanry.

Coates, Walter John (EM10–15 dob 07.09.1893) London Regt.

Codd, Percy John (EM05–08 dob 07.09.1893) R.N., Armoured Car Division, Petty Officer.

Coen, Charles Malcolm (EM11–14 dob 09.08.1895) R.N.V.R. (Invalided out).

Cohen, Arthur B. (EM11–15 dob 25.11.1898) Regiment and rank unknown.

Cohen, Jules Issac (EM10–17 dob 03.08.1898) O.C.U., R.E., 2nd Lt. *[Also listed as 'I. J. Cohen']*.

Cole, Alec Richard (EM07–12 dob 22.10.1895) R.N.A.S.

Cole, George Parnall (EM09–14 dob 26.04.1899) K.O.Y.L.I.

Coles, Bernard (dob 29.08.1895) R.N.R.

Coles, R. St. J., R.E., Lt.

Coles, Stanley (dob 1886) 5th Norfolk Regt., 2nd Lt.

Colgrave, H., London Scottish., Lt.

Collen, Arthur Roland (EM04–12 dob 29.10.1894) R.M.A., att. R.N.A.S., Capt.

Collins, Albert Edward (EM11–12 dob 09.12.1897 dod 21.07.17) R.G.A., Cpl. ✤

Collman, Albert George (dod 10.04.17) Royal West Kent Regt., (Queen's Own). Pte. ✤

Connew, Percy Alexander (EM1889–91 dob 1876 dod 01.12.15) Canadian Contingent. Cpl. ✤

Connor, Rowland W. L. (dob 1883) Army Chaplain Depot, Capt.

Cook, E. M. (EM13–15 dob 13.07.1899) O.C.W.

Cook, Francis George (dob 1891) Manchester Regt., 2nd Lt. *[Also listed as 'F. Cook']*.

Cook, Leslie Amyas (EM09–12 dob 28.04.1897 dod 14.09.17) R.F.A., Gnr. (Wounded) ✤

Cooke-Yarborough, Wilfrid Ernest (dob 1887) Royal Monmouth R.E., 2nd Lt.

Coombs, Gilbert Frank (EM07–12 dob 09.07.1896) Royal Fusiliers.

Cooper, J. F. London Scottish., Sgt.

Corfe, Walter George Frederick (EM06–12 dob 15.12.1893) 3rd Rifle Brigade. 5th Btn. London Regt., (L.R.B.) *[Also listed as both 'W. F. Corfe' and 'W. J. Corfe']*.

Couzens, Cecil Clarke, P & O Mantua (Transport R.N.R.). Asst. Paymaster.

Couzens, Edward Gordon (dob 1887) Northumberland Fusiliers., R.E., 2nd Lt.

Couzens, Reginald Churchill (EM06–08 dob 27.08.1899) R.A.M.C.

Cowling, Harold Edward (EM06–08 dob 15.05.1893) Northumberland Fusiliers, 2nd Lt. *[Also listed as 'H. F. Cowling – 18th Royal Fusiliers and also presumed to be 'Cowling, – Public Sch. Corps']*.

Cowper, Walter Murray (EM09–14 dob 30.11.1899) R.N.A.S., Sub./Lt. *[Also listed only as 'Cowper']*.

Cox, Walter Reginald (EM14–15 dob 27.12.1897 dod 1974) O.C.B., K.O.Y.L.I., 2nd Lt. *[Also listed as 'R. W. Cox']*.

Coxen, Edward John Uniacles (dob 02.11.1889) Egyptian Army, Lt. *[Also listed as 'E. A. U. Coxen']*.

Crampton, Edwin J. (dob 1886) 9th Middlesex Regt.

Cranfield, Wilfred Thomas (EM09–15 dob 01.06.1899) T. R. B., *[Also listed as 'W. T. H. Cranfield']*.

Cresswell, P. T. – R.N.V.R., Sub./Lt.

Crockford, Lewis Charles (dob 1888) R.F.A. *[Also listed as 'L. Crockford']*.

Croft, Charles Leighton (EM12–14 dob 14.07.1897) A.S.C. (Later discharged).

Crook, Harry Arthur George (EM 1900–07 dob 12.06.1891) R.N. (Motor Boat Patrol). *[Also listed as 'H. Crook]*.

Crossle, Frederick (EM08–10) (dob 10.01.1895 dod 27.10.18). Died of influenza. Pte.

Curram, William Edmund (dob 20.05.1894) Somerset Light Infantry.

- D -

Dakin, E. H., 5th London Regt. (London Rifle Brigade). Lt. (Wounded). *(Also listed as 'E. A. Dakin']*.

Dallas, Edward Bernard (EM13–16 dob 20.11.1899) R.A.F., (Wounded). *[Also listed as 'C. B. Dallas']*.

Damen, William Thomas (dob 16.10.1896 dod 12.06.15) 23rd Btn. London Regt. Pte. *[Also listed as 'W. C. Damen']*. Pte. ✤

Dancer, Alfred Christopher (EM07–11 dob 23.02.1893 dod 04.10.17) 8th Royal Fusiliers, 2nd Lt. Dorset Regt., Capt. Awarded M.C. ✤

Dancey, Leslie John (EM13–14 dob 10.04.1898) 24th London Regt.

Dare, George D. (EM06–09 dob 14.09.1892 dod 07.06.18) London Regt., 14th London. L/Cpl. ✤

Davidson, Charles Falconer (dob 21.12.1895 dod 09.01.16) R.F.A., Drv. ✤

Davidson, James Duncan (dob 26.09.1893) 14th King's Canadian Hussars., *[Also listed as 'J. Davidson']*.

Davidson, Ronald Hubert W. (dob 25.06.1891) 2/2nd Home Counties R.F.A., Lt.

Davies, Gwilym Morgan (EM04–09 dob 27.08.1892) 12th Royal Welsh Fusiliers, Lt.

Davis, Frederick Reginald (dob 12.03.1891) British Red Cross.

Davis, K., R.M.A. (Woolwich).

Davis, 16th Btn. The London Regt., (Queen's Westminsters).

Davis, Randall George Henry (EM09–10 dob 09.11.1894) 9th Royal West Kent Regt., 2nd Lt.

Deacon, 28th London Regt. (Artists' Rifles).

Delaforce, George (EM09–17 dob 15.06.1899) O.C.B., London Regt., Queen's Westminster Rifles, 2nd Lt.

Dell, Anthony W. (dob 1887) (Friends' Ambulance Unit)

Dell, Louis Michael (dob 1890 dod 14.07.16) K.S.L.I. 2nd Lt. ✤

Dell, Montague Roger (dob 1892) East Surrey Regt., Awarded M.C. 2nd Lt.

Denman, Frank Christopher (EM08–09 dob 28.05.1894 dod 17.08.17) R.F.A., Awarded M.C. 2nd Lt. (Wounded) ✤

Denvil, H. A., Middlesex Regt., (Wounded and invalided out).

Dequoy, Roger (dob 10.06.1893) 7th Cuirrassiers (French Army) *[Also listed as both 'Degnoi' and 'Deqnoi']*.

Dillon, Ralph Beresford Rupert (EM10–15 dob 01.01.1901) R.N., H.M.S. *Worcester*., Midshipman.

Dilnutt, Edwin John (EM08–09 dob 09.03.1895) 7th Bedfordshire Regt. (att. R.A.F.,). Lt. (POW).

Dilnutt, Eric William (EM08–12 dob 22.08.1896 dod 02.03.16) 14th Royal Fusiliers, Capt. ✤

Dixon, G., Canadian Contingent.

Dixon, Henry Benson (dob 1886) A.S.C.

Doland, Percy Douglas (EM09 dob 29.10.1897) East Surrey Regt. (Wounded) *[Also listed as 'P. Doland']*.

Dolby, Geoffrey Norman (dob 18.12.1895) 16th London Regt. (Queen's Westminsters) Awarded M.C., 2nd Lt.

Dougan, Frank Oliver (EM08–12 dob 20.07.1897) 18th London Regt., (London Irish).

Douglas, William Sholto (EM04–05 dob 23.12.1893 dod 29.10.1969) R.F.C., Lt-Col. Awarded D.F.C. and M.C.

Drew, L. J., R.A.F., 2nd Lt.

Duncan, Frank Montague (EM09–13 dob 06.11.1896) London Regt.

Durst, Thomas Alan (dob 25.11.1889) K.R.R.C., (Wounded). *[Also listed as 'T. Durst']*.

Dwyer, H.A.C.

Dyer, Henry Stephens (dob 1884) 3rd City of London Yeomanry, Sgt.

- E -

Earl, Sidney Edward (EM11–14 dob 08.12.1899 dod 14.10.18) London Regt. Pte. ✤

Edwards, P. R. G., R.F.A.

Edwards, William (dob 1889) London Regt., 2nd Lt. (Wounded).

Elder, William Gardner (Staff 11–15 dob 17.11.1889 dod 10.02.18) 20th London Regt., Lt. (Acting Capt.) (Invalided from Palestine). *[Also listed as 'W. E. Elder']*. ✤

Eley, William Douglas (EM1896 dob 22.05.1883 dod 10.10.16). K.R.R.C., *[Also listed as 'W. Ealey']*. ✤

Elliott, B. L., London Rifle Brigade, 2nd Lt.

Ellis, London Regt.

Ellis, Thomas Henry (EM1910 dob 23.02.1897) 8th Loyal North Lancashire Regt., 2nd Lt., London Scottish (Wounded).

Elliston, Leonard Henry (EM1910 dob 10.11.1900) R.A.F., Cdt. *[Also listed as 'L. H. Ellison']*

Elson, Arthur Bardsley (EM1911 dob 22.11.1897) A.S.C. (Motor Transport). Tank Corps, 2nd Lt. (invalided home).

Entwistle, Thomas (EM08–13 dob 21.12.1896) 16th London Regt., (Queen's Westminsters) Tank Corps., (Wounded) 2nd Lt. Awarded M.C. *[Also listed as 'I. Entwistle']*.

Evans, Hubert William (EM11–13 dob 23.11.1897 dod 24.05.17) Officers' Cadet Btn., The Buffs (The East Kent Regt., 2nd Lt., *[Also listed as 'N. W. Evans']*. (Died of wounds). ✤

Everest, Ernest Arthur (EM11–13 dob 27.05.1899) T.R.B.

Ewington, Gilbert Oswald (dob 1885 dod 01.07.16) London Regt., Rifle Brigade. Rifleman ✤

Ewington, Lionel E., Yeomanry. *[Also listed as 'L. E. Eurington']*.

- F -

Fagan, Herbert Archer (EM 10–13 dob 14.03.1899) The Yorkshire Regt., 2nd Lt., Gurkhas., Lt., Awarded M.C. and Bar.

Fairweather, John Henry (EM12–13 dob 15.03.1898) H.A.C. *[Also listed as 'F. H. Fairweather']*.

Farmer, Alfred Henry (EM10–13 dob 23.05.1897) R.E., (Despatch Rider/Cyclist).

Farrar, Willie Brooks (EM07–09 dob 05.07.1898) Indian Army, 2nd Lt. *[Also listed as 'W. Farrer']*.

Fayer, H. A., R.N.A.S.

Feacey, Alan Stanley (EM09–14 dob 02.10.1897) 26th Royal Fusiliers (Bankers' Btn.) (Wounded) L./Cpl.

Fell, George Frederick (dod 08.01.17) Yeomanry. Pte. ✤

Ferrario, Henry (EM12–15 dob 13.03.1899). R.E.

Feurings, M., R.N.A.S.

Fewings, M., R.A.F.

Field, Reginald Thomas (EM05–12 dob 24.07.1896) 28th London Regt., (Artists' Rifles), 25th London Regt., (Cyclist Section). 2nd Lt.

Finch, Lawrence Henry (dob 15.08.1893) 23rd London Regt. *[Also listed as 'C. H. Finch']*.

Finch, Frank Victor (EM09–12 dob 19.07.1897) Middlesex Regt. *[Also listed as both 'F. V. T. Finch' & 'F. U. T. Finch')*.

Finch, Bernard Thomas (dob 1886) 23rd Btn., London Regt., (Missing). *[Also listed as 'T. Finch']*.

Finch, William Delph (EM11–14 dob 15.01.1899), London Regt., R.N., Paymaster's Clerk.

Fisher, Douglas George (EM10–12 dob 28.11.1896) 13th London Regt., (Princess Louise's Own Kensington) (Invalided from France).

Fisher, Edmund 'Eddie' (EM08–15 dob 27.05.1899 dod 16.11.16) 3rd East Lancashire Regt., 2nd Lt. ✤

Fisher, Edward Henry (dod 09.04.18) King Edward's Horse. 2nd Lt. ✤

Fletcher, Arthur (EM02–08 dob 21.06.1892) A.S.C.M.T.

Fletcher, Frederick James (dob 1883) 9th London Regt., (Queen Victoria Rifles). *[Also listed as 'F. G. Fletcher']*.

Fletcher, Harry Mason (EM07–12 dob 21.05.1896) 18th London Regt., (London Irish) (Wounded) *[Also listed as 'R. M. Fletcher']*.

Fletcher, Richard (EM05–10 dob 07.02.1895) 18th Northumberland Fusiliers, att. R.F.C., 2nd Lt.

Flint, Charles Edward (dob 1887) H.A.C. Bdr. *[Also listed as 'C. Flint']*.

Ford, Ernest Leonard (dob 23.05.1889) R.F.C. *[Also listed as 'E. Ford']*.

Ford, S., R.N.A.S., Sub./Lt.

Fortune, Clifford Dudley (EM10–16 dob 31.05.1900) Gordon Highlanders.

Fowler, Cyril William (dod 26.05.15) London Regt., Pte. ✤

Fox, Donald Leslie R. (EM11–12 dob 04.05.1897) 9th Royal West Surrey Regt., (Queen's). Cpl.

Foxley, Frederick (EM10–14 dob 23.07.1897) London Rifle Brigade, London Regt., (Wounded & invalided out/discharged). *[Also listed as 'F. Forley' & 'H. Foxley']*.

Fricker, Thomas Mastern (EM 1906–09 dod 13.04.17) Royal Fusiliers, Pte. ✤

Frith, Alfred Walter (dob 17.02.1895) 23rd London Regt.

Frost, Harold Owen (dob 1889) Royal West Surrey Regt., 2nd Lt.

Fry, Henry Thomas (EM10–14 dob 09.12.1898) R.F.C.

Fry, L. E. (EM11–16 dob 09.09.1899) London Regt.

Fuller, William George (EM07–12 dob 30.12.1895) Yeomanry (Wounded & invalided out).

Furlong, Dennis Walter (EM08–13 dob 08.07.1897 dod 05.09.1940) 1st Royal Berkshire Regt., (formerly Royal Military College, Sandhurst). Awarded O.B.E. and M.C. [KILLED in Second World War].

- G -

Gabb, Richard George (EM05–09 dob 02.04.1894 dod 06.08.15) 12th East Regt., Essex Regt., 2nd Lt. ✤

Gabb, William John (EM04–11 dob 08.08.1894) Surrey Yeomanry.

Garrow, A., R.F.A.

Gauntlett, C. E. (EM11–16 dob 01.08.1899) London Regt.

Gay, Christopher Frederick (dob 1883) Provisional Btn.

Gearing, Alexander Desmond (EM11–15 dob 20.05.1901) Royal Fusiliers (Sportsman's Btn., Bugler) (Wounded & invalided out).

Gearing, Harold James (EM10–15 dob 08.05.1898) 4th Highland Light Infantry, att. R.F.C., 2nd Lt. and F./O. (Wounded).

Genner, Leopold John Ellacott (EM09–12 dob 24.08.1897) 18th Northumberland Fusiliers, 2nd Lt.

George, Edgar James (dod 07.09.16) 14th London Regt., (London Scottish). *[Also listed as 'E. George']*. Pte. ✤

German, J. (dob 1887) Welsh Regt., Inns of Court O.T.C., 2nd Lt.

German, Oscar Ernest (EM1897–07 dob 21.09.1890) Westminster House, Yeomanry, 2nd Lt.

Gilbert, G. William (Dob 1884) Rough Riders.

Gilbert, Humphrey Frank (EM12–18 dob 23.09.1899) O.C.B., London Regt., 2nd Lt.

Gilbert, L. G., 23rd London Regt.

Gilbert, Roland Stredwick (EM10–15 dob 03.12.1898) R.F.C., 2nd Lt., (POW) [Shot down 11.10.17 . and Mentioned in Despatches].

Gilder, Frank William (EM09 dob 05.02.1898) K.R.R.C.

Giles, Charles Wilfrid [Scott] (EM02–11 dob 24.10.1893 dod 06.02.1982) A.S.C.

Gillett, Peter George (EM12–15 dob 14.07.1898) Royal Scots Dragoon Guards., 2nd Lt. (Formerly Sandhurst).

Gilson, C., 23rd Btn. London Regt.

Gilson, Leslie Thompson (EM10–13 dob 22.03.1897) 23rd London Regt.

Gilson, William T. (EM10–12 dob 09.09.1895) R.F.C., 23rd London Regt.

Glinden, Arthur Richard (dob 18.03.1888) *[Also listed as 'A. Glindon']*.

Glinden, Percy Leslie (dob 26.05.1890) New Zealand Contingent. *[Also listed as 'P Glinden']*.

Glover, Alfred Kendall (dob 1881) A.S.C.

Glover, A. J., 23rd Btn. London Regt.

Glover, Frank Percy Joseph (EM10–15 dob 02.10.1898) 4th East Surrey Regt., Awarded M.C. and Bar. Lt. *[Also listed as 'F P G Glover']*.

Glover, Harry Charles Edwin (dob 1889) R.A.M.C.

Glover, Ronald Everett (EM11–15 dob 25.12.1897) Hussars., (POW).

Goddard, Reginald Stuart (dob 1890) R.N.A.S., Lt.

Godfrey, Harold Charles (EM07–12 dob 04.12.1895) R.F.C., (Formerly 22nd London Regt). (Invalided from France).

Godfrey, William Frank (EM09–14 dob 07.07.1896 dod 03.09.16) 4th North Staffordshire Regt. (The Prince of Wales's) 2nd Lt. ✤

Godwin, Carl (EM1900 dob 18.07.1887) 7th K.R.R.C.

Goodall, Arthur (EM06–11 dob 07.10.1894 dod 20.02.18) 5th Royal West Kent Regt., London Regt., 2nd Lt. (Died of wounds) ✤

Gosling, George Walker (EM10–13 dob 10.10.1898) R.N.V.R. [*Also listed as 'Gosling'*].

Graham, Henry Ernest (EM07–10 dob 24.01.1896) R.E., 1st London Divisional Signal Coy.

Graham, Edward Alfred Osborne (dob 1885) C.A.W.C.

Grattidge, John Edwin (dob 07.10.1901 dod 08.12.18) Mercantile Marine. Apprentice. ✤

Gray, Clarence (EM08–12 dob 05.09.1896) Royal Berkshire Regt. (Wounded).

Greaves, C. C. H. (EM11–13 dob 09.01.1898) Lincs. Regt., 65th Provisional Btn., 2nd Lt.

Greaves, Donald Worrall (dob 1889) R.G.A., 2nd Lt.

Greaves, Vernon Edward Worrall (EM03–09 dob 05.08.1892) R.F.C., Lt., (Formerly 6th West Riding Regt, Duke of Wellington's). (Wounded).

Green, Edgar (dod 10.10.18) Australian Infantry, A.I.F. Pte. (POW) ✤

Green, William Joseph (EM08–13 dob 08.07.1897 dod 08.09.17) 16th London Regt., (Queen's Westminsters) Queen Victoria's Rifles *[Also listed as 'W Green']*. Rifleman. ✤

Greenwood, Reginald Ernest (EM1912 dob 22.05.1898) R.A.F., R.N.A.S., P.F.O. 2nd Lt.

Greetham, William James (EM11–16 dob 14.09.1899). T.R.B., Middlesex Regt.

Griffiths, Hubert (dob 1884) Royal Sussex Regt., 2nd Lt.

Griffiths, Roland (EM1897–07 dob 11.05.1890) R.A.S.C., Lt. *[Also listed as 'R. J. Griffiths']*.

Grimes, Sydney Norton (EM05–08 dob 03.12.1893) *[Also listed as 'S. M. Grimes']*.

Grindley, George Lawrence (EM07–09 dob 27.03.1893) 9th London Regt., (Queen Victoria's Rifles) Cpl.

Grint, Alfred Langham (EM07–10 dob 14.10.1892) London University O.T.C. *[Also listed as 'A. S. Grint']*.

Grove-Price, A., R.N.R.

Grundy, Cecil Boyce (EM05–09 dob 23.03.1894 dod 16.11.15) Middlesex Regt., 2nd Lt. (Died of wounds). ✤

Grundy, Ronald Edwin (EM09–13 dob 06.06.1897 dod 01.07.16) Middlesex Regt., 2nd Lt. ✤

Guille, Sidney Arthur Harold (EM1911 dob 06.12.1899) O.C.B. *[Also listed as 'T. A.H. Guille']*.

Gurrey, Percival (Staff 21–26 dob 06.02.1890 dod 1980).

- H -

Hagues, Charles (dob 23.07.1894) New Zealand Contingent, Cpl., (Invalided from Gallipoli) *[Also listed as 'C. E. Haques']*.

Halford, Robert George (dob 05.06.1908) 2nd City of London Yeomanry (Rough Riders).

Hall, A., R.F.C. 2nd Lt.

Hall, Arthur Edwin (EM07–12 dob 08.01.1898) R.N.A.S., Flt. Sub./ Lt., R.A.F., Lt.

Hall, Leslie William Edward (EM06–13 dob 01.01.1897) 16th London Regt., (Queen's Westminsters).

Hall, William George (EM07–12 dob 13.07.1896 dod 1984) R.F.A., Bdr., 2nd Lt., Awarded M.C. and D.C.M.

Ham, G., Welsh Guards.

Hamilton, Lawrence G. (EM08–10 dob 20.10.1893) 7th Dorset Regt., 2nd Lt.

Hammett, Horace William (EM12–15 dob 12.10.1900) R.F.C., R.A.F.

Hammett, Harold Radmore (EM12–13 dob 16.06.1899) R.N.R.

Hancock, Walter Edward (EM08–12 dob 29.10.1897 dod 19.10.17). Duke of Cornwall's Light Infantry. L./Cpl. ✤

Hann, George Evelyn (EM10–15 dob 06.12.1899) London Regt., Welsh Guards., *[Also listed as 'G. Ham' and 'Hann, G. F.',* 16th London Regt., (Queen's Westminsters)*]*.

Hannam, G. N., R.N.A.S., R.G.A. Lt.

Harding, Frederick John (EM09–12 dob 14.08.1897 dod 22.09.17) East Surrey Regt., Lt. *[Also listed as 'F. G. Harding']*. ✤

Harding, Frederick Leonard (EM11–16 dob 05.03.1900) 16th Middlesex Regt., (Public Sch. Btn.)

Hardy, Harold Montague (dob 1890) The Buffs (The East Kent Regt).

Hardy, Richard Stanley (dob 1890) The Buffs (The East Kent Regt). *[Note – twin brother of above]*.

Hare, Sydney St. George (EM13–15 dob 11.04.1898) 3rd Bedfordshire Regt., Lt. (Wounded and invalided from France). *[Also listed as 'S. G. Hare']*.

Harrington, Frank (dob 1876) R.E. (89th Field Coy.). Lt.

Harris, H. J. (EM1883 dob 05.05.1875). *[Also listed as 'H. Harris']*.

Harris, Roland George (EM07–11 dob 09.01.1895) 16th London Regt., (Queen's Westminsters). Lincolnshire Regt., 2nd Lt.

Harris, Reginald Lewin (EM07–10 dob 07.11.1898) R.M.L.I. Lt.

Harris, William (EM09–11 dob 17.07.1895) Royal Fusiliers, 4th Cameron Highlanders. 2nd Lt.

Harrison, George Henry (EM08–11 dob 14.05.1897) 5th London Regt., (London Rifle Brigade).

Harvey, Cuthbert (EM07–13 dob 23.12.1897) R.F.C.

Harvey, Stanley Alfred George (EM02–11 dob 24.08.1893 dod 21.03.18) 9th Royal Berkshire Regt., Lt. (Wounded) ✤

Harwood, George (EM1900 dob 10.07.1886) Royal Fusiliers.

Hastings, William James (EM06–10 dob 17.09.1893) 14th Notts & Derby Regt., (Sherwood Foresters). Awarded M.C., 2nd Lt.

Hastings, W., 5th Btn. The London Regt., (L.R.B.).

Hatchard, Reginald Warren (EM07–11 dob 27.07.1895) Surrey Yeomanry.

Hawkins, Joseph (EM10–11 dob 18.05.1895) R.E., (Motor Cyclist).

Hawkins, R., Indian Contingent.

Hayes, Ernest James Thomas (EM06–11 dob 02.08.1896) M.G.C., 10th South Lancashire, Lt. (Wounded).

Hayes, Reginald (EM07–11 dob 06.11.1897 dod 22.07.17) 10th South Lancashire Regt., Lt., att. R.F.C., ✤

Heath, Douglas Alan (EM1899–07 dob 18.02.1891 dod 24.12.15) R.A.M.C. Staff Sgt. (Died of wounds). ✤

Heath, John (EM10–17 dob 06.07.1900) London University, O.T.C.

Hedgeland, R. J. T. (EM09–10 dob 08.11.1895) R.N., H.M.S. *Princess Royal* (Engine Room, Boy Artificer).

Heming, Jack Chetward Weston (EM10–16 dob 02.09.1899) R.N.A.S., Sub./Lt., R.F.C.

Henson, Leslie (EM1903–06 dob 03.08.1891 dod 03.12.1957) R.F.C. [Wartime entertainer with the Leslie Henson 'Gaieties.'].

Henwood, Hedley Ernest (EM05–08 dob 12.01.1895) Canadian Contingent, 54th Btn.

Hill, Charles (Staff 29–64 dob 01.07.1899 dod 11.11.1980) Bedfordshire Regt.

Hill, Francis James (EM09–14 dob 04.08.1897) East Surrey Regt.

Hill, John Rawortto (EM10–16 dob 04.02.1900) O.C.W., R.A.F., Lt.

Hillman, William Samuel (EM07–12 dob 18.03.1896 dod 23.03.18) Royal Fusiliers Pte. East Kent Regt., L./Cpl. ✤

Hills, Percy Bernard (EM09–16 dob 06.01.1898) A.S.C.

Hincks, Hubert Oswald (dob 1891) Canadian Contingent, (Wounded) Lt.

Hincks, Percy V. (EM11–18 dob 05.08.1899) O.C.B.

Hinson, D. S., London Wall Rifle Corps.

Hinson, Oliver Stoakley (EM09–12 dob 06.11.1897) H.A.C., Royal Sussex Regt., att. R.F.C. Lt.

Hinton, John William Melville (dob 17.06.1898) Army Veterinary Corps., Sgt.

Hirst, George Littlewood (dob 1890) Monmouthshire Regt.

Hodges, Newton James (EM10–15) London Regt., (POW).

Hodgson, Charles H. (dob 1883) A.S.C., Cpl. *[Also listed as 'Hodson' and 'C. Hodgson']*.

Holding, Cecil E. (dob 1882) R.N. (Invalided out).

Holdsworth, Charles F. (dob 1889) Canadian Contingent *[Also listed as 'C. E. Holdsworth']*. (Wounded).

Holgate, Herbert Cecil Frederick (EM10–15 dob 11.09.1898) 4th East Surrey Regt., att. K.R.R.C. (Wounded & invalided from the Mediterranean/ Salonika). Lt.

Hollands, Frederick Ronald (EM07–12 dob 19.08.1896) 28th London Regt., (Artists', Transport Section), 21st London Regt., (1st Surrey Rifles). 2nd Lt.

Hollands, G. C., R.N.V.R.

Holloway, Philip Edward (EM12–14 dob 25.10.1899 dod 28.08.18) London Regt. (Queen's Westminster Rifles) Rifleman. ✤

Holloway, Sidney George (EM12–14 dob 25.10.1899) London Regt. (Wounded). *[Also listed as 'T. G. Holloway']*.

Holley, Percy J., A.S.C. *[Also listed as 'Percy J. Holly']*.

Holmes, Charles Edward (EM05–11 dob 26.10.1885) R.E.

Holmes, S. W. (EM11–15 dob 10.12.1899) Artists' Rifles., O.C.B.

Holmes, William M. (EM10–11 dob 14.06.1895) Canadian Contingent, 27th Light Horse., Staff Sgt.

Holt, Ernest Edward (EM10–15 dob 15.02.1899) London Regt., L./Cpl.

Hopkins, Archibald Maurice (EM10–15 dob 30.08.1899) London Regt.

Hopkins, John Collier F. (EM12–16 dob 12.05.1898) H.A.C., R.F.C. 2nd Lt.

Hopwood, Gilbert Edmund (EM10–12 dob 10.11.1895) R.A.M.C.

Horswell, Bazil Whittle (EM07–13 dob 22.12.1896 dod 11.10.17) R.N.A.S, Sub./Lt., ✤

Howard, G., R.E., (Despatch Rider).

Howard, William George (EM07–09 dob 26.04.1893 dod 20.12.17) R.G.A., 2nd Lt. ✤

Howgill, Richard John Frederick (EM08–09 dob 21.04.1894) Northumberland Fusiliers, 2nd Lt., (Wounded). *[Also listed as 'R. Howgill']*.

Hoy, Colin (EM08–11 dob 02.11.1898) Regiment and rank unknown.

Hudson, Sidney Rowland (EM08–15 dob 15.06.1899) 5th Royal Fusiliers, 2nd Lt. (Wounded).

Hughes, Alwyn Kerfoot (EM12–13) 16th London Regt., (Queen's Westminsters) (Wounded and missing). (POW). *[Also listed as 'A. Hughes']*.

Hughes, Samuel Gethin (EM10–15 dob 09.08.1898 dod 1988) O.C.B., Yeomanry. *[Also listed as 'T. G. Hughes']*.

Hull, Thomas Arthur (EM10–14 dob 09.02.1899.) London Regt. *[Also listed as 'T. Hull']*

Humphries, R.N.A.S., R.A.F., Cdt.

Hunt, Harold Arthur (dob 1881 dod 03.06.15) Canadian Contingent, Sgt., Mentioned in Despatches, *[Also listed as 'A. A. Hunt']*. ✤

Hutsox, F., Regiment and rank unknown.

Hutson, F., Surrey Yeomanry.

- I -

Ilott, Harold Frederick (EM10–14 dob 15.09.1898) 9th London Regt., (Queen Victoria's Rifles).

Inglis, Brian (EM10–14 dob 28.01.1893) R.A.M.C.

Inkster, Lawrence (EM1900–06 dob 02.05.1891) 10th The Queen's (Royal West Surrey Regt), Lt. [Acting Captain] *[Incorrectly listed as KILLED in the Trinity Term Portcullis 1918 Pro Patria]*. (Wounded). Awarded M.C.

Ive, Sidney George Frederick (EM10–11 dob 09.08.1895 dod 27.04.18) 18th K.R.R.C., I.C.D., L./Cpl. *[Also listed as 'S. Ive']*. ✤

Ives, Alfred Ernest (EM07–12 dob 02.05.1896 dod 29.12.16) The Buffs (The East Kent Regt.) Pte. ✤

Ivy, Robert (EM1891–98 dob 1880 dod 1974) United States Medical Corps.

- J -

Jackson, Alfred Reginald (EM10–14 dob 22.09.1898) R.A.F., (Formerly O.C.W). Lt.

Jackson, Charles John (EM10–11 dob 09.08.1895) 14th London Regt., (London Scottish). R.A.F., 2nd Lt.

Jackson, George Frederick (EM06–10 dob 03.07.1894) Ross and Cromarty Battery (Highland) Mountain Brigade., R.G.A. Lt.

James, Arthur (dod 03.01.17) Yorkshire Regt., Lt. ✤

James, J. S., R.E., 2nd Lt.

Jeffries, Frederick Arthur (EM07–08 dob 20.11.1892) A.S.C. *[Also listed as Jeffries, F. H., Artists' Corps]*.

Jeffries, L. M., 28th London Regt., (Artists' Rifles). Cpl.

Jeffries, T. H., 28th London Regt., (Artists' Rifles).

Jeffries, Vincent Montague (EM1900–09 dob 06.05.1893) 16th London Regt., (Queen's Westminsters).

Jennings, Francis Henry Cuthbert (EM07–10 dob 03.12.1896) 10th Norfolk Regt., 2nd Lt.

Jennings, James Smith (EM07–13 dob 19.01.1897) Regiment and rank unknown.

Johnson, Evelyn Walter James (EM07–13 dob 09.04.1897 dod 20.07.16) 7th Bedfordshire Regt., (att. 19th). 2nd Lt. (Died of wounds). ✤

Johnson, Donald G. (EM09–10 dob 22.09.1892.) 23rd London Regt., Capt. (Wounded).

Jones, Edmund Colin, Hereford Regt., Sgt., (Formerly 15th Middlesex Regt). 2nd Lt.

Jones, John Sharpley (EM03–12) R.E., (1st London Coy), (1st London Divisional Engineers). Lt.

Jones, S. (dob 14.05.1895) R.E.

Joy, John Henry (EM1904 dob 31.05.1893) 10th Norfolk Regt., Lt.

Joyce, Esmund Lionel (EM12–17 dob 26.06.1899) London Regt.

Jubert, Maurice A. C. (EM1908 dob 01.03.1898) R.E. (Formerly 3rd Yorkshire Regt). Lt. (Wounded)

Justice, Herbert Maxwell (EM08–13 dob 22.06.1896) 28th London Regt., (Artists' Rifles), 21st London Regt., (First Surrey Rifles). 2nd Lt.

- K -

Kearney, Edward Marshall Sydney (EM10–15 dob 04.06.1899 dod 27.10.18) East Surrey Regt., R.A.F., 2nd Lt., *[Also listed as 'E. M. T. Hearney']*. ✤

Kearney, Norman Charles (EM04–07 dob 22.07.1891 dod 27.04.18) R.F.C. 2nd Lt., (formerly 10th East Surrey Regt, L./Cpl). *[Also listed as 'N. E. Hearney']*. (Wounded). ✤

Kearney, R. A. M., I.C.D., (Formerly Middlesex Regt). (Twice wounded). Staff Cpl.,

Kelly, D. C. (EM11–14 dob 03.10.1899) 10th Royal West Surrey Regt., (Queen's). Sgt.

Kennedy, R.A.F.

Kennedy, D., South African Contingent, K.R.R.C.

Kennedy, George Cyril (EM12–16 dob 02.09.1900) H.A.C., *[Also listed as 'G. E. Kennedy']*.

Kerridge, George Cecil (EM07–14 dob 29.06.1899) R.A.F.

Kerridge, Roy Sheldrake (EM11–16 dob 03.04.1903) H.M.S. *Worcester*. *[Also listed as 'R. T. Kerridge']*.

Kettley, Arthur George (dod 30.05.16) Australian Contingent, L./Cpl., ✤ (Killed at Hooge).

Kidman, H. J., 14th London Regt., (London Scottish).

Kimber, D., (Missing).

Kimber, Frederick William (EM07–12 dob 02.05.1896 dod 13.11.16) London Regt., (Missing). Pte. ✤

Kimpton, Thomas Douglas (EM07–12 dob 10.04.1896) 15th London Regt., (Civil Service Rifles). ✤

King, Dudley Bertram (EM09–12 dob 15.02.1895).

King, Francis Ferdinand (EM16–22 dob 01.08.1904) Yeomanry, Westminster Dragoons.

Kinck, B. J. H., (Wounded and missing 26.10.16).

Kinnear, Angus MacPherson (EM1901–04 dob 17.07.1893 dod 16.03.17) Mercantile Marine 3rd Engineer S.S. *Narragansett* (sunk by German submarine U–44) ✤

Kinnear, The Reverend J. C., M.A., Awarded M.C., Royal Army Chaplains Department, Lt–Col.

Klasen, C. B. (EM14–15 dob 27.02.1899) London Rifle Brigade.

Knight, Claude Charles A. (EM09–12 dob 14.10.1897) R.E.

Knight, Cecil Francis (EM10–13 dob 27.04.1898) (POW).

Knight, Percy James (EM1908–13 dob 24.10.1896 dod 1985) 11th Loyal North Lancashire Regt., Lt., later Capt.

Knock, Bernard John Henry (EM10–12 dob 10.06.1894) Royal West Surrey Regt., (Wounded and missing 26.10.17)

Knott, Alfred Stocken (EM08–11 dob 19.02.1898) 23rd London Regt., *[Also listed as 'A. Knott']*.

Knott, Percy Harry Rendell (EM08–10) R.E., Despatch Rider (Egypt). *[Also listed as 'P. Knott']*.

- L -

Lampden, Johnny, Regiment and rank unknown.

Lane, Frank Ashton (EM 07–12 dob 08.04.1896 dod 31.07.17) 17th Royal Fusiliers., 18th Btn. King's Liverpool Regt., 2nd Lt., *[Also listed as 'F. P. Lane']*. ✤

Langstaffe, Leonard William (EM07–09 dob 20.09.1892) 11th North Lancashire Regt, 2nd Lt., M.G.C., *[Also listed as 'W. L. Langstaffe']*.

Larcombe, John Norman (EM08–13 dob 20.04.1899) R.G.A.

Larkins, Douglas Molyneux (EM03–08 dob 29.01.1892) 14th West Yorkshire Regt., 2nd Lt.

Latham, John (EM07–09 dob 28.06.1892) Royal Welsh Fusiliers.

Leather, Arthur Sidney (EM09 21.01.1893) R.A.M.C.

Leather, James (EM09–10 dob 04.03.1894) Regiment and rank unknown.

Leather, Bernard (EM12–13 dob 03.12.1896) R.A.M.C., att. K.R.R.C.

Leader, Stanley (EM10–13 dob 23.04.1896) 14th London Regt., (London Scottish). (Formerly 3rd Btn). London Scottish. (Wounded).

Le Burn, Leonard Edwin (EM09–14 dob 29.09.1897) 9th London Regt., (Queen Victoria's Rifles). R.I.R., (Wounded twice).

Le Chavetois, Grantley Adolphe (Staff 1909–12 dob 14.09.1889 dod 22.01.18) No. 1 Officers' Cadet Btn., 22nd London Regt., Act. Capt. (Wounded). Awarded the M.C. ✤

Leech, Edgar James (EM11 dob 12.12.1895) 10th Lincolnshire Regt., 15th Btn., London Regt., (Civil Service Rifles). 2nd Lt.

Leech, George William R. J. (EM09–10 dob 13.06.1894) 5th Yorkshire Regt., 2nd Lt.,

Leeks, L. A. L., London Regt.

Lee, Ralph Langdon (EM12–14 dob 05.04.1903) Regiment and rank unknown. *[Also listed as 'R. Lee'].*

Lee, R. S. (EM11–13 dob 30.05.1896) 20th London Regt., (Formerly Inns of Court O.T.C.) 2nd Lt. *[Also listed as 'R. Lees'].*

Leete, A. J. (EM11–15 dob 10.07.1900) R.F.A. (Wounded). *[Also listed as 'A. J. Leeks'].*

Le Feuvre, Henry Albert (EM13–14 dob 16.12.1899) 4th Staffordshire Regt., att. R.A.F., R.N.A.S, Lt.

Lehrs, G. E., 7th London Regt.

Lenner, K. W. B., 17th Rifle Brigade.

Lewis, John Edward (EM11–16 dob 22.07.1899) Rifle Brigade, T.R.B.

Lewis, Max (EM07–10 dob 14.06.1894) 9th York & Lancaster Regt., Maj.

Lilley, William Galpin (EM09–11 dob 30.10.1896) 19th Notts & Derby Regt., (Sherwood Foresters) 2nd Lt. (Wounded).

Line, Charles Edward (EM04–09 dob 04.03.1893) Royal Sussex Regt., 2nd Lt.

Line, William Wesley (EM04–07 dob 22.05.1891) Royal Fusiliers, 2nd Lt. (POW).

Little, William Hash (EM08–10 dob 21.05.1894) Cyclists' Corps (Putney). *[Also listed as 'W. Little'].*

Loneon, Harold Neville (EM15–16 dob 11.11.1900) R.N., *[Also listed as 'Lonion'].*

Looker, William (EM12–16 dob 04.08.1900) London Rifle Brigade.

Lovelock, William (EM10–16 dob 13.03.1899 dod 26.06.1986) R.G.A.

Luckham, Harold (EM06–10 dob 17.05.1891) East Surrey Regt.

Lumb, John Reginald Bertram Bradley (EM1899–08 dob 27.03.1890) R.A.M.C., Lt., *[Also listed as 'J. R. Lumb'].*

Lumb, Norman Peace Lacy (EM1899–08 dob 26.07.1891) R.A.M.C., Capt.

Lund, S. W. – R.A.M.C., Capt., (Missing). *[Name added to First World War Memorial but later removed after discovery that Lund had survived the war].*

Luttnam, F., 15th London Regt., (Civil Service Rifles).

Lyons, John William (EM1910–13 dob 11.11.1898 dod 1978) K.R.R.C.

- M -

MacBeth, J. E., R.G.A., att. R.F.C., 2nd Lt.

Macbeth, Stanley (dod 15.09.16) 18th London Regt., (London Irish). Lt. ✤

Macey, Reginald George (EM11–14 dob 07.01.1900) Yeomanry.

MackAdam, H. J. (EM11–16 dob 02.12.1894) Royal Fusiliers, Sgt.

MackNess, Reginald Jas E. C. (EM11–16 dob 06.04.1900) Inns of Court O.T.C.

MacRae, D. W., Royal Scots, R.N.V.R. Sub./Lt.

MacRae, R. J., R.N., H.M.S. *Caesar*, Asst. Paymaster.

Male, Charles Edward (EM07–12 dob 29.08.1895) R.E.

Mallinson, P. R. – 14th London Regt., (London Scottish).

Malinson, P., R.F.C. (Wounded).

Mander, Reginald Percy (EM10–12 dob 02.05.1894) 16th Middlesex Regt., (Public Sch. Btn.). M.G.C., 2nd Lt. (Wounded).

Manser, J., Regiment and rank unknown.

Marie, Maurice (EM08–09 dob 08.03.1894). *[Also listed only as 'Marie'].*

Marle, French Army.

Marshall, R., R.N.

Marshall, S., Hussars, Lt.

Marthews, Leonard Gordon (EM10–14 dob 19.08.1898 dod 22.04.18) South Lancashire Regt., Lt. (Died of wounds whilst POW in Germany) ✤

Martin, Regiment and rank unknown.

Martin, Ernest Alfred (EM12–16 dob 13.10.1902) London Regt.

Martin, Leonard Jack (EM13–15 dob 09.06.03) R.N., H.M.S. *Worcester*.

Martindale, Hugh Barnes (EM1899 dob 18.01.1899) Easy Surrey Regt., Capt.

Mason, George (EM10–15 dob 18.02.1899 dod 15.04.18) North Staffordshire Regt., 2nd Lt. ✤

Maule, E. A., 10th Seaforth Highlanders, 2nd Lt.

Mayle, N. L. (EM11–14 dob 06.12.1898) R.A.F., 2nd Lt.

Mayrick, Leonard James (EM10–15 dob 06.12.1898) R.E. L./Cpl.

McIntosh, James Cook (EM11–15 dob 10.07.1900) Edinburgh University O.T.C.

McKnight Eric (EM10–11 dob 30.11.1896) 14th London Regt., L./Cpl. *[Also listed as 'E. A. McKnight'].*

McKnight, Norman (EM1910 dob 15.01.1894) London Regt.

McLellan, P., R.N.A.S., Sub./Lt.

McKellan, W., R.A.F., Lt.

McNish, Roland Leonard Hastings (EM1897–99 dob 16.05.1884) Mercantile Marine. Awarded the D.S.O. First Officer SS *Otaki* (POW).

Meacher, G., Middlesex Regt., Q.M. Sgt.

Meager, Frederick James (EM11–12 dob) R.A.F., *[Also listed as 'F. G. Meager and 'F. J. Meager'].*

Mellstrom, Godfrey C. (EM09–15 dob 18.12.1899) L.U.O.T.C.

Mellstrom, Stephen C. (EM09–17 dob 12.04.1901) L.U.O.T.C. *[Also listed as 'S. C. W. Mellstrom'].*

Mercer, W. H., 12th London Regt., (The Rangers).

Meredith, Charles Aubrey (EM13–15 dob 18.08.1898) R.A.F., 2nd Lt., 26th Royal Fusiliers, Sgt., *[Also listed as 'A. Meredith'].*

Middleton, Alfred Everit (dob 1890) 2nd London Regt., (Royal Fusiliers).

Milner, William (EM06–09 dob 28.04.1894) R.A.M.C.

Mitchell, 16th Btn. The London Regt., (Queen's Westminsters).

Mitchell, George Edward (EM03–08 dob 02.06.1894) R.G.A. 2nd Lt.

Mitchell, Henry Stanley (EM09–14 dob 29.09.1897) R.A.F., R.N.A.S. 2nd Lt., *[Also listed as 'H. T. Mitchell'].*

Moir, Roy Adamson (EM09–12 dob 18.03.1898) R.E.

Monk, F. S. M., R.N.A.S. *[Also listed as 'F. L. M. Monk'].*

Monk, Harry Ivor Montague (EM1906–10 dob 16.06.1898) R.N.A.S.

Monk, Roy Athol Montague (EM08–11 dob 28.06.1898) R.N.R. Midshipman.

Monson, Cyril Archibald (dod 18.05.15) Wiltshire Regt., R.F.A., 2nd Lt. ✤

Montford, Richard Clifford (dob 1886) M.G.C., 2nd Lt.

Moody, William George Musson (EM06–12 dob 10.10.1897) 21st & 25th London Regts. (1st Surrey Rifles) Cyclist., *[Also listed as 'W. G. T. Moody'].*

Moody, William Thomas Charles (EM10–14 dob 05.02.1897) Royal Welsh Fusiliers, 2nd Lt. (Wounded).

Moore, Albert Alexander (EM08–13 dob 15.11.1896 dod 02.06.16) Canadian Mounted Rifles. Pte. ✤ (Killed at Hooge).

Moore, Frederick Harry Bedloe (EM08–14 dob 26.05.1898 dod 04.11.18) London Regt. (Queen Victoria's Rifles) 2nd Lt., (formerly R.A.M.C.) ✤

Moore, John Robert (EM08–13 dob 10.07.1898) T.R.B., Cpl.

Moore, William Arthur (EM08–12 dob 22.02.1900) T.R.B., London Regt.

Morbey, Arthur Cecil (EM06–09 dob 10.04.1893) R.F.C.

Morbey, P. H., London Regt. (Wounded).

Morfey, Howard Lawton (EM12–17 dob 11.10.1900) R.N.R *[Also listed as H. L. Morbey' and 'H. T. Morfey'].*

Morfey, Ronald James (EM1900–07 dob 13.12.1900) Royal Fusiliers, 2nd Lt.

Morgan, William Howell (EM11–13 dob 12.12.1897) R.F.A., 2nd Lt., (Wounded).

Moseley, Herbert James Ritchie (EM1910 dob 07.08.1893 dod 27.06.16) Rifle Brigade, H.A.C., 2nd Lt. *[Also listed as 'J R Moseley' and 'H G Ritchie-Moseley'].* ✤

Mott, Edward James (EM10–16 dob 02.01.1899) R.F.C., R.A.F., Lt.

Mountain, Cyril Robert Wightman (EM06–10 dob 05.06.1896 dod 05.08.17) Cheshire Regt., Capt. ✤

Moxley, Douglas John (EM09–14 dob 07.04.1898) Royal Fusiliers, Cpl. (Invalided from France). *[Also listed as 'D. J. Morley'].*

Munden, John Arthur (EM08–13 dob 27.01.1897) K.R.R.C.

Munford, Robert John (EM09–14 dob 27.01.1898) Royal Fusiliers.

Mussett, William J. (dob 1886) A.S.C., Staff Sgt-Maj.

- N -

Nannam, G. N., R.N.A.S.

Narbeth, Charles Ansley (EM06–09 dob 03.06.1898) R.N.A.S.

Naylor, Ernest John (EM08–16 dob 20.06.1899) R.E., O.C.B., 2nd Lt.

Neale, Colin Francis (EM05–10) (dob 15.10.1895 dod 23.04.17) R.N.V.R., Sub./Lt., *[Also listed as 'C. F. Neal'].* ✤

Neal, Eric Donald (dob 1890) Canadian Contingent.

Neal, G., 16th Middlesex (Public Sch. Btn.)

Neal, Robert Gilbert (dob 08.11.1895) Officers' Cdt Btn., (Royal Fusiliers previous to O.C.B.).

Nerney, John Combes (dob 1890) R.N.A.S., Petty Officer.

Newman, Reginald James (EM06–09 dob 30.06.1892) 6th Btn. Essex Regt., Lt.

Newby, Edwin Valere (EM09–13 dob 09.05.1899) R.N.V.R., (Wounded at Ypres).

Newton, Kenneth Frederick Cecil (EM10–14 dob 01.07.1896 dod 24.04.17) Seaforth Highlanders, Cpl. ✤

Nichol, William Alexander (dob 1888 dod 23.06.17) Australian Contingent. Pte. ✤

Nichols, Alfred William (EM05–09) *[Also listed as 'A. W. Nicholls'].* A.S.C.

Nichols, Claude Aplin (EM1901–1902 dob 29.03.1891) 12th Australian Light Horse Regt., Sign'r., (Wounded).

Nichols, Douglas William Lane (EM1901–1902 dob 04.05.1892 dod 20.08.16) 8th Queen's (Royal West Surrey) Regt., Awarded M.C., Capt. ✤

Nichols, Frederick Joseph (EM07–12 dob 18.06.1896 dod 13.04.18) R.F.C. (Wireless Section) *[Also listed as 'F. Nichols'].* Air Mechanic 1st Class. ✤

Nichols, George William (EM02–09 dob 02.05.1892) R.E., (Despatch Rider). Cpl. *[Also listed as 'G. E. W. Nichols'].*

Nicholls, Hubert Frederick (EM10–13 dob 03.05.1896) Shropshire Light Infantry, att. 22nd Div. Cyclist Corps., Capt. *[Also listed as 'H. F. Nichols'].*

Nicholson, Henry Phillips (EM09–12 dob 09.09.1897 dod 22.08.16) 23rd London Regt. Drummer. ✤

Nicholson, R. J. (EM09–12 dob 07.06.1896) 5th London Regt., (London Rifle Brigade) (Invalided home from France).

Nix, Percy John (EM12–14 dob 27.08.1900) 23rd London Regt. (Invalided out).

Nixon, R. H. (EM09–14 dob 12.05.1898) London Regt. (Wounded).

Noel, Francis Radford (EM04–10 dob 27.03.1892 dod 08.05.18) Australian Contingent, L./Cpl. ✤

Noel, William Percival (EM04–09 dob 15.06.1891) R.E., Sgt., (Formerly R.F.A). Awarded M.M. (Mentioned in Despatches). L./Cpl.

Norris, Frank William (EM10–16 dob 25.05.1899) R.F.C., 2nd Lt.

North, Frederick William (EM07–08 dob 09.05.1894) British Red Cross. *[Also listed as 'F. North'].*

Nunn, E. G. F. (EM11–16 dob 06.11.1899) London Regt. *[Also listed as 'E. G. Nunn'].*

- O -

Ollis, Lawrence Redver (EM14–18 dob 11.10.1899) O.C.B. *[His brother 'A. E. Ollis' appeared on various Pro Patrias, but he wasn't an OE].*

Orchard, Henry 'Harry' (dod 26.09.16) Canadian Contingent., Pte. ✤

Orcheston, Alec Barford (EM09–12 dob 21.11.1897) Middlesex Regt., Royal West Kent Regt. *[Also listed as 'A. B. Orcharton'].*

- P -

Page, Yeomanry.

Page, Percy George (EM09–15 dob 13.10.1897) R.G.A., 2nd Lt., Cpl.

Painter, Edmund John (EM10–11 dob 20.10.1895) 14th London Regt., (London Scottish) (Wounded & invalided out). *[Also listed as 'C. J. Painter'].*

Painter, Oswald Frederick (EM10–14 dob 19.09.1894) 14th London Regt (London Scottish) Cpl. (Wounded). *[Also listed as 'O. F. R. Painter'].*

Parkes, Thomas Gerrard (EM05–08 dob 16.10.1891) 6th Worcester Regt.

Parrott, Charles Stuart Chimney (EM08–11 dob 09.12.1896) M.G.C., *[Also listed as 'C. S. Parrott'].*

Pashley, Frederick Stanley (EM08–11 dob 22.06.1895) 16th London Regt., (Queen's Westminsters).

Paton, H. C., 14th London Regt., (London Scottish).

Paton, John Esplen Falconer (EM08–11 dob 03.11.1894) R.E., Lt. Oxford & Bucks. Light Infantry.

Paton, R. C. E. (EM11–14 dob 31.08.1898) R.A.F.

Paul, Cyril Henry (EM09–15 Dob 16.09.1897) 16th London Regt., (Queen's Westminsters) Cpl.

Payne, Charles Frederick (EM1896–99 dob 1884 dod 11.02.19) L./Cpl., Cpl. Duke of Wellington's (West Riding Regt). (Died of Influenza) ✤

Payne, William George (EM10–14 dob 20.11.1898) R.N.R.

Peacock, Charles Duncombe (EM11–17 dob 23.08.1900) Regiment and rank unknown.

Pearce, Ernest (EM14–15 dob 21.03.1900) Scottish Engineers.

Pearman, Alan (EM14–16 dob 14.09.1900 dod 29.09.18) Australian Contingent. Pte. ✤

Pearne, Edgar Henry (EM10–15 dob 10.12.1898) T.R.B., R.A.F.

Perritt, H., Regiment and rank unknown.

Perry, Charles W. (dob 1888) A.S.C. Sgt-Maj.

Peters, Arthur Edward (EM10–14 dob 09.01.1899) H.A.C. Cpl. (Wounded) *[Also listed as 'A. Peters'].*

Peters, William Hubert (EM12–16 dob 28.07.1898) Sandhurst, then East Kent Regt., Lt. (Retired as unfit through wounds).

Petherbridge, Lawrence Angus Fraser (EM08–15 dob 25.07.1898) 3rd King's Own Scottish Borderers, Lt. (Wounded & invalided from Salonika) *[Also listed as 'L. H. F. Petherbridge'].*

Pettit, 16th Middlesex Regt., (Public Sch. Btn.).

Pettit, Stephen Louis (EM 1903–08 dob 14.07.1895) Royal Fusiliers and R.F.C. (POW).

Petty, Cyril Arthur (dob 1886) Middlesex Regt. *[Also listed as 'C. H. Petty'].*

Phelan, William H. (dob 1877) 1st London Regt., (Royal Fusiliers).

Phillips, London Regt., Cpl.

Pickford, Aston Charles (EM10–13 dob 19.03.1898) R.E. *[Also listed as 'A. C. C. Pickford'].*

Pickford, Harold Langley (EM12–15 dob 10.01.1900) O.C.B., Inns of Court O.T.C.

Pike, Cecil Frank (EM10–15 dob 19.01.1899) T.R.B., Queen's.

Pike, Roy Seymour, R.N.V.R.

Pine, Albert Arthur (EM02–11 dob 15.06.1894 dod 16.01.17) Worcester Regt., Lt., ✤

Pine, Leslie William Tattersall (EM08–14 dob 27.12.1897 dod 18.08.17) Hants Regt., (Formerly 4th North Staffordshire Regt). (Prince of Wales) & Sandhurst, 2nd Lt., (Wounded). ✤

Pine, Reginald Herbert (EM08–14 Dob 01.01.1899) H.A.C.

Pinniger, Robert Remfry (EM09–12 dob 19.04.1895) R.F.C., 1st A.M. Flight Sgt., (Wounded).

Pitcairn, Douglas Neville (dob 1889) 9th Gordon Highlanders, Lt.

Pleace, Robert Arthur (EM07–12 dob 27.11.1895) M.G.C., 14th London Regt., (London Scottish) (Wounded) 2nd Lt.

Pockett, Henry Truebridge (EM07–10 dob 24.01.1893) R.E., (Signal Service).

Pockett, William (EM07–13 dob 17.01.1896) R.N.A.S., R.H.A., (Anti-Aircraft Section).

Pocock, Bernard Langdon Elliott (dob 25.05.1895) London Regt., Capt. *[Also listed as 'B. L. C. Pocock']*.

Pocock, F., 5th London Regt., (London Rifle Brigade). 2nd Lt.

Pocock, Norman Stanley Dean (dob 1892) Calcutta Scottish Volunteers.

Polhill, Clement William (EM06–12 dob 17.09.1895) R.N. (Royal Navy Steward working in sick bay).

Pollock, R. W., Royal West Surrey Regt.

Pomeroy, – 28th London Regt. (Artists' Rifles).

Poole, James Henry (EM06–11 dob 15.09.1894) R.N., (drowned in H.M.S. *Cressy*). ✣

Pope, Frances J. (EM10–16 dob 01.01.1899) West Surrey Regt., (Formerly Sandhurst). 2nd Lt. *[Also listed as F. T. Pope]*.

Pope, William Archer (dob 1892 dod 07.10.16) 10th Royal West Surrey Regt., (Queen's) (formerly 9th London Regt, Queen Victoria's Rifles). Capt., (Wounded). ✣

Porraz, V., French Army.

Potter, Herbert Walter (EM09–14 dob 02.01.1899) A.S.C., Clerk. H.M.S. *Ajax*.

Poundall, J., R.A.M.C.

Poundall, William Arthur (EM08–10 dob 31.12.1892 dod 31.10.17) South Lancashire Regt., att. R.F.C. Capt. Awarded M.C. ✣

Prescott, Frederick William Lloyd (EM10–15 dob 04.12.1899 dod 02.04.18) London Regt., O.C.W., Rifleman. ✣

Prescott, George Edward (EM10–12 dob 20.01.1897) 23rd London Regt.

Price, Frank Seymour (EM06–11 dob 12.05.1897) 26th Royal Fusiliers., (Wounded).

Price, Harold Cuthbert (dob 1890) 5th London Regt., (London Rifle Brigade). 15th Btn. The London Regt., (Civil Service Rifles).

Price, Leonard John Jolliffe (EM05–10 dob 04.10.1893 dod 15.08.16) 15th London Regt., (Civil Service Rifles) K.O.S.B., 2nd Lt. *[Also listed as 'L. J. F. Price']*. ✣

Priestley, Tom Morriss (EM07–08 dob 02.07.1894) Home Front, Board of Trade.

Pringle, Walter Francis (dob 1891) R.F.A.

Prismall, Alan (EM09–18 dob 15.10.1899) O.C.B.

Prismall, Maurice Arthur (EM02–08 dob 08.03.1892) 13th London Regt., (Kensington Btn. Princess Louise's Own). Awarded M.C. Maj. (Wounded).

Pugden, D., L.R.B. (Wounded).

- R -

Ramsden, Leslie Herbert (EM09–12 dob 10.04.1896) 16th London Regt., (Queen's Westminsters).

Ramsey, Douglas Eden Ramsey (dob 1889) 15th London Regt., (Civil Service Rifles).

Randall, Stephen Robert (EM10–14 dob 01.04.1899) Border Regt., 2nd Lt. *[Also listed as 'S. R. Randle']*.

Ranson, Jessie William (dob 1879) 1st Btn., Suffolk Regt., (POW). *[Also listed as 'J. Ransom']*.

Ranson, Stanley Jack (EM00–08 dob 19.03.1893) 16th London Regt., (Queen's Westminsters) (Wounded) Lt., *[Also listed as 'J. Ransom' and 'S. J. Stanley']*.

Rawlings, Frank (EM07–08 dob 09.09.1892) 2nd West Ridings Regt., Cpl.

Reader, Bertram Alec (EM09–13 dob 08.12.1897 dod 15.09.16) 15th London Regt., (Civil Service Rifles). Pte. ✣

Reece, George (EM03–08 dob 30.10.1892) R.F.A, Surrey Yeomanry, *[Also listed as 'G. Rees']*.

Rees, William Thomas (EM08–13 dob 20.08.1896) Surrey Yeomanry R.F.A., *[Also listed as 'W. Reece' and 'W. Rees']*.

Reed, John Robert (dob 1893) R.N.V.R.

Reed, Ronald Stephen (dob 1894) R.N.V.R.

Reid, Oscar Martin (dob 1887) 25th Btn. London Regt.

Relleen, Bernard Evelyn (EM05–08 dob 22.04.1891). Served on Steampship *Appam*.

Rice, Edward Felix (EM07–10 dob 13.07.1893 dod 18.02.17) No. 1 Officers Cdt Btn., late 5th London Regt., London Rifle Brigade., R.E., 2nd Lt. *[Also listed as 'F Rice']*. (Wounded). ✣

Richards, John Henry Sherer (EM11–14 dob 12.04.1897) 9th East Surrey Regt., Lt. (Wounded).

Riches, Andrew Dudley (dob 1888) 21st Royal Fusiliers.

Riches, John Leslie (EM04–10 dob 04.03.1896 dod 15.07.16) Yeomanry, 10th Rough Riders. R.F. L./Cpl. ✣

Rigden, Brian Causes (EM03–09 dob 05.11.1896) O.B.L.I. Capt., (Formerly 5th London Regt. London Rifle Brigade). (Wounded) 2nd Lt., Awarded M.C. *[Also listed as 'D. C. Rigden']*.

Rigden, Walter O'Brian (EM03–09 dob 12.03.1894) R.N.D. (Formerly R.W.D). *[Also listed as 'R. W. Rigden']*.

Rignall, John Richard (EM02–08 dob 06.03.1890) Staff Sgt., Instructor Aldershot.

Riley, Gerald Tattersall (EM04–09 dob 12.12.1893) R.F.C., *[Also listed as 'J. Riley']*.

Ring, F. F., Regiment and rank unknown.

Roberts, John Henry (EM05–14 dob 18.10.1896 dod 15.11.16) H.A.C., L./Cpl. ✣

Robinson, Aylmer St. John (EM05–10 dob 1895) London Regt., 2nd Lt. *[Also listed as 'A. J. Robinson']*.

Robinson, Frank Gilbert (EM06–09 dob 07.02.1893 dod 07.07.16) 4th Northumberland Fusiliers, 2nd Lt. (Temp. Lt.) ✣

Robinson, Ralph Duncan (EM09–11 dob 26.06.1895 dod 07.06.17) 9th Loyal North Lancashire Regt., Capt. (Formerly Royal Fusiliers). (Wounded) ✣

Rodgers, William Henry Eric (EM08–12 dob 25.05.1896). Regiment and rank unknown.

Rogers, George Ronnie (EM10–17 dob 01.12.1898) Suffolk Regt., 2nd Lt.

Roper, Frederick Watts (EM08–13 dob 26.03.1897) R.N.V.R.

Roper, Stuart Edgar (EM1910–1914 dod 29.09.18) M.G.C., Pte. ✣

Ross, Frank Russell (EM13–16 dob 24.01.1894) 14th London Regt., (London Scottish). Wounded.

Ross-Jenkins, Maurice (EM13–16 dob 24.08.1897 dod 16.06.18) Gloucester Regt., 2nd Lt., O.C.B., R.A.F. (Wounded). ✣

Rough, – A.S.C., Q.M. Sgt. [Presumed to be 'Harold Spencer Rouffe' (EM09–10 dob 04.11.1894)].

Royffe, C. N., Regiment and rank unknown.

Royffe, Harold Spencer (EM09–10 dob 04.11.1894) Middlesex Regt., (att. R.F.C.) 2nd Lt.

Ruffle, Harold Percy (EM08–13 dob 26.12.1896) O.C.B., (Formerly 12th London Regt). (Rangers) Sgt. (Invalided from France).

Ruffle, R., York & Lancaster Regt.

Rumford, Cuthbert (EM10–16 dob 01.02.1890) Notts & Derby Regt.

Rundle, R.F.A.

Rundle, Robert William (dob 1892) O.C.B.,

Rush, Colin Charles (EM05–12 dob 08.08.1896) A.S.C. (Transport Section). *[Also listed as 'C. Rush']*.

Rush, Norman James (EM06–16 dob 27.05.1898) R.G.A., Artillery School. 2nd Lt.

Ryley Jr, Harold Buchanan (EM11–13 dob 06.06.1896 dod 05.09.16) 4th North Staffordshire Regt., (Prince of Wales's). 2nd Lt. ✣

Ryley, Harold Buchanan (Headmaster 06–13 dob 18.07.1856 dod 15.12.17) Suffolk Regt., Lt. ✣

- S -

Sach, Kane Charles Burleigh (EM07–09 dob 18.05.1897 dod 01.07.16) Worcester Regt., London Regt., 2nd Lt. *[Also listed as both 'B. Sach' and 'C. B. Sach']*. ✣

Sanders, William Henry (EM09–14 dob 07.03.1898) London Regt., Awarded M.M.

Sanderson, Harold F. (EM09–11 dob 30.10.1895) 28th London Regt., (Artists' Rifles). Lt.

Sanderson, H. T., Railway Transport Officer, Lt.

Sanford, Christopher (EM09–18 dob 28.09.1899) O.C.B.

Sawyer, William Henry (EM10–13 dob 07.10.1899) R.F.C.

Scott, 15th London Regt., (Civil Service Rifles).

Scurfield, Bryan (EM 09–15 dob 22.10.1898 dod 30.09.18) 2nd East Surrey Regt., Lt. (Awarded Order of Military Merit 4th Class Greece and M.C.) ✣

Segar, B. G., O.C.B., 2nd Lt., (Wounded & Invalided out).

Selley, Alan Herbert (EM11–13 dob 20.05.1897) No. 6 O.C.B., Suffolk Regt., 2nd Lt. (Wounded).

Shackleton, Arthur Donald (EM07–12 dob 20.09.1897) R.E. London Electrical Engineers. *[Also listed as 'Shakleton' and 'R. D. Shackleton'].*

Shaw, C., King Edward's Horse, Lt.

Shaw, E. V., Indian Army, Lt.

Shaw, Henry C. (dob 1883) A.O.C., King Edward's Horse, A.O.C. 2nd Lt. ✤

Shaw, Vincent Eric (dob 1888) Notts & Derby Regt., (Sherwood Foresters) 2nd Lt.

Sheppee, Frederick John (EM1885–88 dob 25.04.1873 dod 07.08.15) Australian Infantry. Pte. *[Sheppee was also known as Frederick Johnson, a name he used to enlist because of his age].* ✤

Siese, Arthur Charles Silce (EM10–11 dob 12.11.1897) R.M.A., (Invalided out). *[Also listed as 'A. C. Siese'].*

Simpkins, Percy (EM09–11 dob 03.05.1895) 11th Royal Fusiliers.

Simpson, Victor Leslie (EM06–13 dob 30.11.1896 dod 03.05.17) H.A.C. Pte. (Missing) ✤

Sims, A. W. (EM11–18 dob 02.02.1900) O.C.B.

Sims, J. M. (dod 27.09.18) Suffolk Regt., Cpl., ✤

Sinstadt, Charles F. (EM10–14 dob 11.10.1899) 8th Essex Regt., (Cyclist Section).

Sisterson, Norman Hele (EM04–12 dob 21.05.1895 dod 16.04.18) Northumberland Fusiliers, 2nd Lt. ✤

Skepelhorn, H., Life Guards.

Skertchley, Ernest William EM13–16 dob 26.01.1900) Inns of Court O.T.C.

Skinner, Frank William (EM04–08 dob 05.02.1892 dod 05.05.16) Canadian Contingent, 1st British Columbia Regt., Sign'r., Lt. (Died of wounds). ✤

Skinner, Stuart (EM09–10 dob 19.11.1894) R.F.A., (Wounded) – *[later corrected to 'invalided twice'].*

Slocock, Sydney Lawrence (dob 1891) Army Veterinary Corps., Capt.

Slocombe, Charles Geoffrey (EM06–09 dob 21.07.1893 dod 13.05.17) The Buffs (The 6th East Kent Regt.). Sgt. (Wounded and died as POW) ✤

Slocombe, G. L., Australian Contingent.

Slocombe, Leonard Frederick Martin (EM10–11 dob 19.06.1898) R.A.F. *[Also listed as 'L. M. Slocombe'].*

Slocombe, R. C. M. (EM09–11 dob 23.06.1895) Manchester Regt., 2nd Lt., (Formerly 4th West Surrey Regt). (Wounded at Suvla Bay, August 1915).

Slocombe, Gerald Walter (dob 1888) A.S.C. *[Also listed also as 'G. W. Slowcombe'].*

Smalley, Walter Norman Adam (EM09–15 dob 16.09.1899) R.N.A.S.

Smith, Albert (EM10–15 dob 18.12.1898) London Regt. (POW) *[Also listed as 'A. Smith'].*

Smith, Alfred Martin (EM02–10 dob 12.02.1893) Worcester Regt., Capt., (Wounded in France, invalided from Gallipoli).

Smith, A. R. (EM11–15 dob 18.10.1899) London Regt.

Smith, C. R., Canadian Contingent. 2nd Lt.

Smith, E. A. W. H. (EM11–16 dob 16.09.1899) London Regt.

Smith, Henry Raymond (dob 1889) Canadian Contingent., Sgt.

Smith, Martin, Manchester Regt. 2nd Btn., Lt.

Smith, Geoffrey Cholerton (EM 06–13 dob 07.04.1897 dod 31.07.17) A.S.C. (Horse Transport). att. R.F.C., Lt. (Formerly Royal Military College, Sandhurst). Awarded M.C. ✤

Smith, Wilfred Douglas (EM08–13 dob 08.04.1897) 21st London Regt., (1st Surrey Rifles). 2nd Lt., (Wounded).

Smithard, Richard Glass (EM03–07 dob 1891) K.S.L.I., Awarded D.S.O. and M.C., Maj.

Smythson, Alfred Frank (dob 1887) Lincolnshire Regt.

Southern, Alfred William (EM13–14 dob 03.09.1898) S.A.H.A.

Spencer, Edgar John (EM09–12 dob 28.12.1896) Motor Transport, R.E., (Electrical Section).

Spencer, Harold John (EM04–11 dob 29.10.1896) 15th London Regt., (Civil Service Rifles). Lt.

Spencer, Edward Roland (EM08–12 dob 06.10.1898) R.N.A.S. (Anti–Aircraft Coy). R.F.C.

Spencer, Walter George (dob 1888 dod 26.03.18) 23rd London Regt., Capt. ✤

Spicer, Filmer Blake (dod 06.10.16) The Buffs (The East Kent Regt.). 2nd Lt. ✤

Spiers, Robert (dob 1895).

Squibb, Ernest James (EM09–12 dob 27.04.1898) 23rd London Regt.

Squibb, Harry Thomas (EM08–13 dob 29.09.1898) Middlesex Regt. (Bugler).

Squires, Frank Cornelius (dob 1887) 6th Dorsetshire Regt., 2nd Lt. (Wounded) *[Also listed as 'F. C. Squire'].*

Standing, Richard Clifford (dob 1893) A.S.C. (Despatch Rider).

Stanford, Mark (EM08–10 dob 02.12.1894) East Surrey Regt., Capt., (Formerly 13th London Regt, Kensington Btn. Princess Louise's Own) (Wounded) *[Also listed as 'M. Stanfad'].*

Stanley, Hubert Montague (EM09–14 dob 22.06.1898) London Regt., (Wounded).

Staton, Ronald John (EM12–15 dob 03.10.1900) R.N.R. *[Also listed as 'R. G. Staton'].*

Steer, George John (dob 17.06.1900) O.C.B.

Stephens, Cyril Hayne (EM09–14 dob 09.09.1898) R.N.V.R., H.M.S. *Victoria*, Sub./Lt.

Stephens, George (EM11–12 dob 14.07.1897) 28th London Regt., (Artists' Rifles)., Gloucester Regt., 2nd Lt Awarded M.C.., (Wounded).

Stepto, Cyril Frederick (EM08–13 dob 25.10.1896 dod 07.10.16) London Regt. Pte. (Missing). ✤

Stevens, 14th London Regt., (London Scottish).

Stevens, Cecil Alfred (EM08–14 dob 31.10.1898 dod 31.08.1958) R.F.C. Capt., (Formerly Sandhurst). Awarded M.C. and Bar.

Stevens, J., 14th London Regt., (London Scottish).

Stickland, Francis Norman (EM08–10 dob 06.08.1897) R.F.A., 2nd Lt.

Stickland, Reginald Gordon (EM08–10 dob 03.10.1893) R.F.A., Lt. (Wounded). *[Also listed as 'S. R. Stickland'].*

Stockwell, Ernest Holland [Harold] (EM10–15 dob 23.08.1898 dod 21.03.18). London Regt., Rifleman. ✤

Stoner, George Frank (EM07–10 dob 22.08.1895) British Red Cross (France).

Storr, William Gowland (EM07–10 dob 12.12.1895).

Stuart, Charles (EM09–14 dob 15.07.1898) K.R.R.C.

Stuart, C. A. F., Inns of Court O.T.C., East Surrey Regt., 2nd Lt.

Stutely, Cecil R. (EM11–16 dob 04.11.1899) O.C.B. *[Also listed as 'C. Stutely'].*

Summers, Ranulph Augustus (EM04–08 dob 03.12.1891 dod 28.09.15) 9th Royal Berkshire Regt., 2nd Lt., ✤

Sutcliffe, Ely Godfrey Spencer (dob 1892) A.P.C.

Sutcliffe, John Frederick Sheard (EM07–11 dob 1895) R.E., Cpl. (Wounded). *[Also listed as 'J. F. Sutclife'].*

Sykes, Frederick N. (EM11–15 dob 02.01.1900) O.C.W.

- T -

Taylor, Henry Arthur (dob 1886) Army Pay Corps, Sgt.

Taylor, James John (EM14–18 dob 12.08.1899) O.C.B., Artists' Rifles.

Tcheraz, Greek Army.

Thew, Leslie Ernest (EM11–18 dob 08.10.1899) R.N.A.S. P.F.O., R.A.F., 2nd Lt.

Thomas, Arthur Lewis (dob 1887 dod 24.04.18) Northampton Regt., 2nd Lt., ✤

Thomas, Harold John (EM09–11 dob 30.11.1895) 13th Royal Fusiliers. (Wounded).

Thompson, New Zealand Contingent, 6th Wellington Regt.

Thompson, Eric Langdon (EM07–16 dob 23.03.1898) Royal Berks Regt., 2nd Lt., (Wounded & POW).

Thompson, K., R.N.A.S.

Thomson, Jepthah (dob 1883) R.N.A.S.

Thomson, Rupert Archer (dod 17.06.15) Canadian Infantry (Central Ontario Regt.), L./Cpl., ✤

Thornton, S. H. (EM11–16 dob 27.11.1899) R.A.F., R.N.A.S. P.F.O., Lt.

Threadgold, Cecil Archibald (EM10–15 dob 07.04.1899) R.F.C.

Tier, Alexander V. (dob 1882) R.A.M.C., Staff-Sgt.

Tilson, Ernest George (EM03–08 dob 02.05.1890) 13th London Regt., (Kensington Btn. Princess Louise's Own) (Wounded) *[Also listed as 'Tillson']*.

Titley, Alfred Eric 'Titus' (EM06–16 dob 14.01.1898 dod 03.1961) Devonshire Regt., Awarded M.C. (Wounded) (Mentioned in Despatches). Capt.

Toler, Harry Robert (dob 1889) A.S.C.

Tolley, N. H. (EM11–13 dob 31.01.1898) Record Office., Labour Corps., *[Also listed as 'N. H. Tolly']*.

Tompkins, William James, Australian Contingent.

Toogood, Jack (EM07–12 dob 28.09.1895) No. 4 Officer Cadet Btn. A.P.C., Norfolk Regt., 2nd Lt., later R.A.F. Lt. (Wounded & POW).

Townsend, William (EM10–15 dob 08.09.1898) London Regt. 2nd Lt.

Tremlett, L. J. P. (EM11–18 dob 13.09.1899) Indian Army Cdt., O.C.B., Gentleman Cdt., Quetta.

Tring, C., 16th London Regt., (Queen's Westminsters) (Invalided out). *[Presumed to be 'William Clarence Montague Tring (EM05–09, dob 05.04.1894)]*.

Tring, William Gordon (dob 1893).

Tunks, Albert George (dob 1888) East Surrey Regt.

Turner, Charles Ernest (EM04–10 dob 24.06.1895) 11th Worcester Regt., 2nd Lt. Awarded Croix de Guerre (French award).

Turner, Francis Philip (EM10–13 dob 14.10.1897 dod 08.05.15) 12th Btn., London Regt., (Rangers) Rifleman. (Missing since April, 1915). ✤

Turner, Reginald Reader (EM11–14 dob 24.05.1898) University of London, O.T.C., Tank Corps, 2nd Lt., (Wounded).

Tustain, George Edward (EM09–13 dob 13.06.1898) R.N., A.T.S.S. Midshipman.

- U -

Underwood, Frederick Nelson (EM11–16 dob 21.10.1899 dod 02.07.19) R.N.A.S. P.F.O., R.A.F., 2nd Lt. ✤

Urquhart, Robert (EM09–14 dob 18.12.1897 dod 1975) London Regt., Cameron Highlanders, (Wounded & discharged).

- V -

Vaughan, Hugh William (EM13–14 dob 11.09.1897) 7th Royal West Surrey Regt., (The Queen's). 2nd Lt., (Wounded) (Wounded second time, and missing, believed prisoner in German hands).

Vaughan, James (EM05–08 dob 06.05.1892) The Buffs (8th East Kent Regt.). Maj. Awarded M.C. (POW).

Vaughan, R. W., Royal Fusiliers. *[Presumed to be 'William Vaughan' dob 1897]*.

Vaughan, Stanley (EM08–11 dob 06.01.1895) The Buffs (8th East Kent Regt.). 2nd Lt. (POW. Originally reported as died of wounds but rectified later that he survived).

Villis, Archibald (EM11–15 dob 16.10.1899 dod 18.10.18), Duke of Wellington's (West Riding Regt.), Pte. ✤

Villis, Tom (EM06–11 dob 16.12.1894 dod 11.10.18). R.A.F., Air Mechanic 2nd Class. ✤

Vincent, Henry (dob 1877) R.E., 2nd Lt.

Vincent, Harold J. (dob 1883) R.F.A., Maj. *[Also listed as 'H. G. Vincent']*.

- W -

Waddington, Percy George (EM10–15 dob 06.11.1898) A.O.C. *[Also listed as 'P. S. Waddington']*.

Waghorn, Hugh Colin (EM06–12 dob 05.06.1895) 21st London Regt., (1st Surrey Rifles). R.F.C., Observer. Awarded M.B.E. (Wounded). Lt.

Wagstaffe, Charles Frederick (EM12–16 dob 29.10.1899) R.N.A.S., Awarded D.F.C. Prob. F./O. *[Also listed as 'C. F. A. Wagstaffe']*.

Walker, Frederick A. (EM09–15 dob 31.07.1899) O.C.W., London Regt., (Gassed/wounded).

Walker, George Ernest (EM03–10 dob 02.05.1893 dod 06.06.17). 14th London Regt., (London Scottish/Royal Scots.). Lt. ✤

Walker, Leonard George (EM05–10 dob 18.02.1894) New Zealand Engineers. *[Also listed as 'L. J. Walker']*.

Walker, W. G., 14th Btn. London Regt., London Scottish.

Walker, William James (EM01–07 dob 17.05.1891) 9th Scottish Rifles, 2nd Lt.

Waller, E., K.O.S.B., Capt.

Wallis, Arthur Albert (EM13–14 dob 25.07.1898) 16th London Regt., (Queen's Westminsters). Bugler.

Wallis, Claude Edgar (EM1899–02 dob 1885) Loyal North Lancashire Regt., (POW). Lt. *[Also listed as 'G. Wallis' and 'C. G. Wallis']*.

Wallis, Edward (EM12–16 dob 14.03.1898) R.E., (Signal Service).

Walter, King's Own Scottish Borderers, Capt.

Warren, Frederick P. (dob 1889) R.F.C., (Canada).

Webb, Alfred J. (dob 1889) R.E., or R.G.A., 2nd Lt,. *[Also listed as 'J. Webb' and 'Webb']*.

Webb, Ernest Court (EM10–15 dob 04.10.1898) London Regt.

Welch, Frederick Harry (dob 1890) 2nd Lt. (Invalided at Osborne).

Welsh, Hedley Stephen (EM12–14 dob 24.06.1902) London Regt., London Irish., 2nd Lt., *[Also listed as ' H. Stephen Welsh' and 'H. Welsh']*.

Wells, Capt.

West, Arthur John (EM1886–87 dob 12.04.1873) Surrey Yeomanry, Maj.

West, Gerald William (EM04–09 dob 18.04.1892 dod 25.09.15) Royal Sussex Regt., Lt. ✤

Wheeler, R.N.V.R.

Wheeler, Frank Henry (EM11–13 dob 19.03.1896) R.N.A.S., Electrician.

While, Eric Martin (EM10–13 dob 28.03.1895) Staff Officer, I.D., (Formerly 6th Royal Fusiliers) Lt. (Wounded).

While, Hugh Dickie (EM10–15 dob 03.07.1898) 5th Royal Fusiliers, 2nd Lt., Scots Guards (Wounded).

While, Ivor Austin (EM10–14 dob 27.10.1896 dod 31.08.16) 4th North Staffordshire Regt., (Prince of Wales's). 2nd Lt. ✤

White, Arthur Frederick (EM09–14 dob 06.07.1898) 2nd Lt.

White, Francis George (EM09–14 dob 13.07.1898) H.A.C.

White, Frank Henry (EM11–15 dob 30.01.1899 dod 1955) London Regt., L./Cpl., (POW).

White, Frederick Richard (EM12–17 dob 05.09.1899 dod 09.06.18) 21st Batt. Middlesex Regt., Pte. (Wounded & POW). ✤

White, Gilbert (EM08–13 dob 27.10.1896) H.A.C. (Invalided from France).

White, Harold Norton (dob 1896 dod 06.09.18) 26th Royal Fusiliers, M.G.C., 2nd Lt. *[Also listed as 'H. M. Norton']*. ✤

Whitehead, James Edward (Staff 1909–16 dob 1887 dod 1977) London University O.T.C, R.G.A., (Invalided from France). Lt.

Whittle, B. A., R.A.M.C. (Australian Contingent).

Whittle, Sydney George (dob 1884) H.A.C.

Wicks, Samuel George (EM06–11 dob 03.02.1895) 6th London Regt., L.Cpl., (Wounded). *[Also listed as 'Whicks']*.

Wildey, Cecil Eden (EM11–16 dob 16.08.1899) O.C.B., R.N.A.S., Prob. F./O.

Wildish, Charles Albert (dob 1889) A.O.C.

Wilkins, Henry Sydney (EM07–09, dob 1888) 6th Btn. Gloucester Regt., Capt. *[Also listed as 'S. Wilkins']*.

Williams, W. T. (EM09–14 dob 22.10.1897) R.N.R.

Willis, George Ward (EM09–10 dob 13.12.1897 dod 03.05.17) D.L.I., Pte. *[Also listed as 'G. Wilson]*. ✤

Wilner, W., R.A.M.C.

Wilson, C. J., 16th London Regt., (Queen's Westminsters) Sgt. ✤

Wilson, Eric Edgar Paxton (EM07–10 dob 19.04.1896) R.E. *[Also listed as 'E. Wilson']*

Wilson, H. A. J., R.N.A.S., R.N.V.R. (H.M.S. *Princess Royal*). Lt.

Wilson, Jack Henry G. (EM10–15 dob 21.04.1899) Inns of Court O.T.C.

Wilson, John Vetch (EM06–09 dob 08.10.1892) R.N. Flying Corps, A.S.C. Lt.

Wilson, Montague Percy (EM08–10 dob 17.02.1894) A.S.C. *[Also listed as 'P. M. Wilson']*.

Wilson, Robert Douglas (EM09–13 dob 14.07.1897) 5th London Regt., (London Rifle Brigade). L./Cpl.

Wilson, Robert Philip (EM07–09 dob 06.01.1894 dod 07.08.15) 6th East Yorkshire Regt., 2nd Lt. (Missing since 7 August 1915). ✤

Wingrove, Frank Albert (EM07–11 dob 02.01.1895) R.F.A.

Winsconsey, R.A.M.C.

Wisdom, Colin Matson (EM03–08 dob 29.05.1892 dod 09.04.17) 16th Canadian Contingent. Sgt. ✤

Wise, Frank William (EM11–16 dob 15.05.1900) R.A.F. Cdt.

Wise, Norman Henry (EM09–15 dob 21.01.1898) M.G.C.

Withers, Geoffrey J. L. (EM05–09 dob 28.11.1893) H.A.C. 2nd Lt.

Withers, W. W., 5th Notts & Derby Regt., (Sherwood Foresters). 2nd Lt., R.A.M.C.

Wolfe, Frederick Derrick S. (EM10–13 dob 12.02.1898 dod 10.08.18) London Regt. (L.R.B.), Rifleman. ✤

Wolfe, Russell Sennett (EM10–13 dob 31.12.1899) R.N.V.R., Sub./Lt.

Wood, John (EM06–09 dob 02.04.1893) West Surrey Regt., Lt.

Wood, William Alfred (EM09–13 dob 05.06.1898) 15th London Regt., att. K.R.R.C. (Civil Service Rifles). (Wounded & gassed).

Woodall, Eric (EM07–09, dob 1890) A.S.C. (Wounded). *[Also listed as 'S. E. Woodall'].*

Woodgate, L. C., R.A.M.C.

Woodmansey, Hubert Vernon (dob 1889) 5th London Regt. (L.R.B.). *[Also listed as 'V. Woodmansey'].*

Woodward, Hubert Edwin (EM08–11 dob 10.10.1894 dod 26.04.15) 28th London Regt., (Artists' Rifles), 13th London Regt., (Kensington Btn. Princess Louise's Own). London Regt. (L.R.B.), Rifleman. ✤

Wray, William Theodore (EM08–12 dob 15.11.1896 dod 09.10.16) Royal West Kent Regt., Queen's Westminster Rifles, Rifleman. (Died of wounds). ✤

Wrench, Ernest Bentham (EM10–14 dob 05.10.1896) R.E., O.C.B., Cpl., (Suffered from gas poisoning).

Wright, Cecil Railton (dob 1890) R.N.A.S. Lt./ Cmdr. *[Also listed as 'C. N. R. Wright'].*

Wright, Gerald Francis (dob 1890) 13th London Regt. (Kensington Btn. Princess Louise's Own).

Wright, Paul Henry (EM15–17 dob 14.09.1900) Sussex Regt.

Wyborn, Harry John Gustave (dob 1877 dod 25.03.18) Royal Surrey Regt. & Middlesex Regt. Pte. ✤

- Y -

Yorke, K., Australian Contingent.

Young, Sidney Arthur (EM06–13 dob 17.04.1897) R.A.F., Lt.

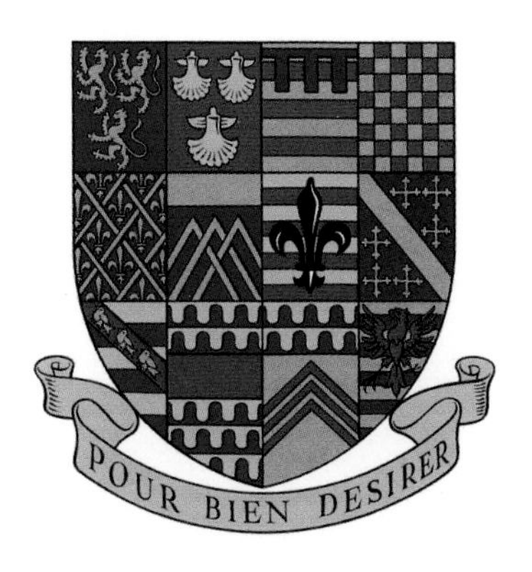

Emanuel School

Second World War
Pro Patria

- A -

Abbott, Frank Louis (EM21–33 dob 12.10.13 dod 2005) O.C.T.U., Middlesex Regt., Capt.

Abraham, Norman Alexander (EM27–31 dob 26.05.19) Intel. Corps., Capt.

Abramson, Nicholas (EM24–32 dob 18.04.13) Intel. Corps., Capt.

Adams, Frederick Prigden (EM26–31 dod 18.03.45) R.N.R., Lt. ✤

Adams, Harold Richard (EM24–31 dob 08.10.12 dod 25.06.1978) R.A.C., East Surrey Regt., Capt.

Adamson, R., Queen's Westminsters, Rifleman.

Adkins, Ernest John (EM1924 dob 01.01.08) R.A.F., P./O.

Alesworth, Frederick Richard (EM29–34 dob 04.03.17) R.E., Capt.

Alesworth, G. – Lt. Regiment unknown.

Allcock, Donald John (EM30–36 dob 01.12.20) (E) R.N.V.R. (Mentioned in Despatches). Sub./Lt.

Allen, David Arnold (EM27–35 dob 29.09.16) Regiment and rank unknown.

Allnutt, Kenneth Samuel (EM36–41 dob 20.05.24) R.A.C., Tpr.

Anderson, Eric Alfred (EM32–38 dob 15.04.21) R.A.S.C., 549 Coy., Cpl.

Anderson, Ronald Percy (EM20–30 dob 02.06.12) R.A., Lt.

Anderson, Jack Cole (EM29–35 dob 20.06.16) Regiment and rank unknown.

Angell, Ernest Henry L. (EM29–36 dob 13.01.20 dod 2006) R.A.O.C., L./Sgt. *[Also listed as 'E. H. Angell'].*

Ansell, George John (EM29–34 dob 13.09.15) R.A., Capt.

Appleby, Gerald William (EM30–36 dob 05.08.20) R.A.F., A.C.2., *[Also listed as 'G. Appleby'].*

Archer, Leonard Charles A. (EM19–22 dob 17.06.05 dod 1984) R.E., Lt.

Armstrong, Drummond L (EM17–22 dob 11.07.05) R.A.O.C., Lt-Col. *[Also listed as 'D. S. Armstrong'].*

Armstrong, James William Douglas (EM29–36 dob 06.06.19 dod 22.02.45) East Surreys, Maj. *[Also listed as 'J. W. B. Douglas'].* ✤

Ashcroft, J. A., R.A.F.V.R., L./A.C.

Assig, Harold Leslie (EM1902 dob 11.05.1895) R.A.F., Wing Comdr [Father of L. F. Assig].

Assig, Leslie Frederick (EM32–35 dob 10.09.19) R.E., Bdr., Sapper. *[Also listed as 'F. L. Assig'].*

Attfield, William Henry (EM36–41 dob 15.02.25) R.C.S., L./Cpl. att. R.N.

Austin, F. W., O.C.T.U., Lt.

Avery, Vernon Harrison (EM30–37 dob 29.07.20) R.C.S., L./Cpl (POW).

Ayers, Stanley John (EM29–33 dob 28.09.15) Regiment and rank unknown.

Ayling, Kenneth (EM34–39) R.A.F.V.R. (dob 1923 dod 07.2006)

Ayris, L., Surrey Yeomanry, Gnr., (Invalided out). *[Also listed as 'F. Ayris'].*

- B -

Badendoch, Kenneth George (EM19–28 dob 06.02.11) Field Security Police/Intel Corps., Cpl. *[Also listed as 'Badenoch' and 'K. R. Badenoch'].*

Bailey, Desmond Ronald Crampton (EM30–40 dob 27.04.22) Royal Fusiliers att. 2nd Btn. Royal Worcestershire, Maj. Awarded the M.C.

Bailey, John Richard Thomas (EM36–43 dob 09.04.25 dod 24.06.2012) R.A.F.

Bailey, William Herbert Crampton (EM25–35 dob 29.10.17) 2nd Lt. (POW).

Baker, Kenneth Croucher (EM30–36 dob 11.05.19 dod 01.12.43) Royal Fusiliers., Capt. (died of wounds). *[Also listed as 'L. C. Baker'].* ✤

Balchin, L. F. J., R.A.O.C., Capt.

Balchin, Spencer J. H. (EM09–15 dod 1975) R.E.M.E., Capt. *[Also listed as 'S. Balchin'].*

Baldwin, G. W. L. (EM27–37 dob 24.01.20) R.D.G., Lt.

Ballam, Raymond Frederick (EM34–36 dob 22.05.19) Cpl.

Ballantine, Robin Douglas (EM33–38 dob 06.05.21) K.O.S.B., Special Duties, London Scottish, Lt. *[Also listed as 'R. S. Battantine' and 'R. S. Battentine'].*

Banbery, John Charles (EM36–42 dob 17.06.25) R.G.H., R.A.C., Tpr. *[Also listed as 'Banbury'].*

Banting, George Gaywood, C.B., C.B.E., (EM09–15 dob 25.02.1898 dod 27.12.1973) R.A.F. Air Vice-Marshal.

Barfield, James Colin (EM20–28 dob 08.02.12) R.N.V.R., Sub./Lt. *[Also listed as 'J. Barfield'].*

Barker, Sidney James (EM29–34) Fleet Air Arm

Barnard, Alexander John (EM36–43 dob 01.02.25) R.N., Ord./Tel., L./Cpl.

Barnes, Allan Francis Charles (EM35–43 dob 10.03.25 dod 2013) Welsh Guards, Gdsman.

Barnes, Thomas Henry (EM31–37 dob 28.01.20) R.C.S., Sign'r. *[Also listed as 'T. Barnes'].*

Barnett, Charles Joseph (EM30–36 dob 14.07.19 dod 22.10.1945) R.A.S.C., Pte. ✤

Barnett, David Norman (EM37–43 dob 01.10.25) Regiment and rank unknown.

Bartlett, Norman Francis (EM35–42 dob 23.05.24) R.A.C., Lt.

Batchelor, G. W., Indian Army, Lt., Gnr., H.A.A., R.A. (A.A).

Baverstock, David John (EM27–33 dob 14.02.16) R.A.S.C., Lt.

Baverstock, James Butham (EM25–32 dob 08.09.14) R.A.S.C., R.E., Capt. *[Also listed as 'G. M. Baverstock'].*

Beeching, Donald (EM38–40 dob 25.02.24 dod 01.03.44) Royal Fusiliers, I.T.C., Fusilier. ✤

Bearne, Frederick John (EM28–34 dob 08.04.16) R.A.F., Cpl.

Belcher, L. F. J. (EM26–28 dob 09.09.12) R.A.O.C., Capt.

Bell, Peter Herbert (EM35–43 dob 27.04.26) Indian Army, Lt.

Bender, R. W. (EM29–38 dob 29.09.20) R.N.V.R., F.A.A., (Fleet Air Arm) *[Also listed as 'A. W. Bender'].*

Bennett, John Stanley (EM37–43 dob 23.09.26) *[Listed as 'J. Bennett'].*

Bennett, Thomas Wyatt (EM19–26 dob 20.08.08 dod 20.12.42) R.A.F.V.R., F./Sgt. *[Also listed as 'T. Bennett'].* ✤

Bennett, Leonard William (EM23–28 dob 30.01.11 dod 26.12.2001) R.A., L./Bdr. (POW).

Berry, Alan Harvey (EM37–43 dob 17.10.25) R.A.F., A.C.2. *[Listed as 'A. Berry'].*

Berry, Richard Charles James (dod 7.04.44) R.A.F.V.R. Flt/Sgt. Spitfire went missing over Chin Hills. ✤

Berwick, Geoffrey Richard (EM31–38 dob 25.04.21) Indian Army, Capt. *[Also listed as 'G. Berwick'].*

Besant, Ronald Cuthbert (EM22–30 dob 06.01.14 dod 11.08.1943) R.A.F., W./O. Awarded the D.F.M. *[Also listed as 'K. C. Besant'].* ✤

Bettley, Frederick Anthony (EM31–37 dob 19.01.20) R.A., (Surrey Yeomanry) 2nd Lt., Gnr., Bdr.

Beverley, Stanley Cecil (EM15–19 dob 31.01.04) R.N.V.R., Lt.

Bevis, William (EM18–29 dob 15.02.12 dod 12.01.2004) R.N.V.R., Lt.

Beyer, Walter George (EM23–30 dob 09.11.11 dod 2013) R.A., R./O.

Bird, Cyril Edward (EM31–34 dob 23.02.18) Regiment and rank unknown.

Blackburn, John (EM23–32 dob 11.01.16) Middlesex Yeomanry, L./Sgt.

Blackburn, Richard H. (EM23–29 dob 28.05.14) Middlesex Yeomanry, Dvr.

Blackmore, Howard Loftus (EM29–35 dob 27.10.17 dod 24.11.1999) R.T.R.

Blair, Kenneth Cecil (EM26–31 dob 28.08.13) R.A., Lt.

Blishen, John Ernest (EM27–34 dob 24.05.16 dod 20.05.1987) R.P.C., Capt. *[Also listed as 'J. G. Blishen'].*

Blogg, R. J., Royal Fusiliers, Capt.

Bloore, Keith Charles (EM30–39 dob 23.03.22) King's African Rifles., Queen's Royal Regt., Capt.

Blow, John Stanley (EM25–33 dob 30.16.19.16) R.A., Sgt., Gnr. *[Also listed as 'G. S. Blow'].*

Blow, Robert Cyril (EM17–26 dob 03.09.09) R.A.F., F./Lt.

Blundell, Adrian Reginald Hugh (EM33–41 dob 07.09.25) R.A.S.C., Pte. *[Also listed as 'A. Blundell'].*

Blunt, Walter Frederick C. (EM32–38 dob 05.07.21) R.A.F., A.C.1. *[Listed as 'W. Blunt'].*

Boswell, Kenneth Amato (EM37–43 dob 25.12.25) R.N., O.S., Cpl.

Bossom, Kenneth Arthur E. (EM37–40 dob 12.05.22) O.C.T.U., R.E., Lt.

Botting, Eric Harold (EM32–37 dob 11.07.1919 dod 25.10.42) L.R.B., Sgt. ✤

Bowler, David Philip (EM35–42 dob 07.01.24). Medical Services.

Bowles, Frank David (EM31–37 dob 18.10.19 dod 02.10.42) R.N., Leading Stoker. ✤

Bradley, Colin (EM24–31 dob 21.08.13) R.A.F., Wing Comdr.

Bradley, C., R.A., (A.A.) L.Sgt.

Bradley, Eric (EM27–32 dob 27.06.16) R.M., Cpl.

Brainwood, Eric Thomas Francis (EM36–37 dob 03.02.20 dod 14.03.41) M.N. Second Radio Officer. *[Also listed as 'Brain, E. T. J.' – M.N., Wireless Opr']*. ✤

Bresler, F., R.E., R.A.S.C., Dvr.

Brook, Henry John (EM28–33 dob 09.01.17 dod 31.10.42) R.A.F., Sgt./Pilot. *[Also listed as 'Henry Brook']*. ✤

Brooks, Percy Mathison (EM07–12 dob 12.08.1895) R.A.F.

Brooks, Walter Paul (EM33–38 dob 13.04.21 dod 16.03.42) R.A.F.V.R., Sgt. ✤

Broom, Michael John Alastair (EM32–33 dob 12.07.25) R.C.S. (S.U.C.) Cdt., Sign'r.

Brown, Thomas Finch (EM07–12 dob 09.03.1896 dod 1983) R.E.M.E., Royal Fusiliers., Cfn.

Bryan, David Norman (EM34–40 dob 06.10.22) O.C.T.U., Indian Army., Lt.

Buckler, R.A.F., Wing Comdr.

Buckridge, Richard Valentine (EM26–30 dob 21.12.12) South Lancs., Lt.

Budgitt, Arthur Edwin (EM19–25 dob 21.06.08 dod 1989) R.A.F.V.R., F./Lt.

Bumstead, Albert Edward (EM33–39 dob 16.01.22) R.A.F., F./Sgt. (POW)

Bunce, Dennis Godfrey (EM35–40 dob 13.07.24) 9th Lancers., Lt. *[Also listed as 'D. J. Bunce – Tpr., Reece. T.C.']*.

Burnie, Thomas Pointer (EM28–34 dob 22.12.15) R.E.M.E.

Burrett, Edward Henry (EM30–36 dob 14.09.19) R.A.F., A.C.1.

Burrett, Frederick Gordon (EM33–40 dob 31.10.21) R.E., Lt., Temp. Capt., and later Acting Maj.

Burrows, Robert (EM31–37 dob 24.04.20) R.A.F.

Burt, D. N., R.A., Pte.

Burt, R. A., O.C.T.U., R.A., Gnr.

Butler, Hugh Joseph (EM16–17 dob 27.08.02) R.A.F., Sqn./Ldr.

- C -

Cabe, – R.A.F., Sgt. A.C.2.

Cadman, Derek William (EM32–40 dob 06.01.23 dod 16.05.41) R.A.F.V.R., A.C.2., *[Also listed as D. J. Cadman]*. ✤

Cadman, Gordon John (EM32–38 dob 13.11.21) R.A.F., L.A.C., F./O., P./O.

Cadman, James Robert (EM30–37 dob 23.02.20) Intel. Corps., Surrey Yeomanry, R.A., Sgt., Gnr., Bombardier.

Cain, Anthony Charles Brian (EM37–42 dob 30.01.26) R.N. *[Also listed as 'A. C. Cain']*.

Caldicott, Lionel Hugh (EM17–22 dob 05.03.08) R.C.S., Maj.

Cameron, David A. (EM37–44 dob 27.09.26) R.A.F., A.C.2.

Cameron, Donald Simpson (EM35–42 dob 12.07.24) R.A.F.V.R., F./O., A.C.2.

Camfield, Donald Alan (Staff 1936–40 dob 15.01.14) R.T.R., O.C.T.U., Intel. Corps., Capt.

Camm, G. J., Queen's Royal Regt., Capt.

Campbell, Malcolm Sinclair (EM26–31 dob 07.07.13) R.A.M.C., Maj.

Candey, Willis John F. (EM37–42 dob 21.01.26) R.N., O./Tel. *[Listed as 'J. Candey']*.

Cannon, Ernest Lindsay (EM24–31 dob 31.07.13) R.A.S.C., Maj.

Capron, Frederick Howard Capsow (EM24–32) R.A.F., A.C.2., Cpl.

Carey, Kenneth Owen (EM38–44 dob 28.09.29 dod 1985) R.C.S., Sign'r.

Carpenter, David John (EM35–39 dob 07.11.23) M.N., Mercantile Marine, (POW – initially reported as 'dead'). *[Also listed as 'D. Carpenter']*.

Carter, Reginald John (EM27–32 dob 29.03.14 dod 03.05.40) R.A.F., P./O. ✤

Carter, Rodney Townsend (EM38–44 dob 19.02.27) R.N., P.S.A.

Carver, David – AKA – Harold Dove (EM15–21 dob 10.08.03 dod 1974) R.A.F., P./O.

Cassie, Guy (EM02–08 dob 26.06.1892 dod 12.08,1960) R.A.O.C., Maj., (Invalided out).

Castle, William Arthur (EM19–24 dob 25.10.07) R.A.F., F./Lt.

Chamberlain, J., Dental Corps., Capt.

Chandler, Alan (EM38–41 dob 24.04.23) R.A.F.

Chandler, Malcolm (EM38–44 dob 07.04.26) R.A.F.

Chandra, G. A. (EM27–30 dob 08.11.14) R.N.V.R., Sub./Lt.

Chandra, N. E. A., R.A.F., F./O.

Chapman, Cecil Blythe (EM20–26 dob 09.12.10) R.E., Sapper (Spr). *[Listed as 'C. Chapman']*.

Chapman, Eric Charles William (EM35–42 dob 21.09.24) R.C.S. (S.U.C). Sign'r. *[Listed as both 'E. C. Chapman' & 'E. G. W. Chapman']*.

Charlton, Peter Ernest (EM35–43 dob 13.04.25) R.I.A.S.C. (Royal Indian Army Service Corps) Capt.

Charman, George Charles (EM35–40 dob 16.12.23) B.O.A.C. *[Listed as 'G. Charman']*.

Cheadle, Dennis Edward (EM26–32 dob 31.10.14) R.A., Lt.

Chick, Donald George (EM35–40 dob 25.09.21) R.I.A.S.C., (formerly R.A.S.C., Royal Northumberland Fusiliers, Indian Army, O.C.T.U., Queen's Royal Regt.). (Mentioned in Despatches). Capt.

Chiles, John Aubrey (EM34–39 dob 24.03.22) R.A.C., Guides Cavalry., Capt. Probyn's Horse 5th King Edward VII's Own Lancers. Mentioned in Despatches.

Church, Dan Ernest (EM36–42 dob 30.08.25) R.C.S., Sign'r.

Church, Richard Ernest (EM27–31 dob 29.11.15 dod 07.09.40) The Buffs, (The Royal East Kent Regiment) L./Cpl. ✤

Cleaver, Donald Vincent (EM31–37 dob 16.08.20) R.A.F., A.C.1. *[Listed as 'D. Cleaver']*.

Cleeve, Stewart Montagu (Music teacher) (dob 20.10.1894 dod 05.01.1993) Recalled for Special Service.

Clinton, Eric Francis (EM19–27 dob 24.05.09) – R.A. (A.A.) Lt. *[Also listed as 'G. F. Clinton]*.

Cloud, Peter Ronald (EM37–43) R.A.F.V.R., (S.U.C.,) A.C.2.

Clutterbuck, Arthur Ronald D'Agnold (EM36–39 dob 07.10.20) R.A.F., P./O., Awarded the D.F.C.

Clutterbuck, Eric John (EM25–42 dob 05.04.25) Military Police, Pte. *[Listed as 'E. Clutterbuck']*.

Cocks, Geoffrey (EM36–41 dob 05.05.25) R.A.F., A.C.2.

Cocks, Horace James (EM25–29 dob 29.02.12) Middlesex Yeomanry, R.C.S., Maj.

Coduri, Charles Arthur (EM22–27 dob 25.03.11 dod 24.03.42) M.N., Able Seaman (Serving in OCANA sunk by U-Boat) *[Also listed as 'C. A. Coduri',– R.A., Gnr.]* ✤

Coe, Percy Peter (EM34–35 dob 27.09.19 dod 09.08.2008) Merchant Navy (M.N.). (POW).

Cole, Frances Alfred John (EM16–23 dob 26.03.08 dod 02.09.1982) Indian Army, Maj.

Cole, John Richard (EM18–26 dob 15.02.07) Loyal Regt., Maj. (Listed as missing, later, POW) *[Also listed as 'F. E. Cole']*.

Cole, Ken Douglas Owen (EM23–28 dob 04.08.12 dod 1980) Middlesex Regt., Lt., (POW).

Coleman, John Gould (EM22–30) Royal Fusiliers,. Maj.

Coleson, Neville Anthony (dob 09.04.25 EM37–42) R.A.F., A.C.2.

Collings, Leonard George (EM26–33 dob 25.05.15 dod 13.03.43) R.A.F.V.R., Sgt.✤

Collins, N. Regiment and rank unknown.

Connell, R.A.O.C., Maj.

Cook, Edwin Neville (EM22–26 dob 24.03.10) Lincoln Regt., Lt.

Cook, Harold Simpson (EM30–33 dob 04.04.16) Queen's Royal Regt., Pte.

Cook, James Norman (EM24–32 dob 12.09.14 dod 10.07.2010) East Lancs. Regt., Maj.

Cook, W. V., R.A.F.

Cook, Leslie Kenneth James (EM23–31 dob 22.06.12) T.A., (General List) Lt., *[Also listed as 'L. J. K. Cooke']*.

Coombs, Kenneth (EM36–41 dob 08.04.25 dod 09.2009) R.N.V.R., A.B., O.S.

Coombs, Richard Joseph (EM41–43 dob 07.06.25)) Cpl., *[Listed as 'J. R. Coombs']*.

Coombs, R. G., R.N.V.R. (F.A.A.) Wireless Opr.

Cooper, Frank Douglas (EM13–22 dob 14.03.05) R.A., Lt.

Cormack, John Alexander (EM17–24 dob 09.10.05) Seaforth Highlanders, (late London Scottish) Capt.

Corney, Leslie (Staff 1945–56 dob 11.12.01) R.C.S., Sign'r.

Cotterill, Hubert Cecil (EM19–25 dob29.12.07) R.A.F., F./Lt. *[Also listed as 'C. Cotterill'].*

Coulthard, Arthur Jacques (EM34–41 dob 20.06.23 dod 10.07.44) R.A.F. Univ. Course. O.C.T.U., Airborne, Parachute Regiment, Cpl. ✤

Cove, Hugh Frederick (EM23–32 dob 01.10.14) R.A., Gnr.

Coward, Richard George (EM37–42 dob 22.03.25). R.N., S./A.

Cowles, George Oliver (EM30–36 dob 10.11.18) R.A. (A.A.). R.E.M.E. Awarded the M.B.E.

Cox, G. F., R.A.F.V.R., A.C.2.

Cox, Stanley John (EM24–29 dob 18.10.12) R.I.N., Paymr–Comdr., *[Listed as 'S. Cox'].*

Crabtree, John Raymond (EM36–43 dob 01.05.25) Sgt.

Craddock, Paul Norman (Staff 49–81 dod 11.09.2003) Intel. Service.

Cripps, Herbert Edwin (EM20–30 dob 20.12.11) R.A.S.C., Lt., *[Also listed as 'R. E. Cripps'].*

Cripps, Norman Maurice (EM23–32 dob 25.10.14) Dental Corps, Capt.

Cronin, Edward Cornelius (EM27–30 dob 30.09.13) R.N., Sub./Lt.

Cross, Howard Gordon (EM32–35 dob 14.12.18 dod 31.05.40) (Mentioned in Despatches). R.C.S., L./Cpl., *[Also listed as 'H. C. Cross'].* ✤

Crump, Charles Ernest (EM26 dob 09.01.15) R.C.S., Lt.

Crump, Ernest Melville Terence (EM35–40 dob 16.12.23) R.C.S., Lt.

Cruse, John Anthony (EM24–33 dob 13.09.13) Education Corps.

Culverwell, Edward R. (EM27–34 dob 15.09.16 dod 13.06.41) R.A.F., Sqn./Ldr. ✤

Cunnell, Lionel Charles (EM20–27 dob 07.06.09) R.A.O.C., Capt.

Curnock, John Robert (EM35–41 dob 06.06.25) R.N. *[Listed as 'J. Curnock'].*

Curnow, Eric Arthur (EM31–35 dod 08.10.43) Leading Aircraftman R.A.F.V.R. ✤

Curtis, Arthur James (EM34–41 dob 22.09.23) R.E., Lt.

Cutler, Philip Joseph (EM33–38 dob 04.05.21) R.A.F., Cpl., A.C.2.

- D -

Daniels, Anthony John (EM32–39 dob 30.06.23) R.I.A.S.C., Lt.

Daniels, A., Royal Sussex., Pte.

Darley, Horace Stanley (EM25–32 dob 03.11.13) R.A.F., Wing Comdr., Awarded the D.S.O.

Darnell, Jack Leslie (EM30–36 dob 27.08.19) R.E.M.E., (Mentioned in Despatches). Sgt.,

Davidson, Alan Hubert (EM30–36 dob 31.01.20) Buffs., London Rifle Brigade., Lt., Rifleman. *[Also listed as 'A. Davidson'].*

Davidson, Gordon Archie (EM28–33 dob 18.08.15) R.N., A.S., A.B. *[Also listed as 'G. A. Davison'].*

Davidson, Stanley Charles (EM21–27 dob 17.01.11) R.A.F., Cpl.

Davis, Andrew Arthur William (EM21 dob 12.02.14) R.A., Lt.

Davies, John Rhys (EM17–23 dob 14.07.06 dod 28.03.2008) 88th H.A.A. Regiment att. Special Boat Squadron.

St. Hill Davies, John William (EM34–37 dob 22.07.20) O.C.T.U., R.A., Lt.

Davies, Harold Francis Parlour (EM35–42 dob 10.09.25 dod 09.08.2003) R.C.S., Pte.

Davis, Derek Maynard (EM34–38 dob 24.02.26) K.R.R.C.

Dawson, Raymond Stanley (EM34–41 dob 15.02.23 dod 23.10.2002) R.A.F., Sgt.

Deacon, W. A. (EM26–31 dob 28.12.14) R.E., B.Q.M.S., Sapper., *[Also listed as 'W. Deacon'].*

Dean, Ernest Henry 'Dixie' (EM32–36 dob 21.10.17) R.A.F., (Mentioned in Despatches). Wing Comdr., Awarded the Greek Distinguished Flying Cross.

Dear, Gordon Stuart (EM34–41 dob 27.05.23 dod 2011) R.N.V.R., Sub./Lt.

Dearmer, Stanley George (EM18–20 dob 28.04.04) R.C.S., Sign'r. *[Also listed as both 'Deamus' & 'Deamur'].*

Deeks, Geoffrey Weymouth (EM31–40 dob 10.01.24) P.T.C., Pte.

Deeks, Henry 'Harry' Barnett (EM20–29 dob 09.06.11 dod 17.06.45) Royal Scots Fus., Maj., Awarded the Croix de Guerre. ✤

Deeks, Joseph Clement (EM13–20 dob 16.08.04) R.A.P.C., R.A.O.C. (Mentioned in Despatches). Lt-Col., Awarded the M.B.E.

Deeks, William Robert (EM30–35 dob 02.07.19) R.A., Sign'r and Gnr.,

Delaforce, George D. (EM09–17 dob 15.06.1899) S.A.A.F., Maj., Awarded the D.S.O.

Derrett, E. H., O.C.T.U. (Indian Army). Cdt.

Derrett, John Duncan M. (EM32–40 dob 30.08.22 dod 2013) R.A. and R.A.M.C., Pte.

Derry, Alan Walter Derry (EM30–39 dob 05.01.21) R.A.F., A.C.1. *[Listed only as 'Derry'].*

Dickins, Norman (EM38–43 dob 01.04.27) R.N., Writer/Prob.

Dilnutt, Eric John (EM33–38 dob 27.08.22) R.N., Sub./Lt. Midshipman, *[Listed as 'E. Dilnutt'].*

Dixon, John Alfred 'Jack' (EM32–37 dob 10.03.21 dod 2006) R.A.F.V.R., Awarded the D.F.C.

Dixon, Robert Leonard (EM35–42 dob 10.06.25) Regiment and rank unknown.

Doe, Herbert John Fust (EM25–31 dob 15.06.14) 140th F.A. Div. R.A.M.C., Pte. *[Listed as 'H. J. F. Dow'].*

Douglas, Lord Sholto (EM04–05 dob 23.12.1893 dod 29.10.1969) R.A.F. G.C.B. [Awarded the M.C. and D.F.C. in the First World War] Air Marshal. C-in-C Fighter Command Autumn 1940–1942.

Downs, Peter (EM35–44 dob 31.07.26) R.C.S., L/Cpl.

Drake, Cyril Langley (EM20–30 dob 29.06.12) Recce Corps.

Dransfield, Stephen John (EM33–39 dob 28.03.21) R.A.F., A.C.2.

Drayton, Leslie D'Aarcy (EM21–28 dob 23.03.11) R.A., Maj.

Dresch, Leonard Alfred (EM32–37 dob 18.02.21) R.T.R., Tpr.

Drew, Phillip Russell (EM30–32 dob 17.12.14 dod 2006) East Surreys, (Mentioned in Despatches). Lt–Col. Awarded the O.B.E.

Dubbins, Reginald Walter (EM29–34 dob 07.12.17) Queen's Royal Regt., L./Cpl.

Duffield, Henry Clive (EM32–35 dob 13.06.18) R.A.F., R.A.T.G., F./O., L.A.C.

Duffield, Leslie Allister (EM32–40 dob 13.09.21) O.C.T.U., R.A., 2nd Lt. (Later Assistant District Comdr, Palestine).

Duffield, Ronald Alan (EM32–35 dob 10.08.19 dod 30.11.42) R.A.F.V.R., Sgt.–Obs. ✤

Duncan, Douglas Albert (EM33–38 dob 06.12.21) R.A.F., P.O., Awarded the D.F.C.

Dunderdale, John (EM36–43 dob 13.04.25) R.A.F.V.R., (S.U.C.) A.C.2.

Dunkin, Reginald Charles Frederick (EM18–28 dob 23.09.10 dod 2009) R.A.S.C., Lt. (Listed as missing later POW) *[Also listed as both 'R. C. E. Dunkin' and 'C. E. Dunkin'].*

Dunning, John Theo (EM29–39 dob 29.11.20) R.M., Lt., (Invalided out).

Durant, Lionel Charles (EM21–25 dob 30.09.09) R.A.M.C., Lt. *[Also listed as 'L. C. Durrant'].*

Durant, Wilfred M Robert (EM25–30 dob 17.07.14) R.A., Lt.

- E -

Elger, Anthony Charles (EM35–39 dob 30.12.21 dod 20.12.42) R.A.F., F./Sgt., *[Also listed as 'A. E. Elger'].* ✤

Elkins, George Edward Albert (EM30–36 dob 12.10.18 dod 19.06.1975) O.C.T.U., R.C.S., Lt.

Elliott, Peter Archibald (EM30–36 dob 15.12.19) O.C.T.U., Cdt.

Embleton, John Frances B. (EM22–28 dob 23.12.20) R.C.S., Lt. *[Also listed as 'J. Embleton'].*

Emes, James Cookdell (EM36–39 dob 21.10.20) R.C.S., Sign'r.

Eusden, Frank Cawton (EM34–41 dob 04.08.24) O.C.T.U., R.M., Lt.

Evans, George Albert (EM32–39 dob 09.09.23 dod 30.12.43) Royal Fusiliers, R.M. Commandos, Lt. ✤

Evans, Gwilyn Morgan (EM30–37 dob 08.07.20) R.A.M.C. Lt.

- F -

Fagan, Herbert Archer (EM10–13 dob 14.03.1897) Gurkha Rifles, Col. Awarded the M.C. and D.S.O.

Fairman, Norman Sydney (EM35–38 dob 04.07.20) Military Police, Probationer then Capt.

Farrow, Lionel Edgar (EM12–19 dob 17.04.02) R.A.F., P./O.

Fawcett, Kenneth Douglas (EM30–36 dob 17.02.21) R.A.F., L.A.C. *[Listed as 'K. Fawcett'].*

Feehally, William Joseph (EM28–30 dob 31.03.12) Northants Regt., Maj., *[Also listed as 'Frehally'].*

Fiducia, Carmelo Michael Francis (EM28–37 dob 08.02.19) R.A.M.C., Lt.

Fielder, Robert Edwin (EM35–41 dob 27.07.24 dod 06.06.44) R.A.S.C. 716 Airborne. Pte. ✤

Finch, Harry Alfred (EM24–28 dob 11.04.12 dod 02.1986) R.A.O.C., Capt. *[Listed as 'H. A. Finch'].*

Finlay, Douglas William (EM38–40 dob 11.06.23) R.A.F. (Univ. Course.) F./Lt., Awarded the D.F.C. (POW).

Firmin, Ralph Johnstone (EM28–36 dob 08.03.18 dod 03.01.2008) R.A., Gnr.

Fitzgerald, Douglas John (EM33–39 dob 18.10.21 dod 30.08.44) R.A.F.V.R., F./Sgt., *[Also listed as 'D. Fitzgerald'].* ✤

Fitzgerald, Kenneth Raymond (EM38–42 dob 04.01.24) R.N., O./S. *[Listed as 'K. Fitzgerald'].*

Fitzgerald, Raymond Charles (EM34–39 dob 28.11.22 dod 30.08.44) R.A.F.V.R., F./Sgt. ✤

Flutter, John Francis (EM25–32 dob 07.03.14) R.C.S., Lt.

Ford, Brian Charles Gelsatt (EM33–40 dob 01.01.24) O.C.T.U., R.E., Lt.

Forster, Douglas William (EM37–40 dob 18.08.26 dod 2008) Norwegian Navy & British Army. Sgt.

Forster, Kenneth Frank (EM34–39 dob 06.06.23) R.A.F.V.R., F./O.

Forward, Frank Cecil (EM32–40 dob 24.06.23) R.N., O.S.

Forward, James Alexander (EM31–37 dob 30.03.20) Intel Corps., Lt.

Fosbrooke, D. C., R.A.F., A.C.2.

Fowle, Colin Arthur Armstrong (EM33–39 dob 02.09.21 dod 09.2002) Middlesex Regt., M.G.T.C., R.A., (A.T.) Capt. and later Maj. in 225 Bty., M 10 Tanks and 381st (A.T.) R.A.

Fowle, Kenneth Geoffrey (EM28–34 dob 26.07.17 dod 02.08.2010) King's (Liverpool) Regt., Capt.

Fox, Anthony Francis Samuel (EM31–39 dob 27.07.20) O.C.T.U., R.T.R., Capt.

Fox, Ord C. (EM34–40 dob 13.07.23) R.E., Pte., Sapper., (Invalided out & discharged). *[Also listed as 'C. O. Fox'].*

Fox, Peter Michael J. (EM34–40 dob 21.11.23) R.A.F.V.R. *[Listed as 'P. M. J. Fox'].*

Fowler, V. H., R.N., O.S.

Francis, Colin Dunstone (EM33–37 dob 24.05.21 dod 30.08.40) R.A.F., P./O. ✤

Francis, John Hampton (EM27–34 dob 02.09.16) R.A.F., F./O.

Fraser – R.A.F., F./O.

Fraser, Ian Charles Stanley (EM37 dob 15.05.26) L./Cpl.

Fraser–Petherbridge, Cedric Alexander (EM19–26 dob 10.05.09) R.A.F.V.R., F./Lt., Awarded the D.F.C. *[Also listed as 'C. A. F. Petherbridge'.]*

Freeman, Derek Gaillard (EM29–34 dob 24.10.15) R.N.V.R., Sub./Lt.

Frost, Richard Charles (EM35–38 dob 24.04.22) R.A.F., P./O., A.C.I., Awarded the D.F.M.

Fuller, Montague William (EM17–22 dob 16.08.05 dod 1998) R.A.F., Wing Comdr.

Furlong, Dennis Walter D.S.O., M.C., O.B.E. (EM08–13 dob 08.07.1897 dod 05.09.40) Royal Berkshire Regt., Brig. Awarded the D.S.O. ✤

- G -

Gabbitas, William Ewart (EM32–38 dob 28.02.21) R.A., Lt.

Gale, O.C.T.U., R.A.C., Cdt.

Galsworthy, Sir Arthur (EM27–34 dob 01.07.16 dod 10.1986) O.C.T.U., Duke of Cornwall's Light Infantry., Intel Corps., S.H.A.E.F., Lt–Col.

Galsworthy, F. J., R.N., Surgeon Lt–Comdr.

Galsworthy, Sir John Edgar (EM28–37 dob 19.06.19 dod 18.05.1992) O.C.T.U., 2nd Lt. (Invalided out). Bletchley Park and Foreign Office.

Gander, Stanley Frank (EM32–39 dob 06.06.21 dod 2005) O.C.T.U., R.E., Lt.

Gardiner, Reginald Charles (EM17–23 dob 05.11.05) P.T.C., Pte.

Gardner, David Boult (EM35–42 dob 25.03.26 dod 27.03.2006) R.N., *[Also listed as 'D. Gander'].*

Gay, Richard Hammond (EM27–34 dob 27.10.15) M.N., 3rd Ofr., *[Also listed as 'R. Gay'].*

Geen, Dennis Victor (EM36–42 dob 15.12.24) R.A., 1st Field Battery, Gnr.

George, Peter Dunkinson (EM1930 dob 09.03.1920) R.A., Capt., *[Listed as 'P. D. Dunkinson'].*

Geraghty, Sir William (EM28–35 dob 12.02.17 dod 05.1977) R.A., Capt.

Gibson, J., R.A.F., F./Lt.

Gibson, Paul Wallace (EM31–34 dob 23.01.19) R.A., Lt. *[Listed as 'P. Gibson'].*

Gilbert, Robert D'Lonay (EM24–25 dob 02.05.09) R.M., R.N., Lt.

Gilder, Frank William (EM09–15 dob 05.02.1898) R.A., Capt.

Giles, F. R. V. (EM26–34 dob 16.04.15) R.A.S.C., Sgt. *[Listed as 'F. Giles'].*

Gimson, Alfred Charles (EM28–36 dob 07.06.17 dod 28.04.1985) Intel Corps., F.S.P., Capt.

Glendenning, Peter Graham (EM32–39 dob 07.09.21) York & Lancaster Regt., att. 5th Green Howards. Lt. (Listed as missing later POW – later escaped). Awarded the M.B.E.

Goalen, Robert Henry W. (EM34–37 dob 08.12.20) R.A., (A.A.) R.T.C., Gnr. *[Also listed as 'R. H. Goaler'].*

Godfrey, Arthur William George (EM28–30 dob 19.07.11) R.A.F., Cpl., A.C.2.

Goff, Gustavus Frederick J. (EM16–25 dob 24.03.08) 503 Coy. (Field) R.E., Maj.

Gold, W. G., R.I.A.S.C., (Mentioned in Despatches). Maj.

Goldsworthy, Basil Martin (EM21–24 dob 11.03.13) R.N., Surgeon., Lt.-Cdr.

Goldsworthy, Francis John (EM21–25 dob 15.05.05 dod 1994) R.N., Dentist on H.M.S. *Maine.*

Goodchild, Reginald Arthur (EM19–27 dob 09.05.08) Singapore Defence Force, Lt. (listed as missing, later POW).

Goodger, Allan Charles – R.A.S.C., Lt. (POW). *[Also listed as R. K. Goodyear]*

Grant, Alan (EM21–29 dob 26.03.10 dod 25.12.1974) R.N.V.R., Lt.

Gray, Robert Austin Ring (EM34–37 dob 16.05.20) R.A.F., Fitter.

Gray, Ronald Douglas (EM31–38 dob 01.11.19) Intel. Corps., R.A., Capt. Bletchley Park.

Gray, Tom Edmond Stone (EM23–29 dob 06.07.11) R.N. Lt., (POW).

Green, Eric Dudley (EM39–40 dob 17.03.22) R.C.S., Capt.

Green, Raymond Joseph (EM36–40 dob 17.02.26) H.M.S. *Worcester*, Cdt.

Green, Andrew James Kitchener (EM26–34 dob 15.09.15) R.A.P.C., A.M.P.C., Pte. *[Also listed as 'A. J. Greene'].*

Greene, Frederick George (EM26–33 dob 03.01.15 dod 1986) R.A.F., Sgt.

Greenslade, Thomas Henry (EM27–34 dob 05.12.15) R.A.F.

Griffiths, John Stanley (EM27–31 dob 19.05.13) R.A.C., Tpr.

Griffiths, Stanley Phillips (EM33–36 dob 09.06.22) R.N. *[Listed as 'S. Griffith'].*

Grundy, John Brownsdon Clowes (EM13–20 and Headmaster 1953–1963 dob 21.04.02 dod 17.07.1987) Intel. Services.

Gurling, Kenneth John (EM32–40 dob 23.05.21 dod 17.06.2002) R.A.M.C., Maj.

- H -

Haining, William (EM24–28 dob 11.04.11 dod 1983) R.A.F.

Hale, Harold Bertram (EM30–37 dob 19.11.20 dod 21.03.43) R.A.F.V.R., F./O. ✤

Halfacre, H. A. G. (EM37–42 dob 27.04.26) Training Btn., Pte.

Halligan, John Edward (EM31–37 dob 23.03.20) East Surreys, Q.R.R., Royal Horse Artillery., Capt. *[Also listed as 'J. E. Halligam'].*

Hamilton, Robert John (EM19–25 dob 22.12.07) R.A.M.C., Maj. *[Listed as both 'R. Hamilton' and 'R. T. Hamilton'].*

Hamilton-Wilkes, Frank Deane (EM23–29 dob 29.04.12 dod 23.08.42) R.A.F.V.R. F./Sgt. ✤

Hammond, Arthur Howard Hammond (EM10–18 dob 04.02.01) Indian Army, Lt. *[Listed as 'H. A Hammond'].*

Hancock, Horace Herbert (EM23–28 dob 22.06.14) Regiment and rank unknown.

Hanks, Harry (staff 1929–48 dob 23.11.01 dod 19.07.1977) R.A.F.V.R., F./Lt.

Hansford, Kenneth Stanley (EM27–36 dob 08.06.18) R.N.V.R., Sub./Lt. *[Also listed as 'K. E. Hansford' and 'R. K. Hansford']*.

Hansford, Leslie Percy H. (EM20 dob 06.07.1911) O.C.T.U., R.A.O.C., Lt. *[Also listed as 'C. P. H. Hansford']*.

Hanscombe, Henry Spencer (EM18–23 dob 28.09.07) R.A.F., A.C.2. *[Listed only as 'Hascombe']*.

Harber, James Frederick (EM30–40 dob 22.08.23) Recce Corps., L./Cpl.

Hardie, Ian Cameron (EM32–38 dob 04.01.21) London Scottish., L./Cpl.

Harding, Philip George (EM26–32 dob 03.11.14) Glos. Regt., Worcester Regt., Capt. *[Listed as 'P. Harding']*. (POW).

Harding, Roy Albert (EM38–45 dob 05.05.27) Intel Corps., Pte.

Hardy, S. A., R.A., Lt.

Hardy, Sydney Campbell (EM23–32 dob 26.05.15) R.A., Gnr.

Harfoot, Brian Thomas Edmund (EM33–38 dob 21.12.18) R.C.S., 2nd London Div. Signals., Capt. *[Also listed as 'B. J. E. Harfoot']*.

Harker, J. L., Recce Corps., 2nd London Div. Signals., L./Cpl.

Harman, Henry Robert (EM28–35 dob 23.08.17) R.A.F., P./O., A.C.2., *[Also listed as 'H. Harman']*.

Hulton Harrap, Victor Edward M. (EM27–29 dob 16.05.14) R.A.F.

Harrington, Derek James (EM26–33 dob 15.04.15 dod 25.05.2001) Queen's Royal Regt., R.A.F., Capt.

Harris, Albert Francis (EM30–36 dob 02.07.19) R.C.S., L./Sgt.

Harris, Charles Michael (EM25–34 dob 11.02.15) R.A.F., Sgt.

Harris, Frederick William (EM33–39 dob 08.08.22) R.A.F., L.A.C.

Harrison, Reginald John (EM27–35 dob 19.06.16 dod 01.03.45) O.C.T.U., K.S.L.I., Maj. ✤

Harry, Charles Philip Spencer (EM32–37 dob 08.08.20) R.A.S.C., Dvr., *[Also listed as 'C. Harry', 'C. S. Harry', also under 'Spencer Harry']*.

Hart, John Frederick (31–37 dob 03.12.19) R.A.F., P./O. (Invalided out).

Hart, Owen William (EM18–21 dob 05.10.08) King's Regt., Lt., *[Listed as 'O Hart']*.

Hart, W., R.A.F. P./O.

Hartly, S., R.A.

Hartnett, William Bernard (EM36–37 dob 21.08.19) R.A.F., F./O., Awarded the D.F.C., *[Also listed as both 'W. Hartnett' and 'Hartrett']*.

Hastings, Leslie R. (EM34–36) R.A.F.V.R., (Mentioned in Despatches). Sqn./Ldr., Awarded the D.F.C. *[Also listed as 'C. R. Hastings']*.

Hawes, Robert Donaldson (EM32–39 dob 13.01.24) R.A.F.V.R., P./O., A.C.2.

Haydock, Brian W. (EM33–44 dob 10.04.26) R.A.F., A.C.2., Cpl.

Haydock, John Lindsay (EM30–42 dob 13.08.23 dod 1947) R.A. (S.U.C.) Lt.

Haydon, David P. (EM14–18 dob 28.04.02) R.E.M.E., Lt–Col.

Hayward, Kenneth 'Rex' (EM19–30 dob 18.06.11 dod 1987) R.P.C., Capt. *[Also listed as 'R. Hayward']*.

Head, Arthur James 'Jimmy' (EM18–24 dob 08.08.06 dod 1976) R.A.O.C., Maj. *[Also listed as 'J. Head']*.

Hearnden, John Frederick (EM36–42 dob 12.10.24) R.N.V.R., Sub./Lt. Midshipman.

Heath, Anthony Eric (EM27 dob 30.12.12) War Office, Capt.

Heath, George Feetham (EM24–28 dob 11.01.15 dod 06.1978) Sharp Shooters, North Africa.

Hedges, Peter Edward (EM36–42 dob 06.04.25) R.N.V.R., Sub./Lt.

Hein, Albert William (EM29–35 dob 09.06.18) O.C.T.U., Maj.

Heming, Jack Chetward Weston (EM10–16 dob 02.09.1899 dod 11.10.1987) R.N.

Henderson, Edmund (EM28–34 dob 15.04.17) R.A.F., W.O.

Henson, Leslie Lincoln (EM03–06 dob 03.08.1891 dod 03.12.1957) E.N.S.A.

Herbage, Sidney James (EM33–40 dob 23.02.25) Royal Warwicks, Capt. *[Also listed as 'P. J. Herbage']*.

Heywood, James Frank (EM22–29 dob 31.05.11) R.N.V.R., Lt. (survived sinking of H.M.S. *Ark Royal*, 1941).

Heywood, Percival Charles (EM27–34 dob 28.05.16) O.C.T.U., Royal Warwicks., Maj.

Hill, Sidney Alfred (EM32–38 dob 21.11.20) London Scottish, Pte.

Hillier, George Henry (EM29–35 dob 17.12.17) Regiment and rank unknown.

Hipkins, Wilfred Stafford (EM12–19 dob 03.02.01 dod 12.02.1982) T.A.R.O., Capt.

Hoare, Douglas Sydney 'Sammy' (EM29–35 dob 22.10.17) R.A.F., F./O. (POW)

Holdbrook, Kenneth (EM25–31 dob 15.05.14) R.A., Lt.

Holland, Basil Herbert (EM35–42 dob 22.03.24) R.A.F.V.R. (S.U.C.) P./O. *[Also listed as 'B. A. Holland']*.

Holland, Norman Joseph (EM1939 dob 10.01.22) R.A. (Surrey) Gnr.

Hollands, Richard Lyntell (EM13–22 dob 29.11.05 dod 1978) R.A.S.C.

Holliman, Kenneth Harold (EM34–40 dob 29.01.24) R.N.V.R. (F.A.A.) Sub./Lt. *[Also listed as 'K. A. Holliman']*.

Holliman, Stanley George (EM33–41 dob 28.05.22) Queen's Royal Regt., (O.C.T.U.) R.E. Capt., Awarded the M.C.

Holt, Alec (EM24–28 dob 17.04.12) R.A., Gnr. (POW).

Hopkins, Frederick William (EM31–38 dob 23.03.20) R.A.P.C., Lt.

Hopkins, Jack, (EM27–34 dob 04.05.16 dod 19.01.1990) Maj.

Hopkins, John Collier F., Rhodesian Territorial

Force. Instructor

Hopkins, L. L., R.C.S., L./Cpl.

Hopkins, Leslie Norman (EM34–40) O.C.T.U., Cdt.

Hopkins, Peter John (EM33–39 dob 16.06.22) Recce Corps., R.A.P.C., Pte., *[Listed as 'P. Hopkins']*.

Hopper, Alec Stanley (EM31–36 dob 09.10.19) 321 Coy. R.E., Sapper., *[Listed as 'A. Stanley']*.

Horlock, Ronald A. (EM33–42 dob 01.09.25) R.A.O.C., Pte.

Horseman, Kenneth (EM29–36 dob 24.11.17) Rifle Brigade, Rifleman. (POW).

Houlden, Ernest Arthur (EM30–35 dob 12.04.17) R.A.S.C., R.A.P.C., Cpl.

Hudson, Sidney Rowland (EM08–15 dob 15.06.1897) T.A., T.D., General List, A.M.P.C., A.P.C., Pioneer Btn., Maj.

Huggett, Frank Edward (EM35–42 dob 25.03.24) R.A.F.V.R., A.C.2.

Huggins, Anthony Gerald Lawrence (EM38–42 dob 30.12.24) R.A.F.V.R., A.C.2.

Hughes, Glyn Morgan (EM34–40 26.11.1923) L./Cpl., *[Listed as 'G. Hughes']*.

Hughes, Richard Ernest (EM27–33 dob 03.01.16) D.C.L.I., Lt.

Hughes, Samuel Gethin (EM10–15 dob 09.08.1898 dod 1988) Leader of a Home Guard unit.

Hunt, Alfred Richard Hefin (EM31–37 dob 20.06.20) R.A., (Signals) Bdr.

Hunt, James Glyn (EM34–40 dob 14.10.22 dod 25.09.44) Royal Welsh Fusiliers, Cpl., *[Listed as 'J. Hunt']*. ✤

Hurden, Roy Kenneth (EM37–42 dob 22.05.26) Nigerian Regiment, Lt.

Hurn, Robert George Douglas (EM40–42 dob 14.06.25) R.N.V.R., (F.A.A.) Sub./Lt., N.A.2.

Hutchins, Harold John (EM21–28 dob 24.09.10 dod 1999) East Lancs. Regt., Maj. Awarded the M.C.

- I -

Inkster, Alan Raymond (EM34–39 dob 12.08.21) R.A.F., A.C.2.

Inkster, Donald Stewart (EM34–42 dob 29.03.25) O.C.T.U., Cdt., R.A.P.C., Lt.

Inkster, Lawrence (EM1900–06 dob 02.05.1899) A.T.C., Flt./Lt., Awarded the M.C in First World War].

Inkster, Lawrence George (EM34–37 dob 16.12.19) Indian Army, London Scottish., Capt.

Irving, Edward Roger (EM34–40 dob 28.12.24) R.A.F.V.R., A.C.2., *[Listed as 'E. B. Irving']*.

Ivy, Robert H. (EM1891–98 dod 1974)

American Medical Corps., Dental Surgeon.

- J -

Jackson, Peter Harold (EM32–38 dob 09.11.20 dod 10.11.43) O.C.T.U., R.A.C, D Squadron, 2nd Special Air Service Regiment (2 S.A.S) Lt., Awarded the M.C. ✤

James, D. G., East Surreys.

James, Hugh S. Gwynne (EM31–33 dob 15.12.15) King's African R., East Surrey Regt., Maj.

Jarvis, W. John Thorning (EM25–32 dob 01.07.1915) R.N. *[Also listed as 'W. G. T. Jarvis'].*

Jeffery, William Michael Squire (EM32–38 dob 21.08.21) O.C.T.U., R.T.R., (Mentioned in Despatches). Capt., (Colonel R.T.R. in1966).

Jenkins, Adrian H. (EM28–33 dob 17.02.17) K.R.R.C., Rifleman.

Jenkins, John Stephen P. (EM35–40 dob 07.01.24) R.A.F., F./Sgt.

Jenrick, John Blackmore (EM36–43 dob 11.09.24) C.Q.M.S. A.M.P.C. (retired). Capt., *[Also listed as 'G. B. Jenrick'].*

Jewell, Richard Arundel (EM20–26 dob 01.10.10) Master builder for Government.

Johnson, Bramwell Frederick Thomas (EM33–39 dob 09.11.21 dod 17.07.41) R.A.F.V.R., Sgt./P., *[Also listed as both 'B. F. Johnson' and 'B. Johnstone'].* ✤

Jones, John William Thomas (EM15–25 dob 30.04.06) R.A.O.C., Capt.

Jones, Maurice Galbraith (EM24–34 dob 14.02.16) O.C.T.U., 2nd Lt., (Invalided out).

Jones, Stanley Lloyd (EM31–37 dob 03.11.19) R.C.S., Sgt. *[Also listed as 'S. C. Jones'].*

Jones, William James (EM20–26 dob 21.11.08 dod 13.06.44) R.A.F.V.R., F./Lt. *[Also listed as 'W. J. F. Jones'].* ✤

Joslin, George (EM23–27 dob 06.09.11) Mercantile Marine. First Officer.

Joyce, Reginald Francis (EM 29–34 dob 19.11.17 dod 11.07.42) K.R.R.C., Rifleman. ✤

- K -

Kearey, A. S., K.O.S.B., Lt., *[Also listed as 'A. S. Keary'].*

Kearney, William Henry (EM24–31) R.A.F., W/C., *[Also listed as 'W. H. Kearny'].*

Kebbell, Peter Davies (EM34–37 dob 26.01.21 dod 15.11.42) Gordon Highlanders, Capt. ✤

Keeler, Ian David (EM25–32 dob 05.06.14) R.I.A.S.C., Maj., *[Listed as 'I. Keeler'].*

Keeling, Cecil F. (EM23–28 dob 12.08.12 dod 27.08.1976) R.A. *[Also listed as 'F. Keeling'].*

Keeling, Thomas Henry (EM22–27 dob 04.12.09) R.A.F., F./O.

Kemp, Alan (EM37–45 dob 25.09.26) R.N., O.S.

Kemp, Tom (EM32–40 dob 28.02.1928 dod 22.12.1993) R.N., O.S.

Kent, Edward Nelson (EM18–25 dob 05.12.06) R.A.S.C., Lt.

Kent, Peter (EM27–32 dob 28.09.15 dod 1985) O.C.T.U., R.E., Lt.

Kentfield, Geoffrey William (EM28–36 dob 30.08.18) East Surreys, Q.R.R., Pte., *[Listed as 'J. Kentfield'].*

Kevis, Dennis James (EM31–35 dob 08.06.19 dod 29.06.42) R.A.O.C., att. 10th Btn. Royal Welch Fusiliers L./Cpl. ✤

Kibble, Frank John (EM18–23 dob 29.10.06 dod 08.01.2005) R.A.F., F./O.

Kiebooms, John Robert (EM32–40 dob 10.08.21) R.I.A.S.C., Indian Army, Queen's Royal Regt., O.C.T.U., Beds & Herts Regt., Maj.

Kimber, Albert Thomas George, R.T.R., Sgt. *[Also listed as 'A. E. Kimber'].* (dod 12.11.43). ✤

Kimber, Kenneth George (EM31–35 dob 26.03.17 dod 09.02.2005) Experimental Officer, Chemical Inspection Dept.

King, Frederick Ernest Royston (EM26–30 dob 17.04.13 dod 19.08.39) R.A.F., F/Lt.

King, H. C. L. (EM21–28 dob 1909 dod 1962) 60th Rifles, K.R.R.C.

King, Ronald Roy (EM32–35 dob 27.12.19) R.A.F., A.C.1.

King, William Arthur (EM left 1935 dod 26.05.40) Royal Warwicks, 2nd Lt. ✤

Kingham, Dennis Frederick (EM27–35 dob 01.07.20) R.C.S., Sign'r.

Kirby, Charles Frederick (EM28–32 dob 05.12.14 dod 15.11.43) R.N.V.R. (Air Branch) (F.A.A) Lt. ✤

Kirk, John Peter (EM32–38 dob 04.02.20) Royal Gurka Rifles, K.O.Y.L.I., (Invalided out). Capt.

Kirkwood, Thomas Miller (EM24–25 dob 30.12.06) Inniskillings, Lt–Col.

Kitt, David Douglas (EM36–40 dob 26.11.1924) R.N., O.S.

Knight, Maurice William (EM30–40 dob 02.08.22) R.N., O.S.

Knight, Philip Sydney (EM33–41 dob 24.09.25) Welsh Guards, Guardsman. *[Listed as 'P. Knight'].*

Kuper, Charles (Headmaster 1964–75 dob 1915 dod 09.08.1975) R.N.

- L -

Laine, John Francis H. (EM34–40 dob 27.07.1923) R.N.V.R., (F.A.A) Sub–Lt.

Laker, A. G., O.C.T.U., Indian Army., Lt.

Lamb, Herbert Gordon (EM22–29 dob 08.03.11 dod 2000) R.N.V.R., Lt., *[Also listed as 'Lambs'].*

Lander, Rollo Thomas (EM30–37 dob 23.02.20) R.C.S., L./Cpl.

Lane, B. A. (EM29–37 dob 08.07.21) Westminster Dragoons., O.C.T.U., R.C.S., Maj. *[Also listed as 'Capt. B. A. Lane'].*

Langley, C. (EM18–23 dob 16.02.07) R.A.F., P./O.

Langton, Norman Robert (EM30–36 dob 30.08.19 dod 19.06.44) R.A.F.V.R., W./O. ✤

Lawrence, Edward Bruce (EM35–36 dob 04.01.19) R.C.S., Sign'r.

Lawrence, Francis (EM35–39 dob 17.04.22) R.N., Lt.

Leader, Vernon Stanley J. (EM38–45 dob 28.02.27) R.A., Gnr.

Lee, Jack (EM24–30 dob 25.08.12 dod 07.06.44) R.A., Beds & Herts Regt., Capt. ✤

Leggett, Cyril Alfred (EM22–29 dob 15.04.13 dod 24.05.41) O/S R.N. H.M.S. *Hood.* ✤

Le Good, Hugh James Felce (EM24–30 dob 12 dod 03.08.1992) R.A.F., Wing Comdr., Awarded the A.F.C., and D.F.C.

Lehmann, Peter (EM29–37 dob 15.12.18 dod 29.10.2006) Air Sea Rescue, R.A.F.

Leiper, Jason Hamilton (EM15–21 dob 11.10.04) Pioneer Corps., Maj., *[Also listed as 'J. R. Leiper'].*

Leiper, Newall (EM19–30 dob 14.07.12) R.A., Dvr.

Lenthall, Wilfrid Harry (EM24–30 dob 15.05.13) L./Cpl.

Le Pelley, J. P., R.N., O.S.

Le Seilleur, O., R.A., Capt.

Lewis, Michael John (EM37–40 dob 13.12.23 dod 11.10.44) 17/21 Lancers., R.A.C., Lt. ✤

Lewis, William Harry (EM36–39 dob 06.09.19) R.A., Gnr., Lt., (POW) *[Also listed as 'W. Lewis' and 'W. A. Lewis'].*

Lightoller, Herbert Brian (EM28–29 dob 19.01.18 dod 04.09.39) F./O., R.A.F.V.R. ✤

Linck, David (EM37–39 dob 01.11.24) M.N.

Lloyd, James B. (EM15–24 dob 10.04.1907) R.A.S.C., C.S.M.

Lockeyear, Peter Claude (EM32–40 dob 04.04.23 dod 30.11.43) R.A.F.V.R., Sgt./Obs., *[Also listed as 'Lockyear'].* ✤

Lofting, Leonard Archer (EM32–37 dob 01.08.21) R.A.F., F./Sgt.

Lovegrove, Charles Edward (EM17–25 dod 1981) Air Ministry, R.A.F.

Lovegrove, Kenneth A. (EM36–43 dob 19.04.25 dod 06.04.2012) R.N.

Lovelock, William (EM10–16 dob 13.03.1899 dod 26.06.1986) Indian Army Ordnance Corps., Maj.

Luckin, R.A.C., Tpr.

Luery, Rupert Aswald (EM23–31 dob 20.12.14) R.A.F., Sgt.

Lumsden, J. Albert (EM39–42 dob 25.07.24) East Surreys, Pte., (Invalided out).

Lyons, John W. (EM1910–13 dod 24.01.1977) Regiment and rank unknown.

- M -

MacDonald, J. V., R.A.F.V.R., P./O.

MacIntosh, Donald Roderick (EM35–42 dob 09.07.24) R.A.F.V.R., A.C.2., Sgt./P.

McKenzie, Alexander V. (EM35–41 dob 21.11.23) Indian Army, Highland Regt., Lt.

MacKenzie, D. (EM19–23 dob 2.03.07) Canadian Army, Maj.

Macrow, Clement Roy (EM17–19 dob 17.07.03 dod 1992) R.A.O.C., Pte., (Invalided out). *[Also listed as 'Mackrow'].*

Maidment, R. E. (EM32–38 dob 13.12.20) R.A.F., A.C.2.

Mairs, James (EM26–32 dob 18.06.15) H.A.C., Pte.

Maltby, *[Presumed to be 'Kenneth Thomas Maltby' EM36–39 dob 07.01.23]*. O.C.T.U., Recce Corps, Cdt.

Mammen, Gerald Sidney (EM37–44 dob 17.12.25) Lancs Fusiliers., Sgt.

Mann, Albert 'Bertie' Sydney (EM27–37 dob 14.06.19 dod 30.12.2009) R.A.F., Wing Comdr., Awarded the D.F.C.

Marks, W. J., O.C.T.U. *[Presumed to be 'Hayward John William Marks EM23–31 dob 27.11.12]*. Cdt

Marrison, W. B., R.A.S.C., Lt.

Marshall, E. A., East Surreys, Pte.

Marshall, L., Q.R.R., Pte.

Marshall, S. A. (EM36–43 dob 25.08.25) Gordon Highlanders, L./Cpl.

Masey, Cecil James (EM29–34 dob 24.07.16) O.C.T.U., R.C.S., Capt.

Mash, Wilfrid Edgar (EM25–30 dob 08.05.12) R.A.O.C., Cpl.

Mason, H. G., R.A.F., L./A.C.

Mason, Peter Herbert (EM22–33 dob 23.10.14) 46th Recce Corps. R.A.C., Capt., Awarded the M.C.

Mason, Percy James (EM15–17 dob 12.10.04) R.A.S.C., Pte.

Mather, John (EM36–44 dob 20.03.26) R.N., O./Tel., L./Cpl.

Matthews, R. E. (EM26–33 dob 27.11.14) 2nd Lt., *[Listed as 'R. Mathews']*.

Matsuyama, Eichi (EM27–32 dob 08.10.15) Canadian Army, Sgt.

Matthews, R. C., Gordon Highlanders, Capt.

Maxwell, Roy (EM37–44 dob 19.02.26 dod 2004) L./Cpl., *[Listed as 'R. D. Maxwell']*.

May, Henry Robert (EM35–41 dob 20.06.24) R.A.F., Sgt.

Maycock, Anthony (Staff dob 02.04.21 dod 16.05.1995) Worcestershire Regiment.

Mayes, Frederick Wortley (EM24–27 dob 11.09.11 dod 30.09.1986) R.A.C..

McCabe, – R.A.F., Sgt., A.C.2.

McDonnell, Michael Herbert Lucas (EM33–38 dob 30.03.21 dod 29.04.43) O.C.T.U., R.T.R. R.A.C. 2nd Lt. ✤

McGregor, John Harvey (EM16–23 dob 12.05.06 dod 19.12.41) R.N. Acting Paymaster Comdr. on HMS *Neptune [Listed as both 'J. McGregor' and 'R. MacGregor']*. ✤

McGregor, Kenneth Robert (EM19–28 dob 09.12.08 dod 07.12.45) Army Educational Corps., Sgt. ✤

McKenzie, Alexander V. (EM35–41 dob 21.11.23) Indian Army, Highland Regt., 2nd Lt.

Mclean, John (dod 14.09.44) R.A.O.C., R.A.C., Lt. (Mentioned in Despatches twice). ✤

McMahon, J., Parachute Coy., Pte.

McMahon, Kenneth (EM31–38 dob 06.06.22) Field Security Corps., Indian Army., Q.R.R., Capt.

McMahon, Thomas Charles (EM31–41 dob 09.05.20) Ind. Parachute Coy, Pte.

McMillan, Eric John (EM33–38 dob 16.04.22 dod 22.10.43) R.A.F.V.R., Sgt. ✤

McMillan, Leonard Henry M. (EM17–24 dob 30.05.06) R.A.F., F./O., *[Also listed as 'L. H. McMillian']*.

McNish, Roland Leonard Hastings (EM1897–99) R.N.R., M.M., Capt., [Awarded the D.S.O. in the First World War]

Mendleson, Lionel (EM37–42) R.A.F.V.R., A.C.2. (dob 23.12.22)

Meredith, Alan Francis (EM28–35 dob 27.08.05) Intel. Corps., R.C.S., M.G.T.C., Capt.

Meredith, Oswald Lake (EM13–19 dob 03.12.1900 dod 1991) R.N., Lt. Comdr.

Meredith, William Lake (EM14–24 dob 27.08.05) R.N.V.R., (Mentioned in Despatches).

Merrett, Frank Hinson (EM31–40 dob 07.01.24) O.C.T.U., Royal West Kents., Lt.

Merrett, F. M., O.C.T.U., Royal Sussex., 2nd Lt.

Meyers, John Frederick (EM18–24 dob 28.09.06) R.A.C., Lt., *[Also listed as 'J. A. Meyers']*.

Miller, James George (EM34–39 dob 18.02.22) 3rd King's Own Hussars, Tpr.

Miller, J. G., East Surrey Regt., R.A.C., Pte.,

Milliken, F. J., R.A.F., F./O., Awarded the D.F.C.

Millist, Charles Jackson (EM31–36) Ox & Bucks Light Infantry and Intel. Services.

Millist, Kenneth Milton (EM31–35 dob 31.03.19 dod 07.04.41) R.A.F., P./O., Awarded the D.F.C. ✤

Millist, Robert Geoffrey (EM31–33) Arctic Convoys.

Mills, Alfred Edward (EM24–32 dob 02.03.13 dod 07.1993) R.E.M.E., Craftsman., R.A.F.

Mitchell, R.A.F.

Mitchell, Leonard John (EM37–44 dob 18.02.26) R.A.F., A.C.2.

Money, Leslie Joseph (EM23–28 dob 21.03.12) M.N., Chief Officer.

Monkhouse, Eric Carl (EM19–28 dob 02.05.11 dod 08.1973) R.N.V.R., Lt. Comdr., Paym'r., *[Also listed as 'G. C. Monkhouse']*.

Moore, G., R.A., Gnr.

Morford, William Douglas (EM23–30 dob 13.03.13) R.A.F., F./O.

Morfey, Ronald James (EM00–07 dob 13.12.1900) R.A., Maj. *[Also listed as 'R. J. Morley']*.

Morrill, Douglas George (EM28–33 dob 08.02.17 dod 18.06.41) L/Cpl R.A.C. ✤

Morris, Herbert Edward (EM23–28 dob 08.10.11 dod 21.02.1945) R.C.S., Cpl. ✤

Mott, Arthur Reginald (EM24–30 dob 28.08.13 dod 13.10.42) R.A.F., Sgt./Pilot. ✤

Mulliner, Peter Owen (EM26–35 dob 12.06.17) R.A.S.C., Capt.

Murphy, Denis William (EM36–43 dob 20.02.25) Royal Scots Fusiliers, R.A., F.B. (S.U.C). Lt.

Murray, Gordon Marr (EM29–37 dob 03.05.21) London Scottish., Pte. and Royal Corps of Signals., Lt.

Murray, Norman William (EM21–27 dob 19.03.12) London Scottish., Lt. *[Also listed as 'N. M. Murray']*.

Murray, Richard Marr (EM21–27) L.D.F., Malaya 2nd Lt., (POW).

- N -

Nargang, Victor Stanley (EM27–33 dob 26.02.14) East African Garrison., K.A.R., Maj.

Naylor, Donald Russell (EM27–34 dob 22.02.16) R.E.M.E., (Mentioned in Despatches). Maj. *[Also listed as 'D. Russell Naylor']*. Awarded the M.B.E.

Neale, Bruce Alan (EM34–40 dob 15.09.29 dod 1996) R.A. (S.U.C.) Lt.

Neale, John Howard (EM31–37 dob 02.04.20) O.C.T.U., R.A., Capt. Awarded the M.C. *[Also listed as 'J A Neale']*.

Neath, Wilfrid Claude (Staff 36–74 dob 09.12.07 dod 14.04.1975) R.A.F.V.R., P./O., *[Also listed as 'W. G. Neath']*. Awarded the D.F.C.

Needham, Kenneth Robin (EM23–29 dob 09.08.12 dod 1995) R.A., Maj. (Chindits).

Neubert, Peter William (EM30–40 dob 27.06.22) F.A.A., L.A.C., *[Also listed as 'P. W. Newbert' and Neubert, D. W., R.N.V.R., (F.A.A.).]*.

Neubert, Robin Geoffrey (EM34–39 dob 10.07.27) R.A.C., Tpr., *[Listed as 'R. Neubert']*.

Newstead, Arthur Robert (EM23–31 dob 03.10.14) Middlesex Regt., Capt., *[Listed as 'A. Newstead']*.

Newton, Percy Alfred (EM30–36 dob 29.10.18 dod 01.10.42) O.C.T.U., Middlesex Regt., Lt. ✤

Nichols, F., R.N., A.B.

Nicholson, Peter Fowles (EM32–37 dob 13.07.20) O.C.T.U., R.E., Capt.

Noble, Brian Robert (EM27–33 dob 26.08.16) R.A.F., Sqn. Ldr. *[Also listed as 'B. Noble' and 'B. H. Noble']*.

Noble, Eric Hughes (EM31–39 dob 10.07.20) O.C.T.U., R.A., Lt.

Noble, James Alexander (EM37–44 dob 30.11.25) R.A.F.V.R., A.C.2., Cpl.

Noble, Roy Beaumont (EM16–23 dob 03.07.04) R.N.V.R., Sub-Lt.

Noble, R. C., R.E., O./Cdt.

Noel, Marcel Paul (EM36–39 dob 19.03.20) R.A.F., F./Lt. *[Also listed as 'M. Noel']*.

Nonweiler, Eric Ronald (EM22–29) 2nd Lt. (POW).

Nussey, S. S. M. (Staff 1938–48 dob 03.08.15) Lincolnshire Regt., Lt., *[Also listed as 'S. S. N. Nussey']*.

- O -

Oliver, Ronald Geoffrey Oliver (Staff 1939–40 dob 10.03.13) F.S.P., L./Cpl. *[Also listed as 'R. Oliver']*.

Orford, Frank (EM36–43 dob 20.07.25) R.A.F., (S.U.C.) Sgt., A.C.2.

Orr, James (EM22–24 dob 17.03.08) R.E.M.E., R.A.O.C., Col.

Orr, Nathaniel Percy (EM22–29 dob 24.12.09 dod 25.02.43) R.A.F.V.R., P./O. ✤

Osborn, Denis Stanley (EM37–44 dob 24.09.26) R.N., O.S.

Owens, Richard Frank (EM31–34 dob 27.08.22 dod 05.11.40) R.N.R. Midshipman, KILLED when HMS *Jervis Bay* sunk. ✤

- P -

Page, Edwin Douglas (EM33–39 dob 28.12.21) Royal Fusiliers., O.C.T.U., 1st Gurkha Rifles., Capt.

Page, Frank Ernest (EM28–30 dob 24.04.13) R.A.F., A.C.I.

Page, Harold Stanley (EM31–39) Royal Berkshire Regt., O.C.T.U., R.A., Capt.

Page, John Joseph Joffre (EM26–33 dob 01.01.15 dod 05.02.2006) R.A.F., Group-Capt.

Page William Leonard (EM31–39 dob 22.04.20 dod 26.12.44) att. 9th Btn. Royal Fusiliers, (B.D.S.) Lt. ✤

Painter, Duncan Frederick Scott (EM33–39 dob 04.09.22 dod 18.01.46) R.A., Sgt. ✤

Palmer, Felix Harvey Spencer (EM20–28 dob 03.05.12 dod 01.09.2005) East Surreys, Q.R.R., Maj. (POW). *[Also listed as 'F. Palmer'].*

Palmer, Geoffrey Blake (EM19–25 dob 06.01.09) New Zealand Medical Service, 5th Field Ambulance, New Zealand Defence Force. (Mentioned in Despatches). Awarded the Greek Silver Medal. Adjutant.

Palmer, Norman Baydges (EM20–28 dob 05.05.11) Kenya Def. Force., Gnr.

Pamplin, Richard Geoffrey (EM15–17 dob 04.06.03) R.A.F., A.C.1.

Parrack, Kenneth Beach (EM22–31 dob 24.12.13) R.A., (A.A.) Lt., Gnr. *[Also listed as 'K. C. Parrack'].*

Parris, Reginald Frank (EM27–32 dob 29.08.16) R.N.V.R., (Motor Boat Patrol) P.O.

Parslow, Charles William Lewis (EM27–33 dob 13.03.16) South Wales Borderers., Capt.

Pearce, Eric John (EM31–39 dob 19.05.21) R.N.V.R., (F.A.A.) (Air Branch) Lt.

Peck, Dennis William (EM34–40 dob 15.07.23) R.C.S., Lt. *[Also listed as 'D. W. Peel'].*

Pendrigh, John Robert (EM34–42 dob 19.03.23) Oxford & Bucks L.I., O.C.T.U., Hampshire Regt., Lt.

Pepper, Leonard Arthur Walter (EM29–35 dob 14.01.18) R.C.S., Sign'r.

Perkins, Alexander Reginald (EM31–34 dob 07.03.18) F.S.C., O.C.T.U., Lt.

Perkins, Stanley Arthur (EM31–38 dob 23.05.20) R.A.M.C., Pte.

Peters, Gordon Henry (EM26–32 dob 12.07.15) R.N.R., Paym'r., Lt.

Peters, John A. Peters (EM14–18 dob 28.03.03) R.N.V.R., Sub./Lt. *[Listed as 'J. Peters'].*

Peters, John Edgar Norris (EM29–36 dob 18.07.19) R.A., Capt.

Petty, Donald Charles (EM38 dob 17.09.27) R.A.F., P./O., *[Listed as 'D. K. Petty'].*

Philip, David Alexander (EM35–39 dob 11.08.23) R.E.M.E., Craftsman.

Phillips, Anthony Heath (EM32–39 dob 16.07.22) R.C.S., Sign'r.

Phillips, Colin Angus (EM37–39 dob 27.05.26) Life Guards, Tpr.

Phillips, Michael Frederick M. (EM30–36 dob 17.03.19) R.A., Capt.

Phillips, M. P., O.C.T.U., R.A. (A.A.) Cdt.

Pickford, John Aston (EM34–41) O.C.T.U., R.E., Lt., *[Also listed as 'J. Pickford'].*

Pike, Seymour Charles 'Peter' (EM33–37 dob 04.02.20 dod 30.03.44) R.N.V.R., PO./ Writer., Sign'r. [Lead Signalman on MGB 314 – Operation Chariot, aka St Nazaire Raid] Awarded the D.S.M. ✤

Pike, Douglas Beauchamp (EM34–39 dob 20.05.1923) Westminster D'gns., Cpl.

Pink, Sidney James (EM35–40 dob 13.04.24) R.A.F.

Pinkham, Eric Nelson (EM25–20 dob 06.09.12) R.A.P.C., Capt.

Pinkham, Ronald Victor (EM31–37 dob 02.10.19) O.C.T.U., Leicestershire Regt., Maj. Awarded the M.C.

Pleats, Donald Sidney (EM28–32 dob 09.06.15) R.A.C., Lt., *[Also listed as 'D. Pleass' and 'D. S. Pleass'].*

Pocock, Leslie Frederick (EM29–35 dob 22.06.18) R.A.M.C., Pte.

Pointon, Cyril William Joseph (EM30–35 dob 26.02.17) R.A.M.C., Pte. (POW).

Poole, Kenneth McDonald (EM30–38 dob 26.09.20) London Scottish, Pte.

Pople, Eric Gordon Morell (EM27–34 dob 06.01.17) London Scottish., O.C.T.U., K.R.R.C., Lt., (POW). *[Listed as 'G. Pople'].*

Poplett, Donald Oliver (EM37–43 dob 28.03.26) R.C.S., Pte.

Poplett, John Humphrey Francis (EM36–40 dob 05.09.22) Queen's Royal Regt., L./Cpl.

Powell, Delwyn James (EM28–36 dob 08.09.17) R.A.F., Sgt.

Prendergast, R. W., R.A.F., P./O., Awarded the D.F.C.

Price, John Sydney (EM24–30 and staff 1946 dob 25.11.11) R.A.F., A.C.1., *[Listed as 'J. Price'].*

Priestman, Eric (EM31–37 dob 27.08.20) R.C.S., Ind. Div. Signals., L./Cpl.

Price, Edward Allen (EM15–21 dob 04.06.03) R.E.M.E., Craftsman. *[Also listed as 'A. E. Prior'].*

Prins, Cornelius Arnold Larenz (Staff 1936–40 dob 17.06.11) Intel. Corps., Capt.

Prior, A. E., R.E.M.E.

Prior, Allen James 'Clem' (EM19–27 dob 09.11.07 dod 14.07.1983) Audit Branch of N.A.A.F.I. & Home Guard.

Prior, Roy Gerald (EM32–38 dob 10.09.21) C.L.Y., O.C.T.U., R.A.C., Sgt. Tpr.

Pritchard, John (EM33–36 dob 28.10.18) O.C.T.U., Cheshire Regt., Lt. *[Also listed as 'Cdt A. Pritchard' and 'Cdt J. Pritcard'].*

Prowse, Arthur Harry Robin (EM32–39 dob 27.02.21 dod 2010) R.A.F., P./O., (POW).

Pusey, Alfred Bateson (EM30–34 dob 10.08.17) Lt.

Pywell, Cecil Percy Dodd (EM28–37 dob 19.06.20) Surrey Yeomanry, Gnr.

- R -

Radford, Alan Charles (EM29–35 dob 15.06.20) R.N., *[Listed as 'A. Radford'].*

Rae, William Arthur (EM36–41 dob 31.03.25) R.M., Lt., Marine., *[Listed as 'W. R. Rae'].*

Rankin, Douglas John (AKA Rosenberg) (EM16–18 dob 24.01.01 dod 01.07.42) N.G.V.R. New Guinea Volunteer Rifles, Rifleman., (POW). ✤

Rayner, Donald John (EM32–38 dob 14.03.22) R.C.S., R.I.A.S.C. Sign'r., Lt.

Razzell, Frederick George (EM26–31 dob 31.08.14 dod 03.1973) R.A., B.S.M.

Reid, Robert Douglas (EM38–41 dob 02.07.24) R.N., O.S.

Richards, A. R., Coldstream Guards, Cpl.

Richards, George Henry H. (EM15–22 dob 30.06.04) Civil Affairs Branch, A.M.P.C., Lt.

Richards, John Henry S. (EM11–14 dob 12.04.1897) R.A.F., Wing Comdr.

Richardson, F., R.A.F.V.R., F./Lt.

Richardson, Gilbert (EM38–43 dob 30.05.27) R.N., O.S.

Richardson, Graham Eric (EM29–36 dob 25.06.19 dod 10.06.40) East Surrey Regt., Q.R.R., Pte. ✤

Richardson, Kenneth Arthur (EM32–39 dob 01.03.22) R.A.F.V.R., L.A.C.

Ridge, John William (EM37–42 dob 29.04.24) R.A.F.V.R., F./Sgt. *[Also listed as' J W Ride]* A.C.2., (S.U.C).

Roberts, Dudley (EM25–32 dob 19.06.14 dod 08.03.2006) R.A.F., P./O.

Roberts, Howard (Staff 1975–1987) R.A., 57th Field Regt., W./O.

Roberts, Jack (EM30–36 dob 01.07.19) R.A.F., Sgt.

Roberts, Kenneth Bryson (EM32–41 dob 07.09.23) Regiment and rank unknown.

Roberts, Leonard Craig (EM16–22 dob 17.11.04) R.E., Maj.

Robinson, Albert Victor (EM35–41 dob 27.03.24) R.N., O.S.

Robinson, Leonard Charles C. (EM24–29 dob 19.08.12) R.A.F., L.A.C.

Robinson, Niall Crichton G. (EM22–31 dob 09.08.14) R.A., Lt., *[Also listed as Axon, N. C. G. (né Robinson)].*

Robinson, Royd (EM26–32 dob 06.07.15) Leicestershire Regt., Lt.

Robinson, Thomas William C. (EM19–25 dob 06.06.08) R.A.F., Wing Comdr.

Roddis, David Leslie (EM32–39 dob 15.01.21) Lt.

Roddis, Peter Archibald (EM32–36 dob 22.06.19) R.A., Gnr.

Rogers, George Ronnie (EM10–17) R.T.R., Maj.

Rogers, Kenneth Walter (EM 40–44 dob 07.03.26) Intel. Corps. Pte.

Rogers, Therold Michael (EM32–38 dob 24.09.21) R.A.S.C., Pte.

Rolls, Gordon Cecil (EM29–34 dob 27.02.18) R.A.F., P./O.

Roots, A. C., R.A.F.

Rose, R., R.A., R.Q., (A.A.) Pte.

Rowdon, Leslie R. H. (EM27–34 dob 24.10.15) R.A., Lt.

Rowdon, Maurice Stanbury (EM33–41 dob 22.09.22 dod 2009) R.A., Capt.

Rowe, Jack Vickery (EM30–37 dob 29.03.21 dod 23.06.41) R.A.F.V.R., Sgt., A.C.2. ✤

Royal, Jack Douglas (EM26–34 dob 17.05.17 dod 18.05.42) R.A.F.V.R., (Mentioned in Despatches). Fl./Lt. *[Also listed as 'J. J. Royal' and 'J. Royal'].* ✤

Royffe, Harold Spencer (EM09–10) M.G.T.C, Capt. *[Also listed as both 'H. S. Roiffe' and 'H. S. Royfe'].*

Royd-Robinson, (EM25–32 dob 06.07.15) Leicester Regt., Lt.

Rubidge, Harold Edwin (EM36–42 dob 25.04.25) Black Watch, L./Cpl.

Runeckles, Gilbert Edmund (EM14–21 dob 19.04.03) R.A.F., Wing Comdr.

Ryder, Richard Stanley (EM30–35 dob 28.10.18 dod 06.09.42) R.A.F.V.R., F./Sgt. ✤

- S -

Sammond, Charles James (EM40–43 dob 11.09.26 dod 14.01.2006) Intel. Corps, R.A.

Sandell, R. E., Lt.

Sandell, M. C., R.A.S.C., Lt.

Sanders, David Walter (EM35–42 dob 24.02.24) O.C.T.U., Cdt.

Sanders, L. G. D., R.A., Gnr.

Sanderson, Harold F. (EM09–11 dob 30.10.1898) R.E., Lt–Col.

Sandi, – R.N.V.R., (F.A.A.) Lt., Awarded the D.S.C.

Sandle, Geoffrey Frederick (EM31–37 dob 30.06.22) R.A.F.

Sandoz, Henri Albert (EM33–39 dob 16.06.22) R.A., Lt.

Sandoz, Marcel Henri (EM28–33 dob 03.09.17) R.E., 217th Coy., Capt.

Sanford, Christopher (EM09–18 dob 28.11.1899) Canadian Army, Lt–Col.

Sanford, John Gurth (EM13–23 dob 11.09.05) R.E., Maj. *[Listed as 'J. Sanford'].*

Sangster, John Laing (EM34–41 dob 21.11.22) Intel. Corps., R.A., L./Cpl., L./Bdr.

Savage, Alan Patrick (EM21–29 dob 09.04.13) R.A.F., W./O., Awarded the D.F.M.

Savitt, Lawrence (EM26–31 dob 16.09.14 dod 13.05.44) R.A., Lt. ✤

Schofield, R.E., Lt.

Scoullar, Donald Alan (EM35–38 dob 05.01.24) R.G.H., Tpr. (POW).

Seabrooke, Dennis Ernest (EM36–41 dob 25.05.25) R.N., O./Cod.

Searle, Harold Nigel Leonard (EM34–41 dob 19.07.24) R.C.S., L./Cpl.

Sewell, Edwin Francis (EM34–39 dob 16.07.23) R.A.F., F./Sgt. *[Listed as 'E. Sewell'].*

Shaddock, Kenneth Charles (EM36–43 dob 24.05.25) L./Sgt.

Shaffi, Lorenzo A. (EM27–30 dob 18.08.12) R.A.F., Sqn./Ldr.

Sharman, Ivan Michael (EM26–33 dob 30.05.14 dod 20.12.2003) Medical Services.

Sharp, Robert Walter (EM35–41 dob 21.02.24 dod 21.01.44) R.A.F.V.R., P./O., *[Also listed as 'Sharpe'].* ✤

Sharvell, George Eltham (EM21–27 dob 14.05.11 dod 11.02.41) R.A.F., P./O. ✤

Shaw, Robert Henry (EM33–41 dob 25.10.24) R.A.F., A.C.2.

Sheerman, Eric John (EM29–32 dob 14.05.14) Royal Warwicks., Pte., *[Listed as 'E. Shearman'].*

Sheerman, Maurice Gordon (EM31–38 dob 13.06.17 dod 03.10.43) R.A.F.V.R., F./O., *[Also listed as 'Shearman'].* ✤

Sheldon, Philip S. (EM23–30 dob 09.05.13) R.E., Capt.

Sheppard, Geoffrey John (EM23–32 dob 24.05.14) R.A.

Sheppard, Kenneth Alfred (EM27–33 dob 22.10.15) R.A.F., A.C.2. *[Also listed as 'K. Sheppard'].*

Shepperd, E., L./Cpl.

Shevel, Ernest George (EM33–33 dob 27.02.21) R.A.F., L.A.C.

Shine, Henry Alfred (EM33–39 dob 19.04.22) R.A., Lt., Gnr.

Shirley, Donald Emerson (EM36–43 dob 06.05.25) R.N., O./S. *[Also listed as 'D. Shirley'].*

Shoosmith, Alec (EM34–35) Westminster Dgns., C.L.Y., Sgt., (POW) *[Also listed as 'R. A. Shoosmith'].*

Short, Gilbert R. (EM14–20 dob 23.01.03) R.A., Lt.

Shotter, John Reginald (EM30–36 dob 13.02.19 dod 04.1977) O.C.T.U., R.A., Capt., *[Also listed as 'J. R. Shooter'].*

Silcott, Ernest Francis (EM36–43 dob 01.11.24) R.N.V.R., (F.A.A.) Lt.

Sim, Hugh Craigie (EM35–41 dob 07.01.22) Inns of Court Regt., R.A.C., Lt., Awarded the M.C.

Simendinger, Ronald Charles (EM32–38 dob 26.01.21) R.A.F., P./O., Awarded the D.F.M.

Simmons, Clifford William Ronald (EM36–42 dob 01.10.24) R.A.F., P./O.

Simmons, Geoffrey Montague (EM34–43 dob 19.04.25) R.A.F.V.R., (S.U.C.) A.C.2., L./Sgt.

Simms, Ronald Edward (EM21–28 dob 14.07.13) R.A., L./Bdr.

Simpkins, Harold Arthur (EM13–20 dob 25.11.01) R.A.F., F./O.

Simpson, Arthur William (EM29–34 dob 27.10.20 dod 04.12.42) R.A.F.V.R., Sgt./Obs. ✤

Simpson, David George (EM29–36 dob 29.03.20) Surrey Yeomanry, R.A., Gnr., Pte.

Simpson, J., R.A., Gnr.

Simpson, James Alexander (EM29–31 dob 10.02.14) R.A.F.V.R., Sqn./Ldr.

Simpson, K., R.A. Gnr.

Simpson, Norman Frederick 'Wally' (EM30–37 dob 29.01.19 dod 27.08.2011) R.A. Gnr., Intel. Corps.

Skillern, Alan Reginald John (EM28–37 dob 28.02.20 dod 17.01.44) 9th Btn. Royal Fusiliers, Maj. ✤

Skinner, William Robert James (EM25–32 dob 31.12.13 dod 1975) Royal Fusiliers, Capt.

Slocock, Sydney Lawrence (EM1903 dob 12.04.1891 dod 25.01.1947) R.A.V.C., Brig. ✤

Slowman, John Barrington (EM32–40 dob 14.12.18) O.C.T.U., Queen's Regt., Capt.

Smalley, Walter Norman Adams (EM09–15 dob 16.09.1899) – R.N.V.R., Sub./Lt. (POW) *[Also listed as 'W. N. A. Smelley'].*

Smeaton, Douglas Malcolm (32–38 dob 18.04.21) R.A.F.V.R., Sgt.

Smeaton, Gordon Rae (EM27–33 dob 21.03.16) R.A.F.V.R., (Mentioned in Despatches). F./O.,

Smith, B., L./Cpl.

Smith, Benjamin Charles (EM31–39 dob 05.12.19) R.A.F., (Medical) F./O.

Smith, Claude Drury (EM31–42 dob 04.02.24 dod 03.08.44) Dgns., R.A.C., Tpr. ✤

Smith, Donald Frederick (EM30–38 dob 22.06.21) R.A.F., L.A.C., *[Also listed as 'D. E. Frederick'].*

Smith, David Vivian Roland (EM36–44 dob 22.09.25) R.N., O.S.

Smith, Edgar Cyril (EM14–16 dob 26.09.04) R.C.S., Sign'r.

Smith, Eric Haydn (EM18–19 dob 30.01.03 dod 24.02.41) R.N.R., Comdr. ✤

Douglas-Smith, Eric Ernest (EM14–20 dob 07.08.02) R.A.S.C., Lt.

Smith, Edward Frederick (EM14–21 dob 27.02.03) R.A.F., Wing Comdr.

Smith, Frank Thomas (Staff EM39–46 dob 15.05.13) Meterological Section, R.A.F., Fire Service.

Smith, G. F., R.A.F., Wing Comdr.

Smith, Geoffrey Victor (EM35–39 dob 02.01.24) R.A.F.V.R., (S.U.C.) A.C.2., R.A.F. P./O.

Smith, Gallienius William (EM35–40 dob 09.06.24 dod 2007) R.N.

Smith, Kenneth Sydney (EM32–37 dob 05.03.21 dod 1985) R.A.F., F./Lt.

Smith, Leonard (EM35–42 dob 05.07.24) R.A.F.V.R., (S.U.C). A.C.2.

Smith, Ralph Harry (EM29–35 dob 23.10.17) Regiment and rank unknown.

Smith, Roy Peter (dob 06.08.23 dod 19.03.1945) R.A.F.V.R., Sgt. ✤

Smith, Stanley Thomas (EM34–38 dob 22.02.21) R.A., Dvr.

Smout, Alan Hilden (EM30–35 dob 09.08.16) Indian Army, Lt.

Smythe, Geoffrey William Bevis (EM35–43 dob 21.01.26) R.N.V.R. (Y Entry) Cdt., *[Also listed as 'B Smythe']*.

Snelling, Cecil James (EM13–18 dob 21.03.02) Queen's Westminsters., K.R.R.C., C.S.M.

Snelling, Thomas Henry (EM21–27 dob 07.05.10 dod 02.09.1985) R.A.F., Wing Comdr., *[Also listed as 'T. D. Snelling']*.

Soan, Alfred Leslie (EM11–15 dob 28.01.02 dod 15.08.43) R.N.V.R., Lt., *[Also listed as 'L. A. Soan' & 'A. L. Soar']*. ✤

Solkhon, John Arthur (EM29–36 dob 06.12.17) R.A.S.C., Maj., *[Also listed as 'A. Solkhon']*. Awarded the M.B.E.

Sollis, James William (EM31–38 dob 21.02.20) R.E.M.E., R.A.O.C., Craftsman.

Somerville, John Peter (EM34–42 dob 11.09.23) R.T.R., R.A.C., Lt., Tpr.

Sparkes, Donald Victor (EM31–37 dob 14.06.20) R.T.R., L./Cpl. *[Also listed as 'R. V. Sparkes']*.

Speeding, Peter Rowland (EM38–42 dob 02.10.24) R.E., Dvr. *[Listed as 'P. Speeding']*.

Spencer, Edward John C. (EM27–33 dob 22.10.15) R.C.S., Maj.

Stacey, Bernard Frederick (EM29–34 dob 16.02.18 dod 15.02.42) P./O R.A.F.V.R., A.C.I., ✤

Standing, Brian (EM32–38 dob 31.01.24) R.A.F., F./Sgt.

Stanford, David Ralph (EM33–43 dob 02.11.25) O.C.T.U., Cdt., Drum–Maj.

Stanford, Raymond Mark (EM31–40 dob 24.07.22 dod 23.12.1995) R.A., E.A.A., Lt.

Stanley, Dennis William (EM35–39 dob 20.11.23) R.M., Cpl.

Stenton, Eric F. (EM29–36 dob 08.07.18) Intel. Corps., Capt.

Stephens, Cyril Noel (EM19–28 dob 25.02.10) Green Howards, The Buffs, (The Royal East Kent Regt.) Capt.

Stevens, Cecil Alfred (EM08–14 dob 31.10.1898 dod 31.08.1958) Air Vice-Marshal, Awarded the C.B.E. [Awarded the M.C. and Bar in the First World War].

Stinton, Leslie Frederick (EM27–31 dob 06.12.13) R.N.V.R., Sub./Lt.

Stockton, David Leonard (EM37–44 dob 14.11.25 dod 10.07.2012) R.N.V.R., (N.I.D.) Midshipman., Intel. Corps. Bletchley Park.

Stone, Kenneth Frank (EM32–39 dob 14.06.21 dod 03.10.43) R.A., Lt. *[Also listed as 'R. F. Stone', Sign'r]*. ✤

Stewart, Alan Chambers (EM27–34 dob 07.02.16 dod 06.1978) R.N.V.R., A.B., *[Also listed as 'A. C. Stuart']*.

Stubbings, Leslie Walter Frederick (EM31–38 dob 04.04.20) O.C.T.U., The Buffs. (The Royal East Kent Regt.) Lt. (POW).

Stubbs, Eric Charles (EM15–24 dob 06.01.06 dod 31.12.1985) Queen's Regt., Middlesex Regt., Capt. (Listed as missing, then POW).

Suffield, Leslie William Day (EM15–23 dob 08.01.06) R.A.F., F./Lt.

Swinstead, Parachute Regt., Tpr.

Swinstead, Edgar Harry (EM33–37 dob 16.08.19) R.A.S.C., Dvr.

- T -

Talbot, Derrick (EM33–39 dob 05.08.22 dod 04.11.1944) R.A.F.V.R., F./O.

Taphouse, F. S., Beds & Herts Regt., Lt.

Taylor, Harold Michael Dennis (EM36–40 dob 03.05.24) Monmouthshires., Pte.

Taylor, John Francis (EM30–34 dob 11.09.16) R.A.F., Sgt.

Taylor, William Henry (EM29–35 dob 04.09.17) King's Own Royal Regiment., att. The Buffs. (The Royal East Kent Regt.) Lt. (POW).

Tester, Maurice Harold (EM23–33 dob 12.05.16) Air Sgt, Air Mechanic, S.A.A.F., Lt.

Tester, Merton Philip (EM30–41 dob 20.05.23) Indian Army., Mahratta L.I., Lt., *[Also listed as 'M. K. Tester']*.

Thomas, Edward Alfred Charles (EM23–31 dob 15.04.15 dod 1995) R.A., Maj., Awarded the M.C.

Thomas, Francis James (EM26–33 dob 02.12.14) R.A., L./Cpl.

Thomas, Francis W. (EM21–30 dob 04.08.13) R.A.F., (Mentioned in Despatches) Sqn./Ldr.,

Thomas, Geoffrey Trevor (EM30–39 dob 21.01.21) Regiment and rank unknown.

Thompson, Alexander L. C. (EM37–44 dob 22.05.26) R.A.F.V.R., A.C.2.

Thompson, F. G. (EM32–38 dob 02.04.21) Royal Fusiliers, Oxford & Bucks L.I., Lt.

Thompson, Geoffrey Malcolm Millard (Staff 1940 dob 09.08.14) Admiralty., *[Also listed as 'G. M. T. Thompson']*.

Thompson, Ronald Vincent (EM32–40 dob 18.03.21) R.A., O.C.T.U., The Buffs (The Royal East Kent Regt.) Capt.

Thompson, S. H., R.A., Sgt.

Thornburn, Urwin 'Ned' (EM24–33 dob 11.06.14) K.S.L.I., T.A. (General List). Maj., Awarded the M.C.

Threadgold, Boris Hainsworth (EM35–42 dob 24.02.24) R.A.F. (S.U.C.) Sgt./Pilot.

Tinker, Arthur John Benyon (EM20–27 dob 07.04.09) Lt.

Titley, Alfred Eric (EM06–16 dob 14.01.1898 dod 03.1961) Devons, T.A. (General List). [Awarded the M.C. in First World War], T.D. Maj.

Titlow, S. R., Life Guards, Tpr.

Toms, Norman Henry (EM19–25 dob 05.02.1908) R.A., Gnr.

Topliss, George Warwick (EM25–31 dob 20.07.14) R.A.F., F./Lt., Awarded the D.F.C. *[Also listed as 'G. W. Topuss']*.

Topliss, John (EM21–25 dob 05.10.1908) R.A., Capt.

Town, Edwin John 'Jack' (EM27–33, Staff 70–81 dob 26.01.16 dod 25.05.1995) R.N.V.R., Sub./Lt.

Townsend, Gordon Eric Victor (EM30–36 dob 29.05.19) R.A.F., F./Lt.

Townsend, Cyril Arthur (EM22–26 dob 30.01.11 dod 1996) R.E., Capt.

Trew, Roderick Frederick Towell (EM22–28 dob 15.11.10) R.A.S.C., R.A.O.C., Lt.

Tucker, Ivan Robert (EM35–42 dob 15.11.10) R.C.S., Gloucestershire Regt., Lt.

Tucknott, Leslie George (EM27–33 dob 05.03.16) Regiment and rank unknown.

Turley, Alick Edward (EM29–34 dob 02.05.18) R.A.F., A.C.1.

Turley, Frederick Charles (EM21–27 dob 29.08.10) R.A.F., A.C.1.

Turley, Robert James (EM20–25 dob 08.12.08) R.A.F., A.C.1.

Turner, Albert (EM15–20 dob 25,10.03) Indian Army, Lt.

Turner, E. G., R.E., Dvr.

Turner, Ernest Geoffrey Roy (EM36–42 dob 28.08.25) Royal Fusiliers, Lt.

Turner, John Reuben (EM12–19 dob 08.02.02 dod 1984) R.C.S., Sign'r.

Twamley, Reginald John (EM24–31 dob 03.12.12) R.A.F., Wing Comdr., Awarded the D.F.C.

Tyack, Francis George (EM18–24 dob 23.06.07) R.E., Lt. *[Also listed as 'Tizack']*.

- U -

Underwood, Lionel George (EM32–38 dob 31.05.21) R.A.C., Lt.

- V -

Vernon, Ernest (EM27–31 dob 25.07.15) R.E., Lt., Sapper.

de Ville, Geoffrey Francis (EM28–30 dob 17.09.19) R.A., Gnr., Pte. *[Listed as 'G. de Ville']*.

Vollaire, G. D., S.A.A.F., *[Also listed as Vollane]*

- W -

Walker, Roy (EM36–43 dob 04.07.25) F.A.A. (U.N.S.C) R.N.V.R., (F.A.A.) Sub./Lt.

Wallace, Allan Forsyth (EM24–33 dob 28.12.15) R.A.M.C., (Mentioned in Despatches). Maj., Awarded the M.C.

Wallis, Stanley Edgar (EM37–44 dob 10.06.26) R.A.C., Tpr.

Ward, Walter Frederick (EM34–39 dob 18.05.23 dod 07.11.1944) R.A.C., Lt. *[Also listed as 'W. Ward']*. ✤

Warner, Stanley Charles (dob 12.06.20 dod 19.07.45) Royal Fusiliers, Capt., Awarded the M.C. ✤

Warren, David John (EM30–37 dob 18.11.18 dod 21.07.2001) Hants. Regt., Maj., [Later Brig] Awarded both Immediate M.C. & D.S.O. *[Also listed as 'D. J. Warner']*.

Warren, Godfrey Philip (EM34–39 dob 29.12.20 dod 2006) Indian Army, Gurkha Regt., O.C.T.U., Capt.

Warren, Harold James (EM22–29 dob 10.03.12) R.E.M.E., Cpl.

Warren, Stewart Albert (EM21–33 dob 27.02.14) R.E., Maj., *[Also listed as 'S. C. Warren']*.

Waterman, Harry Jerem (EM33–36 dob 13.11.19 dod. 04.09.43) O.C.T.U., R.C.S. L./Cpl. (POW). ✣

Wates, Allan Charles (EM19–27 dob 01.03.09 dod 1985) 687 Coy., R.E., Maj.

Wates, Norman Edwards (EM17–21) Mulberry Harbours.

Wates, Sir Ronald Wallace (EM17–23) Mulberry Harbours.

Watkins, J. H., Regiment and rank unknown.

Watson, Sydney Douglas (EM17–21 dob 06.02.04) R.A.F., F./Sgt.

Weatherley, Derek Vivian (EM33–36 Dob 08.06.22) R.N.V.R., Sub./Lt.

Weatherley, Peter (EM36–43 dob 21.01.25) S.S.I.

Webb, D., Sgt. (POW)

Weeks, Roy Keeble (EM33–36 dob 22.06.22 dod 02.08.43) R.N.R., Sub./Lt. *[Also listed as 'R. K. Weekes']*. ✣

Welch, Alexander Edwin (EM27–32 dob 27.02.14) H.A.C., R.A.P.C., Lt., *[Also listed as 'A. E. Welsh']*.

Wells, Frederick Howard (EM25–34 dob 27.12.12) R.A.M.C., Sgt.

West, Arthur John, Chairman of Surrey Territorial Army, Air Force Association, Maj., Awarded the D.S.O., O.B.E., T.D., D.L.

West, Leonard Arthur (EM19–26 dob 21.11.08 dod 23.01.43) P./O. ✣

Weysome, Sidney Wescott (EM17–21 dob 15.04.05) R.A.O.C., Maj., *[Also listed as 'Weysom']*.

Wheeler, Albert Edward (EM27–31 dob 23.09.15) R.A.F., A.C.1.

Wheeler, Allen Earlsman Frederick (EM25–32 dob 06.10.13 dod 28.04.41) R.N., O.S. ✣

Wheeler, Douglas William (EM27–33 dob 13.12.18) R.N., Leading Seaman.

Wheeler, K., Indian Army, Lt.

Wheeler, Kenneth William K. (EM27–30 dob 17.08.19) R.N., A.B.

Bastin–Wheeler, Frank M. (EM33–39 dob 02.01.22) K.R.R.C., Rifleman.

Whelan, Douglas Sydney (EM31–39 dob 01.06.22) R.E., Sapper.

Whitcombe, Herbert Geoffrey Robinson (EM32–36 dob 11.03.20) R.A.S.C., Dvr.

White, John Arthur Evelyn H. (EM28–32 dob 04.08.14) R.A. (Surrey) Gnr.

White, Thomas Edward Charles (EM27–34 dob 24.02.16 dod 11.09.41) R.A., 2nd Lt., *[Also listed as 'T. E. A. White']*. ✣

Whitehead, John (EM26–31 dob 13.10.15) R.A.S.C., Capt.

Whittingham, R. D., Manchester Fus., Lt.

Whittingham, Richard (EM26–33 dob 03.05.15 dod 2003) Indian Army, Capt.

Wildey, Richard Kemp (EM26–35 dob 06.11.16 dod 15.10.42) R.A.F., Wing Comdr., Awarded the D.F.C. ✣

Wilkes, Maurice Frederick (EM36–43 dob 29.04.25) R.N., O./Coder., (Invalided out).

Willett, Arthur Daniel (EM25–33 dob 30.01.15 dod 08.12.43) Beds & Herts Regt., Pte., (Died, Japanese POW). ✣

Willett, John William (EM19–28 dob 16.05.11) R.N.V.R., Lt.

Williams, Michael George W. (EM36–44 dob 13.10.25) R.A., L./Bdr.

Williams, Robert 'Bob' Merion Oliver (EM22–29 dob 30.10.10 dod 2001) R.A.F., P./O. *[Also listed as 'R. M. D. Williams']*.

Wilmot, W., H.A.C., Pte.

Wilmshurst, Trevor Reginald Cyril (EM34–42 dob 25.06.24 dod 23.10.44) R.A.F.V.R., A.C.2. (Drowned). ✣

Wilson, Donald Stanley M. (EM28–35 dob 17.02.18) R.A.S.C., R.A.M.C., A.A.S.C., Sgt.

Wilson, Jack Harry Gough (EM1910 dob 21.04.1899) M.N.

Wiltshear, Owen Edmund (EM24–28 dob 09.07.11) R.A.F., Sqn.Ldr., Awarded the D.F.C. *[Also listed as 'O. Wiltshear']*.

Wiltshear, S. R. (EM25–30 dob 18.02.13) O.C.T.U., Royal West Kent Regt., Lt. *[Also listed as 'S. R. W. Wiltshire']*.

Wintringham, – East Surrey Regt., Q.R.R., Lt.

Wise, Charles (EM08–13 dob 14.07.1898) R.A.S.C., Maj.

Urquhart-Wood, Harry (EM34–41 dob 11.03.23) R.A., L./Bdr.

Woodrow, Joseph Frederick (EM22–27 dob 14.11.10) R.A., Lt.

Wright, Christopher Peter (EM32–38 dob 27.01.21) Royal Fusiliers, Lt.

Wright, Michael Oliver (EM33–38 dob 25.06.28) R.N.V.R., Sub./Lt. *[Also listed as 'M. Q. Wright']*.

- Y -

Yates, Roland Victor Fleming (EM30–32 dob 25.02.15) City of London Yeomanry, Tpr., *[Also listed as 'R. F. V. Yates']*.

Yorke, Stephen Charles Gardner (EM30–36 dob 09.07.19 dod 07.01.47) King's Own Hussars., Middlesex Yeomanry., O.C.T.U., R.A.C., Capt. ✣

Young, Philip Francis Harding (EM30–38 dob 24.07.20) Glider Regt., Sgt., R.A. (A.A. Batt.) Gnr.

Young, Rodney Frederick Harding (EM26–34 dob 04.03.16 dod 25.08.42) R.A.F.V.R., W.O., Awarded the D.F.M. ✣

Yoxall, Thomas Charles (EM25–33 dob 22.09.16) R.A.S.C., Capt.

Edward Kearney

Frederick Underwood

Frederick Wolfe

First World War Roll of Honour

Surname/First name[s]	Rank	Service Number	Date Of Death	Age	Regiment/Service	Nationality	Grave/Memorial Ref.	Cemetery/Memorial Name
ALLEN, HAROLD ALFRED	Private	941	04/08/1916	18	Seaforth Highlanders	United Kingdom	IX. C. 9.	ETAPLES MILITARY CEMETERY
ALLEN, LAWRENCE JOHN MAYNARD	Second Lieutenant		02/07/1916	19	Wiltshire Regiment	United Kingdom	Pier and Face 13 A.	THIEPVAL MEMORIAL
BARBER, HARRY MASON	Second Lieutenant		08/08/1918	24	East Surrey Regiment	United Kingdom	III. H. 11.	BEACON CEMETERY, SAILLY-LAURETTE
BERNARD, GEORGE ROBERT	Second Lieutenant		08/04/1917	29	Royal Engineers	United Kingdom	III. K. 55.	BETHUNE TOWN CEMETERY
BISHOP, CHARLES FREDERICK	Second Lieutenant		04/04/1918	34	Royal Fusiliers	United Kingdom	Bay 3.	ARRAS MEMORIAL
BODLE, CLIFFORD RAYMOND	Rifleman	4366	07/09/1916	25	London Regiment (Queen's Westminster Rifles)	United Kingdom	IX. V. 10.	DANTZIG ALLEY BRITISH CEMETERY, MAMETZ
BOWES, STANLEY WARD	Second Lieutenant		29/09/1915	25	Dorsetshire Regiment	United Kingdom	Panel 76.	LOOS MEMORIAL
BULLIVANT, ROLAND WALTER	Second Lieutenant		01/05/1917	21	Somerset Light Infantry	United Kingdom	III. C. 1.	WIMEREUX COMMUNAL CEMETERY
BURNS, ROBERT	Private	517075	01/12/1917	30	London Regiment (London Scottish)	United Kingdom	IX. B. 13.	GREVILLERS BRITISH CEMETERY
CAHILL, ALBERT EDWARD	Private	87561	10/10/1917	30	Machine Gun Corps (Infantry)	United Kingdom	XI. J. 12.	DOZINGHEM MILITARY CEMETERY
CAIRNS, WILLIAM HARDING	Sergeant	PS/1279	01/07/1916	?	Middlesex Regiment	United Kingdom	A. 80.	HAWTHORN RIDGE CEMETERY No.1, AUCHONVILLERS
CASSIE, LEITH	Second Lieutenant		11/12/1917	27	Argyll and Sutherland Highlanders	United Kingdom	XXVII. D. 16.	LIJSSENTHOEK MILITARY CEMETERY
CASWELL, THOMAS	Lance Corporal	50455	02/01/1917	19	Middlesex Regiment	United Kingdom	IV. G. 31.	PERONNE ROAD CEMETERY, MARICOURT
CHAMBERLAIN, CYRIL JOHN	Second Lieutenant		07/10/1917	24	Rifle Brigade	United Kingdom	Panel 145 to 147.	TYNE COT MEMORIAL
CHANDLER, ARTHUR ERNEST	Rifleman	40900	27/04/1918	18	Rifle Brigade	United Kingdom	I. C. 8.	CROUY BRITISH CEMETERY, CROUY-SUR-SOMME
CHARLES, WILLIAM GEORGE	Rifleman	8913	27/04/1915	25	London Regiment (London Rifle Brigade)	United Kingdom	Panel 52 and 54.	YPRES (MENIN GATE) MEMORIAL
CHITTOCK, CHARLES HENRY	Private	535508	27/11/1917	29	London Regiment (Prince of Wales' s Own Civil Service Rifles)	United Kingdom	Panel 12.	CAMBRAI MEMORIAL, LOUVERVAL
CHUTER, JOHN WILLIAM (JACK)	Flight Sub-Lieutenant		09/06/1917	19	Royal Navy	United Kingdom	1739.	MIKRA BRITISH CEMETERY, KALAMARIA
CLARKE, SEAFORTH St. JOHN	Private	204640	26/03/1918	19	Seaforth Highlanders	United Kingdom	V. F. 24.	DUISANS BRITISH CEMETERY, ETRUN
COLLINS, ALBERT EDWARD	Corporal	69107	21/07/1917	19	Royal Garrison Artillery	United Kingdom	F. 14.	BUS HOUSE CEMETERY
COLLMAN, ALBERT GEORGE	Private	17144	10/04/1917	41	Queen's Own (Royal West Kent Regiment)	United Kingdom	I. H. 21.	BARLIN COMMUNAL CEMETERY EXTENSION
CONNEW, PERCY ALEXANDER	Corporal	108163	01/12/1915	39	Canadian Mounted Rifles	Canadian	II. D. 36.	BERKS CEMETERY EXTENSION
COOK, LESLIE AMYAS	Gunner	L/21778	14/09/1917	20	Royal Field Artillery	United Kingdom	VII. C. 10.	MENDINGHEM MILITARY CEMETERY
CROSSLE, FREDERICK	Private	536396	27/10/1918	23	Royal Army Medical Corps	United Kingdom	G. 7A.	BOIS GUILLAUME COMMUNAL CEMETERY EXTENSION
DAMEN, WILLIAM THOMAS	Private	2028	12/06/1915	18	London Regiment	United Kingdom	II. B. 8.	ABBEVILLE COMMUNAL CEMETERY
DANCER, ALFRED CHRISTOPHER	Captain		04/10/1917	24	Dorsetshire Regiment	United Kingdom	Panel 92.	TYNE COT MEMORIAL
DARE, GEORGE	Lance Corporal	515263	07/06/1918	25	London Regiment (London Scottish)	United Kingdom	IV. H. 50.	AUBIGNY COMMUNAL CEMETERY EXTENSION
DAVIDSON, CHARLES FALCONER	Driver	1503	09/01/1916	20	Royal Field Artillery	United Kingdom	I. F. 26.	NOEUX-LES-MINES COMMUNAL CEMETERY
DELL, LOUIS MICHAEL	Second Lieutenant		14/07/1916	25	King's Shropshire Light Infantry	United Kingdom	Pier and Face 12 A and 12 D.	THIEPVAL MEMORIAL
DENMAN, FRANK CHRISTOPHER	Second Lieutenant		17/08/1917	23	Royal Field Artillery	United Kingdom	I. C. 27.	BLEUET FARM CEMETERY
DILNUTT, ERIC WILLIAM	Captain		02/03/1916	19	Royal Fusiliers	United Kingdom	Panel 25 to 27.	LOOS MEMORIAL
EARL, SIDNEY EDWARD	Private	496357	14/10/1918	18	London Regiment	United Kingdom	C. 5.	SOMER FARM CEMETERY

ELEY, WILLIAM DOUGLAS	Rifleman	C/7442	10/10/1916	33	King's Royal Rifle Corps	United Kingdom	III. D. 5.	WARLENCOURT BRITISH CEMETERY
EVANS, HUBERT WILLIAM	Second Lieutenant		24/05/1917	19	The Buffs (East Kent Regiment)	United Kingdom	XVII. A. 20.	ETAPLES MILITARY CEMETERY
EWINGTON, GILBERT OSWALD	Rifleman	Z/2966	01/07/1916	31	Rifle Brigade	United Kingdom	Pier and Face 16 B and 16 C.	THIEPVAL MEMORIAL
FELL, GEORGE FREDERICK	Private	7117	08/01/1917	21	London Regiment	United Kingdom	VII. E. 4.	RAILWAY DUGOUTS BURIAL GROUND
FISHER, EDMUND 'EDDIE'	Second Lieutenant		16/11/1916	17	East Lancashire Regiment	United Kingdom	C. 19.	WAGGON ROAD CEMETERY, BEAUMONT-HAMEL
FISHER, EDWARD HENRY	Second Lieutenant		09/04/1918	21	1st King Edward's Horse	United Kingdom	Panel 2.	LOOS MEMORIAL
FOWLER, CYRIL WILLIAM	Private	3174	26/05/1915	19	London Regiment	United Kingdom	Panels 45 & 46.	LE TOURET MEMORIAL
FRICKER, THOMAS MASTERN	Private	E/618	13/04/1917	22	Royal Fusiliers	United Kingdom	Bay 3.	ARRAS MEMORIAL
GABB, RICHARD GEORGE	Second Lieutenant		06/08/1915	21	Essex Regiment	United Kingdom	Sp. Mem. C. 238.	TWELVE TREE COPSE CEMETERY
GEORGE, EDGAR JAMES	Private	7272	07/09/1916	25	London Regiment (London Scottish)	United Kingdom	XXXI. L. 6.	SERRE ROAD CEMETERY No.2
GODFREY, WILLIAM FRANK	Second Lieutenant		03/09/1916	20	North Staffordshire Regiment	United Kingdom	VII. L. 10.	DELVILLE WOOD CEMETERY, LONGUEVAL
GOODALL, ARTHUR	Second Lieutenant		20/02/1918	23	London Regiment (The Rangers)	United Kingdom	H. 7. 2589.	WANDSWORTH (EARLSFIELD) CEMETERY
GRATTIDGE, JOHN EDWIN	Apprentice		08/12/1918	17	Mercantile Marine	United Kingdom	Plot XV. Prot. Sect.	VENICE (SAN MICHELE) CEMETERY
GREEN, EDGAR	Private	1705	10/10/1918	25	Australian Infantry, A.I.F.	Australian	XXI. G. 2.	BAGHDAD (NORTH GATE) WAR CEMETERY
GREEN, WILLIAM JOSEPH	Rifleman	391383	08/09/1917	20	London Regiment (Queen Victoria's Rifles)	United Kingdom	X. D. 19.	TYNE COT CEMETERY
GRUNDY, CECIL BOYCE	Second Lieutenant		16/11/1915	21	Middlesex Regiment	United Kingdom	II. L. 3.	BETHUNE TOWN CEMETERY
GRUNDY, RONALD EDWIN	Second Lieutenant		01/07/1916	19	Middlesex Regiment	United Kingdom	Sp. Mem. 6.	OVILLERS MILITARY CEMETERY
HANCOCK, WALTER EDWARD	Lance Corporal	13017	19/10/1917	21	Duke of Cornwall's Light Infantry	United Kingdom	Panel 80 to 82 and 163A.	TYNE COT MEMORIAL
HARDING, FREDERICK JOHN	Second Lieutenant		22/09/1917	19	East Surrey Regiment	United Kingdom	III. F. 27.	ZANTVOORDE BRITISH CEMETERY
HARVEY, STANLEY ALFRED GEORGE	Lieutenant		21/03/1918	24	Royal Berkshire Regiment	United Kingdom	Panel 56 and 57.	POZIERES MEMORIAL
HAYES, REGINALD	Lieutenant		22/07/1917	19	Royal Flying Corps	United Kingdom		ARRAS FLYING SERVICES MEMORIAL
HEATH, DOUGLAS ALAN	Staff Sergeant	33557	24/12/1915	24	Royal Army Medical Corps	United Kingdom	A. 15. 34.	ST. SEVER CEMETERY, ROUEN
HILLMAN, WILLIAM SAMUEL	Private	228820	23/03/1918	21	London Regiment (Royal Fusiliers)	United Kingdom	2. H. 11.	CHAUNY COMMUNAL CEMETERY BRITISH EXTENSION
HOLLOWAY, PHILIP EDWARD	Rifleman	557163	28/08/1918	18	London Regiment (Queen's Westminster Rifles)	United Kingdom	IV. G. 24.	QUEANT ROAD CEMETERY, BUISSY
HORSWELL, BAZIL WHITTLE	Flight Sub-Lieutenant		11/10/1917	22	Royal Naval Air Service	United Kingdom	2 G. 14729.	PADDINGTON CEMETERY
HOWARD, WILLIAM GEORGE	Second Lieutenant		20/12/1917	24	Royal Garrison Artillery	United Kingdom	XIII. A. 6.	NINE ELMS BRITISH CEMETERY
HUNT, HAROLD ARTHUR	Sergeant	81424	03/06/1915	33	Canadian Infantry	Canadian	VIII. A. 65.	BOULOGNE EASTERN CEMETERY
IVE, SIDNEY GEORGE FREDERICK	Lance Corporal	C/6549	27/04/1918	22	King's Royal Rifle Corps	United Kingdom	H. 21. 422.	WANDSWORTH (EARLSFIELD) CEMETERY
IVES, ALFRED ERNEST	Private	6967	29/12/1916	20	London Regiment	United Kingdom	VI. Q. 15.	RAILWAY DUGOUTS BURIAL GROUND
JAMES, ARTHUR	Lieutenant		03/01/1917	31	Yorkshire Regiment	United Kingdom	XI. E. 6.	GUARDS' CEMETERY, LESBOEUFS
JOHNSON, EVELYN WALTER JAMES	Second Lieutenant		20/07/1916	19	Bedfordshire Regiment	United Kingdom	Officers, A. 4. 4.	ST. SEVER CEMETERY, ROUEN
KEARNEY, EDWARD MARSHALL SYDNEY	Second Lieutenant		27/10/1918	19	Royal Air Force	United Kingdom	I. C. 4.	PREMONT BRITISH CEMETERY
KEARNEY, NORMAN CHARLES	Lieutenant		27/04/1918	26	Royal Flying Corps	United Kingdom	D. 5. 138.	WANDSWORTH (PUTNEY VALE) CEMETERY AND CREMATORIUM
KETTLEY, ARTHUR GEORGE	Lance Corporal	2158	30/05/1916	31	Australian Infantry, A.I.F.	Australian	I. H. 27.	RUE-PETILLON MILITARY CEMETERY, FLEURBAIX
KIMBER, FREDERICK WILLIAM	Private	4560	13/11/1916	20	Honourable Artillery Company	United Kingdom	Pier and Face 8 A.	THIEPVAL MEMORIAL

KINNEAR, ANGUS MACPHERSON	Third Engineer		16/03/1917	23	Mercantile Marine	United Kingdom		TOWER HILL MEMORIAL
LANE, FRANK ASHTON	Second Lieutenant		31/07/1917	21	The King's (Liverpool Regiment)	United Kingdom	Panel 4 and 6.	YPRES (MENIN GATE) MEMORIAL
MACBETH, STANLEY	Lieutenant		15/09/1916	36	London Regiment (London Irish Rifles)	United Kingdom	XII. H. 19.	CATERPILLAR VALLEY CEMETERY, LONGUEVAL
MARTHEWS, LEONARD GORDON	Lieutenant		22/04/1918	19	South Lancashire Regiment	United Kingdom	XIII. G. 18.	COLOGNE SOUTHERN CEMETERY
MASON, GEORGE	Second Lieutenant		15/04/1918	19	North Staffordshire Regiment	United Kingdom	Panel 8.	PLOEGSTEERT MEMORIAL
MONSON, CYRIL ARCHIBALD	Second Lieutenant		18/05/1915	28	Wiltshire Regiment	United Kingdom	Panel 33 and 34.	LE TOURET MEMORIAL
MOORE, ALBERT ALEXANDER	Private	108397	02/06/1916	19	1st Canadian Mounted Rifles Battalion	Canadian	Panel 30, 32.	YPRES (MENIN GATE) MEMORIAL
MOORE, FREDERICK HARRY BEDLOE	Second Lieutenant		04/11/1918	20	London Regiment (Queen Victoria's Rifles)	United Kingdom	A.7.	SEBOURG COMMUNAL CEMETERY
MOSELEY, HERBERT JAMES RITCHIE	Second Lieutenant		27/06/1916	22	Rifle Brigade	United Kingdom	I. E. 4.	FAUBOURG D'AMIENS CEMETERY, ARRAS
MOUNTAIN, CYRIL ROBERT WIGHTMAN	Captain		05/08/1917	21	Cheshire Regiment	United Kingdom	Panel 19 - 22.	YPRES (MENIN GATE) MEMORIAL
NEALE, COLIN FRANCIS	Sub-Lieutenant		23/04/1917	22	Royal Naval Volunteer Reserve	United Kingdom	III. H. 39.	ORCHARD DUMP CEMETERY, ARLEUX-EN-GOHELLE
NEWTON, KENNETH FREDERICK CECIL	Corporal	200409	24/04/1917	20	Seaforth Highlanders	United Kingdom	Bay 8.	ARRAS MEMORIAL
NICHOL, WILLIAM ALEXANDER	Private	2645	23/06/1917	28	Australian Infantry, A.I.F.	Australian	II. E. 1.	KANDAHAR FARM CEMETERY
NICHOLS, DOUGLAS WILLIAM LANE	Captain		20/08/1916	23	The Queen's (Royal West Surrey Regiment)	United Kingdom	Pier and Face 5 D and 6 D.	THIEPVAL MEMORIAL
NICHOLS, FREDERICK JOSEPH	Air Mechanic 1st Class	7398	14/04/1918	21	Royal Air Force	United Kingdom	III. B. 27.	AUBIGNY COMMUNAL CEMETERY EXTENSION
NICHOLSON, HENRY PHILLIPS	Drummer	3145	22/08/1916	18	London Regiment	United Kingdom	II. F. 5.	LOUEZ MILITARY CEMETERY, DUISANS
NOEL, FRANCIS RADFORD	Lance Corporal	2373	08/05/1918	24	Australian Infantry, A.I.F.	Australian		VILLERS-BRETONNEUX MEMORIAL
ORCHARD, HENRY 'HARRY'	Private	436835	26/09/1916	39	Canadian Infantry	Canadian		VIMY MEMORIAL
PAYNE, CHARLES FREDERICK	Lance Corporal	235435	11/02/1919	35	Duke of Wellington's (West Riding Regiment)	United Kingdom	XIII. C. 37.	TERLINCTHUN BRITISH CEMETERY, WIMILLE
PEARMAN, ALAN	Private	5091	29/09/1918	18	Australian Infantry, A.I.F.	Australian		VILLERS-BRETONNEUX MEMORIAL
PINE, ALBERT ARTHUR	Lieutenant		16/01/1917	22	Worcestershire Regiment	United Kingdom	XXIV. C. 29.	AMARA WAR CEMETERY
PINE, LESLIE WILLIAM TATTERSALL	Second Lieutenant		18/08/1917	19	Hampshire Regiment	United Kingdom	IV. B. 16.	DOZINGHEM MILITARY CEMETERY
POPE, WILLIAM ARCHER	Captain		07/10/1916	24	The Queen's (Royal West Surrey Regiment)	United Kingdom	III. A. 26.	HEILLY STATION CEMETERY, MERICOURT-L'ABBE
POUNDALL, WILLIAM ARTHUR	Captain		31/10/1917	23	Royal Flying Corps	United Kingdom	I. D. 19.	WHITE HOUSE CEMETERY, ST. JEAN-LES-YPRES
PRESCOTT, FREDERICK WILLIAM LLOYD	Rifleman	554886	02/04/1918	19	London Regiment (Queen's Westminster Rifles)	United Kingdom	III. D. 48.	AUBIGNY COMMUNAL CEMETERY EXTENSION
PRICE, LEONARD JOHN JOLLIFFE	Second Lieutenant		15/08/1916	22	King's Own Scottish Borderers	United Kingdom	VI. H. 1.	ABBEVILLE COMMUNAL CEMETERY
READER, BERTRAM ALEC	Private	3623	15/09/1916	18	London Regiment (Prince of Wales' s Own Civil Service Rifles)	United Kingdom	Pier and Face 13 C.	THIEPVAL MEMORIAL
RICE, EDWARD FELIX	Second Lieutenant		18/02/1917	23	London Regiment (London Rifle Brigade)	United Kingdom	VII. A. 32.	MERVILLE COMMUNAL CEMETERY
RICHES, JOHN LESLIE	Lance Corporal	STK/510	15/07/1916	20	Royal Fusiliers	United Kingdom	Pier and Face 8 C 9 A and 16 A.	THIEPVAL MEMORIAL
ROBERTS, JOHN HENRY	Lance Corporal	4457	15/11/1916	20	Honourable Artillery Company	United Kingdom	Pier and Face 8 A.	THIEPVAL MEMORIAL
ROBINSON, FRANK GILBERT	Lieutenant		07/07/1916	23	Northumberland Fusiliers	United Kingdom	Plot 1. Row B. Grave 45.	CORBIE COMMUNAL CEMETERY EXTENSION
ROBINSON, RALPH DUNCAN	Captain		07/06/1917	21	The Loyal North Lancashire Regiment	United Kingdom	II. P. 13.	ST. QUENTIN CABARET MILITARY CEMETERY
ROPER, STUART EDGAR	Private	132405	29/09/1918	19	Machine Gun Corps (Infantry)	United Kingdom	I. C. 16.	MENIN ROAD SOUTH MILITARY CEMETERY
ROSS-JENKINS, MAURICE	Second Lieutenant		16/06/1918	20	Royal Air Force	United Kingdom	Dancourt German Mil. Cem. Mem. 59.	ROYE NEW BRITISH CEMETERY
RYLEY, HAROLD BUCHANAN	Second Lieutenant		05/09/1916	20	North Staffordshire Regiment	United Kingdom	Pier and Face 14 B and 14 C.	THIEPVAL MEMORIAL

SACH, CHARLES BURLEIGH	Second Lieutenant		01/07/1916	19	London Regiment	United Kingdom	Pier and Face 9 D 9 C 13 C and 12 C.	THIEPVAL MEMORIAL
SCURFIELD, BRYAN	Lieutenant		30/09/1918	19	East Surrey Regiment	United Kingdom	395.	MIKRA BRITISH CEMETERY, KALAMARIA
SHEPPEE, FREDERICK JOHN AKA JOHNSON, FREDERICK	Private	1371	07/08/1915	42	Australian Infantry, A.I.F.	Australian	18.	LONE PINE MEMORIAL
SIMPSON, VICTOR LESLIE	Private	7362	03/05/1917	20	Honourable Artillery Company	United Kingdom	Bay 1.	ARRAS MEMORIAL
SIMS, J M	Corporal	27787	27/09/1918	?	Suffolk Regiment	United Kingdom	K. 14.	LOWRIE CEMETERY, HAVRINCOURT
SISTERSON, NORMAN HELE	Second Lieutenant		16/04/1918	22	Northumberland Fusiliers	United Kingdom	Panel 19 to 23 and 162.	TYNE COT MEMORIAL
SKINNER, FRANK WILLIAM	Lieutenant		05/05/1916	24	Canadian Infantry	Canadian	V. A. 32.	LIJSSENTHOEK MILITARY CEMETERY
SLOCOMBE, CHARLES GEOFFREY	Sergeant	G/13685	13/05/1917	23	The Buffs (East Kent Regiment)	United Kingdom	III. E. 6.	HAMBURG CEMETERY
SMITH, GEOFFREY CHOLERTON	Lieutenant		31/07/1917	20	Royal Flying Corps	United Kingdom	XIV. A. 10.	LIJSSENTHOEK MILITARY CEMETERY
SPENCER, WALTER GEORGE	Captain		26/03/1918	30	London Regiment	United Kingdom	Officers, B. 2. 24.	ST. SEVER CEMETERY, ROUEN
SPICER, FILMER BLAKE	Second Lieutenant		06/10/1916	24	The Buffs (East Kent Regiment)	United Kingdom	I. J. 59.	BARLIN COMMUNAL CEMETERY EXTENSION
STEPTO, CYRIL FREDERICK	Private	532627	07/10/1916	19	London Regiment (Prince of Wales' s Own Civil Service Rifles)	United Kingdom	I. H. 33.	WARLENCOURT BRITISH CEMETERY
STOCKWELL, ERNEST HAROLD	Rifleman	304876	21/03/1918	19	London Regiment (London Rifle Brigade)	United Kingdom	Bay 9.	ARRAS MEMORIAL
SUMMERS, RANULPH AUGUSTUS	Second Lieutenant		28/09/1915	23	Royal Berkshire Regiment	United Kingdom		LOOS MEMORIAL
THOMAS, ARTHUR LEWIS	Second Lieutenant		24/04/1918	32	Northamptonshire Regiment	United Kingdom	Panel 54 to 56.	POZIERES MEMORIAL
THOMSON, RUPERT ARCHER	Lance Corporal	18097	17/06/1915	28	Canadian Infantry (Central Ontario Regiment)	Canadian		VIMY MEMORIAL
TURNER, FRANCIS PHILIP	Rifleman	1908	08/05/1915	17	London Regiment (The Rangers)	United Kingdom	Panel 54.	YPRES (MENIN GATE) MEMORIAL
UNDERWOOD, FREDERICK NELSON	Second Lieutenant		02/07/1919	19	Royal Air Force	United Kingdom	K. 907.	EDINBURGH (COMELY BANK) CEMETERY
VILLIS, ARCHIBALD	Private	33657	18/10/1918	19	Duke of Wellington's (West Riding Regiment)	United Kingdom	D. 31.	YORK CEMETERY, HASPRES, Nord
VILLIS, TOM	Air Mechanic 2nd Class	43405	11/10/1918	24	Royal Air Force	United Kingdom	I. F. 10.	DELSAUX FARM CEMETERY, BEUGNY
WALKER, GEORGE ERNEST	Lieutenant		06/06/1917	24	Royal Scots	United Kingdom	III. H. 19.	BROWN'S COPSE CEMETERY, ROEUX
WEST, GERALD WILLIAM	Lieutenant		25/09/1915	23	Royal Sussex Regiment	United Kingdom	Panel 69 to 73.	LOOS MEMORIAL
WHILE, IVOR AUSTIN	Second Lieutenant		31/08/1916	19	North Staffordshire Regiment	United Kingdom	Pier and Face 14 B and 14 C.	THIEPVAL MEMORIAL
WHITE, FREDERICK RICHARD	Private	54297	09/06/1918	18	Middlesex Regiment	United Kingdom	I. E. 6.	BERLIN SOUTH-WESTERN CEMETERY
WHITE, HAROLD NORTON	Second Lieutenant		06/09/1918	21	Machine Gun Corps (Infantry)	United Kingdom	E. 15.	SUN QUARRY CEMETERY, CHERISY
WILLIS, GEORGE WARD	Private	53153	03/05/1917	24	Durham Light Infantry	United Kingdom	Bay 8.	ARRAS MEMORIAL
WILSON, ROBERT PHILIP	Second Lieutenant		07/08/1915	21	East Yorkshire Regiment	United Kingdom	Panel 51 to 54.	HELLES MEMORIAL
WISDOM, COLIN MATSON	Sergeant	16372	09/04/1917	26	Canadian Infantry	Canadian	Arras Road Cem. Mem. 5.	NINE ELMS MILITARY CEMETERY, THELUS
WOLFE, FREDERICK DERRICK S	Rifleman	303850	10/08/1918	20	London Regiment (London Rifle Brigade)	United Kingdom	IV. C. 10.	VILLERS-BRETONNEUX MILITARY CEMETERY
WOODWARD, HUBERT EDWIN	Rifleman	874	26/04/1915	20	London Regiment (London Rifle Brigade)	United Kingdom	Panel 52 and 54.	YPRES (MENIN GATE) MEMORIAL
WRAY, WILLIAM THEODORE	Rifleman	7135	09/10/1916	19	London Regiment (Queen's Westminster Rifles)	United Kingdom	Pier and Face 13 C.	THIEPVAL MEMORIAL
WYBORN, HARRY JOHN GUSTAVE	Private	G/40458	25/03/1918	41	Middlesex Regiment	United Kingdom	Panel 60 and 61.	POZIERES MEMORIAL
Teachers:								
ELDER, WILLIAM GARDNER	Lieutenant		10/02/1918	28	London Regiment	United Kingdom	1920	ELTHAM (ST. JOHN THE BAPTIST) CHURCHYARD
LE CHAVETOIS, GRANTLEY ADOLPHE	Captain		22/01/1918	30	London Regiment	United Kingdom	27. 25151.	CAMBERWELL OLD CEMETERY
RYLEY, HAROLD BUCHANAN	Lieutenant		15/12/1917	49	Suffolk Regiment	United Kingdom	D. 30.	RAMLEH WAR CEMETERY

EMANUEL SCHOOL

UNVEILING and DEDICATION

OF THE

WAR MEMORIAL

IN THE

CHAPEL

BY

AIR VICE-MARSHAL G. G. BANTING, C.B., C.B.E., (O.E.)

AND

THE REV. A. M. T. DAINTREY (O.E.)
Rector of Sutton and Bignor, Sussex

ON

SATURDAY, 23rd JULY, 1949

Edward Culverwell

Michael McDonnell

Kenneth Stone

Second World War Roll of Honour

Surname	Rank	Service Number	Date Of Death	Age	Regiment/Service	Nationality	Grave/Memorial Ref.	Cemetery/Memorial Name
ADAMS, FREDERICK PRIDGEN	Lieutenant		18/03/1945	29	Royal Naval Reserve	United Kingdom	N. 34.	DIEPPE CANADIAN WAR CEMETERY, HAUTOT-SUR-MER
ARMSTRONG, JAMES WILLIAM DOUGLAS	Major	149357	22/02/1945	25	East Surrey Regiment	United Kingdom	Grave 389.	MALDEN (ST. JOHN THE BAPTIST) CHURCHYARD
BAKER, KENNETH CROUCHER	Captain	71627	01/12/1943	24	Royal Fusiliers (City of London Regiment)	United Kingdom	Plot P.P. Grave 40015.	CROYDON (MITCHAM ROAD) CEMETERY
BARNETT, CHARLES JOSEPH	Private	S/143866	22/10/1945	26	Royal Army Service Corps	United Kingdom	15. A. 3.	KRANJI WAR CEMETERY
BEECHING, DONALD	Fusilier	14368096	01/03/1944	20	Royal Fusiliers (City of London Regiment)	United Kingdom	XVIII. A. 9.	BEACH HEAD WAR CEMETERY, ANZIO
BENNETT, THOMAS WYATT	Flight Sergeant	1378737	20/12/1942	34	Royal Air Force Volunteer Reserve	United Kingdom	Coll. grave 6. G. 2-4.	BERGEN-OP-ZOOM CANADIAN WAR CEMETERY
BERRY, RICHARD CHARLES JAMES	Flight Sergeant	1390084	07/04/1944	23	Royal Air Force Volunteer Reserve	United Kingdom	Column 434.	SINGAPORE MEMORIAL
BESANT, RONALD CUTHBERT	Warrant Officer	580838	11/08/1943	29	Royal Air Force	United Kingdom	Panel 134.	RUNNYMEDE MEMORIAL
BOTTING, ERIC HAROLD	Sergeant	6968254	25/10/1942	23	London Rifle Brigade	United Kingdom	Column 73.	ALAMEIN MEMORIAL
BOWLES, FRANK DAVID	Leading Stoker	C/KX106929	02/10/1942	22	Royal Navy	United Kingdom	C. of E. Plot. Sec. F. Grave 31.	LONDONDERRY CITY CEMETERY
BRAINWOOD, ERIC THOMAS FRANCIS	Second Radio Officer		14/03/1941	21	Merchant Navy	United Kingdom	Panel 118.	TOWER HILL MEMORIAL
BROOK, HENRY JOHN	Sergeant	656868	31/10/1942	25	Royal Air Force	United Kingdom	Row A. Grave 18.	GENDRINGEN ROMAN CATHOLIC CEMETERY
BROOKS, WALTER PAUL	Sergeant	931402	16/03/1942	20	Royal Air Force Volunteer Reserve	United Kingdom	Block A.S. Grave 1418.	WANDSWORTH (PUTNEY VALE) CEMETERY AND CREMATORIUM
CADMAN, DEREK WILLIAM	Aircraftman 2nd Class	1384084	16/05/1941	18	Royal Air Force Volunteer Reserve	United Kingdom	Square 8. Grave 2769.	STREATHAM PARK CEMETERY
CARTER, REGINALD JOHN	Pilot Officer	78271	03/05/1940	26	Royal Air Force	United Kingdom	Panel 23.	SOUTH LONDON CREMATORIUM, MITCHAM
CHURCH, RICHARD ERNEST	Lance Corporal	6290901	07/09/1940	24	The Buffs (Royal East Kent Regiment)	United Kingdom	Sec. R. Grave 2082.	UCKFIELD CEMETERY
CODURI, CHARLES ARTHUR	Able Seaman		24/03/1942	30	Merchant Navy	United Kingdom	Panel 131.	TOWER HILL MEMORIAL
COLLINGS, LEONARD GEORGE	Sergeant	655677	13/03/1943	27	Royal Air Force Volunteer Reserve	United Kingdom	Panel 145.	RUNNYMEDE MEMORIAL
COULTHARD, ARTHUR JACQUES	Lance Corporal	6923991	10/07/1944	21	Parachute Regiment, A.A.C.	United Kingdom	IVA. H. 21.	RANVILLE WAR CEMETERY
CROSS, HOWARD GORDON	Lance Corporal	2579364	31/05/1940	21	Royal Corps of Signals	United Kingdom	Plot 2 Row 15 grave 27.	DUNKIRK TOWN CEMETERY
CULVERWELL, EDWARD	Squadron Leader	33235	13/06/1941	25	Royal Air Force	United Kingdom	Panel 28.	RUNNYMEDE MEMORIAL
CURNOW, ERIC ARTHUR	Leading Aircraftman	912308	08/10/1943	26	Royal Air Force Volunteer Reserve	United Kingdom	1. H. 17.	MADRAS WAR CEMETERY, CHENNAI
DEEKS, HARRY BARNET	Major	47931	17/06/1945	34	Royal Fusiliers (City of London Regiment)	United Kingdom	3A. N. 6.	HAMBURG CEMETERY
DUFFIELD, RONALD ALAN	Sergeant	613125	30/11/1942	23	Royal Air Force	United Kingdom	Block 7. Grave 3.	WANDSWORTH (PUTNEY VALE) CEMETERY AND CREMATORIUM
ELGER, ANTHONY CHARLES	Flight Sergeant	136941	20/12/1942	20	Royal Air Force Volunteer Reserve	United Kingdom	22. B. 2.	BROOKWOOD MILITARY
EVANS, GEORGE ALBERT	Fusilier	4928682	30/12/1943	20	Royal Fusiliers (City of London Regiment)	United Kingdom	V. C, 8.	MINTURNO WAR CEMETERY
FIELDER, ROBERT EDWIN	Private	S/14384200	06/06/1944	19	Royal Army Service Corps	United Kingdom	IVA. C. 6.	RANVILLE WAR CEMETERY
FITZGERALD, DOUGLAS JOHN	Flight Sergeant	1432356	30/08/1944	22	Royal Air Force Volunteer Reserve	United Kingdom	Panel 217.	RUNNYMEDE MEMORIAL
FITZGERALD, RAYMOND CHARLES	Flight Sergeant	1585554	30/08/1944	21	Royal Air Force Volunteer Reserve	United Kingdom	Panel 217.	RUNNYMEDE MEMORIAL
FRANCIS, COLIN DUNSTONE	Pilot Officer	42211	30/08/1940	19	Royal Air Force	United Kingdom	20. E. 18.	BROOKWOOD MILITARY CEMETERY
FURLONG, DENNIS WALTER	Brigadier		05/09/1940	43	General Staff	United Kingdom	Grave 76.	KILHAM CEMETERY

HALE, HAROLD BERTRAM	Flying Officer	179530	21/03/1945	23	Royal Air Force Volunteer Reserve	United Kingdom	2. H. 14.	HANOVER WAR CEMETERY
HAMILTON-WILKES, FRANK DEANE	Flight Sergeant	1166524	23/08/1942	30	Royal Air Force Volunteer Reserve	United Kingdom	Column 249.	ALAMEIN MEMORIAL
HARRISON, REGINALD JOHN	Major	149462	01/03/1945	28	King's Shropshire Light Infantry	United Kingdom	46. D. 1.	REICHSWALD FOREST WAR CEMETERY
HUNT, JAMES GLYN	Corporal	4208295	25/09/1944	21	Royal Welch Fusiliers	United Kingdom	I. D. 8.	VALKENSWAARD WAR CEMETERY
JACKSON, PETER HAROLD	Lieutenant	138196	10/11/1943	23	Royal Armoured Corps and S.A.S.	United Kingdom	VI. E. 39.	BARI WAR CEMETERY
JOHNSON, BRAMWELL FREDERICK THOMAS	Sergeant	1166116	17/07/1941	19	Royal Air Force Volunteer Reserve	United Kingdom	Panel 46.	RUNNYMEDE MEMORIAL
JONES, WILLIAM JAMES	Flight Lieutenant	113952	13/06/1944	35	Royal Air Force Volunteer Reserve	United Kingdom	West. B. 4.	NASSAU WAR CEMETERY
JOYCE, REGINALD FRANCIS	Rifleman	6848223	11/07/1942	24	King's Royal Rifle Corps	United Kingdom	II. D. 12.	PRAGUE WAR CEMETERY
KEBBELL, PETER DAVIES	Captain	109042	15/11/1942	21	Gordon Highlanders	United Kingdom	Grave 502.	NAKURU NORTH CEMETERY
KEVIS, DENNIS JAMES	Lance Corporal	7619857	29/06/1942	23	Royal Army Ordnance Corps	United Kingdom	Sec. E. Grave 36.	BANDON HILL CEMETERY
KIMBER, ALBERT THOMAS GEORGE	Sergeant	421107	12/11/1943	24	Royal Tank Regiment, R.A.C.	United Kingdom	II. D. 30.	SANGRO RIVER WAR CEMETERY
KING, FREDERICK ERNEST ROYSTON	Flight Lieutenant		19/08/1939	27	Royal Air Force	United Kingdom		NO KNOWN GRAVE
KING, WILLIAM ARTHUR	Second Lieutenant	107109	26/05/1940	22	Royal Warwickshire Regiment	United Kingdom	X. 12. 3.	BRUSSELS TOWN CEMETERY
KIRBY, CHARLES FREDERICK	Lieutenant (A)		15/11/1943	28	Royal Naval Volunteer Reserve	United Kingdom	Bay 4, Panel 6.	LEE-ON-SOLENT MEMORIAL
LANGTON, NORMAN ROBERT	Warrant Officer	921402	19/06/1944	24	Royal Air Force Volunteer Reserve	United Kingdom	Block 23. Grave 369.	WANDSWORTH (EARLSFIELD) CEMETERY
LEE, JACK	Captain	177616	07/06/1944	31	Royal Artillery	United Kingdom	Panel 11, Column 1.	BAYEUX MEMORIAL
LEGGETT, CYRIL ALFRED	Ordinary Seaman	P/JX 223834	24/05/1941	28	Royal Navy	United Kingdom	Panel 51, Column 1.	PORTSMOUTH NAVAL MEMORIAL (Died in sinking of HMS Hood)
LEWIS, MICHAEL JOHN	Lieutenant	281970	11/10/1944	20	Royal Armoured Corps	United Kingdom	IV. B. 16.	FLORENCE WAR CEMETERY
LIGHTOLLER, HERBERT BRIAN	Flying Officer	37884	04/09/1939	21	Royal Air Force Volunteer Reserve	United Kingdom	4. B. 13.	SAGE WAR CEMETERY
LOCKEYEAR, PETER CLAUDE	Sergeant	1319254	30/11/1943	20	Royal Air Force Volunteer Reserve	United Kingdom	Block 12. Grave 623.	WANDSWORTH (PUTNEY VALE) CEMETERY AND CREMATORIUM
McDONNELL, MICHAEL HERBERT LUCAS	Lieutenant	193648	29/04/1943	22	Royal Tank Regiment, R.A.C.	United Kingdom	II. E. 14.	MASSICAULT WAR CEMETERY
McGREGOR, JOHN HARVEY	Commander (S)		19/12/1941	35	Royal Navy	United Kingdom	Panel 45, Column 1.	PLYMOUTH NAVAL MEMORIAL
McGREGOR, KENNETH ROBERT	Sergeant	2375528	07/12/1945	36	Army Educational Corps	United Kingdom	VII, C, 200.	CASERTA WAR CEMETERY
McLEAN, JOHN	Lieutenant	193657	14/09/1944	24	Royal Armoured Corps	United Kingdom	XI, G, 9.	CORIANO RIDGE WAR CEMETERY
McMILLAN, ERIC JOHN	Sergeant	1338724	22/10/1943	21	Royal Air Force Volunteer Reserve	United Kingdom	Block 6. Grave 9269.	WANDSWORTH (EARLSFIELD) CEMETERY
MILLIST, KENNETH MILTON	Pilot Officer	42420	07/04/1941	22	Royal Air Force	United Kingdom	Column 241.	ALAMEIN MEMORIAL
MORRILL, DOUGLAS GEORGE	Lance Corporal	328284	18/06/1941	24	Royal Armoured Corps	United Kingdom	5. D. 7.	HALFAYA SOLLUM WAR CEMETERY
MORRIS, HERBERT EDWARD	Corporal	2354744	21/02/1945	33	Royal Corps of Signals	United Kingdom	Plot B. Row 1. Grave 9.	TILBURG (GILZERBAAN) GENERAL CEMETERY
MOTT, ARTHUR REGINALD	Sergeant	657993	13/10/1942	28	Royal Air Force	United Kingdom	Column 262.	ALAMEIN MEMORIAL
NEWTON, PERCY ALFRED	Lieutenant	145629	01/10/1942	23	Middlesex Regiment	United Kingdom	Column 13.	SAI WAN MEMORIAL
ORR, NATHANIEL PERCY	Pilot Officer	139946	25/02/1943	33	Royal Air Force Volunteer Reserve	United Kingdom	Panel 132.	RUNNYMEDE MEMORIAL
OWENS, RICHARD FRANK	Midshipman		05/11/1940	18	Royal Naval Reserve	United Kingdom	40, 1.	CHATHAM NAVAL MEMORIAL
PAGE, WILLIAM LEONARD	Lieutenant	302886	26/12/1944	24	East Surrey Regiment and Royal Fusiliers (City of London Regiment)	United Kingdom	III, B, 5.	FORLI WAR CEMETERY
PAINTER, DUNCAN FREDERICK SCOTT	Sergeant	14215529	18/01/1946	23	Royal Artillery	United Kingdom	5. L. 9.	JAKARTA WAR CEMETERY

PIKE, SEYMOUR CHARLES 'PETER'	Petty Officer Writer	C/LD/X 4732	30/03/1944	24	Royal Naval Volunteer Reserve	United Kingdom	78, 3.	CHATHAM NAVAL MEMORIAL
RANKIN, [AKA ROSENBERG] DOUGLAS JOHN	Rifleman	NGX509	01/07/1942	42	New Guinea Volunteer Rifles	Australian	Panel 30.	RABAUL MEMORIAL
RICHARDSON, GRAHAM ERIC	Private	6145481	10/06/1940	20	East Surrey Regiment	United Kingdom	Grave 3.	LANNOY CUILLERE COMMUNAL CEMETERY
ROWE, JACK VICKERY	Sergeant	912067	23/06/1941	20	Royal Air Force Volunteer Reserve	United Kingdom	Column 243.	ALAMEIN MEMORIAL
ROYAL, JACK DOUGLAS	Flight Lieutenant	82951	18/05/1942	25	Royal Air Force Volunteer Reserve	United Kingdom	Grave 1140.	LOSSIEMOUTH BURIAL GROUND
RYDER, RICHARD STANLEY I.	Flight Sergeant	1267013	06/09/1942	23	Royal Air Force Volunteer Reserve	United Kingdom	Panel 76.	RUNNYMEDE MEMORIAL
SAVITT, LAWRENCE	Lieutenant	182017	13/05/1944	29	Royal Artillery	United Kingdom	I. G. 17.	CASSINO WAR CEMETERY
SHARP, ROBERT WALTER	Pilot Officer	144580	21/01/1944	19	Royal Air Force Volunteer Reserve	United Kingdom	5. B. 34.	BERLIN 1939-1945 WAR CEMETERY
SHARVELL, GEORGE ELTHAM	Pilot Officer	86422	11/02/1941	29	Royal Air Force	United Kingdom	Cremation. Screen Wall Panel 3.	WANDSWORTH (PUTNEY VALE) CEMETERY AND CREMATORIUM
SHEERMAN, MAURICE GORDON	Flying Officer	151328	03/10/1943	26	Royal Air Force Volunteer Reserve	United Kingdom	Grave 108.	LONGWAY CEMETERY (WEST-TERSCHELLING)
SIMPSON, ARTHUR WILLIAM	Flight Sergeant	1380795	04/12/1942	22	Royal Air Force Volunteer Reserve	United Kingdom	Panel 3, Column 2.	MALTA MEMORIAL
SKILLERN, ALAN REGINALD JOHN	Major	75197	17/01/1944	23	Royal Fusiliers (City of London Regiment)	United Kingdom	VII, G, 16.	MINTURNO WAR CEMETERY
SLOCOCK, SYDNEY LAWRENCE	Brigadier		25/01/1947	55	Royal Army Veterinary Corps	United Kingdom	Cremation. Screen Wall Panel 3.	WANDSWORTH (PUTNEY VALE) CEMETERY AND CREMATORIUM
SMITH, CLAUDE DRURY	Trooper	14306309	03/08/1944	20	Royal Armoured Corps	United Kingdom	IV. A. 15.	FONTENAY-LE-PESNEL WAR CEMETERY, TESSEL
SMITH, ERIC HAYDN	Commander		24/02/1941	38	Royal Naval Reserve	United Kingdom	Panel 60, Column 1.	PORTSMOUTH NAVAL MEMORIAL
SMITH, ROY PETER	Sergeant	1395145	19/03/1945	21	Royal Air Force Volunteer Reserve	United Kingdom	13. F. 1.	RHEINBERG WAR CEMETERY
SOAN, ALFRED LESLIE	Lieutenant		15/08/1943	41	Royal Naval Volunteer Reserve	United Kingdom	Sec. W. Grave 13.	SEAFORD CEMETERY
STACEY, BERNARD FREDERICK	Pilot Officer	101225	15/02/1942	24	Royal Air Force Volunteer Reserve	United Kingdom	Column 413.	SINGAPORE MEMORIAL
STONE, KENNETH FRANK	Lieutenant	262920	03/10/1943	22	Royal Artillery	United Kingdom	X. B. 17.	SANGRO RIVER WAR CEMETERY
TALBOT, DERRICK	Flying Officer	152410	04/11/1944	22	Royal Air Force Volunteer Reserve	United Kingdom	Coll. grave 22. A. 8-12.	REICHSWALD FOREST WAR CEMETERY
WARD, WALTER FREDERICK	Lieutenant	292203	07/11/1944	21	Reconnaissance Corps, R.A.C.	United Kingdom	Block K. Grave 552. Screen Wall.	WANDSWORTH (PUTNEY VALE) CEMETERY AND CREMATORIUM
WARNER, STANLEY CHARLES	Captain	90786	19/07/1945	25	Royal Fusiliers (City of London Regiment)	United Kingdom	II. G. 7.	UDINE WAR CEMETERY
WATERMAN, HARRY JEREM	Lance Corporal	2336103	04/09/1943	23	Royal Corps of Signals	United Kingdom	Sp. Mem. 9. M. 4.	KANCHANABURI WAR CEMETERY
WEEKS, ROY KEEBLE	Sub-Lieutenant		02/08/1943	21	Royal Naval Reserve	United Kingdom	Row B. Grave 4.	YEOVILTON CHURCHYARD R.N.A.S. EXTENSION
WEST, LEONARD ARTHUR	Pilot Officer	108946	23/01/1943	33	Royal Air Force Volunteer Reserve	United Kingdom	Column 269.	ALAMEIN MEMORIAL
WHEELER, ALLEN EARLSMAN FREDERICK	Ordinary Seaman	D/JX 254057	28/04/1941	27	Royal Navy	United Kingdom	Grave 41.	TORPOINT (HORSON) CEMETERY
WHITE, THOMAS EDWARD CHARLES	Second Lieutenant	126938	11/09/1941	25	Royal Artillery	United Kingdom	1. C. 2.	SUEZ WAR MEMORIAL CEMETERY
WILDEY, RICHARD KEMP (DICK)	Wing Commander	37437	15/10/1942	25	Royal Air Force	United Kingdom	Coll. grave 5. D. 16-17.	RHEINBERG WAR CEMETERY
WILLETT, ARTHUR DANIEL	Private	5955656	08/12/1943	28	Bedfordshire and Hertfordshire Regiment	United Kingdom	8. M. 45.	KANCHANABURI WAR CEMETERY
WILMSHURST, TREVOR REGINALD CYRIL	Aircraftman 2nd Class	1892536	23/10/1944	20	Royal Air Force Volunteer Reserve	United Kingdom	Column 282.	ALAMEIN MEMORIAL
YORKE, STEPHEN CHARLES GARDNER	Captain	245409	07/01/1947	27	Royal Armoured Corps	United Kingdom	2. C. 20.	MUNSTER HEATH WAR CEMETERY
YOUNG, RODNEY FREDERICK HARDING	Warrant Officer	741708	25/08/1942	26	Royal Air Force Volunteer Reserve	United Kingdom	Allied Plot. Row 2. Grave 36.	THE HAGUE (WESTDUIN) GENERAL CEMETERY

First World War Decorations

Winners of the Distinguished Service Order

Augustus Wieland Bird – 11th East Surrey Regt. (Formerly H.A.C.), R.F.C.

Herbert Archer Fagan – 9/Gurkhas. [Gazetted 27 September 1920]

Roland Leonard Hastings McNish – Mercantile Marine

Richard Glass Smithard – K.S.L.I.

Winners of the Military Cross and Bar

Robert Brown – Royal West Kent Regt.

Herbert Archer Fagan – 5th The Yorkshire Regt.

Frank Percy Joseph Glover – 4th East Surrey Regt.

Cecil Alfred Stevens – R.F.C.

Winners of the Military Cross

Leslie Stuart Clinton – 20th Hussars. (Formerly 23rd London Regt).

Alfred Christopher Dancer – 8th Royal Fusiliers., Dorset Regt.

Montague Roger Dell – East Surrey Regt.

Frank Christopher Denman – R.F.A.

Geoffrey Norman Dolby – 16th London Regt. (Queen's Westminsters).

William Sholto Douglas – R.F.C.

Thomas Entwistle – 16th London Regt. (Queen's Westminsters), Tanks Corps.

Dennis Walter Furlong – 1st Royal Berkshire Regt.

William George Hall – R.F.A.

William James Hastings – 14th Notts & Derby Regt. (Sherwood Foresters).

Lawrence Inkster – 10th The Queen's (Royal West Surrey) Regt.

Rev. J. C. Kinnear – M.A. Royal Army Chaplains' Department.

Douglas William Lane Nichols – 8th The Queen's (Royal West Surrey) Regt.

William Arthur Poundall – South Lancashire Regt., att. R.F.C.

Maurice Arthur Prismall – 13th London Regt. (Kensington Btn. Princess Louise's Own).

Brian Causes Rigden – 5th London Regt. (London Rifle Brigade).

Bryan Scurfield – 2nd East Surrey Regt.

Geoffrey Cholerton Smith – A.S.C. (Horse Transport), att. R.F.C.

Richard Glass Smithard – King's Shropshire Light Infantry.

George Stephens – Gloucester Regt. (Wounded).

Alfred Eric Titley – Devonshire Regt.

James Vaughan – 8th East Kent Regt (The Buffs).

Winners of the Distinguished Conduct Medal

Walter E. T. Chester – Royal Fusiliers.

William George Hall – R.F.A.

Winners of the Distinguished Flying Cross

William Sholto Douglas – R.F.C.

Charles Frederick Wagstaffe – R.N.A.S.

Winners of the Military Medal

William Percival Noel – R.E. (Formerly R.F.A).

William Henry Sanders – London Regt.

Winners of Foreign Awards

Augustus Wieland Bird – 11th East Surrey Regt. (Formerly H.A.C.), R.F.C. The Silver Medal for Military Valour – Italian decoration.

Joseph Dunstan Bradly – Suffolk Regt., att. R.F.C. (Formerly 5th East Kent Regt.), (The Buffs), Croix de Guerre, Belgian Order of Leopold – Belgian decoration.

Bryan Scurfield – 2nd East Surrey Regt., Order of Military Merit 4th Class – Greek decoration.

Charles Ernest Turner – 11th Worcestershire Regiment., Croix de Guerre – French decoration.

Other Awards

Dennis Walter Furlong – 1st Royal Berkshire Regt. Awarded O.B.E.

Hugh Colin Waghorn – 21st London Regt. (1st Surrey Rifles), R.F.C. Awarded M.B.E.

Mentioned in Despatches

Harold Arthur Hunt – Canadian Contingent.

William Percival Noel – R.E., formerly R.F.A.

Alfred Eric Titley – Devonshire Regt.

Second World War Decorations

Winners of the Distinguished Service Order

Horace Stanley Darley – R.A.F.

George D. Delaforce – S.A.A.F.

Dennis Walter Furlong – Royal Berkshire Regt.

David John Warren – Hants. Regt.

Winners of the Distinguished Flying Cross

Arthur Ronald D'Agnold Clutterbuck – R.A.F.

John Alfred 'Jack' Dixon – R.A.F.V.R.

Douglas Albert Duncan – R.A.F.

Douglas William Finlay – R.A.F.

Cedric Alexander Fraser-Petherbridge – R.A.F.V.R.

William Bernard Hartnett – R.A.F.

Leslie R. Hastings – R.A.F.V.R.

Hugh James Felce Le Good – R.A.F.

Albert 'Bertie' Sydney Mann – R.A.F.

F. J. Milliken – R.A.F.

Kenneth Milton Millist – R.A.F.

R. W. Prendergast – R.A.F.

George Warwick Topliss – R.A.F.

Reginald John Twamley – R.A.F.

Richard Kemp Wildey – R.A.F.

Owen Edmund Wiltshear – R.A.F.

Winners of the Military Cross

Desmond Ronald Crampton Bailey – Royal Fusiliers att. Royal Worcestershire.

Stanley George Holliman – R.E.

Harold John Hutchins – East Lancs. Regt.

Peter Harold Jackson – R.T.R., 2 S.A.S.

Peter Herbert Mason – 46th Recce Corps. R.A.C.

John Howard Neale – R.A.

Ronald Victor Pinkham – Leicestershire Regt.

Hugh Craigie Sim – R.A.C.

Edward Alfred Charles Thomas – R.A.

Urwin 'Ned' Thornburn – K.S.L.I.

Allan Forsyth Wallace – R.A.M.C.

Stanley Charles Warner – R.F.

David John Warren – Hants. Regt.

Winner of the Distinguished Service Medal

Seymour Charles 'Peter' Pike – R.N.V.R.

Distinguished Service Cross

Sandi – R.N.V.R. (F.A.A.).

Winners of the Distinguished Flying Medal

Ronald Cuthbert Besant – R.A.F.

Richard Charles Frost – R.A.F.

Alan Patrick Savage – R.A.F.

Ronald Charles Simendinger – R.A.F.

Rodney Frederick Harding Young – R.A.F.V.R.

Winners of Foreign Honours

Ernest Henry 'Dixie' Dean – R.A.F. Greek Distinguished Flying Cross – Greek decoration.

Henry Barnett Deeks – 9th Royal Scots Fus., Croix de Guerre – French decoration.

Hugh James Felce Le Good – R.A.F. Australian Flying Cross – Australian decoration.

Geoffrey Blake Palmer – New Zealand Medical Service, 5th Field Ambulance, New Zealand Defence Force. Greek Silver Medal – Greek decoration.

War related Honours

George G. Banting – R.A.F. Awarded C.B., C.B.E.

George Oliver Cowles – R.E.M.E. Awarded M.B.E.

Joseph Clement Deeks – R.A.O.C., R.A.P.C. Awarded M.B.E. and Legion of Merit.

Phillip Russell Drew – East Surreys. Awarded O.B.E.

Peter Graham Glendenning – York and Lancaster Regt. Awarded M.B.E.

Donald Russell Naylor – R.E.M.E. Awarded M.B.E.

John Arthur Solkhon – R.A.S.C. Awarded M.B.E.

Arthur John West – Chairman of Surrey Territorial Army, Air Force Association. Awarded O.B.E.

Mentioned in Despatches

Donald John Allcock – R.N.V.R., (E).

Donald George Chick – R.I.A.S.C. (formerly R.A.S.C., R. North'd Fus., Indian Army, Queen's Royal Regt).

John Aubrey Chiles – I.A.C.

Howard Gordon Cross – R.C.S.

Jack Leslie Darnell – R.E.M.E.

Ernest Henry 'Dixie' Dean – R.A.F.

Joseph Clement Deeks – R.A.O.C., R.A.P.C.

Phillip Russell Drew – East Surreys.

W. G. Gold – R.I.A.S.C.

Leslie R. Hastings – R.A.F.V.R.

William Michael Squire Jeffery – R.T.R.

John McClean – R.A.O.C., R.T.R. Mentioned in Despatches twice.

William Lake Meredith – R.N.V.R.

Donald Russell Naylor – R.E.M.E.

Geoffrey Blake Palmer – New Zealand Medical Service, 5th Field Ambulance, New Zealand Defence Force.

Jack Douglas Royal – R.A.F.V.R.

Maurice Rowdon – R.A.

Gordon McRae Smeaton – R.A.F.V.R.

Francis W. Thomas – R.A.F.

Allan Forsyth Wallace – R.A.M.C.

Lt. Reginald Goodchild *(Emanuel 1919–1927)*

This card was sent by Reginald Goodchild to his wife in South Africa whilst he was a FEPOW (Far East Prisoner of War) in Thailand during the Second World War to let her know he was alive. Reginald was a talented pupil at Emanuel. He was a School Prefect, House Captain of Wellington, a member of the First Fifteen and First Eight, Secretary of Boats, a Sergeant in the OTC and Editor of The Portcullis. Reginald moved to Singapore where he was Inspector of Schools and Lecturer in English Literature at Raffles College. He enlisted in the Straits Settlement Volunteer Force in the early 1930s rising to the rank of Lieutenant. He was captured when Singapore fell to Japanese forces on 15 February 1942. His wife Frieda May Goodchild, carrying their second child, Jean, was evacuated first to Australia then Durban, South Africa with their daughter Sally. Reginald was forced to work on the building of the infamous Burma-Thai Railway. He was transported to several POW camps whilst a POW and was released on 2 September 1945. The last camp in which he was held was Nakhon Nayok north-east of Bangkok. On his release he wrote to the OEA to say several OEs interned in the Far East had survived their captivity. Reginald, like many who had gone through Japanese POW camps, did not talk about his experiences in post-war years.

Old Emanuel Prisoners of War

First World War

Frederick Roy Ashenden – R.N.V.R. Interned in Holland.

Donald Keith Batstone – R.N.V.R. Interned in Holland.

Edwin John Dilnutt – 7th Bedfordshire Regt., (att. R.A.F.)

Roland Stredwick Gilbert – R.F.C.

Ronald Everett Glover – Hussars.

Edgar Green – 15th Btn., Australian Infantry. Interned in Yosgad, Turkey. Died of Spanish Influenza.

Newton James Hodges – London Regt.

Alwyn Kerfoot Hughes – London Regt., Queen's Westminsters. Minden Camp.

Cecil Francis Knight – details unknown.

William Wesley Line – Royal Fusiliers.

Leonard Gordon Marthews – South Lancashire Regt. Died of wounds in Germany. ✤

Roland Leonard Hastings McNish – R.N.V.R. Six different POW camps including Karlsruhe.

Stephen Louis Pettit – 7th Battalion Royal Fusiliers. R.F.C. POW Constantinople.

Jessie William Ranson – 1st Btn., Suffolk Regt.

Charles Geoffrey Slocombe – 6th East Kent Regt., (Buffs). Wounded and died as POW. ✤

Albert Smith – London Regt.

Lionel Richard Mortimer Strachan – Civilian POW held at Ruhleben.

Eric Langdon Thompson – Royal Berks Regt.

Jack Toogood – No. 4 Officer Cadet Battn. Army Pay Corps., Norfolk Regt., later R.A.F.

Hugh William Vaughan – 7th Royal West Surrey Regt., (The Queen's). Interned in Karlsruhe.

James Vaughan – 8th East Kent Regt., (Buffs).

Stanley Vaughan – 8th East Kent Regt., (Buffs).

Claude Edgar Wallis – Loyal North Lancashire Regt.

Frank Henry White – London Regt.

Frederick Richard White – 21st Btn., Middlesex Regiment. Wounded and POW. ✤

Second World War

Vernon Harrison Avery – R.C.S., Camp 73, Fossoli di Carpi, Italy and Stalag XVIII–A, Austria.

William Herbert Crampton Bailey – Various Camps (FEPOW).

Leonard William Bennett – R.A., Poland.

Albert Edward Bumstead – R.A.F., 1121 Stalag Luft–6 and Stalag Luft–1, Germany.

David John Carpenter – M.N. Milag Nord, Germany.

Percy Peter Coe – M.N., Frontstalag 221.

John Richard Cole – Nagoya (FEPOW).

Ken Douglas Owen Cole – Middlesex Regt., Hong Kong, Nagoya, (FEPOW).

Reginald Charles Frederick Dunkin – R.A.S.C. Various Camps, (FEPOW).

Douglas William Finlay D.F.C. – R.A.F., Stalag Luft–3, Germany and Milag Nord, Germany.

Peter Graham Glendenning – York & Lancaster., att. 5th Green Howards., Campo 49, Fontanellato. Escapee.

Reginald Arthur Goodchild – Singapore Defence Force. Thailand, (FEPOW).

Allan Charles Goodger – R.A.S.C., Oflag VII–Eichstatt, Bavaria, Germany.

Tom Edmond Stone Gray – R.N., Germany.

Philip George Harding – Glos Regt., 1st Btn. Worcester Regt., Italy and Oflag–79, Brunswick, Lower Saxony, Germany.

Douglas Sydney Hoare – R.A.F., Oflag–IXA (An Army camp); Oflag–IXA(H) (RAF Camp); Stalag Luft–I; Oflag–IXA(H); Stalag Luft–XXA; Oflag–IX(H); Oflag–VIB; Oflag–XXIB; Stalag Luft–III; Stalag Luft–IVD

Alec Holt – R.A.

Kenneth Horseman – R.B., Campo P.G 59., Italy and Stalag IV–F Hartmannsdorf, Saxony, Germany.

William Harry Lewis – R.A., Oflag–79, Brunswick, Lower Saxony, Germany.

Richard Marr Murray – L.D.F., Malaya Territorials., Malay, (FEPOW).

Percy Alfred Newton – Middlesex Regt., Hong Kong, (FEPOW) Killed whilst being transported to a Japanese POW camp on the Lisbon Maru, which was sunk by a US Submarine. ✤

Eric Ronald Nonweiler – Thailand, (FEPOW).

Cyril William Joseph Pointon – R.A.M.C., Stalag VIII–B Cieszyn, Poland.

Eric Gordon Morell Pople – K.R.R.C., London Scottish., O.C.T.U. Campo P.G., No 49 P.M., 3200, Italy and Oflag–79, Brunswick, Lower Saxony, Germany.

Felix Harvey Spencer Palmer – East Surrey Regt., Q.R.R., Various Camps, Germany.

Harry Arthur Robin Prowse – R.A.F., Stalag Luft–III, Germany.

Douglas John Rankin (aka Rosenberg)., New Guinea Volunteer Rifles., Killed whilst being transported to Japanese POW camp on Montevideo Maru which was sunk by a US Submarine. (FEPOW). ✤

Donald Alan Scoullar – R.G.H., Oflag–VIIF and Oflag–79, Brunswick, Lower Saxony, Germany.

Alec Shoosmith – Westminster Dgns., C.L.Y., Stalag IV–B Maglberg/Elbe, Brandenburg.

Walter Norman Adams Smalley – R.N.V.R., Hong Kong, (FEPOW).

Leslie Walter Frederick Stubbings – The Royal East Kent Regiment (The Buffs). (Reported in the Summer Term edition of *The Portcullis* but unconfirmed by research).

Eric Charles Stubbs – Queen's Regt., Middlesex Regt., Oflag–VII-B Eichstatt, Bavaria, Germany.

William Henry Taylor – King's Own Royal Regiment, att., The Royal East Kent Regiment (The Buffs)., Oflag–79, Brunswick, Lower Saxony, Germany.

Harry Jerem Waterman – R.C.S., Malaya, (FEPOW)., (Died as POW). ✤

D. Webb – details unknown.

Arthur Daniel Willett – Beds & Herts Regt., (FEPOW). (Died as POW) ✤

Robert Cunningham Williams – (FEPOW).

George Wiseman – Changi Jail (FEPOW).

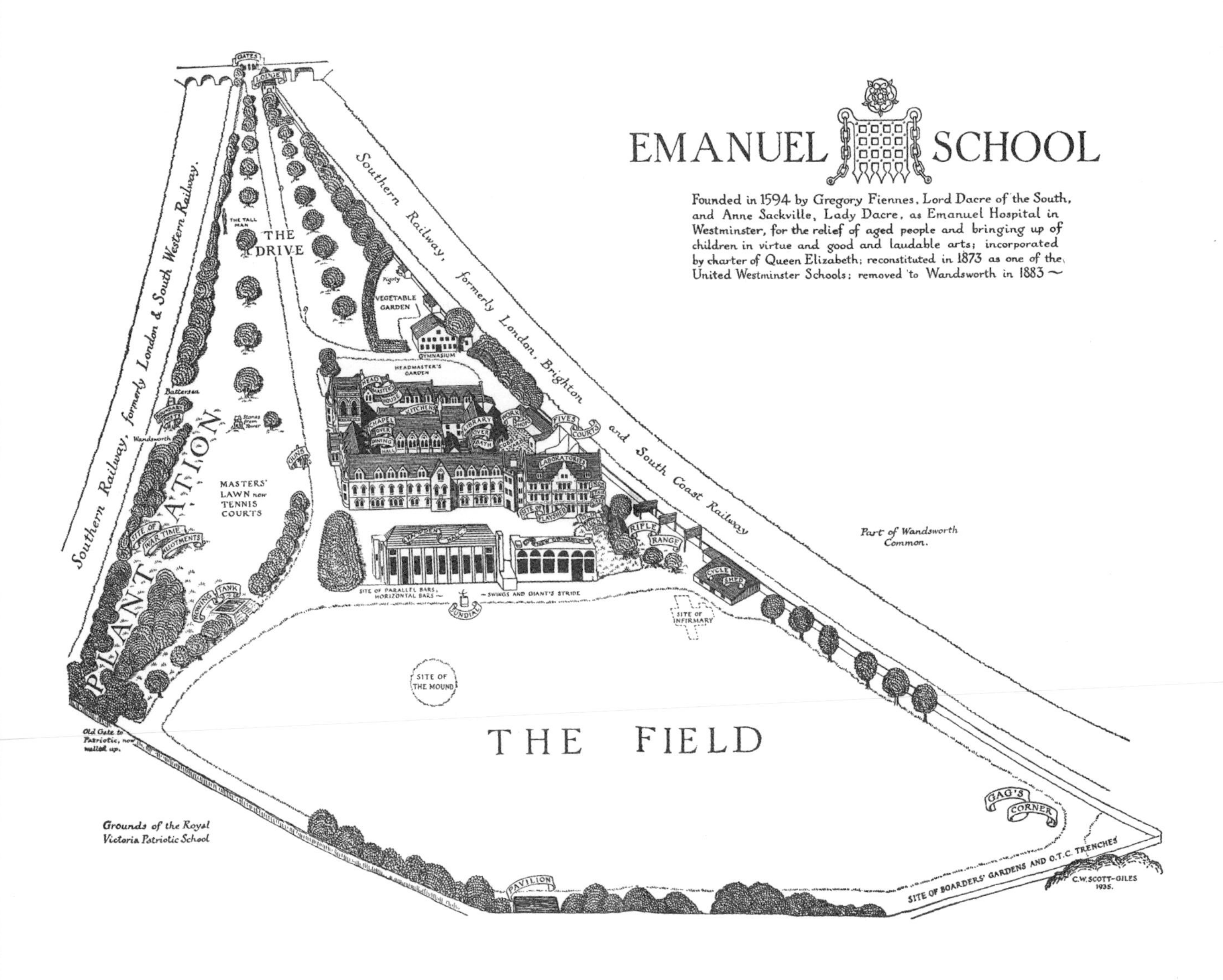

This map appeared in every edition of *The History of Emanuel School* from 1935–1977 and was drawn by the author and OE, C. W. Scott-Giles. It features all the famous School landmarks from the early part of the twentieth century, many of which were included in the Beating of the Bounds ceremonies which were popular from the 1920s to 1950s and were often led by Scott-Giles. The guns which were awarded to the School after the First World War can be seen on the front lawn. They were to remain there for 20 years until they were melted down for the Second World War effort. Behind the guns, close to the railway wall, were allotments where younger boys grew a wide range of vegetables, and often had competitions to see who could grow the largest marrows. The bottom right corner of the map in 'Gag's Corner' (named after an English teacher G. A. Garrington) shows where the OTC practised building trenches in the First World War and the whole area was used to grow wheat for the School's baked bread. To the right hand side is the old 'Rifle Range'. Near the top end of the drive stands 'The Tall Man', who was rumoured to be the ghost of a soldier and who was sighted on 'The Drive' at the end of the First World War.

List of Military and Non-Military Abbreviations which Appear in the Text

AA	Anti-Aircraft
AB	Able Seaman
AC1	Aircraftsman 1st Class
AC2	Aircraftsman 2nd Class
ADC	Aide-de-Camp
AFB	Anti-Frostbite Grease
AFHQ	Allied Forces Headquarters
AGRA	Army Group Royal Artillery
AHQ	Army Headquarters
AM	Air Mechanics
AOC	Air Officer Commanding
AQMG	Assistant Quartermaster General
AQMS	Assistant (or Artificer) Quartermaster Sergeant
ASC	Army Service Corps
ATC	Air Training Corps
ATS	Aircrew Training System
ATT	Attached
AVRE	Armoured Vehicle, Royal Engineers
BBC	British Broadcasting Corporation
BEF	British Expeditionary Force
BHQ	Battalion Headquarters
CB	Companion of the Order of the Bath
CBE	Commander of the Order of the British Empire
CCF	Combined Cadet Force
CEF	Canadian Expeditionary Force
CHQ	Company (or Corps) Headquarters
CIV	City Imperial Volunteers
CO	Commanding Officer
CQMS	Company Quartermaster Sergeant
CSM	Company Sergeant Major
CSR	Civil Service Rifles
DADME	Deputy Assistant Director, Mechanical Engineers
DFC	Distinguished Flying Cross
DFM	Distinguished Flying Medal
DLI	Durham Light Infantry
DSO	Distinguished Service Order
EA	Enemy Aircraft
ENSA	Entertainments National Service Association
FDL	Forward Defended Localities
FEPOWS	Far East Prisoners of War
FOO	Forward Observation Officer
GHQ	General Headquarters
GOC	General Officer Commanding
GPO	General Post Office
GS	Gunshot
GSO	General Staff officer
GSW	Gunshot wound
HAC	Honourable Artillery Company
HCU	Heavy Conversion Unit
HMHS	His Majesty's Hospital Ship
HMS	His Majesty's Ship
HQ	Head Quarters
IAFVR	Indian Air Force Volunteer Reserve
ICRC	International Committee of the Red Cross
IWM	Imperial War Museum
JICFE	Joint Intelligence Committee, Far East
JTC	Junior Training Corps
KAR	King's African Rifles
KRRC	King's Royal Rifle Corps
KSLI	King's Shropshire Light Infantry
LC	Lines of Communication or Landing Craft
LCA	Landing Craft, Assault
LCC	London County Council
LDV	Local Defence Volunteers
LMG	Light Machine Gun
LRB	London Rifle Brigade
MBE	Member of the Order of the British Empire
MC	Military Cross
ME	Middle East
MEDLOC	Mediterranean Lines of Communication
MEF	Mediterranean Expeditionary Force
MG	Machine gun
MGC	Machine Gun Corps
MI	Military intelligence
MID	Mention in Despatches
MKV	Mark V (German Panther tank)
MM	Military Medal
MP	Member of Parliament
MT	Motor Transport
NCO	Non-Commissioned Officer
NWFP	North-West Frontier Province
OBE	Officer of the Order of the British Empire
OC	Officer Commanding
OCB	Officer Cadet Battalion
OCTU	Officer Cadet Training Unit
OE	Old Emanuel
OEA	Old Emanuel Association
OERFC	Old Emanuel Rugby Football Club
OP	Observation Post
OTC	Officers' Training Corps
OTU	Officer Training Unit
PAI Force	Persia and Iraq Command
PNBA	Pilot Navigator Bomb Aimer
PO	Pilot Officer
POW	Prisoner of War
RA	Royal Artillery
RAAF	Royal Australian Air Force
RAC	Royal Armoured Corps
RADAR	Radio Detection and Ranging
RAF	Royal Air Force
RAFVR	Royal Air Force Volunteer Reserve
RAMC	Royal Army Medical Corps
RAOC	Royal Army Ordnance Corps
RAPC	Royal Army Pay Corps
RASC	Royal Army Service Corps
RCAF	Royal Canadian Air Force
RCS	Royal Corps of Signals
RE	Royal Engineers
RE8	First World War Reconnaissance Aircraft
REME	Royal Electrical and Mechanical Engineers
RFA	Royal Field Artillery
RFC	Royal Flying Corps
RFM	Radio Frequency Monitor
RGA	Royal Garrison Artillery
RMA	Royal Marine Artillery
RNAS	Royal Naval Air Service
RNHQ	Royal Navy Headquarters
RPO	Regimental Post Office
RT	Radio Transmission
RTO	Radio Transmission Operator
SASO	Senior Air Staff Officer
SHAEF	Supreme Headquarters, Allied Expeditionary Force
TA	Territorial Army
UN	United Nations
USAAC	US Army Air Force
WRNS	Women's Royal Naval Service
VC	Victoria Cross
VE	Victory in Europe
VJ	Victory in Japan
WO	War Office
YMCA	Young Men's Christian Association

Picture Credits

Legal Disclaimer: The authors have tried to recognise all copyright holders for the images which appear in *Emanuel School at War*, but where it has not been possible to identify copyright holders the authors ask them to make contact so this can be added to future editions.

Chapter 1:
p. 2: Nevil Bursey Hodgson © British Library

Chapter 2:
p. 11: Ryley memorial by kind permission of Jeremy Archer
p. 12: Grantley Adolphe Le Chavetois by kind permission of St. Olave's School

Chapter 3:
p. 20: Daniek Kirmatzis by kind permission of Jayson Singh
p. 34: J. D. Bradly by kind permission of Paul Bradly
p. 35: Portrait of John Burns by kind permission of the National Liberal Club
p. 36: Edgar Burns © British Library
p. 39: 'The Colossus of Battersea' by kind permission and © *Punch Magazine*
p. 42: Edgar Burn's train ticket to Ypres by kind permission and © British Library

Chapter 4 Part I:
pp. 47-60: Grundy letters by kind permission of The Archive of Modern Conflict
pp. 47-60: Paintings and photographs by kind permission of the Grundy family
pp. 68-77: Photos and documents of Charlie Payne by kind permission of Dr. Chris Payne
pp. 78-90: Photos and documents of Alec Reader by kind permission of Doug Goodman. © Reader/Goodman/Collins
pp. 91-102: The Dell Family photographs by kind permission of David Dell and © Religious Society of Friends in Britain
pp. 106-108: George Lyward by kind permission of John Lyward
pp. 109-111: Photographs and documents of Eric Titley by kind permission of Jessica Bolton
pp. 112-121: With thanks to the Trustees of the Imperial War Museums for allowing access to the collection of the Private Papers of Lt. F. P. J. Glover MC and their kind permission for the reproduction of images
p. 122: Photograph of the Hall brothers by kind permission of Colin Hall

Chapter 4 Part II:
pp. 124-130: With thanks to the Trustees of the Imperial War Museums for allowing access to the collection of the Private Papers of Captain Claude Edgar Wallis and their kind permission for the reproduction of images
p. 131: Photo of Leonard Gordon Marthews by kind permission of Stamford Marthews

Chapter 4 Part III:
p. 135: Frank Skinner by kind permission of Lijssenthoek Military Cemetery

Chapter 5
pp. 140-143: Arthur Collen by kind permission of Richard and Rodney Freeman
p. 144: Sir Alfred Butt, 1st Bt, by Lenare, nitrate negative, 23 July 1946. © National Portrait Gallery, London

Chapter 6
pp. 145-149: With thanks to the Trustees of the Imperial War Museums for allowing access to the collection of Air Vice Marshal Banting – The Royal Flying Corps and the Royal Air Force 1914–1950 and their kind permission to reproduce images
pp. 150-157: John C. F. Hopkins by kind permission of Evadne Spickett

Chapter 7
p. 161: Leonard Edwin Fry by kind permission of Chris Fry

Chapter 8
p. 173: Harry Gustave Wyborn by kind permission of Jill Blackbourn

Chapter 9
p. 177: C. W. Scott-Giles by kind permission of Giles Scott-Giles
pp. 182-184: Percy Mathison Brooks by kind permission of the Brooks family
pp. 183-184: Photographs and documents of Lawrence Inkster by kind permission of Donald Inkster
p. 185: R. C. Montford by kind permission of Chris Kenyon

Chapter 10:
p. 186: Adolf Hitler inspecting the Hitler Youth by kind permission of Shirley Blackburn
p. 188: Lt-Col. Charles Hill by kind permission of Dr Charles Hill
pp. 203-204: *Picture Post*, 'Leslie Henson Reviews the Situation' by kind permission of © Getty Images
p. 207-214: Other photographs in the Petersfield section by kind permission of David Palmer and Jim Cleverley
p. 217: Charles James Sammonds by kind permission of Charles James Sammonds
p. 218: Painting of the Market Square in Petersfield in the 1930s by Flora Twort by kind permission of Petersfield Museum and © the Flora Twort Gallery
p. 220: Peter Downs by kind permission of Dennis Geen
pp. 223-226: Allan Barnes's letters by kind permission of Allan Barnes
p. 226: Winston Churchill and Five French boys by kind permission of © Getty Images
p. 227: Memorial of Five French boys crossing the Channel by kind permission of © Nic Maunder Taylor
p. 230: 1946 letter from the King sent to British school children by kind donation of Chris Banwell
p. 232: Reunion photographs by kind permission of Ron Williamson
p. 234: Image of Wates Ltd pre-cast bunks for air-raid shelters by kind permission of Wates Ltd
p. 235: John Henry Mills by kind permission of Val Bowman
p. 236: Portrait of Allan Wheeler by Flora Twort by kind permission of Petersfield Museum and the Flora Twort Gallery
p. 240: William Leonard Page's grave by kind permission of the Royal Fusilier Museum, London
pp. 241-242: Leonard Mitchell by kind permission of Robin Mitchell

Chapter 11
p. 245: John Banting by kind permission and © Estate of Humphrey & Rachel Spender
pp. 246-53: Photographs of Leslie Henson by kind permission of Nicky Henson
p. 248: The Gaities photograph by kind permission of © the Trustees of TACT (formerly the Actors' Orphanage Fund and Actors' Charitable Trust
p. 251: Leslie Henson with Fred and Adele Astaire by kind permission of © Getty Images
p. 252: With thanks to the Trustees of the Imperial War Museums for allowing use of the image (A 15289) © Imperial War Museums
p. 255: The *Otaki* being sunk by the *Moewe*, painted by K. T. Roussell by kind permission of © Archives New Zealand [Archives Reference: AAAC 898 NCWA Q200]
pp. 257-262: Lawrence Inkster by kind permission of Donald Inkster
pp. 263-264: With thanks to the Trustees of the Imperial War Museums for allowing use of the image of Sir Sholto Douglas (Q_069150) © Imperial War Museums
p. 264 Sholto Douglas & Winston Churchill © National Library of Australia. From Album of Wartime Photographs of R. G. Casey, 1940-1947. BibID: 4319630
p. 266 Photo of Dunkirk by kind permission of Jill Loader © Chas Duckhouse and Jill Loader
pp. 266-269: Dennis Furlong by kind permission of Madam Pauline Hunter of Hunterston
p. 271: Cecil Stevens, NPG x185462, by Walter Stoneman, bromide print, 1951 © National Portrait Gallery, London
p. 271: With thanks to the Trustees of the Imperial War Museums for allowing use of the image (CI 001141) © Imperial War Museums

Chapter 12
pp. 274-275 Graham Richardson and Ken Richardson by kind permission of Martin Richardson

Chapter 13
p. 276 Camera-gun film taken from a Supermarine Spitfire Mark I flown by the Commanding Officer of No. 609 Squadron RAF, Squadron Leader H. S. Darley with thanks to the Trustees of the Imperial War Museums for allowing use of the image (CH 1829)
pp. 276-280: The majority of photographs of George Darley by kind permission of David Darley
pp. 283-285: Brian Noble photographs and documents by kind permission of Nigel Noble
p. 288: Tom Morris Priestley by kind permission of Bobbi Crickmore

Chapter 14
pp. 290-293: Richard Kemp Wildey by kind permission of the Peter Wildey

pp. 294-295: Maurice Gordon Sheerman by kind permission of Willem de Jong
pp. 296-300: Gordon Townsend by kind permission of Gordon and Michael Townsend
pp. 301-302: Harold Bertram Hale by kind permission of Steve Bond and Richard Forder and their book *Special Ops Liberators* where this photograph originally appeared
pp. 303-304: Eric John McMillan by kind permission of Sue Mintram-Mason
p. 305: Richard Frost by kind permission of Robert Frost
p. 307: Richard Simendinger by kind permission of Richard Stanton
p. 309: Jack Royal by kind permission of Rachel Barnes

Chapter 15
pp. 312-315: Cecil Keeling by kind permission of The Royal Artillery Museum and Robert Hale Ltd
pp. 316-317: Derek Harrington by kind permission of Peter Harrington
p. 318-319: Geoffrey Victor Smith by kind permission of Mrs Smith and Jill and Peter Grainge
p. 320 John Solkhon by kind permission of Annie Lear Findlay
p. 321: Robert Ivy © University of Pennsylvania
p. 323: Frederick A. Walker by kind permission of John Walker
p. 324: David Bowler portrait by kind permission of Simon Bowler
pp. 324-326: Malcolm Campbell by kind permission of Helen Rowell
p. 327: Vernon Richards by kind permission of © Freedom Press
pp. 329-31: Donald Inkster by kind permission of Donald Inkster
pp. 332-335: Blackburn brothers by kind permission of Shirley Blackburn
p. 336: Colin and Kenneth Fowle by kind permission of Gail Fowle and Jenny Fowle
pp. 336-339: The Page Brothers by kind permission of Nora Page and the Page family

Chapter 16
p. 242: John Howard Neale by kind permission of John Howard Neale, Andrew and Victoria Neale
pp. 350-352: Photographs from the Italian Campaign by kind permission of the Royal Fusilier Museum, London
p. 352 John Coleman by kind permission of Anthony Coleman
p. 353: John Skillern visiting the grave of Alan Skillern by kind permission of John Skillern
pp. 357 Albert Marle laying a wreath at Alan Skillern's grave by kind permission of Albert Marle
pp. 358-359: Bob Deeks by kind permission of Bob Deeks and his family
pp. 360-362: Michael Jeffery by kind permission of Michael Jeffery and his family
p. 363: El Alamein Memorial Service © Daniel Kirmatzis and Richard Deeks
p. 364-369: Harold Stanley Page by kind permission of Kathy Page
pp. 370-374: Holliman brothers by kind permission of the Holliman family
p. 375: Walter Beyer by kind permission of John Beyer
p. 377: Middlesex Regiment by kind permission of John McLoughlin
pp. 378-379: Gordon Burrett by kind permission of Gordon Burrett
p. 378: John Pritchard by kind permission of Shirley Passmore
p. 380: Jack Halligan by kind permission of Jack Halligan
pp. 383-391: Maurice Rowdon by kind permission of Dachiell Rowdon

Chapter 17
pp. 394-397: John Chiles by kind permission of John Chiles
pp. 398-399: Robin Needham by kind permission of Patrick Needham
pp. 402-403: Dennis Geen by kind permission of Dennis Geen
pp. 405-406: Photos of George Darley by kind permission of David Darley
p. 410: Painting of A. S. Mann by William Dring, with thanks to the Trustees of the Imperial War Museums for allowing use of the image (LD 4680) © Imperial War Museums
pp. 411-416: Photographs of Albert 'Bertie' Mann by kind permission of © Patrick and Tim Mann
p. 417: Horace Cocks by kind permission of Brian Cocks
pp. 418-419: William Attfield by kind permission of William Attfield

Chapter 18
pp. 420-421: Robert Fielder by kind permission of Carol Janes and Margaret Wood
pp. 422-427: Brigadier David Warren by kind permission of Richard Warren
pp. 428-432: Urwin Ned Thornburn by kind permission of Tony Thornburn
p. 429: R. J. Harrison by kind permission of Tony Thornburn
pp. 433-435: Allan Barnes by kind permission of Allan Barnes
pp. 436-448: Albert 'Bertie' Mann by kind permission of © Patrick and Tim Mann
pp. 449-450: Philip Russell Drew by kind permission of Nick Drew
pp. 451-453: Gordon Murray by kind permission of Gordon Murray and Rose Mollett
pp. 454-464: All photographs related to the Wates brothers and Mulberry Harbours by kind permission of © Wates Ltd
pp. 465-468: Harold Hutchins by kind permission of Roger Hutchins
p. 467 Harold Hutchins being awarded the MC with thanks to the Trustees of the Imperial War Museums for allowing use of the image © Imperial War Museums
pp. 469-470: John Banbery by kind permission of John Banbery

Chapter 19
p. 473: Ronald Gray's *Brecht: the Dramatist* book cover © Cambridge University Press
pp. 474-477: All photographs and documents by kind permission of N. F. Simpson. One Way Pendulum book cover © Faber and Faber

Chapter 20
p. 483: Douglas Hoare by kind permission of Michael Hoare and Valerie Kelley
pp. 485-493: Bill Taylor by kind permission of Bill Taylor
pp. 494-498: Douglas Hoare by kind permission of Michael Hoare and Valerie Kelley
pp. 499-505: Douglas William Finlay by kind permission of R Derek Finlay
pp. 507-512: Kenneth Horseman by kind permission of Brian Horseman
p. 512: Alec Shoosmith by kind permission of © Kent and Sharpshooters Museum
p. 518: Mark Hanley-Browne and Lord Sebastian Coe © Anthony Murphy
p. 519 Peter and Sebastian Coe by kind permission of Lord Sebastian Coe
p. 519-520: Albert 'Bert' Bumstead by kind permission of © Ian Bumstead

Chapter 21
p. 524-528: Seymour 'Peter' Pike by kind permission of © Patricia Brandon. Robert Ryder's drawing of St. Nazaire Raid by kind permission of © Lyle Ryder
pp. 529-534: Eric Haydn Smith by kind permission of © Michael and Stephen
p. 530 Photo courtesy of State Library of New South Wales
Smith; John Harvey McGregor by kind permission of © John and Richard McGregor; William Bevis by kind permission of © Michael Dickins; Eric Carl Monkhouse by kind permission of © John Monkhouse
p. 536: Leslie Henson's photograph of the Japanese surrender at Singapore by kind permission of © the Trustees of The Actors' Children's Trust (TACT) (formerly the Actors' Orphanage Fund and Actors' Charitable Trust)

Chapter 22
p. 537: A View of Berlin by kind permission of Henry Carpenter

Chapter 23
p. 539: Derek Drury by kind permission of Derek Drury, and Derek Drury as Rowing Master by kind permission of © Roger George Clark

Chapter 24
p. 543: Ernest Tristram Crutchley by kind permission of © National Portrait Gallery, London
p. 544: Derek Davis by kind permission of © Josse Davis and photograph of Derek Davis pottery © Tony Jones
pp. 544-545: Sir Arthur Norman Galsworthy by kind permission of © Sir Anthony Charles Galsworthy
p. 545 Sir John Galsworthy by kind permission of © Michael Galsworthy
p. 546: Reginald Goddard by kind permission of the Goddard family
p. 546: Jack Chetwynd Western Heming by kind permission of Dorothy H. E. Bispham
p. 547: Jack Heming's *Playing for the School*, © Purnell, 1961 and *Lost World of the Colorado*, © Frederick Warne, 1963
p. 548: William Lovelock photograph originally appeared in a vinyl Australian Festival of Music Volume 9. © Festival Records 1972
p. 549: The portrait of Owen Saunders originally appeared in the Biographical Memoirs of Fellows of the Royal Society, Vol. 41 (Nov., 1995), pp. 378-394 Published by the Royal Society. It was supplied by Lady Daphne Saunders

Features
pp. 551-558: Kenneth Clark; Alvar Lidell; Gracie Fields; Henry Moore; Roger George Clark; Albert Speer; Lord Mountbatten of Burma; Douglas Bader; Barnes Wallis; Sir Cecil Beaton; John Snagge: All photos on these pages by kind permission of © Roger George Clark
pp. 559-566: Kurt Langelüddecke by kind permission of © Henrik Langelüddecke
p. 569: Sir Sholto Douglas arrives at Gatow airfield, Berlin, with thanks to the Trustees of the Imperial War Museums for allowing use of the image (CL 3655) © Imperial War Museums

Text Credits

The majority of texts and quoted materials in *Emanuel School at War* have come from previously unpublished documents. Copies of full-length memoirs are now held in the Emanuel School Archive. A full inventory of the Emanuel School Archive War Collection will be published on the School website in due course.

Disclaimer

The authors have taken every effort to contact copyright holders in order to give references and credit quoted materials; the authors will be happy to make corrections to future editions if errors or omissions are brought to their attention.

A Note on Sources

Generally the sources for each article appearing in *Emanuel School at War* are given in the References at the end of each article.

The copyright holders for quoted materials in *Emanuel School at War* are listed below:

Chapter 2

- *The Gallant Headmaster* text © Jeremy Archer 2014.
- *Emanuel Masters in the First World War* – Montagu Cleeve papers Imperial War Museums Accession No. 7310 – The collection is held in the Documents and Sound Department of the Imperial War Museums. Thanks are due to Trustees of the Imperial War Museums for allowing access to the collection and permission to reproduce text.
- *The Colossus of Battersea* – The Papers of John Burns © The British Library Board, (followed by the reference/shelf mark). BL Add MS 46303 f. 19 Sir Edward Grey, Letters to J. Burns: 1898–1914; BL Add MS 46303 f. 12 Clementina Black, Letters to J. Burns: 1891–1914; BL Add MS 46303 f. 15 Emily Hobhouse, Letters to J. Burns: 1900–1914; BL Add MS 46303 f. 60 Anthony W. Dell, of Wandsworth, Letter to J Burns: 1914; BL Add MS 74261 f. 144 Letter from John Collie to John Burns 21 October 1915; BL Add MS 74261 f. 78 Letter to John Edgar Burns, 9 July 1916; BL Add MS 46338, Diaries of John Burns 1916, entry for 9 July 1916; BL Add MS 46338 Diaries of John Burns 1916, entry for 24 August 1916; BL Add MS 74261 f. 83 Letter to John Edgar Burns, 14 August 1916; BL Add MS 74261 f. 87 Letter to John Edgar Burns, 3 September 1916.

Chapter 4 Part I

- *Brothers in Arms* – The Grundy Family letters and papers are held in the Archive of Modern Conflict – digital copies of the Grundy papers are held in the Emanuel School Archive.
- *Charles Frederick Payne* – text © Dr. Chris Payne OBE. A book on Charlie Payne's life is forthcoming.
- *Bertram Alec Reader* – Alec Reader's letters are republished by kind permission of Doug Goodman. The Reader papers are held in the IWM Accession No. Documents 4127. © Reader/Goodman/Collins.
- *The Dell Family* – The Dell papers are republished by kind permission of David Dell. The Dell papers are held in the National Army Museum, Chelsea accession No. 2002-02-1372.
- *With The East Surreys* – Papers of F.P.J. Glover, IWM Accession No. 78/10/1 – The collection is held in the Documents and Sound Department of the Imperial War Museums. Thanks are due to Trustees of the Imperial War Museum for allowing access to the collection and permission to reproduce text.

Chapter 4 Part II

- *Old Emanuel POWs in the First World War* – The extracts in the part of the article on Claude Edgar Wallis are reproduced with permission from The National Archive [TNA], Kew – WO/161/95/61.

Chapter 6

- *George Banting CB, CBE Air Vice-Marshal* – TNA, Kew – Air1/2392/228/11/186 C554385.
- *Dr John Collier Hopkins CMG – British Aviation of the First World War Period: Dr. J. C. F. Hopkins CMG: Experience of a night-flying pilot from home bases, 1917–18; and from Auchel, 1918*, IWM Accession No. 000021 / 06. The collection is held in the Documents and Sound Department of the Imperial War Museums. Thanks are due to Trustees of the Imperial War Museum for allowing access to the collection and permission to reproduce extracts. Extracts from Sholto Douglas, *Years of Combat: The First Volume of the Autobiography of Sholto Douglas, Marshal of the Royal Air Force, Lord Douglas of Kirtleside, GCB, MC, DFC.* © Harper Collins Publishers (UK) Ltd. and © Lord Douglas of Kirtleside, 1963.

Chapter 7

- *Frederick Harry Bedloe Moore* – Text © Tim Goddard.

Chapter 10

- *Lt-Col. Charles Hill OBE, MM, TD, BA* – War memoir of Charles Hill reproduced by kind permission and © Charles Hill (son of Lt. Col. Charles Hill).
- *Emanuel School in Petersfield 1939–1945* – Text © Vaughan Clarke.
- *Bombings and Civilians* – Papers of F.P.J. Glover, IWM Accession No. 78/10/1 – The collection is held in the Documents and Sound Department of the Imperial War Museums. Thanks are due to Trustees of the Imperial War Museums for allowing access to the collection and permission to reproduce text.
- p. 227 quoted text © *Life*.

Chapter 11

- *The Mascot of the Battersea Battalion* – Lawrence Inkster letters reproduced by kind permission of Donald Inkster.
- *Brigadier Dennis Walter Furlong DSO, OBE, MC* – Extracts from Brigadier Dennis Furlong's Dunkirk Diary by kind permission of The Wardrobe – The Rifles Berkshire and Wiltshire Museum.
- Extracts from Sholto Douglas with Robert Wright, Years of Command: The Second Volume of the Autobiography of Sholto Douglas, Marshal of the Royal Air Force, Lord Douglas of Kirtleside GCB, MC, DFC (Collins, 1966). © Harper Collins Publishers (UK) Ltd. and © Lord Douglas of Kirtleside, 1966.

Chapter 12

- *Tragedy in France* – Extracts from Peter Scott Janes and Keith Janes, *Conscript Heroes* (2004), by kind permission and © Keith Janes.

Chapter 13

- *The Battle of Britain* – Emanuel School has a copy of the (unpublished) memoir of Horace 'George' Darley – Extracts reproduced by kind permission and © David Darley.
- *The Battle of Britain* – Harry Arthur Robin Prowse – Combat Report TNA, Kew, AIR/50/167. Extracts from David Ross, Bruce Blanche and William Simpson, *The Greatest Squadron of them All: The definitive history of the 603 (City of Edinburgh) Squadron, RAUXAF*, (Grub Street, 2003) by kind permission of the authors and Grub Street Publishing.

Chapter 14

- *Flight Lieutenant Gordon Eric Victor Townsend* – Emanuel School Archive has a copy of *A Life in the Royal Air Force* (unpublished) by Gordon Townsend. Extracts reproduced by kind permission of Gordon Townsend.
- *Into the Storm – Eric John McMillan* – D. Williams and S. Mintram-Mason, *Into the Storm: the Making of a Bomber Crew* (1998). Extracts reproduced by kind permission of Sue Mintram-Mason.

Chapter 15

- *An Artist's War – Cecil Keeling* – Extracts reproduced by kind permission of Robert Hale Ltd.
- *A Queen's Man – Derek Harrington* – Text © Peter Harrington.
- *So I Joined the Royal Army Pay Corps... A story of delays! by Donald Inkster* – Text © Donald Inkster.

Chapter 16

- *Once a Gunner* – Extracts from John Neale's memoir by kind permission of Andrew Neale.
- *From North Africa to Normandy – Harold Stanley Page* – Letters of Harold Page reproduced by kind permission of Kathy Page.

- *Rome Indeed – Frank Louis Abbott* – An extract of this text © John McLoughlin.
- *Maurice Rowdon* – Extracts from *Of Sins and Winter* and Maurice Rowdon's unpublished memoir by kind permission and © Dachiell Rowdon.
- *Peter Harold Jackson MC* – Extracts from Roy Farran's *Winged Dagger* © Harper Collins Publishers (UK) Ltd. and © Roy Farran 1948.

Chapter 17

- *A Disciplined Service – John Chiles MBE* – John Chiles memoir reproduced by kind permission and © John Chiles.
- *Chindits in Burma – Major Robin Needham* – Major K. R. N. Needham – The 51st Field Regiment R.A. September 1943 to October 1944, Imperial War Museum accession number 80/49/1. The collection is held in the Documents and Sound Department of the Imperial War Museum. Thanks are due to Trustees of the Imperial War Museum for allowing access to the collection and permission to reproduce text.
- *Escape from Singapore – Horace Stanley 'George' Darley DSO* – Emanuel School has a copy of the (unpublished) memoir of Horace 'George' Darley – Extracts reproduced by kind permission and © David Darley.
- *Albert 'Bertie' Sydney Mann DFC* – Extracts from Bertie Mann's unpublished memoir reproduced by kind permission and © Patrick and Tim Mann.

Chapter 18

- *Brigadier David Warren DSO, OBE, MC* – Extracts are from interviews conducted by Conrad Wood and can be located at the Imperial War Museums catalogue Nos. 13041, 02/09/1993 and 12962, 18/01/1993. Thanks are due to Trustees of the Imperial War Museums for allowing access to the collection and permission to reproduce extracts.
- *Albert 'Bertie' Sydney Mann DFC* – Extracts from Bertie Mann's unpublished memoir reproduced by kind permission and © Patrick and Tim Mann.
- *The Wates Brothers in the Second World War* – Extracts from *Wates Sheet News* by kind permission of James Wates CBE.
- *An MC-Winning Rugger Captain – Major Harold John 'Ham' Hutchins MC, 5th East Lancs and 5DCLI* – Text © Roger Hutchins.
- *A Day Out (or so) to Minden* by John Banbery –Text © John Banbery.

Chapter 20

- *William 'Bill' Henry Taylor* – Extracts from Bill Taylor's POW Log Book by kind permission and © Bill Taylor. A digital copy of the Bill Taylor's Log Book is in the Emanuel School Archive.
- Extracts from Richard C. Smith, Hornchurch Scramble: The Definitive Account of the RAF Fighter Airfield, Its Pilots, Groundcrew and Staff, Volume One: 1915 to the End of the Battle of Britain (2002), © Richard C. Smith and Grub Street Publishing.
- *The Cool and Fearless Captain* – Douglas William Finlay – Extracts from Derek Finlay's autobiography *Ten to Take Her Home: The Life and Times of RDF* (2012), by kind permission and © Derek Finlay.
- *Kenneth Horseman* – Extracts from Kenneth Horseman's Second World War Journal by kind permission and © Brian Horseman.
- *Alec Shoosmith* – Extracts from Alec Shoosmith's memoir by kind permission of the Kent & Sharpshooters Museum, Hever Castle.
- *Albert 'Bert' Edward Bumstead* – The Collection of A. E. Bumstead can be consulted in the Emanuel School Archive.
- *A one-man resistance movement – Major Felix Harvey Spencer Palmer CBE* – Extracts from a talk given by Felix Palmer to the Royal British Legion reproduced by kind permission of Hugh Palmer.

Features

- *Roger George Clark's Gallery of Second World War Personalities* – Text © Roger George Clark See Roger's website for contact details – http://rogergeorgeclark.com/index.htm
- *A View from the Other Side of the Hill* – Text © Dr. Henrik Langelüddecke 2014.

Interviews with OE Second World War Veterans

Allan Barnes; John Chiles; William Robert Deeks; Dennis Geen; Stanley George Holliman; Michael Jeffrey; Gordon Murray and William Taylor. Full transcripts of these interviews conducted by Daniel Kirmatzis are available to consult from the Emanuel School Archive – © Daniel Kirmatzis 2014.

Christmas card sent by Eric Titley to his family in 1917.

Select Bibliography

Emanuel School Archive

Daniel Kirmatzis and Tony Jones have been assembling the 'War Collection' of the Emanuel School Archive over a number of years. The 'War Collection' consists of mainly digitised papers and letters relating to the experiences of Emanuel School alumni in the First and Second World Wars.

The Emanuel School Archive holds the digitised collections of the following. Please note that although these documents may be consulted at the Archive the original copyright holder must be contacted for their permission to reproduce any materials, which may incur additional charges payable to the copyright holder. Please see a list of copyright holders in *Further Reading and Text Credits*.

First World War Documents

- *Emanuel School Magazine* (title changed to *The Portcullis* in 1906).
- *The Portcullis* – The School magazine contains a variety of sources. The First World War is covered in both the 'Old Emanuel Notes' and also 'Letters from the Front'. There are also a number of 'war poems' composed by Emanuel pupils that can be found throughout the magazines. *The Portcullis* was produced once a term and information about the First World War can be found from 1914–1923. In the Second World War information about the War can be found in various places from obituaries, poems, short accounts about life in Petersfield and letters from OEs in a section called 'OE Jottings'.

Letters

- Cecil and Ronald Grundy letters and documents.
- Alec Reader letters and documents.
- Louis Michael Dell letters.
- Stanley Arthur George Harvey letters printed in *The Portcullis*.
- Lawrence Inkster letters and documents.

Diaries

- The Diary of William George Hall.

Memoirs

- 'My War 1914–1918' by Lt-Col. Charles Hill.

Miscellaneous

- A scrap book of materials covering the military career of Brigadier Dennis Furlong DSO, MC.

Second World War Documents

Collections

- Evacuation documents – the Emanuel School Archives holds a large number of documents including letters, diaries, memoirs and photographs relating to the School's evacuation to Petersfield 1939–1945. Please contact the Archivist for further details.
- Papers, letters, log books and RAF training materials of Albert 'Bert' Bumstead.
- Papers and POW log book of Douglas Finlay DFC.
- POW log book belonging to William 'Bill' Taylor 1943–1945.
- Letters, manuscripts and papers of Major Urwin 'Ned' Thornburn MC, relating to his research into the part played by the King's Shropshire Light Infantry (KSLI) in the North-West Europe Campaign 1944–1945.
- The letters, papers and log books of Squadron Leader Richard Kemp Wildey DFC.

Letters

- Douglas 'Sammy' Hoare POW letters.
- Seymour Charles 'Peter' Pike letters.

Unpublished Memoirs

- 'A Disciplined Service' by John Chiles MBE.
- 'The memoirs of Group Captain Horace Stanley 'George' Darley' by H. S. George Darley.
- 'So I Joined the Royal Army Pay Corps... A story of delays!' by Donald Inkster.
- 'Once a Gunner' by John Howard Neale MC.
- 'A Life in the Royal Air Force 1940–1946' by Flight Lieutenant Gordon Eric Victor Townsend DFC.

Miscellaneous

- A scrapbook of materials covering the career of Wing Commander Brian Robert Noble.
- 'The Landing – a pencil-written note by A. R. J. Skillern' detailing his experiences before and during the Salerno Landings September 1943.
- Observer's and Air Gunner's Flying Log Book belonging to Harold Bertram Hale, Nos. 12, 101 and 223 Squadrons.
- 'A Queen's Man' – An account of the experiences of Derek Harrington by Peter Harrington.

Interviews with OE Second World War Veterans

Allan Barnes; John Chiles; William Robert Deeks; Dennis Geen; Stanley George Holliman; Michael Jeffrey; Gordon Murray and William Taylor. Full transcripts of these interviews conducted by Daniel Kirmatzis are available to consult from the Emanuel School Archive.

Acknowledgements

Daniel Kirmatzis would like to thank Mark Hanley-Browne, Emanuel Headmaster for employing him as a writer-in-residence in 2014 in order to complete this book. We would like to express our appreciation to the small army of proofreaders including John Hardy, Deputy Head at Emanuel; Rowena Kirton and Myra Jones, and OEs Claude Scott and Geoff Thorne. Their comments have proved invaluable to the overall text and we are extremely grateful to them.

Our deep gratitude goes to Paul Hewitt and Mary Woolley of Battlefield Design who have worked tirelessly with us for over a year giving careful consideration to the way this book is illustrated and laid out. We commend their work to anyone thinking of undertaking such a project.

We would like to thank subscribers to Emanuel School at War, whose generosity enabled this book to be published. The raising of funds for such a book should not be taken lightly and through the indefatigable energy of Sarah Fisher, (Emanuel Development Director 2002–2013) we have been able to produce a fully illustrated volume. Our thanks are due to Sarah for raising the funds needed in such a short period.

Daniel Kirmatzis would especially like to thank Old Emanuels the late Allan Barnes, John Chiles, the late Bob Deeks, Dennis Geen, Stanley Holliman, the late Michael Jeffery, Gordon Murray and Bill Taylor for allowing me to interview them and exploring what were often emotional experiences. Also to Old Emanuels William Attfield, John Banbery, Ronald Gray, Jack Halligan, Donald Inkster and the late Norman Simpson for providing materials relating to their Second World War experiences.

Daniel would like to thank his mother, Efthalia, for her continued support and encouragement throughout the writing of this book. He also wishes to express his deep gratitude to his grandmother Ivy for inspiring his interest in the Second World War with illuminating tales of what life was like on the Home Front. His thanks are also due to Maxine who spent many hours listening to these stories as they were discovered for the first time. Tony would like to thank his wife Regina and daughter Alice for their support throughout the Emanuel School at War Project.

This book has been enriched by contributions from authors who have already researched particular Old Emanuels and masters. Our thanks are due to several individuals for allowing us to reproduce their work: OE Paul Tofi composed the opening poem 'The Emanuel Boys'; Jeremy Archer, whose son Sebastian attended Emanuel, has written about the pre-First World War Emanuel Headmaster Harold Buchanan Ryley; Dr. Chris Payne OBE has written about his grandfather Charlie Payne; Roger Hutchins has written about his father Harold Hutchins; OE Doug Goodman has written about his OE brother Roger's journey to discover what happened to their uncle Alec Reader; Richard and Rodney Freeman have written about their uncle Arthur Collen; Tim Goddard has given his permission to reproduce an article about his relative Frederick Harry Bedloe Moore. OE Nicholas Kerfoot Hughes has written about his father's experiences in the First World War.

We would like to thank the following for giving their permission to reproduce articles and extracts from their works and assisting us in sourcing materials: Vaughan Clarke; OE Vic Townsend; Sue Mintram-Mason; Phillip Stanton; OE Peter Harrington; Gill and Peter Grainge; Helen Rowell; John Skillern; Kathy Page; Andrew and Victoria Neale; David Darley; Tim Mann; Brian Horseman; The Wates family and Marita Mahon of Wates Ltd. for access to the Company's archives and her assistance in sourcing materials; The Grundy family for providing us with photos of the Grundy brothers; Derek and James Finlay for providing materials relating to Derek's brother Douglas Finlay; Peter Wildey for donating his father's Second World War collection to the Emanuel School Archive; The Henson family, in particular Nicky Henson for providing access to his father's film collection at the British Film Institute; Tony Thornburn OBE for donating his father's collection relating to the 4th Battalion, King's Shropshire Light Infantry to the School Archive; and to the many others who have provided us with materials and who have donated to the School Archive.

Daniel Kirmatzis would like to thank the staff of the following institutions for their time and assistance during the course of his research: British Film Institute; Battersea Library; British Library; The Friends House Library; Imperial War Museum; Kent & Sharpshooters Museum; The National Archives, Kew; National Army Museum; National Liberal Club; National Portrait Gallery; Royal Berkshire Regiment Museum; Royal Hampshire Regiment Museum; Royal Fusilier Museum, Tower of London.

In addition to those already mentioned we wish to express our gratitude to the following individuals and institutions in giving their time and supplying materials for *Emanuel School at War*.

A–E

Barbara Adams, Francis Abbott, Phil Ainsworth, Archive of Modern Conflict, Arthur Arnold, Max Arthur, Melissa Atkinson, Rob Avery, Mrs Bailey, Tony Banham, Jeremy Banning, Bansted Memorial Group, Chris Banwell, Stephen Barker, Phyllis Barnes, Lottie Barratt, Eric Bates, Margaret Bell, Ruth Bennett, John Beyer, Walter Beyer, Dave Birrell, Jill Blackbourn, Shirley Blackburn, Eloise Blake, Jessica Bolton, Steve Bond, Nikki Gordon Bowe, Simon Bowler, Val Bowman, Paul Bradly, British Library, Geoffrey Brooks, Andrew Buchanan, Alan Buckingham, Dave Buckley, Ian Bumstead, Patricia Bunkham, Catherine Burns, Gordon Frederick Burrett, Stuart Cameron-Waller, Canadian Great War Project, Henry Carpenter, Peter Clare, Roger George Clark, Jim Cleverley, Brian Cocks, Lord Sebastian Coe, Anthony Coleman, Professor Penelope Corfield, John Cox, Sue Crawshaw, Bobbi Crickmore, Jack Darrah, Mary Davis, Richard Deeks, David Dell, Mrs M. Derrett, Gary Dibden, Colonel Dicken, Stuart Disbrey, Annabel Dixon, Dorset Masonry, Professor Peter Doyle, Philip Dransfield, Derek Drury, Nick Drew, Peter Dudley, Jennifer Eburne, Jeremy Edwards.

F–K

Sheila Fennings, Annie Findlay, Richard Forder, Tony Forrest, Gail Fowle, Jenny Fowle, Freedom Press, Neil A. French, David Friend, Robert Frost, Chris Fry, Sir Anthony Galsworthy, Michael Galsworthy CVO CBE, Getty Images, Michael Gibbs, Roger Goodman, Gill Grainge, Nicola Gray, Ian Greaves, Ben Grundy, Dominic Grundy, Håkan Gustavsson, Hale Books, Colin Hall, Mark Hanley-Browne, John Hardy, Andy Hayward, Peter Henderson Gulliver, Joe Henson, Sara Hersheson, Paul Hewitt, Tony Hill, Michael Hoare, Kwok Ho-Ip, Ronald Horlock, John Howell, Paul Hunt, David Irwin, Carol Janes, Keith Janes, Peter Scott Janes, Elizabeth Jarrett, Shan Johannson, Willem de Jong, Regina Jones, Alice Jones, Valerie Kelley, Marshall Kearney, Chris Kenyon, Les Kerjenski, Stephanie Killingbeck, Henry King, Rhona Kirkwood, Efthalia Kirmatzis, Ivy Kirmatzis, Sarah Kirmatzis, Naomi Klein.

L–R

Helen Langley, Henrik Langelüddecke, Justin Le Good, Robert Lewis, John Lewis-Stempel, Lijsenthoek Military Cemetery, Jill Loader, Maxine Loader, John Lyward, Mike Markland, Albert Marle, Tim Mann, Patrick Mann, Roger Marjoribanks, Albert Marle, Stamford Marthews, Helen Mavin, Roy Maxwell, Nick McCarthy, Paul McCue and the Wandsworth First World War Sub-Committee, John McGregor, Richard McGregor, Ross McNeill, Gene Meieran, Robin Mitchell, Rose Mollett, Boris Mollo, John Monkhouse, National Liberal Club, John Neale, Patrick Needham, New Zealand Ministry of Culture and Heritage, Alan Nichols, Toby Nichols, Ysolde Nichols, Nigel B. Noble OBE, Nora Page and family, David Parton, Shirley Passmore, Hugh Palmer, Marion Parsons, Nicholas Pearman, Dennis William Peck, Kathrin Pieren and the Petersfield Museum, David Pierce, Frank De Planta, Adrian Punacks, Punch Magazine, Paul Reed, Martin Richardson, Simon Roberts, Terry Rogers, Dachiell Rowdon, Lisle Ryder, Ralston Ryder.

S–Z

Charles Sammonds, Professor Nigel Saul, Rob Schäfer, Claude Scott, Giles Scott-Giles, Sir Anthony Seldon, Sevenoaks Memorial, Jeremy Sharp, Jayson Singh, Iris Smith, Mike Smith, Stephen Smith, Neil Smith, Nigel Smith, Evadne Spikett, David Stapley, St. Olave's School, Colin Sutherland, Caroline Sykes, Roland Symons, Emily Symmons, Steve Tagg, Dick Tarrant, Elizabeth Taylor, Nic Maunder Taylor, Mrs Grace Taylor, The Actors' Children's Trust, Alex L. C. Thompson, Andrew Thompson, George Thompson, Jeremy Thompson, Geoffrey Thorne, Robert Townsend, Michael Townsend, Pete Tresadern, David Underdown , John Walker, General Sir Peter Wall GCB CBE ADC Gen, Wandsworth Museum, Richard Warren, James Wates CBE, Brian White, Martin White, Roger White, Elisa Wild, John and Hilary Wilkinson, D. Williams, Lesley Williams, Ronald Williamson, Guy Wiltshear, Margaret Wood, WW2 Talk Forum.

Index